MAKING WORLD DEVELOPMENT WORK

Making World Development Work

Scientific Alternatives to Neoclassical Economic Theory

EDITED BY GRÉGOIRE LECLERC
AND CHARLES A. S. HALL

UNIVERSITY OF NEW MEXICO PRESS

ALBUQUERQUE

13 12 11 10 09 08 07   1 2 3 4 5 6 7

LIBRARY OF CONGRESS CATALOGING-IN-PUBLICATION DATA

Making world development work : scientific alternatives to
neoclassical economic theory / edited by Charles A. S. Hall
and Grégoire Leclerc.
            p. cm.
       Includes bibliographical references and index.
       ISBN-13: 978-0-8263-3733-7 (cloth : alk. paper)
       ISBN-10: 0-8263-3733-3 (cloth : alk. paper)
  1. Economic development.
  2. Neoclassical school of economics.
  3. Science—Methodology.
  I. Hall, Charles A. S.
  II. Leclerc, Grégoire
       HD75.M247 2006
       338.9001—dc22

                     2006019436

DESIGN AND COMPOSITION: *Mina Yamashita*

CONTENTS

Website

Color originals of all figures as well as pictures, emails, and errata can be found at:
http://www.makingworlddevelopmentwork.net
Readers are encouraged to join the discussion forum at that site.

Acknowledgments

This book has benefited from seed funding from the Ecoregional Fund to Support Methodological Initiatives (www.ecoregionalfund.com), through a research project (http://gisweb.ciat.cgiar.org/cross_scale/index.htm) managed by the International Center for Tropical Agriculture (CIAT) in 1997–2000. The project's final workshop brought about three dozen scientists and decision makers to share their views about across-scale systems, and the idea of a new book about science and development was born. In subsequent years the book gained momentum and depth by broadening its scope and by inviting several new authors to contribute their unique experience. Therefore, this book owes a great debt to other funding sources for salaries of scientific staff, support staff, and students, for research grants, and to the generous donation of time, money, and patience from all contributors. The research was supported in part by grants #BSR-8811902, DEB-9411973, DEB-008538, and DEB-0218039 from the National Science Foundation to the Institute of Tropical Ecosystem Studies (IEET), University of Puerto Rico, and the International Institute of Tropical Forestry (IITFR) as part of the Long-Term Ecological Research Program in the Luquillo Experimental Forest. Additional support was provided by the Forest Service U.S. Department of Agriculture) and the University of Puerto Rico. The editors are grateful to all the people who have believed in this book, in particular Jose Ignacio (Nacho) Sanz (CIAT); the administrators at State University of New York College of Environment Science and Forestry (SUNY ESF); Luther Wilson, the director of the University of New Mexico Press; Lincoln Bramwell and Gregory McNamee for a huge editing job at and for the Press; and all the contributors. Finally, we wish to thank SUNY ESF for a sabbatical—and to Ferdinand Bonn for a postdoctoral grant—that allowed Charles Hall and Grégoire Leclerc to meet in Costa Rica in 1995.

Draft copies of the chapters in this book were used for several seminars at SUNY ESF. Charles Hall would like to thank Jacquie Anderson, April Baptiste, Leif Brunet, Leandro Castillo, Amy Chen, Carol Franco, Susana del Granado, Nate Gagnon, Jen Khoury, Kelly Lash, Jenny Lorango, Vincent Lumia, Katie McGohan, Rita Monteiro, David Murphy, Jeff Pacceli, Bobby Powers, Amos Quaye, Heather Root, Abby Sterling, Oksana Titarenko, and Chris Travis for being guinea pigs in his course on tropical development, where they edited and commented upon the material and improved it in many ways.

We dedicate this book and whatever good that might come from it to the poor, with the hope that if development is guided and constrained by science rather than ideology, their lives might be improved.

Abbreviations

ASEAN	Association of Southeast Asian Nations	GIS	Geographic Information Systems
CATIE	Centro Agronómico Tropical de Investigación y Enseñanza (Tropical Agricultural Research and Higher Education Center, Costa Rica)	GNI	gross national income
		GNP	gross national product
		GPS	Global Positioning System
		GPV	gross production value
CEP	Caribbean Environment Program	HDI	Human Development Index
CEPAL	Comisión Económica para América Latina (Economic Commission for Latin America and the Caribbean)	IFAD	International Fund for Agricultural Development
		IFPRI	International Food Policy Research Institute
CGIAR	Consultative Group on International Agriculture Research	IICA	Instituto Interamericano de Cooperación Agropecuaria (Inter-American Institute for Cooperation on Agriculture)
CIA	U.S. Central Intelligence Agency		
CIAT	Centro Internacional de Agricultura Tropical (International Center for Tropical Agriculture)		
		IITA	International Institute of Tropical Agriculture
CIDA	Canadian International Development Agency	ILRI	International Livestock Research Institute
CIMMYT	Centro Internacional de Mejoramiento de Maíz y Trigo (International Maize and Wheat Improvement Center)	IMF	International Monetary Fund
		I-O	input-output
CIRAD	Centre de Coopération Internationale en Recherche Agronomique pour le Développement (Center for International Agricultural Research Development)	IPCC	Intergovernmental Panel on Climate Change
		IRD	Institut de Recherche pour le Développement
		IRRI	International Rice Research Institute
CLUE	Conversion of Land Use and Its Effects Project	LDC	less developed country
		LUCC	land-use/land-cover change
DEM	digital elevation model	LULC	land-use/land-cover
DTM	digital terrain model	MAC	marginal abatement cost
EC	European Commission	MAG	Ministerio de Agricultura y Ganadería (Costa Rica Ministry of Agriculture and Livestock)
EEZ	exclusive environment zone		
EPIC	erosion productivity impact calculator		
EU	European Union	MBL	marginal benefits locally
FAO	Food and Agriculture Organization of the United Nations	MBN	marginal benefit to the nation
		MBR	marginal benefit to the region
G77	group of seventy-seven less developed countries	NASA	U.S. National Aeronautics and Space Administration
GATT	General Agreement on Tariffs and Trade	NCE	neoclassical economics
		NEPAD	New Economic Partnership for African Development
GDP	gross domestic product		

NWE	neoclassical welfare economics
NGO	nongovernmental organization
NIMA	U.S. National Imagery and Mapping Agency
NMFS	U.S. National Marine Fisheries Service
NOAA	U.S. National Oceanic and Atmospheric Administration
OECD	Organization for Economic Cooperation and Development
OEEC	Organization for European Economic Cooperation
OPEC	Organization of Petroleum Exporting Countries
PDF	Project Development Fund
PLUC	potential land-use change
PPA	participatory poverty appraisal
PPO	participatory planning by objectives
PPP	purchasing price parity
REPOSA	Research Program on Sustainability in Agriculture
SAP	structural adjustment program
SCS	U.S. Soil Conservation Service
SOLUS	Sustainable Options for Land Use
SQL	Structured Query Language
TCG	technical coefficients generator
TREES	Tropical Ecosystem Environment Observation by Satellite Project
UN	United Nations
UNDP	United Nations Development Program
UNEP	United Nations Environment Program
UNESCO	United Nations Educational, Scientific and Cultural Organization
UNFPA	United Nations Population Fund
UNHCR	United Nations High Commissioner for Refugees
UNICEF	United Nations International Children's Emergency Fund
UNIDO	United Nations Industrial Development Organization
USAID	U.S. Agency for International Development
USDA	U.S. Department of Agriculture
USEPA	U.S. Environmental Protection Agency
USGS	U.S. Geological Survey
WBI	well-being index
WFP	World Food Program
WHO	World Health Organization
WRI	World Resources Institute
WTO	World Trade Organization
WWF	World Wildlife Fund

PART ONE

Critique of Development Economics and the Need for a Biophysical Alternative

The editors of this book were trained in the natural sciences, focusing on physics and geographic information science (Leclerc) and biology and ecology (Hall). We are used to using the scientific method, to assessing consistency with first principles, to testing hypotheses, and to watching some of our trusted theories crumble under the onslaught of hypothesis testing, model validation, empirical studies, and the rigorous standards of our colleagues. Other theories have stood the test of time, and we can then use them with confidence.

When for practical reasons we began to spend more and more time interacting with economists and their theories, we were astonished to find that although economics is usually considered a social *science*, it seems to have subjected precious little of its main theories to the rigorous gaze of hypothesis construction and testing; neither has it spent much time asking whether the principles and basic assumptions are consistent with the laws of nature. Many economists tell us that the criticism is not fair, because controlled laboratory conditions where such experiments can be undertaken do not exist or are inappropriate. Other economists have decided to confront this problem by engaging in experimental economics, and found that testing even the simplest theories or hypothesis produces a range of results that often contradict mainstream economic thought. From our perspective, if the difficulty in testing economic theories does not keep economists from making policy pronouncements as to how to improve a nation's economy based on them, then how can we believe what they recommend? How can we have any faith in their use?

The following six chapters can be viewed as explicit broadsides at neoclassical economics from the perspective of natural scientists who want economics to be reality-based, rather than theory based, as is the case at the present. We hasten to add that economists have told us that in fact economics has an empirical basis, but we believe this is generally from the perspective of calibrating economic models to existing data rather than undertaking explicit tests of hypotheses. We are modelers. We know that any model in natural science, even an incorrect one, can be fit to reality (as in chapter 1). This is not the same as developing hypotheses that are consistent with first principles and then testing them. In this book, we give many suggestions as to how this might be done, and we expect that biophysical economics, as imperfectly (of necessity, it is early in the game) developed in chapter 6 and elsewhere, should be subject to the same rigorous scientific approach that we wish had been undertaken for neoclassical economics. Mostly we want economists and natural scientists to talk about these things, to argue and develop better models and approaches in the future. The needs of the poor people of the earth and the need to protect the earth demand no less than our best efforts in what is a very difficult business.

Chapter 1

Does the Emperor Have Any Clothes?

An Overview of Scientific Critiques of Neoclassical Economics

Charles A. S. Hall and John Gowdy

Introduction

The fundamental factor influencing the formulation and implementation of development policies and aid in the past four or so decades has been the ascendancy, indeed intellectual dominance, of neoclassical welfare economics (NWE), also known as free market economics, neoliberalism, or neoclassical economics (NCE). Although technically NWE is broader, in most of the rest of this book we use NCE, because it has the broadest usage, although we believe NWE describes the entity more accurately). In a number of ways, all of these are perceived as being the same as, or at least closely linked to, capitalism. In many cases, the economic premises of NWE are presented as national political goals. In the United States, for example, both Democratic and Republican presidents spend considerable time unabashedly selling the virtues of competition, economic growth, and privatization to the rest of the world. The free-market ideology of NWE has become the dominant economic guideline for the developed world, and it is increasingly accepted by, or forced upon, the developing world. There are a number of reasons for the ascendancy of neoliberal economics: (1) the collapse of communism, the principal perceived alternative to capitalism; (2) the role model of the United States, which claims, and appears to many to be, the successful embodiment of neoliberal principles; (3) the fervent belief in the principles of neoclassical economics by a suite of very powerful decision makers in Washington who find these principles sympathetic with their university training, political leanings, and personal economic interests; (4) the intervention of the International Monetary Fund (IMF), World Bank, and other powerful economic actors who were extremely strong advocates of NCE (often for their own ends), and who gained strong bargaining power for intervention in Latin American and other economies because of the increasing foreign debts of many nations; and (5) the domination of neoclassical economics in teaching, research, and the reward system in the economics profession, in part because it is financed by economically powerful groups and other approaches are not. Missing from this list is the argument that NWE works because it correctly describes the economy. We argue that instead NWE and many other conceptual descriptions of real economic systems "work" because for the moment there are abundant energy resources that can be pulled out of the ground to make them work. The enormous net energy surplus we have now allows nearly any intellectual system imagined to in some sense "work," even if the underlying mechanisms incorrectly describe the real system.

Neoclassical economics, as it has evolved since the end of the nineteenth century, has become a new religion that is sweeping the world, one that, like other religions, is based more on faith than on empiricism. In the first part of this book, we attempt to review objectively what is known about the real successes and real failures of neoliberalism. We discuss a number of new studies, using the scientific method where possible, to examine the track record of neoliberal policies in developing countries to see which of their claims seem to be justified and which of them might be better explained from other perspectives. In this endeavor we recognize that the terrain is not easy, the "enemy" is very well entrenched, and the results are rarely unequivocal. We also would like to emphasize that our target is not such simplistic policy issues as whether increased global trade is good or bad (we don't know) or whether economies should be more or less regulated (it depends). Our target instead is whether the way that real economies work is captured by the conceptual and logical models of contemporary economists and their institutions, and whether the blind application of untested theory produced the results advertised by the models. Mostly we believe it critical to open a dialog about development policies based on good science and empirical evidence, and not simply economic or political ideology.

Sources of Criticisms of Contemporary Economics

Even as neoclassical economics sweeps over the world, there is mounting criticism within the economics profession of the very foundations of neoclassical welfare theory, and of policies based on that theory. Recent theoretical work in economics has called into question the neoclassical welfare model. The recent Nobel laureates Joseph Stiglitz and George Ackerlof stress the prevalence of asymmetric information in real world economies, contrary to the neoclassical assumptions of perfect information and perfect competition. Another major breakthrough in economics is the increasing emphasis on empirical research on real human behavior. Another recent Nobel Prize winner, Vernon Smith, has used controlled experiments to demonstrate the ubiquity of "other regarding preferences." Experimental economics has clearly demonstrated that our perception of well-being depends on our standing relative to others, that changes in well-being may be more important than absolute levels, and that notions of fairness are culturally dependent. All of these real observations and experiments undermine the base and legitimacy of the neoclassical model.

Although these criticisms at the level of "high theory" are increasingly well developed and empirically validated, they seem to have made little or no impact on those responsible for the application of economics in the field. At best, day-to-day practitioners have acknowledged some minor problems with the fundamental model, but they insist that these can be patched up by correcting

prices to reflect various "externalities" such as egregious environmental or social damage. But the criticisms currently being generated are fundamental, deep, and go to the core of NWE and as such they call into question the idea that the model can be rehabilitated. In the natural sciences we are familiar with large-scale "paradigm shifts," where fundamental ideas that have been widely accepted and well developed are suddenly found to be quite wrong, leading to the replacement of the entire conceptual basis of a discipline. Some examples include the sixteenth-century replacement of the earth-centered Ptolemaic theory of the solar system with the Copernican/Galilean sun-centered view, and, fifty years ago, the replacement of a static view of continents with that of plate tectonics. Two questions are: do we need, and are we ready for, such a paradigm shift in economics? And if we are prepared intellectually for that task, can we possibly implement it given the enormous intellectual and financial investment in neoclassical economics as it is applied around the world? Our answer to the first question is that it is probably too late for the older economists steeped in neoclassical theory, but there are many younger economists and certainly a vast army of environmental, geological, and physical scientists ready to learn a new economics more consistent with their own empirically based view of the world. The answer to the second is that it would be an extremely difficult and demanding task to implement a new policy approach to economics, even if it could be agreed as to what that should be. The other side of the coin is, however, that it might be much worse not to do so, especially if the plight of the third world degrades substantially, which is likely as oil prices increase over the coming years.

There are essentially three fundamental criticisms of the neoclassical economic paradigm. The first is logical, the second scientific-empirical, and the third social. We review them next.

1) Logical Inconsistencies in the Neoclassical Model

Historically, the question of the distribution of wealth was a central concern of economics (for example, the work of Adam Smith, Alfred Marshall,

Arthur Pigou, and even Vilfredo Pareto). But starting in the 1930s, a new group of economists (including John Hicks, Nicholas Kaldor, and Lionel Robbins) began to develop a positivist approach. Part of the rationale for these changes was that to be a "real" science, economics should become more purely objective, academic, and less political, with the assumption that questions about the desirability of a more equitable income distribution were normative, not positive, and were best left to the political process. This allowed economists to concentrate on efficiency, that is, the ability of economies to turn "scarce" resources into economic wealth. Two important developments fostering this approach were the narrowing of the concept of individual "utility" (well-being or happiness) to "consumption" and the assertion that interpersonal comparisons of utility were unnecessary in constructing a "social welfare function," that is, an estimate of the well-being of society as a whole. Social welfare came to be equated with economic output. If per capita income increased, then society was happier because, theoretically at least, everyone could consume more economic goods. This in turn was based on the seminal ideas of Vilfredo Pareto (1848–1923), who derived the concept of "Pareto optimality," a situation in which no one can be made better off without making someone else worse off. This principle is of limited practical use since almost all public policies help some people and hurt others. To get around this limitation, Hicks and Kaldor came up with the idea of a "potential Pareto improvement" (Kaldor 1939; Hicks 1939). They reasoned that if the gains from a particular economic change were greater than the losses, the gainer could compensate the loser and still come out ahead. The desirability of given economic activity could therefore be measured simply by the change in income for the entire population affected, regardless of whether some people were made much worse off. Thus, academic economists essentially washed their hands of any responsibility for *who* got whatever wealth might be generated by their policies. But an often underappreciated aspect of this approach is that to the economist's mind as long as the compensation to the losers *might* take place then the transaction should go forward even

if the actual compensation never happens. In other words, if someone is made worse off by an economic activity that increases overall wealth, and he is compensated only in theory but not in fact, this is of no concern to welfare economists, who concentrate solely on efficiency. Many of the actual inconsistencies that have fallen out of the application of welfare economics are reviewed by Bromley (1990) and Gowdy (2004).

Economists use income as a proxy for well-being. And in economic jargon and practice, the welfare function is linear and additive. Each individual gains welfare in direct proportion to increases in his or her real disposable income. Thus a given individual will be "better off" by a factor of two if he or she has $2,000 rather than $1,000 to spend (or if prices fall by half). By invoking the potential Pareto improvement criterion and assuming that income equals happiness, an increase in per capita GDP means an increase in social welfare. Thus a gain of $1,000 to a wealthy person is viewed as being as good as a gain of $1,000 to a poor person, and if one individual becomes five times wealthier (say from $1,000 to $5,000), that is as great a social good as five people becoming twice as wealthy (say from $1,000 to $2,000 each). Even worse, society is better off in this assessment if a millionaire's income goes up by $1,000 and a poor person's income goes down by $999. The potential Pareto improvement concept lies behind neoliberal policies, including most development plans that tend to pay most attention to increasing gross national product (GNP) and relatively little to *who* gets the proceeds. As indicated above, the "objective" economists believe that distribution is a political, not economic, question. This of course avoids the contentions within the developing world that development tends to enrich those who have much, while doing little, or even further impoverishing, those who have little. But from the perspective of contemporary neoclassical economics, the task of economic policy is to increase total wealth, leaving distribution for others to worry about. This economic perspective is often enhanced by social notions that people are well off or not in accordance to their own efforts rather than due to factors outside their control. Social Darwinism is alive and well in neoclassical welfare economics. Somewhat ironically, most welfare economists are opposed to state-supported welfare because they perceive most poverty as the failure of the poor themselves.

In absolute contrast to this view, recent empirical research by psychologists and a few economists makes the case that after a certain threshold human welfare and happiness does not increase with income (Frey and Stutzer 2002). Relative income becomes more important than absolute income. Even more fundamentally, other factors such as rich social relationships, health, and security are at least as important to well-being as is more material consumption. Hence, in fact, and in contrast to the NWE linear assumption, supplying poor people with the basic necessities of life generates a greater amount of happiness and welfare with a given amount of money compared to much less happiness or well-being generated by the same amount of money in the hands of someone who already is well off. The extensive research being done in behavioral economics and game theory has completely undermined the "value neutral" assumption at the base of neoclassical welfare economics.

What is especially important is not simply that one of the most important conceptual bases in economics—that social welfare could be determined by simply adding up the incomes of isolated individuals—was incorrect when subjected to empirical testing. Focusing exclusively on isolated individuals allowed neoclassical economists to ignore and even to develop theory contrary to one of the key concepts in neoclassical economic theory—diminishing marginal utility—when formulating development policies. When concentrating solely on increasing GDP, development economists assume that all money gained in a population is of equal value no matter who gets it. But the concept of diminishing marginal utility says that the first unit of anything is more valuable than the second, the second more valuable than the third, and so on. This should apply equally to money, and says that poor people will value a $100 bill in their hands more than a rich person will. Diminishing marginal utility of income was taken for granted by leading economists at the beginning of the last century, such as Alfred Marshall, A. C. Pigou, and John Maynard Keynes, who all recognized that social welfare would increase by redistributing income from the rich to the poor.

Related to the idea that money is "neutral"—that is, a dollar in the hands of a wealthy person is just the same as a dollar in the hands of a poor person—is the idea of money as a universal substitute. In economic models of sustainability, for example, features of the natural world such as rainforests—called natural capital by economists—are valued in monetary units and assumed to be equivalent to human-made manufactured capital. By this sleight of hand, it is good policy to cut down a rainforest and build a chainsaw factory if that increases the value of the total stock of productive capital, even if there are no trees left to cut.

If economics is to be accepted as a real science, its basic assumptions and models must be exposed to rigorous and thoughtful empirical testing and to requirements for consistency. The fact that empirical testing is now taking place in economics represents a revolution in the field and will completely change economics in the coming decades. Results from experimental economics show that the actual human behavior and values that drive people's sense of well-being bear little resemblance to the fundamental assumptions about these same issues as used in neoclassical economic theory. There is a pressing need to subject more of our economic theories to broad, unbiased, and thorough assessments of whether they deliver on what they promise (Gintis 2000; Hall et al. 2001). In particular, the value judgments underlying the concept of "efficiency" need to be thoroughly explored because efficiency is the principal argument used to promote the neoliberal development model (Bromley 1990; see chapter 5).

It is impossible to say what direction economics will take now that its core is in the process of disintegration. But the movement toward interdisciplinary, science-based explanations of consumer and firm behavior, as well as the reaching out of economics beyond simply firms and consumers to the natural world that allows their existence, offers an opportunity to change the simplistic worldview of neoclassical welfare economics toward one taking into account biophysical laws and empirically valid models of human behavior. If economics continues down the path of basing theories on empirical results rather than on ideology, this will offer a source of support for social and environmental responsibility rather than a defense of individual and corporate greed. It will also help economics as a discipline to come to grips with a future of almost certain enormously increased real scarcity of high-quality fuels and of many aspects of environmental quality.

2) Inconsistencies Between the Neoclassical Model and Science

The second main critique of neoclassical economics is that many of its most fundamental assumptions are inconsistent with the laws of nature and the methods of science. Since these ideas are developed fully in chapter 4, we will not repeat them here except to note that it seems quite strange to develop "laws" or principles of economics that are inconsistent with the laws of physics, which to our knowledge have never been broken. Economics, when first developed by the French physiocrats and the Englishmen Adam Smith and David Ricardo, was initially based on biophysical concepts, including the importance of land and its quality for economic production (we might say today largely in terms of intercepting and transforming solar energy) and the importance of human labor (which today we might also view as the energy used in transforming raw materials). Curiously, most economics today gives very little credit or interest to resources, believing instead in the power of market activities to create new resources or at least to find suitable substitutes. For example, the economist Michael Lynch (2002) emphasizes that there have been many past predictions of oil shortages that have not come true, which he believes will continue to be true indefinitely. A recent manifestation of this perspective in terms of the focus of this book is the white paper "Aid to 'poorly performing' countries: A critical review of debates and issues" (Macrae et al. 2004), a comprehensive review of the causes of low economic growth that focuses (appropriately) on government corruption, "economic structure," and so on but essentially does not even mention natural resources or the efficacy of humans in using

them. While it is clear that rich natural resources are hardly any guarantee of prosperity or economic growth, and may in fact get in the way (see chapter 2), countries without any particular resource base have an extremely difficult time in generating enough wealth to escape poverty, especially if they also have significant human population growth. The recent emphasis that countries with very rich natural resources often suffer intense corruption (but some do not) has obscured the fact that countries with very low resources are also not likely to do very well either.

3) Social and Environmental Inadequacies of the Neoclassical Model

Our third principal criticism of contemporary neoclassical welfare economics is social. Since their independence, developing countries have received a great deal of attention from the donor community, and generally have diligently adhered to their neoclassical requirements in terms of investment, public spending, and privatization. A typical case is that of Honduras, which has followed every bit of advice from the United States, yet remains the second-poorest country in the Americas, ahead of only Haiti. Aggressive growth-oriented policies dictated by the developed world have tended not to deliver their promises, but even so developing countries are blamed, usually for their bad policies and bad economic ideas. Ironically, the ideas that are used to run their economies do not come from the developing countries themselves, but from experts trained in the developed world. Success stories seem to be more frequent for countries that did not follow all the advice of the developed world blindly but accepted and rejected advice according to their own context, as any wise person would do (see part 2). Even the United Nations, which is at the core of the global governance agenda, has had virtually no influence in setting international economic policies (WCSDG 2004). This under-performance of the multilateral system may have a simple explanation: while working hand in hand with the World Bank and IMF in promoting economic reform in line with NWE (called "accomplishment # 36"), the United Nations was investing heavily in forty-nine other areas, many of which make considerable sense but are either in total contradiction to NWE principles or else are completely undermined by NWE.

Why, then, have so many developing countries "signed on" to neoliberal economics, given its less than stellar track record and the much greater diversity of economic models that were used, often quite successfully, in the past? As just stated, a lot of the reason has to do with the power of lending and other financial institutions. For a number of reasons many developing countries today have enormous public debt, often related to past development plans. Sometimes it is simply not possible to meet the interest payments that are due, and even when possible it is always difficult and painful. Since it is always difficult to pay the interest, it is usually essentially impossible to pay off the principal, even though often these countries have paid off the equivalent of the principal many times over in never-ending interest payments. Sometimes, due to crop failures, increases in the price of needed imports such as oil, or internal problems it is impossible to pay even interest. The options given for many countries were, in effect, either to go into default, with serious repercussion on economies increasingly dependent upon international trade, or to become subject to "structural adjustment programs" (the instrument of choice for implementing neoliberal principles). The latter meant, essentially, to relinquish governmental control and influence over large sectors of the economy once reserved for the government. In addition, it often meant to turn the workings of the economy over to the IMF or through them to private enterprise, neoclassical economics, and the marketplace, whatever that meant in a given application. Whether the main motivating factor for the IMF and World Bank to promote NCE was that they genuinely thought this would improve the economies so affected or whether it was a means of increasing the probability of their getting back the interest owed to them is a matter of conjecture. Probably both are true. One recent book (Perkins 2004) certainly implicates the latter view from the perspective of an insider.

The degree to which neoclassical economics and neoliberal policies did or did not improve the economies of the countries to which they were applied, indeed even met their own objectives, is rather controversial and subject to whom is doing the analysis. For example, Friedman and Friedman (1980), Bhagwati (2003), and the IMF (1993) have proclaimed unequivocally that the NCE policies were and would be effective and that the countries that did march to the NCE drummer would recover from whatever economic ills they were subject to, and those that did not would not. "Stabilization and structural adjustment programs contribute to debt reduction by helping to reduce deficits in the government budget and the balance of payments, to contain inflation, to stimulate savings, and to generate more resources for investment and debt service" (Gillis et al. 1996:417). We believe that Wolf (2004) effectively gives a less ideological and more empirical defense of free trade and globalization, although that too pays insufficient attention to the biophysical basis for most wealth generation.

The assessments from sources other than the development agencies and hardcore neoliberal economists are far less likely to be positive, and are often bitterly negative. The criticisms tend to come from two camps: first, people concerned about social/economic issues such as who gets the benefits and who gets the costs, and second, from people concerned about the environmental implications. For example, Collins and Lear (1995) argue that it is only through a very selected use of the national statistics that Chile (the poster child for the success of neoclassical economics) appears to have benefited from NCE-based structural adjustment policies. They also report that if the entire time span during which Chile was subject to structural adjustment is taken into account, the economy performed poorly by any reasonable criteria—and, in addition, the workers lost much more relative to the wealthy elite and lost most of their hard-won rights. In the authors' view, structural adjustment was a disaster for most Chileans. A more recent assessment would perhaps not give quite such a pessimistic view of the Chilean economy, but it is clear that much of the success of neoliberalism or whatever is going on is dependent upon the mining of resources such as timber and marine fish. Gray (1998) gives a similar and powerful assessment of the effects of neoliberal policies for England, Mexico, and New

Zealand, focusing on social impacts and the loss of the governments' ability to govern. Annis (1992) and Hansen-Kuhn (1993) argue that neoliberal policies forced upon Costa Rica by the IMF had devastating effects on small farmers and others, as well as the environment, while failing to solve the issues they were supposed to. Reed (1996) and many others have examined the environmental impact of structural adjustment and other neoliberal policies and generally conclude with rather devastating critiques of those activities. Gomeroy and Baumol (2000) argue that, in time, open markets tend to undermine the economies of the more developed nations. Although the issue of whether free markets lead to net gains or losses is far from resolved, and is in the press weekly if not daily, it is clear that even where there are net positive economic benefits, one result seemingly everywhere is that the difference in wealth between rich and poor within any individual country tends to increase (Wolf 2004). Even Paul Samuelson, whom some would say is the ultimate architect of neoclassical economics and certainly the writer of its most famous textbook, has suggested that free trade might not necessarily benefit all concerned (Samuelson 2004).

More generally, it seems that science has rarely been used to test what the gains and losses are. One exception is Montanye (1998), who used the scientific method to test whether the structural adjustment policies imposed upon Costa Rica met the objectives of USAID, the organization that imposed them. She found that mostly they did not, while generating many additional social and environmental problems. Kroeger and Montanye (2000) and Hall (2000) examined the effects of structural adjustment policies in Costa Rica and found many adverse aspects not well represented in most of the development agency reports about structural adjustment. In these authors' view, structural adjustment was tending to deal with the symptoms of Costa Rica's economic problems, and not the root problems of relentlessly increasing population, external debt, land degradation, and dependence upon foreign industrial products that were very sensitive to the price of oil.

Ranis, Stewart, and Ramires (2000) have examined the relationship between GDP and the Human Development Index (HDI), a composite index defined and used by the United Nations to take into account the multidimensional nature of poverty. They studied cross-country statistics for sixty-seven developing countries on three continents and in three time periods (the 1960s, 1970s, and 1980s) in an attempt to find a causal link between the type of development policy (economic growth [EG] versus human development [HD], that is, public expenditure in education, health, and the like) and actual development (as measured either as GDP or HDI). The main question was: is EG precursor to HD, or vice versa? They found that countries emphasizing only one type of policy (EG or HD but not both) were poor performers, the worst choice being a pure EG approach (systematically leading to poor performance in terms of both EG and HD). The winners were countries balancing both types of policies, as any wise person would think. Costa Rica was an exception as it was consistent in focusing more on HD than on EG and managed to sustain improved HD despite slow economic growth. If there was any success of neoliberal policies apparent in Costa Rica, (and that is certainly debatable), it could well be attributed to a high initial investment in education and health.

More recently strong criticisms of the ineffectiveness of our development procedures have even come from within the community of development economists themselves. Both Easterly (2001) and Stiglitz (2001) are senior and respected economists within the development community who have written scathing accounts of the failures of development. In a recent interview, Stiglitz remarks,

> When I went to the World Bank and was asked to look at a developing country's finances, I would always ask myself one question: if I were the head of their Council of Economic Advisors, what would I do to get recovery in their economy? How would I reduce poverty? But it soon became obvious that this was not what the IMF was all about at all. . . . That was not their mindset. They were interested in one thing. They looked at the country and thought, "they need to repay the loans they owe to Western banks. How

do we get that to happen?" So they would never ask, "should we give this developing country a bankruptcy procedure so they can have a fresh start?" They thought that bankruptcy was a violation of the sanctity of contracts, even though every democracy has a bankruptcy law for people who have persistently failed. They were interested in milking money out of the country quickly, not rebuilding it for the long term.

I saw first-hand the devastating effect that globalization can have on developing countries, and especially the poor within those countries. . . . Decisions were often made because of ideology and politics. Many wrong-headed decisions were taken, ones that did not solve the problem at hand but that fit the interests or belief of the people in power. . . . Decisions were made on the basis of what seemed a curious blend of ideology and bad economics, dogma that sometimes seemed to be thinly veiled special interests. It is not just that they often produced bad results: they were antidemocratic.

IMF's remedies failed as often as they worked. IMF structural adjustment programs led to riots and hunger in many countries; even when the results were not so dire, even when they managed to eke out some growth for a while, the results went disproportionately to the better-off, with those at the bottom sometimes facing even greater poverty (Hari 2003).

In the words of the interviewer, Johan Hari, "Of course, the IMF was not willfully malicious, devastating developing economies for fun. No; it had become saturated with a new and extreme ideology which its exponents sincerely believed would help the poor—even though its basic premises were flawed." The IMF was hijacked in the early 1980s by a sect Stiglitz calls "the market fundamentalists," who preach an extreme variant of capitalism that has never been tried anywhere in the developed world. They formed a new "Washington Consensus" between the IMF, World Bank, and United States Treasury about how developing economies should be run, which might be considered neoliberalism taken to the extreme.

But in our opinion, even Stiglitz and Easterly, valuable as their analyses are, have barely scratched the surface of the problems or of the possible solutions to contemporary economics because they still think like economists. To generate real solutions, if any are to be had, it is necessary to step outside economics. In this process we think that the natural sciences have a great deal to offer, and that is what this book is about. The fundamental question is "How do we determine if something is true?"

The world is full of people who proclaim to know what "truth" is. These people include religious, political, and other ideological fanatics, including more than a few economists, who proclaim that they know truth from some sort of ideological base. But to our eyes there is only one procedure that can be counted upon to determine what is true and what is not, and that is the scientific method, through the generation and continual testing of hypotheses. Some argue that the domain of science—the laboratory—is too small, but we think that the scientific method has been vastly underutilized relative to its potential domain, which includes the natural world (of course) but also much of the social world, even such previously unexpected areas as the relation of couples in marriage (Gottman, Swanson, and Swanson 2002) and, as we develop here, entire economies.

Exactly what constitutes science and the scientific method is of course not simple, and not all, and perhaps few, scientific discoveries follow the "official" Baconian pattern of observation, generation of hypotheses, and testing of hypotheses through tests and control. Rather, there are three important aspects that tend to determine whether something is scientific or not. The first is whether the phenomenon of interest is consistent with existing scientific laws and hypotheses, ideally with what are called "first principles," which are the most basic laws of science such as the first and second laws of thermodynamics and the conservation of matter. We have no knowledge of anything that is true that violates these fundamental scientific laws. Second, the relation must be tested—that is, the predictions of the science need to be examined in relation to reality. Third, what we call science (including good social science) must allow predictability: we must be able to make nontrivial predictions and examine the behavior of the actual system against the prediction that we made based on what we think is our known science and our understanding of causes and effects (induction).

This process is done most generally by creating, and then testing, a *model*, which is best defined as "a formalization of our assumptions about a system" (Hall and Day 1977). Such models may or may not live in a computer, but they are sufficiently formalized so as to be explicitly testable. This approach says that what makes science strong, what determines which science is most real, most important, and most useful, is the proper representation of proper mechanisms, repeatability, and consistency of prediction (or explanation), whether or not that prediction is consistent with, for example, one's ideological stance or profit margin. Models are critically important to the development of science, but of course the world is full of both good and also quite poor models. The process of science is the repetitive one of filtering, of understanding how things work well enough to create good models consistent with first principles, testing them to see how good they really are, and then applying them judiciously while keeping track of whether the models' predictions are born out in reality. When our models fail, and they do that more often than they succeed, one can learn from the failures and try to build a better model, but the old model must be scrapped or at lease radically altered. The real strength of good science is not necessarily that it is correct at any given time but that it has a self-correcting quality over time, so that slowly, often painfully, we can approach "truth," such as we humans are able to do that. This book attempts to bring that scientific method to economics in general and to the process of development in particular. In our opinion, this is badly needed as many people and many environments are being devastated by what we believe are the too often inappropriate application of doctrinaire and generally untested or insufficiently tested economic theory. Finally, we cannot underestimate the power of the entrenched interests of those in power. In an insightful article

Makgetla and Sideman (1989) state that where reality and the (neoclassical model) disagree reality is changed politically to be consistent with the model. Thus, powerful economic interests can "make" the neoclassical or whatever other model "work" simply through extreme financial or political power. We need to keep this in mind while we examine and test our economic models and the impacts they have on economies, society, and the environment.

Thus we conclude that there are many reasons that we might want to question the systems of economics that are being used to guide development in the less developed world (and indeed to run the developed countries) from the scientific perspective. This basic issue will arise again and again in the rest of this book, as will our attempts to build another way that we might undertake economics that is more grounded in the biophysical reality of the world.

Acknowledgments

We thank Kent Klitgaard and an anonymous reviewer, both economists, for a critique of an earlier draft, and our graduate students for helping to push us on these issues.

References

Annis, S. 1992. Debt and wrong way resource flows in Costa Rica. *Ethics and International Affairs* 4:107–21.

Bailey, M. N., and D. Farrell. 2004. Exploding the myths of offshoring. www.mckinseyquarterly.com/links/13927.

Bhagwati, J. 2004. *In Defense of Globalization*. New York: Oxford University Press.

Bromley, D. 1990. The ideology of efficiency. *Journal of Environmental Economics and Management* 19:86–107.

Cameron, R. 1997. *A Concise Economic History of the World*. New York: Oxford University Press.

Collins, J., and D. Lear. 1995. *Chile's Free Market Miracle: A Second Look*. Monroe, Ore.: Subterranean Books.

Easterly, W. 2001. *The Elusive Quest for Growth: Economists' Adventures and Misadventures in the Tropics*. Cambridge, Mass.: MIT Press.

Frey, B., and A. Stutzer. 2002. *Happiness and Economics: How the Economy and Institutions Affect Well-Being*. Princeton, N.J.: Princeton University Press.

Friedman, M., and R. Friedman. 1980. *Free to Choose: A Personal Statement*. New York: Harcourt Brace Jovanovich.

Gintis, H. 2000. Beyond *Homo economicus*: Evidence from experimental economics. *Ecological Economics* 35:311–22.

Gomory, R. E., and W. J. Baumol. 2001. *Global Trade and Conflicting National Interests*. Cambridge, Mass.: MIT Press.

Gottman, J., C. Swanson, and K. Swanson. 2002. A general systems approach of marriage: Nonlinear difference equation modeling of marital interaction. *Personality and Social Psychology Review* 6:326–40.

Gowdy, J. 2004. The revolution in welfare economics and its implications for environmental valuation and policy. *Land Economics* 80:239–57.

———. 2005. Toward a new welfare foundation for sustainability. *Ecological Economics* 53:211–22.

Gowdy, J., and J. Erickson. 2005. The approach of ecological economics. *Cambridge Journal of Economics* 29:207–22.

Gray, J. 1998. *False Dawn: The Delusion of Global Capitalism*. London: Granta Books.

Hall, C. A. S. 2004. The myth of sustainable development: Personal reflections on energy, its relation to neoclassical economics, and Stanley Jevons. *Journal of Energy Resources Technology* 126:85–89.

———, ed. 2000. *Quantifying Sustainable Development: The Future of Tropical Economies*. San Diego: Academic Press.

Hall, C. A. S., and J. W. Day. 1977. *Ecosystem Models in Theory and Practice*. New York: Wiley-Interscience.

Hall, C. A. S., C. J. Cleveland, and R. Kaufmann. 1986. *Energy and Resource Quality: The Ecology of the Economic Process*. New York: Wiley-Interscience.

Hall, C. A. S., D. Lindenberger, R. Kummel, T. Kroeger, and W. Eichhorn. 2001. The need to reintegrate the natural sciences with economics. *BioScience* 51, no. 6: 663–73.

Hall, C. A. S., P. Tharakan, J. Hallock, C. Cleveland, and M. Jefferson. 2003. Hydrocarbons and the evolution of human culture. *Nature* 426, no. 6964: 318–22.

Hansen-Kuhn, K. 1993. Sapping the economy: Structural adjustment policies in Costa Rica. *The Ecologist* 23:179–84.

Hari, J. 2003. A writer at large: Hypocrisy and the IMF. *Independent*, London, November 9.

Hicks, J. 1939. The foundations of welfare economics. *Economic Journal* 49:549–52.

International Monetary Fund. 1993. *Economic Adjustment in Low Income Countries: Experience Under the Enhanced Structural Adjustment Facility*. Washington, D.C.: International Monetary Fund.

Kaldor, N. 1939. Welfare propositions of economics and interpersonal comparisons of utility. *Economic Journal* 49:549–52.

Kroeger, T., and D. Montanye. 2000. Effectiveness of structural adjustment policies. In Hall 2000, 665–94.

Lynch, M. C. 2002. Forecasting oil supply: Theory and practice. *Quarterly Review of Economics and Finance* 42:373–89.

Macrae, J. A., O. Shepherd, A. Morrissey, E. Harmer, L-H. Anderson, A. Peron, D. McKay, D. Cammack, and N. Keggombe. 2004. *Aid to "Poorly Performing Countries": A Critical Review of Debates and Issues*. London: Overseas Development Institute.

Makgetla, N. S., and R. Sideman. 1989. The applicability of law and economics to policy making in the third world. *Journal of Economic Issues* 23:35–78.

Montanye, D. 1998. Examining sustainability: An evaluation of USAID policies for agricultural export-led growth in Costa Rica. M.S. thesis, State University of New York.

Pareto, V. 1976. *Manual of Political Economy*. New York: Augustus Kelly.

Perkins, J. 2004. *Confessions of an Economic Hit Man*. San Francisco: Berrett Koehler.

Perlin, J. 1989. *A Forest Journey*. Cambridge, Mass.: Harvard University Press.

Ranis, G., F. Stewart, and A. Ramires. 2000. Economic growth and human development. *World Development* 28, no. 2: 197–219.

Rawls, J. 1971. *A Theory of Justice*. Cambridge, Mass.: Harvard University Press.

Reed, D. 1996. *Structural Adjustment, the Environment, and Sustainable Development*. London: Earthscan.

Samuelson, P. 2004. Where Mills and Ricardo rebut and confirm arguments of mainstream economists supporting globalization. *Journal of Economic Perspectives* 18:135–46.

Stiglitz, J. 2002. *Globalization and Its Discontents*. New York: Norton.

Tainter, J. 1988. *The Collapse of Complex Societies*. New York: Cambridge University Press.

WCSDG. 2004. *A Fair Globalisation: Creating Opportunities for All*. Geneva: World Commission on the Social Dimensions of Globalisation, International Labour Office.

Wolf, M. 2004. *Why Globalization Works*. New Haven, Conn.: Yale University Press.

CHAPTER 2

THE RELATION BETWEEN ECONOMIC DEVELOPMENT AND LAND-USE CHANGE IN THE TROPICS

CHARLES A. S. HALL

Introduction

Many people in the developing world are desperately poor, and this is often exacerbated as populations increase, often in response to well-meaning medical intervention. Most industrial nations have international aid programs whose objective is to alleviate poverty (and reduce mortality), mostly in rural and tropical and always barely industrialized regions, through programs of economic development. But recently there has been some very pungent criticism of the perceived failures of programs of development from both outside and within the development community itself and, in the minds of many, a sense that, overall, programs for economic development in the tropics have failed to deliver.

The objectives of this chapter are to (1) review some of the more important earlier work by mainstream economists on land, (2) express my dissatisfaction with the utility of much of that work for dealing with issues of development, (3) develop some aspects of the qualitative and quantitative biophysical (versus dollar-based) relations of development to resource use and land-use change, (4) summarize the different types of development from a biophysical and cultural perspective, (5) review the intellectual foundations of the concept of development and some of its critics, (6) introduce the use of explicit empirical analysis and hypothesis testing as tools (which are now insufficiently exercised) for assessing and understanding these failures, and (7) consider a new biophysical, systems-oriented perspective, including a hypothesis about why most previous development has tended to fail. I will provide specific and explicit examples to undertake these objectives both here and elsewhere in this book. The reader should be aware that I am not interested in putting a market price on land or resources (hence moving nature inside the economics "box") but rather in putting the entire discipline of economics inside the "box" of the natural world, within which it must operate and without which it could not exist (see Hall et al. 2001). In some senses this chapter is similar to the next, although we developed each independently from our own individual experiences. Given our very different international experiences, it is rather remarkable that we each came up with essentially the same conclusions.

Land from an Economist's View

In response to reviewers' comments, I include an overview of how mainstream economists have treated land and land-use change over time. One reviewer stated, "The paper claims that in economics and other social sciences little attention is paid to resource use, land quality and or other environmental consequences of developmental plans. . . . I am afraid that the author is unaware of the vast literature on this subject in economics. . . . [They] have been extensively studied in environmental economics, [and] natural resource use management." I found that a rather surprising statement, given the moderate amount that I knew about economics, so I undertook a search to try to see what I had missed. Fortunately, I was assisted in this by an excellent review, "The role of land in economic theory," by Hubacek and van den Bergh (2002), two economists with an interest in the relation of contemporary land-use change and economics. I also asked the three economists I know best for their opinion. I first would like to state that I stand by my original analysis, but with a caveat that

I should have said before: I was referring principally to dominant mainstream economics, often called neoclassical, neowelfare, or market economics. While it is certainly true that subdisciplines of economics often do include a more explicit analysis of land and its quality (although, in my experience, rarely in biophysical units such as hectares, soil fertility, and slope, which is the point here), mainstream economics, which influences developing countries most explicitly through policies of structural adjustment and the like, essentially does not consider land in any way except for price or rent. However, I would be the first to admit that this might be open to some substantial interpretation, and I look forward to what others might say. I add finally that my perspective is focused somewhat on economic production and production functions.

I take the liberty of summarizing very briefly Hubacek and van den Bergh's excellent and detailed review. In ancient and medieval times the writers on what we would now call economics certainly focused on land, agricultural potential, and mineral wealth. This emphasis on land was displaced to some degree by the rise of mercantilists, who focused on mineral wealth (principally gold and silver, including the labor to obtain it) as a means for obtaining national power and prestige. The earliest formal economics "school," the physiocrats of eighteenth-century France, thought that land was the only real net source of wealth. They focused their interests there, including on the issue of population growth as a concern since land was finite. The early classical economist Adam Smith certainly found land critical to the production of wealth, although he also focused on the action of labor to win that wealth from the land, a view that continues through most classical economics although with increasingly less emphasis. The concept of rent, which was often the way that subsequent economists viewed land, was introduced in terms of the surplus production of good land that could be delivered to the landowner, generally a person of the upper, or at least landowning, class. The great classical economist David Ricardo focused in large part on the importance of lands of different quality in ultimately determining prices. Somewhat later Mills summarized what is probably the basic belief of Smith and Ricardo, that wealth came from the interaction of land and of labor. Mills also introduced the concept of land as an irreplaceable supplier of important amenities.

As time progressed, the function of land as a producer of wealth had less and less prominence in the writings of economists. Although Marx certainly accepted the basic classical perspective of the importance of land, he emphasized much more the role of labor—as was appropriate in his day, if for no other reason than the rise of industrialization.

The marginal revolution of Jevons, Menge, and Walras, which forms the basis of today's neoclassical economics, focused almost exclusively on human preferences and market transactions and essentially caused the movement of economics as a discipline away from any consideration of land or indeed of resources in general from any perspective except its market price (with some exceptions of course). In the words of Hubacek and van den Bergh, "Neoclassical core economic theory gave less attention to land use, generally regarding it as a production factor of relatively little importance." Later they write, "The theory of production was replaced by the theory of allocation and prices. Physical realities disappeared from the theoretical view." By 1956 Solow had removed land (which sometimes meant natural resources in general) from standard production functions, leaving only capital and labor, which has continued. There was a little activity by economists about land and resources in general in response to the publication in 1972 of *The Limits to Growth*, but most of that was to proclaim that resources were not important inasmuch as they were responsible for only 3 percent or so of GNP. The ecological economist Robert Costanza states that "mainstream economics has largely assumed away space and spatial externalities of economic agents." Thus, if we look at economics in recent times, I think that I am safe to say that economics as a discipline, at least at its core, pays relatively little attention to land as a biophysical entity, and I feel confident that there is an opening for this review of the role of land in economic development that follows. This view is strongly supported in a review by Eric Freyfogle (2003): "To the typical economist studying land . . . the vast writing on land by . . . students from the biological sciences, environmental history and environmental philosophy . . . is irrelevant."

Nevertheless, according to Hubacek and van den Bergh, specialized subfields of economics, such as regional and urban economics, met the demand for explicit spatial analysis "to some extent . . . based on an interaction with other disciplines." In the subfield of spatial economics, "land is not referred to explicitly in spatial economic studies, even when it is the focal point of attention" (31). They quote Schultz as saying, "very little has been done in applying economics to land" and that "economic analysis of land [has been] solely occupied with price signals and shadow prices (rather than historical, institutional and biophysical factors." Economist Kent Klitgaard summarizes the work that has been done as follows:

> For most neoclassical economists solutions to land use problems lie in the domain of allocative efficiency (where price equals marginal costs) that emerge when individual firms (farmers in the case of land use) try to maximize a stream of returns over time. The method is essentially the same whether one is building a factory, draining a wetland, applying pesticides, controlling for erosion etc. The economic issue tends to be to set the discounted stream of expected revenues equal to the discounted stream of costs. If the net present value is positive, go with the project. This is land use economics in a nutshell. Those costs which are not captured in the market are external to the system, and public policy should be designed to internalize these externalities by the most market-like mechanism possible.

If these statements truly reflect the general state of how economists deal with land use and land-use change, then I believe there is plenty of room for what follows. Whether subdisciplines represented by the journals *Land Economics*, *Ecological Economics*, and *Environment and Development Economics* sufficiently fill this gap is not an easy question to answer. A search of titles of all nine years published

of the latter found only three titles that I would construe as relating in any way to biophysical aspects of land. But the economic analyses in these journals, important as they may be, do not appear to me to influence a great deal the core of neoclassical economics except for an increased emphasis on environmental degradation.

A Synthesis of the Evolution of Economic Production Functions Over Time

We see in the preceding review that the source of wealth according to economists and as represented explicitly through their production functions has evolved over time from an emphasis on land to labor to capital. But in my view all of this misses the boat, for each of these factors is related to the dominant energy source for the economy at the time being considered. The energy used through the individual muscular activities of hunter-gatherers generated food directly for them and their families, the labor of artisans likewise generated items exchangeable for food and other commodities, the activities of farmers who cleared forests and planted cultivars of their choice redirected the solar energy of ecosystems to human mouths (hence leading to the importance of land as a source of wealth as emphasized by economists prior to the industrial revolution), and, obviously, the energy of water power and then fossil fuels generated the basis for wealth progressively during the nineteenth and twentieth centuries, such that the landed gentry were progressively replaced by new industrialists at the top of the financial ladder. Thus Quesney was correct for the times in which he lived when the solar energy intercepted by land generated the most wealth, Smith was correct for the times in which he lived when labor was the main way to generate wealth, and then the neoclassical economists properly but incompletely focused on capital, which was a means of using energy through its machines and ancillary equipment to do the job. But what they all missed or at least failed to emphasize was that *energy* did the work of producing wealth, whether from land, labor, or capital-assisted fossil fuels.

I believe that it is simply obvious, once you think about it, that most generally wealth is generated by the application of energy by and through human activity to the exploitation of natural resources. Nature generates the raw materials and the processes that are the basis for wealth, mostly using solar energy, and human-directed work processes, in the sense of physics, are used to bring these materials and sometimes processes into the economy as goods and services. Therefore, if I were to construct a production equation the first element I would consider would be energy (for example, in chapter 4 we show it more important in economic production functions than either capital or labor).

The objectives stated above lead to a requirement for a new type of economics, which I (and others) call *biophysical economics* (see Hall 2000; Hall et al. 2001; Hall and Klitgaard 2006). This is a system of economic thought based not on money (or even money as a proxy for scarce resources) but on laws of energy and actual material transformations and empirical assessments of these and their relation to money. It is an economics that starts with resource capacities, sustained production potential, and human demography and from that examines the actuality and potential of a region for given economic activities, both in toto and per capita. A summary of how to generate a biophysical economics model of a country is given in chapter 6. We are the first to admit that this approach is in its infancy, but we also believe that it is sufficiently developed to have important implications in application (see Hall 2000 for one example).

The Application of This Approach

My main hypothesis is simple but profound: most economic development programs in the tropics have failed to enhance the quality of life of the average person there, and one fundamental reason for the perceived failure of most economic programs is that we have not used the tools of the natural and biophysical sciences adequately to assess the probability of success prior to the initiation of development programs, to understand the constraints that biophysical reality may have on our development schemes, or to analyze the effectiveness of our investment efforts and economic analyses after the fact. Much of this failure derives from the insufficient attention paid to the biophysical attributes of the land involved or of the resources required to undertake successful development of land. As a consequence, we have depended for far too long on economic concepts and theories that, when finally tested against empirical data, have proven to be inadequate at best and immaterial at worst as tools to generate the changes for which they are offered as a guiding rationale. The principal reason these concepts fail is simply that within the human-centered perspective in which economics has evolved, most economists are simply not trained in or do not even know how to think comprehensively about the biophysical reality and constraints within which their plans will succeed or fail. Rather, they often are trained to attribute success or failure of all development to policy or human will rather than biophysical conditions or limits. (I hasten to add that a failure of natural scientists or others to understand the social milieu can be equally important, but that is not the focus here.)

When biophysical science is used to design and guide development, the conclusions are often extremely harsh and distasteful to both practitioners and the people they are trying to help. This, as well as some misleading earlier assessments supposedly negating the importance of the natural sciences (see chapter 4), have made the use of natural science and the scientific method in the development community rare. Yet the realities of good assessments using biophysical economics will not go away just because we do not like the conclusions.

The Link Between Development, Land-Use Change, and Energy Investments

Agricultural development in tropical countries usually starts with a biophysical process—land-use change—an initial removal of natural vegetation followed by a simplification of the ecosystems that were there through a transition to cropland or grazing land. Subsequently (often much later) there may be a transition from agriculturally based subsistence economies to regionally or even globally connected agroindustrial or industrial economies dependent on fossil fuels, above all oil. In many tropical countries this is a process that begins in cities or "insular" industrial centers and gradually moves toward, and eventually transforms, even remote rural regions (Grünbühel et al. 2003) in a way not too different from that described for Europe by Johan-Heinrich von Thünen, considered by many the father of spatial development thought (see chapter 28). This transition is associated with fundamental changes in society as well as the economy in terms of both monetary and biophysical flows. Changes in industrial societies include, among others, increases in the division of labor and the education it requires, rising life expectancy, and a decrease in the number of people in each household. In the last one hundred years, this has meant most fundamentally an increasing reliance on fossil fuels. In subsistence economies only a small part of the production is traded in markets. By far the largest part is produced for household consumption. Integration of subsistence economies into the regional or international market economy of industrial society generally requires that production rely to an increasing extent on inputs bought in the market. This in turn requires that products be sold in markets in order to pay for the inputs needed for production as well as for consumer goods. Thus, industrialization fundamentally also alters a society's metabolism. While material and energy inputs of agricultural societies derive mainly from agriculture and forest use—that is, local land use—industrial societies depend upon materials and energy from geological deposits that are rarely local (Weisz et al. 2001). Over the last century the production of wealth and the use of energy have tended to be extremely closely linked (Hall, Cleveland, and Kaufmann 1986; Smil 2000).

Industrialization also changes the socioeconomic function of land use, above all agriculture. While agriculture is the most important source of net energy in agricultural societies, it tends to be monetarily rather unimportant in rich industrial societies where such products may be imported easily from abroad if domestic production proves to be uneconomical (Krausmann and Haberl 2002). Contemporary development, seen as a rapid transition from agricultural subsistence economies to industrial societies, therefore implies far-reaching changes in many aspects of society-nature

relations, above all land use and fuel dependence, or a transition from a solar-based to an increasingly fossil fuel–based economy.

One might say that the principal cause of land-use change is, by definition, development, and this implies *investments of energy and money* in that development. For example, the massive deforestation and other large-scale land-use changes seen in the tropics in the past several decades are often associated with economic development, whether that development was derived from local, national, or international private or public financial resources. To my knowledge, no one has attempted to examine explicitly links between investments for development, including the economic concepts related to such investment, and rates, patterns, or causes of land-use change except for isolated case studies. In a way this is strange, because there is an enormous effort and literature on development—from the World Bank and its critics, for example—and more recently there is a growing but independent literature from the land use–change community attempting to understand the root causes of land-use change, especially tropical deforestation. Geist and Lambin (2001) and Lambin (1997) review some 152 case histories of deforestation from ninety-five earlier articles and attempt to determine what were the most important drivers in each case. These authors conclude, not surprisingly, that it is hard to point to any specific single factor as principally responsible for this deforestation, and the second paper chides the use of "simplistic" single factor causations. Rather, most commonly several factors, demographic, economic, and institutional among them, operate in tandem. This is in agreement with the earlier conclusions from the deforestation–global carbon analysis group of researchers that deforestation has many causes, although in their analyses underlying all proximate causes is long-term population growth (Richards and Flint 1994; Cornell and Hall 2001). Geist and Lambin's conclusion that "population pressures in the form of population increases due to high fertility is clearly not the major underlying driving force at the scale of a few decades when taken as a direct cause in isolation from other factors" seems to me to be disingenuous by biasing their case against the conclusions of the global carbon scientists and even their own earlier statement that the "human population dynamics (even when limited to no more than two decades), in combination with other drivers, is reported to underlie . . . 61 percent . . . of all cases of deforestation." I would say that whatever the proximate causes of deforestation, over the longer run more people, and more people per unit of developed land, are responsible for virtually all other proximate causes of continued investment in deforestation and other land-use change. To limit the consideration of population growth to no more than two decades seems most disingenuous when in most tropical regions populations and all of their effects have essentially doubled every thirty or so years during most of the last one to two centuries. In what may be our best historic data, Richards and Flint (1994) did find a very regular correlation between population density over time and forest area for Southeast Asia, although the per capita impact decreased progressively as populations increased from less than one to more than ten persons per hectare.

Curiously, the words "investments" or "development" barely appear in these two, or other, summaries of the causes of land-use change, although Geist and Lambin state that "economic development policies underlie about one third of the deforestation cases" (2001:39). In this statement, however, the authors appear to be considering only government-type investments and not private investments for logging roads or agricultural expansion. So it is not possible to conclude from these otherwise comprehensive and useful analyses the actual degree to which formal development schemes of some kind are part of the process of land-use change.

My own view is that monetary investment—that is, explicit development—is required to cause most of the land-use change in most of the examples given by Geist and Lambin with the exception of those driven by desperate poverty, war, or artisanal logging. Development investments, public or private, usually are required for and accelerate the actual land transformation, and development aid (and sometimes investments) often flow into a region because the people are in some sense poor.

One leading reason for poverty is that populations have grown up to, or beyond, the limits of the existing resource base they have access to. In other words, I believe that, despite many proximate causes of land-use change, in the long run population growth generates both the needs (lowered income from decreasing resources per capita) and the means (either their collective efforts or savings or attention from governmental or donor agencies) that are the immediate cause for the investments that lead to most land-use/land-cover change. And I think of investments as a diversion of energy—either human muscles or fossil fuels—from consumption to the exploitation of more resources with the expectation of greater economic gain in the future. Thus, development is explicitly a biophysical process from human population growth that transforms the type of plants that intercept solar energy to the increased use of fossil fuels and their derivatives such as fertilizer.

What Development Is: Monetary Investments as Energy Investments

As do most economists, I view money as something with essentially no intrinsic value but an agreed upon medium useful for facilitating exchange, that is, a generalized claim on available goods and services (Dohan 1977). Another view from a classical economics perspective is that money is a means of calibrating the value of commodities depending upon the characteristics of the stocks of nature from which they came and the human labor required. I differ in that I believe that money would have no value if it were not backed by energy: cut off the money to an economy and it would continue to function, perhaps quite differently and much more awkwardly, but with much the same wealth produced. Cut off the energy, and even if money were available the economy would quickly grind to a halt. For it is the energy behind the money that gives it real purchasing power. If more money is printed or otherwise let into society without a concomitant increase in work done, then all one gets is inflation. The Spanish found this when they trebled the amount of gold and silver in Europe by bringing it from the Americas; they thus cut money's per-unit value to one-third, for the work done in Europe by the sun, foresters, farmers, and so on had not changed (Cameron 1997). In personal terms, you trade your own time and physical work (including the energy you direct either directly or through your financial decisions) for a paycheck, with the assumption that energy will be used in other parts of the society so that goods and services will be available to give meaning to that paycheck.

If you have money (which has no intrinsic value), we as a society have agreed to use or redirect energy toward those goods and activities represented by how the holder of money (individually and collectively) chooses to spend it. If the holder of money chooses to purchase a new car, energy will be used (or had been used in the past in anticipation of the purchase) to mine iron and copper, generate plastics from coal and oil, and so on to create the final product, the automobile. If the holder of the money chooses to invest it into development, then energy (and resources in general) will be redirected toward clearing land, constructing buildings and machinery, training engineers or salespersons, or whatever is needed to make the development occur. Without energy investments, there would be no development. And, in most of the developing world, without energy investment there would be no land clearing, no construction, no planting of commercial crops. So monetary investments, energy use, and land-use change tend to be fundamentally linked through the process of development.

Most economists do not think that way. Todaro and Smith (2003) define development as traditionally used as "the capacity of a national economy, whose initial economic condition has been more or less static for a long time, to generate and sustain an annual increase in its gross national product (GNP or the similar measurement of GDP, gross domestic product) at rates of perhaps 5% to 7% or more." That index is sometimes divided by population to give per capita rates, which would account for the dilution of economic growth by population growth. They also develop the more recent view that encompasses social goals as well as economic ones, including better education, higher standards of health and nutrition, less poverty, a cleaner environment, and a richer cultural life

(Wade 2001). More generally, development (and its sometime associate foreign aid, or just aid) tends today to mean attempts to increase human welfare through monetary investments, that is, the transfer of money from richer countries to poorer countries with (normally) the aim of increasing economic activity, nominally in the poorer country. This may be done through private (non-governmental organizations; NGO) entities seeking profit or public or NGO entities seeking to aid the people in the recipient countries.

But an increasing body of literature states that it is imprecise at best and erroneous at worst to think of *any* economic activity simply in monetary or labor terms (see Sen 1983; Cleveland 1991; Hall 1992; Hall et al. 2001; Wackernagel 2004). Rather, because virtually all economic activity must be accompanied by biophysical activity, including energy flow, material transformations, and, generally, land-use transformation, it is important to consider and perhaps measure development in terms of these biophysical impacts. Thus we must always think about development from a perspective consistent with the general concepts of both biophysical economics and societal metabolism. To me, "development" means mostly changes in land and energy use over time—the transition from mostly subsistence agricultural societies to industrial production relying on fossil energy integrated into the global economy, and ultimately continued generation of new industrial infrastructure within already developed countries. Through such actions, energy-intensive machines, activities, and operations, from chainsaws to bulldozers to fertilizers to purified silicon to the construction of new buildings to the training of doctors or teachers, are transferred from the developed world to the less-developed world.

So although development obviously requires an initial investment of money, it also implies investing energy. Or perhaps it is better to put it the other way around, for it is possible to have development of agriculture by tribal shifting cultivators without money involved, but the opposite is not possible. Since most development today involves investing both money (which is how most people think about it) and energy, that perspective works well. For my purposes development will be used here to refer to any enhanced economic activity, especially in poorer countries, that occurs from deliberate public or private actions, including especially monetary movements or policies and the energy investments those entail with the end result that there are significant changes in land and/or fossil energy use. There is usually a roughly one-for-one relation between increases in GDP and energy use over time, at least since 1960 (Ko, Hall, and Lopez 1998; Tharakan, Kroeger, and Hall 2001). The actors range from individual farmers to local businesspersons to regional or national governments to, increasingly, international corporations, governmental agencies, and NGOs. The total area of land cleared in the tropics, which is roughly the less-developed world, has been summarized by Myers (1980), Detwiler and Hall (1988), The Food and Agriculture Organization (FAO 2000), and Achard et al. (2002; see chapter 24). It is not known how much of the inducement for this land clearing is from which sources (international versus national versus local or public versus private sources of investment funds). And there are other important ways to think about development. The United Nations, for example, is increasingly making a differentiation between growth—that is, quantitative expansion of an economy, as measured by GDP—and development, meaning a qualitative increase in health, education, and so on, measured by the human development index (HDI), which may or may not be associated with the expansion of the economy.

Types of Investments

I define five types, or perhaps better, five gradations or even five "flavors," of development in terms of their general usage and their impact on land use.

Land clearing for new subsistence agriculture due to growing population

The type of development with the longest history, indeed since at least the dawn of agriculture, is clearing natural vegetation to prepare land while simplifying the ecosystems to redirect the solar energy to some human-directed subsistence or economic activity, primarily growing crops or grazing animals. As human populations expanded, due in part to the energy surplus generated from this redirection of the energy flow to satisfy human wants and needs, more land is needed (or the management on the existing developed land needed to be intensified through more labor or inputs). If the energy and resources were available to clear or otherwise modify the land, more and more hectares were changed into what humans want. Until recently, the energy required for this type of development came principally from human labor, although we cannot ignore entirely the earlier solar energies used by the natural ecosystems that built the soil. More recently, the energy required has come principally from the petroleum to run chain saws and bulldozers, which has enhanced human muscle power dramatically. In the distant past this slow, inexorable process cleared enormous tracts of forests in, for example, ancient Greece, India, China, and southern Mexico (Perlin 1989; Ponting 1991; Williams 2003). Sometimes this process would occur as cycles of forest clearing followed by temporary agricultural riches on the new soils, destruction and depletion of those soils, and collapse of civilization (Tainter 1988; Perlin 1989; Ponting 1993; Diamond 2005). In several of the regions mentioned above the cycle was repeated as many as three times. In general, this process of land clearing occurred from the dawn of agriculture until 1950, at which time globally there was relatively little land left to develop that was worth developing for agriculture (Brown 1996). Since that time, increases in agricultural production have occurred principally through increasing per hectare yields through technology such as plant breeding, mostly with the assistance of energy-intensive nitrogen fertilizer.

A special case of this earlier development process is that of shifting cultivation, where agricultural production is maintained by continuously bringing new forested land into production, cropping that land for several years, and then abandoning it for one to three decades (Conklin 1961; see reviews in Hall et al. 1984 and Cornell and Hall 2001). The process is called "shifting cultivation" because the land actually being cropped at any time shifts from one geographical location to another. Shifting cultivation, at least the traditional type (along with some paddy rice and some riparian agriculture, where the soil is periodically rejuvenated by human efforts or river flooding) may be one of the few examples of truly sustainable agriculture. Most other agriculture depends upon depleting soils, fossil fuels, or both. A more recent variant is "advancing front" shifting cultivation, where traditional cultivators are pushed off their ancestral land by more or less permanent development caused by people with greater social or financial power (Myers 1998).

Where human populations continue to increase over time, a point is reached where there is no longer enough land available to support human activities in this extensive system, as the people cannot afford to leave much land fallow. When this occurs one of three things can happen: the civilization can overuse their soil and collapse (Tainter 1990), successful, more intensive nonindustrial agricultural systems can be generated, at last for a while (see Geertz 1963; Boserup 1965, 1991; Netting 1993), or, more recently, land productivity can be enhanced through the industrialization of agriculture (Odum 1973; Hall 2000). There is much argument about the degree to which each of these three factors will dominate into the future.

Economic development in response to financial investments

Our second use of the word "development," and the one used most commonly today, refers to making financial investments to increase the material standard of living of a group of people, most commonly in a poorer nation, by increasing economic activity in that country through specific projects, often of an extractive nature. This type of development, often called "economic development" or "agricultural development," is almost inevitably associated with land-use change, although these words are generally not dominant in the development literature. They tend also to be associated with an increased use of fossil fuels to undertake the actual development or to maintain the cash flow. The source of the original investment monies can be from internal resources such as taxes or loans from the nation's own banks, loans from international banks, or gifts from richer countries. From a biophysical perspective, when a bank advances a loan that money tends to be used to divert petroleum (or

other fuels, and also petroleum-derived substances such as fertilizers, as well as labor and materials) from other uses to the development project. Such a concept of development is occasionally divided into "growth," which is *quantitative* expansion of an economy, and "*qualitative* development" defined as an increase in the quality of life, for example as measured by health statistics, access to good government, freedom from fear, religious opportunities, and so on. A thoughtful, well-meaning, and extremely ambitious example of the need for both types of development (qualitative and quantitative) is the Brundtland Report, which advocated large transfers of money from the "Northern" developed world to the "Southern" less-developed world with the objective of bringing the material standard of living of the south up to that of "Europe in the 1970s" (World Commission on Environment and Development 1987).

Expansion of trade

A third type of development is the process of enhancing the economic interaction of a region with the rest of the world to develop its trade. As the less-developed world modernizes, there is a great increase in the need for foreign exchange to pay for fuels, machinery, and computers. Many less-developed nations have few sophisticated products to trade with the developed world but need foreign exchange to purchase anything from abroad (see Hall 2000). Consequently, any increase in trade generally means the increased exploitation of timber, minerals, or agricultural products, or sometimes the construction of assembly plants or fancy hotels, all of which generate land-use change, and most of which require an increase in the use of energy. What this tends to mean today energetically is that the investment money is used to purchase fossil fuels and the machines or products that use them to exploit the earth or soil to generate trade items including oil, minerals and soybeans. How it affects land use depends upon how diffuse or concentrated the resources are, and what needs to be done to access them. The terms of trade—that is, the relative prices of purchased versus exported commodities—are critically important to the developing country (see Hall, Cleveland, and Kaufmann 1986, chapter 9; Brown 1996; Hall 2000). For example, the price of coffee in 2000 was as low as any time in the previous fifty years, even after correcting for inflation, so more land has to be devoted to coffee production to pay for a ton of oil. Meanwhile agronomists continue to improve coffee production technology with the hope that it will solve all problems for coffee growers.

The consequences of relatively small investments in opening up a region to, say, the exploitation of timber for trade often has enormous secondary land-use consequences as landless farmers follow the new roads into the regions made available by the road, and in fact a number of investigators believe this to be the major mechanism leading to the conversion of forested land to agriculture (Goodland and Irwin 1974; Myers 1999).

Disaster relief

A fourth source of investment money for developing countries, which may or may not be considered under the rubric "development," is emergency aid: food, clothing, shelter, and so on brought into a region suffering from some calamity such as war, drought, earthquakes, or flooding. This is of little interest to us here other than to say how important such aid is in reducing human suffering and that such aid helps keep people and economies alive, with one result being that in whatever ways they have been affecting the land they will be able to continue to do so into the future. A critique of some aspects of this type of aid is given in Hancock (1989).

Conservation investments

Finally, in recent years the concept of development has been expanded to include direct transfer of funds from conservation organizations into poorer countries to enhance conservation objectives. In contrast to the previous ones, this type of development tends to keep land in its natural state, although it may simply displace development activities to some other location. Two important ones come to mind: the 1990 Dutch government purchase of $33 million of outstanding Costa Rican debt in response for agreements to protect nature (these are called "debt for nature swaps"), and the ongoing purchase of tropical forestland by industrial countries as part of "carbon offset" programs (Niles et al. 2002).

Most of these five development activities are associated with land-use change, both directly and indirectly: directly through changing the nature of the land cover on the site that is being developed, and indirectly through a plethora of activities including the mining of materials such as timber, limestone, and iron for buildings to be constructed on that site; the development of agriculture to support whatever people will then move to the developed site; the extraction of oil and other fuels to allow all of these activities; and so on. This concept is of course the basis for the idea of the "ecological footprint" (Wackernagel 2004), and that approach, while not applied explicitly to development as far as I know, probably gives us the best ideas as to how much land is required in different cultures per new person added. Probably land use occurs both directly and indirectly from all of these types of development with the exception of rebuilding an existing city, wherein only the offsite activities affect land-use change. Since most development occurs in order to, in some way, serve people, in some ultimate sense it is population growth (and increasing per capita affluence) that is behind most development, whether it is directly to get a place to live or to grow food to eat, or indirectly to produce more food or timber for the growing population of a distant city. For example, Hall et al. (1995) estimated the total amount of land and other resources that would be required to support each new American born in the 1990s over his or her lifetime. The entire issue is more complex of course and is probably best thought of using the IPAT equation: Impact = population number times per capita impact times some technology factor. But an in-depth consideration of these issues is beyond the present discussion.

A Brief History of Development Investments

"Investments" means the diversion of available effort or money, and the resources it represents, from immediate consumption to the construction of some kind of infrastructure or program that has the likelihood of returning additional money or resources in the future. The concept of investment for development of land is probably as old as civilization itself, and certainly early Greek and Roman governments spent considerable portions of their revenue to encourage forest cutting, agricultural production, and so on (Cameron 1997). In the Western world, the concept of investment was tremendously constrained by the biblical injunction against usury and the concept of Jubilee—after every fifty years, all debts were cancelled and land and property returned to their original owners. It was not until St. Augustine discriminated between usury, which was a sin, and interest, which was the time value of money, that real investments were possible. This opened the possibilities for investment banking and the explosion of all sorts of human economic and cultural activities that we associate with the Renaissance, as well as, of course, the considerable land-use change induced with those activities. Most important was the investment activities of the Medici family of Florence and the Fugger family in Germany. We have no large-scale land-use map from that time, but it certainly would seem that these activities accelerated deforestation and land-use change in Europe (Perlin 1989; Ponting 1993). For the first time money itself could be used as a tool to generate other money, and that was mostly through encouraging resource exploitation. As the concept of mercantilism developed, those involved were probably increasingly insulated from the fact that most of the wealth was gained through extraction or exploitation of the earth, including for most cash crops. Instead, the transactions themselves increasingly became the focus of these early investments.

Most of these early investments were by kings or nobility to enable war or encourage the further development of armies and war machines, often with the expectation of booty, or to develop or maintain administrative infrastructure and pay for the often brutal training of labor that would allow a colonial country to extract more resources and hence money from the colonized country. Thus it can hardly be said that Spain's or England's investments in oceangoing fleets or the development of mining facilities in Bolivia or Rhodesia had the

interests of the people of those countries at heart, so it is better to just consider these investments as exploitation for the benefit of the colonial country. The implications of these past investments on land use are often enormous. For example, the tremendous erosion of ancient lake-bottom soils over millions of hectares near Tarija, Bolivia, is widely thought to be a consequence of the removal of the forest cover there for pit props for the silver mines at Potosi, hundreds of miles away. More generally, investments in mines for production of coinage or military apparatus resulted in enormous deforestation in, for example, Crete, the Peloponnesian Peninsula of Greece, England, and Sweden (Perlin 1989). The resultant energy crisis in Sweden led to the emigration of tens of thousands of Swedes to the United States and subsequent deforestation of the American Midwest.

Development for the Nominal Benefit of the Receiving Nation

The modern concept of developmental aid that is intended to benefit principally the recipient country was born following World War II with the great success of the Marshall Plan that rebuilt Germany and other European countries and encouraged their development as nonmilitaristic democracies. This model was in response to the fact that the reparations that Germany had to pay to France and England following World War I impoverished a proud people, led to an enormous devaluation of the German mark (so that the reparations could be paid more easily—but simultaneously wiping out everyone's savings), and, in the opinion of many, set up the conditions for the rise of Nazism. In this case, the development funds and the international banking structures engendered by the Marshall Plan were critical to rebuilding a shattered Europe. Probably the impact on land use was not large, since the land had been cleared for centuries and subject to many previous destructive wars.

A second factor encouraging an increase in development aid during the twentieth century was the general dismantling of the British and other European colonial systems following World War II. Many of the colonial administrators had developed affection and concern for those people they had been administering. They thought it critical to invest in training the local people, and the development of their needed infrastructure, so that the country would not fall apart when the colonial country left or, more cynically, so that they could continue extracting resources. This training was done reasonably well, for example, by England when leaving India, but in other regions, notoriously Belgium in the Congo, it was not done at all and the only infrastructure constructed was for the purpose of brutal exploitation of people and resources, including rubber and ivory from elephants (Ewans 2002). The basic idea of development aid for modernization spread throughout other non-colonial but relatively wealthy nations, and the leading aid-providing nations generally have been northern European and, at least until recently, the United States. Meanwhile religious and other nongovernmental organizations (NGOs) for development were created and expanded, and supplied aid in various forms.

International development aid as a major economic entity was greatly accelerated during the Cold War, when it was observed that (apparently) the forced "savings" and hence investments of the Soviet Union resulted in a tremendous growth in that country's GDP. The feeling among many in the Kennedy and Johnson administrations was that if the United States did not enhance their economic well-being, many third world nations would look to the Soviet Union (or their communist economic model) for help (Easterly 2002). Thus, the provision of aid generally was associated with meeting other national objectives of the suppliers. This perspective of the benefits flowing to the supplier of the money has been enhanced by the fact that "strings" were often added to aid packages requiring that the money be spent in the country supplying the aid. Hence, the real aid went from the governments of the developed countries to their own tractor, fertilizer, and machinery companies, and that pattern has tended to continue. For example, Costa Rica received about $1 billion of development aid from the United States from 1950 to 1998, when it was discontinued, but Costa Rica now purchases about $1 billion of trade items from the United States *each year* (Hall et al. 2000).

A new issue in the development field is the sustainability of that development. The annual publications of the World Bank, for example, use the words "sustainable development" frequently. What sustainability really means, though, is often confusing. Goodland and Daly (1996) have decreased some of that confusion by pointing out that what is called sustainable depends entirely upon the group doing the naming. "Sustainable" can mean social, economic, or environmental (including the resource base) continuation, and one or another of these types of sustainability is often bought at the expense of one or more of the other types. In this chapter we are principally interested in sustainability as the maintenance of the resource base upon which an economy might be maintained.

A Review of Models of Development: The Use and Non-use of Science

As the importance of the concept of development increased from the 1950s through about 1990, Western countries and their economists tended to base their ideas and theories as to *how* to enhance the development process in less-developed countries on some relatively abstract economic principle or theory. Fortunately or not, there generally seems to be someone in charge in the developing countries who will ally themselves with the dominant theories or philosophies of development economists. An important issue is that the ideas that are applied to the developing world tend to come from the general economic and political milieu of the developed countries that supply the aid, so that Sweden's rationales might be different from that of the United States. Thus, if we are to understand land use and other activities that have taken place in the developing world as a consequence of development monies, we also have to understand what has been going on intellectually in the economic circles of the developed world.

The neoclassical or neoliberal model

As also stated in chapter 1, the most fundamental factor that has influenced the pattern and process of development aid in the past three or so decades has been the ascendancy, indeed intellectual

---

Table 2.1. Assumptions of the neoclassical model

The following are some standard assumptions of neoclassical economics that are made so that economic models are workable (that is, conceptually and analytically tractable). To my knowledge, few or none of them have been tested empirically or comprehensively, especially within a developmental context.

Perfect markets exist, which implies:
  Buyers and sellers (agents) have perfect information about the present and future;
  There is perfect homogeneity and divisibility of goods produced;
  There is totally free entry into the markets by any agent;
  There is an infinite number of agents on both the supply and the demand side

Economic agents maximize utility. Agents are rational, which means they make decisions only by the criteria of maximizing their monetary utility and profits.

If there are occasionally some external effects in production and/or consumption,
  they can always be identified and internalized.

The markets deal with factors of production that are:
  fully employed
  perfectly mobile from one sector to another
  perfectly reactive to marginal changes in the economy

Markets mechanistically and automatically adjust to changes in economic conditions, and thus reversibility is always possible.

(From Hall 1990, with thanks to Andrea Baranzini, Department of Economics, University of Geneva. See also chapter 3.)

---

dominance, of neoclassical economics (NCE), also known, more or less according to how it was applied, as free market economics, monetarism, or neoliberalism. This has become the dominant social and economic paradigm for the developed world's economies. In many cases the premises of this model are put forth as more or less indistinguishable from democracy even though the two concepts are completely distinct entities. For example, "free markets" are often mentioned in conjunction with "freedom" although each is a quite independent entity. Neoclassical principles are often put forth as if it were proven beyond doubt that the neoliberal principles ultimately generate economic benefits for all concerned, although data to support that perspective seems

painfully thin, and also is contradicted by many other studies as partially developed below.

Explicit criticisms of the neoclassical model include Hall et al. (2001; see chapter 4,). I might also point out that the model is based on the assumptions given in table 2.1. The reader can judge whether these assumptions are routinely met in any given situation.

In the United States, the term *liberal* means mostly socially liberal, vaguely leftish. In other parts of the world, such as Europe and Argentina, it means "liberal mercantilism," or free market and vaguely rightist, deriving its meaning from earlier times when liberal denoted the interests of the mercantile class versus those of the king, who may have had much less interest than businessmen in a large amount of trade beyond the borders of his country. The concepts associated with the second definition of liberal have existed for many decades or centuries and were of interest to Ricardo and other early economists. They have been formalized and codified especially by the economics department of the University of Chicago under the leadership and influence of Milton Friedman and others (Friedman 1972; Friedman and Friedman 1980). Curiously, the term *liberal* has not been especially associated with the relatively pro-business American Republican party. Such issues about "rightist" and leftist" economic policy are probably most important from our perspective for determining the allocation of land, energy, and environmental resources among socioeconomic groups, since all economic decisions are ultimately manifest in how and to what degree resources are exploited, and who incurs the benefits and costs of such policies.

The possible reasons for the political ascendancy of free marketism and, more generally, neoclassical economics were given in the introduction to this section. Whatever the reason, they are the dominant economic force and philosophy in the world now and the cynic might say that this is indeed the environment in which economics takes place. In addition, neoclassical economics was often thrust upon, for example, Latin American economies because of the increasing foreign debts of many of those nations. In effect, the options given for many countries were either to go into default, with serious repercussion on economies or trade, or accept the neoliberal policies that were often thrust upon them. This was most generally put forth in a package that the International Monetary Fund (IMF), among others, called "structural adjustment," which meant reducing government spending, decreasing trade barriers, and enhancing export crops.

The explicit use of this approach through the 1980s and 1990s, especially by development banks, has been formalized in the "Washington consensus" or "pillars of structural adjustment" ("Washington consensus" is a term coined in 1990 by John Williamson of the Institute for International Economics; *Economist* 2003), which, despite some acute criticisms, has been used explicitly to guide development in, for example, much of Latin America and the Philippines. There were ten points to the "consensus": fiscal discipline, redirection of public expenditure (toward private activities), tax reform, competitive exchange rates, secure property rights, deregulation, trade liberalization, privatization, elimination of barriers to foreign direct investment, and financial liberalization. Now, of course, how each of these ten concepts is actualized and implemented leaves a lot of latitude to the practitioner, but it is safe to say that in general the focus was toward reducing government, increasing privatization, increasing access to and by external markets, and generally implementing and consolidating the basic concepts and doctrines of neoclassical economics. To my knowledge, the efficacy of these ten points has never been tested in a comprehensive and scientific manner, and the many problems associated with it are identified even in the supportive article in the *Economist*.

In addition, of course, what objectives do we wish to pursue and do these "pillars" lead to them? One of the leading critics of simply increasing growth for its own sake has been economics Nobel Laureate A. Sen, who stated clearly, "I believe the real limita- tions of traditional development economics arose not from the choice of means to the end of economic growth, but in the insufficient recognition that economic growth was no more than a means to some other objectives. . . . Ultimately, the process of economic development has to be concerned with what people can or cannot do, e.g. whether they can live long, escape avoidable morbidity, be well nourished, be able to read and write and communicate, take part in literary and scientific pursuits, and so forth. It has to do, in Marx's words, with 'replacing the domination of circumstances and chance over individuals by the domination of individuals over chance and circumstances'" (Sen 1983).

Such policies have many other consequences beyond those they are supposed to encourage. In some cases there were extremely large impacts on land use as a result of neoliberal development policies—for example, to encourage exports. In Costa Rica, the central government, the World Bank, and the United States Agency for International Development (USAID) encouraged various exports to increase the production of commodities of value in international commerce and, incidentally, to insure interest flows based on outstanding debt to the banks (Annis 1990; Hansen-Kuhn 1993). Chief among these activities was the investment of some $20–30 million (in 1970 dollars) in forest clearing to produce more pastures. This was a major contributor to the deforestation of Costa Rica, where undisturbed forests went from 86 percent of the land area in 1940 to 17 percent in 1983. The increase in pasture alone was from about 12 percent of the national area in 1950, when the investment program was started, to about 37 percent in 1984, roughly when the program was discontinued (Sanchez-Azofeifa 2000). Meanwhile existing pastureland in dry Guanacaste province, the classic center of cattle raising, was returning to dry forest because there was little other economic or social incentive to raise cattle. In other words, deforestation for new pastures was encouraged while other pasture areas were being abandoned. This is a particularly graphic example of how investment policies imposed from outside encouraged land-use change. Interestingly, because cattle raising is land intensive but less energy intensive than raising most crops, this policy did not increase energy requirements as much as did other investment strategies. Nevertheless, the limits of this approach appear to have been reached for Costa Rica and most professional pasture analysts are recommending fertilizer and other input-intensive strategies for the future (see Ibrahim, Abarca, and Flores 2000). Most sectors of the economy, among them the production of domestic grains and export crops such as coffee and bananas, tourism and other services, manufacturing, transportation, waste control, and so on, were quite dependent upon imported energy and petrochemicals. The general economy produced about $70 (in 1985 dollars) of economic activity per gigajoule of energy. This ratio essentially did not change from 1970 to 1995 (Hall 2000).

Such structural adjustment programs were often instituted without a "level playing field," as, for example, Costa Rica and the Philippines were required to reduce their trade barriers for imported corn and reduce their subsidies to their own corn farmers while the United States and Europe were subsidizing their own corn and other agricultural production with many hundreds of billions of dollars (see Kroeger and Montanye 2000; Myers 1998).

It is not clear at all that these approaches generally or perhaps even ever achieved their stated objectives of helping the target countries and especially the poor of those countries. As of this writing, there were especially adverse reactions of poorer people to these and related policies in Bolivia, which resulted in its president's having to seek asylum in the United States. In a commentary in the prestigious *Los Angeles Times* of October 19, 2003, Keith Slack of the NGO Oxfam wrote,

But the issues raised by Bolivia's "gas war" will not go away; they will only become more important throughout the region as plans to further liberalize trade and investment move inexorably forward. Bolivia is a stark illustration of the damage caused by unchecked economic liberalization in Latin America. In the mid-1980s, at the behest of the International Money Fund, Bolivia slashed its public payroll and opened up its natural resource sectors, the traditional basis of the country's economy, to foreign investment. Inflation, which had once run as high as 24,000%, plummeted and economic growth surged as state-owned enterprises were privatized. But Bolivia's poor, indigenous peoples were left behind. Profits from the oil, gas, and mining sectors either exited the country or ended up in the pockets of its minority white elites. Bolivia's experience mirrors that of Peru, Ecuador, and Colombia. According to many analysts such as Slack, a number of urgent changes must be made in how South America manages its natural resources in order to reverse the dangerous trend toward civil strife and state instability in the region. International agencies must not force countries like Bolivia to open their resource sectors to foreign investment in exchange for aid. They should instead help governments better manage the social and environmental effects these investments have on poor, native populations.

Even Paul Samuelson, generally credited as one of the most consistent and erudite defendants of the neoclassical paradigm, has recently questioned whether in fact globalization and free trade are necessarily in the interests of all involved (Samuelson 2004).

Science and development models

The rationale, or at least the model, of development used by the development agencies often seems surreal to many natural scientists. For some reason when humans enter the picture being analyzed or considered it seems that often the scientific method is left behind. One might think that the resource opportunities might be examined, the objectives for development stated explicitly, concepts and approaches devised to reach those objectives generated, and then, most important, the actual subsequent economic experience of the region be examined against the objectives, and the results subject to large amounts of publication, argument, and thought. If the objectives were met then one might have at least some sense that the development plan worked. This might be done for a series of areas where the development approach had been tried and some statistics applied to see how well the approach worked. While this is not sufficient to say that a given plan is scientifically sound, it is certainly a good start. For example, Dawn Montanye (1998) took the development plan for Costa Rica devised by the USAID, rephrased its objectives as hypotheses, and tested the hypotheses to see whether the structural adjustment policies imposed upon Costa Rica achieved them. She found that for the most part they did not, and that in addition the policies generated a series of other environmental and social problems not foreseen in the documents presented before the implementation of their plan. This kind of explicit scientific assessment of development models is all too rare.

While this particular exercise demonstrated neither that the overall intervention was successful not (quite) the contrary, it certainly did demonstrate what objectives were not met and which components of the development plan clearly did not work, an important issue when the interventions are generally viewed as onerous by those effected.

One obvious requirement for development models in the future should be that their goals be stated explicitly as testable hypotheses, and then that the results of the policies should be examined from the perspective of these hypotheses. Although we have heard on occasion from economists that such models are surrounded by complex parameters and that we might not expect them to be so simply tested, if they are not necessarily expected to work, why then should we use them for policy? Given our interest here in land-use change, each of those analyses should include hypotheses about how land cover and land use are affected by the policies.

Critiques from development economists themselves

We have two other excellent opportunities to examine the effectiveness of developmental models because of two recent and important books on development written by economists who have had a great deal of experience with development from positions of extreme involvement and decision-making importance. These books are by William Easterly and Joseph Stiglitz. Easterly (2001), reviewing past models of development, states that the "Domar" growth model remains the "most widely applied growth model in economic history." Curiously, Domar derived this model originally as part of an esoteric debate about the business cycle, and it was not intended to have anything to do with development. The version used in development states that "GDP growth will be proportional to the share of investment spending in GDP" (often equated to investments in machines). Evsey Domar himself later disavowed any faith in his model as used for investment planning, but development economists took ahold of that model, added in foreign aid investment spending to savings, and renamed it the Harrod-Domar model (we present the details of this model, as well as other well-known development models, in chapter 3). That model, like many others, has taken on a life of its own and has been used again and again as a guide to development. Easterly noted that nobody had checked Domar's model "against actual experience" (in itself a surprising admission by an economist and a further justification of the previous paragraph), but then he undertook that test himself by examining savings rate and subsequent growth for eighty-eight less-developed nations over thirty years. He found that "there was no statistical association between growth in one four year period and investment in the previous four year period" with the possible exception of four countries (Hong Kong, Malta, Morocco, and Tunisia). Hence, we find by this development economist's own assessment the most generally used model for development had been completely untested, and when in fact he did test it, it generally failed to predict the growth that actually took place. This is a classic case of what economists call "mixed evidence." Yet it had been the basis of development policy, the investment of untold billions of dollars, and almost unimaginable impacts on people, land use, and resources for decades.

In a review of Easterly's book, Cassidy (2002a) summarizes results of similar analyses by Boone, who found no relation between aid and economic growth, although a more sophisticated later analysis by Burnside and Dollar (2000) found that when corrections were made for an "index of economic management" there was some small correlation of aid and growth. Easterly also reviews the Rostow model, which included five stages, including a "takeoff" term, and is related to the Domar model. However, even Rostow had to admit that his model could explain at most three of the fifteen nations to which it was applied, and other analysts found an even lower predictability. Finally, Easterly reviews the Solow model, the neoclassical workhorse in which development is a function of technical innovation. That model also had few empirical confirmations to recommend it, something that does not surprise me given that the model does not include the energy required to make the technical innovations work! So one wonders where the science of development is. Billions of dollars have been spent on attempts to increase economic prosperity without any particular empirical evidence that such investments achieve their objectives, at least according to Easterly. But almost certainly most of these money flows affected resource and land use in one way or another.

Part of the reason that development appears to generate the desired economic outcome only rarely is that the economic models used are based only on money, and not on the biophysical reality that gives (or does not give) the money meaning (Hall et al. 2001). For example, U.S. development aid to the Costa Rican banana industry encouraged the expansion of banana plantations (with accompanied deforestation)—and the increased reliance of that industry on industrial inputs from the developed countries. The net effect was that for every dollar's worth of bananas sold at dockside, about fifty cents' worth of industrial inputs are required, greatly decreasing the profitability to Costa Rica. Meanwhile, USAID was also encouraging the growth of the Ecuadorian banana industry, so that when the newly encouraged Costa Rican bananas reached the market they found the market more or less flooded with Ecuadorian bananas.

There is also some earlier economic literature that explicitly criticizes developmental concepts as a road to helping the poor countries. One example is the so-called Prebish-Singer thesis, which states that a country's orientation toward primary product exports such as raw materials or agricultural products (which most developing countries have) will result in degrading terms of trade over time, which will in turn result in the long-term transfer of income from poorer to richer countries (Prebish 1950; Singer 1950). This is because the demand for, say, bananas will saturate relative quickly in the richer, lower-population-growth countries (for we can eat only so many bananas) while the demand for industrial consumer goods by the poor, aspiring countries with higher population growth is much larger. But these ideas are rarely if ever considered by contemporary development economists, even if they seem to be verified (e.g., for coffee and bananas in Hall 2000).

Increased Trade and Globalization

Most development or international economic policy seems to be guided by a faith in some kind of economic ideology, which seems to take the place of a scientifically supported concept. Most notably, there is today a very strong sense that "free market" and other neoliberal approaches to development and to economies in general will generate greater growth of economies and in general more economic benefits to all affected (see Bhagwati 2004). I am unaware of any comprehensive assessment of many countries over long time periods, especially during changing ideologies, to see if this is true as a rule. On the other hand, a number of quite pungent analyses of development failures also are available from more of a social and conventional economic perspective (see, for example, Bello, Kinley, and Elinson 1982; Annis 1990; Hanson-Kuhn 1993; Bello 1994; Collins and Lear 1995; Gray 1998; MacEwan 1999; see review in Kroeger and Montanye 2000). A complete assessment of the benefits and costs of this trade liberalization is beyond the scope of this chapter, but it is clear that the benefits are not always as forthcoming as once promised. Any truth-seeking person who believes in the efficiency of increased trade and globalization should spend some time with these publications.

The neoliberal development models depend on the concept of the supposed unalloyed benefits that would flow from increasing trade more or less anywhere and everywhere. This concept stems from, originally, the eighteenth-century economist Ricardo's concept of "comparative advantage," meaning that each region should specialize in the production of whatever products that its climate, natural resources, labor supply, or whatever makes it especially well suited for. Ricardo, a classical economist, thought this concept should be used only for particular circumstances and should not include the free flow of the investment capital, although these ideas seem to be forgotten today. The concept has had enormous encouragement in the past three decades from the general increase in the internationalization of corporations and, more generally, international trade. This "comparative advantage" concept has been taken to its logical extreme in contemporary neoliberal economics, where the idea is to reduce or eliminate barriers to trade wherever they may be. In principle, this is supposed to benefit all concerned, although there may be an initial period of "adjustment" as, for example, Mexican or Costa Rican farmers learn that they cannot compete against (subsidized) grain

from the United States. Meanwhile the implications of the expansion of international trade on land use remain as large, complex, and various as the changes in trade itself. One thing is clear, however: as the international economy itself has expanded, the use of resources and changes in land use have expanded more or less in proportion to them (see Richards and Flint 1994; Ko, Hall, and Lopez 1998; Tharakan, Kroeger, and Hall 2001).

More recent criticism of the issue of globalization, or at least of what it has become in the hands of its most powerful actors, has come from within the discipline of development economics itself. Joseph Stiglitz is a professor of economics at Columbia University, a Nobel Prize winner in economics, and someone with a great deal of experience in international finance. He was, for example, one of President Bill Clinton's chief economists and was also chief economist at the World Bank in the late 1990s. In the words of one reviewer (Cassidy 2001b), "According to Stiglitz, the rich countries have hijacked globalization, using as weapons the I.M.F., the world trade organization, and other international bodies that are supposed to act in the interests of all countries. These institutions 'all too often are closely aligned with the commercial and financial interests of those in the advanced industrial countries . . . to benefit the few at the expense of the poor.' The governments of the rich countries have pushed developing nations to open their borders to computers and banking services but continued to protect their own farmers and textile workers from the cheap food and clothes that the poor countries produce."

In Stiglitz's own words, "The critics of globalization accuse Western countries of hypocrisy, and the critics are right." Stiglitz also credits the demonstrators against the World Bank in Prague, Seattle, Washington, and Genoa as being important agents in bringing the attention of the world to the bad things generated by globalization. Another review of Stiglitz's book states that Stiglitz "painted a picture [of] how rampant arrogance, simplistic nostrums and disdain for foreign political reality doomed globalization. He argues that in the hands of the Washington brain trust, globalization became a neoimperialist force that left hundreds of millions of people worse off in 2000 than they were in 1990."

Thus we find in the writings of development economists themselves a rather poor track record for each of the major economic models of development that have been put forth, including at least some important aspects of the "free market" neoliberal model that is currently in favor. In fact, there are many economists, including Stiglitz and Easterly, but also the Nobel Prize winner Sen and many others, who are very critical of the mindless application of neoliberal or other "modern" economic approaches. But in my opinion although the thoughts of these economists are important and welcome they do not go nearly far enough, and the reason is that what needs to be done is to *not* start from *any* economic model and then, as these critics argue, tinker with the model to deal with the perceived problems. Rather, what is needed is to start anew from a biophysical perspective, examine the possibilities, the strengths and weaknesses of the landscape itself, and then develop the possible economics from that base.

For example, if one is considering the development of some export crop, it is critical to understand what the potential production of that crop is based on biophysical limitations and then examine what inputs from the industrial world would be required to make that crop yield sufficiently for it to be economically viable, and what would be the impact of those actions on other resources of the region, for example if forests had to be cut or if chemicals leached from the operations were to impact local fisheries. One might also ask whether the land is better used for production of domestic or export crops from many perspectives. Then an extremely important issue is to ask the people affected themselves what they perceive to be issues (if any) defining their own poverty, and what steps they might think useful for moving away from that poverty. At this point it is quite reasonable to assess the monetary costs and gains from all aspects of this operation, and that might be one important aspect of the assessment. In other words, I have no argument with using economic assessments, and in fact believe it critical. But that is very different from using the concept that there should be no interference with

using market criteria or open markets alone to guide all decisions, or that leaving all decisions to the market will negate the importance of the other information needed to understand and respond to the problems of poverty (or anything else). While it is not possible to say at this time that a perfect, or even sufficient biophysical model exists, a guide to actually undertaking a biophysical analysis for a region or a nation is presented in chapter 6, and a comprehensive analysis of an entire country (Costa Rica) using the biophysical approach is found in Hall (2000) and the summary of that in chapter 9.

How Important Are Rich Natural Resources for Successful Development?

If economic policies by themselves are not clearly successful in generating economic development, then what is? It would seem obvious that countries with a rich endowment of natural resources should be the best candidates for development, but the reality is far more complex. Of course, the United States is so wealthy largely because of its tremendous initial endowment of soil, water, timber, fish, coal, oil, and so on, especially when considered on a per capita basis. But the results of such an assessment are not as clear for much of the world. Japan and South Korea are resource-poor countries that are models of successful development, although both are huge importers of energy, timber, and food from the rest of the world. There are some arguments that having large quantities of natural resources or effective international trade actually *decreases* the ability to develop successfully (see Fishman 2002). The arguments are fundamentally that overreliance on resource extraction industries generates disincentives to develop other aspects of the economy and invites corruption, military adventurism, and interventions from powerful foreign companies that may or may not have the interest of the local population as a goal. For example, Nigeria and Ecuador have large oil resources, but the economic development in each country is rather minimal, at least in terms of improving the life of the average citizen in the region where the oil is being exploited. Additionally the indigenous people living in the Niger River delta and the Ecuadorian

Amazon have suffered enormously from the environmental effects of spilled oil and other aspects of the oil development, but have gained little from the enormous proceeds of selling the oil. In each of these examples, there are also important questions about external multinational companies coming in, exploiting the oil, and then departing with most of the money. There are in addition political issues about the distribution of what relatively little money is left behind between the provinces with the oil and the provinces with the most political power.

There are other studies that seem to indicate that rich natural resources (especially mineral wealth) are not necessarily the blessing one would think. According to a review by Izursa and Tilley (2005), resource-rich (compared to resource-poor) countries did more poorly economically (Sachs and Warner 1997); had per capita incomes that grew two to three times slower between 1960 and 1990 (Auty 1997, 1998); had stunted manufacturing sectors (Auty and Mikesell 1999); have a less diversified economy (Duncan 1993); are more prone to political problems and experience a slower growth in technical skills (Wood and Berge 1997); suffer higher levels of corruption (Karl 1997); and have a higher degree of inequality (Leamer et al. 1998). Of course, without these resources, it is unlikely that any country would be growing economically.

In an excellent report undertaken by the director of the World Bank's research arm, the history of a nation, in terms of its inability to avoid civil war or to develop economically, was highly correlated with the availability or not of valuable resources that could be exploited and exported relatively easily by insurgent groups, providing a source of money for arms and armies (Collier and Hoeffler 2002). Examples include diamonds and oil that were used to finance Jonas Savimbi's decades-long but inconclusive guerrilla insurgency, and the rich natural resources of Zaire that were used to finance various insurgencies.

But there are counterexamples to that pattern too. Where you have relatively good government, that is, with relatively little corruption and one that is focused on meeting the needs of the people and dedicated to a relatively equitable distribution of wealth, large endowments of natural resources

can lead to tremendous economic development that is relatively widely shared. For example, the huge oil and gas resources of Malaysia, again especially as expressed on a per capita basis, have been very important in the economic development of that country, under the remarkable leadership of Muhathir Mohamad in the 1990s. Another interesting aspect of Mohamad is his strong critique of unfettered free markets and "dogmas of global capitalism," and his insistence on the importance of the role of government (Mohamad 1998). Likewise, Ko (chapter 7) reviews the importance of good cooperation between government and private industry in the successful development of Korea. Mexico, despite some very large incidents of corruption, has also developed reasonably well, based in large part on oil resources. In all three countries there remains a large difference between rich and poor, and the development has had very large impacts on land cover and water quality, but it also seems that there have been serious efforts to use the oil revenues for national development and affordable health services that reach a large portion of the poor. Thus, a huge caveat is that the resources are important to general economic development only in the presence of good government committed to relatively equitable use of the proceeds of the sale or use of the resources and political stability. Both of these tend to be frequently in short supply in the developing world.

Of course, there are other important resources that are not readily sold on international markets, such as good-quality soil and water. These are often critically useful for development, and their absence often paralyzes it, for the first thing a country must do is feed its people. But even good agricultural land can lead to mischief as well as well-being, as is the case for heroin poppies in Afghanistan or Cambodia, or coca leaves in Columbia. Each of these has fed extremely repressive and bloody wars.

Thus the answer to the question about the importance of resources, good government, or any other factor is not easy or simplistic, and, borrowing from Jared Diamond, perhaps the way to think about the requirements for development is through the "Anna Karenina principle." This concept is named after the first line in Leo Tolstoy's great novel, which states that all good marriages are good in the same way, but that each bad marriage is bad in its own unique way. In other words, all good marriages have a list of characteristics that must be met: fidelity or mutual acceptance of something else, attraction between mates, reasonable financial security, mutual respect, and so on. A bad marriage misses at least one of these, and that can happen in many ways. Likewise, we can say that successful developments all have some similar characteristics including stable, relatively incorrupt political and financial institutions; a development plan that makes sense; reasonably equitable distribution of the fruits of economic activity, including the development; a sustainable resource base for that development; and a means by which individuals are given incentives to contribute to the success of the investments. If a country does not have an adequate energy base, then it must have something to trade for the needed energy. Thus, one of the most critical components of this "good marriage" that leads to successful development is that it be reasonably sustainable physically.

The Critical Issue of Population

This book will come back again and again to the critical importance of the biophysical element population growth, an issue that continuous to resurface despite the efforts of many in the United States and elsewhere to suppress its importance. Birdsall, Kelley, and Sinding (2001) have undertaken a review of the issue of population and economic welfare and concluded that population is almost always extremely important in issues of development and economic activity, despite the efforts of many to suppress this issue.

For example, despite large efforts by outside aid communities to increase Costa Rican per capita wealth it has been nearly constant for thirty years. The basic reason appears to be that the human population growth, increasing at nearly 3 percent per year, is similar to the rate of the increase in the use of the energy that generates new GDP. When we examined many developing countries we have found an increase in per capita wealth only where energy use per capita has exceeded population growth, in for example Korea and Malaysia

(Ko, Hall, and Lemus 1998; Tharakan, Kroeger, and Hall 2001). Because the generation of wealth is so closely correlated with the use of energy in countries such as Costa Rica, where population growth has equaled or exceeded energy growth empirically people have not become more wealthy, as of necessity all of the energy growth is spread out among the increased number of people. Of course, arguments can and have been made that somehow more people will lead to more wealth production, but we find this unconvincing for most modern less-developed (and other) countries. I believe that, for example, the work of Boserup and her allies has been extremely misleading. She states, with rather limited empirical evidence, that "the acceleration of population growth in the Third World revived old Malthusian fears. We have seen, however, that in many earlier periods, the response to population growth was intensification of land use, and this experience was repeated in recent years" (Boserup 1981:200). Her implication is clearly that one need not worry much about population growth, inasmuch as somehow food production per hectare can always be increased. While in fact this has often happened, the increase since about 1950 is almost always associated with an increase of agro-inputs such as fertilizers and pesticides, and it is the need for foreign exchange for these products that is a large component of increasing debt and all the misery that entails (see chapters 5 and 6). Had the industrialization of agriculture proceeded (as it would have) and populations remained stable, I believe that those people would be much better off. It is my opinion that ideas like Boserup's have been a very important reason that many developing countries remain poor. I recognize that there are other opinions, but I need to see much better biophysical analysis than I have to accept them. In chapter 12, Rudriksha Rai explicitly tests the Boserup hypothesis for Nepal.

Conclusion

I conclude that my first hypothesis—that most economic development programs in the tropics have failed, and have done so because in large part because we have not used the tools of the natural and biophysical sciences adequately—is supported by most assessments of the social critics of development aid, my own detailed analysis of the literature, specific case histories, and important development economists themselves. If there is an extensive countervailing empirical base, I have not been able to find it, nor is it mentioned in the extensive literature used in this paper. It is time to rethink the concept of investments in development, how we use economics in that process, and how we can develop a better system of economics for development starting with a biophysical basis.

Nevertheless, these investments affect land and resource use profoundly, and although land-use change has many causes, nearly all of them can be related to the concept of investment. Yet land-use analysts rarely, if ever, think about investment as a cause of land use change, and people in the international development agencies certainly do not think often about the land-use change or enhanced requirements for energy that are occasioned by their investments or their policies. This chapter has begun an analysis of how land-use change is related to investments, how both are related to increasing use of nonrenewable resources, how the investment community has tended to model the supposed effects of investments, and how in at least one country very large investments were unable to improve the material standard of living of the people because population growth, interacting with limited high-quality land, imposed a severe constraint on efforts to increase per capita wealth (see also Birdsall, Kelley, and Sinding 2001). Although there is plenty of land per capita in Costa Rica (more than one hectare per person), there is not nearly enough good land to feed even the existing population, even when not including the land needed to grow the export crops to pay for the inputs necessary to achieve the relatively high yields needed because of population growth. Thus there are enormous biophysical constraints, including land quality constraints, on the economic possibilities of this and most other countries. I believe that if our biophysical analysis were extended to other countries, many that are not thought to be overpopulated would in fact be found to be so.

One of the apparent failures of previous economic development plans is that they were often implicitly based on rather poorly thought-out economic or industrial expansion. Part of the problem, I believe, is that the current dominant economic model (the neoclassical model) is inadequate to the task because it does not examine the resource possibilities and constraints of proposed policies. One important aspect of this situation is that because of the increasing energy dependence of most investment activities the net foreign exchange generated by many investments is bled out of the country as necessary costs for the required inputs, as in the case of Costa Rican bananas. Thus, many development plans increase gross—but much less net—economic activity, and it is the net that benefits the people supposedly being helped. Poorer-quality land, which tends to be that land not yet developed, requires a proportionately larger share of investments to get economic yield (Hall et al. 2001). These are possible reasons for the apparent failure of so many development projects, despite the good intentions of the investors, as remarked upon by academic critics and development economists themselves (Eviatar 2004).

I do not believe these problems of development, including the often horrendous impacts on land use and the intensification of chemical use, can be resolved solely, or perhaps even at all, within the aegis of neoclassical economics. I believe that the merging field of biophysical economics offers many useful tools that might be broadened into a new base for economics (see Hall 2000; Hall et al. 2001; Hall 2006), although its application will be difficult because there are so few people trained in the required biophysical approach, including a systems perspective, but also in integrating a knowledge of soils, ecology, agronomy, hydrology, and so on with economics. One reason that the dominant economic models are so popular may be because they so often require almost no real knowledge of the area to which they are applied: one only has to sit back and "let the market decide." While this is satisfying to people who believe in the power of markets or distrust institutions for guidance of investment decisions, it seems to me that the track record of neoliberal economics is demonstrably quite poor as applied to international development. In addition, there are complex social factors that need to be addressed, and for which at least some aspects of monetary analysis (what are the financial incentives? who gains and who loses?) is necessary. I do not yet see this fusion occurring, but it seems to me to be essential.

The relatively few tropical areas that have made the "transition" to a wealthy, or at least not poor, state (Puerto Rico, Malaysia) generally have combined reasonably good government (itself often a short commodity in the tropics) with a secure and expanding energy base (sometimes subsidized from outside, as in the case of Puerto Rico) that grows more rapidly than the population. As partly detailed above there is an increasing virulent literature that holds neoliberal/neoclassical economics at least partly to blame for the failures of development including the exacerbation of income differences within a nation, a failure of the poor to rise out of poverty, and an accelerated environmental destruction. In a way, we have received too often the bad aspects of development (the destruction of forests and land) without receiving too much in the way of benefits. The problem of much of the tropics is that resources, especially agricultural resources, are rather meager and the populations are growing rapidly. These are both biophysical realities. The (false) promise of economic growth championed by too many investors has diverted attention from the necessity of population control, resource protection, and avoidance of debt. Instead, with an emphasis on growth and investments that supposedly return more than they cost (but often do not), and a de-emphasis on the critical importance of population control, many well-meaning economists from the developed world have helped the poor countries avoid seeing the unpleasant but necessary reality that there may not be magic silver bullets out there waiting to offer them economic salvation. Meanwhile, much economic development that has taken place is simply resource extraction to feed the greed of powerful elites from both inside and outside the country being developed (Perkins 2004).

Increasingly, I am reminded of the old pictures of the Spanish conquistadors arriving in the New World, dressed in their armor and steel swords, and always with a priest holding up a cross off to the side. I suppose that for many of the Spaniards, the saving of the Indians' souls was worth the incredible misery they imposed upon them (although the Indians were rarely consulted on this—and to my knowledge their souls have not reported on how they are doing). Today Europeans of various stripes (including many of other ethnicities who have swallowed European and American neoclassical economics) interact increasingly with the developing world, sometimes to the benefit of those who live there but more often to the impoverishment of them, their lands, their forests, and their fish. I see these Europeans again landing on the shores of the unsuspecting or powerless natives, with their armaments and the new priests, now called economists, holding the new bible of neoclassical economics up high, justifying in their minds whatever carnage they are, again, letting loose upon these lands.

I believe that biophysical models that deal explicitly with the reality of the resources base available, the human population and its growth, and the limits of the land, water, and air to assimilate the wastes so generated are essential to understanding the potential, or lack thereof, for development. It is essential that we develop comprehensive integrated models that combine (with as little political or disciplinary baggage as possible) quantitative economic, social, and biophysical analyses of past and future economic activity. A systems approach needs to be used to evaluate how any policy might affect economic, social, and environmental sustainability and what the trade-offs might be. Such an approach is given in the simulation model provided with Hall et al. (2000) and chapter 6 in this volume, and such an approach must include the possibilities and constraints generated by land quality and actual and potential land use as well as the necessity for the (generally imported) energy and other inputs required to implement any economic development plan. These models can probably be combined in some way with more traditional economic models, but as to exactly how that might be done (beyond the simple correlations with GDP that we use commonly) I am not yet sure. Finally, I am convinced that using a serious scientific approach will result in less destruction to whatever wild lands remain because their truly marginal economic value would be realized. What to do with the increasing numbers of humans until populations stabilize or decline, if they ever do? For me, the answer is for countries to make their investments in the cities, to turn them into good places to live, with plenty of meaningful jobs, with proper services and amenities, and with housing close to where people work so that elaborate transportation systems are not required. This, too, would help to reduce land development. Whether it is possible to institute such a plan in today's market economies is another matter that I leave up to others. All of these issues will be much more difficult to deal with as global oil production reaches its peak and begins to decline.

Acknowledgments

I thank Laura Schmitt, Aman Luthra, Myrna Hall, Jae-Young Ko, David Pimentel, Abby Sterling, and Helmut Haberl for discussions and critiques on these issues, as well as a series of anonymous reviewers, not all of whom agreed with my fundamental premises. This chapter is reprinted with permission from Environmental Development and Sustainability (2006) 8:19-53

References

Achard, F., H. D. Eva, H-J. Stibig, P. Mayaux, J. Gallego, T. Richards, and J-P. Malingreau. 2002. Determination of deforestation rates of the world's humid tropical forests. *Science* 297:999–1002.

Annis, S. 1990. Debt and wrong way resource flow in Costa Rica. *Ethics and International Affairs* 4:107–21.

Auty, R. M. 1997. Natural resources, the state and development strategy. *Journal of International Development* 9:651–53.

———. 1998. Resource development and economic development: Improving the performance of resource rich countries. *UNU/WIDER Research for Action* 44.

Auty, R. M., and R. F. Mikesell. 1999. *Sustainable Development of Mineral Economies*. Oxford: Oxford University Press.

Bello, W. 1994. *Dark Victory: The US, Structural Adjustment, and Global Poverty*. London: Pluto Press.

Bello, W., D. Kinley, and E. Elinson. 1982. *Development Debacle: The World Bank in the Philippines*. San Francisco: Transnational Institute.

Bhagwati, J. 2003. *In Defense of Globalization*. Oxford: Oxford University Press.

Birdsall, N. A., C. Kelley, and S. W. Sinding. 2001. *Population Matters: Demographic Change, Economic Growth, and Poverty in the Developing World*. New York: Oxford University Press.

Boserup, E. 1965. *The Conditions of Agricultural Growth: The Economics of Agricultural Change Under Population Pressure*. Chicago: Aldine.

———. 1981. *Population and Technological Change*. Chicago: University of Chicago Press.

———. 1993. *Economics and Demography in Development*. Baltimore: Johns Hopkins University Press.

Brown, L. 1996. The acceleration of history. In *State of the World 1996*, 3–20. New York: Norton.

Brown, M. T., H. T. Odum, R. C. Murphy, R. A. Christiansen, S. J. Doherty, T. R. McClanahan, and S. E. Tennenbaum. 1995. Rediscovering of the world. In C. A. S. Hall, ed., *Maximum Power*, 216–50. Niwot: University Press of Colorado.

Burnside, C., and D. Dollar. 2000. Aid, policies and growth. *American Economic Review* 90, no. 4: 847–68.

Cameron, R. 1997. *A Concise Economic History of the World*. 3d ed. New York: Oxford University Press.

Cassidy, J. 2002a. Helping hands: How foreign aid could help everybody. *New Yorker*, March 18.

———. 2002b. Master of disaster. *New Yorker*, July 15.

Cleveland, C. 1991. Natural resource scarcity and growth revisited: Economic and Biophysical perspectives. In R. Costanza, ed., *Ecological Economics: The Science and Management of Sustainability*, 289–317. New York: Columbia University Press.

Collier, P., and A. Hoeffler. 2002. On the incidence of civil war in Africa. *Journal of Conflict Resolution* 46, no. 1: 13–28.

Collins, J., and J. Lear. 1995. *Chile's Free Market Miracle: A Second Look*. Monroe, Ore.: Subterranean Books.

Conklin, H. C. 1961. The study of shifting cultivation. *Current Anthropology* 2:27–61.

Cornell, J., and C. A. S. Hall. 2001. Shifting cultivation. In D. Pimentel, ed., *Encyclopedia of Agriculture*, 763–67. New York: Marcel Dekker.

Detwiler, P., and C. A. S. Hall. 1988. Tropical forests and the global carbon cycle. *Science* 239:42–47.

Diamond, J. 2005. *Collapse*. New York: Viking Penguin.

Dohan, M. 1977. Economic values and natural ecosystems. In C. Hall and J. Day, eds., *Ecosystem Modeling in Theory and Practice*, 134–71. New York: Wiley-Interscience.

Duncan, R. C. 1993. Agricultural export prospects for sub-Saharan Africa. *Development Policy Review* 11:31–45.

Easterly, W. 2001. *The Elusive Quest for Growth: Economists' Adventures and Misadventures in the Tropics*. Cambridge, Mass.: MIT Press.

Economist. 2003. Wanted, a new regional agenda for economic growth. *The Economist*, April 24.

Eviatar, D. 2004. Spend $150 billion per year to cure world poverty. *New York Times Magazine*, November 7.

Ewans, M. 2002. *European unity, African Catastrophe: Leopold II, the Congo Free State and Its Aftermath.* London: Routledge Curzon.

Fishman, T. C. 2002. Making a killing: The myth of capital's good intentions. *Harper's*, August 2002.

Freyfogle, E. T. 2003. Private land made (too) simple. *Environmental Law Reporter* 33:10,155–59.

Friedman, M. 1972. *Capitalism and Freedom*. Chicago: University of Chicago Press.

Friedman, M., and R. Freidman. 1980. *Free to Choose: A Personal Statement.* New York: Harcourt Brace Jovanovich.

Geertz, C. 1963. *Agricultural Involution*. Berkeley: University of California Press.

Geist, H., and E. F. Lambin. 2001. What drives tropical deforestation? Land Use and Land Cover Change Report Series 4, International human dimensions programme on global environmental change. International Geosphere-Biosphere Program.

———. 2002. Proximate and underlying causes of tropical deforestation. *BioScience* 52:143–50.

Goodland, R., and H. Daly. 1996. Environmental sustainability: Universal and non-negotiable. *Ecological Applications* 6:1002–27.

Goodland, R., and H. S. Irwin. 1974. An ecological discussion of the environmental impact of the highway construction program in the Amazon Basin. *Landscape Planning* 1:123–254.

Gray, J. 1998. *False Dawn: Delusions of Global Capitalism.* London: Granta Books.

Grünbühel, C. M., H. Haberl, H. Schandl, and V. Winiwarter. 2003. Socio-economic metabolism and colonization of natural processes in SangSaeng village: Material and energy flows, land use, and cultural change in northeast Thailand. *Human Ecology* 31, no. 1: 53–86.

Hall, C. A. S. 1992. Economic development or developing economics: What are our priorities? In M. K. Wali and J. S. Singh, eds., *Environmental Rehabilitation*, 1:101–26. Amsterdam: Elsevier.

———. 2001. Sanctioning resource depletion: Economic development and neo-classical economics. *The Ecologist* 20:99–104.

———, ed. 2000. *Quantifying Sustainable Development: The Future of Tropical Economies.* San Diego: Academic Press.

Hall, C. A. S. and Klitgaard, K. 2006. The need for a new biophisically-based paradigm in economics for the second half of the age of oil. *Journal of Transdisciplinary Research* 1:4–22

Hall, C. A. S., C. J. Cleveland, and R. K. Kaufmann. 1986. *Energy and Resource Quality: The Ecology of the Economic Process*. New York: Wiley-Interscience.

Hall, C. A. S., R. P. Detwiler, P. Bogdonoff, and S. Underhill. 1985. Land use change and carbon exchange in the tropics: I. Detailed estimates for Costa Rica, Panama, Peru and Bolivia. *Environmental Management* 9:313–34.

Hall, C. A. S., J-Y. Ko, C-L. Lee, and H. Q. Wang. 1998. Ricardo lives: The inverse relation of resource exploitation intensity and efficiency in Costa Rican agriculture and its relation to sustainable development. In *Advances in Energy Studies, Energy Flows in Ecology and Economy*, 355–70. Rome: Musis.

Hall, C. A. S, D. Lindenberger, R. Kummel, T. Kroeger, and W. Eichhorn. 2001. The need to reintegrate the natural sciences with economics. *BioScience* 51, no. 6: 663–73.

Hall, C. A. S., R. G. Pontius Jr., L. Coleman, and J-Y. Ko. 1995. The environmental consequences of having a baby in the United States. *Population and Environment* 15, no. 6: 505–23.

Hancock, G. 1989. *Lords of Poverty*. New York: Atlantic Monthly Press.

Hansen-Kuhn, K. 1993. Sapping the economy: Structural adjustment policies in Costa Rica. *The Ecologist* 23:179–84.

Hoogvelt, A. 1997. *Globalization and the Postcolonial World: The New Political Economy of Development*. Baltimore: Johns Hopkins University Press.

Hubacek, K., and J. van den Bergh. 2000. The role of land in economic theory. Interim report IR-02-037. International Institute of Applied Systems Analysis, Laxenburg, Austria.

Ibrahim, M., S. Abarca, and O. Flores. 2000. Geographic synthesis of data on Costa Rican pastures and their potential for improvement. In Hall 2000, 423–48.

Izursa, J-L., and D. R. Tilley. 2005. Energy analysis of Bolivia's natural gas. In M. T. Brown et al., eds., *Energy Synthesis III*, 551–61. Gainesville: University of Florida Center for Environmental Policy.

Karl, T. L. 1997. *The Paradox of Plenty: Oil Booms, Venezuela and Other Petro-States*. Berkeley: University of California Press.

Ko, J-Y., C. A. S. Hall, and Lopez. 1998. Resource use rates and efficiency as indicators of regional sustainability: An examination of five countries. *Environmental Monitoring and Assessment* 51:571–93.

Krausmann, F., and H. Haberl. 2002. The process of industrialization from the perspective of energetic metabolism: Socioeconomic energy flows in Austria 1830–1995. *Ecological Economics* 41, no. 2: 177–201.

Kroeger, T., and D. Montanye. 2000. Effectiveness of structural adjustment policies. In Hall 2000, 665–94.

Lambin, E. E. 1997. Modeling and monitoring land cover changes in tropical regions. *Progress in Physical Geography* 21:375–93.

Leamer, E. E., H. Maul, S. Rodriguez, and P. Schott. 1998. Does resource abundance increase Latin American income inequality. *Journal of Developmental Economics* 59:3–42.

MacEwan, A. 1999. *Neo-liberalism or Democracy*. London: Zed Books.

Mohamad, M. 1998. Call me a heretic if you like: Malaysia is not going to prostrate itself to the dogmas of global capitalism. *Time*, September 21.

Montanye, D. R. 1998. Examining sustainability: An evaluation of USAID's agricultural export-led growth in Costa Rica. Master's thesis, State University of New York.

Myers, N. 1998. Lifting the veil on perverse subsidies. *Nature* 392:327–28.

———. 2005. *Conversion of Tropical Moist Forests*. Washington, D.C.: National Academy of Sciences.

Netting, R. M. 1993. *Smallholders, Householders: Farm Families and the Ecology of Intensive, Sustainable Agriculture*. Stanford, Calif.: Stanford University Press.

Niles, J. O., S. Brown, J. Pretty, A. Ball, and J. Fay. 2002. Potential carbon mitigation and income in developing nations from changes in use and management of agricultural and forested lands. *Philosophical Transactions of the Royal Society of London A* 360:1621–39.

Odum, H. 1973. *Environment, Power and Society*. New York: Wiley-Interscience.

Pareto, V. 1971. *Manual of Political Economy*. New York: Augustus Kelly.

Perlin, J. 1989. *A Forest Journey*. Cambridge, Mass.: Harvard University Press.

Ponting, C. 1991. *A Green History of the Earth*. London: Penguin.

Prebish, R. 1950. *The Economic Development of Latin America and Its Principal Problems*. New York: United Nations.

Reed, D., ed. 1996. *Structural Adjustment, the Environment and Sustainable Development*. London: Earthscan.

Repetto, R. 1988. *The Forest for the Trees? Government Policies and the Misuse of Forest Resources*. Washington, D.C.: World Resources Institute.

Richards, J. F., and E. P. Flint. 1994. A century of land use change in South and Southeast Asia. In V. Dale, ed., *Effects of Land Use Change on Atmospheric CO_2 Concentrations: South and Southeast Asia as a Case History*, 15–57. New York: Springer.

Sachs, J., and A. M. Warner. 1997. *Natural Resource Abundance and Economic Growth*. Cambridge, Mass.: Center for International Development and Harvard Institute for International Development.

Samuelson, P. 2004. Where Mills and Ricardo rebut and confirm arguments of mainstream economists supporting globalization. *Journal of Economic Perspectives* 18:135–46.

Sanchez-Azofeifa, A. G. 2000. Land use and land cover change in Costa Rica. In Hall 2000, 473–501.

Sen, A. 1983. Development: Which way now? *The Economic Journal* 93 (December): 745–62.

Singer, H. W. 1950. The distribution of gains between borrowing and investing countries. *American Economic Review* 40:473–85.

Smil, V. 2000. *Energy at the Crossroads*. Cambridge, Mass.: MIT Press.

Stiglitz, J. 2002. *Globalization and Its Discontents*. New York: Norton.

Tainter, J. 1990. *The Collapse of Complex Systems*. New York: Cambridge University Press.

Tharakan, P., T. Kroeger, and C. A. S. Hall. 2001. 25 years of industrial development: A study of resource use rates and macro-efficiency indicators for five Asian countries. *Environmental Science and Policy* 4:319–32.

Todaro, M. P., and S. C. Smith. 2003. *Economic Development*. 8th ed. Boston: Addison-Wesley.

Wackernagel, M. 2004. World-Wide Fund for Nature International (WWF), Global Footprint Network, UNEP World Conservation Monitoring Centre, 2004, Living Planet Report 2004. Gland, Switzerland: WWF.

Wade, R. H. 2001. Making the World Development Report 2000: Attacking poverty. *World Development* 29, no. 8: 1435–42.

Weisz, H., M. Fischer-Kowalski, C. M. Grünbühel, H. Haberl, F. Krausmann, and V. Winiwarter. 2001. Global environmental change and historical transitions. *Innovation: The European Journal of Social Science Research* 14, no. 2: 117–42.

Williams, M. 2003. *Deforesting the Earth: From Prehistory to Global Crisis*. Chicago: University of Chicago Press.

Wood, A., and K. Berge. 1997. Exporting manufactures: Human resources, natural resources and trade policy. *Journal of Developmental Studies* 34:35–59.

World Commission on Environment and Development. 1987. *Our Common Future*. New York: Oxford University Press.

CHAPTER 3

A BRIEF HISTORY OF INTERNATIONAL DEVELOPMENT

Models and Foreign Aid

GRÉGOIRE LECLERC

In the old story, the peasant goes to the priest for advice on saving his dying chickens.

The priest recommends prayer, but the chickens continue to die. The priest then recommends

music for the chicken coop, but the deaths continue unabated. Pondering again, the priest

recommends repainting the chicken coop in bright colors. Finally, all the chickens die.

"What a shame," the priest tells the peasant. "I had so many more good ideas."

—Joseph Sachs

What Is Development?

Recently a French colleague turned up in my office and asked if I knew a good definition of "development." To my own astonishment and guilt, I realized that I didn't have a clear answer, even after having spent the last ten years working for international agricultural research centers[1] in developing countries. I could only say (more or less and after a lot of side comments), "a country is developing when it moves in the direction desired by its people." I had the feeling, however, that my line of reasoning was quite weak and absolutely not mainstream. Later I turned to books and Web sites of renowned development organizations with the conviction that the real experts will have come to a consensus on a good definition. Unfortunately, it was not the case: I found pages of text *about* development but no single self-contained sentence telling clearly what it was.

Until recently the words "development" and "economic growth"[2] were interchangeable, and mainstream economists were confident that the notions conveyed by these words were equivalent in practice. While development organizations realize more and more the multidimensionality of development and the problems of a purely economic definition, working to improve the economy and the private sector is still the main goal of development efforts.

An archetypical definition of—that is, about—development, which relates to most international aid projects, reads as follows: "development occurs with the reduction and elimination of poverty, inequality and unemployment within a growing economy." If we put aside the economic component of this definition, we could conclude that, strictly speaking, development has *not* occurred in the United States: poverty and unemployment are omnipresent and stable, and inequality has reached absurdly high levels unseen since the so-called Golden Age[3] in the decades surrounding 1900. But there has been economic growth in the United States, and even if the economy has been sluggish in recent years the prospects for future growth are good,[4] and this alone is probably enough officially to qualify a country as "developed."[5]

Since the year 2000 the United Nations, the International Monetary Fund (IMF), and the

World Bank have agreed on international development goals for eliminating poverty, improvements in health and education, and protection of the environment (see www.developmentgoals.org). In this context, development aid means helping a (tolerable) proportion of people get over a series of (tolerable) thresholds of poverty, health, and education, while helping to sustain the provision of environmental goods and services. Obviously, what is considered an acceptable threshold for a shelter in Mali has nothing to do with what we, developed people, can imagine, but we can sleep well if we are convinced that a good number of "them" are happy with the shelter they have. Eradication of poverty will mean, in this context, that nobody will have to live with less than a dollar per day. Thus the world's two billion or so poorest people could have their incomes doubled for one year if two billionaires chose to do that with their money.

Development suggests that a situation can be improved. But when can we honestly say that there is an improvement when we see one? Can the proliferation of suburbs, shopping malls, and parking lots in developed countries be called good development? Is it unmistakably clear that the exodus from the city to make the countryside a playground for urban dwellers is the better choice for a society? One thing is undeniable: there is more than one way to go forward in time. Isn't it true that average Swedes, with their social programs and 70 percent tax rate, do at least as well as average Britons, with their wild privatizations? Can we imagine France being forced by donors to slash their "inefficient" state programs, fire 50 percent of the civil servants while privatizing boldly? It is not very easy, therefore, to understand the logic that pushes development banks to promote essentially the "economic growth" solution that unquestionably increases the difference between rich and poor. But we can find clues by looking at the history of development and development aid.

Why Has Development Been Turned Over to Economists and Their Values?

Many good economists have done superb research on development, and many are solicited to lead (or shed their expertise on) large development projects.[6] Certainly, economists are useful agents in the process of development. But should they be the only or principal actors? It is not easy to understand why economists have become the de facto reference for everything related to development. The literature on poverty, institutions, and environment (when it has to be valued) is dominated by the economic paradigm. Indeed many scientists have made timid suggestions that development has a geographical or regional dimension (including many authors in this book), many social scientists have advanced the idea of a plural reality and the dangers of prejudice and generalization (see part 4), ecologists and natural scientists maintain that the environment is not properly taken into account in development policy no matter how much externalities are internalized, and even renowned economists question economic foundations and approaches (Sachs 1996; Easterly 2001; Stiglitz 2002). Compared to an average economist, however, even the best natural scientist has virtually no authority in the development world.[7] My suggestion as to how this perhaps not very effectual group has garnered so much power is that development requires money, and those who control the money especially trust economists because they speak the same language and are intellectual brothers and sisters.

The story of the World Development Report 2000/2001 (WDR 2001) is eloquent about the great divide between economists and non-economist social scientists when it comes to poverty analysis and poverty alleviation strategies.[8] We can equally easily find examples of fundamental disagreements between ecologists and environment economists (O'Neill, Kahn, and Russell 1998). Even within the prolific economic research body of the developed world, we find innovations that have led to bioeconomic models (see chapters 13 and 31), evolutionary economics, cooperative microeconomics, agent-based models (see chapter 13), and the like, but these ideas are far from being as influential as mainstream neoclassical economics (NCE).

So: what is development? In the case of a country, perhaps the citizens themselves should have the right to build the future they envision (see chapter 35), and development aid should respect

---

Box 3.1. "Development" in the dictionary

\De*vel*op*ment\, n. [Cf. F. développement.]

- gradual advancement or growth through a series of progressive changes; also, the result of developing, or a developed state.[9]
- *Synonyms*: development, evolution, progress. These nouns mean a progression from a simpler or lower to a more advanced, mature, or complex form or stage: *the development of an idea into reality; the evolution of a plant from a seed; attempts made to foster social progress.*[10]
- a process in which something passes by degrees to a more advanced or mature stage; "the development of his ideas took many years"; "the evolution of Greek civilization."[11]

---

[9] Webster's Revised Unabridged Dictionary, 1996, 1998, MICRA, Inc.

[10] The American Heritage Dictionary of the English Language, Fourth Edition, Houghton Mifflin Company

[11] WordNet 1.6, 1997 Princeton University

---

this choice. And who knows, maybe a better model for growth could emerge if we let the brains of developing countries think about it their own way. Therefore, I would like to suggest a simple, non-economic definition of what development *should* be: "Development is the process of change toward the future desired by those targeted."

Development Aid

The onset of international development[12] can probably be traced to early colonial times, when businessmen realized that the workforce they needed had to have a minimum level of health and knowledge to be cost-effective. Missionaries motivated by the firm conviction that their God was better for the local populations than whatever the alternative was accompanied the businessmen. Both joined efforts to domesticate the locals, integrate them in the production chain, and provide them with an adequate level of "humanity" (the resisting ones being marginalized or slaughtered). Fortunately, these rough times are virtually over, at least from the perspective of being officially sanctioned. However, the same underlying paradigm is still very much alive[13] (see also chapters 1 and 2).

We present next a brief history of "modern" development aid, also called international development, from the perspective of economics, agriculture, and to a lesser extent environment.

We unfold the origin of Bretton Woods institutions and the United Nations, the green revolution, and nature NGOs. The means and ends of development aid evolved with these institutions and with a changing geopolitical environment: the post–World War II period, the Cold War, the 1973 and 1979 energy crises, and the rise of globalization. The debt crisis in 1980, following and caused largely by the oil crises, left the door open to neoliberal interventions, with the United Nations supposedly acting as a safety net. Then emerged global environmental concerns, the promotion of local governance, and, at the turn of the new millennium, a critical assessment of our successes and failures of the past and a commitment for real results in the future. Yet all of this cannot be understood without understanding certain prior events.

The Beginning of Modern Development Aid
1945–50

Just before the end of World War II, U.S. President Franklin D. Roosevelt organized a monetary and financial meeting in a New Hampshire hotel called Bretton Woods. The meeting, which was sponsored by the recently created United Nations, was attended by representatives of many countries and by a group of institutions (which are also called

"Bretton Woods institutions"), which included the International Bank of Reconstruction, the IMF, and the General Agreement on Tariffs and Trade (GATT). These institutions also form the World Trade Organizations or WTO. The participants shaped a new concept of assistance to economically weak countries, many of which were still struggling with colonialism or a colonial heritage. The beginning of modern development aid coincides with the addition of the word "development" to the name of the International Bank of Reconstruction, known today as the World Bank. The foundations of modern development aid were laid down within the five years that followed.

The Truman Doctrine[14] of 1947 marked the beginning of the Cold War: the United States was committed to help any country threatened by communism, while the Soviet bloc was committed to just the opposite. This help was effectively done with major investments in development aid, military cooperation programs, and direct intervention in many third world countries.[15] For helping the recovery of Europe, the United States adopted a law that led to the five-year Marshall Plan[16] and created the Economic Cooperation Agency. The law was designed to transform a public gesture of help into benefits for the United States and became the reference for future aid programs. Two measures were particularly powerful: a form of credit that benefited more the supplier of aid than the recipient, and the obligation that both parties agree on the use of aid and its repayment. In the case of Europe, it led to the creation, in 1948, of the Organization for European Economic Cooperation (OEEC). Seventeen countries—including Germany and Italy—signed the agreement, which became the prelude and experimental basis for a full codevelopment agreement among industrialized countries.[17]

In 1944 the Rockefeller Foundation and the Mexican government helped to start what would trigger the U.S.-led green revolution.[18] They asked Norman Borlaug, a plant pathologist at the University of Minnesota, to work in Mexico on a project to increase the productivity of wheat. It became a long-term collaborative program with the Mexican government. Borlaug and his team developed, by plant breeding, new varieties of wheat that essentially diverted the energy of growing plants to the generation of many fat kernels rather than into growing tall. They also created plants more resistant to pests. It was also the early days of chemical fertilizers, to which dwarf varieties were particularly responsive.[19] The figures are impressive: in 1944, Mexico was importing half its wheat; in 1956 it was self-sufficient in wheat production; and in 1964 it was exporting half a million tons of wheat. Meanwhile, forty-four governments agreed on creating the Food and Agriculture Organization (FAO) as a specialized United Nations agency.

As the industrialization era was taking off in soon-to-be developed countries, many wealthy people started to worry about unexpected side effects of development: destruction of nature and the miserable urban existence for many workers. Just before World War I, naturalist Paul Sarazin, head of the nongovernmental organization (NGO) Ligue Suisse de Protection de la Nature, and Theodore Roosevelt had been strongly promoting the idea of a union of government and NGOs for the protection of nature. The idea was on hold during World War I and World War II, but then reemerged at the initiative of prominent biologist Julian Huxley, head of the newly created United Nations Educational, Scientific and Cultural Organization (UNESCO), with headquarters in Paris. In November 1948 the French government conveyed a meeting in Fontainebleau that gave birth to the International Union for the Protection of Nature, a loose-knit network of nature organizations that would quickly change its name to the International Union for the Conservation of Nature (IUCN) while strengthening its scientific bases through voluntary networks of experts. Nature organizations in time became mostly involved in all aspects of development related to protected areas and endangered species.

Institutionalization of Development Aid

On December 14, 1946, the United Nations (which was barely operating) adopted Resolution 58, which authorized the funding of technical assistance activities for developing countries. Resolution 200, adopted on December 4, 1948, established assistance to less developed countries (LDC) in the form of sectoral technical advisory services.[20] It officially endorsed the supply of "expertise" in connection with the LDCs' economic development programs. Consequently, it marked the beginning of a broad recognition of an international body with the power to plan and assist a country's development from the outside (and with an outsider's viewpoint).

The famous Point IV Program of U. S. President Truman's second inaugural address on January 20, 1949, summarizes well the main thrusts of development aid of the time:

> Developed countries have the technical knowledge to help relieve suffering of the people of "primitive" LDCs and let them aspire for peace, freedom, and a better life.
>
> We aim at helping the free people of the world [read noncommunist] to raise the industrial capacity of LDCs. Greater production is key to prosperity and peace.
>
> We will promote cooperation of business, private capital, agriculture, and labor of many developed countries through the United Nations.[21]
>
> We have a new way of doing development based on the concepts of democratic fair-dealing.

U. S. Development aid was essentially perceived as a transfer of a Western ideology and development model toward noncommunist LDCs. It is this line of reasoning that triggered the green revolution. By talking about "fair-dealing," on one hand, while promoting, on the other hand, a flow of capital and technology toward LDCs that was entirely controlled by free world developed countries, Truman gave the opening salvo to the modern development aid crusade. Since this dual objective strategy is still in use, we can say either that Truman was a visionary or that our attitude has progressed very little since World War II.

1950–55

Nevertheless, Truman had to convince the Congress not to cut the Point IV budget and brought forward his main concerns in a note on the appropriation for foreign aid[22] of August 25, 1950:

> The importance of the Point IV appropriation in the struggle against communist imperialism cannot be overemphasized. Although the amount involved is relatively small in terms of dollars, the Point IV program has come to be a symbol of hope for millions of people all over the world. In countries where the choice between communist totalitarianism and the free way of life is in the balance, this program can tip the scales toward the way of freedom. The advance agents of the communist conspiracy loudly promise the peoples of these countries a better way of life. We know that communism cannot deliver on these promises. We know that the way of freedom actually can and will provide a better life for people everywhere.

On the side of the communist bloc there were equally convincing arguments being shaped about development aid—which was also taking the form of technology transfers, capital investment, and military cooperation—as a good way to promote an ideology and provide a good level of control over other nations.

While the two superpowers were positioning themselves in the developing world, the United Nations was building its expertise capacity for sectoral analysis and technical assistance. Discussions on a special program of technical assistance financed from voluntary contributions became viable when the United States bought into it. The Expanded Program of Technical Assistance (EPTA) was formally established, and it started operations in July 1950. In a 1951 report, EPTA described LDCs as dual societies where a traditional sector feeds labor into a modern (and modernizing) one, and economists of the so-called postwar consensus, such as Arthur Lewis, developed the models needed to help aid policy makers. It recommended development aid programs aiming at reinforcing the modern sectors. This was in line with the general trend in turning to the interventionist state as a key policy instrument to development (Ranis 2004).

In the 1950s and 1960s, policy makers were looking for an industrial revolution in LDCs (Ranis 2004). They deployed a wealth of policy instruments based on of the idea of "import substitution," the replacement of foreign goods and services with substitutes produced within the country. This usually involved government subsidies and tariff barriers to protect local industries, as well as overvalued local currency to make easier the purchase of foreign goods and capital controls. This lead to widespread shift of aid resources from the farmers toward the political elite and a new breed of nonagricultural entrepreneurs (often the same political people).

Concurrently with this neoindustrial optimism, the 1950s, 1960s, and early 1970s were also a period of widespread international concern that many developing countries would inevitably succumb to famine.[23] In 1950, a cooperative agricultural development program, similar to that developed in 1944 in Mexico by the Rockefeller Foundation, began in Colombia. It would become CIAT in 1967, and it focused on cassava, rice, beans, and forages. In 1955–56, Chile, Ecuador, and India begin participation in similar agriculture programs of the Rockefeller Foundation. This green revolution took the form of an innovative combination of international and adaptive domestic research.

1955–60

The problems of U.S. involvement in Asia[24] and domestic priorities (such as the steel workers strikes) slowed down the implementation of Point IV. In the early 1950s, European agriculture had recovered from World War II, leaving the United States with enormous crop surpluses; the U.S. Congress, under pressure from the powerful farm lobby, proposed using the aid channel to help stabilize the domestic prices by dumping the surpluses in the developing world. The Food for Peace program was authorized in 1954, and the United States, quickly followed by Canada and other developed countries including the USSR, flooded LDCs indiscriminately with food, with the help of charitable organizations. The result would be the dismantlement of much of the LDCs own food-producing agriculture.

Soon the underdeveloped world started to boil under the pressure of the two blocs and decided it was time to establish a stronger position in relation to aid programs. The famous 1955 Bandung Conference clearly helped to forge the modern identity politics of race, religion, and nationality for African and Asian states. In addition to a clear nonalignment position[25] and the birth of "pan-" ideologies,[26] it had a practical consequence: the official endorsement of the concepts of underdevelopment and development aid. The conference ultimately led to the establishment of the Nonaligned Movement in 1961 and later to the G77, a group of seventy-seven LDCs.

Under pressure from the LDCs, the United Nations created its Special Fund, meant to finance larger and longer projects than its technical assistance branch, but smaller than the Bretton Woods ones. The United Nations' Conference on Trade and Development, held every four years since 1964 and meant as a counter-power to the GATT, never managed to change the main rules of international trade as defined by the superpowers. It would take thirteen years for the petroleum-producing LDCs, who first met in 1960 to create the Organization of Petroleum Exporting Countries (OPEC), to have an influence on the price regulation of oil.

As the world was moving into the era of the so-called Washington Consensus with neoliberal development policies, the role of technology in generating growth was being reconsidered with a new start for neoclassical growth theory based on the importance of capital investments as the implementation of that technology, and on the work of Robert Solow, which considered capital as adjustment variable and eventually replaced Harrod-Domar as an economic model to guide development.

1960–65

Meanwhile, the Organization for European Economic Cooperation expanded to take in all industrialized countries and became in 1961 the Organization for Economic Cooperation and Development (OECD), a platform for spreading the neoliberal beliefs. Every year, 600,000 high-ranking civil servants from LDCs meet in

OECD offices for consultation, training, and, one might say, inculcation of neoliberal ideology. The main function of OECD Development Assistance Committee is to keep an eye on the harmonization of aid policies within a neoliberal structural adjustment frame. It is not surprising, therefore, to find that the domestic policies of LDCs are profoundly grounded in neoclassical economics.

In 1960 the United Nations announced the Development Decade and a plan aiming at the economic "takeoff" of LDCs within the next ten years (for example, by putting in place the "pre conditions for development"). The industrialized countries established their own development aid agency and NGOs started to get involved in the private development aid field.[27] The World Bank started its "development planning" period (Sachs 1996) using models such as Harrod-Domar that focused on the flow of resources, capital investments (both domestic and foreign), and a limited role of technology and population dynamics.

The United Nations provided a platform for LDCs concerned about the better articulation, negotiation, and promotion of their collective economic and technical cooperation interests. In 1964, 77 developing countries signed the "Joint Declaration of the Seventy-Seven Countries," which was issued at the end of the first session of the United Nations Conference on Trade and Development (UNCTAD) in Geneva. The membership of the G77 had now increased to 135 countries but kept its original name.

The International Rice Research Institute (IRRI), the first of what is now a system of sixteen international agricultural centers, was established in the Philippines in 1960. It modeled its methods on Borlaug's work with wheat. It is a little-known fact that there was a China-led green revolution in Asia as well. China's researchers had created semi-dwarf rice varieties a little before (and independently) of the international plant breeding centers, and adoption of these varieties was already widespread when the centers' varieties started to be used (Dalrymple 1986).

1965–73

In 1966 the United Nations had incorporated most of today's large international organizations: the United Nations Development Program (UNDP—the merging of EPTA and United Nations Special Fund), the United Nations Industrial Development Organization (UNIDO), the Food and Agriculture Organization (FAO), the World Food Program (WFP), the International Fund for Agricultural Development (IFAD), the United Nations Educational, Scientific and Cultural Organization (UNESCO), the United Nations International Children's Emergency Fund (UNICEF), and the United Nations High Commissioner for Refugees (UNHCR).

Given the favorable funding environment, research centers specializing in development, either university-based or governmental, started to burgeon within the developed world. In 1965 Borlaug moved his attention from Mexico to India and Pakistan, where he continued his variety improvement work and launched a massive education campaign to get the farmers to use the new varieties. Three other major green revolution centers were founded in 1966–67: the International Maize and Wheat Improvement Center (CIMMYT) in Mexico, the International Institute of Tropical Agriculture (IITA) in Nigeria, and the International Center for Tropical Agriculture (CIAT) in Colombia. In 1971 the World Bank, which had already established "consultative groups" for individual countries, led the efforts to create the Consultative Group on International Agriculture Research (CGIAR), whose mission was to develop improved food crop varieties for the developing world. Beginning with IRRI, CIMMYT, IITA, and CIAT, which were initially funded by the Rockefeller Foundation and Ford Foundation, the CGIAR grew to sixteen centers (with much more diversified research interests) supported by thirty-nine international donors. The 1970s can also be seen as the World Bank "basic needs" era (Sachs 1996).

At the end of the 1960s, it became clear that most development donors were eager to finance projects focusing on the environment. In 1968, Sweden had suggested a United Nations conference to discuss the environment, and the idea materialized in 1972 as Stockholm's first Conference on the Human Environment and the creation of the United Nations Environment Program (UNEP).[28] In the following years, UNEP was at the heart of several environmental conventions and the source of funding of a wealth of integrated development projects. The idea of *sustainable development* was burgeoning. However, modern development aid focuses on economic growth, or poverty, or protection of nature (in that order of importance) but very rarely these three dimensions simultaneously.[29] By the time of the first energy crisis, the worldwide institutionalization of all aspects of development aid had been achieved.

The Failed New International Economic Order
1973–80

Thanks to the Arab-Israeli war, OPEC managed to be the first group of LDCs to impose a higher price for oil.[30] Given the absolute dependency of its economy on energy consumption (Cleveland et al. 1984), the United States was facing its most serious post–World War II crisis. The problem was worse for the less-developed countries. By the beginning of the first oil crisis, in 1973, LDCs' debt had risen to $110 billion while their share of world trade went down from 21 percent in 1960 to 18 percent. Despairing third world countries had started to believe that they could reshape a world economy dominated by Bretton Woods institutions. During its general assembly in April 1973, the United Nations held an extraordinary meeting on the problems of development and cooperation and the urgency of a change of the rules of the game. The proposal was in accordance with the NCE tradition: it included the rise in raw material prices (negotiated by cartels of LDCs), accompanied by a debt reduction and more favorable conditions for technology transfer. It also aimed at a revision of the international division of labor and the buildup of self-reliant national economies. The declaration and action program on the establishment of a "new international economic order" was accepted by consensus and raised high hopes for the LDCs.[31]

Developed countries quickly adapted to this situation, which appeared initially against their interests, by suggesting a different interpretation of the "new international economic order" that better suited their needs. They devised a redeployment strategy that got full support from the World Bank and the IMF: the idea was to increase the profits of firms by capitalizing on the LDCs' cheap manpower and natural resources by relocating their own subsidiaries there. It is worth noting that the United States formerly had cheap energy and expensive manpower (and the technology to use the cheap energy for high labor productivity); when energy prices became the same around the world there was no longer an advantage for firms to be located in the United States and corporations went global. In the rounds of negotiation that followed, LDCs realized that they needed the established system for their personal interests and that perhaps a collective action was not that great after all, and they accepted the redeployment idea. A massive movement of the manufacturing facilities that were owned by, and had been formerly located in, the developed countries occurred. National companies became international entities overnight.

In 1975, the capitalist and communist blocs started the dialogue for a rapprochement, which raised hope for a fairer treatment of LDCs. Gelinas (1994) reports well the spirit of the time. Commenting on the conversion of the two enemies into partners conniving in the exclusion of weak nations, the wise old Chou En-Lai, a Chinese revolutionary and communist leader (1898–1976), referred to the African saying, "When two elephants fight, it's the grass that suffers." But, he added wittily, "when they make love, the grass suffers nonetheless." The moral of the story is that the grass must never rely on a superpower to better its lot.

1980–90

In August 1982, during the world recession of 1982 that reduced demand for exports from LDCs, forty LDCs were in arrears in their interest payments when the Mexican government and the IMF announced that the country could no longer meet interest payments on its $80 billion debt.[32] The debt crisis of the LDCs had started and, in the year that followed, twenty-seven other countries were renegotiating the terms of their loans.

The pace of LDCs' growth had been steady at around 5 percent annually since 1960, stimulating capitalization in LDCs through large loans by international banks[33] and the redeployment of multinationals. The spread of financial services contributed to the emergence of a new international market system, the Eurodollar market system, which pooled enough funds to allow development banks to undertake loans to developing countries on a much larger scale. The sharp rise in oil prices generated inflationary pressure in the industrial world (and even a world recession), which in turn had the effect of raising the cost of imported goods for LDCs (because capitalization was more expensive) and led to their need for larger loans.[34] Meanwhile, oil-exporting countries were generating enormous profits in "petrodollars," more than they could possibly spend, which were redirected into the Eurodollar pool through dollar-denominated bank deposits (Curry 1999). Money, like any commodity, responds to supply and demand, and the price of a loan (the interest rate) declined to around 2 percent per year. So financially strapped developing countries borrowed huge amounts from the banks. Therefore, the Eurodollar system continued to be perceived as an infinite pool of funds (just like a virgin lake is believed to have an infinite production of fish—until the sudden and irreversible drop in the fish population triggered by greedy fishermen) and banks continued to promote loans to LDCs. Two-thirds of the debt of LDCs was tied to long-term credit with a floating interest rate—that is, the London Interbank Offering Rates (LIBOR)—and therefore very vulnerable to changes in the macroeconomic condition of industrialized countries. In fact, as of the early 1980s the petrodollars disappeared, and interest rates shot up to roughly 10 percent. The poor nations were hammered.

In 1979 the IMF and the World Bank established new structural adjustment programs (SAPs) to which LDCs had to conform in order to renegotiate their loans or contract new ones. The idea was to guarantee repayment of the debt via a more "efficient" structure based in large part on neoliberal economic doctrine. The SAPs forced LDCs to modify their governmental, economic, and commercial structures to the requirements of global markets, and yet the results were—again—more than disappointing, to say the least.[35] Most World Bank projects had to adhere to the structural adjustment dogma, although in some cases safety nets were deployed to protect that part of the population that would be affected negatively the most.

Meanwhile, the United Nations produced the Brundtland report ("Our Common Future"), which articulated what became the Agenda 21 and the principles of the Rio declaration in 1992, two documents outlining key policies to achieve sustainable development (that is, "development that meets the needs of present generations without compromising the ability of future generations to meet their own needs"). Agenda 21 and the Rio declarations led to two legally binding conventions: Biodiversity and Climate Change. This is probably the greatest victory of natural scientists about influencing development.

1990–2005

The industrialized countries began to care less about the ethics of their doings because they were backed by a "fair" and "rigorous" economic discourse based on neoliberal principles. In theory, neoliberal policies would lead to "efficiency," and "efficiency" would lead to a resolution of many problems including environmental ones (see chapter 5; see also Hall 2004). Supposedly it was not in their interest to leave a LDC with a clear comparative advantage over the industrial world or to get in a position to negotiate other rules of the game. Until 1989, LDCs were not a threat to industrial countries except for a failed attempt by OPEC in 1973.

Middle East countries knew that oil was the industrialized nations' Achilles' heel (particularly the energy-hungry United States). The U.S.-led first Gulf War was a primer in geopolitics: a coalition of developed countries aiming at the containment of a third world country. This demonstration of force, which was repeated by a British-American team in 2003, announced a new face for North-South cooperation: the model of free enterprise/minimum government had to be guaranteed by muscled and intimidating interventions. To many eyes, the spectrum of colonial methods was back onto the scene.

In the 1990s the role of the multinationals and of national agricultural research programs in LDCs had become so strong[36] that in order to survive, the CGIAR, the group of international agricultural research centers that were the main players of the green revolution, was forced to broaden their scope beyond the traditional sectors, to rely more than ever on partnerships and on the development of transgenic crops such as vitamin A–rich golden rice. Although many say that without the green revolution it would have been impossible to feed the world's growing population with the same land area, there are downsides: first, the widespread use of chemical fertilizers made the agricultural sector totally dependent on petroleum; second, the use of single "best" varieties has eroded the world's crop genetic resources while making whole countries vulnerable to new pests or diseases. Finally, transgenic crops are presented as the new solution for eliminating world hunger.

Protests against structural adjustment programs started as early as 1985 (mostly in universities) but took strength during the 1990s. The pages of newspapers, magazines, and academic journals are filled with critical analysis of structural adjustment, yet it seems difficult to demonstrate the efficacy of alternatives, which are easy to find or invent, but difficult to demonstrate. As in this book, the criticism is easy, but the resolution is difficult! Meanwhile the GATT became the World Trade Organization (WTO) in 1994, to which even communist China adhered in 2002. Neoliberal policies, whether they worked or not (and for whom?) became ever more firmly entrenched.

In 1996 the Heavily Indebted Poor Countries (HIPC) debt initiative, a strategy proposed by the World Bank and IMF to lower debt of extremely poor countries to sustainable levels, was agreed upon by governments around the world. It uses projections of the capacity to pay, based on net present value of exports and imports, of LDCs pursuing IMF and World Bank–supported neoliberal adjustment and reform programs (with an added emphasis on spending for health and education)

to determine a "decision point" where part of the debt can be canceled. To qualify, LDCs must have a near-crisis debt level, must have a track record of neoliberal policies, and must have developed a Poverty Reduction Strategy Paper (PRSP). The latter is still very closely related to the structural adjustment of the past; however, increased importance is given to improving institutions' efficiency to help make new welfare economics promises happen, along the lines of North (1990).

The World Bank is now moving to expand its private sector operations, partly because demand for standard loans to nations has stagnated in recent years, but mainly because it is highly profitable.[37] The governments of LDCs prepare their PRSPs, to which the development of private-sector operations and the quest for economic growth remain central. Curiously, the $32 billion debt of all heavily indebted poor countries, which is one of the main obstacles to poverty reduction in these countries, could be eliminated instantly by the surplus generated by the World Bank and the IMF (Kapoor 2003). But according to their experts, it would be a "moral hazard" to do so.

Ten years after Rio, the participants of the earth summit in Johannesburg had to face that the Agenda 21 had fallen short of its promises, with poverty deepening and environmental degradation worsening. Johannesburg did not produce spectacular outcomes, no agreement or treaties, but rather a down-to-earth action plan with emphasis on free trade, increased development assistance, good governance, partnerships, and results.

Some well-educated (and often populist) leaders of the LDCs have started to object openly to either the foundation or the application of conceptual models imported from the north. In a World Bank meeting in Hong Kong in 1997, Malaysian president Mahatir put the blame on foreign currency speculators for the 1997 collapse of Asian markets; he also suggested that bad development policies are promoted by developed countries because they fear the true competition that full development will ultimately bring. Note that many authors attribute the good results of Korea and Taiwan to muscled government interventions aimed at helping an inexperienced entrepreneurial class.

African nations have devised a vision for Africa and an implementation plan for becoming an economic bloc by 2028 (very much like the European Union, with its own money), the New Economic Partnership for African Development (NEPAD), a theoretical blend of macroeconomic policies and local realities. In 2002 the United States and the European Union were criticized by Brazil for breaking WTO rules by subsidizing their cotton producers (cotton is a commodity for which Brazil and Africa have a clear competitive advantage).[38] The left-wing politician Luiz Ignacio Lula da Silva was elected to the presidency in a landslide to develop a Brazilian solution to his country's extreme poverty and inequality.

At the turn of the new millennium the world's leaders agreed to a series of measurable goals for development (and not only growth), which are now known as the *millennium development goals*: to eliminate world poverty by the year 2015; to achieve universal primary education; to promote gender equality and empower women; to reduce child mortality; to improve maternal health; to combat HIV/AIDS and other diseases; and to ensure environmental sustainability. Since then all major donor agencies have used them to orient their strategies. Progress toward the millennium development goals is monitored via a framework of eight goals, eighteen targets, and forty-eight indicators accessible on the United Nations website (http://millenniumindicators.un.org/unsd/mi/mi_goals.asp) and graphically on the World Bank website (www.developmentgoals.org). Whether the continued increased use and influence of the neoliberal model works for or against these goals seems not to have been asked.

The Influential Development Models

Economics is the only field in which two people can get a Nobel Prize for saying exactly the opposite thing.[39]

In this section, we undertake the tricky task of extracting the essence of the models that have shaped development,[40] the very same models that decision makers have in their mind when they deal with development and which seem inaccessible to the rest of us. Wherever possible, we provide a graphical or mathematical representation of the models, so as to dissipate the aura of complexity in which development economics evolves and make it less intimidating. We also try to highlight the discrepancies between models and some of the problems associated with them.

Economics having been at the center stage of development, it is not surprising that most development models are economic models. A look at the history of economic thought shows a myriad of schools with different viewpoints on how the economy operates.[41] An abundant and fascinating literature exists on the subject; here we limit ourselves to a rapid sketch of this influential discipline.

Classical Economics

With the publication of his monumental work *The Wealth of Nations*, Adam Smith (1776) established the framework of the classical school of political economy (and probably economics as a discipline as well). Focusing on individual income, he states that capital, land, and labor were the pillars of nation's wealth. He introduced his famous "laissez-faire" and "invisible hand" to illustrate his conviction that a self-regulating market mechanism, operating through individual self-interests, will automatically produce the greatest benefits to society as a whole. What is less remembered is that in his first book, *The Theory of Moral Sentiments*, he made a very strong case for the proper role of governments in regulating economic activity.

David Ricardo was more interested in the distribution of income and emphasized the conflict between labor and capital, on one hand, and land (which is in fixed supply but variable quality, the better land being used first—hence his law of diminishing returns) on the other. He was the main contributor to the formalization of classical analysis. He put forward the famous theory of *comparative advantage* in foreign trade whereas each region should focus in producing whatever goods could be produced best there based on the climate, skills of the workers, or natural resources. So if Scotland produced wool best and Portugal wine best, it made the most sense for Scotland not to produce wine but to trade wool for wine and, in theory, everybody would be better off. This is the origin of the arguments for free trade, although a careful reading of Ricardo shows many caveats rarely considered by the advocates of free trade, for example that capital should not flow across national borders.

Thomas Malthus, in addition to his population theory, used the idea of diminishing returns to explain low living standards (and therefore the unlikelihood of the better society that Smith foresaw), and questioned the automatic tendency of a market economy to produce full employment.

John Stuart Mill was a social commentator who confronted the classical economic assumptions with his own observations on the unpleasant evolution of a society being industrialized. Mill worked on a reinterpretation of the nature of economic law (his theory of value), which challenged the classical assumption that uninterrupted economic expansion was a goal of such obvious importance that it required no justification. Departing from the classical tradition, he also emphasized the role of the state as a "civilizer" as well as a stabilizer of economic activity.

Marxist Economics

A contemporary of Mill, Karl Marx saw capitalism as a transitory phase of development: capitalism would ultimately destroy itself and be followed by a world without private property. Marx believed that all production belongs to workers and not to capitalistic investors because, he believed, workers produce all value in society. He saw the divergence among economists as an expression of problems latent with capitalism: "The more the antagonistic character comes to light, the more the economists, the scientific representatives of bourgeois production, find themselves in conflict with their own theory; and different schools arises." His main contribution to economic thought was to demonstrate that the economic reality, society at large, and history are inseparable: economic "laws" are specific to particular stages in history, and the discovery of such laws governs the unfolding of history itself. Marx's doctrines became the rallying point of many developing countries (such as China, Nicaragua, El Salvador, and Cuba). Although Marxists theories,

or at least their imperfect political manifestation in the Soviet Union and elsewhere, seem largely discredited now he remains an amazingly insightful and thoughtful commentator on economics and capitalism (Cassidy 2002).

The Marginalists (1870–1930), the Paretians (1910–50), and the Development of Neoclassical Economics

Classical economists assumed that the costs of production (and especially labor) were determining prices. The marginalists put forward the premises of neoclassical economics and generated "the marginal revolution": that prices also depended on demand, and therefore on consumer's satisfaction. The concept of diminishing marginal utility was put forward by William Stanley Jevons, Carl Menger, and Léon Walras, to pin down the character of demand (thus the term "marginalist").

The "Paretians" are the flock of economists who built on Vilfredo Pareto's *Manual of Political Economy* (1906), particularly his analysis of economic optimization via mathematical programming techniques. This included the "New Welfare Economics" of the late 1930s (see chapter 1), which sought to connect efficiency to competitive equilibria and define a "social optimum," that is, which Pareto-optimal allocation is the best.

The classical economists, Marshall, Pigou, and even Pareto, were concerned about distribution and what constituted a "fair" society. The new welfare economists Kaldor, Hicks, and Robbins revived the concept of Pareto efficiency (that is, an outcome is more efficient if at least one person is made better off and nobody is made worse off) while abandoning concerns of equity (and leaving that to government, whether in fact it did so, therefore making economics as a discipline more "objective" and "scientific") in order to concentrate only on efficiency. Central to this is the so-called Kaldor-Hicks efficiency, where a more efficient outcome can leave some people worse off (this was possible if those who are made better off could in theory compensate those who are made worse off and lead to a Pareto optimal outcome). In terms of "development" policies, the result was that nothing mattered except increasing total (or per capita) GDP, because (theoretically) a higher GDP could make it possible to pay for other goals such as better education, health care, and environmental protection. The fact that these other goals were seldom achieved was blamed on corruption, mismanagement, lack of property rights, and so on, never on the inherent tendency of capitalism to generate inequality. Chapter 1 reviews some of the additional problems of all these assumptions.

The crux of neoclassical economics (NCE) is therefore the analysis of the behavior of the market system and the mechanisms within it through which equilibrium (a perfect balance between supply and demand) could be produced. The focus is on microeconomics, the study of economic behavior of households, firms, and industries—assuming that the "natural value" of a good is determined only by its subjective scarcity, that is, the degree to which people's desire for that good exceeds its availability. In this view, firms are not producing goods that consumers buy: it is "utilities" that are exchanged. This innovation bypassed the quest for the laws of motion of society, and favored the development of a conceptually simpler, more formal, and unified formalism. In effect, the neoclassical story is best captured by supply-demand curves in price-quantity space, and the introduction of subjective scarcity that provides the human ingredients that were necessary to elevate the theory to, in the minds of many, the level of a universal law.

Ironically, neoclassical economists were largely inspired by natural scientists, as they aimed for developing a "pure" economic science, complete with abstract mathematical models and controlled experimental conditions.[42] This gave an aura of universality and respectability to the subject but led to an increased disconnection with the real world. In contrast with the natural sciences, however, was that this economic theory gained a normative and prescriptive status without having to rely on confirming data: the theory being perfect, it was the world that was imperfect and had to adapt. Efficient allocation of resources (in neoclassical economics terms) became not only socially desirable but the human being's main goal.

In 1936 John Maynard Keynes published his *General Theory of Employment, Interests and Money*, in which he defended the thesis of necessary government intervention to stabilize the economy, such as decreasing taxes to increase people's spending when the economy was depressed, or increasing taxes to reduce inflation when the economy was "overheated." His analytic framework on the determinants of total spending is still at the heart of modern macroeconomic analysis.

While the core of NCE remains the same, several schools of thought emerged with different viewpoints about macroeconomics, money, dynamics, mathematics, and so forth. Fonseca and Ussher identify the Austrian school (Austria, 1870s–1930s; America, 1970s–now); the Lausanne (Walrasian) school (Swiss-French-Italian, 1870s–90s); the Lausanne (Paretian) school (Italy 1900–1920; Chicago, Harvard, France 1930s–40s); the Cambridge (Marshallian) school (Britain, 1890s–1930s); the Stockholm school (Sweden, 1920s–30s); the Chicago school (America, Version I, an eclectic mix of schools, 1920s–40s; Version II, more distinct, with Monetarists and New Classicals, 1960s–80s; see also chapter 11); and the Neo-Walrasian school (worldwide, 1950s–80s).

In relation to the underdeveloped world, NCE has emerged as the dominant paradigm for development aid, where it takes two prominent forms. In the first, the free exchange of utilities is believed to be frustrated by factors such as land tenure, religion, tribal affiliation, or caste, as many "imperfections" that had to be eliminated (together with government interventions). In the second, which is inspired by Keynes, neoclassical economists are less confident in the capacity of free markets in the LDC to produce the good results expected from the theory, and therefore assign to the state the task of adjusting the prices of productive factors (wages, interest and exchange rates, and so forth) in order to come closer to the optimum solution.

Supply and Demand Model (Market Economic Model)

The supply and demand model, the basic workhorse of economics, is used extensively in development, to justify bilateral aid, to negotiate within the World Trade Organization (WTO), or to design

---

Box 3.2. The demand function

The demand function (also called "demand") depicts the association between the price of a good and the maximum quantity of that good that a consumer or group of consumers are willing (or able) to buy at that price, *ceteris paribus* (that is, holding all the other influencing variables—tastes, income, prices of related goods, expectations, and number of buyers—constant at some given level) under perfect information, within a given period of time.

The demand function for good X is:

$$X^D = f(P_X, P_s, P_c, I, T, Pop, I^E, P_X^E)$$

Where:

X^D = quantity demanded
P_X = price of X
P_s = price of substitute for X
P_c = price of complements of X
I = Income of the buyer
T = taste for X, level of desire of X
Pop = population in market, or "market size."
I^E = expected future income of the buyer
P_X^E = expected future price of X

The *law of demand* (also called "law of diminishing marginal utility") states:

$$\frac{\partial P_X}{\partial X^D} < 0$$

Note that a change in price (P_X) or quantity (X) causes a movement *along* the demand curve for X. Only a change in one of the *ceteris paribus* demand variables causes a *shift* of the entire demand curve, that is, an increase or decrease in demand.

---

sectoral policies. Understanding this model is important as many apparently weird decisions are based on the arithmetic of market economic models in price-quantity space.

Demand

While the idea of a demand function was first put forward by Charles d'Avenant (1699), Augustin Cournot (1838) was the first to draw a demand and supply curve as an algebraic function in price-quantity space.[43] Cournot believed that goods were required for a particular purpose so demand had to be deduced from empirical fact[44] by plotting actual price and quantity-sold data and fitting a line through the points (figure 3.1a). Therefore his

demand function was *not* the demand function in the modern sense (see box 3.2), although he assumed that the demand function was continuous and assumed that it was downward-sloping (*loi de débit*). Also, he assumed that goods were produced for a *purpose*, and not only to create demand.

Modern economists have given a broader meaning to the idea of a demand: demand functions depict the conceptual relationship between price and the quantity *sought* by buyers. They expect that buyers would want to purchase more of a particular good at a lower price than at higher one. Therefore a modern demand function can have any functional form and, because of assumed decreasing marginal utility, is believed to have a negative slope: buying a

---

Box 3.3: The supply function

The supply function (also called "supply") describes the relation between a good's price and the maximum quantity that a producer or group of producers are willing (or able) to sell at that price, *ceteris paribus*, under perfect competition, within a given period.

The supply function for good X is:

$$X^s = g\,(\,P_X,\ P_{fp},\ P_{ap},\ S,\ N,\ P_X^E\,)$$

Where:

X^s = quantity supplied
P_X = price of X
P_{fp} = price of factors of production for X
P_{ap} = alternatives in production ("opportunity cost")
S = technical knowledge
N = number of competing firms in the market
P_X^E = expected future price of X

The *law of supply* states that:

$$\frac{\partial P_X}{\partial X^S} > 0$$

Note that only a change in price (P_X) or quantity (X) causes a movement *along* the supply curve for X. A change in one of the *ceteris paribus* supply variables causes a *shift* of the entire supply curve—an increase or decrease in supply. And total benefits must exceed total cost.

---

second car does not double your happiness (you will perhaps buy an extra one if it is cheaper, otherwise you will prefer to spend that money on something else). This premise leads to the establishment of the influential *law of demand*, which states that the relationship between a good's price and the quantity demanded of that good is negative.[45]

Supply

Imagine a world where many companies are producing and selling similar goods, are not profit maximizers, and know little (or do not care much) about each other's prices and markets. Each industry has its own production cost, stores, and clients, and therefore sells its goods at a price that they think is OK (and make a reasonable profit).[46] If we plot actual production data for a given time period on an XY graph, the number of goods produced along the X-axis, and the selling price along the Y-axis, we would obtain a cloud of points[47] through which we could fit a supply curve à la Cournot.[48]

In its modern (neoclassical) sense, a supply curve is believed to have a gentle positive slope (but it can be negative or constant for some industries), which means that to produce more shoes the firm has to spend more, because the raw material is limited, or because they would prefer to spend the extra money on something else than producing an extra good (because they fear, say, that they would not be able to sell it). Note that because the curve is drawn for units of a good, the price on the vertical axis represents what economists call the *opportunity cost*, or *marginal cost*, for producing an extra unit of that good. The astute reader might notice that the assumptions of this curve are opposite what one might assume from another basic economic "law," that of decreasing unit costs with increasing scale.

Any functional form for the supply curve can be assumed in modern economics (figure 3.2), but they generally must conform to the influential law of supply, which states that the slope of the supply curve is positive. Note that for some industries the slope is negative, which can make it difficult to define an intersection with a demand curve.

Interaction of supply and demand and the generation of price

When supply and demand curves for a good are plotted on the same graph (figure 3.1d), we get the whole picture of how sellers and buyers (economic "society") interact around that good. The net social benefit for a given quantity of that good is the difference between supply and demand: demand shows how much individual buyers in society are willing to forgo to get a unit of that good, while supply shows how much individual sellers have to forego to produce a unit of that good. This is valid as long as (1) buyers receive all the benefits; (2) sellers assume all the costs; (3) society agrees that such goods should be produced; and (4) benefits and costs are counted as being of equal social importance regardless of whom they may fall.

Producers will be willing to produce more of a good as long as there are buyers willing to forgo something else to get a certain quantity of that good, that is, up to the point where the curves intersect. Therefore, in a competitive market system, the price paid and quantity produced will tend to be the intersection of the demand and supply curve (the equilibrium). The equilibrium price, where supply equals demand, is called the "market clearing" price. An interesting property to keep in mind is that the social value of small changes in quantity of a good is equal to the market clearing price times the (small) change in quantity. This property is heavily used in cost-benefit analysis.

Figure 3.2 shows various supply and demand curves that appear in the literature (omitting cases where the law of supply or demand would be broken). Supply and demand curves are extremely difficult to obtain from actual data, given the large dispersion of points in price-quantity space, the relative imperfections of markets, and the fact that often it is the market clearing price for a given time period that is known, which forces one to rely on time series (and relax assumptions) to recover plausible curves (from various equilibrium points). Therefore, the use of supply-and-demand curves is often rather theoretical (or dogmatic), with major efforts by econometricians to estimate their validity, and the inevitable "identification problem." One can easily imagine that everything can be explained by demand and supply when one can arbitrarily choose their shapes, shift them to the right or the left (or up and down) according to plausible arguments, and test the validity of the model—when we are lucky—with incomplete data.[49]

Demand and supply curves have become the basic workhorse of NCE and macroeconomic economic forecasting.[50] Figure 3.3 shows how, for example, inflation can be explained (1) by a shift of the supply curve ("cost push inflation") or (2) by a shift in the demand curve ("demand pull inflation"). Note the funny bent shapes (e.g., top left) to take into account some threshold in buyers' or sellers' behavior. Figure 3.3c helps to understand why the price of commodities has the tendency to drop with adoption of improved technology (shift of the supply curve to the right—for example, the use of fertilizers or government subsidies). In that case even if income increases and demand increases (shift of the demand curve to the right), the market clearing price will still be lower; which happens because the demand curve is believed to be steeper than the supply curve, and because the demand curve for commodities is believed to be quite insensitive to an increase in income—the shift of the demand curve is not important (in economic jargon: commodities have a "low income elasticity on demand").

Problems

So the assessment of supply and demand is trivial and should not be questioned? Perhaps not—there are objections. Even a cursory examination of the above supply-and-demand curves used in actual economic cases indicates that there is no reliable single mathematical function upon which one can hope to build a bulletproof case (or run your country's economy). Other problems follow.

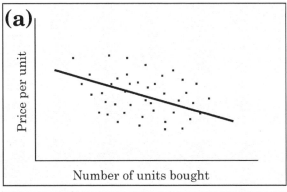

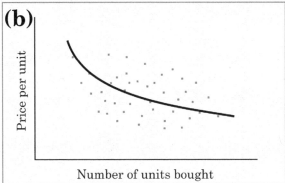

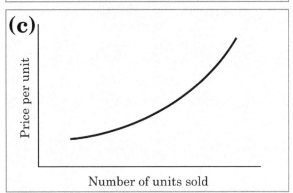

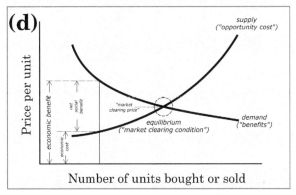

Figure 3.1. (a) A hypothetical example of Cournot's (1838) empirically derived demand curve; (b) a hypothetical modern demand curve that could be fitted through the points of (a); (c) a hypothetical modern supply curve; (d) interaction of supply and demand: equilibrium price/quantity (based on Dohan 1990).

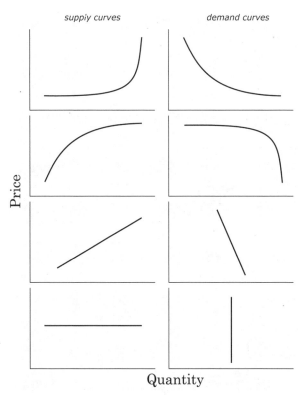

Figure 3.2. Supply and demand curves: a sample of functional forms found in the literature. The analysis of the interaction of curves of various functional forms is at the core of a large body of NCE economics and econometric work.

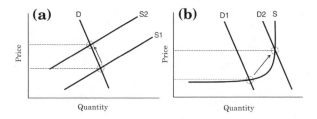

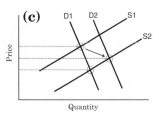

Figure 3.3. Examples of analysis of supply and demand: (a) inflation explained by a shift in supply ("cost push inflation"); (b) inflation explained by a shift in demand ("demand pull inflation"); (c) drop of commodity price explained by a shift in supply (better technology, subsidies) that is not compensated by demand: commodities are often necessities, and therefore people do not need much more of it even if it is cheaper (steep downward slope, low income "elasticity" on demand).

The identification problem.

The econometrician's job is to make quantitative estimates of economic variables and relationships among them. For example, demand and supply curves (which are essential for market economics forecasting) can be obtained from time series of market price/quantity data, assuming that this data represent the intersection of various demand and supply functions that move according to changing *ceteris paribus* variables with time. If one knows that it is demand that has shifted while supply stayed constant, a demand curve can be estimated, and vice versa, assuming that the shape of these functions does not change with time. The most likely situation is that both supply and demand shift and change, which yields a pattern of points in price-quantity space that is virtually impossible to analyze except with overly simplistic assumptions and some nonmathematical interpretation of ancillary information. The outcome of an honest analysis of actual data is eventually that the econometrician will be unable to distinguish the supply from the demand curve or estimate the shape of either. This is the identification problem (Myoung-jea 2002). Most, if not all, economic models suffer from this problem.

The assumptions.

Perfect competition (supply), perfect information (demand) are conditions difficult to meet in practice (information is biased by advertising and other mass media, variations of product qualities or brands exist, as do monopolies, delays in the diffusion of price information, etc.).

The perfect-competition assumption implies that supply or demand curves cannot exist! In effect, under perfect competition the supply-and-demand diagram shrinks instantly to the equilibrium point, so you can have either perfect competition or demand/supply curves, but not both.

There must be many sellers or buyers for a supply or a demand curve to exist, and no individual seller or buyer must believe that he alone can influence price: he moves along the supply or demand curve and chooses the price he wants (hence the term "price takers"). This assumption is often false in the case of sellers.

Buyers and sellers must be clearly separate groups (note that the only factor that is common to buyers and sellers is price—see boxes 3.2 and 3.3). Therefore, when one factor changes, it affects supply or demand, but not both.

The model needs well-defined private property rights (we see now why this is such a big issue in development aid). It falls apart in the case of common property goods (such as ocean fish, communal land, and public forests), because the costs of production or the benefits of harvesting are not necessarily fair (as they would be, as we must believe by now, in a perfect market system!).

Even if the assumptions are not met, the model is said to be right, because it is believed to predict correctly the *direction* of change in many cases (for example, the increase of the price of roses just before Valentine's Day).

The economic "laws."

In the natural sciences, a theory must be backed by undisputable experimental evidence to qualify as a *law*. Apparently this is not the case of the law of supply and the law of demand and other economic laws (such as Walras's law) that seem to be more in the realm of *statements*, for which experimental proofs are always questionable and many exceptions can be found easily. The psychological effect of calling something a law is, however, extremely strong: we think it represents something that is "true." If a phenomenon appears to contradict a law, then something is wrong with the measurement or with the behavior of nature, not the law. Therefore when economists say that the "market fails"[51] or is "imperfect," or that some goods are "inferior,"[52] the message they send is that the market doesn't behave as it should, and that we need to do something to change the way the world operates.

Demand and Supply in Development

It is clear that nearly all aspects of bilateral and multilateral commerce and trade with LDCs have been done with supply and demand models. In the 1980s, however, a coalition of economists and politicians started to promote a more proactive approach to boost productivity: *supply-side economics*.

Supply-side economists are convinced, based on their supply-demand models, that the focus should be on the level of total aggregate supply of goods and services: supply creates demand,[53] and this market behavior maximizes social benefits. Therefore, they argue that the role of government is to promote policies that create an environment where competition and free enterprise prosper, and to abandon policies related to demand (for example, social security and Medicare): industries drive the economic wagon, not consumers. Many influential businessmen and politicians who adhered to supply-side economics did so not to promote a more efficient society, but rather to abolish a government that they hated.

Supply-side policies are therefore microeconomic policies that aim to change the underlying structure of the economy and are at the heart of the neoliberal approach to development. This approach occupied a central position in the United States during the Reagan era, and inevitably splashed on U.S.-based multilateral organizations such as the World Bank and the IMF, taking the shape of structural adjustment programs.[54] However, while many supply-side measures were dropped (for the United States) during Clinton mandates, the World Bank and the IMF have continued to require that pure supply-side economics is implemented in LDCs; with the result that the idea of inevitable and necessary economic reforms that favor supply-side economics is now much better accepted in most LDCs that it was during the Lomé convention in 1989.

Supply-side economics concentrates on increasing the supply of goods and services (by denationalization, deregulation, contracting out), and on increasing the supply of labor (by abolition of trade unions, minimum wage, and taxes). There are many objections to this approach even within the economics corpus, particularly Keynesians. But so far, the widely acknowledged problems of supply-side economics have not affected the way development aid is being done in large part in its image.

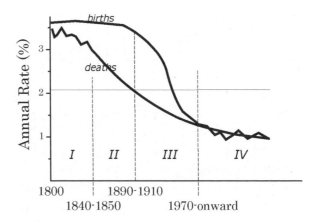

Figure 3.4. Population dynamics in Western Europe and Malthusian phases.

Population and Development

In 1798, Thomas Malthus,[55] in his *Essay on the Principle of Population*, expressed his concern about demographic problems in England. His thesis was that population growth would eventually exert such a pressure on resources that it would irreversibly lead to general reduction of wealth. Malthusian thinking is based on two main hypotheses. The first one is that population growth is exogenous; it is exponential or explosive. The second one states that the productivity of the land for subsistence goods is limited, that is, increasing arithmetically: the best land is used first (and will eventually become degraded), forcing the exploitation of lower-quality land. This imbalance results in chronic low wages that leave most people living under the poverty line.

According to the Malthusian thesis, the demography of developed countries has gone through four stages (see figure 3.4): in phase 1 there is a high population growth rate but also a high mortality rate, in equilibrium; in phase 2 the death rate decreases (this is when there is the maximum demographic growth),[56] which corresponds to a demographic *transition* period; in phase 3 the birth rate decreases as a result of progress; and in phase 4 (where developed countries stand now) population reaches a new equilibrium where both the birth rate and the mortality rate are low (because the cost of a child is greater than its benefits). Development experts believe that LDCs are in a transition period (phases 2–3) similar to the one observed for developed countries in the nineteenth century. It is projected that almost all of the world's demographic growth of the next thirty years will take place in LDCs, whose population will go from 4.8 billion now to probably 7.2 billion by 2030.

Taking a standpoint opposite to Malthusian and neo-Malthusian[57] theories, Boserup (1965) says that demographic growth is key to modernization and economic development: a strong demographic pressure on natural resources forces adaptation and creativity (see also chapter 12). Countries with abundant natural resources and low population density can be trapped into poverty. A revisionist wave of the 1980s held that a large and growing young population is more inclined to take risks and promote innovations while benefiting from economies of scale, which are essential ingredients to productivity growth and rapid development. This was indeed supported by various econometric studies in the 1970s and 1980s, as well as by the "limits to growth" or "Club of Rome" models.

Most economists think now that the pessimistic Malthusian thesis is wrong: many economists promote the idea that productivity is unbounded, that technology will keep up with the needs (the main constrain being labor); and population growth is believed to be eventually endogenous, which is to say, the rate of growth is regulated internally (population ultimately reaches an equilibrium state).[58] However, even the sign of the relationship between demography and development is still the subject of controversy. Leading economic demographers now suggest that rapid population growth hinders economic development through decreasing the per capita resources and increasing general environmental degradation, and that demographic policies are needed (Birdsall, Kelley, and Sinding 2001). For most economists, however, environmental degradation is not a real problem, because either technology is capable of coping with it or it is not reflected in market price, and therefore it does not have to be taken into account explicitly by the models.

Since 85 percent of the world population will live in LDCs by 2025, it is important to understand better how demography is linked to development. More than a prior condition to development or the reason for its failure, population dynamics is interlocked with economic dynamics and natural resources. While unbounded population growth can be critical in the context of a slow economy and little resources to tap into, strong population dynamics in itself is not necessarily an obstacle to economic growth when natural resources or opportunities abound. Obviously, given the large importance of cheap petroleum related to agricultural productivity increases, a future where "the end of cheap oil" is a strong possibility implies that resource constraints may have a whole new general importance.

Mobility (Dualist) Models

Rural exodus, accelerated urbanization, and international migration are observed characteristics (or side effects) of development. Bhrada and Brandao (1993) have reviewed empirical and theoretical work on urbanization and found that the main drivers were at two levels: macroeconomic and microeconomic. The macroeconomic level involves a lower demand for agricultural products, while progress in technologies was more important for sectors associated with urban centers. The authors also found that a pattern of rural exodus seems to be related more to the deterioration of living conditions in rural areas than to the attractiveness of the city. The microeconomic drivers are associated with geographical (territorial) imbalances of sectoral productivity (see chapter 32), which are critically dependent on accessibility (see chapters 28 and 29).

An essential point to address is the capacity of developing economies to absorb (or live without) a workforce "freed" by a modernizing agriculture in a competitive world. The overflow goes in unemployment, the informal economy, or brain drain and international migration.[59]

The Lewis Model
Overview.
The Lewis model of a capitalistic system (Lewis 1954) is based on the dualist view of LDCs: a traditional sector (low labor productivity) and a modern sector (high labor productivity). It supposes an unlimited supply of low-paid labor (from the rural areas) that feeds the modern sector with no increase

Box 3.4. The Harris-Todaro model

Agricultural production X_A:

$$X_A = q\,(L_A,\, T,\, K_A), \text{ with q'} > 0,\, \text{q''} > 0$$

where L_A is the agricultural labor, T is the land, and K_A the agricultural capital. T and K_A are supposed fixed therefore q' and q'', the change and rate of change, respectively, of agricultural productivity, depend only on agricultural labor.

Urban production (manufacturing) X_M:

$$X_M = f\,(L_M,\, K_M), \text{ with q'} > 0,\, \text{q''} > 0$$

where L_M is the manufacturing labor and K_M the capital labor. K_M is supposed fixed therefore q' and q'', the change and rate of change, respectively, of manufacturing productivity, depend only on manufacturing labor.

Prices of agricultural goods P:

$$P = p\,(X_M / X_A), \text{ with p'} > 0$$

The price of agricultural goods is set by internal exchanges (manufactured goods versus agricultural goods).

Real agricultural wage W_A:

$$W_A = P \times \text{q'} = P \times \frac{\Delta X_A}{\Delta L_A}$$

Real urban wage W_M:

$$W_M \geq \text{Min}W$$

Note: if there is enough supply of labor then $W_M = \text{Min}W$

Expected urban wage *We/M*:

$$W_M^e = MW \times \frac{L_M}{L_U}$$

L_M/L_U is the probability of finding a manufacturing job in the city (L_U is the total active urban population).

Equilibrium condition:

$$W_A = W_U^e$$

with a constraint on labor, where total labor L is supposed fixed:

$$L_A + L_U = L$$

At equilibrium rural exodus stops because urban wages are not attractive, but this causes urban unemployment ($L_M/L_U > 1$).

in wages. Profits go entirely into capital accumulation, and some are reinvested, which increases the productive potential of the modern sector and calls for more labor. Therefore, there will be a gradual erosion of the traditional sector and simultaneously a reinforcement of the modern sector.

Problems.

The model supposes that taking out labor from rural areas will have no effect on agricultural productivity. Massive exodus can destructure the rural sector and lead to the collapse of agriculture; therefore, the transfer of labor can be costly. Moreover, if wages stay at the subsistence level, who is going to buy the products of the modern sector? Provided they are not entirely for exports, we should therefore observe a substitution of capital for higher wages, which is not taken into account by the model. Moreover, we observe an increase of urban unemployment in LDCs, which the model does not explain.

The Harris-Todaro model
Overview

The probabilistic theory of Harris and Todaro (Todaro 1969; Harris and Todaro 1970) addresses the urban unemployment contradiction of the dualist view. Two mechanisms are necessary for the demonstration:

> The level of rural wages depends on the "marginal productivity of labor"—the increase of productivity obtained by a given increase of labor.
> Urban wages are fixed to a minimum level (e.g. by law). However, if this minimum is set too high it will create urban unemployment.

The city will become attractive to farmers if the expected wages there are higher than the agricultural wages.[60] At equilibrium (zero migration), the model leads to the existence of urban unemployment.

Box 3.4 (see page 59) presents a formalization of the Harris-Todaro model.

Problems.

The problem with the model obviously stands in its simplifying assumptions. It supposes a fixed capital when LDCs actually invest in infrastructure by borrowing from international banks. In addition, it supposes that migration has no cost. The so-called Todaro paradox emerges when measures aiming at reducing urban unemployment, such as direct subsidies to urban employment, have the opposite effect: they can stimulate rural exodus to the city and increase urban unemployment. Policy analysts would want to counterbalance this effect by controlling migration in order to keep urban unemployment at a tolerable level. Few will question the simplifying assumptions (fixed capital or total labor, probability of finding a job, etc.) either because they want to avoid addressing a problem that cannot be solved theoretically, or because they ignore that another policy will invalidate the assumptions (for example, if there are massive, externally funded injections of capital in the agricultural or manufacturing sector).

International migrations

Econometric studies have shown that when industrialized countries have implemented protectionist measures aiming at reducing their imports, there was an increase of immigration from LDCs because of the higher demand for labor and because of attractive wages,[61] which can be explained by a Harris-Todaro–like model. Liberalization of the economy can also increase international migration: an increase of income per capita in LDCs can promote migration (because it pushes further the monetary cost constraint) as long as the nonmonetary costs of migration (distance to the family, difference in culture, etc.) is compensated by higher wages. Therefore, everything is possible, and there is always something that can be explained by a simple model! But the fact that there are important international migrations (some 120 million people in 1996, according to Zlontnik [1998]) challenges the neoclassical theory of international trade, which is based on a representation where the production factors are not mobile (i.e. the Heckscher-Ohlin-Samuelson model).

Growth Models: Investment, Competition, Subjectivity, and Determinism

Rosenstein-Rodan (1943), in a paper that is believed to have pioneered development economics, put forward the need for a balanced growth helped by a *big push*, a muscled and diversified investment strategy. The analysis starts with the identification of potential obstacles to growth: on the demand side, the internal market is believed to be too small with respect to the production potential, while on the supply side the major problem are the bottlenecks in the productivity chain. The proposed *big push* strategy is twofold: in addition to targeted investments meant to fill gaps and exploit complementarities in the production chain, it promotes investments in broad-base projects that will be beneficial to a large number of economic agents (roads, electricity, dams). Note that the big push has been modeled formally only in recent years (Murphy, Shleifer, and Vishny 1989), while the concepts put forward by Rosenstein-Rodan had been applied since World War II.

Building on the same idea of a balanced growth theory and capital accumulation, some economists such as Nurkes (who builds on Rosenstein's work) insist on the timing and compatibility of rhythms of different sectors, while Rostow proposes a deterministic development scheme independent of timing. Similarly, the Harrod-Domar model and the neoclassical growth model have both played a major role in development despite their apparent contradiction about the influence of capital stock (that is, savings; see chapter 2). These models are described in the next sections.

Rostow stages of growth
Overview.

In his 1960 book *The Stages of Economic Growth*, American economic historian Walt Whitman Rostow suggested that all countries have to go through a specific sequence of five stages of economic development. LDCs would be just like industrialized countries were a long time ago. The interest of the approach has been to identify breakpoints, or milestones, in the development process and highlight the need for investment. The determinism of the approach is not as strict as it appears:

society can be jammed in a vicious circle—and this determines the duration of a development stage—until something triggers the transition to another stage. The Rostow model provided the foundation for much of the development planning in the early days of the USAID.

Stage 1: Traditional society.

The economy is similar to the one prevailing during the Middle Ages: dominated by subsistence activities, in particular agriculture. Trade is carried out by exchanging goods for other goods. There is virtually no savings or accumulation of capital and production is labor intensive. Feudality and religion block all change.

Stage 2: Transitional stage.

Societies get more open; people start to free themselves from the feudal or religious schemes and entrepreneurs appear. People fully realize the existence of terrestrial time, which modifies their behavior with respect to present and future consumption and stimulates savings. Technical progress and specialization generate surpluses for trading. There is an emergence of a transport infrastructure to support internal trade, while external trade concentrates on primary products. It is believed that the Harrod-Domar model applies to this phase (Easterly 2001).

Stage 3: Takeoff.

Takeoff is a short phase (a few decades) where growth becomes self-sustaining. Industrialization increases, and so does rural exodus. The level of investment reaches over 10 percent of GNP. Transformation industries appear and workers receive salaries. The economic transitions are accompanied by the evolution of new political and social institutions that boosts confidence in industrialization.

Stage 4: Drive to maturity.

The economy is experimenting with structural changes and is diversifying into new areas due to technological innovation. The secondary sector is consolidated, the economy is producing a wide range of goods and services, and there is less reliance on imports. Protest movements are more frequent as social requests become legitimate.

Stage 5: High mass consumption.
The economy is geared toward mass consumption. The consumer durable industries flourish. The service sector becomes increasingly dominant. Wages are higher, and working conditions improve.

According to Rostow, development requires substantial capital investment. For the economies of LDCs to grow, the right conditions for such investment would have to be created. If aid is given or foreign direct investment occurs at stage 3, the economy needs to have reached stage 2. If stage 2 has been reached, then injections of investment may lead to rapid growth.

Problems.

The idea of a deterministic, linear, ahistorical, and hierarchical development scheme inspired by Western culture seems not to be applicable to actual LDCs. The preconditions for growth and international context are vastly different now than they were when presently industrialized countries were LDCs. The target of high mass consumption is also poorly founded. Like many of the other models of economic developments, it is essentially a growth model and does not address the issue of development in the wider context. Finally, it is contradictory with a dualist view (that is, where a traditional society coexists with a modern one such as India).

The Harrod-Domar model
Overview.

The Harrod-Domar model has been used extensively in development economics. Stiglitz (2001) and Easterly (2001) argue that most development aid for infrastructure is related to this model. The reason for its widespread use is twofold: first, it is so simple that it easily fits into one's head; second, it is operational when it comes to evaluate funding requirements.

The model supposes a stable relationship between production Y and capital K:

$$Y = m \cdot K$$

where m is a constant. This can be rewritten as:

$$\Delta Y = m \cdot \Delta K$$

In economics terms, the growth rate can be expressed as the product of the investment rate by the marginal productivity of capital:

$$g = \frac{\Delta Y}{Y} = \frac{\Delta K}{Y} \cdot \frac{\Delta Y}{\Delta K} = i \cdot m$$

Where the growth rate g is given by:

$$g = \frac{\Delta Y}{Y}$$

The investment rate i is given by:

$$i = \frac{\Delta K}{Y}$$

The marginal productivity of capital m (how much increase of productivity results from a given increase in capital investment) is given by:

$$m = \frac{\Delta Y}{\Delta K} = \frac{1}{k}$$

k is the ICOR (incremental capital-output ratio), which is defined (for convenience) as the inverse of m.

We define the saving rate s as the proportion of production going into savings:

$$s = \frac{S}{Y}$$

In a closed economy, investment is equal to savings; therefore growth is equal to the ratio of savings rate s to ICOR:

$$g = \frac{s}{k}$$

Therefore, in the Harrod-Domar model, economic growth results from a capacity to mobilize savings (s), which will be transformed into capital investments, which in turn increase production with a given efficiency (m).[62]

With the hypothesis of constant ICOR, growth is linearly related to saving rate. This is also very operational. For example:

> To have a rough estimate of growth, just compare the saving rate to the ICOR.
>
> Given a goal for growth (e.g. 3 percent) one can estimate how much investment in capital is needed and therefore how much foreign aid is required given the level of domestic savings.
>
> One can also calculate the impact of domestic savings on growth.

Problems.

The main problem is that capital-output ratio is considered an exogenous variable, and therefore the steady state is unstable (there is no equilibrium in the price-quantity space); therefore, recommendations based on this model are in contradiction with NCE.

Nevertheless, it is by reference to this model that major investments in infrastructure (such as Ghana's Akosombo hydroelectric dam) are being justified. It is not clear how such investments clash or are canceled by strong NCE measures imposed upon the country (such as Solow's model, which considers capital as an endogenous variable).

As usual, there are no data to validate the model (Easterly 2001). And in fact, when it was tested against actual reality, its predictions generally failed (see chapter 2).

Neoclassical Economics: An Answer to the Water-Diamond Paradox

Isn't it strange that diamonds (which are quite useless) are much more expensive than water (which is essential to all life forms)? That problem bothered the classical economists, too, and they were unable to give a reasonable answer to that diamonds-versus-water paradox, saying, inadequately, that diamonds are more expensive because they are costlier to produce. The neoclassical solution, on the other hand, is that diamonds are more valuable because they are scarcer than water, and people will attribute a lot of value to at least their first few liters of water, but because there are so many

liters per person available the average cost is quite low. While these two answers may look like two sides of the same coin,[63] neoclassical theory of value insists on the concept of *subjective scarcity*, that is, scarcity as perceived by consumers: the values of goods depend on their relative scarcity, which in turn depends on subjective desires.[64] In NCE, the integration of subjective scarcity and demand is mainly done through the concept of *diminishing marginal utility*, that is, that equal increments of a good yield diminishing increments of utility.[65] This concept was covered in detail in the context of supply and demand models.

However, rather than consolidate one NCE theory, economists have developed several independent schools of thought, often themselves divided, which resulted in divergent conceptual models of how various elements of markets operate and in a great confusion for the rest of us. However, the building blocks of NCE are the same for every school of thought.

The Neoclassical model of growth

The neoclassical model of growth includes assumptions on technology, supply of inputs, markets, and behavior of firms; the dynamics of an economy over time is obtained by finding the equilibrium solution.

Technology.

Aggregate production function:

$$Y = F(K, L)$$

where K is capital and L labor and Y as defined above, production. (Note that labor is better seen as *effective* labor by multiplying by $A(t)$, which is a labor-increasing technology factor; we use AL to denote effective labor.)[66]

Aggregate output is produced with a *neoclassical* technology:

Decreasing marginal products in capital and labor:

$$\frac{\partial F}{\partial K} > 0 \, , \frac{\partial^2 F}{\partial K^2} < 0 \qquad \frac{\partial F}{\partial AL} > 0, \frac{\partial^2 F}{\partial AL^2} < 0$$

which means that the slope of the production function is always positive and decreasing (since the double derivative is negative); *Constant return to scale*

$$F(\lambda K, \lambda AL) = \lambda F(K, AL)$$

which means that the size of the economy does not matter (production of all firms is directly proportional to the production of one average firm), and therefore all decisions made by an archetypical firm characterize the productive behavior of the whole economy.

Inada conditions.

A function $f(x)$ satisfies the Inada conditions if: $f(0) = 0$; $f(\text{infinity}) = \text{infinity}$; $f(0) = \text{infinity}$; and $f(\text{infinity}) = 0$. the first condition means in our context that capital (or labor) are essential; the second means that capital (or labor) are not limiting factors; the third is that the increase in productivity is very large for small investments or little labor, i.e. the marginal product of capital ($\frac{\partial F}{\partial K}$) or labor ($\frac{\partial F}{\partial K}$) approaches infinity when capital (or labor) goes to o; the fourth is that the increase in productivity is very small when capital or labor are very large, i.e. the marginal product of capital ($\frac{\partial F}{\partial K}$) or labor ($\frac{\partial F}{\partial K}$) approaches o as capital (or labor) goes to infinity (see figure 3.5 for an example of a function that satisfies the Inada conditions).

Markets are competitive and in equilibrium. The main implication of these two assumptions is that at any time, output is determined entirely by the supply of productive inputs (labor and capital), and that the behavior of aggregate variables over time is determined by household consumption/saving and work/leisure choices.

The supply of inputs.

Inputs are owned by households in the economy
Capital $K(t)$ is given by the *law of motion of capital*:

$$\frac{dK(t)}{dt} = I(t) - \delta \cdot K(t)$$

where δ = rate of depreciation;
$I(t)$ = Investment
Labor: Each household supplies $l(t)$ units of labor in production activities (which are optimized); therefore, for a country $L(t) = l(t) \cdot N(t)$, where $N(t)$ is the number of households (increases with time due to population growth). Therefore

$$\frac{dL(t)/dt}{L(t)} = n + \frac{dl(t)/dt}{l(t)}$$

where n is the population growth rate.

$$\frac{dN(t)/dt}{N(t)}$$

Markets.

There are competitive markets for production. Prices are market clear prices: they adjust to equalize supply and demand—that is, consumption $C(t)$ and investment $I(t)$.

Behavior of firms

Firms are competitive and profit maximizers, that is, profit-seeking, for a given time period t:

$$\max(F(K, AL) - RK - wL)$$

where R and w, the real price of inputs, are given. Note that $R = dF/dK$, and $w = A\, dF/dAL$, also called "factor demands," are obtained.

Equilibrium.

Equilibrium depends on functions of time: $Y(t)$, $K(t)$, $L(t)$, $A(t)$, $C(t)$, $I(t)$, $w(t)$ and $R(t)$. Firms must behave optimally, and market must "clear," i.e. the process adjusts so that:

$$Y(t) = C(t) + I(t)$$

(production = consumption + investment)
The *Law of motion of capital* becomes:

$$\frac{dK(t)}{dt} = F(K(t), AL(t)) - C(t) - \delta \cdot K(t)$$

which is rewritten in per unit of labor ($1/L$), i.e. $k = K/L$, $c = C/L$, $y = Y/L$:

$$\frac{dk(t)}{dt} = F(k(t), A(t)) - c(t) - \left(\delta + n + \frac{dl(t)}{dt}\right)k(t)$$

which characterize the behavior of the economy over time. *l(t)* and *c(t)* depend on household choices (labor used for production activites and consumption) that are made under constraints (usually budget constraints):

$$Y = F(K,AL) = RK + (w/A) \, AL = RK + wL$$

If we divide by *N* (number of households), we obtain the budget constraint at the household level:

$$ly = lF(k,A) = Rlk + wl$$

Problems.

Necoclassical economists promised a purer, more scientific explanation of how an economy operates. However, the very notion of marginal utility, on which neoclassical economics (NCE) is based, is hardly a scientific concept, because it is not "refutable," to take Karl Popper's approach (Popper 1963). Stigler (1950) notes, "Had specific tests been made of the implications of theories, the unfruitfulness of the ruling utility theory as a source of hypotheses in demand would soon have become apparent." It also suffers from the same problems of demand and supply models.

The neoclassical models represent the micro foundations approach to macroeconomics. They assume that an entire country's or even the world's economy can be represented by the kinds of production function developed for the individual firm. However, the neoclassical production function does not describe firm behavior properly, and as a description of a national economy it is a bad joke. The model does not work unless we assume perfect competition, constant returns to scale, and full employment of resources. Particularly problematic is the marginal productivity theory of distribution (Miller 2000).

A comprehensive critique of NCE (and of the New Welfare Economics) is given in chapters 1 and 4. Despite all its weaknesses, NCE has managed to displace virtually every other theory in economics.

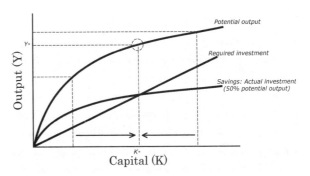

Figure 3.5: the Solow model of neoclassical growth. Equilibrium is reached where the required investment curve intersects with the actual investment curve (which is a constant fraction of the potential output function).

The neoclassical growth workhorse: Solow

The Solow model (for which the American economist Robert Solow was awarded the Nobel Prize in economics in 1987) was first conceived to analyze economic growth in relation to technology. Solow considers the capital-output ratio of the Harrod-Domar model as endogenous and indeed uses it as the adjusting variable that would allow reaching equilibrium. It has been and is still extensively used in the evaluation of international aid programs (Stiglitz 2002; Ranis 2004).

Following NCE, the main building block is the production function *Y=F(K,L)*. Solow's solution, which seeks an infinite time horizon, is obtained by making simple assumptions about the behavior of consumption (linear function of income), labor supply ("inelastic," which is to say, "constant"), and technology (labor-augmenting technology grows —exogenously—at a constant rate).

Depreciation of *K* is assumed a constant fraction of the capital stock, e.g. 5 percent/year. The depre-ciation line in *Y/K* space (or, in a more general setting, the requirement line) is a straight line (with slope 0.05). To determine investment (savings), Solow supposes there is no government and no trade with other countries, and that investment equals savings, which is a fixed share *s* of income (that is, a proportion of *Y*—50 percent in figure 3.5).

The basic version of the Solow model assumes an individual labor supply normalized and constant (*l(t)*=1). Therefore labor force is equal to population, *L(t)* = *N(t)*, (which grows at a rate *n*); Solow thus allows only the capital to vary. To identify the level of income (or output Y) this economy generates in the long run, we need to find out the capital stock maintained in long-run equilibrium.

According to the neoclassical model capital grows when households (or firms) invest and it is lost due to depreciation (or some of the capital becomes obsolete). The capital stock remains unchanged if investment equals (offsets) depreciation; this situation is called a steady state. It represents the long-run outcome the economy will eventually achieve starting from any initial condition. Prior to that point economists talk about *transitional economics*. k^* is called the *steady-state capital stock*, and γ^* is called the *steady-state income*.

At equilibrium, for a given time t and per unit of effective labor:

$$(1+n)(1+\gamma)\hat{k}_{t+1} = s \cdot F(\hat{k}(t), AL = 1) + (1-\delta)\hat{k}_t$$

Where $\hat{k} = \dfrac{K}{AL}$ (capital per unit of effective labor), s is the savings rate, n the population growth rate, and γ the rate of technical change dA/dt.

It can be shown that the widely used Cobb-Douglas production function ($Y = K^\alpha \cdot H^{1-\alpha}$) is neoclassical: it has constant return to scale, decreasing marginal product in each input, and Inada conditions. Using this production function, the temporal behavior of capital and GDP (and many other interesting variables) can be predicted:

a) capital per effective unit of labor $\hat{k} = \dfrac{K}{AL}$

$$\frac{1}{k} \cdot \frac{dk}{dt} = \frac{1}{\hat{k}} \cdot \frac{d\hat{k}}{dt} + \gamma$$

=> the higher the rate of technology change, the higher the growth of capital (It also applies to the steady state).

b) GDP per capita (i.e. $Y/N = y$):

$$\frac{1}{y} \cdot \frac{dy}{dt} = \alpha \cdot \frac{1}{k} \cdot \frac{dk}{dt} + (1-\alpha) \cdot \gamma$$

(α is the exponent in the Cobb-Douglas function)

=> the higher the growth of k, the higher the GDP growth. (This also applies to the steady state.)

It is easy to imagine that many decision-makers or policy analysts will memorize Solow's conclusions and use them as much as they can even if the basic assumptions do not apply.

Problems.

In contradiction to the Harrod-Domar model, Solow supposes that savings behavior has no influence on long-term growth: capital is not an exogenous factor, but a variable that is influenced by the environment and by the economic policy. Capital being rare in LDCs, and therefore more "expensive" according to NCE, labor-intensive production will be favored, which results in an ICOR that is lower than in developed countries, where capital is "cheaper." Note that the cost of imported capital can also be artificially influenced by exchange rates.

Solow suggests that long-term growth is determined mainly by demographic and technology variables. He does not include any variable related to an economic behavior: ICOR has no effect, except during the transition phase; accumulation has a meaning only until capital stock is optimal, and this value is bounded since ICOR is increasing with development. Therefore, Solow suggests that there is a natural convergence of economies, that LDCs' economies get closer and closer to the ones of developed countries without government intervention and policies. Empirical studies show that, unfortunately, convergence occurs for only a minority of LDCs.

Many studies have shown that energy is more important than either capital or labor (the only two factors that economists normally include in their Cobb-Douglass production functions) in determining economic productivity (see Hall et al. 2001). So, to use the language of physicists and engineers, we have to ask whether the basic economic equations have been *properly specified*. Our answer is absolutely not.

Box 5: A note on the genesis of policies

In its most basic definition, a public policy is a governmental action program in a given sector of society or a given geographical space. A policy can therefore be sectoral (e.g., agricultural policy) or territorial (e.g., regional development).

Nevertheless, a public policy is also a social mediation process, as the object of each policy is to take care of imbalances or inconsistencies between a sector and other sectors, or between a sector and society. In this case we would say that the object of a public policy is the management of global/sectoral linkages. The analysis of public policy as mediation or bargaining process is more in the domain of existing relationships between collective action from civil society social groups and the state.

Public policy does not appear to result from decisions elaborated rationally in ministerial bodies, that is, based on objectives that are both clear and well hierarchical. Instead, the construction and implementation of public policies result more from vigorous wrestling exercises between different ideologies (e.g., vision of the world) or objectives (e.g., vision of the future) given a series of constraints (real or stated). In addition policies are neither cast in stone as players that were ineffective in having their voice heard during the design phase will elaborate strategies to bypass or undermine them, therefore reducing their effectiveness.

Traditionally natural scientists have either ignored policies (possibly because of the connection with politics) or have naively adhered to a rational/positivist paradigm where policies are perceived as well instrumentalized, designed for clear purposes and building on data, models, and expert knowledge. Similarly, economists play a key role in policy design, yet the way natural sciences are accounted for in economic theory is flawed: (1) it may not pass any formal test against hard data, and (2) it is highly questionable in the context of societies that have deep cultural and traditional roots, common-pool resources, and social-environmental linkages (e.g., in sub-Saharan Africa).

Development and Sectoral Policies

It is common to analyze the production structure of a nation by dividing it into 3 sectors: the primary sector, with activities related to the exploitation of natural resources (agriculture, fishing, forestry, and in some cases mining and oil); the secondary sector, covering industries; and the tertiary sector, including services. Production is therefore analyzed in terms of value-added or in terms of active population (see chapter 20). It is also common to see development as a gradual transition from a state where the production system is dominated by the primary sector to a state where services prevail. This transition is tentatively explained by a modification of the supply-demand function according to the benefits that are expected for a given productive activity. It then becomes straightforward to apply NCE models in for the design of sectoral policies.

The main thrust of agricultural policies corresponds to the view that farmers are profit-maximizing individual agents interacting with a financial/technical system. They essentially involve aspects of (1) land tenure ("agrarian reform"), (2) technology (mechanization, fertilizers and biological improvement of crops, technical assistance), and (3) commerce (price policies, trade).

The main axes of policies related to industrial development include (1) heavy industries, which required considerable investment with the promise, according to Harrod-Domar, of large returns; (2) import-substituting industries; and (3) promotions of exports. Its is clear that industrial policies have to be accompanied by an assortment of powerful financial and commercial instruments that are doomed to be tainted by the flavor of the day in politics and development economics.

The informal sector, dominant in LDCs, has a different nature. Some analysts see in the informal sector the symptoms of the profound crisis characterizing the traditional sectors. Others see, to the contrary, the emergence of a powerful economy in perfect agreement with the neoclassical doctrine, and the best prepared to support the effects of deregulation and privatization.

Finance and Development

Given the weight of growth models in development aid, it is not surprising to find the important role of finance in the experiment. The Harrod-Domar model insists on the importance of savings and investment for growth, and development banks have heavily and consciously used this concept for their evaluation of LDC investment projects. The results are mixed, however: countries with high saving rates have not necessarily experienced strong growth (Thailand's 4.5 percent average annual growth since 1980 versus Costa Rica's 0.25 percent annual growth during the same period) and not all countries with similar growth have had similar investment rate (Malaysia versus Chile). Some say that these "anomalies" have been caused by restrictive financial measures (such as lowering interest rates) during the 1960s and 1970s. This is essentially why the IMF and the World Bank triggered the "structural adjustment" tide of the 1980s, which produced in the short term a macroeconomic context that was antagonistic to increased savings and investment in LDCs (ironically, the result is opposite to Harrod-Domar's conditions for growth): "optimal" external financing became risky, either because of higher debt, or because of vulnerability to external shocks. In this unstable context even concepts that seem intuitively valid (for example, the Keynesian "law of consumption": the share of consumption decreases as revenues are higher) have to be reexamined.

Structural adjustment programs have also been accompanied by powerful monetary policies aimed at improving the balance of payments. Several theories contributed to their development. The *theory of critical elasticities* establishes a relationship between exchange rate and commercial balance: the Marshall-Lerner-Robinson theorem,[67] which states that devaluation improves commercial balance as long as the sum of price-elasticities of exports is greater than one (a condition difficult to find for most LDCs exports, which have low elasticities). The tautological *absorption thesis* sustains that devaluation is not sufficient, that equilibrium is reached only if internal spending is reduced (hence the term "contraction"); since the private sector is assumed to reach equilibrium naturally, policy makers had as their objective justification of cuts in government spending. The generalization of the absorption thesis to all transactions related to the balance of payments (including demand and supply of money) puts the money market at the center of the stage.[68]

The Polak model (or IMF monetary model)

The first model of reference for macroeconomic stabilization plans promoted by the IMF was proposed by Polak in 1950. Since then it has been at the core of the analysis leading to IMF conditionality, i.e. the policy actions that a borrowing country must take to have access to IMF credit. Like the models of supply-demand and Harrod-Domar, its success comes from its simplicity and how it facilitates the evaluation of financial requirements.

Considering price-takers in a small open economy with no access to financial markets (that is, demand for money such as IMF credit is the only motive for transaction), the system consists of a dynamic system of four equations:

1) demand for money:

$$Md = k \cdot P \cdot Y$$

where P is the general price level and Y country's real income. k corresponds to the inverse of the *velocity of circulation of money*.

2) supply of money:

$$Ms = C + R$$

where C is the domestic credit to banking system and to the state and R the country's foreign reserves.

3) Exchange rate:

$$P = e \cdot Pf$$

where e is the exchange rate and Pf the foreign prices.

4) Equilibrium:

$$Md = Ms$$

We obtain an equation that describes the conditions for equilibrium of foreign reserves:

$$R = k \cdot e \cdot Pf \cdot Y - C$$

Therefore the increase in foreign reserves (i.e. $\Delta R > 0$) depends on 3 factors that are controlled directly or indirectly by macroeconomic policy: devaluation of domestic currency ($\Delta e > 0$), restriction of internal credit ($\Delta C > 0$), and increase of supply ($\Delta Y > 0$). One can easily recognize the ingredients of IMF conditionality. This model is still very much alive today as monetary targets continue to serve as performance criteria or benchmarks essential for renegotiation of loans.

There is a good correlation between growth and the variables linked to the financial (and banking) system (Goldsmith 1969), but an adequate financial system is not necessarily a requisite to growth: it could well be the opposite! Microfinance and informal financing embodies an important and often dominant share of the economic activity of LDCs; this would be related to traditional society, or a rational response to an inefficient state or financing system, or a safety net to structural adjustments. The variables affecting savings/investment are believed to be:

Exports per capita GNP is a good indicator of the public savings rate: in countries where the fiscal system is rudimentary, it is easier to apply taxes on imports and exports that on other goods and services.

The effect of the capital flow is not obvious, as external investments can substitute for domestic savings instead of complementing it.

Dependency ratio (inactive/active) is correlated to savings: a young population has little savings.

Financial and monetary policies: Interest rates, geographic distribution of intermediaries (such as the banking system), taxation, maturity of financial system.

Energy and Development

I cannot resist the temptation to end this chapter by describing Hall's model of development, which is little known and to my knowledge has never been officially used for development policy, and which perhaps future historians of economics will find as faulty as the models reviewed here. This model is based on the empirical observation that almost everywhere economic development is almost one for one with an increase in energy use (e.g., Hall and Ko 1995; Ko, Hall, and Lemus 1998; Tharakan, Kroeger, and Hall 2001). Where energy use increases at a rate greater than the population, as was the case for Korea (1970–95), per capita wealth increases. Where population growth is the same as the growth in energy use, then populations stay at the same level of wealth, as is the case in Costa Rica (Hall 2000). Where populations grow more rapidly than energy use, people get poorer, as in the case of Zambia. Of course, this model leaves unanswered what factors cause or can cause energy use to increase, and assumes that any new energy is used wisely. Still, this model does seem to work for all countries (with a few minor exceptions such as Singapore) where it has been examined, so as an empiricist and believer in the importance of energy I will believe in it for the moment. This model also warns us that the future may be bleak for development because of the incipient peak in global oil production and th environmental impact of energy use. As such it requires us again to bring the issues of population and natural resources to center stage.

Conclusion

This historical and model-centered perspective highlights an unexpected phenomenon: the smooth transition of descriptive, academic economic statements to normative ones that irreversibly shape our mind and our society. Karl Marx had already foreseen the risk that the imposition of bourgeois conceptual models could have on the evolution of society, and he proposed radical measures to prevent it.

Instead of the fairer society that most human beings want, we observe endemic hunger, increased inequalities, a widening gap between developed and less developed countries, enormous profits of the "pro-poor" World Bank and the IMF, and ad hoc interventionist wars. The problem is that we do not know how the world would be without development models and development aid.

Development models are contradictory: some promote savings, others trade, others supply, others money markets, some are based on the analysis of the history of Western societies, others pop up from nowhere. Few, if any, are formally validated by data; "when an economist says the evidence is *mixed*, he means that theory says one thing and data says the opposite."[69] Nevertheless development conceptual models are well alive and unanimously accepted: the Harris-Todaro model on rural-urban migration, the NCE supply and demand, Rostow's stages of growth, and so on. Hall (1988) reports a similar phenomenon with poorly validated ecological models (predator-prey, fish population dynamics, etc.) and for economics (Hall 1990, 1992, 2000; Hall et al. 2001).

However, the problem is not just in the economic science, which has been extremely prolific, rigorous, and innovative. The problem lies in the use that businessmen and politicians make of it, the easy way they ignore model assumptions and range of validity, and the way they can live with contradictions, "mixed evidence," and stagnation or collapse of LDCs' economies. Then a simple conceptual model becomes a powerful and dangerous weapon when it materializes in development policies. Indeed using several contradictory conceptual models according to what is more profitable is even more powerful—for example, funding large dams (which have all been failures in LDCs and benefit only those who build the dam) while promoting policies that consider capital as an endogenous variable. Consequently, everything seems to support the hypothesis that it is a plain profit-maximizing strategy that has motivated the ways of interacting with LDCs.

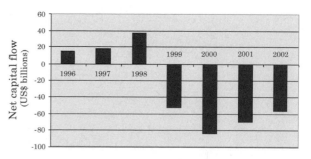

Figure 3.6: Net capital flows to all developing countries (1998–2002) ($billion).

Recent findings on capital assets seem to confirm this hypothesis. Instead of the "trickle-down" effect of NCE development policies—that is, the flow of capital from where it is plentiful to where it is scarce—the reverse is happening (Pettifor 2003): since 1999 there is a net flow in the range of $50–$80 billion from the poorest countries to the richest ones (the "Hoover effect") (Figure 3.6).

Adam Smith wrote in 1755, "Little else is requisite to carry a state to the highest degrees of opulence from the lowest barbarism, but peace, easy taxes, and tolerable administration of justice." Perhaps it is time to think that the world is complex, adaptive, and that no simple recipe will work? International development should be about social and political empowerment, not only money efficiency. It should be accomplished through learning, organization, adequate resources intelligently managed, innovation, and ethics, not simply with economic models.

Acknowledgments

Thanks are due to the numerous people who put their ideas, writings, and realizations into the public domain. I owe special thanks to Charlie Hall for giving me a reprint of his paper on ecological models (Hall 1988) back in 1995 and for animated discussions with him about economics, science, and development, which inspired me to write this chapter. Comments from John Gowdy were greatly appreciated.

Notes

1. For agricultural research centers, development has traditionally been associated with "producing more food." Now, with the genetically modified organisms lobby,

modern agricultural research for development is roughly equivalent to "producing more food with more vitamins."

2. Increase of the ability of a country to produce goods and services.

3. Inequality also implies a separation of perceived realities between the poor and the powerful: "The rich have always been different people than you and me," writes F. Scott Fitzgerald in *The Great Gatsby*, to which Ernest Hemingway once rejoined, "Yes, they have more money."

4. My opinion is that mechanisms for fair redistribution of wealth, put in place after the Second World War until the 1980s, have done far more to help the developed economies than economic theories.

5. Together with a level of poverty or corruption that citizens can tolerate—in other words, that do not compromise the economy.

6. In fact, when there is a lot of money involved, economists are believed to be better prepared.

7. Ironically many economists complain that nobody listens to them! However it is clear that structural adjustment is a "victory" of NCE theory.

8. In two words, accepting a broader, non-economic definition of poverty would have triggered harsh critics toward the approach of the World Bank, and therefore there was extreme pressure to modify the message of the World Development Report—which was meant to be neutral—to suit the World Bank's interests. A compromise solution is the WDR 2000 that went to press.

9. Webster's Revised Unabridged Dictionary, 1996, 1998, MICRA, Inc.

10. The American Heritage Dictionary of the English Language, Fourth Edition, Houghton Mifflin Company

11. WordNet 1.6, 1997 Princeton University.

12. This section is largely inspired from Gélinas (1994).

13. In fact, the present situation has evolved from the colonies and therefore has retained certain of their characteristics.

14. On March 12, 1947, U.S. President Truman requested appropriation for $400 million before a joint session of Congress to fight the spread of communism in Greece and Turkey. This so-called Truman Doctrine received the backing of most of the Republican members of Congress in accordance with the bipartisan foreign policy, which was in effect during most of the Truman administration. (http://www.trumanlibrary.org/truman-2.htm)

15. Korea, Taiwan, Palestine, and Southeast Asia were assisted within the Point IV program.

16. After U.S. Secretary of State George C. Marshall (1880–1959).

17. In 1961 the OEEC became the Organisation for Economic Cooperation and Development (OECD).

18. A term made up by the USAID director in 1968.

19. Robert Herdt, head of the Rockefeller Foundation agricultural division in 1997, emphasizes in his words the role of fertilizers: "Today fertilizer, produced by the industrial sector, is an important source of food."

20. The scope of *regional* advisory services was established by Resolution 2803 on December 14, 1971.

21. In July and August 1950 the U.S. Congress would adopt the Act for International Development and the Foreign Economic Assistance Act, which allowed bilateral aid agreements with LDCs.

22. www.trumanlibrary.org/trumanpapers/pppus/1950/220.htm.

23. Japan already was deeply concerned with population and hunger issues before World War II and believed that research for development was necessary (www.ipss.go.jp/English/info-e/history.html).

24. Korean War, China.

25. As India Prime Minister Nehru said during the Bandung Conference, "We do not agree with the communist teachings, we do not agree with the anti-communist teachings, because they are both based on wrong principles."

26. Pan-Africanism, pan-Arabism, and pan-Islam, for example.

27. There are now more than 24,000 NGOs active at the international level.

28. The main focus of UNEP is to address the relationships between the economy, the environment, and people, and the promotion of environment science and information.

29. In most modern projects that put forward the crux of sustainable development, the main thrusts are still one of these dimensions depending on the disciplinary area of the organization writing the proposal. Interaction with other dimensions—e.g., agricultural technology as drivers of poverty reduction—is often assumed. Truly integrated, unbiased projects are rare.

30. Oil prices quadrupled in 1973–74. OPEC revenues increased from $14 to $70 billion between 1972 and 1974.

31. The apparent success of NCE recipes in the West led LDC authorities to enthusiastically endorse the growth prospects of open economies.

32. Ten years before, the debt from all LDCs totaled $110 billion.

33. The Harrod-Domar model establishes a direct relationship between capitalization and growth.

34. In addition, commodity prices for LDCs exports dropped because of the recession. But this effect is smaller:

the balance of trade has always been much more in favor of the industrial countries.

35. For example, Honduras diligently followed the rules of SAPs since 1980, and governments have genuinely believed in the benefits of a strong collaboration with the United States (being for example a base for the contras war in Nicaragua, as well as a banana republic owned by Dole and Chiquita). In 1999, immediately after Hurricane Mitch destroyed the banana plantations near San Pedro Sula, where 20,000 people were employed, Chiquita alone fired 5,500 out of 6,500 banana workers. Moral: there is little room for ethics in business, and a sustained relationship with multinationals is no guarantee for a decent treatment during a crisis.

36. The budget of EMBRAPA, Brazil's agricultural research department, is now larger than the whole CGIAR budget.

37. The private sector arm of the World Bank (the IFC) has posted double-digit growth rates. The World Bank profits have increased from $1.2 billion in 1996 to $5.3 billion in 2003.

38. The demand was dismissed during the WTO 2003 negotiation round, and 25,000 influential cotton farmers in the United States will keep 2 million poor West African farmers hostage by encouraging U.S. cotton tariffs. It is estimated that the income of 1 billion people from LDCs depends on cotton.

39. A classic economist's joke, which has a variant: "Economics is the only field in which two people can share a Nobel Prize for saying opposing things." Specifically, Myrdal and Hayek shared the Nobel prize in 1974 "for their pioneering work in the theory of money and economic fluctuations and for their penetrating analysis of the interdependence of economic, social and institutional phenomena."

40. This section is largely inspired from Montalieu T (2001), *Economie du développement*.

41. The reader is encouraged to look at Gonçalo L. Fonseca and Leanne J. Ussher's Web site, http://cepa.newschool.edu/het/home.htm, for in-depth history of economic thought.

42. The Hayek Nobel prize lecture is particularly eloquent on the problem of economics aspiring to the recognition of the physical sciences, on the validation of economic theories, and on the non-usefulness of mathematical economics. "I prefer true but imperfect knowledge, even if it leaves much undetermined and unpredictable, to a pretence of exact knowledge that is likely to be false" (http://www.nobel.se/economics/laureates/1974/hayek-lecture.html).

43. Cournot, who earned a doctorate in physics, has also introduced the concepts of marginal revenue and cost, profit-maximizing firm, monopoly, duopoly, and perfect competition.

44. As he notes, the "accessory ideas of utility, scarcity, and suitability to the needs and enjoyments of mankind . . . are variable and by nature indeterminate, and consequently ill suited for the foundation of a scientific theory" (Cournot 1838:10).

45. It is largely beyond the scope of this book, if not impossible, to list all the dogma and pseudo laws of economics. We can, however, mention the concept of "Normal goods," for which demand increases—upward *shift* of the demand curve—as income increases, and "Inferior goods," for which demand decreases as income increases.

46. While it is intuitive to think that decisions to buy depend on price, decisions to produce consider the true variable to be the price at which a given quantity can be sold. Indeed, the producer knows his costs of production for any given quantity and has to guess on the selling price in order to cover his costs.

When he moved from Guatemala—where people are skilled bargainers—to Costa Rica, a Guatemalan friend went to the town's open market to buy vegetables from a farmer. He told the farmer that he would buy his potatoes at the same price as his neighbor, who was selling his at 25 *colones* less per kilo. The reply was, "If you want to pay that price, you just have to buy from him."

47. We pose this hypothesis because in theory, in case of a competitive market the supply (or demand) curve collapses into a single point (this is the main objection raised by the Austrian school).

48. Note that classical economists theorized that prices are determined by the costs of production.

49. An economist is a trained professional paid to guess wrong about the economy. An econometrician is a trained professional paid to use computers to guess wrong about the economy (a classic economist's joke).

50. Note that the model is not restricted to goods: it is also used to analyze demand and supply of labor, services, and so forth.

51. In many circumstances the market falls short in uncovering the social costs and benefits of a good, and therefore the optimum price is not reached: this is called "market failure." Generally this is due to (1) incomplete specification of property rights, (2) common goods, (3) transaction costs, (4) option demand (value of choice at some future time; consumers are uncertain about their needs), and (5) imperfect information.

52. This is because the slope of the demand curve is positive.

53. They reaffirmed Say's Law: supply creates its own demand. In other words, production of goods and services must precede their utilization, overproduction of any particular good being impossible in a free market.

54. Structural adjustment describes the process of reforming LDCs' economies and institutions in order to maximize per capita economic growth. Its theoretical foundations are models of the balance of payments (import exports) and the reduction of inflation. SAPs generally require countries to devalue their currencies against the dollar; lift import and export restrictions; balance their budgets and not overspend; and remove price controls and state subsidies.

55. Malthus (1766–1834) was a clergyman who was concerned by the decline of living conditions in nineteenth-century England. He believed the decline was due to a demographic explosion with its roots in the irresponsibility of the lower classes.

56. It is believed that the decrease of mortality rate is due to advances in health care (technology), while the change of birth rate needs a change in mentalities, which takes more time.

57. In addition to green revolution precepts that are clearly Malthusian, we can cite Leibenstein's (1957) theory based on the comparison of the economic growth and the population growth curves. The only way to achieve development (to go from a "subsistence" point to an "existence" point, to use Leibenstein's terms) is to implement restrictive population policies that will force the population growth to be lower than the economic growth.

58. It is difficult to avoid thinking that Malthus may have been right: no rich country has had a population growth rate higher than 1 percent in the last hundred years, and even so, every rich country has virtually depleted its own natural resources base. And whether near-future exhaustion of cheap oil will have a large impact might bring Malthus right back into our laps, whether we want that or not.

59. Note that without international immigration, the U.S. economy would certainly not be what it is.

60. The reverse is not true: the rural sector is not attractive to urban people.

61. This may explain part of U.S. growth: to maintain the low-cost immigration to enforce protectionist measures while maintaining the young workforce necessary for innovation.

62. Remember this and you can decide how much to loan to an LDC as easily as a bank manager does. You also hear from time to time in the news how countries compare in terms of capacity for savings: this is Harrod-Domar model in action.

63. "[T]he value of [precious] metals has, in all ages and nations, arisen chiefly from their scarcity, and that their scarcity has arisen from the very small quantities of them which nature has any where deposited in one place, from the hard and intractable substance with which she has almost every where surrounded those small quantities, and consequently from the labor and expence [*sic*] which are every where necessary in order to penetrate and get at them" (A. Smith 1776:563).

64. To take Lionel Robbins's (1932:46) famous example, bad eggs may be "rare," but if people do not desire bad eggs, then even one bad egg is already "too many" in their eyes and thus will not have much value.

65. Daniel Bernoulli use this concept to solve the St. Petersburg paradox: he assumed that the willingness of being richer by $2 million is not twice as high as being richer by $1 million.

66. Hall et al. (1986) have shown that labor productivity in the United States from 1900 to 1984 was very highly correlated with the increase in energy used per worker hour during that time interval.

67. The theorem is named after three neoclassical economists who discovered it independently: Alfred Marshall (1842–1924), Abba Lerner (1903–82), and Joan Robinson (1903–83).

68. It is exactly to these policies that Malaysian president Mahatir attributed the collapse of Asian markets in 1997.

69. Another classic economist's joke.

References

Birdsall, N., A. C. Kelley, and S. W. Sinding. 2001. *Population Matters: Demographic Change, Economic Growth, and Poverty in the Developing World*. New York: Oxford University Press.

Boserup, E. *Population and Technical Change: A Study of Long-term Trends*. Chicago: University of Chicago Press.

Brabda, D., and A. S. Brandao. 1993. Urbanization, agricultural development and land allocation. *World Bank Discussion Papers* 201.

Cleveland, C., C. Constanza, C. A. S. Hall, and R. Kaufmann. 1984. Energy and the United States economy: A biophysical perspective. *Science* 225:890–97.

Cournot, A. 1838. *Principes de la théorie des richesses*. Paris: Hachette.

Curry, T. 1999. The LDC debt crisis. www.fdic.gov/bank/historical/history/contents.html.

Dalrymple, D. G. 1986. *Development and Spread of High-Yielding Rice Varieties in Developing Countries*. Washington, D.C.: USAID.

Easterly, W. 2001. *The Elusive Quest for Growth: An Economist's Adventures in the Tropics*. Cambridge, Mass.: MIT Press.

Gélinas, J. B. 1994. *Et si le Tiers-Monde s'autofinançait: de l'endettement à l'épargne*. Paris: Les Editions Ecosociété.

Hall, C. A. S. 1988. An assessment of several of the historically most influential theoretical models used in ecology and of the data provided in their support. *Ecological Modelling* 43:5–31.

———. 1990. Sanctioning resource depletion: Economic development and neo-classical economics. *The Ecologist* 20:61–66.

———. 1992. Economic development or developing economics: What are our priorities? In M. K. Wali and J. S. Singh, eds., *Environmental Rehabilitation*, 1:101–26. Amsterdam: Elsevier.

———. 2004. The myth of sustainable development: Personal reflections on energy, its relation to neoclassical economics, and Stanley Jevons. *Journal of Energy Resources Technology* 126:86–89.

———, ed. 2000. *Quantifying Sustainable Development*. San Diego: Academic Press.

Hall, C. A. S., and J.-Y. Ko. 2005. The myth of efficiency through market economics: A biophysical analysis of tropical economies, especially with respect to energy and water. In M. Bonnell, ed., *Land, Water and Forests in the Tropics*, 40–58. UNESCO.

Hall, C. A. S., C. J. Cleveland, and R. Kaufmann. 1984. *Energy and Resource Quality: The Ecology of the Economic Process*. New York: Wiley-Interscience.

Hall, C. A. S., D. Lindenberger, R. Kummel, T. Kroeger, and W. Eichhorn. 2001. The need to reintegrate the natural sciences with economics. *BioScience* 51, no. 6: 663–73.

Harris, J. R., and M. P. Todaro. 1970. Migration, unemployment and development: A two sector analysis. *American Economic Review* 60:126–42.

Kapoor, S. 2003. Can the World Bank and IMF cancel 100% of HIPC debt? www.jubileeresearch.org/analysis/reports/jubilee_canceldebt.pdf.

Ko, J. Y., C. A. S. Hall, and L. L. Lemus. 1998. Resource use rates and efficiency as indicators of regional sustainability: An examination of five countries. *Environmental Monitoring and Assessment* 51:571–93.

Lewis, B. 1954. *Economic Development with Unlimited Supply of Labor*. Manchester: Manchester School of Economics.

Miller, R. A. 2000. Ten cheaper spades. *Journal of Economic Education* 31, no. 2: 119–30.

Montalieu, T. 2001. *Economie du développement*. Paris: Breal.

Murphy, K., A. Shleifer, and R. Vishny. 1989. Industrialization and the big push. *Journal of Political Economy* 97:1003–26.

Myoung-jea, L. 2002. *Panel Data Econometrics: Methods-of-moments and Limited Dependent Variables*. San Diego: Academic Press.

North, D. C. 1990. *Institutions, Institutional Change and Economic Performance*. New York: Cambridge University Press.

O'Neill, R. V., J. R. Kahn, and C. S. Russell. 1998. Economics and ecology: The need for detente in conservation ecology. *Conservation Ecology* 2, no. 1: 4.

Pettifor, A. 2003. *Real World Economic Outlook, 2003: The Legacy of Globalization*. London: Palgrave MacMillan.

Popper, K. R. 1963. *Conjectures and Refutations*. New York: Harper & Row.

Ranis, G. 2004. The evolution of development thinking: Theory and policy. Center Discussion Paper 886, Economic Growth Center, Yale University.

Rosenstein-Rodan, P. N. 1943. Problems of industrialisation of eastern and southern Europe. *Economic Journal* 43:202–11.

Rostow, W. W. 1960. *The Stages of Economic Growth: A Non-Communist Manifesto*. London: Cambridge University Press.

Sachs, J. 1996. Growth in Africa: It can be done. *The Economist*, 29 June 1996.

Stigler, G. J. 1950a. The development of utility theory I. *Journal of Political Economy* 58, no. 4: 307–27.

———. 1950b. The development of utility theory II. *Journal of Political Economy* 58, no. 5: 373–96.

Stiglitz, J. E. 2002. *Globalization and Its Discontents*. New York: Norton.

Tharakan, P., T. Kroeger, and C. A. S. Hall. 2001. 25 years of industrial development: A study of resource use rates and macro-efficiency indicators for five Asian countries. *Environmental Science and Policy* 4: 319–32.

Todaro, M. P. 1969. A model of labor migration and urban unemployment in LDCs. *American Economic Review* 59:138–48.

WDR. 2001. *World Development Report 2000–2001: Attacking Poverty*. New York: Oxford University Press.

Zlontnik, H. 1998. International migration 1965–1996: An overview. *Population and Development Review* 24, no. 3: 429–68.

CHAPTER 4

THE NEED TO REINTEGRATE THE NATURAL SCIENCES WITH ECONOMICS

CHARLES A. S. HALL, DIETMAR LINDENBERGER,

REINER KÜMMEL, TIMM KROEGER,

AND WOLFGANG EICHHORN

How long will researchers working in adjoining fields . . . abstain from expressing serious

concern about the splendid isolation in which academic economics now finds itself?

—Wassily Leontief

The question is extremely important, because economics is the foundation upon which most decisions affecting agriculture, fisheries, and the environment and, indeed, most aspects of our daily lives are based. Natural scientists, including biological scientists, may have particular views on this or that economic policy, but few question the legitimacy of economics as a tool. We believe, paraphrasing the great Prussian military historian Karl von Clausewitz, that economics is too important to leave to the economists and that natural scientists should not leave the procedure by which we do economics up to the economists alone. Instead, natural scientists must contribute to a new discourse about the means, methods, and ends of economics.

This chapter is a response to Leontief's question. It is essential that economics be based on sound principles, and that the policies that are generated have a solid foundation. Neoclassical economics, that form of economics derived in the mid-nineteenth century and the one that prevails today, focuses on problems related to value decisions, the behavior of economic actors, and the working of markets. These problems belong to the sphere of the social sciences (many of whom,

incidentally, have their own problems with neoclassical economic theory; see, for example, Marris 1992). But the wealth that is distributed in the markets must be produced in the hard sphere of the material world, where all operations must obey the laws and principles of physics, chemistry, and biology. Our concern is that many production models of economics are not based upon these laws and principles; in fact, they tend to ignore them (Georgescu-Roegen 1971; Daly 1973, 1977; Kümmel et al. 1985; Leontief 1982; Cleveland et al. 1984; Hall, Cleveland, and Kaufmann 1986; Hall 1992, 2000).

This disregard of the biophysical aspects of production by economists was not the rule historically. Quesnay and other members of the eighteenth-century French physiocrat school focused on the use of solar radiation by biotic organisms and the role of land in generating wealth by capturing this energy through agricultural production. The classical economics of Adam Smith, David Ricardo, and Karl Marx was interested in both the physical origin and the distribution of wealth (Smith 1937; Ricardo 1891; Marx 1906). Podolinsky, Geddes, Soddy, and Hogben were biological and physical scientists of the nineteenth and early twentieth centuries who thought deeply about economic issues (Martinez-Alier 1987; Christensen 1989; Cleveland and Ruth 1997). Thus we find the degree to which neoclassical economics has displaced classical economics curious and almost a historical accident. The primary reason for the displacement of classical economics by the neoclassical school was the superior mathematical rigor of neoclassical economics and the development of the marginal utility theory, which solved the "water versus diamonds" paradox that classical economics could not. But the underlying biophysical perspective of Smith and Ricardo was not brought along with the new mathematical elegance of the "marginal revolution."

Consequently, major decisions that affect millions of people and most of the world's ecosystems are based on neoclassical economic models that, although internally consistent and mathematically sophisticated, ignore or are not sufficiently consistent with the basic laws of nature. This leads to the failure of those economic policies that run against these laws and endanger sustainable development. In this chapter we examine this issue in more detail, making a case for including the laws of nature in economic theory and analysis and in the policies derived from this theory as carefully and explicitly as the assumptions on human preferences and choices. Both natural scientists and even some economists have been leveling severe criticisms at the basis of neoclassical economics for many years (Soddy 1926; Boulding 1966; Georgescu-Roegen 1966, 1971; Daly 1973; Binswanger and Ledergerber 1974; Cleveland et al. 1984; Hall, Cleveland, and Kaufmann 1986; Ayres 1996, 1999). These criticisms, however, are largely ignored by neoclassical economists, and the rest of the scientific community seems to be largely unaware of them. We believe that it is time to exhume these criticisms and add to them more recent analytic work that gives them even greater validity.

Past criticisms of neoclassical economics from the perspective of natural scientists can be summarized under three fundamental arguments:

1. The structure of the basic neoclassical model is unrealistic because it is not based on the biophysical world and the laws governing it, especially thermodynamics.
2. The boundaries of analysis are inappropriate because they do not include the real processes of the biosphere that provide the material and energy inputs, the waste sinks, and the necessary milieu for the economic process.
3. The basic assumptions underlying the models used have not been put forth as testable hypotheses but rather as givens.

We substantiate these three criticisms in the pages that follow, then present a new model of industrial production that we believe further supports our criticisms and our assessment of the importance of energy. In this new model, the output of the economic system and the maintenance of its components depend on continuous input of energy into the system, as is true for all organisms and ecosystems.

Critique of Neoclassical Economics

Anything as important in industrial life as power deserves more attention than it has yet received from economists. . . . A theory of production that will really explain how wealth is produced must analyze the contribution of the element energy.
—F. G. Tryon

The decisive mistake of traditional economics . . . is the disregard of energy as a factor of production.
—H. C. Binswanger and E. Ledergerber

Argument 1: Thermodynamics

Contemporary economics pays only marginal attention to the first and second laws of thermodnamics. This is a serious conceptual flaw and an obstacle to designing economic policies that can successfully meet the challenges of pollution, resource scarcity, and unemployment. The two laws say: Nothing happens in the world without energy conversion and entropy production, with the consequence that every process of industrial and biotic production requires the input of energy. Because of the unavoidable entropy production the valuable part of energy (called exergy) is transformed into useless heat at the temperature of the environment (called anergy), and usually matter is dissipated, too. This results in pollution and, eventually, the exhaustion of the higher-grade resources of fossil fuels and raw materials. Human labor, living on food, has been, and continues to be, replaced (at least in part) by energy-driven machines in the routine production of goods and services.

Although the first and second laws of thermodynamics are the most thoroughly tested and validated laws of nature and state explicitly that it is impossible to have a perpetual motion machine—that is, a machine that performs work without the input of exergy—the basic economic model *is* a perpetual motion machine, with no limits (figure 4.1a). Most economists have accepted that incomplete model as the basis for their analysis and have relegated energy and other resources to unimportance in their analysis (e.g., Denison 1979, 1984). This attitude was fixed in the minds of most economists by the analysis of Barnett and Morse, who found no indication of increasing scarcity of raw materials, as determined by their inflation-corrected price, for the first half of the twentieth century (Barnett and Morse 1963; Smith 1989).

Their analysis, although cited by nearly all economists interested in the depletion issue, was nevertheless seriously incomplete. Cleveland showed that the only reason that decreasing concentrations and qualities of resources were not translated into higher prices for constant quality was because of the decreasing price of energy and its increasing use in the exploitation of increasingly lower-grade reserves in the United States and elsewhere (Cleveland 1991). Thus, although economists have argued that natural resources are not important to the economy, the truth is that it is only *because* of the abundant availability of many natural resources that economics can assign them low monetary value despite their critical importance to economic production.

The perspective of the Nobel laureate in economics Robert M. Solow is interesting. In 1974 he

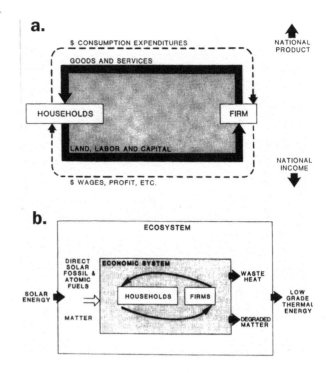

Figure 4.1. Two views of the economy. (a) The neoclassical view of how economies work. Households sell or rent land, natural resources, labor, and capital to firms in exchange for rent, wages, and profit (factor payments). Firms combine the factors of production and produce goods and services in return for consumption expenditures, investment, government expenditures, and net exports. This view represents, essentially, a perpetual motion machine. (b) Our perspective, based on a biophysical viewpoint, of the minimum changes required to make figure a conform to reality. We have added the basic energy and material inputs and outputs that are essential if the economic processes represented in figure a are to take place (based on Daly 1977).

considered the possibility that "the world can, in effect, get along without natural resources" because of the technological options for the substitution of other factors for non-renewable resources: he noted, however, that if "real output per unit of resources is effectively bounded—cannot exceed some upper limit of productivity which in turn is not too far from where we are now—then catastrophe is unavoidable" (Solow 1974:11). More recently, Solow states, "It is of the essence that production cannot take place without some use of natural resources" (Solow 1992, 1993). Clearly, there is need for more analytical and empirical work on the relation between economic production and natural resources, especially energy but also all aspects of the supportive contributions of the biosphere. We believe that the attempt simply to put a monetary value on these services, although useful in some respects, is insufficient to resolve the issue, if only because such values are based on human perceptions that, in turn, are developed on the basis of imperfect information and, all too often, myopia.

Why Does Neoclassical Economics Assign a Low Value to Natural Resources?

The conventional neoclassical view of the low importance of energy and materials dates back to the first stages in the development of neoclassical economics. Initially, the focus was not so much on the generation of wealth as on its distribution and the "efficiency of markets." Consequently, the early thinkers started with a model of pure exchange of goods without considering their production. With a set of mathematical assumptions on "rational consumer behavior," it was shown that through the exchange of goods in markets an equilibrium results in which all consumers maximize their utility in the sense that it is not possible to improve the situation of a single consumer without worsening the situation of at least one other consumer (the so-called Pareto optimum). This benefit of (perfect) markets is generally considered as *the* foundation of free market-economics. It shows why markets, where "greedy" individuals meet, work at all. But later, when the model was extended to include production, the problem of the physical generation of wealth was coupled, inseparably, to the problem of the distribution of wealth as a consequence of the model structure: in the neoclassical equilibrium, with the assumption of profit-maximizing entrepreneurial behavior, factor productivities by definition had to be equal to factor prices. This means that in the resulting model, the weights with which the production factors contribute to the physical generation of wealth are determined by the factor cost share of each factor. In other words, observations on contemporary social structure and entrepreneurial behaviors are used to draw inferences concerning the physical importance of production factors.

Here lies the historical source of the economists' underestimation of the production factor energy, because in advanced industrial market economies the cost of energy, on the average, is only 5 to 6 percent of the total factor cost (Baron 1997). Therefore, economists tend either to neglect energy as a factor of production altogether or to argue that the contribution of a change of energy input to the change of output is equal only to energy's small cost share of 5 to 6 percent (Denison 1979, 1984). However, it can be argued that energy has a small share in total production costs not because it is relatively less important than capital or labor as a production factor, but rather because the free work of the biosphere and the geosphere has been abundant and cheap: moreover, not all costs of its use are reflected in its market price (this is the problem of "externalities"). That energy actually has more leverage was demonstrated by the effect of the two energy price explosions in the years 1973–75 and 1979–1981 on economic growth (Cleveland et al. 1984; Jorgenson 1984, 1988).

Neoclassical models that do not include energy cannot explain the empirically observed growth of output by the growth of the factor inputs labor and capital. There always remains a large unexplained growth residual that is formally attributed to what economists call "technological progress." "This . . . has led to a criticism of the neoclassical model: it is a theory of growth that leaves the main factor in economic growth unexplained" (Solow 1994). As we will argue, weighting a factor by its cost-share is an incorrect approach in growth theory. Likewise, the finite emission-absorption capacity of the biosphere is vastly more important to future economic production than its present (often zero) price indicates.

The human economy uses fossil and other fuels to support and empower labor and to produce and utilize capital, just as organisms and ecosystems use solar-derived energy to produce and maintain biomass and biotic functions. Labor productivity has been correlated highly with increasing energy use per worker. This has been especially critical in agriculture (Hall, Cleveland, and Kaufmann 1986). Energy, capital, and labor are combined in human economies to upgrade natural resources (generated by natural energy flows) to useful goods and services. Therefore economic production, like biotic production, can be viewed as the process of upgrading matter into highly ordered (thermodynamically improbable) structures, both

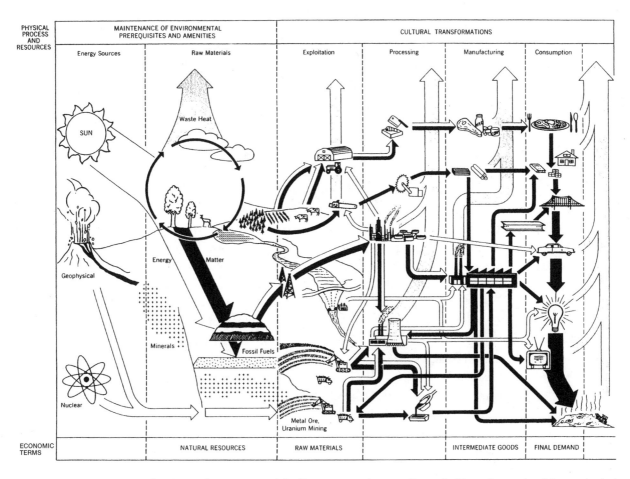

Figure 4.2. A more comprehensive and accurate model of how economies actually work. Natural energies drive geological, biological, and chemical cycles that produce natural resources and public service functions. Extractive sectors use economic energies to exploit natural resources and convert them to raw materials. Raw materials are used by manufacturing and other intermediate sectors to produce final goods and services. These final goods and services are distributed by the commercial sector to final demand. Eventually, nonrecycled materials and waste heat return to the environment as waste products. We believe this diagram to be the minimum model of how a real economy works.

physical structures and information. Where one speaks of "adding value" at successive stages of production, one may also speak of "adding order" to matter through the use of free energy (exergy). The perspective of examining economics in the "hard sphere" of physical production, where energy and material stocks and flows are important, is called *biophysical* economics. It *must* complement the social sphere perspective.

Argument 2: Boundaries

Another problem with the basic model used in neo-classical economics (figure 4.1a) is that it does not include boundaries that in any way indicate the physical requirements or effects of economic activities. We believe that at a minimum figure 4.1a should

be reconstructed as figure 4.1b to include necessary resources and generation of wastes, and the necessity for the economic process to occur in within the large system, the biosphere (Daly 1977; Cleveland, Hall, and Kaufman 1984; Dung 1992; Ayres 1996: Dasgupta, Levin, and Lubchenco 2000). Taking this assessment one step further, we believe that something like figure 4.2 is the diagram that should be used to represent the actual physical aspects of an economy's working. It shows the necessity of the biosphere for the first steps of economic production and as a milieu for all subsequent steps. Figure 4.2 further emphasizes the flow of energy and matter across the boundary separating the reservoirs of these gifts of nature from the realm of cultural transformation within which subboundaries indicate the different stages of their subsequent transformation into the goods and services of final demand. Some such diagram should be presented to every student in an introductory economics course so that the way the economic process operates in the real world is properly understood.

Argument 3: Validation

Natural scientists expect theoretical models to be tested before applied or developed further. Unfortunately, economic policy with far-reaching consequences is often based on economic models that, although elegant and widely accepted, are not validated (Daly 1977; Cleveland et al. 1984; Dung 1992; Ayres 1996). Empirical tests to validate economic models are undertaken even less frequently in the developing countries where these models are followed regularly. As Nobel laureate in economics Wassily Leontief has noted, many economic models are unable "to advance, in any perceptible way, a systematic understanding of the structure and the operations of a real economic system"; instead, they are based on "sets of more or less plausible but entirely arbitrary assumptions" leading to "precisely stated but irrelevant theoretical conclusions" (Leontief 1982).

Most people who are not economists do not appreciate the degree to which contemporary econoics is laden with arbitrary assumptions. Nominally objective operations, such as determining the least cost for a project, evaluating costs and benefits, or calculating the total cost of a project, normally use explicit and supposedly objective economic criteria. In theory, all economists might come up with the same conclusions to a given problem. In fact, such "objective" analyses, based on arbitrary and convenient assumptions, produce logically and mathematically tractable—but not necessarily realistic—models. Where there have been empirical analyses (of, for example, consumer choice), the results frequently have shown that the behavior of real people in experimental or laboratory situations were quite different from the assumptions of a given neoclassical model (Schoemaker 1982; Smith 1989; Hall 1991; see also chapter 1). This is not surprising, because social science models of human behavior sometimes apply and sometimes they do not, depending upon which modeled subset of the infinite set of human behavioral patterns is matched by the actual group of people to which the model is applied. On the other hand, the authority economists often assign to their "physics-based" models is somewhat perplexing, because unavoidably fuzzy economic models do not become precise just because they emulate the mathematical rigor of physics.

For example, Hamiltonians are used in economics in analogy to the Hamiltonians in physics. In fact, in physics a Hamiltonian is an energy function representing the sum of kinetic and potential energy in a system from which one can derive the equations of motion of the particles of the system. In neoclassical production theory, the price vector is given by the gradient of the output in the space of the production factors. This corresponds *formally* to the vector of a conservative physical force, which is given by the gradient of potential energy in real space (Mirowski 1989). This formal analogy would result only in an appropriate description of economic situations if the economy evolved in a state of equilibrium characterized by a profit maximum that lies in the interior—not on the boundary—of the factor space accessible to the production system, according to its state of technology. However, as we show in the next section, this equilibrium has not been satisfied during three decades of industrial evolution in the United States, Japan, and Germany under the reign of low energy prices. Rather, the economies have been sliding downhill on the slope of the cost mountain inclined toward the cost minimum in the state of total automation. This state is characterized by minimum input of expensive labor and maximum input of cheap energy combined with highly automated capital. Because of technological constraints, this cost minimum has not been reached (Kümmel et al. 1985).

Validation also proves difficult or impossible because both classical and neoclassical theories were originally developed using concepts of production factors as they existed in agrarian societies. These theories have been transferred more or less unchanged to applications in the modern industrial world. Very often no provisions have been added to the basic theory for industrialization and its consequences.

The Importance of Energy to Economic Production

In industrial economies the capital stock consists of all energy conversion devices and the installations and buildings necessary for their operation and protection. Its fundamental components are heat-engines and transistors (formerly mechanical switches, relays, and electronic valves), activated by energy and handled by labor. They provide the average citizen of the industrially developed countries with services that are energetically equivalent to those of ten to thirty hard-laboring people—"energy slaves," if you will. These numbers would more than triple if one included energy for room and process heat. In 1995 primary energy consumption per capita and day was 133 kWh in Germany and 270 kWh in the United States. This would correspond numerically to more than forty and ninety energy slaves per capita in Germany and the United States, respectively, each one delivering about 3 kWh per day. Huge armies of energy slaves create our wealth.

In order to demonstrate the economic importance of energy quantitatively we present an econometric analysis of economic growth over three decades for the United States, Japan, and Germany (Kümmel 1980, 1982, 1989; Kümmel et al. 1985; Kümmel, Lindenberger, and Eichhorn 2000). This analysis shows how the proper inclusion of energy removes much of the unexplained residuals encountered by neoclassical theory.

We make the fundamental assumption that wealth, as represented by the output Q of value added, is created by the cooperation of the production factors capital K, labor L, and energy E in conjunction with creativity Cr. Raw materials are the passive partners of the production process. They are critically important but do not contribute by themselves to the generation of value added. Their monetary value is not included in the national accounts' empirical time series on value added, which we compare our theoretical results. However, if materials become scarce in spite of recycling, growth will be constrained. In systems in which catalytic processes play a quantitative role, one might consider treating the catalytic material as a factor distinct from the capital stock.

Creativity is that specifically human contribution to economic evolution that cannot be made by any machine capable of learning and cannot be realized by changing factor combinations. Creativity contributes ideas, inventions, value judgments, and decisions. Creativity's influence may be weak in the short run but important in the long run. In fact, creativity often has been about finding ways to increase energy subsidies for a task.

Q is of necessity measured in inflation-corrected monetary units, and so is K, whereas appropriate measures for E are petajoules per year and for L man-hours worked per year. E and L are obtained from the national energy and labor statistics and K and Q from the national accounts. Ideally, one would like to measure K by the amount of work performance and information processing that capital stock is capable of delivering when totally activated by energy and labor. Likewise, the output Q might be measured by the work performance and information processing necessary for its generation. The detailed, quantitative technological definitions of K and Q are given by Kümmel (1980, 1982; see also Kümmel, Lindenberger, and Eichhorn 2000). However, these physical measurements of K and Q are not available. Therefore, we assume proportionality between them and the constant currency data. We normalize all variables to their values (Q_0, K_0, L_0, E_0) for a base year. For a quantitative analysis of growth we employ production functions $q = q[k(t), l(t), e(t); t]$, which describe the evolution of the normalized output $q = Q/Q_0$ as the normalized inputs of capital, $k = K/K_0$, labor, $l = L/L_0$, and energy, $e = E/E_0$ change with time t. We allow for an explicit time-dependence of q in order to model the effects of creativity.[1] We calculate production functions from the following growth equation that relates the (infinitesimal) relative change of the normalized output, dq/q, to the relative changes of the normalized inputs, dk/k, dl/l, de/e, and creativity's action:

$$(4.1) \quad dq/q = \alpha\,(dk/k) + \beta\,(dl/l) + \gamma\,(de/e) + Cr$$

α, β, and γ are called the *elasticities of production* of capital, labor, and energy in the language of economics. They measure the productive powers of the factors in the sense that (roughly speaking) they give the percentage of output change when the corresponding inputs change by 1 percent. They, and Cr, involve the partial derivatives of q.[2] If one can approximately neglect the explicit time-dependence of q, as we will do for the moment, one has $Cr = 0$.

Our procedure for calculating the production function from equation 4.1 differs in one essential point from that of neoclassical economics: We do not set α, β, and γ equal to the *cost* shares of capital, labor, and energy in total factor cost. These stipulated equalities of elasticities of production and cost shares are the result of the fundamental hypotheses underlying the neoclassical equilibrium model. Instead, we determine these coefficients differently using standard economic analysis with a set of three differential equations representing the integrability conditions of the production function.[3]

The simplest non-constant solutions of these equations with technologically meaningful boundary conditions are:

$$\alpha = a_0(l + e)/k, \quad \beta = a_0(c_0(l/e) - l/k)$$

and $\gamma = 1 - \alpha - \beta$ with technology parameters a_0 and c_0.[4] Here, a_0 gives the weight with which the ratio of labor to capital and energy to capital contribute to the productive power of capital, and c_0 indicates the energy demand $e_t = c_0 k_t(q)$ of the fully utilized capital stock $k_t(q_t)$ that would be required to generate the fraction q_t of output accessible to fully automated production with virtually no labor while the production $(q - q_t)$ is saturated: (then β goes to zero as e and k approach e_t and k_t). If one inserts these elasticities of production into equation (4.1) and integrates, with $Cr = 0$, one obtains the (first) LINEX production function:

$$(4.2) \quad q = q_0 e \exp[a_0(2 - (l + e)/k) + a_0 c_0(l/e - 1)],$$

which depends *lin*early on energy and *exp*onentially on quotients of capital, labor, and energy.

The integration constant q_0 is the third technology parameter of the theory. Its changes indicate changes in the monetary valuation of the original basket of goods and services making up the output-unit Q_0. Activities of creativity Cr that lead to an explicit time-dependence of the production function can be modeled by allowing a_0, c_0, and q_0 to change in time. The elasticities of production, α, β, and γ, must be non-negative to make sense economically. This poses important restrictions on the admissible factor quotients in α, β, and equation 4.2. (Integration of equation (4.1) with the constants α_0, β_0, and $\gamma_0 = 1 - \alpha_0 - \beta_0$, yields the energy dependent Cobb-Douglas production function:

$$q = q_0 k^{a0} l^{\beta_0} e^{1 - \alpha_0 - \beta_0}$$

This function, however, violates the laws of thermodynamics because it allows for the almost complete substitution of energy by capital. Thus it should be avoided in scenarios for the future.) Our model incorporates the limits to substitution, thanks to the restrictions on α, β, and γ. The LINEX function is of the type "variable elasticities of substitution." Its relation to the frequently used translog function has been discussed by Kümmel et al. (1985).

We tested our energy-dependent production function (equation 4.2) with empirical data, examining the sectors "Industries" of the United States and Japan and the West German manufacturing sector ("Warenproduzierendes Gewerbe"). (The sectors "Industries" are defined by the "System of National Accounts" and include the services-producing sectors). We were able to obtain consistent sets of data for these sectors, which produce about 80, 90, and 50 percent, respectively, of gross domestic product. When we inserted the numerical values for the technology parameters indicated in figure 4.3 and the annual empirical inputs of k, l, and e for the United States from 1960 to 1993, Japan from 1965 to 1992, and West Germany from 1960 to 1989 into the LINEX function, we obtained the theoretical outputs shown in figure 4.3, together with the annual empirical outputs. For each country the numerical values of the three technology parameters have been determined by fitting the LINEX function to the empirical time series of output before and after 1977, using the Levenberg-Marquardt method (see Press, Flannery, and Teukolsky 1992). This results in the different sets of a_0, c_0, and q_0 shown in figure 4.3, that is, a time dependence of the parameters between 1977 and 1978.

Results

The LINEX functions, which include the production factor energy, reproduce the output of all three production systems for all years considered with only minor residuals, including the recessions caused by the two major energy crises. Energy crises were triggered by the first and second oil-price explosions in 1973–75 and 1979–81, in the wake of the Yom Kippur war between Israel and its Arab neighbors and the war between Iraq and Iran, respectively. The influence of creativity in response to the oil price increase shows in the reduction of the energy demand of the capital stock, c_0, and the enhancement of capital's productive power by the enhanced a_0 after 1977. These shifts of technology parameters are the results of the decisions of governments and entrepreneurs to invest in energy conservation technologies after the shock of the first oil-price explosion. Structural changes toward less energy-intensive economic activities played a role as well.

Of course, the limitation of the parametric time changes to one year is a consequence of our simple modeling of creativity's action as a single one-year pulse. If one goes a step further—that is, assumes that creativity is always active and modeled the transitions between the different values of a_0 and c_0 before and after the energy crises using continuous functions of time—the discrepancies between the theoretical and empirical U.S. curves after 1985 disappear and the results for Japan and Germany remain practically the same (Henn 2000).[5] In any case, in the short run the changes caused by creativity are small compared to the changes caused by the changing combinations of capital, labor, and energy. Therefore, creativity's influence, and thus any time dependence of the production function, can be neglected during time spans of at least a decade. Even without any parameter readjustments between 1977 and 1978 the evolution of production in Germany and Japan during three decades is reproduced by the LINEX function with residuals of less than 10 percent (Kümmel, Lindenberger, and Eichhorn 2000). Other energy-dependent production functions with mathematically simpler (i.e., constant) or

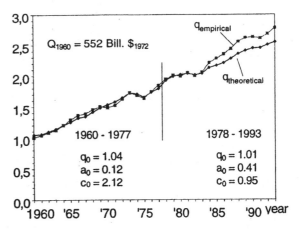

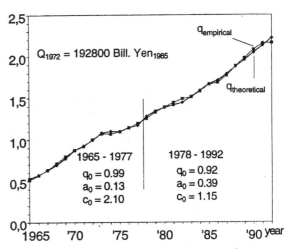

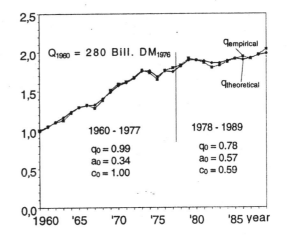

Figure 4.3. Theoretical (diamonds) and empirical (squares) growth of annual industrial production $q = Q/Q_0$ in the United States ($Q_0 = Q_{1960}$), top, Japan ($Q_0 = Q_{1972}$), middle, and West Germany ($Q_0 = Q_{1960}$), bottom. In all three systems the overall growth of the capital stock k is similar to the overall growth of the output q, and the ups and downs of energy inputs e and outputs q occur at the same times. Labor l rises in the United States, stays nearly constant in Japan, and decreases in West Germany.

more complicated elasticities of production yield quantitatively and qualitatively similar results (Lindenberger 2000).[6]

The results of our analysis also demonstrate in all three cases that the productive power of energy is more important than that of capital or labor, and nearly an order of magnitude larger than the 5 percent share of energy cost in total factor cost. This follows from the time-averaged LINEX elasticities of production of capital, labor, and energy, which are:

1. for the United States:
   $(\bar{\alpha} = 0.36, \bar{\beta} = 0.10, \bar{\gamma} = 0.54)$,
2. for Japan:
   $(\bar{\alpha} = 0.34, \bar{\beta} = 0.21, \bar{\gamma} = 0.45)$, and
3. for West Germany[7]:
   $(\bar{\alpha} = 0.45, \bar{\beta} = 0.05, \bar{\gamma} = 0.50)$

In addition, the time-averaged elasticity of production of labor, β, is much smaller than labor's cost share (typically 0.70). In industrialized countries such as the United States, energy commands about 5 percent, labor about 70 percent, and capital about 25 percent of total factor cost. This means that one of the fundamental assumptions of neoclassical equilibrium economics—that is, the equality of elasticities of production and cost shares—has not been satisfied under the conditions of production prevailing in the United States, Japan, and Germany over the last three decades. Rather, under the pressure to minimize cost, these economies have been driven into substituting cheap, powerful energy (in combination with increasingly automated capital) for expensive labor, which is weak economically in the sense that its elasticities of production are much smaller than that of energy. This substitution of energy for labor takes time because of technical constraints on the progress of automation, the demand for those products and services that cannot be produced in a totally automated fashion, and still-existing and respected laws and agreements. Therefore, the economies of the industrial countries have not yet reached the absolute cost minimum.

Some Social Implications of Our Analysis

If one accepts the importance of a biophysical basis for economics, then our analysis has some important implications for economics and for society.

1. *The replacement of expensive labor in routine jobs with the combination of cheap energy and capital stock is likely to continue under the present incentive structure.* This combination also reinforces the trend toward globalization, because goods and services produced in low-wage countries can be transported cheaply to high-wage countries. Thus, high unemployment (in most high-wage countries) will continue if the disparities between the productive powers and cost shares of labor and energy are not removed (for example by adjusting fiscal policy). Certainly, the low price of fossil fuels relative to their productive power generates large profits. But, as is well known, it also prevents the market penetration of large-scale energy conserving and nonfossil energy technologies, which could lower the demand for fossil fuels and relieve some of the burden of pollution. We therefore believe that the problems of unemployment, resource depletion, and pollution can be attacked successfully only if the pivotal role of energy as a factor of production is properly taken into account in economic and social policy.

2. *Price does not always reflect scarcity and economic importance.* Scarcity of a resource must be defined in terms of both short- and long-term resource availability. Price, the economist's usual metric of scarcity, reflects many important aspects of scarcity poorly because it is often based on short-term market values. Most important, as Norgaard (1990) and Reynolds (1999) show, is that uncertainty about the size of the base of a resource can obscure the actual trend in scarcity of that resource, with the result that "empirical data on cost and price . . . do not necessarily imply decreasing scarcity" (Reynolds

1999:165). As an example of this phenomenon, in mid-1999 the real price of oil was at nearly its lowest level ever, despite the fact that most estimates of the time at which global oil production would peak ranged from 2000 to 2020 (Kerr 1998; Cleveland 1999).

3. *The concept and implementation of sustainable development as interpreted and advocated by most economists must be thought through much more carefully, given the requirement for energy and materials for all economic activity* (see Hall 2000 for a detailed analysis of Costa Rica). Energy is in fact disproportionately more important in terms of its impact on the economy than its monetary value suggests, as evidenced by the events of the 1970s (inflation, stock market decisions, reduced economic output, and so on), which appear to be reoccurring to some degree in 2000 partly in response to a similar proportional increase in the price of oil. Fundamentally, current societal infrastructure has been built and maintained on the basis of abundant, cheap supplies of high-quality energy—that is, energy characterized by the large amount of energy delivered to society per unit of energy invested in this delivery through exploration and development or through trade of goods for imported energy (Hall, Cleveland, and Kaufmann 1986).

4. *In developing nations, investment policies based on neoclassical economic analyses encourage borrowing from developed countries and hence growing indebtedness.* Pressure to service the debt encourages the quick extraction of resources to generate a cash flow so that payments of interest and repayment of principal can be maintained. In the meantime, the long-term productivity of the region may be destroyed. But those assessments are not included in neoclassical analyses; in the rare cases where resources are included in the analysis, their value is heavily discounted. For example, many tropical countries sell their forest products at a price far below their worth (Repetto 1988; Hall 2000), and the Russian government has been talked into abolishing its export tax on fossil fuels, which was the last source of secure revenues for highly indebted Russia. Developing countries and nations in transition to market economies should attribute more importance to their natural resources than they presently do under the influence of the reigning economic theory.

5. *Humans tend to seek political explanations for events that in fact may have been precipitated by biophysical causes.* For example, Reynolds (2000) shows how the sharp decline in the former Soviet Union's oil production may have precipitated the economic crises that led to the collapse of the Soviet Union.

Some Biological Implications of Our Analyses

Economies, just like ecosystems—or any system—can be represented as stocks and flows of material and energy, with human material welfare largely a function of the per capita availability of these stocks and flows. Present agricultural technologies, most wildlife management and conservation programs, and perhaps biomedical technology are as dependant upon the availability of cheap energy as anything else. For example, most increases in agricultural productivity have not come from genetics alone. In fact, for many crops there appears to be essentially no increase in gross photosynthesis but rather an increase in only the proportion of photosynthate that goes to the parts we eat, often seeds, while the organs and functions of the wild plant (e.g., growing roots to take up more roots and water, generating secondary compounded for insect defense) are increasingly supplied by industrially derived inputs from outside the plant (Smil 2000). In addition, the efficiency of agriculture tends to be increasingly related to the intensity of use of land area or fertilizer (Hall, Cleveland, and Kaufmann 1986; Hall 2000).

Human material well-being is derived essentially by redirecting energy stocks and flows from what natural selection and the accidents of geology dictated to ends determined by human needs and, increasingly, desires. Now some 40 percent to 60 percent of global primary production is exploited, in one way or another, by the human economy (Vitousek et al. 1986, 1987).

Outlook: The Challenge of Constructing a Model That Includes the Biophysical Basis of the Economy

Existing "economic" models cannot effectively represent a total economy because none has a biophysical basis; some attempts to produce such a model have been made, however. First, there are very detailed and comprehensive models of the flow of energy through each sector of the U.S. economy (Hannon 1982). But these do not include the flows of nature (such as the energy associated with the hydrological cycle, flows of rivers, solar energy, photosynthesis, and other important components of the economic system). Another approach, one that garners considerable controversy, does include the energy flows of nature and the human economy: this is *emergy* (with an *m*) analysis, which also attempts to give each energy flow a weighting according to its quality (Odum 1996). This approach has been applied at an aggregated level to national economies and used as the basis for policy recommendations (Brown et al. 1995). Finally, evolutionary economics looks for ways to model the economic process by combining nature's principle of self-organization with the growth of human knowledge and innovations (Witt 1997; Faber and Proops 1998).[8]

We must conclude, however, that a truly useful and acceptable model that includes the biophysical basis of the economy is probably still far in the future. What then is the utility of bringing a biophysical perspective into economics? We believe that it is overwhelmingly heuristic. By thinking about economies as they actually are (figures 4.1b or 4.2) instead of how we might conceptualize them for analytic ease and tractability (figure 4.1a) we can teach a new generation of economists about the real operations of human economies and the various links to the "economies" of the natural world. We believe that doing so is especially important because science leads us to understand that there are at least constraints, and possibly even limits, to growth. Future generations of economists probably will not be able to treat such issues as overpopulation, oil and groundwater depletion, and changes in the composition of the atmosphere and the biosphere simply as "externalities" to be given a price and rolled into the larger analysis; these will have to be treated as fundamental components of the total economic model. We do not understand how that can be done without starting from a biophysical basis. We challenge a new generation of economists and natural scientists to think from this perspective.

Acknowledgments

This chapter is a reprint, with some modifications, of C. Hall, D. Lindenberger, R. Kümmel, T. Kroeger, and W. Eichhorn, "The need to reintegrate the natural sciences with economics," *BioScience* 51, no. 8 (2001): 663–73. We thank Rick Beal, Bart Daly, Jae-Young Ko, and Paul Christensen for discussions, Julian Henn for analytic help, and the Denman "Foundation" for providing a nice place to work.

References

Ayres, R. U. 1996. Limits to the growth paradigm. *Ecological Economics* 19:117–34.

———. 1999. The minimum complexity of endogenous growth models: The role of physical resource flows and technology. Working paper, INSEAD, Fontainebleau.

Barnett, H. J., and C. Morse. 1963. *Scarcity and Growth: The Economics of Natural Resources Availability.* Baltimore: Johns Hopkins University Press.

Baron, R. 1997. Competitive issues related to carbon/energy taxation. Annex I Expert Group on the United Framework Convention on Climate Change. Working paper 14, ECON-Energy, Paris.

Binswanger, H. C., and E. Ledergerber. 1974. Bremsung des Energiezuwachses als Mittel der Wachstumskontrolle. In J. Wolff, ed., *Wirtschaftspolitiken der Umweltkrise,* 117–25. Stuttgart: DVA.

Boulding, K. E. 1966. *Environmental Quality in a Growing Economy.* Washington, D.C.: Resources for the Future.

Brown, M. T., H. T. Odum, R. C. Murphy, R. A. Christianson, S. J. Doherty, T. R. McClanahan, and S. E. Tennenbaum. 1995. Redefining the world. In C. A. S. Hall, ed., *Maximum Power: The Ideas and Applications of H. T. Odum,* 216–50. Niwot: University Press of Colorado.

Christensen, P. 1989. Historical roots for ecological economics: Bio-physical versus allocative approaches. *Ecological Economics* 1:17–36.

Cleveland, C. J. 1991. Natural resource scarcity and economic growth revisited: Economic and biophysical perspectives. In R. Costanza, ed., *Ecological Economics: The Science and Management of Sustainability,* 289–317. New York: Columbia University Press.

———. 1999. Presentation to Bank of America Securities energy conference, Houston, Texas, 29 June.

Cleveland, C. J., and M. Ruth 1997. When, where, and by how much do biophysical limits constrain the economic process? A survey of Nicholas Georgescu-Roegen's contribution to ecological economics. *Ecological Economics* 22:203–23.

Cleveland, C. J., R. Costanza, C. A. S. Hall, and R. K. Kaufmann. 1984. Energy and the US economy: A biophysical perspective. *Science* 225:890–97.

Daly, H. E. 1977. *Steady-State Economics.* San Francisco: W. H. Freeman.

———, ed. 1973. *Toward a Steady-state Economy.* San Francisco: Freeman.

Dasgupta, P., S. Levin, and J. Lubchenco. 2000. Economic pathways to ecological sustainability. *BioScience* 50:339–45.

Denison, E. F. 1979. Explanations of declining productivity growth. *Survey of Current Business* 59, no. 8, Part II: 1–24.

———. 1984. Accounting for slower economic growth. In J. W. Kendrick, ed., *International Comparisons of Productivity and Causes of the Slowdown,* 1–45. Cambridge, Mass.: Ballinger.

Dung, T. H. 1992. Consumption, production and technological progress: A unified entropic approach. *Ecological Economics* 6:195–210.

Faber, M., and J. L. R. Proops. 1998. *Evolution, Time, Production and the Environment.* 3d ed. Berlin: Springer-Verlag.

Georgescu-Roegen, N. 1971. *The Entropy Law and the Economic Process.* Cambridge, Mass.: Harvard University Press.

———, ed. 1966. *Analytical Economic Issues and Problems.* Cambridge, Mass.: Harvard University Press.

Hall, C. A. S. 1991. An idiosyncratic assessment of the role of mathematical models in environmental sciences. *Environment International* 17:507–17.

———. 1992. Economic development or developing economics? In M. Wali, ed., *Ecosystem Rehabilitation in Theory and Practice,* 1:101–26. The Hague: SPB.

———, ed. 2000. *Quantifying Sustainable Development: The Future of Tropical Economies.* San Diego: Academic Press.

Hall, C. A. S., C. J. Cleveland, and R. K. Kaufmann. 1986. *Energy and Resource Quality: The Ecology of the Economic Process.* New York: Wiley-Interscience.

Hannon, B. 1981. Analysis of the energy cost of economic activities: 1963–2000. Energy Research Group Doc. 316, University of Illinois.

Henn, J. 2000. Die Produktionsmachtigkeit von Energie und Kreativität: Eine Zeitreihenanalyse für Deutschland, Japan und die USA. Diplomarbeit, Universität Wurzburg, Germany.

Jorgenson, D. W. 1984. The role of energy in productivity growth. *American Economic Review* 74, no. 2: 26–30.

———. 1988. Productivity and economic growth in Japan and the United States. *American Economic Review* 78:217–22.

Kaufmann, R. K. 1997. Assessing the DICE model: Uncertainty associated with the emission and retention of greenhouse gases. *Climatic Change* 35:435–48.

Kerr, R. A. 1998. The next oil crisis looms large—and perhaps close. *Science* 281:1128–31.

Kroeger, T., and D. Montanye. 2000. An assessment of the effects of structural adjustment policies in the United States. In Hall 2000, 665–94.

Kümmel, R. 1980. *Growth Dynamics of the Energy Dependent Economy*. Cambridge, Mass.: Oelgeschlager, Gunn and Hain.

————. 1982. The impact of energy on industrial growth. *Energy: The International Journal* 7:189–203.

————. 1989. Energy as a factor of production and entropy as a pollution indicator in macroeconomic modelling. *Ecological Economics* 1:161–80.

Kümmel, R., and W. Strassl. 1985. Changing energy prices, information technology, and industrial growth. In W. Van Gool and J. J. C. Bruggink, eds., *Energy and Time in the Economic and Physical Sciences*, 175–94. Amsterdam: North Holland.

Kümmel, R., D. Lindenberger, and W. Eichhorn. 2000. The productive power of energy and economic evolution. *Indian Journal of Applied Economics* 12:231–62.

Kümmel, R., W. Strassl, A. Gossner, and W. Eichhorn. 1985. Technical progress and energy dependent production functions. *Z. Nationalökonomie/Journal of Economics* 45:285–311.

Leontief, W. 1982. Academic economics. *Science* 217:104.

Lindenberger, D. 1999. *Wachstumdynamik industriellier Volkswirktschafften: Energieabhängige Produktsfunktionen und ein faktorpreisgesteuertes Optimierungsmodell*. Marburg, Germany: Metropolis.

Marris, R. 1992. Implications for economics. In M. Egidi, R. Marris, and R. Viale, eds., *Economics, Bounded Rationality, and the Cognitive Revolution*, 197–212. Brookfield, Vt.: Edward Elgar.

Martinez-Alier, J. 1987. *Ecological Economics: Energy, Environment and Society*. Oxford: Blackwell.

Marx, K. 1906. *Capital*. New York: Modern Library.

Mirowski, P. 1989. *More Heat Than Light*. Cambridge: Cambridge University Press.

Norgaard, R. 1990. Economic indicators of resource scarcity: A critical essay. *Journal of Environmental Economics and Management* 19:19–25.

Odum, H. T. 1996. *Environmental Accounting: Energy and Environmental Decision Making*. New York: Wiley and Sons.

Press, W. H., B. Y. Flannery, and S. A. Teukolsky. 1992. *Numerical Recipes in C*. Cambridge: Cambridge University Press.

Repetto, R. 1988. *The Forest for the Trees? Government Policies and the Misuse of Forest Resources*. Washington, D.C.: World Resource Institute.

Reynolds, D. B. 1999. The mineral economy: How prices and costs can falsely signal decreasing scarcity. *Ecological Economics* 31:155–66.

————. 2000. Soviet economic decline: Did an oil crisis cause the transition in the Soviet Union? *Journal of Energy and Development* 24:65–92.

Ricardo, D. 1891. *The Principles of Political Economy and Taxation*. London: G. Bells and Sons.

Roberts, P. C. 1982. Energy and value. *Energy Policy* 10:171–80.

Schoemaker, P. J. H. 1982. The expected utility model: Its variants, purposes, evidence and limitations. *Journal of Economic Literature* 20:529–63.

Smil, V. 2000. *Feeding the World: A Challenge for the Twenty-first Century*. Cambridge, Mass.: MIT Press.

Smith, A. 1937. *An Inquiry Into the Nature and Causes of the Wealth of Nations*. New York: Modern Library.

Smith, V. K. 1989. Theory, experiment and economics. *Journal of Economic Perspectives* 3:151.

Soddy, F. 1926. *Wealth, Virtual Wealth and Debt*. New York: Dutton.

Solow, R. M. 1974. The economics of resources or the resources of economics. *American Economic Review* 66:1–14.

————. 1992. *An Almost Practical Step Toward Sustainability*. Washington, D.C.: Resources for the Future.

————. 1993. Policies for economic growth. In A. Knoester and A. Wellink, eds., *Tinbergen Lectures on Economic Policy*, 127–44. Amsterdam: North-Holland.

————. 1994. Perspectives on growth theory. *Journal of Economic Perspectives* 8:45–54.

Tryon, F. G. 1927. An index of consumption of fuels and water power. *Journal of the American Statistical Association* 22:271–82.

Vitousek, P. M., P. R. Ehrlich, A. H. Ehrlich, and P. A. Matson. 1986. Human appropriation of the products of photosynthesis. *BioScience* 35:368–73.

Vitousek, P. M., H. A. Mooney, J. Lubchenco, and J. M. Melillo. 1997. Human domination of earth's ecosystems. *Science* 227:494–99.

Witt, U. 1997. Self organization and economics: What is new? *Structural Change and Economic Dynamics* 8:489.

Notes

1. The constraints on economic growth due to entropy production (Kümmel 1980, 1982, 1989; Kümmel et al. 1985) will not be considered in this analysis of the past.

2. Equation 4.1 results from the total differential of the production function. The elasticities of production are α $(k,l,e) \equiv k/q$ $(\partial q/\partial k)$, β $(k,l,e) \equiv l/q(\partial q/\partial l)$, γ $(k,l,e) \equiv e/q$ $(\partial q/\partial e)$, and the term due to the creativity-induced explicit time dependence of the production function is $Cr = (t/q)$ $(\partial q/\partial t)$ (d/t).

3. The differential equations result from the requirement that the second-order mixed derivatives of the production function with respect to the production factors are equal. With the assumption of constant returns to scale: $\gamma = 1 - \alpha - \beta$, the differential equation for α is k $(\partial \alpha/\partial k)$ $+ l$ $(\partial \alpha/\partial l)$ $+ e$ $(\partial \alpha/\partial e) = 0$, the equation for β has identical structure, and the coupling equation reads l $(\partial \alpha/\partial l) = k$ $(\partial \beta/\partial k)$. The most general solutions of the first two equations are $\alpha = f$ $(l/k, e/k)$ and $\beta = g$ $(l/k, e/k)$, with arbitrary differentiable functions f and g. The boundary conditions that would unequivocally determine the solutions of this system of partial differential equations would require knowledge of β on a surface and of α on a curve in k,l,e space. It is practically impossible to obtain such knowledge. Therefore, one has to chose approximate or asymptotic boundary conditions.

4. These solutions take into account the possible approach to the state of total automation, as described in the paragraph below equation 4.2, and the condition that α must vanish if $(l + e) / k$ goes to zero: with zero labor and energy, that is, zero capacity utilization of capital, capital growth cannot contribute to output growth. These "asymmetric" boundary conditions lead to the "asymmetric" solutions of the symmetric set of differential equations. When we tested other boundary conditions and more sophisticated elasticities of production with the corresponding "higher" LINEX functions the quantitative results did not change significantly (Kümmel et al. 1985; Lindenberger 2000).

5. Yet another modeling of creativity's action is possible for West Germany, where we know the time-series of the share of electricity $El(t)$ in end-energy consumption: If one replaces e by $[1 + El(t)]e$ in the LINEX production function and determines the three technology parameters by only one fitting procedure for the time from 1960 to 1989, one obtains a theoretical output that is barely discernible from the one in figure 4.3, bottom (Kümmel, Lindenberger, and Eichhorn 2000). This is consistent with the observation that normally efficiency improvements require more electrical devices and confirms the view that electrification and technological progress are closely interrelated (Jorgenson 1984).

6. Like the Deutsche Bundesbank (Federal Reserve Bank of Germany 1996) in its macroeconomic multi-country model, we prefer here the standard econometric quality measures, namely the coefficients of determination R^2 (the "best" possible value is 1.0), and the Durbin Watson coefficients of autocorrelation dw (the "best" possible value is 2.0). The R^2 and dw pertinent to the LINEX functions in figure 4.3 are for West Germany 1960–77 (0.991 and 1.23), 1978–89 (0.782 and 0.96); for Japan 1965–77 (0.995 and 1.22), 1978–92 (0.992 and 1.15); and for the United States, 0.983 and 0.65 during 1960–1977, and very small values during 1978–1993. In Julian Henn's innovation-diffusion model with continuously decreasing $c_0(t)$ and increasing $a_0(t)$—not shown in figure 4.3—one finds for the United States $R^2 > 0.99$ and $dw = 0.56$ for the time 1960–93; for Japan and Germany, the R^2 and the dw are better than 0.993 and 1.57 for the whole length of observation times. The technology parameters have been determined with the help of the Levenberg-Marquardt method (see Press, Flannery, and Teukolsky 1992).

The positive autocorrelations are due to the unavoidable approximations for the boundary conditions on the elasticities of production (see note 3) and, as a consequence, the necessarily approximate character of the production functions. When estimating the gross domestic product of the United States, Japan, and Germany between 1974 and 1995, using a translog-type production function, the econometricians of the Deutsche Bundesbank (1996) obtained 0.997, 0.995, and 0.96 for R^2 and 0.42, 0.32, and 0.24 for dw, respectively.

7. The time-averaged LINEX elasticities are approximately equal to the constant elasticities of production of the energy-dependent Cobb-Douglas production function $q = q = q_0 k^{\alpha_0} l^{\beta_0} e^{1-\alpha_0-\beta_0}$ that also fits reasonably well to the empirical data. Thus, energy-augmented Cobb-Douglas functions approximate LINEX functions on past growth-paths in factor space that, of course, did not violate the physical limits to substitution.

8. An opportunity of starting this process was offered by the seminar "Economic Growth—Driving Forces and Constraints in the Perspective of Economics and the Sciences" of the WE-Heraeus Foundation, 22–25 October 2005, Bad Honnef, Germany.

CHAPTER 5

THE MYTH OF EFFICIENCY THROUGH MARKET ECONOMICS

A Biophysical Analysis of Tropical Economies

CHARLES A. S. HALL AND JAE-YOUNG KO

Introduction

Tropical countries, in general, are changing much more rapidly than temperate ones. This is true with respect to population numbers, deforestation, economic growth (both positive and, occasionally, negative), influence of trade, and, in general, various other aspects of globalization (World Bank 1998). At the same time, most tropical countries remain especially vulnerable to both natural and manmade disasters (Hurricane Mitch in Central America and the 1998 Asian economic "meltdown" serve as ready examples). Within this context of uncertainty, "sustainability" remains an obvious and a highly desired goal for many, as is obvious in the promotional tourist literature of many tropical countries, such as Costa Rica. Similarly, one hears from various quarters of the desirability of improving "efficiency," and of the concept that with high levels of development, environmental improvements are not only possible but also likely (e.g., the environmental Kutznets curve; see Rothman and deBruyn 1998). Often these are seen as important rationales for far-reaching programs, such as the structural adjustment programs implemented in many tropical countries by the World Bank and International Monetary Fund (Lélé 1991; Taylor 1993), and even for large-scale conservation programs (Goodland et al. 1990).

The Concept of Sustainability

What would constitute this sustainability, if indeed it could be achieved? In fact, it turns out to be remarkably hard to characterize sustainability explicitly, despite thousands of references in the literature (a search for "sustainable development" on Amazon.com turned up 2,103 references in 2006).

Sustainable development is an extremely attractive concept, and since it is rarely defined explicitly, it allows nearly everyone to define it in a way to have one's desired cake and often to eat it, too.

There are at least nine basic definitions of sustainability (OTA 1994). Most can be categorized as examples of three basic perspectives on sustainability, each of which are advocated by particular groups (Goodland and Daly 1996). These are:

Economic sustainability, important to many of those focused on the material welfare of various groups.

Social or cultural sustainability, used especially by anthropologists, and some others, and generally in reference to sustainability of cultures.

Environmental sustainability, generally favored by those concerned about resource depletion, deforestation, loss of biodiversity, or the impacts of pollution.

The curious thing about these three concepts of sustainability is that they are often at variance with one another; that is, each one can be obtained only with at least some expense to one or both of the others. In addition, advocates of one perspective tend to be uninterested in or oblivious to the perspectives of the others.

The Concept of Efficiency

Another important concept in these deliberations is that of "efficiency." Efficiency—like motherhood—is golden, in that everyone is in favor of it, but, the meaning of efficiency, like sustainability, is different in the minds of different beholders, and these differences have large implications for what it is we might be attempting to achieve, and at what expense to the other possible objectives. Most generally, efficiency is output over input, each of which can be defined in various ways. Three basic definitions of efficiency are pertinent to our present interests:

> **Engineering efficiency**, which often means energy output over energy input, such as mechanical work or electrical power out over steam or coal in for a steam engine.
>
> **Neoclassical economic efficiency**, which is generally perceived as low price per unit for a particular good or service (implying relatively small monetary inputs and hence efficient use of all resources used to generate that good or service). Or, more generally, as a disparaging term used for the perceived lack of efficiency in some economic system or activity. "a major goal of economists is the efficiency function . . . objectives should be pursued in the most resource efficient fashion" (McGuigen et al. 2002).
>
> **Biophysical economic efficiency**, somewhat of a hybrid, generally perceived as economic output over energy or material input.

The first and the third are normally given formally and mathematically, the second less commonly so, but it certainly could be represented as dollar cost of product over dollar cost of all inputs.

There is a widespread belief that efficiency has improved over time, especially recently, and that much greater improvements are possible in the near future if we put our minds and policies to that (Ausubel 1996). In fact, it is not hard to find examples of this occurring. For example, by some accounts, the biophysical economic efficiency of the U.S. economy has increased by some 24 percent since 1973 (Schipper and Howarth 1990; Wernick et al. 1996). An alternative perspective is based on Howard Odum's concepts (e.g., Odum 1971) that economic activity and its increment are nearly universally associated with energy use and with increases in energy use.

Determining when or whether an increase in efficiency has happened following development or economic reform is a notoriously slippery thing for getting an explicit measure. For one thing, it is difficult to ask, "efficient relative to what?" And when comparing prices, only one of the many problems requiring correction is that of general or commodity-specific inflation over time. For these and other reasons, there seems to have been remarkably little testing by economists of whether our economies are in fact becoming more efficient. In other words the most important reason given by economists as to why we should be using neoclassical economics, that we want to increase efficiency, remains at best a theoretical concept that has essentially not been tested, or certainly not tested routinely. In their behalf one might argue that the low and sometimes declining prices of many routine consumer goods is evidence arguing that whatever economic policies and practices are in place are, in fact, working. But then prices may be declining for various other reasons, including that energy-intensive mass production and outsourcing to areas with lower labor costs or less rigorous pollution standards do indeed, not surprisingly, lower production costs, at least while oil is cheap.

One can argue that since many Latin American countries have been under tremendous pressure since roughly 1990 to "liberalize" their economies, especially those countries such as Costa Rica that have been subject to structural adjustment, then if indeed structural adjustment does lead to efficiency this should be obvious from the data before and after structural adjustment. If this is not observed, it seems hard to argue that structural adjustment or market liberalization in general has led to efficiency.

In this chapter, we examine the biophysical economic efficiency—that is, resources required per unit economic product—for a series of tropical countries to see if there is any indication of increase in efficiency by which we turn raw materials into economic wealth. Our focus is energy, forest products, and water, because we believe these to be among the most fundamental and those that are likely to change. We use time series where possible, as well as comparison across nations. More formally, our hypothesis is that over time, technological progress has operated to decrease the resource intensity of economic activity. We will accept this hypothesis if the ratio of inflation-corrected gross domestic product (GDP) per resource input, in tons or other physical units, increases over time for the nations examined. We will reject this hypothesis if there is a clear correlation (with a conservative R^2 of 0.5 or higher) of resource use and economic production, both across nations and for individual nations over time, or if resource use increases while economic product stagnates.

We have attempted to make this analysis as simple and straightforward as possible. Nevertheless, we must first acknowledge (although not necessarily deal with) some potential problems with such a simple analysis. The issues include *boundaries* (how far back do you follow energy inputs—do you include the energy required to, for example, grow the food to support labor?), *convertibility* (should you express purchasing power in terms of local buying power, where prices may be low, or as an ability to purchase goods in dollars on the international market?), and *comprehensiveness* (should you include energy flows of nature?).

Some critics of international corporations argue that the way economic efficiency—that is, "correct" prices, which generally means low prices—is achieved is often by means that are socially or environmentally injurious, such as low wages or not taking care of residual pollutants. Likewise, there can be a problem with deriving reliable biophysical economic efficiency since, for example, a car manufactured and sold in the United States is apt to have been built with steel (the particularly energy-demanding component) made in Brazil, South Korea, or elsewhere. Since there is more value added from finishing the product than from generating the raw materials, this would make the United States look relatively energy-efficient and South Korea relatively energy-intensive (Ko 2000). In reality, all analyses are to some degree incomplete. For example, should we include the prorated energy cost of manufacturing, or indeed developing, the steam engine or computer chip or even the workers? How about the energy cost of obtaining the energy required to run the engine? Probably

the best way to deal with these issues is to acknowledge that there is no one best set of boundaries to work within, and thus to define the boundaries carefully and perhaps undertake analyses from several perspectives. But that is impossible on this scale of research, and so we simply assume that national boundaries and annual values (the criteria by which most of the data are maintained) are sufficient for our purposes.

Methods

We chose four countries from Africa, Asia, and Latin America, respectively, to represent a variety of overall characteristics of demography, economic development, and natural resource stocks of the tropical countries (table 5.1). There are large differences in economic level among the nations. The World Bank (1997) has given estimates for "natural capital" for all countries, which includes pasture land, crop land, timber resources, non-timber forest resources, protected areas, and subsoil assets. The natural capital of Malaysia and Venezuela are high, due mostly to large petroleum reserves in these countries. Kenya, India, and the Philippines have relatively low natural endowments. African countries have the highest recorded population growth rates for the last three decades. Asian countries are the most crowded regions among the three continents. Population growth in most of these countries has been higher than the world average for the 1990s. Thus we believe that we have chosen a suite of contrasting nations to examine our efficiency hypothesis. However, most of the selected countries had to implement neoliberal policies (structural development programs) to some degree in order to obtain loans from development banks; therefore, we can test empirically the success of these policies in the generation of an efficient economy.

The main source of the time series data for our study was the World Resources Institute's (WRI) 1998–99 data set, which compiles environmental and resource information published by several international agencies, including the United Nations and the World Bank. Additionally, we downloaded agricultural data from the Food and Agriculture Organization (FAO) Internet Web site.

Table 5.1. A comparison of twelve countries in relation to their economic output, demographic conditions, and natural capital assets

Countries	GDP per capita, 2000 (1995 US $)	Natural capital per capita (US $)	Population density, 1970 (per sq km)	Population density, 2000 (per sq km)	Population growth, 1990-95 (percent)
Africa					
Kenya	328	1,730	20	53	2.91
Nigeria	255	n/a	58	139	3.00
Senegal	608	5,300	22	49	2.52
Zambia	404	5,490	6	13	2.24
Asia					
India	463	3,910	184	342	1.76
Malaysia	4,808	11,820	33	71	2.37
Philippines	1,173	2,730	122	257	2.20
Thailand	2,828	7,600	70	119	0.94
Latin America					
Brazil	4,626	7,060	11	20	1.44
Columbia	2,289	6,100	22	41	1.88
Costa Rica	3,911	7,860	34	76	2.41
Venezuela	3,301	20,820	12	27	2.27
World			34	46	1.48

Source: World Bank. World Development Index (WDI), (http://publications.worldbank.org/subscriptions/WDI/); World Bank, *Expanding the Measure of Wealth: Indicators of Environmentally Sustainable Development* (Washington, D.C., 1997), 34–38; World Bank, *World Development 1998–99: Knowledge for Development* (1998).

The most comprehensive analysis of water use by various countries that we are aware of is found in Gleick (1998). He has reviewed the available data on water input (through rain, inflowing rivers and groundwater pumpage) for most of the nations of the world. Gleick (1998) also gives summaries of extraction of water for agriculture, industrial, and domestic purposes. Vorosmarty and Sahagian (2000) reach similar conclusions about the world distribution of per capita water and water shortages. Unfortunately, Gleick's data are generally for one year only, normally roughly 1990. Vorosmarty and Sahagian's projections, based on climate change and growth in human populations, are that whatever one's conclusions might be for 2000 the problems are likely to be much more severe into the future, due mostly to human population growth. Thus we can assume that our conclusions, based on Gleick's data, are in some ways conservative (but see discussion).

Economic Analysis

We used time series of gross domestic product (GDP) as an index of economic output for all countries. GDP figures presented in this study were corrected for inflation and different currencies by using the constant 1987 U.S. dollar–based GDP, and we used total commercial energy consumption (in heat units uncorrected for quality, so that more economically potent electricity gets the same rating per unit as does coal for the same countries). Energy qualities of different energy sources are not adjusted, so that more economically potent electricity gets the same rating per heat unit as coal) for the same countries. Quality corrections would probably make for stronger correlations, so in this sense this analysis is again conservative, as primary electricity tends to be increasing as a proportion of total energy use.

Using these two data sets, we traced the pattern of per capita energy consumption versus per capita GDP for the countries from 1970 to 1995. Finally, we calculated each year the energy efficiency of national economies by dividing constant dollar GDP by commercial energy use.

Agricultural Analysis

We measured the *fertilizer efficiency* of cereal production as an index of agricultural efficiency. This was calculated by dividing the total cereal production by the NPK fertilizer used on all cereals (barley, corn, rice, sorghum, wheat, etc.). This was not easy as no year-by-year numbers are kept on fertilizer use on specific crops. To estimate the fertilizer input to cereals, we used the following procedures:

1. We calculated the ratio of fertilizer for "total cereals" to "total crops" for the only year available from *Fertilizer Use by Crop* (FAO 1999), which was derived from questionnaires sent to national governments who returned the data (for example, the fertilizer consumption ratio of total cereals over total crops for the "index" year for each country was 41.7 percent for Kenya in 1991, 9.4 percent for Malaysia in 1995, and 32.0 percent for Brazil in 1991).

2. The total fertilizer used for all crops collectively, the yield of all cereals, the area harvested for all cereals, and area of "arable and permanent crops" are available for each year from the agricultural statistics of FAO through the web site of FAO (http://faostat. fao.org).

3. From 1 and 2, we estimated fertilizer used for cereal production for each year by multiplying the total annual national fertilizer use by the ratio of fertilizer used on all cereals to total national fertilizer used for the index year, based on the assumption that the index year's ratio is applicable to the entire research period.

4. From 2 and 3, we estimated fertilizer input (kg/ha) for cereals by dividing the estimated fertilizer use for all cereals by the area harvested for all cereals.

5. From 2 and 4, we estimated fertilizer efficiency, a ratio of cereal production over fertilizer input, for each country during the research period.

Water Analysis

The problem for our analysis is that Gleick's (1998) data are for various individual years, and there are no year-by-year data. Thus we were able to examine only the correlation of water use and economic activity (GDP) of different nations, where GDP was corrected for inflation and to the year of the availability of water data. We compared the sum of the quantities used in the categories "domestic" and "industrial" to values for inflation-corrected GDP for the same year.

Forest Analysis

We were able to derive deforestation rates and extraction or exports of forest products for only some of the countries that we have considered. Our sources included the United Nations Environmental Program (UNEP), Global Environmental Outlook 2000 (available from http://www.unep. org/Geo2000/english/index.htm), and Verissimo et al. (1997).

Results

Contrary to our hypothesis, our results show no general pattern of increased efficiency (decreased resource use intensity per unit economic output) over time in any way or for any of the parameters we have measured. More frequently, we find approximately linear increases in resource use with increased economic activity or, less frequently, a decreased efficiency over time, especially as intensity of use increases.

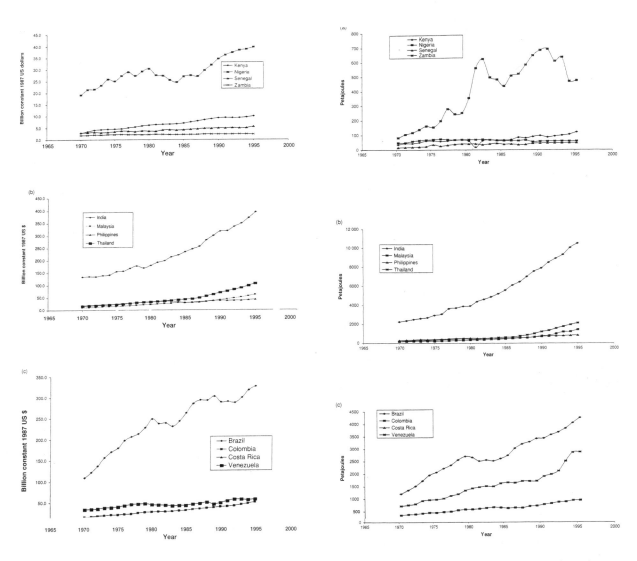

Figure 5.1. Gross domestic product, 1975–95. (a) Africa, (b) Asia, (c) Latin America.

Figure 5.2. Annual energy use, 1970–95. (a) Africa, (b) Asia, (c) Latin America.

Energy Use and Economic Activity

In general, there is a continuing pattern of increased energy use over time, similar to the increase in GDP (figures 5.1 and 5.2), with the general exception that neither GDP nor commercial energy consumption has increased much in Africa during the period examined, and there was a significant drop in energy use in Zambia (figures 5.2 and 5.3). Both economic activity and commercial energy consumption has increased, especially in Asian countries, as shown most markedly in Malaysia and Thailand (figures 5.2 and 5.3).

Per capita energy consumption has decreased or increased only slightly for most countries, with the exception of Malaysia, Thailand, and Venezuela, where per capita energy use has increased significantly (figure 5.4). Thus, most of the increases in energy use are due simply to expanding populations.

There were in general very high positive correlations (often with R^2 from 0.8 to 0.99) for economic activity and energy use for each nation over time, although the correlations were not relatively strong in Africa. The correlations were even higher, often reaching virtually 1.0, when economic

Table 5.2. Determinants of economic growth in the countries, 1970–95

A. The proposed equation: GDP = a[ENGCONS] + b[POP] + c*

Country	Equation			Adj. R-square	Durbin-Watson
Africa					
Kenya	GDP = 0.079	ENGCONS + 0.336	POP − 0.99	0.986	0.42
Nigeria	GDP = − 0.317	ENGCONS + 0.437	POP − 4.82	0.876	0.53
Senegal	GDP = 1.334	ENGCONS + 0.156	POP − 0.028	0.962	1.17
Zambia	GDP = 0.549	ENGCONS + 0.082	POP − 1.285	0.791	1.20
Asia					
India	GDP = 1.932	ENGCONS − 0.6733	POP + 144.9	0.995	1.01
Malaysia	GDP = 1.889	ENGCONS + 1.0623	POP − 6.089	0.994	1.66
Philippines	GDP = 1.042	ENGCONS + 0.5319	POP − 3.655	0.952	0.32
Thailand	GDP = 2.006	ENGCONS + 1.6478	POP − 66.849	0.989	0.35
Latin America					
Brazil	GDP = 2.71	ENGCONS + 2.6625	POP − 150.83	0.982	0.52
Columbia	GDP = 1.801	ENGCONS + 1.9320	POP − 37.215	0.993	0.47
Costa Rica	GDP = 3.040	ENGCONS + 1.7476	POP − 1.9830	0.977	1.12
Venezuela	GDP = − 0.1533	ENGCONS + 2.898	POP + 19.962	0.885	0.62

GDP = Gross Domestic Product in billion constant 1995 US $
ENGCONS = total commercial energy consumption in million tonne of oil equivalent
POP = total population in million
* All regression analyses are significant at p=0.0001.

B. (Excluding population) The proposed equation: GDP = a[ENGCONS] + b*

Country	Equation		Adj. R-square	Durbin-Watson
Africa				
Kenya	GDP = 0.911	ENGCONS − 3.455	0.978	0.56
Nigeria	GDP = 0.270	ENGCONS + 5.978	0.819	0.31
Senegal	GDP = 1.840	ENGCONS − 0.057	0.961	1.36
Zambia	GDP = 0.341	ENGCONS + 1.794	0.790	1.11
Asia				
India	GDP = 1.045	ENGCONS − 94.81	0.984	0.23
Malaysia	GDP = 2.174	ENGCONS + 5.327	0.994	1.83
Philippines	GDP = 1.783	ENGCONS + 14.14	0.948	0.42
Thailand	GDP = 2.552	ENGCONS − 3.284	0.980	0.19
Latin America				
Brazil	GDP = 4.531	ENGCONS − 17.63	0.975	0.31
Columbia	GDP = 3.890	ENGCONS − 21.35	0.982	0.56
Costa Rica	GDP = 4.716	ENGCONS − 0.374	0.963	1.46
Venezuela	GDP = 0.837	ENGCONS − 31.49	0.835	0.72

* All regression analyses are significant at p = 0.0001.

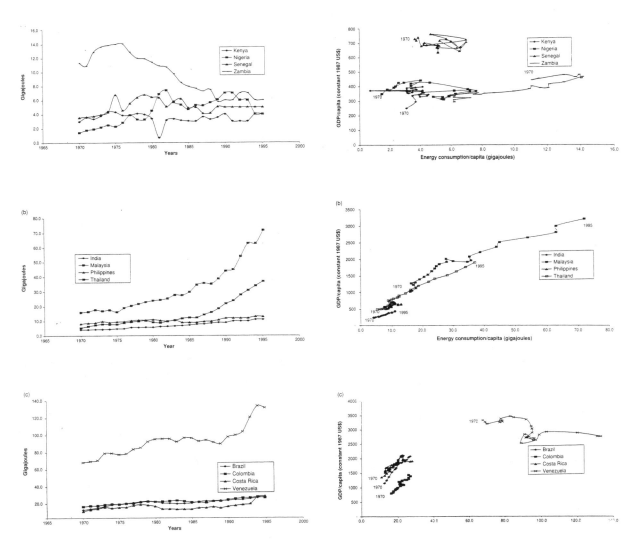

Figure 5.3. Commercial energy consumption per capita, 1970–95. (a) Africa, (b) Asia, (c) Latin America.

Figure 5.4. Per capita GDP versus per capita energy consumption, 1970–95. (a) Africa, (b) Asia, (c) Latin America.

activity was regressed against both human population levels and energy use. However, the correlations of the African countries were lower than other continents, especially in Zambia. Further, in Nigeria and Venezuela the correlations were negative after population was added, which probably has a lot to do with their role as oil producers.

In most countries, increases in energy use are matched fairly closely by population growth so there is little, if any, increase in energy use per capita (figure 5.4). The same pattern is true for economic growth: growth in the economy is roughly the same as population growth, so there has been little change in per capita inflation-corrected GDP (table 5.2). Per capita GDP has declined in Zambia, increased slightly in Kenya, and has been steady in the other two African nations. The four Asian nations show a clear increase in both energy use and economic activity, with the increase of per capita energy use strongest for Malaysia (figure 5.4). Brazil, Colombia, and Costa Rica also had relatively small increases in both per capita energy use and economic activity, implying that population growth has swallowed most of the potential

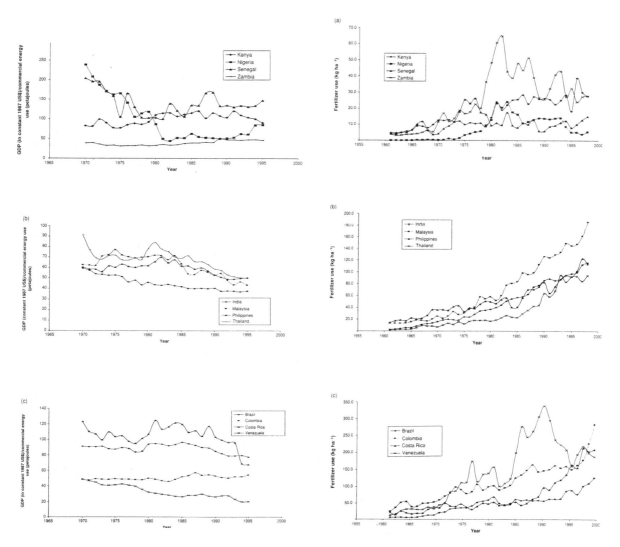

Figure 5.5. Energy efficiency of national economy, 1970–95. (a) Africa, (b) Asia, (c) Latin America.

Figure 5.6. Ratio of total fertilizer use to cultivated area for total cereals, 1961–98. (a) Africa, (b) Asia, (c) Latin America.

economic enhancement that might follow from an increase in energy use. Venezuela and Nigeria used more energy while economic activity decreased, consistent with perspectives given in chapter 2 about how resource-rich nations might be less efficient in generating wealth.

In general, there was a strong correlation between increases (or decreases) in economic activity and energy use, so that energy efficiency (GDP/energy) of national economies in many countries show little change over time. There are exceptions, and energy efficiency *decreased* especially for Nigeria

and all Asian countries. Increases in efficiency occurred for Zambia (figure 5.5). In sum, we did not see any consistent pattern of increasing energy efficiencies for eleven of the twelve countries. Zambia's increasing energy efficiency, the exception, was accompanied by economic depression.

Agricultural Efficiency

The intensity of fertilizer use (kg/ha) increased in most countries throughout the study period except for Nigeria, Senegal, and Venezuela, where there was a decline after roughly the 1970s or 1980s

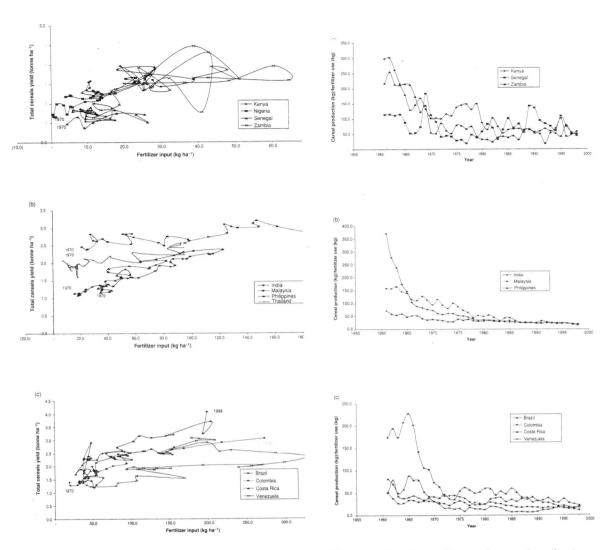

Figure 5.7. Cereal yield versus fertilizer input, 1970–98. (a) Africa, (b) Asia, (c) Latin America.

Figure 5.8. Fertilizer efficiency for cereal production, 1961–98. (a) Africa, (b) Asia, (c) Latin America.

(figure 5.6). Overall, the cereal output for each country over time did not increase as rapidly as fertilizer input, almost certainly in response to yield saturations (figure 5.7). There was no evidence at all for any increase in the efficiency with which fertilizer was turned into food, and, at very high levels of application, as in Zambia in some years, strong evidence for a decrease in efficiency with time (figure 5.8). This is probably also a general function of increasing expansion of land in agriculture over time, which tends to mean that land of increasingly poor quality is brought into production, generally lowering the average quality of land in production (Hall and Hall 1993; Hall et al. 1998). An additional possibility is that erosion is, over time, reducing the intrinsic quality of land to generate yield, and that fertilizer is less able to compensate for this over time.

Water Analysis

There is a positive linear relation between water use and economic activity among the twelve nations examined (figure 5.9). Poor and dry countries use less water, while relatively wealthy countries

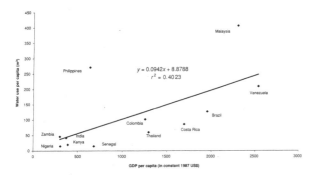

Figure 5.9. Water demand versus GDP per capita for domestic and industrial use per capita (Gleick 1998). Data are for 1990, except Nigeria (1987), Senegal (1987), and Zambia (1994).

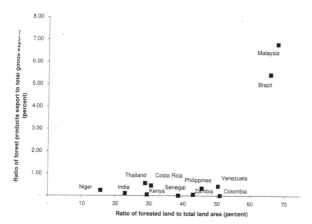

Figure 5.10. Ratio of forest products exports versus ratio of forested land for 1994.

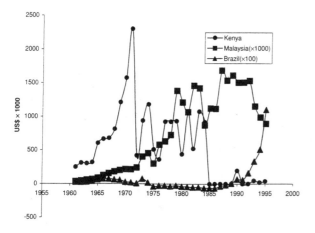

Figure 5.11. Net export of roundwood, 1961–95.

use more water. The Philippines and Malaysia, both relatively wet countries, stand out for using more water at a given level of GDP.

Deforestation and Use of Forest Products

There is a positive but relatively weak correlation between deforestation or export of roundwood (figure 5.9; correlation not shown) and economic growth. In addition, there tends to be some relation between economic growth and the production of wood (in this case roundwood) (Figure 5.10). However, this weak relation is influenced very much by the remaining area of forest land left to be exploited (e.g., Brazil) and by policy (e.g., Kenya and, more recently Malaysia have instituted very strict policies to restrict the cutting of remaining natural forests), although these policies are of course influenced by the depletion of available timber (figure 5.11).

Discussion

For most countries, especially in Asia and in Latin America, there is a close relation of changes in GDP per capita and in energy use per capita. Nevertheless, increasing energy use does not guarantee increasing wealth, as is clear from the case of Zambia. Thus increasing energy use appears to be a necessary but not sufficient component of increasing wealth. Another apparent condition is that energy use must increase more rapidly than population growth, or else, such as in Senegal or the Philippines, the population growth swallows any increase in economic activity, and per capita wealth falls.

This pattern implies the continuing importance of energy increases for increased economic activity (Hall et al. 2003). Interestingly the amount of energy used per unit GDP produced and the slope of energy increase as GDP increases are similar for all countries in Asia and all countries in Latin America except Venezuela. The large oil-producing countries of Venezuela and Nigeria show unusual patterns conceivably related to their oil extraction becoming more energy intensive as the best resources are used first. Other African countries show an increase in energy use per capita with little or no increase in GDP implying increasingly less efficient economies—for unknown reasons.

In Africa, as elsewhere, there is no increase in per capita wealth without an increase in per capita energy use. These findings would seem to indicate that energy availability and population policy are far more important than fiscal or monetary policy for enhancing a nation's material wealth, although social/governmental stability or effectiveness is also required.

In India and the Philippines, per capita economic activity barely increased despite enormous increases in energy use because of equally large population growth. In Malaysia, by contrast, energy use increased much more rapidly than population and an increase in per capita GDP occurred. This is probably related to Malaysia having become a leading nation in energy production, despite its small population of 22 million. In Thailand, a similar pattern occurred, although not quite as strong. In Latin America, most countries had only small increases in both per capita wealth and per capita energy use.

In sum, populations have increased steadily in most countries while periodically significant economic challenges, including oil shocks, debt, and resultant International Monetary Fund (IMF) impacts, have decreased economic activities and sometimes decreased energy consumption. Any reduced energy or fertilizer consumption appears to be driven not by technological developments leading to efficiency, as is commonly believed, but rather by economic constriction. Thus we found no clear pattern of decreasing energy, water, or fertilizer use per unit of economic activity for any of the countries we have examined. The simplest summary is this. Resource (or at least energy) use expands at about the rate of economic growth, and different countries use resources in rough proportion to their economic activity. Hence our results do not lend any particular support to the idea that technology or some other factor is allowing economies to expand without having an impact on resource consumption or the environment, at least with respect to these resources that we have examined. If anything our data shows the contrary, that resource use efficiency in many countries has *decreased*. It also shows that there are no examples of per capita wealth increasing if populations grow more rapidly than resources can be mobilized, at least within the countries we have examined. We conclude that an economy is largely a biophysical phenomenon, and economic theories or policies that do not consider this are doomed to failure and will continue to exacerbate their dismal record in most of the developing world (see Hall 2000; Hall et al. 1986; Hall et al. 2001).

Does Increased Efficiency Lead to Reduced Resource Use?

There are many who argue that increased efficiency is necessary for reduction in the environmental impact of economic activity. Yet even where engineering efforts or market pressures have in fact increased the efficiency of individual processes, such as where fuel is turned into mechanical work or even wealth, this does not necessarily lead to resource efficiency in the sense of using less, as the lower price may encourage increased use of the resource; this is known as Jevons's paradox after Stanley Jevons (Jevons 1865; Hall 2004).

Where neoclassical market economics has led to lower prices (and we do not argue that) it is often as a consequence of few buyers (e.g., for bananas or other resources) and many sellers, a situation analogous to Marx's arguments that the capitalist system pushes down the price—but not the value—of labor. From our perspective, this is not efficiency but a transfer of costs from consumers to laborers. In the context of a globalized world, then what we are observing would reflect an exploitation of natural resources of less-developed countries not by their own population but by richer countries. The problem would be exacerbated by the absence of self-regulation mechanisms that might take place within a nation.

Implications for Water Management in the Humid Tropics

If there is to be development, and unless there is an enormous change from past patterns, more energy will be used, and more water will be used both in general and specifically for energy projects. This argues, in agreement with Vorosmarty and Sahagian (2000), that the future of water availability and quality will depend more on "global change" in human population and affluence than in, for example, possible climate change, although the latter may exacerbate or ameliorate the former. This phenomenon cannot be examined well without time series analysis of economic activity and water use for individual countries. Gleick is now undertaking such an analysis, with preliminary results showing two different patterns: many countries continue to use water in proportion to their economic activity while in others economic growth is continuing without a significant increase in water use.

The Forest Situation in Kenya, Malaysia, and Brazil

Most of the forests in Africa have been reduced by increasing demands for wood products, including roundwood. The consumption of forest products nearly doubled for the period 1970–94, but domestic production has been maintained only through increased logging with virtually no effective measures for sustainable forestry management (UNEP 2000). The uncontrolled logging industry in Kenya was able to export roundwood while meeting domestic needs during the 1970s. However, it did so by exhausting its forest resources so that the country had become a net importer of roundwood by the 1990s (as did Costa Rica). Unfortunately, the pressures on African forests are likely to continue due to the increasing human populations in urban zones who need construction timber and charcoal.

Much of the primary forests in Asian nations have been depleted through serious deforestation, and many Asian nations have been trying to reduce deforestation by employing forest plantations (UNEP 2000) or by restricting logging of the remaining natural forests, as has been done in Malaysia, for example.

In Brazil, 15 million hectares of forest area disappeared from 1988 to 1997 due to clearing for cropland and livestock farming, construction of roads, and other infrastructure development. The deforestation increased between 1994 and 1995, with 2.9 million new hectares affected. The logging industry continues to expand without proper governmental planning or regulations (Verissimo et al. 1997). Roundwood exports from Brazil may well collapse in the near future as happened in Kenya

through either depletion or policy intervention in advance of that.

Conclusions

The most important policy implication of this analysis (and see also Ko et al. 1998; Hall 2000; Tharakan et al. 2001) is that we found no empirical support for the commonly heard statement that neoclassical or market economics will lead to efficiency in the use of productive resources. This is especially true if efficiency is defined as we do: the quantity of material, energy, and so forth required to undertake a unit of economic production (see also Rothman and de Bruyn 1998). Thus we believe that the efficiency argument can no longer be used to argue for the use of neoclassical economics.

If this is true, and the efficiency argument can no longer be used to justify the uncritical application of neoclassical economics, then why do we use it? This question is explored in some depth in the original paper from which this chapter was derived (where we ask whether neoclassical economics is sometimes used as an excuse to plunder), and also in chapters 9 and 11 of this volume, but we certainly need to focus more explicitly on who gets what when neoclassical economics is put forth as a recipe for ailing economies. And, of course, we need a full biophysical assessment of what economic development is possible and might have the best returns. For that we turn to the next chapter.

Acknowledgments

This chapter is reprinted with slight modifications and with permission from Michael Bunnel, ed., *Soil, Water and Forests in the Tropics* (UNESCO 2005). We thank Michael Bunnel and Celia Kirby for editorial suggestions and Timm Kroeger for more precise economic definitions, and Kelly Lash for editing suggestions.

References

Ausubel, J. H. 1996. Can technology spare the Earth? *American Scientist* 84:166–78.

Barnett, H., and C. Morse. 1963. *Scarcity and Growth: The Economics of Natural Resource Availability*. Baltimore: Johns Hopkins University Press.

Bromley, D. W. 1998. The ideology of efficiency: Searching for a theory of policy analysis. *Journal of Environmental Economics and Management* 19:86–107.

Cleveland, C. J. 1991. Physical and economic aspects of natural resource scarcity: The cost of oil supply in the lower 48 United States, 1936–1987. *Resources and Energy* 13:163–88.

Costanza, R. 1980. Embodied energy and economic valuation. *Science* 210:1219–24.

FAO. 1992. *Fertilizer Use by Crop*. Rome: FAO.

Gleick, P. H. 1998. *The World's Water 1998–1999: The Biennial Report on Freshwater Resources*. Washington, D.C.: Island Press.

Goodland, R., and H. Daly. 1996. Environmental sustainability: Universal and non-negotiable. *Ecological Applications* 6:1002–17.

Goodland, R. J. A., E. O. A. Asibey, J. C. Post, and M. B. Dyson. 1990. Tropical moist forest management: The urgency of transition to sustainability. *Environmental Conservation* 17, no. 4: 303–18.

Hall, C.A. S. 2004. The myth of sustainable development: Personal reflections on energy, its relation to neoclassical economics, and Stanley Jevons. *Journal of Energy Resources Technology* 126:85–89.

———, ed. 2000. *Quantifying Sustainable Development:The Future of Tropical Economies*. San Diego: Academic Press.

Hall, C. A. S., and M. Hall. 1993. The efficiency of land and energy use in tropical economies and agriculture. *Agriculture, Ecosystems and Environment* 46:1–30.

Hall, C. A. S., C. J. Cleveland, and R. K. Kaufmann. 1986. *Energy and Resource Quality: The Ecology of the Economic Process*. New York: Wiley-Interscience.

Hall, C. A. S., J-Y. Ko, C-L. Lee, and H. Wang. 1998. Ricardo lives: The inverse relation of resource exploitation intensity and efficiency in Costa Rican agriculture and its relation to sustainable development. In S. Ulgiadi, ed., *Advances in Energy Studies: Energy Flows in Ecology and Economy*, 355–70. Rome: Musis.

Hall, C. A. S., D. Lindenberger, R. Kummel, T. Kroeger, and W. Eichhorn. 2001. The need to reintegrate the natural sciences with economics. *BioScience* 51:663–73.

Hall, C. A. S., P. Tharakan, J. Hallock, C. Cleveland, and M. Jefferson. 2003. Hydrocarbons and the evolution of human culture. *Nature* 426:318–22.

Jevons, W. S. 1985. *The Coal Question: An Inquiry Concerning the Progress of the Nations*. New York: A. M. Kelley.

Ko, J-Y. 2000. An integrated assessment of energy and resource efficiency trends at regional, national, and international scales. Ph.D. dissertation, State University of New York. Syracuse, N. Y.

Ko, J-Y, C. A. S. Hall, and L. G. L. Lemus. 1998. Resource use rates and efficiency as indicators of regional sustainability: An examination of five countries. *Environmental Monitoring and Assessment* 51:571–93.

Kruseman, G. 2000. Bio-economic household modelling for agricultural intensification. Mansholt Graduate Studies No. 20, Wageningen University.

Lélé, S. M. 1991. Sustainable development: A critical review. *World Development* 19:607–21.

McGuigen, J. R., R. C. Moyers, and F. H. de B. Harris. 2002. *Managerial Economics: Applications, Strategy and Tactics*. Cincinnati: South Western Press.

Odum, H. T. 1971. *Environment, Power and Society*. New York: Wiley-Interscience.

OTA. 1994. Perspectives of the Role of Science and Technology in Sustainable Development. OTA-ENV-609. Washington, D.C.: Office of Technology Assessment, U. S. Congress.

Rothman, D., and S. de Bruyn. 1998. The Environmental Kuznets Curve. *Ecological Economics* 25:143–46.

Schipper, L., and R. B. Howarth. 1990. United States energy use from 1973 to 1987: The impacts of improved efficiency. *Annual Review of Energy* 15:455–504.

Stern, D. 2004. Environmental Kuznets curves. In C. Cleveland, ed., *Encyclopedia of Energy*, 2:517–25. The Hague: Elsevier.

Taylor, L. 1993. The world bank and the environment: The world development report 1992. *World Development* 21, no. 5: 869–81.

Tharakian, P., T. Kroeger, and C. A. S. Hall. 2001. Twenty-five years of industrial development: A study of resource use rates and macro-efficiency indicators for five Asian countries. *Environmental Science and Policy* 4:319–32.

United Nations Environmental Program (UNEP). 2000. *Global Environmental Outlook 2000*. www.unep.org/Geo2000/english/index.htm.

Verissimo, A., C. S. Junior, S. Stone, and C. Uhl. 1997. Zoning of timber extraction in the Brazilian Amazon. *Conservation Biology* 12:128–36.

Vörösmarty, C., and D. Sahagian. 2000. Anthropogenic disturbance of the terrestrial water cycle. *BioScience* 50:753–65.

Wernick, I. K., R. Herman, S. Govind, and J. H. Ausubel. 1996. Materialization and dematerialization: Measures and trends. *Daedalus* 125, no. 3: 171–98.

World Bank. 1997. *Expanding the Measure of Wealth: Indicators of Environmentally Sustainable Development*. New York: World Bank.

———. 1998. *World Development 1998–99: Knowledge for Development*. New York: World Bank.

CHAPTER 6

How to Construct a Biophysical Economic Model for a Country or Region That Can Be Used for Rapid Appraisal of Development Potential

Charles A. S. Hall and Grégoire Leclerc

It seems imperative that we as individuals who care about the human condition and about nature create a new way to undertake developmental economics and perhaps economics in general. The reasons that this is so important have been reviewed in previous chapters. They include our dissatisfaction with the intellectual foundations of conventional economic models used in development and of the results that have occurred with their use; the general sense of many development economists themselves that conventional economics has failed; the need to do something that will work; the concern that most knowledgeable people have that the future, and especially the future of most developing nations, will be much more constrained by the "end of cheap oil"; and the need to protect whatever nature is left. We try to develop such a model in this chapter, summarizing certain approaches and even successes of the past, and use a biophysical basis to try to generate a synthesis to help the reader. Our approach is integrated with the analyses in Hall (2000), as well as several chapters in this book, where case histories and examples of successful applications are developed. We are not foolish enough to believe that we can in one fell swoop cure all the economic problems that generations of traditional economists have not been able to, but we believe that we do provide a useful basis here for beginning that process and for generating useful results now for field workers.

The fundamental assumption for biophysical economics is that we must maintain, to the degree humanly possible, the fundamental integrity of the earth and its major physical and biotic systems, for without that it is not possible to have the human economy continue indefinitely. It is not something that can simply be discounted away. Most important, as we perceive things now, are reliable and safe energy supplies and protecting the atmosphere. To do these things requires ultimately noncarbonaceous fuels and a reinvention of the concept of economic growth. We recognize that it is extremely unlikely that either of these things will happen any time soon, although the second may be forced upon us sooner than we think if the impacts of the end of cheap oil are as severe as most believe. Nevertheless, we wish to proceed with our analysis while we keep the idea of these ultimate issues on the back burner.

We undertake this analysis with the full understanding that conventional (neoclassical) economics, for whatever its limitations, is an extremely well developed and integrated approach where, in general, the players are well entrenched and agree upon the rules. And we acknowledge that their influence is increasing in the applied world, even as many academic economists step back from the pure model. For example, computable general equilibrium (CGE) models, which are pure applications of neoclassical economics (NCE), are increasingly used in World Trade Organization (WTO) negotiation rounds that affect billions of lives. In addition, conventional economics has been developed in such a way (for example, by emphasizing money rather than energy, demography, and other resources as we do) as to appear to be a logical extension of the day-to-day economics with which we are all familiar. These are significant hurdles to overcome for those of us who believe that a more useful and accurate economics can be developed. Nevertheless, we perceive the importance of this to be so great as to require our best efforts to do so. A point in our favor is that we know that we are not alone in challenging NCE, and our best allies may be some of the economists themselves, especially those who spend their time in the realities of the developing world (see chapter 1).

We have spent considerable time in the past developing a biophysical assessment for the country of Costa Rica (Hall 2000), and much of what follows is based on our experience in that assessment. That book has twenty-six chapters with detailed assessments of essentially all important aspects of the Costa Rican economy and environment. It has in addition (on a CD bundled with the book) a comprehensive and user-friendly dynamic model that we think is extremely important in communicating biophysical information and assessments to both other professionals and also to lay people. The basic idea of this model and its user interface is that there is a central image—that of the country of Costa Rica, shown with the mountains visible in a three-dimensional representation, with ten small graphs around the edge with lots of different information that is plotted over time (past and future). You watch the rather amazing deforestation unfold in the central image, and the green, forested country turns to agriculture and pastures represented in yellow while the numbers of humans, cows, hectares of used and degraded lands, and so on grow nearly exponentially on the graphs around the margin.

One characteristic of these analyses—which may be good or bad, depending upon your point of view—is that there is (usually) no attempt to reduce the various different information sets to a single scalar (such as is usually the objective in, for example, money-based economic cost-benefit analyses). Rather, the idea is to put all of the dynamic information—including land use, demography, the environment, and the economy—on the screen simultaneously, then let the user or decision maker (or the people affected) decide whether they prefer the actual path of development (by whatever criteria they choose) or might rather have

something else. This approach can be particularly effective when integrated with historical patterns of, say, land use. Most people living in Costa Rica today are too young to understand how much their country has changed in one human lifetime, but they can see that clearly—and are often amazed—when they see this as an *n*-dimensional visualization. Thus, most of the rest of this chapter is a discussion of what kind of information you might want to include and how you interact with it (this can also be done, depending on the situation, in some simpler analytic structure such as a spreadsheet).

A rough guess as to the total cost of developing the kind of overall biophysical analysis for a small to medium-sized developing country is on the order of $1 million, assuming that you are undertaking this analysis with competent and not greedy investigators and that the biophysical and economic database is well developed, as was the case for Costa Rica. Our assessment of Costa Rica (Hall 2000) was done on a small fraction of that, although much of the work was subsidized with sabbatical pay from Hall's university, essentially free graduate student help, other projects that had already been funded, and the data, interest, skills, and good will of numerous Costa Ricans. Most of the examples we give here are aimed at such a national level, although the biophysical approach that we are advocating is in theory applicable at any regional level that the investigator might choose. The most important scale issue is that much of the data that is generally most readily available is only suitable for national-level analyses (or at most at the scale of large regions).

Other Related Biophysical Approaches

Before we give our own approach, we think it useful to review a number of other biophysical approaches that have been developed either to evaluate specific environmental impacts of economic activity or for some other explicit reason. While these approaches do not give the full and comprehensive environmental and economic analysis that we advocate, we think it important to review them, for they can be very useful supplements to the analysis that we give below.

We would also like to emphasize that our attempts to build a biophysical assessment is only marginally related to most of what is being done under the aegis of "environmental economics," or even the bulk of the activity in "ecological economics" (a field in which we consider ourselves a member). Although the goal of environmental economics (and a substantial part of ecological economics) is to integrate the environment into economic analyses, in fact it has been mostly about putting a dollar price tag on all kinds of environmental objects and services, and while we applaud such analyses that is not at all our objective here. One basic reason for this is that we believe that the dollar or other monetary unit is basically defined in market situations for nonessentials, the demand for which hardly represents real human wants and needs because it is often tremendously influenced by advertising. In addition, dollar values often give extremely poor information about basic resources: for example, as wild salmon increasingly are disappearing and are hence of less and less value to our society, their price goes up, indicating they are becoming more valuable than when they were cheap and abundant!

Hence, we believe that giving a dollar value to many things is often a rather poor estimate of the value of our most prized things, including our relations to those people close to us, justice before the law, and the maintenance of natural environments and the milieu of Earth that allows us to exist here in the first place. In fact, all of these are under assault by dollar-based aspects of our economy, and hence in our opinion dollar-based criteria are not appropriate for making assessments of the value of nature or our most essential resources. That said, we of course realize that we live in a money-based world where many things must be valued in monetary units for routine day-to-day transactions. So we try to walk an appropriate tightrope between using and not using monetary estimates.

However, there is much else that is good and interesting in the emerging transdisciplinary field of "ecological economics," defined by Costanza in the inaugural volume of the journal by that name as "all areas where ecology and economics overlap." Much of ecological economics is a radical departure from environmental economics, and analysis of the interdependence and coevolution of human economies and their natural ecosystems (economics being a strict subsystem of human ecology).

The first assessment procedure we review is called *ecological footprint analysis*. The idea, developed by William Rees and Mathis Wackernagel (see www.footprintnetwork.org), is to examine the environmental requirements for a person or a given region (for our purposes a social and economic unit such as a country or city) in terms of the quantity of land required to support the activities on that area considered. For example, they found that the land area required to support the needs of the city of Vancouver, Canada, was about eighteen times the land area of the city itself. This included land areas needed for growing crops and producing cows, fish, and other animals consumed; growing timber; mining minerals and so on (about half the area required); as well as assimilating the sewage, toxins, CO_2, and other wastes produced (the other half). Such assessments always show that the areas actually in use supporting people are much greater than the areas the humans actually occupy, and give lie to those who say that the Earth can support much larger human populations (or even the present level) indefinitely. They conclude that about three Earths are needed for today's population and level of affluence if we are to live on income rather than by running down capital. Over time, the authors have developed and refined their methodology impressively, and made its use on their Web site very straightforward and easy. Because they trace back virtually all the major material substances used by different groups of people their complete list of material used constitutes a ready-made list of the biophysical materials required to support an economy. What they have not done yet is to relate the materials required to the level of monetary activity; neither have they addressed the specific case of developing countries. Once this is done, we will have one rather good biophysical assessment at our fingertips.

The second approach is to undertake *energy analysis*, which in its many variants means essentially, how much energy does it take to undertake various economic activities? These methods were developed most importantly at the University of Illinois in the 1970s by Bruce Hannon, Clark Bullard, and Robert Herendeen, and were applied to most aspects of our economy, including agriculture, manufacturing, provision of services, and so on. A feature of these studies was that they calculated not only the direct energy used (such as the energy used in a tractor factory to make the tractor) but the indirect energies as well (the energy to mine and refine the iron, plastics, and so on used by the tractor factory). As a rough estimate, about half the energy used to make some product sold in "final demand" occurs in obtaining and refining the raw materials. Summaries of the results of such studies are given in Herendeen and Bullard (1975), Hall, Cleveland, and Kaufmann (1984), and Cleveland (2004). An important aspect of this research is that the numbers are old, as there has been little government funding of such energy research for decades as energy analysis has fallen into political disfavor, or more accurately, indifference, because in the minds of many (but not us) the market has resolved the energy issues of the 1970s and will continue to do it (with the help of technology). However a recent study by Carnegie Mellon has updated these analyses, and these estimates are readily available on their Web site (http://eiolca.net/). Sergio Ulgaldi and his students at the University of Siena are putting together a Web-based system for calculating the material costs for many different commodities (for example a new building) including the associated environmental costs.

Howard Odum, Mark Brown, and others have argued that while this kind of energy analysis is useful, it is incomplete because it does not take into account the environmental energies required to manufacture something or correct for the fact that different types of energies have different qualities. For example, a kilojoule (kJ) of electricity has value to society beyond its ability to simply heat water, and hence more value than a kJ of coal, because of its special properties and because it takes about three heat units of coal in a power plant to produce one unit of electricity, the rest more or less of necessity being released into the air and water. Likewise, a kJ of sugar fixed by a plant has more

value than a kJ of the sunlight that made it and so on. Odum has generated the idea of *embodied energy*, or more explicitly *Emergy* (with an *m*, as in energy memory, a concept analogous to the embodied labor, or total energy required to make, in a manufactured item) as a term to reflect the various qualities of energy. Odum and his student Mark Brown have developed an extensive accounting scheme to measure this and to compute the quantities of *emergy* required to make, or cause to happen, many things (Odum 1988). *Transformity* is a word used to evaluate the different qualities of different types of energy. An advantage of this approach is that although it is obvious that we want to account for the oil used to manufacture something, we are missing altogether the large quantities of environmental energies that are just as much needed to make it. These energies include, for example, the energy used to distill freshwater from the sea and lift it to mountaintops, which allows it to form rivers and hence become available to plants and to humans. Likewise, the sun runs photosynthesis and everything that derives from that, even though we do not pay Mother Nature for either the water or many of the products of photosynthesis. In addition it includes in the analysis an emergy assessment of the environmental services *forgone* because of the activity in question. While the idea is tremendously appealing to us (see Brown 2004), and the comprehensiveness essential in our view, the difficulty in estimating transformities makes its use less desirable to some (see Herendeen 2004). This same difficulty, however, may be an opportunity for opening an exciting new field of research.

From a rather different perspective, an interesting new approach for trying to deal with the dynamic nature of real economic systems versus the static view of the neoclassical economics is found in Driesen (2003). Driesen is a lawyer interested in improving the efficacy (effectiveness) and efficiency by which we achieve improvements in the environment. The neoclassical model usually treats environmental protection as a *static* efficiency problem. The policy maker seeks to adopt the environmental regulation that will balance costs and benefits. This point of view assumes, wrongly, that costs and benefits remain static. In fact, environmental problems grow over time as population and consumption increase. And the costs of regulatory compliance can decline in response to regulations, as firms seek to innovate and compete to reduce costs. Furthermore, environmental law must always take into account the ability of powerful firms to help shape administration of the law. In Driesen's view, an *economic dynamic* approach is needed. This approach evaluates the direction of change over time and designs laws that carefully cope with those changes. It designs law to create appropriate incentives to rein in destructive tendencies rather than to seek an equilibrium that never exists. And it requires careful evaluation of how economic incentives can undermine or support the goals of environmental protection, given the bounded rationality of both firms and government actors. While this approach is not explicit to either neoclassical or biophysical or any other specific economics, it is different and promising enough to us to include it here.

It may be that all of these techniques are measuring something quite similar, and that their utility may converge. Their use has not been compared often, but for example, Hall, Brown, and Wackernagel (2000) compared the carrying capacity of Costa Rica for humans using a comprehensive economic approach that went well beyond market costs, as well as two biophysical assessments: ecological footprints and emergy analysis. The results of the three approaches were very similar to the common question they were asked to address (how many people could be supported sustainably in Costa Rica), giving hope that we are approaching a true cost using both biophysical and comprehensive economic analysis. However, although each of these procedures is helpful in assessing a biophysical economic analysis, we still feel that it is useful to generate a more explicit summary as to how we can undertake biophysical economics. We do this below, meanwhile looking forward with perhaps excessive optimism to the day when scientists and policy makers agree on a set of integrated assessment procedures. There are movements under way as we write this by Richard Lawrence, Cutler Cleveland, Phillip Bogdonoff, and others to integrate all these assessment procedures into one online and professionally maintained site, but this will require time and

money, two commodities generally in short supply these days for such research, in part because of the dominance of those who believe in market rather than analyzed/computed/negotiated solutions to resource issues. Nevertheless, we look forward to the time in the not-too-distant future when, as part of the biophysical analysis of any item or activity, all that would be necessary would be to go to one Web site, maintained by skilled professionals, and type in the quantity (in tons or dollars of a particular year) to get all of the material, energy, emergy, footprint, environmental degradation, and so on associated with that economic activity. Later this can be done for different countries or international corporate entities to give more explicit values. Perhaps some day there will be a label on your breakfast cereal that gives, in addition to calories and sodium per serving, an assessment of the fuel and solar energy and land required to make it as well as the soil and biodiversity loss, maybe all summarized in terms of some common evaluative metric such as emergy.

Explicit Procedures for Creating a Biophysical Economic Analysis

While we wait for this future Web-based interactive synthesis, there is a great deal of quantitative analysis we can do, and in fact that can help provide the basis for this Web synthesis. We base what follows on Hall (2000). The assessment therein includes extensive discussion of our (and others') biophysical approaches with contributors and our extensive previous experience with assessing land-use change (e.g., Detwiler and Hall 1988). We also base our assessments on simply living for much of our lives in the developing tropics (especially Leclerc, who has done everything to escape his native Canadian winters), and reading a large number of newspapers and scientific papers there. Hall (2000) represents the most serious attempt to date to develop a complete biophysical economics model of a national economy, which we summarize and extend in this chapter and in chapter 9. The present book gives many additional specific examples of the methodology including scientific approaches, methods, and tools to help do the job at any level of organization. The only issue is that for many developing nations much of the data is most readily available at the national level.

We are the first to recognize that developing a biophysical analysis of an economy is a very imperfect activity, that we are just learning how to undertake such analyses, and that there are many changes that will be developed over time. Nevertheless, we have found that this approach in part or in full has served us and our colleagues and students well for analyzing many basic characteristics of a country or a region. We believe that it will be especially useful (compared to conventional economics) in assessing what might be optimal economic choices as we enter the "second half of the age of oil," that is, as oil production reaches its peak or peaks and begins its inevitable decline in parallel with an increased demand from transition economies.

We next give a formula for undertaking routine biophysical economic analysis for a rapid assessment of development, together with a series of suggestions as to how to use this process to help construct better development schemes. We propose a methodology that unfolds in four steps that can be put simply as follows:

Step 1: State your objectives (with the right people)

Step 2: Assemble a database of critical biophysical parameters

Step 3: Make an assessment of critical economic parameters

Step 4: Explore alternative futures with those concerned

Although there is some logic in following these steps sequentially, it is better to look at this process as four iterative, successively refined phases. We assume that after these steps are taken into account for devising a development scheme, money will flow in the right directions, schools will be built, equipped, and populated, and institutions will improve. Nevertheless, we are also quite aware of the potential for, say, corrupt leaders to undermine this kind of effort. Does the use of explicit and open science make corruption less possible? We think so, but we do not really know. Part of what must be done is the professionalization of all government institutions and personnel, including accountants, and a larger injection of the scientific process into government itself (see part 7).

Step 1: State Your Objectives (with the Right People)

It is not possible to undertake a journey, no matter how sophisticated your vehicle, if you do not know where you are going (unless of course your objective is simply the activity itself). So the first thing to do in undertaking a biophysical assessment is to ponder, discuss, and then state explicitly your objectives. Often people confound problems and objectives. An objective should not be a series of problem-solving activities, it should be seen as a long-term desired future condition. For the Costa Rica study (see chapter 9), the main objective was to determine to what degree, and in what ways, the country was or could become sustainable. This led logically to the next set of objectives, which was then to determine what we meant by sustainability, which in turn led to some interesting literature that showed that very different people had very different perspectives on what sustainability meant, most of which were antithetical to each other.

A second part of this analysis is to examine what other objectives people had in the past for related issues and how well these were achieved. In other words, a review of pertinent literature both for the region being analyzed and of past public and private development projects and their objectives, procedures, and successes and failures. Many of these analyses use (or should use) time-series data of economic, agricultural, or other information (see Hall 2000, chapter 4). It simply is not possible to understand whether whatever plan you are undertaking is successful or not unless you have a yardstick of the past trends over time to compare it to.

Very often the objectives will be stated in social, economic, or environmental terms. Given that we agree with that perspective, the reader might be curious why we then focus so much on the biophysical aspects of analysis. The answer is simple: we believe that social, economic, and environmental issues must all be addressed and, where possible, resolved within the context of the biophysical systems within which they must take place. It is very easy to list the various things that you would like to have: higher incomes, less pollution, greater welfare, and so on. For the developing world, these and other objectives are very often not met, which means that there are serious constraints. Some, of course, are social, and we include here especially corruption and the very unequal distribution of whatever wealth is available. But much of what gets in the way of achieving one's social or economic objectives is biophysical, including resource availability, climatic constraints, and biophysical mismanagement including, for example, overfishing, soil erosion, fuel limitations, and inability to generate foreign exchange. Perhaps most important is a sense that there will be many trade-offs or opportunity costs, and that these trade-offs will often be made more obvious through a biophysical assessment. For example, if foreign exchange to buy oil is limited, then each new project that uses oil should be examined relative to its ability to provide it.

The biophysical aspects of development especially have been neglected during decades of NCE policies. Therefore, the biophysical context must be restored in mainstream thinking, possibly as the framework within which the social and economic possibilities are considered. Hence our biophysical emphasis, although we in no way wish to diminish the importance of the social, political, and economic elements. In fact, we believe that the reader will find that most of our work tries to integrate the biophysical and the social sciences toward attempting to meet their objectives.

If we are interested not only in the progress of science but also in its impact in the development of the country studied, then we have to find the right people to develop the models with. These people will help at many levels: to clarify the objective, to obtain the data (not easy in many developing countries), to provide key insights to interpreting the data and for prospective analysis, to make the connection with policy so that we can extend its use beyond that of scientific paper (i.e., step 4). If we are all involved from the start in developing an analytic model, such as in "companion modeling" (Barreteau et al. 2003) or "integrated natural resources management" (Hagmann et al. 2002),

there is a good chance that we learn from each other and end up with a model (or a family of models) that is not only more relevant but one that will continue to be used and developed for policy making. Allan and Holland (chapter 22) and Beaulieu et al. (chapter 35) give several hints about how to identify *who* you should work with and *how* to connect to a development process. A good starting point is to do a stakeholders' analysis and work, with the right people, on a shared vision for the country or region. This is where genuine objectives will appear more clearly to all, and when the collective learning process will begin.

Step 2: Assemble a Database of Critical Biophysical Parameters

Assessing the natural resources base

The first step in undertaking biophysical analyses (once past time trends of pertinent data have been prepared) is normally to determine the physical characteristics of the country or region being analyzed. Such analyses are far easier than in the past due to the increased availability of good digital summaries compared to twenty years ago. (The use and synthesis of this information is another matter.) An example of how such a database has been developed is given in chapter 17. The best way to do this is to generate an assessment of the physical resources of the region in question. This information includes both energy and non-energy resources.

Energy resources.

An essential requirement is a summary of energy resources, including any known oil, gas, and coal deposits; assessments of what might be found in the future (see the reviews in EIA or ASPO); developed and potential hydroelectric, solar, and wind power (for which you need meteorological information); biomass possibilities; and so on. In all of these assessments it is important to realize that in general the better resources were developed first, such that increased exploitation may be more energy and monetarily expensive. For all of these generate a time series of their use (Hall 2000, figure 4.5).

But different types of energy have different properties or qualities, and often it is useful to take that into account. Generally, the data available will be in the form of heat units (BTUs, kilowatt hours, kilocalories, or the most commonly accepted units used today, Joules). By heat units we mean that the energy is measured by its ability to heat water; for example, one kilocalorie (kCal) is the energy required to heat one liter of water and increase its temperature by one degree centigrade. These units are all intraconvertible, and there is no real difference among them (although kilowatt hours is most commonly used for the heat value of electricity, which has a different quality when used to do something besides heating water). Each of these terms is of the same quality, meaning that no particular value is given to the energy except for its ability to heat water. Fossil fuels (coal, oil, and natural gas) are most explicitly well measured by their heat values (because we burn them to use them), although each has its own particular qualities (oil is readily transportable, gas is the cleanest, and so on). Sometimes data on biomass are also provided, usually again in heat units. The energy supplied from nuclear and hydropower, however, is as electricity, which is usually considered of higher quality as shown in part by our willingness to pay roughly three times more for electricity as for an equivalent heat value of fossil energy such as oil. A good way to think about this is that we (society) are willing to trade roughly three heat units (MJoule or kCal) of fossil (or nuclear) energy for one unit of electric energy (as heat) in our fossil-fueled electricity plants, which of necessity requires that the other roughly two-thirds of the energy in the fuel is lost as heat either up the smokestack or to the necessary cooling water drawn from an adjacent river, lake, or ocean. In other words, there is a huge opportunity (and conversion) cost to generate electricity from fossil or nuclear fuels. Additionally we need to undertake an assessment of the various environmental energies that must be supplied for the economy to work properly. As stated above this can be done most comprehensively using an emergy analysis (Odum 1996).

Non-energy natural resources.

Similar assessments are required for natural resources that are not energy sources, such as:

1. Non-fuel mineral resources, such as metal ores. The important components of this are the size of the reserve (in tons), the quality (percent metal in ore, both at present and as exploitation proceeds), the depth and ease of extraction, the energy cost of extraction of different amounts, and so on. Since usually the best grades were used first, the remaining resources may not be as cheaply or profitably exploited as was once the case. Because the exploitation of minerals often occasions significant pollution, any such impacts, and a social and monetary estimate of that damage, must be made before the project begins. These issues must be considered in addition to expected market prices and other routine economic factors. (See Youngquist 1997.)

2. Water resources, both quantitatively and qualitatively, first in overview and then spatially. Some of the information that needs to be generated or summarized includes rainfall and flow of major rivers (both as a mean and for drought and wet years), groundwater resources and their vulnerability to depletion/salinization, evapotranspiration and soil moisture over space and time, water-body volumes and pollution levels, and so on. (See chapter 14 and Hall 2000, chapters 9, 10, and CD.)

3. Land resources for examining agricultural (and other) potential:
   a soil map, ideally with the soil units related to crop productivity, and including where possible potential and actual erosion (see chapters 16 and 23)
   a digital elevation map (see Hall 2000, chapter 8)
   a land use map

Taking demography into account

We believe that fundamental to what one is trying to achieve with almost any biophysical model is a proper representation of human demography, in part to examine per capita economic results and to assess population pressure on resources. While the mothers of the developing world are well aware of the problems caused by unbounded population growth in their neighborhoods, there are few demographers in the field compared to sociologists, anthropologists, agronomists, geographers, and the like. This is probably because in recent years the adaptation capacity of people and the environment has been overemphasized. Excellent data sets exist for less-developed countries (LDCs), from nationwide census data every five or ten years. Yearly estimates can be interpolated from excellent data sets available from demographic and health surveys. Other data are conveniently summarized by the Food and Agricultural Organization (FAO) of the United Nations.

For analysis of the future it is necessary to generate a demographic model based on actual demographic data. One simple model is:

$$P_t = P_0 \, e^{rt}$$

where P is the population level (normally in millions), P_t is the population at time t years into the future, P_0 is the population at some initial time t, e is the natural logarithm (= 2.718), and r is the "intrinsic rate of growth," the rate at which the population is growing or, better, is expected to grow. The value r (in units of proportion of the existing population per year) is the birth rate (b) minus the death rate (d). Hence the term e^{rt} is a number that will usually be greater than 1.0 and will be the factor by which the population is larger (relative to the initial population) over time. The doubling time of a population can be calculated by dividing the number 70 by the growth rate expressed as a percentage, so for example a population with a 2 percent per year growth rate will double in thirty-five years. This simple model is often reasonably accurate, at least for developing countries and within the restrictions of knowing the value of r, for at least a few decades.

But there have been many who believe that to continue to use an exponentially growing model is seriously flawed, as populations cannot grow exponentially indefinitely as they would run out of food, resources, and/or space (i.e. carrying capacity). Some models, attempting to represent that fact, will assume or simulate some sort of empirical plateau, (in other words, r diminishes) or saturation of growth. A logistic, or S-shaped curve, is used often

to simulate that saturation effect (see chapter 8). Although the logistic equation is simple and has some perhaps good logic behind it, in fact few populations in nature follow that pattern and attempts to use that model to predict human populations in the past failed miserably (Hall 1988). The debate between population "explosionists" and "implosionists" is still alive (because the data support either view equally well), and while the S-curve is still the most widely used model for making human population projections in LDCs (see www.prb.org), the beginning of the plateau could be put at any time after 2050.

Both the exponential and the logistic model have a number of liabilities including that they are not sensitive to changing values of r over time and are insensitive to more detailed demographics, such as the number of prereproductive versus postreproductive females, and of course it is for only one geographical unit. More accurate, or at least sensitive, models can be made using what is known as a Leslie matrix, which is usually computed numerically. A simple example in programming pseudo-code (which can be easily transformed to a specific computer code) is given in table 6.1. Data for all of the world's countries can be obtained from FAO or the CIA database. Additional demographic information can be developed, including poverty assessments (see chapter 20), labor productivity, adaptation and migrations (see chapters 8, 12, and 31).

Localizing infrastructures

Additional geographical information needs to be developed on the location and extent of built infrastructure, including cities, villages, transportation, industries, ports, airports, protected areas, land tenure (private and public), and so on (see chapters 28 and 29). These can be built into additional geographic information systems (GIS) data layers, as is well understood from conventional GIS analyses. This information is vital for understanding the accessibility of resources to populations and as drivers for predicting land-use change. Often our overall objective is to simulate how future land use, economic, and food security scenarios might be influenced by demography, erosion, policy, climate change, roads, and so on.

Table 6.1. A Simple Leslie Matrix program

DICTIONARY:

AgeClass	=	age class of the human population (1 equals all people before their first birthday; 2 = all people between their first and second birthday; . . .)
PopNum (Year, AgeClass)	=	population number for each age class for each year. This state variable is updated for each simulated year.
DeathRate (AgeClass)	=	Age-specific death rate (constant over simulation period)
BirthRate (AgeClass)	=	number of births per year per female in given age class (this may be known only on average, and is constant for entire simulation period).
TotalBirths	=	total births in a given simulated year
Births	=	births for a given age class and a given year
ReprodPop	=	number of females in age to reproduce (i.e. between 15 and 50)

PSEUDO CODE:

```
#Read in initial population numbers (in thousands or millions) & age-specific death rates (assume 80 is oldest
year people live or at least reproduce):
for AgeClass from 1 to 80 {
       read PopNum(Year = 1, AgeClass), DeathRate(AgeClass), BirthRate(AgeClass)
}
#compute population levels by age class by updating PopNum data annually for 50 simulated years
for Year from 1 to 50 {
       PopNum(Year,AgeClass=1) = TotalBirths # i.e. Births from end of last year considered age class one
       for AgeClass from 2 to 80 {
               PopNum(Year,AgeClass) = PopNum(Year – 1,AgeClass – 1) – DeathRate(AgeClass)
               if AgeClass between 15 and 50 then {
                       ReprodPop = ReprodPop + PopNum(Year,AgeClass)
                       Births = ReprodPop * BirthRate(AgeClass)
                       TotalBirths = TotalBirths + Births
               }
       }
# write simulated population number for each simulated year
       for AgeClass from 1 to 80 {
               write Year, PopNum(Year,AgeClass)
       }
}
```

Step 3: Make an Assessment of Critical Economic Parameters Over Time
Generating an empirical economic summary

The first step is to undertake an assessment of the current economy and its recent history. There are a number of locations to find this information, but probably the easiest is to get the data off the Internet. Good sources are the large multilateral organizations (such as the FAO, UNDP, and WTO), NGOs (WRI, IUCN), and the unavoidable World Bank. Several organizations, such as the CIA and *The Economist* (www.cia.gov/cia/publications/factbook/index.html; www.economist.com/countries), provide good country fact sheets. As the digital divide between the developed and less-developed countries gets narrower, more and more data from LDC government sites are available. These government sites often contain key documents on policies, feasibility studies, law texts, economic summaries, and so on. Travel books are quite useful to get a grasp of a country's idiosyncrasies. A problem with many sites is the lack of time-series data, which makes the FAO data (especially the country profiles), dating back to 1961, probably the most generally useful.

From this information a time series of economic activity can be graphed (e.g., chapter 5). Some data that we suggest should be considered include a time series of basic monetary economic information, including gross domestic product (GDP) and import/export figures. Beside the fact that they are basic economic indicators, these numbers also have a large influence on foreign development policy.

GDP over time.

While analyses of any raw GDP data almost always show a rapid increase over time, this is very misleading, for much of the increase is due to inflation. So the first thing to do is to correct the data for inflation, normally by expressing all data in terms of monetary units for one year, for example "2000 dollars" or "2004 pesos." This is done by using "implicit price deflators" (the easiest ones can be found in the *Statistical Abstracts of the United States*). This is especially useful when dealing in U.S. dollars, although it is more accurate to use corrections implicit for the country in question. In the United States and many other countries there are also more specific correctors for different sectors of the economy, for example for energy and for food.

A second step is sometimes required, which is to make an additional correction for purchasing price parity (PPP). If a nation's GDP is corrected from inflation relative to the U.S. dollar, as it often is, it is also necessary to correct for the fact that the increase in prices expressed in dollars does not reflect the fact that there is often far less inflation for local products such as food than for imported computers or fuel paid for in dollars. On the other hand, if you are interested in the issue of how much it costs for importing oil (which must be paid for in dollars or Euros) then correcting for PPP is not useful. Since for many developing countries the inflation rate applied to dollars is considerably greater than the rate applied to local items, this can be an important issue.

To express the meaning of the GDP changes (corrected as appropriate) in terms of how it affects the average person's ability to purchase goods and services, the total national GDP needs to be corrected to per capita values. The total national GDP tells little about how well individuals in that country are doing in terms of their own economic welfare or purchasing power. Dividing the total wealth production by the number of people gives per capita wealth, which is roughly proportional to at least some important aspects of the average person's material well-being. To do this, one simply divides the total GDP (corrected as above) by the number of people in the country for that year to get the per capita GDP (see Hall 2000, figure 4.2). This results in a decrease in the effect of GDP increases, and in many cases where the population increases more rapidly than the GDP, people, on average, get poorer.

Even per capita changes do not tell the whole story, for most of the GDP may go to only a relatively few people. One way to examine this issue is to use or compute the "Gini index," conceived by the Italian statistician Corrado Gini, which is the ratio of what income (or other economic assets) the richest 20 percent get over the proportion that the poorest 20 percent get. For example if the richest 20 percent get 40 percent of the income and the poorest 20 percent get 10 percent, the Gini index would be 4.0. More complex indexes are also available.

Imports, exports, and their difference.

An extremely important aspect of sustainability is whether a nation is able to do whatever economic activity it does without going into international debt, which tends to be a killer aspect of development that leads many otherwise excellent development schemes into failure. Since the desire for foreign products, both those essential for the development of food production and also luxury items, requires payment in foreign exchange (dollars or Euros), it is essential for a country to export enough to pay for these items. The alternative is foreign debt, which in many countries is more or less the largest problem in making an economy that works. Costa Rica, for example, needs to use about 15 percent of the foreign exchange it generates through the sales of bananas, coffee, and tourist services simply to pay for interest on its foreign debt. It uses perhaps another 20 percent of the foreign exchange it earns to pay foreign countries for the industrial products that it needs for the generation of the exports (for example, the fertilizers, plastics, and fuels required to make bananas). Since there are enormous demands in Costa Rica for imported items (from cars, buses, and trucks to fuel to run them to computers to apples) and a rather limited international demand (or more properly a huge oversupply) of bananas and coffee, then it is really tough for countries like Costa Rica not to get into debt. On top of this, governments often borrow from external banks to make payrolls or provide social services. While Costa Rica has done much better than many countries (including the United States) in not running up external debt, it is a very difficult issue. Hence it is useful to plot imports, exports, and their difference, as well as debt and its accumulation or decrease over time (see Hall 2000, figure 4.10). The latter is especially important in the recent debate of debt cancellation of heavily indebted developing countries (see chapter 3).

Another issue that contributes to a large difference between imports and exports is that developing countries tend to be desperate for development capital, and that capital is rarely available internally. So, for example, Costa Rica needs more electric power as its economy grows, and that can be supplied by developing more hydropower. But the Costa Rican government does not have the investment capital for that. So Japanese power companies are more than happy to build the hydropower plants that are needed because they are happy to collect the revenue from those plants. The problem is solved, sort of, but there is a new revenue flow out of the country. The point is that development projects need to be examined from the perspective not only of their promised gains but also of their costs, including, of course, their costs and gains to whom.

Undertaking a biophysical assessment of the current economy

The next major step is to look at the biophysical resources needed to make the economy do what it does, and presumably, to do more of the same in the future (to prepare for step 4). Since we also have developed time series of economic activity and also time series of energy used we can quite easily develop the energy intensity, which is the energy used per unit of economic activity, either for the economy as a whole or for some aspect of interest. This is the first step required to understand the biophysical resources needed for the operation of the economy. A similar concept (actually the inverse) is assessing the *efficiency* of an economy, something we have discussed in the previous chapter. In general, efficiency is the output of a process divided by the input (see Hall 2000, figure 4.5, which has both expressed as per capita). *Efficacy*, a similar-sounding but very different term, is the effectiveness of some activity regardless of the efficiency—in other words it is getting the job done. For example, we might say that the U.S. economy is very efficacious—that is, it produces a great deal of goods and services. But its efficiency, the total dollar value of its output compared to the quantity of energy used to generate that wealth, is rather low compared to many other nations. This straightforward measure of efficiency that we might want to calculate is the output of the economy divided by its energy input, which, if we have the information derived above, we can do very easily in a spreadsheet or computer program. The efficiency of the economy can be seen by the ratio of the two, and the changing efficiency by the changing slope of that line (see Hall 2000, figure 4.5).

Depending upon the objectives of the study, other indexes can be used, such as imported versus domestic energy or GNP per unit of water, or agricultural production per unit of energy or fertilizer used, or GNP per unit foreign exchange gained or lost, or many other objectives. When we have done these analyses in the past, we have often found that GDP increases more or less in step with energy, water, fertilizer use, and so on, so that efficiency does not change much over time (see chapter 5). This has important implications for the economic aspect of efficiency—for if efficiency is not increasing, that implies that the only way to generate wealth is through the further exploitation of resources, something that has ultimately serious environmental and supply implications.

Much more detailed analyses interweaving all sectors of economic activity can be undertaken through the use of input-output matrices (see chapter 32). These are specially useful for analyzing development scenarios where the relative weight of each sector is likely to change rapidly.

An important aspect of a biophysical (or any) assessment is that there are often not clear ways to achieve several goals at once, and one is left with tradeoffs. Several of the chapters (e.g., 13, 23 and 35) in this book are focused on that issue. Finally, development projects that were once very good often crash over time, as is classically illustrated with wild fisheries and aquaculture (chapters 26 and 27). These crashes are often, but not always, predicted through fisheries science (taking into account climate change and its effect on sea surface temperature, for example), but never, to our knowledge, through market assessments alone.

Predicting the future energy needs of a society

Presumably, any such biophysical analysis will show that the economy of the region is moderately to very energy-intensive and that any expansion of the economy is likely to be even more so. Most present development is based on oil. Thus future expansion of an economy presupposes the physical and economic availability of oil or at least some other equally useful form of energy, if that exists (which we doubt). It suffices to watch the frantic activity that accompanies unexpected oil price changes (especially when the price increases) to understand that petroleum plays a central role in an economy. After all, globalization started just after the first oil crisis (see chapter 3), and since then governments and firms do everything possible to maintain low oil price.

At present there are about thirty-eight oil-exporting nations. The economies of most of the smaller and medium-sized exporters are becoming themselves much more energy intensive over time, and most will become net importers themselves within decades as their own domestic use intercepts their production. Thus it is important now to consider how, if economies are to be expanded, that might be done in a way that makes them less dependent on perhaps unreliable or at least very expensive future

oil supplies. This is an issue not normally considered within conventional economics, inasmuch as the present price of oil (determined by the market or as a result of muscled negotiations or interventions) makes this energy a seemingly attractive choice. But we feel it important to go beyond that mentality. The first six years of the twenty-first century saw great price increases in the price of oil, although correcting for inflation, the average cost was only about two-thirds of the maximum price in the 1970s. One of our colleagues in Great Britain said that he felt he was standing on the shore of the North Sea, and although the storm had not hit yet, the first large waves were starting to roll in. In other words, the price increases that we have observed in the recent past are only a small sign of what lies ahead as the world truly approaches the end of cheap oil. What this will mean for the world can only be guessed at, but for nations of the developing world that do not produce oil, the impact is likely to be enormous as populations and economies that had expanded based on cheap oil have the rug pulled out from under them. It will not be a pretty sight.

Predicting land-use change

An important part of many assessments of the future capacity of a nation or a region for providing economic or environmental services is how much land is available in different categories (this is loosely related to the concept of ecological footprint). The principal tools for doing this are several computer models that start with one map of land use for a given year and then make assessments of future land use based on rates and patterns of development. Both rates and patterns can be derived statistically from existing patterns that can be extracted digitally from one or more existing maps of land use. The model that we know best for doing this, not surprisingly, is one that was derived by one of the authors (see Hall et al. 1995; Pontius, Cornell, and Hall 1995). This model, called GEOMOD, has been simplified and bundled with the most recent version of IDRISI, a commercial software package with powerful modules for assessing and predicting patterns of land use. Not surprisingly, GEOMOD shares the features of many other land use models, some of which are described in detail in this book (chapters 15, 17, 31); the following example illustrates what a land-use prediction model based on GEOMOD can do (see also chapter 18).

One might start with, for example, a map of the forested versus nonforested region of Costa Rica, as we did in our original analysis. Looking out airplane windows while flying over many regions of the tropics, especially the hilly or mountainous tropics, we have seen that development tended to start along rivers, often at lower elevations, and then to work progressively upstream and upslope over time, with the development usually proceeding from one already developed place to an adjacent forested one. This is consistent with the idea that farmers will develop land in a way that represents the most favorable energy return on investment, that is, with the highest potential for agricultural production (usually soils near a river on flatter land) with the least effort or energy investment on their part (hence adjacent properties on flatter land). Our first assessments used a DEM (digital elevation model) to represent topography, with originally the land represented as a checkerboard of one-kilometer-by-one-kilometer cells, each cell being labeled either as "forest" or "nonforest" (i.e., developed) (see Hall et al. 1995; Hall et al. 2000). We would provide GEOMOD with an initial or startup map with a given pattern of forest and nonforest (or with more categories). GEOMOD uses a search window to examine the eight (or sometimes more) cells around each developed cell and determine which cells are likely to be developed. If there was an undeveloped (forested) cell next to a developed cell, then we have an "edge," and that forested cell was a candidate for development. This was done for the entire forest/nonforest map, meanwhile keeping track of the elevation and/or slope for each candidate cell. Then enough of the lowest-elevation (and/or flattest) cells were developed to meet the proscribed rate of development expected for that time step (usually one year). Over time this process resulted in the spread of development upstream and upslope, simulating a basic pattern by which humans use land in Costa Rica. The final project comprises maps of future land use that can be discussed with planners.

It is useful to reexamine, on a regular basis, our assumptions on farmer's decision-making rules. This typically involves interviews and surveys in the field. Often we find that what we thought initially was wrong, even if it seemed perfectly logical. For example, the main cabbage production areas in Nepal are rocky high-altitude slopes, classified as "not suitable for agriculture" by Western planners. Chapter 21 gives a striking example of such a misconception, which can have serious consequences for policy.

Over time, variants of GEOMOD have been developed that can use many different properties of the environment (distance from roads or cities, soil types, and so on) that give the option of undertaking much more sophisticated assessments and predictions of land-use change. Several chapters in this volume use GIS and related spatial-analysis techniques to examine geographical aspects of development and development possibilities, often while paying special attention to scale issues. All of these chapters show the incredible role that geographical analyses linked with computers now play in virtually every aspect of examining development issues.

Predicting net economic output as a function of land type

All land does not have the same capacity for economic production, and this is especially true when specific uses are examined. For example, Hartshorn et al. (1982) determined that for Costa Rica only about 19 percent of the total land area was flat and fertile enough to be utilized for any use, including specifically row crop agriculture, which would be likely to cause irreparable damage if applied to other land categories (in other words, if the land was too steep, then erosion would destroy the potential for production in a relatively short time). Another 9 percent of the land was suitable for pastures, and another 16 percent for tree crops such as coffee, which causes less erosion because of its continuous cover. The rest of the country, more than 56 percent, should have no human use at all except for forestry that would maintain tree cover. In fact far more than 56 percent of the country has already been developed for agriculture, pastures, or urban areas.

Farmers and many other humans are well aware of what land is best to use for various purposes and tend to use the best land first, as is represented by the farmer's choices given in the preceding example for GEOMOD. Thus, over time the land available for development tended to be of poorer and poorer quality, as represented in the pioneering work of David Ricardo (1817). What this means for development is that average values of crop production cannot be used to forecast what the yields might be for some development project. For example, coffee can be grown anywhere in Costa Rica. But high-quality coffee, of which Costa Rica has some of the best, requires very explicit environmental conditions (precipitation, temperature, soil, and so on) to get high yields. We found that for Costa Rica as of 1990 nearly all of the land that was best for growing Arabica coffee already had it growing there (or was covered by urbanized areas), and that if there were to be increased coffee production, yields of high-quality coffee would probably be less or else more energy-intensive than the average of what was occurring already. This is an example of what has been called, variously, diminishing returns to investment or declining (energy or other) return on energy investment as the best resources are used. We found, quite remarkably, that for most crops any increase in area of land cropped would produce an instantaneous reduction in yield per hectare, as the land being used for production would be, on average, of lower quality (Hall 2000, figure 12.4e).

In any land-use model we have to make sure, however, that the decision rules that we put in the model are rules that land users actually follow. This generally implies running interviews and surveys in the field. Examples of such ground truth checks are given in chapters 13, 15, 20, 21, 30, and 31. One of the best ways to challenge and restate our hypotheses is to go in the field and talk to land users.

Assessing the costs and benefits of a development scheme

If there is a plan for development, then the next step is to assess the energy, material, and other resource requirements for the projects that will enable that plan, including its monitoring/evaluation/feedback components. While this can be an extremely difficult and comprehensive issue (especially if the environment is to be taken into account) and there are not yet easy formulas for how to undertake it, one can turn to life cycle assessment (LCA) software, which provides careful input (e.g., costs of materials required, allocation rules) and output (e.g., impact assessment, what-if scenarios) evaluations. These evaluations can be converted to energy and emergy analyses in a very simple and flexible way (Bargigli et al. 2006), a far cry from the old days of undertaking such calculations by hand (see Hall et al. 1986). Recently, the United Nations Environment Program (UNEP) and the Society for Environmental Toxicology and Chemistry (SETAC) launched the Life Cycle Initiative, which aims to put LCA into effective practice by providing information publications, training modules, and free software (lcinitiative. unep.fr). By assessing the benefits of the plan (in direct relation to the objectives and using the simulation results of step 4), and the incremental costs to reach the objectives, we have everything in hand to mobilize the funds and the people needed and start the process.

Including social assessments

As we stated in step 1, many of the issues that are most important to people interested in development are social and economic. There is no easy formula for integrating the biophysical and the socioeconomic approaches, although much can be undertaken with an open mind, a willingness to work outside of one's own discipline, and, perhaps most important, an ability to find and work with others from other disciplines. Persistent attempts by economists to put a dollar value to "social capital," just as they do with the environment, are enterprises that we believe are seriously flawed and doomed to fail. Many of the chapters that follow are especially good at attempting to integrate biophysical and socioeconomic approaches (e.g. chapters 21, 31 and 35).

Step 4: Explore Alternative Futures with Those Concerned

A final step in undertaking a thorough assessment of the biophysical possibilities and constraints of a region is to examine alternative future environments in which one's decisions might be played out. While predictions and trends are developed in step 2 and 3 as integral parts of any biophysical assessment for objectives stated in step 1, prospective analysis plays a fundamental role in shaping the development of a country. However, it is poorly done at best, policy makers having to juggle with too many parameters and being forced to use shortcuts, which opens the door to misconceptions and prejudice, wrong interpretation of the data, and shortsighted emergency measures. Swartz (1996) describes the critical role of scenario analysis for positioning ourselves properly into the future. Scenarios are not predictions or forecasting: they are "vehicles for helping people to learn, alternative images of the future, to change the managerial view of reality." At the core of any managerial view is the concept of objectives (i.e., step 1). However, in the approach that we propose, objectives are not cast in stone: prospective analysis helps to revisit these objectives and modify them if needed.

At the core of prospective analysis, one can easily imagine an environment to run and discuss comprehensive simulations of the future based on the previous three steps. It can contain some or all of the entities included above plus whatever other elements the user feels appropriate, including elements of neoclassical economic analysis, and the results can be compared or even integrated. We believe especially in the development of good graphics and real-time simulations for communication to stakeholders.

Many people are extremely suspicious of any such simulation models. How can scientists even start to think that they can predict the future? In some cases we find that suspicions arise from the common acceptances of some kind of "butterfly effect," or, to the contrary, that only God can predict the future. A perception shared by knowledgeable environmental scientists is that the Club of Rome "limits to growth" model (Meadows et al. 1972), which predicted some rather severe oscillations in basic world characteristics, was a colossal failure because these oscillations had to be unpredictable owing to the multiplicity of factors involved. What is almost not known is that if one draws a timeline

on the bottom of their "standard run," and if one assumes that "resources" is well represented by petroleum and "pollutants" by global sulfur or CO_2, then as of 2004 the model is almost exactly on course (Meadows, Randers, and Behrens 2004). Whether the violent oscillations that the model predicts for 2025 will come to pass remains to be seen, but we can say, so far so good after thirty-five years! We think that formalizing one's knowledge and assumptions through modeling is a critical approach that needs to be undertaken much more with the decision makers of the developing countries in the future.

We must also face the fact that whatever good we might be able to do with the approach that we advocate can be undermined, like anything else, by the corruption and unresponsiveness of government in much of the developing (and developed) world. We have no magic solution to this, although we are confident in the positive impact of a neutral and transparent scientific approach. But the main problem that we scientists face is that we are generally not very good at communicating our results to the public, have little financial or political power, and therefore we have limited influence on the decisions that affect our society. This is where good computer graphics showing to the general populace the past and projected future aspects of their economies and environments as a function of whatever policies are implemented can be key. We believe that political debates about the future might be carried out with the aid of good computer simulations and visualizations shown on national television; it would be very interesting if the promises of the candidates were subject to modeling reality checks to see what was in fact possible, and at what cost.

Making the right decisions

Most people who are involved with such a comprehensive analysis are interested in implementing the results in what is normally called policy. Since policy design is an iterative, cyclic process (see box 3.5), it is important for all who care to be involved from the beginning. From decision makers (and ideally from the general affected populace as well) the scientist or economist can get a much clearer idea of desired ends (which might be quite different from what the scientist or economist assumes). In turn, the decision maker can learn to have a systemic, longer-term, realistic perspective for his or her country.

"Hybrid" forums (Callon, Lascoumes, and Barthes 2001), where scientists, decision makers, and citizens meet and address development problems, are a proven vehicle for collective learning and commitment for a better future. Too few developing countries, however, have the necessary conditions for such democratic governance exercises. However, the use of dynamic graphs that can convey to the user possible futures as a function of policy today and resource realities is critical in a highly politicized, lobbied, and manipulated developing world. With the new insights gained from the entire process given above, we can reexamine if and where conventional economics has failed and propose amendments to neoclassical economics–based policy or develop an entire new perspective based on the analyses we have given. It is a big charge to develop an entirely new economics. But we think it critical, and what we have here is a formal start. Throughout the entire process of undertaking biophysical economic assessments and development plans, the scientific method must be used, theories need to be advanced in a way consistent with first principles, hypotheses need to be generated and tested, and so on (Hall and Klitgaard 2006). The final arbiter of the correctness of our analyses is not whether this or that theory is the basis for our efforts, but whether our predictions and policy prescriptions correspond to observations. This closes the loop on what is our basic wish: to bring the scientific method to developmental economics.

References

Bargigli, S., M. Raugei, and S. Ulgiati. 2006. Nested emergy analyses: Moving ahead from the spreadsheet platform. In M. T. Brown, ed., *Proceedings of the 4th Biennial Emergy Research Conference*, Gainesville, Florida, 19–21 January 2006.

Barreteau, O., M. Antona, P. d'Aquino, S. Aubert, S. Boissau, F. Bousquet, W. Daré, M. Etienne, C. Le Page, R. Mathevet, G. Trébuil, and J. Weber. 2003. Our companion modelling approach. http://jasss.soc.surrey.ac.uk/6/2/1.html.

Brown, M. 2004. Energy quality, emergy, transformity: The contributions of H. T. Odum to quantifying and understanding systems. *Ecological Modelling* 178:201–14.

Brown, M., M. Wackernagel, and C. A. S. Hall. 2000. Comparable estimates of sustainability: Economic, resource base, ecological footprint and emergy. *Ecological Economics* 19:219–36.

Callon, M., P. Lascoumes, and Y. Barthes, eds. 2001. *Agir dans un monde incertain: Essai sur la démocratie technique*. Paris: Seuil.

Cleveland, C. J. 2004. *The Encyclopedia of Energy*. Amsterdam: Elsevier.

Detwiler, P., and C. A. S. Hall 1988. Tropical forests and the global carbon cycle. *Science* 239:42–47.

Driesen, D. 2003. *The Economic Dynamics of Environmental Law*. Cambridge, Mass.: MIT Press.

Hagmann, J., E. Chuma, K. Murwiea, M. Connolly, and P. Ficarelli. 2002. Success factors in integrated natural resource management R&D: Lessons from practice. *Conservation Ecology* 5, no. 2: 29.

Hall, C. A. S. 1988. An evaluation of several of the most important theoretical models in ecology and of the data used in their support. *Ecological Modeling* 43:5–31.

———, ed. 2000. *Quantifying Sustainable Development: The Future of Tropical Economies*. San Diego: Academic Press.

Hall, C. A. S., C. J. Cleveland, and R. Kaufmann. 1984. *Energy and Resource Quality: The Ecology of the Economic Process*. New York: Wiley-Interscience.

Hall, C. A. S., H. Tian, Y. Qi, G. Pontius, and J. Cornell. 1995. Modeling spatial and temporal patterns of tropical land use change. *Journal of Biogeography* 22:753–57.

Hall, M., C. A. S. Hall, and M. Taylor. 2000. Geographical modeling: The synthesis of GIS and simulation modeling. In Hall 2000, 177–204.

Hall and Klitgaard. 2006. The need for a new biophysi-
cally-based paradigm in economics for the second
half of the age of oil. Journal of Transdisciplinary
Research. 1:4–22.

Hartshorn, G., et al. 1982. *Costa Rica: Country
Environmental Profile*. San José, Costa Rica: Tropical
Sciences Center.

Herendeen, R. 2004. Energy analysis and emergy analysis:
A comparison. *Ecological Modelling* 178: 227–238.

Herendeen, R., and C. Bullard. 1975. The energy costs of
goods and services, 1963 and 1967. *Energy Policy* 3:268.

Meadows, D. H., D. L. Meadows, J. Randers, and W.
Behrens. 1972. *The Limits to Growth*. New York:
Universe Press.

Meadows, D. L., J. Randers, and W. Behrens. 2004. *The
Limits to Growth: A New Look*. White River Junction,
Vt.: Chelsea Green.

Odum, H. T. 1988. Self organization, transformation and
information. *Science* 242:1132–39.

———. 1996. *Environmental Accounting, Emergy, and
Environmental Decision Making*. New York: Wiley.

Pontius, R. G., Jr., J. Cornell, and C. A. S. Hall. 1995.
Modeling the spatial pattern of land-use change with
GEOMOD2: Application and validation for Costa
Rica. *Agriculture, Ecosystems & Environment* 85, nos.
1–3: 191–203.

Ricardo, D. 1817. *On the Principles of Political Economy and
Taxation*. London: John Murray.

Swartz, P. 1996. *The Art of the Long View: Planning for the
Future in an Uncertain World*. New York: Doubleday.

Worldwide Fund for Nature International (WWF). 2004.
Living Planet Report 2004. Gland, Switzerland:
WWF.

Youngquist, W. 1997. *Geodestinies: The Inevitable Control of
Earth Resources over Nations and Individuals*. Portland,
Ore.: National Book Company.

PART TWO

NATIONAL SUCCESS STORIES, NATIONAL FAILURES, AND A LOT OF AMBIGUITY

From roughly 1490 through about 1945, the dominant force in what we now call the developing world was colonialism. The wealthier and more powerful military nations of the world (generally meaning European nations) tended to view the rest of the world as their own property or fiefdoms to colonize, exploit economically (including the practice of slavery, which did not end formally until the middle of the nineteenth century), convert religiously, and in some cases "improve." The reasons for the European dominance of other, sometimes more fully developed, cultures are interestingly explained in Diamond (1998) and Crosby (1986), among others. What colonialism meant to many people in the developing world was generally that they had little say about the conditions of much of their life and that they spent much of their life undertaking more or less hard and distasteful physical work for relatively little economic benefit to themselves—but of much benefit to the colonizers. However, in many cases their lot might have been little different without colonists as they may have had the same relation to the elites of their own region. Humans have had historically a great propensity to exploit others for their own benefit. An important question is whether much of economic development today is really so very different. From the perspective of at least some observers (such as John Perkins in *Confessions of an Economic Hit Man*), neocolonialism is alive and well and marching forward under the new banner of neoliberal economics. More generally, however, there is a sense that the interaction of the developed world with the less-developed world has not helped the latter too much because of ineptness rather than the objectives of the approach used. This is the view put forth in William Easterly's *White Man's Burden*. Easterly believes that much of

the $2.3 trillion the North has spent on foreign aid for the South has produced precious few results. Like the good economist he is, he attributes most of the reasons to concepts central to economic thinking, such as inadequately utilizing personal incentives. He also emphasized the need to replace excessive planning with more "searching" for solutions utilizing locals who know the specifics of their economy. While his perspective is very useful and probably correct, there still is a huge gulf between how most economists are trained to think—which focuses on economic policy changes—and our perception of the need to bring a down-to-earth biophysical assessment and the use of the scientific method into the analysis.

This section examines the success, or lack thereof, of development for six countries that are, or were, considered "less developed," most of which are in the tropics or subtropics and most of which were former colonies, either explicitly or de facto. Perhaps it is more accurate to say that these countries run the gauntlet of "very successful" to "not very successful," at least from the perspective of whether their per capita wealth increased. More generally, there are few examples of real success stories outside of Asia (and not too many there, either). The clear successes would include Puerto Rico, Korea, and Malaysia. Puerto Rico is a very special case as it is heavily influenced, and subsidized, by the main U.S. economy. Aspects of this special relation include the highly successful operation bootstrap program in the 1950s, U.S. tourism, extremely high oil imports, and the location there of many high tech industries—in part due to heavy investment in higher education and in part to (initially) lax labor and environmental laws. Korea has become much more wealthy based on a very successful program of heavy industrialization.

Malaysia has also been quite successful due in part to enormous natural gas reserves, relatively low population density, relatively honest government, and remarkable leadership of Mahatmir Mohamad (including his refusal to knuckle under to the International Monetary Fund during the "Asian Meltdown" of 1997). Malaysia has generated a vibrant and relatively wealthy society that is increasing its housing and economic opportunities for broad sectors of the population.

More commonly most tropical countries are not especially successful in their efforts for development. Sub-Saharan Africa (especially Niger) remains chronically poor, and the prevalence of hunger in this region is increasing despite massive development programs. The reasons include political instability, corruption and poor leadership, poorly designed development programs, low agricultural productivity, and, in some cases, just too many people for too few resources.

The following section includes national summaries for six countries, authored or coauthored by nationals of those countries. One, South Korea (chapter 7, by Jae-Young Ko), is generally considered a development success story. Two, Costa Rica (chapter 9, by Charles Hall and Carlos León Pérez) and the Philippines (chapter 10, by Aileen Guzman and Laura Schmitt), while hardly failures, are more recalcitrant to development attempts. Another, Argentina (chapter 11, by Charles Hall and his Argentinean colleagues Pablo Daniel Matossian, Claudio Ghersa, Jorge Calvo, and Clara Olmedo), was once very wealthy but has recently had some really hard times. Two more, Niger (chapter 8, by Mamadou Chetima and Grégoire Leclerc) and Nepal (chapter 12, by Rudriksha Parajuli), remain extremely poor.

Development, as measured by an increase in GDP per capita, has been an elusive goal for most of these countries (except South Korea). But when measured by the human development index (HDI), which includes economic as well as health and other statistics, development seems to be occurring, slowly but surely, at a worldwide scale. The following figure shows the evolution of the HDI from 1975 to 2001: (a) for the countries treated in this section, and (b) for all countries. What we see in the rightmost graph are a series of lines that are more or less parallel going up slowly, although many trend lines start declining in the 1980s. So we do not observe convergence (that is, the gap between the rich and the poor does not narrow), which should be the aim of development aid. Nevertheless, if we are to believe the HDI data, it appears that lives can be made better even while per capita GDP stagnates.

This concept is shown by the cases of Korea and Nepal, which demonstrate that an improvement in the human condition is possible regardless of the level of the economy, Korea being an example of success among the better-off countries (HDI above median), while Nepal may be an example of what can be achieved for a mostly agricultural country in the poorer half. Both countries have sustained a strong improvement of their HDI since 1975.

Paul Krugman, in a *New York Times* editorial of November 22, 2003, seeking good news in economics among a plethora of bad, observes that unlike the situation in the mid-1970s, when he was a graduate student, there is indeed some good economic news about the developing world. He says that there are a number of real success stories, based on export-led growth, but gives only Korea, China, and "parts of India" as examples. While it is true that many people in these countries are quite better off than they were, it is also true that they are large countries with excellent educational systems, many graduate students studying abroad, and a remaining majority of really poor people. They also tend to be countries that do not particularly follow the dictates of the neoclassical model. Korea is a special case examined here. But export-led growth is hardly a universal panacea. Krugman comments, "Latin America has signally failed to reproduced (parts of) Asia's success: Latin countries have liberalized, privatized and deregulated with results ranging from disappointing to catastrophic." Chapter 11 looks into this issue in Argentina in some detail.

The HDI for the Philippines is average, while Niger consistently remains at the bottom (with most sub-Saharan Africa countries). Argentina and Costa Rica more or less follow the same path, stagnating during the 1980s but catching up in the last decade (until the crash of Argentina in about

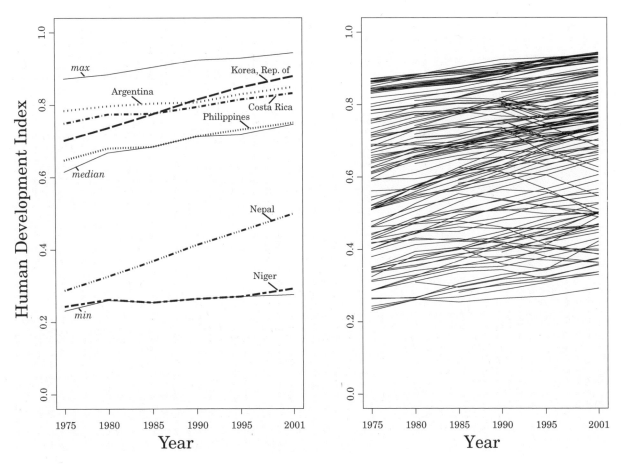

Figure Overview 1. Trends for the human development index (HDI). Left: for the countries summarized in this section. Solid lines represent minimum, median, and maximum values of worldwide HDI data. Right: HDI trends for all countries.

2000). What is striking is the collapse of human development for many countries that were once on the right track (Tanzania, Botswana, Congo, Zimbabwe, Kenya, Ivory Coast, Malawi, Zambia). Is this a side effect of wars, AIDS, or the structural adjustment of the 1980s, or is it that these heavily populated countries have reached the limit of their biophysical potential?

In all of these countries, there is no clear increased upward trend perceptible during the first decade of structural adjustment programs (SAPs), roughly the 1980s, which would suggest that if these policies work it is not clear from this index. A recent World Bank study, reported in *The Economist* of November 6, 2003, on the distribution of wealth in poor countries concluded that in Latin America (with the exception of Brazil and perhaps Mexico) the distribution of wealth was becoming somewhat less equitable, such that the richest tenth among

Latin Americans earn 48 percent of total income, while the poorest tenth earn just 1.6 percent. The equivalent figures for rich countries are 29.1 percent and 2.5 percent. In other terms, the average Gini coefficient for Latin American countries increased from 50.5 to 51.4 over the 1990s; thus, inequality rose slightly. The article asks, "Why is Latin America so unequal? Have the 'neo-liberal' policies implemented in many countries in the region over the past 15 years or so made matters worse, as critics often assert? What could be done to reduce inequality." But it provides no answers beyond an increase in education for the poor, which itself is very inequitably available.

We believe that many of these questions can be answered more fully by adding in a comprehensive biophysical analysis and more of the natural sciences to conventional economics. The rest of this book attempts to begin this process.

References

Crosby, A. 1986. *Ecological Imperialism: The Biological Expansion of Europe, 900–1900.* New York: Cambridge University Press.

Diamond, J. 1998. *Guns, Germs, and Steel.: The Fates of Human Societies.* New York: Norton.

Easterly, W. 2005. *White Man's Burden: Why the West's Efforts to Aid the Rest Have Done So Much Ill and So Little Good.* New York: Penguin Press.

Perkins, J. 2004. *Confessions of an Economic Hit Man.* San Francisco: Berrett-Kohler.

CHAPTER 7

THE SOUTH KOREAN EXPERIENCE IN ECONOMIC DEVELOPMENT

JAE-YOUNG KO

Introduction

In the three decades following the end of the World War II, many countries in Africa, Asia, and Latin America declared independence from their former colonial masters. These countries have since tended to follow two broadly different development models: centrally controlled socialism (or sometimes totalitarianism) versus a market economy for economic development. Foreign aid from the wealthy Western countries to poor countries has continued for the last six decades, influenced strongly by theoretical frameworks of development economics (e.g., Myrdal 1957; Hirschman 1958). However, development in most of these countries has failed, and most are still under a vicious cycle of economic poverty—poverty leads to little purchasing power, malnourishment, poor housing, poor health, little education, low agricultural and economic productivity, low income, and poverty, each reinforcing the others (Martinussen 1997). Meanwhile the economic gap between rich countries and poor countries has widened, not narrowed (UNDP 1999). Only a few nations in East Asia (e.g., Malaysia, South Korea, and Taiwan) have made impressive economic development. What went wrong? Why have noble ideas of foreign aid not worked well for most countries? Why has development worked well in a few? Complex situations across the world have provided many examples to provide material for the controversies and debates over development models, the role of international agencies such as World Bank, and the governing capacity of the developing countries themselves (see chapter 1).

Korea, formerly a colony of Japan, has had a rather more successful experience. This chapter provides an assessment of and explanation for the successful economic development of South Korea since the 1960s. Korea was once one of the newly independent poor countries in the world, poorer in the 1950s than India and the Philippines. Its problems included a very high and increasing population density, exacerbated by the mountainous terrain, which severely limits agricultural area, and quite meager national resources. Nevertheless, it has been able to accomplish quite successful development, certainly by comparison to most other countries that have emerged from colonialism.

Korea was traditionally a monarchy. It was governed subsequently by imperialist Japan from 1910 to 1945. According to agreements between the United States and Russia at the end of the World War II, the Korean peninsula was divided into South and North Korea. South Korea was placed under trust governance by U.S. troops and North Korea by the Russian army for the period 1945–48. South Korea, like other poor developing countries, experienced huge political turmoil during the trust governance. The confusions between old values and newly imported values (monarchy versus republic government), ideological conflicts (pro–United States versus pro–Soviet Union), and economic ideology (capitalism versus socialism) had generated serious social problems among Koreans (Cumings 1981; Merrill 1989). Political assassinations and labor strikes were frequent. Under the supervision of the United Nations, general elections were held for congress and the presidency to establish the first republic government in South Korea in 1948. However, the unrest continued during the First Republic.

The Korean War broke out in 1950 and ended in 1953 with a truce treaty between the United States, China, and North Korea. More than six million Koreans were killed or captured by opposite sides during this war, and much of the existing industrial infrastructure was destroyed (Steinberg 1989). During and after the Korean War, Korea was governed by the notoriously corrupt and ineffectual First Republic, fashioned in large part by the United States and headed by a very strong president. A student-led civilian uprising in 1960 toppled this government. The Second Republic was established after general elections during the same year. The new republic adopted the British parliamentary system, in which small political parties set up a coalition government, based on the belief that the concentrated presidential power of the first republic was the source of corruption and impotent government. The changes in the political system, however, could not make by themselves a politically stable and economically growing nation. During the Second Republic (1960–61), there were more than two thousand demonstrations by students and labor union members asking for rapid reforms, involving some 900,000 participants (Steinberg 1989:55). The civilian government was not able to provide strong governing power to handle diverse demands from the people.

In 1961, the Second Republic was toppled by a military coup led by General Park Chung-Hee, who argued that the action had to be undertaken in order to purify a corrupt government and save the country from the continuing threat of North Korea. General Park became the president after organizing his own political party and changing the national constitution in 1963. Park was a strong president until he died in 1979, surviving several reelections and a change of constitution. He introduced systematic economic and social planning, and the implementation of these programs continued from 1962 until today under his strong leadership. His selected programs were forcefully implemented, and they resulted in impressive economic development.

By the beginning of the twenty-first century, South Korea had become one of the rich OECD member countries, making globally competitive industrial goods and exporting them to the global market. The World Bank named Korea as one of the "high performing Asian economies (HPAEs)" (World Bank 1993). Clearly Koreans under Park had broken the vicious circle of economic poverty and achieved significant economic development. But how did they do it, since many other countries were trying to do the same thing during the same time and most failed?

In this chapter, I try to explain how South Korea was successful in its development. First, I give a snapshot of economic development in Korea, and explain that development broadly from the three most important aspects: (1) the domestic situation, focusing on historical nationalism and Confucian cultural factors, (2) the international political economy, and (3) the development and implementation of appropriate policies (figure 7.1). Finally, I explore some new challenges under the growing trend of globalization.

Each of these factors appears to me to be critical in understanding successful versus unsuccessful development, and as such helps explain the general failure of both the broad brush investment approach to development (that is, the Domar or the Rostow approach) described in chapters 2 and 3 and, perhaps, the general failure of globalization and neoliberal economics occurring today to raise the standard of living of the average person. The importance of the cultural domestic situation may explain why an economic policy from a successful case may not work well in other countries. Successful economic policies are probably attributable largely to each country's unique historical and cultural circumstances, and this provides unique challenges for policy making and implementation. My discussion of the international political economy helps to explain the external environment to which a country must adapt as it generates and implements economic development plans. Finally, I discuss the critical role of government as an active agent in initiating development programs, and how government can handle possible challenges in implementing successful programs.

Indicators of Economic Development

The overall economic growth in South Korea for the last four decades, expressed in gross domestic product (GDP) in "real" or constant 1995 U.S. dollars, is impressive. The GDP of the entire

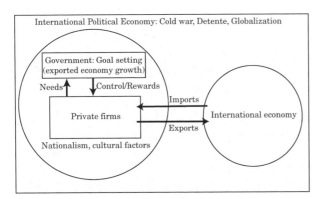

Figure 7.1. An explanatory framework for Korean economic development. The Korean experience is a combined result of domestic characteristics of strong nationalism and helpful cultural factors; a favorable international political economic situation during the most critical years; and the strong government's proper policy formulation and forceful implementation linked to private firms' aggressive entrepreneurship. Source: WDI Online.

Table 7.1. Socioeconomic changes of South Korea, 1960–2000

Year	GDP per capita (constant 1995 US $)	Death rate (per 1,000 people)	Fertility rate (births per woman)	Life expectancy (years)	Population growth (annual %)
1960	$1,325	13.5	5.67	54.2	2.8
1970	$2,283	9.4	4.27	59.9	2.1
1980	$3,910	6.4	2.56	66.8	1.6
1990	$7,967	6.3	1.77	70.3	0.9
2000	$13,199	5.7	1.43	73.3	0.7

Source: World Bank (2000)

country grew from $33 billion in 1960 to $73 billion in 1970, $149 billion in 1980, $342 billion in 1990, and $620 billion in 2000. Of greater importance, per capita real GDP increased from $1,325 for 1960 to $13,199 in 2000 (table 7.1). The tenfold increased economic output per person over time has contributed significantly to the material well-being of Koreans. The death rate has been reduced significantly over the last five decades, and Koreans now live nineteen years longer than the previous generation. The population growth rate has continuously slowed down, as the fertility rate has dropped from 5.67 births per woman in 1960 to 1.43 in 2000. Table 7.1 illustrates clearly that Koreans escaped the typical demographic pattern of developing countries (high birth rate, high population growth) and instead joined the pattern typical of developed countries (high life expectancy, low population growth). Thus, an increasing number of Koreans did not swallow Korea's economic growth. This is especially important now, since the overall economic growth rate of the economy has slowed somewhat.

The Korean economy had very high grow rates of real GDP compared to other developing countries, 9.9 percent for the period 1965–80, and 9.7 percent for 1980–89, which can be compared to the Philippines (5.9 percent and 0.7 percent),

Costa Rica (6.3 percent and 2.8 percent), and Mexico (6.5 percent and 0.7 percent) (World Bank 1991:206–7).

The structure of the Korean economy also changed greatly during this period from a solar-based to a fossil fuel–based economy. In the 1960s, agriculture was the dominant sector in Korea, considerably larger than manufacturing. However, the importance of the manufacturing sector grew rapidly until today. The annual growth rate of the manufacturing sector was 18.7 percent during the period 1965–80, compared to 3.0 percent growth for the agricultural sector (World Bank 1991:207).

Most of the economic growth was attributable to increasing imports of natural resources to be processed as well as machines for manufacturing activities, leading to the increasing exports of manufactured goods to the global economy (figure 7.2). The ratio of trade to national economic output was less than 20 percent of GDP in 1960, but increased to 37.7 percent in 1970, 73.3 percent in 1980, 59.4 percent in 1990, and 86.5 percent in 2000. Exports grew from 3.2 percent in 1960 to 13.8 percent in 1970, 32.7 percent in 1980, 29.1 percent in 1990, and 44.8 percent 2000 (World Bank 2000). The composition of the country's exports also changed rapidly over this period, from raw materials to light manufactures

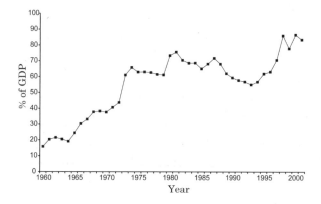

Figure 7.2. Trade trend of South Korea, 1960–2001.
Source: WDI Online.

to heavy industrial products to information and technological products.

Deep-Rooted Nationalism and Confucianism among Koreans

Unlike other newly independent nations across the globe after World War II, there was already a strong sense of national identity among Koreans, which made nation building much easier than in other developing countries. Koreans have over five thousand years of national history, mainly encompassing the Korean peninsula. Koreans have built homogeneous ethnic, cultural, and national identities throughout the years. The five hundred years of the Chosun dynasty (1392–1910) especially built a strong sense of national identity among the people. The dynasty had developed a central administration system, in which the central kingdom dispatched administrators to local provinces. The administrators were selected through a civil service exam, testing mainly Confucian virtues.

Other factors besides relative ethnic homogeneity that contributed to a strong sense of nationality were the Korean language and the Korean phonetic alphabet (Hangul), which was devised by Korea's King Sejong in A.D. 1446. That alphabet contributed significantly to an improved literacy rate among Koreans and to building national identity. Even though the historical Chinese cultural powers, introduced through trade and from numerous wars, had been sometimes overwhelming, the Koreans maintained their identity through the indigenous Hangul alphabet (Diamond 1999:333),

even after the arrival of the United States after World War II.

The three years of foreign governance (1945–48) after World War II planted seeds for two different economies: the centrally controlled economy of North Korea and the market-driven economy of South Korea. During these three years, significant political instabilities continued between procommunist groups and conservative groups in South Korea. However, the conflicts were not large enough to destroy the nationalism among Koreans, but instead generated confusion about the direction that newly independent South Korea should take: a socialist or a capitalist South Korea. The Korean War generated massive human losses among civilians and soldiers in combat. The war also made significant changes in Korea, and the impacts are still significant today. Politically, the war contributed to a clear ideological foundation of South Korea. Pro–North Korean groups were purged by the South Korean government or escaped to the north during the war. The same happened in North Korea. Thus, after the war, South Korea made it clear that it had and would pursue a democratic, market-oriented governance. This has remained its national ideology, which has been rarely challenged through today. Economically, the Korean War had broken down the economic bases of existing wealthy economic elites (the owners of lands and factories), who had survived and prospered during the Japanese colonial days.

The lasting nationalism among Koreans, the stable national ideology, and the reduced economic power of private sectors after the Korean War provided an environment for a strong central government. The Park government used nationalism as a base for pursuing economic programs beginning in the 1960s. The government also initiated several non-economic programs to support its economic programs. First, the government supported programs to build and maintain a strong nationalism. The Korean government asked people to work not just for their own self-interests but also for national interests. The South Korean flag was found in virtually every office and factory, and workers rose to attention, facing the flag, when the national anthem was played each morning and evening. Posters and pamphlets containing work-exalting slogans were found on the walls of workplaces and on street billboards. National campaigns stressing both the need for diligent work and meeting export targets were also promoted through the mass media (Kim and Park 2003).

The Park government emphasized industrializing the economy as a national approach to become an affluent modern society. More exports were emphasized over short-term profits to manufacturing companies. For example, the Korean government announced in 1973 a long-term national goal of achieving a per capita income of $1,000 and exports of $10 billion by 1981. Specific economic goals, such as "one billion dollar exports" and "ten percent economic growth," were promoted as national goals shared among most Koreans, who had a strong motivation for a better life after their war-torn poor lives. A campaign of "can-do-spirit" was also initiated to raise morale among people. Militaristic expressions and slogans were also used to motivate workers, including the notions of a "trade war," "export warriors," and "exports as total war," which forced Korean workers to work twelve hours a day in assembly lines and take days off only every other Sunday. Work was also promoted through awards and prizes. Both the monthly and annual awards and prizes were given out to productive workers at award ceremonies at the company, industry, and national levels.

The South Korean government could ask the Korean people to submit to specific additional harsh working conditions because the concept was supported by a broadly agreed upon national goal of export-oriented economic development. First, Koreans in the manufacturing sector worked on average more than fifty hours per week until 2000 (ILO 2002). Second, the Korean government tried to keep wage levels low to support the manufacturing companies. The government intervened in wage negotiation between employers and employees. Wade and Kim (1978:100) estimate that in the 1960s Korean labor productivity was higher than American in light industries such as textiles and electronics because Korean labor cost was only around 20 percent of U.S. labor cost. The newly installed manufacturing machines imported

mostly from Japan and the United States produced high-quality goods, while workers were expected to work long hours with low wages. Third, the Korean government maintained its social spending at minimum levels during the 1960s to 1980s. For example, expenditures on social insurance, public health, public assistance, welfare, and veterans' relief represented only 0.97 percent of GNP in 1973 (Cumings 1984). Finally, the government did not allow for any discussion of expanding the role of labor unions in economic activities. The government could and did suppress the activities of pro-labor unions as pro–North Korean activity and initiated harsh punishments on labor organizers. Even though labor union workers argued for better treatment, the Korean government tended to marginalize their efforts, making Korean labor abundant, cheap, and unorganized during the 1960s and 1970s.

Another ideological factor is Confucianism, which traditionally has been strong in Korea, even after the idea of republic government was introduced in the 1950s. Traditional Confucian values include respect for authorities and elders, loyalty, and the importance of education and diligence. These values were transferred to the new industrial society in Korea. Family loyalty was transformed into company loyalty; diligence for self-cultivation was changed to working hard for one's workplace, and domestic paternalism was adapted to a modern industrial society. Themes of harmony, solidarity, and cooperation among employees were adopted as mottos or slogans of a vast majority of South Korean companies (Kim and Park 2003).

One of the impacts of Confucianism is that the labor union was a second choice as a negotiation channel between employer and employees. Most workers preferred to be treated as a family member, rather than combative labor union workers. Korean companies exercised a paternalistic sway over workers with company dormitories, recreation and hospital facilities, uniforms, and company songs. Additionally, the anticommunist (anti–North Korea) political logic of South Korean government produced an outcome in which organized labor (equated with communism) was systematically weakened (Gills 2000).

Table 7.2. An international comparison of comparative CEO compensation relative to average employee

Country	CEO compensation as a multiple of average employee compensation
Brazil	57
Venezuela	54
Argentina	48
Britain	25
Thailand	23
Korea	11
Japan	10
United States	365

Wahlgren (2001)

Table 7.3. Per capita income (1972) and median years of education of young adults (25–34 age group) for selected countries (circa 1970)

Country	Per capita income (US $)	Median years education
Korea	310	6.76
Argentina	1,290	7.39
Chile	800	6.70
India	110	0.70
Indonesia	90	2.35
Iraq	370	0.55
Libya	1,830	0.64
Mexico	750	4.13
United States	5,590	12.54
Zambia	380	0.97

Modified from Wade and Kim (1978:128)

Another effect of Confucian culture is a relatively narrow wage gap between the top-level managers and low-level employees. For example, the average gap between U.S. chief executive officers and employees is 365, while Korea's is only 11 (table 7.2) (Wahlgren 2001). The American culture of self-interest and greed as civic virtue allows CEOs to get extremely higher compensations compared to low-level workers in the United States (Phillips 2002).

A combined effect of the Confucian tradition and poverty after the Korean War was a remarkable commitment to education among Koreans. Its school enrollments, for example, are comparable to those found in countries with per capita income levels twice and even more than its own (table 7.3). In 1970, median years of education in Korea were 6.76 for young adults (ages 25–34) and per capita income was roughly $300, while, for example, in Algeria (per capita income, $430) it was 0.65 years for the same age group; in Zambia ($480) it was 0.97 years, and in Iraq ($370) it was 0.55. It is apparent in any case that the intense commitment to education was and still is seen by large numbers of Korean parents and students as a means to social mobility and a better life (Wade and Kim 1978).

The Confucian cultural tradition has made government bureaucratic jobs valuable and attractive to smart and ambitious young college graduates who were willing to take a higher civil service exam. Those who pass the exam are appointed to middle-level jobs in central government and become dedicated to socioeconomic planning. The bureaucrats have not been captives of the private economic sectors, at least relative to much of the rest of the world, but have been able to initiate independent economic policies, which has encouraged or sometimes forced private companies to follow the national economic strategies. When these bureaucrats retire, they often join the private companies with which they have maintained relationships, as board members or top-level managers, to utilize their expertise developed through their careers in the government.

The Context of the International Political Economy

Historically, the targets of Western colonial powers have been the natural resources in the third world such as gold or oil (Stravrianos 1981; Clark 1990; Yergin 1991). Unlike many countries in Africa or

Latin America, Korea does not have much in the way of natural resources attractive to foreign companies. After World War II, the Japanese colonial government withdrew from the Korean peninsula. After World War II, South Korea belonged to the hegemonic power of the United States (Cumings 1984). Economically, some American speculators had shown an interest in minerals (such as the relatively modest deposits of gold and tungsten) in the Korean peninsula since the late nineteenth century. There were, however, no policy-level actions from the United States to acquire mineral rights or any systematic support for the interests of individual Americans in Korea. Nor did American companies see Korea as attractive markets, leading to low levels of direct investment (Cumings 1990). Strategically, however, the growing concerns of the Cold War with the communist regimes including Russia and Mainland China, led to the United States' initiating and maintaining the division of the Korean peninsula as a way to contain expansion of communist power in the northeastern Asia after the end of the World War II. This was done by stationing U.S. troops there and establishing a pro-American government in South Korea (Cumings 1984). This containment policy has continued to the present. Thus the United States thought of the Korean peninsula as militarily, but not as economically, important. The discrepancy between military and economic interests generated an inconsistent policy of the United States toward South Korea for the period 1945–50, but at least insured that U.S. corporations did not especially intervene in the Korean economy.

U.S. troops came to South Korea in 1945 and governed the country until 1948. The republic government was established in that year, and the United States withdrew its troops from Korea in 1949, even after the Korean president asked repeatedly for their continued presence. Dean Acheson, then the secretary of state, implied that South Korea was excluded from the American defense perimeter in Asia in January 1950, one of the triggers of the North Korean invasion of South Korea in June 1950 (Cumings 1990).

The Korean War was the main event that forced the United States to recognize the importance of Korea in maintaining its containment policy against the communist powers in Asia. After the Korean War, the United States provided economic and military aid to Korea, while stationing military troops in Korea, to make Korea a strong ally under its hegemony in the Northeast Asia. The Cold War continued between the Western and the Eastern powers during the 1960s, which also forced the United States to continue economic and military aid to Korea. South Korea had received some $6 billion in economic grants and loans from the United States during the period 1963–78, compared with $6.89 billion for all of Africa, and $14.8 billion for all of Latin America, during the same period (Cumings 1984). Further, the United States tolerated specifics of Korean policies as long as the Korean government set up policies and implemented them within the U.S. hegemony (e.g., export-oriented economy over import substitution), because the United States wanted to have a stable Korean government (Cumings 1984).

Strong nationalism among Koreans, relatively weak domestic economic power, and U.S. toleration in domestic masters led to the development of a strong state in Korea, which could mobilize national resources (that is, such natural resources as there were, as well as technology and labor) and support private companies' vigorous efforts in international market under a strong leader. By the mid-1960s, Korea had become a bureaucratic-authoritarian industrializing regime with a strong central governmental power that could maintain its stability even with rapid economic and social changes occurring (Cumings 1984). This is another factor that explains the stability of the Park regime over about two decades. Park maintained his presidency against internal and external threats over eighteen years until he died in 1979.

The détente mode in the 1970s, initiated by U.S. President Richard Nixon, provided another change for the Korean government. The weakening military support from the United States forced the Korean government to become more self-reliant militarily, and the state under President Park's personal direction began to commit extensive funds to develop the heavy metallurgical, chemical, and defense industries required to generate modern weapons of war. This in turn allowed Korea to begin to generate various heavy industries, including shipbuilding, construction equipment, and chemicals. Korean heavy industrial products with names such as Hyundai and Daewoo joined light industrial products such as Samsung and LG as names familiar to Americans.

Economic Policies and Implementation

Korea started export-led industrialization in the early 1960s, which has been the fundamental pattern until today. A description of how the Korean government has set up and implemented econo-mic development plans from the 1960s to 2000 follows.

Period 1 (1961–80)
The decision-making process in government

After becoming the national leader after his military coup, Park concentrated all political, economic, and social forces under his command. He formed a strong ruling political party, the Democratic Republican Party, to support politically his ideas of Korean development. He formed the Economic Planning Board (EPB) in 1960, combining both planning and budgeting in one office headed by the deputy prime minister for an effective economic planning. The Ministry of Finance had control over the central bank, which consolidated the cooperatives and the agricultural banks.

The Park government played a central role in orchestrating export-led growth. Technocrats, who were recruited mostly through a higher civil service exam, had been influenced by economic ideologies that emphasize the advantages of the private sector and export-led growth. Some of the technocrats were educated in the United States in the principles of a market economy. Technocrats designed economic policy, which was followed by a strong implementation with high-level political support.

Park forced the formation of a single, umbrella labor union and then controlled it as a way to control labor costs to support private businesses, including the manufacturing sectors. Labor organization was utilized for a symbolic and formal process to influence negotiations of wage and labor

conditions between employers and employees across the country. Further, Park eliminated elected local governments, substituting instead a highly centralized, appointed command system, to increase the influence of central government to local governments.

Five-year economic plans

The Korean government implemented its economic plans thorough a series of five-year economic plans, which selected sectors of the economy as targets of economic growth and channeled financial and other support to those selected industrial sectors. The first five-year economic development plan was implemented from 1962 to 1966. The major directions of the first plan were to (1) secure energy supply sources (especially important for Korea, which had virtually no fossil fuel), (2) expand basic industries and infrastructure, (3) improve the balance of payments performance, and (4) promote technology. The second five-year plan (1967–71) aimed at (1) self-sufficiency in food, (2) family planning and population control, and (3) improved technology. The third plan (1972–76) targeted (1) promoting heavy and chemical industries and (2) improving technology. The fourth plan (1977–81) included (1) self-sufficiency in investment capital, (2) increased investment for science and technology, and (3) increased competitiveness in international markets. The fifth plan (1982–86) focused on (1) controlling inflation and (2) overcoming energy constraints. The sixth plan (1987–91) was designed to (1) stabilize inflation and (2) balance regional and rural development (for detailed information, see Song 1990).

The changing directions of the five-year plan over time reflected changing policy agendas in economic development. In the early 1960s, the disparity between rural areas and urban areas was not significant. However, the continued increase in the role of manufacturing sectors caused increasing disparity between regions and income classes. Although the government sector played the dominant role in the 1960s, the power of the private sector has increased relative to the government. Additionally, the objectives of the planning also reflected changing international situations. The détente mode in the 1970s following the partial withdrawal of U.S. troops from Korea pushed the Korean government to consider self-defense against threats from North Korea. As a way to counter the changing international situations, the Korean government promoted heavy and chemical industries during the third five-year planning period, even though American advisors resisted these heavy industries, which, however, have produced steel, supertankers, and automobiles that have consistently competed strongly with American products. Provisions for more financial loans, special depreciation allowances, low tax rates, and better public services and administrative support were arranged for the private companies that started the heavy and chemical industries. However, the focused investment on heavy industries also caused significant problems with foreign debts, even with the Korean government's effort to increase already high domestic savings.

Closeness between the business and government sectors

Park strongly supported the strategy of economic development through increased exports of manufactured goods. He organized the Monthly Export Promotion Conference in 1962, and he moderated these meetings between high-ranking officials in government and business leaders, in which export targets were discussed and bureaucratic impediments to achieving those targets removed. The president also recognized successful businessmen with medals and citations, which were effective motivators for increasing exports abroad. Larger Korean firms were assigned annual export targets by the government, and the export targets were seen by firms as virtual orders or assigned missions (Song 1990:71), because rewards of public recognition were linked to institutional credit available on most favorable terms. Companies that failed to fulfill government-set objectives could lose access to bank credit, forcing them to seek credit on the curb, or informal, market at double or more the interests rates and thus, making them uncompetitive, because the government had a complete monopoly on all institutional credit. As a result, the Korean government could extract and channel resources to targeted industries (Haggard and

Cheng 1987). It was a very effective, although not necessarily democratic, system.

Control of financial flow, debt management, and domestic savings

Foreign investment in Korea was virtually nonexistent before 1962, when a law to encourage it was enacted. The first foreign bank opened its branch in 1967. Continuous efforts since that date have resulted in cumulative foreign direct investments of about $2.6 billion—a very small amount given the size of the Korean economy (gross national product in 1987 of $115 billion) and the amounts that foreign firms have invested elsewhere. About half of that investment has come from Japan. American investment was not significant. The low level of interest from foreign countries was attributable to Korean government restrictions and economic uncertainties because of business cycles, constant international tension along the Demilitarized Zone, and fear of internal unrest or violence. In Korea, in contrast to Brazil and Mexico, direct foreign investment played a negligible role during the 1960s. Korea was regarded as too small in market size and too politically risky to attract investment interest (Haggard and Cheng 1987). For example, the share of foreign-invested firms' export to total exports of Korea was 18.3 percent for 1978, while that of Mexico was 37 percent for 1977 (Haggard and Cheng 1987:93).

Korea had to borrow from international capital markets such as the World Bank instead. Its gross external debt was $46.8 billion by 1984 (Haggard and Cheng 1987). Debt has played an important role in financing Korea's development. Thus, Korea has faced periodic debt servicing problems and the level of indebtedness became a major policy and political concern in the early 1980s, largely in response to the large increase of doing business following the oil price increases in 1973 and 1979, in addition to purchasing manufacturing machines, which made exported goods. But it has not faced the massive rescheduling and wrenching debt-related adjustments that has faced the Latin American countries because the success of its exports has allowed South Korea to get terms equal to or better than those granted the large Latin American borrowers while keeping its debt service ration substantially lower (Haggard and Cheng 1987). Banks in Korea were also owned by the government. The EPB controlled domestic credit and favored certain export-oriented firms, and it mediated foreign credit through licensing schemes. Thus, the central government maintained control of access to investment capital.

Another important source of financial resources was domestic savings. The Korean government has continued to make a nationwide drive for people to increase their savings, creating an annual festival to award people who made deposits relatively higher than their peers. For example, all secondary school students were expected to have their own savings accounts at banks, which coordinated the establishment of those accounts with the schools, and to make a weekly deposit from their allowances. When they graduated, they were able to receive the principal and interest. From the banks' view, this was a source of stable savings, because there was an extremely low probability of withdrawing deposits by students until graduation, except when they transferred schools. The domestic savings' contribution to the national economy until the 1960s was quite low. The ratio of gross domestic savings to GDP was only 2 percent in 1960 (figure 7.3). South Korea was ranked forty-ninth among the fifty less-developed countries (LDCs) surveyed in the ratio of gross domestic savings to GDP for the period 1950–65 (Wade and Kim 1978:94). However, the savings drive resulted in significant capital formation over time. In 1966 the savings contribution to GDP was 12.5 percent and has increased to 1990 with 36.5 percent. The increasing savings has increased domestic investment significantly. In 1969, domestic sources (private and governmental) accounted for 58.8 percent of gross domestic investment; in 1970, 60 percent; in 1971, 56.9 percent (Wade and Kim 1978:104). Thus the Korean economy has become increasingly self-sustaining as a consequence of its enlarged capacity to generate and mobilize internal savings to support its own economic development plan. Before the significant domestic savings and domestic investment were realized since the late 1960s, foreign aid, especially from the United States, was significant for the South Korean

Figure 7.3. Gross domestic savings. Source: WDI Online.

economy. For example, the official development assistance and official aid for 1960 was $250 million, which contributed to 56.9 percent of gross capital formation for the same year. Foreign aid continued until 1983 (World Bank 2000).

Period 2 (1981–97)

After Park's unexpected death in 1979, South Korea experienced political instability and economic difficulties. Close ties with business had corrupted some government officials. Labor union groups, which the government had closely monitored and pressured, started to claim due compensations in wage increases and human rights. Further, there was an urgent need for structural adjustments in the economy because of the policies favoring heavy industry over the production of domestic consumer goods, and the relatively neglected agricultural sector was in disarray. In 1980, for the first time since the Korean War, there was an economic contraction as gross national production dropped by 5.2 percent. There were also systematic problems in the Korean economy. Protectionism (high tariffs on imported goods) was high, technology transfer from foreign companies was proceeding very slowly, the internal market was comparatively small for the type of products produced, purchasing power was unequally distributed, and Korea was beginning to experience diminishing labor advantages as wages rose because of labor shortages.

As exports grew, Korea was confronted with increasing external pressure for the liberalization of trade. Trade tensions had long existed between the United States and Korea, with textiles, footwear,

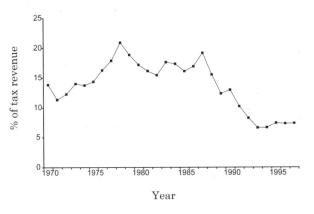

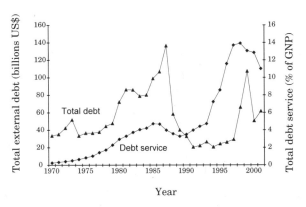

Figure 7.4. Import duties of South Korea, 1970–97.
Source: WDI Online.

Figure 7.5. Total debt and debt services, 1970–2001.
Source: WDI Online.

steel, color televisions, and other products figuring in acerbic negotiations on dumping, subsidization, quotas, and orderly marketing agreements. In response, Korea reduced tariffs and other barriers for increased imports in 1981 (figure 7.4). Korean firms also started to invest in U.S. plants and industries for the production of a variety of household products and in other countries, such as Bangladesh, where labor was far cheaper, and in industries such as textiles, the export of which was limited by quotas.

As exports grew, so too did imports. This increase was necessary, mainly because of a growing and more affluent population that demanded consumer products, but also because Korea must import much of the raw materials for the goods it exports and components it is unable to produce for other products. Further, imports of agricultural products has increased due to declined economic output in the domestic agricultural sector, the increased population, and changing tastes that include a passion for wheat-based pizza. In 1985, Korea imported $2.8 billion in agricultural commodities (about 10 percent of all imports), including 2.9 million tons of wheat, 3 million tons of corn, and 885,000 tons of soybean products. Korea's self-sufficiency in food has continued to decline. This rate was 71.6 percent for 1985 but dropped to 56.8 percent in 2001 (KNSO 2003). One interesting thing is that the self-sufficiency in rice, which is the principal cereal of the Korean diet, was 102.7 percent in 2001, because the consumption of rice in Korea has been declining even more rapidly

than its declining production, reflecting the changing taste of Koreans toward a Western-style diet. Major foreign borrowing was required to finance growth and adjustments, and to increase employment. The debt for Korea reached $46 billion in the mid-1980s, the fourth largest debt among developing countries, and larger per capita than Brazil's (figure 7.5). Because of Korea's export success, foreign bankers did not regard this burden as untoward but were skeptical of higher levels.

The growing complexity of the Korean economy also prompted many in government and in the private sector to call for less governmental interference in economic affairs. The government liberalized the banking system, ending the state's monopoly. Nonbanking financial institutions, such as insurance and credit associations, were recognized and began to play a major role in credit allocations. But the liberalization plans were implemented only slowly; the *chaebols* expanded their influence into financial markets by buying banks and financial institutions, effectively impeding the liberalization efforts.

Period 3 (1998–)

The Korean government requested an International Monetary Fund (IMF) bailout on November 13, 1997, in response to the contagious financial crisis that spread through Southeast Asia. After nego-tiation with the IMF delegation, the Korean government adopted the IMF recommendations for economic "structural adjustment" for an increasingly open free market economy. The IMF

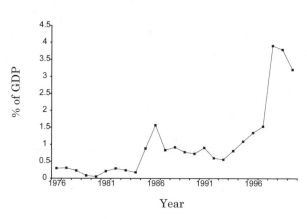

Figure 7.6. Foreign direct investment in South Korea, 1976–2000. Source: WDI Online.

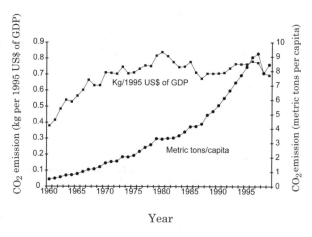

Figure 7.7. South Korean CO_2 emissions, 1960–99. Source: WDI Online.

initiatives dismantled the residual element of the bureaucratic-authoritarian industrializing regime: weakened government role, increased global trade, decreased barriers for financial markets against foreign funds, and privatization. Thus, foreign direct investment increased after the IMF, but financial control by the government was reduced significantly (figure 7.6). Now the Korean economy has improved and paid back the money borrowed from the IMF. However, the consequences of the IMF recommendations are controversial (Stiglitz 2002).

Challenges Ahead: Globalization

It seems quite clear that the long-term political stability under President Park was quite critical for Korean economic development. However, other authoritarian regimes in Latin America, including Brazil's military government (1964–85), Pinochet's Chile (1973–90), Uruguay (1973–90), and Argentina (1976–83), and in Asia, including Marcos's Philippines (1965–86), did not make similar economic development like Korea. Furthermore, while Koreans received financial aid from the United States, some countries in Latin America (El Salvador, Honduras) also received generous aid from the United States in the 1980s. But they did not result in effective economic development.

I argue that the vital components for successful Korean development were principally the macro variables of: (1) high education; (2) high savings among Koreans; (3) strong national identity,

which kept Koreans from arguing too much among themselves about financial compensation; (4) a set of proper micro programs implemented through a series of five-year plans by a strong Korean government that cooperated very closely with industry leaders; and (5) an international political economy that Koreans could adjust to, or exploit, favorably. The costs were that Koreans experienced tough labor conditions and were asked to endure human rights abuses by government. After the death of the strong president, the main strategy of economic development based on strong government was challenged during the next president's reign and during the IMF intervention. The Korean government's role as an intermediary between international financial markets and local productive investment, arguably the source of their former success, has diminished significantly. Meanwhile, for whatever reason, the growth of the Korean economy has slowed, although it is still relatively large compared to much of the rest of the world.

Globalization, which can be defined as deregulation, financial liberalization, and privatization (van Wolferen 2002), provided serious challenges to developing countries. Due to increasing globalization and the IMF recommendations, the Korean government has cut government controls in the stock market and other financial capital flows. Now it is exposed to rapid or uncertain money flow of the world global market. In addition, there are many "little Koreas" that have implemented among themselves, something like the Japanese/Korean

Table 7.4. A comparison of peak air quality statistics between Seoul and New York City for 2000

Category	Seoul	New York City
CO (ppm)[1]	8.4	4
Pb ($\mu g/m^3$)[2]	0.08	0.02
NO_2 (ppm)[3]	0.234	0.038
O_3 (ppm)[4]	0.146	0.12
PM_{10} ($\mu g/m^3$)[5]	378.	57.
SO_2 (ppm)[6]	0.053	0.043

Source: Ministry of Environment, Republic of Korea (2001); US EPA (2000).

1. Highest one-hour mean concentration for Seoul, highest second maximum non-overlapping eight-hour concentration for New York City.
2. Quarterly maximum for New York City.
3. Highest one-hour mean concentration for Seoul, highest arithmetic mean concentration for New York City.
4. Highest one-hour mean concentration for Seoul; highest second daily maximum 1-hour concentration for New York City.
5. Highest one-hour mean concentration for Seoul; highest second maximum 24-hour concentration for New York City.
6. Highest one-hour mean concentration for Seoul; highest second maximum 24-hour concentration for New York City.

model of industrial development, and now compete directly with Korean products. These include Taiwan, Singapore, and, increasingly, China itself. Korea was at the right place at the right time with the right economic development plan. Now it is just another player on the world market, where the past advantages of low labor costs and clever ideas have a lot of competition. Whether Korea can successfully manage the changes remains to be seen.

Environmental Costs of Korea's Success

Korea generated its remarkable economic progress mostly through intelligent industrialization, which had clear targets and clear markets in mind, and that is basically export-driven economic development. Government-controlled labor movements and a focus on manufacturing competitive goods in international market worked well. But the focus moved from labor-intensive goods to heavy industrial goods (e.g., shipbuilding, steel manufacture), which are highly energy intensive. The CO_2 intensity of national economic output had increased rapidly up to the 1980s, when the bases of heavy industries were established. The CO_2 emission from economic activities has been increasing rapidly from 0.5 metric tons per capita in 1960 to 9.2 metric tons in 1996, associated with a larger economy and a more affluent society (figure 7.7). The increased economic activity of Korea has been almost one for one with increased use of energy, with little or no increase in efficiency (Ko et al. 1998).

Environmental quality has not been actively considered for the last four decades. The environmental impacts of economic activities have increased significantly: air and water quality has worsened, and the production of toxic wastes has increased. South Koreans are now experiencing the results of neglected environmental issues. Table 7.4 illustrates the air quality problem in Seoul, the capital of South Korea, with a comparison to New

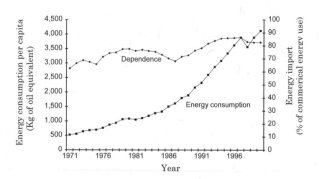

Figure 7.8. Commercial energy consumption and dependence on foreign sources. Source: WDI Online.

York City. People in Seoul struggle with multiple impacts of worsened air quality, and broad environmental problems.

Another potential problem is that because Korea imports most of its commercial energy sources from foreign countries (oil from the Middle East and natural gas from Indonesia), it is very vulnerable to energy price increases and supply disruptions. As of 2000, about 83 percent of commercial energy was imported from abroad, and energy consumption has been increasing continuously (figure 7.8). Thus, it is another big challenge for South Koreans to acquire enough energy in sustainable ways from foreign countries, along with other economic issues of globalization.

In conclusion, Korea has been very fortunate in that, for a variety of reasons, development there worked. Curiously, however, nearly all aspects of the initial "Korean model"—including strong government leadership and intervention, internal cooperation versus competition, protectionism of early industries, subsidy of internal agriculture, and large government investment in education—are more or less the direct opposite of what is called for in the broad brush of neoliberalism. Whether this is transferable to other countries is of course debatable, but as such it hardly argues for the unmitigated effectiveness of the models now most persistently advocated.

References

Clark, J. G. 1990. *The Political Economy of World Energy.* Chapel Hill: University of North Carolina Press.

Cumings, B. 1981. *The Origins of the Korean War.* Princeton, N.J.: Princeton University Press.

———. 1984. The origins and development of the Northeast Asian political economy: Industrial sectors, product cycles, and political consequences. *International Organization* 38:1–40.

———. 1990. *The Origins of the Korean War*, vol. 2. Princeton, N.J.: Princeton University Press.

Diamond, J. 1999. *Guns, Germs, and Steel: The Fates of Human Societies.* New York: Norton.

Frieden, J. 1987. Third world indebted industrialization: International finance and state capitalism in Mexico, Brazil, Algeria, and South Korea. In J. A. Frieden and D. A. Lake, eds., *International Political Economy*, 298–318. New York: St. Martin's.

Gills, B. K. 2000. The crisis of postwar East Asian capitalism: American power, democracy and the vicissitudes of globalization. *Review of International Studies* 26:381–403.

Haggard, S., and T. Cheng. 1987. State and foreign capital in the East Asian NICs. In F. C. Deyo, ed., *The Political Economy of the New Asian Industrialism*, 84–135. Ithaca, N.Y.: Cornell University Press.

Hirschman, A. O. 1958. *The Strategy of Economic Development.* New Haven, Conn.: Yale University Press.

ILO (International Labor Office). 2002. LABORSTA. http://laborsta.ilo.org.

Kim, A. E., and G-S. Park. 2003. Nationalism, Confucianism, work ethic and industrialization in South Korea. *Journal of Contemporary Asia* 33:37–49.

Kim, J. 1997. The future of Korea in the world trading system. *Korea and World Affairs* 21, no. 2: 236–53.

KNSO (Korea National Statistical Office). 2002. *Statistical Handbook of Korea 2002.*

Ko, J., C. A. S. Hall, and L. G. Lemus. 1998. Resource use rates and efficiency as indicators of regional sustainability: An examination of five countries. *Environmental Monitoring and Assessment* 51:571–93.

Martinussen, J. 1997. *Society, State and Market.* London: Zed Books.

Merrill, J. 1989. *Korea: The Peninsular Origins of the War.* Newark: University of Delaware Press.

Ministry of Environment, South Korea. 2001. *Environmental Statistics Yearbook.* Seoul: Ministry of Environment.

Myrdal, G. 1957. *Economic Theory and Under-Developed Regions*. London: Gerald Duckworth.

Phillips, K. 2002. *Wealth and Democracy*. New York: Broadway Books.

Song, B-N. 1990. *The Rise of The Korean Economy*. Hong Kong: Oxford University Press.

Stavrianos, L. S. 1981. *Global Rift*. New York: William Morrow.

Steinberg, D. I. 1989. *The Republic of Korea*. Boulder, Colo.: Westview.

Stiglitz, J. E. 2002. *Globalization and Its Discontents*. New York: Norton.

UNDP (United Nations Development Program). 1999. *Human Development Report 1999*. New York: Oxford University Press.

US EPA (United States Environmental Protection Agency). 2000. Latest findings on national air quality: 2000 status and trends. http://www.epa.gov/air/aqtrndoo.

Van Wolferen, K. 2002. Conceptual challenges of a globalizing economy. In H. van Ginkel, B. Barrett, J. Court, and J. Velasquez, eds., *Human Development and the Environment: Challenges for the United Nations in the New Millennium*, 33–44. Tokyo: United Nations University Press.

Wade, L. L., and B. S. Kim. 1978. *Economic Development of South Korea*. New York: Praeger.

Wahlgren, E. 2001. Spreading the Yankee way of pay. *Business Week*, April 18.

World Bank. 1991. *World Development Report 1991*. New York: Oxford University Press.

———. 1993. *The East Asian Miracle*. New York: Oxford University Press.

———. 2000. World Bank WDI Online. http://publications.worldbank.org.

Yergin, D. 1991. *The Prize*. New York: Touchstone.

CHAPTER 8

The Myth of Development

Examples from the Republic of Niger

Mamadou Mai Kassoua Chetima and Grégoire Leclerc

Introduction

The Republic of Niger belongs to the group of countries at the bottom of every scale of classification of countries in terms of development, and at the top of the line in terms of food insecurity. The United Nation's Development Program (UNDP) ranked Niger as 171st out of 172 nations in its Human Development Index (HDI) in 2002. Biophysical and geoclimatic conditions have set the stage for this situation, but a failure in planning and development policies appears to have exacerbated it. "A particular harsh climate and inhospitable geographical features, a completely land-locked situation—such are, broadly speaking, the underlying economic realities of the Republic of Niger. The country's economy is still largely at the mercy of vagaries of the climate, being based principally on agriculture and livestock raising." This is what can be read in the section on Niger, on the University of Pennsylvania African Studies fact sheet.

About two thirds of the country is covered by desert, and more than 75 percent of its population (about 12 million and growing at a current rate of 3.2 percent per year) is confined to less than 12 percent of the total area of the country (about 1.2 million km2), which is the only land that is arable (FAO 2003), for an effective population density of about one person per hectare. The aridity of the climate, which is characterized by low and erratic rainfall and instability of seasons, calls for the development of alternate production systems that could reduce vulnerability to the frequent droughts and resulting famines. The problem is that it is not clear what that strategy might be.

Historical Background

Before colonization, many kingdoms and empires formed political units, and the current concept of "country" was literally unknown in sub-Saharan Africa. The French colonized the area known today as the Republic of Niger. They subordinated the formal political units and created different geopolitical entities within the new country, which did not always recognize the former alliances and/or tributaries (Guillemin 1983; Lund 1998). But in general, the traditional system was conserved to a certain extent. Villages were still ruled by village chiefs, a group of villages constituted a canton that was ruled by canton chief, and sometimes many cantons formed a sultanate or province (Lund and Husseling 1999). At the top was the French administration, which made sure that the local leader provided allegiance to France. After independence in 1960, the administrative units created by France were maintained as centers of decision, and chieftaincy became a traditional power, while the new elite trained under French supervision came to rule the new state.

The Uranium Boom and Some of Its Effects

Niger does not have much in the way of abundant natural resources, but it does have high-grade uranium ore. When in the 1960s the French government decided that it too had to have nuclear bombs, it turned to Niger for the required uranium. France sent in teams of engineers and mining supervisors, who improved the roads and spent a lot of money. By 1971, France (in partnership with Japan and Spain later) bought the uranium at what was a very high price for the people of Niger. This provided a bonanza in terms of foreign exchange, and the government and the people began to have dreams of relative wealth. The government built schools and hospitals, but also huge buildings in the capital city, Niamey, to "beautify" the image of the country and attract most of the regional conferences. Some Nigeriens became rather wealthy. It seems that nobody worried about the growing population because the overall wealth of the country appeared to be growing. But then, in 1990, the Cold War was over, and the price of uranium dropped dramatically on the market as demand decreased. The French, who had exclusivity on Niger's uranium, were less in need of it. The bonanza dried up and Niger went back to relying on what it had always had, agriculture. Niger held its first democratic elections in 1993, which were quickly followed by coups (in 1996 and 1999), and a transition to the French-style semi-presidential system in place today. While much effort was put into having a working government since independence, the population had grown more than twofold, and there had been no increase in the amount of good land. But was there any concern about the possibility that food security may never be achieved in Niger? The answer is simply no.

Rural Development

In general there are two ways to increase food production in a country where agriculture is already a widespread activity: (1) increase the productivity of existing agricultural land through provision of additional mineral fertilizers and water and (2) bring into productivity marginal land previously thought improper for agriculture. Both ways require huge investments in terms of capital and/or labor, one more or less than the other, depending on the circumstances of investment. Which of the options is best for the Republic of Niger? The answer depends greatly on the biophysical conditions of the site, the degree to which it can be reclaimed, and how long the intensification can be supported, among other factors.

Various projects have been implemented in Niger to intensify and/or extend agriculture in the broad sense of the term (cropping, animal husbandry, fishery, and forestry), which contributes

40 percent to the gross domestic product (GDP) and occupies about 80 percent of the population. These projects took various forms, including irrigation schemes based on surface water, the building of modern wells or the modernization of existing ones for pastoralism, and afforestation projects to provide forest resources. Were these successful? How did they affect the people back then? Alternatively, did most of the agricultural development take place without aid programs? How did international aid affect the life of peasant farmers in the short and long terms?

A Development Project in Practice

Since independence, there have been many "modern" development programs for Niger. Very few, if any, were funded exclusively by the public funds of Niger. Rather, most of the money came from external "development" agencies. Some had the larger part of their budget derived from the state's budget (which largely come from taxes paid by the population), and others required only symbolic state participation, which often consisted of only human resources and/or infrastructures.

An example of what might be considered a "classic" development project in the Republic of Niger is this one, implemented in the late 1980s with the aim of reducing food insecurity for the communities living in the project area. The project was funded by the International Fund for Agricultural Development (IFAD) and jointly financed by the World Food Program (WFP), UNDP, French and Dutch volunteer organizations, the government of Niger, and program beneficiaries. The project opted for intensification of agriculture to produce cash crops through an irrigation scheme along the Komadugu River in the eastern part of the country. This project took place within a traditional land use system that had relatively low yields but that had been relatively sustainable for thousands of years. With the development project, a semi-modern, very productive type of agriculture replaced this traditional use.

Usually, valleys are considered as having the best agricultural potential, where additional investment will result in even higher return. Therefore, the IFAD chose the valleys, already the best agricultural land, for their project, perhaps to insure that it would work. Some of the problems that the IFAD project was supposed to address were linked principally to water management in traditional farms, especially pepper (*Capsicum* spp.), farms. The project engineers determined that there was a high loss of irrigation water through the traditional canals because most of the water infiltrates the soil before reaching the cropped plots. In addition, that water was exposed to evaporation because it flowed very slowly in the ditches, and irrigation in general was very labor intensive. IFAD reports that "663 hectares of individual plots as well as the 18 community plots were created under the project." By building water reservoirs and cemented canals, river water was rendered more available, the time that the water took to reach the plants was reduced, and less water was lost. Providing motor pumps made irrigation more effective and put more water on the plants. The life of the peasant farmers was made much easier (IFAD 2003).

The high potential of the valley land allowed intensification and yielded returns proportional to the investments. At first, any addition of inputs resulted in high returns, and most farmers who had contracted loans increased their production. Since the activity was highly profitable, farmers diverted their efforts away from subsistence production toward commercial production because their harvest could easily be sold to provide sufficient food and cover other needs.

However, there were some unanticipated side effects. The farmer, who had contracted a loan to afford a motor pump, had to produce more than needed for his household to pay back the loan within the predetermined time. This required each to contract additional loans to purchase fertilizer, because there was no possibility to extend land area, but only to demand more from the same land. He also had to buy gasoline for the pump.

Meanwhile, at the international level, the initial increase in the demand for uranium had affected the earnings of the public funds in the country, with a consequent reduction of services provided by the government to the population, which included many subsidies to agricultural inputs, education, and public health. Therefore, at the household level there was an increase in the need for cash. Family size had increased because of the initial improved situation for the farmers, including the encouragement of additional wives and children for the most affluent. IFAD reports that one of the beneficiary farmers stated that he could "even think about getting married" after the success of his farming activities through the help of the project (IFAD 2003). But then the demand for uranium evaporated.

Analysis

In reality, the development project described above was not successful. The extra water increased yields for a while but that, and the increase in chemical fertilizers, ended by building up salinization in the soil, making it unfit for valuable crops. Also, the planting of the same cultivars (for export) in the river valleys year after year favored the buildup of pathogens and insect pests, requiring pesticides and higher investments. But when pests and other farming problems arose, the project was completed and closed, leaving the farmers with new problems to deal with. Two antagonistic phenomena were occurring at the same time: The increase of the need to produce more and the decrease in the possibility of producing more. The result was a sad reality: the goose which had been laying golden (or at least silver) eggs every day for a thousand years has been killed, only one golden egg was found inside her, and her life having been taken away, no more eggs would be laid. That is what happened to the best agricultural lands along the Komadugu River, and there are no more magical formulas by which to expand our agriculture. There are more mouths to feed, but no new prime farmland.

Demographic analysis of the Republic of Niger shows that the population has been increasing at an accelerating rate, based on official data available from the 1970s. A population survey conducted in 1977 estimated the population of the country at 4.2 million with a growth rate of 2.77 percent. By 1988, the population had increased to 7.2 million with a growth rate of 3.32 percent (CNEDD 1998). In 2002, the population was estimated at a little below 12 million (FAO 2003). The Republic of Niger has one of the highest rates of fecundity, 7.6 percent in comparison to an average of 6.3

for Africa, and 3.6 for the world (University of Hohenheim 2003). Similarly, in 1979 the total area under subsistence farming in Niger was 3.2 million hectares, which was increased to 3.5 million hectares in 1984, and it was 7 millions hectares in 1994. Today, it is estimated to be 10 million hectares (FAO 2003; CNEDD 1998). In short, within three decades, there was a threefold increase in both human population and cropland (the latter being of lower quality and in drier areas).

Sahelian agriculture is often qualified as unsustainable because it is essentially relying on fallow to rebuild soil fertility. The main solution promoted by agronomists, which is to combine mineral fertilizers with incorporation of organic matter (through crop rotation), has not been adopted by small farmers. In Niger, with such an exploding demography and consequently increased pressure on the land, the fallow period is reduced more and more in time and space, and soil fertility declines steadily (Pieri 1989). This affects not only crops (cereals) but also pastoralism and, as we will see, rural exodus.

Niger muddles along by expanding cultivation and animal husbandry on increasingly marginal land, but this often affects the wild animals, which today have disappeared completely from most of the regions. Wildlife habitat currently protected with some relatively rigorous enforcement essentially consists of a ridiculously small portion of the southwest of the country, where no farming is allowed, the "parc du W" created in the 1950s. Some other regions have also been classified as natural wildlife habitat, and hunting is officially prohibited, but without any measures to enforce either that or protection from the encroaching agriculture. The level of encroachment of agriculture is doubly serious, inasmuch as it also affects pastoralism, which for long has been the only subsistence activity of some portions of the population, and a backup in case of crop failure for most farmers. Today, for the average resident of Niger, it is very difficult to make a living. As agriculture and herding move into the increasingly arid north, the Sahara desert advances, probably due not only to local human activity but also to global climate change, squeezing the wild animals onto less and less land. But is there any light at the horizon?

Ruas and Cattin (1991) have developed a simple modeling tool to investigate the combined effect of technological change, land degradation, and demography in Sahelian countries for the period 1990–2040. We decided to use this tool to explore scenarios for the future of Niger given the harsh constraints that the country faces. The model has three components: demographic transition; land and labor productivity; and food security and rural exodus.

The demographic transition component is based on a standard S-curve or logistic model (see chapter 6), which, for Niger looks more like an exponential given the high population growth rate since 1990 and the fact that there is no indication that this rate is going to decrease substantially in the next forty years. The model was calibrated on demographic data prior to 1990, and it is not possible to modify these parameters in the software implementation. Urban and rural population is modeled separately.

The land and labor productivity component also uses S-curves to simulate the change of these parameters in time. Land productivity, or yields, is the production per unit surface of land that is cultivated. This can be affected by gradual adoption (or rejection) of technological practices (improved seeds, fertilizers, and so on), or with degradation (or improvement) of soil fertility. Labor productivity, which is the area cultivated per capita, can be affected by mechanization, crowding, and other factors. The model assumes that the agricultural labor force is equal to the labor force of the total rural population, since land and labor productivity are not necessarily independent; as the transition to mechanization can be accompanied by an improvement in land productivity (better control of the crop calendar, improving the soil structure, and so on). In the model these two components of agricultural intensification can be modified independently by changing the starting point (e.g., yield in 1990) and the endpoint (e.g., yield in 2040) of the S-curves. The other parameters of the curve are calibrated in such a way that 99 percent of the transition takes place between 1990 and 2040, and 90 percent between 2000 and 2030. If a yield-doubling technology has been successfully

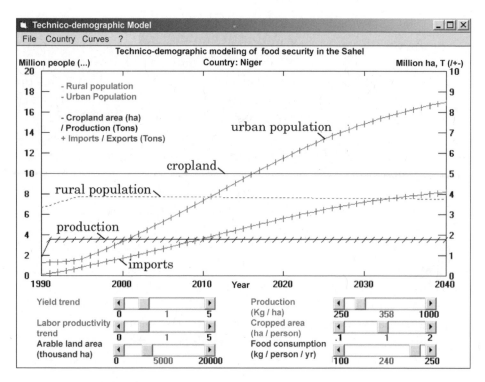

Figure 8.1. Baseline scenario using only arable land for cultivation. See website for color originals.

adopted between 1990 and 2040, yields in 2040 are effectively twice those of 1990. On the other hand if land degradation cannot be stopped and technology is not there to counterbalance the loss of yields, one can simulate that by setting a yield in 2040 that would be, say, half the one of 1990. Although the model assumes that all arable land has been used (which is a fact in most of the Sahel and true for Niger), a fraction of the population is still moving into marginal land with much lower productivity. This can be simulated by changing both the available land surface and the average yield of all land (arable and marginal).

The model assumes that the country aims at producing enough food to feed its own population. Therefore, all agricultural production in excess (after all the rural population is fed) goes to urban populations, and in turn all remaining surpluses are exported. The reverse also applies: if domestic agricultural production is not sufficient to feed the population, food must be imported. Food security is also the main driver of rural exodus that the model considers. Since Sahelian rural agriculture is essentially subsistence agriculture (cereals, tubers, and starches), the model assumes that someone living in rural areas will stay there as long as the land

can support him or her. The model permits specifying per capita food consumption, and assumes it remains constant. This is supported by recent data that show only a slight decrease (5.5 percent) in per capita total caloric intake since 1978 (FAO commodity projections, various years).

The results for the baseline scenario for Niger are given in figure 8.1. We use a typical value for per capita food consumption of 240 kg/year, a cereal yield of 358 kg/ha (www.earthtrends.org), and labor productivity of one hectare farmed per capita (www.nationmaster.com). The model results suggest that all of the five million hectares of arable land have been totally cultivated already (which is true), and therefore rural exodus is already on the rise, such that 22 percent of the population lives in urban areas. If nothing is done to improve yields or labor productivity (and if yields and available land stay constant), the urban population of Niger is expected to reach 65 percent of the total population by 2040, and the country would have to import about four million tons of cereals to feed twenty-five million people (it would sustain only 30 percent of the population with its own production). Only 65 percent of rural population would be working the land in 2040 (down from 75 percent

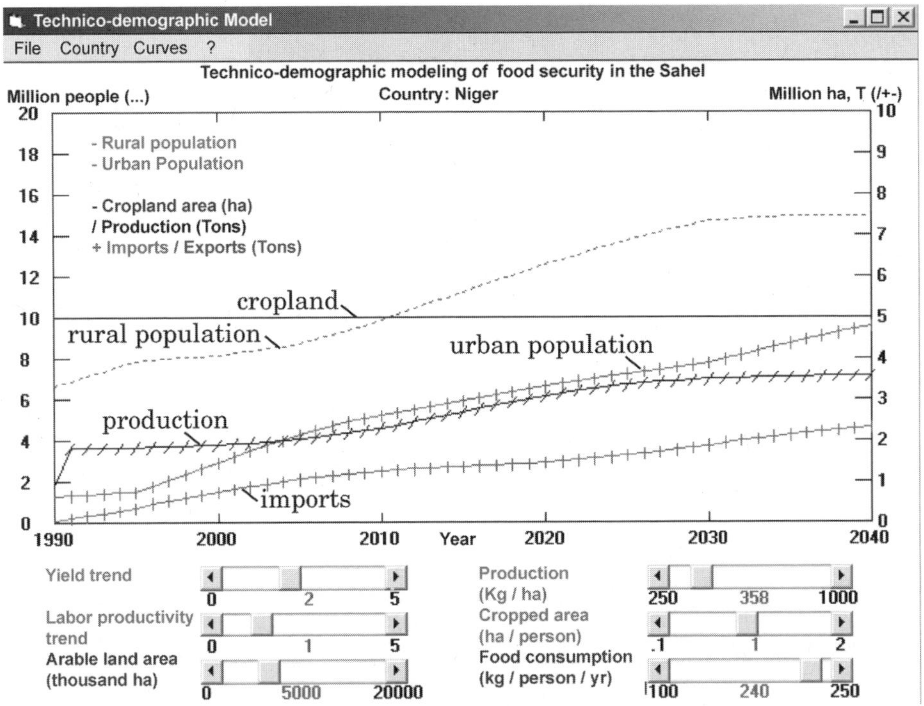

Figure 8.2. Effect of doubling yields over the period 1990–2040.

in 1990). Note that imports and urban/rural ratio are slightly overestimated for 2004. A separate model constructed independently by Chetima gave broadly similar results but emphasized the increasing vulnerability of the population to periodic droughts, especially in newly colonized areas. The model was validated in a sense by the extreme droughts and loss of life in 2005.

But let us be overly optimistic and suppose that that some technology will progressively be adopted to intensify agriculture in all available arable land, and that the yields would have doubled in the 1990–2040 period (see dotted black line on figure 8.2). The picture looks much less catastrophic. The proportion of urban population would saturate to about 40 percent around 2010, but the rural exodus would continue, and Niger would still have to import about 40 percent of its cereals (two million tons), while only 35 percent of the rural population would be working the land. Under this scenario, Niger authorities would have about twenty-five years until they have to deal with a population of twenty-five million and the exhaustion of the possibility of bringing new good land into production. But even this optimistic view with large gains in yields is rather illusory, since there has been

virtually no change in cereal yields in the past forty years. The required change would need very large and sustained interventions for improving soil and water management practices and the promotion of the use of better crop varieties. Another option could be to induce a change in the diet, and include more tubers, which are produced with yields of eight tons per hectare. But changing a diet is a very slow process (just like changing reproductive behavior) and could have seriously adverse dietary effects. And if development projects have failed in the recent past, what are the chances that they succeed in the near future?

A plausible scenario is that labor productivity could be increased within the 1990–2040 period by better management of weeds, more use of animal traction for cropping, increased technical knowledge, and so forth. Unfortunately, if this is not accompanied by a change in yields this will have virtually no effect except to decrease the number of people who are involved with farming, something that is not particularly useful in a region with precious little alternative employment. We end up instead with a situation similar to the baseline scenario.

A more realistic scenario for the long term, which is already visible, is that the rural population

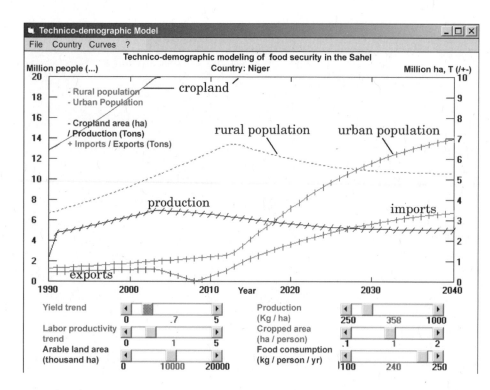

Figure 8.3. Effect of doubling land area for agriculture by developing marginal land.

would increasingly move and expand into increasingly marginal land. This movement would almost certainly result in decreased mean yields unless cropland expansion also moves over protected areas (which are often not strictly protected and whose status could eventually be changed by the state), in which case overall yields could possibly be maintained. This is assuming that the protected areas have higher fertility than marginal land (which they should have if the areas were relatively pristine and rigorously protected and suitable for agriculture, which is not the case in the "parc du W"). The results are shown in figure 8.3, where we run the model with the assumption that the available land is twice the area of arable land (i.e., estimated cultivated land in 2005) and yields in 2040 are at 70 percent of their 1990 level (because of the decreasing average productivity of the land). The model predicts that, although the explosive rural exodus ceases around 2010, it is nevertheless much more marked than in the baseline scenario. The model predicts that the urban population increases from 16 percent of the national total to 58 percent in just twenty-five years, and the country would have to import 40 percent of its cereals. In addition, 95 percent of the rural workforce would be

working the land in 2040, after a drop to 75 percent around 2010. In this case, as in the baseline case, an increase of labor productivity of 50 percent changes the picture only marginally. In both cases there would be important changes to be expected in the next decade in Niger, and the authorities should be prepared to face it.

Conclusion

Does our chapter bring any new information to the various technocrats working in the agricultural, the environment, and rural development fields in Niger? Probably not, as all know the basic facts and deal with a day-to-day reality that is difficult to conceal: Niger is a beautiful but not especially productive land where the false hopes for sustained development in the past generated more people than can be sustained on its own resources, regardless of possible (and often costly) technologies. However, even these professionals, and certainly some of the well-meaning people in NGOs, may not be fully aware of the difficulty of the challenges that await them even during the next few decades. As we saw during summer of 2005, it is increasingly becoming difficult to deal with regularly occurring events such as locust plagues and droughts.

Meanwhile, people, especially in the rural areas, continue to have large families because they confer status, because they love children, and because they believe, or would like to believe, the promises of the developmental experts who have new ideas and schemes and technologies for increasing agricultural production or the economy in general. But in fact, most or all of the development schemes, like the one outlined above, have given little lasting results and none that compensates for the population growth, bounded land productivity, and landlocked geography. The issue is made worse by the fact that the recent increases in the price of oil have reached even into the middle of Africa, making fertilizers increasingly unaffordable. What is needed is for the people and the government in Niger to look the facts in the eye and accept that the possibilities of economic growth are very limited. They have to understand that there is no silver bullet and take drastic measures to reverse the trends. Then the people of Niger will make the best of what they have—as they always have.

References

CNEDD. 1998. *Plan National de l'Environnement1'Envi ronnement Pour un Développement Durable*. Niamey: SE/CNEDD.

FAO (Food and Agriculture Organization). 2003. Grassland and Pasture Crops, Country Pasture/Forage Resource Profiles: Niger. www.fao.org.

Guillemin, J. 1983. Chefferie traditionnelle et administration publique au Niger. *Mois en Afrique* 213–14: 115–24.

IFAD. 2003. www.ifad.org/media/success/niger.htm.

Lund, C. 1998. Struggles for land and political power: On the politicization of land tenure and disputes in Niger. *Journal of Legal Pluralism* 40:1–22.

Pieri, C. 1989. *Fertilité des terres de savanes: Bilan de trente de recherche et de développement agricole au sud du Sahara.* Paris: Ministère de la coopération.

Ruas, J.-F., and M. Benoit-Cattin. 1991. Modélisation technico-économique des futurs alimentaires du Burkina Faso. *Cahiers de la Recherche Développement* 29.

Sacks, M. R. 2003. Cotton being unloaded from a truck in Pala, Mayo-Kebbi Prefecture. http://lcweb2.1oc.gov/frd/cs/tdtoc.html.

Salifou, A. 1981. La chefferie du Niger revue et corrigée par le colonisateur. *Afrique Histoire* 1:30–34.

Thebaud, B. 2001. Droits de communage ("Commons") et pastoralisme au Sahel: Quel avenir pour les eleveurs Saheliens? In A. T. Benjaminsen and C. Lund, eds., *Politics, Property and Production in the West African Sahel: Understanding Natural Resources Management*, 163–81. Stockholm: Nordic Africa Institute.

University of Hohenheim. 2003. Niger-Benin. www.uni-hohenheim.de/~atlas308/startpages/page2/english/content/title_en.htm.

University of Pennsylvania. 2003. African Studies fact sheet: Niger. www.sas.upenn.edu/African_Studies/Country_Specific/niger_info.html.

USAID. 2003. www.usaid.gov/our_work/humanitarian_assistance/ffp/rffp/bellmon_profiles/bellmon_profile_niger_dec_02.pdf.

CHAPTER 9

ASSESSING THE POSSIBILITY OF SUSTAINABLE DEVELOPMENT IN COSTA RICA

CHARLES A. S. HALL AND CARLOS LEÓN PÉREZ

Introduction

About a decade ago, author (Charles Hall) decided to take a good hard look at the possibilities for developing some kind of real sustainability, including sustainability in land use, in the tropics. He chose the country of Costa Rica, because it was generally regarded as a rich agricultural country as well as possessing many other natural resources, including especially very high biodiversity; it had a strong reputation for sustainability within conservation circles; its president had announced that they would make their country a "laboratory for sustainability"; and the sophisticated state of Costa Rican science meant that there was a great availability of data (Figures-Olson 1996). He felt that if any place could be sustainable, it would be Costa Rica. He moved there, a place he was already very familiar with, for nearly a year and met many wonderful people who were interested in similar questions, the most marvelous of whom were Carlos León, a native of Costa Rica, and Grégoire Leclerc, a brilliant French Canadian tired of snow and ice, who joined him in his quest.

The result was a thick book with many contributors besides ourselves, many of them Costa Ricans (Hall 2000). This was the beginning of my professional engagement in the issue of economic development, since it turned out that almost everything about Costa Rica, other than its remnant natural environments but including their destruction, is related to issues of development, either too little or too much or, most generally, the wrong kind.

This chapter is distilled from Hall (2000), especially chapters 2 and 26 and the sources therein, including especially Seligson (1980), Janzen (1983), Gundmundson (1986), and Holl, Daly, and Ehrlich (1993). It is a summary of the main points we learned about development in Costa Rica and the possibilities of sustainability.

A Short History of Development in Costa Rica

In pre-Columbian times, the area that is now the country of Costa Rica supported a substantial human population. It was a crossroad of trade routes and the meeting place of Mesoamerican and South American cultures. At that time, an important agricultural division corresponded to linguistic and ethnic differences. In the northwest, in what is now the province of Guanacaste, lived the Chorotega, a people whose primary agricultural crop was maize, which they ground and made into tortillas or combined with chocolate to make the drink called *chicha*. The rest of Costa Rica was occupied by the Huetares and Talamancas along the Atlantic coast and in the central highlands, and the Diquis of the Terraba Valley. Their basic food crops were yucca, other tubers, and the pejibaye palm.

At the time of the Spanish conquest, beginning in 1560, much of the Atlantic coast was cultivated, probably principally by shifting cultivators. Before the arrival of the Europeans, the indigenous peoples of the Latin American continent, like those of tropical regions around the world, maintained the fertility of their gardens—and, incidentally, the ecological integrity of the environment and the productivity of soils—through a variety of low-intensity but land-requiring techniques. These included shifting cultivation, mountain terracing, paddy culture, crop rotation, and interplanting of different types of crops. Shifting cultivators, for the most important example, cut forest vegetation and allowed it to dry—and then they burned it, preparing for the crops a sunny place with nutrients in the ash. These fields (also called milpas or swiddens) were planted with many agricultural varieties for several years, after which the plot was abandoned for a new one.

In retrospect, we can consider these techniques as more or less environmentally sound, although that is probably as much a function of relatively low human population density as any intrinsic virtue of shifting cultivation. The diversified plantings provided a habitat somewhat like that of the natural vegetation while maintaining to some degree a natural balance between pests and their natural predators. People lived within this system for thousands of years, so it was to some large degree sustainable. There were no huge empires such as existed in Mexico to the north or Peru to the south.

The Colonial Period

In about 1550, when the first Spanish settlers arrived, the Indian population of Costa Rica was estimated to be from seventeen thousand to eighty thousand (depending upon one's interpretation of the early Spanish records). Within a few years this was reduced by as much as 95 percent by war, disease, and slavery. The Indian cultures were lost, the fields were abandoned, and the forest reclaimed most of their once-cultivated areas.

In Costa Rican academic circles there is currently a debate over the settlement pattern and socioeconomic structure of the colonial period. The issue is the degree to which Costa Rica followed the traditional Spanish pattern of settlement characteristic of most of the New World.

For much of Latin America, many institutions perpetuated the medieval, stratified class structure of Iberia, most especially what is called *el latifundio*, a feudal agrarian system based economically on monoculture and socially on class stratification. This implies extensive and inefficient use of labor and land as well as a lack of concern for preserving the quality of the land. It promotes monoculture of crops for export, for therein lie the greatest profits. A main economic activity was, in the Spanish tradition, cattle raising, which required large land holdings but little investment, especially in the dry

areas. From the time of the first colonial settlement, the system reserved landownership (and thus power and wealth) to the European colonists and their descendants. The system remains intact in much of Latin America, but probably less powerfully in Costa Rica, where land reform has occurred and there has been traditionally a relatively large emphasis on egalitarianism.

The Advent of Real Development: Coffee and Bananas

Whether pre-coffee Costa Rica was egalitarian or not is debatable, but with the advent of full-scale coffee culture in about 1830 there arrived direct exploitive relations between coffee barons and small holders and laborers, the birth of a true laborer class called *jornaleros*, and something that we might consider as economic development. By the middle of the nineteenth century, Costa Rica was exporting four thousand tons of coffee beans and was the world's leading exporter of coffee, a commodity that originated in northeastern Africa. Great Britain was the financier of this conversion from subsistence farming to the production of a major export crop. The principal beneficiaries of this new industry were a small elite group tracing their heritage to the conquistadors (whether or not that was actually true) but deriving their power from the land. They grew coffee, but, more important, processed it in production units called *beneficios* and controlled the exports. Social divisions became increasingly important based on who owned the beneficios. The incentive to grow coffee probably marked the beginning of serious forest cutting in Costa Rica, as for the first time large land holdings had value.

The next phase in development and land-use change can be attributed to an American named Minor Keith, who, in the late 1800s, built a railroad from the Meseta Central to Limon on the Atlantic coast to facilitate the export of coffee. He then received land from the Costa Rican government, on which he established banana plantations. This was the beginning of the United Fruit Company. With growing U.S. investment in Central America and with U.S. military interventions to protect those investments, Costa Rica became a classic example

---

Table 9.1. Some important economic development schemes for Costa Rica

(a) The provision of British capital for coffee development in the 1800s.

(b) The construction of railroads, docking facilities, and other infrastructure to encourage banana production in the late 1800s and throughout the 1900s, mostly by North American companies.

(c) The encouragement of coffee production for United States troops (and civilians) during World War II.

(d) Investments in banana plantations by United Fruit and others throughout this century.

(e) General foreign aid from the developed world, including especially for agricultural research and development (for example, through the U.S. Agency for International Development [USAID] and the center for tropical agriculture research and training [CATIE]).

(f) Loans from the World Bank, the International Monetary Fund (IMF), and other organizations for the development of export cattle production, especially in the 1950s and 1960s.

(g) Loans for general development during the economic crises at the beginning of the 1980s. (These were often used to maintain government services rather than to develop new production.)

(h) Structural adjustment, meaning many things but including emphasis on "nontraditional exports" such as cut flowers and ferns, macadamia nuts, and fresh fruits during the early 1990s.

(i) A government (and private) reemphasis on traditional exports during the late 1990s, although overlapping with continued emphasis on nontraditional crops.

(j) A government (and private) focus on tourism and ecotourism, especially since about the mid-1980s.

(k) Government subsidies for foreign-financed high-tech industries in the mid-1990s.

(from Hall 2000:51–52)

---

of a neocolonial banana republic—although, it is important to note, while (mostly) maintaining its own sovereignty. This period marks the beginning of the transition between two competitive forms of agricultural organization—production for use or subsistence cropping, and production for exchange or cash cropping. Nevertheless, Costa Rica remained a relatively equitable society, in large part because of very successful and popular governmental programs in health care, education, and agricultural extension that were available to essentially all citizens. In addition, the main agricultural activity, both for food crops and for export crops (with the exception of bananas and sugarcane) remained small family units. Over time agriculture and especially cattle ranching expanded, in part in response to international development schemes (table 9.1), most of which—besides coffee and bananas—have been at best only marginally successful for the country as a whole. More recently, agriculture has become somewhat less important and manufacturing and especially services more so, but it still employs directly and indirectly nearly a half of Costa Ricans and generates about one-quarter of the country's wealth.

Costa Rica Today

Costa Rica is in many respects a green tropical paradise. Because of its mountains and its closeness to two oceans, it receives a great deal of rain, and this rain keeps much of the country, both forests and agricultural fields, very green. The high mountains also provide a tremendous range of climatological and hence ecological conditions, which are reflected in very high biodiversity. Costa Rica has other attributes of an earthly paradise: because of the mountains the temperature is generally very comfortable over much of the nation, because the country is a peaceful democracy with no army there is peace, because of a strong commitment to health care and other aspects of social welfare both natives and tourists generally feel very safe and secure, because of a reasonably healthy economy and subsidies from more northerly countries the standard of living is relatively high for the tropics (a GDP $3,000–4,000 per capita per year in 2000). The life expectancy of 74.7 years is very high by nearly any country's standards, and infant mortality is a low 15.3 per 1,000 live births. Corruption, the bane of so many governments in Latin America, is or at least was, relatively rare. However, in 2006 the last three presidents were on trial for corruption.

But there are broad problems within Costa Rica, starting with serious, continuing, although probably decreasing deforestation (see Sader and Joyce 1985). As of the mid-1990s the population growth rate was 2.4 percent per year, which, if continued, translates into a population of 3.5 million in 1990 that may grow to 6 million in 2015. Costa Ricans are now importing about 30 percent of the food calories they eat, and this proportion is increasing year by year, implying serious difficulties for feeding Costa Ricans in the future. In addition, social conditions for children are now changing dramatically. Despite very large infusions of foreign aid and development funds Costa Rica had a $3 billion foreign economic debt as of 1995, which exceeds the annual gross domestic product and is amongst the highest per capita debt/earnings load in the world. The country, traditionally and still basically middle class, is becoming increasingly a nation of extremes. Huge new houses of a sort rarely seen in the past are now common at the outskirts of many small cities, and for the first time there are large slums, for example at Paraiso. Severe air pollution is a daily occurrence in San José, and most rivers below their forested headlands are heavily polluted with sewage, garbage, and agricultural wastes. New fast-food restaurants are contributing large quantities of paper trash to once clean city streets, and life seems increasingly crowded and frantic. Visitors who are familiar with the "old" Costa Rica and who returned in the 1990s and after find a very rapidly changing nation. Fifty airplane flights a day bring in tourists and travelers to the international airport. Many people are optimistic that the tourist industry, which in 1994 passed bananas as the major source of foreign exchange, will save the Costa Rican economy, which continues to be plagued by debt. Government seems increasingly impotent because of the mounting debt and the stringent requirements that the lenders are placing on the government in order to attempt to recover their money.

Nevertheless, borrowing continues, and the debt increases with every increase in the price of oil or decrease in the markets for bananas.

Very expensive hotels are being built, especially along the Pacific Coast, and a new jetport in the middle of nowhere brings tourists in directly from such cities as Minneapolis. Ecotourism, although only a small part of all tourism, is rapidly becoming more important and gives hope that development and the generation of foreign exchange can be made compatible with preserving Costa Rica's unique and wonderful natural resources. The government is very interested in preserving and expanding the national parks, which constitute about a quarter of the land area of the country. A controversial fee system is charging foreigners some twenty-five times more than Costa Rican nationals to visit national parks, and this money is being used to refurbish and maintain the magnificent national parks. Nontraditional export crops, including macadamia nuts, specialty fruits, and cut flowers and ferns, expanded rapidly in the 1990s due to the ready availability of air shipping and the encouragement of financial institutions, but have not been the panacea some thought. Cattle raising in the northwest is decreasing rapidly as the sons of cattle ranchers seek their fortunes in the largest city, San José, so that at least here the forests are recovering to some degree.

The San José metropolitan area has now spread without much in the way of borders to encompass many once independent cities and towns, and this area, once the prime coffee growing area for the country, is now a metropolis of more than a million people. The changes are certainly a two-edged sword. San José, traditionally a clean, easygoing, and quiet city is clogged with traffic, commerce, and U.S.-style fast food restaurants. There are many new jobs in the service industries, but air pollution during rush hour in the dry season can be nearly as bad as anywhere in the world. Two enormous, even by U.S. standards, shopping malls were built recently in the suburb of San Pedro.

Advertisements for these and other new shopping malls are almost universally focused on products such as luxury foods and automobiles that are not produced in Costa Rica. Consumption seems much more obvious than production. Security systems are, more or less for the first time in the 1990s, big sellers. Slum areas are growing rapidly. Many traditional farmers can no longer afford rents in rural areas and are forced to move their families to the slums while they take a bus to work on plantations.

Social mores are changing rapidly. Costa Ricans tend to be Roman Catholic, and traditionally very religious and family-oriented. But television and urbanization are changing that, and many young people derive their values from popular soap operas that promote luxury consumption and romance with no consequences, such as pregnancy. Now the majority of babies are born to mothers who have no husbands, and the outlook for many of these children is bleak indeed. The population growth rate, which had declined by 50 percent from 1960 to 1975, remains at a plateau of about 3.2 percent since then, and babies are increasingly born to poor people. Immigration from poorer parts of Central America supplies an important part of the population growth.

Governmental and private debt continues to increase, the latter accelerated by the ready availability of credit on charge cards. The smoothly operating and universally admired systems of health, education, and other social services is threatened by governmental insolvency, and foreign creditors are demanding tightened government fiscal "responsibility" through structural adjustment programs, while the need for governmental services expands. Meanwhile serious crimes such as bank robberies and even murders, until recently essentially unheard of, occur, sometimes weekly. The distribution of wealth, once extremely equitable, especially by Central American standards, is now increasingly inequitable, and very fancy houses are no longer rare.

Where does the new money come from? Nearly every Costa Rican has an explanation. Large-scale government corruption is thought not the source. A popular view, hard to nail down, is that increasingly drug money is passing through Costa Rica. Or maybe it is just that the process of industrialization and free marketism, like other past patterns of large-scale social change, has created winners and losers. The winners win big, and the losers lose big.

Thus there are new opportunities and problems facing Costa Rica, in a sense similar to past problems and opportunities. Costa Rica has a modern, relatively sophisticated population with needs and desires for industrial products that cannot possibly all be produced in Costa Rica. In the past this problem has been resolved by increasing the export of tropical agricultural products. Costa Rica has a sufficiently diverse climate that more or less perfect conditions can be found for each tropical (and many temperate) crops. Thus in the past excellent conditions for the growing of coffee and bananas were found, and the export of these crops allowed Costa Rica to modernize and maintain a moderately high standard of living. New questions concern the degree to which Costa Rica is or is not approaching the limits of its ability to grow and export these crops profitably, and whether there are new sources of foreign exchange.

Industrialization, Energy Prices, and Debt

Perhaps the overriding issue for Costa Rica and many other developing nations is how to pay for the industrial inputs required for modernization. Hall's interest in Costa Rica was initiated when visiting Costa Rica for the first time in the mid-1970s as part of a program to model tropical deforestation. He was astonished to find that Costa Rica had been affected far more by the increase in fuel prices following the "energy crises" of 1973 (and 1979) than had the United States. Due to population increases, the country had become dependent upon energy-intensive industrial inputs to its agriculture and could not do without them lest the people starve, although they could not pay the price increases either. The mechanism and reason for this is developed below, but in many ways Costa Rica had become a thoroughly industrialized nation. The inputs were paid for through debt (money was cheap to borrow in the 1970s and early 1980s due to the surplus of "petrodollars" from oil-exporting countries in international banks). But then interest rates went from 2 percent to 10 percent a year, and it became impossible for Costa Rica to retire the principal, or in some cases even pay the interest owed, as in the default of 1992. Thus Costa Rica (and many other countries) is still paying for the energy price increases of the 1970s through huge interest payments on the principal mostly acquired at that time.

At this time, there appear to be three possible ways to continue to pay for needed industrial inputs: (1) the expansion of exports of tropical crops and (via tourism) use of natural ecosystems, (2) further industrialization, and (3) debt. The expansion of coffee and banana production in other countries makes the first difficult. Further industrialization in some ways makes sense because there is plenty of land and skilled and semiskilled labor available, and because Costa Rica makes sense to many investors because of its relatively low wages, well-educated population, and stable political climate. It does not make sense because Costa Rica does not have indigenous fuel (except for hydropower), other industrial raw materials, or a high-tech industrial base. This approach also has its insecurities. For example, there was an expansion of shirt making in Costa Rica in the mid-1990s. Foreign exchange generated from textiles went from near zero in 1985 to $600 million a year in 1995, and then declined precipitously. It is not clear how much more such expansion is likely, since that textile expansion was based on a one-time decision in the United States to find a market for surplus cotton. How can a nation control its destiny when so much is dependent upon the outside world of

markets? The third "solution" is the least desirable but in fact is what happened.

Structural Adjustment

Meanwhile much of daily life and political activity in Costa Rica in the 1980s and 1990s became dominated by "structural adjustment," a package of economic restrictions imposed by loan-granting institutions such as USAID (Annis 1990; Korten 1993; Hanson-Kuhn 1993). The trigger for this was that Costa Rica, beset with flat or decreasing prices for its exports and increasing prices for fuel and industrial products, was unable to meet its debt obligations and went into default in 1992. Costa Rica went to the International Monetary Fund, "the lender of last resort." The intended purpose of structural adjustment was to change the "structure" of the Costa Rican economy to reduce debt and increase revenues, especially in hard currencies from overseas. These changes included privatizing agricultural loan–granting agencies; reducing government spending, including subsidies for domestic food production and highly popular health and education services; encouraging the importation of food grains from the United States; reducing import and export tariffs to encourage all international trade; and favoring export crops at the expense of subsistence crops. According to most investigators who have examined the effects of this plan, the consequences of these harsh new regulations have been devastating to many small Costa Rican farmers, who can no longer compete with cheap (and government-subsidized) wheat from the United States or afford fertilizers for the export-oriented agriculture. Who came out ahead from these changes? Again, according to these investigators it is the already wealthy, including exporters of nontraditional products, importers, and those linked to the financial-services sectors. Whatever the case, it is clear that structural adjustment did not meet its principle objective of reducing the trade deficit, which in fact increased from $135 million in 1984 to $569 million in 1992, or the debt, which increased from $2 billion to $4 billion (despite a $1 billion forgiveness) during the same period.

What alternatives are left? In the mid-1990s, President Figures Olsen billed Costa Rica as a "green economy," and there was considerable hope that new industries could be generated to produce much-needed foreign exchange with relatively little destruction of the resource base. Critics argue that Costa Rica will become "green" only to the degree that it is economically useful to do so. Much actual data in fact argues that Costa Rica is quite the opposite, for deforestation continues, polluting industries are encouraged, and most indexes of environmental quality are decreasing. Perhaps it is fairest to say that many in Costa Rica would like to build a green economy, but that with falling agricultural revenues, an increasing population, and increasing debts, the nation must do whatever it can to maintain the health of the public sector. If that can be green, so much the better. If not, well, human needs take precedence. One possible bright spot is the development of a huge Intel chip manufacturing plant in Costa Rica, which has spawned many nearby high-tech industries. Unfortunately, the plant opened just before the collapse of high-tech stocks in 2000, so returns have been less than hoped.

In conclusion, we can see that the development cup of Costa Rica is either half empty or half full, depending upon your point of view and which aspects you choose to emphasize. The economy is still better than that of most of its neighbors, but high-paying jobs are scarce, debt persist, and many needed governmental services were lost. More accurately, it is best to say that the future of Costa Rica is very uncertain. We believe that the full examination of this question requires a much fuller biophysical analysis of what might be developed, how much, at what cost, and to what degree is it industrially based and hence vulnerable to oil price changes. An important component of our analysis is that the actual resource base is not static but changes over time. It is increased through technology and fossil energy use, and it is depleted as a function of the total quantity developed and as a function of exploitation and history of use (e.g. Hall 2000, chapters 4, 5, and 12). For example there is a very clear inverse relation between the amount of land planted in each crop each year and the yield per hectare of that crop—as more land is planted the mean yield goes down, apparently in a Ricardian response to the use of land of lower average fertility.

Thus if developmental plans call for increased plantings of a given crop, or crops in general, one can expect mean yields to decrease. This is a particularly important aspect that cannot be captured by most economic models that are based on a static representation of the economic system, and that often do not treat resources with any degree of sophistication if, indeed, they are treated at all.

Summary of Results

Thus, what we found, rather to our surprise, was that Costa Rica was very far removed from sustainable. The principal reasons are given below, and the details are summarized in chapter 26 of Hall (2000).

The human population of Costa Rica is dependent upon imports for from a quarter to a third of their food calories. Our calculations indicate that even if all of the land thought suitable for agriculture were devoted simply to domestic food crops it probably would not be possible to feed even the current population, let alone the projected increases. Thus the population base is simply too large for the land to be used in any sense sustainably. Within this suite of problems, we found a certain amount of self-delusion. For example, Costa Rica prides itself on being self sufficient in terms of dairy products. While this is literally true, the largest of many large agricultural imports in the 1990s were cattle feed concentrates.

Although the agricultural infrastructure of Costa Rica is very sophisticated and there are many who hold out a great deal of promise for enhanced productivity per hectare, yields for most crops have not been increasing since about 1985. This is the case despite the fact that yield per hectare had been increasing more or less steadily from 1960 to 1985 or so, in response to agrotechnology (which was mostly an increase in the use of energy-intensive fertilizers and other agrochemicals). However, even during this relatively favorable earlier time the yield per unit fertilizer used for all crops declined, indicating a decline in the efficiency with which inputs generate crops. A second clear finding is that over the period for which we had good data (1960–96) there was a clear inverse relation between yield per hectare and the area of each crop planted in each year. The implication of this relation is that if and as the Costa Rican population continues to grow and more agricultural land is needed either for food production or for growing more export crops for more foreign exchange, mean crop yields and fertilizer efficiency will continue to decrease.

One implication of the increased use of industrial inputs is that the cost of those inputs for export crops eats greatly into the foreign exchange earned by their sale. For example, the $600 million worth of bananas exported in the 1990s (bananas are usually the largest source of foreign exchange for the nation) requires nearly $300 million of imported agrochemicals, plastics, trucks, fuels, and so on to get it to the dockside. Thus although the gross foreign exchange earned from bananas is $600 million, the net foreign exchange is only about half that.

A fundamental biophysical reason for the low yield in Costa Rica, one that technology or economic policy cannot overcome, is that within the tropics there is never a season with short nights and long days, indeed with less than an eleven-hour night. Most of the energy fixed by a green plant goes for its own maintenance metabolism. During the day, photosynthesis more than compensates for this energy drain, but at night respiration robs some of the net production of the day. High agricultural yields (greater than two or three tons per hectare) generally are obtainable only in temperate regions where relatively long nights during the growing season do not rob crop plants of much of the day's energy profit.

A finer-grained analysis indicated a tremendous dependence of agricultural productivity on climatic conditions. Thus, although coffee can be grown nearly anywhere in Costa Rica, high yields can be obtained only in a very restricted set of rainfall and temperature conditions. One implication of this is that although there is a great deal of land in Costa Rica available that might be used for the expansion of agriculture, there is little land left where one might expect good yields, at least for the crops that we have examined (sugarcane may be an exception).

The implications of all this is that food production for the four million or so existing Costa

Ricans has become inextricably tied up with fossil fuel–derived (and hence nonrenewable) inputs from the industrial world, and it is likely to continue to be so. There simply is not enough land of sufficient quality in the country to grow the food needed for this many people without the industrial inputs, and most of the land is eroded and/or "tired" and thus cannot produce much food without intensive fertilization. In addition, the need to generate foreign exchange to pay for fuels and other industrial products means that a great deal of land has been deforested and degraded to generate beef, bananas, and coffee for export. In addition, the enormous increase in agrochemical use has left Costa Rica with a very high rate of human health impacts from pesticide poisoning, dead coral reefs that may have been killed by pesticide applications, and the need to abandon agricultural production on large regions of soil (for example, in the southwest, former banana plantations) because of past overuse of hard pesticides. One consequence of the absolute dependence upon industrial inputs for agriculture was the tremendous debt derived in large part from the oil price increases in the 1970s. This continues to be nearly impossible to pay off, and the servicing of this debt (mostly interest) consumes large quantities of scarce foreign exchange, and the use of much of the best agricultural land, to generate that foreign exchange. While many new schemes have been promoted in recent decades for broadening the economic base of Costa Rica and adding to sustainability, most are hardly new and have been no panacea.

Meanwhile, the basic Costa Rican international staples of coffee, bananas, sugar, and beef continue to be important, especially for export, but their total value has not kept pace with either population growth or the renewed increase in the price of oil in the mid-2000s, diluting this importance. Tourism may be an exception, but because of its high import dependence (microbuses, fuel, bathroom fixtures, and so on, not to mention the necessity of cheap jet fuel), its net contribution to the economy is difficult to judge.

Despite large efforts by outside aid communities to increase it, Costa Rican per capita wealth has been essentially constant for thirty years. The basic reason appears to be that the human population growth, increasing at nearly 3 percent per year, is similar to the rate of increase in the use of the energy that generates new GDP. When we examined many developing countries, we found an increase in per capita wealth only where energy use per capita has exceeded population growth—in, for example, Korea and Malaysia (e.g., Ko, Hall, and Lemus 1998; Tharakan, Kroeger, and Hall 2001).

We also examined the efficacy of neoliberal development policies using the methods of the natural sciences and applied them to study development policies in Costa Rica (Montanye 1998; see table 9.1). We have done this by restating the development objectives of the World Bank, the IMF, and USAID (generally given as a rationale for some policy, such as part of programs of "structural adjustment") as hypotheses ("if this policy is adopted the following results will occur") and then testing whether or not the objectives were obtained in years following the implementation of the policy. Most generally, we found that in fact the economic objectives were not met, and that there were other unintended but negative effects of the implemented changes, many of which were reflected in degradation of land quality through deforestation and an increased use of chemicals.

Therefore Costa Rica, as a nation with no fossil fuels, has been, continues to be, and almost certainly will become even more dependent upon imported fossil fuels and their derivatives such as agrochemicals. This dependence is a large component of the inability of Costa Rica to balance its external monetary accounts, and may become much more of a problem in a future in which we believe that oil will be scarcer and much more expensive. A hint of that occurred with the price increases in 2000 and 2005, which wiped out the hard-won improvements in debt retirement of the previous few years.

Although the most rapid period of deforestation has ceased with the cessation of World Bank investment funds, deforestation continues in some areas as poor people desperate for lands encroach upon remaining forested lands, including those within national parks. On the other hand, as the productivity of unimproved pastures declines and as ranching becomes a less attractive alternative for young men, forests are returning to some formerly deforested regions in, for example, Guanacaste Province.

If we look at the increasing dependence of Costa Rica on nonrenewable resources and the possibly of severe supply disruptions in the future, the possibility of anything resembling sustainability of present infrastructure, let alone "sustainable growth," appears rather small. There are already too many people to feed without industrial inputs, which must be imported at great cost. A further conclusion is that growth, both of populations and of economies, undermines future sustainability because new technologies have not in fact decreased per capita dependence upon finite resources, including land. If one wanted to contribute to the future welfare of Costa Ricans, the most important development issue to deal with is not expansion of the economy but the number of future Costa Ricans. How this might be done is the business of Costa Ricans, but at a minimum it is critical to enhance educational and health programs so that young people have more options than pregnancy. This is exactly the opposite of what happened when structural adjustment was implemented and government programs diminished. In our opinion, the development economists made a bad issue worse because of a misguided faith in neoliberal economics, rather than a careful assessment of biophysical reality.

References

Annis, S. 1990. Debt and wrong way resource flows in Costa Rica. *Ethics and International Affairs* 4:105–21.

Figures-Olsen, J. M. 1996. Sustainable development: A new challenge for Costa Rica. *SAIS Review* 16:187–202.

Gudmundson, L. 1986. *Costa Rica Before Coffee*. Baton Rouge: Louisiana State University Press.

Hall, C. A. S., ed. 2000. *Quantifying Sustainable Development: The Future of Tropical Economies*. San Diego: Academic Press.

Hansen-Kuhn, K. 1993. Sapping the economy: Structural adjustment policies in Costa Rica. *The Ecologist* 23:179–84.

Holl, K. D., G. C. Daly, and P. R. Ehrlich. 1993. The fertility plateau in Costa Rica: A review of causes and remedies. *Environmental Conservation* 20:317–23.

Janzen, D. H. 1983. *Costa Rican Natural History*. Chicago: University of Chicago Press.

Ko, J-Y., C. A. S. Hall, and L. L. Lemus. 1993. Resource use rates and efficiency as indicators of regional sustainability: An examination of five countries. *Environmental Monitoring and Assessment* 51:571–93.

Korten, A. 1993. Cultivating disaster: Structural adjustment and Costa Rican agriculture. *Multinational Monitor*, July–August, 20–22.

Sader, S. A., and A. T. Joyce. 1988. Deforestation rates and trends in Costa Rica, 1940 to 1983. *Biotropica* 20:11–19.

Seliger, M. A. 1980. *Peasants of Costa Rica and the Development of Agrarian Capitalism*. Madison: University of Wisconsin Press.

Tharakan, P., T. Kroeger, and C. A. S. Hall. 2001. Twenty-five years of industrial development: A study of resource use rates and macro-efficiency indicators for five Asian countries. *Environmental Science and Policy* 4:319–32.

CHAPTER 10

PUTTING DEVELOPMENT IN PERSPECTIVE

Colonial and Neocolonial Dynamics in the Philippines

AILEEN GUZMAN AND LAURA SCHMITT

Introduction: The Sick Man of Asia

To many economists, the Philippines is a development puzzle (Balisacan and Hill 2003). Immediately after World War II, it had one of the highest economic growth rates in Southeast Asia, but now it is lagging behind its neighbors with a growth rate that has barely hit 3 percent per capita since 1980 and has not been consistently positive for more than four years in a row (figure 10.1). Although measures of per capita gross national income (GNI, which is approximately equivalent to GDP) place the Philippines squarely in the middle of the developing-country spectrum (table 10.1), during the economy's most export-oriented period—1986 to the present—per capita GDP in the Philippines (adjusted for inflation) did not grow (figure 10.2). In fact, the Philippines' open trade policy has resulted in a consistently negative trade balance (figure 10.3), and heavy borrowing throughout the 1970s and 1980s meant that a consistently high portion of GDP is swallowed up by foreign debt payments. Some Philippine analysts have labeled the country "the Sick Man of Asia."

The "sickness" takes many forms. The standard of living index, a measure of government and private consumption of nonmilitary goods, fell from 1970 to 1989—an indication of the Philippines' highly U.S.-subsidized militarization (figure 10.4). The incidence of poverty has declined across the country since the 1980s, but the magnitude of this decline has varied widely (a 39 percent decline in urban areas versus a 22 percent decline in the rural areas) (Balisacan 2003). In addition, these figures refer to poverty measured by household expenditure, which does not take into account many nonmarket factors on which families depend for their welfare, such as the health of the country's ecosystems. The income ratio of the wealthiest 10 percent of Filipinos compared to the poorest 10 percent of Filipinos has increased over the last decade

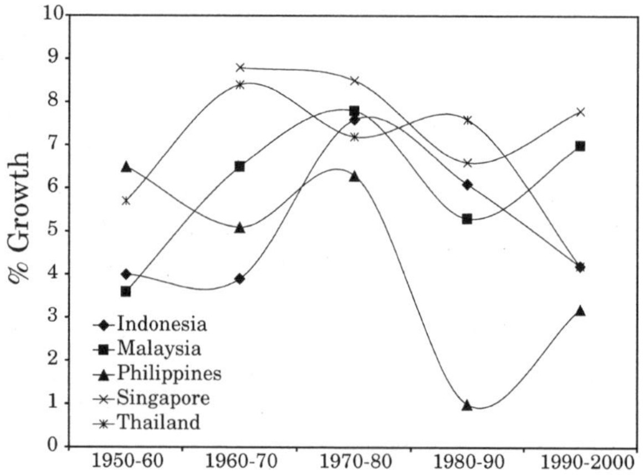

Figure 10.1. Average growth of GDP in Southeast Asia by decade, 1950–2000. Source: Balisacan and Hill (2003).

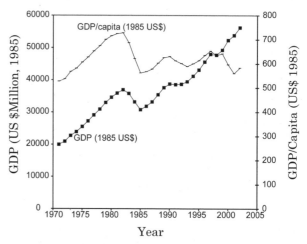

Figure 10.2. GDP per capita in constant 1996 US dollars for Southeast Asian nations, 1970–2000.

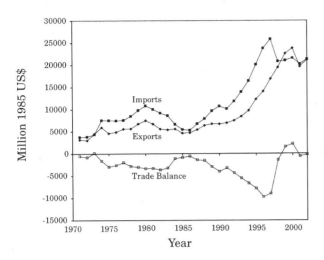

Figure 10.3. Philippine trade balance, 1985 (in US$ millions), 1970–2002.

Country	GNI/capita
Japan	35610
Costa Rica	4060
Malaysia	3330
Thailand	1940
Ecuador	1240
Philippines	1030
Indonesia	690
India	460
Kenya	350
Nigeria	290
Niger	180
Malawi	160

Table 10.1: Real GNI per capita, current U.S. dollars, in selected countries, 2001

Source: World Development Indicators (World Bank)

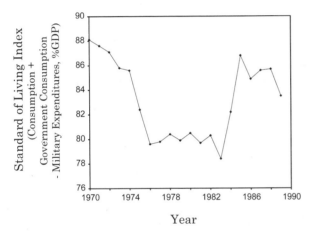

Figure 10.4. Standard of Living Index, 1970–1990. The index is calculated as (consumption + government consumption – military expenditure) as a percentage of GDP.

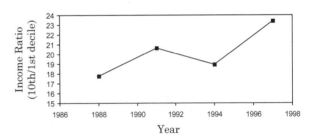

Figure 10.5. Income ratio of the wealthiest 10 percent of Filipinos to the poorest 10 percent of Filipinos, 1988–97.

(figure 10.5), giving the Philippines one of the highest rates of income inequality in Southeast Asia, as measured by the Gini coefficient (figure 10.6). According to a *Philippine Daily Inquirer* article of June 2, 2002, a Congressional committee found that 15 million Filipino children were malnourished. This represents an increase of 2.6 percent from 1996 numbers. Shantytowns, pollution, and overcrowding continue to plague the Philippines' urban areas. Population growth rates are among the highest in Southeast Asia (Herrin and Pernia 2003). Deforestation, erosion, and coral reef destruction are trends environmentalists decry (Tujan 2000).

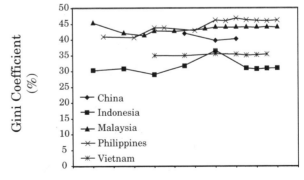

Figure 10.6. Gini coefficient of income inequality for selected Asian countries, 1982–2002.

This litany of woes is shared with many countries in the developing world. What makes the Philippines unique is that it was not supposed to be this way for the former American colony. The Philippines, more than most countries, has had its economy and society shaped from the beginning by Western economists—first under Spanish control, then the American colonial regime, wherein it had exclusive trading relations with the United States, and finally under the auspices and assistance of the World Bank and International Monetary Fund. According to modern economists, the country has done just about everything right. It has lowered trade barriers, devalued its currency, liberalized its financial markets, promoted exports, and kept wages low. Yet the Philippines is still far from developed, compared to its Asian neighbors (notably Malaysia) that defied IMF policies during the 1997 financial crisis (Stiglitz 2002).

The reasons behind the Philippines' underdeveloped state may be a puzzle for economists, who typically concern themselves with the efficient allocation of resources *given individuals' initial resource endowments*, rather than with how these initial endowments came to be, or whether they are just (Gowdy and O'Hara 1995). However, the authors believe that the causes of the Philippines' struggle with development are fairly clear, once one examines the country's colonial and neocolonial past. This chapter does not propose to solve the puzzle of the Philippines' failure to join the ranks of its more developed Asian neighbors, but it does aim to shed light on certain aspects of the country's current economic and environmental situation that have their roots in historical structures.

Two theses are advanced. The first holds that the seemingly major changes in the Philippines' economy throughout its history (and especially in the past hundred years) have largely served to perpetuate the same foreign/Filipino elite economic and political power centers that existed since the Spanish conquest. In this sense, economic reforms have not been true reforms—they have perpetuated the status quo. This has had the dual effect of preventing poor Filipinos from experiencing the benefits of economic expansion, and stifling competition that might promote the growth of domestic industry (ironically, as fostering competition was one of the aims of World Bank Structural Adjustment Loans to the Philippines [Broad 1988]).

The second thesis is that the Philippines' natural resource base has been unsustainably degraded through polices that originated in the colonial period and persist today—again as the result of perpetuated power structures. This chapter will demonstrate how the entrance of the Philippines into the international market has been hampered by a natural resource deficit incurred during the Spanish and American colonial periods.

Why are natural resources important for development? Some development economists claim that they are not; they point to the other "Asian tiger" countries, such as Korea and Singapore, which seemingly have been able to industrialize with few natural resources. They might say that natural resource depletion in the Philippines is no barrier to its entering the world market as a successful manufacturing or services economy. Indeed, the services sector of the Philippine economy is growing faster than any other (Balisacan and Hill 2003). Even if the Philippines were able to boost GDP in the services sector, however, we believe that several key issues would remain unaddressed, namely (1) the welfare of poor farmers who depend on natural resources for their livelihood and who have no access to the market; (2) environmental destruction wrought by resource depletion that continues to worsen; (3) unequal distribution of wealth and political power that causes the Philippine business sector to be noncompetitive; and (4) foreign debt that cripples economic growth and creates an avenue for foreign control of the Philippine economy. We believe that these concerns are an important legacy of the Philippines' colonial past, which must be addressed under any development strategy. In addition, the services sector of the Philippines is much more energy intensive than the extractive or manufacturing sectors.

In our study of the trends in natural resource and economic development in the Philippines, we begin with a discussion of the country's precolonial past.

Precolonial Life in the Philippines

Dr. Frito Voss, a German scientist, disputes the theory that during the Pleistocene or Ice Age land bridges connected the Philippines to mainland China (Agoncillo 1990; Scott 1984). Another theory used to explain the peopling of the Philippines is that of wave migration, which has been accepted for years by scholars as the major means of the peopling of the Philippines (Salcedo 1967; Beyer 1947). Recent scholars have challenged the theory, and have opined that the theory was formed using flawed methodological approaches and that there is no archaeological evidence to support wave migration (Jocano 1967). Scholars agree that the Filipino race is a result of multiracial interaction; however, the process of formation is still debated (Jocano 1975).

The ancient Filipinos believed in the existence of an almighty creator called Bathalang MayKapal as well as the presence of other deities in particular environmental and soul spirits. The deities played a role in the day-to-day activities of the people, thus the existence of gods for various activities (harvest, sowing, and so on). Deities were also attributed to diseases and illnesses a person or a community suffered. Accordingly, recovery from an illness was based on appeasing the deities. This belief system led ancient Filipinos to respect everything that had to do with their daily lives. Nature was venerated; plants, animals, and even the land were adored (Agoncillo and Alfonso 1960).

Life in the precolonial Philippines centered on the *barangay*, which was the basic form of government. A barangay was independent from its neighbors and thus was free to set its own rules and follow its own justice system based on customs and traditions of the community. The barangay was generally a grouping based on kinship, and was ruled by a chieftain commonly known as the *datu*. The datu was responsible for administering the day-to-day governance of the people. A council of elders usually assisted the chief especially in deciding over crucial matters.

Precolonial settlements were scattered in many parts of the country. There was no central government for the country's more than 7,100 islands. The degree of governance varied from locality to locality. An alliance of barangays also existed, which can be likened to a loose confederation mostly for defense purposes.

In the precolonial government, the people were classified into three categories, namely: (1) the *maharlikas* (nobles), (2) *timawa* (freemen), and (3) slaves. The nobility was the ruling class and usually had the fewest members. The slaves were classified into two groups. The first type (*aliping namamahay*) owned houses and went to the noble's house for servitude, while the second type (*aliping sagigilid*) stayed in the noble's house. Indebtedness and war were the usual reasons for slavery. It should be noted that during this time, one's position in society was not permanent. Anyone could become a chief, provided he had the ability and strength to lead.

Precolonial Economy

Economy during the ancient times was dominated by subsistence agriculture. Filipinos produced rice, hemp, coconuts, sugarcane, cotton, fruits, and vegetables. The techniques used for farming varied from sophisticated irrigation in the Mountain Province to the north to mere use of wood implements and *kaingin*, or slash and burn, in most parts of the country. Agriculture and fishing were considered community activities, meaning that the owner of the land would call on his community members to help plant and harvest his land. The owner did not pay the workers but instead provided food for them, and the fruits of their labor would be divided among those who helped (Arcilla 1971).

Land was both privately and publicly owned. Privately owned land was administered by the datu but owned by the community, and was located in fertile areas (Collins 1989). People could till these lands provided they paid the datu some sort of tribute (Agoncillo 1966). Public lands were usually located in semiarable and upland areas and could be cultivated by anyone.

Domestic trade existed between barangays and the usual trade routes were the river systems and the seas. Ships from Luzon would sail all the way to Cebu, Bohol, and Butuan in the south to conduct trade with the southerners, using a barter system (Agoncillo 1966). Among the products traded were woven baskets, textiles, small furniture, knives, and other utensils.

Aside from a flourishing domestic trade, foreign trade also existed during the precolonial times. Trade between mainland China and the Philippine islands began in the ninth century. Arab traders through the port of Canton brought products from the Philippines to China. By the middle of the fourteenth century, the Philippines traded with other countries as well as China, among them Siam, Japan, and Annam (Agoncillo and Alfonso 1960).

Early Colonial Structure of Life (1521–1898)

On March 16, 1521, Ferdinand Magellan "discovered" the Philippines and claimed the islands for the king of Spain. However, it was only in 1565 that the country was formally annexed as a colony of Spain and the first permanent Spanish settlement was founded in Cebu, Philippines. The Spanish king appointed Miguel Lopez de Legazpi as the first governor-general of the Philippines.

The conquest of the Philippines by the Spaniards is characterized by the use of the sword and the cross. The sword symbolizes the forceful subjugation of the Filipinos and the ruthless suppression of any form of resistance. The cross symbolizes the peaceful dominance of the Spaniards over their conquests through the conversion of the Filipinos from a pagan religious belief to Christianity.

The coming of the Spaniards ended freedom for the Filipinos and likewise ended the way of life that existed in the Philippines prior to colonization. The westerners introduced a central government system, wherein the barangay existed as the smallest political unit. Unlike the precolonial barangay, which had the power not only to govern the people but also to execute judicial and legislative powers, the colonial barangay was only allowed to oversee the day-to-day activities of its constituents.

The governor-general, who resided in Manila, exercised executive powers, while the Royal Audiencia or Supreme Court executed judicial powers. The introduction of this central government system was also a means to unify the fragmented island groups by force.

Spanish colonization also entailed the formation of settlements by force. The Spaniards concentrated the sparse and dispersed populations into settlements known as *visitas*. To identify each *visita* and its inhabitants, the Spaniards assigned a uniform surname, consequently changing the names of the native inhabitants. Various visitas then made up the towns or pueblos.

Towns or pueblos were formed according to a single settlement pattern known as the town-plaza complex. The town plaza complex dictated a pattern wherein important institutions like the church and municipal hall were built around a town plaza. The house of the Spanish supervisor, or *principalia*, was also located near this center. The prestige of an individual was directly proportional to his house's distance from the town plaza. This formation defined the pattern of urbanization in the Philippines.

The Encomienda System

The *encomienda* system began in 1570, when Legazpi distributed land to loyal Spanish subjects through a decree from the king of Spain (Filipinia Book Guild 1965). The idea was that the king was delegating his authority to individuals or institutions. Therefore, in a sense, the encomienda was intended to be a public office rather than a land grant. However, it effectively became the latter (Agoncillo 1966).

The encomienda system became a tool of Spanish administration. The colony was divided into various administrative units, which in turn became known as encomiendas, which were administered by the *encomendero*. The precolonial elite became the landed class and would later be part of the colonial local elite known as the principalia. The ordinary people became landless subjects and were subject to further oppression.

The system was used effectively for extracting tributes and forced labor among Filipinos. The encomienda system infuriated the Filipinos, who bore all the burden of paying tribute. Aside from being alienated from the land they tilled and once owned communally, the Filipinos were forced to work extra hours to pay their tribute to the encomendero.

Because of its negative effects, the Spaniards finally abolished the encomienda system toward the end of the eighteenth century. It left a lasting legacy by introducing the concept of private property and assigning land and all rights associated with it to individuals.

The Galleon Trade

The transpacific galleon trade operated between China and Mexico. Goods from China were brought to Manila and then to Acapulco, and vice versa. Manila acted as the transshipment point in the trade that came from China and other parts of Asia. Among the major products traded were Chinese silk and porcelain. Silver from Mexico was brought back to China. This trade lasted until 1815. The galleon trade allowed the establishment of a flourishing shipping industry in the Philippines; however, massive destruction of Philippine forests was attributed to the galleon trade, especially in areas where the ports were located (Arcilla 1971). The galleon trades are also blamed for the lack of development of agriculture and industry in the Philippines during the Spanish colonial period (Agoncillo and Alfonso 1960).

Cash Crops and the Hacienda System

The Philippines was administered through Mexico, and the colony was heavily subsidized. The galleon trade was the colony's main source of income. Spain's loss of Mexico brought the end of the galleon trade and highlighted the need for an alternative source of funds.

The colonial government soon shifted to cash crops. Crops such as sugar, abaca (Manila hemp), and indigo were grown for export. Groups such as the Sociedad Económica de Amigos del País, organized by the colonial government in 1778, and the Royal Philippine Company, which was set up in 1785, paved the way for the establishment of a new business. Rich Filipinos as well as Spaniards acquired lands and developed these lands for agricultural purposes. Export crops soon replaced crops raised for local consumption. This also resulted in the massive conversion of lands to serve export needs. It is believed that the present-day hacienda system evolved during this period.

The Tobacco Monopoly

Strapped for cash, the colonial government was forced to install measures to raise funds. In 1780, a Spanish royal decree established a government monopoly in the tobacco industry. This raised substantial money for the colonial government. Tobacco factories also employed many Filipinos; however, corruption and abuses forced the abolition of the monopoly in 1882.

The Royal Company

The Spanish government established the Royal Company in 1785 to facilitate trade between the colony and Spain and to develop the Philippines' natural resources. The company suffered its own setbacks due to management incompetence of Spanish officials, leading to financial losses. The company was abolished in 1834.

The establishment of the company, however, led to the further development of Philippine agriculture, especially sugar. The company designated around 4 percent of its income for the development of agriculture.

Further Opening of the Philippines to the World Market

The development of the free market in Europe during the eighteenth century in the context of laissez-faire forced the Spanish government to open the Philippine market in 1789. This brought trade with foreigners, especially with the Germans, English, and Americans. Ports in Pangasinan, Iloilo, Zamboanga, Cebu, Legazpi, and Tacloban were opened to facilitate further trade. Corresponding transportation and communication infrastructure was also developed to support the growing trade. For instance, a telegraph communication system was established in 1888 through an undersea cable between Zambales and the British Colony of Hong Kong.

The opening of the Philippines had an effect on both the economic and political aspects of Filipino life. The country was exposed to a stronger influence of the world market. Industry sectors developed as a response to world demand rather than domestic needs. The colonial economy was therefore vulnerable to changes and fluctuations in world market. This pattern of development continued in the American period.

Economic Development During the Spanish Era

Various policies intended to generate income for the colony were implemented during the Spanish Era in the Philippines. These policies included the encomienda system, the tobacco monopoly, the trade galleons, cash crops, and others (discussed in some detail in the preceding sections). However, these efforts can be summarized as restrictive, monopolistic, and oppressive, and they led to the decline of indigenous agriculture and the abandonment of cottage industries that flourished prior to the arrival of the Spaniards (Agoncillo 1968).

The decline of agriculture and the abandonment of industries can be attributed to the Spanish failure to enforce a positive economic policy in the Philippines. The Spanish provided no means for the Filipinos to meet the high taxes imposed on them. Instead of providing lands, seeds, and tools for farming, able-bodied Filipinos were taken away from their lands and families and forced to work for Spain in shipyards or as rowers for galleons or as hacienda cash-crop laborers. Cottage industries that thrived prior to the arrival of the Spaniards such as basket and textile weaving were neglected due to non-market-friendly strategies such as monopolies, price fixing below actual market prices, and the difficulty of getting permits to open shops and other factories. Domestic and foreign trade also declined due to unchecked raids and piracy (Agoncillo and Alfonso 1960).

Before the arrival of the Spanish, Filipinos venerated nature (both animals and plants and the land) and considered nature as an integral part of their belief system and way of life. Natural resources were exploited sustainably, and only that which was needed was taken from nature. However, the removal of Filipinos from their lands alienated them from the very nature and land that they once venerated and subsequently led to the overexploitation of natural resources that began with the Spanish colonization and accelerated during the American colonial period.

The American Colonial Period (1898–1946)

Spain ceded the Philippines to the United States on December 10, 1898, through the Treaty of Paris for a price of $20 million. McKinley, then president of the United States, issued his "Benevolent Assimilation Proclamation" on December 21, 1898. The proclamation was the first official indication of America's intention to stay in the Philippines. In the same proclamation, the president instructed the U.S. military to extend American sovereignty over the Philippines by force.

With the breakout of Filipino-American hostilities, the Americans pushed for the control of Luzon. They then proceeded with the conquest of the Visayas and gained the sympathy of the wealthy inhabitants of Negros Island, who welcomed the colonizers.

In Mindanao, the Americans made peace with the Muslims through the Bates Treaty. Through the treaty, the Americans recognized the rights and dignities of the Sultan of Jolo and its datus. The treaty further provided the sultan the right to free, unlimited, and duty-free trade under the American flag and monthly compensation in Mexican dollars.

The Bates Treaty was part of the American strategy to neutralize the Muslims of the south and allow the Americans to concentrate on pacifying the colonial resistance in Luzon. The capture of the leaders of the resistance movement led to the end of the struggle against the United States; however, sporadic fighting continued and the Americans continued to suppress displays of Filipino nationalism (Agoncillo and Alfonso 1960).

The Americans soon established a colonial government with the Philippine Act of 1902, granting Filipinos "limited" freedom. When U.S. President Roosevelt declared that election preconditions had been fulfilled, the Filipinos prepared for the election of the Philippine Assembly on July 30, 1907.

The Jones Act of 1916 provided the first basis of Philippine independence. It stipulated that the independence would be given "as soon as a stable government can be established therein." A Senate and Congress that were composed solely of Filipinos replaced the Philippine Assembly.

Education

The establishment of a public school system was one of the most important developments in the colonial history of the Philippines. During the Spanish regime, only rich Filipinos were able to send their children to school. With the creation of the public school system, almost all Filipinos could go to school, and literacy rates dramatically increased. From 1899 to 1900 there were about a hundred thousand children enrolled in primary school. The Department of Public Instruction, created in December 1901, was established to help set up schools in the Philippines and to train future teachers. Filipinos were also sent to the United States for training to augment the small number of American teachers in the Philippines.

Health

An important impact of American colonialism was the improved health conditions. The Americans established public hospitals (around 138 by 1935, aside from private and army hospitals) and leprosaria to help Filipinos fight epidemics such as cholera and smallpox and diseases such as beriberi, tuberculosis, malaria, leprosy, and dysentery. Health education was also introduced in public schools. The improvements in health can be attested to by the decrease in death rates from 30.50 percent in 1898 to 20.94 percent in 1915. It should also be noted that birth rates decreased from 47.60 percent in 1898 to 38.61 percent in 1915 (Agoncillo and Alfonso 1960).

The position of women in society also improved during the time of the Americans. Women were given the right of suffrage and the right to seek public office. They were encouraged to go to college, taught to participate in family and community affairs, and admitted into government service.

Economy and Agriculture

During the Spanish era, Spain claimed all lands of the Philippines as belonging to the king under the Regalian Doctrine of Ownership. This same doctrine was used by the Americans to claim ownership over the Philippines. Only lands that had proper documentation from the Spanish colonial government were honored as being privately owned.

This doctrine justified the American claim of over 90 percent of Philippine lands (Lynch 1983). This policy continued to displace indigenous Filipinos, who before the coming of the Spaniards were the "communal owners" of the land.

Private lands were determined through the Land Registration Act of 1902 and all unregistered lands were declared public lands according to the Public Land Act of 1905. The Cadastral Act of 1907 facilitated land titling.

The Americans established the Bureau of Agriculture in 1902 to guide the development of agriculture in the Philippines. In 1903, cultivated lands covered more than a million hectares; this amount doubled in 1918 and increased to more than four million hectares in 1935.

In a report submitted to the president of the United States in 1900, it was mentioned that the Philippines was rich in mineral resources; however, the Spaniards failed to exploit these resources to their full potential. Therefore, it was the task of the new colonial powers to explore the potential of these resources (Philippine Commission 1900). The New Mining Law of 1905 allowed for the free and open exploitation of Philippine mineral resources.

Trade

Trade also flourished during the American colonial period. In 1909, the Payne-Aldich Tariff Act provided for limited free trade with the U.S. By 1929, Philippine trade with the United States was PhP 623,214,234 ($1 = 2 PhP) compared to its world trade of PhP 68,079,136 in 1898—a more than 800 percent increase. Industries such as sugar mills, coconut oil mills, textile factories, distilleries, mining, and rope manufacturing were also established.

The Philippine Commonwealth (1935–1946)

The Tydings-McDuffie Law of 1934 established the Philippine Commonwealth in 1935 and set Philippine independence for ten years later. It also called for a constitutional convention, drafting of the constitution, and the ratification and election of officers. The act also set the duty-free quota of specific Philippine products and limited

Filipino immigration to the United States during the Commonwealth period. It also subjected Philippine products to full rates of U.S. tariffs after independence (Agoncillo 1968). The act allowed Americans to use the Philippines as a refueling station until the end of the Philippine Commonwealth (Simbulan 1989).

The government faced problems of political and economic instability. The problem of stability is also associated with the evolution of a new nation. Difficulties with national defense, civil service, and the establishment of a popular government specifically haunted the commonwealth.

Economic Development During the American Era

Economic development during the American era can be summarized as artificial and extractive. The growth especially in foreign trade that was experienced by the Philippines during this time was a result of the free-trade agreement between the Philippines and the United States. Philippine total exports in 1938 were 231,590,554 PhP; out of these exports, 178,889,989 PhP landed in the United States (Dept. of Agriculture and Commerce 1939). Philippine products could compete very well with products from other countries because of the Philippines' favored relationship with the United States. Products such as tobacco and sugar could enter the United States without tariffs or quotas. Because of this favored relationship, other foreign markets were not explored. Products demanded by the American market were the only ones produced and manufactured in the Philippines. Thus, the Philippine market became dependent on the United States.

The Philippine market focused on the production of raw materials coming from the rich natural resources of the country. The top ten exports of the Philippines were cash crops and minerals. Manufacturing industries such as drugs, steel, or finished products were neglected, as these products could be imported cheaply from the United States.

Although the Philippines had a flourishing foreign trade, domestic trade was still slow and controlled by foreigners. During the Commonwealth era, 50 percent of domestic trade was owned by Chinese, 20 percent by the Japanese, 5 percent by other foreigners, and only 25 percent by Filipinos (Agoncillo and Alfonso 1960).

Postwar, Pre–Martial Law Development
The Roxas Administration, 1946–48

At the end of World War II, reconstruction and rehabilitation became serious concerns. Manila was one of the war's most devastated cities next to Warsaw, with 10 percent of its buildings totally destroyed and another 15 percent partially destroyed. Agricultural activities were greatly hampered when animals used in plowing the fields were killed as a result of war. Industries were also destroyed. Currency became scarce, and Japanese money used during the occupation became worthless. Educational systems had to be revised in order to respond to the changing times.

The Philippine Trade Relations Act, known as the Bell Trade Act, was approved in 1946 to define a new free trade relationship between the Philippines and the United States. From January 1, 1946, to July 3, 1954, Philippine exports such as sugar, tobacco, and coconut oil were not subject to tariffs provided these goods did not exceed the quotas set by the United States. The act also stipulated that preferences for Philippine products would be gradually removed after 1954, and duties would be imposed at a rate of 5 percent annually until 100 percent duty was reached by 1973.

The Bell Trade Act required that Americans be provided with "parity rights." This meant that Americans had equal rights with Filipinos to exploit the natural resources of the Philippines. The granting of parity rights required the amendment of the 1935 Philippine Constitution (Constantino 1966, 1972; Agoncillo and Alfonso 1960).

The Bell Trade Act was further tied with the Treaty of General Relations passed by the American Congress on July 4, 1946. It called for American surrender of sovereign rights to the Philippine Republic except for the military bases. The act also required the Philippines to assume debts and obligations incurred under the colonial rule and honor the terms of the Treaty of Paris. It also stipulated that no war repatriation in excess of $500 should be paid to the Philippines unless the "parity rights" were approved.

During this period, the Philippines banked on a program of increased production that also meant to improve agriculture. Upon the recommendation of the Philippines-U.S. Agricultural Mission of 1946, mechanization was implemented. Only partial mechanization was implemented for fear that full mechanization would disenfranchise many farm workers (Agoncillo 1968).

The Rehabilitation Finance Corporation (RFC now the Development Bank of the Philippines) was also set up to assist individuals and private corporations start businesses after the war.

Another important development in this era was the signing of the RP-U.S. Military Bases Agreement and the U.S. Military Assistance Agreement on March 14 and 21, 1947, respectively. The latter was responsible for the development of the Philippine military including training and provision of supplies and equipment.

While the United States "loosened" its direct political control by granting the Philippines independence, the postcolonial treaty defined the Filipino-American relationship with strong U.S. military presence. The economic grip of the United States in the Philippines continued, reinforced by political treaties. The Philippine economy remained agrarian and "industrial development" was related solely to the extraction of natural resources. Economically, the Philippines was still in the hands of the Americans—thus, the transformation of the country from a colony to a neo-colony.

The Quirino Administration, 1948–53

The sudden death of Roxas brought Quirino to the presidency. The program of Quirino can be summed up as a restoration of peace, order, and confidence in the government.

This period was characterized by peasant unrest, a result of centuries of discontent and oppression. Peasant uprisings were prominent in Central Luzon. Quirino attempted to make peace with the rebels, but succeeded in negotiating only a few months' cessation of hostilities.

The continuing hostilities left scores of civilians caught in the crossfire, so the government created a body to attend to their needs. The administration also bought land and resold it to farmers at easy terms to encourage them to own land. Inflation also hit the country during this period and became the basis of raising the minimum wage, except for agricultural wages. The program of the Quirino administration did not significantly change the character of the Philippine agrarian economy.

One important policy that has shaped the Philippines' current relationship with the United States is the Mutual Defense Treaty signed on August 30, 1951. This treaty stipulates that each party would act to "meet the common dangers in accordance with its constitutional process."

Magsaysay, 1953–57

Magsaysay's program was centered on the security of the "common man" or *tao*. His administration is still remembered today for putting down the Huk (peasant) rebellion. Magasaysay banked on a program of rural improvement to address peasant unrest. A Land Tenure Reform Law was enacted, whereby the government pledged to buy large land estates and resell the land to tenants. Roads and bridges were constructed and credit-support programs for farmers were established. Water systems in towns and barrios were also built. Mobile health units were sent to the barrios to provide free medical services. Campaigns against malaria as well as educational programs to educate Filipinos about malaria were implemented.

The Social Security System Act of 1957 was also passed to provide security for employees and workers in case of death, accident, or illness through compensation packages. Efforts were made to reform the educational system toward scientific and economic advancement.

On December 15, 1954, the Laurel-Lanley Agreement was signed. This provided for the increase of Philippine duties on American goods and the decrease of American duties on imported goods from the Philippines. Despite the popularity of Magsaysay's social programs, the country's economic structure did not really change.

Garcia, 1957–61

The death of Magsaysay paved the way for Garcia's ascendancy. Garcia's best-known endeavor was the

"Filipino First" policy. This represented a protectionist move to spur the growth of small Filipino businesses (Constantino and Constantino 1978).

Another significant contribution of Garcia was the approval of the establishment of the International Rice Research Institute (IRRI) in 1960 through funds provided by the Ford and Rockefeller Foundations. IRRI was supposed to increase the rice production of the Philippines, which it did; however, some critics have claimed that the establishment of IRRI has simply brought commercial interests and input-intensive agriculture to the countryside (Escala 1993).

Macapagal, 1961–64

The Macapagal administration was quick to deregulate trade, reversing the partial protectionism of the Garcia administration. This decontrol policy had detrimental effects on the neo-colonial situation of the Philippines.

Another policy of Macapagal for the improvement of the plight of poor Filipinos was land reform. His critics felt that Macapagal was too slow and too timid to implement a full-scale land reform program in the Philippines, and he eventually lost the trust of the poor, as their dreams of genuine reform were not met (Macapagal 1968).

Development during the years between World War II and martial law can be characterized as rebuilding and adjustment amid the newly gained independence of the country. During the first few years after independence, the Philippine government focused its attention on rebuilding the institutions and buildings that were destroyed during the war. This was also a time of unrest especially for the peasants who demanded to have their own lands to till.

Independence meant that the Philippines lost its most favored nation status with the United States. This meant that the country's exports to the United States were subjected to tariffs and quotas. This was a huge blow to the country's foreign trade, since it lost a large chunk of its export market. Being dependent on the American market for such a long time, the country was unable to find a new market for its surplus products. At the same time, the Philippines was unable to compete or find a niche for itself in the world market. Industries under the colonial era had not been developed to maximize efficiency or minimize imports of raw industrial goods. Domestic trade remained in the hands of foreigners, and this situation was aggravated by the passage of the parity rights agreement between the United States and the Philippines (Agoncillo and Alfonso 1960).

Almost all presidents during the era before martial law had programs to address the peasant problem or the land reform question. However, they were unable to implement genuine agrarian reform. By the end of Macapagal's term, demand for land was still a big problem in the Philippines (Macapagal 1968).

Likewise, development during the period before martial law was not continuous. Each president had a different program or priority. No matter how good the previous development plans were, there was no guarantee that the next president would continue or follow up on that policy. Every Philippine president wanted to be remembered for his policy and not as someone who followed the previous president's policies.

The Marcos Years, 1965–86

The infamous Ferdinand Marcos ran for president on a platform that included an array of populist concerns, including land reform, wage increases, and trade protectionism. He was elected in 1965 and used payoffs and threats to win again in 1969 (Guillermo and Guillermo-Almirante 1999). Faced with increasing popular discontent, sparked largely by worsening economic conditions—and a failure to implement his campaign platform—Marcos declared martial law in September 1972. The subsequent fourteen years were a dark period for the Philippines in terms of poor economic conditions, human rights violations, and environmental destruction. Far from sanctioning Marcos for his abusive policies, however, international lending institutions continued to heap loans upon the administration, and by 1976 the Philippines was one of the World Bank's top ten loan recipients (Broad 1988).

Under the guise of promoting Philippine agricultural self-sufficiency, Marcos gained political patronage by artificially supporting collapsing crop markets, such as the sugarcane industry (Lopez-Gonzaga 1994). Throughout his tenure, Marcos gradually relaxed trade restrictions, especially in the industrial sector, but he was not moving fast enough for the World Bank, which imposed a structural adjustment loan on the country in 1980 (Broad 1988). During Marcos's presidency, the most heavily protected agricultural product was sugar, a capital-intensive crop grown primarily by large landowners, some of whom were Marcos's political allies (David 2003; Lopez-Gonzaga 1987). It could be argued, therefore, that Marcos's agricultural protectionism policy was not friendly to the poor.

Neither was industrial trade liberalization. The establishment of export processing zones (EPZs) accelerated during the Marcos years, bringing more foreign investment to selected tax-exempt areas mostly located near Manila and the U.S. military bases. The growth in the materials manufacturing sector during the 1980s was in value-added products made from semiprocessed materials such as cloth, metal, and semiconductor chips (Broad and Cavanagh 1993). As a result, net flows of foreign direct investment have remained low in the Philippines, and were even negative in 1980—although the country was exporting more goods, it had to pay for the semiprocessed materials to make them (figure 10.7). This value-added process also had a negative impact on the trade balance and prevented the development of backward linkages that might have promoted the growth of native Philippine industries, already crippled by the competitive advantages of Marcos cronies. Economists have since questioned the long-term sustainability of EPZs, which at the time were highly touted by the World Bank (Hill 2003). To lure foreign companies to the EPZs, the Philippine government eliminated the minimum wage and forbade strikes and unionizing in these areas, ensuring the exploitation of poor urban workers (Broad and Cavanagh 1993).

Deforestation trends (figure 10.8) continued under Marcos, who provided a variation on the old logging theme by granting timber concessions for purposes of political patronage. Corruption was

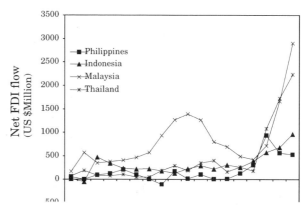

Figure 10.7. Net FDI flow in selected Southeast Asian countries, 1973–90. Source: Mercado-Aldaba (1994).

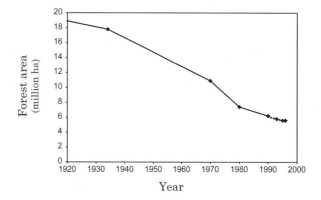

Figure 10.8 Forest area in the Philippines (million hectares), 1920–2000.

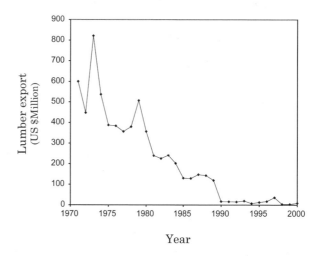

Figure 10.9. Lumber exports (in US$ millions), 1970–2000.

rampant in the forest industry. Despite this, the World Bank 1976 country report on the Philippines recommended increased lumbering as a means of generating foreign exchange (Cheetham 1976). The graph of Philippine timber exports over time clearly shows that this was not a sustainable strategy (figure 10.9). Meanwhile, continued incursion of roads into the forested uplands—for purposes of military containment as well as infrastructure development—encouraged the landless poor to settle and clear the land (Bello et al. 1982).

Free Trade: Good for What Ails You?

In February 1986, Ferdinand Marcos was ousted from his totalitarian presidency by a diverse popular coalition that included businesspeople and politicians, the Catholic Church, and members of the radical left. The economy was in shambles and burdened with enormous debt. Private lenders and the World Bank had been willing, even eager, to lend money to the Marcos regime during the economic boom of the 1970s. However, when the oil price shocks hit the global economy in the later years of that decade, the foreign capital pouring into the Philippines could no longer cover the substantial economic losses incurred partly through the corruption and cronyism of the political elite and partly through the country's export-oriented strategy. In 1984 the IMF (in collaboration with the World Bank) imposed a process of structural adjustments on the economy in a desperate attempt to placate foreign lenders, who were becoming uneasy with the economic downturn and growing political unrest caused by the assassination of a major opposition leader, Benigno Aquino. This induced a severe recession and arguably paved the way for the success of the People Power revolt against Marcos (de Dios and Hutchcroft 2003).

Corazon Aquino, Benigno Aquino's widow, took over the presidency and immediately found herself torn between the populist demands of the coalition that swept her to power and the clamoring of the international debtors who wanted their money repaid. In possibly the most significant decision of her presidency, Aquino decided to take on the Marcos regime's debt completely and unconditionally, in spite of the possibly fraudulent nature

of many of the debts acquired by her predecessor (de Dios and Hutchcroft 2003). This began the period of further liberalization of the Philippine economy under new negotiations between Aquino and the IMF, followed by negotiated reduction of interest rates on debts owed to other foreign creditors (Dohner 1989). In return for these concessions, Aquino pledged her assistance in advancing the main goals of the neoliberal economic agenda, ostensibly to open up the country to the full benefits of the global marketplace and to induce economic growth. The most important of these goals concerned the relaxation of trade barriers and the provision of incentives to foreign investment, policies that have continued through the current presidency of Gloria Macapagal-Arroyo, daughter of former president Diosdado Macapagal. Although the success of free trade as a development strategy in the Philippines is far from obvious, no serious alternatives have yet been proposed. In fact, ASEAN (Association of Southeast Asian Nations, of which the Philippines is a member) is currently making a strong move toward further trade liberalization through discussions with China.

One concession made by Aquino to poor rural Filipinos was her agrarian reform program. Although Marcos put together an impressive reform agenda on paper during his regime, the implementation of the program was an almost complete failure. "Land to the tiller" became a rallying cry of the Aquino administration, and she proposed a phased process of turning sharecroppers into leaseholders, encouraging "voluntary" land sharing, and redistributing large landholdings. The program contained many loopholes, and wealthy landowners were often able to use their political leverage to back out of redistribution requirements. In addition, some analysts have observed that the upper limit for exemption from the plan was five hectares, larger than that of successful land reform programs in Japan and South Korea (Griffin 2001). Today, the program still has many critics, and it has been more successful in some areas (such as central Luzon) than others (such as the highly class-stratified island of Negros). Obstacles to land reform implementation currently include inadequate funding for the program, rapid turnover and lukewarm commitment of the DAR (Department of Agrarian Reform) secretary, bureaucratic corruption, and the wielding of political, economic, and military force by wealthy landowners (Riedinger 1995).

Toward Sustainability? Natural Resources and Development in the Philippines

The ecological economist Herman Daly coined the term "strong sustainability" to indicate the essential contribution that natural resources make to economic production (Daly 1995). Although functions commonly used by economists to describe production take natural resources, labor, and capital investment to be substitutes, ecologists do not believe that this is the case. They point out that no amount of money or current technology, for example, can provide certain functions that tropical forests provide for free, including the protection of upland soil systems, the preservation of biodiversity, localized climate control, and cultural and aesthetic functions.

The Philippines is an agricultural economy, meaning that currently the production and processing of agricultural products, including the manufacturing of agricultural inputs and processed foods, account for 40 percent of GDP and two-thirds of the country's labor force (David 2003). The protection of the Philippines' natural resource base is therefore essential for the long-term sustainability and growth of the country's economy, or at least for the maintenance of its poorest citizens' livelihood. Yet current practices continue the colonial institutions that have degraded these resources. The monopoly of political power in the hands of the landed elite impedes the ability of government and NGOs to stop corruption and the exploitation of loopholes in environmental law (Broad and Cavanagh 1993). This is a direct consequence of the Spanish land consolidation process, and the hierarchical class structure that was promoted and exploited by the United States to gain control over the economy during colonization, as mentioned earlier.

Environmentalists have long been leery of unrestricted free trade, in part because of concerns that inviting multinational corporations into a developing country with a weak regulatory structure leads to uncontrolled pollution and the destruction of natural resources (Daly 1993). In fact, scaling back expenditures on public services such as environmental regulation and enforcement is part of the IMF's structural adjustment policy that accompanies trade liberalization. Legislation such as the Philippine Mining Act of 1995 has been roundly criticized by environmentalists for its nearly unlimited granting of timbering rights to mining corporations and lack of specific protocol for containing and managing toxic waste tailings ponds (CBCP 1998). Although some nongovernmental organizations are doing an admirable job of addressing these issues in their local contexts, they have been less successful in challenging the policies that are at the root of the problem.

The industrialization of agriculture that began in the Philippines with the promotion of export crops during the Spanish era also has environmental consequences. As the Philippines has entered the global agricultural economy, the land planted in subsistence crops (mostly corn and rice) has been declining, while land planted in export crops like fruits, tobacco, and coconut has risen. This has happened to the greatest extent in Mindanao, where multinational corporations like Dole and Del Monte have established enormous banana and pineapple plantations (Feranil 1998). Fruit trees are less erosive than grain crops, and this shift in cropping practices may help conserve soil (Coxhead 2000). However, with the exception of coconut, export crops require much more intensive fertilizer application than rice and corn (table 10.2). A 1990 report issued by the International Fertilizer Development Center indicates that in the Philippines sugarcane, an export crop, is over-fertilized, while maize, a subsistence crop, is under-fertilized (Martinez 1990). Intensive fertilizer use has been linked to groundwater contamination and increased soil acidity, more examples of environmental externalities that do not enter the economic analysis when the viability of industrialized agriculture is examined. Large monoculture plantations also require pesticide and herbicide inputs to protect them from infestations, and these chemicals have detrimental effects on the environment, not to mention the health of the workers who apply them (Naylor 1994).

Table 10.2. Fertilizer application by crop, 2001

Commodity	Area (000 ha.)	Area fertilized (%)	N Rate (kg/ha)	P₂O₅	K₂O
Coconut	3,077	30	20	15	10
Coffee	137	40	75	35	40
Fruits	943	50	75	35	40
Maize	2,507	80	58	16	10
Oil Palm	15	80	75	25	70
Rice	4,037	85	51	15	11
Sugarcane	375	80	85	55	30
Tobacco	44	80	75	20	55
Vegetables	560	60	85	25	50

Source: FAO

Since the green revolution in the 1960s, the Philippines has been pursuing an input-intensive agricultural strategy that is dependent on imported energy. This is evident when one examines fertilizer use trends, which have been growing nearly exponentially in the last several decades. Ecologists and some economists are concerned about the sustainability of agricultural systems that require ever-increasing amounts of nonrenewable energy to maintain their viability (Hall et al. 2000; Chapman and Barker 1991). Yield per kilogram of fertilizer added has been declining in the Philippines since the green revolution, indicating the inability of fertilizer to make up for increasingly nutrient-depleted and eroded soil (figure 10.10). In the late 1970s, the Philippines' debt ballooned at least partly as a result of OPEC-induced petroleum price fluctuations (de Dios and Hutchcroft 2003). If the price of oil were to rise significantly, as many experts predict it will, the country's agricultural production and economic stability would be endangered.

When all of the external costs of export-oriented agriculture are considered, the economic benefits of adopting it as a strategy lessen significantly, and may even be negative—if "export-oriented agriculture" in the Philippine context continues to mean, as it has historically, large-scale, chemically intensive operations. The GATT and other trade liberalization policies create a climate favorable

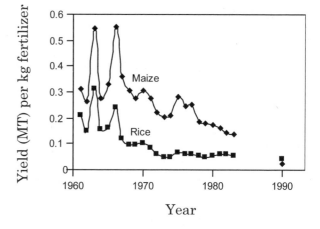

Figure 10.10. Rice and maize yields (MT) per kg fertilizer input, 1960–90.

to exporters and detrimental to farms producing crops for local markets (Guzman 2000). In many areas of the Philippines, those who grow export crops tend to be large-scale farmers, and those who grow locally consumed crops tend to be small-scale farmers (NSO 1991). This is a relic of the colonial land tenure system, as described previously. Wealthy families have a centuries-long history of economic domination in the Philippines, which has given them access to the political influence necessary to prevent a more equitable distribution of their assets through land reform (Riedinger 1995). The colonial legacy, coupled with the current liberalization of agricultural

Table 10.3. Forest destruction by cause, 1980–94

Year	Total (ha)	Kaingin	Forest fire	Illegal logging	Pests and diseases	Other
1980	32,640	6,302	18,324	7,348	112	554
1981	24,605	5,826	12,471	6,108	200	
1982	16,654	3,286	8,063	4,954	351	
1983	121,326	2,241	117,951	1,015	119	
1984	4,895	1,137	3,177	478	6	97
1985	14,632	941	11,743	1,918	30	
1986	7,682	1,991	4,257	90	1,344	
1987	7,146	570	5,386	676	2	512
1988	10,255	2,914	423	4,474		2,444
1989	12,814	4,683	675	1,727	218	5,511
1991	7,233	759	5,872	72		530
1992	12,806	86	12,720			
1993	17,862	90	15,330			2,442
1994	10,342	1,529	7,720	107		986

Source: DENR Planning and Policy Service

trade, creates an economic structure that is detrimental to small, primarily poor, farmers, environmentally unsound, and unsustainable.

Recently, there has been significant discussion about reforestation in the Philippines. The Philippine Department of Environment and Natural Resources (DENR) has received more World Bank funds than any other government branch, and it is earmarking funds specifically for NGOs to establish community-based, participatory reforestation projects (Malayang 2000). These projects have had mixed success. Some have failed because of their authoritarian, top-down management style; others have run into trouble with corruption, a ubiquitous problem (Severino 2000). Deforestation proceeds in the Philippines, albeit at reduced rates, in spite of these programs (see figure 10.9). This is because semi-legal and sloppily enforced logging contracts issued by the government are the primary cause of deforestation (Tujan 2000). The Philippine government blames shifting agriculturalist ("Kaingin") for the continued destruction of the country's forest resources, but their own data do not bear out this conclusion (table 10.3). Programs therefore target poor upland communities in an attempt at reeducation, when perhaps the resources would be more effectively spent on the enforcement of logging restrictions.

What the history of Philippine development tells us is that the Philippines is at a disadvantage in terms of natural resource endowments as it struggles to enter the world economy. The deforested state of Philippine uplands causes landslides, flash floods, extensive erosion from agricultural fields, and sedimentation of rivers and coastal waters, the costs of which have yet to be quantified in either ecological or economic terms (Tujan 2000). Large landholdings planted in energy-intensive export crops continue to dominate the fertile lowlands, channeling the landless poor into the ecologically sensitive uplands. In addition, the biodiversity of the native forest and the potential for revenue from sustainable logging or harvesting of non-timber forest products has been destroyed in all but a few remote locations (Broad and Cavanagh 1993). The Filipino people are suffering from decreased agricultural productivity, economic damage from extreme weather events, and unquantifiable cultural and aesthetic losses from deforestation and skewed land distribution—because of decisions most Filipinos did not participate in making, and a colonial power structure that has survived to the present day.

Conclusion: The Past Lives

Novelist William Faulkner once said, "The past is not dead. It is not even past." This is a particularly apt summation of the influence that historical forces exert on the Philippines' present state of development. From the establishment of the Spanish encomienda system to the opening of the Philippine economy to the world market and the extractive and destructive nature of most income-generating projects in the country, the Philippines' past determines its present position in the world economy. Meanwhile the population continues to grow.

References

Agoncillo, T. A. 1966. *Philippine History*. Manila: Inang Wika.

———. 1990. *History of the Filipino People*. Quezon City: Garotech Publishing.

Agoncillo, T. A., and O. M. Alfonso. 1960. *A Short History of the Filipino People*. Quezon City: University of the Philippines Press.

Arcilla, J. S. 1971. *An Introduction to Philippine History*. Quezon City: Ateneo de Manila University Press.

Balisacan, A. M. 2003. Poverty and inequality. In Balisacan and Hill 2003, 311–41.

Balisacan, A. M., and H. Hill. 2003. *The Philippine Economy*. Quezon City: Ateneo de Manila University Press.

Bello, W., D. Kinley, and E. Elinson. 1982. *Development Debacle: The World Bank in the Philippines*. San Francisco: Institute for Food and Development Policy.

Beyer, H. O. 1947. Outline review of Philippine archeology by islands and provinces. *Philippine Journal of Science* 77 (July–August).

Broad, R. 1988. *Unequal Alliance: The World Bank, the International Monetary Fund, and the Philippines*. Berkeley: University of California Press.

Broad, R., and J. Cavanagh. 1993. *Plundering Paradise: The Struggle for the Environment in the Philippines*. Berkeley: University of California Press.

CBCP (Catholic Bishops Conference of the Philippines). 1998. Statement of Concern on the Mining Act of 1995.

Chapman, D., and R. Barker. 1991. Environmental protection, resource depletion, and the sustainability of developing country agriculture. *Economic Development and Cultural Change* 39, no. 4: 723–37.

Cheetham, R. J. 1976. *The Philippines: Priorities and Prospects for Development*. Washington, D.C: World Bank.

Collins, J. 1989. *Philippines: Fire on the Rim*. San Francisco: Food First.

Constantino, R. 1966. *The Making of a Filipino: A Story of Philippine Colonial Politics*. Quezon City: Malaya Books.

———. 1972. *The Filipinos in the Philippines and Other Essays by Renato Constantino*. Quezon City: Malaya Books.

Constantino, R., and L. R. Constantino. 1978. *The Philippines: A Continuing Past*. Quezon City: Foundation for Nationalist Studies.

Coxhead, I. 2000. Consequences of a food security strategy for economic welfare, income distribution and land degradation: The Philippine case. *World Development* 28, no. 1: 111–28.

Daly, H. E. 1993. The perils of free trade. *Scientific American*, November 1993, 50–57.

———. 1995. On Wilfred Beckerman's critique of sustainable development. *Environmental Values* 4:49–55.

David, C. C. 2003. Agriculture. In Balisacan and Hill 2003, 175–218.

De Dios, E. S., and P. D. Hutchcroft. 2003. Political economy. In Balisacan and Hill 2003, 45–73.

Department of Agriculture. 1939. *Facts and Figures About the Philippines*. Manila: Bureau of Printing.

Dohner, R. S. 1989. *Philippine External Debt: Burdens, Possibilities and Prospects*. New York: Asia Society.

Escala, S., Jr. 1993. Dilemmas and debacles: Analysis of Philippine upland underdevelopment. M.S. thesis, State University of New York.

Feranil, S., Jr. 1998. *The Philippine Banana Industry: Confronting the Challenge of Agrarian Reform*. Quezon City: Philippine Peasant Institute.

Filipinia Book Guild. 1965. *The Colonization and Conquest of the Philippines by Spain*. Manila: Filipinia Book Guild.

Geertz, C. 1963. *Agricultural Involution: The Processes of Ecological Change in Indonesia*. Berkeley: University of California Press.

Gowdy, J. M., and S. O'Hara. 1995. *Economic Theory for Environmentalists*. Delray Beach, Fla.: St. Lucie Press.

Griffin, K. 2001. Poverty and land distribution: Cases of land reform in Asia. In H. R. Morales Jr., J. Putzel, F. Lara Jr., E. Quitoriano, and A. Miclat-Teves, eds., *Power in the Village: Agrarian Reform, Rural Politics, Institutional Change and Globalization*, 17–38. Quezon City: University of the Philippines Press.

Guillermo, R., and S. Guillermo-Almirante. 1999. *Philippine History and Government*. Manila: IBON Foundation.

Guzman, R. B. 2000. The GATT agreement on agriculture: Final blow to Philippine farms? In A. Tujan Jr., ed., *The Impact of the WTO Agreement on Agriculture*, 27–64. Manila: IBON Foundation.

Hall, C. A. S., J. Vargas, O. Saenz, W. Ravenscroft, and J. Ko. 2000. Data on sustainability in Costa Rica: Time series analysis of population, land use, economics, energy and efficiency. In C. A. S. Hall, ed., *Quantifying Sustainable Development: The Future of Tropical Economies*, 91–120. San Diego: Academic Press.

Herrin, A. N., and E. M. Pernia. 2003. Population, human resources and employment. In Balisacan and Hill 2003, 283–310.

Hill, H. 2003. Industry. In Balisacan and Hill 2003, 219–53.

Jocano, F. L. 1967. Beyer's theory on Filipino prehistory and culture: An alternative approach to the problem. In Zamora 1967, 128–50.

———. 1975. *Question and Challenges in Philippine Prehistory*. Quezon City: University of the Philippines Press.

Karnow, S. 1989. *In Our Image: America's Empire in the Philippines*. New York: Random House.

Lopez-Gonzaga, V. B. 1987. *Capital Expansion, Frontier Development and the Rise of Monocrop Economy in Negros (1850–1898)*. Bacolod, Philippines: SRC-Negrense Studies Program.

———. 1994. *Land of Hope, Land of Want: A Socioeconomic History of Negros (1571–1985)*. Quezon City: Philippine National Historical Society.

Macapagal, D. 1968. *A Stone for the Edifice: Memoirs of a President*. Quezon City: MAC Publishing House.

Malayang, Ben S., III. 2000. The changing role of government in forest protection. In Utting 2000, 40–66.

Martinez, A. 1990. *Fertilizer Use Statistics and Crop Yields*. Muscle Shoals, Ala.: International Fertilizer Development Center.

Mercado-Aldaba, R. A. 1994. *Foreign Direct Investment in the Philippines: A Reassessment*. Manila: Philippine Institute for Development Studies.

Naylor, R. 1994. Herbicide use in Asian rice production. *World Development* 22, no. 1: 55–70.

NSO (National Statistics Office, Republic of the Philippines). 1991. Census of Agriculture Final Report. Manila: RPNSO.

Philippine Commission. 1900. Report of the Philippine Commission. Washington, D.C.: U.S. Government Printing Office.

Riedinger, J. M. 1995. *Agrarian Reform in the Philippines: Democratic Transition and Redistributive Reform*. Stanford, Calif.: Stanford University Press.

Salcedo, J. 1967. H. Otley Beyer: Anthropology and the Philippines. In Zamora 1967, 1–6.

Schirmer, D. B., and S. R. Shalom, eds. 1987. *The Philippines Reader: A History of Colonialism, Neocolonialism, Dictatorship, and Resistance*. Quezon City: Ken.

Scott, W. H. 1984. *Prehispanic Source Materials for the Study of Philippine History*. Quezon City: New Day Publishers.

Severino, H. G. 2000. The role of local stakeholders in forest protection. In Utting 2000, 84–116.

Stiglitz, J. E. 2002. *Globalization and Its Discontents*. New York: Norton.

Tujan, A., Jr., ed. 2000. *The State of the Philippine Environment*. Manila: IBON Foundation.

Utting, P., ed. 2000. *Forest Policy and Politics in the Philippines: The Dynamics of Participatory Conservation*. Quezon City: Ateneo de Manila University Press.

Vitug, M. D., and G. M. Gloria. 2000. *Under the Crescent Moon: Rebellion in Mindanao*. Quezon City: Ateneo Center for Social Policy & Public Affairs.

Zamora, M. D., ed. 1967. *Studies in Philippine Anthropology*. Quezon City: Phoenix Press.

CHAPTER 11

IS THE ARGENTINE NATIONAL ECONOMY BEING DESTROYED BY THE DEPARTMENT OF ECONOMICS OF THE UNIVERSITY OF CHICAGO?

CHARLES A. S. HALL, PABLO DANIEL MATOSSIAN, CLAUDIO GHERSA,

JORGE CALVO, AND CLARA OLMEDO

Introduction

Neoclassical economics (NCE), also known as free market economics, monetarism, or neoliberalism, has become the dominant social paradigm for the world's economies. In many cases its economic premises are presented as national political goals; for example, U.S. President Bill Clinton spent considerable time unabashedly selling the virtues of neoclassical economics to the rest of the world.

In the United States, "liberal" means mostly socially liberal, vaguely leftish. In Europe and Argentina "liberal" means "liberal mercantilism," or free market and vaguely rightist, deriving its meaning from earlier times when "liberal" meant the interests of the mercantile class versus those of the king, who may have had much less interest in a large amount of trade beyond the borders of his country. The concepts associated with the second definition of liberal have existed for many decades or centuries and were of interest to Ricardo and other early economists. They have been formalized and codified especially by the economics department of the University of Chicago under the leadership and influence of Milton Friedman. Curiously, the term liberal has not been especially associated with the relatively pro-business Republican Party. Such questions about economic policy are important for determining, among other things, the allocation of energy and environmental resources, since all economic decisions are ultimately manifest in how and to what degree resources are exploited and who incurs the benefits and costs of such policies.

Increasingly, free marketism and, more generally, neoclassical economics have become the dominant economic guideline for the Latin American developing world. There are a number of reasons for this: (1) the unresolved economic problems associated with other economic systems; (2) the "fall" of communism, the only perceived real alternative to capitalism that was available to most of the world; (3) the role model, encouragement, and apparent economic success of the United States, which claimed, and appeared to some to be, the successful embodiment of the neoclassical model; and (4) the intervention of the IMF, World Bank, USAID, and other powerful economic actors that were extremely strong advocates of NCE (often for their own ends), and who gained strong bargaining power for intervention in Latin American economies because of the debts of many nations. In effect, the options given for many countries were either to go into default, with serious repercussion on economies increasingly dependent upon international trade, or to become subject to "structural adjustment." This meant essentially to relinquish governmental control and influence over large sectors of the economy and turn the workings of the economy over to private enterprise, neoclassical economics, and the marketplace, whatever that meant. Whether the main motivating factor for the IMF and World Bank to promote NCE was that they genuinely thought this would improve the economies so affected or whether it was a means of increasing the probability of their getting back the money owed to them is a matter of conjecture. Probably both are true.

The degree to which neoclassical economics and neoliberal policies did or did not improve the economies of the countries to which they were applied and indeed even met their own objectives is rather controversial and subject to whoever is doing the analysis. For example, Friedman and Friedman (1980), Bhagwati (1993), and the International Monetary Fund (1999) have unequivocally proclaimed that the NCE policies would be or were effective and that the countries that did march to the NCE drummer would recover from whatever their economic ills were, while those that did not would not (see also the review in David, Dirven, and Vogelgesang 2000). "Stabilization and structural adjustment programs contribute to debt reduction by helping to reduce deficits in the government budget and the balance of payments, to contain inflation, to stimulate savings, and to generate more resources for investment and debt service" (Gillis et al. 1996:417).

Most of the pronouncements of the virtues of NCE appear to come from neoclassical economists, the agencies that employ NCE, or occasionally from government agencies associated with governments that are enamored with NCE. The assessments from other sources are less likely to be positive and are often bitterly negative. For example, Collins and Lear (1995) argue in "Chile's economic miracle: a second look" that it is only through a very selected use of the national statistics that Chile appears to have benefited from NCE-based structural adjustment policies. They also report that if the entire time span during which Chile was subject to structural adjustment is taken into account, the economy not only performed very poorly by any reasonable criteria but workers also lost much more relative to the wealthy elite, as well as many of their hard-won rights. In the authors' view, structural adjustment was a disaster for most Chileans. Gray (1998) gives a similar and powerful assessment of the effects of neoliberal policies for England, Mexico, and New Zealand, focusing on social impacts and the loss of those governments' ability to govern. David, Dirven, and Vogelgesang (2000) examined the behavior of Latin American agriculture in response to liberal economic policies and found relatively few positive and many

negative consequences. Montanye (1998) found that structural adjustment policies imposed upon Costa Rica met few of their own objectives while generating many additional social and environmental problems. Kroeger and Montanye (2000) and Hall (2000) examined the effects of structural adjustments in Costa Rica and found many adverse aspects not well represented in most of the agency reports about structural adjustment. In their view, structural adjustment tended to deal with the symptoms of Costa Rica's economic problems and not the root problems of relentlessly increasing population, external debt, land degradation, and dependence upon foreign industrial products that were very sensitive to the price of oil.

We believe that it is a legitimate scientific concern to attempt to apply the scientific method to determining to what degree structural adjustment policies do or do not meet their own objectives while also examining quantitatively other effects and impacts, positive or negative. Given the very strong sentiments, often negative, expressed by many Argentines (and other Latin Americans) about structural adjustment we believe it important to move the discussion of these issues into the arena of relatively objective, quantitative assessment. Our model for such analyses is Montanye (1998), which develops a methodology for examining explicitly whether the objectives of structural adjustment were met. Montanye set up the objectives as a series of hypotheses and then tested whether they occurred. We present the IMF structural adjustment program for Argentina (such as we can find it) here; we view the objectives or expected outcomes of the plan (given in parentheses) as testable hypotheses.

1. Monetary reform, through the convertibility law, subsequently supplemented by the new charter of the Central Bank (would stabilize the currency by reducing inflation).
2. Fiscal reform, initially through a sharp improvement in the administration of the tax system and a redefinition of the tax system and later through a redefinition of tax instruments and rate (would shift the tax burden away from businesses, especially

those concerned with imports and exports, to encourage international trade).

3. Public sector reform, through debt restructuring, civil service reform, fiscal restructuring, and an "ambitious and successful plan of divestiture and deregulation of factor and product markets" (would reduce government expenditures and enterprise ownership, while the newly privatized companies improved efficiency of services and generated tax revenues).

4. Social security reform, allowing for a new capitalization mechanism operated by the private sector (would shift the pension system to the private sector).

5. Trade reform (would eliminate export taxes and most quantitative restrictions on imports, and reduce the level and range of import tariffs).

These actions collectively were expected to generate a stable economic climate, friendly to international trade, that would increase over-all economic welfare by increasing foreign investments and hence business activities and GNP, while increasing the efficiency of the delivery of services and reduce international debt.

A Brief Economic History of Modern Argentina

Argentina has been traditionally among the world's relatively wealthy nations, and at the beginning of the twentieth century it was the wealthiest. Until about 1950 that wealth was generated principally through agriculture. The peak in wealth that occurred during a period between 1875 and 1930 was created through the export of grain and cattle under the cropping/grazing system that predominated in the vast Pampas region. The Pampas are extensive plains originally covered by grasslands with very fertile soils (mollisols) derived principally from windblown sediments (loess) from the Andes Mountains (Hall et al. 1992). How these grasslands were transformed into an agricultural mosaic from the arrival of the Europeans through the twentieth century is described in detail by several authors who cover a wide range of socioeconomic,

agronomic, and ecological aspects (Giberti 1961; Cortes Conde 1979; Solbrig 1997; Ghersa, Martínez-Ghersa, and León 1998). Hall et al. (1992) describe this transformation as having three phases: (1) The expansion of the area used for arable farming, approximately 1875–1935; (2) a phase of stagnation, 1935–52; and (3) a phase of increase of total production of grains, which persists until the present. An important fact about the Pampas, which constitutes about 90 percent of Argentine agricultural land, is that the majority is too sandy, poorly drained, or otherwise inappropriate for continuous agriculture (Solbrig 1997). Only about 12.4 percent is suitable for continuous crops and another 25 to 50 percent for agriculture rotated with livestock. At least 25 percent is not suitable at all for any agriculture (Solbrig 1997).

Phase 1, 1875–1915: Expansion and Wealth Based on Solar Energy Alone

At the beginning of this first phase, which followed the defeat and virtual elimination of the fierce Native American populations, the land was owned by relatively few individuals as a residue of the original Spanish colonialist approach of awarding land in huge units to those aligned with early governments. These landowners dictated developments in land use at their economic convenience, which differed across the region. In the northern portion of the Pampas, some of these landowners started to develop agricultural colonies and sold or rented to small agriculturalists. The Argentine government encouraged immigration from other countries, which landowners encouraged as well because the value of their land increased as colonization progressed. Both the colonies and tenant farms rented by large establishments expanded rapidly along with the area planted to crops such as wheat, linseed, and maize, which increased from 0.1 to 4.5 Mha between 1875 and 1900. Expansion continued until the 1930s, giving rise to a management system that Sabato (1980) describes as standing on three legs: the grazing of cattle on alfalfa and other pastures, the growing of crops by tenant farmers, and the harvesting of the crops by migratory labor, which came over regularly from Europe to take part in the wheat and maize harvests.

The expansion of the railway system from less than 1,000 km in 1872 to over 27,000 km in 1910 also played an important role in the spread of cropping. World War I was an important factor in the determination of the end of this phase, due to the recall of laborers who were reservists in the Italian army. Although at the end of this period Argentina was a wealthy country, exports of the cropping and grazing system contributed mostly to the wealth of a relatively few urban Argentines, including the large landowners in particular, and the benefits to many of those laborers who played such an important role in generating this wealth were rather less obvious.

Phase 2, 1920–55: Exploiting Agriculture to Generate Industrial Infrastructure

With the start of the Great Depression and the associated contraction in world trade, prices for grain dropped to one-half of their pre-Depression values (Coscia 1983), and a government price-support scheme had to be introduced to mitigate the plight of the grain producers. Total area sown and yields responded little to the low prices (figure 11.1), possibly because of the lack of alternatives for the grain producer, so that the main effect was a cessation of the earlier growth of the area under cropping (Hall et al. 1992).

When World War II started, meat and wool once again offered better returns than grain. The situation of the tenant farmers who grew much of the grain became so desperate that in 1942 legislation was enacted reducing and freezing the rents paid by tenants and sharecroppers, and forbidding their eviction. (This law was replaced in 1967, although the changes in tenure continued during its twenty-five-year life span.) Although the tenant could now graze cattle on as much as 40 percent of the land under his control (Barsky and Murmis 1986), an important effect of this legislation was the effective suspension of the legume-based pasture cropping rotations for those parts of large holdings let to tenants. Previously alfalfa had improved nitrogen availability for crops and the physical characteristics of soils, allowing for better water storage and root crop development (Senigagliesi, Garcia, and Galetto 1984; Barberis et al. 1985; Maddonni

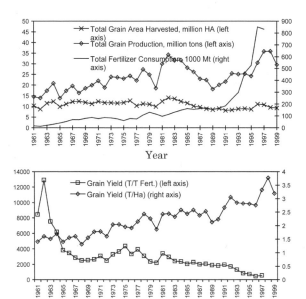

Figure 11.1. Time series data on Argentine grain. Top graph, area planted, total production, and total national fertilizer use. Bottom graph, efficiency as tons per ha and tons per ton fertilizer over time (assuming that 70 percent of fertilizer was used on grain).

et al. 1998). Subsequently, the suppression of the legume-based pasture cropping rotations appears to have had a negative effect on soil fertility.

In the early parts of the twentieth century, considerable wealth accumulated from the rich agriculture that was used to develop urban industries in order to substitute domestic products for expensive imports (Alexander 1995). Argentina became a highly industrialized nation, especially in the Frondizi administration of 1958–62, and developed sophisticated construction, automobile, machinery, and appliance industries. This industrial development and its relatively high wages encouraged both emigration from the Pampas and the drying up of sources of migratory labor from provinces outside the Pampas, which gradually had replaced European with native Argentine migratory labor. This dramatic reduction in available labor led to increasing difficulties at harvest time because of the undercapitalized and undermechanized production systems.

Government policies toward agriculture in the postwar years also accentuated agricultural stagnation. Government monopolization of grain exports kept costs to the producer low, and little foreign exchange was available for the import of agricultural machinery. Both policies had the effect of delaying mechanization relative to the industrial world. An additional burden was the restriction on the use of family labor during harvest time imposed by strong labor unions, which aggravated the harvest bottleneck. The lowest agricultural production was reached in the early 1950s when a combination of climatic events and excessive exports in relation to the harvest finally brought the problem to urban Argentina (Barsky and Murmis 1986). For the first time since the start of the wheat boom in 1875, the country had insufficient wheat to feed her population, and the army was called to help bring in the next harvest (Hall et al. 1992). This forced the government to change its policies toward agriculture. The rural crisis could no longer be ignored, grain prices were increased, and the national banking system allocated long-term credits that were particularly oriented for acquisition of machinery, including from the government-initiated domestic tractor industry.

Phase 3, 1955–2000: Industrialization and More Debt

It is difficult to derive a simple explanation for the enormously complex social, economic, and agronomic changes that occurred during this period because of the general lack of hard data and the complexity of the interrelations among them (Hall et al. 1992). Probably the most critical issue was the spread of tractors and combine harvesters, followed by an increase in their horsepower, both of which increased labor productivity enormously. Before mechanization, a two-hundred-hectare farm strained the resources of a large family, but subsequently one person could prepare the soil and plant more than eight hundred hectares with a large tractor (Coscia 1983). Combine harvesting and the bulk handling of grain reduced man-hours used per hectare fivefold to twelvefold (Coscia 1983). Inflated rural credit played a key role for machinery purchases and encouraging the cropping boom (Sabato 1980).

Coal imported from Europe was the principal source of industrial energy until World War II, when domestic natural gas, hydroelectric power, and domestic coal became important. Electrical energy supplies are now based on two large hydroelectric dams that supply more than 70 percent of Argentine consumption. Natural gas and nuclear plants supply the remainder. At present, and especially since 1991, Argentina is exporting oil, natural gas, and electric power to its neighbors Chile, Brazil, and Bolivia. The continuous development of Argentina's energy system increased the input for agriculture. Diesel fuel was taxed less than gasoline to provide relatively cheap fuel for agriculture and transport. Average horsepower of tractors sold has increased from 34 HP in 1950 to more than 100 in the 1980s (Huici 1986). The Pampas responded to mechanization with increased yields per hectare (figure 11.1) (Ghersa, Perelman, and di Bella 1997; Satorre and Slafer 1999). Fertilizer application was very restricted until the mid-1990s.

A downside to the mechanization and yield increase per hectare, especially in the last two decades, is thought to be a decrease in soil fertility (Ghersa and Martínez-Ghersa 1991; Vigglizzo and Roberto 1998). Whereas in the past a person with a horse could plow perhaps 30 ha in a day, this increased to 100 ha with an early tractor and 500 ha today. In the past land had to wait its turn to be plowed; today it is perhaps more accurate to say that a tractor is always awaiting more land. Because of this increased capacity, about 14 Mha of land is plowed each year and only 36 Mha is left for grazing, which affects the soil much less (Solbrig 1996). Large quantities of soil were lost from much of the Pampas during this period, often at more than 1 cm per year (i.e., 3 percent of 30 cm) (Casas 1998). Soil degradation caused by continued land use, including compaction, a particular problem with loess soil, reduced the capacity of the soil to produce maize to about 80 percent of earlier levels (Solbrig 1996; Maddonni et al. 1998). In addition, soy, an extremely erosive crop, was grown increasingly for export starting in about 1980. This high soil erosion rate and a decline in corn yield created an awareness of the problem among farmers, who have increasingly adopted the "zero tillage" system developed in the United States (de la Fuente et al. 1999). To illustrate the importance of this change, the area of land cropped in the Pampas has been roughly stable at about 14 Mha since 1920 (figure

11.1). In 1989–90 only 92,000 ha were sown using zero tillage, of which 87 percent was soybeans. By 1995–96 nearly 3 million ha were sown this way, about 20 percent of the cropped area of the Pampas, of which 72 percent was soybeans. Other crops such as maize and sunflowers also are planted increasingly using zero tillage (Solbrig 1996). In some areas where there is enough rain (about 300 mm) the percentage is as high as 50 percent (Solbrig 1996; Ghersa et al. 2000).

National and International Variables Affecting Cropping

At all times during the development of farming in the Pampas, virtually all the grain produced entered the cash economy. Export markets for agricultural produce have always been very influential in determining the partitioning of land use between grazing and cropping and the mix of grain produced. Roughly 50 percent of most grain crops are exported, although the proportion is higher for soy and for oilseeds. Argentina is at present a major contributor to world trade in many grain-related commodities (around 5 percent in wheat and soybeans and 30 percent in sunflower oil). Nevertheless, Argentine farmers rarely have received full value of the nation's remarkable agricultural potential because of storage problems and generally depressed global prices for grain. It is only through increasing labor efficiency—through industrialization based on cheap energy—that farmers are able to make a profit at all.

Agricultural products typically represent about three quarters of the value of Argentine exports, and from 50 to 90 percent of these are Pampean products (CEPAL 1985). The relative contributions of livestock and grain crops to the value of these exports varied over the years. It remained fairly close to a 1:1 ratio between 1925 and 1969, then changed sharply to reach about 80 percent for crops in the years 1982 to 1984 (Sabato 1980; CEPAL 1985) and 90 percent in the 1990s. Cropping on the Pampas has been influenced greatly by government manipulation of grain prices by various mechanisms. There was probably a net flow of funds to grain producers from the introduction of the price support scheme in 1933 through World War II, but thereafter grain farming was used as a net source

of cash for industrialization. In contrast, livestock husbandry received more consistent tax exemptions and favorable credit conditions. Coscia (1983) suggests that between 1951 and 1980 the Argentine wheat producer received, on average, slightly less than 60 percent of the price paid to the U.S. producer, the balance going mostly for export taxes (Miro 1986). Nevertheless, during the 1980s high levels of exports were encouraged by the very weak currency relative to the consuming countries.

The Linkage of Debt, Economic Instability, and Structural Adjustment

During this entire period of increase in agricultural production and, in general, massive production of wealth, Argentina had not balanced its external monetary accounts for various political and social reasons. This was done both to maintain its development rate, which has been remarkably high by international standards in the last two decades, and especially to maintain consumption (including interest on earlier debt). For this reason, the Argentine government had exhausted its credit borrowing from commercial banks and in 1991 had to turn to the International Monetary Fund, generally considered the borrower of last resort. The IMF agreed to loan Argentina some $2.5 billion initially, and more subsequently, but required that Argentina submit to structural adjustment in return. The officers and techniques of the IMF were for the most part indistinguishable from the neoclassical economics approach as formalized and promulgated by the faculty of the University of Chicago (e.g., Friedman 1972; Friedman and Friedman 1980; Bhagwati 1993). Simultaneously, the Argentine government, including both legislative bodies, responded with enthusiasm to the structural adjustment concepts by enacting additional legislation consistent with the IMF-imposed ones.

Structural adjustment for Argentina meant in effect decreasing government expenditures and ownership, cutting worker's benefits, encouraging foreign investment and imports through reduced tariffs, while, perhaps less clearly, encouraging exports, especially by cutting internal production costs. Government services such as health, education, and especially workers' benefits were decreased.

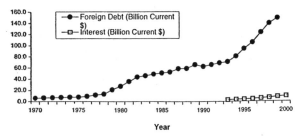

Figure 11.2. Foreign debt and interest on it.

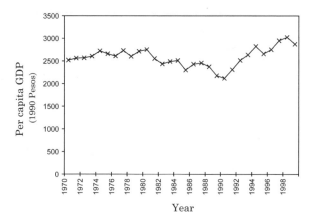

Figure 11.3. Per capita real GDP, Argentina, 1970–99. The values for 2002 and 2003 declined enormously to about half of the values given here.

One of the ways that this took place was through privatization, a process through which formerly state-owned industries were sold to private companies, which often instituted smaller employment and lower wages and worker benefits. An important part of the debt owed by the government (more than 60 percent) has been bought by citizens (especially by elder citizens) in the form of "bonuses" through the social security system, making the citizens the real borrowers while making the government look as if it were paying off debt (although in essence it was just transferring debt). Structural adjustment also meant that export crops such as corn and soy were increased dramatically. Although beef is a more valuable commodity per kilogram than grains or pulses, beef production per hectare is low, roughly 200 kg per yr. Crop production, on the other hand, tends to range from about 1 to 5 tons per ha, allowing a roughly 500 to 2,500 percent increase in production per ha (or about half that in dollars) compared to beef. Thus the IMF encouraged the conversion of pastureland to crop production, resulting in greatly increased exports and hence income of foreign exchange,

but in erosion as well. By 1992 this increased income was generating enough revenue to pay the interest but not to reduce the principal owed on the Argentine international debt (figure 11.2). During the early phase of structural adjustment, Argentina attracted a great deal of foreign investment capital, mostly because of a new environment that appeared favorable for foreign business. Simultaneously, many large international companies such as McDonalds and Wal-Mart moved into Argentina, encouraged by the lowering or elimination of tariffs and by favorable trade terms.

Results of Structural Adjustment

We next examine whether the objectives of the IMF have been gained by testing their original hypotheses, or rather their objectives rephrased as hypotheses.

1. Stabilize the currency by reducing inflation: Hypothesis supported—the inflation rate dropped quickly to very close to zero, greatly strengthening the peso relative to many other currencies.

2. Shift the tax burden away from businesses, especially those concerned with imports and exports, to encourage international trade. Hypothesis supported—large amounts of investment capital from overseas entered the new business-friendly environment of Argentina.

3. Reduce government expenditures and improve efficiency of services. Hypothesis partially supported—the government did in fact sell off many of its core industries and some industries appeared more efficient as they focused on their particular objective, for example by reducing the numbers of many workers. These industries included docks, energy, and telephones. However, "efficient" implies that prices should lower, yet prices for privatized tolls and telephone service in Argentina in 2000 were two to four times higher than those in many other countries. Meanwhile, there was a crisis in health care, dramatized by the suicide of Argentina's most prominent physician

in protest against the adverse effects of privatization in health care.

4. Shift the pension system to the private sector. Eliminate export taxes and most quantitative restrictions on imports, and the reduction of the level and range of import tariffs. Hypothesis supported—the pension system was privatized. Exports increased from about 6 to about 9 percent of GDP.

Overall Objective/Hypothesis

These actions collectively were expected to generate a stable economic climate friendly to international trade that would increase overall economic welfare by increasing GNP, increase the efficiency of the delivery of services, and reduce international debt. Hypothesis partially supported: The economic conditions as measured by the GDP increased (figure 11.3), but only for a relatively short time (four years).

Subsequently, the growth of the economy has been uneven and sometimes negative, as in 1995 and 1999. Overall economic growth has been about the same as population growth, so that per capita income has remained nearly the same in the decade since the initiation of structural adjustment as it was in the 1970s.

Adverse Effects of IMF

Although many of the explicit objectives of the structural adjustment plan were in fact obtained, giving "scientific" support to the concept that the structural development plans were in fact improving the economy, there were other, perhaps unanticipated effects of the structural policies that detracted from their overall effectiveness in improving the economy. These included:

1. As the peso strengthened, Argentine products became relatively expensive abroad and foreign (notably Brazilian) products became much cheaper in Argentina. The net effect was to decrease greatly the demand for products made in Argentina. This affected, even gutted, nearly all industries except food, and greatly decreased the income of the average middle-class Argentine. For example, the Argentine tourism industry lost many of its own vacationers to Brazil as well as others from other South American countries. Tires made in Argentina began to sell for twice the price as for the same brands made in Brazil, where laborers were paid in the devalued but still domestically useful Brazilian currency. Auto-parts supply companies particularly were affected. For example, in 1990 seven international brand-name tire companies produced tires in Argentina. By 1999, all had moved to Brazil. In general, domestic costs for local businesspeople inflated by 30 to 80 percent while receipts from international sales did not inflate at all. Argentina essentially ceased to export manufactured goods.

2. The GDP grew at a high level for only about four years, followed by several severe recessions in 1995 and 1999 (figure 11.3). Per capita GDP increased little or none over this period. It is not clear how much of the increase in GDP is real and sustainable. Some came from accounting changes that added in some formerly excluded black market activities. Other increases come from selling off national assets. For example, YPF (Yacimientos Petroliferos Fiscales, the national petroleum company) increased the level of oil and gas extraction by 66 percent between 1985 and 1995 (Ciccari, Prado, and Romero 1997). Meanwhile, the value of petroleum exported increased by nearly a factor of four from 1991 to 1997, adding about $2.5 billion to GDP.

3. The distribution of that GDP was increasingly inequitable, with unemployment increasing from roughly 7 percent to as high as 20 percent and underemployment also increasing. For example, YPF employed 1,436 workers in the province of Santa Cruz in northern Patagonia in 1991, 350 in 1993, and 250 in 1997, even as it was increasing production. While we were writing this chapter, there were many

demonstrations of workers in Argentina against the "Chicago boys" and their national associates, including one of 80,000 people at the Casa Rosada, the president's house. According to one poll, in Argentina public support for privatization fell from 52 percent in 1989 to 17 percent in the middle of 2000 (*The Economist*, July 15, 2000).

4. Although the value of exports increased, partly due to the low prices for agricultural products, imports increased more rapidly than exports. The effect was that Argentina's balance of trade deteriorated, exacerbating debt and the debt crisis that had been the impetus for structural reform (figure 11.2). During this period, about 10 percent of the total GDP each year went abroad to pay for debt service, while outstanding debt did not decrease—in fact, it increased.

5. Although there was a great acceleration of foreign investment into Argentina, it is not yet clear how much of that investment helped the average Argentine. Large retail corporations such as Wal-Mart that sell standard consumer goods from all over the world may bring relatively cheap consumer goods into the reach of the average Argentine, but they operate equally to pull foreign exchange out of the country, since few of the products sold are produced in Argentina. Likewise, many large international automobile manufacturing corporations purchased machine parts from well-established external suppliers, rather than from within Argentina, as had been the case before with domestic manufacturers.

6. As national unemployment approached 20 percent and the difference in wealth between the rich and the poor was greatly exacerbated, many social conditions declined seriously. The World Bank (1999) reported that more than 36 percent (13.4 million) of Argentina's people lived under the poverty line in the late 1990s, and 8.6 percent (3.2 million) lived under indigent conditions. Much of the decline is related directly to structural adjustment; for example, the convertibility plan in 1993 helped to decrease poverty to 20 percent, but after 1994 the situation changed. Now the top 20 percent of the population receives over 50 percent of total income, the lower 20 percent about 5 percent (World Bank 1999). In 1990 the richest 10 percent of Argentines earned fifteen times the income of the poorest 10 percent. By 1999 it was almost twenty-four times. Many people think this increase in inequality to be the most important consequence of the neoliberal policies.

7. Buenos Aires, where in 1986 serious crimes against individuals were almost unknown, had become a dangerous city by 1999 as desperate individuals sought money for themselves and their families. These social impacts are extremely severe and seem to flow directly from the structural adjustment policies.

8. The free market conditions generated favored large international enterprises. One result was an increasing import of intermediate products for production from large international suppliers, generally outside Argentina, which destroyed a large proportion of the small and intermediate industries in Argentina. Iñiguez (1997) observes that "the big national companies and the *empresas transancionales* [ETs, or transnational businesses] took advantage of the privatizations," which meant the concentration of capital in few hands and the destruction of medium and small enterprises, the ones with lower levels of technology (and hence not readily competitive) and that were also labor-intensive. Following structural adjustments, the ETs fired more than 25 percent of their workforce. Because the ETs are more capital-intensive than local companies, they had less demand for labor force. Thus, out of each $1 million ETs invest in Argentina, only 2.8 employment positions were created, less than 50 percent of the rate for local companies.

Because ETs import more than local companies, seventy cents of each dollar of profits are sent out of Argentina. The ETs are now a majority of the five hundred *grandes compañías* (major companies) in Argentina and are responsible for 76 percent of the production of these companies (INDEC 1999). This analysis shows that although the large financial activity of these companies can contribute greatly to the increase in GDP, they do so in ways that increase money drain, unemployment, and levels of poverty in Argentina.

9. With the privatization of the public social services, the government reduced the fiscal deficit by on one hand reducing the levels of employment in those sectors, and on the other hand not having to pay for the social services once provided by the public companies. Despite the savings in government expenditures, external debt was not decreased (figure 11.2). Meanwhile, the government no longer received income from those profitable industries that had been sold off.

10. In 1994 the international interest rate began to increase, which meant the departure of financial capital from Argentina and other Latin American countries. The new government rallying cry was *mercados o economías emergentes*—markets or emerging economies, as if these were the only choices. As Iñiguez (1997) says, "this shows the weakness of the model." It was based on an *economía de casino*; the international financial capital went for higher interest rates (temporarily in Asia), not for long-term productive investments. The departure of international financial capital at that time produced uncertainty for investors in Argentine projects, generating a massive withdrawal of their savings. It generated a financial crisis in the country.

Discussion

When we examine the objectives of the IMF as hypotheses, we see that all of the five "pillars" or target achievements of the structural adjustment plan might be considered "realized" in some sense. However the other side of the coin associated with each successful achievement is the additional adverse effects given previously, which tend not to be discussed by the advocates of the IMF structural adjustment or by other advocates of neoliberalism either before or after the fact, although they continue to push for the enactment of such structural adjustments around the world. Finally, we see that the debt schedule of the World Bank was met each and every year, although debt was not reduced. Most average Argentines without hesitation blame the severe economic conditions, worse than many can remember, on neoliberal economic policies imposed by "the Chicago boys of the North" or their domestic advocates. How well aimed is this blame?

In essence, the idea behind privatization was to exchange state industries for external debt. That is why most of the public enterprises were sold to international companies. Privatization was indeed a way of getting rid of "inefficient" enterprises (oil, gas, telephone, transport), where sometimes "inefficient" meant inadequate in supplying public needs (such as telephones) while sometimes it meant expensive, because Argentine workers tended to have large benefits. At the same time, the sales were meant to get money for the government and pay the outstanding debt. In practice, privatization was necessary to balance (in theory) the public budget because the state never had taken responsibility earlier for running those enterprises according to good international business standards. With the great pressure of the debt on the national economy, the privatization strategy allowed the multinationals to buy enterprises at prices far below the market cost, and corruption was one of the main features of the process (Nudler 1998). Thus, with privatization the government allowed the international companies to get extraordinary levels of profit. The government received $59.7 billion from this convertibility plan from 1991 to 1997, which it used for interest on debt and capital amortization, but during the same period the government borrowed $63.5 billion, which means that the external debt not only did not diminish but increased substantially. So much for selling off the state-owned enterprises to pay the debt.

Environmental Effects of Enhanced Exports

The economic growth that occurred both in the past and in recent decades was at the expense of Argentine natural resources, especially those of the Pampas, but it is much less clear that structural adjustment by itself particularly enhanced that degradation beyond enhancing the exports of crops, petroleum, and fish. Historically, the first major environmental impact of economic activity in Argentina was the destruction of the natural grasslands caused by the expansion of the cropping frontiers starting in 1875. This activity developed the present agricultural mosaic, and the ensuing erosion, which was often severe. For Argentina this period could be said to be equivalent to today's globalization, with open markets and the movement of people from Argentina to Europe and vice versa, which allowed exports to bloom. This developed tremendous wealth, which benefited mostly the few large landowners and the urban communities around the ports. Today Argentina has consolidated its democracy and in the last two decades has been going through a new period of economic growth and wealth accumulation, based not on the increase of agricultural area but of yield through energy-intensive technologies, with whatever pollution that entails. In a sense, the stagnation phase that occurred after World War II and the policies that delayed mechanization and fertilizer use delayed the impact of industrialization on the soil resource base. Both in the past and today the wealth obtained was concentrated in the hands of a very few—large landholders, city dwellers, and corporations.

Other resources have been affected similarly. For example, the hake (*Merluccia*) fisheries of the Atlantic coast are Argentina's most valuable fisheries and a significant source of export earnings. Part of the enhanced exports recommended by the World Bank plan were to be supplied by increased exports of these fish. Fisheries managers said that the fishery could sustain a harvest of no more than

Figure 11.4. Argentinean imports and exports, 1980–98.

400,000 tons per year, but political pressures, including that from the IMF, pushed that limit up to 1,200,000 tons for the two years before the fisheries collapsed.

For many Argentines, global climate change is not some abstract concept but a daily and decade-by-decade experience. Some of the real climate change hazards that Argentina has to cope with include clear temperature increases in most of the country of at least several degrees centigrade and (perhaps) more floods and droughts caused by changes in the patterns of isohyets, ozone layer depletion in the south, and perhaps soil drying in Patagonia. Although there seems to be little direct relation between economic activities in Argentina, which are small on the global scale, and the changes in climate observed there, these changes are completely within our understanding of the probable effects of continued atmospheric changes brought about by global industrialization. Hence we might say that if globalization and increased international trade is indeed as effective as advertised, it will increase global wealth and, especially, trade, necessitating increased consumption of fossil fuel while contributing to greenhouse gas warming and drying impacts in locations such as Argentina (IPCC 1995; Rind et al. 1990).

The Basis of Enhanced GDP

An intriguing question is how the structural adjustment programs have increased the Argentine GDP. Many would argue that the neoclassical principles simply work as intended, and that the stabilized currency and decreased business taxes have enhanced the Argentine environment for business. But in fact there may be other reasons as given above. If Argentina has greatly increased its foreign sales of oil, gas, unprocessed fish, wood, etc. as raw materials (versus value-added industrial products) it is, in effect, trading outstanding current foreign monetary debt for future resources and hence monetary debt as these resources are depleted. The increased production of oil for export generated about $2.5 billion more GDP in the late 1990s compared to the early 1990s, about 5 percent of the increase in Argentina's GDP during the same time. A barrel of oil generates roughly eight times the income when run through an economy compared to its direct sales value. In addition, these industries employ far fewer people per unit GDP derived, leading to large unemployment even during times of increasing wealth. Earlier governments were keeping many of these resources "in reserve," either deliberately or accidentally, so the development and overdevelopment of these now can make the economy look good at least temporarily. In addition, there has been an extremely large influx of foreign capital investment that may have showed up in some way as GDP. A major research agenda now is to determine how the per capita GDP can increase by 40 percent while the number of people employed drops from 93 to 80 percent of the population.

Is It Fair to Blame Structural Adjustment and Neoclassical Economics?

It is clear that neoclassical economics is not the only, or perhaps even the principal, reason for Argentina's economic and social problems, nor the sole cause of natural resource degradation. But it seems fair to consider that neoclassical economics (or its equivalent before it was named) during both the early stages of agricultural development in the Pampas and again more recently has coincided with environmental degradation and unevenness of wealth distribution in two independent historical periods. It is also reasonable to think that high rates of development at the expense of natural resource exploitation (e.g., soil and energy) may contribute to an unsustainable Argentina, and to an unsustainable

globe. It is also interesting to note that some of this wealth was used to develop industries, and that led to positive feedback, increasing energy consumption. But globalization has also served as a means to enhance widespread soil conservation through the spread of knowledge about no till agriculture, and, what is more important, an awareness of the effects caused by high rates of wealth development.

The final question is whether the (few) inarguably good results from the structural adjustment plan could have been obtained in part or entirely without the many adverse impacts. Is structural adjustment just trading one set of problems for another? For example, how necessary is neoclassical economics to make the changes necessary to stabilize currencies? Even some of our most noted traditional economists are beginning to ask whether, for example, government-directed Keynesian economics might have some utility after all (see Krugman 2000). Certainly the problem of inflation and governments debasing currency (as was the case in ancient Rome) is hardly a new one, and hardly requires the entire grab bag of neoclassical economic theory or massive restructuring of economies for its resolution (Harl 1996).

A second critical issue in Argentina and in other places is how the spoils of restructuring are divided. If restructuring sells industries developed with public investments to particular individuals at fire-sale prices, who are those individuals, and what did they have to do with initiating restructuring in the first place? How much has restructuring benefited the total number of people in that economy versus just a relatively small subset of economic actors outside of the economy being restructured? The latter point brings to mind the general history of Latin America, where various foreigners over time, from Spanish conquistadors to Boston banana barons, have "invaded" and made off with resources. Frequently these individuals, often seen as heroes in their times but as pillagers today, were accompanied by various priests who would sanctify the rapacious activity in the name of some higher cause, be it saving souls or manifest destiny. Are the "Chicago boys" analogous new priests who sanctify the rape of Argentina's resources by wealthy elites either inside or outside the country? Obviously, there are many possible answers to that question, and we do not pretend to know ourselves. But it seems to us that these issues need to be addressed to a much greater degree both outside and inside departments of economics, where it does seem to us that many practitioners tend to believe rather too strongly in the virtues of whatever suite of economic principles, such as neoclassical economics, they promulgate. We are of the opinion that much more natural science can be brought to bear on these issues, which over time may leave us with at least some partial answers that are not accessible through conventional neoclassical economics (Hall 2000). Thus we leave the reader with this critical question: Are there ways by which we can gain the benefits of structural adjustment without the severe social costs and the enhanced resource depletion that often accompany them? Certainly we need more insight into these issues than can be gleaned from neoclassical economics alone.

Postscript

In August 2001, the Argentine economy "crashed," leading to a huge loss of income and employment, roughly 25 percent in each case. The economy has slowly and painfully recovered but continues to struggle. Meanwhile, oil production peaked in 1999, and as of 2006 Argentina no longer exports oil. The economy is held together by a massive expansion of soybean farming and exports, which currently uses energy equivalent to about 15 to 30 percent of Argentina's oil production. Argentina remains a country with enormous potential—and enormous problems.

Acknowledgments

This chapter was originally published in S. Ulgiati, M. T. Brown, M. Giampietro, R. A. Herendeen, and K. Mayumi, eds., *Advances in Energy Studies* (Padua, Italy: Servizi Grafici Editoriali, 2001). We thank Carri Gala, Oscar Giayetto, Timm Kroeger, Jessica Lambert, Patricia F. Thompson, Jerry Mead, Dawn Montanye, Amy Richmond, Jeff Lyng, and Jae-Young Ko for help in finding and preparing the data used herein.

References

Alexander, R. J. 1995. Import substitution in Latin America in retrospect. In J. L. Dietz, ed., *Latin America's Economic Development: Confronting Crisis*, 159–66. Boulder, Colo.: Lynne Rienner.

Barberis, L., E. Chamorro, C. Baumann-Fonay, D. Zourarakis, D. Canova, and S. Urricarriet. 1985. Respuesta del cultivo de maiz a la fertilización nitrogenada en la pampa ondulada. Campanas 1980/81–1983/84. II. Modelos predictivos y explicativos. *Revista Facultad de Agronomia de Buenos Aires* 6:65–84.

Barsky, O., and M. Murmis. 1986. *Elementos para el análisis de las transformaciones de la región pampeana*. Buenos Aires: CISEA.

Bhagwati, J. 1993. The case for free trade. *Scientific American* 268, no. 5: 42–49.

Casas, R. R. 1998. Causas y evidencias de la degradación de los suelos en la región pampeana. In Solbrig and Veinesman 1998, 99–129.

CEPAL (UN Economic Commission for Latin America and the Caribbean). 1985. *Principales consecuencias socio-económicas de la división regional de la actividad agrícola*. Buenos Aires: CEPAL.

Cerruti, M. 2000. Economic reform, structural adjustment and female labor force participation in Buenos Aires, Argentina. *World Development* 28:879–91.

Cicciari, M. R., M. Prado, and J. Romero. 1997. Caracterización de la dinámica económica de la cuenca del golfo San Jorge en los Andes 90. In A. Salvia and M. Anaia, eds., *La Patagonia privatizada: Crisis, cambia estructurales en el sistema regional Patagonia y sus impactos en los mercados de trabajo*, 221–40. Buenos Aires: Centros do estudios Avanzados Oficina de Publicaciones del CBC, Universidad de Buenos Aires.

Collins, J., and J. Lear. 1995. *Chile's Free Market Miracle: A Second Look*. Monroe, Ore.: Food First Books.

Cortés Conde, R. 1979. *El progreso argentino*. Buenos Aires: Editorial Sudamericana.

Coscia, A. A. 1983. *Segunda revolución agrícola en la región pampeana*. Buenos Aires: CADIA.

David, M. B. de A., M. Dirven, and F. Vogelgesang. 2000. The impact of the new economic model on Latin America's agriculture. *World Development* 20:1673–88.

de la Fuente, E., S. A. Suarez, C. M. Ghersa, and R. J. C. León. 1999. Soybean weed community: Relationships with cultural history and crop yield. *Agronomy Journal* 91:234–41.

Friedman, M. 1972. *Capitalism and Freedom*. Chicago: University of Chicago Press.

Friedman, M., and R. Friedman. 1980. *Free to Choose: A Personal Statement*. New York: Harcourt Brace Jovanovich.

Ghersa, C. M., and M. A. Martínez-Ghersa. 1991. Cambios ecológicos en los agrosistemas de la pampa ondulada: Efectos de la introducción de la soja. *Investigación y Ciencia* 5:182–88.

Ghersa, C. M., M. A. Martínez-Ghersa, and R. J. C. León. 1998. Cambios en el paisaje pampeano y sus efectos sobre los sistemas soporte de vida. In Solbrig and Veinesman 1998, 38–71.

Ghersa, C. M., M. M. Omacini, D. Ferraro, M. A. Martínez-Ghersa, S. Perelman, and H. C. E. Giberti. 1961. *Historia económica de la ganadería argentina*. Buenos Aires: Solar/Hachette.

Ghersa, C. M., M. Omacini, D. Ferraro, M. A. Martínez-Ghersa, S. Perelman, E. H. Satorre, and A. Soriano. 2000. Estimación de indicadores de sustentabilidad de los sistemas mixtos de producción en la Pampa Interior. *Revista argentina de producción animal* 20, no. 1: 49–66.

Ghersa, C. M., S. Perelman, and C. di Bella. 1997. Comparación fractal de la variación temporal del rendimiento del trigo y del maíz en EEUU, Australia y Argentina. Proc XVIII Argentine Ecology Meeting, Buenos Aires.

Gillis, M., D. H. Perkins, M. Roemer, and D. R. Snodgrass. 1996. *Economics of Development*. 4th ed. New York: Norton.

Gray, J. 1998. *False Dawn: The Delusion of Global Capitalism*. London: Granta Books.

Hall, A. J., C. M. Rebella, C. M. Ghersa, and J. P. Culot. 1992. Field crop systems of the pampas. In C. J. Pearson, ed., *Ecosystems of the World: Field Crop Ecosystems*, 413–50. Amsterdam: Elsevier.

Hall, C. A. S. 1992. Economic development or developing economics? In M. Wali, ed., *Ecosystem Rehabilitation*, 101–26. The Hague: SPB.

———, ed. 2000. *Quantifying Sustainable Development: The Future of Tropical Economies*. San Diego: Academic Press.

Harl, K. W. 1996. *Coinage in the Roman Economy, 300 B.C. to A.D. 700*. Baltimore: Johns Hopkins University Press.

Huici, N. 1986. *Requerimientos de semilla y fertilizantes y maquinaria para la expansión agrícola en 1985/1990*. Buenos Aires: CISEA.

INDEC. 1999. Ministerio de Economia, Anuario Estadistico de la Republico Argentina.

Iñiguez, A. 1997. Las dimensiones del empleo en la Argentina. In E. Villanueva, ed., *Empleo y globalización: La nueva cuestión social en la Argentina*, 61–103. Buenos Aires: Universidad Nacional de Quilmas.

IPCC (Intergovernmental Panel on Climate Change). 1995. *Climate Change*. Cambridge: Cambridge University Press.

Kroeger, T., and D. Montanye. 2000. An assessment of the effectiveness of structural adjustment in Costa Rica. In Hall 2000, 665–94.

Krugman, P. 2000. Green cheese rules. *New York Times*, June 4, 2000.

Maddonni, G. A., S. Urricariet, C. M. Ghersa, and R. Lavado. 1998. Assessing soil quality in the rolling pampas using soil properties and maize characteristics. *Agronomy Journal* 91:280–87.

Miro, D. 1986. Producción y comercio de granos. La limitante de infraestructura. *Bolsa de Cereales, Numero estadístico 1986*, 6–37.

Montanye, D. 1998. Examining sustainability: An evaluation of USAID policies for agricultural export-led growth in Costa Rica. M.S. thesis, State University of New York.

Nudler, J. 1998. Estallido rigurosamente. *Vigilado*, November 10, 1998.

Rind, D. R., D. Goldberg, J. Hansen, C. Rosensweig, and R. Ruedy. 1990. Potential evapotranspiration and the likelihood of future drought. *Journal of Geophysical Research* 95:9,983–10,004.

Sabato, J. F. 1980. La pampa prodiga. Claves de una frustración. Buenos Aires: CISEA.

Satorre, E. H., and G. A. Slafer. 1999. *Wheat: Ecology and Physiology of Yield Determination*. New York: Haworth Press.

Senigagliesi, C., R. Garcia, and M. L. de Galetto. 1984. Evaluación de la respuesta del maíz a la fertilización nitrogenada y fosfatada en el area centro-norte de Buneos Aires y sur de Santa Fe. Proc. III Congreso Nacional de Maíz.

Solbrig, O. T. 1996. *Towards a Sustainable Pampas Agriculture: Past Performance and Prospective Analysis*. Cambridge, Mass.: David Rockefeller Center for Latin America Studies, Harvard University.

Solbrig, O. T., and L. Veinesman. 1998. *Hacia una agricultura productiva y sustentable en la pampa*. Buenos Aires: DRCLAS and CPIA.

Solbrig, O. T., and E. Viglizzo. 2000. *Sustainable Farming in the Argentine Pampas: History, Society, Economy and Ecology*. Cambridge, Mass.: David Rockefeller Center for Latin America Studies, Harvard University.

Viglizzo, E. F., and Z. E. Roberto. 1998. On trade-offs in low input agroecosystems. *Agricultural Systems* 56:253–64.

CHAPTER 12

TESTING BOSERUP

An Analysis of the Relation between Human Population Growth

and Cereal Supply in Nepal

RUDRIKSHA RAI PARAJULI

Introduction

Global food production has increased in recent years, due principally not to more hectares in production but to increased yields per hectare in response to "the green revolution" and other technical improvements. However, the demand for food has also increased about as much due to continued population growth, economic growth, and dietary change (Harris 1996). As part of this trend, agriculture has been expanded and especially intensified in developing countries in an attempt to feed their growing populations. But these intensified practices also have resulted in a loss of soil productivity by erosion and nutrient depletion in many areas (Brown 1981), increasing use of marginal land, the destruction of forests and pastures, and the loss of wildlife (Maikhuri, Rao, and Semwal 2001).

According to the World Food Summit in 1996, food security is a situation in which "all people at all times have physical and economic access to sufficient, safe and nutritious food to meet their dietary needs, and food preference for an active and healthy life" (Short 2001:1). It implies the capability of a country to provide an assured, adequate, accessible, and affordable food supply to meet the nutritional demands of all social groups and individuals. In the case of Nepal, my own country, hunger and undernourishment are prevalent. The number of hungry people rose from 3.5 million to 5 million from 1977 to 1999 (FAO 2000). According to Wasti (2002:2), "the food inadequacy is indicated by the percentage of population undernourished i.e. the people within a population whose dietary energy intake lies below their minimum requirements." In Nepal, 20–34

percent of the population is undernourished by this definition, and 47 percent of the total households consume less than the required amount of calories (2,250 calories per person per day) (FAO 2002; MOA 2001). Micronutrient-deficiency diseases such as anemia, iodine deficiency disorder, and Vitamin A deficiency are widely prevalent (Wasti 2002). In addition, hunger and poverty are among the contributing factors to the political conflicts and the increase in insurgent activities in hunger- and poverty-stricken areas of Nepal. The very low per capita income means that Nepal cannot possibly purchase most of its food; it must grow it.

The problem of hunger and undernourishment could be due to lack of purchasing capacity of people because hunger can also be a cause of poverty. According to the FAO (2002), countries with severe undernourishment problems are defined as having their population surviving on less than one dollar per day. In Nepal this would be about 38 percent of the population (MOA 2001). Hunger can be treated quickly by increasing the food supply, but poverty reduction is a much longer process of socioeconomic development. Abolishment of hunger can reduce undernourishment and diseases caused by the deficiency of food nutrients, and produce a healthier and more productive population.

This chapter reviews the development possibilities for Nepal, focusing on the actual biophysical resources for Nepal and the question as to whether the Nepalese population can increase their own food production in an increasingly crowded land. I frame this question within the context of testing quantitatively the "Boserup hypothesis," which

Figure 12.1. Political map of Nepal.

has been very influential in shaping people's ideas about development.

Overview of Nepal

Nepal is a small developing subtropical country in South Asia, bordered by India to the east, west, and south and China to the north. Its total land area is 14,718,000 hectares (56,827 mi²). The topography varies from the plains of the flatlands in the south to the deep valleys and high mountains in the north. As shown in the map developed by the International Center for Integrated Mountain Development (figure 12.1), Nepal has five physiographic regions from south to north, identified as terai, siwalik, hill, high mountain, and high Himalaya. The hill category occupies the largest percentage of land area (29.15 percent), followed by high Himalaya (23.94 percent), high mountain (20.39 percent), terai (13.68 percent), and siwalik (12.85 percent). The terai and siwalik together make up the more commonly used term terai, which is at 100–500 m elevation. The hill region extends from 500 to 4,000 m, and the mountains extend as high as 8848 m.

The terai has the largest percentage of cultivable land (40 percent) and is the most populated region. Of the total land area in the hill region, only 4.2 percent is cultivable because it comprises several mountain ranges, with only a little area in fertile valleys and basins with a temperate climate. The mountain region is rocky with an alpine climate. It covers 35 percent of the land area of the country, of which only 2 percent is suitable for cultivation. It comprises ice-covered massifs, rolling uplands, and snowfields and includes the highest peak in the world, Mount Everest. It has the lowest population concentration of the three regions and the least agricultural activity.

Nepal is an agricultural country, and more than two-thirds of the population is involved in agriculture. Although the human population is increasing rapidly at the rate of 2.3 percent per year (i.e., doubling each thirty years) the proportion engaged in agriculture nevertheless is declining (MOP 2000). According to FAO (1987) the agriculture population in Nepal declined from more than 92 percent of the total population in 1965 to 1987 to about 82 percent in 2001. Agriculture is traditional and mostly rain fed, as only 36 percent of the agriculture land is irrigated. An estimate based on fertilizer sales in Nepal shows that 40 percent of fertilizer is used for wheat cultivation, followed by rice (35 percent), maize (10 percent), and the rest (15 percent) is used for potatoes and other crops (FAO 2002). Besides chemical fertilizers, farmers also use farmyard manure. For example, in rice cultivation, one-third of nutrients is supplied by farmyard manure (MOA 2000). In 2001, agriculture contributed about 38 percent to GDP, compared to industries (23 percent) and services (39 percent; CBS 2002). Tourism is one of the important sources of earning foreign exchange in Nepal. In the fiscal year 2000–2001, the commerce, restaurant, and hotel sector contributed approximately 9.6 percent of the total GDP (CBS 2002).

Rice, maize, wheat, barley, millet, potato, oil seeds (plants with oil-containing seeds used for oil extraction), jute, vegetables, and tea are the major crops cultivated in Nepal; among them, rice, maize, wheat, millet, and barley are the staple foods. Agriculture depends heavily on animal power (48 percent), followed by human power (30 percent), and then mechanical sources such as small tractors contribute the rest (22 percent) (Shrestha 1998). Rapid population growth has resulted in small landholdings (0.95 ha on average), and skewed land distribution (more than 50 percent of households own only 6.6 percent of the total cultivated land, more than two-thirds of the households own less than a hectare, and about 10 percent of the households are landless) (MOP 2000).

Cereals provide nearly 90 percent of the food calories. More than half of the agriculture land in Nepal is used for the production of cereals, 55 percent for rice, most of the rest for wheat and corn. The rice is grown most extensively in terai (88 percent), followed by hills (10 percent) and high-altitude cold regions (2 percent). Maize is grown in hills (70 percent), terai (22 percent), and high hills

(8 percent), and wheat is extensively grown in terai as well as in the hill region. Millet and barley are produced in the higher parts of the hill region and in the mountain region.

The Boserup Hypothesis and Nepal

Rapid population growth is perceived by some investigators as one of the major causes of impoverishment and starvation in much of the world. The first principle on population growth given in 1798 by Malthus in his *Essay on Population* states that "population, *when unchecked*, increases in a geometrical ratio while the means of subsistence at most increases in an arithmetical ratio; hence, population tends to increase up to the limits of the means subsistence." However, there are many criticisms of Malthus's view, for the population of the earth has increased many times since he wrote his book, and starvation (as a percentage of all people) is probably no worse than in his day and may be much less. One of the most prominent criticisms of Malthus's idea is given by Esther Boserup (1965), and many others have picked up her rather optimistic perspective on population growth. In the introduction to *The Conditions of Agricultural Growth*, she writes, "population growth is here regarded as the independent variable which in its turn is a major factor determining agricultural developments" (11). She has emphasized that as population grows, people will develop technologies to enhance food production.

In her 1981 book *Population and Technological Change*, Boserup writes, "Thus, the increase of population within an area provides an incentive to replace natural resources by labor and capital" (6). In this book she reviews agricultural change and agricultural technology and finds, not surprisingly, that as population densities increase people use more technologies including, explicitly, fertilizer. She adds, "The acceleration of population growth in the Third World revived old Malthusian fears. We have seen, however, that in many earlier periods, the response to population growth was intensification of land use, and this experience was repeated in recent decades. In step with the increase of world population, intensive systems of agriculture replaced extensive systems in larger parts of the world. Not only population but also rates of (intensification) growth have accelerated" (200). She makes no mention that I could find that such intensification might have negative impacts on environment, dependency (on for example industrial countries as sources of fertilizer), increased erosion, or the sustainability of agriculture. Similarly, Simon (1981) also considers moderate human population growth as "conducive" for economic development in a capitalist system.

Ahmed (1984), however, found that the population growth in Bangladesh did not increase per capita agricultural output. He ascribes this to lack of technological and physical facilities and poverty among peasant communities. Hence, as proposed by Demeny (1979), population growth can be considered as a hindrance to economic development, especially in developing countries.

A number of studies have shown the adverse effects of population growth. Population expansion degrades agriculture production by converting cropland to nonfarm use such as cities, and through elimination of fallow, initiating human migration, and contributing to urban sprawl (Brown 1981; Thapa and Weber 1999), and thus use of suboptimal land (Hall 2000). It also changes resource utilization patterns and may lead to degradation of forestland and grazing land and a loss of biotic diversity. For example, a study done in different Himalayan regions of India by Negi, Bhatt, and Todaria (1999), and another by Maikhuri, Rao, and Semwal (2001), showed that the causes of deforestation were increasing human and bovine population. Similarly, Pandey and Singh (1984) have demonstrated that subsistence agriculture and forest degradation is detrimental to agriculture as well as to water management in hill areas because agriculture depends on the energy and nutrients carried in from the forest.

One way in which population growth might support an increase in agriculture productivity is by providing labor in labor-intensive agriculture systems, especially in developing countries (Ahmed 1984). Moreover, population pressure could inspire farmers to adopt agriculture technologies and innovations (Hooper 1976; Sankhyan et al. 2000; Bilsborrow and Carr 2001). But the

adoption of modern agriculture technologies has sometimes been shown to cause environmental disasters, genetic loss of crops, and loss of indigenous knowledge (Konar 1996; Upreti and Upreti 2002; Altieri and Anderson 1986). It certainly leads to an increase in dependency of developing countries on imported agrochemicals needed for intensification. This in turn generates an increased need for exports to get foreign exchange to pay for the technological inputs and the oil from the industrial world, and hence makes these countries very sensitive to oil prices (Hall 2000). Endogenous technological changes were not sufficient to solve the problem of food scarcity in Bangladesh because the population growth rate was higher than the growth rate of agricultural production (Kabir and Chowdhary 1982).

A number of ways have been identified to overcome the pressure of overpopulation and food instability. One of them is the diversification of the source of income by cultivating export crops (Norse 1992), although in developing countries export crop production can put more pressure on their economies by displacing subsistence agriculture from prime land and by increasing the expenditure on imports of fertilizer and food crops (Hall 2000).

The better way to approach this dilemma would be to develop an agriculture system that is based on the ecological, economical, and sociocultural factors of a country (Loomis 1976). However, this must also consider the socioeconomic factors, which could be regional or global, governed by market conditions and terms of tariffs and trade; these are often influenced by the costs of energy, raw materials, and labor (Blum 1998). According to Kaosa-ard and Rerkasem (2000), continued increase in agriculture production depends on the availability and the quality of natural resources and the way they are utilized in the production process; therefore, technology management and government intervention determine agriculture sustainability. Developing countries need to emphasize long-term investments in research, infrastructure, and institutional innovations to overcome uneven food production in different regions of the country, and to determine the optimum combinations of crops (Barker and Chapman 1990; Ruttan 1997; Randhawa and Abrol 1990). However they must also realistically deal with the biophysical limits of the landscape being considered.

South Asia and sub-Saharan Africa often have severe food insecurity problems, and L. C. Smith and his colleagues (1999) believe that poverty is the main cause of food insecurity in South Asia. Exceptions exist; despite population pressure, China and India have entered the stage of food self-sufficiency and, in the case of India, even exports. This appears to be based in large part on the extensive use of their large supplies of fossil fuels to generate fertilizers. But Nepal has no fossil fuels, and it has not been able to produce sufficient food to feed the growing population (CBS 2001). The cause of insufficient agriculture production may be the low use of agriculture inputs or perhaps a lack of initiatives among producers to adopt agriculture technologies and innovations due to financial constraints, as well as a lack of technical support. It could be that Nepalese suffer from poverty because they cannot generate any surplus food that can be used for exports and then use that foreign exchange for importing inputs and using them to enhance cultivation, or it may be simply that Nepal does not have land that responds well to improvement through fertilizers or other means. Certainly given the general poverty of Nepal and the lack of resources that most of the rest of the world wants (except for mountain trekking), Nepal has no option but to produce its own food.

Objectives

The purpose of this research is to test the general conclusion of Boserup for Nepal. Since I felt that her assumptions about population growth were not quite explicit enough to test formally, I restated her basic ideas as testable hypotheses:

1. Population growth results in increased productivity per unit land area and this increase is enough to feed the growing population.
2. Agricultural intensification can continue to feed the growing population of Nepal. Among many possible methods of

intensification of agriculture, I will test the second hypothesis by examining the effects of increased use of fertilizer in cereal production because fertilizers are usually the most important factor in increasing yield (Brown 1981).

As part of that test I will:
   a. compare the growth of both human populations and cereal production in Nepal from 1961 to 2000.
   b. determine the efficiency of land and fertilizer use for cereal production in Nepal from 1961 to 2000.
   c. develop a simulation model to predict the growth of human population from 1982 to 2031 in Nepal and cereal production from 1961 to 2031 with increased fertilizer use.

Materials and Methods

I tested the first hypothesis, which states that population growth results in an increase in agriculture productivity per unit of land, by dividing the total cereal produced by the total population for each year from 1961 to 2000. I also divided total cereal production (corrected for 25 percent loss to pests) by the product of the number of people times their minimum cereal requirements (assuming that all of their food comes from cereals), which is 0.3 ton per person according to Hall and Hall (1993) and Shrestha (1998). Finally, I developed a FORTRAN simulation model to predict population growth and cereals production, and their ratio, until the year 2031. The first hypothesis is supported if the cereal production per person stayed constant or increased while the agriculture population increased and secondarily if the total cereal produced was able to fulfill cereal requirements of the population both empirically until the year 2001 and through simulation until 2031.

I tested the second hypothesis by examining the relation of cereal production to fertilizer use from 1961 to 2001.

Sources of Data

It is difficult to get primary data and information on Nepal that are reliable, comprehensive, and usable. This assessment is based on data found on the Internet, in professional literature, and in research reports, especially statistical data from FAO and the databases of the Statistical Bureau of Nepal. I have used as many resources as possible to compare and verify them.

The data on Nepal's population of 1981 were derived from the Statistical Year Book of Nepal, 2001 (CBS 2001) and from the publications of Nepal's Ministry of Population and Environment, 2000 (www.mope.gov.np). The principal data on the agriculture systems (land use, crop yield, and fertilizer use) were derived from FAOSTAT, the Statistical Database of the Food and Agricultural Organization of the United Nations (www.fao.org/DOCREP/004/AB988E/ab988e06.htm). I assumed that rice, maize, and wheat make up 90 percent of the total cereals produced, 74 percent of the total cropped area, and 85 percent of total fertilizer used.

I determined the efficiency of fertilizer use for rice, maize, and wheat and the efficiency of land use for rice, maize, wheat, millet, and barley using the procedure of Hall and his colleagues (Hall et al. 1998; Hall et al. 2000), which is done by dividing yield by fertilizer input (each determined for each crop for each year).

Simulation of Population and Cereal Production

A model is an abstraction or simplification of a system; it is the formalization of our knowledge about a system or process. A predictive or simulation model attempts to represent quantitatively relatively well-known systems allowing simulation of the future or hypothetical states (Hall and Day 1977). The model predictions can be compared with field data for validation. The model is presented in brief here. Details can be found in Rai (2003).

Population model

I developed NepalSim, a computer simulation model of both the human population and the cereal production of Nepal. The population simulation is based on a Leslie Matrix (see box 6.1), and it extrapolates future populations based on an initial age-structured population and age class–dependent survivorship and fecundity values (Box 6.1, Hall 2000). I used the latest available age and sex structure data, which was 1981 (CBS 2001). I calculated fecundity or total fertility rate from the age-specific fertility rate per 1,000 women of 1981 (MOP 2000).

The survivorship is calculated from the death rate of each age class (MOP 2000). I performed a sensitivity analysis by reducing the death rate and fecundity values between 1 and 5 percent of the values I had originally used for simulation.

Agricultural model

The model simulated the production of rice, maize, and wheat as a function of fertilizer use and area of production for seventy years starting from 1961 while including changes in fertilizer used, area of cereal production, erosion, and yield of cereals without fertilizer. The simulation was computed following the procedure of Hall (2000, chapter 5 and code on the associated CD).

The relation of yield to fertilizer input in Nepal is complex and not easy to calculate. The empirical patterns of fertilizer use and cereal production are complex but show that the relatively low inputs of fertilizer prior to 1985 were not accompanied by any substantial increase in yield; in fact yield often declined. Since then, fertilizer use increased dramatically and yields sometimes increased and as often decreased, at least at the national level (figures 12.2, 12.3, 12.4). Third- and fourth-order polynomials of cereal yield versus fertilizer tended to give very low and nonintuitive R^2s, indicating very poor response to fertilizers and difficulties in deriving half saturation coefficients for modeling. It is possible that crops in Nepal just don't particularly respond to fertilizers. For modeling purpose I referred to Goletti (2001), who has estimated that in Nepal, rice gives a maximum yield with about 148 kg/ha of chemical nutrient added, after which yield starts to decline. Based on this, I assumed that the half saturation constants are 74 kg per ha for rice, 40 kg /ha for maize, and 80 kg per ha for wheat. After that, more fertilizer leads to some small increased production.

There was a decline in yield per unit area from 1965 to the mid-1980s, despite a rapidly increased

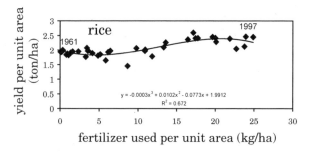

Figure 12.2. The ambiguous relation between chemical fertilizer use and yields of rice production in Nepal, 1961–2000.

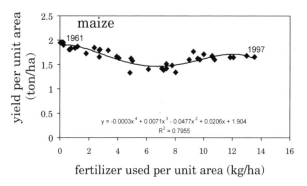

Figure 12.3. The ambiguous relation between chemical fertilizer use and yields of maize production in Nepal, 1961–2000.

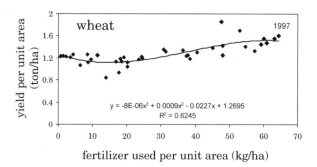

Figure 12.4. The ambiguous relation between chemical fertilizer use and yields of wheat production in Nepal, 1961–2000.

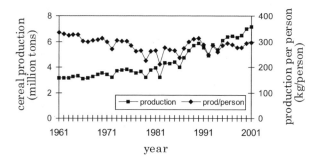

Figure 12.5. Agricultural production and production per person.

use of fertilizer per unit area. One likely explanation for the failure for the yield to increase was due to the effects of soil erosion, as that is a large issue in the often steep fields of Nepal. In other words, the fertilizer used before the mid-1980s compensated for the loss of soil fertility but contributed to no increased yield. I assumed the yield of rice in 1986 (1.78 ton/ha) as the base yield. From 1961 to about 1985 there was a decline of approximately 31 percent in agriculture yield per ha, which I assumed was due to soil erosion. Thus I assumed that agricultural productivity decreases at the rate of about 1 percent per year when fertilizer applications are below about 20 kg/ha. According to one estimate 5–200 metric ton/ha/year of soil is lost every year in Nepal, during the rainy season, depending on land use and landform (Shrestha 1998); however there is not any estimate on how this affects the productivity of crops.

Cereal production decreases when the lands of lower intrinsic quality are used. I represent agricultural land quality by a numerical factor (1 = best,

0.5 = medium, 0 = worst) (Hall 2000). Since farmers use the best land first, the productivity in additional, new agricultural land would be less. I assume that any new agricultural land would be of lower quality than the average of what is used to date, which I represent by a quality of factor of 0.5.

The terai region has alluvial soil, so it is more fertile than hills and mountain regions. Similarly, due to slope and rugged landscape, the hill region is more prone to erosion. There are not any recent data on land area used in cereal production in terai, hills, and mountains and there are none on soil erosion; hence I did not specify independent land quality factors and erosion factors for terai, hill, and mountain.

A significant quantity of cereals is lost after harvesting. Globally, the loss varies from 10–40 percent of total cereals produced, depending on the crop, the country/place, climatic region, and the method of measurement of loss (FAO 2000; Pimentel 1997). For instance, for rice it varies between 10 percent and 37 percent of all rice grown in Southeast

Asia (FAO 2000). I assumed that in Nepal about 25 percent of the predicted cereal production is lost after harvesting.

Finally, I multiplied the total cereal production (TCPROD) by 1.1 to estimate production of all crops, and by 0.85 to correct for moisture content. Since a person requires about a third of a ton of dry grain per year to meet basic caloric requirements, I then multiplied the results by three to get the number of people that could be fed from grains in a year (figure 12.5). Since grains make up most of the food of the Nepalese people, this number can then be compared directly with the simulated or actual number of people to estimate whether or not the population can be fed.

Results

Neither my hypothesis that population growth results in increased productivity per unit land area nor my hypothesis that domestic cereal production would feed the growing population of Nepal with increased use of fertilizer was supported, based on both my empirical and my simulation results. Specifically, my empirical research showed that in Nepal the cereal supply has grown at a rate slightly lower than the human population (figure 12.6). Simulation results suggest that the situation is likely to get much worse in the future, mostly because of projected increased populations but also because empirically the crops are not responding well to additional fertilizers.

Thus, contrary to Boserup's view that population grows independent of food supply (1965, 1981), there was very little increase in the agriculture productivity from 1961 to 2001 and a decrease in the per capita rate. Reinforcing these results are: first, Nepal has had a deficit in cereal production for more than thirty years; second, it has been importing food and animals to fulfill the food demands of the country; third, Nepal needs its nonagricultural land as forests and grazing land; and fourth, Nepal is basically unable to pay for increasing agro-technologies of any kind because of poverty and debt. Finally, my simulation results suggest that if Nepal's population continues to grow at the current rate, then the future cereal production would not able to supply the growing

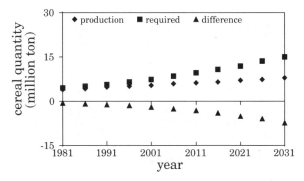

Figure 12.6. Cereal requirements and cereal production in Nepal. Data from 1981 to 2001, simulation subsequently.

population even if more fertilizer was available. In other words Boserup's basic concept does not work at the national scale in Nepal.

Land Use and Efficiency of Land Use by Agriculture

Agricultural land, defined as the sum of land under temporary crops, permanent crops, and permanent pasture expanded by 0.99 million ha from 3.53 million ha in 1961 to 4.52 million ha in 1994 while forestland decreased by 1.32 million ha. Total land in cereal production increased from 1.71 million ha in 1961 to 3.3 million ha in 2000, a 92 percent increase. The total production of cereals increased from 3.17 million metric tons (mt) in 1961 to 3.93 mt in 1981 to 6.99 million mt in 2000 (table 12.1). Mean cereal yield was 1.85 ton/ha in 1961 but decreased to about 1.69 in the 1980s and then increased to 2.12 ton/ha in 2000, about a 15 percent increase, with a 93 percent increase in the area of production. The yield for 1961–2000 increased for rice (1.94–2.6 ton/ha) and wheat (1.23–1.85 ton/ha) but decreased for maize (1.95–1.76 ton/ha). As shown in figures 12.7–9, cereal yields per ha increased significantly only after about 1985.

Agriculture land per person decreased from 0.37 ha per person in 1961 to 0.28 in 1981 to 0.20 ha per person in 2000. The cereal production per person was 335 kg per person in 1961 but that decreased to 311 in 1990 and further declined to 293 kg per person in 2000 (figure 12.5).

Based on the assumption that a person needs 0.3 tons of cereal grain per year to meet his or her total dietary needs (Hall and Hall 1993; Shrestha

Table 12.1. Actual population and actual and required cereal production in Nepal 1961–2000

Year	Population (million)	Capacity to feed (million)	Difference (million)	Cereal production (million tons)	Cereals requirement (million tons)	Surplus/deficit (million tons)	Production per person (kg/person)
1961	9.44	9.50	0.06	3.17	2.83	0.34	335.49
1962	9.62	9.53	−0.09	3.18	2.89	0.29	330.11
1963	9.82	9.54	−0.27	3.18	2.94	0.24	324.15
1964	10.01	9.84	−0.17	3.28	3.00	0.28	327.52
1965	10.21	10.01	−0.21	3.34	3.06	0.27	326.61
1966	10.42	9.38	−1.04	3.13	3.12	0.00	300.15
1967	10.63	9.50	−1.13	3.17	3.19	−0.02	297.89
1968	10.85	9.88	−0.97	3.29	3.25	0.04	303.54
1969	11.08	10.25	−0.83	3.42	3.32	0.09	308.44
1970	11.33	10.67	−0.66	3.56	3.40	0.16	313.93
1971	11.59	10.35	−1.24	3.45	3.48	−0.03	297.65
1972	11.88	9.65	−2.23	3.22	3.56	−0.35	270.84
1973	12.17	11.13	−1.05	3.71	3.65	0.06	304.65
1974	12.48	11.27	−1.22	3.76	3.74	0.01	300.87
1975	12.80	11.55	−1.24	3.85	3.84	0.01	300.98
1976	13.12	11.20	−1.92	3.73	3.94	−0.20	284.60
1977	13.45	10.60	−2.84	3.53	4.03	−0.50	262.87
1978	13.79	10.95	−2.84	3.65	4.14	−0.49	264.69
1979	14.14	9.58	−4.56	3.19	4.24	−1.05	225.90
1980	14.50	11.38	−3.12	3.79	4.35	−0.56	261.56
1981	14.88	11.80	−3.07	3.93	4.46	−0.53	264.44
1982	15.26	9.66	−5.60	3.22	4.58	−1.36	211.03
1983	15.67	12.93	−2.73	4.31	4.70	−0.39	275.17
1984	16.08	12.93	−3.15	4.31	4.82	−0.51	268.03
1985	16.50	13.12	−3.38	4.37	4.95	−0.58	265.00
1986	16.94	12.00	−4.94	4.00	5.08	−1.08	236.15
1987	17.38	14.28	−3.10	4.76	5.21	−0.45	273.83
1988	17.83	15.92	−1.91	5.31	5.35	−0.04	297.57
1989	18.30	17.02	−1.28	5.67	5.49	0.18	310.01
1990	18.77	17.54	−1.23	5.85	5.63	0.22	311.48
1991	19.26	16.56	−2.70	5.52	5.78	−0.26	286.66
1992	19.75	14.71	−5.04	4.90	5.92	−1.02	248.22
1993	20.25	17.32	−2.93	5.77	6.08	−0.30	285.07
1994	20.76	16.12	−4.63	5.37	6.23	−0.85	258.92
1995	21.27	18.23	−3.04	6.08	6.38	−0.30	285.72
1996	21.79	19.10	−2.69	6.37	6.54	−0.17	292.17
1997	22.32	19.25	−3.07	6.42	6.69	−0.28	287.51
1998	22.85	18.99	−3.85	6.33	6.85	−0.52	277.11
1999	23.39	19.40	−3.99	6.47	7.02	−0.55	276.47
2000	23.80	20.96	−2.85	6.99	7.14	−0.16	293.47

Source: FAO (2000).

Table 12.2. Simulated population, 1981–2031

Year	Breeding population (million)	Total births (million)	Total deaths (thousand)	Total population (million)
1981	7.07	2.16	0.00	15.02
1986	8.15	2.49	262.41	16.78
1991	9.59	2.93	298.40	19.08
1996	11.01	3.37	340.67	21.78
2001	12.20	3.73	386.88	24.74
2006	13.53	4.14	439.01	28.07
2011	15.13	4.63	494.39	31.61
2016	17.17	5.25	556.11	35.55
2021	19.19	5.87	625.37	39.98
2026	21.14	6.46	702.00	44.88
2031	23.45	7.17	786.54	50.29

1998), and the assumption that 20 percent of the crop is lost to pests, the cereal requirement of the population of Nepal was 2.83 million tons in 1961, which increased to 4.46 million tons in 1981 and to 7.14 million tons in 2000. During this time, the cereal actually produced was 3.17 million tons in 1961 (indicating a surplus then), 3.93 million tons in 1981, and 6.99 million tons in 2000, indicating a change from cereal sufficiency to inadequacy. There has been a deficit almost every year after the 1970s, except in 1989 (when there was a surplus of 180,000 tons) and in 1990 (when there was a surplus of 220,000 tons). In other words, the cereals produced in 1961 could feed 9.5 million people, 11.8 million in 1981, and 20.96 million in 2000, while the population in the corresponding years was 9.44 million, 14.88, and 23.8 million; hence almost every year since 1961 to 2000, the cereals produced were not sufficient for the rapidly growing population. In 1981, the cereals produced could not feed 3 million people, while in 2000 2.84 million people had a serious deficiency of cereals.

Efficiency of Fertilizer Use by Agriculture

Total national chemical fertilizer used increased from 149 mt in 1961 to 121.5 thousand mt in 1998, but then decreased to 76 thousand mt in 2000. Total national chemical fertilizer used per unit area

has been increasing for both all crops and the three main cereal crops, although it declined in 1999 and 2000. I calculated that its use per unit area of total cereals (national average) increased from less than 0.07 kg/ha in 1961 to more than 8.8 kg/ha in 1981 and to more than 23 kg/ha in 1991. It increased to more than 31.8 kg/ha in 1998 but declined to less than 19.6 kg/ha in 2000.

Nepalese crops do not respond well to fertilizers (figures 12.2–4). The yield per unit fertilizer used for rice, maize, and wheat decreased in Nepal from 1980 to 2001. Production per unit fertilizer for rice decreased from 313 kg/ha in 1980 to 138 in 1990 but increased to 151.5 kg/ha in 2000. Maize productivity declined from 331 kg/ha to 170 in 1990 but increased to 190 kg/ha in 2000. Wheat productivity decreased from 49 kg/ha in 1980 to 29 in 1990 but increased to 38.93 kg/ha in 2000. Efficiency decreases as more fertilizer is added and increases as fertilizer use is decreased. Thus, contrary to Boserup, increased population and the resultant increased technification leads to a decrease in efficiency.

Population and Cereal Simulations

My simulation results showed that if the birth and death rates of 1981 continue into the future Nepal's population of 14.9 million in 1981 would increase

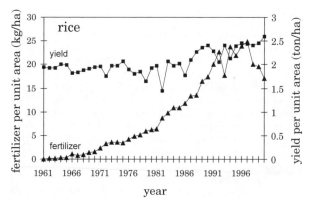

Figure 12.7. Chemical fertilizer per unit area and yield of rice in Nepal, 1961–2000.

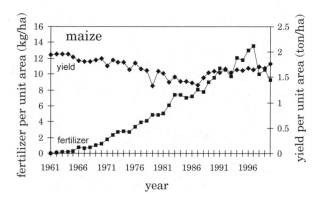

Figure 12.8. Chemical fertilizer per unit area and yield of maize in Nepal, 1961–2000.

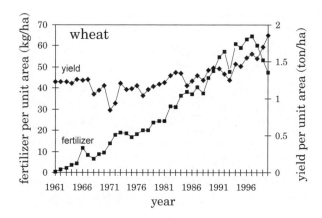

Figure 12.9. Chemical fertilizer per unit area and yield of wheat in Nepal, 1961–2000.

to 24.74 million in 2001, 31.61 million in 2011, and 50.29 in 2031 (table 12.2). This was partially validated using actual population data that showed a population in 2000 of 23.8 million.

The continuing gap between birth and death rates, even though both are declining, meant that the population continued to increase even as the birth rate declined, and because the number of people to which the birthrate is applied is still increasing the actual number of new Nepalese continues to increase each year.

The agriculture model predicted that the total cereal production would increase from 5.84 million tons in 2001 to 8.34 million tons in 2031, which could feed 11.79 million people in 1981, 16.37 million people in 2001, and 23.4 million people in 2031. The simulated populations of the corresponding years were 15.02 million, 24.74 and 50.29 million respectively. Thus the food deficiency will increase greatly if the population continues to increase as predicted (figure 12.6).

The simulated population of 1981 (15.02 million) would require 4.51 million tons of cereals that increased to 7.42 million tons for the population of 2001 (24.74 million) and to 15.09 million tons for 50.29 million people in 2031 while the cereals produced in these corresponding years to 2001 were 3.93 million tons, 5.46, and 7.8 million tons respectively, which is not sufficient to fulfill the cereal demand. Similarly, the capacity of simulated cereals to feed the simulated population is very low. Population is expanding and is predicted to continue expanding geometrically, while food production is increasing linearly, hence the difference. In 2031, cereals could feed 23.4 million people, but according to my simulation there will be 50.29 million people in 2031. The production of cereals per person was 262 kg per person in 1981 but declined to 221 in 2001 and to 155 kg per person in 2031.

Sensitivity Analysis

I performed sensitivity analysis to find out how sensitive my model prediction is to changes in fecundity and death rate. Since the most likely scenario is that I have overestimated both birth and death rates I found that a reduction of 4 percent in both the fecundity and death rate in 1981 gives populations of 24.28 million in 2001, which increases to 30.74 in 2011 and to 47.81 million in 2031. These would be 98 percent, 97 percent, and 95 percent of the original estimates.

Discussion

Despite a significant decline in the ratio between per capita cereal production and per capita requirements in Nepal, the population has continued to expand, apparently because the gap is filled in by other food sources (such as potatoes, root vegetables, and meat) and by imported foods. Since half of the population has an income of less than one dollar per day, it is apparent that not all people were able to fulfill their daily caloric requirements with food sources other than cereals; this could be a reason why food scarcity is more prevalent among poor, deprived, and disadvantaged communities.

This study has demonstrated that decreasing food supply per person, agriculture land per person, and other resources such as fertilizer have not affected the growth of the human population of Nepal. Another important issue is that, unlike Boserup's view, population growth did not increase per capita agriculture productivity. Clearly there has been little or no increase in per hectare yields with more people and in fact it has decreased. The actual human population growth rate in Nepal has remained stable at 2.3 percent per year since 1998. Hence there are two solutions: either control population growth or increase cereal production by increasing fertilizer use and expanding irrigation facilities. However, my fertilizer analysis suggests that the latter will not work.

This study did not look into finding all the possible reasons behind this failure for agriculture productivity to increase; however, it found that poverty among farmers is one of them. Rapid population growth resulted in a decline in per capita agriculture land and per capita cereal production. Previous studies also have shown that a major proportion of Nepalese farmers were unable to adopt new agriculture technologies, particularly chemical fertilizers, due to problems of cash flow and inefficient distribution mechanisms (Goletti 2000). In addition, my analysis indicated that crops in Nepal do not respond well to fertilizers,

so we may be dealing with true biophysical limitations of the land. Additionally, the proportion of the population engaged in agriculture is declining and total agriculture productivity may be affected as people abandon their agricultural land in search of better and profitable job opportunities. This is an important issue, and it needs further study.

The fertility rate of the human population appears not particularly affected by the food shortage but more by the socioeconomic institutions that consider children as future security for parents and invaluable labor in traditional labor-intensive agriculture, especially as farmers expand agriculture in marginal areas in an attempt to increase food production per person.

Grigg (1976) found that the development of agriculture in Nepal is limited by the socioeconomic situation of farmers as well as the difficult rugged landscape of Nepal. Most farmers are still following old, traditional methods of farming and have not been able to adopt modern agriculture technologies, and so farm mechanization is limited to richer farmers on the terai plain. For example, 75 percent of all farmers were well aware of the modern inputs and their value even in early 1970s. Nevertheless, only about 12 percent actually used them even though there were credit programs to support farmers. The farmers were hesitant to take risks due to the high cost of farm machinery, fuel, fertilizers, and pesticides and the problems of commercialization, which made adoption difficult and risky (HMG 1970). Hence the population continued to expand with very little modernization of agriculture because the population density is so great there cannot be sufficient cereal surpluses that would be needed to pay for the new inputs to agriculture.

Yet, in the early 1970s, the introduction of agriculture technologies and innovations had visible effects on Nepalese society. The gap between the rich and poor farmers had enlarged because it is usually only the relatively well-off farmers who are able to adopt modern technologies and innovations and who in fact get credit benefit and receive other facilities intended to support poor farmers. This situation, which is archetypical of developing countries engaging in the green revolution, led to rich farmers producing lots of relatively low-cost cereals that undersell others.

The increase in agricultural land is often achieved by forest clearing, which on the one hand affects human livelihood directly by depleting the timber and non-timber forest resources and through the effects of increasing flooding, and on the other hand affects agro-ecosystems by disturbing the natural process of soil fertility restoration. This is further evidence that Boserup's ideas cannot work in Nepal.

The use of chemical fertilizers appears to have become essential in Nepalese agriculture to counteract the effects of erosion and to enhance the productivity, although the cost of using chemical fertilizer is huge in Nepal, as it has neither any domestic fertilizer production plant nor hardly any means of paying for imports. This study found that in 1999–2000 Nepal spent approximately $9.85 million to import fertilizer at the cost of approximately $714 per metric ton (CBS 2001). Similarly, in 1999–2000 farmers spent one dollar per kilogram of fertilizer, which is interesting as more than 42 percent of the total population in Nepal earns $0.30 or less per day (Shrestha 1998).

Previous research has shown that Nepal's use of fertilizer has declined to 16.8 kg per hectare in 1999/00 (MOA 2000; CBS 2000), as compared to 94 kg per hectare in India (Golleti 2001). The maximum national average consumption was recorded at 35 kg per hectare per year in 1994/95 (MOA 2000). The rapid decline in fertilizer use after 1995 was due to the removal of the fertilizer subsidy (MOA 2000), which in return was induced by difficult economic conditions in Asia. Although there is a discrepancy in Nepal's fertilizer statistics maintained by different national and international organizations (Goletti 2001), the amount of chemical fertilizer used per unit of land is very low. The reasons have been identified as due to difficult terrain, unavailability of fertilizer, and especially poverty among farmers.

Most of the uncultivated land in Nepal is marginal with poor soils, which if developed would require costly irrigation and water management systems, and costly measures to enrich the soil. In addition, clearing of forests in search of potential agricultural land would cause environmental damage including land degradation, erosion, and climate changes, not to mention the loss of timber and non-timber forest resources that Nepalese subsistence livelihood is dependent upon. Hence, insufficient per capita land and marginal agriculture among poor farmers are the reasons for low agriculture production and food scarcity, and these in turn can be based on high population levels and rapid population growth.

Conclusion

This study has investigated the relation between population growth and cereal supply in Nepal. The analysis of the trends of population growth and agriculture productivity, specifically that of cereals (rice, maize, wheat, barley, and millet) indicates that Nepal's population has been growing rapidly, but Nepal has not been able to increase the agriculture productivity as rapidly. In fact, the population growth rate is so great that even with increased chemical fertilizer use it is very unlikely that enough cereals can be produced to feed the growing population. This does not support my (that is, Boserup's) hypothesis underlying the study that population growth increases agriculture productivity. Perhaps her ideas once were applicable to Nepal when human populations were much less, but they certainly are not for the period examined.

I have argued that any positive effects of population growth is insignificant in the case of Nepal, as the rate of population growth has outstripped the rate of cereal production and decreased per capita income of farmers. Farmers have not been able to adopt agriculture technologies of agriculture intensification, including use of chemical fertilizers to enhance agriculture production, because fertilizers do not work well in Nepal (possibly due to the long nights of the subtropical environment; see Hall 2000, chapter 12) and because farmers cannot afford them. Nepal imported 50,000 tons of cereals and also received a food aid of 240,700 tons of cereals in 1998 (FAO 2000), which compensated for about 14 percent of the cereal deficit that year. Considering Nepal's deteriorating economy, another important issue that needs further study is how long Nepal can support population growth with food importation and food aid.

But the most important way that Nepal can solve these crises is to increase its efforts for population control and conduct education and awareness programs on population control. The Nepalese government and its teachers must conduct such programs on population control because one of the reasons of continued population growth in Nepal is its socioeconomic structure and its cultural and religious beliefs. In addition, the government should focus on generating other opportunities and initiatives for the young people, especially women, to delay early motherhood. I am hopeful that this study will assist Nepal's planners and decision makers to develop strategies for balancing population and sustained food production.

This research was based on limited data and information; particularly in the simulation model, I have many assumptions to derive the parameters and variables, hence with better measurement and metrics the model prediction can be improved and made more realistic. I intend to do this over the next decade.

References

Ahmed, A. 1984. *Agricultural Stagnation Under Population Pressure: The Case of Bangladesh*. Dacca: Vikash.

Alteri, M. A., and M. K. Anderson. 1986. An ecological basis for the development of alternative agricultural systems for small farmers in the third world. *Journal of Alternative Agriculture* 1:20–38.

Barker, R., and D. Chapman. 1990. The economics of sustainable agricultural systems in developing countries. In Edwards et al. 1990, 478–94.

Bilsborrow, R. E., and D. L. Carr. 2001. Population, agricultural land use, and the environment in developing countries. In D. R. Lee and C. B. Barrett, eds., *Tradeoff or Synergies? Agricultural Intensification, Economic Development and the Environment*, 35–56. Oxford: CAB International.

Blum, W. E. H. 1998. Sustainability and land use. In G. E. D'Souza and T. G. Gebremedhin, eds., *Sustainability in Agriculture and Rural Development*, 171–91. Brookfield, Vt.: Ashgate.

Boserup, E. 1965. *The Conditions of Agricultural Growth*. London: Allen and Unwin.

———. 1981. *Population and Technological Change: A Study of Long-Term Trends*. Chicago: University of Chicago Press.

Brown, L. 1981. World population growth, soil erosion, and food security. *Science* 214, no. 27: 195–214.

CBS. 2000–2002. Statistical Year Book of Nepal, Central Bureau of Statistics, Nepal.

Clark, C. 1967. *Population Growth and Land Use*. London: Macmillan.

Demeny, P. 1979. On the end of the population explosion. *Population and Development Review* 5, no. 1: 141–69.

Edwards, C. A., R. Lal, P. Madden, R. H. Miller, and G. House, eds. 1990. *Sustainable Agriculture Systems*. Iowa City: Soil and Water Conservation Society.

FAO. 2000–2002. FAO Statistics. http://www.fao.org.

Goletti, F. 2001. The impact of fertilizer subsidy removal in Nepal. Discussion Paper No. 1. Agricultural Sector Performance Review, ADB TA 3536-NEP.

Grigg, D. B. 1976. Population pressure and agricultural change. *Progress in Geography* 8:135–76.

Hall, C. A. S., ed. 2000. *Quantifying Sustainable Development: The Future of Tropical Economies*. San Diego: Academic Press.

Hall, C. A. S., and J. W. Day, eds. 1977. *Ecosystem Modeling in Theory and Practice: An Introduction with Case Histories*. New York: Wiley-Interscience.

Hall, C. A. S., and M. Hall. 1993. The efficiency of land and energy use in tropical economies and agriculture. *Agriculture, Ecosystems and Environment* 46:1–30.

Hall, C. A. S., J. Ko, C. Lee, and H. Wang. 1998. Ricardo lives: The inverse relation of resource exploitation intensity and efficiency in Costa Rican agriculture and its relation to sustainable development. In S. Ulgaldi, ed., *Advances in Energy Studies: Energy Flows in Ecology and Economy*, 355–70. Rome: Musis.

Hall, C. A. S., C. Leon, W. Ravenscroft, and H. Wang. 2000. Temporal and spatial overview of Costa Rican agricultural production. In Hall 2000, 349–401.

Harris, J. M. 1996. World agricultural futures: Regional sustainability and ecological limits. *Ecological Economics* 17:95–116.

HMG. 1970. *Agriculture Report*. Katmandu: His Majesty's Government of Nepal.

Hooper, W. D. 1976. The development of agriculture in developing countries. *Scientific American* 235, no. 3: 197–205.

Kabir, M., and A. A. Chowdhary. 1982. Population growth and food production in Bangladesh. Dacca: Center for Population Studies Occasional Paper 4.

Kaosa-ard, M. S., and B. Rerkasem. 2000. *The Growth and Sustainability of Agriculture in Asia*. Oxford: Oxford University Press.

Konar, D. N. 1996. Population growth, agricultural development and the problem of environment in India. In K. C. Roy, R. K. Sen, and C. A. Tisdell, eds., *Environment and Sustainable Agricultural Development: Concepts, General Issues, Constraints and Strategies*, 101–11. Delhi: International Institute of Development Studies.

Loomis, R. S. 1976. Agricultural systems. *Scientific American* 235, no. 3: 99–105.

Maikhuri, R. K., K. S. Rao, and R. L. Semwal. 2001. Changing scenario of Himalayan agro ecosystems: Loss of agro biodiversity, an indicator of environmental change in Central Himalaya, India. *The Environmentalist* 21:23–39.

MOA. 1998–2001. Fertilizer Unit. Ministry of Agriculture, Nepal.

MOF. 1999. Ministry of Finance, Nepal.

MOP. 2000. Ministry of Population and Environment. Nepal. www.mope.gov.np.

Negi, A. K., B. P. Bhatt, and N. P. Todaria. 1999. Local population impacts on the forests of Garhwal Himalaya, India. *The Environmentalist* 19:293–303.

Norse, D. 1992. A new strategy for feeding a crowded planet. *Environment* 34, no. 5: 6–11, 32–39.

Pandey, U., and J. S. Singh. 1984. Energy-flow relationship between agro- and forest ecosystems in Central Himalaya. *Environmental Conservation* 11, no. 1: 45–53.

Pimentel, D. 1980. Environmental and economic costs of soil erosion and conservation benefits. *Science* 267:1117–23.

Pimentel, D., and M. Pimentel. 1996. *Food, Energy and Society*. Boulder: University Press of Colorado.

Pimentel, D., E. C. Terhune, R. Dyson-Hudson, S. Rochereau, R. Samis, E. A. Smith, D. Denman, D. Reifschneder, and M. Shepard. 1976. Land degradation: Effects on food and energy resources. *Science* 194:149–55.

PRB. 2002. Population Reference Bureau. www.prb.com.

Rai, R. 2003. An analysis of the relation of human population growth and cereal production in Nepal. M.S. thesis, State University of New York.

Randhawa, N. S., and I. P. Abrol. 1990. Sustaining agriculture: The Indian scene. In Edwards et al. 1990, 438–52.

Ruttan, V. W. 1997. Sustainable growth in agricultural production: Poetry, policy, and science. In S. A. Vosti and T. Reardon, eds., *Sustainability, Growth and Poverty Alleviation: A Policy and Agro-ecological Perspective*, 19–33. Baltimore: Johns Hopkins University Press.

Sankhyan, P. L., N. Gurung, B. L. Sitaula, and O. Hofstad. 2000. Bio-economic modeling of land use and forest degradation at watershed level in Nepal. *Agriculture Ecosystem & Environment* 3:1–12.

Seddon, D. 1987. *Nepal: A State of Poverty*. New Delhi: Vikas.

Shrestha, D. 1998. *Agriculture Mechanization and Management*. Katmandu: Country Report of Nepal.

Short, C. 2001. Food insecurity: A symptom of poverty. Paper delivered at the Sustainable Food Security for All by 2020 Conference, September 4–6, Bonn, Germany.

Smith, L. C., A. E. El Obeid, and H. H. Jensen. 1999. The geography and causes of food insecurity in developing countries. *Agricultural Economics* 22:199–215.

Thapa, G. B., and K. E. Weber. 1999. Population and environment in the hills of Nepal. *Asia-Pacific Population Journal* 4:2.

Upreti, B. R., and Y. G. Upreti. 2002. Factors leading to agro-biodiversity loss in developing countries: The case of Nepal. *Biodiversity and Conservation* 11:1607–21.

Wasti, P. C. 2002. Feeding the hungry: A challenging task. *The Rising Nepal*, July 15.

Weeks, J. R. 1974. *Population: An Introduction to Concepts and Issues*. 4th ed. Belmont, Calif.: Wadsworth.

PART THREE

Science for Development

Building Biophysical Models of Development Potential

Over the years, biophysical scientists have developed theory and applied a wealth of biophysical methods and tools to real problems in the developing world, working with farmers and policy makers. Yet little is known of these efforts outside the development research community. This and subsequent sections give a series of examples in which biophysical science, sometimes alone, sometimes in conjunction with economics, has been applied to issues of development in Latin America. The subjects chosen are familiar ones to people working in development: land use, land quality, soils, water availability, erosion, and the consequences of developing suboptimal land. Chapter 13 suggests a simple method to examine the trade-offs between erosion and income in a small watershed in Honduras using a spatial bioeconomic model. Chapter 14 develops a spatial model for water availability and management, predicting, for example, how far families in Honduras will have to walk to get water in wet seasons and dry, a means of helping to assess where and how water supply schemes would benefit the people who need it the most. Chapters 15 and 16 summarize part of what was a very comprehensive and sophisticated program of agricultural and land-use analysis by a Dutch group from the University of Waginengen;

the latter chapter derives a soil classification system more useful to agronomists. Chapter 17 generates a model of how development in the coastal region of Venezuela is likely to evolve and therefore to contribute to the probability of additional landslides that have already had devastating effects on the communities of this region. Chapter 18 extends this concept of modeling land-use change to comprehensive work for estimating where land-use change will occur in Latin America. Finally, chapter 19 specifies the components of a comprehensive yet simple mathematical model to simulate the evolution of food production and consumption in Eritrea, an example of what we might consider "rapid assessment" for a developing nation, as discussed in chapter 6.

In all cases, a main point of the analysis is that one has to pay much attention to the geographical and biophysical factors of an environment and to the interrelationships between them before one undertakes development—whether that development is perceived as good or bad. Failure to take all important parameters into account can lead to the collapse of whole agroecosystems. New computer-based tools provide useful and straightforward ways to analyze these complex issues and help provide sound recommendations to decision makers.

CHAPTER 13

TRADE-OFFS BETWEEN INCOME AND EROSION IN A SMALL WATERSHED

GIS and Economic Modeling in the Río Jalapa Watershed, Honduras

BRUNO BARBIER, ALEXANDER HERNÁNDEZ,

ORLANDO MEJIA, AND SAMUEL RIVERA

Introduction

Honduras has a long history of problems related to watershed management. In the late 1980s, the output of the El Níspero hydroelectric dam had to be reduced by 50 percent due to sedimentation problems. During early 1994, the El Cajón hydroelectric dam reduced its operation due to high sedimentation rates and a severe drought that affected this area. The resulting power shortages cost $20 million each month in lost industrial production (Gollin 1994). In 1998, when Hurricane Mitch hit Honduras, floods and landslides took more than eleven thousand lives. Millions of dollars were lost in infrastructure damages. In all cases, the press accused deforestation and the general mismanagement of the hillsides by farmers and loggers as well as the inaction of the government.

There are now many watershed management projects in Honduras financed by major as well as small donors. These projects dedicate themselves to reforestation and to community management. Most of these projects use GIS to define and promote sustainable land use. The many methods that have been implemented to determine best land use have focused on biophysical variables such as soils, slope, and climate, with little consideration for socioeconomic variables such as profitability, distance to roads, and population density, making the recommendations difficult to implement (Richter 1995).

Another difficulty of these projects is the compromise between economic factors and the environment. Win-win situations might occur, but in most cases there is a trade-off between productivity and environmental conservation. To calculate such trade-offs, one needs to assess the effect of different options on both productivity and the environment. Scientists have developed different tools that help establish such relations. These decision support tools have become sufficiently reliable to be used in a given environment. The combination of GIS and optimization models can help to determine loss of income while reducing erosion in a watershed.

Why use an optimization model to predict farmers' behavior? Economists believe that farmers are rational and that their decisions are based upon a utility maximization framework. Thus, an optimization model is likely to predict farmers' behavior. In Honduras, as in most developing countries, a watershed is mainly controlled by the decisions made by private owners and very little by government. Many conflicts may occur if watershed management plans are not designed to propose land uses that maximize individuals' incomes. This is one more reason why watershed models should add a profit-maximizing objective to the biophysical variables (Beaulieu and Benneth 1998).

Characterization of Honduras

Honduras, located in the middle of Central America (figure 13.1), is characterized by a wet climate in the north and a semiarid climate in the south. Precipitation is irregular north and south. More than half of Honduras might experience rainfalls of greater than 300 mm in twenty-four hours (Hargreaves 1992). Approximately 46 percent

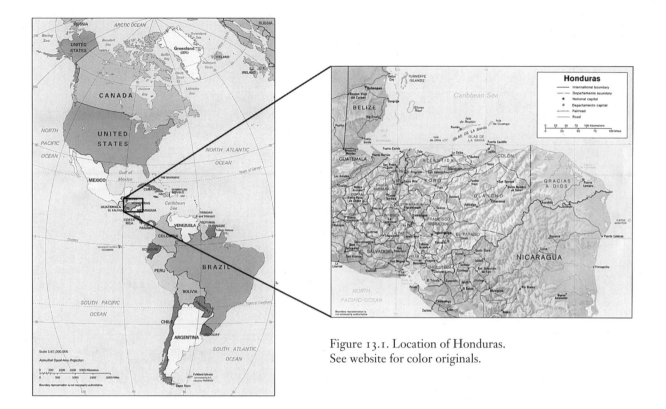

Figure 13.1. Location of Honduras.
See website for color originals.

of the country is still covered by forests (Rivera, Martínez, and Sabillón 1999), although other land uses such as agriculture and cattle ranching are spreading fast.

In Honduras, most soils are classified as having a high to very high erosion risk. In addition, the terrain is steep, with 75 percent of the territory having slopes greater than 30 percent. Most soils are underlain by poorly permeable material so that deep percolation of water is limited, increasing run-off (Hargreaves 1992). Erodible soils, steep terrain, runoff, and bad practices combine to produce a great deal of erosion, which is increasing even as water quality is declining at an accelerated rate (OAS-UNAH 1992; Government of Honduras 1991).

The Study Area

The Río Jalapa watershed is typical of central Honduras. It is an upper second-order watershed of the El Cajón watershed, which supplies 57 percent of the electricity used in Honduras. The Jalapa watershed has abundant water resources (Hargreaves 1992). The annual discharge from the major streams is used for domestic consumption and livestock,

but very little for agriculture (Gutierrez 1992).

The Jalapa watershed covers an area of 2,509 hectares (Hernandez 1999). In 1994, the total population of the watershed was around two thousand people. The population density is around eighty persons per square kilometer and is increasing at almost 3 percent annually, which means that the population is likely to double during the next twenty years. This population is entirely rural, and the vast majority lives below the poverty limit.

The landscape topography of the watershed is rugged (figure 13.2). Tributaries are generally enclosed in narrow V-shaped valleys and possess a dendritic drainage pattern. Soils of the upper watershed, which originated from limestone, are fertile. Soils of the medium and lower watershed, which originated from clay stone, are much less fertile (Simmons and Castellanos 1969). Only a small valley in the lower watershed has fertile alluvial soils. Most of these soils have slow water percolation, especially in the upland areas leading to more surface runoff (Hargreaves 1992).

The annual mean temperature varies from 22 to 24 Celsius (Hargreaves 1992). The climate consists of a dry season (higher temperature values occur from March to April) and a rainy season (higher temperature values occur from May to December) (Hirt, Lara, and Hasemann 1989). Rainfall in the valleys is approximately 1,200 mm per year, while upland forest-covered areas receive an annual average of 2,000 mm (Hirt, Lara, and Hasemann 1989). Because of soil quality and rainfall, the upper part of the watershed is totally cultivated, while the middle part is occupied by forest. A small valley in the lower watershed is left mostly for extensive pasture. Most of the farming consists of semi-subsistence farming. The closest town is one hour away, making commercialization difficult. The crops are mostly maize and beans. Coffee production is limited. Agriculture covers about one-third of the watershed area (Hernandez 1999).

The forest, which covers 65 percent of the watershed, includes two types of trees: pine trees in the central part of the watershed and broadleaf trees located mainly in the very upper part of the watershed (figure 13.2). The pine trees are *Pinus oocarpa*, which is adequate for timber production. The broadleaf trees are usually deciduous species of oak (*Quercus* sp.) suitable only for fuelwood and fences (Hernandez 1999).

Methodology

Our methodology was to use an optimizing model combined with GIS data from the watershed to determine which combination of land-use options (agriculture, pasture, coffee, pine forest, broadleaf forest) would maximize the profit of the community living in the watershed. Aerial photographs and maps of properties were used to determine homogenous land units (HLU) of a few hectares based on slope, altitude, access to market, and land tenure. These HLU then became the input of the model. We present the data, then the way the HLU are calculated, and then the optimization model.

Survey Data

We conducted a small survey with sixteen typical farms drawn from a typology based on farm size to determine key variables (prices, costs,performance, requirements, and availability of labor and capital).

Figure 13.2. Agricultural production and forest cover in the upper part of the Río Jalapa watershed.

We selected additional data from the national agriculture census of 1993 with the purpose of comparing and/or assuring the quality of the information obtained during the surveys. We also revised the forest management plan document from 1996 prepared by the forestry agency. The information obtained included productivity per ha per year for each type of use.

Homogenous Land Units

For the purpose of the present study, seventy-two HLU types were established. Four variables and their combinations were considered to settle them (table 13.1).

We digitized a topographic map (1:50,000 scale) containing twenty-meter altitude contours to generate the digital elevation model (DEM). Slope polygon cover was generated by mathematical derivation from the DEM. Altitude polygons resulted from the topology intersection (digital) of the watershed boundaries and the contours representing the altitude classes mentioned above.

Three buffers of distance to a road were obtained by digitizing visible roads in a digital aerial photograph, collecting field data using a GPS (Global Positioning System) device to verify what had been digitized. We created a few buffers around the roads according to the distances from the road (0.5, 1.0, and more than 1.0 km). The information about land tenure was digitized from cadastral maps (1:50,000 scale). The four layers

<table>
<tr><td colspan="5">**Table 13.1. Choice variables to determine the Homogenous Land Units**</td></tr>
</table>

Variables	Variable Codes & Description			
	1	**2**	**3**	**4**
Slope	0 to 15%	15.1 to 30%	30.1 to 45%	More than 45%
Altitude	Less than 800 masl*	801 to 1200 masl	More than 1200 masl	
Distance to a road	Less than 500 m.	501 to 1000m.	More than 1000m.	
Land tenure	National	Private		

* meters above sea level

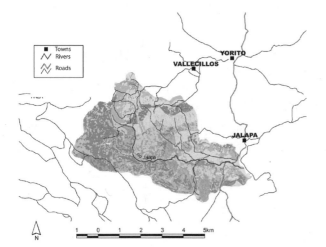

Figure 13.3. Map of the seventy-two homogenous land units of the Jalapa watershed. The highest elevation is toward the west (left) and the lowest toward the east (right).

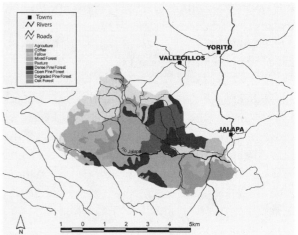

Figure 13.4. Land-use map for the Río Jalapa watershed, based on areal photo interpretation.

(slope, altitude, distance, and tenure) were spatially overlaid in order to obtain seventy-two combinations that would lead to the HLUs (figure 13.3).

Each HLU has a different productivity based on data from the 1993 national census (DGECH 1994). Productivity is higher at higher altitude and on flatter soils. For maize, for example, yields ranged from 700 kilos to 2 tons per hectare. The land-use map was generated from the visual interpretation and definition of the different classes that were screen digitized from the aerial photographs (figure 13.4). This cover was then checked by collecting field samples and spotting the field with a GPS device.

The Bioeconomic Model

Bioeconomic models link economic behavioral models such as mathematical programming with biophysical components such as erosion, soil fertility, and water or soil-nutrients balances. For further information on these models, see Barbier and Bergeron (1999) and Kruseman (2000). For a partial review, see Oriade and Dillon (1997).

In this study, the bioeconomic model maximizes the income of the whole watershed as if it were one large farm. The model is static, and we are looking at average year. We do not consider investment time in this exercise. The different competing activities are the different land uses. The constraints of the model are land, labor, capital, and grain consumption by the population. Land is divided into seventy-two HLUs. Labor, capital, and consumption are divided by the three main sectors of the watershed, which we distinguished according to altitudes.

Below we present the equations of the model. The subscripts of the variables are c for the nine possible land uses, s for the three slopes, a for the three altitudes, b for the three buffers (determined by various distances from the roads), and o for the two land tenures.

Objective funtion =

$$Max \sum_{c=1}^{C}\sum_{s=1}^{S}\sum_{a=1}^{A}\sum_{b=1}^{B}\sum_{o=1}^{O} n_{c,s,a,b,o} \cdot X_{c,s,a,b,o} - u_a \cdot G_a$$

The model maximizes the sum of net incomes (n) from the different land uses (of area X) less the cost of grain (G) purchased for a given price (u) outside of the watershed. This last variable gives the opportunity to the model to move away from subsistence production to generate cash crops if it is economically more interesting. The unit of the equation above is in local currency.

Constraint on land area =

$$\sum_{c=1}^{C} X_{c,s,a,b,o} \leq UTH_{s,a,b,o}$$

The area of each land use has to be less than the available area (UTH). The unit of the equation above is in hectares.

Constraint on labor =

$$\sum_{c=1}^{C}\sum_{s=1}^{S}\sum_{b=1}^{B}\sum_{o=1}^{O} lab_{c,s,a,b,o} \cdot X_{c,s,a,b,o} \leq disp \cdot POP_a$$

The labor requirement for each hectare of land use (lab) has to be less than the available labor at the different altitudes ($disp$) multiplied by the population (POP) within each altitude range. Labor requirements for the land uses located within the buffer closest to the road is less than for the same land uses located further from the road. The unit of the equation above is in days of labor.

Constraint on inputs =

$$\sum_{c=1}^{C}\sum_{s=1}^{S}\sum_{b=1}^{B}\sum_{o=1}^{O} inp_{c,s,a,b,o} \cdot X_{c,s,a,b,o} \leq CAP_a$$

Each type of land use requires different types of inputs or investment (*inp*). Their sum has to be less than the available cash of the population living at each of the three altitudes (*CAP*). The unit of the equation above is the lempira, the local currency.

Constraint on consumption =

$$\sum_{c=1}^{C}\sum_{s=1}^{S}\sum_{b=1}^{B}\sum_{o=1}^{O} y_{c,s,a,b,o} \cdot X_{c,s,a,b,o} + G_a \geq cons \cdot POP_a$$

Per capita grain consumption (*cons*) multiplied by the population (*POP*) has to be satisfied by own grain production represented by yields (*y*) multiplied by the area (*X*) or by grain purchase (*G*). The unit of the equation is one ton of grain.

Soil erosion =

$$\sum_{c=1}^{C}\sum_{s=1}^{S}\sum_{a=1}^{A}\sum_{b=1}^{B}\sum_{o=1}^{O} eros_{c,s,a,b,o} \cdot X_{c,s,a,b,o} = EROSION$$

We consider that total erosion (*EROSION*) is the sum of the erosion occurring in each hectare of land use (*eros*) multiplied by the area in this land use (*X*). The unit of the equation above is one ton of soil.

We solved the problem of maximizing the income of the watershed (i.e. the objective function) under constraints with a mathematical programming algorithm. The solution shows the optimal combination of land uses for the whole watershed. If the model is correctly specified, the results are usually close to what farmers already do, which is not surprising since farmers in reality have little choice given the strong constraints they face. If the model is able to reproduce farmers' reactions to various external conditions, we can run new scenarios. For instance, we changed the maximum possible level of erosion as if the manager of the hydroelectric dam downstream decided that this watershed has to reduce the quantity of eroded soil. Since one line of the model sums up the erosion within the watershed, we can bind the model

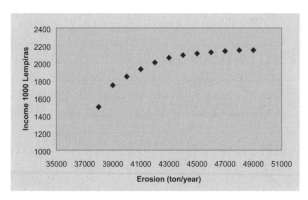

Figure 13.5. Trade-off between simulated erosion and simulated incomes in the Río Jalapa watershed.

to less than a given amount of erosion. The model will look for a less erosive optimal land use.

Results and Conclusion

The optimal-simulated land use turned out to be similar to the actual land use. As in reality, the crops are located in the upper watershed, close to the road. The rest of the land is mainly used for pine trees and pastures. This landscape is explained by the low population density of the watershed, by the difficulty in carrying the products to the road, and by the quality of the soils in each region. Simulated erosion reaches 50,000 tons per year for the whole watershed. This represents 20 tons/ha on average, but the cropped area causes much of the erosion while the other land uses show little erosion. When we start to impose a restriction on erosion levels, the model changes for less erosive land uses such as

pasture and coffee, but income starts to decrease.

When we plot different erosion levels with the resulting incomes we get the curve of the trade-off between the two variables (figure 13.5). It shows a characteristic upward and concave curve. This curve suggests that with the current technology it would be relatively easy to reduce the erosion in the watershed by almost 20 percent without reducing farmers' incomes much. The company running the hydroelectric dam could easily compensate farmers for this loss.

Saturation of income appears to occur around 40,000 tons of erosion. There is little probability of producing less than 37,000 tons per year of erosion because such land use does not generate enough income. If we want to reduce erosion, cropping is no longer possible, and the alternative land uses are not profitable enough to buy food.

Without being a clear win-win situation for both the farmer and the environment, the form of the curve is encouraging for watershed management projects. Alternatives such as coffee production can help significantly in reducing erosion while maintaining incomes. But to reduce erosion to less than 20 percent of present, one will need to think about more expensive means.

This modeling framework can be applied rapidly in different watersheds. The necessary data can be collected in a few weeks. It can help project managers and even communities compare different land-use options and predict their impact on incomes and the environment.

References

Barbier, B., and G. Bergeron. 1999. Impact of policy interventions on land management in Honduras: Results of a bioeconomic model. *Agricultural Systems* 60:1–16.

Beaulieu, J., and D. Benneth. 1998. Ecological-economic modeling on a watershed basis: A case study of the Cache River of Southern Illinois. Southern Illinois University.

Chaves, H. M. L., and M. A. Nearing. 1996. Uncertainty analysis of the WEPP soil erosion model. Transaction of the American Society of Agricultural Engineers, Research Note Int–305.

COHDEFOR. 1996. Plan de acción forestal de largo plazo 1996–2015. PLANFOR. Borrador. Unidad de Planificación Institucional. Tegucigalpa: AFE-COHDEFOR.

DGECH (Dirección General de Estadísticas y Censos de Honduras). 1994. *Tercero censo agropecuario nacional.* Tegucigalpa: DGECH.

Gobierno de Honduras. 1984. Reglamento General Forestal. *La Gaceta.*

———. *Agenda ambiental de Honduras.* 2nd ed. Tegucigalpa: Gobierno de Honduras, 1991.

Gollin, J. D. 1994. Trees down, lights out in Honduras. *Christian Science Monitor*, November 15, 1994.

Government of Honduras. 1991. Honduras: Environmental agenda. UNCED National Reports, 1994. Directory of Country Environmental Studies Data Base. Record 366.

Gutiérrez, L. A. 1992. *Diagnóstico de las cuencas hidrográficas de Honduras: Informe de consultaría.* Tegucigalpa: Banco Interamericano de Desarrollo.

Hargreaves, G. 1992. Hydrometeorologic data for Honduran water resources development. Dept. of Biological and Irrigation Engineering, Utah State University.

Hirt, K., G. Lara, and G. Hasemann. 1989. Archaeological research in the El Cajon region. University of Pittsburgh—Instituto Hondureño de Antropología.

Humphrey, C. 1997. *Honduras Handbook.* Portland, Ore.: Moon Travel Handbooks.

Kruseman, G. 2000. Bio-economic household modelling for agricultural intensification. Manshold Graduate School of Social Sciences, Wageningen University.

OAS-UNAH. 1992. *La cuenca del río Choluteca.* Tegucigalpa: Ediciones Saz.

Oriade, C. A., and C. A. Dillon. 1997. Developments in biophysical and bioeconomic simulation of agricultural systems: A review. *Agricultural Economics* 17:45–58.

Rivera, S., L. M. Martínez, and G. Sabillón 1998. Multitemporal analysis of the deforestation in Honduras. Watershed Science Unit, Utah State University.

Simmons, C., and V. Castellanos. 1969. Informe al Gobierno de Honduras sobre los suelos de Honduras. Rome: FAO.

Chapter 14

Simulation Modeling for Characterizing Strategic Streamwater Availability in the Tascalapa River Watershed, Honduras

Joep Luijten and Ron Knapp

Introduction

Growing demand on available water resources caused by general population growth and movement of people to increasingly marginal areas is increasingly a major threat to food security, human health, and natural ecosystems throughout the world. An estimated 1.4 billion people, amounting to a quarter of the world population, or a third of the population in developing countries, live in regions that will experience severe water scarcity by 2025 (Seckler, Barker, and Amarasinghe 1999; Vorosmarty and Sahagian 2000). People are particularly at risk in regions of steep-slope hillsides, exemplified by many areas in Latin America. Small-scale farming is the predominant economic activity and means of food supply in these hillside areas. Small streams are the primary or only source of water to meet domestic, industrial, and agricultural water needs in these areas, but people have only very limited means of managing water resources.

Several studies have been conducted to quantify fresh water availability on a national level, ranking countries according to their per capita available annual water resources (AWR) (Falkenmark, Lundqvist, and Widstrand 1989; Raskin et al. 1997; Seckler et al. 1998). Falkenmark, Lundqvist, and Widstrand (1989) considered freshwater shortages local and rare for AWR values above 1,700 m³ per capita, whereas water availability was considered a primary constraint to life for AWR values less than 500 m³ per capita. With the exception of Peru, the sample of Latin American countries in table 14.1 considerably exceeds the threshold, suggesting an abundance of available fresh water and enough

leeway to expand water use in the future in those countries. However, water availability is distributed in a spatially and temporally heterogeneous manner in patterns that may differ from water needs. The data in table 14.1, therefore, do not provide any insight to water security at spatial scales smaller than a country, for example, a small watershed.

We studied water availability in one such watershed, the Tascalapa River watershed in Honduras, during the late 1990s as part of the Hillsides Program of the International Center for Tropical Agriculture (CIAT), in Cali, Colombia (CIAT 1997; Knapp et al. 1998). The first stage for planning development projects in this watershed included a three-day Participatory Planning by Objective (PPO) workshop, held on February 3–6, 1998, in Lago de Yojoa, Cortés, Honduras. The workshop brought together a broad group of stakeholders: local farmers, community groups, agricultural extension agencies, and regional government officials. The specific objectives of this workshop were to identify current problems in the Tascalapa River watershed as they relate to both natural resources management and aspects of well-being in general, to formulate specific development objectives, generate integrated development plans, specify a clear vision of responsibilities and expected results, and coordinate all activities (CLODEST 1998).

Workshop participants brainstormed about a wide range of issues and problems in the watersheds, including deforestation, land burning, soil erosion, water resources, fuel sources, human health, lack of income and development opportunities, and limited access to markets (CLODEST 1998). They

Table 14.1. Basic statistics on population and water availability in selected Latin American countries with a high percentage of the area under steep-slope agriculture

Country	Steep area[a] (%)	Population[b] (million)	AWR[c] (km^3)	Per capita AWR (10^3 m^3)
Bolivia	40	8.33	300	36.0
Colombia	40	42.11	1,070	25.4
Costa Rica	70	4.02	95	23.6
El Salvador	75	6.28	19	3.0
Ecuador	65	12.65	314	24.8
Guatemala	75	11.39	116	10.2
Honduras	80	6.42	63.4	9.9
Nicaragua	80	5.07	175	34.5
Peru	50	25.66	40	1.6
Venezuela	70	24.17	1,317	54.5

[a] Percent of the area under agriculture with slopes > 30 percent (CIAT 1996).
[b] Estimated 2000 population according to United Nations (1999) medium growth projection.
[c] Source: Seckler, Barker, and Amarasinghe (1998).

mentioned the following specific concerns related to water resources: (1) a decrease in the amount of potable water as well as diminished water quality caused by contamination; (2) the construction of "personal reservoirs" and unregulated water extraction for irrigation that could reduce downstream-water availability to levels below water needs; (3) the deforestation and lack of ground cover that may alter the hydrological behavior of the watershed, resulting in less predictable river flow rates and higher peak flow rates; (4) the strong seasonal variation in precipitation was causing some natural springs in the watershed to dry up and, as a result, watercourses to become less numerous and their beginning points to move down slope. Poor families that were not connected to piped drinking water and farmers without good irrigation equipment were most affected by reduced accessibility to water. It is also important to note that downstream communities have the advantage of benefiting from a larger catchment area, and thus higher streamflow, but they may also experience the cumulative effects (such as pollution) of any

changes in land and water resources management that occur at higher elevations.

It also became apparent from the PPO workshop that local assumptions might not always be adequate when addressing problems that are related to complex landscape processes (CIAT 1993). Water resources management problems at a watershed level can be understood and addressed better through analysis and negotiations that incorporate effects across traditional community boundaries (Knapp et al. 1999). Information technology and simulation modeling tools offer major opportunities to help scientists and local stakeholders understand landscape processes better and improve natural resources management (CIAT 2001). Geographical information systems (GIS), in combination with simulation modeling of hydrological processes, can help provide basic information about the "state of water resources," and how they change over space and time (Burrough and McDonnell 1998). Specific aspects that could be analyzed include (1) the interdependencies between land use and streamwater flow in different parts

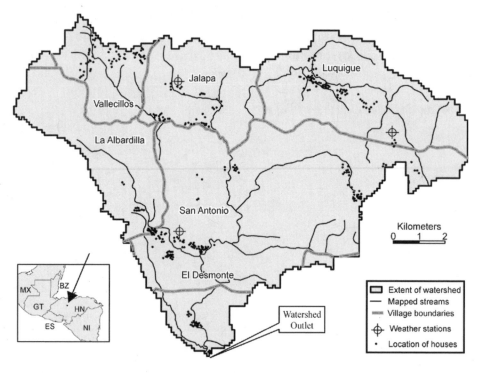

Figure 14.1. Geographical location of the Tascalapa River watershed in the department of Yoro, Honduras. Watershed boundaries were delineated from a 100-m digital elevation model.

of the watersheds; (2) the possible consequences of changes in land use/land cover, dam construction, and water extraction on water availability in downstream communities; (3) stream linkages throughout the watershed; and (4) the variation in household-level access to streams.

We developed a GIS-based simulation methodology for analyzing and synthesizing these aspects (Luijten et al. 2003). We applied this methodology earlier to assess the potential changes in water availability and water security under alternative development pathways in a hillside watershed in Colombia (Luijten, Jones, and Knapp 2000; Luijten, Knapp, and Jones 2001). This chapter presents the lessons we learned from application of the simulation methodology in the Tascalapa River watershed and discusses how the simulation results can be used to support local water resources management negotiations and planning.

Materials and Methods

We used our simulation methodology to characterize the temporal and spatial variation in streamwater availability, location of streams, and accessibility to streams in the Tascalapa River watershed. We carried out a base simulation using actual weather

data that described the actual situation in the late 1990s, and a second simulation using twenty-five years of stochastically generated weather for better computation of long-term averages and probabilities related to water availability. This section provides detailed information about the watershed, the hydrological simulation model, the different types of analyses, and the input data that were used.

Description of the Tascalapa River Watershed

The Tascalapa River watershed is located between longitude 87°22′–87°11′ W and latitude 14°56′–15°04′ N, in the province (*departamento*) of Yoro, Honduras (figure 14.1). The watershed includes all or parts of the villages (*aldeas*) of Vallecillos, Luiquigue, Jalapa (municipality of Yorito), La Albardilla, San Antonio, and El Desmonte (municipality of Sulaco). The total area of the watershed as delineated from a 100-m resolution digital elevation model (DEM) is about 12,200 ha. Elevation ranges from near 1800 m above mean sea level in the mountains to below 500 m in the central valley. The landscape is very steep: only 7 percent of the area has slopes less than 5 degrees, and half the area has slopes greater than 23 degrees, reaching 60 degrees

Table 14.2. Classification of streamwater availability and corresponding flow rates at the outlet of the Tascalapa River watershed[a]

Availability	Flow Rate		Typical water use
	Per hectare (l s^{-1} ha^{-1})	At outlet [b] (l s^{-1})	
Very low	< 0.08	< 960	Domestic use (people, animals) and irrigation of a 10 × 10 m plot per farm. Subsistence level.
Low	0.08–0.20	960–2400	Domestic use and irrigation of 0.5 ha land per farm. Self-sufficiency level.
Medium	0.20–0.32	2400–3840	Higher domestic use. Irrigation of 8.1–10 ha land per farm. Medium level of productivity.
High	> 0.32	> 3840	Abundant domestic use. Irrigation of the whole farm. Maximum level of productivity.

[a] Adapted from Luijten (1999).
[b] The flow rates (third column) were computed by multiplying the corresponding per-hectare flow rate (second column) by the catchment area, rounded to 12,000 ha.

in some locations (based on a 10-m DEM). The landscape is heterogeneous with many small plots of natural forest, bush scrub, pasture, and various crops. The main production activity is subsistence farming by smallholders, with some cash cropping and livestock production. Industrial activity is limited to the processing of maize and beans in small plants and on some farms.

The watershed has a number of landscape characteristics that are important within the context of this study. First, and most important, it is a headwater watershed; there is no run-on from adjacent areas. Streamwater flows are generally low, and unlike many regions in the United States and Europe, streamwater originates from the areas where people live and agricultural and industrial activities take place. Second, a significant minority of the poorest families, and those living at the fringes of the watershed, gathers water directly from streams to provide for their domestic, agricultural, and industrial water demands. Third, precipitation is irregular and varies strongly with seasons. Consequently, streamflow rates and the locations of streams vary over time and space. And fourth, significant differences in land cover throughout the watershed, and to a lesser extent in precipitation, could result in

differences in how and the degree to which different parts of the watershed contribute to streamwater.

Spatial Water Budget Model

We used the spatial water budget model (SWBM), a continuous, distributed-parameter watershed scale model that simulates water supply and demand over space and time on a daily basis using GIS raster structures (Luijten, Jones, and Knapp 2002). Processes that are simulated by SWBM are: (1) a land-unit water balance, (2) surface runoff and lateral flow to streams, (3) a streamwater flow balance, (4) water storage behind dams and in small manmade reservoirs, and (5) water extraction from reservoirs and streams for domestic, agricultural, and industrial uses. A stream is represented by a series of connected grid cells, each of which receives an accumulated flow beyond some threshold. Canopy interception, evapotranspiration, surface runoff, and drainage from the root zone to deeper groundwater are calculated as part of the land-unit water balance. All these processes, as well as routing of surface runoff as it flows downslope and lateral flow toward streams, are governed by empirical equations (Luijten, Jones, and Knapp 2000; Luijten, Knapp, and Jones 2001).

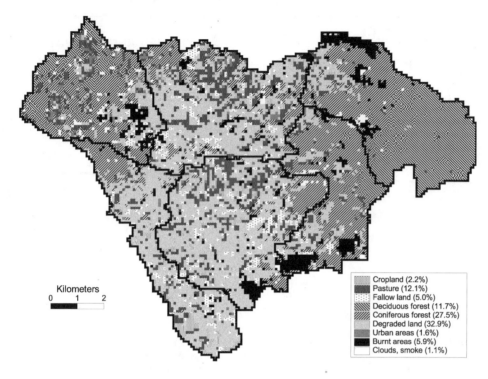

Figure 14.2. Land cover in the Tascalapa River watershed, based on 1986 data. The solid lines are the boundaries of the six zones that were used for the analysis.

Cropland (2.2%)
Pasture (12.1%)
Fallow land (5.0%)
Deciduous forest (11.7%)
Coniferous forest (27.5%)
Degraded land (32.9%)
Urban areas (1.6%)
Burnt areas (5.9%)
Clouds, smoke (1.1%)

Kilometers
0 1 2

Simulation of water supply required input data on topography, land cover, basic soil properties, and daily weather. Addition input data would be needed for the simulation of water use and the operation of dams; however, these processes were not simulated here. Required weather data consist of daily solar radiation, rainfall, and minimum and maximum temperatures (either measured or stochastically generated). Spatially variable grids of the four weather variables can be calculated by the model on a daily basis by (1) a spatial interpolation of weather data from multiple weather stations or by (2) combining weather data from one station with grids of the long-term, monthly averages of the four weather variables. We used the second method for our simulation runs.

The model was designed specifically for the needs and resources of developing countries in Latin America and the Caribbean, but can be applied in other areas as well. A more detailed scientific description of the model and the processes it simulates can be found in Luijten (1999), Luijten, Jones, and Knapp (2000), and Luijten, Knapp, and Jones (2000, 2001). SWBM is made available as an ArcView GIS 3.2 extension along with a user's manual (Luijten, Jones, and Knapp 2002) as part of the International Consortium on

Agricultural Systems Approaches toolkit (www. icasa.net/toolkit).

Overview of Simulation Analyses

First, we used SWBM to simulate water availability (before water use) in the Tascalapa River watershed from January 1, 1996, to December 31, 1999. This period includes the occurrence of Hurricane Mitch, from October 27 to November 1, 1998. Water reaches a stream as surface runoff (fast flow) and base flow (slow subsurface flow). Both flow components were calculated separately each day. Water availability at the watershed outlet was categorized as very low, low, medium, or high, based on a specific per-hectare flow rate threshold (table 14.2). This classification was similar to one that Luijten (1999) applied to a hillside watershed in Colombia, with the classification adjusted for the estimated differences in population densities and areas of the watersheds. Simulated streamflow rates at the outlet were also compared to measured flow rates for a few days in 1998 for which such measurements were available.

Results from the 1996–99 simulation run were not useful for computing statistics of average long-term water availability and flow rates because the simulated period was too short and included an

Table 14.3. Area, dominant land cover types, average slope, average runoff curve number (CN), and average annual rainfall, for six zones in the Tascalapa River watershed

Zone [a]	Area (ha)	Dominant Land Cover	Slope [c] (degrees)	CN[b,c] (-)	Rainfall (mm yr⁻¹)
1. North-west	1,779	Coniferous forest, pasture	18.7	66.9	1,277
2. North-central	2,415	Degraded land, pasture	15.8	76.1	1,244
3. North-east	2,292	Deciduous forest, coniferous forest	14.2	62.1	1,153
4. East	1,597	Coniferous forest, degraded land	14.8	65.7	1,165
5. South-central	2,509	Degraded land, pasture	13.4	77.5	1,204
6. South-west	1,563	Degraded land, coniferous forest	11.7	77.7	1,228
TOTAL	12,155	Degraded land, coniferous forest	14.8	71.3	1,211

[a] The boundaries of these zones are indicated in figure 14.2.

[b] The U.S. Soil Conservation Service runoff curve number is a dimensionless number between 0 and 100 that is used to calculate the amount of daily rainfall that becomes surface runoff (USDA-SCS, 1972). The curve numbers given here are those for Antecedent Moisture Conditions II, i.e., an average case, with a five-day antecedent rainfall amount between 0.5 and 1.5 inches.

[c] Average slope and curve numbers were derived from, resp., 100 m DEM and land cover data.

extreme weather event. Therefore, another simulation run was carried out using generated daily weather data for a period of twenty-five years, yielding streamflow data for a total of 9,131 days. These days were ranked by flow rate at the watershed outlet to identify the 1, 10, 50, 90, and 99 (flow rate) percentile days. Only the simulation results for these five selected days were further analyzed. Keep in mind that the 50 percent day is the day with the median river flow rate, but this flow rate may be quite different from the average flow rate over the twenty-five-year period. For each of the five selected days we looked at (1) the average location of streams, (2) the distance from houses to the nearest stream, and (3) the probabilities associated with the aforementioned water availability categorization, by month. Any grid cell was considered a stream cell if its accumulated flow rate (i.e., the net receiving flow from its upstream contributing area) exceeded 10 l·s⁻¹. With this threshold, simulated streams in the wet season compared well to streams on existing maps. Accessibility to streams was then computed based on the Euclidian (shortest) distance to the

stream network, using stream thresholds of both 10 l·s⁻¹ and 50 l·s⁻¹.

Last, we divided the watershed into six zones based on subwatersheds and major differences in land cover (figure 14.2). We looked how differences in land cover, average slope, and annual rainfall among the zones (table 14.3) might affect the relative water yield of each zone. Here, we defined "water yield" as the net amount of water (precipitation minus evapotranspiration) that reaches a stream via surface runoff or subsurface flow in a specific period. Each zone's relative water yield was computed as the ratio of the average monthly per-hectare water yield of the zone and the average monthly per-hectare water yield of the watershed as a whole. The SCS curve numbers in table 14.3 are used by SWBM to compute the fraction of daily precipitation that becomes surface runoff (Luijten, Jones, and Knapp 2000). Higher curve numbers result in more surface runoff and less infiltration to deeper soil layers. Steeper slopes will increase the flow rate of both surface runoff and base flow toward streams.

Table 14.4. Measured monthly rainfall (mm) in the Tascalapa River watershed[a]

Year	Jan	Feb	Mar	Apr	May	Jun	Jul	Aug	Sep	Oct	Nov	Dec	Year
1996	—	—	26	34	183	150	270	158	159	177	145	18	—
1997	55	28	17	31	25	271	154	104	166	56	70	27	1,004
1998	44	0	16	11	53	125	144	219	227	546[b]	155	14	1,554
1999	119	94	25	15	153	161	337	—	—	—	—	—	—
Mean	71	36	21	23	103	177	219	160	184	159	110	20	1,283

[a] Averages from daily measurements from the Lagunitas, El Guaco, and San Antonio weather stations.
[b] The higher values in October and November 1998 were caused by Hurricane Mitch, which occurred from October 27 through November 1. The amount of rainfall that fell on those six days was not accounted for in the calculation of the monthly and annual averages.

Data

Elevation and land cover

A digital elevation model is a representation of elevation of the landscape in the form of a matrix for use by raster-based GIS (Burrough and McDonnell 1998). A 50 m resolution DEM of the watershed was previously created at CIAT (Knapp et al. 1999) and used for water routing. The ArcView GIS Spatial Analyst (ESRI 1996) was used to resample the DEM to 100 m resolution, fill any topographic depressions that could impair the calculation of water flows, compute the flow direction, delineate streams using a minimum flow rate of 10 l·s⁻¹, and delineate subwatersheds. We found a resolution of 100 m to be the maximum though still an adequate resolution to represent the steep topography and correctly delineate streams. Land cover (figure 14.2) was based on a classification of 1986 Landsat Thematic Mapper imagery at 30 m resolution (Cox 1998). We resampled this classification at 100 m using a maximum area criterion—that is, the most frequent land use type was assigned to the aggregated grid cell.

Weather data

SWBM required daily precipitation, solar radiation, and minimum and maximum temperatures. Two weather data sources were available for this study. The first source was measured daily precipitation from three weather stations in the region (see figure 14.1), which was the only type of measured weather data available from within the watershed.

Unfortunately, there were significant gaps of missing data in all three data sets, though there was a measurement available from at least one station for each day from February 17, 1996, and July 24, 1999. Therefore, daily rainfall measurements of the three stations were averaged and assigned to the approximate center point of the three weather stations. Rainfall varied strongly within seasons, ranging from an average low of 21 mm in February to an average high of 219 mm in July (table 14.4). Extreme weather events occurred in 1998: no rainfall at all was measured in February of that year, and it remained below average in the five months thereafter, and Hurricane Mitch caused excessive rainfall of about 546 mm at the end of October, 60 percent of which fell within five days.

The second set of weather data was long-term average monthly precipitation, minimum temperature, and maximum temperatures, available in the form of grids (a total of thirty six) with a cell size of 900 m grids. These grids were part of a larger data set that covered most of Central America and was generated from the CIAT climate database. Smooth monthly climate grids at 100 m resolution were generated for the Tascalapa watershed by an inverse-distance-weighting spatial interpolation of the center points of the original grid data. Long-term average monthly precipitation and temperatures are given in table 14.5, and the spatial variation in the annual averages is mapped in figure 14.3.

The annual average minimum temperature is 15.5° C, but this varies from 11.2° C in the higher

Table 14.5. Long-term average monthly minimum temperature (Tmin, °C), maximum temperature (Tmax, °C), precipitation (Precip, mm), and number of rainy days per month (Nrain) in the Tascalapa River watershed

Year	Jan	Feb	Mar	Apr	May	Jun	Jul	Aug	Sep	Oct	Nov	Dec	Year
Tmin[a]	13.0	13.1	14.6	16.0	17.3	17.1	16.4	16.6	16.8	16.4	14.9	13.8	15.5
Tmax	25.8	27.3	30.1	31.0	30.9	29.1	28.3	28.5	28.5	27.0	25.7	25.3	28.1
Precip	30	25	21	45	140	175	155	155	206	149	67	43	1,211
Nrain[b]	4.0	3.6	4.1	5.6	11.6	15.9	14.1	14.2	18.8	15.7	8.4	5.7	10.1

[a] The temperatures and precipitation were determined from the long-term average monthly grids.

[b] The number of rainy days in each month was not readily available, but this data was essential to make a useful WeatherMan climate parameter file. Rainy days were estimated from the daily precipitation measurements for the years 1996–99, but corrected for the difference in the average monthly rainfall in 1996–99 (the "mean" row in table 14.4) and the long-term average monthly rainfall (the "precip" row in this table). This correction made use of a monthly regression function between the number of rainy days and the precipitation amount.

elevation in the east and western parts of the watershed to 18.2° C in the south-central valley. The annual average maximum temperature is 28.1° C, and varies from 24.0° C to 30.9° C. The spatial variation in the minimum and maximum temperatures in figure 14.3 is very similar because both temperatures are dependent on elevation. Precipitation in the region is bimodal; two consecutive rainy seasons peak in June and September, and the first four months of the year are very dry. Rainfall also varies significantly over space. Average annual precipitation is highest in the northwest (1,290 mm) and gradually decreases in southeastern direction to a low of 1,115 mm. However, the direction of the gradient changes over time. Visual inspection of monthly data showed that it decreases in eastward direction from May through September (wet season), southward from November though February (end of the wet season through the beginning of dry season), and it is in a transitional southeastern direction in all other months.

Both sets of weather data were used to generate a WeatherMan climate parameter file (Pickering et al. 1994). Measured rainfall during the week of Hurricane Mitch was left out because of its extremity. The WeatherMan software was then used

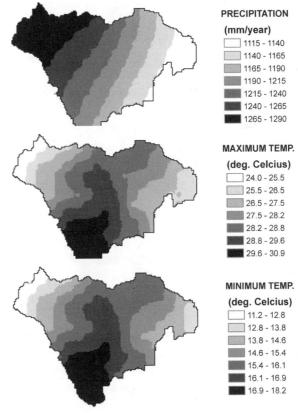

Figure 14.3. Long-term average annual precipitation and daily maximum and minimum temperatures throughout the Tascalapa River watershed (interpolated surfaces at 100 m resolution).

Table 14.6. Population of the Tascalapa River watershed, by village, for the entire village and for the part of the village that is located within watershed boundaries

Village (aldea)	Village population		Within watershed boundaries	
	Actual in 1988[a]	Estimated in 2000[b]	% houses[c]	Estimated in 2000[d]
San Antonio	2,510	3,476	78.6	2,731
Luquigue	971	1,345	86.1	1,158
Jalapa	608	842	94.1	792
Vallecillos	928	1,285	49.6	637
El Desmonte	1,609	2,228	22.3	497
La Albardilla	1,097	1,519	32.5	493
San Juan	961	1,331	0.0	0
La Esperanza	742	1,028	0.0	0
Total	9,426	13,054	48.3	6,308

[a] Source: 1988 Honduran Housing and Population Census (Knapp et al. 1998).
[b] Estimated, based on growth rates of 2.7 percent in 1988, 2.7 percent in 1993, and 3.0 percent in 1998.
[c] Determined from digitized locations of houses from topographic map sheets.
[d] Estimated from the spatial distribution of houses.

to generate daily minimum and maximum temperatures and solar radiation for all days in 1996 through 1999, as well as to fill in missing precipitation data for the first 47 days of 1996 and the last 260 days of 1999. This resulted in a complete set of daily weather data for years 1996 through 1999. In addition, we generated another set of twenty-five years of daily weather (which did not include the 1996–99 data).

Demographic data

The 1988 Honduran Population and Housing Census was the most recent and complete data set about every person and household in Honduras. The entire census database was recreated in digital form by CIAT from original Honduran governmental sources (Knapp et al. 1998). Population numbers were reported at the village (aldea) level, the smallest administrative unit in Honduras (table 14.6). Georeferenced locations of houses were digitized from scale 1:50,000 topographic map sheets of the 1970s and early 1980s. Because we did not have more recent map sheets or any

other information about specific house locations, we assumed that the spatial distribution of houses throughout the landscape—particularly the typical clustering near village centers and along major roads and streams—did not change significantly over time. Note that this assumption is not the same as an assumption of no population growth. Under our assumption, population growth would essentially be reflected by an increase in the number of persons per household rather than by an increase of the number of households over time.

Using the census data, we estimated the 2000 population of the Tascalapa River watershed in three steps. First, the 2000 population of each village was estimated (table 14.6, third column), assuming the population growth rate in the watershed was similar to that of the nation as a whole: 2.7 percent in 1988, 2.7 percent in 1993, and 3.0 percent in 1998 (a net increase of 38.5 percent over the twelve-year period). Second, the percentage of the houses of each village that is located within the watershed boundaries was computed from the digitized house locations (table 14.6, fourth column).

The overall average of 48.3 percent corresponded to 482 houses. While we recognize that the house data set was older than the census data, and that it contained considerably less houses than one would expect given the population counts and an average of five to six persons per household, it was the only data of this kind available to us. Third, the number of inhabitants of each village within the watershed boundaries in 2000 was estimated by multiplying the outcomes of the previous two analysis steps, resulting in a total watershed population of 6,308 (table 14.6, fifth column). This estimated population was used for categorizing streamwater availability. The house locations were used also to compute household-level accessibility to streams.

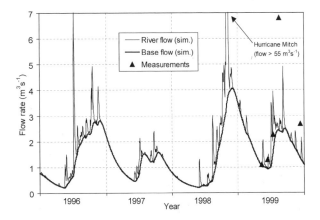

Figure 14.4. Simulated river flow and its base flow component (m³·s⁻¹) at the outlet of the Tascalapa River watershed, 1 January 1996–31 December 1999, with a few measured flow rates.

Streamflow measurements

Streamflow measurements taken near the watershed outlet were available for only a few days in 1999: 1.09 m³·s⁻¹ on May 12, 1.29 m³·s⁻¹ on June 12, 2.26 m³·s⁻¹ on July 14, 6.81 m³·s⁻¹ on August 15, 11.01 m³·s⁻¹ on September 11, 10.57 m³·s⁻¹ on October 16, 10.32 m³·s⁻¹ on November 13, and 2.68 m³·s⁻¹ on December 11. These measurements were insufficient for adequate calibration of the SWBM model because that required daily flow measurements for a longer period. Therefore, SWBM was calibrated based on Joep Luijten's experience with application of the model in other hillside watersheds throughout Latin America (Luijten 1999; Luijten et al. 2000), for which daily series of streamflow measurements data were available. While we acknowledge that this is not an optimal way to conduct a hydrological modeling exercise, it represents what was possible given the limited availability of data.

Results

This section presents the results of the simulation analysis. Four major aspects of water availability that we looked at are each presented in a separate subsection. The results will illustrate by means of simple graphs and basic tabular data that simulated streamwater availability varied significantly over space and time. For example, when comparing a very dry day and a very wet day, we found that the difference in river flow rate at the outlet as well as

in the combined length of all streams was about a factor four. A small fraction (about 10 percent) of the households was within one or two hundred meters of a stream all year around, whereas some households were several kilometers away from the nearest stream in every dry season. Differences in land cover throughout the watershed also resulted in quite a variation in the amount of rainfall that reached a stream between different parts of the watershed.

Simulated Streamwater Availability

Simulated river flow from 1996 to 1999 showed high peak flows and fairly rapid retention of surface runoff after rainy periods (figure 14.4). The average simulated river flow rate at the watershed outlet was 1863 l·s⁻¹, but it more than doubled or even tripled during periods of heavy rainfall whereas it decreased below 500 l·s⁻¹ in April and May of every year, except in 1999. The simulated river flow rate during Hurricane Mitch was over 55 m³·s⁻¹ (off-scale in figure 14.4). The hurricane recharged the deeper soil layers till capacity, which resulted in a higher than average base flow rate during the entire first half of 1999. The minimum river flow occurred slightly after the start of first of the seasonal rains. This can be explained as follows. The first rains resulted in little surface runoff and low infiltration to the deeper soil layers; most of the precipitation that reached the surface was absorbed by the dry soil of the root zone. It took, therefore, between

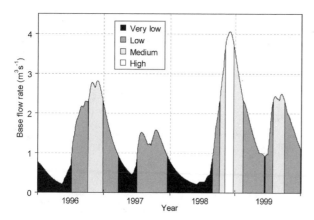

Figure 14.5. Water availability classification based on the simulated base flow, 1996–1999.

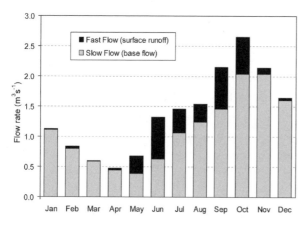

Figure 14.6. Simulated fast flow (surface runoff) and slow flow (base flow) components, based on the simulation of twenty-five years using generated weather data, and averaged by month.

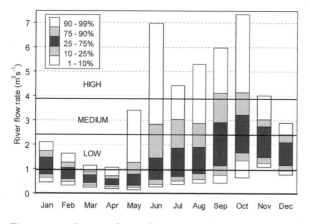

Figure 14.7. Range of river flow rates and corresponding probabilities classes in the Tascalapa River, averaged by month, based on twenty-five years of daily weather data, ranked by simulated river flow rate at the watershed outlet. The percentiles apply to days, not to flow rates. Flow rates for the 1 percent of days with the lowest flow rate and 1 percent of days with the highest flow rates are not shown.

one and three weeks before river flow rates actually started increasing, depending on the intensity and frequency of the rains. The model simulated lower flow rates well compared to the few available flow measurements, but it somewhat underestimated the high flows. It should be noted, however, that the model was not designed to simulate peak flow (Luijten 1999). Such capability would require the model to operate on a time step smaller than one day, such as an hour.

Simulated water availability was classified as very low during the first half of 1996, the second quarter of 1997, and the first half of 1998 (figure 14.5). Note that this classification was based on the base flow rate, not the river flow rate. Base flow is particularly important during the dry season because, unlike surface runoff, it is continuous water flow and in the dry seasons the only significant source of streamwater. The thicker, smoother line in figure 14.4 also indicates the base flow component of the river flow. The difference in base flow between the wet and dry seasons was a factor of 3 to 4. Over the four-year period, 75.4 percent of the simulated river flow reached a stream as base flow. These results may not reflect the long-term average situation well because the simulation period was relatively short and Hurricane Mitch occurred.

The second, twenty-five-year simulation run resulted in a lower average river flow rate of 1388 l·s⁻¹, some 80.7 percent of which was base flow. On average, surface runoff contributed most to river flow during the wet months of July through October, whereas there was hardly any surface runoff in March and April (figure 14.6). The range of simulated river flow rates in figure 14.7 shows the significant variation between seasons as well as within some months. The dark gray section of each bar represents the range of river flow rates for 50 percent of the days in that month, and the light gray sections for an additional 30 percent of the days (15 percent on the higher end and 15 percent on the lower end). These results showed that there was a higher than 99 percent probability that streamwater availability was "low" from January through April, and a higher than 90 percent probability that it was "very low" in March and April.

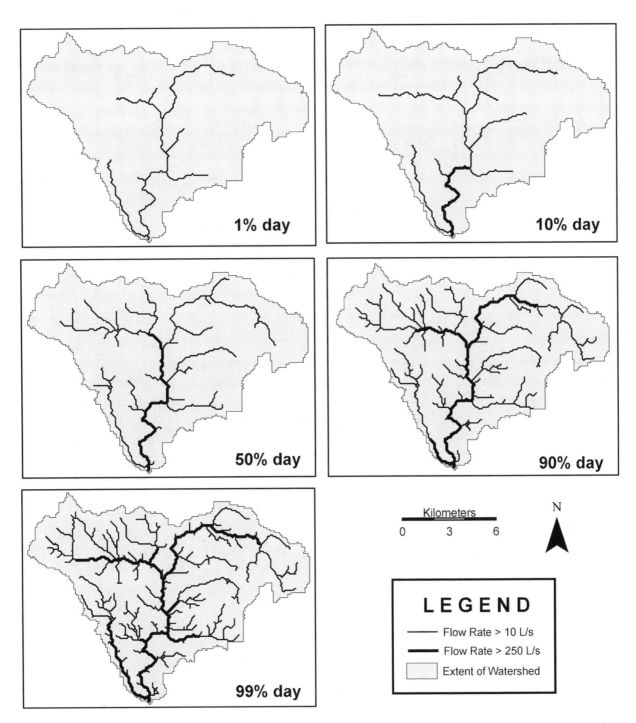

Figure 14.8. Simulated location of streams on the 1 percent, 10 percent, 50 percent, 90 percent, and 99 percent of the days of the year as ranked by flow rates at the Tascalapa River watershed outlet, averaged for twenty-five years.

Table 14.7. Basic statistics of the stream networks in the Tascalapa River watershed for the 1 percent, 10 percent, 50 percent, 90 percent and 99 percent days as ranked by flow rate at the watershed outlet[a]

Watershed characteristic	days ranking				
	1%	10%	50%	90%	99%
Flow rate at outlet, $m^{-3} \cdot s^{-1}$	0.23	0.40	1.06	2.88	5.48
Combined length of streams, km	36	48	81	130	168
Mean stream density, $m \cdot ha^{-1}$	3.0	4.0	6.7	10.7	13.8
Mean distance to stream, m	1,550	1,004	535	304	240

[a] These statistics were computed from the stream networks shown in figure 14.8, using a streamflow threshold of 10 $l \cdot s^{-1}$. Stream density was calculated based on a watershed area of 12,155 ha.

Variation of Stream Networks Over Time

The extent of the stream network varied significantly throughout the year (figure 14.8). For example, the "1 percent day" graph in figure 14.8 shows that 1 percent of the simulated days of the year had as few streams as shown or even fewer, and 99 percent of the days had more streams. Small streams dried up and beginning points where there is some streamwater move down slope substantially during the dry seasons, although numerous transitory streams could be found during and immediately after days with heavy rainfall. On the median (50 percent) day, the combined length of all streams was 81 km, the stream density was 6.7 $m \cdot ha^{-1}$, and the flow rate was 1060 $l \cdot s^{-1}$ (table 14.7). Notice the difference between an average flow rate of 1,388 $l \cdot s^{-1}$. The difference between the combined length of all streams on the 1 percent and 99 percent days (a very dry and very wet day, respectively) was about a factor of four (table 14.7). When flow rates were low, the combined length of the streams and the stream density were low, too, and the average distance to the nearest stream was high.

Household Accessibility to Streams

Accessibility to streams varied throughout the year because of the dynamics of stream location. On average (50 percent day), half of the households were located within 280 m of streams, though some were as far away as 1.7 km (figure 14.9). The farthest any person or household-based livestock would have to walk to a stream on the 99 percent day (high streamflow and many streams) was 730 m. On a 1 percent day (low streamflow and fewer streams), however, only 60 percent of the households were within 1 km of a stream and some were as far away as 4.4 km. These distances generally more than doubled when we considered only streams with a flow rate of at least 50 $l \cdot s^{-1}$. Curves for the 90 percent day are not shown in figure 14.9 because these curves were very close to those of the 99 percent day. A comparison between the household locations in figure 14.1 and the stream networks in figure 14.8 shows that the people in the fringes of the watershed (and in particular those living in the village of Vallecillos and in the eastern part of San Antonio) are most unfortunate because these are the regions where streams dry up the fastest.

Water Yields from Different Zones of the Watershed

Depending on the time of the year, the simulated per-hectare water yields for the six zones varied between 40 percent and 140 percent of the average water yield for the watershed as a whole (figure 14.10). Thus, a value of 100 percent means that the zone's per-hectare water yield was the same as the average for the watershed as a whole in that month.

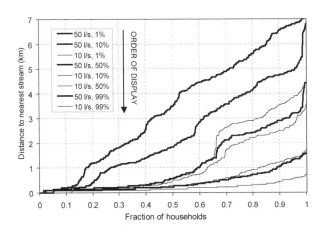

Figure 14.9. Cumulative distribution of accessibility to the nearest stream for flow rate thresholds of 10 l·s⁻¹ and 50 l·s⁻¹, and the 1 percent, 10 percent, 50 percent, and 99 percent days shown in figure 14.8, averaged for twenty-five years.

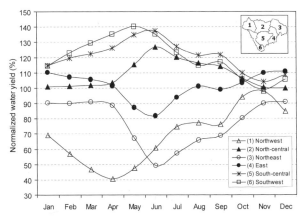

Figure 14.10. Per-hectare water yield of six zones in the Tascalapa River watershed (see inset), as a percentage of per-hectare water yield of the watershed as a whole, averaged for twenty-five years.

The differences between zones were smallest near the end of year (second rainy season) but they increased throughout the dry season until in the middle of first rainy season (May–June). Averaged over the year, simulated relative water yields were lowest in the northwest zone (68.9 percent of the watershed average) and the northeast zone (77.5 percent), despite the fact that precipitation in the northwest zone was higher than in all other zones (table 14.3). Forest and pasture are the dominant land cover types in both zones (table 14.3), which resulted in fairly high interception of rainfall by vegetation and high losses of water through evapotranspiration. On the other hand, degraded land is most dominant in the southwest and the south-central zones. This kept evapotranspiration rates low, resulting in the highest average annual relative water yields (respectively, 120.3 percent and 120.7 percent of the watershed average). These higher relative water yields do not necessarily imply a more favorable situation because degraded land promoted the discharge of precipitation as surface runoff rather than base flow. This higher surface runoff could result in more erosion and sediment transport into streams.

Discussion and Conclusion

Several major assumptions had to be made for this simulation study, most of which are related to the

SWBM model and to limited availability of data. The model was based on empirical relations, and it was not designed for describing the physical routing of water based on mechanistic processes or for engineering design of specific hydrologic projects (Luijten, Knapp, and Jones 2001). For example, streams were delineated based on a fixed streamflow threshold of 10 l·s⁻¹. Weather data had to be generated using monthly long-term averages for the region because few measured data were available. We assumed that the spatial distribution of houses in the watershed (in particular the typical clustering in villages and near roads and streams) was about the same as it was two decades ago. All of these can be improved, although that is unlikely to change the simulation results much. This study was also limited in that we neither included actual water use in the analysis nor analyzed water supply and demand under alternative development scenarios. A true scenario analysis could be an interesting follow-up study.

SWBM fills the gap between the current needs and resources of rural communities throughout developing countries who need help now, and the very large data demands of established, more complex hydrological models designed for data resources and applications in developed countries. Examples of such models are the agricultural nonpoint source pollution model (AGNPS; Bingner and Theurer

2001), the soil and water assessment tool (SWAT; Neitsch et al., 2001), and better assessment science integrating point and nonpoint sources model (BASINS; Lahlou et al. 1998). Nevertheless, the capabilities and applicability of SWBM extend well beyond those presented in this paper (for details, see Luijten, Jones, and Knapp 2000, 2002; Luijten, Knapp, and Jones 2001).

The simulation results given here provided basic quantitative information about several aspects of water availability that had not been studied before and that can be used readily to guide investments. Our results showed that many households in the Tascalapa River watershed are unfavorably located with respect to stream access. These people may have to go far to get water if they do not have access to piped drinking water. Crops may also suffer if the fields are insufficiently irrigated during periods of droughts. Let us assume, for instance, a hypothetical development goal that everyone in the watershed should have access to water within 2 km distance during 99 percent of the time. Today, about one-fourth of the households did not meet this criterion if streams were the only source of water. Development projects could focus on ensuring that these households have an alternative means of water supply, such as piped water, wells, or tanks that can store water for longer periods.

Knowledge about the land cover–induced differences in per-hectare water yields of different parts of the watershed also could be used by planners for setting targets related to land conservation, promoting or discouraging certain land cover changes over parts of the watershed, or limiting water extraction when streamflows are low. Decision-makers may also want to set goals for minimum streamflow rates at different locations in the watershed so that all farm families have access to water within a set distance from their homes during the driest months. Such flow requirements have further implications: are complexes of dams and reservoirs necessary? How large should they be? What are acceptable targets for water extraction? What land cover changes are an acceptable compromise between meeting land conservation goals, providing for local food production needs, and reducing risks for water shortages for future generations? Should people be living in the headwater areas anyway or should these areas be left in their natural state?

We presented results of this study at a workshop held in San Jose, Costa Rica, in July 2000, which was attended by CIAT scientists, academics, agricultural planners, and government officials from the study area. Partial results of the study were also included in the form of multiple images in the Honduran community–based decision support system (Swindell 2000). Workshop participants' responses to this methodology and our specific results were very encouraging. They indicated that this type of GIS-based quantitative information could supplement local knowledge and provides a powerful means of stimulating group discussions and creating a sense of community in the areas where they work and live.

The scale of data and analysis can greatly affect our ability to detect and understand phenomena and relationships that characterized the environment (Nelson 2001). Although water may not be considered scarce in Honduras on a national scale (see table 14.1), many people in fact experience some degree of reduced water availability during part of the year if you look at the right spatial scale. But the "right scale" may vary throughout Honduras, and it may be quite different between countries. It may be the watershed level, maybe the village level, or maybe the farm level. A water security study, therefore, should include an assessment of which biophysical, socioeconomic, and institutional factors actually affect water availability, and at what spatial scale these factors operate and water resources management decisions are being made. The analysis methodology presented in this paper was a tool that helped us understand the processes that affect strategic water availability on the watershed level better, over space and time. The value of GIS-based simulation is that the results are quantitative and unambiguous. The results can be helpful for negotiating desired future conditions, understanding the tradeoffs that are required to reach desired future conditions, and helping multi-institutional alliances become proactive and improve water resources management for local communities.

Acknowledgments

This study was part of the International Center for Tropical Agriculture's project on Methodologies for Integrating Spatial Scales in a Data Rich Environment and was supported by the Trust Fund for Methodological Support to Ecoregional Programs. We thank Nacho Sanz and Grégoire Leclerc for their assistance and managerial support, which that made this study possible.

References

Bingner, R. L., and F. D. Theurer. 2001. AGNPS 98: A suite of water quality models for watershed use. In *Proceedings of the Sediment: Monitoring, Modeling, and Management*, vii:1–8. 7th Federal Interagency Sedimentation Conference, Reno, Nevada, 25–29 March.

Burrough, P. A., and R. A. McDonnell. 1998. *Principles of Geographic Information Systems*. New York: Oxford University Press.

CIAT. 1993. Informe del taller de planificación (Workshop on Participatory Planning by Objective). Programa de Desarrollo Sostenible en Laderas. International Center for Tropical Agriculture (CIAT), Cali, Colombia, 15–19 March.

———. 1996. CIAT Hillsides Program, Annual Report 1994–1995. International Center for Tropical Agriculture (CIAT), Cali, Colombia.

———. 1997. Community-led management of watershed resources in hillside agro-ecosystems of Latin America. Annual highlights for project PE-3. Cali, Colombia.

———. 2001. Nurturing rural livelihood in the tropics: A summary of CIAT's 2001–2010 strategic plan. Cali, Colombia.

CLODEST (Comité para el Desarrollo Sostenible de la Cuenca del Río Tascalapa). 1998. Memoria del taller planificación participativa por objectos. Lago de Yojoa, Cortes, 3–6 February 1998. Yorito, Departamento de Yoro, Honduras.

Cox, J. A. 1998. Land characterization of Honduras. Technical report. International Center for Tropical Agriculture (CIAT), Cali, Colombia.

ESRI. 1996. Using the ArcView Spatial Analyst. Advanced spatial analysis using raster and vector data. Environmental Systems Research Institute, Redlands, Calif.

Falkenmark, M., J. Lundqvist, and C. Widstrand. 1989. Macro-scale water scarcity requires micro-scale approaches: Aspects of vulnerability in semi-arid development. *Natural Resources Forum* 13, no. 4: 258–67.

Hoogenboom, G., C. Leon, D. Rossiter, and P. van Laake. 2000. Biophysical agricultural assessment and management models for developing countries. In C. A. S. Hall, ed., *Quantifying Sustainable Development: The Future of Tropical Economies*, 349–402. San Diego: Academic Press.

Knapp, E. B., J. A. Ashby, H. M. Ravnborg, and W. C. Bell. 1999. A landscape that unites: Community-led management of Andean watershed resources. In R. Lal, ed., *Integrated Watershed Management in the Global Ecosystem*, 125–44. Boca Raton, Fla.: CRC Press.

Knapp, E. B., W. C. Bell, G. Leclerc, H. Ravnborg-Munk, J. A. Cox, A. Nelson, P. Couillaud, S. Nath, G. Rosenberg, B. P. Verma, and D. Nute. 1998. Methodologies for integrating data across geographic scales in a data-rich environment: Examples from Honduras. Paper presented at the workshop Methodological Research at the Ecoregional Level, ISNAR, The Hague, 20–22 April.

Lahlou, M., L. Shoemaker, S. Choudhury, R. Elmer, A. Hu, H. Manguerra, and A. Parker. 1998. BASINS version 2.0 user's manual. Washington, D.C.: United States Environmental Protection Agency.

Luijten, J. C. 1999. A tool for community-based water resources management in hillside watersheds. Ph.D. dissertation, University of Florida.

Luijten, J. C., J. W. Jones, and E. B. Knapp. 2000. Dynamic modeling of water availability in the Cabuyal River, Colombia: The impact of land cover change on the hydrological balance. *Advances in Environmental Monitoring and Modeling* 1, no. 1: 36–60.

———. 2002. Spatial Water Budget Model and Hydrological Tools: An ArcView GIS extension. Version 1.3 user's manual. Agricultural and Biological Engineering Department, University of Florida, and International Center for Tropical Agriculture (CIAT), Cali, Colombia.

Luijten, J. C., E. B. Knapp, and J. W. Jones. 2001. A tool for community-based assessment of the implication of development on water security in hillside watersheds. *Agricultural Systems* 70, nos. 2–3: 603–22.

Luijten, J. C., E. B. Knapp, S. I. Sanz, and J. W. Jones. 2003. A role for GIS-based simulation for empowering local stakeholders in water resources negotiations in developing countries: Case studies for two rural hillside watersheds in Honduras and Colombia. *Water Policy* 5, no. 3: 213–36.

Neitsch, S. L., J. G. Arnold, J. R. Kiniry, and J. R. Williams. 2001. Soil and Water Assessment Tool, version 2000, user's manual. Grassland, Soil and Water Research Laboratory, Agricultural Research Service, and Blackland Research Center, Texas Agricultural Experiment Stations, Temple.

Nelson, A., 2001. Analysing data across geographic scales in Honduras: Detecting levels of organisation within systems. *Agriculture, Ecosystems & Environment* 85:107–31.

Pickering, N. B., J. W. Hansen, J. W. Jones, C. M. Wells, V. K. Chan, and D. C. Godwin. 1994. WeatherMan: A utility for managing and generating daily weather data. *Agronomy Journal* 86:332–37.

Raskin, P., P. Gleick, P. Kirshen, G. Pontius, and K. Strzepek. 1997. *Water Futures: Assessment of Long-range Pattern and Problems*. Stockholm: Stockholm Environment Institute.

Seckler, D., U. Amarasinghe, D. Molden, R. de Silva, and R. Barker. 1998. World water demand and supply, 1990 to 2025: Scenarios and issues. Colombo, Sri Lanka: International Water Management Institute.

Seckler, D., D. Barker, and U. Amarasinghe. 1999. Water scarcity in the twenty-first century. *International Journal of Water Resources Development* 15, no. 1: 29–42.

Swindell, J. 2000. Community based decision support systems in Honduras: Developing an internet based tutorial for end users. Paper presented at the Rural Research Conference of the Royal Institution of Chartered Surveyors (ROOTS), 2000 conference, 6–7 April, Ashford, England.

United Nations. 1999. *World Population Prospects. The 1998 Revision*, vol. 1, *Comprehensive Tables*. New York: UN Department of Economic and Social Affairs, Population Division.

USDA-SCS. 1972. *National Engineering Handbook*, section 4, *Hydrology*. Washington, D.C.: U.S. Department of Agriculture.

Vörösmarty, C., and D. Sahagian. 2000. Anthropogenic disturbance of the terrestrial water cycle. *BioScience* 50:753–65.

CHAPTER 15

THE APPLICATION OF LAND USE–ANALYSIS TOOLS
ACROSS DIFFERENT SCALES
TO THE ATLANTIC ZONE OF COSTA RICA
Hans G. P. Jansen

Introduction

Regional development intrinsically is related to the way in which the land is used. Given the rising awareness of the multiple trade-offs involved in decision making regarding the use of available land resources (Griffon et al. 1999), policy makers face the complex task of accommodating multiple objectives of an increasing number of stakeholders in regional development. This implies a need for tools that can be employed to provide insights into the opportunities and limitations to land use. Such tools should be capable of quantifying trade-offs between socioeconomic, sustainability-related, and environmental policy objectives.

In Costa Rica, questions and problems surrounding the policy debate related to agricultural-sector development vary according to the changing biophysical and socioeconomic conditions of the area being considered, in this case the Atlantic Zone* (see figure 15.1), the particular stakeholders involved, and the time frame as well as the geographical scale of analysis. In addition, the problems perceived by the various stakeholders may differ considerably: they include the short-term problems with which farmers and plantation owners are confronted; the medium-term questions on which policy makers tend to focus; and the long-term problems that draw the attention of environmental protection and nature conservation agencies.

The Atlantic Zone constitutes an area of the humid tropical lowlands of about 500,000 ha. The topography is flat. Rainfall is high (3,000–7,000 mm per year) without a dry period (Gómez 1986). Soils are mostly andosols and inceptisols but vary highly in fertility and drainage conditions (Wielemaker and Vogel 1993). From a socioeconomic point of view, the area is characterized by its colonization history, relatively low average population density (about 60 persons/km²) but high population growth (> 4 percent annual) and an expanding but still limited road infrastructure outside the main regional centers (Nieuwenhuyse et al. 2000). Land use is dominated by declining forest areas, extensive beef cattle holdings, and large banana plantations, besides a large number of smallholders growing a variety of crops both inside and outside state-organized settlements. Rapid structural transformations were and are taking place in the ecological, agricultural, and socioeconomic conditions of the region, in part responding to various structural adjustment programs (Jiménez 1998).

Even though the Atlantic Zone was not a prime focus of attention for policy makers in the capital city of San José until recently, political interest in the area has grown as a result of the increasingly conflicting policy objectives concerning agricultural production, environmental quality, and the establishment and maintenance of nature reserves. Since the early 1990s, questions and problems increasingly center on the following priority issues:

Sustainability of current farm practices: conversion of forests to agricultural land (especially pastures) has led to considerable soil nutrient mining and therefore land

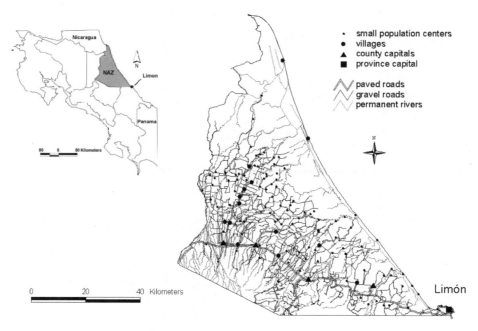

small population centers
villages
county capitals
province capital

paved roads
gravel roads
permanent rivers

Figure 15.1. Location of
the Atlantic Zone (NAZ)
and its main rivers, roads,
and villages. See website
for color originals.

Limón

degradation (Bouman et al. 1999; Bulte et
al. 2000).

Structural adjustment: the various structural
adjustment programs (SAPs) implemented
since 1987 have emphasized production
of both traditional and nontraditional
export crops and stimulated higher usage
of chemical inputs (fertilizer and pesticides), which in turn has led to increased
environmental damage, human health
problems, and increased need for foreign
exchange (Jansen et al. 1998 and chapter 9).

Conservation of forest resources: the increasing awareness of the multifunctional character and associated values of forest lands
has led to the development of a number
of innovative schemes and policies aimed
at capturing some of these values (Bulte,
Joenje, and Jansen 2000; Jansen et al.
2001).

Technological change: as of the late 1990s,
agricultural policy places increased
emphasis on food security without compromising export-led agricultural growth:
efficient production of domestically consumed food crops and livestock products is
promoted through increased attention to
new technologies aimed at increasing the

competitiveness of small and medium-
scale farms (SEPSA 1997).

Infrastructure investments: the need is
increasingly recognized for measures
aimed at strengthening the ability of
farmers to market their produce, including
extension and upgrading of the currently
highly variable road network (Jansen
and Van Tilburg 1996; Roebeling et al.
2000b).

This chapter offers a summary account of a
range of interdisciplinary methodologies for land
use analysis that can help decision makers address
each of the above issues in a more systematic and
quantitative manner. The series of methodologies
was developed over a twelve-year period (1986–
98) in Costa Rica by a collaborative research program (called REPOSA; Research Program on
Sustainability in Agriculture) between Wageningen
University and Research Center (WUR) of the
Netherlands; the Tropical Agricultural Research
and Higher Education Center (CATIE) in Costa
Rica; and the Costa Rican Ministry of Agriculture
and Livestock (MAG). The methodologies are
highly interdisciplinary and span a number of geographical scales (ranging from the field level to the
national level) and are therefore relevant for a wide

Table 15.1. Methodologies for land use analysis on different scales developed and used by REPOSA

Nature of methodology (nickname)	Scale of operation	Characterization and methods	Principal objective	Key outputs	Policy relevance
Projective (CLUE)	Region	Statistical (regression, GIS)	Projection of likely future trends in land cover	Likely future developments in land cover according to user-specified changes in land use drivers	Contributes to understanding of relationships between the environment and land use by demonstrating the spatially explicit effects of important general or ecurrent changes in land cover at the regional or national level
Explorative biophysical (SOLUS)	Region	Biophysical (expert systems, LP, GIS)	Exploration of biophysical options for agricultural land use	Technological options and trade-off analysis between biophysical goals only	Generates insights into the possibilities and ultimate biophysical limitations of regional land use. ("biophysical space")
Explorative bioeconomic (SOLUS)	Region	Bioeconomic (expert systems, LP, econometrics, GIS	Exploration of options for land use under combined biophysical and socioeconomic constraints	Technological options and trade-off analysis and aggregate policy effects	Generates insights into the possibilities and limitations of regional agricultural development in relation to policy goals ("policy space")
Predictive (UNA-DLV)	Farm type and region	Bioeconomic (expert systems, LP, econometrics, GIS)	Short-term prediction of policy effects on farmers' land use decisions	Technological options and farmers' reactions plus policy effectiveness (partial and aggregate)	Reveals effectiveness of policy measures in inducing adoption of desired land use systems at the regional level as well as at the farm-type level
Predictive (SEM)	Country and region	SEM (LP, econometrics, GIS)	Short-term prediction of policy effects on land use allocation between regions	Quantification of trade flows plus policy effectiveness	Quantification of policy effects on quantity and distribution between regions and between consumers and producers) of societal welfare
Generation of land use systems (TCGs)	Plot/field	Expert systems (process-based and expert knowledge, literature, field experiments)	Quantification of input-output relationships for a large number of land use systems in expert systems, to be used as building blocks in explorative and predictive methodologies	Quantification of input-output relationships	Inputs into the SOLUS and UNA-DLV methodologies but can also be used as stand-alone tools for evaluating technologies at the farm level
Prototyping (BANMAN)	Farm	Precision farming (GIS plus farm data plus field experiments)	On farm decision support based on principles of prototyping	Adjustments in farm management	Generates insights into the input-output relations of precision agriculture at the farm level for bananas

range of decision makers. Concepts of systems analysis and information technology play a pivotal role in each of the methodologies. Together, they form a unique toolbox that deserves ample use in the process of agricultural policy design and evaluation (Bouma et al. 2000).

The next section offers a brief description of each of the methodologies. The third section explains the linkages between the different methodologies, provides some examples, and discusses their complementary role as tools that can assist decision making on various scales. The final section discusses some of the lessons learned for successful design, application, and transfer of interdisciplinary, systems-based land use analysis methodologies for policy support.

Methodologies for the Evaluation of Land Use at Different Scales

The various methodologies for land use analysis at different scales developed by REPOSA have a number of important common characteristics. First, their development has been mostly an interdisciplinary effort, with the involvement of both the biophysical sciences (soil science, agronomy, animal husbandry, physical geography) and the social sciences (economics, marketing, rural sociology). Second, information and communication technology, concepts originating in systems analysis, and geographical information systems (GIS) all play an important role. Third, and perhaps most important, they all serve the ultimate goal of policy support, albeit at different scale levels (plot, farm, region, country).

While most of the analytical methodologies presented in this chapter are meant to operate at the regional level (the level at which planners, policy makers, and regulatory agencies tend to focus their attention), regional considerations cannot be addressed in isolation from the possible alternatives at lower-scale levels, including the likely decisions involved in farm-level operations. Moreover, regional development is intrinsically linked to higher-scale levels such as the whole nation. Therefore, the methodologies developed by REPOSA take into account these different scales of operation, which has led to a number of important

associated distinctions in terms of the methodologies' nature, scale of operation, tools and methods used, main objective, and key outputs delivered (table 15.1). Partially building on Van Ittersum et al. (1998), the methodologies for land-use analysis discussed in this chapter can be usefully classified into five groups: (1) projective, (2) explorative, (3) predictive, (4) generative, and (5) prototyping.

Projective Land-Use Analysis: The CLUE Methodology

The CLUE (Conversion of Land Use and its Effects) methodology starts with current land use and then generates likely developments in future regional land use (or national land use in case of countrywide applications) according to different scenarios based on statistical regression analysis that relates changes in land covers to so-called land-use drivers (e.g., climate, soil, topography, population, urbanization, market access, income). This statistical description of land use patterns by a set of drivers is done at different grid levels making use of a GIS (Kok and Veldkamp 2000, 2001). Possible future land use patterns are generated by changing the values of the land-use drivers, either by extrapolating past trends or by projecting certain expectations about their future developments (e.g., changes in regional commodity demand based on changes in population and income). A somewhat similar approach has been used by Pontius et al. (2001); see also chapter 18. As an example for the Atlantic Zone, CLUE predicted that pastures would largely replace forests (due to strong growth in national demand for beef and milk as well as growth in beef exports) and become limited to areas unfavorable for agriculture or national parks, both of which are mostly located in the northern part of the Atlantic Zone (figure 15.2). As a policy tool, the type of analysis that CLUE is able to provide is useful in two respects. First, it allows policy makers to obtain a first and relatively uncomplicated insight as to what would be likely changes in regional land use if current and past trends simply continued in the future (up to about twenty years ahead), without any "structural breaks" such as changes in technologies, major social disruptions, and the like.

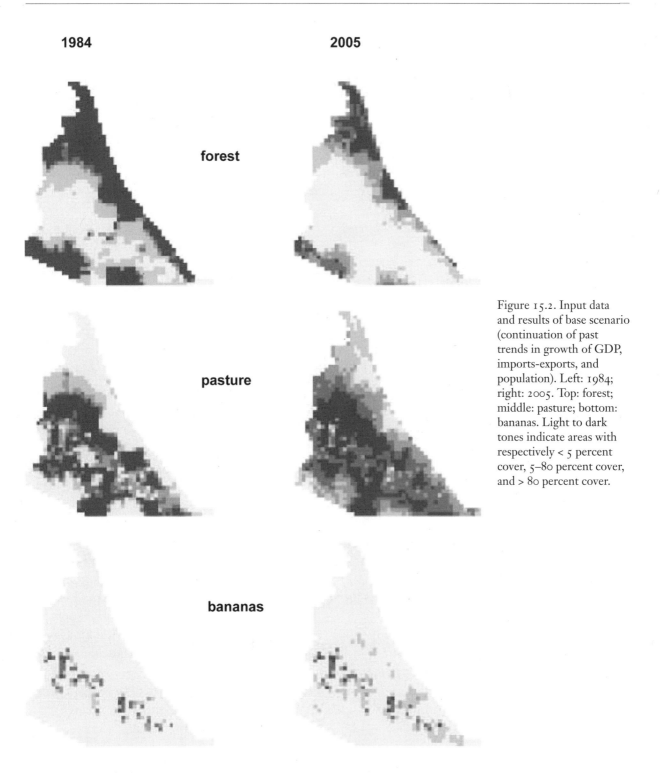

Figure 15.2. Input data and results of base scenario (continuation of past trends in growth of GDP, imports-exports, and population). Left: 1984; right: 2005. Top: forest; middle: pasture; bottom: bananas. Light to dark tones indicate areas with respectively < 5 percent cover, 5–80 percent cover, and > 80 percent cover.

Second, since the pixel (or raster) is the basic spatial unit employed in the CLUE methodology, it employs the results obtained at different spatial aggregation levels to allocate land use in a spatially explicit way using a statistically determined allocation module (Verburg et al. 1999)

Explorative Land-Use Analysis: The SOLUS Methodology

A shortcoming of the CLUE methodology is its lack of causality: that is, current land-use trends and conditions are not explained. This absence of explicit relations of changes in land use with underlying biophysical and/or socioeconomic processes

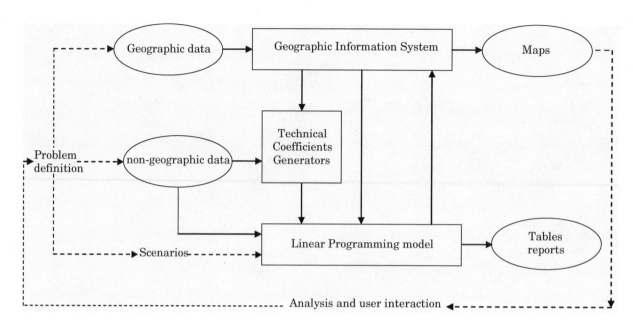

Figure 15.3. Structure of the SOLUS methodology. Rectangles represent models or tools; ovals are data; names without boxes are activities; solid lines are flows of data; dotted lines are flows of information.

is addressed by the SOLUS (Sustainable Options for Land Use) methodology for regional land-use analysis (figure 15.3). The SOLUS methodology allows for the exploration of the aggregate effects of alternative policies on both efficiency and noneconomic (environmental and sustainability) objectives at the regional level (including quantification of trade-offs between policy objectives), with a relatively long time horizon (twenty to thirty years; Bouman et al. 1999). SOLUS makes use of a bioeconomic agricultural sector model of the linear programming (LP) type that incorporates the labor market as well as a multimarket structure for commodities, each of which can be produced by a wide spectrum of alternative land-use systems with specified technologies (Jansen et al. 2005).

Such technological options for land use are generated by two expert systems (so-called technical coefficient generators or TCGs; see Hengsdijk et al. 1999), one for crops and forests (Hengsdijk et al. 1998) and the other for pasture-based cattle systems (Bouman, Nieuwenhuyse, and Hengsdijk 1998). Both expert systems describe a large number of agricultural production technologies by systematically quantifying input-output (I-O) coefficients of their corresponding land use systems at the plot level (usually on a per ha basis).

These I-O coefficients are referred to as technical coefficients and relate to benefits and costs, yields and labor requirements, as well as to sustainability indicators such as soil nutrient depletion and environmental damage resulting from the use of pesticides. Technical coefficients are fed into the LP model that optimizes for one or more objectives (such as maximization of the sum of consumer and producer surplus or employment maximization or minimization of environmental damage resulting from the use of chemical inputs), subject to a number of biophysical and socioeconomic constraints. Such constraints may relate to either resource endowments (and are therefore mostly absolute—for instance, availability of soil resources) or to specific policy measures (normative because user-defined, such as taxation of pesticides or zero soil nutrient balances).

In SOLUS there is a semi-automated flow of data between the GIS, the TCGs, and the LP sector model (Bouman, Nieuwenhuyse, et al. 1998). Other salient characteristics of the SOLUS methodology are the geographic explicit delineation of land and labor resources through a GIS; the incorporation of endogenous prices of outputs and labor; and the variation of output prices according to quality of roads and distance to markets. Output price

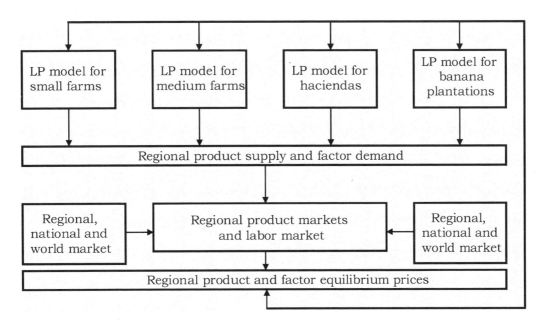

Figure 15.4. Multiple farm structure of the UNA-DLV projective land-use analysis methodology.

variation is related to the size of the region, while endogenous prices and wages are necessary because the supply originating in the region is capable of influencing prices and wages. Explorations carried out with the SOLUS methodology may focus on the quantification of the ultimate biophysical constraints on land use by excluding socioeconomic factors (Bessembinder et al. 2000). Alternatively, explorations may focus on the options for agricultural development under explicitly simulated socioeconomic conditions, such as product demand, labor supply, and the like. Another useful feature of the SOLUS methodology is that it can be fruitfully used for simulation of the potential effects on land use, income, and sustainability of an introduction of new technologies or agricultural policy measures (Jansen et al. 2001; Schipper et al. 2000).

Predictive Land-Use Analysis
The UNA-DLV methodology

Unlike the explorative SOLUS land use–analysis methodology, the UNA-DLV methodology incorporates farm(er) behavior and is suitable for making more precise predictions about the likely short-term (< 5 years) effects of policy measures on farmers' land-use decisions. Although it is based on individual farm models, it can also be used

for regional analysis of farmers' policy reactions, since the results of the individual farm type models are linked with market equilibrium conditions for each product (Roebeling et al. 2000a; figure 15.4). Technical coefficients of different crop and livestock production systems and technologies are generated by the same expert systems also used in SOLUS. These coefficients are incorporated into bioeconomic LP models, one for each of four representative types of producers in the Atlantic Zone of Costa Rica ("farm types"): households with small farms (< 20 ha), households with medium farms (20–50 ha), extensive beef cattle farms or haciendas (> 50 ha), and banana plantations (> 200 ha). These farm types were identified according to dominant land use and perceived objectives, making use of the latest agricultural census (DGEC 1987). Even though each of the farm-type models is of the LP type, they differ significantly in terms of their overall structure, objective functions, resource endowments, and other restrictions.

In the models for small and medium farms, optimization takes place for income and utility objectives. Net farm income is maximized subject to credit constraints, production technologies, consumption requirements, and initial farm characteristics and resource availability. Subsequently, utility (obtained through consumption and leisure) is maximized subject to net farm income. Utility functions are derived from the National Household Income and Expenditure Survey (DGEC 1990).

Economic decision making on extensive haciendas is guided by a long-term income objective, consisting of the net returns from beef production and the terminal value of the land (Roebeling et al. 1998). Consequently, the dynamic LP model for haciendas evaluates technologies for pasture-based beef cattle production according to an income objective, and subject to resource and cash flow constraints. Dynamic properties of the LP model for haciendas include multiperiod livestock activities, and a savings and investment module within the ten-year planning horizon (Roebeling et al. 1998). Restrictions are defined by the hacienda's initial resource availabilities that are allowed to change over time due to investment options in land and cattle.

The banana plantation model is a LP model that analyzes the production side to determine technology choice. Since banana plantations are guided primarily by a profit objective (Roebeling et al. 2000a), a range of alternative banana production technologies (each with its own unique set of I-O coefficients) is evaluated according to an objective function that represents profit maximization, subject to availability of certain resources.

Even though single farm decisions do not affect product and factor prices, at the regional level total product supply and factor demand of all farms in the region may affect subsequent equilibrium prices. This implies that prices, while exogenous at the individual farm level, may become endogenous at the regional level. In the UNA-DLV methodology, partial model results for the different farm types are used to determine total regional product supply and factor demand through weighted aggregation, based on the actual number of farms per farm type according to census data. Regional product supply is subsequently confronted with the product demand functions faced by producers in the region (derived from Geurts et al. 1997). These supply and demand functions are then used to determine regional equilibrium prices for each product. The latter are plugged back into the partial farm type models, from which new supply quantities are

calculated. This iterative procedure is repeated until product prices deviate less than 1 percent from corresponding prices determined in the previous iteration, indicating that the region's agricultural sector simulated by the various farm type models is in equilibrium.

Spatial equilibrium modeling

The spatial equilibrium modeling (SEM) methodology is also of a predictive nature and used for analyzing the spatial patterns of agricultural production and land use, demand, trade flows, pricing, and social welfare. While addressing both the regional and the national levels, the SEM methodology differs from the other methodologies discussed in this chapter in two aspects: first, it is not an entirely new methodology (e.g., Takayama and Judge 1964); second, it lies completely in the domain of economists, with little or no involvement of other disciplines. The SEM methodology consists of an economic optimization model (again of the LP type) that is used to assess the short-term (1–5 years) effects of policy decisions (e.g., free trade measures, investments in infrastructure, technological progress) on agricultural supply, demand, domestic (interregional) and international trade, and social welfare. The model maximizes social welfare, defined as the sum of producer and consumer surplus resulting from domestic demand and supply of commodities, plus exports earnings, minus imports costs, and minus total transport costs involved in trade flows of commodities between supply and demand regions. Restrictions include supply and demand restrictions, commodity balances, and land resource restrictions. In this way the SEM simulates competitive market equilibrium for commodities in regions, where commodity prices are equal to their marginal costs. Regional demand elasticities are derived from Geurts et al. (1997), who used data from the latest household expenditure survey (DGEC 1990). Supply elasticities are based on the standard Nerlove model (Roebeling et al. 2000b). Transportation costs between regions as well as to major export harbors were calculated using data on road infrastructure stored in a GIS, which were used as input in econometric estimation of regression models that relate transportation costs to geographical distances and road qualities (Jansen and Stoorvogel 1998). The SEM considered the six governmental planning regions in Costa Rica plus "the rest of the world" to account for exports and imports (figure 15.5). A total of seventeen major agricultural products (fifteen crops, along with beef and milk) were included, selected on the basis of their relative importance (at the national level) in terms of cultivated area and value of production. The model was calibrated for the year 1995.

The innovative aspect of the SEM modeling framework in the Costa Rican application lies in the successful sequence of data collection followed by the use of solid econometric methods to estimate both supply and demand response, combined with the use of a GIS and econometrics to estimate transport cost models. This type of work is still quite scarce when applied to small developing countries.

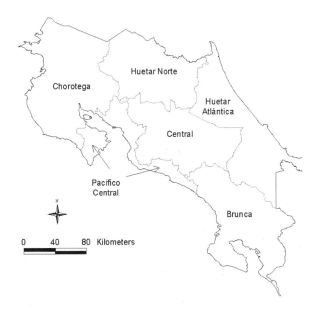

Figure 15.5. Planning regions in Costa Rica.

Generation of Land-Use Systems: Technical Coefficient Generators

Technical coefficient generators (TCGs) are expert systems that operationalize agroecological concepts and principles to quantify land use systems at the field level in the form of so-called technical coefficients that can be used directly in LP models. Technical coefficients represent inputs and outputs of land-use systems that reflect either systems currently practiced by farmers (actual land use systems) or new alternative ones that are technically feasible and sustainable from a biophysical point of view, but most likely not yet widely practiced. Alternative systems are supposed to use inputs more efficiently than actual systems due to assumed future efficiency gains in production (De Wit 1979). They are also sustainable in the sense of maintaining their productivity levels over time, which in the application for the Atlantic Zone means sufficiently high fertilizer levels in order to guarantee closed soil nutrient balances (or zero net soil nutrient losses). Alternative land use systems are generated based on the integration of systems-analytical knowledge of the physical, chemical, physiological, and ecological processes involved; standard agronomic and animal husbandry data; and expert knowledge (Hengsdijk et al. 1999).

TCGs therefore do not involve farmer participation or on-farm research explicitly. Main inputs quantified include costs, labor requirements, fertilizer use, and application of crop protection agents. Outputs are production and a number of associated environmental indicators such as soil nutrient balances (zero for alternative systems) and an environmental damage index for biocides.

Prototyping: The BanMan System

Finally, the BanMan (Banana Management) precision agriculture methodology developed in Costa Rica illustrates the concept of prototyping in designing new types of land use systems (Stoorvogel et al. 2000). Prototyping refers to the design of production technologies through an interactive process between scientists and farmers and involves on-farm development and application of support systems in which the economic and ecological consequences of changes in the production structure of a land-use system are analyzed by evaluating the economic and agronomic management decisions on the farm (Vereijken 1997). Typically for precision agriculture, management specifically addresses within-farm spatial and temporal variability in soil conditions, pest and disease pressure including associated chemical use, and crop yield. In the specific case of BanMan, the main objective was to facilitate a more environment-friendly way

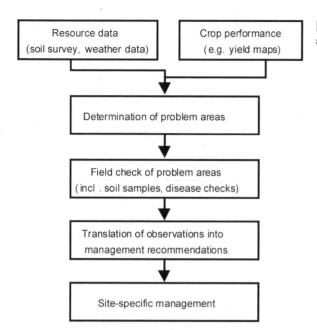

[left] Figure 15.6. A low-tech approach to precision agriculture. Source: Stoorvogel et al. (2000).

Figure 15.7. Regression hot spot maps for bananas (left) and forest (right). Dark areas indicate where regression values exceed actual data values and strong dynamics are to be expected. The opposite holds for grey areas. In grey areas regression values and actual values are similar (less than 10 percent difference). Grid size is 2 × 2 km.

of producing bananas while maintaining its economic viability. Although precision agriculture is often based on advanced equipment, information technology, and deterministic simulation models, in tropical environments and for perennial crops advanced equipment and simulation models are not always available. Therefore, BanMan was developed using a low-tech approach to precision agriculture, combining information technology and knowledge of the owner and manager of the farm (figure 15.6).

Complementarity Between Methodologies and Illustrations of Their Relevance for Policy

Rather than independent entities, the methodologies developed by REPOSA form a coherent toolbox aimed at supporting agricultural policy on different scales and in this sense are highly complementary in terms of their policy relevance (see also table 15.1, last column). Despite differences among methodologies in terms of the type of questions that can be addressed as well as scale and time horizon of analysis, all of them allow the use of the concept of scenario development, defined as the analysis of possible future land use given certain expected changes in land-use drivers (the projective methodology) or certain objectives and policy measures (explorative and predictive

methodologies). Together, the methodologies are able to address issues related to likely changes in future land use assuming that current relationships among land use and its drivers will continue to hold in the future (CLUE); options for future land use that, despite their technological advantages, are not currently feasible mainly as a result of the prevailing socioeconomic environment (SOLUS); and effective agricultural policies to induce farmers to make socially desirable adjustments in their land use (UNA-DLV).

Projective Land-Use Analysis

Information about future land use developments that are likely to take place under ceteris paribus conditions, as produced by the CLUE methodology, obviously is highly relevant to policy makers. Besides answering the question of what might happen under certain scenario assumptions, CLUE can also answer the questions where this is most likely to happen. By subtracting the observed land cover in a particular year from the predicted regression cover of the same year, CLUE is able to generate insight into both the timing and the location of possible hot spots in regional development, and to provide policy makers with an approximation about the possible future pathways of land use dynamics (Kok and Veldkamp 2000). An example of such hot spots based on the year 1984

Table 15.2. Economic and environmental effects of alternative ways of taxing pesticide use

Type of pesticide	Flat tax	Tax A	Tax B	Tax C
		Progressive tax regimes		
Slightly toxic	100%	20%	20%	10%
Medium toxic	100%	50%	50%	30%
Very toxic	100%	200%	100%	150%
Indicators (% change relative to base run)				
Economic surplus	−18.7	−4.3	−4.1	−2.2
Environmental damage	−4.0	−81.9	−1.5	−81.9

(which is the most recent year for which agricultural census data are available) is given in figure 15.7, which shows that the potential dynamics of land use change for bananas are more concentrated geographically than for forest dynamics, since bananas require much more specific conditions than forests. Detailed knowledge about likely future changes in land use enables policy makers to better anticipate and plan their decisions regarding socioeconomic investments (e.g., infrastructure), environmental legislation, and so forth.

Explorative Land-Use Analysis

A limitation of the CLUE methodology is that discontinuities in certain forcing or driving variables (especially policy changes and technological progress) and hence trends cannot be taken into account. Thus, to go beyond using the past as a sole measure for predicting the future, one needs to combine societal desires with biophysical constraints and technical options in terms of alternative production systems (Bouma et al. 2000). The SOLUS methodology facilitates the exploration of land use options by allowing new (that is, currently not practiced) land-use systems, as generated by the TCGs, to enter the analysis, and by including explicit optimization of land use for well-defined policy objectives (Bouman, Schipper, et al. 1998).

SOLUS has been fruitfully used in two distinctly different approaches toward regional land use analysis. On the one hand, Bessembinder et al.

(2000) employed SOLUS for the exploration of the ultimate biophysical limits to production, revealing land use options beyond current and future socioeconomic constraints. On the other hand, Schipper et al. (2000) were interested in the combined effect of biophysical and socioeconomic constraints, showing how strategically advantageous biophysical possibilities are limited by current or projected socioeconomic constraints such as size of the market, labor availability, credit requirements, and so on. By quantifying the trade-offs among the various dimensions of biophysical sustainability and socioeconomic parameters in the medium to long run (as in Schipper et al. 2000), the SOLUS methodology holds the potential to make policy debates more transparent and improve general understanding about the possibilities and limitations of agricultural development. As examples of using SOLUS to help in agricultural policy design, consider the following two environmental protection policies: increased taxation of pesticides (scenario 1) and increased incentives for the conservation of natural forests (scenario 2). The effects of each of these two policy scenarios can be compared to a so-called base run that mimics the actual prevailing land-use pattern in the Atlantic Zone in the year 1996 as well as the current policy structure. Scenario 1 examines the difference in impact between a flat tax and a progressive tax. While the flat tax consists of a percentage markup on the price of each pesticide that is equal for all types of pesticides, the markup in the progressive tax

Table 15.3. Effect of subsidies on natural forest land					
Subsidy level ($ ha^{-1}year^{-1})	0	40	110	120	130
Change in forest land (10^3 ha)	0	0	0	35	115

is different for each type of pesticide and linked to the environmental damage caused by a specific pesticide, expressed as an index that takes into account quantities of active ingredients used as well as their degree of toxicity and persistence in the environment (Jansen et al. 1995). Table 15.2 shows that taxing all pesticides at a uniform rate of 100 percent leads to a reduction in environmental damage of only 4 percent while reducing the economic surplus by nearly one-fifth. In contrast, a progressive tax regime, where different tax rates are applied to three categories of pesticides depending on their degree of toxicity, results in an 80 percent reduction in damage to the environment, while at the same time preserving up to 98 percent of the economic surplus.

The second example analyzes the effect of a policy that subsidizes forest regrowth through the allocation of premiums to natural forest land use. Sustainable exploitation of natural forests in the Atlantic Zone yields only a small return, about $20 ha^{-1}y^{-1} (Bulte, Joenje, and Jansen 2000). Land that is farmed yields returns from $120 (beef cattle on natural pastures) to $2,000 (banana plantations) per year. According to the simulations, a subsidy of $110 ha^{-1}y^{-1} is not sufficient to induce landowners to maintain their natural forests (table 15.3). On the other hand, a subsidy of $120 ha^{-1}y^{-1} would lead to an increase in forest area of about 35,000 ha and a subsidy of $130 ha^{-1}y^{-1} would result in an additional 115,000 ha of natural forest, mainly by inducing farmers to convert pastures back into forest. The current subsidy level ($40 ha^{-1}y^{-1}) has been largely effective in protecting forest stands on land that has low opportunity costs (mostly land that is unsuitable for agricultural use). However, even though Costa Rican law does not allow conversion of natural forests to agricultural land, the current payment level provides insufficient incentives for conservation of forest on lands with higher agricultural potential. Examples of other scenario types exploring the effects of quantitative limits on pesticide use, wage increases, changes in the interest rate, and technological progress are given in Jansen et al. (2001) and Schipper et al. (2000).

Predictive Land-Use Analysis

Often policy makers are particularly interested in the effects of short-term policy on farmers' land-use decisions. This requires modeling the behavior of those who ultimately make decisions about land use explicitly in the context of a methodology whose principle output is information regarding the relative effectiveness of alternative policy measures to reach a certain desired land use pattern. Predictive methodologies allow researchers to evaluate a wide spectrum of policy instruments, including price and market policies, taxes, subsidies, infrastructural improvements, reduced transaction costs, research and extension policies, and financial, trade, and exchange rate measures. The UNA-DLV methodology is operational at both the farm level (through the development and use of a farm typology) as well as at the regional level (through the incorporation of market clearing mechanisms; figure 15.2). The policy relevance of the UNA-DLV methodology can be illustrated by an example that relates to soil degradation. Actual land use patterns in the Atlantic Zone as of 1996 are unsustainable as expressed in an average nitrogen depletion of about 50 kg ha^{-1}yr^{-1}, mainly caused by soil mining in beef cattle ranching (Jansen et al. 2001). This points to the need for the technical change in the form of improved pasture technologies, such as fertilized improved grass species and grass-legume mixtures that have less negative soil nutrient balances. The UNA-DLV methodology is able to simulate the effects

Table 15.4. Technological change simulation with the UNA-DLV methodology: Farm level results

Farm types	Simulation with actual technologies only				Simulation with both actual and alternative technologies			
	Small	Medium	Hacienda	Banana	Small	Medium	Hacienda	Banana
Production structure (ha)								
Banana	—	—	—	127.3	—	—	—	169.7
Other crops	2.8	4.8	—	—	3.7	4.9	—	—
Pastures:	0.8	26.5	190.3	—	0.9	20.8	211.9	—
Natural	0.8	26.5	190.3	—	0.7	9.6	99.8	
Fertilized	0.0	0.0	0.0	—	0.2	11.2	112.1	—
Fallow	5.3	7.8	—	99.0	4.3	13.5	—	56.6
Livestock (animal units)	1.0	75.2	304.3	—	1.1	58.7	341.7	—
Depletion of N (kg ha^{-1} yr^{-1})	160	31	50	140	94	46	49	0

Table 15.5. Technological change simulation with the UNA-DLV methodology: Regional results

	Unit	Simulation with actual technologies only		Simulation with both actual and improved technologies	
		#	%	#	%
Economic surplus	US $ 10^6	172		219	
Cultivated area					
Pastures:	ha 10^3	203	60	211	62
Natural	ha 10^3	203	60	99	29
Fertilized	ha 10^3	0	0	112	33
Grass-legume	ha 10^3	0	0	0	0
Forest	ha 10^3	82	24	59	17
Crops	ha 10^3	55	16	69	21
Number of animals	AU 10^3	285		280	
Labor use	days/month 10^3	856	86	885	89
Depletion of N (crops and pasture areas only)	kg/ha	127		46	

of this type of technical change by incorporating such sustainable technologies into the expert systems (TCGs). Results at the farm-type level (table 15.4) show a general shift toward more sustainable production practices as a result of increased beef production per unit of land that is more than sufficient to compensate for the cost of the initial investment and increased operational costs. In addition to economic benefits, this type of technical change would result in environmental benefits as well: for example, haciendas would convert about 50 percent of their natural pasture land into improved fertilized pastures, leading to a significant reduction in soil nitrogen–depletion levels.

Model results for the whole Atlantic Zone (table 15.5) show that pastures are the dominant actual land use (60 percent of agricultural area), with natural forest area next (24 percent) followed by crops (16 percent). If alternative production systems such as fertilized pastures, more efficient palm heart technologies, and improved banana management schemes are implemented, both crop

**Table 15.6. Effects of trade liberalization and road investments
on welfare of producers, consumers, and society**

	Change relative to base run (10^6)	
	Trade liberalization	Reduction in transport costs
Producer surplus	5.1	23.6
Consumer surplus	37.3	0.5
Social welfare	42.4	24.1

and pasture areas expand at the expense of the adjacent forest area. In this case technological change results in reduced soil nitrogen depletion and rising economic surplus, a win-win situation from the viewpoint of agriculture. This general conclusion is not surprising. The alternative technologies incorporated in the TCGs are more productive and more sustainable than the technologies currently used. They were generated in this way, given the agronomic possibilities, not only theoretically, but also as observed by current practices on the best farms.

The SEM methodology also predicts the short-term effects of alternative policies on land use, but with a focus on the quantification of trade flows and changes in aggregate welfare at both the regional and national levels. As indicated before, disciplines other than economics are not incorporated explicitly in the SEM framework, even though soils and agronomy do enter the picture implicitly via supply response reactions that differ by region due to differences in biophysical conditions (Roebeling et al. 2000b). Two important policy simulations that can be performed with a SEM are trade liberalization and road investments. The former can be simulated by abolishing tariff and nontariff measures, that is, letting producers face (f.o.b.) world market export prices, while confronting consumers with (c.i.f.) world market import prices. Investments in road infrastructure can be expected to lead to lower transport costs (20 percent taken as an example here). The effects of these measures are evaluated relative to a so-called base scenario that works with actual producer and consumer prices and estimated transportation costs as explained earlier. Table 15.6 shows a summary

of the simulation results in welfare terms (see Roebeling et al. 2000b for more detailed results in terms of changes in land use and value of production and trade flows). Trade liberalization leads to a larger welfare increase than infrastructure investments and favors mostly consumers (who now have access to cheaper products from abroad), whereas producers are the main beneficiaries from lower transport costs (even though part of the cost savings is passed on to consumers).

Finally, it is worth noting that besides the SEM and UNA-DLV methodologies, the SOLUS methodology can also be used to some extent as a predictive methodology at the regional level because it addresses aggregate producer (and consumer) behavior. Unlike the UNA-DLV methodology, however, the SOLUS methodology does not incorporate farm types and therefore does not model farmer behavior explicitly. Instead, the subregions within the Atlantic Zone are treated as single farms having the maximization of aggregate economic surplus (consisting of the sum of the producer and consumer surplus in each market) as their objective function. Ignoring farm types has been shown to be a source of aggregation bias (Jansen and Stoorvogel 1998), stressing the complementarity of explorative and predictive land use methodologies at the regional level.

Designing Land-Use Systems

An important aspect of the explorative (SOLUS) and predictive (UNA-DLV) land use methodologies is that alternative land-use systems can be defined at the plot level. Describing alternative land-use systems and subsequently quantifying their inputs and outputs allows the transition from

Table 15.7. Examples of technical coefficients

| Type of land use system | Cassava | | Palm heart | |
| | Actual | Improved | Actual | Improved |
Herbicide level	high	high	high	Low
Outputs				
Prime quality product (kg ha⁻¹)	5,100	12,750	65,277	65,277
Second quality product (kg ha⁻¹)	2,550	6,375	11,519	11,519
Third quality product (kg ha⁻¹)	850	2,125	0	0
Δ soil N stock (kg ha⁻¹)	−54	0	0	0
Inputs				
Nitrogen fertilizers (kg N ha⁻¹)	0	290	713	713
Biocides (kg a.i. ha⁻¹)	1.2	2.2	56	53
Environmental damage index for biocides (ha⁻¹)	4,007	4,051	2,563	476
Labor requirements (d ha⁻¹)	34.1	67.4	193	210
Total costs ($ ha⁻¹)	118	621	9,528	9,487
Fertilizer costs ($ ha⁻¹)	0	465	1,868	1,868
Biocide costs ($ ha⁻¹)	50	63	1,684	1,644

Source: Adapted from Hengsdijk et al. (2000)

projective (extrapolative) modeling to explorative and predictive modeling. The so-called TCGs provide the plot-level building blocks that can be integrated in both the explorative (SOLUS) and predictive (UNA-DLV) methodologies that address larger spatial scales, ranging from a single farm type to an entire region. TCGs are also useful as stand-alone tools in addition to their use as input into explorative and predictive land use methodologies. The Costa Rican Ministry of Agriculture's extension service has used TCGs for ex ante analysis of the technical efficiency of land-use systems; for performing cost-benefit analysis; and for quantifying trade-offs among socioeconomic, agronomic, and environmental indicators at the field level (Hengsdijk et al. 1999). Table 15.7 shows examples of technical coefficients for cassava and palm heart.

Precision Agriculture and Prototyping

The development of the Banman system by Stoorvogel et al. (2000) involved continuous and close cooperation with a national (independent) banana producer and the National Banana Corporation. The aim is to look for complementarity between economic and biophysical sustainability at the farm level, thus providing decision support for farm enterprises by means of identification of land-use systems that increase farmers' profits while at the same time reducing environmental contamination. Once the input-output relationships of such land-use systems are firmly established and validated, they can be incorporated in the TCGs. SOLUS can subsequently be used to explore the feasibility and the consequences (e.g., in terms of agricultural income or pollution of the environment) of such new land-use systems at the regional level.

Lessons Learned for Research Design and Stakeholder Involvement

REPOSA's experience, spanning more than a decade of development and application of methodologies of land-use analysis for policy support, provides two important lessons that have applicability beyond that of the specific Costa Rican case studies. The first lesson relates to the structure and content of land-use analysis methodologies in which extensive use is made of quantitative models and information technology, while the second lesson relates to stakeholder interaction and the transfer process of such methodologies (Jansen and Azofeifa 2000).

Research Design

In order for tools for land-use analysis to be useful for policy makers, they should have a multidisciplinary and multiscale character, involving both the biophysical and the social sciences (particularly economics) while taking explicit account of the multiple levels at which land-use decisions are being made and influenced. This implies the necessity of a team effort in which each and every team member is fully aware of the necessity and unique contributions of the other members and disciplines, thus aiming toward a true integration of the biophysical sciences with economics (Hall et al. 2001). Moreover, if such tools for land-use analysis are to play an important role in evaluating policies for sustainable agricultural production and regional development, these tools should be made more transparent for policy makers and other stakeholders, as well as more user-friendly for analysts. Finding the right balance between scientific rigor and practical usability constitutes a major challenge for future research. With hindsight, REPOSA has probably given too little attention to the transferability aspect during the decade-long development of its "toolbox" of methodologies for land-use analysis on different scales.

Stakeholder Involvement

The ultimate purpose of land-use analysis at the subregional, regional, or national level is to support policy decisions. Therefore, policy makers and stakeholders with an interest in the area under study should ideally be active participants in any land-use analysis. Having said that, however, the second lesson learned is that unlike in prototyping, where scientists and farmers together experiment in finding new forms of land use, the methodologies of land-use analysis should be in a relatively advanced stage of development before end-users can actively be involved. In this way, losing the interest of potential users will be avoided. A substantial investment in training potential users also is usually essential to generate a sufficient level of understanding regarding the effective use of interdisciplinary, quantitative land-use analysis tools, as well as to achieve the accompanying knowledge transfer. Finally, to ensure that scenario analyses carried out bear relevance in the policy arena and address issues that decision makers consider as priorities, regular consultation with policy makers and other stakeholders is necessary, as has been the case in an application of SOLUS at the watershed level in close cooperation with the Costa Rican Ministry of Agriculture (Mera-Orcés 1999).

Acknowledgments

The author wishes to recognize the seminal contributions regarding methodology development made by the other members of the REPOSA team, including Bas Bouman, Rob Schipper, Huib Hengsdijk, André Nieuwenhuyse, Peter Roebeling, and Jetse Stoorvogel.

References

Bessembinder, J., M. K. van Ittersum, R. A. Schipper, B. A. M. Bouman, H. Hengsdijk, and A. Nieuwenhuyse. 2000. Exploring future land use options: Combining biophysical considerations and societal objectives. In Bouman et al. 2000, 145–69. Dordrecht: Kluwer Academic.

Bouma, J., H. G. P. Jansen, A. Kuyvenhoven, M. K. van Ittersum, and B. A. M. Bouman. 2000. Introduction. Bouman et al. 2000, 1–7.

Bouman, B. A. M, H. G. P. Jansen, R. A. Schipper, H. Hengsdijk, and A. B. Nieuwenhuyse, eds. 2000. *Tools for Land Use Analysis on Different Scales.* Dordrecht: Kluwer Academic.

Bouman, B. A. M., H. G. P. Jansen, R. A. Schipper, A. N. Nieuwenhuyse, H. Hengsdijk, and J. Bouma. 1999. A framework for integrated biophysical and economic land use analysis at different scales. *Agriculture, Ecosystems & Environment* 75, nos. 1–2: 55–73.

Bouman, B. A. M., A. Nieuwenhuyse, and H. Hengsdijk. 1998. PASTOR: A technical coefficient generator for pasture and livestock systems in the humid tropics, version 2.0. Quantitative Approaches in Systems Analysis No. 18. Wageningen, Netherlands: AB-DLO / C. T. de Wit Graduate School for Production Ecology.

Bouman, B. A. M., A. Nieuwenhuyse, R. A. Schipper, H. Hengsdijk, and H. G. P. Jansen. 1998. An integrated methodology for sustainable land use exploration using GIS. In *Proceedings of the First International Conference on Geospatial Information in Agriculture and Forestry*, 2:230–37. Ann Arbor: ERIM International.

Bouman, B. A. M., R. A. Schipper, A. Nieuwenhuyse, H. Hengsdijk, and H. G. P. Jansen. 1998. Quantifying economic and biophysical sustainability trade-offs in land use exploration at the regional level: A case study for the Northern Atlantic Zone of Costa Rica. *Ecological Modelling* 114: 95–109.

Bulte, E., B. A. M. Bouman, R. J. Plant, A. N. Nieuwenhuyse, and H. G. P. Jansen. 2000. The economics of soil nutrient stocks and cattle ranching in the tropics: Optimal pasture degradation in humid Costa Rica. *European Review of Agricultural Economics* 27, no. 2: 207–26.

Bulte, E., M. Joenje, and H. G. P. Jansen. 2000. Is there too much or too little forest in the Atlantic Zone of Costa Rica? *Canadian Journal of Forest Research* 30:495–506.

De Wit, C. T. 1979. The efficient use of land, labour and energy in agriculture. *Agricultural Systems* 5:279–87.

DGEC (Dirección General de Estadística y Censos). 1987. Censo agropecuario 1984. Ministerio de Economía, Industria y Comercio, San José, Costa Rica.

———. 1990. Metodología. Encuesta Nacional de Ingresos y Gastos de los Hogares, Informe No. 2. Ministerio de Economía, Industria y Comercio, San José, Costa Rica.

Geurts, J. A. M. M., H. G. P. Jansen, and A. Van Tilburg. 1997. Domestic demand for food in Costa Rica: A double hurdle analysis. Informe técnico 286, CATIE, Turrialba, Costa Rica.

Gómez, L. D. 1986. *Vegetación de Costa Rica*. San José: EUNED.

Griffon, M., T. Price, H. G. P. Jansen, and P. Bindraban. 1999. *The Multifunctional Character of Agriculture*. Rome: FAO.

Hall, C., D. Lindenberger, R. Kummel, T. Kroeger, and W. Eichhorn. 2001. The need to reintegrate the natural sciences with economics. *BioScience* 51, no. 8: 663–73.

Hengsdijk, H., B. A. M. Bouman, A. Nieuwenhuyse, and H. G. P. Jansen. 1999. Quantification of land use systems using technical coefficient generators: A case study for the Northern Atlantic Zone of Costa Rica. *Agricultural Systems* 61:109–21.

Hengsdijk, H., A. Nieuwenhuyse, and B. A. M. Bouman. 1998. LUCTOR: Land crop technical coefficient generator. A model to quantify cropping systems in the northern Atlantic Zone of Costa Rica. Version 2.0. Wageningen, Netherlands: AB-DLO / C.T. de Wit Graduate School for Production Ecology.

Jansen, D. M., J. J. Stoorvogel, and R. A. Schipper. 1995. Using sustainability indicators in agricultural land use analysis: An example from Costa Rica. *Netherlands Journal of Agricultural Science* 43:61–82.

Jansen, H. G. P., and R. Azofeifa. 2000. Lessons derived from a decade of collaborative land use analysis in Costa Rica by the Research Program on Sustainability in Agriculture (REPOSA). In *Interactive North-South Research for Development with special attention for Natural Resources Management*, 61–79. Amsterdam: Royal Netherlands Academy of Arts and Sciences.

Jansen, H. G. P., and J. J. Stoorvogel. 1998. Quantification of aggregation bias in regional agricultural land use models: Application to Guácimo county, Costa Rica. *Agricultural Systems* 58:417–39.

Jansen, H. G. P., and A. van Tilburg. 1996. *Agricultural Marketing in the Atlantic Zone of Costa Rica: A Production, Consumption and Trade Study of Agricultural Commodities Produced by Small and Medium-Scale Farmers*. Turrialba, Costa Rica: CATIE.

Jansen, H. G. P., B. A. M. Bouman, R. Schipper, H. Hengsdijk, and A. Nieuwenhuyse. 2005. An interdisciplinary approach to regional land use analysis using GIS, with applications to the Atlantic Zone of Costa Rica. *Agricultural Economics* 32:87–104.

Jansen, H. G. P., R. A. Schipper, P. Roebeling, E. H. Bulte, H. Hengsdijk, B. A. M. Bouman, and A. Nieuwenhuyse. 2001. Alternative approaches to the economics of soil nutrient depletion in Costa Rica: Exploratory, predictive and normative bio-economic models. In N. Heerink, H. van Keulen, and M. Kuiper, eds., *Economic Policy and Sustainable Land Use: Recent Advances in Quantitative Analysis for Developing Countries*, 211–37. Heidelberg: Physica-Verlag.

Jansen, H. G. P., E. Uytewaal, and J. Stoorvogel. 1998. Health externalities and pesticide use in the Atlantic Zone of Costa Rica: An economic evaluation. Guapiles, Costa Rica: REPOSA.

Jiménez, R., ed. 1998. *Estabilidad y desarrollo económico en Costa Rica: Las reformas pendientes*. San José: Academia de Centroamerica.

Kok, K., and T. Veldkamp. 2000. Using the CLUE framework to model changes in land use on multiple scales. In Bouman et al. 2000, 35–63.

————. 2001. Evaluating the impact of spatial scales on land use pattern analysis in Central America. *Agriculture, Ecosystems and Environment* 85:205–21.

Mera-Orcés, V. 1999. Evaluación de la transferencia de la metodología SOLUS (de REPOSA) al Ministero de Agricultura y Ganadería (MAG), Costa Rica. Turrialba, Costa Rica: REPOSA.

Nieuwenhuyse, A., B. A. M. Bouman, H. G. P. Jansen, R. A. Schipper, and R. Alfaro. 2000. The physical and socioeconomic setting: The northern Atlantic Zone of Costa Rica. In Bouman et al. 2000, 9–34.

Pontius, R. G., Jr., J. D. Cornell, and C. A. S. Hall. 2001. Modeling the spatial pattern of land-use change with GEOMOD2: Application and validation with Costa Rica. *Agriculture, Ecosystems and Environment* 85:1–13.

Roebeling, P. C., H. G. P. Jansen, R. A. Schipper, F. Sáenz, E. Castro, R. Ruben, H. Hengsdijk, and B. A. M. Bouman. 2000a. Farm modeling for policy analysis on the farm and regional level. In Bouman et al. 2000, 171–98.

Roebeling, P. C., H. G. P. Jansen, A. van Tilburg, and R. A. Schipper. 2000b. Spatial equilibrium modeling for evaluating inter-regional trade flows, land use and agricultural policy. In Bouman et al. 2000, 65–96.

Roebeling, P. C., R. Ruben, and F. Sáenz. 1998. Políticas agrarias para la intensificación sostenible del sector ganadero: Una aplicación en la Zona Atlántica de Costa Rica. In E. Castro and R. Ruben, eds., *Políticas agrarias para el uso sostenible de la tierra y la seguridad alimentaria en Costa Rica*, 156–74. Heredia, Costa Rica: UNA-CINPE / WAU-DLV.

Schipper, R. A., B. A. M. Bouman, H. G. P. Jansen, H. Hengsdijk, and A. Nieuwenhuyse. 2000. Integrated biophysical and socio-economic analysis of regional land use. In Bouman et al. 2000, 115–44.

SEPSA (Secretaría Ejecutiva de Planificación Sectorial Agropecuaria). 1997. *Políticas del sector agropecuario (revisión y ajuste)*. San José: Ministry of Agriculture and Livestock (MAG).

Stoorvogel, J. J., R. A. Orlich, R. Vargas, and J. Bouma. 2000. Linking information technology and farmer knowledge in a decision support system for improved banana cultivation. In Bouman et al. 2000, 199–212.

Takayama, Y., and G. G. Judge. 1964. Spatial equilibrium and quadratic programming. *Journal of Farm Economics* 46, no. 1: 67–93.

Van Ittersum, M. K., R. Rabbinge, and H. C. Van Latesteijn. 1998. Exploratory land use studies and their role in strategic policy making. *Agricultural Systems* 58:309–30.

Verburg, P. H., G. H. J. De Koning, K. Kok, A. Veldkamp, and J. Bouma. 1999. A spatially explicit allocation procedure for modelling the pattern of land use change based upon actual land use. *Ecological Modelling* 116:45–61.

Vereijken, P. 1997. A methodological way of prototyping integrated and ecological arable farming systems (I/EAFS) in interaction with pilot farms. *European Journal of Agronomy* 7:235–50.

Wielemaker, W. G., and A. W. Vogel. 1993. *Un sistema de información de suelos y tierras para la Zona Atlántica de Costa Rica*. Guápiles, Costa Rica: REPOSA.

CHAPTER 16

Deriving Land-Quality Indicators from the Landscape Units Used in Soils Surveys

Jeroen M. Schoorl, Tom Veldkamp, and Johan Bouma

Introduction

One of the largest problems faced by development schemes is incomplete knowledge about the potential that different soils have for agricultural production. Much of this problem can be attributed to soil taxonomy because soil taxonomy schemes, as they presently exist, are inadequate for assisting development. They give too much emphasis to soil genesis (origin) and too little to soil properties relevant for production. In order to address this shortcoming, the concept of *soil quality* has been introduced. Soil quality was defined by Karlen et al. (1997) as: "the fitness of a specific kind of soil to function within its capacity and within natural and managed ecosystem boundaries, to sustain plant and animal productivity, maintain water and air quality and support human health and habitation."

Many studies have been made about soil quality (e.g., Doran and Jones 1996), but there is not yet a well-defined universal methodology to derive soil quality indicators. Doran and Jones present four physical, four chemical, and three biological indicators, which, according to the authors, together represent a minimal data set that can characterize soil quality, but they gave no examples. Gomez et al. (1996) define six soil-quality indicators and give minimum or threshold values for determining sustainability of agricultural systems at the farm level. They imply that a greater degree of sustainability corresponds with higher soil qualities. Doran and Jones list other examples of soil quality studies, including a series of soil characteristics that can be used as indicators of soil quality, but no study yet really addresses the broad spirit or scope of the definition advanced in Karlen et al. (1997).

Soils, as described in soil surveys, are 3-D entities with a distinct spatial distribution. Soils are also dynamic, and can change significantly within decades in response to differences in vegetation (Van Breemen 1998), landscape processes (Schoorl and Veldkamp 2001), or management (Droogers and Bouma 1997). When dealing with such multidimensional systems, the issue of scale becomes relevant. A scale can be defined as a range of frequencies for spatial and temporal observations. Resolution below a given scale implies faster and smaller frequencies, which we call noise, and resolution above a given scale implies slower and larger frequencies, which we call "events." Together they define the range of observation frequencies. Actors and processes that operate at the same scale interact strongly with each other, but the organization and context of these interactions are determined by the cross-scale organization of the system (Peterson et al. 1998).

In general, processes of interest to humans operate at characteristic intermediate temporal and spatial scales (Holling 1992). Biophysical processes that control plant physiology and morphology often dominate with small, rapid scales. At larger and often slower scales (fields and catchments), crop-weed competition for nutrients, light, and water dominate. At the largest, landscape, scale, climate, and geomorphologic processes determine the structure and dynamics of agroecosystems (O'Neill et al. 1991). All these processes produce scale-specific patterns, which are under natural conditions self-organizing in nature. Examples are the observed relations between climate and soil zones for continents and soil-landscape elements (*catenas*) within these zones. This implies that one might need different parameters/factors for the different spatial and temporal scales when characterizing soil quality. It is thus necessary to determine systematically at which scale level which property and related process is relevant. Soils are often studied at two important spatial scales: the agroecological zone, often associated with soil groups, and the more detailed soil series, which often coincide in extent with farms and their fields.

The overall objective of this study is to generate a more useful scheme for using spatial data on soils to help to design development projects. Specifically, we:

> Review the traditional concept of soil quality, including a consideration of the effects of spatial scales and the many nonsoil factors that interact with soil quality to determine crop yields.
> Recommend the replacement of the term *soil quality* with *land quality* (LQ), which also takes into account local climate.
> Define a new operational expression of land quality based on crop yield that takes into account the effects of climate, land utilization type, and management and the definition of a general reference level.
> Illustrate the land quality concept with several case studies.
> Suggest further studies to broaden the concept of land quality.

The Traditional Concept of Soil Quality

A number of general considerations have to be made when defining soil quality. These include: Any fitness of a soil for a particular function depends strongly on climate conditions, which vary not only among different agroecological climate zones but also, of course, at any given location during the years. "Fitness for function" will often mean that a given soil can still produce crops under relatively adverse weather conditions in contrast to surrounding soils that may suffer severe yield losses. Implicitly, the latter soils have a "lower" quality. Because of the importance of weather and climate, some suggest the use of land quality (LQ) rather than soil quality. We agree, especially because land occurs in a landscape and soil processes are strongly affected by their landscape position (Hall and Olson 1991). The tendency by some to consider the "functioning" of a soil in terms of one-dimensional

vertical process characteristics is incorrect in a landscape context (Veldkamp et al. 2001).

Problems with Defining Soil Function

"Fitness for function" is tied closely to what the land is to be used for, and this is not included in the existing definition of soil quality. Obviously the function is different when the soil is supporting natural vegetation in natural ecosystems than it is when used for agricultural production of plants and animals. Maintaining or enhancing water and air quality requires certain qualities while maintaining "human health and habitation" may require very different characteristics to be suitable for housing, bicycle paths, and recreation facilities. Each of these functions has very different requirements, which hardly can be combined into a single indicator. Thus, it is necessary to specify the use when defining LQ. In this chapter we use agricultural production as the most important land use when defining LQ, but the principle can be applied to other uses.

Different types of management also can make a big difference in soil quality of a specific kind of soil (Pennock, Anderson, and de Jong 1994). Droogers and Bouma (1997) developed the terms *genoforms* (natural soils) and *phenoforms* (soils changed because of human actions) within soil series to express the effect of soil management on soil properties. Management may have both short- and long-term effects. A given type of tillage under wet conditions may lead to compaction and high bulk densities, while better tillage practices might have resulted in lower and more desirable bulk densities. Thus, bulk density by itself is a poor indicator of soil quality in the short term, even though it is frequently used. Organic matter contents represent a more stable and significant indicator because it can only be changed through long-term management (e.g., Doran and Parkin 1996; Droogers and Bouma 1997; Sonneveld, Bouma, and Veldkamp 2002).

Soil quality also needs to be defined in relation to a reference level because its significance is derived from the fact that the quality of a given soil is either higher or lower than that of another one. An absolute reference level would be quite attractive to allow comparisons among all soils rather than comparisons one by one, but that cannot be defined generally yet. Gomez et al. (1996) were able to do this locally when they expressed their six indicators (soil depth, organic C, permanent ground cover, yield, profit, and frequency of crop failure) in terms of deviations from average values in the community.

Most papers struggling with the definition of soil quality focus on actual soil or crop conditions that have been measured or observed in the field. But as stated before, actual quality for a given function is affected not only by varying weather conditions and types of management but also by a host of socioeconomic conditions. For the soil quality concept to be of value in promoting better soil quality and soil use in the future, a focus on potential crop production would be helpful to provide a point of reference. This would also stimulate practical use of the quality concept. A statement about how much soil quality can be improved, and what it takes to achieve this, is much more interesting than a statement that soil quality is low! Dynamic simulation modeling, as suggested by Harris et al. (1996) and as applied by Bouma and Droogers (1998), can be a useful tool here to define potential production and water-limited yield while assuming that all other factors affecting production, such as fertility status and pests and diseases, are nonlimiting.

Another problem is the size of the units by which we classify soil. Typically, soil type is characterized on a field or farm level. Larger units, specifically soil series that normally cover tens of square kilometers, would be better candidates for our evaluations. Therefore, it would be logical to make use of, for example, the completed soil survey of the United States, in which soil series have been well defined, or of other similarly developed international soil classification schemes. Thus, rather than having to consider organic matter content, bulk density, soil physical characteristics, cation exchange, pH, and microbiological properties in a general manner, it would be better to consider them as characteristics of a given soil series. Such series, incidentally, occur within a given climatic zone and in characteristic landscape positions. The system could be applied to both genoforms and well-defined phenoforms, which may act significantly

differently. The link between defining soil limitations and soil suitabilities for a series of land utilization types (Bouma 1989) is intriguing when connecting the soil quality aspect with soil series.

Soils now tend to be defined in terms of their limitations. Perhaps it would be better to say that soil quality is the inverse of soil limitations for a given use as they are defined in common soil surveys. In other words, when a soil has severe limitations for growing wheat, does that imply that soil quality for growing wheat is low or merely that that particular soil does not receive enough rain or management? It is interesting that the link between soil limitations as defined by soil survey and soil quality has not been made so far.

The soil quality issue normally is considered in the literature in a manner that is independent of scale. Characteristically "soil" has been considered as a pedon (soil profile column) of limited dimensions. In reality soils occur not only in fields and farms but also as extended entities occurring as patterns in landscapes. Thus, it is more logical to link the soil quality concept to the landscape and not only to an individual soil. This could be attractive for policy issues because spatial scales have not been considered when defining soil quality so far, hence an analysis of such potential scale effects is given in this chapter.

Soil Quality and Crop Yield

Actual crop yields are governed by many factors other than the soil and landscape factors, including climate, management, and so on. Therefore, researchers generally use potential yield values when defining soil quality, rather than using measured yield values. It is more advisable to analyze first which factors govern yield at any particular location to be able to better interpret empirical values obtained and suggest alternative management approaches to the production process. We will therefore review papers that link actual crop productions to factors that turn out to be most important in determining yield variability.

Factors that determine potential yield

At the level of the agroecological zone (tens to hundreds of square kilometers), climate plays a prominent role. The spatial variability is often gradual and given conditions apply to large areas, while in contrast the temporal variability is often rapid and perceived as a risk factor by farmers. As such, this temporal variability can strongly determine small-scale processes and management decisions. Clear examples are found in the low input agriculture in the West African Sahel (Prudencio 1993; Brouwer and Bouma 1997; chapter 8).

Thus agroecological zones determine what crops might be planted there, while the relative rapid temporal climatic conditions (yearly, seasonal, and daily) will affect the final choice of crops and its management by local farmers. The soil usually plays a more important role at local levels than at the agroecological scale level. A practical way to address scale issues is to combine spatial and temporal dynamics within agriculture by focusing on production. Consequently, yield reflects the crop choice, local environmental conditions, and the crop's performance (the net effect of a particular growing season).

Production potentials are calculated using crop physiology and climate data. The general disadvantage of production potentials is that they are derived from a modeling exercise and as such cannot be measured and/or verified in the field. However, when standard procedures are defined to define potential production, they can be used to provide an absolute and attractive point of reference (e.g. Penning de Vries, Rabbinge, and Groot 1997).

Factors that determine actual yields

Actual yields are also important when considering LQ. The problem with actual yields is that many nonsoil/climate factors usually cause the actual yield to be far below the theoretical production potential, the so-called yield gap. An analysis of the causes of yield-gaps can give insight into yield-determining and yield-limiting factors. When certain soil or land related factors are found to be yield-limiting, they should be subject to more in-depth analysis and characterization, as they are crucial for defining measures to close the yield gap.

Both socioeconomic and biophysical factors (excluding radiation and water availability) are known to contribute to the yield gap. In order to unravel possible scale effects in actual agronomic production, a system analysis can be made for different spatial scales by keeping the extent (studied area) constant but by changing the resolution of the spatial units. We will put special emphasis on the role of biophysical (climate, geomorphology, and soil) factors in determining the yield levels.

Methods and Data

We focus on developing LQs for agricultural production taking into account the considerations of the previous sections and our focus on agriculture. If we had considered LQ for, say, nature, construction, or recreation, we would have needed a different approach. We did not consider soil characteristics separately when defining LQ but assumed that a given type of soil will function similarly in different locations but in a given ecological climate zone. Thus we use each taxonomic type of soil as a "carrier of information." Consequently, this approach can be followed only when soil surveys and soil classifications are available. However, such surveys are available in many countries, so why not use them? An organic matter content or bulk density value has more meaning when it is tied to a given soil type than a loose number.

We use this available soil information within dynamic simulation models to calculate crop yields as a function of different weather conditions in different years and different rates of fertilization. We also calculate associated leaching rates of agrochemicals to balance production against environmental side effects. Furthermore, use of dynamic simulation also allows creation of an absolute reference level for LQ, in the way that they generate general estimates of potential production as governed by temperature, radiation, and crop characteristics. This model is sensitive not only to the soil type (expressed as the genoform) but also to different phenoforms, which formed through different types of management.

We first discuss a number of soil-centered case studies. We illustrate that the role of soil and climate is very dependent on scale and context or country. Then, we analyze the relation of crop production to agronomic and socioeconomic factors at different spatial scales to provide some background data for an effective definition of LQs.

Land Qualities of Some Major Soils in the Tropics

We defined LQ for both the genoform and several phenoforms for seven major land units in the humid tropics and the seasonally dry subtropics and tropics. Two phenoforms reflect unfavorable effects of management in terms of compaction and water erosion, and one phenoform reflects favorable effects in terms of liming of acid soil, resulting in deeper rooting. Penning de Vries, Rabbinge, and Groot (1997) and Hoogenboom et al. (2000) used simulation models to calculate potential production in terms of grain-equivalents. Potential production represents a ceiling as it reflects the effects of radiation and temperatures while assuming that water and nutrient supply are optimal and pests and diseases do not occur. In addition, water-limited yields were calculated based on the natural available water capacity of the soil, as governed by rainfall and uptake in the rooting zone, under the same assumptions as stated above. The LQ thus obtained reflects characteristic soil-related properties, including natural soil water regimes. Thus, an expression is obtained for "fitness for function," based on core functions of the soil relative to needs of crop plants (Karlen et al. 1997). Rooting depths and water-holding capacities were estimated by studying soil profile descriptions and texture (Bouma, Batjes, and Groot 1998; Bouma 2002). LQs were defined as the ratio between potential and water-limited production multiplied by 100 to avoid decimal values.

Land Qualities of a Prime Agricultural Soil in the Netherlands

We also analyzed a prime agricultural soil in the Netherlands, a loamy, mixed, mesic typic fluvaquent. A total of three phenoforms were studied (Droogers and Bouma 1997) of which only CONV and BIO are discussed here. CONV represents a conventional, high-tech arable farming, and BIO represents "biological" farming, which implies in this case over sixty years of cultivation without application of agrochemicals but with use of organic manure. Consequently, the organic matter content of the surface soil of BIO phenoform was about 2 percent higher than the one of CONV. We used the simulation model WAVE to calculate yields and leaching of nitrates for a thirty-year period as a function of different fertilization rates. We present the results as probability curves, which express the probabilities of exceedance rather than just averages. This expression represents the goal "to maintain water quality and to support human health" (Karlen et al. 1997). LQs were expressed as the ratio of potential production to the higher productions that would be obtained if certain probabilities for nitrate leaching would exceed the threshold values.

Land Qualities and Crop Yields in Costa Rica

Recently, more emphasis in global change research has been put on land use/cover change LUCC (Turner et al. 1995; Lambin et al. 1999). As a result of this LUCC research, more high-quality georeferenced databases have become available. We have been associated with one of these research projects, CLUE (Conversion of Land Use and Its Effects, http://www.cluemodel.nl). This project has yielded a wealth of agronomic data for a series of tropical countries. For one of these countries, Costa Rica (1984), spatially distributed yield data for coffee, bananas, maize, rice, and beans and for potential controlling factors have been studied (Veldkamp and Fresco 1997). These potential controlling factors affecting yield variability were selected from both socioeconomic (infrastructure, population, education) and biophysical (climate, geomorphology, soil) data. We analyzed this data set with multiple regression analysis at two different spatial resolutions (7.5 × 7.5 and 37.5 × 37.5 km).

A spatially explicit data set of calculated water-limited yield potentials for Maize, Rice, and Beans was also available at a 55 × 55 km resolution. These potential yields have been calculated using the IMAGE-2 framework, a global integrated assessment model that uses yield potentials to estimate future land use patterns (Alcamo 1994). Climate data are based on the International Institute of Applied Systems Analysis (IIASA) climate data set (Leemans and Cramer 1991). In order to identify

Table 16.1. Potential yield for cereals and LQ values for seven tropical soils

Soil type	Country	Pot. Prod. Tons Dry matter/ha/yr	Rel. Land Quality Water Limited	Pheno-form Erosion	Pheno-form Compaction	Pheno-form Liming	Absolute Land Quality Water Limited
1 Ferric Acrisol	China	13	96	85	75	100	32
2 Orthic Ferralsol	Indonesia	18	90	75	70	100	39
3 Cambic Arenosol	Colombia	12	96	80	72	100	31
4 Ferric Luvisol	Nigeria	14	90	75	55	90	32
5 Ferralic Arenosol	Nigeria	14	85	70	50	85	30
6 Orthic Acrisol	China	8	90	50	85	100	20
7 Orthic Ferralsol	Zambia	23	50	40	30	50	27

the role of climate in determining yields, a multiple regression analysis of calculated water-limited yields was made for Costa Rica (Veldkamp, Zuidema, and Fresco 1996).

Results and Discussion

LQ Values of Some Major Tropical Genoforms and Phenoforms of Major Land Units

Results of the calculations of potential cereal yields and derived LQs of seven major soils of the tropics at the field/pedon level are presented in table 16.1. Potential productions are indicated as well as relative LQ values for the seven genoforms, to allow comparisons among phenoforms. The relatively high LQ values in table 16.1 reflect wet tropical conditions in most of the soils. The exception is soil 7, which has an annual precipitation of only 114 mm with a resulting LQ of only 50. However, with adequate rainfall this soil would have produced the highest yields of all. LQs for the three phenoforms indicate both the negative impact on LQ of erosion and compaction, and the positive impact of liming of acid soils, which is likely to result in deeper rooting.

Under the assumed conditions, the effects of compaction are larger than those of erosion. Of course, different conditions can occur in individual fields where infiltration rate, water holding capacity of the root zone, and rooting depth may vary. Since liming has a positive effect in acid soils (higher LQ), less-acidic soils 4, 5, and 7 (table 16.1) do show a lower LQ (negative effects of limited liming).

A further problem with this analysis is that the use of water-limited yields for estimating land qualities implies that soil fertility is adequately sufficient. This is, of course, often not the case and actual yield gaps may be larger. If data were available real yields could be introduced into the equation, rather than the theoretical water-limited yield. This will show how large the total yield gap is for a detailed statistical analysis for Costa Rica, which define factors that actually determine yields, allowing the identification of measures that can be effective in closing the yield gap.

The LQ of these seven soils are put in a global perspective by calculating absolute land qualities, comparing water-limited yields with the maximum global (European) potential production value of 41.4 tons dry matter/ha/yr. LQs are then relatively low, hovering in the 20–40 range.

The Trade-off of Yield and Environmental Quality of a Prime Agricultural Soil

Droogers and Bouma (1997) summarized results of the simulations of the trade-offs between yields and associated nitrate leaching rates at the field/pedon level when more fertilizer is used in the Netherlands (figure 16.1). Cumulative probabilities are shown for yields that are associated with different levels of probability that nitrate leaching will exceed environmental thresholds, as specified in the law. Lines for exceeding the standards for 10 percent, 3 percent, and 0 percent of the years are shown. Yields are reduced strongly as the probability of exceeding the threshold decreases. The two phenoforms BIO and CONV characteristically react differently: the higher organic matter content in BIO implies that the reduction in yield is less as the strictness of the leaching criteria is increased. This, certainly, expresses an element of quality, as land users perceive it, in that soils with high organic quality are less likely to leach nitrogen at high application levels. LQs can be defined, using data as presented in figure 16.1, only when a certain probability is defined for both yield and leaching risk.

Potential production for spring wheat could reach up to 8,400 kg/ha/yr. If enough N fertilizer is added to generate a probability of 20 percent, that production on BIO soils is greater than 7,500 kg, corresponds with a probability that the threshold for nitrate leaching to the groundwater is exceeded in 10 percent of the years. The corresponding yield for CONV is 7,060 kg. When we reduce nitrogen fertilization rates so that the probability that the nitrate leaching threshold is exceeded is only 3 percent, corresponding yields are reduced to 6,100 kg and 5,080 kg/ha, respectively. When the leaching standards are never exceeded, yields are reduced to 5,100 kg and 2,800 kg/ha, respectively.

The proposed LQ indicator value is different for the two phenoforms being distinguished. For example, the indicator will be 89, 73, and 61 for BIO, corresponding with probabilities for exceeding nitrate leaching standards of 10 percent, 3 percent, and 0 percent respectively. This arbitrarily assumes a yield level that has a probability of 20 percent of being exceeded. Corresponding values for CONV are 84, 60, and 33. Thus, it is clear that the higher organic matter content of BIO has favorable effects. When the probabilities for exceeding nitrate leaching standards are set at 3 percent, the LQ value for BIO is 73 and 60 for CONV.

This example demonstrates that an LQ value can be selected only after decisions have been made on the selection of probability levels in terms of yields and values not to exceed for nitrate leaching. Thus, the user is forced to make a choice. Research

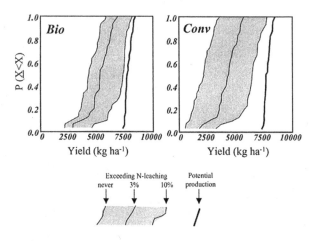

Figure 16.1. Probabilities that yields of wheat are exceeded as a function of three probabilities that the threshold value for nitrate leaching to the groundwater is exceeded as well. Data are based on simulations for a thirty-year period for a prime agricultural soil in the Netherlands using a wide range of fertilization rates.

provides a range of options that expresses the trade-offs involved, but the choice needs to be made by the user, not by the researcher.

Crop Yields as a Function of Soil Conditions and Other Factors in Costa Rica

Three climatic variables, mean temperature in May, mean precipitation in January, and mean precipitation in October explain more than 74.4 percent of the variability in water-limited yields for maize, rice, and beans in Costa Rica (table 16.2). The majority of the yield variability is related to within-cell (55×55 km) variability of climate and a relative minor part to the climate differences within the country as described by the coarse cells. These results confirm the dominant role of spatial variability in climate for determining potential yields at a high aggregated scale level. However, this coarse resolution might exaggerate its role because, as we stated previously, we know that climate is a dominant yield factor at high aggregated scales like agroecological zones (see also Hall 2000, chapter 12).

We also analyzed the variability in yield of coffee, bananas, maize, rice, and beans within Costa Rica in 1984 based on spatially explicit agronomic census data on yields (Veldkamp and Fresco 1997). Figure 16.2 gives the spatial distribution of these

Table 16.2. Regression model fits of water-limited yields for maize, rice, and beans in Costa Rica as explained by climatic variables, mean temperature in May, mean precipitation in January and October

Crop	Climatic model R^2	Local, within cell variability Part R^2	Regional, between cells variability Part. R^2
Maize	83.4%	74.6%	8.8%
Rice	78.1%	53.4%	24.7%
Beans	74.4%	65.5%	8.9%

Spatial resolution 55 km * 55 km. After Veldkamp, Zuidema, and Fresco (1996)

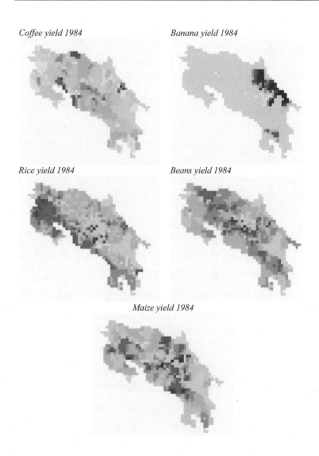

Coffee yield 1984

Banana yield 1984

Rice yield 1984

Beans yield 1984

Maize yield 1984

Figure 16.2. Summary of empirical yield patterns for coffee, bananas, maize, beans, and rice in Costa Rica 1984 derived from census data. Data is given at the 7.5 km resolution from grid-processed census data (after Veldkamp and Fresco 1997).

yields in 1984, the darker the grid the higher the average yield. Table 16.3 gives the results from multiple regression analysis valid for a spatial resolution of 7.5 × 7.5 km. Yield variability was examined against both socioeconomic (infrastructure, population, education) and biophysical (climate, geomorphology, soil) factors. All crops studied showed significant correlations (at the 0.05 level) with significant contributions from both socioeconomic and biophysical factors. Model fits (coefficients of determination) were relatively poor for coffee and banana yields (around 13–14 percent) to fair for the annual crop yields of maize, rice, and beans (ranging from 29 to 37 percent). The relative contribution of the land- and climate-related factors within the model ranged from 0.20 for coffee yield to 0.93 for rice yields, illustrating the complex interactions within land-use systems (Turner et al. 1995).

When the exercise is repeated for the same data set but aggregated to coarser spatial units (37.5 × 37.5 km), there is a considerable increase in model performance, with the exception of coffee and banana yields (table 16.4). At this aggregation level coefficients of determination range explain from 52.9 percent of the variability for bean yields to 63.8 percent for maize and 72.3 percent for rice. The contribution of biophysical factors has generally increased compared to the socioeconomic factors with the exception of coffee yield. Soils continue to play a significant role at both spatial scales. Soil properties play a role in determining the yield variability of maize, rice,

Table 16.3. Regression models at the 7.5 km resolution (significant at the 0.05 level) for the relation of yield variability to biophysical and socioeconomic factors in Costa Rica 1984 for selected crops

Spatial resolution: 7.5 × 7.5 km	Coffee yield	Banana yield	Maize yield	Rice yield	Bean yield
Overall model fit	13.1%	14.2%	29.2%	37.1%	26.3%
Socioeconomic factors	10.5% (0.80)	5.7% (0.40)	13.7% (0.47)	2.5% (0.07)	16.5% (0.63)
Biophysical factors	2.6% (0.20)	8.5% (0.60)	15.5% (0.53)	34.6% (0.93)	9.8% (0.37)
Climate	1.8% (0.14)	8.5% (0.60)	9.8% (0.34)	31.1% (0.84)	0.6% (0.02)
Geomorphology	—	—	1.3% (0.04)	0.9% (0.02)	1.8% (0.07)
Soil	0.8% (0.06)	—	4.4% (0.15)	2.6% (0.07)	7.4% (0.28)

The partial R^2 values of the independent factors are listed. The relative factor weights within the regression model are given between parentheses.

Table 16.4. Regression models for the 37.5 km resolution (significant at the 0.05 level) for the relation of yield variability to biophysical and socioeconomic factors in Costa Rica 1984 for selected crops

Spatial resolution: 37.5 × 37.5 km	Coffee yield	Banana yield	Maize yield	Rice yield	Bean yield
Overall Model fit	14.7%	11.6%	63.8%	72.3%	52.9%
Socioeconomic Factors	14.7% (1.00)	—	18.7% (0.29)	—	29.5% (0.56)
Biophysical Factors:	—	11.6% (1.00)	45.1% (0.71)	72.3% (1.00)	23.4% (0.44)
Climate	—	11.6% (1.00)	26.3% (0.41)	58.7% (0.81)	—
Geomorphology	—	—	6.9% (0.11)	—	7.7% (0.15)
Soil	—	—	11.9% (0.19)	13.6% (0.19)	15.7% (0.29)

The partial R^2 values of the independent factors are listed. The relative factor weights within the regression model are given between parentheses.

and beans at both spatial scales studied. For coffee and bananas soil type is less important, probably related to the fact that these cash crops are grown on the better soils and receive more input anyway. At a more detailed level, the plantation field level, soils are known to be the most important variable explaining local variability in yield (Veldkamp et al. 1990).

The Costa Rica example illustrates clearly the scale dependence of the yield-explaining regression models. The general tendency at the scale levels used is that at more aggregated spatial scales an increase in model performance can be observed and the climate component becomes more important. This is probably simply because climate is more likely to vary at the coarser scales.

A similar study for Ecuador in 1991 (De Koning, Veldkamp, and Fresco 1998) demonstrated that socioeconomic factors dominate the yield variability there, while a case study for Honduras (Kok and Veldkamp 2001) demonstrated the opposite, a mainly biophysical-dominated system. Apparently, Costa Rica is intermediate, with both groups contributing to an explanation of patterns. We have demonstrated here that if one wants to use actual agronomic production as a measure of LQ, a quantification of important factors is required in order to calculate the relative contribution of LQs such as soil, geomorphology, and climate-related properties. It is obvious from the Costa Rican case that although soils tend to always be somewhat important, they are almost never the most important factor in determining the actual variability in yields of annual crops.

This picture might change significantly when a study is made at the field/pedon level, as illustrated by the success of precision farming, where within a regional climate type soil type can be most important (Bouma 1997). The advantage of the approach that we used is that it identifies the relevant LQ indicators at a regional scale. Once identified, they can serve as a measure of the quality of the soils/land under consideration at specified scale levels for specific land utilization types (crops). It is important to emphasize that these quality indicators are always both land use– and scale-dependent and that their relevance can change over time.

The disadvantage of some aspects of the approaches that we have used so far is that a lot of data are needed, ideally for multiple growing seasons, which are rarely available. Furthermore, high-resolution data are usually extremely scarce or nonexistent, limiting such an application to a very coarse scale. The most limiting aspect of these difficult-to-derive actual yields is the fact that the exploration of future options and scenarios becomes impossible (Veldkamp and Lambin 2001). However, the use of a scale- and land use–specific analysis of the relevance and productivity of soils and other land properties (quality) might open up the means for strategic "niche management" at various scales.

Conclusions and Recommendations

An important objective when defining LQs is effective communication of soil information to other scientists and to a wide variety of soil users. This chapter provided an example to illustrate (1) how existing soil information can be made more useful by considering LQ, (2) the need to specify the land

use for which the LQ is defined, and (3) how this might be done.

We gave examples for crop production for seven major soil types in the tropics. The results illustrate that potential yield and water-limited production levels are key elements of the LQ. When the LQ values are applied to a single local soil genoform, they can be used to predict real production levels. The LQ equation can also be expanded to represent yield as a function of varying management by farmers and of various socioeconomic conditions. The yield gap that remains shows how much room for improvement of production exists and how this relates to other soils in other areas. The statistical analysis of yield as a function of various factors, including the soil and climate, as illustrated above for Costa Rica, is essential to pinpoint measures that have the potential of being effective in closing the yield gap. The scale-dependent outcomes suggest that a multiscale approach might be most feasible as often applied in population biology (Milne 1991) and land use–change modeling (Veldkamp and Lambin 2001).

The example of agricultural production for a prime agricultural soil in the Netherlands showed the trade-offs between production and environmental effects at the field level, including a specific number to reflect the effects of management, as expressed by the phenoforms. For example the superior performance of the organic "BIO" phenoform relative to the conventional "CONV" phenoform could be quantified and used to improve the numeric value of the LQ. This can be important, for example in Western Europe, when discussing the merits of organic versus conventional farming. Furthermore, by expressing LQs for different soil types (both genoforms and phenoforms) in relation to, for example, environmental hazards such as nitrate leaching, decision makers can actually direct their measures to stimulate or discourage certain farming strategies and to quantify possible results on different soil types. To summarize, the following final conclusions and recommendations:

We prefer the term *land quality* (LQ) over the term *soil quality*, because it reflects the importance of climate that plays a crucial role in the performance of the soil, and because soils cannot be considered as isolated pedons but have to be considered as integrated parts of landscapes (natural gradients of water, nutrients, catena positions, and so on).

Land use has to be specified when defining LQ as the quality depends on what the land is, can, or will be used for. The focus in this study was on agricultural production and the LQ for single soil types has been quantified as the ratio between calculated water-limited and potential yield, multiplied by 100. We distinguished both genoforms and phenoforms for seven major land units of the tropics, while also expressing the effects of soil-degradation and soil improvement as an example.

Measured production can be compared to potential or water-limited production, to give an indication of the local yield gap, which reflects the effects of soil conditions and many other socioeconomic and agronomic factors, as was illustrated with a case study from Costa Rica. These factors can be used to help to decide how to close the yield gap.

Land qualities have been presented in earlier literature only for individual soils. We have expanded the use of LQs to different scales, for example, from field to regional levels.

More detailed models can be used to express LQs from the perspective of their impact on the trade-offs between water-limited yield and the probability of nitrate leaching. Thus, in order to define LQs the user must make a selection from the yield versus nitrate-leaching probabilities. Research offers a set of options from which a choice can be made.

Defining scale-specific LQs for major land units in the world would be helpful to communicate soil expertise more effectively to the outside world.

References

Alcamo, J., ed. 1994. IMAGE-2 Special Issue. *Water, Air and Soil Pollution* 76.

Bouma, J. 1989. Using soil survey data for quantitative land evaluation. *Advances in Soil Science* 9:225–39.

———. 1997. Precision agriculture: Introduction to the spatial and temporal variability of environmental quality. In *Precision Agriculture: Spatial and Temporal Variability of Environmental Quality*, 5–13. New York: Wiley.

———. 2002. Land quality indicators of sustainable land management across scales. *Agriculture Ecosystems and Environment* 88:129–36.

Bouma, J., and P. Droogers. 1998. A procedure to derive land quality indicators for sustainable agricultural production. *Geoderma* 85:103–10.

Bouma, J., N. H. Batjes, and J. J. R. Groot. 1998. Exploring land quality effects on world food supply. *Geoderma* 86:43–59.

Brouwer, J., and J. Bouma. 1997. Soil and crop growth variability in the Sahel: Highlights of research (1990–95) at ICRISAT Sahelian Center. Information Bulletin 49.

De Koning, G. H. J., A. Veldkamp, and L. O. Fresco. 1998. Land use in Ecuador: A statistical analysis at different aggregation levels. *Agriculture, Ecosystems and Environment* 70:231–47.

Doran, J. W., and A. J. Jones, eds. 1996. *Methods for Assessing Soil Quality*. Madison, Wis.: Soil Science Society of America.

Doran, J. W., and T. B. Parkin. 1996. Quantitative indicators of soil quality: A minimum data set. In Doran and Jones, 1996, 25–38.

Droogers, P., and J. Bouma. 1997. Soil survey input in exploratory modelling of sustainable soil management practices. *Soil Science Society of America Journal* 61:1704–10.

Gomez, A. A., D. E. Kelly, J. K. Syers, and K. J. Coughlan. 1996. Measuring sustainability of agricultural systems at the farm level. In Doran and Jones 1996, 401–9.

Hall, C. A. S., ed. 2000. *Quantifying Sustainable Development: The Future of Tropical Economies*. San Diego: Academic Press.

Hall, G. F., and C. G. Olson. 1991. Predicting variability of soils from landscape models. In M. Musbauch and L. P. Wilding, eds., *Spatial Variabilities of Soils and Landforms*, 9–24. Madison, Wis.: Soil Science Society of America.

Harris, R. F., D. L. Karlen, and D. J. Mulla. 1996. A conceptual framework for assessment and management of soil quality and health. In Doran and Jones 1996, 61–82.

Holling, C. S. 1992. Cross-scale morphology, geometry and dynamics of ecosystems. *Ecological Monographs* 62:447–502.

Hoogenboom, G. C., Leon D. Rossiter, and P. Van Laake. 2000. Biophysical agricultural assessment and management models for developing countries. In Hall, C A. S., ed 2000. *Quantifying Sustainable Development: The Future of Tropical Economies*. San Diego: Academic Press.

Karlen, D. L., M. J. Mausbach, J. W. Doran, R. G. Cline, R. F. Harris, and G. E. Schuman. 1997. Soil quality: A concept, definition and framework for evaluation. *Soil Science Society of America Journal* 61:4–10.

Kok, K., and A. Veldkamp. 2001. Evaluating impact of spatial scales on land use pattern analysis in Central America. *Agriculture, Ecosystems & Environment* 85:205–21.

Lambin, E. F., X. Baulies, N. Bockstael, G. Fischer, T. Krug, R. Leemans, E. F. Moran, R. R. Rindfuss, Y. Sato, D. Skole, B. L. Turner, and C. Vogel. 1999. Land-Use and Land-Cover Change (LUCC) Implementation Strategy. IGBP Report 48. Stockholm: IGBP Secretariat.

Leemans, R., and W. Cramer. 1991. *The IIASA Database for Mean Monthly Values of Temperature, Precipitation and Cloudiness on a Global Terrestrial Grid*. Laxenburg, Austria: International Institute of Applied Systems Analysis.

Milne, B. T. 1991. Heterogeneity as a multi-scale characteristic of landscapes. In J. Kolasa and S. T. A. Pickett, eds., *Ecological Heterogeneity*, 69–84. Berlin: Springer-Verlag.

O'Neill, R., S. J. Turner, V. I. Cullinam, D. P. Coffin, T. Cook, W. Conley, J. Brunt, J. M. Thomas, M. R. Concley, and J. Gosz. 1991. Multiple landscape scales: An intersite comparison. *Landscape Ecology* 5:137–44.

Penning de Vries, F. W. T., R. Rabbinge, and J. J. R. Groot. 1997. Potential and attainable food production and food security in different regions. *Philosophical Transactions of the Royal Society of London* B 352:917–28.

Pennock, D. J., D. W. Anderson, and E. de Jong. 1994. Landscape-scale change in indicators of soil quality due to cultivation in Saskatchewan, Canada. *Geoderma* 64:1–19.

Peterson, G., C. R. Allen, and C. S. Holling. 1998. Ecological resilience, biodiversity, and scale. *Ecosystems* 1:6–18.

Prudencio, C. Y. 1993. Ring management of soils and crops in the West African semi-arid tropics: The case of the Mossi farming system in Burkina Faso. *Agriculture, Ecosystems and Environment* 47:237–64.

Schoorl, J. M., and A. Veldkamp. 2001. Linking land use and landscape process modelling: A case study for the Alora region (SE Spain). *Agriculture Ecosystems and Environment* 85:281–93.

Sonneveld, M. P. W., J. Bouma, and A. Veldkamp. 2002. Refining soil survey information for a Dutch soil series using land use history. *Soil Use and Management* 18:157–63.

Turner, B. L., D. Skole, S. Sanderson, G. Fischer, L. Fresco, and R. Leemans. 1995. Land-use and Land-cover Change. IGBP Report No. 35. Stockholm: IGBP Secretariat.

Van Breemen, N. 1998. Plant-induced soil changes: Processes and feedbacks. *Biogeochemistry* 42:1–252.

Veldkamp, A., and L. O. Fresco. 1997. Reconstructing land use drivers and their spatial scale dependence for Costa Rica (1973 and 1984). *Agricultural Systems* 55:19–43.

Veldkamp, A., and E. F. Lambin. 2001. Predicting land use change. *Agriculture Ecosystems and Environment* 85:1–6.

Veldkamp A., K. Kok, G. H. J. De Koning, J. M. Schoorl, M. P. W. Sonneveld, and P. H. Verburg. 2001. Multi-scale system approaches in agronomic research at the landscape level. *Soil and Tillage Research* 58:129–40.

Veldkamp, A., G. Zuidema, and L. O. Fresco. 1996. A model analysis of the terrestrial vegetation model of IMAGE 2.0 for Costa Rica. *Ecological Modelling* 93:263–73.

Veldkamp, E., E. J. Huising, A. Stein, and J. Bouma. 1990. Variation of measured banana yields in a Costa Rican plantation as explained by soil survey and thematic mapper data. *Geoderma* 47:337–48.

Chapter 17

Modeling Land-Use Dynamics
with Geographical Data

The Case of Intervened Ecosystems in the Central Mountain Range of Venezuela

Felipe Baritto, Mario A. Piedra, and Gilberto Páez

Introduction

Over the past decades, the central northern part of Venezuela has undergone tremendous development pressure, placing a great deal of stress on the local natural ecosystems. After major landslides affected the region in 1999, many issues regarding the importance of understanding, predicting, and guiding land-use change came to the fore. In this research we were interested in modeling land-use change processes in the region. Our interest in and ability to model this complex process has increased recently because of enhanced monitoring coupled with increased computational capabilities to collect, use, and analyze large amounts of new georeferenced data (Lambin 1997).

Economists' interest in assessing regional land use can be traced to Johan-Heinrich von Thünen's original ideas of agricultural land rent. Von Thünen's static analysis was concerned with the optimal distribution of rural land uses—specifically different types of crops and forests—around a market town. Alonso (1964) applied von Thünen's ideas to develop his urban land market theory, which explained the behavior of people choosing their residential locations and the resulting spatial structure of an urban area (Briassoulis 2000:37). Diverse authors have followed both veins of research to investigate changes in land use as a function of various socioeconomic, biophysical, and political factors. These factors have been generally called *driving forces* in the scientific literature (Berry et al. 1996; Turner, Wear, and Flamm 1996; Wear, Turner, and Flamm 1996; Bockstael 1996; Veldkamp and Fresco 1997a, 1997b). Chomitz and Gray (1996) applied this agricultural land rent theoretical framework, aiming at better understanding of the complex process of deforestation in the tropics. They developed a spatial explicit link between land use, road accessibility, and site characteristics to enhance their empirical analysis. Further research by Mertens and Lambin (2000), Mertens et al. (2000), and Mertens, Forni, and Lambin (2001) has also modeled deforestation using economic and site variables as key factors to explain changes in the rural landscape. Hall et al. (1995) and Pontius, Cornell, and Hall (2001) have developed models explaining land-use change, principally the conversion of forested land to nonforested land, as a function of biophysical (i.e., elevation, slope, and the like) as well as socioeconomic factors.

This chapter, although within the general tradition of the others in this book, differs from previous research by addressing land-use dynamics in the unique setting associated with urban expansion, rather than simply modeling deforestation. Our interest in the urban-rural interface is prompted by the rapid expansion of urban centers in parts of Latin America at the expense of agricultural and forested areas. This process is expected to continue as population expands and the region becomes more urbanized.

This chapter begins by developing the theoretical economic assumptions that appear to explain land-use choice. Then, it adds a dynamic component through the use of Markovian transitional probabilistic matrices (*MTPM*) to assess the impact of relevant but unobservable factors varying though time on the transitional probabilities of land conversion. Next we present the study area,

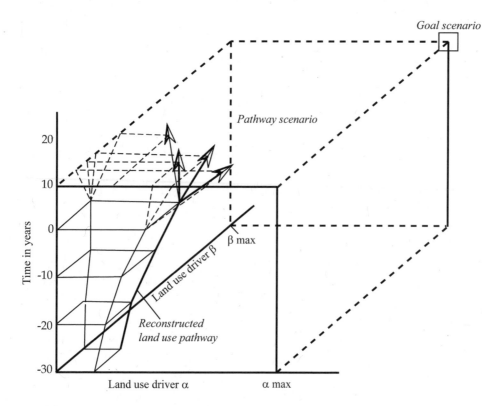

Figure 17.1. Forecast of land-use condition scenarios through time as a function of the intensity of a specific driving force. Source: Veldkamp and Fresco (1997a).

Land-Use Dynamics

The evolutionary process of land-use change can be represented by modeling land-use transitions over time. This approach may yield a truer picture of the dynamic time-spatial process than following a static line of work. It is also a superior approach because modeling land-use change is quite a complex issue in which time plays a central role (Mertens and Lambin 2001). Veldkamp and Fresco summarize their proposition on how the evolutionary process of land use works. The pathway—that is, the route from one land-use type to another over time—can be interpreted as the development route (Veldkamp and Fresco 1997a; figure 17.1) followed by society over time. Implicitly the sign and magnitude of each driver's effect is assumed constant over time on the reconstructed land-use pathway. We believe that it would be better to consider this concept a testable hypothesis that might yield different answers depending on the time-scale of the analysis chosen.

From an econometric standpoint, reconstructing the pathway (that is the function of land-use conversion over space and time) based upon remote sensing data is not an easy task. Economists have followed two possible routes when initially conceptualizing the problem. The first, taken by Bockstael (1996), uses static choice specifications for land conversion decisions when urbanization and other normative factors matter; the second, developed by Nelson and Hellerstein (1997) and Chomitz and Gray (1996), models explicitly the link between parcel characteristics and cost of access to production decisions. Given that both theoretical approaches are based on agricultural land rent theory and the fact that land-use conversion to urban uses has been the main transition observed in the study area, this chapter follows Bockstael's (1996) conceptualization of the land use–choice problem.

The changes in land-use choice can be thought of as follows: if the land use for *Parcel A* changes from *state i* to *state j*, then:

$$(17.1) \quad PV_{Ajt/i} - CS_{Ajt/i} \geq PV_{Amt/i} - CS_{Amt/i}$$

where, $PV_{Ajt/i}$ is the net present value of the future stream of returns to parcel A in state j at time t. $CS_{Ajt/i}$ is the cost of converting the parcel A

from state i to state j. Land uses are defined by m = $1 \ldots M$ (including i and j), and t is time at any particular point in time. It is clear that the benefits of change are zero if the land use remains the same—for example, $PV_{Ajt/i} = 0$ if $i = j$; therefore, to record a change, it is assumed that the parcel was in state i at time $t–1$. The decision weighting the value of contrasting PV and CS is not known to the modeler. Rather, only the outcome of the land-use choice is the aspect observed, not the net returns associated with that choice. In order to model this hypothetical decision it is assumed that (PV–CS) has two components, a systematic component φ that at least in principle can be modeled, and a random component γ. Therefore, the probability that parcel A, which is in land use i at time $t–1$, will be found in land use j at time t is given by:

(17.2) $\text{Prob} \left(\varphi_{Ajt/i} + \gamma_{Ajt/i} > \varphi_{Amt/i} + \gamma_{Amt/i} \right)$

If we assume M land uses, and if γ is assumed to be distributed according to a Weibull distribution, then (17.2) can yield easily a multinomial logit (ML) specification,

(17.3) $\text{Prob}_{AM} = \dfrac{e^{V_M \beta_j}}{\sum\limits_m e^{V_M \beta_i}}$

where V_M may contain, depending on data availability, three sets of variables: G (site-specific geographic variables), A (cost-of-access variables), and S (spatial effects geography variables) (Nelson and Hellerstein 1997). With equation 17.3, we can assess the marginal effects of the variables contained in V_M and therefore develop the following hypothesis based on our theoretical underpinnings:

> Land-use transitions are regulated by physical restrictions of the environment and by factors of socioeconomic and regulatory character as depicted in equation 17.3.
> The sign of the effects of the driving forces are consistent in shaping land-use transitions over time.

One key aspect in choosing an ML as a modeling tool is that it allows testing for parameter stability, which is a central hypothesis in this research.

Choosing this specification, however, oversimplifies land-use choice because the future stream of benefits and/or costs of conversion are not known with certainty (Chomitz and Gray 1996), and information about it, as well as perceptions about it, might differ across the population (Bockstael 1996) and over time.

To address land-use stability over time, we resorted to MTPMs as a way to incorporate temporal changes (Bell 1974; Bell and Hinojosa 1977; Mueller and Middleton 1994). To undertake this analysis, several land uses at different points in time have to be clearly and consistently identified. For a certain instant (t_b), land-use classification defines only the state of the landscape in static terms, so that landscape variability found in a particular year is only spatial, not temporal information. Based on the initial classification of land uses on a map, a nominal categorical variable LU can be created (there is not a specific order in the values that takes the variable), representing the different land-use alternatives defined previously as $m = 1 \ldots M$ (including i and j):

(17.4) $LU = \{1, \ldots, M\}$

The possible transitions from LU_i to LU_j between two points in time (t_b, t_{b+1}) generates a squared matrix with dimensions $I = 1, 2, 3, \ldots,$ M rows and $j = 1, 2, 3, \ldots, M$ columns, composed by $m^2 = M \times M$ possible combinations of changes from one state to another, where n_{ij} represents the frequency of each transition event in the sample. Because the transition toward any land use category at time t_{b+1} depends on the previous use in time period t_b, the conditional probability $p_{(j|i)}$ will be:

(17.5) $p_{j|i} = \dfrac{n_{ij}}{n_{i+}}$

In this way, the matrix presented in table 17.1 represents the possible Markovian transitional probability matrix between two points in time. The values $p_{(j|i)}$ represent the probability that a cell of the landscape with initial use i in t_b will pass to another state j by the next moment in time. The diagonal of this matrix represents the stability of the system—that is, the uses that do not change over time.

Table 17.1. Markovian transitional probabilities matrix (MTPM) for land-use changes between two points in time

t_h \ t_{h+1}		LU_j				$pi+$
		1	2		J	↓
LU_i	1	$p(1\mid 1)$	$p(2\mid 1)$	. . .	$p(J\mid 1)$	1.0
	2	$p(1\mid 2)$	$p(2\mid 2)$	. . .	. . .	. . .
	. . .	. . .	. . .	. . .	. . .	. . .
	I	$p(1\mid I)$	. . .	. . .	$p(J\mid I)$	1.0

Table 17.2. Conventional classification of land-use patterns

Class	Use/cover	Description
1	Non-defined cover	Exposed soils, scarcely covered areas, and others
2	Urban use	Used with residential purposes with or without planning
3	Agricultural use	Permanent and subsistence agriculture in the hillsides
4	Secondary vegetation	Resulting cover after agricultural intervention and abandonment
5	Grassy cover	Includes savannas of the upper parts of basins
6	Bushy cover	*Matorrales* and *espinares* in the low coastal part of the study area
7	Forest cover	Dense and high forests and forests located near rivers and creeks

Spatial data on land use was available for our study area for the years 1958, 1973, 1983, and 1994. We identified seven land uses based upon land uses reported by MARN (1996) from Landsat satellite imagery and field verification (table 17.2).

However, the elaboration of MTPMs for each of the two different points in time [$MTPM_{(1958-73)}$, $MTPM_{(1973-83)}$ and $MTPM_{(1983-94)}$] revealed that not all the forty-nine possible transitions occurred in the sampled periods, and furthermore, some transition alternatives had a very low probability of occurrence. Therefore, to track the most relevant transitions explaining the evolution in the landscape, as shown by the historical maps, a new categorical variable (Y) was created. Figure 17.2 presents the five transitions ($Y = \{1, 2, 3, 4, 5\}$) deemed more appropriate for modeling the evolutionary process of land-use change. The persistence

of a given land use between two points in time ($t_h \rightarrow t_{h+1}$), identified in figure 17.2 as $1\rightarrow1$; $2\rightarrow2$; $3\rightarrow3$; $4\rightarrow4$; $5\rightarrow5$; $6\rightarrow6$; $7\rightarrow7$, was considered as a valid transition option. In this sense, the fact that a certain use in the t_h instant continues to be the same in the following time step (t_{h+1}) expressed its stability in time despite the existence of factors promoting the probability of transitions to other categories in the following period.

Study Area

The study area is located in the northern part of La Costa Mountain Range in Venezuela, adjacent to the Caribbean Sea (figure 17.3). It is the most populated section of Vargas State. The UTM coordinates are 720.000–745.150 E and between 1.165.900 and 1.175.400 N, zone 19, covering an area of 159.3 km². In this section of the country, the

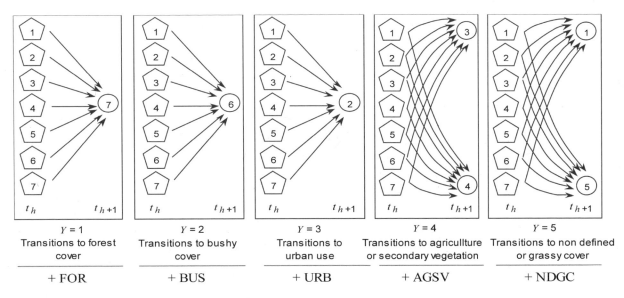

Figure 17.2. Transition possibilities selected (*Y*) between two points in time. The states represented inside each square are referred to as the possible land uses for each point in the set LU = {1,2,3,4,5,6,7}.

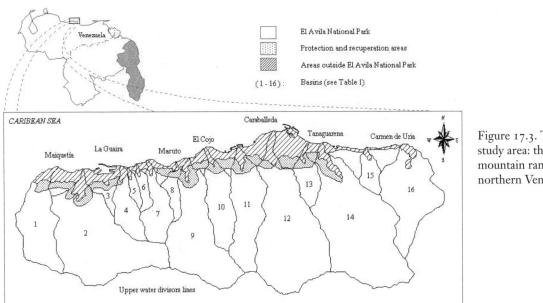

Figure 17.3. The study area: the central mountain range in northern Venezuela.

mountain range is characterized by an abrupt relief reaching considerable differences in elevation in short horizontal distances, and by the occurrence of torrential rainfall (Pérez 1987). Floods and landslides linked to torrential rains have occurred in the region throughout history. Particularly important are the landslide events for the years 1798, 1914, 1938, 1944, 1948, 1949, and 1951 (Singer, Rojas, and Lugo 1983; CAF 2000; García and Perdomo 2000) and the most recent one in 1999. The study area also includes a portion of El Avila National Park and the heavily populated areas located in the coastal lower parts, from Carmen de Uria to Maiquetía in an east-west direction and from the coastline to the upper water dividing line of the basins in a north-south direction (figure 17.3).

Materials and Methods

We gathered information regarding historical land uses and driving forces related to the La Costa

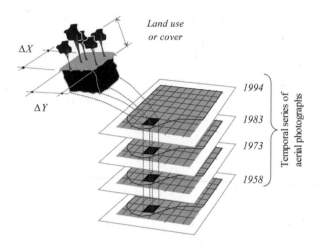

Figure 17.4. Graphic representation of the basic information unit defined for the study.

range. This information was processed in the appropriate GIS formats to carry out the econometric modeling.

Basic Information Unit

The basic information unit for our analysis represents a parcel of land of 20 × 20 m (0.04 ha) (figure 17.4). There are 398,250 of these cells in the study area of 15,930 ha, each referenced to a grid-cells system in turn chosen for the scale used (1:25,000). Each of these cells represents an entity with its own physical and geographical characteristics (slope, altitude, and land cover represented in different data layers), and subject to differential effects of anthropogenic and regulatory factors.

Data Analysis and Interpretation

We gathered information regarding historical land uses from two different sources. For the years 1958, 1973, and 1983, interpretations of black and white aerial photographs were used. For 1994, orthocorrected digital color mosaic aerial photographs were available (table 17.3). We digitalized and georeferenced the aerial photographs by using a second-order polynomial correction algorithm, with a base in the orthocorrected 1994 mosaic and including the largest possible quantity of common ground control points as reference (GCP > 50). The individual views were integrated in layers for every year using Erdas software (Erdas 1997).

Unfortunately, even these procedures for geometric correction of aerial photographs do not eliminate the distortion of this type of remote sensor. Whenever possible, only the central portion of each photograph was used when the overlapping among views allowed it. In areas located at the lower and flatter parts of the La Costa range, the RMS error reported was deemed acceptable for the scale used (RMS between 2 and 4 meters). At higher elevations the error was larger but because these areas are mainly covered with forest vegetation, the displacement error did not affect the interpretation greatly.

Due to the deformation in the aerial photograph mosaics mentioned before, the spatial interpretation of the older photographs was carried out by using the orthocorrected mosaic of 1994 as the reference point. Visualization of the interpreted and the orthocorrected mosaics was done simultaneously by linking both windows through its coordinates. Each point was examined on the computer screen to diminish the displacement error based on common references (crossings of roads, creeks, rivers, and so on). Those points with significant displacement or uncertain land-use classification were eliminated.

Sampling Procedure

In econometric studies using GIS data, the primary goal for establishing a sampling procedure seeks to minimize spatial autocorrelation among land uses or among explanatory variables. For a detailed description of spatial issues limiting econometric analysis in this context, see Nelson and Hellerstein (1997). The second goal was to minimize the use of points with land-use classification uncertainty, which is a critical factor when dealing with several decades and two different data sources, as this chapter attempts to do. We follow a random sampling strategy that is better suited to overcome the inherent limitations in time-spatial GIS data mentioned above. A list of $n_{initial}$ = 5000 random samples based on coordinates (X,Y) was generated with a computer algorithm. Sample size (1.25 percent of the original data set) was at best arbitrary but certainly satisfies the restriction that no two sample points (pixels) are neighbors (see Haining 1990). Further,

Table 17.3. Basic information of aerial photographs

Year	Mission	Scale	Views
1958[a]	030412	1:25.000[c]	017, 019, 020, 022, 023, 024, 025, 026, 102, 104, 106, 173
1973[a]	0304109	1:16.000[c]	002, 004, 006, 008, 010, 011, 012, 023, 025, 027, 029, 031, 033, 035
1983[a]	0304167	1:20.000[c]	310, 312, 314, 316, 317, 319, 321, 323, 343, 345, 927, 928, 929, 931, 933, 935, 938
1994[b]	Cartocentro	1:25.000	6847IV (NO, NE, SO, SE)

[a] Individual views of black and white aerial photographs (MARN 1996).
[b] Orthocorrected mosaic of color aerial photographs.
[c] Average scale of individual views.

Table 17.4. Incident factors matrix (*X*) regulating land-use transitions

	Factor	Unit	Specification
X_1	Slope (SLOPE)	Degrees	Terrain inclination
X_2	Altitude (ALT)	mas[a] 1/1000	With respect to the average sea level
X_3	Annual precipitation regime (PRECIP)	Annual regime mm/1000	Proxy of agricultural potentiality
X_4	Previous land use (LU_{t-1})	Use type (*UT*)	Land use or cover in the previous instant (t_b)
X_5	Distance to roads (DISTR)	Km	Horizontal distance to roads
X_6	El Avila National Park (PARK)	0,1 dummy	0 = Outside PARK 1 = Inside PARK
X_7	Distance to water courses (DREN)	Km	Horizontal distance to the drainage network

[a] Meters above sea level.

after eliminating those pixels with significant displacement or uncertain land use, the final sample size was fixed at n_{final} = 3,770 pixels (0.96 percent of the original data set). Choosing an arbitrary sample size leads to the critical issue of sample representativeness. We verified the adequacy of the sample in two ways. First, we examined the variance (s^2) of all land uses in relation to sample size. Results indicate a stabilization of land-use sampling variance at n = 2000; therefore, a sample size of 3,770 points was deemed initially appropriate. Second, we verified that the proportion of sampled land uses is approximately the same as in the original data set.

Spatial Driving Forces

Information regarding theoretical spatial driving forces—as depicted in equation 17.3—was gathered from basic and thematic cartography, originally at a 1:25,000 scale, based on the cartographic sheets 6847-IV(NW, NE, SW, and SE). The information was then converted to digital format and those variables of interest were processed using ArcView software (ESRI 1996). To obtain slopes and altitude values, a digital terrain model (DTM) was constructed using information of contours and drainages contained on cartographic sheets. A summary of the final spatial driving forces is presented

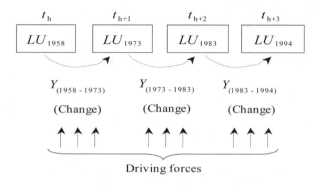

Figure 17.5. Diagram of the time-spatial land-use change process and its relation to the driving forces considered.

in table 17.4. Variables include parcel-specific characteristics (slope, altitude, and precipitation), a regulatory variable representing the presence of the Avila National Park; socioeconomic variables such as distance to roads and previous land use; and finally a variable linked to vulnerability (distance to drainages) given the historical record of landslides along the natural drainage systems in the region. All thematic information was converted to a raster format with cell resolution of 20 × 20 meters. The specific information for each sample unit ($n = 3770$) was then obtained by a transformation of the definitive coordinates (X,Y) to a grid of floating points (see figure 17.4). The thematic information of each point (X,Y) was gathered using the COMBINE command of ArcInfo software.

Land-Use Transition Models

Figure 17.5 presents the main transition probabilities between two points in time and their relationship with the set of spatial driving forces.

Notice that we were forced to model transitions at irregular time intervals given data availability. Because the model chosen is an ML with $k = \{1, 2, 3 \ldots, M\}$ categories, it is necessary to construct $M-1$ nonredundant logits among the dependent variable to remove an indeterminacy in it (Greene 1993:666). We chose the lowest value as the reference ($m = 1$), considering p_{+FOR} (as in figure 17.2) as a common denominator in all the expressions. The only reason we chose transition to forest cover (+FOR) to normalize was for the fact that forest cover encompasses the largest proportion of the total area under study and represents the baseline

land use in the park. The normalization yields the following group of estimated parameters:

$$L_{(2|1)} = \ln\left[\frac{p_{(+BUS)}}{p_{(+FOR)}}\right] = \hat{\beta}_{01} + \hat{\beta}_{11}x_1 + K + \hat{\beta}_{71}x_7$$

$$L_{(3|1)} = \ln\left[\frac{p_{(+URB)}}{p_{(+FOR)}}\right] = \hat{\beta}_{02} + \hat{\beta}_{12}x_1 + K + \hat{\beta}_{72}x_7$$

$$L_{(4|1)} = \ln\left[\frac{p_{(+AGSV)}}{p_{(+FOR)}}\right] = \hat{\beta}_{03} + \hat{\beta}_{13}x_1 + K + \hat{\beta}_{73}x_7$$

$$L_{(5|1)} = \ln\left[\frac{p_{(+NDGC)}}{p_{(+FOR)}}\right] = \hat{\beta}_{04} + \hat{\beta}_{14}x_1 + K + \hat{\beta}_{74}x_7$$

where $L_{(j|i)}$ represents the empirical models for the transitions possibilities selected (Y) between two points in time (see figure 17.2). The βs capture the sign and significance of the effect of the driving forces in the transitions modeled. We developed three (see figure 17.6) transition models to attempt to explain land-use change among the four sampling points (1958–73, 1973–83, and 1983–94). The parameters for these models were estimated using the econometric software LIMDEP (Greene 1998). A catch with multinomial specifications is that a direct economic interpretation of the estimated beta coefficients—beyond sign and significance—is difficult without prior knowledge of the land use chosen for normalization. Therefore, in order to come up with a better understanding of the influence of the independent variables on transitional probabilities we differentiated the density functions (i.e., $L_{(j|i)}$) with respect to the independent variables (i.e. X_i) at their means to obtain what is called the marginal effects (ME) for the β_k parameters (see Green 1993:666). Marginal effects represent the marginal contribution to the transition probability by a unitary change in the independent variable x.

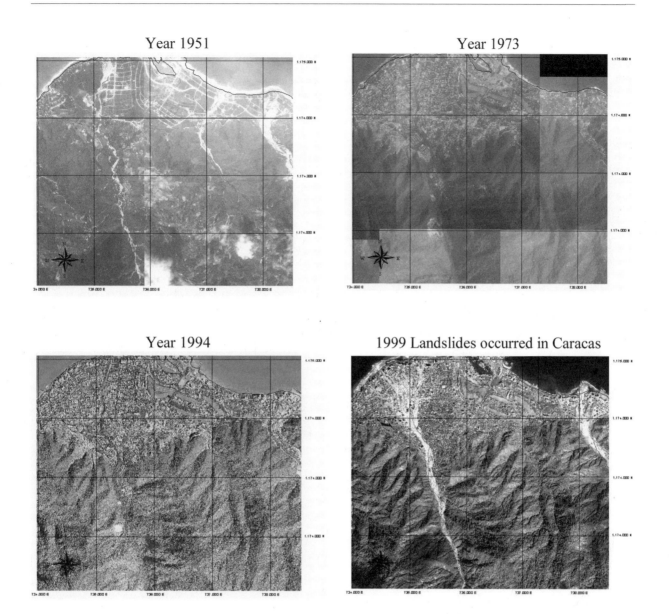

Figure 17.6. Land-use conversion to urban uses in the Carabadella Sector from 1951 to 1999. See website for color originals.

Temporal Stability of Estimated Parameters

To test for parameter stability, two additional time-accumulative transitional models were developed. They differ in their time horizon from the first one previously estimated (for the period 1958–73).

The test was carried out following a standard likelihood ratio (LR) test procedure. The null hypothesis assumes no significant differences in the estimated parameters at two different points in time (that is, the parameters are stable). The alternative hypothesis is that at least one of the parameters is significantly different. The statistic used is:

$$(17.13) \quad LR = -2 \, (LML \text{ model2} - LML \text{ model1})$$

Where LML model1 = logarithm of the maximum likelihood value in time t and LML model2 = logarithm of the maximum likelihood in time $t + 1$. This test has an χ^2 distribution with degrees of freedom equal to the number of parameters being compared (28 degrees of freedom in this case).

Results and Discussion

We found that land-use dynamics have been characterized by a general transition from nonurban to urban uses in the lower parts, whereas stability and

Table 17.5. Summary of land-use classification plus proportion estimates for each land-use category

Land-use class		Estimated proportion of the total area for each land use category (%)							
		1958		1973		1983		1994	
Identification	UT	$p_{1958} = \hat{P}_{1958}$		$p_{1973} = \hat{P}_{1973}$		$p_{1983} = \hat{P}_{1983}$		$p_{1994} = \hat{P}_{1994}$	
Nondefined cover (NDC)	1	5.8	± 0.012	2.5	± 0.008	1.1	± 0.005	0.7	± 0.005
Urban use (URB)	2	3.3	± 0.013	8.5	± 0.021	10.2	± 0.023	12.3	± 0.025
Agricultural use (AGR)	3	12.2	± 0.025	8.2	± 0.020	4.7	± 0.015	3.4	± 0.013
Secondary vegetation (SV)	4	0.7	± 0.006	6.3	± 0.022	8.8	± 0.021	10.3	± 0.022
Grass cover (GC)	5	2.5	± 0.011	1.8	± 0.012	1.9	± 0.009	1.8	± 0.009
Bushy cover (BC)	6	17.5	± 0.028	14.8	± 0.032	14.3	± 0.025	12.8	± 0.024
Forest cover (FC)	7	57.9	± 0.040	58.0	± 0.056	59.0	± 0.040	58.7	± 0.040
TOTALS		100		100		100		100	

recovery of natural ecosystems have been the norm in the middle to upper parts of the watershed. We also found that land-use transitions—except to urban uses—are regulated by physical restrictions of the environment and by factors of socioeconomic and regulatory character.

Land-Use Dynamics

Table 17.5 presents descriptive statistics for land-use classification in 1958, 1973, 1983, and 1994. Our analysis found that the area of forests was relatively stable throughout time, whereas there were significant changes in urban and agricultural uses, as well as in secondary vegetation. It is especially clear that uses related to agriculture have diminished over time, which may have prompted secondary vegetation growth. The interpretation of our aerial photographs (figure 17.7) for 1958—the baseline—indicates that by the time the Avila National Park was created the middle and upper parts of the watersheds studied were significantly impacted by human activities. There were dispersed patches of forest clearing, which we interpreted as evidence of deforestation, and large areas with uncovered soils or scarce covering vegetation. This kind of pattern has been associated with the construction of buildings in the lower parts of the watersheds and roads in the highest parts.

Table 17.6. Proportion of pixels (as percentage) in the sample correctly forecast in five transitional models

Transition	1958–73	1973–83	1983–94
+FOR	90.6	97.9	98.5
+BUS	26.1	75.1	82.5
+URB	82.5	87.3	88.1
+AGSV	53.8	95.5	92.1
+NDGC	1.9	1.8	2.2

It is also possible that some of these areas classified as deforested or covered with scarce vegetation may be related to massive landslides that occurred in the region in 1951. In subsequent years, though, most of the upper areas recovered with either secondary vegetation or forests. This is an indicator that there was a gradual abandonment of agricultural activities within the Avila National Park boundaries. A different development pattern took place at the lower planes. In 1958 a significant part of the lowlands was dedicated to agricultural uses. Aerial photographs evidence showed however, that agricultural uses were replaced mostly by urban uses in subsequent decades (figure 17.7).

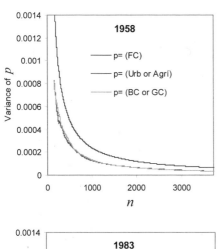

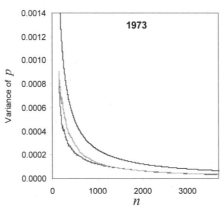

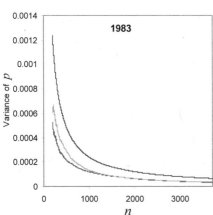

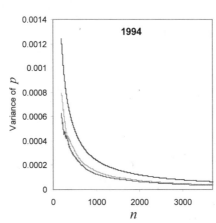

Figure 17.7. Sampling variance of five land uses for the years 1958, 1973, 1983 and 1994.

Land-Use Transition Models

All land-use transition models were highly significant ($P < 0.01$), indicating that the chosen driving forces explain reasonably well the observed transitions for the time periods considered. The overall precision—measured as the proportion of pixels in the sample correctly forecast by the model—was 71.3 percent, 90.5 percent, and 91.9 percent for the periods 1958–73, 1973–83, and 1983–94, respectively. More specifically, transitions to forest and bushy cover, and to agriculture and urban uses, were estimated with higher precision in all transition models. But the model predicted the spatial occurrence of grassy and scarcely covered areas poorly (table 17.6).

Marginal Effects on Transitions to Urban Use

Contrary to our expectations, none of the explanatory variables was significant for explaining the transition probabilities to urban uses at any particular point in time (tables 17.7, 17.8, and 17.9).

It was expected that changes to urban uses would be seriously influenced by the physical restrictions of the terrain. Restrictions on urban sprawl were expected to be more stringent in areas with steeply sloped terrain and the presence of regulatory factors such as national park boundaries or the proximity to water courses. However, our results clearly show this was not the case. Therefore, urban sprawl occurred over a wide range of conditions. Results clearly suggested that there has been an autonomous urban growth not regulated by physical-natural restrictions, such as slope, either for legal or regulatory factors or for the adjacency to previously developed regions.

Marginal Effects on Transitions to Agricultural Use and Secondary Vegetation Cover

For all periods, transition probabilities to agricultural uses and secondary vegetation (+AGSV) were positively and significantly influenced by factors such as altitude and the protection of El Avila

Table 17.7. Magnitude and significance of the marginal effects for each of the variables hypothesized as land use–change drivers (1958–73)

					$ME = \partial L_j / \partial X_i$			
Transition to:	Intercept	SLOPE	ALT	PRECIP	LU-58	DISTR	PARK	DREN
+FOR $p_{(Y=1)}$	−0.8474 **	0.0024 **	0.0332 N.S.	0.8041 **	0.1169 **	0.1253 **	0.0009 N.S.	−0.8148 **
+BUS $p_{(Y=2)}$	0.7547 **	−0.0013 N.S.	−0.1533 **	−0.7385 **	−0.0248 **	−0.0418 **	0.0959 **	0.2781 **
+URB $p_{(Y=3)}$	3.4×10^{-7} N.S.	$−7.1 \times 10^{-8}$ N.S.	$−1.9 \times 10^{-5}$ N.S.	8.2×10^{-6} N.S.	$−3.9 \times 10^{-7}$ N.S.	$−5.9 \times 10^{-6}$ N.S.	$−1.9 \times 10^{-7}$ N.S.	3.9×10^{-6} N.S.
+AGSV $p_{(Y=4)}$	−0.0703 N.S.	−0.0002 N.S.	0.1544 **	0.0286 N.S.	−0.0735 **	−0.0429 **	0.1749 **	0.4049 **
+NDGC $p_{(Y=5)}$	0.1630 **	−0.0009 **	0.0322 N.S.	−0.0943 **	−0.0187 **	−0.0406 **	−0.0799 **	0.1318 **

** = Significant ($P \leq 0.05$); N.S. = Nonsignificant ($P > 0.05$); $P \,|Z| > z$.

Table 17.8. Magnitude and significance of the marginal effects for each of the variables hypothesized as land use–change drivers (1973–83)

					$ME = \partial L_j / \partial X_i$			
Transition to:	Intercept	SLOPE	ALT	PRECIP	LU-73	DISTR	PARK	DREN
+FOR $p_{(Y=1)}$	−5.1889 **	0.0008 N.S.	−0.2671 **	3.0980 **	0.6484 **	0.05878 N.S.	0.0130 N.S.	−0.9583 **
+BUS $p_{(Y=2)}$	3.9359 **	−0.0019 N.S.	−0.1120 N.S.	−2.1335 **	−0.4139 **	−0.0218 N.S.	−0.0194 **	0.8281 **
+URB $p_{(Y=3)}$	3.3×10^{-5} N.S.	$−1.8 \times 10^{-5}$ N.S.	$−7.7 \times 10^{-5}$ N.S.	2.9×10^{-5} N.S.	$−8.4 \times 10^{-6}$ N.S.	$−2.8 \times 10^{-5}$ N.S.	$−4.2 \times 10^{-6}$ N.S.	2.3×10^{-6} N.S.
+AGSV $p_{(Y=4)}$	0.8295 **	0.0011 N.S.	0.2772 **	0.6794 **	−0.1733 **	−0.0128 N.S.	0.2231 **	0.1443 N.S.
+NDGC $p_{(Y=5)}$	0.4235 **	9.1×10^{-5} N.S.	0.1020 **	−0.2851 **	−0.0612 **	−0.0241 **	−0.0425 **	−0.0141 N.S.

** = Significant ($P \leq 0.05$); N.S. = Nonsignificant ($P > 0.05$); $P \,|Z| > z$.

Table 17.9. Magnitude and significance of the marginal effects for each of the variables hypothesized as land use–change drivers (1983–94)

					$ME = \partial L_j / \partial X_i$			
Transition to:	Intercept	SLOPE	ALT	PRECIP	LU-83	DISTR	PARK	DREN
+FOR $p_{(Y=1)}$	−3.2818 **	0.0010 N.S.	−0.1180 N.S.	0.7971 **	0.5343 **	0.0596 **	0.0055 N.S.	−0.1788 N.S.
+BUS $p_{(Y=2)}$	1.8343 **	−0.0013 N.S.	−0.3356 **	−0.5179 **	−0.1577 **	0.0159 N.S.	−0.1408 N.S.	0.3453 N.S.
+URB $p_{(Y=3)}$	1.3×10^{-5} N.S.	$−8.2 \times 10^{-8}$ N.S.	$−3.7 \times 10^{-5}$ N.S.	1.5×10^{-5} N.S.	$−3.3 \times 10^{-6}$ N.S.	$−1.6 \times 10^{-5}$ N.S.	1.9×10^{-6} N.S.	$−4.1 \times 10^{-6}$ N.S.
+AGSV $p_{(Y=4)}$	0.9758 **	0.0006 N.S.	0.3269 **	−0.1963 N.S.	−0.2884 **	−0.0332 N.S.	0.2838 **	−0.0939 N.S.
+NDGC $p_{(Y=5)}$	0.4717 **	−0.0003 N.S.	0.1268 **	−0.0829 N.S.	−0.0883 **	−0.0422 **	−0.1485 **	−0.0726 N.S.

** = Significant ($P \leq 0.05$); N.S. = Nonsignificant ($P > 0.05$); $P \,|Z| > z$.

National Park. Cornell (in Hall 2000) also showed the importance of national parks in influencing where development occurs. Table 17.6 shows that a decrease in agriculture use is correlated with an increase in secondary vegetation (*SV*) and forest cover (*FC*), especially at higher elevations, from 1958 to 1973. As a result, it is possible to infer that both altitude and the presence of the park helped the natural ecosystem recovery in the middle and upper parts of the basin. Results also indicate that distance to roads in the first period had a significantly negative effect on transition probabilities to agricultural uses and secondary vegetation, but its significance was lost in the subsequent periods. It could be interpreted as if the distance to roads became less important for agricultural uses once the establishment of the park and urbanization took place.

Marginal Effects on Transitions to Forest

Transitions to forest cover were not influenced significantly by the presence of the protected area in any period; however, transitions to forest were positively and significantly influenced by the land use of previous periods. In other words, forested areas were more likely to be forest in the next period than something else. Likewise, transitions to forest cover increased with annual precipitation and slope. This suggests that the steeper the slope and the larger the amount of annual precipitation, the more likely one was to encounter forest cover in any particular plot. Distance to roads was always positively correlated with the likelihood of the transition of forests to other land uses; however, it was significant only for 1958–73 and 1983–94. These results concurred with previous studies that found that larger distance to roads make it more likely to encounter forest cover in any particular plot (Chomitz and Gray 1996; Mertens and Lambin 2000; Mertens, Forni, and Lambin 2001; Mertens et al. 2000).

Marginal Effects on Transitions to Bushy Cover

For all periods, a higher precipitation regime and higher altitudes had significant negative effects on transitions to bushy cover. Likewise, land use in the

previous period had a significantly negative effect on bushy vegetation. In other words, bushy areas were less likely to remain as bushy than were other land cover types. This could be explained by two different reasons. First, the urbanization process tended to take place on low and drier land on which this type of vegetation was present. Second, it was associated with the presence of the Avila National Park on the upper lands of the watershed. The park encompasses higher elevations and wet climates favoring forest recovery.

Marginal Effects on Transitions to Grassy Cover or Scarcely Covered Areas

These uses represent a very small fraction of the area under study (table 17.6). Therefore, the transition models had a very limited capacity to predict their spatial distribution (table 17.7). Even though some important significant relations were found, they will not be discussed due to the lack of adequate predictability of the estimated models. In similar studies results do indicate that some land uses cannot be properly explained by the models (see Turner, Wear, and Flamm 1996; Chomitz and Gray 1996; Nelson and Hellerstein 1997). The more land uses are incorporated, the greater the risk some land uses would be poorly explained.

Persistence of Land Uses

Tables 17.10–17.12 indicate that most changes in land use took place from 1958 to 1973. It was the most active regarding land-use dynamics. The two following periods (1973–83 and 1983–94) revealed a general tendency toward land-use stability. This converging state to equilibrium is reflected by the ever growing transitional probabilistic values in the diagonal of the tables. Most of the land conversion to urban uses took place from 1958 to 1973. The undefined and scarcely vegetation-covered areas had a high probability of being converted to urban uses. This could be explained by the abundance of both at the lower parts of the studied area on which urbanization took place.

Markovian transitional probabilities for urban uses were close to one in the diagonal, indicating that for all periods there was virtually no transition from urban to any other land-use. This suggests

Table 17.10. Markovian transition probabilities matrix (MTPM) for 1958–73

1958	LU$_i$	LU$_j$	1973 NDGC	URB	AGR	SV	GC	BC	FC	p_{i+} ↓
	NDGC	1	0.227	0.309	0.005	0.005	0.050	0.195	0.209	1.0
	URB	2	0.000	**0.968**	0.000	0.000	0.000	0.032	0.000	1.0
	AGR	3	0.004	0.024	**0.361**	0.315	0.002	0.024	0.270	1.0
	SV	4	0.000	0.000	0.179	**0.143**	0.000	0.036	0.643	1.0
	GC	5	0.010	0.354	0.083	0.000	**0.365**	0.094	0.094	1.0
	BC	6	0.058	0.121	0.032	0.015	0.014	**0.618**	0.142	1.0
	FC	7	0.002	0.003	0.049	0.035	0.005	0.037	**0.868**	1.0

Table 17.11. Markovian transition probabilities matrix (MTPM) for 1973–83

1973	LU$_i$	LU$_j$	1983 NDGC	URB	AGR	SV	GC	BC	FC	p_{i+} ↓
	NDGC	1	**0.417**	0.198	0.021	0.000	0.104	0.177	0.083	1.0
	URB	2	0.000	**1.000**	0.000	0.000	0.000	0.000	0.000	1.0
	AGR	3	0.000	0.006	**0.549**	0.308	0.003	0.016	0.117	1.0
	SV	4	0.000	0.000	0.000	**0.996**	0.000	0.000	0.004	1.0
	GC	5	0.000	0.090	0.015	0.000	**0.881**	0.015	0.000	1.0
	BC	6	0.000	0.063	0.000	0.002	0.002	**0.928**	0.005	1.0
	FC	7	0.000	0.001	0.003	0.000	0.000	0.000	**0.996**	1.0

Table 17.12. Markovian transition probabilities matrix (MTPM) for 1983–94

1994	LU$_i$	LU$_j$	1994 NDGC	URB	AGR	SV	GC	BC	FC	p_{i+} ↓
	NDGC	1	**0.575**	0.200	0.000	0.000	0.075	0.100	0.050	1.0
	URB	2	0.000	**0.997**	0.000	0.000	0.000	0.003	0.000	1.0
	AGR	3	0.000	0.000	**0.601**	0.354	0.000	0.017	0.028	1.0
	SV	4	0.000	0.000	0.015	**0.928**	0.000	0.003	0.054	1.0
	GC	5	0.000	0.070	0.028	0.000	**0.845**	0.042	0.014	1.0
	BC	6	0.009	0.109	0.009	0.004	0.006	**0.848**	0.015	1.0
	FC	7	0.000	0.004	0.005	0.007	0.000	0.005	**0.979**	1.0

Table 17.13. Test for stability of parameter estimates (β_k)

Model	Period	LML[a]	
A	1958 to 1973	−2,998.01	
B	1958 to 1983	−1,671.44	
C	1958 to 1994	−1,489.80	

	Comparisons	LR[b]	$P(\beta^2_{gl=28})$
A vs. B	1958–73 vs. 1973–83	2,653.13	< 0.01
B vs. C	1973–83 vs. 1983–94	363.29	< 0.01
A vs. C	1958–73 vs. 1983–94	3,016.42	< 0.01

[a] *LML*: Logarithm of the maximum likelihood value.
[b] *LR*: Likelihood ratio.

that once large-scale human intervention—through increased urbanization—takes place, it may not be reversible, even if the areas have shown to be highly vulnerable to disasters within the historical record. Agriculture is decreasingly important over time in the regional spatial distribution (from 12 percent to 3 percent of total area in thirty-six years; see table 17.6); however, those agricultural uses that survive showed an increased persistence (0.361, 0.549, and 0.601).

Temporal Stability of Parameters

The tests related to the stability of parameters over time are presented in table 17.13. Statistically significant differences ($P < 0.01$) were found in overall parameter estimates for all transitional models. This finding clearly suggests that the different driving variables are statistically different in their importance for determining transitions to some or all land-use changes. Likewise, as this paper attempts to explain, some land-use transitions over a long period have only transient spatial effects while others have a continuous influence. Overall, most variables had a positive effect on land-use change, but their relative importance over time was different. These results are at odds with Veldkamp and Fresco's proposition of a constant effect of the driver on the time-spatial function of land conversion.

Conclusion

There has been a clear tendency toward stability in land-use and recovery of natural ecosystems in the middle to upper parts of the study area. Compared to 1958, the impact of human intervention on the upper protected forested lands has been negligible, whereas it has been quite important on the lower lands of the watershed due to disorganized urbanization. This general stability is particularly important for forest cover, which represents the largest proportion of land use.

The creation of El Avila National Park appears to have had a significant positive effect on forest cover due to reduction of agriculture in the upper lands, but afforded no buffering effect protecting other uses located at the lower sections of the basin. The effectiveness of the park against urban sprawl in the upper lands can better be explained by the steeply sloped terrain it was intended to protect.

Urban sprawl is definitely the most important land-use change identified. It increased from 3.3 percent to 12.3 percent of the total area over thirty-six years. The fact that land-use transitions to urban use were not regulated either by physical terrain restrictions or by socioeconomic factors suggests an autonomous growth, not explained by the model, of commuting zones of nearby Caracas such as La Guaira and Caraballeda. This lack of explanatory power of the variables we chose to explain urban expansion may be due to our failure to include other important demographic and economic variables such as population growth, unemployment levels, changes in macroeconomic policies, and the like, that might explain land-use dynamics at the urban level. Furthermore, an increase from 3.3 percent to 12.3 percent of spatial occurrence as "city" suggests a relatively large migration process to a region with limited space for human settlement, which yielded a disorganized urban growth. This also may have played a large role in changing people's perceptions of the importance of physical and normative factors regulating human settlements in highly vulnerable areas.

The Venezuelan experience has shown that available space near the urban frontier can be easily taken and transformed to new urban uses regardless of its suitability. Settlement was independent of accessibility, vulnerability, characteristics of the relief, and whether it could/not be located within the national park boundaries. This latest aspect is of greatest importance because it suggests that protected areas not effectively "protected" may rather enhance urbanization of "free access" lands. If current tendencies in population growth continue, they may yield a further demand shift for urban land uses in unsuitable places.

In summary, all land-use transitions—except to urban uses—were regulated by physical restrictions of the environment and by factors of a socioeconomic nature such as park boundaries, previous land use, distance to roads and drainages. The consistency in the sign of the marginal effects attributed to the driving forces in shaping land-use transitions over time supports Veldkamp and Fresco's proposition presented in figure 17.1. However, statistical differences in the magnitude of the marginal effects suggest that in this region the importance of selected drivers may change over time and hence must be used very carefully in predicting future land-use changes.

Acknowledgments

We thank Sergio Velásquez and Alexander Salas at CATIE's GIS laboratory for their support in processing the GIS information. We would also like to express our gratitude to Miguel Carriquiry from IICA and the personnel of the Ministerio del Ambiente y de los Recursos Naturales and the Servicio Autónomo de Geografía y Cartografía Nacional of Venezuela. This research was partially financed by a CATIE-SIDA-Goteborg University agreement.

References

Alonso, W. 1962. *Location and Land Use: Towards a General Theory of Land Rent*. Cambridge, Mass.: Harvard University Press.

Baritto, F. S. 2000. Dinámica de factores asociados al uso de la tierra e implicaciones sobre el colapso ambiental de 1999 en la costa norte de Venezuela. M.S. thesis, Centro Agronómico Tropical de Investigación y Enseñanza (CATIE), Turrialba, Costa Rica.

Bell, E. J. 1974. Markov analysis of land use change: An application of stochastic processes to remotely sensed data. *Socio-Economic Planning Sciences* 8:311–16.

Bell, E. J., and R. C. Hinojosa. 1977. Markov analysis of land-use change: Continuous time and stationary processes. *Socio-Economic Planning Sciences* 11:13–17.

Berry, M., R. Flamm, B. Hazen, and R. McIntyre. 1999. The land-use change analysis system (LUCAS) for evaluating landscape management decisions. http://citeseer.ist.psu.edu/berry94landuse.html.

Bockstael, N. 1996. Modeling economics and ecology: The importance of a spatial perspective. *American Journal of Agricultural Economics* 78, no. 5: 1168–80.

Briassoulis, H. 2000. Analysis of land use change: Theoretical and modeling approaches. www.rri.wvu.edu/webBook/Briassoulis/contents.htm.

Chomitz, K. M., and D. A. Gray. 1996. Roads, land use, and deforestation: A spatial model applied to Belize. *World Bank Economic Review* 10:487–512.

Corporación Andina de Fomento (CAF). 2000. *Efectos de las lluvias caídas en Venezuela en diciembre de 1999*. Caracas: CDB.

Dervis, K., J. de Melo, and S. Robinson. 1982. *General Equilibrium Models for Development Policy*. Cambridge: Cambridge University Press.

Erdas. 1997. *Erdas Field Guide*. 4th ed. Norcross, Ga.: Erdas.

ESRI. 1996. *Using ArcView GIS*. Redlands, Calif.: ESRI.

García, L. F., and E. Perdomo. 2000. Situación meteorológica generadora de las inundaciones y flujo de lodo en el nor-centro de Venezuela, con especial énfasis en la Costa Norte (16 de diciembre de 1999). Conference report, Caracas, May 2000.

Greene, W. H. 1993. *Econometric Analysis.* 2nd ed. Macmillan, New York.

———. 1998. LIMDEP Version 7.0. User's Manual. Rev. ed. New York: Econometric Software.

Haining, R. 1990. *Spatial Data Analysis in the Social and Environmental Sciences.* Cambridge: Cambridge University Press.

Hall, C. A. S., ed. 2000. *Quantifying Sustainable Development: The Future of Tropical Economies.* San Diego: Academic Press.

Lambin, E. 1997. Modeling and monitoring land-cover change processes in tropical regions. *Progress in Physical Geography* 21:375–93.

Mertens, B., and E. Lambin. 2000. Land-cover-change trajectories in southern Cameroon. *Annals of the Association of American Geographers* 90, no. 3: 467–94.

Mertens, B., E. Forni, and F. Lambin. 2001. Prediction of the impact of logging activities on forest cover: A case study in the east province of Cameroon. *Journal of Environmental Management* 62, no. 1: 16–36.

Mertens, B., W. Sundelin, O. Ndoye, and E. Lambin. 2000. Impact of macroeconomic change on deforestation in south Cameroon: Integration of household survey and remotely-sensed data. *World Development* 28, no. 6: 983–99.

Ministerio del Ambiente y de los Recursos Naturales (MARN). 1996. *Memoria descriptiva del Mapa de Vegetación del Parque Nacional El Avila, Distrito Federal y Estado Miranda.* Caracas: MARN.

Mueller, M., and J. Middleton. 1994. A Markov model of land-use change dynamics in the Niagara region, Ontario, Canada. *Landscape Ecology* 9, no. 2: 152–57.

Nelson, G., and D. Hellerstein. 1997. Do roads cause deforestation? Using satellite images in econometric analysis of land use. *American Journal of Agricultural Economics* 79:80–88.

Pérez H., D. 1987. El problema de las inundaciones en Venezuela. Report, Universidad Central de Venezuela.

Pontius, R. G., Jr., J. Cornell, and C. Hall. 2001. Modeling the spatial pattern of land-use change with GEOMOD2: Application and validation for Costa Rica. *Agriculture, Ecosystems & Environment* 85, nos. 1–3: 191–203.

Sadoulet, E., and A. de Janvry. 1995. *Quantitative Development Policy Analysis.* Baltimore: Johns Hopkins University Press.

Sanderson, S., and L. Pritchard Jr. 1993. The human dynamic of land-use and land cover change in comparative perspective. www.cdf.ufl.edu/cp06933/readings/sndrprit.html.

Singer, A., C. Rojas, and M. Lugo. 1983. *Inventario Nacional de Riesgos Geológicos.* Caracas: Fundación Venezolana de Investigaciones Sismológicas.

Turner, D., D. Wear, and R. Flamm. 1996. Land ownership and land-cover change in the southern Appalachian highlands and the Olympic Peninsula. *Ecological Applications* 6, no. 4: 1150–72.

Veldkamp, A., and L. O. Fresco. 1997a. Exploring land use scenarios: An alternative approach based on actual land use. *Agricultural Systems* 55, no. 1: 1–17.

———. 1997b. Reconstructing land use drivers and their spatial scale dependence for Costa Rica (1973 and 1984). *Agricultural Systems* 55, no. 1: 19–43.

Wear, D., M. Turner, and R. Flamm. 1996. Ecosystem management with multiple owners: Landscape dynamics in a southern Appalachian watershed. *Ecological Applications* 6, no. 4: 1173–88.

CHAPTER 18

SCALE ISSUES IN DEVELOPING A DEFORESTATION BASELINE FOR THE REGION OF THE NOEL KEMPFF MERCADO CLIMATE ACTION PROJECT, BOLIVIA

MYRNA H. P. HALL, AARON DUSHKU, AND SANDRA BROWN

Introduction

Development in the tropics usually is associated with deforestation, and it is important to understand the dimensions of this development, its driving factors, and possible mitigation schemes. Global interest in tropical forests is more and more focused on their role in the global carbon cycle from the perspective of carbon emissions produced by deforestation (e.g., Detwiler and Hall 1988) and their potential role to store carbon (e.g. Brown et al. 1993), as well as concern for conservation of species and ecosystems. Climate Action Projects (CAPs) in the developing tropics, financed by the developed world, are put forth as one means to satisfy both carbon emission offsets and conservation of threatened ecosystems (Brown, Masera, and Sathaye 2000). Forest conservation, or averted deforesta-tion, CAPs currently are not eligible activities under the Kyoto Protocol mostly due to the perceived uncertainties in determining key elements of a project cycle, particularly the baseline or the business-as-usual deforestation rate and pattern. However, many developing countries, and investors, continue to be interested in developing forest conservation projects given the potential for such projects to slow or even reverse high rates of deforestation while at the same time generating credible greenhouse gas (GHG) emission reductions.

For averted deforestation projects (and for all carbon sequestration projects) carbon credits can be earned only for that carbon that is in addition to a business-as-usual baseline. In an effort to develop reliable methods for projecting deforestation

baselines at various scales, we have recently applied the land use–change model GEOMOD (Hall et al. 1995a; Pontius, Cornell, and Hall 2001) to a number of sites in Latin America (Brown 2002; Brown et al. 2006). Our approach is sensitive to larger regional patterns of change, and hence we were able to use it to analyze deforestation in six areas of Central and South America and to project what would happen to these landscapes if no measures to limit deforestation were implemented.

For each analysis, we generally have worked with data sets provided to us by project partners and in the process have discovered that both map scale and scale of analysis play a significant role in identifying both spatial land-use pattern and rate drivers, depending on the degree of human development already occurring in a region. We found that it is often difficult to capture the trajectory of change fully if the scale of analysis is limited to the local or even regional scale of interest, because the factors that drive land-use change are often operative at a scale larger than the locality affected. In this chapter we explain how we developed a methodology to capture development pressure in the region of the Noel Kempff Mercado National Park (NKMNP), a frontier environment in northeastern Bolivia. We also show how the establishment of credible baselines in such locales will require analysis of both coarse- and fine-grained spatial data.

The Spatio-temporal Modeling Approach

In this study we applied spatially georeferenced modeling, using socioeconomic, demographic, and

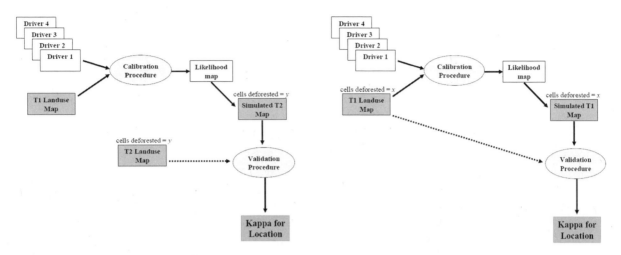

Figure 18.1. Flowchart for GEOMOD showing how empirical knowledge in the form of maps is used to weight spatial pattern drivers and how the simulated map derived from the weighted likelihood map is validated against the "actual" landscape, (a) where two points in time are available; (b) where only one point in time is available. The kappa-for-location index indicates which driver set explains most of the spatial variation of land-use change between two points in time.

biophysical drivers, to project the likely future state of land use in the already established Noel Kempff Mercado Climate Action Project and surrounding region. The results of the spatial modeling approach that we focus on here are compared to other methodologies and reported in Brown et al. (2006).

Spatial modeling, as we define it (Hall, Hall, and Taylor 2000), is the application of a numerical simulation model that uses spatially distributed data to simulate landscape dynamics. In the case of land use–change modeling it implies that the spatial distribution of various factors, such as topography, plays an important role in determining where humans exploit the landscape. Spatial models of future land-use change require two types of parameters—those that project *how rapidly* and those that indicate *where* the land-use changes will take place—that is, the rate and location of change. To project the future location of land development and thus a baseline of changes in carbon stocks, we applied GEOMOD, developed by researchers at SUNY College of Environmental Science and Forestry (Hall et al. 1995a, 1995b; Pontius et al. 2000) and now available in IDRISI software (Eastman 1999). Based on the "maximum power principle" (Odum 1983) the model assumes and then tests whether those factors that are most likely to impact an individual's energy return on investment (EROI) (Hall, Cleveland, and Kaufmann

1986) are statistically significant in explaining human settlement and land development patterns. These factors can include biophysical determinants such as topographic position (elevation and steepness of slope), distance from rivers, soil type, and/or socioeconomic factors such as infrastructure, already established settlements, distance to roads and markets, density of population engaged in agriculture and forestry, and other census-based information, if available, as long as it is spatially referenced. GEOMOD creates a potential land use–change (PLUC) "suitability" map that weighs cells that are candidates for development based on how much land of each category of each spatially distributed factor is already developed at time one, the calibration period. It then generates a validation map for time two by selecting from the PLUC map the highest weighted cells (figure 18.1). The factor-based PLUC map can be thought of as a development suitability map with the highest numbers assigned to those cells with the highest likelihood of deforestation to nonforest use based on human preference. Finally it computes the statistical fit between the simulated and actual land-use maps for the validation period using the kappa-for-quantity and kappa-for-location indexes (Pontius 2000). Once the set of drivers yielding the "best" kappa measure has been derived, GEOMOD simulates the future business as usual (BAU) landscape. The model allows for regional stratification to capture, for instance, different government policies in different political units that would affect and/or effect land clearing and land tenure. It also includes the option to impose, or not, the adjacency or contiguity rule in simulation. This rule can limit land clearing to areas that are located next to land units already cleared. The search-window distance used to impose contiguity around already developed land can be adjusted to capture the difference between, say, clearing for shifting cultivation and clearing for industrialized agriculture.

Out of a growing concern for the impact of tropical deforestation on the accumulation of atmospheric CO_2, a number of methodologies have been developed to derive expected rates of future forest losses. These include (1) the Forest Resource Assessment (FRA) program of the United Nations Food and Agriculture Organization (FAO 1993), which developed a model to correlate "forest cover change in time with other variables including population density and population growth for the corresponding period" and estimates deforestation by country or political units, such as departments or municipalities, as a function of population density and/or population growth trajectories; and (2) the Landsat Pathfinder Program, whose goal is to establish long-term, medium- to high-resolution spatial data sets for particular regional and global applications to global change research (Skole and Tucker 1993). The Humid Tropical Forest Project, a working group of the Pathfinder Program, from which the most important data used in this analysis were acquired, focuses in particular on moist tropical forest regions. Time-series analysis of these data was an integral part of our rate derivation. For other methodologies explored across the six climate action projects mentioned above, see Brown et al. (2006).

One of the strengths of GEOMOD is its use of validation procedures to compare simulated results to actual landscapes to derive the most statistically robust set of factors upon which to make future projections. We advocate complete separation of the calibration and validation data sets, which is necessary to test goodness of fit of validation. Realistically, due to the high cost of image classification, projects are sometimes limited to the use of only one satellite-derived land-use map. In this case, the goodness of fit is determined by comparing a simulated map that is created from a model calibrated from the same time period as the validation map. This type of validation is called goodness of fit of calibration. Researchers at Clark University have determined that the expected goodness of fit of calibration is always better than that of validation. However, goodness of fit of calibration is particularly useful in determining which model performs best in capturing the trends for the given time period (Pontius and Pacheco 2005).

A number of statistical approaches are available to test model accuracy (Costanza 1989; Pontius and Schneider 2002). To ensure accurate prediction of land use–change location and hence the carbon emission/reduction potential of those locations we applied the "kappa-for-location" index ($K_{location}$) (Pontius 2000) as our validation measure. The $K_{location}$ index is the measure of agreement between two maps that tells us to what degree the model has accurately located the map categories compared to either a random assignment of categories, where $K_{location} = 0.0$, or a perfect assignment, where $K_{location} = 1.0$.

Both the location of forest conversion and the quantity of that conversion must be captured as accurately as possible to make reliable projections into the future. We often rely on the deforestation rate observed from analysis of remotely sensed information in the form of land-use change maps. This can be misleading if data are available from only two points in time, or impossible if only one point in time exists. Even if multiple snapshots of deforestation exist, trying to derive correlation between that change and socioeconomic trends is problematic in the developing tropics given that few time-series data sets of the latter exist, particularly at the regional or local scale. Comparison of the amount of land converted in an area versus corresponding population growth is another, and common, means to derive the rate of land development, but here too problems exist if the population record does not correspond to the extent of the area under analysis. In the developing world a

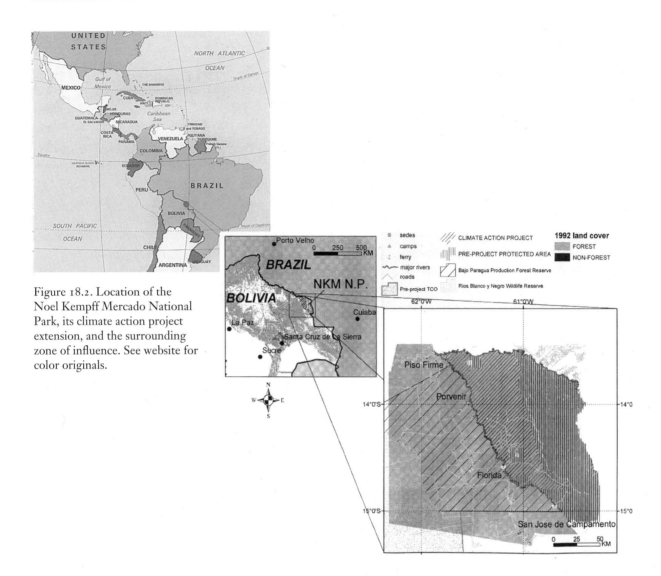

Figure 18.2. Location of the Noel Kempff Mercado National Park, its climate action project extension, and the surrounding zone of influence. See website for color originals.

high correlation between the two often is found, especially at regional and countrywide scales (Myers 1993; Cropper and Griffiths 1994; Brown et al. 2006). However, in an intensely energy-subsidized environment, where land is not necessarily being cleared for livelihood, this may or may not be the case. We have found in both developed and developing countries that using local population growth as a predictor of future deforestation in areas situated at some distance from urban areas misses the potential "threat" of development to that area that will eventually arrive from outside the boundary of analysis (Tyrrell, Hall, and Sampson 2004). We propose that both colonization in the developing world and urban sprawl in the developed world are captured better through analysis of remotely sensed imagery across concentric growth zones increasing in distance from population nodes, than through the use of population and socioeconomic data at the local scale. We developed this methodology for the analysis that follows.

The Region of Interest

The 634,000 ha Noel Kempff Mercado Climate Action Project, located in eastern Bolivia (figure 18.2) was implemented in 1997 with the goal of emissions avoidance through forest conservation. An extension of the existing Noel Kempff Mercado National Park, it is the largest pilot carbon mitigation project to date. The project was initiated in 1997 by the Nature Conservancy (TNC), the government of Bolivia, Fundación Amigos de la Naturaleza (FAN), American Electric Power, BP Amoco, and PacifiCorp. With a $9.6 million

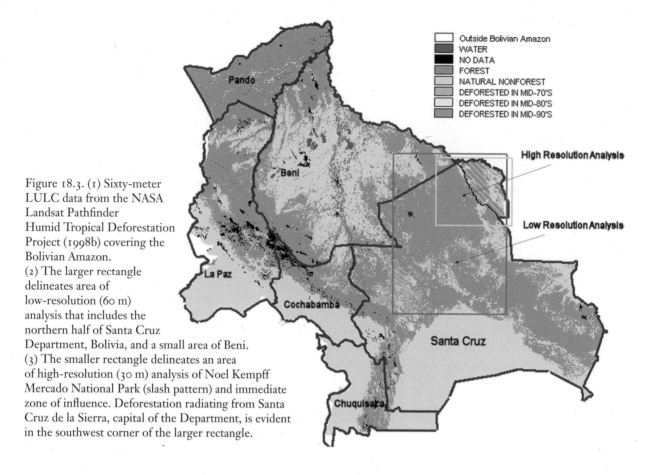

Figure 18.3. (1) Sixty-meter LULC data from the NASA Landsat Pathfinder Humid Tropical Deforestation Project (1998b) covering the Bolivian Amazon. (2) The larger rectangle delineates area of low-resolution (60 m) analysis that includes the northern half of Santa Cruz Department, Bolivia, and a small area of Beni. (3) The smaller rectangle delineates an area of high-resolution (30 m) analysis of Noel Kempff Mercado National Park (slash pattern) and immediate zone of influence. Deforestation radiating from Santa Cruz de la Sierra, capital of the Department, is evident in the southwest corner of the larger rectangle.

investment for the first ten of thirty years, the project area consists of lowland tropical moist forest, flooded forests, savanna, flooded savanna, and gallery forest that are home to 130 mammal species, 620 bird species, and 70 reptile species. The major vehicle for establishment of the park extension was the purchase of logging concession rights. Local colleagues view the major deforestation drivers as expansion of cattle ranching by the local population and possibly from neighboring Brazil, as well as new settlements by people from the Bolivian highlands. The original national park and its CAP extension, delineated in figure 18.2, lie in a remote, frontier environment.

Objectives/Hypothesis

The primary objective of this analysis was to determine the land-use and carbon baseline for the Noel Kempff CAP (NKCAP) and its surrounding region. We hypothesized that it would be possible to (1) create credible baselines using publicly available, lower- versus higher-resolution data sets, thus

reducing the cost to project implementers; and (2) establish regional, versus project-specific, baselines that would reduce transaction costs.

The Application of GEOMOD to Predict the "Without Project" Carbon Baseline at Two Different Scales

Department-wide Analysis Using Publicly Available Information

For our department-scale analysis, in which we were attempting to develop a baseline for as large a region as possible, we selected the northern half of the department of Santa Cruz (and a small area of the department of Beni) for analysis (the larger rectangle of figure 18.3). We selected this area for several reasons: (1) it encompasses the NKCAP; (2) it does not cross country boundaries; (3) it is an area with abundant forests of similar composition to those found within the NKCAP; (4) it is the area of most rapid population growth and deforestation in the country of Bolivia and thus a likely region for additional projects; and (5) we had good spatial

Table 18.1. Publicly available data used on department-wide (low resolution, small map scale) analysis

Description	Areal Extent	Date	Source
WWF ecoregions	all Bolivia	unknown	WWF (Olson et al. 2001)
Provincial boundaries	all Bolivia	unknown	ESRI
500m dtm coverage	study area	unknown	Computamaps.com
Settlement centers	study area	unknown	Digital Chart of the World (Penn State)
Roads	study area	unknown	Digital Chart of the World (Penn State)
Rivers	study area	unknown	Digital Chart of the World (Penn State)
LULC map of Amazonian Bolivia (60m res.)	Amazonian Bolivia	70s-80s-90s	Pathfinder Program / University of Maryland

All data were reprojected to a customized projection we called "Bolivia."

coverage of land-use change from 1975 to 1995 for this area. The region encompasses 112,000 km² of primarily lowland tropical evergreen and semi-evergreen forest.

Data, data source, and metadata for department-wide analysis

All of the data used for analysis of this region were acquired via the Internet on publicly accessible Web sites (table 18.1). Generally these data were based on maps of 1:1,000,000 scale, except the digital elevation model (1:500,000), and were gridded to match the forest change data set, which was derived from LANDSAT multispectral scanner (MSS) and thematic mapper (TM5) satellite imagery, of 80 meter and 30 meter resolution respectively, resampled to a common 60 × 60 meter grid cell resolution. The latter data set, from the NASA Landsat Pathfinder Humid Tropical Deforestation Project (NASA 1998a, 1998b), formed the core information for this study.

Derivation of weighted potential land-use change map

We derived seven candidate driver maps from the raw information described above. These included Euclidian distance to both roads and rivers and a cost-distance map (UNSD 1997; Eastman 1999; Chomitz and Gray 1997) to both the city of Santa Cruz and the city of Trinidad, individually and combined. The cost-distance map is a combination of a measure of the friction, or difficulty of traversing an area based on its terrain and vegetation, plus its accessibility in terms of distance from existing transportation corridors or communities. Because we could not test our assumptions about energy use to traverse different types of terrain and vegetation cover in this part of Bolivia directly, we assigned to all land cover classifications a base friction value of 50 and to all other features a value relative to that base. Rivers, because of the difficulty in crossing them, were given high friction values (500) while inland water body shorelines were given frictions of 1,000. We assigned frictions of 1 to road connectors within urbanized area polygons and single-track railroads, frictions of 2 to dual lane and divided highways, and frictions of 5 to primary and secondary roads. Slopes, due to the scale of the DEM and because most of this region is relatively flat, and land cover types were not analyzed although they add additional energy cost and/or time. Additional spatial pattern drivers included World Wildlife Fund Ecozones and elevation. All were calibrated against the 1985 land-use map in GEOMOD.

A potential land-use change (PLUC) map, calibrated with all of seven drivers, produced a simulated 1995 land-use land-cover (LULC) map

■ OUT OF ANALYSIS
□ REMAINING FOREST
■ NONFOREST IN 1995

Figure 18.4. Simulated 1995 deforestation (left) versus actual 1995 deforestation (right) in the northern half of the Department of Santa Cruz, Bolivia; 96 percent correct, $K_{location}$ statistic = 0.31.

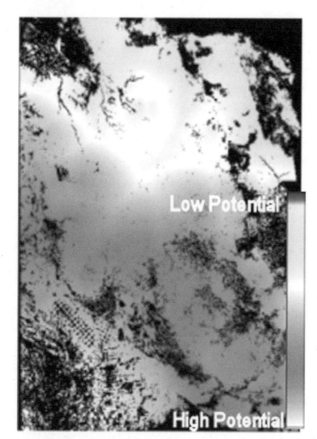

Figure 18.5. Final weighted potential land use–change (PLUC) map yielding the highest $K_{location}$ based on three drivers: distance to Sta. Cruz de la Sierra, distance to roads, and distance to prior disturbance, used to simulate the 2000–2030 baseline.

that was validated against the actual 1995 map. This simulated map yielded a $K_{location}$ statistic of 0.189, meaning that the model is performing only 19 percent better than would a random deforestation model, that is, one with no knowledge of past patterns. We achieved the highest $K_{location}$ index (0.31) using a combination of distance to previous disturbance, distance to roads, and distance to Santa Cruz. The simulated results, when compared to the actual 1995 landscape (figure 18.4), indicate the overwhelming influence of "distance to Santa Cruz" as the spatial determinant. We verified this using principal components analysis (PCA) to compare the relative importance of these three factors. These results show that in 1985 "distance to Santa Cruz" with an eigenvalue of 0.69 was more than twice as important as the other two drivers in capturing the spatial distribution of development at that time. "Distance to 1975 disturbance" produced a weight of 0.30 and "distance to roads" only 0.01. The composite 3-factor weighted PLUC map (figure 18.5), which guided the final baseline simulation, illustrates this.

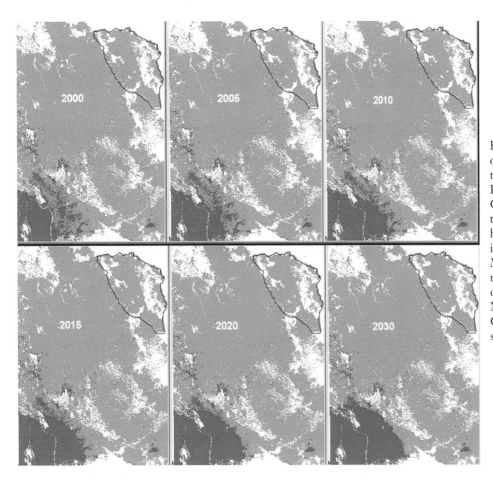

Figure 18.6. Extrapolation of land clearing (dark) to the year 2030 in the Department of Santa Cruz. In spite of the fact that some deforestation has already occurred in the Noel Kempff Mercado region, the model produces no future deforestation in either the Noel Kempff Mercado CAP or its immediate surroundings.

Derivation of department-wide deforestation rate

The rate of deforestation between 1975 and 1995 was derived from the Pathfinder maps for all of the Bolivian Amazon. It can be projected forward to 2030 using either a conservative linearly extrapolated rate ($R^2 = 0.973$) or a somewhat better fit aggressive exponential rate ($R^2 = 0.998$). We applied the more conservative rate, which amounts to approximately 28,218 ha per year.

Department-wide simulation results

We simulated maps of deforestation for the years 2000, 2005, 2010, 2015, 2020, 2025, and 2030 (figure 18.6) for the study area using the conservative rate, and the best-fit 3-factor PLUC map. Due to the overwhelming influence of distance from Santa Cruz in explaining past trends, all of the predicted change occurs in increasing distance from the capital, with much of the change occurring as infill. The model deforests an additional

987,627 hectares by the year 2030. This represents an 8 percent decrease in 1995 forest cover in the department of Santa Cruz. In the region of the NKCAP, however, no deforestation was predicted by this analysis. Even if the better-fit exponential deforestation trend had been used one can see through comparison of the linear-based results (figure 18.6) and the PLUC map (figure 18.5) that the conservative simulation reaches only partially into the most highly weighted southwest region of the latter, and therefore, no cells in the region of the project would be vulnerable to deforestation anytime in the next fifty years.

Discussion of department-wide simulation results

A $K_{location}$ of 0.31 indicates that for the period 1985 to 1995 the model is performing 31 percent better than a random cell selection but still far short of a perfect simulation ($K_{location} = 1.00$), which could occur only if the model had perfect knowledge of past patterns. The inability of the drivers to return a higher kappa can be attributed largely to the scale mismatch between most of the drivers tested (1:1,000,000) and that of the land-use/land cover maps whose grid cell resolution (60 × 60 meter) corresponds roughly to a regional map scale of 1:100,000. The model does not capture the subtleties of settlement patterns existing in this area. It simulates the general location of the government-organized development projects at increasing distance from Santa Cruz where land is available, but fails to mimic either the regular block pattern of these developments, or the "Swiss cheese" pattern of isolated clearings, which are evident in the 1995 map (figure 18.4). Interestingly, when we tested heuristically derived weightings—that is, weighting cells in monotonically increasing distance from various features, as opposed to weighting them based on the actual number of cells deforested at each distance interval—we received a slightly higher kappa-for-location (0.34). This can be interpreted to mean that we lack sufficient biophysical or cadastral mapping at the appropriate scale to explain the siting of government planned projects or the biophysical-socioeconomic conditions guiding the historic choices of individual farmers. It can also indicate that the pattern of development is so random that there is no way to explain it empirically. The lack of publicly available detailed road information, in particular, and the overwhelming significance of the two major pattern determinants, which are not mutually independent, caused the model to select land close to the capital, particularly the fallow lands and road corridors of the government development projects.

We believe that deforestation will take place farther from Santa Cruz than projected by these results and we know that the pattern is much more complex. Small areas of forest clearing, detected on higher-resolution maps, and evident to some degree in the Pathfinder data, have generally been lost through cell aggregation from 30 m² to 60 m². This limits the ability of the model to "grow" development off existing "seeds," or to generate new pioneering locations of development that may threaten the forests of the NKCAP in the future.

In the case of the seemingly random, individual settlement pattern, evidenced in the satellite-derived land-use maps, the fact that the highest $K_{location}$ was derived using heuristically as opposed to empirically derived drivers is indicative of the lack of biophysical drivers that reveal the ecological conditions that attract farmers to, or repel them from, certain areas. Previous analyses, where the data set at countrywide scale was rich, found that life zones and soils explained much of the pattern of deforestation in, for example, Costa Rica, including most especially the "jump" phenomenon that found noncontiguous ideal locations for new agricultural development (Hall et al. 1995a; Pontius et al. 2000). In the case of the more regular, government-organized pattern, our analysis lacked a map of government-planned agricultural development projects. We did consult the official Bolivian potential land-use designation map, which is intended in the broad sense as a zoning map to control resource extraction, but as we will show, this policy map does not always reflect reality.

In conclusion, without independent driver variables derived from maps of the same map scale as the land-use map, it is very difficult to "explain" or "mimic" the LULC dynamic for the region and impossible to capture the baseline for the NKCAP. We, therefore, cannot recommend the use of 1:1,000,000 scale publicly available global data sets for estimating either regional or project-specific baselines. The department-wide LULC data set and the application of GEOMOD to it, however, has been most useful in helping identify the overall pattern and advance of the human population in the Bolivian lowlands in concentric rings emanating from its capital, Santa Cruz de la Sierra. This information we subsequently put to use as we zoomed in to the project-level scale described next.

Project-scale Analysis
Using Finer-grained Data

Our second analysis zoomed in to an area covering 3,726,000 ha in the northeast corner of the original study area. This area comprises the expanded Noel Kempff Mercado National Park and its zone of influence in Bolivia (figures 18.2 and 18.3).

Table 18.2 Metadata for maps employed in local-scale analysis

Name of map	Decription	Source	Extent	Date of data collection	Initial projection information
PAC	30 m resolution of vegetation map of NKM project area	Museo Noel Kempff Mercado/ Winrock International	NKM expansion zone only	1996	Utm-20s
Veg_nkm	30 m resolution vegetation map of greater NKM region	Museo Noel Kempff Mercado	WRS 230–69, 230–70, 229–70	1992	Utm-20s
Roads	Road network taken from NIMA topo map and digitized 2000 Landsat imagery	Museo Noel Kempff Mercado	All greater NKM and Concepción region	2000	Utm-20s
Towns	Town locations taken from NIMA topo map and digitized 2000 Landsat imagery	Museo Noel Kempff Mercado	All greater NKM and Concepción region	2000	Utm-20s
Rivers	Rivers network taken from NIMA topo map and digitized 2000 Landsat imagery	Museo Noel Kempff Mercado	Within NKM national park Concepción area	2000	Utm-20s
Camps	Point locations of lumber camps	Fundación Amigos de la naturaleza	Greater NKM region	1996	Utm-20s
Ferry	Point location of river ferries	Fundación Amigos de la naturaleza	Greater NKM region	1996	Utm-20s
WWF Ecoregions	1:1,000,000 WWF designated Ecoregions (dry forest, wet forest, savanna)	www.geographynetwork.com/free.cfm	Global	1999	latlong
Elevation	Elevation map derived from 500m DTM	Computamaps, 2001	Utm-20s tile	2001	Utm-20s
Pathfinder	60 m resolution forest-nonforest map of Bolivian Amazon from "NASA pathfinder humid tropical deforestation project" archive at University of Maryland	Pathfinder Project	All of Bolivian Amazon	Mid-70s, mid-80s mid-90s	Sinusoidal

Data, data source, and metadata for local scale analysis

The LULC base map for this windowed region was a classified mosaic of three Landsat TM scenes (30 m × 30 m resolution) (for full color see http://v1.winrock.org/general/publications/ecocoop.pdf). The scenes were captured in 1992 with some 1995 information incorporated in areas obscured by cloud cover in the 1992 images. The region is characterized by 9 percent savanna, 49 percent deciduous or semi-deciduous forest, of which 41 percent is considered tall inundated forest, 27 percent tall evergreen forest, and 9 percent short inundated evergreen forest. These classes were collapsed into forest and nonforest categories. We included savanna in the forest category because it

Table 18.3. Final spatial pattern drivers analyzed

Driver	Number of Categories	Interval Distance (m)	Min. Value (m)	Max. Value (m)
WWF Ecoregions	3	n/a	n/a	n/a
DEM	41	10	210	620
Distance to major rivers	100	1,315	0	131,500
Distance to roads	100	442	0	44,200
Distance to major towns	100	1,331	0	133,100
Distance to likely seeds of 1992 disturbance	100	1,317	0	131,700
Distance to towns	100	857	0	85,700
Distance to camps	100	1,361	0	136,100
Distance to forest edge	100	480	0	48,000

is often used for farming or livestock raising; hence, "forested" cells can be interpreted as candidates for alteration from natural vegetation to human use and "nonforest" as already disturbed areas. According to this classification, by 1992 only 0.15 percent of the region had been deforested for agriculture/pasture, timber extraction, or residential use.

The Museo Noel Kempff Mercado digitized roads, rivers, and towns from 1:24,000 U.S. National Imagery and Mapping Agency (NIMA) topographical maps and 2000 Landsat ETM+ satellite images (table 18.2). The Fundación Amigos de la Naturaleza (FAN) provided equally detailed coverage of former lumber camps and ferry crossings. We used the same public domain 500-meter interval elevation map and the WWF ecoregions maps (Olson et al. 2001) as for the department-wide analysis. A map of vegetation types and corresponding measures of their carbon stocks within the NKCAP area, based on extensive fieldwork, formed the basis of the carbon baseline analysis for the project area (Brown et al. 2000).

Derivation of project-scale driver weighting and final potential land-use change map

From these vector layers, we created and analyzed nine spatial pattern driver raster-format maps in order to create the final weighted PLUC map (table

18.3). The major rivers included the Río Paragua and Río Itañez. The seeds were digitized points where it appeared likely, based on evidence in the 1992 map, that deforestation may have started when humans first came to the area. To create a distance from forest edge map (Pontius and Pacheco 2005), factors that give people easier access to the forest interior, such as roads, major rivers, savanna edge, towns, and lumber camps, were incorporated. We identified the four major centers of commercial and political importance in the park area: Piso Firme, Porvenir, Florida, and San José de Campamento. Cost-distance maps, discussed earlier, incorporated friction values for different road surfaces, river crossings, railroads, and land cover types relative to each other. Slopes were not incorporated into the friction values because the area in general is quite flat, and the roads are constructed on the flattest terrain. However, the river's role as an effective barrier to the movement of people from one side to another was sufficiently conveyed by FAN representatives to encourage us to include the cost-distance map in the analyses without knowing true cost. WWF ecoregions in this region included savanna, dry forest, and moist forest.

Based on PCA of the nine factors analyzed, elevation, ecozones, and distance to forest edge were equally important (15 percent each) in explaining

Figure 18.7. Potential land-use-change map for the project-scale local area analysis ranked low (dark) to high (light) based on empirical human settlement preferences. The importance of alluvial soils is obvious.

the 1992 land-use pattern, followed by distance to roads and distance to major rivers (each 12 percent), distance to towns and distance to lumber camps (each 9 percent), distance to original seeds of development (8 percent) and distance to the most important commercial centers (7 percent). Starting from a Time 0 (prehuman) landscape and simulating to 1992, we tested fifty-two different combinations to derive the best $K_{location}$ statistic upon validation against the actual 1992 forest/nonforest map. The final PLUC map employed is illustrated in figure 18.7. When all nine determinant factors were combined, the model yielded a moderate $K_{location}$ of 0.34 upon validation against the 1992 land-use map. However, this metric penalizes for missing the target by even 30 meters (one cell). When we applied the "neighborhood" validation technique described in Pontius et al. (2004), we achieved a $K_{location}$ of 1.0, indicating a "perfect" simulation if the model selected cells for deforestation within 120 meters of cells actually deforested. Use of this technique is warranted, based on the concept of spatial auto-correlation, which accounts for the fact that spatial attributes tend to cluster. What this means is that even with high-resolution data, the model cannot select precisely every 30 m² cell of change; however, it is able to do so perfectly within 120 m of actual deforested areas, which seemed intuitively pretty good to us, and which indicates the highest "certainty" or truest scale of our projections.

The final PLUC map does not indicate how many cells will be converted in, for example, each five-year time period of our simulated future landscape, but only where that development is most and least likely to occur. Because we needed a plausible deforestation rate for an area where there was inadequate historical deforestation data (LULC for only one point in time) we returned to the regional scale, longer-term data set (three points in time) to derive either a population-versus-deforestation rate, or to determine when the apparent Santa Cruz wave of deforestation, detected in our department-wide analysis, would reach the Noel Kempff region.

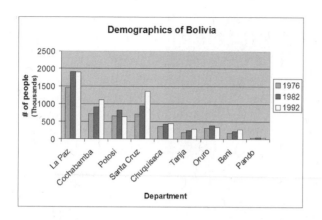

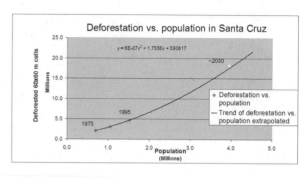

Figure 18.8. Population statistics for Bolivian Departments. Source: *Statesman's Yearbook 2000*.

Figure 18.9. Department of Santa Cruz deforestation as a function of population growth based on the analysis of 1970s, 1980s, and 1990s data. Population extrapolated to 2030 using Santa Cruz population trend ($y = 564. x^2 -2.2 \times 10^6 x + 2.14 \times 10^9$, $r^2 = 0.9995$). Source: *Statesman's Yearbook 2000* for population; Landsat Pathfinder maps for quantity of deforested 60 m × 60 m grid cells.

Derivation of project-scale deforestation rate

Within the project-scale window, we needed to derive a realistic deforestation rate. Because high-resolution satellite imagery exists for only one point in time for this area, it was impossible to observe change over time at that resolution. A number of possible rate extrapolations were considered. The first, described earlier, was FAO population-correlated type model. Using data for the years 1950, 1976, 1982, and 1992 (*Statesman's Yearbook*) we found a decline of population in the Andean highlands (the department of La Paz), and an increase in the lowlands, particularly in the department of Santa Cruz (figure 18.8). This exodus from the highlands is attributed to the decline of the mining industry, declining soil fertility, and availability of lowland agriculturally suitable soil. Plotting each department's population versus 1975, 1985, and 1995 forest cover from the Pathfinder data set, we found significant correlation between population growth and decline in forest cover throughout the Amazon with the exception of the department of Pando. Using this correlation we projected the population trend in the department of Santa Cruz (figure 18.9) to the year 2030. This results in a projected department-wide population increase of 2.5 million people and would yield an expected deforestation of 6,347,656 ha in the department

of Santa Cruz. This represents a 23 percent loss of the 1995 forest. This estimate, does not, however, tell us if any of those 6 million-plus ha would be located in the vicinity of the NKCAP. Unrealistically we could have applied this rate to the 1992 forest lying within the project-scale window, which would yield 866,000 ha of deforestation by 2030.

A second method, relying solely on time-series analysis of the Pathfinder satellite images for all of the department of Santa Cruz, revealed a twenty-year trend that projected to 2030 would represent a 17.38 percent loss of forest. Applied to the forested area of the project-scale window, this would result in 654,722 ha of forest lost within the region of the NKCAP and its zone of influence. A third method, applied specifically to the area of interest, involved windowing the Pathfinder image to the same extent as the project-scale analytical window to determine how much change occurred in just this part of the department from 1975 to 1995. A best-fit trend projected to 2030 results in a 0.07 percent deforestation rate, or a loss of only 2,327 ha of forest.

Because Bolivian colleagues who know this area well can testify to the increasing number of immigrants to the region, not only from the cold and arid highlands but also from neighboring Brazil, it was our decision to use an "advancing wave" extrapola-

Figure 18.10. City of Sta. Cruz de la Sierra (photograph by Myrna Hall).

Figure 18.11. 100 km rings used for analysis of deforestation as a function of distance from Santa Cruz.

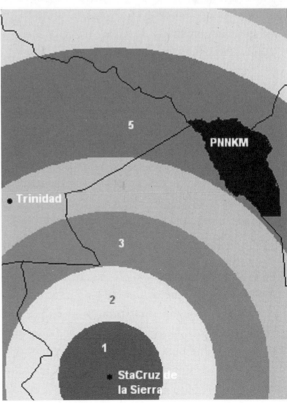
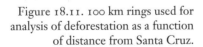

Table 18.4. Percent deforested in each 100km ring from Santa Cruz de la Sierra

Historical Years	1885	1900	1905	1910	1915	1920	1925	1930	1940	1945	1950	1975	1985	1995
Zone 1 backcast	0.003	0.2	0.5	0.9	1.5	2.2	3.2	4.5	8.1	10.4	*13.2*	28.3	38.6	51.50
Zone 1 actual												28.2	38.6	51.5
Zone 2 actual												*3.60*	7.00	*13.3*
Zone 3 actual												*0.60*	1.35	*3.28*
Zone 4 actual												0.21	0.32	*0.60*
Zone 5 actual												0.20	0.21	0.43
Advancing wave" Zone 4 rate	0.32	0.43	0.62	0.77	0.35	2.21	3.28	4.73	7.00	11.10	13.34			
Advancing wave" Zone 5 rate	0.21	0.32	0.43	0.62	0.77	1.35	2.21	3.28	4.73	7.00	11.10			
Simulation years			1995	2000	2005	2010	2015	2020	2030	2035	2040			

The best-fit equation for the Zone 1 (1975–95 data) when backcast, yields a trend line upon which other values for other zones fall (see italics) $y = 2 \times 10^{-7} x^{3.155}$, $R^2 = 0.9998$; y = proportion deforested; x = time.

tion (on the Bolivian side of the border only) as the best indicator of potential development and forest loss in the NKCAP region. Visual analysis of the Pathfinder Data set and the significance of distance from Santa Cruz in our department-wide analysis revealed deforestation radiating over time from the capital of Santa Cruz. The city, from its beginnings, has self-organized in concentric rings that represent stages or epochs of expanding development. It is common for citizens of Santa Cruz to identify where they live by the sequential ring number (see figure 18.10). Based on this pattern and the high population-deforestation correlation, the question became when and how fast the wave of population-driven deforestation emanating from the capital of Santa Cruz would reach the northeast frontier of

the department, where the NKCAP is located. To answer this question, we constructed 100 km concentric rings radiating from Santa Cruz de la Sierra (figure 18.11) and used the Pathfinder data set to calculate the percent of land that was deforested in each zone at each mapped time period (mid-1970s to mid-1990s). We found that by 1995 the first 100 km zone had lost 51 percent of its original vegetative cover, whereas in zone 5, where the NKCAP is located, only 0.43 percent had been removed (table 18.4). In zones 4 and 3 the percent deforested in 1995 (0.6 percent and 3 pe

rcent respectively) is approximately equal to the percentage deforested twenty years earlier in the zones 100 km closer to Santa Cruz de la Sierra, namely, zones 3 and 2 respectively. Zone 5, in 1995,

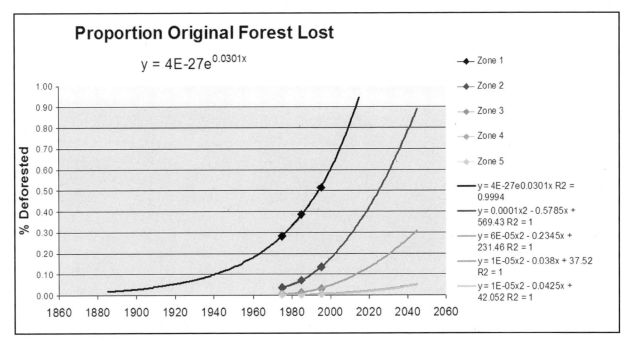

Figure 18.12. Proportion of forest lost in each 100 km zone.

is about five years behind zone 4.

When a trend line for each zone is fit to the 1975–95 data points, little deforestation is predicted for zone 5 (figure 18.12). However, when we projected the zone 1 data back in time we found that the percents deforested for zones 2–5 can be located on the zone 1 best-fit curve and that the zone 2 1995 value occurred in about 1950 of the zone 1 trend (table 18.4). This reinforced our assumption that there is a predictable deforestation trend over time radiating out from the department capital to zone 5, the NCAP region. To test this further, we slipped each zone's three data points into a location on this curve working backward from the zone 1 1950s trend location that corresponds to the zone 2 1995 percent deforested value (table 18.4). When all zones were plotted together as a function of time (figure 18.13), we found that zone 1's power function ($y = 2 \times 10^{-7} x^{3.155}$, where y = percent of the original forest cover deforested and x = time) visually fits the data points. This process also revealed that zones 2 and 3 are deforesting at a slightly faster rate than earlier years along the zone 1 trend, and that there appears to be a threshold of acceleration. Fitting a curve to all the points (not shown) produced an equation ($y = 6 \times 10^{-5} x^2 - 0.0025x + 0.0195$, $R^2 = 0.9942$, where y = percent deforested of the origi-

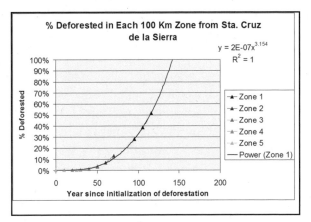

Figure 18.13. Percent deforested data points for all five zones. Trend line represents Zone 1 back and forward cast using power function.

nal forest cover and x = year) that can be used to project future deforestation across zones. This shall be referred to as the "advancing wave" trend line. Using this curve, Zone 5 in the mid-1990s was as deforested as the capital region was around 1905 (table 18.4). Although the city of Santa Cruz de la Sierra was founded in 1560 and was prosperous through the late 1880s, primarily due to rubber export, both the city and the department were relatively isolated from the rest of the country and world. The program instituted after the 1952 popular uprising, offering cheap land to highlanders and building a paved road from the nation's capital of

Table 18.5. Rate projections (%)

Trend year	Advancing wave rate across all zones	Zone 4 deforestation rate	Zone 5 deforestation rate	Projection year	Zone 4 deforested cells	Zone 5 deforested cells	Proportion of zones 4 & 5 located in PNNKM window	60 m pixels converted to 30 m pixels	Resolution adjustment (60m to 30m cells)	Total ha deforested in region
				1992						5,740
1905	0.0043	0.0062	0.0043	1995	86,270	34,483	7,237	28,948	77,291	6,956
1910	0.0062	0.0078	0.0062	2000	109,117	49,015	9,463	37,852	101,065	9,096
1915	0.0078	0.0135	0.0078	2005	188,278	61,996	15,034	60,138	160,567	14,451
1920	0.0135	0.0236	0.0135	2010	330,148	106,972	26,263	105,053	280,493	25,244
1925	0.0236	0.0328	0.0236	2015	459,182	187,577	38,751	155,005	413,862	37,248
1930	0.0328	0.0490	0.0328	2020	685,477	260,888	56,752	227,010	606,116	54,550
1935	0.0490	0.0700	0.0490	2025	979,523	389,460	82,052	328,207	876,314	78,868
1940	0.0700	0.1150	0.0700	2030	1,608,773	556,525	129,999	519,996	1,388,388	124,955
1945	0.1150	0.1334	0.1150	2035	1,866,064	914,039	166,176	664,705	1,774,762	159,729
1950	0.1334	0.1549	0.1334	2040	2,166,366	1,060,221	192,866	771,466	2,059,813	185,383

La Paz in the highlands to Santa Cruz de la Sierra to facilitate population redistribution, marked the real beginning in the department of timber extraction and deforestation for land to raise cash crops.

We used the "across zone" empirical percents deforested, upon which the "advancing wave" trend line is based, to estimate the quantity of deforestation (1996–2030) in the two zones (4 and 5 of the 60 m data set) that crossed our study area (tables 18.4 and 18.5). Five-year rates, where missing, were calculated from the best-fit zones 2–5 model. We multiplied these results by the proportion of all zone 4 and zone 5 deforested cells from the 1995 Pathfinder map that lay inside the project-scale analysis window. This was necessary because deforestation is not evenly distributed across a zone. In 1995 the proportion of zone 4 forests lying within the windowed region is 26 percent of all zone 4 and 63 percent of zone 5, but the proportion of zone 4 deforested cells within the window is only 0.061 and in zone 5 is 0.057. A second adjustment for scale differences was required because the deforested quantities were based on the coarser-resolution Pathfinder data. The deforestation percentage for 1992, interpolated from the "advancing wave" trend line, is 0.056 percent of the windowed area, or 21.55 km², whereas the higher resolution (30 × 30 meter) 1992 land cover/land-use map indicates that 0.15 percent of the area, or 57.40

km², were deforested. Therefore we adjusted the quantity predicted by the coarser-scale "advancing wave" trend by 2.67 (57.40/21.55), which is the proportion of the high-resolution (local scale) area (ha) deforested in 1992 to the low-resolution area interpolated for 1992.

Project-scale Simulation

We simulated the business-as-usual baseline to the year 2030 (figure 18.14) by applying the deforestation rate derived from our "advancing wave" analysis to the best-fit PLUC map, assuming no new roads nor government nor private agricultural development projects are built. In essence we applied what we learned from our large window results with respect to department-wide development rates and patterns and adjusted it using local finer-resolution data to project more accurately how much change and where that change can be expected in this heretofore relatively undisturbed frontier environment.

Results of predictions of land area cleared and resulting carbon emissions

In the Noel Kempff Mercado project area we predict 9,256 hectares of forest clearing between 1997 and 2026, with significant jumps in 2012, 2017, and 2026 (figure 18.15). An additional 1787 ha of *cerrado* and *pantano* will be disturbed. Inundated

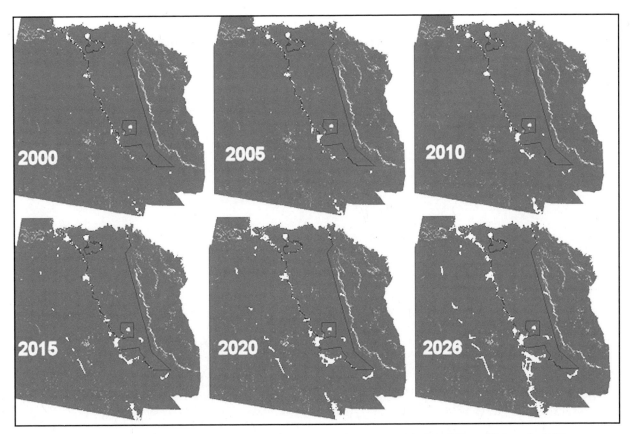

Figure 18.14. Project-scale land-use change simulation results for the region of the Noel Kempff Mercado CAP. Black = forest; white = deforested; gray = noncandidate cells.

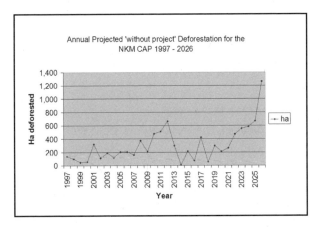

Figure 18.15. Projected ha deforested per year in the Noel Kempff Mercado CAP.

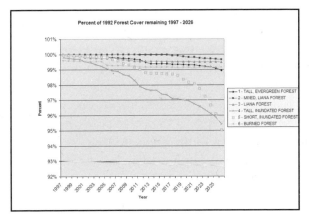

Figure 18.16. Projected loss of original vegetation over time in the Noel Kempff Mercado CAP.

Table 18.6. Comparison of rate effect on baseline area

Projected 2030 deforestation in the PNNKM region

2030 projected	ha	Rate	Source of Rate Derivation	Compared to "advancing wave" rate (x)	Comparison to highest rate	Comparison to lowest rate
Forest	2899824	23.00%	Santa Cruz Dept. Defor. vs. population analysis	7.27	1.00	328.57
Nonforest	866181					
Forest	3111284	17.39%	Pathfinder change analysis for Santa Cruz	5.49	0.76	248.36
Nonforest	654722					
Forest	3763370	0.07%	Pathfinder change analysis for project-scale window	0.02	0.0030	1.00
Nonforest	2636					
Forest	3646791	3.17%	100 km zone "advancing wave" analysis	1.00	0.14	45.22
Nonforest	119215					

forest, both tall and short, will suffer greater losses of original forested area than other types (figure 18.16). Cumulative carbon emissions over thirty years total 1,647,014 tons with an average of 59,900 tons total and 114 t/ha lost per year. Estimated carbon emissions include CO_2 derived from above- and below-ground living and dead biomass plus 8 percent of soil carbon up to five years after cutting (Brown et al. 2000).

Regionally, between 1997 and 2026, the model predicts 80,700 ha to be deforested. This means that the deforestation predicted within the CAP is 13.68 percent of the deforestation predicted in the region over the life of the project. Extending projections to 2030, regionally, we expect a loss of 119,215 ha of original 1992 vegetative cover, which is 3.17 percent of the original forest cover in the area of analysis. The impact on various forest types is not projected by the model to be uniform across the landscape. The high riverine forest is predicted to lose up to 38 percent of its original area, pioneer riverine up to 27 percent, and inundated savanna 20 percent. All other forest types would experience a loss of between 1 percent and 6 percent. For those forest classes for which we have carbon numbers (Brown et al. 2000)—tall evergreen, short inundated, and tall inundated—the conversion amounts to 6,708,833 tons of carbon; 21,919 ha of these three forest types are predicted by the model

to be cleared over the project period. Due to a lack of more than one period of high-resolution LULC data before the onset of the project, we could not easily test our rate projections with, for example, the $K_{location}$ metric. We have tested a number of potential rate derivation methodologies, however, and feel that the one chosen captures the dynamics of the region better than the others, especially given new activity in the region (see latest developments below). Clearly, if a simple baseline projection, without the spatial model, were used, and the same 3.17 percent loss of forest were applied evenly to all forest types, for these three forest types only an estimated 14,926 ha would be cleared. This would represent a 32 percent underestimate of carbon released to the atmosphere. If we had used the department-wide population vs. deforestation rate (23 percent) or the department-wide Pathfinder-detected rate (17 percent) and applied it to this region the number of ha deforested between 1992 and 2030 would have equaled 866,181 and 654,722 respectively (7.27 or 5.49 times that which we have projected) with significantly more carbon emissions (table 18.6). The advantages of spatial modeling versus other types of baseline derivation are developed more fully in Brown et al. (2006).

Discussion of Results at Both Scales

We hypothesized that the LULC change for a specified area of the earth's surface should be similar regardless of the scale of analysis and the resolution and scale of the data. Although the data sets employed were not completely equal, thus preventing a perfect test, we still must reject this hypothesis for reasons that follow. On the other hand, we have shown that, as also hypothesized, it is possible to create large regional baselines for project planning if the land-cover data matches the grain of the spatial pattern driver data sets, and if a good estimate of rate of change can be derived. Use of the publicly available Pathfinder data sets was key to this latter component.

With respect to rejection of our first hypothesis, using the lower-resolution, smaller map scale data set, applied at the scale of the department, we did not project *any* deforestation in the Noel Kempff region by the year 2030, whereas using our zone analysis for the entire province and adjusting the rate from the coarser data set to the actual deforestation observed locally, we estimated that approximately 3.16 percent of the area will be deforested by 2030. This difference is caused by a number of factors. Data derived at different scales or aggregated to different grid cell resolutions will yield considerable differences in deforestation estimates. The Pathfinder maps showed much less deforestation in the region by 1995 than did the higher-resolution 1992 local land cover map. This may be caused by lower satellite sensor pixel resolution where many small areas of clearing exist, or perhaps partial clearings can be overwhelmed by the reflectance of the surrounding forest cover and are, therefore, eliminated, or they are lost due to spatial aggregation effects encountered particularly when maps are resampled to different resolution or smoothed using a 3 × 3 window to remove noise in the data. We know that the 1985 and 1995 Landsat TM-derived maps, which are of high resolution, were aggregated to provide a match with lower-resolution MSS data gathered from earlier sensors (1970s). Small clearings are lost in this process. The scale at which data are captured affects not only the detection of the rate of deforestation but also the analysis of historical patterns. In the department-wide study, the use of publicly available, lower-resolution information derived from maps at a scale

of mostly 1:1,000,000 did not allow us to assess adequately the influence of these factors on land-use change when mapped at 60 m × 60 m ground resolution. However, such lower-resolution data did allow us to quantify the rate parameter that was crucial for modeling at the project scale. If we had applied the same zonal technique to the lower-resolution data set, we would perhaps have been able to project some deforestation in the Noel Kempff zone but, as we have shown, this would still have resulted in a significant underestimate of the true rate because the coarser 1990s map captured only 39 percent of the deforestation found in the 1992 higher-resolution LULC map. Furthermore, the lack of higher-resolution spatial-pattern driver data, such as roads, for the entire region, even with zonal rate analysis, would limit the model's ability to mimic the local pattern.

Our simulations did not exclude any lands held in common by indigenous communities, nor other protected or designated lands. This is based on our assumption that little policing is possible or effective in this environment. For example, at the time of the writing of this chapter, we received word from local colleagues that a colony of immigrants from the Bolivian highlands was illegally taking up residence on the southern outskirts of the project area (figure 18.17) in an area predicted by GEOMOD to experience some deforestation as early as 2015 (figure 18.14). This action was illegal in the sense that under the national land-use plan this land was set aside for forestry. Each of ninety families had been given five hundred hectares to develop according to their livelihood needs. If we had excluded this region from the potential for deforestation in our simulations based on the official national land-use potentiality map, we would have severely underestimated local land-use change. Rather, this activity is not unexpected by the model and in fact supports our "advancing wave" assumption. On the other hand, Cornell (2000) has shown that at least in Costa Rica, where government is reasonably able, forest reserves, national parks, and the like can have significant influence on land-use change patterns and that their inclusion in the modeling process can improve validation statistics considerably. It is our recommendation, therefore, that the

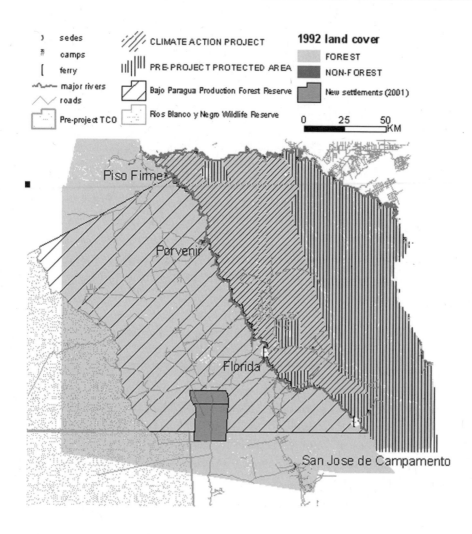

Figure 18.17. New illegal settlements (lower block) of ninety families resettled from the Bolivian highlands in 2001.

issue of whether to exclude reserves and parks from baseline analysis needs to be determined according to the policing resources and land tenure situation of each country.

The $K_{location}$ index presented here is our maximum certainty. Over the thirty-eight years that were modeled, this could decrease. Other less expected events, due to, say, market or climatic events, cannot be foretold. To enhance certainty over time, it is straightforward to input the new factors (for example, new settlements as new seeds) as they occur and run the simulations again. A system that learns and adjusts over time could be used by policy analysts and decision makers to refine and update baseline estimates.

Conclusions

The spatial modeling approach is a highly useful tool for projecting where and at what rate defor-

estation is likely to occur in the future. The spatial modeling approach, when employed prior to selection of future project areas, is also useful for locating those areas most immediately threatened by human activity. However, to derive the most realistic pattern and rate of deforestation expected, it may be necessary to apply a spatial model at two scales of analysis. What we have seen is that in areas already under considerable development pressure, such as in zone 1 of our analysis, which is close to Santa Cruz de la Sierra, it is fairly easy to detect both the rate and location of areas traditionally preferred by humans for development. However, in more remote, less developed regions, time-series analysis focused on the local region can miss what is coming.

For frontier environments, we have shown the importance of using data from two scales and developed an explicit zone-analysis methodology for telescoping from one to the other to project the magnitude of development pressure that may not be evident from examination of just the localized environment, even when examined over the last twenty, fifty, or even one hundred years. After all, who would have predicted the development of the region to the west of the Appalachians from local data as of 1750? However, an examination of the wave advancing from the coast to the mountains east of the Appalachians would have given a pretty good clue as to what was in store for the areas to the west.

We had hypothesized that the use of GEO-MOD, in particular, removes some of the "counter-factual uncertainty" (Moura-Costa 2001; Kerr 2001) inherent in other methods used to estimate baseline scenarios, because of its kappa-for-location statistic. Although there remains uncertainty in all model projections due to unforeseen factors, we have shown through the rigorous testing of individual drivers, and combinations of drivers, that if additional information is not scale appropriate it may not necessarily enhance the modeler's ability to capture the true future landscape dynamic. In the case of the department-wide, low-resolution analysis, we had to discard most of the drivers and were left with only three, one of which (distance to roads) explained very little of the pattern. The analysis was overwhelmed by the distance to Santa Cruz factor, which did not allow us to mimic the salt-and-pepper deforestation pattern in the hinterlands, but which was very important in shaping our approach to deriving the rate of deforestation over time across the department. The analytical power of the $K_{location}$ statistic to eliminate uncertainty, or "unveil" false assumptions is highly useful, therefore, in deriving the most realistic and robust baseline possible. When that is used and even crudely integrated at several scales, we believe that the results are much more probable simulations.

Acknowledgments

Funding for this work was provided by a Cooperative Agreement between Winrock International (WI) and the U.S. Environmental Protection Agency (USEPA) (ID No. CR 827293-01-0 and XA-83052101; Sandra Brown, principal investigator, and Ken Andrasko, project officer). We wish to thank Charles Hall, Gil Pontius, Pablo Pacheco, and Kiran Batchu, Marc Steininger (Conservation International), Richard Vaca (FAN), Bill Stanley (The Nature Conservancy), Tim Killeen (Museo Noel Kempff Mercado), and the Global Land Cover Facility (GLCF) and affiliated ESIP Partnership organizations from which we received data used for this investigation.

References

Brown, S. 2002. Land use and forests, carbon monitoring, and global change. Cooperative agreement between Winrock International and the EPA, CR 827293-01-0. www.winrock.org/ecosystems/files/Summary%20of%20project—Brown%202002.pdf.

Brown, S., M. Burnham, M. Delaney, R. Vaca, M. Powell, and A. Moreno. 2000. Issues and challenges for forest-based carbon-offset projects: A case study of the Noel Kempff climate action project in Bolivia. *Mitigation and Adaptation Strategies for Global Change* 5:99–121.

Brown, S., M. Hall, K. Andrasko, F. Ruiz, W. Marzoli, G. Guerrero, O. Masera, A. Dushku, B. DeJong, and J. Cornell. 2006. Baselines for land-use change in the tropics: Application to avoided deforestation projects. *Adaptation and Mitigation Strategies for Global Change*, in press.

Brown, S., L. R. Iverson, A. Prasad, and D. Liu. 1993. Geographical distributions of carbon in biomass and soils of tropical Asian forests. *Geocarto International* 4:45–59.

Brown, S., O. Masera, and J. Sathaye. 2000. Project-based activities. In R. Watson, I. Noble, and D. Verardo, eds., *Land Use, Land-Use Change, and Forestry: Special Report to the Intergovernmental Panel on Climate Change*, 283–338. New York: Cambridge University Press.

Chomitz, K., and D. Gray. 1996. Roads, land use, and deforestation: A spatial model applied to Belize. *World Bank Economic Review* 16, no. 3: 487–512.

Computamaps. 2001. http://www.computamaps.com/freedata.shtml.

Cornell, J. 2000. Assessing the role of parks for protecting forest resources using GIS and spatial modeling. In Hall 2000, 543–60.

Costanza, R. 1989. Model goodness of fit: A multiple resolution procedure. *Ecological Modeling* 47:199–215.

Cropper, M., and C. Griffiths. 1994. The interaction of population growth and environmental quality.

American Economic Review 84, no. 2: 250–54.

Detwiler, R. P., and C. A. S. Hall. 1988. Tropical forests and the global carbon budget. *Science* 239:42–47.

Eastman, J. R. 1999. *Idrisi32 Guide to GIS and Image Processing*, vol. 2. Worcester, Mass.: Clark Labs.

FAO. 1993. Forest resources assessment 1990: Tropical countries. FAO Forestry Paper 112.

Hall, C. A. S., ed. 2000. *Quantifying Sustainable Development: The Future of Tropical Economies*. San Diego: Academic Press.

Hall, C. A. S., C. J. Cleveland, and R. C. Kaufmann. 1986. *Energy and Resource Quality: The Ecology of the Economic Process*. New York: Wiley-Interscience.

Hall, C. A. S., H. Tian, Y. Qi, R. G. Pontius, J. Cornell, and J. Uhlig. 1995a. Spatially explicit models of land-use change and their application to the tropics. *DOE Research Summary* 31.

———. 1995b. Modeling spatial and temporal patterns of tropical land use change. *Journal of Biogeography* 22:753–57.

Hall, M. H. P., and A. Dushku. 2002. Description of GEOMOD and application to the Noel Kempff project area. Report to Winrock International.

Hall, M. H. P, C. A. S. Hall, and M. R. Taylor. 2000. Geographical modeling: The synthesis of GIS and simulation modeling. In Hall 2000, 177–202.

Kerr, S. 2001. Seeing the forest and saving the trees: Tropical land use change and global climate policy. www.rff.org/disc_papers/PDF_files/0126.pdf.

Lambin, E. F. 1997. Modeling and monitoring land-cover change processes in tropical regions. *Progress in Physical Geography* 21:375–93.

Moura-Costa, P. 2001. Elements of a certification system for forestry-based greenhouse gas mitigation projects. www.rff.org/disc_papers/PDF_files/0126.pdf.

Myers, N. 1993. Tropical forests: The main deforestation fronts. *Environmental Conservation* 20, no. 1: 9–16.

NASA Landsat Pathfinder Humid Tropical Deforestation Project. 1998a. www.geog.umd.edu/tropical/method.html.

———. 1998b. http://www.geog.umd.edu/tropical/bolivia.html.

Odum, H. T. 1983. *Systems Ecology*. New York: Wiley-Interscience.

Olson, D. M., E. Dinerstein, E. D. Wikramanayake, N. D. Burgess, G. V. N. Powell, E. C. Underwood, J. A. D'Amico, et al. 2001. Terrestrial ecoregions of the world: A new map of life on Earth. *Bioscience* 51, no.

11: 933–38.

Pontius, R. G., Jr. 2000. Quantification error versus location error in comparison of categorical maps. *Photogrammetric Engineering & Remote Sensing* 66, no. 8: 1011–16.

Pontius, R. G., Jr., and P. Pacheco. 2005. Calibration and validation of a model of forest disturbance in the Western Ghats, India 1920–1990. *GeoJournal* 61, no. 4: 325–34.

Pontius, R. G., Jr., and L. Schneider. 2001. Land-use change model validation by a ROC method for the Ipswich watershed, Massachusetts, USA. *Agriculture, Ecosystems & Environment* 85, nos. 1–3: 239–48.

Pontius, R. G., Jr., L. Claessens, C. Hopkinson Jr., A. Marzouk, E. B. Rastetter, L. C. Schneider, and J. Vallino. 2000. Scenarios of land-use change and nitrogen release in the Ipswich watershed, Massachusetts, USA. *Proceedings of the 4th International Conference on Integrating GIS and Environmental Modeling (GIS/EM4)*, Banff, Alberta.

Pontius, R. G., Jr., J. Cornell, and C. Hall. 2001. Modeling the spatial pattern of land-use change with GEOMOD: Application and validation for Costa Rica. *Agriculture, Ecosystems & Environment* 85, nos. 1–3: 191–203.

Pontius, R. G., Jr., D. Huffaker, and K. Denman. 2004. Useful techniques of validation for spatially explicit land-change models. *Ecological Modelling* 179, no. 4: 445–61.

Skole, D., and C. Tucker. 1993. Tropical deforestation and habitat fragmentation in the Amazon: Satellite data from 1978 to 1988. *Science* 260:1905–9.

Statesman's Yearbook. 2000. New York: St. Martin's.

Tyrrell, M., M. Hall, and R. N. Sampson. 2004. Dynamic models of land use change: Developing tools, techniques, and talents for effective conservation action. http://research.yale.edu/gisf/ppf/dynamic_models/index.html.

UNSD (United Nations Statistics Department). 1997. Applications of geographical information systems (GIS) for population and related statistics. www.

Chapter 19

A Preliminary Simulation of the Potential
for Sustainability in Eritrea

Rick E. Beal

un.org/Depts/unsd/demotss/intro2.htm.
Introduction

Eritrea, a small country located in East Africa, is that continent's newest nation. A thirty-year war for independence from Ethiopia has hindered development greatly and the country had required food subsidies for nine of the first ten years since independence. Eritrea currently has a policy for developing agricultural self-sufficiency. The potential success of this policy is dependent on overcoming a number of biophysical constraints, including poor soils, low rainfall, high erosion rates, and whether the high annual rate of population growth continues. Additionally, the sustainability of energy production is unknown, although energy consumption in the form of electricity has been increasing 10 percent annually and the main source of energy, biomass, is extremely constrained by the limited forest cover.

Simulation models at the national scale allow one to develop and refine systems-analysis techniques and tools to integrate biophysical, economic, and social considerations into straightforward and useful models for policy. Moreover, biophysical economic simulation models can incorporate spatial resource requirements and constraints that can help us in the assessment of which economic policies are likely to be successful and which are likely to fail. The impact of the spatial distribution of gradients such as rain, temperature, soil type, elevation, and population can be used to evaluate the biophysical constraints on large-scale economic policy decisions (Hall 2000).

Methods

I generated a model called ERISP4, written in FORTRAN77, that calculates the population growth, agricultural production, energy use, deforestation, and estimated costs of agricultural production for a hundred-year period in Eritrea starting in 1998. Additionally, the model simulates the expansion of agriculture in two-dimensional space based on the principle that farmers will choose to utilize the best agricultural lands first, as proposed by Ricardo (1817). The agricultural expansion model utilizes two digital maps of soil fertility (IGADD 1994) and a digital rainfall map (Woldu and Van Buskirk 1997). Additional data used was derived from (www.sas.upenn.edu/African_Studies/Country_Specific/erit_gov.html).

ERISP4 consists of fourteen individual subunits, eleven of them FORTRAN subroutines:

Population growth: I used population data for 1993–97 from the Food and Agriculture Organization of the United Nations (FAO 1999). Population rates varied slightly for all year intervals but were generally close to 2.5 percent, although rates nearer to independence (1993 and 1994) were higher due to the return of refugees. On the other hand, most UN projections assume a decrease in population growth rates. I used an arbitrary but probably not unrealistic value of 2.3 percent to account for these factors and assumed a constant population growth rate throughout the simulation. The model also assumes that human settlements take up no room.

Calories required: The total amount of kilocalories required (REQUIR) by the population was calculated in subroutine CALOR using the equation:

$$REQUIR = Population \times 2,600 \times 365$$

Where 2,600 is equal to the number of kcal required by one human each day based on the UN recommended daily calorie intake for an active adult (Collins 1982; Wilkie and Perkal 1985) and 365 equals the number of days in a year.

Stochastic cloud cover: Little data on annual solar variability was available, so I assumed from speaking with Eritreans and personal knowledge of Eritrean weather that very little change would be observed year to year in the amount of light present during the growing season (there are usually no clouds at all in the last half of the growing season). The model generates annual sunlight (SOLAR) that fluctuates between a maximum of 1.0 (full sunlight for plant growth) and 0.9 (a cloudy year). The SOLAR values are used to calculate crop production.

Stochastic rain variation: Variability in rainfall is extremely important in dry Eritrea. I obtained rainfall data from the African Data Dissemination Service (1999). Data were recorded in millimeters per dekad (ten days) for eighty-six sites. I summed the data for all thirty-six decades to calculate rainfall for each year. Data were incomplete for many years. Generally, I used only rainfall data from complete years. I used this data to make a rainfall time series. To gain a relative estimate of total rainfall variation from year to year, I summed data from sites that were within the grain belt of the country. I used this graph as a representation of the possible rain level variability within Eritrea (the minimum is approximately 38 percent of the maximum from within the time series that I had). The results were compared to time series of crop yields, specifically cereal yield. Additionally, I attempted to quantify the response of grain yields to rainfall by regressing crop yields on rainfall and found that a change in rain of 1.0 percent elicits a change in crop yield of 1.3272 percent. The simulation model uses a random number generator to produce numbers ranging between 0.0 (highest rainfall) and 0.38 (lowest rainfall) representing the observed 38 percent variability in rainfall. The rainfall variation value is multiplied by 1.3272, which represents the crop yield response per unit of rainfall change (see above) that range from 0.0 to 0.5044. The result is subtracted from 1 to generate rain-derived crop yield variation values from 1 (highest rainfall and high crop yields) to 0.4956

(drought conditions and lowest crop yields). The numerical result is used to calculate crop yields (see below).

Agricultural expansion: The amount of new land that is put into agriculture at the beginning of each simulated year is dependent on how effectively crop yields satisfied calorie requirements during the previous year. The model uses the formula:

New Land = Old Land × The Proportional Food Deficit

where the proportional food deficit is equal to the required food calories for the previous year/the food calories produced during the previous year. One of the simulation model's main assumptions is that Eritrea will increase crop production by expanding the amount of agricultural land utilized, either through the voluntary actions of individual farmers or a government program. This assumption comes from the fact that just before 2000 Eritrea was farming only 5 percent of its land area while over 20 percent of the land is very suitable for crop production. Furthermore, potentially 60 percent of the land area could be used for farming, although with much lower returns. Recent large-scale agricultural expansion policies promoted by the government also indicate that this will be a long-term strategy for achieving food self-sufficiency (see below). Agricultural expansion is determined in subroutine LAND. The model increases agricultural land utilized if the previous year's calorie requirements of the population were not met by the calories produced by agriculture. If requirements were met, the model uses the same amount of land and locations of agriculture as the previous year. If requirements were not met, the simulation model increases agricultural land using the above equation. These rates varied between 0.0 percent and 300 percent annually during the first ten years of the simulation.

The model, based essentially on Hall et al. (1995), assumes that farmers will pick the best-yielding land first. A series of search windows spreads agriculture from existing agricultural pixels within a digital map representing a relative agricultural fertility index (SFERT) based on rainfall and soil fertility (see below). The model locates the most fertile underdeveloped land near to existing agricultural lands and designates the land as new agricultural land in order to calculate erosion and agricultural yield for that pixel in subsequent subunits in the program.

SFERT was constructed by multiplying a raster map that represents the relative crop response to annual rainfall (RAINLV) by the sum of two soil maps derived from an FAO database (IGADD 1994): UPSOILS and UPMOD.

Relative fertility for a pixel = (rainfall/800) × ((UPSOILS) + 0.7(UPMOD))

UPSOILS equals the percentage of soil defined by the FAO as good for upland crops and UPMOD equals the percentage of soil in which upland crops grow moderately well as described by the FAO. RAINLV was generated from an annual digital rainfall map created by Woldu and van Buskirk (1997) divided by 800 mm (the amount of rainfall assumed to allow for near-maximal growth for upland crops). The digital map UPMOD was multiplied by a factor of 0.7 (representing an optimistic 30 percent decrease in crop yields) to account for the relative lower fertility of these more marginal lands. I restricted agricultural expansion to lands that have altitudes of between 0 and 2800 meters and with annual rainfalls of greater than 200 mm based on data from Tesema (1998), USAID (1999), and IGADD (1994).

Erosion: The model calculates the loss of soil fertility each year from the combined effects of erosion and nutrient loss through harvest effects each year in the subroutine ERODE. The model simulates cumulative effects with a factor that reduces crop yields for all pixels that are located in agricultural lands by a conservative 0.5 percent per year (Pimentel 1987; Hall 2000). This rate is most likely an underestimate and simulations with higher factors were performed (*see* crop production). It is likely that this underestimates the high erosion rates observed in Eritrea where there are low vegetative levels, seasonal rains, and much steep terrain. Preliminary estimates for actual annual crop yield losses due to erosion range from 0.5 percent to as high as 2.5 percent.

Fertilizer intensity: Total fertilizer use (nitrogen and phosphorus) was available for Eritrea be-

tween 1993 and 1997. Fertilizer intensity increased there from 10–25 percent annually. I assumed a 10 percent annual increase in fertilizer intensity for years after 1997 (FERFAQ) in the subroutine FERT to simulate a program of agricultural intensification. I also set an upper limit of twelve times the current fertilizer intensity since higher additions of fertilizer inputs had minimal impacts in a sensitivity analysis. Even this level of fertilizer application is well above those of most developing countries and would be at saturation levels for Ethiopian crops. For years after 1997, the proportion of fertilizer used on each individual crop type remains constant.

Crop production: Agricultural production is calculated by subroutine AGPROD. The model assumes that only five crops (representing 75 percent of annual historical production and extrapolated to 100 percent) are grown (sorghum, maize, wheat, pulses, and barley). Livestock production is also simulated. The outer loop of the subroutine locates pixels that are identified as agricultural land while the inner alters crop type to calculate yield for each agricultural pixel (five crop types).

Crop yield (YIELD) is determined individually for each pixel using the equation

$$\text{YIELD} = (\text{SFERT} \times \text{SL} \times \text{RF} \times (([V_{max},c] \\ \times ([\text{FERT},N] / ([K_s,c,N] + [\text{FERT},N])) \\ \times ([\text{FERT},P] / ([K_s,c,P] + [\text{FERT},P]))) + \\ [\text{RESID},c] \times \text{ERO}) \times \text{PER}$$

SFERT stands for the relative fertility of a pixel, based on annual average rainfall and inherent soil fertility; SL stands for the stochastic amount of sunlight (see cloud cover); RF is equal to the stochastic rainfall variation; $[V_{max},c]$ is the maximum growth for each individual crop c; $[\text{FERT},N]$ and $[\text{FERT},P]$ are the concentrations in kg/ha of N and P fertilizers respectively; $[K_s,c,N]$ and $[K_s,c,P]$ are the concentrations of fertilizers N and P that elicit half maximal growth for each crop c; $[\text{RESID},c]$ is the residual fertility of Eritrean soils for each crop c; and ERO is the cumulative yield decrease caused by erosion. The percent composition (PER) of each of the five crops in a pixel is dependent on the region of the country in which the pixel is located. An FAO survey divided Eritrea into fifty-six independent crop zones, each possessing a unique composition of crops (IGADD 1994). Yield is calculated using a Michaelis-Menten equation simulating response to nitrogen and phosphorus fertilizers for each individual crop type (*see* crop fertilizer response).

Additionally, YIELD is modified by sunlight, rainfall, the relative fertility of the land classes, and erosion. The relative fertility of land (SFERT; see agricultural expansion), sunlight (SL; see stochastic cloud cover), and rainfall (RF; see stochastic rain variation) may range from 1 (favorable for crops) to 0 (unfavorable to crops). Specifically, the erosion factor for each pixel is less than or equal to one and functions to lower yields by decreasing the residual fertility of land (RESID). Agricultural production for each pixel (APROD) is then calculated by multiplying YIELD by percentage of that land that the particular crop type occupies (PER) within the pixel. Total production (TOTPRD) is calculated by summing the agricultural production in all agricultural pixels. Livestock production is determined separately. The model assumes a starting livestock production (i.e., harvest) of 28,000 Mt (1997 levels). The model increases livestock production at a steady historical rate of approximately 10 percent per year, with a maximum production of fourteen times this amount.

I converted crop and livestock production from Mt to kcal by multiplying by 3.5 million and 5.0 million respectively based on calculations in Hall (2000). The moisture content of crops is approximated as 15 percent while no adjustment for moisture content of livestock is made. The calorie deficit (CALDEF) is determined by subtracting the national required calories (REQUIR) by the calories produced (TOTCAL). CALDEF is finally converted to the amount of humans requiring food imports (HUMCST) by dividing by 2,600 Kcal (daily minimum) × 365 days.

Crop fertilizer response: All agricultural data are from the FAO website (1999) unless otherwise stated. I determined total production and area harvested for five specific crops: maize, sorghum, pulses, barley, and wheat. Sorghum fertilizer intensity was unavailable so I substituted data for teff, a local grain that I felt would be similar. Hence,

sorghum yields per kg of fertilizer per hectare were calculated. Data for millet might be preferable but were not available.

Fertilizer usage was recorded originally as total national consumption for all crops. In order to calculate crop-specific usage, I derived estimates of crop-specific fertilization rates by way of an equation deemed acceptable by the International Fertilizer Research Institute (Hall 2000, chapter 12), which assumes that the fraction of fertilizer used on a given crop per fraction of total land area in that crop remained constant throughout the period analyzed. The equation requires values for the crop-specific rates for one year, and is as follows:

$$F_{c,yr} = [(F_{c,b}/F_{t,b})/(A_{c,b}/A_{t,b}] \times (A_{c,yr}/A_{t,yr}) \times F_{t,yr},$$

Where F is fertilizer consumption in tons, c denotes the specific crop of interest, yr stands for the year of interest, b refers to the base year, t represents total area of all crops or total amount of fertilizer used, and A is area. The ratio $[(F_{c,b}/F_{t,b})/(A_{c,b}/A_{t,b}]$ is assumed to remain constant for any crop (i.e., constant rate ratios). I determined the fertilizer input per hectare by dividing the result of the equation above by the land area for that crop. Crop-specific fertilization rates were not available for any year in Eritrea, and data from Ethiopia were used to determine the proportion of total fertilizer used on each crop. I believe this approach is valid because of the similarity in land and agricultural practices between the two countries and close physical proximity, although I also note that the main agricultural area of Ethiopia is somewhat wetter and cooler and has different soils. I also used these ratios to determine crop responses to fertilization based on data from Ethiopia, where there was a thirty-six-year time series available. I believe this to be a more dependable reflection of crop response to fertilization than whatever could be derived from the very limited data from Eritrea.

Both nitrogen and phosphorus were analyzed as all nitrogenous fertilizer and phosphate fertilizer, the only two classes of fertilizer reported for Eritrea (Ethiopia had minor applications of potassium). I used Ethiopian crop response to fertilizers as representative of Eritrean crop response to fertilizers as described above. I plotted crop yield against fertilizer input for both nitrogen and phosphorus to obtain maximum crop response (Vmax), half-maximal rate fertilizer concentration (Ks), and the residual yield with no fertilizer inputs (RESID). All crops appeared to be reaching fertilizer saturation. I adjusted Vmax for the fertility of the soil without fertilizer using the formula:

$$Vmax = Vmax–RESID$$

Where RESID is equal to yield per hectare with no fertilizer inputs. Vmax results were 1.1, 1.2, 0.6, 1.0, and 0.7 Mt/ha for sorghum, maize, barley, wheat, and pulses respectively. Nitrogen Ks results were 3, 1.5, 2, 4, and 0.1 kg/ha, and phosphorus Ks results were 3, 2, 2, 5, and 0.4 kg/ha for the same crops. Crop RESID results were 0.6, 0.8, 0.8, 0.6, and 0.6 Mt/ha respectively. These constants were used to calculate Eritrean crop production using a Michaelis-Menten type response formula described above.

Costs of inputs: The total yearly dollar cost for agricultural inputs (TOTCST) is divided into three parts: fertilizer costs (FERCST), pesticide costs (PSTCST), and cost for agricultural machinery (MCHCST). Statistics for agricultural inputs were incomplete (FAO), especially for years prior to 1998. Total agricultural land area for 1998 and 1999 was estimated by adding unconfirmed reports of 44,000 ha and 100,000 ha increases to the 1997 reported level of 393,000 ha for totals of 437,000 ha and 537,000 ha for 1998 and 1999 respectively.

I determined machinery costs per hectare for tractors and harvester-threshers by dividing the total 1998 import costs of each machine type by the increase in number of units for 1998 versus the number of units for 1997. The cost of tractors was $11,000 each and for harvester-threshers $3,000 each. I calculated the number of harvester-threshers required for land expansion by dividing the increases in harvester-threshers and tractors in 1998 (33 and 173) by the increase in land use (44,000 ha) to calculate 0.00075 harvester-threshers/new ha and 0.004 tractors/new ha. These amounts were multiplied by the cost of the machinery to obtain a rate of $2.25/new ha and $44.00/new ha for harvester-threshers and tractors respectively. Approximately $300,000 of the total

agricultural-based imports were not accounted for within direct FAO machine costs, so I assumed it to be for parts and maintenance costs ($0.70/total ha).

The data available for fertilizer use were recorded only as the quantity of imports without import price. I estimated price indirectly using available Ethiopian data for fertilizer imports. Ethiopia paid $905/Mt for nitrogen in 1997 and $90/Mt for phosphate in 1991. I multiplied the quantities of fertilizers imported by Eritrea in 1997 (5,000 Mt nitrogen and 1,000 Mt phosphorus) by the Ethiopian fertilizer prices to obtain a total cost for fertilizer ($4,615,000). The total fertilizer cost was divided by the total agricultural land in 1997 (393,000 ha) to calculate a rate of $11.75 fertilizer/total ha. Likewise, I determined pesticide costs by dividing the total pesticide costs for 1998 ($3,700,000) by the total land area used to obtain a rate of $8.50 of pesticide/total agricultural ha. The following equations are used to calculate the costs of machinery, pesticides, and fertilizers for total land:

$$MCHCST = (\$2.25 + \$44.00) \times New\ Land$$
$$+ (\$0.70) \times Total\ Land,$$
$$PSTCST = \$8.50 \times Total\ Land,$$
$$FERCST = \$11.75 \times Total\ Land/$$
$$\%\ Fertilizer\ Increase.$$

$$Total\ costs\ of\ all\ agricultural\ inputs =$$
$$MCHCST + PSTCST + FERCST$$

Accumulated cost (DEBT) is equal to the sum of the total costs for all years.

Energy use: I obtained data on energy use per year, along with electrical use by sector, from the Eritrean Energy, Resource, and Development webpage. Actual energy consumption rates before 1997 were unavailable but were extrapolated back using the current rate of increase in electrical use (10 percent) and current population growth rate. For years after 1997 the model assumes that electrical and fossil fuel rates will continue to increase 10 percent annually (rising affluence), while all forms of energy use will increase by the same rate as the population (2.3 percent). The model sets an upper limit on fossil fuel and electrical use at one hundred times the current rate, equal to current U.S. energy use levels, thus assuming eventually a

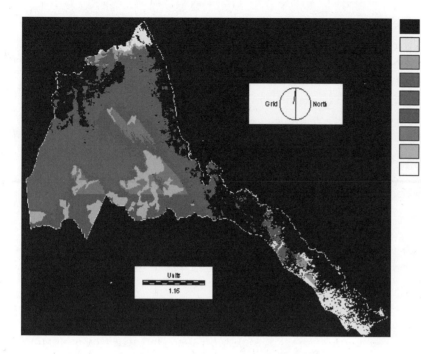

Figure 19.1. Simulated expansion of agriculture into lower-quality regions in Eritrea over a ten-year period of intense development. By 2007 all potential agricultural lands are utilized. White = Eritrean border; grey areas = agricultural land expansion over time; black = no crops or outside border (1998 is actual data). See http://web.syr.edu/~rebeal/EriPage2.html for originals.

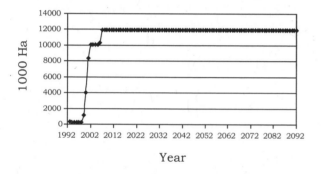

Figure 19. 2. Graphical representation of simulated expansion of agriculture in Eritrea over time.

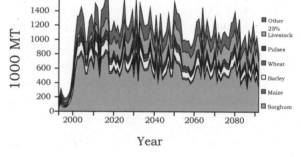

Figure 19.3. Predicted yields for five crops and livestock in Eritrea over a hundred-year period. A stochastic weather function varies year-to-year crop yields. The downward trend in the graph is due to an erosion function.

very high level of affluence.

Deforestation: FAO provided data of forested land for the years of 1993 and 1994. Forested land for 1997 was described as around 5 percent of total area by government estimates with a 10 percent annual decrease (Gebremedhin 1996). Government estimates were in agreement with FAO statistics, so I subtracted 10 percent of total hectares per year from 1994 levels to calculate forest levels for 1995–97. The model assumes an annual decrease of 10 percent of remaining forested land for years after 1997 as well, since the effects of both reforestation campaigns and increasing population are not clearly understood.

Results

The simulation model predicts that Eritrea may be nearing its biophysical carrying capacity already. Eritrea could run out of useable arable land by as early as 2007 under a scenario of maximum agricultural development for agricultural self-sufficiency (figure 19.1 and 19.2). The model predicts that agricultural land probably will be expanded in the central highlands first followed by the northern highlands and then the southern deserts (figure 19.1). This is due mainly to the low annual rainfall outside of the central highlands as well as the rocky terrain in the northern highlands. The simulation predicts that crop production initially will rise as land and fertilizer use expand (figure 19.3). However, the initial high rates of growth in total national crop yields eventually decline due to the utilization of less fertile lands for agriculture. Crop yields reach a maximum of approximately 1,200,000 Mt after only eight years. Additional increases in yields due to agricultural expansion and intensification are negligible as all good land would be in use and responses to fertilizers would be asymptotic.

Sorghum makes up the highest percentage of yields of the five crops. This reflects my assumption, based on historical data, that sorghum makes up a high percentage of agricultural crops in Eritrea, and it reflects the simulated agricultural expansion that moves progressively into lower-altitude regions of lower annual rainfall. Farmers in these drier regions favor lowland crops such as sorghum.

The results show that variation in rainfall could alter crop yields greatly if irrigation is not expanded as indicated by the large year-to-year variation in simulated crop yields (figure 19.3). The simulation also demonstrates the possible long-term effects of erosion on crop production. Total simulated crop production begins to decrease by 2020 due to the cumulative effect of erosion increases as shown by the declining trend in total production over time (figure 19.3). The model assumes a conservative annual erosion rate of 0.5 percent, which is likely to be an underestimation of the particularly high erosion rate found in Eritrea (see above). It is unlikely that Eritrean agriculture will remain sustainable if present erosion rates continue.

The number of people potentially supported by agriculture peaks in 2010, then decreases over time due to all arable land's already being utilized after only ten years of the simulation, the decreasing response of crops to fertilizers, and the increasing cumulative effect of erosion. The simulation shows that agricultural production in Eritrea will not be able to support the projected population after the year 2020. Although a conservative estimation of population growth was used in the simulation (2.3 percent), the results indicate that the population of Eritrea could reach 30 million by 2092 if the

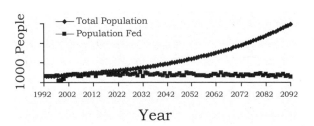

Figure 19.4. The simulated population of Eritrea over time (diamonds). The simulation uses the present growth rate of 2.3 percent. Population sustained by simulated Eritrean crop production (squares).

estimated current population growth rate were to continue. However, the simulated crop yields would support a maximum of only 5 million Eritreans, assuming a daily intake of 2,600 kcal/person/day. Moreover, the annual population supported by Eritrean agriculture would be affected greatly by the large annual variations in rainfall, including the possible effects of global climate change. Three-quarters of the population could require external food subsidies by 2075 based on the caloric productive content of Eritrean crops as indicated by the difference between the population requirements and the population supported by crop production (figure 19.4).

The slight dip observed in the number of people sustained by agriculture in figure 19.3 is a result of two main factors. The first is that Eritrea has supported up to 50 percent of its population using food subsidies historically (1993–97) and because the formula that controls agricultural expansion is dependent on the amount of agricultural land utilized in previous years. Since agricultural lands traditionally made up less than 5.0 percent of total land area in the years from 1993 to 1997, the amount of new land calculated by the agricultural expansion formula causes a slight lag in expansion during the first few years of the simulation. Hence, both factors combine to cause a dip in population sustained by food calories.

Eritrean agriculture may be unsustainable even sooner than this simulation suggests because of the enormous costs of agricultural inputs. Yearly costs of foreign inputs to agriculture could reach close to

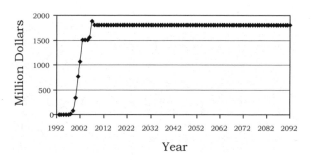

Figure 19.5 The simulated annual costs of agricultural inputs in Eritrea. Costs extrapolated from FAO statistics on Eritrean agriculture. Annual costs of agriculture may reach $1.8 billion by 2008.

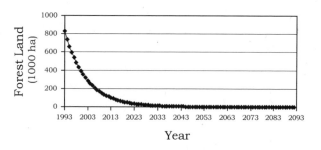

Figure 19.7. Forest land area in Eritrea over time. Deforestation algorithm based on observed reduction of 10 percent annually.

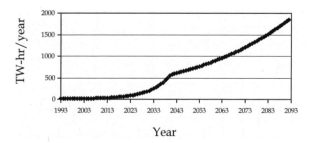

Figure 19.6. Simulated energy use in Eritrea over time. The rate of energy consumption is based on extrapolated population growth and a 10 percent annual increase in affluence.

$2 billion annually by 2008, as extrapolated from FAO statistics (figure 19.5). Foreign agricultural inputs include nitrogen and phosphorus fertilizers and machinery including tractors and harvester-threshers and their maintenance. Large amounts of foreign exchange would be needed to purchase these inputs to maintain the maximal levels of crop production. Other sectors of the economy would need to generate the necessary foreign exchange, since crop production would be fully utilized to sustain the Eritrean population. This would seem unlikely, since the entire Eritrean GDP was only $2.9 billion in 1999 (CIA 2000). Additionally, as we reach "the end of cheap oil," the prices of energy-intensive fertilizers relative to exports for Eritrea will increase enormously.

It is also unclear whether Eritrea will be able to meet the energy needs of its people if energy use continues to increase. Energy use increases quickly in the model, driven by population growth and affluence growth. Affluence reaches U.S. stan-

dards by 2040 at the inflection point in figure 19.6. Afterward, growth in energy use is driven by population growth only. Energy use conceivably could increase by eight orders of magnitude by 2092 as both population and affluence increase. However, it is not clear where this energy would come from, since Eritrea has few developed energy resources of its own other than forests. In fact, nearly 80 percent of Eritrea's present energy needs are met by biomass consumption. Such a system is unsustainable on biomass in a country with less than 4 percent of its land area in forests and where the demands for biomass have decreased forest cover by nearly 10 percent annually. The simulation model predicts that Eritrea could lose all forest cover by 2030 if the current rates of deforestation continue (figure 19.7). One possible resource would be the steady and intense winds at the Southern end of the Red Sea, but utilizing this would require large monetary and energy investments in windmills, and Eritrea simply does not have either.

Discussion

The results of this preliminary simulation show that agricultural production in Eritrea will not be able to support the projected population after the year 2020, even using a series of optimistic parameters. Although many of the simulated results are not precise, the qualitative implications of the analysis are almost certainly accurate: high rates of population growth are not sustainable by any conceivable development scheme. The only issue is exactly when the situation will become totally unsustainable. Eritrea appears to be closing in on its biophysical carrying capacity already, even if it is possible to intensify agricultural inputs greatly. This is due mainly to the high growth rate of the population combined with the biophysical limitations of water, soils, and biomass in this dry country.

The rate of agricultural expansion required to support the population over time without food imports is probably much too great to occur. However, the actual rate of agricultural expansion that could be maintained by the country is unclear at this time. An additional problem facing plans for Eritrean development is that the energy demands of the population will be unsustainable in a system supported mainly by biomass.

These results suggest that any hope for sustainability, indeed for any decent economic situation, requires stabilization of the population; erosion control must continue to have a high priority in national development; and it might be more economically efficient for Eritrea to develop sectors of its economy with a competitive advantage over other countries in the world market (i.e., manufacturing) to generate the foreign exchange necessary to import the required food calories. An economic policy that promotes growth in industry and trade seems possible considering that these sectors were projected to grow by 8–10 percent annually before the second war with Ethiopia in 1998.

Because future sustainability may depend on the generation of foreign exchange through industry and trade, it will be necessary to construct subunits within the model to simulate these economic components. However, even policies that concentrate on the growth of industry and trade will be unable to remain sustainable in the long run unless population growth is adequately controlled. Moreover, the energy needs to support such growth is limited by the energy constraints of the country. Eritrea has no fossil fuels, and although it has significant solar and wind resources, these remain underdeveloped. It is unlikely that a state possessing relatively few developed energy resources but a high dependency on energy will remain sustainable.

The assumptions of the model, although simplified, have allowed for the parameterization of many of the components and algorithms used in the simulation, facilitating future improvements in accuracy. Due to data limitations in the initial stages of model generation, future development of the agricultural component of the model will focus on expanding the number of crops simulated in the model and allowing for different levels of agricultural intensity. This will allow the user to choose different levels of agricultural intensity with different spatial distributions, enabling the user to maximize economic efficiency. Additionally, I will be adding subunits that will simulate natural ecosystems. Natural ecosystems such as forests will be under intense pressure due to an ever-increasing population. This will be due to humankind's need to expand food production and both energy-use and building materials. The long-term goal of this project will be to create a tool that decision makers will be able use to test the possible results of proposed development policies. Moreover, the model will include a number of biophysical constraints often overlooked in traditional economic models.

The agricultural outlook is bleak. Because of this, and because of my personal concern resulting from my Peace Corps experience in Eritrea and subsequent interactions with individual Eritreans and the seemingly very positive environment suggested by the regime of President Isaias Afwerki, I began to consider other possibilities. Circumstances united me, Charles Hall (coeditor of this volume), and Admiral Dino Naschetti, chief of research for the Italian navy. We looked at other resources that Eritrea might have. Due to the shape of the southern end of the Red Sea, there are near-constant, very strong winds in Eritrea, prevailing to the south. This is a world-class resource for windmills as reported by Van Buskirk and others (1996). That power could be used both locally and to generate hydrogen from adjacent seawater for some possible future hydrogen economy. The Italian navy is interested in this for three reasons: First, Eritrea was formerly an Italian colony, and maintains many close ties. Second, Italy is a rich country located near many poorer countries, and its navy has a big job trying to discourage illegal immigrants. The navy has concluded that it would be better to improve the local economies of these poorer countries than to police their emigrants. Third, new generation Italian submarines will be operating (very quietly) on hydrogen used in fuel cells. It seemed worth a try, and we had begun to recruit Italian donors, among them cities such as La Spezia and Italian windmill manufacturers. Unfortunately, in 2001 the politics of Eritrea changed, and this and other development projects were shelved.

Preliminary FAO agricultural studies of Eritrea in 2005 show that cereal yields will be sufficient to cover only 15 percent of the annual national cereal requirements. In fact, in the previous twelve years, only an average of about 30 percent of the annual national cereal requirements were covered by Eritrean agriculture (FAO 2005). These facts, in part, validate the major findings of this report. These are, essentially, that regardless of whatever good aspirations, personal energies, and political institutions one brings to the task, the actual possibilities must take into account the biophysical limitations of the land available.

References

CIA. 2000. World Fact Book 2000. www.cia.gov/cia/publications/factbook/geos/er.htm.

Collins, J. 1982. *What Difference Would a Revolution Make? Food and Farming in the New Nicaragua.* San Francisco: Institute for Food and Development Policy.

FAO. 2005. FAO/WFP crop and food supply assessment mission to Eritrea. www.fao.org/documents/show_cdr.asp?url_file=/docrep/007/J3959e/J3959e00.htm.

Gebremedhin, T. 1996. *Beyond Survival: The Economic Challenges of Agriculture and Development in Post-Independence Eritrea.* Asmara: Red Sea Press.

Hall, C.A.S., ed. 2000. *Quantifying Sustainable Development.* San Diego: Academic Press.

Hall, C.A.S., H. Tian, Y. Qi, G. Pontius, and J. Cornell. 1995. Modeling spatial and temporal patterns of tropical land use change. *Journal of Biogeography* 22: 753–57.

IGADD. 1994. CPSZ Viewer-2000: Crop Production System Zone Database Version 1.01.

IMF. 1999. Eritrea: Selected issues (1999). www.inf.org.

Pimentel, D. 1987. Soil erosion effects on farm economics. In J. M. Harlin and G. M. Berardi, eds., *Agricultural Soil Loss: Processes, Policies, and Prospects,* 217–41. Boulder, Colo.: Westview.

Ricardo, D. 1817. *The Principles of Political Economy and Taxation.* London: G. Bell and Sons.

Tesema, C. 1998. The Tef culture: Agroecology of Tef. http://wam.umd.edu/~tes/tef/agroeco.html.

USAID. 1999. USAID famine early warning system. www.fews.org/horn/fewshorn.html.

Van Buskirk, R., K. Garbosi, and K. Kello. 1996. Preliminary Wind Energy Resources Assessment for Eritrea, http://www.punchdown.org/rub/wind/WindREP796.html.

Van Buskirk, R. 2000. Eritrea Climate, Environment, and Technology Site. www.punchdown.org.rvb.

Wilkie, J. W., and A. Perkal, eds. 1985. *Statistical Abstract of Latin America* 23. Los Angeles: UCLA Latin American Center.

Woldu, T., and R. Van Buskirk. 1997. Remote sensing of biomass production, radiation distributions, and rainfall patterns. Senior thesis report, University of Asmara.

PART FOUR

Science for Development

Developing Social Models and Parameters

This section focuses on the adaptative capacity of people and society and how that relates to biophysical constraints and possibilities. Anthropologists, rural sociologists, and other social scientists (we will put economists aside for the moment—see part 6 of the book) often have an in-depth expertise of the terrain and are aware of the great diversity of representations, approaches, values, and modes of organization of human communities.

Social scientists have to deal with the overwhelming complexity of humans in the diversity of their actions and their potentials, which is a formidable challenge. Many end up telling stories, in a form that goes from fascinating essays to impenetrable jargon, and avoid generalization at all cost; they tend to ask "how" and not "why." Others will adopt a more "positivist" attitude, which is characteristic of the natural sciences. They will dissect a problem from multiple perspectives, and if and only if they feel that at least several are adequate to explain their observations will they attempt generalizations while including a careful assessment of their domain of validity (rural sociologists are notably cautious); and while they acknowledge that a true complex system is irreducible (that is, its global properties are critically dependent on all

the variables), they will try to simplify, characterize, and parameterize it. The three chapters of this section correspond to the second approach, the first being written by a physicist in a venture with rural sociology (and therefore very methodological in essence), the other two by rural sociologists having a bias toward quantification.

The purpose of most development is, at least ostensibly, to help the poor. But who are poor? What is it that they need? How do we insure that our best efforts in fact reach the people who need the most? And what is the role of science and modern scientific tools in this process? Chapter 20, by Grégoire Leclerc, attempts an answer to these questions. In chapter 21, Helle Munk Ravnborg and Jorge E. Rubiano challenge, with supporting quantitative analysis, the view of many agronomists and planners that the biophysical condition of land is the main determinant of land use. The success of development depends on the adequacy of the instruments put in place with respect to the people concerned. In chapter 22, Susan Allan and Dean Holland propose a simple method for constructing an empirical scale for assessing social capital, thus ensuring that the right social technology is planted in the right social soil.

CHAPTER 20

IMPROVING POVERTY-REDUCTION POLICIES, PART 1

Deriving Classic and Local Poverty Indicators

GRÉGOIRE LECLERC

Introduction

The objectives of development normally are to help the poor. But who are the poor, and how can we find where they live? How do we reach them in our development attempts? It is surprising to realize that these apparently simple questions have yet to be answered objectively even after billions of dollars have been invested in development programs. Typically, poverty is measured by computing how far a number of households stand with respect to a "poverty line" (e. g. the price of a minimum food basket). Based on this concept many economic analyses have "shown" that increased food production should have a positive impact on alleviation of the world's poverty (rural and urban population taken as a whole, in a pareto optimum). As a result (and the fear that countless developing countries people would succumb to famine because of high population growth) the Food and Agriculture Organization and the Consultative Group for International Agricultural research centers (CGIAR) have focused on alleviating hunger and poverty primarily through increases in food production, which made them key actors in the green revolution.

While the World Bank was funding most of the green revolution programs, its bilateral programs relied on essentially two poverty alleviation strategies: promoting structural adjustment programs (SAP) in developing countries and funding programs (mostly as a safety net to the SAP) on credit and infrastructure to protect that part of their population deemed vulnerable to the adjustment.

In more recent years, the linkage between these implicit and quasi-one-dimensional assumptions and the broader human conditions of well-being and poverty have been called into question.[1] This resulted in most development organizations' committing to a better understanding of the causes and dynamics of poverty and venturing into a much more complex domain than anticipated. On the other hand, there is increased concern about the relevance of a process traditionally engaged in by various development actors and about the best paths that lead to poverty alleviation. Apparently, the success of poverty alleviation programs is hardly related to factors that were used for their design. This perspective contradicts the accepted logical-positivist view that technical knowledge about poverty is linked directly to the policy message (McGee and Brock 2001). Technical knowledge, however, remains very influential in decision making, while the same poverty diagnostics procedures based on an economist's viewpoint continue to be the ones favored for development policy.

For example, the World Bank, after a self-assessment of the low efficiency of its former poverty-reduction strategy (and partly in response to worldwide criticism), seems to be willing to move toward a more integrated approach. A good example of the new World Bank paradigm comes in the form of a large-scale study referred to as *Voices of the Poor*, an unprecedented effort to gather, using participatory methods, the perceptions and aspirations of sixty thousand poor men and women from sixty countries. Unfortunately, not much seems to have happened since the final reports were written, and the standard procedure to estimate global poverty rates remains simply the $1 (or sometimes $2) per capita per day threshold (World Bank 2001).[2]

In parallel, most development NGOs, which have traditionally opted for bottom-up approaches focusing on local development—while rejecting World Bank–type poverty alleviation programs designed from the top—are now asking for better information and science to achieve impact beyond the intervention areas and to connect their work with broader-scale initiatives (Webb, Woo, and Sant'Anna 1995).

Finally, many governments of developing countries have set up highly targeted and uniform policy instruments to fight poverty that are adjusted to local conditions (e.g., through their own poverty estimates and poverty maps) as well as to the requirements of development banks.

Consequently, it is extremely difficult to do a nationwide characterization of poverty (or its alleviation programs) that is acknowledged as appropriate by all development players. On the one hand, specific surveys (e.g., living standards measurement surveys, or LSMS) are not only expensive and time consuming, but are also biased toward a first-world economist's view. Participatory poverty assessments, or PPA (Grandin 1988), are also extremely time-consuming and therefore generally done in only a few communities, are often affected by reliability problems (Bergeron, Sutkover, and Medina Banegas 1998), and generally cannot be extrapolated beyond the study sites.

On the other hand, comprehensible information is available nationwide from surveys such as housing and agricultural censuses. These censuses are done with the purpose of characterizing demography and agriculture (to help governments and banks) and not specifically to estimate poverty.[3] Several studies, mostly from World Bank researchers, have linked surveys such as the LSMS to censuses via regressions (a method known as small area estimations) to improve the geographical detail and comprehensiveness of poverty maps (Hentschel et al. 1998; see also Henninger 1998 and Davis 2003 for reviews of poverty mapping methods). Censuses are so detailed, however, that it should be possible to connect them with full local assessments such as PPAs and, taking advantage of their wide geographical coverage, map the local knowledge at the scale of the country.

The focus of this chapter and its counterpart, chapter 36, is to summarize our work that does just that for Honduras. I examine methodological issues related to the characterization, measurement, representation, and geography of poverty. Although a large body of literature can be found on the subject, traditional methods address facets of poverty not easily related to agriculture and natural resource–management decision making (Carvalho and White 1997). In 1997, the International Center for Tropical Agriculture (CIAT) embarked on a research project to define a unique approach linking commonly used ad hoc measurements with geographical representations of poverty from community-level, locally constructed well-being rankings (Ravnborg 1999) to standardized maps of national-level rankings. Contrary to proposing a single, unifying poverty index, such as proportion of population below a given income value, we support the design of indexes that target the specific needs of various decision makers, including Ravnborg's well-being index. This poses, however, a formidable challenge. In effect, a prerequisite for catalyzing collective action is a shared vision, and shared visions cannot be created and communicated using unrelated component images. Adopting a standard poverty measure helps everyone to rally to the same perception (for good and bad), while these different viewpoints on poverty that I propose to explore will have to be exchanged and discussed to catalyze collective action. We (myself and colleagues such as Ravnborg) take the position that poverty reduction is a process where several viewpoints (hence poverty measures and representations) must be compared and argued.

In this chapter I start by showing how the richness of raw (political unit–level) national census data can be used to produce nationwide poverty indexes tailored to particular needs. I then introduce the results of the independent study by Ravnborg (1999) where locally relevant indicators of well-being were determined by analyzing information collected through participatory exercises in ninety Honduran villages. I then link these two independent, ad hoc databases, one derived from national censuses and the other from village-level questionnaires, by standardizing the unit of analysis. The result can be viewed as an example of a common knowledge base that can help bridge the communication gap between national perspectives and local community perspectives, in which affordable information technology plays a key role.

In chapter 36, I examine methodological issues for contrasting several representations of poverty indicators (including the ones derived here) for various aggregation levels and classification choices to illustrate the effect they may have on poverty alleviation policy. I complete the study by describing a prototype of a simple, user-friendly interface to raw census data to allow others to represent poverty in various ways and explore without restraint from the World Wide Web.

Materials and Methods
The Honduras Population, Housing, and Agriculture Censuses

Compared to other poor countries, Honduras has an exceptional national dataset. The 1988 Honduras population and housing censuses are the most recent and complete data set available about every single person and household in the country. They give a panorama of the composition of Honduran society and of the life conditions of its inhabitants in 1988. They contain answers that the 4,255,105 individuals—the entire population—gave on a given Sunday (29 May 1988) to questions related to their education level, profession or vocation, family composition, age, mortality, migration, housing type and construction materials, ownership type, water supply, assets, and so forth. In total, there were forty-two variables for 891,298 households and forty-nine for each individual, in addition to nine variables related to administrative localization of the household. The data-collection phase of population and housing censuses takes only one day, but it takes years to prepare and another year before the first results are published.

The 1993 Honduras Agricultural census is the most exhaustive data set related to agriculture. It covers all farms[4] in Honduras (317,199, to be precise) and was updated by the 2001 census.[5] In total, 161 variables covered landownership, agricultural production, technology, and labor, as well as 6 variables about the farmer and 8 variables related to administrative localization of the farm. The data collection, coordinated by the Secretariado de Planificación (SECPLAN)[6] in accordance with the Ministry of Natural Resources, was conducted from 26 April to 15 May 1993. Data on number and area of holdings, land tenure, and land use, shown below, refer to the 1989 Survey. Data on temporary and permanent crops refer to the period 1 May 1992–30 April 1993. Data on livestock numbers refer to 25 April 1993. Many people state that agricultural censuses are error-prone, as farmers will avoid giving to government officials detailed information that would give the government a chance to invade their privacy. Because census information comes without an error estimate, it is impossible to know the accuracy of census information without a "true" sample to use for comparison. In the absence of an exhaustive accuracy check of the census, assessments (and improvements) should be done on a case-by-case basis. For example, we show in this chapter that censuses were accurate enough to provide good well-being estimates at the village level.

The census results are compiled at the municipality (*municipio*) and department (*departamento*) levels in tables distributed within several thick books (RH 1989–90a, 1989–90b, 1994b). This tradition is likely to evolve, as more developed Latin American countries are delivering municipality-level census data via the internet or on CD.

In 1996, the Statistics Bureau of Honduras provided us with a unique opportunity: access to the complete censuses in a raw, unit-level format, which we loaded into a large MySQL database. Confidentiality was partially fulfilled by omitting the names of the individuals. However, geographical coding was still too fine to prevent disclosure of information about individuals (Duke-Williams and Rees 1998). The population and housing censuses are linked through a twenty-three-digit household ID, which unfortunately has no connection to the agricultural twelve-digit one (at the farm level). This means that we cannot join the three censuses at household/farm level, but at one level above, that is, the village. The three censuses are loaded as fifteen tables (one for population, one for housing, and thirteen for agriculture) that occupy a total of 790 MB, which can be held on one DVD disk. The tables are indexed through household or farm ID to speed up queries from linked tables.

The basic geographical database that we wished to link to the censuses consist of a *departamento* coverage (18 departments as polygons, scale 1:100,000), a *municipio* coverage (292 municipalities as polygons, scale 1:100,000), and an *aldea* coverage from SECPLAN (3,729 villages as points, scale 1:50,000; there are 3,742 villages in the census)[7]. To make representations at all administrative levels uniform, point coverages were also generated from the centroids of the departamento and municipio coverages, and a polygon coverage representing the area of influence of villages was created from the aldea point coverage (see chapter 28).

Deriving Compound Indexes from Raw Census Data
Background

The methodology we followed here draws from the traditional index of "unsatisfied basic needs" (UBN) and its cousin, the Human Development Index (HDI-UNDP 2000). The UBN approach has been adopted for at least eleven countries in Latin America because it incorporates important variables for the formulation of social policies (Boltvinik 1996). In the case of Honduras, SECPLAN made the first use of census data for poverty targeting in 1990 and developed the methodology in the following years (RH 1996). However, the U.S.-inspired "national security doctrine" during the 1980s stifled academic freedom and led to the abandonment of micro-level economic or social analyses, especially about rural areas, in favor of "letting the market resolve all issues," resulting in a shortage of information (Thorpe 1993).

I would like to emphasize that our choice of poverty indicators is not meant to be unique (or the best, or that of CIAT), and that the indicators selected are mainly illustrative. Many prefer UBNs, but censuses are so rich that many other indexes can be defined to suit particular needs: for example, poverty line indexes such as the FGR (Foster, Greer, and Thorbecke 1984) or "decomposable inequality" indexes such as the one proposed by Theil (1989). They can be adapted or even twisted to highlight a particular interest or perspective or aggregation level.

UBN methods involve the selection of a certain number of indicators that form a representative set of basic needs, the definition of a normative threshold (i.e., minimum criteria to be satisfied for each need), and the combination into poverty indexes and head counts. Therefore, according to this approach, poverty is linked to the deficiency or deprivation of the goods and services necessary to sustain life at an absolute minimum standard. In the Latin American practice, the UBNs are generally a set of poverty-related factual indicators that include a large number of people sharing a room; improvised or inadequate housing; inadequate water supply and inadequate sewer systems; low school attendance for children; and inadequate household capacity to generate income. Other factors such as lack of participation in collective decisions, social marginalization, and powerlessness are thought to be implicitly correlated to UBNs, and therefore no attempt is made to measure these dimensions separately.

The Honduras social investment fund (FHIS) uses its own index based on UBNs (sometimes complemented by a malnutrition index) for targeting the projects for its poverty reduction program (RH 1994a, 2001; Webb, Woo, and Sant'Anna 1996); many outside FHIS use this index, too. I examine in chapter 36 how the risk of leakage and undercoverage is related to the choice of indicators and to the way they are computed. I emphasize the need, depending on the situation, for a system to help the computation of customized poverty indexes, with a rigorous and standard framework in parallel that would allow cross-country comparisons.

Methodology for deriving an index of unsatisfied basic needs (UBN)

We followed a scheme very close to the one adopted in the elaboration of Bolivia's *Mapa de pobreza* (RB 1995), a multi-institutional effort that took advantage of unit-level census data to produce a very complete set of poverty data and maps for Bolivia. More details can be found in Oyana et al. (1998) and Couillaud (1998). The UBN index derived would fall into the "generalized-improved" (UBN-GI; see Boltvinik 1997) category, since they include a wide range of variables such as non-land assets or education. The UBNs are computed for each household and then aggregated at the village, municipality, or department level by counting the fraction of the population in a particular UBN stratum. In the equation below, the variables selected to build the UBNs are labeled x_j, the subscript j representing the household, and x the variable. For certain variables, such as the education level of a household j, the value is computed for the household from the value for each individual i forming the household. Only the 1988 population and housing censuses, linked at the household level, were used to derive these indicators.

First, we have to define x^*, the *normative threshold (or acceptable value) for variable x*. This is where the knowledge of the area and the local/national context play a crucial role. It is also at this step where subjectivity (and gross errors) are most likely to occur and lead to diverging conclusions. For the current example, the normative threshold that we used for a given variable was derived as the *average value of that variable for the country*. In that sense, the particular poverty measure that we are developing here corresponds roughly to a measure of equity (i.e., a value relative to the national average), which can help orient internal social adjustments (if this is what the governing elite wants to happen).

Second, we define an *index of failure to obtain x** for household j, cx_j, as follows:

$$cx_j = 1 - \frac{x_j}{x^*}$$

The cx are then normalized between -1 and $+1$ to allow comparison: if $cx_j < 0$, we divide cx_j by $\min(cx)$ and if $cx_j > 0$, cx_j is divided by $\max(cx)$. In other words, cx_j is a normalized distance between current condition and the condition defined by x^*.

The compound indexes UBN3 (a combination of three indexes) and UBN4 (a combination of 4 indexes that is closer to UNDP HDI) are obtained for each household by averaging several more specific indexes, which themselves are the result of the combination of more basic ones (i.e., the cx). This is detailed below (see also figure 20.1).

For each household j, we define:

$$UBN3_j = \frac{(CV_j + CSIB_j + CIA_j)}{3}$$

$$UBN4_j = \frac{(CV_j + CSIB_j + CIA_j + RE_j)}{4}$$

where:

CV_j = lack of housing size and quality
$CSIB_j$ = lack of basic services and energy
CIA_j = lack of non-land assets
RE_j = lack of education

Note that no information on land tenure appears in the population and housing censuses (but it does in the agricultural one).

CV_j, the *index of lack of housing size and quality*, was derived from an index of the size of the house CEV_j, and from an index of housing quality CMV_j:

$$CV_j = \frac{(CMV_j + CEV_j)}{2}$$

CMV_j is the average between lack of wall quality (cm_j), roof quality (ct_j), and floor quality (cp_j). A dirt floor, for example, indicates a lack of floor quality. $CSIB_j$, the *index of lack of basic services and energy sources*, is the average between the lack of basic services CSB_j, and of energy deficiency CE_j:

$$CSIB_j = \frac{(CSB_j + CE_j)}{2}$$

CSB_j is computed as the average of water source quality cag_j, lack of water supply infrastructure ctu_j, and lack of latrines csa_j. CE_j is the average between the lack of electricity cal_j and of fuel cco_j (fuelwood excluded).

CIA_j, the *index of lack of non-land assets*, is derived from three indicators: the lack of household appliances (CBA_j), of means of transportation (CTA_j), and telecommunication (CCA_j). The first is the average of lack of sewing machine, refrigerator, and stove. The second is the average of lack of car, of motorcycle/moped, and of bicycle. The third is the average of the index of lack of radio and television. CIA_j is then computed as:

$$CIA_j = 0.25 \times CBA_j + 0.4 \times CTA_j + 0.35 \times CCA_j$$

The choice of weight in this equation is clearly a question of preferences or interests.

RE_j, the *index of lack of education* for each household, is computed from data from individuals i belonging to household j. The index of success of the individual within the household, $ane_{i,j}$, is computed as follows:

$$ane_{i,j} = \frac{ap_{i,j} + as_{i,j}}{ap* + as*} \cdot al_{i,j}$$

where:

   $ap_{i,j}$ is the number of years of schooling
   $as_{i,j}$ is the index of school attendance in
      function of age,
   $al_{i,j}$ is the index of literacy
   $ap*$ is the normative threshold for school
      attendance in function of age,
   $as*$ is the normative threshold for student
      status.

The index of education deficiency for each individual, $re_{i,j}$ is given by:

$$re_{i,j} = 1 - ane_{i,j}$$

Finally, RE_j is computed as the average of the $re_{i,j}$ for household j.

Before proceeding further, I would like to emphasize that indicators chosen to be included must have an objective social existence, which—ideally—would have to be validated by the poor themselves. Ravnborg (1999) describes a methodology to obtain indicators in a participatory way, which I describe briefly later. Many have accepted the view that the idea of absolute need has no sense in societies in a constant process of change and adaptation, and therefore discredit any attempt to quantify poverty. Others, such as Pradhan and Ravallion (2000), are finding innovative ways to obtain a subjective poverty line from qualitative assessments of perceived consumption. By using a normative threshold defined by a country

average, we tend to examine equity issues and adjust to the reality of a country, which may be safer than imposing our perception of an absolute threshold. Still, doing so poses the hypothesis that there is one reality for all of Honduras, one scale of values, and this can lead to gross errors. For example, not having an automobile in a region where transportation is done on waterways is not necessarily a disadvantage (while having a motorized boat is definitely a plus), but there is no information about ownership of a boat in the censuses.

Aggregation of household-level indexes

Household indexes georeferenced for each village can be aggregated and mapped at virtually any scale given predetermined boundaries: it can be village, watershed, or area of influence of a village, municipality, department, or country. Aggregation, which is a necessary step to protect the privacy of census information (Duke-Williams and Rees 1998), also synthesizes and reduces the volume of data to a more manageable level. For poverty indexes or any of their components, we can produce mean or median values, or count the proportion of a given population considered as poor.

In order to illustrate our process, we chose a headcount approach: we estimate the proportion of households where UBN is between 0.4 and 1 (i.e., the proportion of households where unmet basic needs is in the lowest 20 percentile range). Two indexes (which we call PUBN3 and PUBN4) are obtained from UBN3 and UBN4, respectively, for various aggregation levels. We did this only when we could characterize the poverty index for more than 50 percent of the households in a given village. In effect, there are cases where the data are not complete and do not allow us to compute an index from all the variables. For example, we found that regions of high population density are more error-prone (Leclerc, Nelson, and Knapp 2000). Our results are presented in the results section.

This approach should be generally useful for those who wish to experiment and to use census data to its full potential. All the steps to process unit-level data into UBNs can be realized through a series of Structured Query Language (SQL) scripts that allow full automation. In addition,

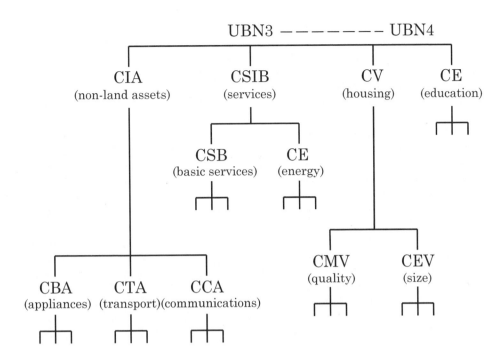

Figure 20.1. Schematic representation of the hierarchy of our Unsatisfied Basic Needs Index (UBN). UBN4 is essentially the same as UBN3, but includes an additional indicator related to education.

there is very little effort required to put the power of the raw census in the hands of any user through the Internet. Thus a simple Web-based interface can provide to a remote user the capacity to produce a poverty index for a special-purpose thematic criterion, through SQL queries with any variables of interest, any weights or ways of combining them, and the choice of any aggregation level, on a central computing facility (Openshaw 1995). An example of low-cost, user-friendly Web interface to unit census data is introduced in chapter 36.

Poverty indexes do not necessarily have to be UBNs. Other indexes, such as innovative ones based on local perceptions, can also be processed from census data, as I shall describe in the next sections.

The Well-being Index, Based on Local Perceptions

The work of Ravnborg (1999) on the identification, extrapolation, and quantification of local perceptions of poverty (or its antithesis, well-being) is certainly a breakthrough for the derivation of alternative regional poverty profiles. Ravnborg conducted a traditional participatory well-being ranking study,[8] but with a fundamental element added: selecting study sites as a designed experiment to allow for extrapolation to areas different than the ones studied. This was a strategy to avoid what

Rhoades (1999), in his essay about participatory methodologies, describes as "the social underdesign of projects." Instead of seeking representative subjects—that is, finding "average" villages in which to conduct the study—the aim was to select a large set of contrasting villages. This would maximize the chance of obtaining all possible indicators (and therefore ensure that we do not miss anyone, even if in the minority), but also would allow the investigators to conclude, if some indicators are found across all communities despite their dissimilarities, that these indicators are generic (or at least valid for all communities from which the sample was taken).

Obtaining well-being indicators that can be extrapolated

First, Ravnborg made assumptions with respect to factors that would influence poverty in Honduras, and selected ninety villages in three departments according to a maximum variability strategy (figure 20.2).[9]

In each village Ravnborg worked with three to five informants of different age, gender, occupation, and ethnicity to avoid the informant-related bias typical of participatory studies (Bergeron, Sutkover, and Medina Banegas 1998). The informants were asked to examine a set of cards, each of which represented a household, and to group the cards

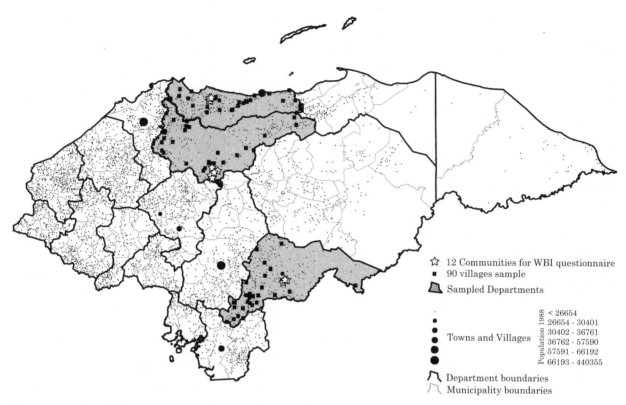

Figure 20.2. Map of Honduras, showing departments sampled by Ravnborg (1999) (shaded), the ninety villages where she obtained the well-being indicators (large squares), and the twelve villages where she used the well-being questionnaire (stars).

into a few stacks according to their perception of the well-being[10] or quality of life of the households. Generally, one will end up with three stacks (not poor, not-so-poor, and poor) according to how each informant perceives poverty, and then the informant describes their content. Strictly speaking, the groupings and the descriptions are valid only for the informant's community and cannot be extrapolated to other ones.

The set of all informant's descriptions were the base for the identifications of well-being indicators. From the 316 descriptions of well-being obtained, Ravnborg extracted almost 400 indicators, which were subsequently reinterpreted and reduced to 11. These indicators were subsequently transformed into quantifiable ones, such as housing, market access, or health (table 20.1). Therefore, Ravnborg found a way to quantify local perceptions of well-being by means of a simple household questionnaire that asks participants to score eleven indicators (I will later refer to this as the well-being questionnaire). The resulting well-being index (*WBI*) is simply the average of the score of all indicators that apply for

that household. Once all *WBI* are obtained, the distribution is split into three categories (highest, middle, lowest) in order to reflect as much as possible the well-being categories defined by the informants (not poor, not so poor, poor). The well-being questionnaire is straightforward, uses simple words, and takes only fifteen to thirty minutes to complete for each household, and can be used to obtain quickly and inexpensively a poverty profile for a region of interest.

Ravnborg ends up with an index that does not look drastically different from other published ones (such as UBNs), but that has a major advantage: it is constructed entirely from the perceptions that the poor have about their own poverty. In a way, it is a message from the poor about what really matters to them, which they are addressing to decision makers. For example, the poor seem to care more about farming and less about sewage or drinking water, quite a different perception from UBNs! The extrapolation and mapping of the well-being index is no more than a translation of this message into a language more familiar to policy makers.

Table 20.1. Summary of indicators of local perceptions of well-being

Indicator	Score	Description
Land Ownership	33	The household owns 4 *manzanas* (1 manzana = 0.7 ha) or more, or has land in pasture or gives land in rent to other farmers
	67	Household owns land but fewer than 4 manzanas (2.8 ha) and doesn't have land in pasture or land in rent to other farmers
	100	Household does not own land or only owns the house and land upon which it stands
Sell day labor	33	Nobody in the household works as a day laborer and the housewife does not do housework for other families or prepare food to sell
	67	Someone in the household works as a day laborer but either for fewer than nine months or for more than nine months but fewer than three times a week
	100	Someone in the household works full-time for more than nine months a year as a day laborer or the housewife does housework for other families or sells prepared food
Income	33	Someone in the household is a professional, a businessman, or a merchant, or children or other relatives send remittances
	67	Someone in the household is a skilled worker but no one in the household is a professional, businessman, or merchant, and the household receives no remittances
	100	No one in the household is a professional, businessman, merchant, or skilled laborer, and the household receives no remittances
Hire day labor	33	Household contracts day labor
	67	Household does not contract day labor
Cattle ownership	33	The household has cattle
	67	The household does not have cattle
Animal ownership	33	The household owns horses, pigs, or oxen
	67	Household owns chickens but not horses, pigs, or oxen
	100	Household owns no animals
Housing	33	Household owns its own house and it is of good quality
	67	Household owns its own house but it is not of good quality
	100	Household owns its own house but it is of very poor quality or does not own its own house
Market participation	33	Household grows coffee or cacao, or household does not buy basic grains and sells half or more of its production of basic grains
	67	Household does not grow coffee but buys and sells basic grains, or the household does not buy basic grains and sells less than half of its production
	100	Household does not grow coffee or cacao, and buys basic grains in addition to using all of its production for home consumption
Money	33	Household has a savings account or makes loans to others
	67	Household does not save or make loans
Health	67	No one in the house was sick or if someone were sick he/she paid for adequate health care either with own money or by selling assets
	100	Someone in the household has health problems and they were treated by asking relatives for money, borrowing money, or by going to the herbalist, or they were untreated for lack of money
Food security	67	Household has not experienced a food shortage, or did for less than a week and solved it without having to ask others for food or money, to reduce number of meals, or to send the wife or children out to work
	100	Household experienced a food shortage for more than a week, or of less than a week but then had to solve it by asking for food, by borrowing money, or by sending wife and children out to work

A higher score is associated with a condition with less wealth. The overall well-being index is the average of scores for all indicators.

A poverty profile for selected communities

The well-being questionnaire has been employed by Ravnborg and her team to quantify the well-being of 768 households, as part of a larger study to identify factors that lead to certain preferences related to agriculture and NRM (Ravnborg 2002; see also chapter 21). The households were selected at random and belong to twelve communities (between 12 and 55 households per village) distributed among three hillside watersheds located in distinctly different social and climatic environments (see figure 20.2). This sampling design allows deriving statistically valid poverty profiles for each sampled village and watershed. Ravnborg gave us access to the database obtained, which allowed us to validate the extrapolation of the well-being index (*WBI*) to the entire country (see next section).

It appears that the well-being index obtained by Ravnborg follows a normal distribution with standard deviations in the order of 0.17 (*WBI* on a 0–1 scale). This will help us improve our capacity to predict proportions of poor based on the average value of the *WBI* (see the appendix).

Computing a Well-being Index from Secondary Data

The question is now to examine how I will obtain the locally derived indicators of poverty from ancillary information such as censuses. Two approaches are possible. The first is to explain the *WBI* with census data (i.e., regression);[12] the other is to compute it directly by averaging individual indicators.

Because of the constraints with our datasets,[13] I chose to compute a village average well-being index. It is obtained as the average of well-being indexes for each household of the village:[14]

$$WBIc = \text{mean}(WBIc)$$

Therefore I did not adjust, or calibrate, from the *WBI* data obtained by Ravnborg, like in a regression model (see Bigman et al. 1999 for a model-based validation), but validated my results a posteriori. In the next section I show how I succeed in deriving an index from the census data, which covers the entire country, that agrees with Ravnborg's well-being index.

Computing the Well-being Index with Proxy Variables Obtained from the Census

We can obtain two hundred variables from the population, housing, and agricultural censuses taken together, and I should be able to obtain a good approximation of Ravnborg's eleven indicators from these (table 20.1). However, Ravnborg used a rather strict definition of how these indicators are quantified into two or three categories and combined to give the well-being index. The well-being questionnaire has well-defined questions that allow well-defined calculations in this context, but not necessarily in the context of the censuses. Let us take the example of Ravnborg's indicator of health in Table 20-2.

Clearly, it is impossible to find this exact indicator in the censuses. The population census would be an appropriate source for a proxy and I used it, in fact, to compute an indicator that had no resemblance to this description. The proxy that I used for health is typical for poverty estimates, but I found poor correlation with the locally defined health indicator for the twelve villages, as expected.

A simpler example is cattle ownership as shown in Table 20.3. This indicator can easily be found in the agricultural census, but we have to be aware those agricultural censuses are notably error

---

Table 20.2. Well-being indicator related to health (from table 20.1)

Indicator	Score	Description
Health	67	No one in the house was sick, or if someone were sick he/she paid for adequate health care either with his or her own money or by selling assets
	100	Someone in the household has health problems and they were treated by asking relatives for money, borrowing money, or by going to the herbalist, or they were untreated for lack of money

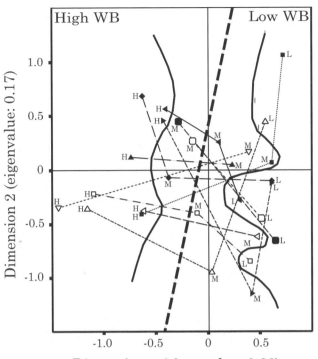

◁ Hire day labour	
△ Land ownership	
○ Health	
▫ Market involvement	
▶ Sell day labor	
◀ Income	
▽ Cattle ownership	
▲ Money	
◆ Housing quality	
▪ Animals ownership	
● Food security	

Figure 20.3. Homogeneity plots (from Ravnborg et al. 1999) showing the contribution of indicators to well-being levels High (H), Medium (M), and Low (L) in a reduced dimensionality. The thick solid line represents an approximate boundary to separate the H, M, and L categories. The dashed line is the approximate boundary between the higher and lower well-being (*WB*).

Table 20.3. Well-being indicator related to cattle ownership (from table 20.1)

Indicator	Score	Description
Cattle ownership	33	The household has cattle
	67	The household does not have cattle

prone. The farmer may declare fewer cows than he actually owns to avoid taxes; in fact the larger the wealth, the higher the probability of lying on assets (RH 1994a). In addition, the agricultural census was designed to provide reliable information at the municipal level, so data from individual farms must be used with care.

To increase the reliability of census-based proxies, I had to simplify Ravnborg's indicators. I redefined each of the eleven indicators so that they represent only two levels, lower and higher well-being, and assign them a value of 1 and 0, respectively. In other words, I have set a threshold that marks the boundary between lower well-being and higher well-being for each indicator. This did not

change significantly the value of *WBI* (when scaled within 0–1 instead of Ravnborg's 33–100 range) and simplifies our task considerably.

I reinterpreted Ravnborg's homogeneity plots[15] (figure 20.3) to obtain an indication of what this threshold can be for each indicator. I delimited the boundary between Ravnborg's lower, middle, and higher well-being categories (thick solid line),[16] and by drawing a line between the two boundaries I could estimate the midpoint value that separates the higher and lower well-being (dashed line) for each indicator.[17]

If we take the example of cattle ownership, the boundary between the poorer and the richer corresponds to only one cow (since the division is much closer to the low well-being category), so the proportion of poorer farmers, according to this indicator only, is the number of farmers with no cows divided by the total number of farmers. The proportion is also equal to the average value for this indicator when it is scaled in the 0–1 range.

I screened the census to identify which variables would provide proxies—that is, indicators that most closely resembled Ravnborg's eleven indicators (see Table 20.1) and ended with nine *Ic*s ("Indicator from Census"), summarized in table 20.4. Four proxies can be obtained from the

Table 20.4. Proxies of Ravnborg (1999) well-being indicators, obtained from the 1988 population and housing census and the 1993 agriculture census of Honduras

Ravnborg's well-being Indicator	My Census variable (proxy)	Source (census)
Cattle ownership	Total cattle heads	Agriculture 93
Hire day labor	Total workers with pay	Agriculture 93
Landownership	Size of exploitation	Agriculture 93
Health	Number of children dead/total number of children; urban or rural area	Population 88
Sell day labor	Relation to head of family; activity; class of activity; Urban or rural area; Total hours worked/number of people in household	Population 88
Housing	Ownership; Roof material, Walls material; Floor material; Urban or rural area	Housing 88
Animal ownership	Total number of pigs, horses, oxen, mules, chicken, hens, sheep, other poultry, rabbits	Agriculture 93
Market participation	Production of permanent crops, other annual crops; quantity of basic grains sold/Production of basic grains	Agriculture 93
Income	Occupation code; urban or rural area	Population 88

population and housing censuses and five from the agricultural census.[18] In the case of the population and housing censuses, I restricted the calculation to rural households, identified as such in the censuses.[19] This accounted, in 1988, for approximately 60 percent of the total Honduras population and 70–80 percent of the poor (RH 1994a). All farms of the agricultural census were assumed to be rural ones.

If both censuses could be joined at household level, it would be possible to compute a *WBI* for each household and then compute summary values for various levels of aggregation. But this is not the case: the agricultural census is independent of the other two, and all three are necessary.[20] However, since the *WBI* is a linear combination of indicators, I can compute a *WBIc* for each village (that is, the average of well-being index from census *Ic*) from the mean of each indicator:

$$WBIc = \text{mean}(Ic_1, Ic_2, \ldots Ic_9)$$

Results

My main results are that the indexes most usually used to characterize poverty did not, in fact, do a particularly good job of that, while a different index derived from census data and the perceptions of the people themselves on agriculture, population, and housing information did. The results are detailed throughout this section.

The census-based unsatisfied basic needs (UBN), which are typical of poverty measures used by decision makers, did correlate well with published poverty measures for Honduras, which was to be expected since the same census data and the perception of the people themselves and essentially the same method were used. It appears, however, that the composition of the indicator matters more than we may think: correlation between $PUBN_3$ and $PUBN_4$ was only 0.83 at village level, despite the fact that $PUBN_4$ is identical to $PUBN_3$ except for an additional education parameter, and the fact that both indexes are computed from the same census data. This means that 17 percent of the people who we think are poor according to one index are not poor according to another, almost identical one. This is not very surprising, inasmuch as many regions, especially remote rural areas, may simply lack schools or access to education while land quality and use may be similar. Similarly, the regional pattern of poverty changes rapidly and, in extreme cases, almost arbitrarily with the choice of poverty indicator.

Table 20.5. Correlation coefficients between population and housing census indicators, computed from municipality-level data

	CV (housing)	CSIB (services)	CIA (non-land assets)	CE (education)
CV	1	0.79	0.76	0.70
CSIB	0.79	1	0.58	0.51
CIA	0.76	0.58	1	0.59
CE	0.70	0.51	0.59	1

I also found that the UBNs were correlated only weakly, at the village level, to actual household well-being indexes (*WBI*) as obtained by Ravnborg, which raises the question of relevance of standard estimates for targeting: the poor people as defined by top-down UBNs are apparently not the ones that populations think they need the most.

On the other hand the village-average well-being index that I computed from both agricultural and population/housing censuses coincided extremely well ($R^2=0.9$) with actual village data collected by Ravnborg in 1999. This attests to the robustness of my method, given the fact that two censuses were combined (thus a possibility of multiplying the errors), and given the time lag of five to nine years between the census data and the validation data. But these promising results also revealed some other not-so-good ones: there has been little improvement in the condition of the rural poor, as measured from the viewpoint of local perceptions, during the 1990s. Therefore the Honduras structural adjustment programs of the 1980s and '90s (Thorpe 1993), and the safety nets that were put in place to counterbalance their possible negative impacts, have apparently not resulted in any improvement of rural well-being.

Census-based UBNs and Their Comparison with the WBI

The results of aggregation of our basic UBNs obtained from the census at the village, municipality, and department levels are presented in figure 20.4. For more clarity at the village level, I complemented the point representation with a polygon representation (figure 20.5d) that corresponds to the area of influence of the village (see chapter 28).

I have chosen to represent the PUBNs by quantiles because it corresponds better to the way funding is allocated by governments at a given target level. I also chose a double-ended chromatic scale where the hue/saturation combination is greater at the extremes of the distribution, to highlight the poorest (bright red-orange) and the richest (bright blue—See website for color originals). One can immediately see that depending on the scale, or on the poverty index chosen, the map (and the message it conveys) changes noticeably even for closely related indexes such as PUBN3 and PUBN4 (UBN4 includes an education attainment index in addition to the same indicators that form UBN3). If we compare the village-level maps one can also observe that investments in education (which lead to PUBN4) results in a distribution of better-off villages that is more clustered in some departments than in the case of PUBN3. This shows, apparently, that some departments have received more education assistance than others.

We can also investigate how certain variables such as the ones used for the definition of the UBNs are related. For example, we found that housing is an indicator that explains between 70 percent and 80 percent of other factors by analyzing the correlation at municipality level ($n = 291$) between housing (CV), services (CSIB), assets (CIA), and education (CE) (table 20.5).

We compared our UBNs to another published summary of poverty measures for which we have municipal-level data, the FHIS (1992). Although our UBNs are consistently higher than the FHIS, the results are strongly correlated (particularly PUBN3). This is not surprising, since the same census data has provided a large part of the

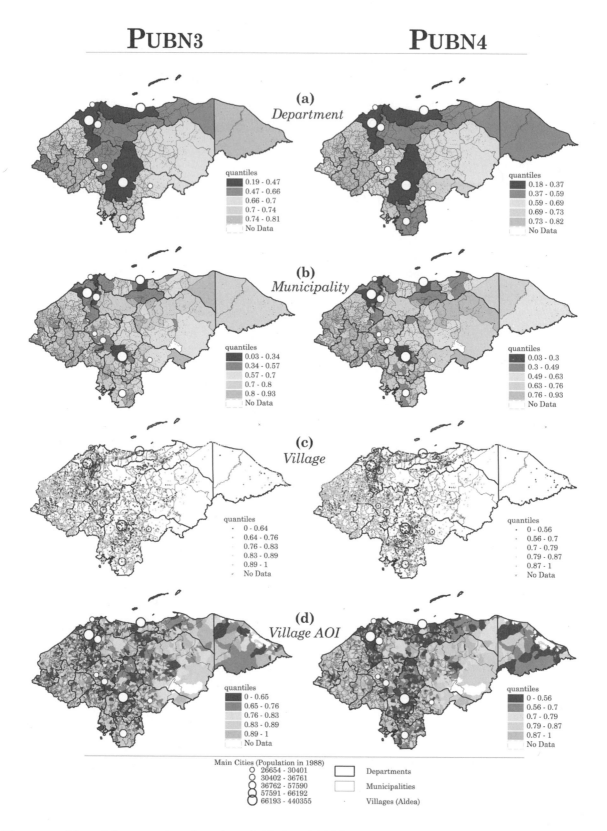

Figure 20.4. Maps of the proportion of poor households (i.e. which UBN3 or UBN4 is greater than 0.4) at village, municipality, and department levels. Legend categories are defined as quantiles of the distributions (higher values mean poorer relative to the total population).

information used by FHIS and the method they used is based on similarly defined UBNs.

I also compared the *WBI* computed from well-being questionnaires by Ravnborg (*WBI*q) with the PUBN3 and PUBN4 at the village level (figure 20.5). On the horizontal scale, I have plotted the proportion of households having the lowest well-being level, for each of the twelve communities where questionnaire data was obtained. We observe some correlation, but the match is poor and the slope of the regression is not equal to one: the proportions of poor coincide at the high-end of the horizontal scale (i.e. for the villages with more perceived poverty, UBNs are more accurate) while our UBNs tend to give a much higher proportion of poor at the low end of the horizontal scale (i.e., villages with less perceived poverty). This means that UBNs do not grasp well the variation of perceived well-being. It is quite alarming to realize how crudely poverty measures estimated using UBNs (most of the official ones) relate to the perceived poverty in these twelve communities.[21]

The problem of a low correlation between different poverty indicators has been observed in numerous cases (Henninger 1998; Davis 2003; see also chapter 36). The perceived exactness of census data and the technical, somehow linear nature of data processing give many of us the confidence to draw conclusions that will look absolutely valid, but in fact will be as biased as others.

Validation of Census-based Village-average WBI Estimates

I am aware that the local well-being indicators that I am trying to model are semi-quantitative, the quality of our census-based proxy indicators (table 20.4) is variable (and this variability is virtually unknown), and one can legitimately question their validity for extrapolation. However, I found that several indicators that compose the well-being index correlate well with our results for the twelve communities for which the well-being questionnaire data have been collected, and that an excellent match was obtained in the case of the overall well-being index *WBI*. Because of the random sampling and the large sample size, the comparison of distributions of *WBI*q (i.e. from

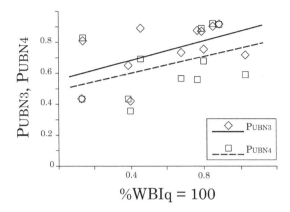

Figure 20.5. Scatter plot of the census-based PUBN3 and PUBN4 versus the proportion of households classified by informants in the poorest well-being category.

WBI questionnaire) and *WBI*c (i.e. from census data) for these villages is possible and is statistically significant.[22]

I checked the validity of the nine indicators that compose the census-derived well-being index (the first three rows of figure 20.6), and of the overall well-being index (the last row of figure 20.6 corresponds to the average of three sets of indicators). For each indicator, two graphs are presented. On the scatter plot (leftmost graph), both axes represent the average value for the indicator (scaled between 0 and 1): the x-axis corresponds to the 1997 well-being questionnaire (let us call them *I*q, "Indicator from questionnaire"), and the y-axis to the *I*c from either the 1988 population and housing census or the 1993 agricultural census. The dotted line indicates what is expected in case of a perfect match, while the solid line corresponds to a robust regression through the points (with equal weight). On the rightmost plot, the box plots[23] correspond to the 1997 well-being data (*I*q), to the *I*c, and to the absolute value of the difference between *I*c and *I*q.

We will explore the plots of figure 20.6 from left to right by row. Note that lower values on the scales correspond to a higher well-being situation. The results for the nine indicators (first three rows of figure 20.6), are analyzed below.

Sell day labor: the results from the population and housing census are lower and have a narrower distribution than observed in the well-being questionnaire data. This means that people engage more in day labor than what we can deduce from the population and housing census. Possibly this is related to a deliberately wrong answer due to a fear of being taxed (or of doing something wrong), or to the nature of the census question that was pointing more toward a permanent working status than a possibly temporal one.

Income: the results from the population and housing census consistently underestimate the sources of income from sources other than agriculture.

Cattle ownership: the results from the agricultural census reflect the well-being questionnaire data accurately, which makes this indicator quite reliable. Note that the robust regression is fooled by a particular alignment of data points, possibly because of the low dispersion of both indicators.

Health: the results from the population and housing census are much more scattered than the well-being questionnaire data, and this probably proves our failure to find a suitable proxy for health in the census. However, average values are very close but this is possibly coincidental.

Housing: the results from the housing census are close to the well-being questionnaire data, except for one outlier, which makes this Ic a reliable indicator. Apparently housing quality has not changed much during the 1988–97 period.

Animal ownership: the results from the agricultural census are close to the well-being questionnaire data, making this indicator an accurate and reliable one.

Hire day labor: the results from the agricultural census seem to consistently underestimate the proportion of people hiring day labor. This can be explained by the fact that the agricultural census was done in April, at the end of the dry (cropping) season, when demand for day labor is low (the question related to the one-month period preceding the census). The well-being data were collected between March and October 1997 and therefore reflect the temporal and geographical diversity of the day labor market better and the fact that even poor people may hire day labor some time during the year.

Land ownership: the results from the agricultural census span a broader range than the well-being questionnaire data, which possibly indicates a failure, in the agricultural census sampling, to correctly include the landless, or a fear from the latter to declare their actual landownership status to government officials.

Market participation: the results from the agricultural census follow a distribution similar to the well-being questionnaire data but aligns quite poorly on the ideal match line.

Our results for the well-being index are shown on the last row of figure 20.6. On the scatter plots, the y-axis represents the $WBIc$ (the average value of several Ics; see equation 20.11), while the x-axis represents the average value of the WBI as obtained from the well-being questionnaire, $WBIq$. The first scatter plot (figure 20.6j) corresponds to the average of all nine Ics. To investigate the effect of doubtful proxies on the resulting $WBIc$, I took out the Ic corresponding to indicator Hire day labor and computed another $WBIc$ (figure 20.6k), then took out another Ic again that corresponds to Health (figure 20.6i). In all three cases, the data points align very well on the ideal line (left plot, dotted line) and have similar ranges (right plot), which means that WBI obtained from the well-being questionnaire in 1997 are accurately reproduced by 1988–93 census data (with a relative error of less than 10 percent). Therefore, I can conclude that there has been little, if any, improvement in the condition of the rural poor, as measured from the viewpoint of perceptions, during this five-to-nine-year period.

Note that no adjustment was necessary: our results come from the raw calculations from carefully chosen unit-level census data. By averaging several

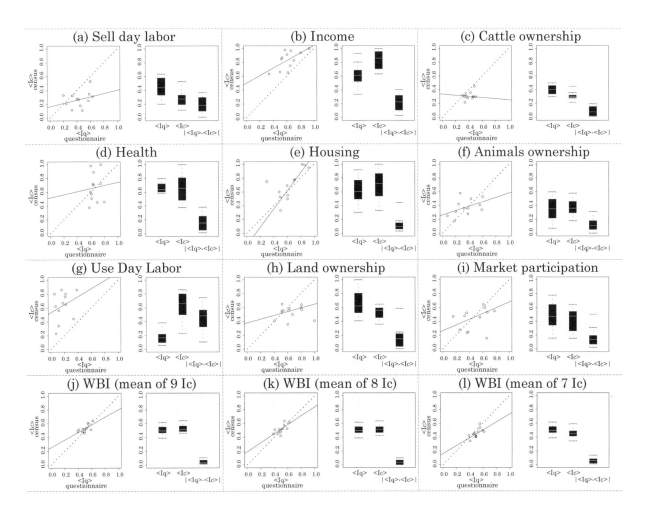

Figure 20.6. Scatterplots and box plots of average values of indicators from the census (vertical scale) versus values obtained with a well-being questionnaire in twelve communities. (a)–(i): *Ic* versus *Iq*; (j)–(l): *WBIc* versus *WBIq*.

indicators we reduce the effect of their respective errors and end up with a more robust, accurate, and meaningful measure of well-being, which can be extrapolated to all villages for which raw census information exists. In slow-developing countries such as Honduras, therefore, old censuses can retain a lot of value and can be exploited to extract good information for policy analysis and design.

Extrapolation Domain for the Well-being Index

Now that we have a well-being index computed for virtually all villages of Honduras, it is tempting to use our results beyond the domain they were designed to address, namely, the three sampled departments. It would be naïve to think that the well-being indicators would be automatically valid

for all villages that present a combination of factors that can be used to select the sample. In effect, people living in coastal villages, or in jungle villages in eastern Honduras, live another reality than the one we observe in the sampled villages, no matter what data (of variable quality) we may have for these villages. On the other hand, it seems reasonable that the indicators of the appendix apply to more villages than the ones of the three departments of the sample.

How can we draw the boundary of the extrapolation domain? I can assume that households with a typology similar to a sampled one will have a perception of poverty that is grasped properly by the indicators of the appendix. The question is therefore: can we construct a valid typology of households—and, by extension, of villages—from our database, and can we assess objectively the similarity of two households or villages? Technically, this would imply selecting a series of variables for the household, and then performing a cluster analysis. Some of these variables should reflect the structure of the neighborhood and some regional influences. The number of clusters chosen, that is, the number of household types, may be decided empirically or according to a given statistical measure. Given the number of steps required and the assumptions involved, the risk of completely missing important indicators is real, and massaging our databases more will not help to reduce it. Expert knowledge may be a better alternative, but again, how can we be sure we are not extrapolating based on anecdote or prejudice?

Apparently, the safest way to be absolutely sure that our results apply beyond the three departments sampled is to select a sample that is more diverse thematically (probably some more factors than the six originally chosen) and geographically (to acknowledge the reality of regions). Within this sample, the participatory work to obtain locally relevant indicators would have to be completed. The process should be iterative: once the indicators are obtained, the relevance of the factors to select the sample is evaluated, which may lead to a readjustment of the sample. Once we are sure of the indicators and of their quantification into indexes, we can locate proxies in the censuses and redo the calculations.

Well-being Index Profiles for the Country

If we take the definition of Lok-Dessalen (1995), a poverty profile is an analytical tool that summarizes poverty-related information and attempts to answer questions such as what are the poor, why are they poor, and where do they live. Doing a full profile nationwide is clearly beyond the scope of this chapter and vastly exceeds the competence of the author. However, I show in this section and in chapter 36 how we can contribute to the *process* of building a regional poverty profile by assembling, mapping, and processing census-based information. A municipal-level profile, for example, can be useful for a local elected official who requires a snapshot of the distribution of village-level poverty

in his jurisdiction. I will therefore explore in this section a few ways of summarizing poverty data such as the indicators produced above, to provide that information at a level of detail suitable for municipal, regional, or national decision making.

I start with the *WBIc* computed for all villages for which census data was available to define all nine indicators (3,712 villages out of a total of 3,729, and 291 municipalities out of 292). As I noted before, the population and housing and the agricultural censuses cannot be joined at household/farm level; therefore, I cannot construct a poverty profile from well-being values at the household level. Even if we could link the censuses at this level, household/farm information may not be accurate enough to provide a reliable profile for small villages. However, I can produce, based on indicators aggregated at the village level, a reliable profile for higher levels.

Because I have four indicators from the population and housing census (where the basic unit is the household) and five from the agricultural census (where the basic unit is the farm), the village-level *WBIc* can be aggregated (by averaging) to municipality and department level as follows:

$$< WBIc > = \frac{1}{N} \sum_{j} (n_j < WBIc >_j)$$

Where

$$n_j = \text{number of households in village } j$$

And

$$N = \sum_{j} n_j$$

the sum running on all villages j within the aggregation unit (municipality or department).

It is more common to see poverty profiles expressed, not in terms of average values of an indicator, but as a headcount index, that is, the number or proportion of people in poverty as defined with respect to a threshold value for a given indicator. PUBN3 and PUBN4 are examples of such indexes, which we were able to compute because they are based on the population and housing censuses,

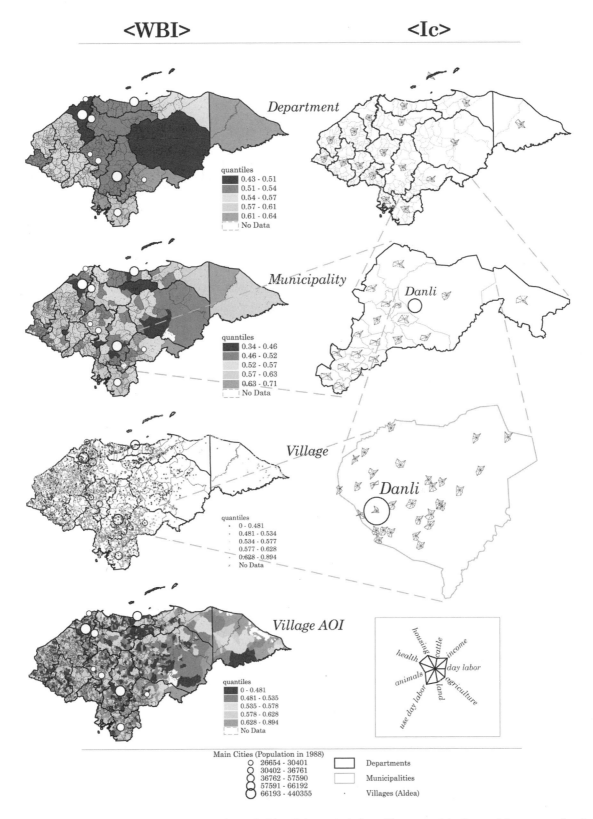

Figure 20.7. Left: Maps of the *WBIc* (average household well-being index) at village, municipality, and department levels; legend categories are chosen as quantiles of the distributions (higher values mean households are poorer in average). Right: starplots, in a geographical context, of average values of household-level *Ic*; each branch of the star corresponds to one of the nine local dimensions of poverty found in the census.

which are joined at household level. It is not the case of the *WBI*, for which, unfortunately, I could obtain only average values for the villages because the three censuses were needed and could not be joined at the household level (there was no way to identify which farm in the agricultural census corresponds to a given household in the other ones). In the appendix I describe how one can produce useful headcount indexes based on the *WBI*, given a few assumptions on the shape of the distribution of household *WBI* in a village. In essence, I find that for villages showing a relatively broad range of household poverty headcount indexes are linearly related to average values.

Figure 20.7 presents a series of maps displaying various representations of the *WBIc*.[24] On the left I have chosen the same representation as in the case of figure 20.4: aggregation at the department and municipal level of village-level *WBIc*, which is represented both as points (village center) and polygons (village area of influence), and five categories defined as the quantiles of the *WBIc* distributions, which give a good idea of how investments may be allocated geographically. I also used the same double-ended chromatic scale with darker saturated colors at the extremes. On the right, I have produced "geographical star plots" for the department, municipal, and village-level *Ic*, which allows us to grasp instantly how the nine dimensions of poverty described by the nine *Ics* contribute to an overall *WBIc*. For each star, the length a branch is proportional to the *Ic* for one indicator: the longer the branch, the poorer the department, municipality, or village along that dimension; star area is proportional to the *WBIc*. Regional patterns emerge naturally through exploration of the shape and geographical distribution of star plots.[25] This new type of plot, which has not been reported before in the literature, can improve significantly the efficiency of communicating of multidimensional data in a geographical context and help to adapt regional development strategies to the local reality.

Discussion

Census data are large and exhaustive household surveys, and as such are suitable for a broad range of microeconomic analyses (King and Bolsdon 1997; Deaton 1997). While it was not particularly challenging to demonstrate the feasibility of computing classic poverty indicators from raw census data (it is however very difficult to obtain access to this data), the extrapolation of locally derived poverty indicators to the scale of a country was never attempted before. The accepted view concerning the results of a participatory poverty appraisal (PPA) is that extrapolation depends exclusively on empirical generalization (Shaeffer 2001). Indeed, Ravnborg (1999) obtained eleven local indicators that could be safely used to describe poverty in three Honduras departments, but the added statistical design and subsequent analysis provided a way to quantify these indicators. By using field data collected in 1999 as a reference, that is, well-being indexes obtained from interviews by Ravnborg, I found that census-based well-being indexes were 90 percent accurate, while commonly used UBNs failed to reproduce local poverty perceptions. Therefore, when properly designed, participatory poverty appraisals can give results well beyond what we usually see.

Although the maps produced for the various indicators at various levels of aggregation do show similarities (we try to measure poverty incidence after all), they are sufficiently different to justify questioning the relevance of the whole poverty measurement exercise. Not only do the indicators chosen give a different view of the poverty, but also the way these indicators are displayed or aggregated has tremendous influence on perceived distributions. This perception in turn is key to policy design, which will have a direct impact on the incidence of poverty. This difficulty calls for a serious commitment by the scientific community to work on reliable, unbiased ways to produce and use indicators and maps.

Indicators also change with scale; therefore, decision makers have to be aware of this bias. The tables below show the correlation coefficients obtained between poverty indicators that are either different (table 20.6a) or computed at various aggregation levels (table 20.6b).

Correlation between poverty indicators UBN3 (or UBN4) and *WBI* is quite low (0.38–0.63), which

Table 20.6a. Correlation coefficients between various poverty indicators computed at a given aggregation level

	WBI		PUBN4		PUBN3	
	Municipality	Department	Municipality	Department	Municipality	Department
Village	0.6	0.37	0.67	0.61	0.5	0.36
Municipality		0.62		0.81		0.66

Table 20.6b. Correlation coefficients between a given poverty indicator computed at various aggregation levels

	Village		Municipality		Department	
	PUBN4	PUBN3	PUBN4	PUBN3	PUBN4	PUBN3
WBI	0.38	0.44	0.43	0.48	0.55	0.63
PUBN4		0.84		0.91		0.96

was to be expected given the large difference in the concepts underlying the construction of these indicators. Given the fact UBN4 uses exactly the same data and basic needs indicators as UBN3, the only difference being that UBN4 has an additional indicator of education, it is surprising to see that correlation between UBN3 and UBN4 is not higher (0.84 at village level). This is explained by the fact that education is poorly correlated to access to services and non-land assets (table 20.5). However, the most striking result is that there is such a low correlation between aggregation levels even for the same indicator, for example, 0.36 between department and village level PUBN3. This is due to the variability of an indicator (which is often a spatial variability); for example, when an indicator at village level varies a lot within a department, a poor correlation is found between village and department data. This gives a hint on the validity at household level of a policy based on data aggregated at higher levels.

McGee (1999) has compared side to side the poverty levels obtained via a PPA and via a classic approach used by the Colombian government to target its social programs. The PPA that she used elicited the views of poor people through standard well-being ranking (like Ravnborg's), while the

"official" view was given by SISBEN's family poverty indicator, a weighted multicriteria index obtained through a household questionnaire (Castaño and Moreno 1994). She obtained a Spearman's rank order correlation test of 0.44 for the village of Uribe ($n = 87$), which is on the same order of magnitude as the village-level correlation that I find between PUBN3 or PUBN4 and *WBI*. This means (roughly) that both studies confirm that more than 50 percent of the households (or the villages, in our case) are likely to disapprove of the allocation of government spending for the poor.

Other studies have also highlighted the fact that the distribution of poverty is extremely sensitive to the choice of poverty indicators (Boltvinik 1996; Glewwe and Gaag 1988). In chapter 36 I show that the spatial distribution of poverty patterns is also very sensitive to classification strategies. It is alarming to realize that decisions that will affect poor people's lives are made on such unstable foundations. But the most insidious effect may be that most decision makers are too confident about the absolute correctness of their analysis, because they use accurate data and very reasonable indicators. Few decision makers have realized this risk, probably because it is onerous and painful to compute and compare many indicators, it is annoying to find such a low correlation between these extremely rational and accurate indicators, and it is difficult to explain why there are differences and to justify the choice of one indicator over another.

The challenge to empower people to extract meaningful information from census data is greater than we thought initially. The poorest municipalities are almost guaranteed to receive aid money, and every local elected official would strongly defend the indicator that favors his municipality. An informed elite having access to data can easily tweak and massage an indicator that will give the answer more suitable to them (for instance, one rich landowner will have access to credit because his farm is located in a priority municipality). Giving universal access to micro-data raises the issue of confidentiality but solves the one of transparency.

In chapter 36 I address in more detail these issues of poverty measures and representations in the context of policy design and community empowerment.

Conclusion

Everyone agrees that poverty is multidimensional and complex and that poverty estimates are subjective. Despite this apparent consensus, analysts are constantly urged to provide one summary number, one poverty index that will fill all expectations, on which reforms can be based or investments be targeted. The "$1/person/day" formula is a good example of such a one-dimensional yet extremely influential indicator. One may agree on such a number by default, because it is too complicated or time consuming to define and compute a poverty measure tailored to diverse needs and share it with other players. I showed that it is not difficult to quickly derive more complex indicators in a flexible way as long as highly disaggregated data is accessible.

On the other hand, poor farmers, who are living with another reality of poverty than that of policy makers, may not see some social investments such as latrines as a good way to end their poverty. This has been recognized by Cornell University and the MacArthur Foundation, which have brought together poverty analysts with different backgrounds, from rural sociology to neoclassical economics, to examine the complementarities and divergences of quantitative and qualitative approaches to poverty appraisal (Kanbur et al. 2001). The work that I have presented here links a measure of locally relevant indicators to nationwide databases, showing one way to achieve this synergy. It can contribute to bridging the knowledge gap between decision makers and poor farmers because it provides a quantifiable means for the necessary "self-critical epistemological awareness" (Chambers 1997) in developing a common language for poverty. In order to fully achieve this potential, poverty appraisal has to be part of a development process where alternative, legitimate knowledge is embedded in the policy making process.

It must remain clear that I do not pretend that the UBNs or the local well-being indicators presented here are "right" or "better": they are different representations of the same reality, or rather possible reality, and are as biased as others. However, the well-being index has two strengths: it is the viewpoint of the poverty by the poor themselves, so taking it into account into policy will results in more impact and less potential conflicts; and, as I proved, it can be computed accurately from census data.

The empirical sensitivity analysis of UBNs done in this chapter, both in terms of their calculation and in terms of their representation in map form (see also chapter 36), implies that most poverty targeting is ineffective as it is currently done, and that serious work is needed to (1) address the problem of error and bias in poverty estimates and representation; (2) bring to decision makers and analysts the richness of raw census data and powerful tools to process them; and (3) embed the perception of the poor in policy design.

Since all representations acquire their best value when contrasted, socialized, and shared between all players, it is essential to let the poor participate in the debate, and mapping their own viewpoint is one way to do that. Another possibility is to add new questions to the periodic censuses, asking what the poor themselves consider important. In other words, poverty measurement, representation, policy, and action issues are inseparable. This is addressed in chapter 36, where I explore the issue

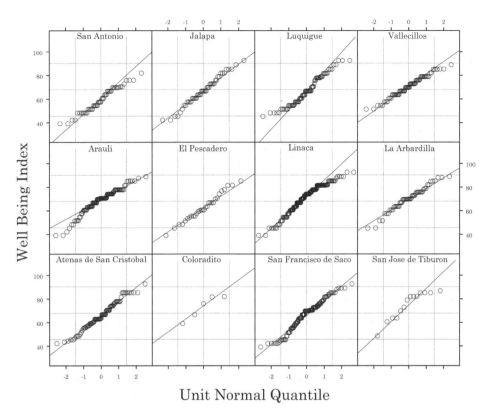

Figure 20.8. Q-Q plots to verify condition of normality: quantiles of the *well-being* index (vertical axis) versus quantiles of a standard normal distribution.

of representation of poverty indicators and provide some methodological clues about contrasting and harmonizing them.

Appendix: Distribution of WBI and Aggregate Indicators

It is more common to see poverty profiles expressed not in terms of average values of an indicator but as a headcount index, that is, the proportion of people in poverty, as defined with respect to a threshold value for a given indicator. PUBN3 and PUBN4 are examples of such indexes, which we were able to compute because they are based on population and housing censuses that are joined at household level. This is not the case of the *WBI*, for which, unfortunately, we could obtain only average values for the villages because the three censuses were needed and could not be joined at household level. However, we can produce useful headcount indexes based on the *WBI* if we know the shape of the distribution of household *WBI* in a village.

Some hypothesis with a great extrapolation potential can be drawn from detailed analysis of the actual distribution of indicators and well-being levels at various aggregation levels. We used *WBI*, the raw well-being index (before it is classified into three categories) to generate a series of qq-plots, displayed in figure 20.8. The vertical scale (which is the one defined by Ravnborg) goes from 33 (higher well-being) to 100 (lower well-being), and the horizontal scale represents the quantiles of a standard distribution. It appears that the *WBI* distributions can be modeled adequately by a normal distribution (data points generally adjust on the qq-line), which has similar standard deviations (slope of the qq-line is similar) in the range 0.13–0.20 (when the *WBIq* are scaled in the range 0–1). This will help us assess our capacity to predict proportions of poor based on the average value of the *WBI*.

For more clarity in the discussion, we will rescale the *WBI* between 0 and 1 instead of 33 and 100. On the last row of figure 20.9a (based on Ravnborg household data) we can see that the proportion of households with a *WBIq* greater than a certain threshold (which we will call *PWBIq*) is linearly related to the *WBIq*, with little relative error (7 percent in case of a threshold of 0.5, i.e. proportion of household with *WBI* < 0.5). We could

(a)

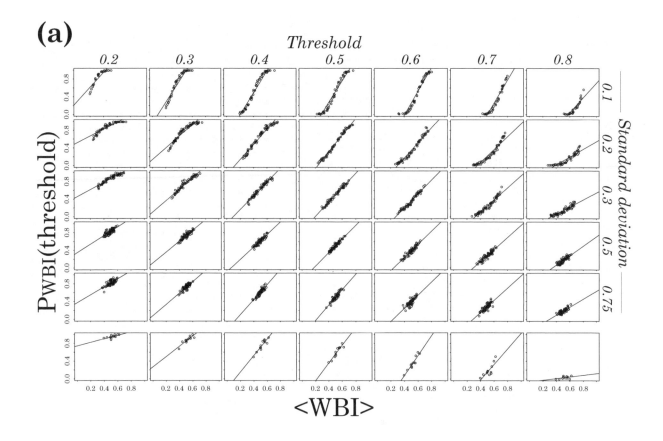

(b)

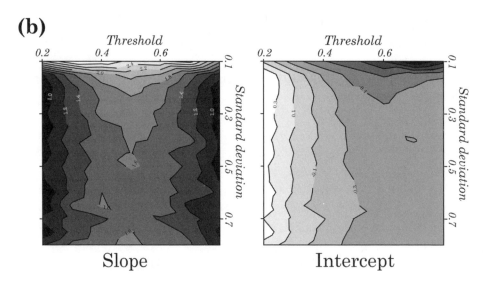

Figure 20.9. (a) Proportion of households for which *WBI* (*PWBI*) is greater than threshold (*T*), in function of *WBI*, first five rows: for simulated distributions of width standard deviation (*S*); last row: actual *PWBIq*(*T*) versus *WBIq* for data collected in twelve communities, for various *T*. (b) 2D maps of slope and intercept of regression line between simulated *PWBI*(*T*) and *WBI* showing the variation of the parameters in function of *T* and *S*.

Table 20.7a. PWBI(T) = aWBI + b: Simulated Regression parameters and estimated relative error (WBI is scaled between 0 and 1)

Threshold (T)	a	b	Error (WBIq) Median	3rd quantile	Error (simulations) median	3rd quantile
0.3	1.30	+0.11	10.6	12.7	4.7	8.2
0.4	1.61	−0.17	10.7	14.9	4.6	8.1
0.5	1.72	−0.36	12.9	15.2	5.0	9.6
0.6	1.61	−0.44	20.6	32.4	8.8	17.2
0.7	1.32	−0.42	59.8	122.7	12.9	30.1

Table 20.7b. *PWBIq*(T) = *aWBIq* + b: Regression parameters for questionnaire data and estimated relative error (*WBI* is scaled between 0 and 1)

Threshold (T)	a	b	Error (*WBIq*) Median	3rd quantile	Error (simulations) median	3rd quantile
0.3	1.17	0.27	2.9	5.3	13.7	19.8
0.4	1.86	−0.22	4.2	7.3	13.6	18.5
0.5	2.00	−0.44	6.1	9.7	11.1	18.6
0.6	2.23	−0.81	13.0	17.9	20.6	32.4
0.7	1.74	−0.72	23.0	74.8	37.4	90.1

use the linear regression parameters to predict, for all Honduras villages, the proportion of poor based on their average *WBIc*, but this would overlook important assumptions that have to be tested beforehand. First, we are certain that not all villages in Honduras have a distribution of *WBI* similar to the ones of the twelve communities. Second, we do not know if the correlation between *PWBIq* and *WBIq* is good by coincidence or if it represents some remarkable property that we can safely rely on. Computer simulations can help explore the possibilities and assess the domain of the feasible.

Our strategy was to generate random populations of household *WBI* from normal distributions of various widths and means and examine the relationship between the *PWBI* computed from these populations and the mean *WBI*. In other words, we have generated a large sample of values from a population having a given mean in the range 0.2–0.8 and a given width. Values of generated *WBI* were truncated to stay within the range 0–1, which approximates the effect of

skewed populations near the extremes. The *WBI* and *PWBI* are then computed from each distribution and for threshold values ranging from 0.2 to 0.8. The effect of the width of the distribution was evaluated by varying the standard deviation from 0.1 to 0.75.

The results of the simulations, which explore the capacity to compute a headcount index based on average values, for various distributions, are summarized in figure 20.9. We can observe from the first five rows of figure 20.9a that when the distribution of *WBI* is not too narrow, the *PWBI* and *WBI* are linearly related, with a slope and intercept that do not vary much for a given threshold value (figure 20.9b). The slope does not even change much with respect to the threshold. If we assume that the actual distribution of *WBI* within a village cannot be narrower than the ones we observed (figure 20.8), we can use our regression results for prediction. Table 20.7a reports the average value of the slope and of the intercept obtained for *WBI* distribution width ranging from 0.15 to 0.5. Table

20.7b reports the slope and intercept obtained from the *WBIq* (see last row of figure 20.9a). For a threshold of 0.5, we could predict the *PWBIq* from *WBIq* with 87 percent accuracy (instead of 94 percent); in addition, *PWBI* from simulated data could be predicted within 5 percent. On the other hand, if we use regression parameters from the *WBIq* we are confident, for the 0.5 threshold, that we can predict *PWBI* from *WBI* within 18.6 percent in 75 percent of the cases. However, we should be very careful of using any regression parameters for thresholds above 0.6.

We are in a position to produce useful head-count indexes based on the *WBI* as long as we make a few assumptions on the shape of the distribution of household *WBI* in a village.

There is no substitute to databases that are joined at household level but we will always need important data sets for which only average values exist, and it would be possible to do more with it provided we have good information on the distribution of disaggregated data (even without access to it).

Aggregation of *PWBI* will be done as follows:

$$PWBIc = \tfrac{1}{N} \sum_j n_j PWBIc_j$$

Acknowledgments

I would like to thank the Dirección General de Estadística y Censo of Honduras for giving us access to the unit-level census data used in this study; to SECPLAN, which provided the georeferenced village database; and to Elisabeth Barona, Hector Barreto, Patrice Couillaud, Pedro Jimenez, Andrew Nelson, and Tonny Oyana for their contribution to the work presented here. Special thanks are due to Helle Ravnborg, who gave us access to her household database and to her experience on well-being concepts and measurement, and to Bronson (Ron) Knapp for the intellectual leadership he has always demonstrated.

This work has been partly funded by the Consultative Group for International Agricultural Research, the Dutch Trust Fund for methodological support to ecoregional programs, and the Inter-American Development Bank.

Notes

1. Throughout this chapter, unless specifically noted, "poverty" and "well-being" will be used interchangeably to refer to a broadly defined but intuitively acknowledged human socioeconomic condition.

2. It is not clear how the results of the World Bank's top-notch research are actually influencing World Bank loans to developing countries.

3. In fact, census questionnaires include questions directly related to income (salary, agricultural production), but the information obtained is believed to be extremely inaccurate, especially in the higher-income segments.

4. The statistical unit adopted was the agricultural holding, defined as all land of at least 0.21 ha, totally or partially used for agriculture or livestock rearing, made up of one or more parcels laying in the same municipality, kept under a single management, without regard to title or legal form.

5. In 2001, Honduras obtained soft loans totaling $8 million to support the sixteenth national population census and the fifteenth national housing census. The Instituto Nacional de Estadísticas carried out the census in July 2001, together with an executing agency created for this purpose.

6. Now defunct and replaced by the National Statistics Institutes (INE), which is independent of SECPLAN.

7. Departments have not changed since 1957, but municipios and villages are constantly evolving: in the period 1974–93, eight new municipios were created. We have found two slightly different official codings of municipalities for 1988–93 and were unable to obtain confirmation about which is correct; therefore, we used the coding by DGEC. Moreover, there is one municipality for which no census information exists. The village coverage prepared by SECPLAN was more difficult to check for consistency, gazetteers being outdated and no other coverage being available for cross-comparison. We checked the village coverage in several steps. First, we did a spatial join with the municipality coverage, which allowed us to pinpoint villages that were coded as part of a different municipio than the one they were actually located in. Next, we evaluated the proximity of villages, which could not be too small (e.g., 300m), and also manually checked official gazetteers. We then assigned a quality code to each village (Couillaud 1998). The overall accuracy of the village coverage is very good: only 147 villages had inconsistent codes, the confusion being mainly between aldeas and *caserios*. The caserio level (i.e., hamlet) is an even more detailed level found in the census (a village is made up of

five to ten caserios, and there are 25,533 caserios in the census), but no official map exists or is likely to in the near future. However, one could think that it could be done for a region of interest; a mayor could want to construct such a map for the municipality.

8. The well-being ranking is a participatory technique for obtaining insights into local perceptions of well-being—and by inference, poverty (Grandin 1988). See also chapter 21 for an application of well-being ranking as a variable to analyze in relation to soil management and land-use choice.

9. A series of villages was selected so as to represent as many combinations of six factors as possible: altitude, basic services (education and water), population density, ethnicity, gender composition, and travel time to urban centers (> 2,000 inhabitants). She obtained these factors from census data and the GIS database for all Honduran villages, and a sample of ninety villages in three departments was chosen to express maximum variability.

10. "Well-being" is a neutral concept, in contrast to "poverty."

11. Only two categories were sufficient to characterize this indicator.

12. For the regression approach I could compute, for each household, a *WBI* in function of a series of explanatory variables found in the census for this household (such as income, housing quality, and agricultural productivity). This could be done by multiple regression between the *WBI* obtained from the questionnaire (which I will label *WBIq*), and census variables, provided I have census data for each household where the *WBI* questionnaire has been filled. An example of this approach, based on a consumption model, is given by Hentschel et al. (1998). There are also many variants of the small area estimation method that use this approach. In the case of poverty (beyond the consumption proxy used by these authors), we can imagine that such a model would be extremely complex (and nonlinear), and we might not have enough data to calibrate it properly.

13. In order to respect confidentiality, we cannot locate, in the census, the exact households that were surveyed by Ravnborg and her team; therefore, we cannot calibrate our model at the household level. This is a similar situation as experienced by Bigman et al. (1999) for poverty targeting in Burkina Faso: the household consumption data was obtained from a priority survey (PS) of sample communities, and the only data available for extrapolation outside the PS sample were mean values of explanatory variables.

14. This is valid even if there are missing values for the *WBIc* as long as the missing values are not used to compute the mean.

15. A homogeneity plot is a reduced-dimension representation for qualitative data. In this case, the 11-dimensional space (defined by the eleven indicators) is reduced to 2, the qualitative data being transformed into objects with metric properties and plotted. The closer two points are from each other on the plot, the more similar the variables are; variables appearing far from the origin are more important. See chapter 21 for an explanation of homogeneity analysis (also known as multiple correspondence analysis) and other optimum scaling techniques.

16. As we can see, the distinction between the higher and middle is much better defined (straighter boundary) than between the middle and lower well-being categories. Prediction of middle well-being would certainly generate confusion with the lower well-being.

17. I found that most of the time, this division occurs between one of the well-being categories and the next one, but in some cases it falls within the middle of one (e.g., market involvement, health, source of income). Note that the descriptions of middle and high well-being indicators (see appendix) are more complex than the low well-being one, which is to be expected since low well-being households have access to less options than the better-off ones.

18. There are two indicators that I was not able to obtain from any census: money and food security. The latter seems to be well correlated with health (lines are parallel in figure 20.3), while questions related to income are known to be particularly error-prone; therefore I supposed that ignoring these two indicators was not critical.

19. When the population of a village was less than two thousand, all households were considered as rural. For cities with a population above two thousand people, we have no information about the criteria used to discriminate rural and urban households and some confusion persists (RH 1994a). An analysis of the population and housing census data has shown that some localities with rural characteristics have been classified as urban in the census, and vice versa (RH 1994a).

20. By looking at the distribution of variables in the two-dimensional space of the homogeneity plot (figure 20.3) and having in mind which census provides a value for these variables (table 20.3), we see that all censuses are needed to cover the full range in both dimensions. This means that using a proxy indicator *Ic* from one census only will only give a partial and biased estimate of well-being; therefore all censuses are necessary and complementary.

21. One may think that this is because there is a substantial difference between data collection periods of the Population and Housing census (1988) and of the well-being questionnaire (1997). However it appears that rural

poverty levels have changed very little during this nine-year period (UNDP 2000; RH 2001), which I confirm later in this chapter.

22.   However, one must keep in mind that five and nine years had passed, respectively, between the time the well-being questionnaire was filled (1997) and the time of the agricultural and of the population and housing censuses. This would account at least for some of the discrepancies between computed and observed values of indicators.

23.   The box plot of figure 20.6 is interpreted as follows: the solid black box represents ± one standard deviation about the mean, while the white line inside shows the median. The whiskers are drawn to the nearest value not beyond a standard span from the quartiles.

24.   Note that because the *PWBI* and *WBI* are linearly related (see appendix), maps produced from both indexes will look the same.

25.   For example (see village-level starplots of figure 20.7), the rural households of the city of Danly (white circle) are markedly different in terms of the composition of *WBI* from the other villages of the municipality; more own land or have bigger farms, use day labor, and have a high agricultural production. The villages in the eastern part of the municipality are similar in terms of composition of *WBI*.

References

Bergeron, G., M. S. Sutkover, and J. M. Medina Banegas. 1998. How reliable are group informant ratings? A test of food security rating in Honduras. Discussion Paper No 43, Food Consumption and Nutrition Division, IFPRI.

Bigman, D., S. Dercon, D. Guillaume, and M. Lambotte. 1999. Community targeting for poverty reduction in Burkina Faso. CES Discussion Paper Series, DPS 99.10, Center for Economic Studies, Leuven.

Boltvinik, J. 1996. Poverty in Latin America: A critical analysis of three studies. *International Social Sciences Journal* 148:245–60.

———. 1997. Poverty measurement methods: An overview. United Nations Development Program (UNDP), Social Development and Poverty Elimination Division (SEPED) Series on Poverty Reduction. www.undp.org/poverty/publications/pov_red/.

Carvalho, S., and H. White. 1997. Combining the quantitative and qualitative approaches to poverty measurement and analysis: The practice and potential. World Bank Technical Paper No. 366. Washington, D.C.: World Bank.

Castaño, E., and H. Moreno. 1994. Metodología estadística del modelo de ponderaciones del Sistema de Selección de Beneficiarios de Programas Sociales (SISBEN). Misión de Apoyo a la Descentralización y Focalización de los Servicios Sociales (Misión Social), Departamento Nacional de Planeación.

Chambers, R. 1997. *Whose Reality Counts? Putting the First Last.* London: Intermediate Technology Publications.

Couillaud, P. 1998. Data handling: Census data codes and geocodes. CIAT Technical Report, PE4 project.

Davis, B., 2003. Choosing a method for poverty mapping, FAO. www.povertymap.net/publications/doc/CMPM DAVIS 13 apr03 sec.pdf.

Deaton, A. 1997. *The Analysis of Household Surveys: A Microeconomic Approach to Development Policy.* Baltimore: Johns Hopkins University Press.

Duke-Williams, O., and P. Rees, 1998. Can census offices publish statistics for more than one small area geography? An analysis of the differencing problem in statistical disclosure. *International Journal of Geographical Information Science* 12, no. 6: 579–605.

FHIS (Fondo Hondureño de Inversión Social). 1992. Presupuesto de inversión 1992–1993. Tegucigalpa: Presidencia de la Republica de Honduras.

Foster, J., J. Greer, and E. Thorbecke. 1984. A class of decomposable poverty measures. *Econometrica* 52:761–65.

Glewwe, P., and J. van der Gaag. 1988. *Confronting Poverty in Developing Countries: Definitions, Information, and Policies.* Washington, D.C.: World Bank.

Grandin, B. 1988. *Wealth Ranking in Smallholder Communities: A Field Manual.* London: Intermediate Technology Publications.

Henninger, N. 1998. *Mapping and Geographic Analysis of Human Welfare and Poverty: Review and Assessment.* Washington, D.C.: World Resources Institute.

Hentschel, J., J. Lanjouw, P. Lanjouw, and J. Poggi. 1998. Combining survey data with census data to construct spatially disaggregated poverty maps: A case study of Ecuador. *World Bank Economic Review* 14, no. 1: 147–65.

Kanbur, R., R. Chambers, P. Petesch, N. Uphoff, F. Bourguignon, D. Sahn, C. Moser, et al. 2001. Qualitative and quantitative poverty appraisal: Complementarities, tensions and the way forward. Contributions to a workshop held at Cornell University, 15–16 March 2001.

King, D., and D. Bolsdon. 1998. Using the SARs to add policy value to household projections. *Environment and Planning A* 30:867–80.

Leclerc, G., A. Nelson, and E. B. Knapp. 2000. Extension of GIS through poverty mapping: The use of unit-level census data. In M. Kokubun, S. Ushida, and K. Tsurumi, eds., *JIRCAS International Symposium Series No. 8: The 6th JIRCAS International Symposium—GIS applications for Agro-Environmental Issues in Developing Regions*, 163–82. Tsukuba, Japan: JIRCAS/MAFF.

Lok-Dessaliens, R. 1995. *Poverty Profiles: Interpreting the Data*. New York: United Nations Development Profile.

McGee, R. 1999. Technical, objective, equitable and uniform? A critique of the Colombian system for the selection of beneficiaries of social programs, SISBEN. http://idpm.man.ac.uk/idpm/diswp57.pdf.

McGee, R., and K. Brock. 2001. From poverty assessment to policy changes: Actors and data. www.ids.ac.uk/ids/bookshop/wp/wp133.pdf.

Openshaw, S. 1995. The future of the census. In S. Openshaw, ed., *The Census User's Handbook*, 389–411. London: Longman.

Oyana, T., P. Couillaud, G. Leclerc, R. Knapp, and W. Bell. 1998. Processing social indicators at individual and household level, and their aggregation at different scales. Technical paper, International Center for Tropical Agriculture (CIAT), Cali, Colombia.

Pradhan, M., and M. Ravallion. 2000. Measuring poverty using qualitative perceptions of consumption adequacy. *Review of Economics and Statistics* 82, no. 3: 462–71.

Ravnborg, H. M. 1999. Assessing rural poverty: A practical method for identifying, extrapolating, and quantifying local perceptions of rural poverty. Technical paper, International Center for Tropical Agriculture (CIAT), Cali, Colombia.

———. 2002. Poverty and soil management: Evidence of relationships from three Honduran watersheds. *Society and Natural Resources* 15, no. 6: 523–40.

RB (República de Bolivia). 1995. Mapa de pobreza: Una guía para la acción social. La Paz: República de Bolivia.

RH (República de Honduras). 1989–1990a. Secretaria de Planificacion, Coordinacion y Presupuesto (SECPLAN), 1988 censo nacional de poblacion y vivienda.

———. 1989–90b. República de Honduras, Dirección General de Estadistica y Censos. Censo nacional de vivienda 1988.

———. 1994a. Honduras, Libro Q: Potencial, Potencialidad y focalización municipal. SECPLAN. Proyecto SECPLAN/OIT/FNUAP—HON/90/P03: Políticas de población, pobreza y empleo.

———. 1994b. Censo Nacional Agropecuario 1993.

———. 2001. *Estrategia para la reducción de la pobreza*. Tegucigalpa: República de Honduras.

Rhoades, R. E. 1998. Participatory watershed research and management: Where the shadow falls. London: Sustainable Agriculture and Rural Livelihoods Programme.

Robinson, A. H. 1950. Ecological correlation and the behavior of individuals. *American Sociological Review* 15:351–57.

Schaeffer, P. 2001. Difficulties in combining income/consumption and participatory approaches to poverty: Issues and examples. www.people.cornell.edu/pages/sk145/papersw/QQZ.pdf.

Theil, H. 1989. The measurement of inequality by components of income. *Economics Letters* 42:197–99.

Thorpe, A. 1993. Honduras: The new economic model and poverty. In V. Bulmer-Thomas, ed., *The New Economic Model in Latin America and Its Impact on Income Distribution and Poverty*, 223–48. New York: St Martin's.

UNDP. 2000. Human Development Report 2000: Human rights and human development. www.undp.org/hdr2000.

Webb, A. K. V., L. K. Woo, and M. Sant'Anna. 1995. The participation of non-governmental organizations in poverty alleviation: A case study of the Honduras social investment fund. World Bank Discussion Paper 295.

World Bank. 2001. *Poverty Trends and Voices of the Poor*. 4th ed. Washington, D.C.: World Bank.

CHAPTER 21

FARMERS' DECISION MAKING ON LAND USE

The Importance of Soil Conditions in the Case of the

Río Cabuyal Watershed of Colombia

HELLE MUNK RAVNBORG AND JORGE E. RUBIANO

Introduction

Development thinking, which in many ways forms the basis for development interventions and research, is full of narratives about human behavior and its motives. Some of these narratives—or commonly agreed-upon assumptions—about what motivates and sustains certain types of behavior are well founded, but others are not. One of the important roles of social sciences in development is to understand the motives and incentives that underlie human behavior and thus to examine critically the foundations of the narratives that help shape development interventions. This chapter illustrates the process of critically and rigorously examining the foundations of one of these narratives, namely the assumption that land-use management is primarily based on knowledge of biophysical conditions and consequently that improving this knowledge would lead to improved land-use management.

Many studies provide evidence of farmers' detailed knowledge of their soils and of their ability to draw agronomic management implications from this knowledge (Talawar 1996; Talawar and Rhoades 1998). As a classic example, Rounce (1949) and Malcolm (1953) documented the soil taxonomy of the Wasukuma people in Northwestern Tanzania, encompassing nine major soil classes and specific management practices associated with each soil type. Among the most important descriptors upon which farmers base their soil classification are soil color, soil texture, and soil structure (Rounce 1949; Malcolm 1953; Ravnborg 1992; Bellon and Taylor 1993; Zimmerer 1994; de Kool, 1996). Such "folk" soil taxonomies have been found to correlate well with acknowledged scientific descriptions of soil properties. As an example, in a study from Chiapas, Mexico, farmers identified and ranked by quality four main classes of soils. Analysis of samples taken from these soils with respect to properties such as pH, organic matter content, and texture showed a significant correlation between these properties and farmers' quality rankings of the soils (Bellon and Taylor 1993).

Given this ability of farmers to distinguish different soil types, it is generally hypothesized that farmers would select the best soils for cultivation while leaving poorer soils under forest or natural pasture. As soils gradually degrade as a consequence of cultivation, crop choice should change from more-demanding crops such as maize and beans to less-demanding crops such as cassava, before the soil is finally put under fallow to regenerate fertility. Such hypotheses also guide mainstream land capability analysis and land-use planning, which tend to be based primarily upon soil and climatic data (Brinkman 1994; Alfaro et al. 1994), though attempts have been made to also include economic and social factors (FAO 1976; Rossiter and van Wambeke 1993).

However, soil properties, and more generally biophysical properties, are not the only factors recognized in farmers' decision-making process with respect to land use and crop choice. Other factors, such as market opportunities and input requirements versus availability, also play important roles (Talawar and Rhoades 1998).

This chapter examines the importance of biophysical conditions versus other factors, such as market concerns, access to productive resources, and overall objectives, that enter into farmers' decision making with respect to land use—that is, choice of land cover (forest, fallow, pasture, or type of crop). It does so based on a case study conducted in the Andean hillsides of southwestern Colombia.

Materials and Methods

In order to enable the critical examination of the assumption of knowledge of biophysical conditions being important to farmers' decision making on land use, it is important to identify concepts and concerns that are meaningful and relevant to farmers rather than simply adopting predefined concepts and concerns. Thus, we follow a sequence of steps of inquiry in order to obtain insight into the kind of observations of biophysical conditions that different types of farmers make, the concepts they use, and the implications this knowledge ideally should have on land-use management, and finally to understand how biophysical knowledge enters along with other concerns into real-life decision making on land use and to remove as much as possible the biases associated with the researcher's a priori concepts and hypotheses. These methods include well-being rankings, semi-structured group interviews, and the conducting of a pictorial questionnaire survey, followed by nonparametric statistical analysis.

The Study Area

The Río Cabuyal watershed (see figure 21.1) is situated in the Andes in southwestern Colombia at altitudes ranging from 1,200–2,200 meters above sea level and covers an area of approximately 7,000 hectares. Annual rainfall is just below 2,000 mm, with a pronounced dry spell from June to August. Steep slopes and varied topography characterize the area. Based on a digital terrain model, half of the Río Cabuyal watershed is estimated to have slopes of more than 30 percent and an additional third of the area to have slopes between 12 and 30 percent (Urbano et al. 1995). Pedology is also highly variable: highly eroded, red soils are often found side by side with deep, black soils. Overall, the soils of the area are characterized as acid soils of volcanic origin and poor fertility. Around two-thirds of the farmers use fertilizer, particularly chicken manure, which is sold commercially in the area and is preferred to chemical fertilizers for most crops.

The Río Cabuyal watershed houses a multiethnic population. Páez Indians have the longest history in the area and constitute 20 percent of the population; mestizos, or Caucanos as they are also called, constitute 65 percent of the population. (This and the following descriptive information is based on the 1997 Río Cabuyal poverty monitoring survey or the 1993 Río Cabuyal household census). The mestizos came to settle in the area from other parts of Cauca around the turn of the nineteenth century (Rappaport 1990). The remaining 15 percent of the population is made up of a mixed group of people, including Guambiano Indians and mestizos coming from other parts of Colombia, who all have a more recent history in the area. The watershed is densely populated (100 persons per km²), although there are substantial variations throughout (see figure 21.1). Virtually all land is titled. Small-scale farming, often combined with day-laboring on local small-scale farms, provides the main source of income in the area. The average farm size is 3.6 hectares, with half of the households owning 2 hectares or less. Barely 10 percent of the households are landless, and an additional 8 percent are virtually landless, having a total farm size of less than 0.5 hectare. Renting land is of negligible importance in the area, practiced by only 1 percent of the households, whereas caretaker cultivation is more common, with an estimated 10 percent of the households earning their living as caretakers.

The principal crops grown are coffee, plantain (intercropped with coffee), cassava, maize, beans, and tomatoes. In the upper part of the watershed above 1,600–1,700 m, fruits are also grown. Livestock production is of minor importance, and only 14 percent of the households own cattle. The Pan-American Highway cuts across the middle of the watershed, giving the population in the mid- and to some extent low-altitude areas good access to markets in neighboring townships as well as in the bigger cities of Popayán and Cali. The majority of farmers sell at least part of their production. More than 90 percent of the households sell at least one of the principal crops mentioned above.

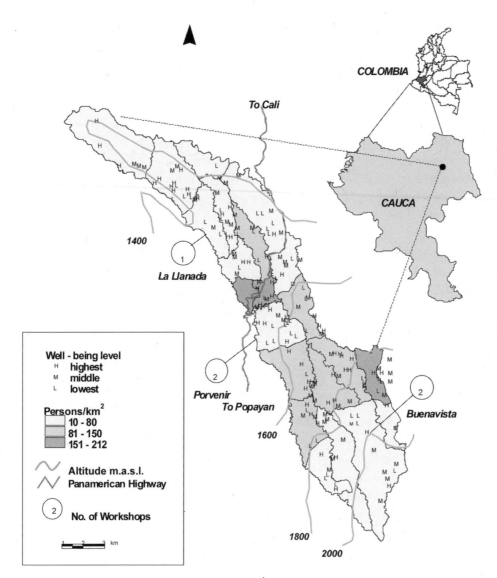

Figure 21.1. Location of Río Cabuyal watershed, altitude zones, population density, location of workshops, and location and well-being level of interviewed households.

Besides coffee, which is the main cash crop, 71 percent of the households sell beans, cassava, maize, plantain, or tomatoes. On average, 80 percent of the families have access to piped drinking water and virtually all households use firewood as the primary fuel for cooking.

Data Collection

As a first step toward gaining insight into farmer decision making related to land use, we organized a series of workshops with groups of farmers in three different locations at different altitudes (< 1,500 m; 1,500–1,700 m; > 1,700 m) and thus differing with respect to agroecological conditions, accessibility, and population density (see figure 21.1).

Prior to the workshops, we conducted a study to develop a poverty profile of the Río Cabuyal population, based on a methodology for developing regional poverty profiles based on local perceptions (Ravnborg et al. 1999). The basis for this methodology is the identification of local perceptions of poverty using the well-being ranking technique described by Grandin (1988), which allows the inquiry into local perceptions of well-being and poverty. These perceptions are subsequently translated into indicators. In the case of Río Cabuyal, we found that well-being indicators covered three domains: (1) dependency on others for livelihood security, (2) degree of basic needs satisfaction, and (3) ownership of assets and resources. Based on these indicators, we formulated questions that could be included into a household questionnaire, and we developed a scoring system so that each household would obtain a score on each indicator depending on its answer to the questions in the questionnaire. For each household, the scores obtained on each of the indicators are then combined as an arithmetic mean into a well-being index. Finally, with a view to the entire population of households, well-being categories—that is, threshold values—are defined on the basis of the well-being index. Following this procedure, qualitative perceptions of well-being and poverty are turned into a single and absolute though locally informed measure of poverty.

Following this procedure, we identified three well-being categories, of which the highest level of well-being applied to 23 percent of the households, implying, among other things, having cattle or nonagricultural sources of income, good-quality housing, and absence of periods of food shortage. At the other end of the well-being scale, 31 percent of the households were categorized as suffering the lowest level of well-being, implying dependence on day-laboring on neighboring farms for a considerable part of their livelihood, owning little land, and facing regular periods of food shortage. Finally, 46 percent of the households were categorized as having a middle level of well-being, for many implying earning their livelihood through farming their own land, at times supplemented by day-laboring on neighboring farms, only rarely facing periods of food shortage and experiencing an intermediate housing quality.

We arranged two workshops in each of the three locations: one including participants enjoying highest and middle level of well-being; and one including participants from households enduring the lowest level of well-being. To obtain local plot descriptors, we asked workshop participants to describe what they perceived to be different types of plots, using a *maqueta*, a three-dimensional scale model of the Río Cabuyal watershed (Rubiano et al. 1997) as a reference point. Subsequently, with reference to these descriptors, we asked workshop participants to identify three contrasting plots on the *maqueta*. Each of these

plots was then visited and participants were asked to explain the decision-making process: the objectives, concerns, and reasons that had led to the actual land use of the specific plot. The reasons we obtained through these discussions were subsequently written onto individual cards and grouped into four sets, corresponding to the four main land-use types (crops, fallow, pasture, and forest). Because well-being in Río Cabuyal is closely associated with access to productive resources such as land, labor, and capital (Ravnborg and Guerrero 1996), having separate workshops allowed us to explore whether well-being or access to productive resources is associated with the objectives farmers pursue, the knowledge upon which decisions are based, and the actual decisions made by farmers.

Based on the insight gained through these workshops about the conceptual and logical framework within which farmer decision-making takes place, we developed a pictorial questionnaire (figure 21.2). The aim of the questionnaire was, with reference to specific plots, to collect quantifiable information about (1) land cover (forest, fallow, pasture, or crop); (2) biophysical conditions; (3) the management for a given plot; and (4) the reason for choosing a specific type of land cover for a given plot. In this way, obtaining plot-specific data on all of these four aspects, we will then be able to statistically assess the relations among them with reference to specific land-use types.

One questionnaire sheet is to be filled for each plot included in the sample. The respondent is asked first to indicate the relevant land-use type. Moving clockwise around the images on the questionnaire sheet and putting circles around the relevant options, the respondent is then asked to indicate the biophysical conditions of the plot, its previous use, and the actual management given to the plot, in terms of input and labor use. Following this, we ask an open-ended question concerning reasons for choosing a specific crop. As the final step in the questionnaire, the respondent is asked to rank the pre-identified reasons—which we had put onto cards—corresponding to the actual land-use type according to their importance for making a specific choice, into three

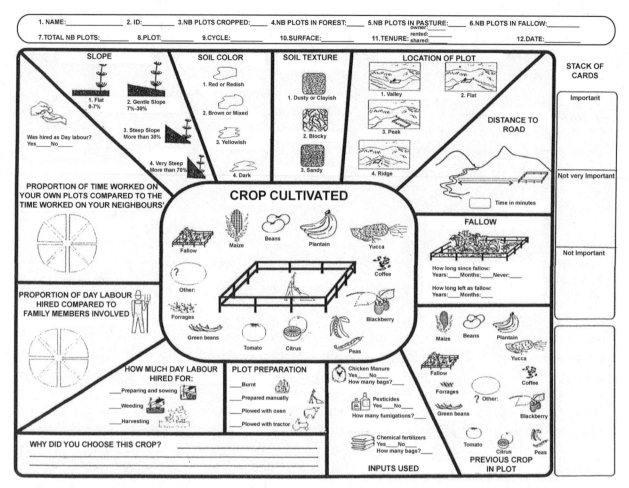

Figure 21.2. Pictorial questionnaire developed for the Río Cabuyal decision-making study. The questionnaire was developed and produced in Spanish only.

categories: 1: important; 2: less important; and 3: unimportant. If the reason mentioned under the open-ended question is not already included among the cards, it is written down and given the rank "1" (important).

We drew a sample of 198 households (corresponding to 17 percent of the households in Río Cabuyal), stratified according to well-being and altitude zone from the Río Cabuyal watershed population. For each household, we included a maximum of four plots in the sample, with one questionnaire sheet to be filled for each plot. For each household, we tried as much as possible to obtain information about plots under land use that were both important to them and as diverse as possible. For households having more than four plots, the respondent was asked to select four plots, representing different uses, as the plots to be included

in the sample. Households with plots under uses other than crops—fallow, pasture, and forest—were asked to select one or two plots representing such uses, however, with a maximum of one plot per land-use type other than crops. With respect to plots under crops, households were asked to select the plots they considered most important to them, while at the same time representing different crops, to obtain variation within each household. The average number of plots owned per household is 3.4 and the average plot size is just below one hectare. Each questionnaire sheet took approximately twenty to twenty-five minutes to fill in.

In total, 532 plots were included in the sample, of which 281 plots were under crops, 54 plots under pasture, 117 plots fallow, and 80 plots under forest cover. The sample represents 13 percent of the land area owned by all households in Río Cabuyal

Table 21.1. Description of sample plots as compared with total number of plots owned by sample households, by land-use type

Land-use type	Number of plots in sample	Total number of plots owned by sample households	Average number of plots owned by sample households	Sample plots as percentage of total number of plots owned by sample houeholds	Percentage of households with all their plots included in the sample	Percentage of sample households owning plots
Crops	281	404	2.0	70	61	96
Pasture	54	62	0.3	87	86	29
Fallow	117	134	0.7	87	88	63
Forest	80	83	0.4	96	96	42
All uses	532	683	3.4	78	58	—

watershed. Table 21.1 provides a description of the coverage of the sample plots compared with the total number of plots owned by the sample households. Considering only the plots under crop cultivation (= 281 plots), the crop distribution for the sample resembles that for all crop plots in the Río Cabuyal watershed (= 2,522 plots) with approximately half the plots under coffee. The main difference is that the sample has a preponderance of plots on which cassava is grown as a monocrop (20 percent in sample versus 12 percent in Río Cabuyal watershed) and of plots under tomato cultivation (7 percent in sample versus 2 percent in Río Cabuyal watershed). Since household respondents selected plots under different crops, as well as plots they considered most important, this reflects the value attached to cassava and tomatoes by farmers as compared to crop combinations such as grains (maize and beans) and cassava grown in association with grains.

The location of the households was georeferenced using aerial photographs. Figure 21.1 shows the location of the 198 households included in the survey differentiated by well-being level. Since most plots are situated close to the homestead, this gives a good indication of the location of the plots.

Data Analysis

The questionnaire data was entered into a database and analyzed using the Statistical Package for Social Sciences, SPSS, version 10.0. A stepwise data-reducing analytical strategy was adopted in order to first construct and then correlate composite variables representing well-being level,[1] soil quality, and reason for crop choice as well as variables directly available from the questionnaire survey.

Optimal scaling procedures were used to construct the variables soil quality and reason for crop choice. Optimal scaling procedures,[2] or multivariate dimension reduction techniques, explore the relationships between two or more variables by representing these in a few dimensions. Using the iterative alternating least square technique, object scores are calculated, corresponding to the coordinates of the point representing the object along the dimensions included in the solution. As these object scores have metric properties, optimal scaling procedures perform a quantification of qualitative data and the object scores can be used as input variables for other procedures requiring interval data. In this study, the object scores were used as input variables for a cluster analysis, using the K-means cluster analysis procedure. Optimal scaling procedures also produce quantifications of the categories of input variables by computing the averages of the scores for the sites in each category.

In the present study, *nonlinear principal component analysis*, which allows the examination of any combination of categorical, ordinal, and numerical variables, is used to compute the soil condition variable. *Homogeneity analysis*, also known as multiple correspondence analysis, in which all variables processed are categorical, is used to compute the variables that summarize the reasons explicitly stated for crop choice. Mutual correlations between these composite variables and variables directly available from the ques-tionnaire database were explored both through optimal scaling procedures and through the detailed analysis of two-way contingency tables.

Results

As a first attempt toward illustrating the importance of soil conditions relative to other factors influencing farmers' choices of land use, table 21.2 lists the reasons mentioned by farmers during the questionnaire interviews as influencing their decision to leave a particular plot in forest, fallow, pasture, or under a specific crop. Table 21.2 also shows the ranks assigned to these reasons as a measure of importance.

Judging from table 21.2, the importance of soil conditions is most notable for the decision to leave a plot in forest. With a combined score of 60, the reason *to protect the soil* ranked as the third most important reason for leaving a plot in forest, as compared to a score of 69 for the most important reason, *to protect the water*.

For plots lying fallow, reasons related to soil conditions ranked second (*restore fertility*) and third (*time for fallow in cropping cycle*). Yet, in the area, fallow is known to be a means to regenerate soil fertility. Therefore, it is surprising that reasons related to regenerating soil fertility did not rank highest among the reasons for leaving a plot fallow. The most important reason for leaving a plot fallow was lack of economic resources for inputs including labor necessary for cultivation.

Reasons related to soil conditions seem to be of least importance for leaving plots under pasture or under a specific crop. The reason *the soil doesn't serve for crops* ranked fourth among the five reasons offered for leaving a plot under pasture, whereas the reasons ranked as most important related directly to the short-term economic gains of pasture-related enterprises.

With respect to crop choice, none of the reasons directly relate crop choice to the soil conditions, and only two reasons, *doesn't require a lot of inputs* and *having a crop that improves the soil*, relate indirectly to soil conditions. This in itself is not sufficient to rule out the importance of soil conditions for crop choice. Like climate, farmers might very well consider soil conditions as *given* at the moment of deciding upon land use. Certain land-use types or crops may simply be discarded *prior* to the explicit decision-making process *due to* the *known* actual soil conditions.[3] In such cases, we should then be able to detect significant correlations between soil conditions on one hand and choice of land-use type or crop on the other. The remaining part of this section examines the extent to which this is the case.

Soil Conditions as Implicitly Correlated with Farmers' Choice of Land-use Type

To analyze the relations between soil conditions and farmers' actual choices of land-use type, we first computed a new soil conditions variable based on farmers' explicit descriptors. Then we relied on correlation analyses to assess the importance of soil conditions on decisions about land use.

Establishing a soil-conditions variable

During the workshops held prior to the questionnaire survey, we found that farmers characterize soil conditions according to descriptors such as soil color (black, reddish, yellow, or brown) and soil structure/texture (sandy, clayish, dusty, or lumpy) as well as according to the plot's location in the landscape and its slope. They expressed clear preferences in favor of black or brown, lumpy soils located on flat or gentle slopes.[4] We found no difference, relative to their well-being level, with respect to farmers' ability to classify soils or to characterize soil conditions. These local descriptors were included as variables in the questionnaire survey (figure 21.2) and can therefore be analyzed statistically.

In order to group the plots according to perceived soil condition, we used the variables soil color, soil texture, plot location, and terrain slope for a nonlinear principal components analysis, and classified the resulting scores for the plots into four clusters.[5] Table 21.3 summarizes the characteristics of these clusters ranking from best to worst soil conditions, according to the constituting variables.

Table 21. 2: Reasons for choosing specific land-use type and crop, ranked in terms of importance, by land-use type

	Number of times ranked as important (score1 = 1) [1]	Number of times ranked as less important (score2 = 2) [2]	Number of times ranked as unimportant (score3 = 3) [3]	Combined score ([1] / score1) + ([2] / score2) + ([3] / score3)
Reasons for leaving plots under forest (n = 78 plots)				
To protect the water	65	0	13	69
To have firewood and building materials	54	13	11	64
To protect the soil	41	37	0	60
To give shade	19	44	15	46
Haven't had time to cut it down	0	7	71	27
The soil doesn't serve for crops	0	4	74	27
We are paid to conserve the forest	0	4	74	27
Reasons for leaving plots under fallow (n = 110 plots)				
Lack of money for inputs *and* laborers	69	8	33	84
Restore fertility	50	14	46	72
Time for fallow in cropping cycle	32	14	64	60
Prefer to cultivate other plots	21	31	58	56
Lack of time for planting/laborers	18	23	69	53
Pays better to day-labor	9	18	83	46
Drought/climate	0	16	94	39
Low crop prices	0	8	102	38
Lack of seeds	0	6	104	38
Reasons for keeping plots under pasture (n = 54 plots)				
Feed for horses	30	12	12	40
Feed for cattle	31	7	16	40
Livestock pays better	27	7	20	37
The soil doesn't serve for crops	0	11	43	20
Haven't had time to plant a crop	0	9	45	20
Reasons for crop choice (n = 281 plots)				
Having products for sale	205	31	44	235
Doesn't require a lot of inputs	169	48	63	214
Having a crop for home consumption	153	85	42	210
The crop has a secured buyer	148	78	54	205
The crop is easier to sell than other crops	138	75	67	198
Having a crop that is easier to transport	119	102	59	190
Doesn't require so much work	101	79	100	174
The crop doesn't cause health problems	99	118	63	179
Having a crop that pays better	98	62	120	169
Having a short season crop	62	53	165	144
Having a crop that improves the soil	58	69	153	144
The crop has no fixed planting season	57	57	166	141
The crop that can be harvested all year	40	29	211	125
The crop has a stable price	18	10	252	107

Frequency of ranks and combined score. Soil-related reasons are indicated in italics.

Table 21.3. Description of soil condition clusters according to soil color, texture, location, and slope (n = 532 plots)

Descriptor *characteristic*	Soil condition cluster			
	Best (n =112) (%)	Good (n = 82) (%)	Fair (n = 236) (%)	Worst (n = 102) (%)
Soil color *black; brown; red; yellow*	black (95)	brown (59) black (31)	black (80)	red (74) black (20)
Soil texture *dusty; lumpy; sandy*	dusty (50) lumpy (29)	dusty (82)	dusty (62) sandy (21)	lumpy (52) dusty (36)
Location *hillside; plain; ridge; valley/depression*	plain (62) valley/depression (34)	ridge (50) hillside (34)	hillside (86)	hillside (86)
Slope *0–7%; 7–30%; 30–70%; >70%*	7–30% (54) 0–7% (38)	7–30% (50) 30–70% (38)	7–30% (45) 30–70% (44)	30–70% (59) 7–30% (27)

Percentages in brackets indicate the proportion of the plots contained in the cluster for which the characteristic applies. Only the most dominant characteristics are included in the table, however, so that 75 percent of the plots contained in each cluster are described according to each descriptor.

The cluster representing the best soil conditions is characterized by black, dusty or lumpy soils located on relatively flat plains. The good soils are located on sloping ridges or hillsides and are brown to black, dusty soils, whereas the fair soils are black, dusty or sandy soils located on slightly steeper hillsides. Finally, the worst soils are the predominantly red lumpy to dusty soils located on very steep hillsides. Of the households with more than one plot included in the sample, 71 percent had plots with different soil conditions or types, which means that soil conditions vary within a few hundred meters in this area.

Examining the relationship between land-use type and soil conditions

We analyzed the relation between soil conditions and farmers' actual choices of land-use type using this new soil conditions variable. Table 21.4 presents the results of this analysis. It shows that a slightly higher proportion of forest plots (51 percent) than plots under other land-use types (42–45 percent) is situated on fair soils, and that a slightly higher proportion of plots lying fallow (23 percent) is found on the worst soils (as compared with 18–19 percent of the plots under other land-use

types). Overall, however, no significant association is found between land-use type and soil conditions. This indicates that other factors than soil conditions dominate when farmers make decisions about land use for a particular plot.

Thus, to explore which other factors influence farmers' choice of land use and relate the importance of these factors to that of soil conditions, we included three more variables in the analysis. The first of these is the distance to the plot, based on the assumption that the closer the plot to the farmer's home, the more intensive the use (i.e., cropping). The second variable is total farm size, based on the assumption that the bigger the farm, the more likely a farmer would be to choose uses other than cropping. The final variable is household well-being level, based on the assumption that farmers enjoying higher levels of well-being will more likely choose uses such as pasture that require not only sufficient land but also other resources such as livestock.[6]

Examining the correlation between these variables with farmers' actual choice of land use, significant correlation emerged between farmers' actual choice of land use and total farm size and well-being level, while we found no significant relation

Table 21.4. Soil conditions (soil-based clusters) by land-use type (n = 532)

Soil condition	Crops (n = 281)	Pasture (n = 54)	Fallow (n = 117)	Forest (n = 80)	All land-use types (n = 532)
Best soils	22	19	19	23	21
Good soils	18	20	13	8	15
Fair soils	42	43	45	51	44
Worst soils	18	19	23	19	19
All soil conditions	100	100	100	100	100

Observed significance level of Pearson chi-square: p = 0.464 (not significant)

Table 21.5. Correlation between variables that potentially may determine decisions on land use (n = 532)

Variables	Land use (crop; fallow; pasture; forest)	Distance (< 5 min; 5–10 min; 10–20 min; > 20 min)	Total farm size (< 1 ha; 1–3 ha; 3–6 ha; > 6 ha)	Well-being level (highest; middle; lowest)
Distance (< 5 min; 5–10 min; 10–20 min; > 20 min)	ns ($p = 0.146$) [crop < 5 min] [forest > 20 min]			
Total farm size (< 1 ha; 1–3 ha; 3–6 ha; > 6 ha)	ns ($p = 0.65$) [crop = < 1 ha] [pasture 3–6 ha and > 6 ha]	ns ($p = 0.093$) [> 20 min > 6 ha]		
Well-being level (highest; middle; lowest)	* ($p = 0.015$) [crop—lowest] [pasture—highest] [forest—highest]	* ($p = 0.014$) [< 5 min—lowest] [10–20 min—highest] [> 20 min—middle]	*** ($p < 0.001$) m [< 1 ha—lowest] [3–6 ha—middle and highest] [> 6 ha—highest]	
Soil quality (best; good; fair; worst)	ns ($p = 0.464$) [fallow—worst] [forest—fair]	ns ($p = 0.387$) [> 20 min—worst] [> 20 min—best]	ns ($p = 0.275$)	ns ($p = 0.280$) [lowest—worst] [highest—good and fair]

Summary of two-way contingency tables between the variables actual land use, soil conditions, distance to plot from road, total farm size, and well-being level: Pearson chi-square and, in square brackets, associations between options with frequencies notably higher than expected.

between land-use type and distance to the plot. Small farms are more likely to be used for crops, particularly those of one hectare or less.[7] Conversely, the likelihood of a plot being under forest or pasture increases with farm size.[8] No significant association was found between fallow and total farm size. Table 21.5 summarizes the results of pairwise correlations between the variables included in the analysis of land use.

We found a similar pattern of association between land-use type and well-being level. The likelihood of plots being under pasture or forest is significantly greater on farms displaying the highest well-being level, whereas the likelihood of

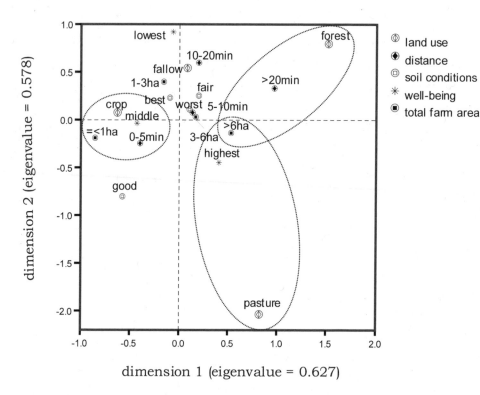

Figure 21.3. Land-use type correlated by soil conditions, distance (in minutes) from road, total farm area, and household well-being level (*n* = 532). Category quantifications (centroids) resulting from nonlinear canonical correlation analysis.

cropping is significantly greater for plots belonging to households of middle and particularly the lowest well-being level. Again, no significant association emerges between the use of fallow and well-being level.

Finally, we found no overall significant correlation between land use and distance to the plot. Yet, one fifth (21 percent) of the forest plots are situated more than twenty minutes' walk from home, while the same is true for only 10–13 percent of the plots under other uses.

Although we found no overall correlation between land-use type on one hand and soil conditions or distance to the plot on the other, partial association between these variables might still exist. To explore whether such an association exists while considering simultaneously all the potential determinants (total farm size, well-being level, distance to plots, and soil conditions),[9] we entered these variables into a nonlinear canonical correlation analysis, which allows the examination of correlation between two or more sets of variables. We entered the variables as two sets: One set contained the potential determinants for farmers' choice of land-use type, while the other contained the variable representing the observed land use. By entering all the potential determinant variables as one set, the effects of association between these variables—such as that between well-being level and total farm size—are minimized, while focusing on the correlation with the second set, namely farmers' actual choice of land-use type.

Figure 21.3 shows the category quantifications graph resulting from this analysis. Each point in the figure corresponds to the average of all plot scores for a given category (indicated by the label). The closer the points, the more likely it is that they correspond to the same plots, and the farther a point is from the origin the better the corresponding variable discriminates the plots.

Looking first at the land-use types farthest from the origin, figure 21.3 indicates that the choice to leave a plot under forest is most strongly associated with the plot's position relative to the road (> 20 minutes walk) and to a lesser extent with farm size (> 6 hectares). Plots under pasture are more likely to be large farms (> 6 hectares) with good soil conditions owned by a farmer of the highest well-being level. Also the choice to have a plot under crops is associated with good soil conditions, particularly

Table 21.6. Soil conditions (soil-based clusters) by actual crop (coffee, cassava, grains, tomatoes)* (n = 249)

Soil-conditions clusters	Actual crop grown				
	Coffee (n = 138)	Cassava (n = 70)	Grains (n = 20)	Tomatoes (n = 21)	Total (n = 249)
Best soil conditions	17	20	15	14	18
Good soil conditions	17	23	10	29	19
Fair soil conditions	45	40	55	43	44
Worst soil conditions	21	17	20	14	19
All soil conditions	100	100	100	100 ·	100

Observed significance level of Pearson chi-square = 0.855 (not significant)

for households with a middle level of well-being; with very small or small farms (< 1 hectare or 1–3 hectares); and with being situated close to the road (0–5 minutes walk). Finally, plots under fallow appear to be associated with moderate distance from the road (10–20 minutes walk), with low well-being households, and with small farms (1–3 hectares).

Apart from a single data-point representing good soil conditions, which appears to be associated with plots under crops and pasture, all the points representing specific soil conditions are located very close to the origin. This indicates that soil conditions are not significantly correlated with any specific land-use type, supporting the conclusion drawn from table 21.4. Rather, farmers' choice of land use appears to be conditioned by total farm size (pasture, crops, forest), level of well-being (pasture, crops, fallow) and distance to the plot from the road (forest, fallow, crops).

In conclusion, both the reasons explicitly stated by farmers for choosing a specific land-use type as well as our efforts to disclose an implicit correlation between land-use type and soil conditions suggest that soil conditions are of only marginal importance in determining farmers' actual choice of land-use type. Rather, farmers' choices concerning land use appear to be determined by their well-being level, which in turn is associated with total farm size and distance to the plot from the road. To poorer farmers, of whom very few own livestock, it makes little sense to leave a plot under pasture. Moreover, farmers with small farms have little choice but to plant crops to satisfy household needs, even though

soil conditions may dictate their plot(s) would be better suited to pasture or forest. Finally, farmers tend to choose the most labor-intensive land-use type—that is, crops—for their most accessible plots and the least intensive land-use type—forest—for the most distant plots. Thus, at the time of actual decision making, these concerns override soil conditions as determinants of land use.

Soil Conditions as an Implicit Determinant for Farmers' Crop Choices

In this section we undertake an analysis similar to that of the previous section, but instead of looking at determinants of land-use choice, we narrow our focus and examine the factors that affect farmers' choice of crops.

Examining the relation between crop choice and soil conditions

In the workshops held prior to the pictorial questionnaire survey, farmers had described the existence of decision-making rules such as "red soils being good for cassava while bad for coffee" or "valley bottom soils being good for maize." Hence, crop choice was described as related, at least partly, to soil conditions. Yet, although grains (maize and beans) appear slightly more likely to be cultivated on fair soils than the other crops, no significant association was found in the analysis of the association between soil conditions and farmers' actual crop choice (table 21.6). Note that the same classification of soil conditions was used for analyzing crop choice as for the analysis of land-use type.[10]

Table 21.7. Description of reason clusters (n = 280 plots)

Characteristic	Reason cluster			
	Short cycle, marketable (n = 43) (%)	Secure market, low input and flexible labor requirements (n = 163) (%)	Secure market, year-round income and environmentally sound (n = 36) (%)	Home consumption and low input requirements (n = 38) (%)
Having products for sale	♦♦♦ (72)	♦♦♦ (88)	♦♦♦ (69) ♦♦ (22)	♦ (79)
Easier to sell than other crops	♦♦♦ (40) ♦ (33)	♦♦♦ (60) ♦♦ (33)	♦♦♦ (64) ♦♦ (19)	♦ (92)
Pays better than other crops	♦ (67) ♦♦ (21)	♦♦♦ (46) ♦ (31)	♦♦♦ (47) ♦♦ (36)	♦ (92)
Secured buyer	♦♦♦ (47) ♦ (30)	♦♦♦ (60) ♦♦ (36)	♦♦♦ (83)	♦ (87)
Stable price	♦ (98)	♦ (98)	♦♦♦ (47) ♦ (39)	♦ (97)
Easier to transport	♦♦ (47) ♦ (30)	♦♦♦ (53) ♦♦ (41)	♦♦♦ (58) ♦♦ (31)	♦ (84)
Short season	♦♦♦ (56) ♦ (42)	♦ (70)	♦♦♦ (42) ♦ (31)	♦ (58) ♦♦ (24)
No fixed planting season	♦ (63) ♦♦♦ (23)	♦♦♦ (71)	♦♦♦ (44) ♦♦ (33)	♦ (42) ♦♦♦ (40)
Harvested all year round	♦ (88)	♦ (84)	♦♦♦ (69) ♦ (19)	♦ (76)
Doesn't require a lot of inputs	♦ (86)	♦♦♦ (72)	♦ (33) ♦♦♦ (44)	♦♦♦ (79)
Doesn't require a lot of labor input	♦ (95)	♦♦♦ (42) ♦♦ (31)	♦♦♦ (44) ♦♦ (36)	♦♦♦ (45) ♦ (36)
Doesn't cause health problems	♦ (51) ♦♦ (26)	♦♦ (48) ♦♦♦ (33)	♦♦♦ (56) ♦♦ (25)	♦♦ (53) ♦♦♦ (40)
Helps to improve the soil	♦ (54) ♦♦♦ (33)	♦ (62) ♦♦ (25)	♦♦ (53) ♦♦♦ (28)	♦ (58) ♦♦♦ (32)
Serves for home consumption	♦ (37) ♦♦ (33)	♦♦♦ (53) ♦♦ (39)	♦♦♦ (58) ♦ (25)	♦♦♦ (84)

The importance of the reason is indicated by diamonds, so that ♦♦♦ indicates "important"; ♦♦ indicates "less important," and ♦ indicates "unimportant." The numbers in brackets indicate the proportion of the plots that correspond to the cluster, showing the relative importance of the reasons mentioned. When the most prominent level of importance accounts for at least 70 percent of the plots contained in the cluster, only the percentage for that level of importance is included in the table. The shaded areas indicate the concerns that best characterize the clusters.

Without questioning the agronomic logic of the soils-related decision-making guidelines stated in the workshops, table 21.6 indicates that such rules may only be normative in the sense that in the actual decision-making process with respect to crop choice, the importance of soil conditions is overshadowed by other concerns.

Only the four major crops are included in the analysis due to the low frequency of the remaining crops: sugarcane, blackberries, plantain (most commonly grown in association with coffee and only rarely in sole stands), and sisal.

As a first step toward identifying which factors other than soils might influence farmers' crop choice, we took a closer look at the reasons, ranked by importance, motivating crop choice, as obtained with the questionnaire survey. Referring to table 21.2, fourteen reasons potentially motivating a

Table 21.8. Correlation between variables that potentially may determine crop choice (n = 248)

Variables	Crop (coffee; cassava; grains; tomato)	Distance (< 5 min; 5–10 min; 10–20 min; > 20 min)	Total farm size (< 1 ha; 1–3 ha; 3–6 ha; > 6 ha)	Well-being level (highest; middle; lowest)	Soil quality (best; good; fair; worst)
Distance (< 5 min; 5–10 min; 10–20 min; > 20 min)	ns (p = 0.165) [cassava-10–20 min]				
Total farm size (< 1 ha; 1–3 ha; 3–6 ha; > 6 ha)	* (p = 0.014) [coffee < 1 ha] [cassava > 6 ha] [tomato 3–6 ha]	ns (p = 0.244) [< 5 min 3–6 ha] [5–10 min 1–3 ha]			
Well-being level (highest; middle; lowest)	ns (p = 0.288) [coffee—lowest]	ns (p = 0.104) [< 5 min—lowest]	*** (p < 0.001) [< 1 ha—lowest] [3–6 ha—highest] [> 6 ha—highest]		
Soil quality (best; good; fair; worst)	ns (p = 0.855)	ns (p = 0.718) [< 5 min—good and fair]	ns (p = 0.311) [< 1 ha—worst] [3–6 ha—fair]	ns (p = 0.314) [lowest—worst]	
Reason for crop choice (short cycle/market; market/low input; market/year-round; home/low input)	*** (p < 0.001) [coffee—market/low input and market/year round] [grains—home/low input] [tomato—short cycle/market]	ns (p = 0.081) [5–10 min—short cycle/market]	ns (p = 0.128) [< 1 ha—market/ low input]	ns (p = 0.117) [lowest—market /low input]	ns (p = 0.309) [worst—market/ low input]

Summary of two-way contingency tables between the variables actual crop choice, soil conditions, distance to plot from road, total farm size, well-being level, reasons for crop choice: Pearson chi-square and, in square brackets, associations between options with frequencies notably higher than expected.

particular choice of crop had been ranked as either important, less important, or unimportant. Hence, to discover possible patterns of association between these reasons and their level of importance, and to reduce the data to a number of different sets of concerns motivating individual crop choice, we relied on a homogeneity analysis of the ranked reasons for a crop choice, followed by a cluster analysis to group these reasons into four representative clusters. We chose a three-dimensional solution, which allowed us to identify three main thrusts of farmers for their choice of crop. Reasons related to marketing such as *having a product for sale* and *having a crop with secured buyer* discriminate most along the first of these dimensions, whereas in the second dimension, the best discriminants are the reasons related to stability, for example, *having a crop with a stable price* and *having a crop that can be harvested all year*

round. Finally, the third dimension is associated with reasons related to input requirements, most notably with *having a crop that doesn't require a lot of inputs.*

The composition of the four-reasons clusters is described in table 21.7. The first cluster comprises plots for which having a short seasonal crop for sale was the overriding motivation for crop choice, whereas no importance was attached to input use or risks of applying pesticides. The second and most common set of concerns, applying to more than half of the plots, relates to having a cash crop with an easy and secure market, combined with low input requirements and a flexible planting season. For the plots contained in the third cluster, having a cash crop with an easy and secure market is also an important concern motivating crop choice. In addition, however, the input requirements of the

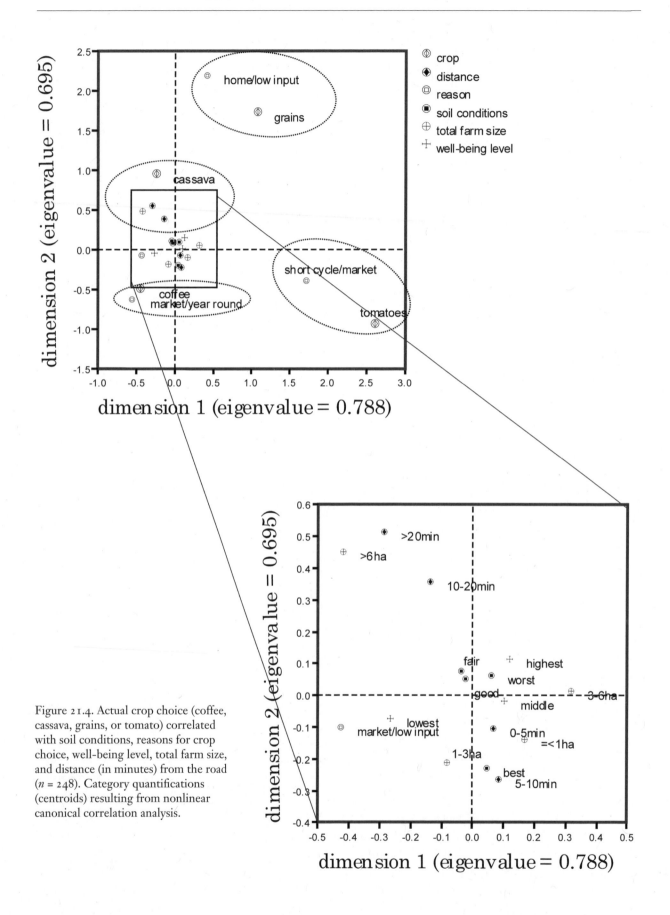

Figure 21.4. Actual crop choice (coffee, cassava, grains, or tomato) correlated with soil conditions, reasons for crop choice, well-being level, total farm size, and distance (in minutes) from the road (*n* = 248). Category quantifications (centroids) resulting from nonlinear canonical correlation analysis.

crop are considered less important whereas price stability and being able to harvest and thus obtain income on a year-round basis are dominating concerns. Finally, the fourth cluster is composed of plots where no importance is attached to market-related features. Instead, the concerns motivating crop choice relate to cropping for home consumption and to low input requirements. The concerns motivating farmers' crop choice do not appear to be associated with the household's level of well-being since no significant correlation was found between these two variables ($p = 0.117$).

Actual choice of crop is strongly associated with the reasons clusters (table 21.8). Thus, the choices to grow coffee and cassava are primarily associated with having a crop for which a secure market exists and that is not too demanding in terms of input and labor use. The choice to grow tomatoes, on the other hand, is associated with the wish to have a short cycle and marketable crop. Finally, the decision to grow basic grains (maize and beans) is associated with having crops for home consumption with low input requirements and, to a lesser extent, with having a short-cycle marketable crop.

In addition to the explicit concerns motivating farmers' crop choice reflected in the reason variable, other factors such as distance of the plot, total farm size, and household well-being level can be expected to influence farmers' choice of crop.

Pairwise correlations between each of these variables on one hand and actual crop choice (coffee, cassava, grains, and tomatoes) on the other show that only total farm size is significantly associated with farmers' crop choice. Table 21.8 summarizes the results of pairwise correlations between the variables included in the analysis of crop choice.

Tomatoes and cassava appear to be crops associated with moderately large to large farms. More than half of all tomato plots belong to moderately large farms (3–6 hectares); the same is true for only 21–35 percent of the plots under other crops. Thirty percent of all cassava plots are found on farms larger than 6 hectares as compared with 5–25 percent of plots under other crops. Although no overall significant association is found with the other variables, there is a tendency for cassava to be planted on more distant plots (10–20 and > 20

minutes' walk from the road). Forty percent of the plots under cassava are situated more than 10 minutes' walking from the road as compared to 10–27 percent of the plots under other crops. Finally, coffee becomes a more likely crop choice as well-being decreases. Half of the plots belonging to the households with the highest level of well-being are under coffee, as compared with two-thirds of the plots belonging to households with the lowest level of well-being.

As in the case of farmers' choice of land-use type, we explored the possibility of partial associations by defining two sets of variables to include in a nonlinear canonical correlation analysis. The first of these sets consists of all the variables representing factors that potentially might influence farmers' crop choice: soil conditions, reasons mentioned that motivate crop choice, total farm size, household well-being level, and distance of the plot from the road. The second set consists of a single variable representing farmers' actual crop choice (only plots under coffee, cassava, grains, or tomatoes are included in the analysis). Figure 21.4 shows the category quantification graph resulting from the analysis (including an enlargement of the area near the origin).

Figure 21.4, which should be interpreted in the same way as figure 21.3, confirms the close association (described on the basis of the pairwise analysis above) between crop choice and the set of reasons motivating crop choice (i.e., the reasons clusters): tomatoes are associated with the wish to have a short-cycle, marketable crop; grains with having crops for home consumption with low input requirements; and coffee with the wish to have a marketable crop providing a year-round income. Only plots under cassava appear to be associated with factors others than those reflected in the reason variable—namely with distance of the plot from the road (cassava being grown on the more distant plots) and with total farm size (being more likely on large farms)—as was also revealed in the pairwise analysis. Even more pronounced than in the analysis of factors influencing choice of land-use type, all the points representing different sets of soil conditions are situated close to the origin, indicating the lack of association between soil conditions and farmers' crop choice. Despite the existence of significant pairwise correlation between well-being level and actual crop choice, even the importance of household well-being level appears negligible when other factors, most notably reasons motivating crop choice, are included in the analysis.

In conclusion, both the reasons explicitly stated as motivating crop choice and the detailed analysis of two-way contingency tables between the variables suggest that concerns with the market opportunities existing for specific crops (short-cycle crops or year-round, stable markets) and with the input requirements of the specific crops, and to a lesser extent with farm size, strongly influence farmers in their choices of crops for a specific plot. Soil conditions as well as household well-being level are of marginal importance.

Conclusions

In this chapter we have critically examined the relevance of the widely accepted assumption that soil conditions are an important factor in shaping farmers' choices of land type, by analyzing data related to farmer's choice to leave a particular plot in forest, fallow, pasture, or a specific crop type.

The workshops that we conducted in the Río Cabuyal watershed in the Colombian Andes showed that farmers distinguish different soil types and know what would be the *ideal* land use for each soil type. However, our examination of farmers' actual decision making suggests that the importance of soil conditions is only *nominal* in the sense that at the time of actual decisions on land use or crop type, other concerns outweigh soil conditions. This is supported by two pieces of evidence.

First, in the questionnaire survey, soil conditions were explicitly mentioned as having only some importance for deciding to keep a plot in forest and to a lesser extent in fallow, while they were hardly mentioned as important for choosing a specific crop or leaving a plot under pasture. Even in the case of forest and fallow, other reasons given were related to protecting water sources (in the case of forest) and lack of economic resources (in the case of fallow) were ranked as more important.

Second, in the statistical analysis of the questionnaire data, the importance of soil conditions as a determinant both of overall land-use type and of specific crop choice was found to be almost negligible. Rather farmers' actual choice of land-use type was found to be associated with total farm size and well-being level, whereas the actual choice of crop for a given plot was found to be closely associated with concerns related to marketability and the input and labor requirements of a given crop. The importance of market and input-related concerns did not relate to household well-being level. Acknowledging that farmers, due to the importance attached to concerns such as having certain land-use types and crops and thereby market opportunities within their portfolios, are conscious of making suboptimal land-use and crop choice from the point of view of soil conditions, it becomes important to explore to what extent farmers take measures to compensate for such suboptimal choices. This is a topic for further research.

The study reported in this chapter is a case study, and as such it cannot conclusively discard the importance of soil conditions as a determinant in farmers' decision-making process on land use. However, it seriously questions the widespread emphasis given to soil conditions in external interventions related to land management. It also questions the often limited attention paid to socioeconomic factors in land-use planning, which we found to be significantly more prominent in explaining farmers' actual land use than soil conditions.

Rather than designing development interventions to enhance farmers' knowledge of soil conditions, two implications for the design of development interventions thus emerge from this conclusion. First, emphasis should be directed at assisting farmers in developing feasible measures to compensate for land-use choices, which from an environmental or agronomic point of view are suboptimal. Second, more emphasis should be directed at understanding how different sets of market conditions affect the sustainability of land management and how to promote environmentally friendly market conditions.

Acknowledgments

The authors wish to thank Ron Knapp, Grégoire Leclerc, and Charles Hall for their valuable and stimulating comments on earlier drafts of this chapter. We are also grateful to Liliana Mosquera, who assisted us in carrying out the survey. Financial support for the study was provided by the Danish International Development Assistance (Danida) and is gratefully acknowledged.

Notes

1. As already described, the variable *well-being level* had been established on the basis of a previous survey—the 1993 Río Cabuyal household census survey.

2. Optimal scaling procedures quantify a mix of categorical, ordinal, and interval data by assigning numerical values to the cases and categories, using the iterative alternating least-squares method. The object scores are calculated so that objects within one category are plotted close together whereas objects in different categories are plotted far apart, and the category quantifications are the average or centroids of the object scores of the objects in that category. The optimal scaling procedures available in SPSS (version 10.0) were developed by the Department of Data Theory at the University of Leiden (SPSS, 1999).

3. If, for example, a farmer is aware that he has only red and very coarsely textured soils, he rules out planting coffee from the very beginning and only considers whether to grow tomatoes or cassava—crops that he thinks would do relatively well on the soil type in question. Thus, in the explicit decision-making process, soil type does not enter as a factor although it did enter as a concern prior to the explicit decision-making process.

4. Soil color and soil structure/texture are used as indicators of soil quality as these characteristics relate to the soil's ability to retain water as well as nutrients. The preference for flat or gentle slopes is explained by the ease of working the soil.

5. We selected a two-dimensional solution for the nonlinear PCA, followed by a k-means cluster analysis.

6. It should be noted that well-being level and total farm size are closely associated (see table 21.5), farm area being one of seven variables constituting household well-being.

7. Two-thirds of the plots belonging to farms of one hectare or less are under crops, compared with 56 percent of the plots belonging to 1–3 hectare farms and 45 percent of the plots belonging to farms bigger than six hectares.

8. One fifth of the plots belonging to farms larger than six hectares are under forest, whereas this is the case for only 7 percent of the smallest farms and 15–16 percent of the middle-sized farms. With respect to pasture, 15 percent of the plots belonging to the largest farms are under pasture, whereas this is the case for as little as 5 percent for the smallest farms.

9. It should be noted that no significant correlation was found between soil conditions and well-being level ($p = 0.28$) or total farm size ($p = 0.533$).

10. This is valid since the plots under crop cultivation show a distribution of the four variables constituting the constructed soil conditions variable similar to that of the total sample, which was used for clustering.

References

Alfaro, R., J. Bouma, L. O. Fresco, D. M. Jansen, S. B. Kroonenberg, A. C. J. van Leeuwen, R. A. Schipper, R. J. Sevenhuyse, J. J. Stoorvogel, and V. Watson. 1994. Sustainable land use planning in Costa Rica: A methodological case study on farm and regional level. In Fresco et al. 1994, 183–202.

Bellon, M. R., and J. E. Taylor. 1993. 'Folk' soil taxonomy and the partial adoption of new seed varieties. *Economic Development and Cultural Change* 41, no. 4: 763–86.

Brinkman, R. 1994. Recent developments in land use planning, with special reference to FAO. In Fresco et al. 1994, 11–21.

de Kool, S. 1996. Exploring soil health through local indicators and scientific parameters. M.Sc. thesis, Wageningen Agricultural University.

FAO. 1976. A framework for land evaluation. FAO Soils Bulletin 32. Rome: FAO.

Fresco, L. O., L. Stroosnijder, J. Bouma, and H. van Keulen, eds. 1994. *The Future of the Land: Mobilising and Integrating Knowledge for Land Use Options.* Chichester: Wiley.

Grandin, B. 1988. *Wealth Ranking in Smallholder Communities: A Field Manual.* London: Intermediate Technology Publications.

Malcolm, D. W. 1953. *Sukumaland: An African People and Their Country.* Oxford: Oxford University Press.

Rappaport, J. 1990. *The Politics of Memory: Native Historical Interpretation in the Colombian Andes.* Cambridge: Cambridge University Press.

Ravnborg, H. M. 1992. Sensing sustainability: Farmers as soil resource managers. CDR Working Paper 92.6. Copenhagen: Centre for Development Research.

Ravnborg, H. M., and M. P. Guerrero. 1996. Poverty profiles for designing and evaluating rural research and development activities. In *CIAT Hillsides Program Annual Report, 1994–1995*, 165–202. Cali, Colombia: Centro Internacional de Agricultura Tropical.

Ravnborg, H. M., R. M. Escolán, M. P. Guerrero, M. A. Méndez, F. Mendoza, E. M. de Páez, and F. Motta. 1999. Developing regional poverty profiles based on local perceptions. CIAT Publication no. 291. Cali, Colombia: Centro Internacional de Agricultura Tropical.

Rossiter, D. G., and A. R. van Wambeke. 1993. Automated Land Evaluation System, ALES Version 4 User's Manual. Cornell University Department of Soil, Crop and Atmospheric Sciences.

Rounce, N. V. 1949. *The Agriculture of the Cultivation Steppe: Department of Agriculture, Tanganyika Territory.* Cape Town: Longmans, Green and Co.

Rubiano, J., M. Vidal, and M. O. Fiscué. 1997. *Como construir modelos tri-dimensionales de cuencas hidrograficas: Un manual para entidades que trabajan con comunidades.* Pescador, Colombia: Consorcio

interinstitucional para una Agricultura Sostenible in Laderas (CIPASLA).

SPSS. 1994. SPSS Categories 6.1. Chicago: SPSS Inc.

Talawar, S. 1996. Local soil classification and management practices: Bibliographic review. Laboratory of Agricultural and Natural Resource Anthropology, University of Georgia.

Talawar, S., and R. E. Rhoades. 1998. Scientific and local classification and management of soils. *Agriculture and Human Values* 15, no. 1: 3–14.

Urbano, P., J. Rubiano, W. B. Bell, and E. B. Knapp. 1995. Cambios en el uso de la tierra como posible indicador de un desarrollo sostenible en una zona de laderas—subcuenca del Río Cabuyal, Cauca, Colombia. Paper presented September 7–9, 1995 at the IV Congreso AESIG, Barcelona.

Zimmerer, K. S. 1994. Local soil knowledge: Answering basic questions in highland Bolivia. *Journal of Soil and Water Conservation* 1:29.

CHAPTER 22

CHOOSING SOCIAL TECHNOLOGIES EMPIRICALLY

SUSAN ALLAN AND DEAN HOLLAND

Introduction

Development professionals are increasingly using collective action to address aspects of natural resource management (NRM). This means managing people, as well as nature. The organizational structures that we know about form the "social technologies" available to us, such as catchment coordinating committees, production cooperatives, and local research groups. Sometimes these groups are spectacularly successful, and sometimes they are notoriously unsuccessful. The challenge is to know what factors indicate their chances of success from the outset.

We argue that development science has been here before. Development professionals have already learned that for biophysical technologies, such as new plant varieties and new NRM practices, success depends on a diagnosis of what type of technology is appropriate to a given natural, economic, and social environment. Development professionals have created an arsenal of participatory and nonparticipatory tools to do such diagnoses. In other words, we are already empirical about the development and choice of biophysical technologies. We argue that there is a need to create such empirical approaches to the development and choice of *social* technologies.

This chapter suggests empirical ways of finding a group structure that is appropriate to (1) the *tasks* to be carried out, and (2) the *level of social capital* in the community. We give a range of possible ways of organizing for collective action, and we ask how much social capital each type of organization needs. We propose a scale that ranks organizational types by the amount of social capital needed to sustain them. We then present a framework for understanding the elements of social capital as applied to collective action, a framework that can give us a rough answer to the question of how much social

capital we have. Finally, we discuss key issues for development professionals when applying social technologies to the NRM challenges faced by their organization.

Why Is an Empirical Approach to Social Capital Important to Development Interventions?

The term "social capital" helps us to understand the theory and practice of people working together. As a term that is used across disciplines, social capital legitimates the consideration of the social resources that a society, community, or group can harness for its own development. For over a decade, the term has been gaining prominence in many fields of the social sciences. It is now entering the natural sciences through participatory and people-centered approaches to research.

Biophysical technologies need minimum levels of money (financial capital) and natural resources (natural capital) to implement. After lessons from the last century, it is rarer now to find projects or policies that rely on expensive technologies for the poor, or recommend nutrient-demanding crops on poor soils. Such approaches would require continued outside support to be maintained, and when the support goes, the technology is abandoned. Yet the track record of development projects suggests that development professionals continue to promote group structures that require high social capital to people who are currently poor in social capital. The results are similar: without continued outside support such as provision of leadership or financial resources, both the group and the collective tasks are abandoned.

It is not that social capital is more important than other elements of development. Instead, our observation is that social capital is often the capital around which development approaches are the *least empirical*. Hence, social capital failures or misunderstandings are increasingly causing development interventions to falter. Development professionals already have a greater degree of shared vocabulary and understanding for the other capitals, and a broader set of tools for understanding which types of intervention are appropriate where. We have ways of becoming aware of conditions of poverty, or a lack of infrastructure, or poor formal literacy, and we have tools (both participatory and nonparticipatory) to respond to these. But do we know how to find out how much social capital a community has? Do we know what types of group structure are appropriate to achieve a collective task given different levels of trust or hope in a community? These are the central questions of this chapter.

Being empirical about social capital makes explicit and purposeful many of the decisions associated with entering a community and engaging in development interventions. For example, in an area with low social capital that requires a complex task, we can ask if we have the time and resources to build social capital before attempting the task. We can ask if we need to partner with other development agencies. We can ask if this is the right time to do this type of intervention in this place, or if we should come back later or pick another place. Without an empirical analysis of the amount of social capital present and the amount required for a particular task or group structure, key decisions about the nature of development interventions may be made implicitly, based on the amount of funding available, and when the funder needs the project completed. But it is better to have explicit empirical information.

To tackle the question of how much social capital is needed for what types of intervention, we propose a scale of group structures that may be appropriate to different levels of social capital. First, we turn to what we mean by that term.

What Do We Mean by Social Capital?

The trust and hope mentioned in the preceding paragraphs are two elements commonly associated with social capital, but there are many definitions of social capital. Here we choose a practical one:

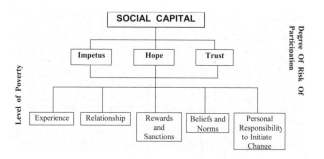

Figure 22.1. Factors affecting people's decisions to get involved and stay involved in collective action (from Allan 2000). We define social capital as being made of these factors.

social capital is those things necessary for collective action. Its measure is not absolute, but concerned with the question, "Have we got *enough* social capital to support the tasks we want to do together and the structures we will need to organize our work?" This perspective is very different from the "let the individual and the market decide" perspective that has permeated much of development policies.

From this starting point, Allan (2000) researched the elements of social capital that people associated with this practical definition, and the results are summarized in figure 22.1. Allan (2000) found social capital to be made up of three major components: (1) the impetus for people to work together, (2) the amount of trust between individuals, and (3) the hope they held that their lives could be improved through collective action. These in turn depended on five elements: (1) experiences of collective action (both positive and negative), (2) the degree of personal responsibility for making change and people's perceptions of this in others, (3) the rewards and sanctions around collective action, (4) the relationships among people, and (5) the beliefs and norms that people held and the degree to which these are shared, particularly regarding which issues are private issues and which can be dealt with in public.

Organizations are built not from these elements, but from scores of piecemeal decisions by individuals to get involved, and once involved, to relate and share tasks based on the perceived or agreed roles and responsibilities of each participant (Wilson 1987). The elements in figure 22.1

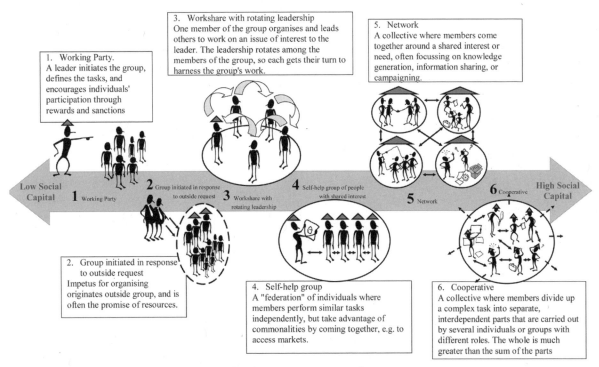

Figure 22.2. A proposed scale of social capital and group structures in the Ucayali region of Peru. Key: ▲ Denotes leadership of task.

are proposed as those things that influence such individual decisions.

In addition to these eight elements, two contextual factors were identified that affected people's ability to engage in communal activities. These were: (1) individuals' experiences of poverty and (2) their perception of the risk of participation. International and local nongovernmental organizations (NGOs) have demonstrated the valuable role that organizations of the poor have in sustainable development. It is therefore ironic that participation in these organizations involves a degree of risk that can discourage involvement by the poor. Richer people can afford more of the risks associated with group activity than can poorer people. These may include a loss of their investment of resources and effort, damage to their property or crops by negligent workers during shared work activities, or involvement in a scheme that overcommits their resources and leaves them indebted. The predominance of a day-to-day survival mode among the poor is also not conducive to collective processes focused on long-term rewards. Poverty therefore has a significant impact on the nature and extent of each of the elements of social capital.

The presence of social capital is not necessarily positive. The same ties that bind also exclude (Narayan 1999:5). Onyx and Bullen (2000) show how social capital is not related to tolerance of others. Instead, the unity of a group may be based on intolerance and exclusion of others. At the extreme, such attitudes lead to arrogance, inflated self-importance, and wars self-justified by the supposedly superior genes or civilizations of the aggressor group. Nevertheless, the elements of social capital provide a framework through which we can better understand the extent and nature of social interaction between residents of the communities with which we work. This understanding informs decisions about where, with whom, and how we should work.

How Much Social Capital Do We Need?

We propose that the more social capital a group of people has, the greater the range of structures the group can adopt, and the more complex the collective tasks it can address. Based on empirical findings by Allan (2000), figure 22.2 illustrates this relationship, suggesting that a working party with a leader needs little social capital, while a successful example of what we term a "cooperative" is one of the most advanced forms of organization, requiring a high level of social capital. In addition, more complex group structures may need a broader range of the elements of social capital that are named in figure 22.1. A group that can successfully operate as a cooperative is likely also to have enough social capital to operate at any of the lower levels. The scale is described below, with details and examples of the different group types following figure 22.2. Then we suggest how to use the scale to inform your work.

The group types presented on the scale are those encountered by the authors, largely during research conducted in Pucallpa, Peru (Allan 2000). The types were identified through a convergent interview process (Dick 1998), and refined through feedback from the people represented in the groups. The rank order of the group types on the scale represents our interpretation of the breadth and depth of the elements of social capital required to sustain the groups, based on the interview data and further feedback from workshops with the participants.

Figure 22.2 does not include a definitive list of the possible group structures for collective work, but gives the reader some broad prototypes that can be related to groups that the reader knows. The boundaries between the group types are not firm; the differences between them may be questions of degree rather than type. Similarly, the names that we have given the group types are arbitrary: what we term a "cooperative" may not relate to what others think of as a cooperative. It is the descriptions of interactions in the groups, not the names of the group types, that carry the meaning. Each of these prototypes can be imagined in other contexts: a different rural setting, an urban setting, or in one's office with colleagues. It can be particularly instructive to try to apply them in our own social groups. They can apply to geographical communities, or to communities of interest, such as parents of schoolchildren.

The scale is intended to be a practical "framework," or an interpretive lens through which it is possible to look at a community to make sense of how people are working together. The scale does not *define* the reality of the forms of collective organization present in a community, so it would not be valid to look at an existing group to try to make it fit one of the prototypes on the scale. Instead the question to ask ourselves is: Does the scale help us to make sense of the activities of the community with which we intend to work, and thereby assist us in knowing what to do next?

By focusing on social capital alone, we are squeezing the possible group structures onto a single dimension, and of necessity losing much of their individuality and meaning. Other factors also affect the amount of social capital that is needed to sustain a particular group structure, such as the amount of investment needed by members, and the risks of failure. A cooperative that underpins the livelihoods of its members will need more social capital than a cooperative that brings less-tangible rewards.

Organizations may also be maintained by financial, human, or physical capital. Financial capital is the catalyst for many organizational forms and can buy collective action, though rarely in a sustainable form. Individuals' skills, knowledge, and technical abilities (human capital) are key factors for groups to work and achieve tasks. The availability of accessible and appropriate physical infrastructure (physical capital) as shared work and meeting space has a tangible bearing on community members' engagement in a project. All of the capitals are enablers of development and important to include in any analysis that informs development action.

By their nature, the types of organizations suggested here are culture-specific. For example, some cultures are more tolerant of hierarchical structures that reflect authority or power differentials existing between people in family and community life. Hence, the types of organizations and their order on the scale may vary between places and cultures. The scale does not imply a linear progression between the prototypes.

The individual group types are described below, with examples from Allan (2000).

1. Working Party

A *trabajo comunal*, or day of community work, is a common form of communal labor in communities of the Ucayali region of Peru. Community leaders call on the labor of residents for tasks such as cleaning the village commons, maintaining local walkways, and assisting with the construction or repair of village amenities such as a health center, school building, or local roads. Often these communal workdays represent the in-kind contributions of a community to a project from an NGO or government agency. Community members who do not participate face monetary fines or penalty workdays; in some communities, members are fined up to two days' work for failing to attend a trabajo comunal.

> The results of the work are for the benefit of the community as a whole.
>
> All community members are required to participate.
>
> There may be sanctions/penalties for community members who do not participate.
>
> The work event is organized through the initiative of a community leader (although the need for the work may be widely acknowledged).
>
> Participants invest only their time. They are not responsible for the initiation, planning, or management of the work.
>
> A shared sense of responsibility for the maintenance and betterment of the community is advantageous to this form of organization, but not essential, especially in the presence of sanctions.

The key element of social capital for this form of organizing is *rewards and sanctions*.

In order to improve the effectiveness of community working parties we can focus on strengthening *relationships* between community members and cultivating members' *sense of responsibility* for their community.

2. Group Initiated in Response to Outside Interests

Ecomusas are local agricultural committees established throughout the Ucayali region by the Peruvian Department of Agriculture. These committees provide the government with an avenue through which it can distribute the benefits of its programs. For example, individual farmers must be members of an Ecomusa to be eligible to receive credit in the form of seed or other agricultural inputs. The expressed intention of the Ecomusas was that they play an active part in the development of the agricultural sector. The reality, however, was that the majority functioned as little more than a list of the names of residents who desired access to available resources. Despite the receipt of substantial startup funds equivalent to US$600, and access to the assistance of the local extension worker, the majority of groups were unable to develop projects of their own. This was largely because they lacked: (1) a shared agenda around which to organize, (2) trust among members, especially in relation to the management of common funds, (3) experience of group work at the level of complexity required, and (4) a belief that it is the responsibility of each member, and not solely of the government, to work for change. In this context, most Ecomusas lacked the social capital necessary to be an effective structure to deliver the outcomes for which they were intended.

> Impetus for this type of organizing originates outside the community or group and may be in response to the availability of external resources or services.
>
> The resources and benefits are available to all group members, and distribution of the received resource may be the main function of the group.
>
> Some participants may be involved just to access the resources, and their commitment ends here.
>
> Members typically lack experience of group management and planning and may need technical support to expand the purpose and functions of their group.

Group membership is limited to an investment of time to attend meetings.

Typically, these groups centralize power and decision making in a small committee. The responsibility for the management of the resource and the maintenance of the group structure is not shared equally among members.

Relationships among group members may be weak, and injecting resources into the group in the absence of transparent accountability and clear and participatory decision-making processes may erode trust between members.

The key elements of social capital are the external sources of *impetus* for organizing, and the associated tangible *rewards*. To develop such a group into a vehicle more capable of sustainable action, it may be necessary to generate an internal, *locally owned impetus* for working together and increase the *responsibility* that individual members will take for the group.

3. Workshare with Rotating Leadership

The *minga* is a common structure for organizing communal work among farmers in the lowland rainforests of Peru. The difficult task of clearing primary or secondary forest for cultivation, the long distances between many farmers' homes and their fields, the short crop cycles, the rapid growth of weeds, and the narrow windows of opportunity presented by the weather impose time constraints on farmers. Thus it is common practice for a group of farmers from the same village to work together on a rotational basis to better care for the crops of the group members. A minga is organized by a member in need of assistance. He or she is obligated to provide lunch and refreshments to the other members of the minga. Members rarely receive financial payment for their work. Their reward is the reciprocal future assistance they become eligible to receive by participating. Mingas usually involve a group of farmers with good relationships and some history of working together. Occasionally, when there is a lot to achieve, a minga will be broadened to include other community members. However

many farmers expressed their reluctance to invite others, as they were not able to control quality or how others worked. This often resulted in a greater risk for the farmer as crops were damaged or efforts needed to be repeated.

The strength of this form of organizing is the reciprocal and rotating nature of its system of rewards and benefits. Each minga has a direct beneficiary—the member who is presently receiving the assistance. The other group members are indirect beneficiaries, receiving payment or in-kind rewards (a meal) for their participation on that occasion. However, they participate with the expectation that they, in turn, will be the direct recipient of the group's assistance.

Mingas require members to trust each other's intention to undertake quality work, care for the property of the recipient as if it were their own, and to do their share of the work.

People need to share good relationships to form an effective minga group. Often they are extended family members, neighbors, and friends.

Each member is personally responsible for returning the efforts of others by participating in other's mingas.

Shared need and/or interests provide the impetus to form the group.

Leadership of the group rotates between members as they take responsibility for organizing a minga to assist them.

People who have not had their efforts reciprocated by others, or who are unhappy with the quality of assistance they have received, may be reluctant to engage in this form of organizing.

The elements of social capital key to this form of organizing are *relationships*, *trust*, *personal responsibility*, and *rewards*. Experience strongly affects people's willingness to participate in this form of communal activity.

4. Self-help Group Formed by People with Shared Interests

A group of Shipibo women, members of an indigenous Amazonian tribe from the river community of Puerto Bethel in Peru, were working together on the production and marketing of their handicrafts. For many Shipibos, the production of handicrafts, using traditional methods of hand painting and stitching, was their primary work and source of cash income. The women of Puerto Bethel shared the problem of the lack of a market for their products. Their closest market, Pucallpa, is up to six hours' travel by boat and already inundated with Shipibo products. One of the women, Delia, had experience traveling and living in other communities within Peru and had developed a number of contacts with vendors of handicrafts in tourist towns. Upon returning to live in her village and encountering the shared difficulty of market access, she initiated a group around handicrafts.

Group members had self-selected on the basis of their relationships with others and their intention to produce quality handicrafts. Although each woman individually produced her products for sale, group members trained and supported each other. On the basis of her contacts, Delia was responsible for taking the products to market, selling them, and negotiating new orders. To fulfill this role required that the others trust her to negotiate a good price and to pay them what she received. However, Delia was not a middleman, ordering and selling the products. She was an equal producing member of the group. In order for the group to function effectively, group members shared a commitment to the group and responsibilities of decision making, planning, and working to fill their orders. There were also benefits of strengthened friendships as the women chatted together while they worked.

Their social capital allowed these women to work together in a way that would otherwise not be possible.

The impetus to organize comes from community members who share a common interest or need. However, it may be only one or two people with prior experience of collective work who take the initiative to test if others are interested in forming a group.

Members' participation is motivated by the hope that they will be able to achieve their goals and improve their situation.

The rewards of the group are available to all members.

This form of organizing requires good relationships among group members and their ability to trust one another.

There are substantial risks of participation as members invest money, time, materials, and the fruits of their labor in the group.

Participation demands a high level of personal responsibility and commitment, as the group's progress and success depends on the actions, inputs, and abilities of each member.

Group members share responsibility for decision making, planning, and managing the affairs of the group. However, it is unlikely that members' experience of group work is equal. The knowledge of how to manage and support a group may be limited to one or a few members. These members create opportunities for others to build skills and confidence and to fulfill their role as equal participants.

Personal responsibility, *hope*, and *trusting relationships* between group members are the elements of social capital key to the effective functioning of this type of organization. We can work to strengthen the effectiveness and sustainability of groups of interest by encouraging cooperative group management and creating opportunities for group members to gain positive *experiences* of collective action.

5. Network

Workers from a range of disciplines are increasingly drawing on professional networks to access feedback on and strengthen their practice. Peers from a range of professional backgrounds working in agricultural research in 1999 formed a network for strengthening their practice in relation to working with stakeholder groups. The shared objectives of the network were:

> to share experiences and develop analyses about aspects of group work that individuals alone would find difficult to analyze, and through this,
> to strengthen the planning and implementation of research interventions involving collective work.

Network members were based in four countries within Central and South America. This required members to invest their own funds and time to participate. To achieve their objectives, members needed to be honest and open about their experiences and the difficulties they faced when working with groups. Such vulnerability was made possible due to the strength of the relationships among members, and the commitment each had to the learning process. Participation also required trust that members would not plagiarize one another's research results.

Although the network members worked with very different stakeholders (with farmers, national researchers, or local peoples' organizations) and brought different content specialties, they shared the methodology of group work. Through networking, scientists gained insights into their own practice and jointly contributed to their organization's understanding of processes of collective work.

> The impetus to form a network arises from a common issue or need. It may emerge from the potential members themselves or be influenced by outside interests.
> There are clear benefits for participation such as improved access to information, contacts, markets, support and resources, and increased power to influence policy, funding, or political decisions.
> Relationships are the foundation of a network. They are at the heart of its growth or diminution.
> Sanctions take the form of lost opportunities and self-exclusion from the network of relationships formed.

> Risks associated with participation include a lack of reciprocity by other members and the potential for each member to make exclusive use of information and resources for his or her own gain.
> Members need to trust each other to work primarily in the interests of the whole and to share information and other resources as appropriate.
> The type and amount of each member's investment depends on the nature of the network.
> Networks are based on a belief in the power of the collective. The presence of shared hope and a vision for change are important.
> The roles and responsibilities of membership are clear and members are expected to fulfill them. This requires members to take personal responsibility for their own active participation.
> The strength of a network is in the range of experiences, perspectives, and skills that its members bring to the whole.
> This structure is also indicative of how extended family units may organize themselves for business or livelihood development.

Key to the formation and effective functioning of networks are a *shared issue or need*, *clear benefits*, *trusting relationships*, and a commitment to participate actively. As network members gain experience of working together and their confidence in their collective ability increases, they may evolve to receive funds and provide services to their members. Such a transition would require a marked increase in the personal responsibility of members and in their investment of time to group activities.

The centrality of relationships means that networks are an ideal organizational form for bridging differences in position, status, roles, and function. For example a fair trade network may involve those in direct production and processing, technical and group support functions, buyers, vendors, and government policy makers all working together for the same ends.

6. Cooperative

Six residents of a squatter community in Los Baños, Philippines, established the Papalika Cooperative in 1996. The cooperative makes paper and recycled paper products as a venture to increase the livelihoods of its members. Papalika's members formed close relationships through their involvement in the development of a community preschool program with a local nongovernmental organization, the Cahbriba Foundation. This experience gave them hope that they could work together for change on more issues than the education of their children. The need for a secure livelihood, coupled with demands for the ongoing maintenance of the school, provided the impetus for them to initiate the cooperative.

Initially, individuals' sights were set on unrealistic gain. Expectations of the tangible (financial) benefits they would receive were unrealistic for the time frame. Although this resulted in a decrease in membership, those who remained shared a vision and a long-term commitment to the group. Members had to delay their gratification in terms of rewards, as the cooperative members could not be paid on a daily basis for their work, only at the completion of the order and its sale. However, their poverty and the urgency of basic needs soon led them to modify this arrangement. Most members received a minimal rate of pay per day and their share of the profits later.

The varied nature of the cooperative's tasks also defined the membership. Men were needed to cut the heavy-duty cardboard; someone with good written and verbal skills was needed for marketing and forming business contacts; another with flair for product design; others for painting, gluing, and packaging tasks were also required. As the sophistication of the tasks and the size of orders increased, members needed to develop new skills (budgeting, accounting, business registration, and the like). For this training they enlisted the support of a local NGO, solicited funds from the regional government, and sent members on practical training courses and business development seminars offered by other organizations.

A close working environment, the interdependency of their tasks, and shared decision making and responsibility for the progress of the group strengthened the relationships and trust between members.

The Papalika Cooperative became a mainstay of the local community. It donated 10 percent of its profits to the local school and supported the development of many other group activities, and its members have been invited to speak about their cooperative in other communities.

> The impetus for collective action comes from the mutual interests of the community members.
>
> People who have established relationships form the group.
>
> Members share a vision for change, and therefore the hope that they are able to achieve more by working together.
>
> Cooperatives require high levels of trust between members. Each person's contribution is needed to achieve the goal as members fulfill different but complementary roles. This contrasts with the self-help group of interest.
>
> The rewards of participation are available to all group members. These benefits emerge from both the tasks of the group (e.g., access to markets, higher produce prices, access to credit and machinery, technical input) and the process of participating (e.g., strengthened relationships and networks, improved skills in group management, opportunities for further collaboration on issues of importance, increased self-confidence and technical skills).
>
> Cooperatives depend on each member's personal commitment to the group and therefore require a high level of personal responsibility to function.
>
> There is a potentially high risk of participation as each member invests substantial personal resources in the cooperative. The investments may be time, money, or materials.
>
> The responsibilities and decisions of the group are shared equally among members;

a cooperative functions on the belief that all its members are equal.

Many members are already likely to have experience of participation in group processes.

Because of their high level of activity and their members' commitment to change, cooperatives often provide the impetus for a range of other communal activities within their communities.

Key elements of social capital necessary for cooperatives include a high level of *personal responsibility* to initiate and actively participate in the collective process, good interpersonal *relationships*, a culture of *trust*, and members with *established group work skills*, as well as *clear benefits* and a well-defined *vision for change*. All are indicative of cooperatives. Thus, the development and maintenance of a cooperative requires a high level of social capital between members. It is likely that it will also require a long-term and intensive investment of support by research or development professionals associated with the project to achieve both the tasks at hand and the group-work process.

Applying the Scale: The Relationship of Social Capital, Task, and Group Structure

There are a number of ways to apply the scale of social capital and group structures to development interventions:

We can do a quick and dirty social capital analysis in a community by estimating where the types of collective action that currently exist might fall on the scale. A complicating factor is that the existence of groups in an area is also an accident of history. Groups arise where they have a purpose, and this may have been the presence of something (or somebody) to unite against. This analysis also says nothing about the relationships between the group members and the people outside the group, which may be conflictual.

We can evaluate how much social capital a proposed structure requires to see if it would be feasible in a particular site.

We can use it to share insights into our work with other researchers and development professionals as it provides a common language for discussing collective action.

We can use the scale to help identify those areas of social capital that need to be strengthened before we can move to higher levels of sophistication and complexity in collective action.

Henderson and Thomas (1980:169) suggest that there are two important variables relevant to forming groups: (1) the extent of social interaction and activity already existing in a community and (2) the nature of the issue around which the group wants to form. An analysis of social capital and the identification of existing forms of collective action tell us how it may be possible to work collectively now. An analysis of the needs and priorities of the community, checked against the mandate, skills, and resources of our organization, tells us what we will do together. By considering both the nature of our task and the ways in which people feel comfortable working together, we are able to identify an appropriate structure for collective action.

Where we are now + What we want to do =
Appropriate group structure
(social capital analysis + existing group
structures) + (needs analysis) =
Group structure

As development professionals, we need to have a broad knowledge and understanding of the different organizational forms that exist and what kinds of tasks they are appropriate for; otherwise we will be trammeled into following a blueprint (Korten 1988). How we structure our group depends on such things as the abilities and experiences of the group members, the amount of time and effort they are willing to contribute, and the strength of their relationships. It also depends on the extent to which people *need* to work together to achieve their goals.

It is often difficult to strike the right balance between available social capital, the task at hand, and a structure for organizing. We can easily overburden group members by saddling them with a structure that requires a lot of maintenance and that is unnecessarily complex for the task. This results in a displacement of group goals and the disillusionment of members with group work. Two common pitfalls we may encounter are:

> when there is not enough social capital to maintain a particular structure; and
> when we elect the wrong structure for the task.

Consider the hypothetical example of the collective management of a natural resource such as fish stocks. We represent an organization scoping the options for development interventions.

> There is likely to be a variety of stakeholders with competing interests on a number of levels. The management of these relationships and interests, both within and between communities, is a complex and difficult task.
> The sustainability of the management strategy may be dependent upon elements of social capital such as the willingness of individuals to act responsibly in the interests of the whole, trust that others will honor the agreement by doing the same, clear incen-tives for participating and sanctions for not, open and accountable relationships between the stakeholders, and the hope that through cooperation, change is possible. Thus, the task demands a high level of social capital.
> In addition, the need for such communal management often arises in areas of environmental sensitivity and where communities may have little or no experience of collective work.

What group structure would be appropriate here? The available social capital and degree of complexity of the task are contradictory.

We can propose a number of options:

> We could bring everyone to the table, establish a network of key stakeholders, agree on a fisheries policy with a clear policing strategy and sanctions, and meet occasionally to monitor it. *(network)*
> The community leaders could lobby the regional and national governments to intervene with research and policy solutions. *(network)*
> We could plan to circumvent the problem through the development of supplementary projects with local research institutions and nongovernmental organizations such as fish farming ponds. *(Groups initiated by outside interests/ or cooperatives)*
> Or we could seek funding for the establishment of an integrated research and development project to do all of the above with the help of outside expertise and training. *(a little bit of everything)*

Or we could take a step back and pause . . .

> Where is the impetus for action coming from? Is it coming from higher authorities, from the fishing cooperatives whose livelihoods are at stake, or from community members who see the availability of a major food source rapidly declining? What do the stakeholders see as potential areas of change and a focus for action? Do they see the issue as a systems problem, an issue of poisoning from insecticides used on the riverbanks, silting of the river due to excessive clearing and resultant erosion, or overfishing? At what level do the stakeholders currently work together (i.e., what structures are we sure they can support with their existing level of social capital)? For example, do they have the shared analysis, trusting relationships, and clearly visible benefits to work together in a network?

We might conclude that any intervention will require a large investment of time and resources in order to build up the social and human capital necessary for sustainable change. The scenario also suggests that a process of intervention will need to be multifaceted, working concurrently on a number of themes and levels, and occur over the long term. Such an integrated intervention will require a large degree of experience and expertise on our part, especially in relation to the management of the group processes and structure.

These conclusions suggest three options for our organization that may seem inadequate in light of our original goal of the collective management of fish stocks. They are:

> to commit ourselves to a long-term strategy and develop a partnership with other organizations that are able to complement our abilities;
> to decide to contribute what we can, electing one piece of the puzzle and being realistic about the potential impact of our intervention;
> to acknowledge that we do not have the expertise, time, and resources to invest in this site and issue and to support the community to look for someone who does.

This example highlights the complexity we are often confronted with when making decisions about which strategy and method we will use for our research or development interventions. If we ignore the insights into collective action that an analysis of social capital provides, we are at risk of selecting a group structure that is possible, but inadequate for the task, or embarking on a path of action that cannot now be achieved and that is likely to result in a negative experience for the group members. By adopting an empirical approach to the selection of an appropriate social technology, we will begin the intervention with a realistic analysis of community members' abilities to work together. We can then build experience and social capital as we move from one achievable task to the next. This is a more manageable and sustainable strategy for change. Problems of increasing complexity will be able to be addressed as the community's social capital grows.

Conclusion

Scientists and social development professionals need to assist communities in selecting the most appropriate structure for working together when their interventions involve collective methodologies. The scale of social capital and group structures proposed in figure 22.2 is a tool for supporting this decision-making process.

Our observation is that projects frequently diagnose what social technology is needed in an area without diagnosing what is currently possible. Networks and cooperatives, the two most sophisticated organizational structures, offer tremendous potential for collective action but are two of the most demanding social technologies available. Much effort is needed to maintain their structures, and this comes on top of the effort needed for the task at hand. Unless existing social capital is strong, the transaction costs of holding the group together can eclipse the task itself. Where the social capital is low, effective networks and cooperatives can still eventually be built, but we argue that the challenge is the gradual buildup of social capital first; it is a community development challenge, not a natural resource management challenge. If trust is not yet strong enough in a community to support the interdependence necessary for a cooperative, perhaps a self-help group might be a more appropriate structure to start from.

We argue that a task should be addressed with the simplest structure possible. To form a committee complete with president, treasurer, and other officers to address a very simple function wastes resources and energy.

To apply the scale to our research or development interventions, two inputs are needed: the current level of social capital in the community and the nature of the task we are planning to undertake. The scale illustrates how different levels of social capital support different group structures. Similarly, different tasks require different types and amounts of social capital and are therefore dependent on different structures.

We do not argue that social capital is more important than other capitals for development. Clearly, all are involved. We argue instead that social capital is often the capital about which we are least empirical when planning interventions. While it is possible to see poverty in people, soils, skills, and infrastructure, and we have tools to develop interventions that are appropriate to these conditions, it may be harder to see poverty of trust, hope, and impetus. We may overestimate the social capital present.

Acknowledgments

The research on which this chapter is based was supported by the International Center for Tropical Agriculture (CIAT), Cali, Colombia, during 1999–2000.

References

Allan, S. 2000. How to use social capital for sustainable collective action in agricultural research and development work. Unpublished manuscript. International Center for Tropical Agriculture, Cali, Colombia.

Dick, B. 1998. Convergent interviewing: A technique for qualitative data collection. www.scu.edu.au/schools/gcm/ar/arp/iview.html.

Henderson, P., and D. Thomas. 1980. *Skills in Neighbourhood Work*. 2nd ed. London: Unwin Hyman.

Korten, D. 1980. Community organisation and rural development: A learning process approach. *Public Administration Review* 40, no. 5: 480–511.

Narayan, D. 1999. *Bonds and Bridges: Social Capital and Poverty*. New York: World Bank.

Onyx, J., and P. Bullen. 2000. Sources of Social Capital. In I. Winter, ed., *Social Capital and Public Policy in Australia*, 105–35. Melbourne: Australian Institute of Family Studies.

Wilson, W. O. 1987. *The Truly Disadvantaged*. Chicago: University of Chicago Press.

PART FIVE

SCIENCE FOR DEVELOPMENT
*Assessing and Mitigating Environmental Impact
and Its Economic Consequences*

One of the principal ways that the poor are impacted by development is that development itself is often the principal cause of local environmental contamination and degradation. Such impacts include soil erosion; the decline of fish populations; the increased release of fertilizers, pesticides, and other agrochemicals into waterways; the release of all kinds of pollutants from industrial activities; the loss of valuable natural forests; and the degradation of air quality in urban areas. Economists often call such impacts "externalities" because their very real costs are usually not included in market prices, as the market has no way (unless forced) to either generate a price for them or to collect that price from producer or consumer. Externalities are real costs and benefits to society, but since they usually are not part of the decision-making process one can expect suboptimal decisions at least some of the time. Good economics will try to internalize the externalities by adding them to the costs of production (see chapter 6, and also parts 3 and 6). But the very word *externality* implies to many that they are somehow secondary, not embedded in the real process, an afterthought and marginal relative to other parameters involved in the decision to buy. We believe that these effects, rather than being external, are as much a product of the process being considered as are the bananas or consumer goods being produced.

These impacts—some from carelessness, some from greed of factory owners, some from ignorance, and some the more or less inevitable by-products of the development activity—are rarely entered into the economic balance sheets (there are, increasingly, important exceptions), and as

such often give a more favorable assessment to developmental projects than would be the case if environmental degradation were included into the assessments. Most assessments of such impacts come from science, and most often government- or NGO-sponsored research (and, increasingly, consulting firms), rather than from the perpetrator. Thus a very clear role for science is in identifying, quantifying, and, ideally, reducing the cost and increasing the benefits of the "externalities" of the process of economic development.

The chapters in this section tackle several of the most important environmental impacts of development in the tropics: soil erosion, deforestation, contamination by pesticides, and degradation of ocean and coastal resources. David Pimentel (chapter 23) is an authority on many aspects of the environment, especially aspects related to soil erosion. Hugh Eva and Frederic Achard (chapter 24) have been undertaking high-profile assessments of tropical deforestation at a global scale, and Carlos Hernández, Jane Yeomans, and Tim Kasten (chapter 25) have completed many important studies for decades that identify and reduce the environmental impacts of agriculture in Costa Rica. In chapter 26, marine biologist Gary Sharp and systems ecologist Charles Hall make a thorough assessment of the capacity of free markets to stimulate sustainable management of fish resources, an area of prime importance for developing countries. Rod McNeil (chapter 27), an authority on shrimp aquaculture intensification, examines the effects of the "blue revolution" on this major export of developing countries.

CHAPTER 23

SOIL EROSION

A Food and Environmental Threat

DAVID PIMENTEL

Introduction

The loss of soil from land surfaces by erosion is widespread globally and adversely affects the productivity of all natural ecosystems as well as agricultural, forest, and rangeland ecosystems (Lal and Stewart 1990; Pimentel 1993; Pimentel et al. 1995; Pimentel and Kounang 1998). Concurrent with and often because of the escalating human population, the problems of soil erosion, water availability, energy, and loss of biodiversity rank atop the list of environmental concerns throughout the world.

Future world populations will require ever-increasing food supplies. Given that more than 99.7 percent of human food comes from the land (FAO 1998), while less than 0.3 percent comes from oceans and other aquatic ecosystems, maintaining and augmenting the world food supply depends on the productivity and quality of all soils. The changes inflicted on soils by human-induced erosion over many years are significant and have resulted in valuable land becoming unproductive and often eventually abandoned (Pimentel et al. 1995; Young 1998). Simply put, soil erosion diminishes soil quality and thereby reduces the productivity of natural, agricultural, and forest ecosystems (Pimentel and Kounang 1998; Pimentel 2001). In addition, the valuable diversity of plants, animals, and microbes in the soil is damaged (Pimentel et al. 1995).

This chapter evaluates the diverse factors that cause soil erosion. The extent of damages associated with soil erosion is analyzed, with an emphasis on the impact these have on future human food security as well as the natural environment.

Causes of Erosion

Erosion occurs when soil is left exposed to rain or wind energy. Raindrops hit exposed soil with

Figure 23.1. About 50 mm of soil blown from cropland in Kansas during the winter of 1995–96. Photo: E. L Skidmore, USDA, Manhattan, Kansas.

great energy and easily dislodge the soil particles from the surface. In this way, raindrops remove a thin film of soil from the land surface and create what is termed sheet erosion. This erosion is the dominant form of soil degradation (Troeh, Hobbs, and Donahue 1991; Oldeman 1997). The impact of soil erosion is intensified on sloping land, where often more than half of the surface soil is carried away as the water splashes downhill into valleys and waterways. Wind energy also has the great power to dislodge surface soil particles and transport them great distances. A strong example of this was the wind erosion in Kansas during the winter of 1995–96, when it was relatively dry and windy. Then approximately 65 t/ha was eroded from this

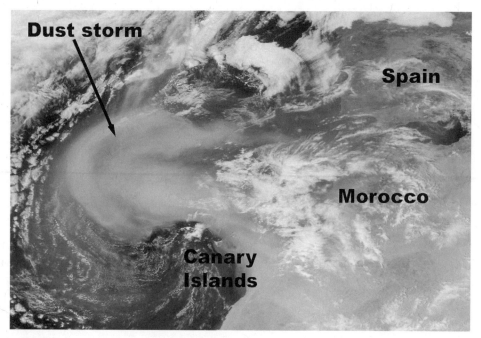

Dust storm

Spain

Morocco

Canary Islands

Figure 23.2. Cloud of soil from Africa being blown across the Atlantic Ocean (imagery by SeaWIFS Project, NASA/Goddard Space Flight Center and ORBIMAGE, 2000).

valuable cropland during one winter (figure 23.1). Wind energy is strong enough to propel soil particles thousands of miles. Figure 23.2, a photograph by NASA, shows a cloud of soil being blown from Africa to South America and North America. Most of the soil particles, however, are lost to the ocean.

Soil Structure

The structure of soil influences the ease with which it can be eroded. Soils with medium to fine texture, low organic matter content, and weak structural development are most easily eroded (Bajracharya and Lal 1992). Typically these soils have low water infiltration rates and, therefore, are subject to high rates of water erosion, the soil particles easily displaced by wind energy.

The Role of Vegetative Cover

Land areas covered by plant biomass, living or dead, are reasonably well protected and experience relatively little soil erosion because raindrop and wind energy are dissipated by the biomass layer and the topsoil is held together by biomass (SWAG 2002; Agriculture California 2002). Myers (1993) estimated that erosion was seventy-five times greater in agriculture than in natural forest areas. For another example, in Utah and Montana, as the amount of ground cover decreased from 100 percent to less

than 1 percent, erosion rates increased approximately two hundred times (Trimble and Mendel 1995). In forested areas, a minimum of 60 percent forest cover is necessary to prevent serious soil erosion and landslides (Singh and Kaur 1989; Haigh et al. 1995; Forest Conservation Act 2002). This is a special problem in the tropics today due to the extensive removal of forests for crop and pastures, which is followed by extensive soil erosion.

Loss of soil vegetative cover is especially widespread in developing countries where population densities are high, and agricultural practices often are inadequate to protect top soils. Richards and Flint (1994) found a strong relation between natural forest cover (and its inverse, agricultural land) and population density for many countries over time in Southeast Asia (figure 23.3). In addition, cooking and heating there frequently depend on the burning of harvested crop residues for fuel. For example, about 60 percent of crop residues in China and 90 percent in Bangladesh routinely are stripped from the land and burned for fuel (Wen 1993). In areas where fuelwood and other biomass are scarce, even the roots of grasses and shrubs are collected and burned (McLaughlin 1991). All these practices (except deforestation for pasture) leave the soil barren and fully exposed to rain and wind forces of erosion.

Land Topography

The topography of a given landscape, its rainfall and/or wind, and exposure, all combine to influence its susceptibility to erosion. In the Philippines, where more than 58 percent of the land has a slope of greater than 11 percent, and in Jamaica, where 52 percent of the land has a slope greater than 20 percent, soil erosion rates as high as 400 t/ha/yr have been reported (Lal and Stewart 1990). Erosion rates are especially high on marginal and steep lands that have been converted from forests to agriculture to replace the already eroded, unproductive cropland (Lal and Stewart 1990). In addition, under arid conditions and with relatively strong winds as much as 5,600 t/ha/yr of soil has been reported lost in an arid region of India (Gupta and Raina 1996).

Other Disturbances
That Cause Soil Erosion

Although worldwide agricultural production produces about three-quarters of the soil erosion, erosion also occurs whenever humans remove vegetative cover (Lal and Stewart 1990; FAO 2002). The construction of roads, logging staging areas, parking lots, and buildings are examples. Although the rate of erosion from construction sites is high and may range from 20 to 500 t/ha/yr, such erosion is relatively brief, generally lasting only while the land surface is disturbed. Then once the land surface is seeded to grass, or the vegetation regrows naturally, erosion decreases (IECA 1991). However, if the soil remains covered by buildings, parking lots, and roads, the area is lost for vegetation production and consequently water runoff in adjacent areas increases. The presence of cattle in and around streams generally increases the erosion of their banks. For example, a Wisconsin stream area inhabited by cattle lost about 60 t/yr of soil along each kilometer of stream length (Trimble 1994; Trimble and Mendel 1995).

Natural ecosystems also suffer erosion losses. This is especially evident along stream banks, where erosion occurs naturally from the powerful action of adjacent moving water. Increased soil losses occur on steep slopes (30 percent or more), when a stream cuts through adjacent land. Even on relatively flat

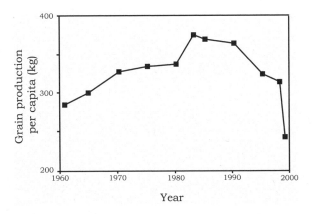

Figure 23.3. Cereal grain production per capita in the world from 1961 to 2000 (FAO 1961–2000; *Quarterly Bulletin of Statistics* 1–13).

land with only a 2 percent slope, stream banks are eroded, especially during heavy rains and flooding. Soil erosion accompanies landslides and earthquakes (Bruijnzeel 1990; McTainish 1993). Landslides, in which layers of soil are dislodged and move downhill, are usually associated with diverse human activities, such as the construction of roads and buildings and the removal of forests. For example, in the Luquillo Forest of Puerto Rico, the naturally high landslide rate was greatly enhanced within several hundred meters of roads, even decades after the roads were constructed (Larson and Parks 1997). Overall, the erosion impact from earthquakes is small mainly because these events are relatively rare. However, when earthquakes occur, massive amounts of soil, including crops and forests, are affected in area hillsides and in surrounding areas. Nevertheless, overall Scatena, Planos-Gutierrez, and Schellekens (2005) report that, to the surprise of tropical hydrologists, recent reviews of the data indicate that when really heavy rains occur, as was the case with Hurricane Mitch in Central America, it matters little to the rate of erosion what the land use of a watershed was before the rain—essentially everything in the floodplain is flooded and eroded.

Assessing Soil Erosion

Although soil erosion has been taking place very slowly in natural ecosystems throughout geologic time, its cumulative impacts on soil quality over billions of years is significant. Worldwide, erosion rates in natural ecosystems range from a low of 0.001–2 t/ha/yr on relatively flat land with grass and/or forest cover to rates ranging from 1–5 t/ha/yr in mountainous regions with normal vegetative cover (Patric 2002). Yet even low rates of erosion sustained over billions of years result in the displacement of enormous quantities of soil and the erosion of great mountains. For example, over a period of one hundred years at an erosion loss rate of only 2 t/ha/yr on 10 ha, erosion will deposit on lowlands the soil equivalent of about 1 hectare of land with a soil depth of 15 cm. In addition, eroded soil frequently accumulates in valleys forming vast alluvial plains. The large deltas of the world, such as that of the Nile and the Mississippi, are the result of millennia of erosion (Solliday 1997).

Myers (1993) reports that approximately 75 billion tons of fertile soils are lost from world agricultural systems each year, with much less erosion occurring in natural ecosystems. I believe that the 75 billion tons is probably a conservative value. Soil scientists Lal and Stewart (1990) and Wen (1997) report 6.6 billion tons of soil per year are lost in India alone and 5.5 billion tons in China alone. Considering these two countries together occupy only 13 percent of the world's total land area, the estimated 75 billion tons of soil lost per year worldwide seems conservative. The amount of soil lost in the United States is estimated to be about 3 billion tons per year (Carnell 2001).

Loss of Productivity in Managed Ecosystems

Approximately 50 percent of the earth's land surface is devoted to agriculture; of this, about one-third is planted to crops and two-thirds to grazing lands (USDA 2001). Forests occupy about 20 percent of the land area (WRI 1997). Of these two areas, cropland is more susceptible to erosion because of frequent cultivation of the soils and because the vegetation is often removed before crops are planted. This practice exposes the soil to wind and rain energy. In addition, cropland is often left without vegetation between plantings. This practice intensifies erosion on agricultural land.

Worldwide cropland

The amount of arable land (2 billion ha) that has been used in the past for crop production and then abandoned by humans since farming began is actually greater than the nearly 1.5 billion hectares of world arable land now under cultivation (Lal 1990, 1994). Such land, once biologically and economically productive, now not only produces little biomass but also has lost considerable diversity of the plants, animals, and microbes it once supported (Pimentel et al. 1992; Heywood 1995). Currently, about 80 percent of the world's agricultural land suffers moderate to severe erosion, while only 10 percent experiences slight erosion (Pimentel 1993; Speth 1994; Lal 1994). Worldwide, erosion on cropland averages about 30 t/ha/yr and ranges from 0.5 to 400 t/ha/yr (Pimentel et al. 1995). As a result of this erosion, about 30 percent of the world's arable land has become unproductive during the last forty years, and much of that has been abandoned for agricultural use (WRI 1994; Kendall and Pimentel 1994). Thus we may say that, in a sense, agricultural development is a process that changes land from once diverse and variously productive natural ecosystems into a source of very productive economic activity for a period of time and then leaves behind land of very little value to humans or indeed most other species.

Worldwide, soil erosion losses are highest in the agroecosystems of Asia, Africa, and South America, averaging 30 to 40 t/ha/yr of soil loss (Pimentel et al. 1995). This is due in part to the heavy rains that tend to occur in the tropics, but also to the high rural population densities there and the low priority of long-range thinking in many developing countries. In such countries, soil erosion is particularly severe on small farms, which are often located on marginal lands where the soil quality is poor and the topography is frequently steep. In addition, the poor farmers tend to raise row crops, such as corn. Row crops are productive but highly susceptible to erosion because the vegetation does not cover the entire soil surface (Southgate and Whitaker 1992; Stone and Moore 1997). In Nicaragua, the government instituted soil erosion programs on small farmers' lands to protect the water supply for the city of Managua. But the local farmers destroyed the erosion-resisting structures and put the land back into cultivation because they could not afford not to use the 5 to 10 percent of the land that was taken out of production (Alfens et al. 1996). In the Sierra Region of Ecuador, 60 percent of the cropland recently was abandoned because erosion and inappropriate agricultural practices left the land devastated by water and wind erosion (Southgate and Whitaker 1992). Similar problems are evident in the Amazonian region of South America, especially where vast forested areas are being cleared to provide more land for crops and livestock production.

U.S. cropland

The lowest erosion rates on cropland occur in the United States and Europe, where they average about 9 t/ha/yr (USDA 2000a, 2000b). However, these low rates of erosion greatly exceed the average rate of natural soil formation from the parent material; under agricultural conditions that range from 0.5 to 1 t/ha/yr (Troeh and Thompson 1993; Lal 1994; Pimentel et al. 1995; Young 1998; Sundquist 2000). This means that 90 percent of U.S. cropland now is losing soil faster than its sustainable replacement rate (USDA 2000a, 2000b).

Soil erosion is severe in some of the most productive agricultural ecosystems in the United States. For example, one-half the fertile topsoil of Iowa has been lost during the last 150 years of farming because of erosion (Risser 1981; Klee 1991). These high rates of erosion continue there at a rate of about 30 t/ha/yr because of both the rolling hill topography and the type of agriculture practiced (USDA 1989). Similarly, 40 percent of the rich soil of the Palouse region in the northwestern United States has been lost during the past hundred years of cultivation (Ebbert and Roe 1998). In both of these regions, intensive agriculture is employed and monocultural plantings are common. Also, many of these fields are left unplanted during the late fall and winter months, further exposing the soil to erosion. About 400,000 ha of valuable cropland are abandoned in the United States each year because rain and wind erosion has made them unproductive. The economic impact of soil erosion is significant. Uri (2001) estimates that soil erosion in the United States costs the nation about $37.6 billion each year in loss of productivity.

Pasture and rangeland

In contrast to the average soil loss of 9 t/ha/yr from U.S. cropland, U.S. pastures lose only about 2.5 t/ha/yr (USDA 1995). However, erosion rates on pastures intensify whenever overgrazing is allowed to occur. Even in the United States, about 75 percent of nonfederal lands require conservation treatments to improve grazing pressure (Johnson 1995). More than half of the rangelands, including those on nonfederal and federal lands, are now overgrazed and have become subject to high erosion rates (Bailey 1996; Campbell 1998). Although erosion rates on U.S. cropland have decreased during the past two decades, the erosion rate on rangelands remains relatively high at about 13 t/ha/yr (USDA 1995). Even higher erosion rates are typical on more than half of the world's rangelands (WRI 1994). In many developing countries, heavy grazing by sheep and goats has removed most of the vegetative cover, exposing the soil to severe erosion. In Africa, about 80 percent of the pasture and rangeland areas are seriously eroded and degraded by soil erosion (UN-NADAF 1996). The prime causes of this are overgrazing and the practice of removing crop residues for cooking fuel, exacerbated, of course, by population increases.

Forest land

In stable forest ecosystems, where soil is protected by vegetation, erosion rates are very low, ranging from only 0.004 to 0.05 t/ha/yr (Roose 1988; Lal 1994). Tree leaves and branches not only intercept and diminish rain and wind energy, but also cover the soil under the trees to protect the soil further. However, this changes dramatically when forests are cleared for crop production or pasture (Daily 1996). For example, in Ecuador, the Ministry of Agriculture and Livestock reported that 84 percent of the soils in the hilly, forested northeastern part of the country should never have been cleared for pastures because of the high erodibility of the soils, their limited fertility, and overall poor soil type that resulted (Southgate and Whitaker 1992). A similar assessment was given for Costa Rica by Hartshorn et al. (1982).

Effects of Erosion on Ecosystems

As I have said, soil erosion reduces the productivity of terrestrial ecosystems. In order of importance, soil erosion also (1) increases water runoff thereby decreasing the water infiltration and the water-storage capacity of the soil (Troeh, Hobbs, and Donahue 1991; Pimentel et al. 1995; Jones, Lal, and Huggins 1997); (2) removes organic matter and essential plant nutrients from the soil, which are lost from that system; and (3) reduces soil depth. These changes not only inhibit vegetative growth but (4) reduce the presence of valuable biota and the overall biodiversity in the soil (Troeh, Hobbs, and Donahue 1991; Pimentel et al. 1995). Because these factors interact with one another, it is almost impossible to separate the specific impacts of one factor from another. For example, the loss of soil organic matter increases water runoff, which reduces water-storage capacity, which diminishes nutrient levels in the soil and also reduces the natural biota biomass and the biodiversity of ecosystems (Lal and Stewart 1990; Jones, Lal, and Huggins 1997).

Water availability

Water is a prime limiting factor of productivity in all terrestrial ecosystems because all vegetation requires enormous quantities of water for its growth and for the production of fruit (Falkenmark 1989; Pimentel et al. 1997). For example, one hectare of corn or wheat will transpire more than 5 to 7 million liters of water each growing season (Klocke et al. 1996; Pimentel et al. 1997) and lose an additional 2 million liters of water by evaporation from the soil (Donahue, Follett, and Tulloch 1990; Pimentel et al. 1997). During erosion by rainfall, the amount of water runoff increases significantly, so that less water enters the soil and less water is available to support the growing vegetation.

In contrast to uneroded soils, moderately eroded soils absorb 10–300 mm less water per hectare per year from rainfall. This represents a decrease of 7 percent to 44 percent in the amount of water available for vegetation growth (Wendt, Alberts, and Helmers 1986; Murphee and McGregor 1991). A water runoff rate of about 30 percent of a total rainfall of 800 mm can result in significant water shortages for crops, like corn, and ultimately low crop yield (Pimentel et al. 2003). When soil water availability for an agricultural ecosystem is reduced by from 20 percent to 40 percent in the soil, plant biomass productivity is reduced from 10 percent to 25 percent depending also on total rainfall, soil type, slope, and other factors (Evans et al. 1997). Major reductions in plant biomass not only diminish crop yields but also adversely affect the overall species diversity within the ecosystem (Heywood 1995; Walsh and Rowe 2001).

Nutrient loss

Eroded soil carries away vital plant nutrients such as nitrogen, phosphorus, potassium, and calcium. Typically, eroding soil, which tends to be the surface portion, contains about three times more nutrients than are found in the deeper remaining soil (Young 1989). A ton of fertile topsoil averages 1–6 kg of nitrogen, 1–3 kg of phosphorus, and 2–30 kg of potassium, whereas the soil on eroded land has average nitrogen levels of only 0.1–0.5 kg per ton (Troeh, Hobbs, and Donahue 1991). When nutrient resources are so depleted by erosion, plant growth is stunted and overall productivity declines (Lal and Stewart 1990; Pimentel et al. 1995). Nutrient-deficient soils produce 15 percent to 30 percent lower crop yields than uneroded soils (Olson and Nizeyimana 1988; Schertz et al. 1989; Langdale et al. 1992). To offset the nutrient loss erosion inflicts on crop production, large quantities of fertilizers are applied where farmers can afford this. Troeh, Hobbs, and Donahue (1991) estimate that the lost soil nutrients cost U.S. agriculture $20 billion annually. If the soil base is relatively deep, about 300 mm, and if only from 10 to 20 tons of soil is lost per hectare per year, the lost nutrients can be replaced with the application of commercial fertilizers and/or livestock manure (Pimentel et al. 1995). However, this replacement strategy is expensive for the farmer and nation and usually not affordable to poor farmers. Not only are the fertilizer inputs fossil-energy dependent, these chemicals can harm human health and pollute the environment (NAS 2002).

Soil organic matter

Fertile soils typically contain about 100 tons of organic matter per hectare (or 4 percent of the total soil weight) (Follett, Gupta, and Hunt 1987; Young 1990; Sundquist 2000). About 95 percent of the soil nitrogen and 25–50 percent of the phosphorus is contained in the soil organic matter (Allison 1973). Because most of the soil organic matter is found close to the soil surface as decaying leaves and stems, erosion decreases soil organic matter significantly. Both wind and water erosion remove the fine organic particles in the soil selectively, leaving behind large soil particles and stones. Several studies have demonstrated that the soil removed by either erosion is 1.3–5 times richer in organic matter than the remaining soil left behind (Allison 1973; Lal and Stewart 1990). The reduction of soil organic matter can affect yields. For example, a loss of from 1.4 percent to 0.9 percent lowered the yield potential for grain by 50 percent (Libert 1995; Sundquist 2000).

Soil organic matter is a valuable resource because it facilitates the formation of soil aggregates and thereby increases soil porosity. The improved soil structure in turn facilitates water infiltration and ultimately the overall productivity of the soil (Langdale et al. 1992). In addition, organic matter aids cation exchange, enhances plant root growth, and stimulates the increase of important soil biota (Allison 1973). Thus once the organic matter layer is depleted, the productivity of the ecosystem, as measured by plant biomass, declines both because of the degraded soil structure and the depletion of nutrients contained in the organic matter. In addition to low yields, the total biomass of the biota and overall biodiversity of these ecosystems is substantially reduced (Heywood 1995; Walsh and Rowe 2001; Lazaroff 2001). Collectively and independently, the diverse impacts of erosion reduce crop biomass both because of degraded soil structure and nutrient depletion. For example, erosion reduced corn productivity by 9–18 percent in Indiana, 0 to 24 percent in Illinois and Indiana, 25 percent–65 percent in the southern piedmont of Georgia, and

21 percent in Michigan (Olson and Nizeyimana 1988; Mokma and Sietz 1992; Weesies 1994). In the Philippines, erosion has caused declines in corn production by as much as 80 percent (Dregne 1992) over rates of the mid-1980s. This was the case despite increases in the quantity of fertilizer and other amendments applied.

Soil depth

Growing plants require soils of adequate depth in which to extend their roots. Various soil biota, such as earthworms, also require a specific soil depth (Pimentel et al. 1995). Thus, when soil depth is substantially reduced by erosion from 30 cm to less than 1 cm, plant root space is minimal, and not only is plant production reduced but also some valuable soil biota disappear.

Biomass and biodiversity

The biological diversity existing into any ecosystem is directly related to the amount of living and nonliving organic matter present in the ecosystem (Wright 1990; Heywood 1995; Walsh and Rowe 2001; Lazaroff 2001). As mentioned, by diminishing soil organic matter and soil quality, erosion reduces overall biomass and productivity. Ultimately, this has a profound effect on the diversity of plants, animals, and microbes present in an entire ecosystem. Numerous positive associations have been established between biomass abundance and species diversity (Elton 1927; Odum 1978; Sugden and Rands 1990). Vegetation is the main component of ecosystem biomass and provides the vital resources required by both animals and microbes for their survival. This relationship is summarized in table 23.1. Along with plants and animals, microbes are a vital component of the soil and constitute a large percentage of the soil biomass. One square meter of soil may support about 200,000 arthropods, plus billions of microbes (Wood 1989; Lee and Foster 1991). A hectare of productive soil may have a biomass of invertebrates and microbes weighing up to 10,000 kg/ha (table 23.1). In addition, soil bacteria and fungi add 4,000 to 5,000 species and in this way contribute significantly to the biodiversity especially in moist, organic forest soils (Heywood 1995).

Table 23.1. Biomass of various organisms per hectare in a temperate region pasture

Organism	Biomass (kg fresh weight)
Plants	20,000
Fungi	4,000
Bacteria	3,000
Arthropods	1,000
Annelids	1,320
Protozoa	380
Algae	200
Nematodes	120
Mammals	1.2
Birds	.3

Source: Pimentel et al. (1992)

There is a positive relation between biomass and biodiversity that was confirmed in field experiments with collards in which arthropod species diversity rose fourfold in the experimental plots with the highest collard biomass compared with control collard plots (Pimentel and Warneke 1989). Reports suggest that when biomass was increased threefold, the number of species increased sixteenfold (Ecology 2002). In a study of bird populations, a strong correlation between plant biomass productivity and bird species diversity was reported when a hundredfold increase in plant biomass yielded a tenfold increase in bird diversity (Wright 1990).

Erosion rates that are ten to twenty times above the sustainability rate (soil formation rates of less than 0.5 to 1 t/ha/yr) decrease the diversity and abundance of soil organisms (Atlavinyte 1965). In contrast, agricultural practices that control erosion and maintain adequate soil organic matter favor the proliferation of soil biota (Reid 1985; FAO 2001). For example, the application of organic matter or manure enhances the biodiversity in soil (Agriculture Canada 2002; IFPRI 2002). Species diversity of macrofauna (mostly arthropods) increased 16 percent when organic manure was added to experimental wheat plots in the former USSR (Bohac and Pokarzhevsky 1987). Similarly, species diversity of macrofauna (mostly arthropods) more than doubled when organic manure was added to grassland plots in Japan (Kitazawa and Kitazawa 1980), and increased tenfold in Hungarian agricultural land (Olah-Zsupos and Helmeczi 1987).

Soil erosion has indirect effects on ecosystems that may be nearly as damaging as the direct effects of reducing plant biomass productivity. For example, Tilman and Downing (1994) found that the stability and biodiversity of grasslands were significantly reduced when the number of plant species were experimentally reduced. They reported that as plant species richness decreased from twenty-five species to five or fewer species, the grassland became less resistant to drought. The total amount of biomass declined more than fourfold. The overall result was that the grassland was more susceptible to drought conditions and required more time to recover its productivity than had occurred when an abundance of plant species was present.

Sometimes soil erosion causes the loss of a keystone species, and its absence may have a cascading effect on the survival of a wide array of species within the ecosystem. Species that act as keystone species include the dominant plant types, such as oaks, that maintain the biomass productivity and structural integrity of the ecosystem; predators and parasites that control the feeding pressure of some organisms on major plants; pollinators of various vital plants in the ecosystem; seed dispersers; as well as the plants and animals that provide a habitat required by other essential species, such as biological nitrogen-fixers (Heywood 1995; Daily 1996). Thus, in diverse ways, the normal activities within an ecosystem may be interrupted when keystone species are altered significantly. The damages inflicted can be severe especially in agroecosystems when, for example, pollinators are drastically reduced and/or even eliminated and there is little or no reproduction in the plants (Pimentel et al. 1997).

Soil biota perform many beneficial activities that improve soil quality and ultimately its productivity (Witt 1997; FAO 2001). For example, soil biota recycle basic nutrients required by plants for their growth (Pimentel et al. 1995). In addition, the tunneling and burrowing activities of earthworms and other soil biota enhance productivity by increasing water infiltration into the soil (Witt 1997). Earthworms, for instance, may produce up to 220 tunnel openings per m² (3 to 5 mm in diameter). These channels enable water to rapidly infiltrate the soil (Anderson 1988; Edwards and Bater 1992).

Other soil biota also contribute to soil formation and productivity by mixing the soil components, enhancing aggregate stability, and preventing soil crusting. This churning and mixing of the upper soil redistributes nutrients, aerates the soil, exposes substrate to the climate for soil formation, and increases infiltration rates, thus making the soil favorable for increased soil formation and plant productivity. Earthworms bring between 10 and 500 t/ha/yr of soil from underground to the soil surface (Lavelle 1983; Lee 1985), while some insects, such as ants, may bring 34 t/ha/yr of soil to the surface (Zacharias and Grube 1984; Lockaby and Adams 1985; Hawkins 2002). In arid regions, species such as the Negev desert snail (*Euchordrus* spp.) also help form soil by consuming lichens and the rocks on which the lichens are growing (Shachak, Jones, and Brand 1995). This snail activity helps form about 1,000 kg of soil per hectare per year, which is equal to the annual soil formation rate by windborne deposits.

Sediments and Windblown Soil Particles

The effects of erosion reach far beyond the local impact on rainfed agricultural and forestry ecosystems into surrounding or even distant environments (Gray and Leiser 1989; FEMAT 1993; Ziemer 1998). For example, large amounts of eroded soil are deposited in streams, lakes, and other ecosystems. The USDA (1989) reports that 60 percent of the water-eroded soil ends up in U.S. streams. Similarly, approximately 2 billion tons/year of soil are transported down China's Yellow River into the Yellow Sea (Lal and Stewart 1990; McLaughlin 1993; Zhang et al. 1997). The most costly off-site damages occur when soil particles enter lake and river systems (Lal and Stewart 1990; Martin 1997; Watershed 2002). Of the billions of tons of soil lost from U.S. and world cropland, nearly two-thirds ultimately is deposited in lakes and rivers (USDA 1989; Pimentel 1997). In some areas, heavy sedimentation leads to river and lake flooding, since the water has nowhere else to go (Myers 1993). For example, some of the flooding that occurred in the midwestern United States during the summer of 1993 was caused by increased sediment deposition in the Mississippi and Missouri rivers and their tributaries. These deposits raised the waterways, making them more prone to overflowing and flooding. Sediments disrupt and harm aquatic ecosystems by contaminating the water with soil particles and the fertilizer and pesticide chemicals they contain (Clark 1987). Siltation of reservoirs and dams reduces water storage, increases the maintenance cost of dams, and shortens the lifetime of reservoirs (Pimentel et al. 1995).

Wind-eroded soil also causes off-site damage because soil particles propelled by strong winds act as abrasives and air pollutants (WEI 2002; Agriculture Canada 2002b). Estimates are that soil particles cause about $8 billion in damages each year by sandblasting U.S. automobiles and buildings (Huszar and Piper 1985; SCS 1993; Pimentel et al. 1995). A prime example of the environmental impact of wind erosion occurs in the United States, where wind erosion rates average 13 t/ha/yr and sometimes reach as much as 56 t/ha/yr (Pimentel and Kounang 1998; Ecology Action 2002). Yearly off-site erosion costs in New Mexico, including health and property damage, are estimated to reach $465 million (Huszar and Piper 1985). The off-site damage from wind erosion in the United States is estimated to cost nearly $10 billion each year (Pimentel et al. 1995). The long-range transport of dust by wind even has implications for health worldwide. Griffin, Kellogg, and Shinn (2001) report that about twenty species of human-infectious disease organisms, such as anthrax and tuberculosis, are carried easily in the soil particles transported by the wind.

Soil erosion contributes to global warming, because CO_2 is added to the atmosphere when the enormous amounts of biomass carbon in the soil are oxidized (Phillips, White, and Johnson 1993; Lal et al. 1999; Lal 2001; Walsh and Rowe 2001). One hectare of soil may contain about 100 tons of organic matter or biomass. The subsequent oxidation and release of CO_2 into the atmosphere as the soil organic matter oxidizes contributes to the global warming problem along with other atmospheric pollutants (Phillips, White, and Johnson 1993). In fact, a feedback mechanism may exist wherein increased global warming intensifies rainfall, which in turn increases erosion and continues the cycle (Lal 2002).

Managing Soil Erosion
Conservation Technologies and Research

Estimates are that agricultural land degradation alone can be expected to depress world food production approximately 30 percent during the next twenty-five-year period (Buringh 1989) or fifty-year period (Kendall and Pimentel 1994). These forecasts emphasize the need to implement known soil conservation techniques. These techniques include the use of biomass mulches, crop rotations, no-till, ridge-till, added grass strips, shelterbelts, contour row-crop planting, and various combinations of these. All of these techniques require keeping the land protected from wind and rainfall energy by using some form of vegetative cover on the land (Troeh, Hobbs, and Donahue 1991; Pimentel 1993; Pimentel et al. 1995). In the United States during the past decade, soil-erosion rates on croplands have been reduced by nearly 25 percent using various soil-conservation technologies such as no-till agriculture (USDA 1989, 1994, 2000a, 2000b). Yet, even with this decline, soil is still being lost on croplands nine times above its sustainability rate (USDA 2000a, 2000b). Unfortunately, soil erosion rates on rangelands have not declined during this same decade and remain at about thirteen times sustainability (USDA 1995).

Soil erosion is known to affect water runoff, soil water-holding capacity, soil organic matter, nutrients, soil depth, and soil biota. All of these influence soil productivity in natural and managed ecosystems. Little is known about the ecology of the interactions of the various soil factors and their interdependency (Lal and Stewart 1990; Pimentel 1993). The effects of soil erosion on the productivity of both natural and managed ecosystems require serious research to develop effective soil and water conservation measures. Farmers will need incentives to implement conservation methods fully.

Productive Soils and Food Security

There is no doubt that soil erosion is a critical environmental problem throughout the world's terrestrial ecosystems. Erosion is a slow insidious process. Indeed one millimeter of soil, easily lost in just one rainstorm or windstorm, is so minute that its loss goes unnoticed. Yet this loss of soil over a hectare of cropland amounts to 15 tons per hectare. Replenishing this amount of soil under agricultural conditions (where possible) requires approximately twenty years, but meanwhile this soil is increasingly less able to support crop growth. Simultaneously, equally important losses of water, nutrients, soil organic matter, and soil biota are occurring. Forest, rangeland, and natural ecosystems are harmed when soil loss is ignored.

Concerning future food security, where cropland degradation is allowed to occur, crop productivity is significantly reduced. Shortages of cropland are already having negative impacts on world food production (Brown 1997). For example, the Food and Agricultural Organization (FAO) of the United Nations reports that the availability of food per capita has been declining for nearly two decades, based on available cereal grains (FAO 1961–2000) (figure 23.3). Cereal grains make up 80 percent to 90 percent of the world's food. Although grain yields per hectare in both developed and developing countries are still increasing, these increases are slowing while the world population continues to escalate. Now, and in the future decades, crop yields must be shared with more and more people (FAO 1961–2000; PRB 2001).

Worldwide, soil erosion continues unabated while the human population and its requirements for food, fiber, and other resources expand geometrically. Indeed, achieving future food security for all people depends on conserving fertile soil, water, energy, and biological resources. Careful management of all of these vital resources deserves high priority to ensure the effective protection of our agricultural and natural ecosystems. If conservation is ignored, the three billion malnourished people in the world will grow in number and per capita food will continue to decline.

Soil Erosion and Development

If one were to ask what has been the relation of this critically important issue and the concept and practice of economic development as it is normally practiced, the most accurate answer would be, essentially, there is none. Development plans are generally formulated by economists, who use discount rates in undertaking their analyses. If soil issues are included in the assessment (a rarity), the importance of erosion, an issue that is small next year but hugely important over decades, tends to be discounted to a negligible component of the overall assessment. Since most development schemes for the developing world are focused at least in part on enhancing export crops, which are often (for example, in the case of cotton, sugarcane, and bananas) especially erosion-causing (although perhaps not as much as maize or other annual row crops used for subsistence), it is likely that the general impact of development is to make the issue of erosion worse, although perhaps for a "good" cause, that is, generating foreign exchange. In fact, if you look into the two most important new (and good) books on economic development by economists themselves (Easterly and Stiglitz; see chapter 1) you do not even find the words "soil," "erosion," or even "energy" or "water" in the index. I believe that this is just one way in which mainstream economics fails to evaluate properly what is really most important to developing countries. That, and the lack of focus and concern on population growth, which lies behind most of the problems presented in this chapter, virtually ensure that most past economic development plans could not possibly have worked to solve the problems of developing countries.

References

Agriculture California. 2002. Control of soil erosion. http//res2.agr.ca/ecorc/program3/pub/status/control.htm.

Agriculture Canada. 2002a. Range management. www/agr.gc.ca/pfra/land/range.htm.

———. 2002b. Wind particles and health. http://res2.agr.ca/research-recherche/science/Healthy_Air4d.html.

Alfens, K. L., M. A. DeFranco, S. Glomsrod, and T. Johnson. 1996. The cost of soil erosion in Nicaragua. *Ecological Economics* 16:129–46.

Allison, F. E. 1973. *Soil Organic Matter and Its Role in Crop Production.* New York: Elsevier.

Anderson, J. M. 1988. Spatiotemporal effects of invertebrates on soil processes. *Biological Fertility of Soils* 6:216–27.

Atlavinyte, O. 1965. The effect of erosion on the population of earthworms (Lumbricidae) in soils under different crops. *Pedobiologia* 5:178–88.

Bailey, A. W. 1996. Managing Canadian rangelands as a sustainable resource: Policy issues. *Proceedings of the Fifth International Rangeland Congress*, Salt Lake City, 23–28 July 1995.

Bajracharya, R. M., and R. Lal. 1992. Seasonal soil loss and erodibility variation on a Miamian silt loam soil. *Soil Science Society of America Journal* 56, no. 5: 1560–65.

Bohac, J., and A. Pokarzhevsky. 1987. Effect of manure and NPK on soil macrofauna in chernozem soil. In J. Szegi, ed., *Soil Biology and Conservation of Biosphere*, 15–19. Budapest: Akademiai Kiado.

Brown, L. R. 1997. *The Agricultural Link: How Environmental Deterioration Could Disrupt Economic Progress.* Washington, D.C.: Worldwatch Institute.

Bruijnzeel, L. A. 1990. *Hydrology of Moist Tropical Forests and Effects of Conversion: A State of Knowledge Review.* Amsterdam: Free University and UNESCO.

Buringh, P. 1989. Availability of agricultural land for crop and livestock production. In Pimentel and Hall 1989, 70–85.

Campbell, L. C. 1998. Managing soil fertility decline. *Journal of Crop Production* 1, no. 2: 29–52.

Carnell, B. 2001. Soil erosion. www.overpopulation.com/fag/natural_resources/food/soil_erosion.html.

Clark, E. H. 1987. Soil erosion: Offsite environmental effects. In J. M. Harlin and G. M. Bernardi, eds., *Soil Loss: Processes, Policies, and Prospects*, 59–89. Boulder, Colo.: Westview.

Daily, G. 1996. *Nature's Services: Societal Dependence on Natural Ecosystems.* Washington, D.C.: Island Press.

Donahue, R. H., R. H. Follett, and R. N. Tulloch. 1990. *Our Soils and Their Management.* Danville, Ill.: Interstate.

Dregne, H. E. 1992. Erosion and soil productivity in Asia. *Journal of Soil Water Conservation* 47:8–13.

Ebbert, J. C., and R. D. Roe. 1998. Soil erosion in the Palouse River basin: Indications of improvement. U.S. Geological Survey Fact Sheet FS-069-98.

Ecology. 2002. Biodiversity, productivity, and overyielding. http://web.utk.edu/~cuixu/School/ecology_debate/biodiversity.htm.

Ecology Action. 2002. Soil. www.growbiointensive.org/ biointensive/soil.html.

Edwards, C. A., and J. E. Bater. 1992. The use of earthworms in environmental management. *Soil Biology and Biochemistry* 24:1683–89.

Elton, C. S. 1927. *Animal Ecology*. London: Sidgwick and Jackson.

Evans, R., D. K. Cassel, and R. E. Sneed. 1997. Soil, water, and crop characteristic important to irrigation scheduling. www.bae.ncsu.edu/programs/extension/ evans/ag452–1.html.

Falkenmark, M. 1989. Water scarcity and food production. In Pimentel and Hall 1989, 164–91.

FAO. 1961–2000. Quarterly bulletin of statistics. *FAO Quarterly Bulletin of Statistics* 1–13.

———. 1998. Food balance sheet. http://armanncorn:98iv ysub@faostat.fao.org/lim . . . ap.pl.

———. 2001. Soil. www.fao.org/ag/AGL/agll/soilbiod/ casecall.htm.

———. 2002. Restoring the land. www.fao.org/inpho/ vlibrary/u8480e/U8480E0d.htm.

FEMAT. 1993. Forest ecosystem management assessment team report. Sponsored by the USDA Forest Service, U.S. Environmental Protection Agency, USDOI Bureau of Land Management, National Park Service, Portland, Oregon.

Follett, R. F., S. C. Gupta, and P. G. Hunt. 1987. Conservation practices: Relation to the management of plant nutrients for crop production. In *Soil Fertility and Organic Matter as Critical Components of Production Systems*, 19–51. Madison, Wis.: Soil Science Society of America and American Society of Agronomy.

Forest Conservation Act. 2002. Riparian forest buffer panel (Bay Area regulatory programs). www. riparianbuffers.umd.edu/manuals/regulatory.html+60 %25+forest+soil+conservation&hl=en&ie=UTF-8.

Gray, D. M., and A. T. Leiser. 1989. *Biotechnical Slope Protection and Erosion Control*. Malabar, Fla.: Krieger.

Griffin, D. W., C. A. Kellogg, and E. A. Shinn. 2001. Dust in the wind: Long range transport of dust in the atmosphere and its implications for global public and ecosystem health. *Global Change & Human Health* 2, no. 1: 20–33.

Gupta, J. P., and P. Raina. 1996. Wind erosion and its control in hot arid areas of Rajasthan. In B. Buerkert, B. E. Allison, and M. von Oppen, eds., *Wind Erosion in West Africa: The Problem and Its Control*, 209–18. Berlin: Margraf Verlag.

Haigh, M. J., J. S. Rawat, S. K. Bartarya, and S. P. Rai. 1995. Interactions between forest and landslide activity along new highways in the Kumaun Himalaya. *Forest Ecology and Management* 78, nos. 1–3: 173–89.

Hartshorn, G. L., A. Hartshorne, L. D. Atmella, A. Gomez, R. Mata, R. Morales, D. Ocampo, C. Pool, C. Quesada, R. Solera, G. Solarzano, G. Stiles, J. Tosi, A. Umana, C. Villalobos, and R. Wells. 1982. *Costa Rica: Country Environmental Profile*. San José, Costa Rica: Tropical Sciences Center.

Hawkins, L. 2002. Ants. www.suite101.com/article.cfm/ homeschooling_science_fun/69922.

Heywood, V. H. 1995. *Global Biodiversity Assessment*. Cambridge: Cambridge University Press.

Huszar, P. C., and S. L. Piper. 1985. Off-site costs of wind erosion in New Mexico. In *Off-Site Costs of Soil Erosion: The Proceedings of a Symposium*, 143–66. Washington, D.C.: Conservation Foundation.

IECA. 1991. *Erosion Control: A Global Perspective*. Proceedings of Conference XXII, International Erosion Control Association, Steamboat Springs, Colorado.

IFPRI. 2002. Effective strategies for reducing hunger, poverty, and environmental degradation in Ethiopian Highlands. www.ifpri.cgiar.org/media/ifi_results.htm.

Johnson, P. W. 1995. *Agriculture*. Washington, D.C.: U.S. Government Printing Office.

Jones, A. J., R. Lal, and D. R. Huggins. 1997. Soil erosion and productivity research: A regional approach. *American Journal of Alternative Agriculture* 12, no. 4: 183–92.

Kendall, H. W., and D. Pimentel. 1994. Constraints on the expansion of the global food supply. *Ambio* 23:198–205.

Kitazawa, Y., and T. Kitazawa. 1980. Influence of application of a fungicide, an insecticide, and compost upon soil biotic community. In D. L. Sindal, ed., *Soil Biology as Related to Land Use Practices*, 94–99. Washington, D.C.: Environmental Protection Agency.

Klee, G. A. 1991. *Conservation of Natural Resources*. Englewood Cliffs, N.J.: Prentice-Hall.

Klocke, N. L., K. G. Hubbard, W. L. Kranz, and D. G. Watts. 1996. Evapotranspiration (ET) or crop water use. University of Nebraska, Cooperative Extension. www.ianr.unl.edu/pubs/irrigation/g992.htm.

Lal, R. 1990. Soil erosion and land degradation: The global risks. In R. Lal and B. A. Stewart, eds., *Soil Degradation*, 129–72. New York: Springer-Verlag.

———. 1994. Water management in various crop production systems related to soil tillage. *Soil and Tillage Research* 30:169–85.

———. 2001. World cropland soils as a source of sink for atmospheric carbon. *Advances in Agronomy* 71:145–91.

———. 2002. One answer for cleaner air, water: Better agricultural practices. www.acs.ohio-state.edu/units/research/archive/sequest.htm.

Lal, R., and B. A. Stewart, eds. 1990. *Soil Degradation.* New York: Springer-Verlag.

Lal, R., R. F. Follett, J. Kimble, and C. V. Cole. 1999. Managing U.S. cropland to sequester carbon in soil. *Journal of Soil and Water Conservation* 54, no. 1: 374–81.

Langdale, G. W., L. T. West, R. R. Bruce, W. P. Miller, and A. W. Thomas. 1992. Restoration of eroded soil with conservation tillage. *Soil Technology* 5:81–90.

Larson, M. C., and J. E. Parks. 1997. How wide is a road? The association of roads and mass wasting in a forested tropical environment. *Earth Surface Processes and Landforms* 22:835–48.

Lavelle, P. 1983. The soil fauna of tropical savannas. II. The earthworms. *Ecosystems of the World* 13:485–504.

Lazaroff, C. 2001. Biodiversity gives carbon sinks a boost. Environment News Service, April 13, 2001.

Lee, E., and R. C. Foster. 1991. Soil fauna and soil structure. *Australian Journal of Soil Research* 29:745–76.

Lee, K. E. 1985. *Earthworms: Their Ecology and Relationships with Soils and Land Use.* Orlando, Fla.: Academic Press.

Libert, B. 1995. *The Environmental Heritage of Soviet Agriculture.* Oxford: CAB International.

Lockaby, B. G., and J. C. Adams. 1985. Pedoturbation of a forest soil by fire ants. *Journal of the Soil Science Society of America* 49:220–23.

Martin, P. 1997. Sediments and erosion. www.gov.mb.ca/environ/pages/publs97/cwgtext/sediment.html.

McLaughlin, L. 1991. Soil conservation planning in the People's Republic of China: An alternative approach. Ph.D. dissertation, Cornell University.

———. 1993. A case study in Dingxi County, Gansu Province, China. In Pimentel 1993, 87–107.

McTainish, G., and C. Boughton. 1993. *Land Degradation Processes in Australia.* Melbourne: Longman Cheshire.

Mokma, D. L., and M. A. Sietz. 1992. Effects of soil erosion on corn yields on Marlette soils in south-central Michigan. *Journal of Soil and Water Conservation* 47:325–27.

Murphee, C. E., and K. C. McGregor. 1991. Runoff and sediment yield from a flatland watershed in soybeans. *Transactions of the American Society of Agricultural Engineers* 34:407–11.

Myers, N. 1993. *Gaia: An Atlas of Planet Management.* New York: Anchor/Doubleday.

NAS. 2002. *New Frontiers in Agriculture.* Washington, D.C.: National Academy of Sciences.

Odum, E. P. 1978. *Fundamentals of Ecology.* New York: Saunders.

Olah-Zsupos, A., and B. Helmeczi. 1987. The effect of soil conditioners on soil microorganisms. In J. Szegi, ed., *Soil Biology and Conservation of the Biosphere,* 829–37. Budapest: Akademiai Kiado.

Oldeman, L. R. 1997. Soil degradation: A threat to food security? Paper presented at the International Conference on Time Ecology, 6–9 April 1997, Tutzing, Germany.

Olson, K. R., and E. Nizeyimana. 1988. Effects of soil erosion on corn yields of seven Illinois soils. *Journal of Production Agriculture* 1:13–19.

Patric, J. 2002. Forest erosion rates. http://syllabus.syr.edu/esf/rdbriggs/for345/erosion.htm.

Phillips, D. L., D. White, and B. Johnson. 1993. Implications of climate change scenarios for soil erosion potential in the USA. *Land Degradation and Rehabilitation* 4:61–72.

Pimentel, D. 1997. Soil erosion. *Environment* 39, no. 10: 4–5.

———. 2001. The limitations of biomass energy. *Encyclopedia on Physical Science and Technology,* 159–71. San Diego: Academic Press.

———, ed. 1993. *World Soil Erosion and Conservation.* Cambridge: Cambridge University Press.

Pimentel, D., and C. W. Hall, eds. 1989. *Food and Natural Resources.* San Diego: Academic Press.

Pimentel, D., and N. Kounang. 1998. Ecology of soil erosion in ecosystems. *Ecosystems* 1:416–26.

Pimentel, D., and A. Warneke. 1989. Ecological effects of manure, sewage sludge, and other organic wastes on arthropod populations. *Agricultural Zoology Review* 3:1–30.

Pimentel, D., C. Harvey, P. Resosudarmo, K. Sinclair, D. Kurz, M. McNair, S. Crist, L. Shpritz, L. Fitton, R. Saffouri, and R. Blair. 1995. Environmental and economic costs of soil erosion and conservation benefits. *Science* 267:1117–23.

Pimentel, D., J. Houser, E. Preiss, O. White, H. Fang, L. Mesnick, T. Barsky, S. Tariche, J. Schreck, and S. Alpert. 1997. Water resources: Agriculture, the environment, and society. *BioScience* 47, no. 2: 97–106.

Pimentel, D., U. Stachow, D. A. Takacs, H. W. Brubaker, A. R. Dumas, J. J. Meaney, J. O'Neil, D. E. Onsi, and D. B. Corzilius. 1992. Conserving biological diversity in agricultural/forestry systems. *BioScience* 42:354–62.

PRB. 2002. World population data sheet. Washington, D.C.: Population Reference Bureau.

Reid, W. S. 1985. Regional effects of soil erosion on crop productivity—northeast. In R. F. Follett and B. A. Stewart, eds., *Soil Erosion and Crop Productivity*, 235–50. Madison, Wis.: American Society of Agronomy.

Richards, J., and B. Flint. 1994. A century of land-use change in South and Southeast Asia. In V. H. Dale, ed., *Effect of Land-use Change on Atmospheric CO₂ Concentrations: South and Southeast Asia as a Case Study*, 15–57. New York: Springer-Verlag.

Risser, J. 1981. A renewed threat of soil erosion: It's worse than the Dust Bowl. *Smithsonian* 11: 120–22, 124, 126–30.

Roose, E. 1988. Soil and water conservation lessons from steep-slope farming in French speaking countries of Africa. In *Conservation Farming on Steep Lands*, 130–31. Ankeny, Iowa: Soil and Water Conservation Society.

Scatena, F. N., E. O. Planos-Gutierrez, and J. Schellekens. 2005. Natural disturbance and the hydrology of the humid tropics. In M. Bonnell and L. A. Bruijnzeel, eds., *Forest, Water and People in the Humid Tropics*, 489–512. New York: Cambridge University Press.

Schertz, D. L., W. C. Moldenhauer, S. J. Livingston, G. A. Weesies, and E. A. Hintz. 1989. Effect of past soil erosion on crop productivity in Indiana. *Journal of Soil and Water Conservation* 44, no. 6: 604–8.

SCS. 1993. Wind erosion report (Nov. 1992–May 1993). Washington, D.C.: U.S. Soil Conservation Service.

Shachak, M., C. G. Jones, and S. Brand. 1995. The role of animals in an arid ecosystem: Snails and isopods as controllers of soil formation, erosion and desalinization. In H. P. Blume and S. M. Berkowicz, eds., *Arid Ecosystems*, 37–50. Cremlingen-Destedt, Germany: Catena Verlag.

Singh, T. V., and J. Kaur. 1989. *Studies in Himalayan Ecology and Development Strategies*. New Delhi: Himalayan Books.

Solliday, L. 1997. Sediment transport of an estuary. http:// bellnetweb.brc.tamus.edu/sediment.htm.

Southgate, D., and M. Whitaker. 1992. Promoting resource degradation in Latin America: Tropical deforestation, soil erosion, and coastal ecosystem disturbance in Ecuador. *Economic Development and Cultural Change* 40, no. 4: 787–807.

Speth, J. G. 1994. Towards an effective and operational international convention on desertification. New York: United Nations, International Convention on Desertification.

Stone, R. P. and N. Moore. 1997. Control of soil erosion. www.gov.pm.ca/OMAFRA/english/crops/facts/95–089.htm.

Sugden, A. M., and G. F. Rands. 1990. The ecology of temperate and cereal fields. *Trends in Ecology and Evolution* 5:205–6.

Sundquist, B. 2000. Topsoil loss: Causes, effects, and implications—A global perspective. 4th ed. www.alltel.net/~bsundquist1.

SWAG. 2002. Principles of erosion and sediment control. www.watershedrestoration.org/erosion.htm.

Tilman, D., and J. A. Downing. 1994. Biodiversity and stability in grasslands. *Nature* 367:363–65.

Trimble, S. W. 1994. Erosional effects of cattle on stream banks in Tennessee, USA. *Landforms* 19:451–64.

Trimble, S. W., and A. C. Mendel. 1995. The cow as a geomorphic agent: A critical review. *Geomorphology* 13:233–53.

Troeh, F. R., and L. M. Thompson. 1993. *Soils and Soil Fertility*. 5th ed. New York: Oxford University Press.

Troeh, F. R, J. A. Hobbs, and R. L. Donahue. 1991. *Soil and Water Conservation*. Englewood Cliffs, N.J.: Prentice-Hall.

UN-NADAF. 1996. UN-NADAF mid-term review: Focus on key sectors: Environment. *Africa Recovery* 10, no. 2: 23.

Uri, N. D. 2001. Agriculture and the environment: The problem of soil erosion. *Journal of Sustainable Agriculture* 16, no. 4: 71–91.

USDA. 1989. *The Second RCA Appraisal: Soil, Water, and Related Resources on Nonfederal Land in the United States*. Washington, D.C.: U.S. Department of Agriculture.

———. 1994. Summary report, 1992 National Resources Inventory. Washington, D.C.: Soil Conservation Service.

———. 1995. *National Resources Inventory: A Summary of Natural Resource Trends in the U.S. Between 1982 and 1992*. Washington, D.C.: USDA Natural Resources Service.

———. 2000a. Changes in average annual soil erosion by water on cropland and CRP land, 1992–1997. Natural Resources Conservation Service, USDA. (Revised April 2000.)

———. 2000b. Changes in average annual soil erosion by wind on cropland and CRP land, 1992–1997. Natural Resources Conservation Service, USDA. (Revised December 2000.)

———. 2001. *Agricultural Statistics*. Washington, D.C.: U.S. Department of Agriculture.

Walsh, K. N., and M. S. Rowe. 2001. Biodiversity increases ecosystems' ability to absorb CO_2 and nitrogen. www.bnl.gov/bnlweb/pubaf/pr/2001bnlpro41101.htm.

Watershed. 2002. Watershed conditions: Cumulative watershed effects. www.krisweb.com/watershd/impacts.htm.

Weesies, G. A., S. J. Livingston, W. D. Hosteter, and D. L. Schertz. 1994. Effect of soil erosion on crop yield in Indiana: Results of a 10 year study. *Journal of Soil and Water Conservation* 49, no. 6: 597–600.

WEI. 2002. Wind erosion impacts. www.cahe.wsu.edu/~cp3/erosion/erosion.html.

Wen, D. 1993. Soil erosion and conservation in China. In D. Pimentel, *Soil Erosion and Conservation*, 63–86.

———. 1997. *Agriculture in China: Water and Energy Resources*. Shenyang: Institute of Applied Ecology, Chinese Academy of Sciences.

Wendt, R. C., E. E. Alberts, and A. T. Helmers. 1986. Variability of runoff and soil loss from fallow experimental plots. *Soil Science Society of America Journal* 50:730–36.

WHO. 2000. Malnutrition worldwide. www.who.int/nut/malnutrition_worldwide.htm.

Witt, B. 1997. Using soil fauna to improve soil health. www.hort.agri.umn.edu/h5015/97papers/witt.html.

Wood, M. 1989. *Soil Biology*. New York: Blackie, Chapman and Hall.

WRI. 1994. *World Resources 1994–95: People and the Environment*. World Resources Institute. New York: Oxford University Press.

———. 1997. *Last Frontier Forests: Ecosystems and Economies on the Edge*. New York: Oxford University Press.

Wright, D. H. 1990. Human impacts on energy flow through natural ecosystems, and replications for species endangerment. *Ambio* 19:189–94.

Young, A. 1989. *Agroforestry for Soil Conservation*. Wallingford, England: CAB International.

———. 1990. Agroforestry, environment and sustainability. *Outlook for Agriculture* 19:155–60.

———. 1998. *Land Resources: Now and for the Future*. Cambridge: Cambridge University Press.

Zacharias, T. P., and A. H. Grube. 1984. An economic evaluation of weed control methods used in combination with crop rotations: A stochastic dominance approach. *North Central Journal of Agricultural Economics* 6:113–20.

Zhang, X., D. E. Walling, T. A. Quine, and A. Wen. 1997. Use of reservoir deposits and caesium-137 measurements to investigate the erosional response of a small drainage basin in the rolling loess plateau region of China. *Land Degradation and Development* 8:1–16.

Ziemer, R. R. 1998. Flooding and stormflows. In R. R. Ziemer, ed., *Proceedings of the Conference on Coastal Watersheds: The Caspar Creek Story*, 15–24. Albany, California: Pacific Southwest Research Station, Forest Service, U.S. Department of Agriculture.

CHAPTER 24

Assessing and Highlighting Forest Change in the Tropics Using Multiscale Data Sets

Hugh Eva and Frédéric Ashard

Introduction

For a number of years there has been a growing concern in the scientific community about the rapid changes in tropical forest ecosystems. The potential consequences of these changes with respect to carbon budgets and climate change (Detwiler and Hall 1988; Gash and Nobre 1996; Zhang, McGuffie, and Henderson-Sellers 1996; Melillo et al. 1996; Steudler et al. 1996), loss of habitat and fear of species extinction (Skole and Tucker 1993; Turner 1996; Prance and Elias 1976), and erosion of indigenous people's rights and ways of living (Vickers 1994; Redford and Padoch 1992), combined with concerns of resource mismanagement and depletion (Myers 1996), have drawn increased attention to the fate of tropical forest ecosystems. The scientific community has called for an intensive effort to highlight and document areas of rapid land-cover change (Turner et al. 1995). These concerns are reflected both in international conventions (IPCC 1996) and in bilateral government actions to reduce the impact of deforestation. The European Union has a stated policy of supporting sustainable forest management and therefore spends several hundred million euros on tropical forest initiatives each year (Shepherd et al. 1998). However, severe criticism has been leveled that aid funding has been counterproductive (Rainforest Foundation 1998), inasmuch as the perceived solutions for rural development are often at odds with forest conservation. One of the most striking examples of this is the extension and improvement of the road systems in the forest domain (FAO 1999; Laurance et al. 2001).

In such circumstances, the provision of timely and accurate data on the tropical forest extent and its changes can help to formulate conservation policies and maximize their impact, and at the same time can serve as an important input into development planning. The Food and Agricultural Organization (FAO) of the United Nations, which has a mandate to collect and publish global forest statistics, would be in theory such a data source (FAO 2001); however, these data are often difficult to compare between countries due to different classification systems, are not spatially explicit, and in some cases are simply extrapolations of historical data (Matthews 2001).

The Joint Research Center of the European Commission initiated the Tropical Ecosystem Environment Observation by Satellite (TREES) project in 1991 to develop a system for the monitoring of the extent, condition, and dynamics of the tropical forest belt at a global level. A crucial goal for the project was to develop techniques for highlighting areas undergoing rapid forest change so that appropriate political action and funding might be efficiently targeted (Malingreau et al. 1995).

Over the last twenty years the use of observation satellites has become more commonplace as a remote sensing tool for documenting and estimating changes in land cover. The observations are carried out at different scales: there are fine spatial resolution observations from Landsat Thematic Mapper, for example, where a restricted scene of around 200 km width can be observed at a resolution of 30 m for a selected site once a month; there are also coarse spatial resolution observations from

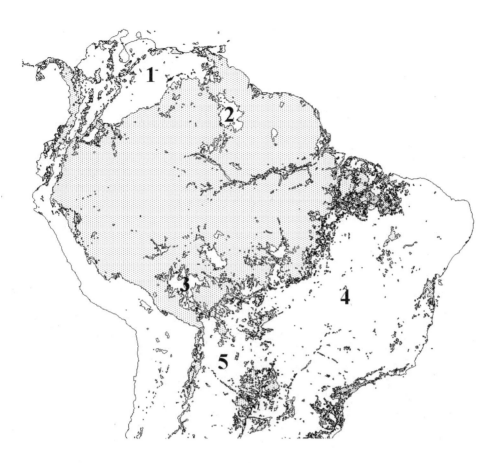

Figure 24.1. The distribution of moist forest in tropical South America (hashed). The main savanna regions are (1) the llanos of Venezuela, (2) Rio Branco, (3) Mojos, (4) Cerrado, and (5) Chaco.

NOAA's advanced very high-resolution radiometer (AVHRR), where regional to continental scenes are acquired daily but with a poor spatial definition, at a resolution of about 1 km.

While in theory a comprehensive coverage of the tropics using high spatial resolution data would reveal in detail the full extent of deforestation occurring at any one time, in practice the availability of imagery, the costs of acquisition and processing, and the huge amounts of data involved limit such efforts at global levels. The lack of sufficient imagery arises because cloud cover frequently obscures the target area in the tropics, and for a number of regions no ground stations exist, so that on-board satellite data storage is required. The latter depend on the space agencies, or on a paying customer.

Coarse spatial resolution remote sensing data have the advantage of giving daily synoptic views over large, often inaccessible areas, allowing phenological analysis of the data. In many cases, near real-time data can be obtained, either through a local receiving station or through the space agencies via the World Wide Web. On the other

hand, these data do not have sufficient spatial resolution to determine land-cover area change estimates accurately.

In this chapter we describe the methods used to highlight areas of land-cover change in the humid forests of tropical South America, which contains about half of the world's remaining rainforest (Achard et al. 2002). Our objective was to use regional maps of forest cover and fire incidence, both derived from coarse resolution satellite data, in conjunction with expert opinion to highlight the major deforestation fronts in tropical South America. The resulting maps can be used to target projects aimed at supporting sustainable forest management accurately, to support public administration, to monitor the integrity of national parks and indigenous lands, and to focus studies that aim to measure forest change in these "hotspots."

Our study encompasses the humid tropical forests of South America, which stretch from the Darien Gap in northwestern Colombia down the Choco, and across the Orinoco basin and Amazonian basins to the Guyanas (figure 24.1). On its eastern and southern edge the forest is bordered by the Brazilian *cerrado* and the Bolivian *chaco*, originally areas of dry forest and savanna, now predominantly agricultural. South of the equator, the western edge of the forest is delimited by the Andes mountain range. Within the vast humid forest domain of South America several large savannahs exist, notably the llanos of Colombia and Venezuela, the llanos de Mojos of Bolivia, and the Rio Branco/Rupunumi/Gran Sabana on the frontier of Brazil, Guyana, and Venezuela.

While much of the area of dry forest had been exploited and converted to agriculture in colonial times, the humid forest areas have remained intact until the post–World War II period. Since then, major land-use changes have occurred due to economic growth and outmigration. The latter has arisen for a number of reasons: isolation from markets and employment opportunities, lack of cultivable land, drought and civil disturbances, and few opportunities for producing cash crops (Preston 1996). The main migratory trends into the forest frontiers have been from the northeast of Brazil and from the Andes. In a number of countries the process has been encouraged by government grants, subsidies, and infrastructure improvements (Fearnside 1983; Nepstad et al. 1997). General economic growth at the national level has also stimulated these infrastructure improvements, leading to the construction and upgrading of ports and roads as well as increased mineral exploration and exploitation, all of which combine to make easier access to—and export from—the forested regions. The FAO forest area statistics show that the annual average net change rate for tropical South America between 1990 and 2000 was of the order of 0.4 percent; however, the data are not specifically spatially located, remaining aggregated at the country level (FAO 2001).

There is a need therefore to provide decision makers with explicit information as to just where deforestation is occurring, along with comparative rates for the particular hotspots.

Method

To produce our deforestation hotspot map we created two layers of thematic information: a map of forest cover (the TREES map) and a map of fire activity. These data were then used by experts at a workshop to locate deforestation fronts considered active during the 1990s. We created the TREES forest map of tropical South America using 1 km spatial resolution satellite data from the NOAA-AVHRR sensor (Kidwell 1991). These data were geometrically registered to Plate Carée projection and analyzed, using a combination of multidate spectral information and expert interpretation, to map three principal land-cover classes—forest, nonforest, and fragmented forest (D'Souza, Malingreau, and Eva 1995). The images were acquired in 1992, predominantly in the dry season, when cloud-free data are more frequent. The resultant map (Eva et al. 1999) is available in both paper and digital formats.

We also produced the maps of fire activity over South America for the 1992–93 period from the NOAA-AVHRR. This sensor is equipped with a middle infrared sensor (3.7 μm wavelength), sensitive to temperatures at which vegetation fires occur. The fires are extracted automatically from the satellite data using a contextual algorithm that detects high thermal anomalies, which are contrasted against the land cover (Flasse and Ceccato 1996). The database used was the Global Fire Product, produced at the Joint Research Center (Dwyer, Grégoire, and Malingreau 1998). These data were overlaid on the forest maps, so that areas of fires occurring in the forest domain were highlighted.

In November 1997, we organized a workshop at the Joint Research Center to bring together regional and international experts on tropical forest. Among the experts were representatives from the FAO, from INPE (the Brazilian National Space Research Agency), and CIAT (Center for Research on Tropical Agriculture). The objective was to solicit the locations of major deforestation hotspots in the tropics. Using their own knowledge and the TREES maps of forest and fire distribution, the experts delineated the locations on the TREES maps (Achard et al. 1998). These were then hand-digitized and entered into a GIS.

A sampling grid of 60 km hexagons was placed over the TREES map, and a hotness index was obtained for each of these grid cells by calculating

Figure 24.2. The location of the deforestation hotspots in tropical South America.

Relative hotness

Warm   Hot

the proportion of forest that lay within a hotspot in the respective cell. To provide a quantitative index, we weighted the resulting hotspot index by the FAO national estimates of net forest change rates for the 1990–95 period (FAO 1997). In this way we attempted to reduce any subjective influences that may have arisen between experts from different countries. The resulting hotspot index map is shown in figure 24.2.

We then carried out two tests on the hotspot map: one test to validate it, another to see if it could be replaced simply by using a map of forest fires. To validate this map we used a sample set of higher-resolution Landsat Thematic Mapper image pairs, acquired at two dates in the 1990s. The dates of acquisition we set to be as close to 1990

and 1997 as possible. Forty-five validation sites were selected using a random stratified sampling scheme, designed to select more observation sites in the hotspots than in the cold spots (Richards et al. 2000).

For each of the forty-five scenes, a land-cover-change map was produced, giving the annual deforestation rate normalized to a reference period of mid-June 1990 to mid-June 1997 by linear extrapolation. For each sample site, we used regression analysis to compare the actual deforestation that occurred during the 1990 to 1997 period, with both the hotness index and the number of fires that occurred within the scene. The degree of correlation and the associated probability (P) between the data (N samples) is given by the Pearson coefficient

Table 1: Deforestation rates for selected hotspots in South America

Country	Annual deforestation rate (%)
Brazil	
Country rate	0.40
Mato Grosso	1.90
Rondonia	2.10
Acre	4.40
Ecuador	
Country rate	1.20
Tumbes	1.50
Napo	1.40
Bolivia	
Country rate	0.30
Santa Cruz	1.00
Colombia	
Country rate	0.40
Florencia	4.50
Peru	
Country rate	0.40
Pulcallpa	0.58

Note: The country rate comes from the FAO (2001). The selected hotspot rates come from the TREES sample sites.

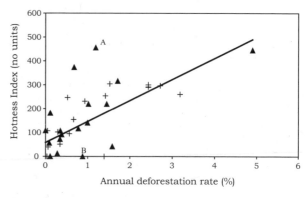

Figure 24.3. Scatter plot for forty-three validation sample sites, relating the hotness index to the annual deforestation rate (1990–97). The Brazilian sites are indicated by crosses, the non-Brazilian sites by triangles. Note the wide variance of the later sites. Point A (Huanuco) has a lower deforestation rate than would be predicted given its high hotness index, while point B (Santa Marta) points to a missed hotspot, with a zero hotness index, but a relatively high deforestation rate.

(R). From these samples we also estimated the deforestation rates for the major hotspots by computing the ratio of the forest change for sites within each hotspot to the total forest within these sites.

Results

We found an overall correlation between our predicted "hotness" index for each sample site and the measured deforestation rate that occurred in the 1990s (Pearson coefficient $R = 0.63$: $N = 45$: $P = 0.998$). This correlation is improved (figure 24.3) if only sites with forest areas greater than 20,000 ha are considered (Pearson coefficient $R = 0.689$: $N = 43$: $P = 0.998$). This removes sites that have a high deforestation rate but are insignificant in that they contain little forest. At the same time the correlation is higher if only Brazilian sites are considered (Pearson coefficient $R = 0.78$: $N = 20$: $P = 0.998$). We note from the graph (figure 24.3)

that the hotness index tends to reach a plateau for Brazilian sites.

Our analysis of fire data detected by satellite in 1992–93 (total number of fires) and the annual average deforestation area also shows a good correlation (Pearson coefficient of $R = 0.68$: $N = 45$: $P = 0.998$). A major outlier (point A, figure 24.4) is caused by the large number of fires that occur in the savanna area that falls in this sample site. Removal of this point increases the correlation ($R = 0.81$) and points to the general need for masking out natural savanna areas in the analysis (Eva and Lambin 2000). Analysis of Brazilian sites shows a similar improved result (Pearson coefficient of $R = 0.92$: $N = 20$: $P = 0.998$). However, when we examine the non-Brazilian sites, we find no correlation between fire and deforestation.

We also assessed the relative deforestation in the major hotspot areas (table 24.1). As we would expect, the deforestation rates in the hotspots are well in excess of nationally reported figures. We note that the Brazilian hotspots have far higher rates of deforestation than the hotspots found in the Andean countries.

Discussion

While the major deforestation hotspot areas derived from coarse-resolution satellite data and expert

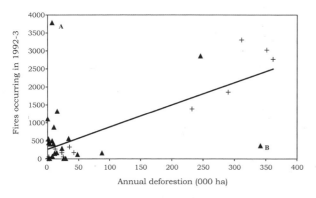

Figure 24.4. Scatter plot showing the relationship between fire activity (number of active fires during the one-year period 1992–93) and annual deforested areas per site. Note point A, which includes a savanna area, where high fire activity is not (and cannot be) accompanied by deforestation, and point B, in the hyper-humid zone, where high deforestation is not accompanied by fires. The Brazilian sites are indicated by crosses, non-Brazilian sites by triangles.

opinion have been shown to be correct, some caution is needed inasmuch as it has not been possible to test all the hotspots. The large "arc of deforestation" on the southeastern edge of the Amazon forest is shown to be the largest contiguous area of forest exploitation in the region. On the western edge of the Amazon basin, the foothills of the Andes are a second major area of activity, but with a lower rate of deforestation. The spatial patterns of the deforestation processes and the land-management techniques are different in both cases. Within the Brazilian hotspot, clear-cutting for large pasture, selective logging followed by clearance, and large colonization schemes are the main vectors of deforestation, with fire almost always used as a clearance tool. In the Andean hotspots, while colonization schemes have played a role in some areas, shifting cultivation carried out by smallholders is the main cause of forest removal. At the same time, fire is used less frequently for clearance. We found that the satellite-derived fire data, while appropriate for highlighting deforestation in the semi-evergreen forest belt of Brazil and Bolivia, was inappropriate for the Andean ecosystems. A combination of land-use practices and humidity means that fire is not an indicator of deforestation. This is demonstrated in Colombia, where the colonization scheme in Florencia (point B on figure 24.3) exhibited high

deforestation but no fire activity. The area is in the hyperhumid climate zone with more than 3,000 mm of rain a year; thus "cut and mulch" is a more appropriate land-cover conversion technique than "slash and burn."

The analysis of the Brazilian data set shows a plateau is reached where deforestation rates increase while the hotness index is saturated. This arises from the differences in spatial resolutions of data sets involved. The deforestation is measured at fine spatial resolutions with a pixel cell of 30 m. The hotness index is derived from low spatial resolution data with a pixel cell of 1 km. At a certain point areas that are already significantly deforested are classed as nonforest by this 1 km satellite data, as over 50 percent of the pixel is already deforested; however, the remainder of the pixel in fact remains forested and is undergoing a continuing fast deforestation. This occurs predominantly in areas where a high fragmentation pattern is seen (e.g., Rondonia). As new data from medium-resolution satellite sensors become available (e.g., MODIS at 250 m resolution), the ability to detect finer spatial fragmentation of forest will be possible.

The specific hotspots often have much higher deforestation rates than the national averages, with some hotspots having between five and ten times the national figure. The implications of this are that deforestation is spatially concentrated and that within the hotspots there is no sustainable forest management. Under these circumstances a continual degradation, fragmentation, and clearance will occur until the hotspots are fully converted to agricultural and/or abandoned land. If development and economic growth continue, new hotspots will appear.

The application of our method in a real-time operational system will allow policy makers to have a clear geographical indication of where the main deforestation areas are occurring, and where new deforestation fronts are appearing. Such a monitoring system would facilitate a more realistic planning of forest reserves and biological corridors and a method for ensuring the integrity of such zones. The information would also serve governments and potential donors, giving them essential background data so as to perform environmental impact studies for rural development projects. At the same time, research on the initiators and drivers of deforestation, such as infrastructure improvements, tax incentives, and land availability, can be spatially explicit rather than static, national comparisons (Deacon 1994; Koop and Tole 1997). As new sources of remote sensing data become available online in near-real time, the potential for regular updates on deforestation fronts becomes more attainable. This potential will provide policy makers, aid donors, scientists, groups representing indigenous peoples, and local administrators with accurate data with which to formulate and enforce sustainable forest management in the context of rural development.

Acknowledgments

The authors would like to acknowledge the help and expertise of the individuals and institutions that took part in the TREES project and the financial support provided by the Global Environment Unit of the EC Directorate for Environment.

References

Achard, F., H. Eva, A. Glinni, P. Mayaux, T. Richards, and H. J. Stibig. 1998. *Identification of Deforestation Hot Spot Areas in the Humid Tropics*. Luxembourg: European Commission.

Achard, F., H. Eva, H. J. Stibig, P. Mayaux, J. Gallego, T. Richards, and J. P. Malingreau. 2002. Determination of deforestation rates of the world's humid tropical forests. *Science* 297:999–1003.

Deacon, R. T. 1994. Deforestation and the rule of law in a cross-section of countries. *Land Economics* 70:414–30.

Detwiler, R. P., and C. A. S. Hall. 1988. Tropical forests and the global carbon cycle. *Science* 239:42–47.

D'Souza, G., J. P. Malingreau, and H. D. Eva. 1995. *Tropical Forest Cover of South and Central America as Derived from Analyses of NOAA-AVHRR Data*. Luxembourg: European Commission.

Dwyer, E., J.-M. Grégoire, and J. P. Malingreau. 1998. A global analysis of vegetation fires using satellite images: Spatial and temporal dynamics. *Ambio* 27:175–81.

Eva, H. D., and E. F. Lambin. 2000. Fires and land-cover change in the tropics: A remote sensing analysis at the landscape scale. *Journal of Biogeography* 27:765–76.

Eva, H. D., A. Glinni, P. Janvier, and C. Blair-Myers.

1999. *Vegetation Map of South America, Scale 1/5M*. Luxembourg: European Commission.

FAO. 1999 *Road Infrastructures in Tropical Forests: Road to Development or Road to Destruction*. Rome: FAO.

———. 2001. *Global Forest Resources Assessment 2000, Main Report*. Rome: FAO.

Fearnside, P. M. 1983. Land-use trends in the Brazilian Amazon region as factors in accelerating deforestation. *Environmental Conservation* 10:141–48.

Flasse, S. P., and P. Ceccato. 1996. A contextual algorithm for AVHRR fire detection. *International Journal of Remote Sensing* 17:419–24.

Gash, J. H. C., and C. A. Nobre. 1997. Climatic effects of Amazonian deforestation: Some results from ABRACOS. *Bulletin of the American Meteorological Society* 78:823–30.

IPCC. 1996. *Climate Change 1995: The Science of Climate Change*. Cambridge: Cambridge University Press.

Kidwell, K. B. 1991. *NOAA Polar Orbiter Data (TIROS N, NOAA-6, NOAA-7, NOAA-8, NOAA-9, NOAA-10, NOAA-11, NOAA-12) Users Guide*. Washington, D.C.: NOAA.

Koop, G., and L. Tole. 1997. Measuring differential forest outcomes: A tale of two countries. *World Development* 25:2043–56.

Laurance, W. F., M. A. Cochrane, S. Bergen, P. M. Fearnside, P. Delamonica, C. Barber, S. D'Angelo, and T. Fernandes. 2001. The future of the Brazilian Amazon. *Science* 291:438–39.

Malingreau, J. P., F. Achard, G. D'Souza, H. J. Stibig, J. D'Souza, C. Estreguil, and H. Eva. 1995. AVHRR for global tropical forest monitoring: The lessons of the TREES project. *Remote Sensing Reviews* 12:29–40.

Matthews, E. 2001. *Understanding the FRA 2000*. Washington, D.C.: WRI.

Mayaux, P., and E. Lambin. 1995. Estimation of tropical forest area from coarse spatial resolution data: A two-step correction function for proportional errors due to spatial aggregation. *Remote Sensing of the Environment* 53:1–16.

Melillo, J. M., R. A. Houghton, D. W. Kicklighter, and A. D. McGuire. 1996. Tropical deforestation and the global carbon budget. *Annual Review of Energy and the Environment* 21:293–310.

Myers, N. 1996. The world's forests: Problems and potentials. *Environmental Conservation* 23:156–69.

Nepstad, D. C., C. A. Klink, C. Uhl, I. C. Vieira, P. A. Lefebvre, M. Pedlowski, E. Matricardi, G. Negreiros, I. F. Brown, E. Amaral, A. Homma, and R. Walker. 1997. Land-use in Amazonia and the cerrado of Brazil. *Ciencia e Cultura* 49:73–86.

Prance, G. T., and T. S. Elias. 1976. *Extinction Is Forever*. New York: New York Botanical Garden.

Preston, D. 1996. *Latin America Development*. London: Longman.

Rainforest Foundation. 1998 *Out of Commission: The Environmental and Social Impacts of European Union Development Funding in Tropical Forest Areas*. London: Rainforest Foundation.

Redford, K. H., and C. Padoch. 1992. *Conservation of Neotropical Forest*. New York: Columbia University Press.

Richards, T., J. Gallego, and F. Achard. 2000. Sampling for forest cover change assessment at the pan-tropical scale. *International Journal of Remote Sensing* 6–7:1473–90.

Shepherd, G., D. Brown, M. Richards, and K. Schreckenberg. 1998. *The EU Tropical Forest Sourcebook*. London: Overseas Development Institute.

Skole, D., and C. J. Tucker. 1993. Tropical deforestation and habitat fragmentation in the Amazon: Satellite data from 1978 to 1988. *Science* 260:1905–10.

Steudler, P. A., J. M. Melillo, B. J. Feigl, C. Neill, M. C. Piccolo, and C. C. Cerri. 1996. Consequence of forest-to-pasture conversion on CH4 fluxes in the Brazilian Amazon basin. *Journal of Geophysical Research* 101:18, 547–554.

Turner, B. L., D. Skole, S. Sanderson, G. Fischer, L. Fresco, and R. Leemans. 1995. *Land-use and Land-cover Change: Science/Research Plan*. Stockholm: International Geosphere-Biosphere Programme.

Turner, I. M. 1996. Species loss in fragments of tropical rain forest: A review of the evidence. *Journal of Applied Ecology* 33:200–209.

Vickers, W. T. 1994. From opportunism to nascent conservation: The case of the Siona-Secoya. *Human Nature* 5:307–37.

Zhang, H., K. McGuffie, and A. Henderson-Sellers. 1996. Impacts of tropical deforestation. Part II: The role of large-scale dynamics. *Journal of Climate* 9:2498–2521.

Chapter 25

Reducing Pesticide Runoff to the Caribbean Sea

A Formidable Regional Challenge

Carlos E. Hernández, Jane C. Yeomans, and Tim Kasten

What is lost cannot be recovered, but we can—and we must—change our ways to protect and ·

restore what remains of the natural system that sustains us, if we are to prosper as a species.

—Sylvia Earle

Introduction

Agriculture is a vital activity for the well-being of humanity. Even though it is practiced at a local level, it both uses nutrients from the local, national, regional, and global levels and provides nutrients needed to support human populations at all of them. With human populations increasing at 1 to 2 percent per year in many developed nations and in some developing nations at more than 3 percent per year, demands for food are constantly increasing (UNFPA 2002). The productivity per area of arable land must increase in order to match the demand with supply (Helling 1993).

Arable land resources are considered a renewable resource as long as good "stewardship" is practiced. However, high-quality arable land is a finite resource, and the use of marginal land for agriculture is undesirable since the demand for nutrients exceeds its capacity and, in due time, it degrades and becomes nonrenewable. Fortunately, lands that are marginal for agriculture use are prime lands for other appropriate uses, which provide vital global environmental services (Helling 1993). A good example of providing vital environmental services is the land that is marginal for agriculture in the humid tropical forests. These forests sequester carbon and provide a vital filtration mechanism to the atmosphere as well as hosting the great majority of the earth's biodiversity, an invaluable treasure indispensable to the survival of humanity.

In this ecosystem, if the land is deforested and used for agriculture, the fragile soil fertility is lost very quickly due to the extreme climate conditions. In time, this depleted land cannot provide the required nutrient supply, and it no longer provides the original carbon sequestering service to the globe or the habitat necessary for all the species that once lived there (Piel 1992; Panayotou 1993).

The "green revolution" was a strategy designed to increase the productivity of arable land. It entailed monocultures, which provided higher yields but also optimal conditions for the growth and development of pests. In response, agrochemical applications, especially pesticides and fertilizers, became a generalized management practice. This approach has been used very intensively in the humid tropical regions of Latin America (FAO 1995). This increased use of pesticides was a successful technology because the response or return on investment was good in the short term. However, this practice has degenerated into an uncontrolled and indiscriminate use of these agrochemicals under the philosophy of "If little is good, more is better." One of the most relevant reasons for the extensive use of pesticides is the estimated amount of crop losses due to pests such as insects, nematodes, diseases, and weeds. Despite the global application of approximately 3,000,000 MT of pesticides each year, pests destroy more than 40 percent of the world's crop production (Pimentel 1997). It is estimated,

Table 25.1. Characteristics of the countries of the MCB

	Nicaragua	Costa Rica	Panama	Colombia
Caribbean coastline	463 km	208 km	1169 km	1600 km
Total land area	124,528 km²	51,276 km²	77,082 km²	1,141,748 km²
Area draining into MCB	96 percent	46 percent	23 percent	70 percent
Population growth rate	1.85 percent	1.89 percent	2.84 percent	1.53 percent
Total population (2000)	5,201,300	3,768,900	2,774,000	40,824,000
Population influencing the region	92 percent	4.6 percent	11 percent	90 percent

Source: Hernández, Yeomans, and Kasten (2001)

however, that pests could destroy as much as 50–60 percent of worldwide crop production if pesticide controls were not utilized (Pimentel 1998).

There were very few voices raised alerting the public to the biological and environmental health risk involved in the abusive application of pesticides, first called technical advances and later archetype management practices. For example, there is evidence that some of these chemicals accumulate in plant and animal tissue, and that eventually they may work their way up through the food chain, posing a risk to human health. Studies show that in the world today there are over sixty-five thousand synthetic chemicals in use and that approximately ten thousand are regularly applied. Of these, only about 2 percent have adequate risk assessment information (McCarthy and Shugart 1990).

There is also evidence that a considerable amount of applied pesticides is transported out of the application zones by surface runoff and leaching and is deposited in streams and rivers. These watercourses eventually reach the sea, causing effects at a local, national, regional, and global level. The National Oceanic and Atmospheric Administration (McKay, Mulvaney, and Thorne-Miller 2000) recognizes eight major causes of environmental change and degradation in oceans. Two of these, chemical pollution and nutrient pollution, can be related directly to agricultural activities. Excessive agrochemical applications leading to chemical pollution can cause poisoning, chronic diseases, reproduction failure, or deformities in marine life. Excessive fertilization, and hence

nutrient pollution, increases algae growth, oxygen depletion, water turbidity, and loss of species (McKay, Mulvaney, and Thorne-Miller 2000).

The strategies to solve the problem of pesticide movement out of the application zone must be handled at a watershed level. However, the solution—the application of best management practices—must be applied at a farm level. Consequently, the additional costs and investments due to the application of best management practices apply at a local level. Nevertheless, the benefits are enjoyed at a local, national, regional, and global level. In order to provide an incentive for the individual farmer to apply better management practices now, it is necessary to distribute the cost among all the beneficiaries. The question is how to measure this benefit at each level, and how to allocate the costs proportionately to each level. Policies need to be set at all levels, and this entails multilateral negotiations.

This chapter explores possible joint solutions to the problem of pesticide movement out of the application zone, and subsequent natural water resources contamination, in a specific subregion of the Caribbean Sea, the Mesoamerican Caribbean Basin (MCB).

The Mesoamerican Caribbean Basin (MCB)

The MCB can be described as a basin of the Caribbean Sea that is shaped by the countries of Nicaragua, Costa Rica, Panama, and Colombia. To understand the importance of and interest in the

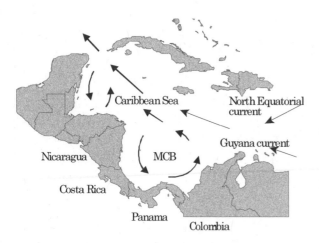

Figure 25.1. Ocean surface circulation patterns in the MCB (adapted from Ogden 2001 and satellite imagery).

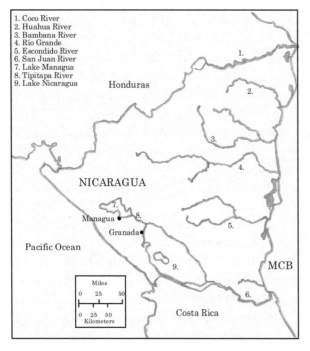

Figure 25.2. Major watercourses that drain into the MCB from Nicaragua.

Figure 25.3. Major watercourses that drain into the MCB from Costa Rica.

MCB, it is necessary to examine the ocean currents that affect it, the four countries that shape it, and the rivers that drain into it from these countries.

The northeastern geotropic winds, which generate current speeds of 0.1 m/s–0.3 m/s, are the driving force for the ocean current in the MCB. This current is derived from a junction of the Guyana current and the North Equatorial current, which intensifies as it enters the Caribbean Sea (figure 25.1). As this current interacts with the continental platform, it produces a cyclic spin-off that varies in radius depending on the time of the year. This cyclic spin-off changes the direction of the current toward the southeast, passing along the coasts of Nicaragua, Costa Rica, and Panama. Then, it turns north as it passes along the coast of Colombia, completing a circular pattern. The Colombian navy has documented this phenomenon using buoys (figure 25.1). These buoys are traced via satellite, demonstrating that the currents completely circle this region approximately every two months.

In total, this Caribbean current passes by more than 3,000 km of coastline in the four countries (table 25.1). As a result, the runoff from land base–generated pollution from any of these four countries has a cumulative and cyclic effect, and in the end, affects all four countries. Furthermore, as the cyclic current meets the main northeastern current, the pollutants may enter this main current as well, and affect the rest of the region, which is in contact with the Caribbean Sea. Therefore, the actions, or the lack of actions, taken by one of the four countries forming the MCB affects not only the other three countries, but also the rest of the Caribbean Sea region.

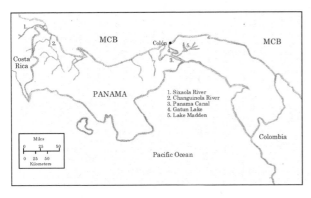

Figure 25.4. Major watercourses that drain into the MCB from Panama.

Figure 25.5. Major watercourses that drain into the MCB from Colombia.

There are many geophysical and climatic characteristics that are common to the four countries forming the MCB. The Pacific Ocean and the Caribbean Sea wash the shores of all four countries. The coastal plains of the Pacific side are very narrow compared to those on the Caribbean side. The geography is generally rugged and mountainous with numerous volcanoes. Tectonic movements are frequent. The temperature varies according to altitude rather than latitude and there are no distinct temperature seasons, although in some parts there are distinct wet and dry seasons. The Caribbean side experiences twice as much rain as the Pacific side. As a result, the watershed areas that drain into the Caribbean Sea are generally larger and collect more water. Runoff is considerably higher as well, due to the ruggedness of the terrain and the amount of rain, and especially in the cases of deforestation and absence of ground cover.

The major watercourses that drain into the MCB, from the four countries forming the MCB, are the following:

> the Coco, Grande, Bambana, and Escondido rivers, located in Nicaragua (figure 25.2),
> the San Juan River, which marks the boundary between Nicaragua and Costa Rica and serves as the final drainage for Lake Managua and Lake Nicaragua (figures 25.2 and 25.3),
> the Tortuguero, Parismina, Pacuare, and Estrella rivers, located in Costa Rica (figure 25.3),

> the Sixaola River, which marks the boundary between Costa Rica and Panama (figures 25.3 and 25.4),
> the Changuinola River in Panama (figure 25.4),
> the Panama Canal with Gatun and Lake Madden (figure 25.4), and
> the Magdalena, including its tributary, the Cauca River, and the Atrato and Sinú rivers, in Colombia (figure 25.5).

Of these, the most significant watercourses are the Panama Canal, the San Juan River, and the Magdalena River. The land mass of these four countries is close to 1.4 million km², and in total 69 percent drains toward the MCB (table 25.1).

The population is increasing at a growth rate of more than 1.5 percent per year in all four countries (table 25.1). There is also a large concentration of the population of these countries in urban environments, with over 40 percent living in cities. With the exception of Colombia, as will be discussed later, most of the large population centers in these countries are located near the Pacific Ocean side. In many cases, the best agricultural lands are being destroyed by the growth of these cities, and farmers are beginning to look for substitute arable land that may be purchased at a feasible cost. The Caribbean coastal plains are sparsely populated and are covered mainly by forests. The largest cities located on the Caribbean side are Limón, Costa Rica (pop. 67,000 in 2000) (figure 25.3), and Colón, Panama (pop. 54,600) (figure 25.4).

When discussing demographics, Nicaragua deserves a special mention. The Caribbean coastal plains comprise about 50 percent of the territory. They are not heavily populated (less than 5 percent of the population) and few crops are grown. The part of the territory with the greatest concentration of population and crops is close to the Pacific Ocean. The capital city, Managua (pop. 1.5 million), is located on Lake Managua, and other large Nicaraguan cities, such as Granada (pop. 70,000), are located on the shores of Lake Nicaragua. The uniqueness of this situation is that Lake Managua is connected to Lake Nicaragua by the Tipitapa River and all three drain not to the Pacific Ocean, but toward the MCB through the San Juan River (figures 25.2 and 25.3). In addition, most of the arable lands in this country, although closer to the Pacific coast, also drain toward both lakes and eventually into the MCB (MARENA 2000).

As stated previously, most of the large population centers in these countries are located near the Pacific Ocean side. In contrast to the other three countries that form the MCB, however, the largest cities in Colombia are located along the Cauca and Magdalena rivers and their tributaries, which drain through the Magdalena River to the Caribbean Sea (figure 25.5). The major cities are Bogota (pop. 5 million), Medellin (pop. 1.6 million), Cartagena (pop. 707,000), Cali (pop. 1.7 million), and Barranquilla (pop. 1 million) (Hómez Sánchez et al. 2000).

The Problem

According to the Caribbean Environmental Program (CEP) of the United Nations Environmental Program (UNEP) report on land-based sources of pollution in this region, the following characteristics of the four countries (UNEP 1994) set the stage for our analysis:

The watersheds that drain into the MCB support many types of human activity, and all human activity generates waste.

Close to 80 percent of the sewage water generated by urban areas is deposited in rivers without treatment.

Solid waste management, where it exists, is deficient, and leachates from solid waste deposit are often untreated.

There are more illegal than legal open-air dumps.

Many industries dump untreated or partially treated water into rivers, lakes, and the Caribbean Sea.

Pesticides are widely used, often without following appropriate guidelines.

Wind drift is a possible vehicle to transport gases and pesticides to bodies of water.

Rain is considerable, deforestation is rampant, urbanization is spiraling, drainage systems are increasing, and these conditions accelerate runoff into bodies of water and leaching into groundwater, which eventually reaches the Caribbean Sea.

There are insufficient funds being invested in pollution control.

The laws and regulations concerning pollution control and abatement are lacking, confusing, and often assign overlapping functions to different agencies, and as a result do not provide protection from pollution.

The government structures charged with control and enforcement are not functioning at the efficacy levels required, and are not adequately controlling the dumping or runoff of pollutants into the bodies of water.

The result is that the MCB is a common regional sink for land base–generated pollutants, and unilateral actions may alleviate the effects but cannot

Table 25.2. Levels of pesticides detected in waterways of the MCB region

Countries	Colombia (μg/L)		Costa Rica (ng/L)		Nicaragua (ng/L)
Pesticides	Sinú and tributaries	Magdalena and tributaries	Streams connecting to the Suerte	Suerte	San Juan
Insecticides					
Metamidophos	40.3				
Carbofuran			800	500	
Chlorpyrifos		2.80	100		
Malathion	6.72	10.85; 6.51			129.2
Terbufos			200		77.3
Endosulfan	12.40; 19.80; 30.20	30.20; 116.60; 3.04			
Fungicide					
Chlorothalonil			1000	500	

For Colombia, see Hómez Sánchez et al. (2000); for Costa Rica, see Castillo, Ruepert, and Solís (2000); for Nicaragua, see MARENA (2000).

minimize them. Therefore, the problem is a regional problem and a strategic alliance among the four countries is needed if the problem is to be solved.

It is clear that pesticides are an important source of pollution, but not the only source. Untreated sewage and oil spills are also priority areas, and may even have a higher priority than pesticide pollution (UNEP 1994). Separate programs are under way to address these problems. However, since the publication of Rachael Carson's *Silent Spring* in 1962, public concern for the environmental and health effects of pesticides have become widespread and a global priority (Carlson and Wetzstein 1993). This project caters to this legitimate public perception, and it has the challenge to validate this concern quantitatively.

The Use of Pesticides in the MCB Region

There is evidence that chemical pollutants, specifically pesticides, are being transported to the MCB and that these chemicals may be affecting its marine environment (Espinoza González 1997; Ramírez 1998; Soto 1998; McKay, Mulvaney, and Thorne-Miller 2000). Runoff, leaching, and wind drift from land-based agricultural activities and disease-vector control operations are assumed the primary vehicles for these pollutants to reach the sea, via the major watercourses that drain into this basin. All these watercourses contribute with different pollutants, in the end forming a chemical cocktail that is deposited in the MCB.

Significant work has been done in this region over the past two decades evaluating the effects of pesticides on nontarget organisms, and transportation away from the point of application to soils and surface and groundwaters. However, very little has been done to organize the information produced by these studies. Many times it is not possible to compare data from various studies because different methods were used for data collection and analyses. As well, the data collected may be for internal use by the organization or institute who funded the study and the information is not available to others who may have an interest in the results. Another problem is funding, which may not be sufficient for making results available to the public.

Results of various studies concerning the presence of pesticides in waterways of the MCB region are presented in table 25.2. The insecticides and fungicide studied are those are commonly used for

Table 25.3. Total area (ha) planted to the principal crops in the MCB area of each country

Crop	Nicaragua	Costa Rica	Panama	Colombia	Total
Coffee	86,025	17,315	3,900	900,000	1,007,240
Rice	74,764	13,382	6,180	403,000	497,326
Beans	125,219	16,200	190	121,000	262,609
Corn	215,888	2,250	3,050		221,188
Sugarcane	19,941	12,010	128	174,000	206,079
Potatoes	2,100	3,063		165,000	170,163
Palm				148,000	148,000
Vegetables				98,000	98,000
Banana		46,233	7,000	40,500	93,733
Cotton				47,500	47,500
Sorghum	40,802				40,802
Oranges		18,750			18,750
Plantain		7,900	450	14,100	22,450
Heart of Palm		11,250			11,250
Ornamentals/ Flowers		2,250		6,000	8,250
Cocoa			5,000		5,000
Pineapple		3,572			3,572
Tobacco	3,511				3,511
Sesame seed	1,768				1,768
Peanut	901				901
Ginger		890			890
Soybean	880				880
Total	571,799	155,065	25,898	2,117,100	2,869,862

various crops in the region, as will be discussed later. It can be seen that high levels of insecticides have been detected in two major rivers, and their tributaries, in Colombia. Much lower levels of the insecticides and one fungicide were detected in waterways in Costa Rica and Nicaragua.

To identify the causes of and possible solutions to the movement of these chemical pollutants, it is necessary to analyze in detail the land-base origin of their source and for this, the rational territorial unit is the watershed. However, the reasons why users often apply inappropriate technologies for pesticide use are extremely complex and entail national and regional elements. Furthermore, the causes may have social/cultural, economic, and environmental considerations. This section looks at common characteristics of the four countries, the differences that exist among them, and the effect these characteristics have on the problem of movement of pesticides to the Caribbean Sea.

Agriculture is critical to the economies of the countries of the MCB area, which produces a significant portion of the world's coffee (12 percent), plantains (10 percent), fresh fruits (9 percent), and bananas (8 percent) and significant quantities of pineapples, sugarcane, ginger, oil palm, and flowers (FAO 2001). Even with the increase in tourism in this region during the past decade, export-oriented agricultural production remains the main source of foreign exchange earnings. In Nicaragua, the agricultural sector provides approximately 32 percent of Gross National Product (GNP) (MARENA 2000), in Colombia 19 percent (Hómez Sánchez et al. 2000), in Costa Rica 18 percent (MINAE 2000), and in Panama 7 percent (Espinoza González 2000).

The increasing demands for food in the cities and the decreasing availability of arable land have created pressure to colonize the Caribbean coastal plains. Therefore, this region is becoming the agricultural frontier of Nicaragua, Costa Rica, and Panama, and there is an inherent risk that pesticide use will increase. Of the four countries, Colombia, because of its territorial size and demographics, has the greatest risk of contributing pollutants to the Caribbean Sea.

In the MCB area, these four countries cultivate close to 3,000,000 ha of crops (table 25.3) (Contraloría General de la República 1999; MAGFOR 1999; Ministerio de Agricultura y Desarrollo Rural 1998; SEPSA 2000). Coffee, rice, beans, and sugarcane are major crops for Colombia, Costa Rica, and Nicaragua. Bananas and plantains grown for export purposes are important to Costa Rica, Panama, and Colombia and are typically grown in the MCB area. Corn and sorghum are also important crops for Nicaragua, while flowers and ornamentals are increasingly important export crops for Colombia and Costa Rica.

All the aforementioned crops grown in these four countries are vulnerable to pests and production strategies include the use of pesticides. Taking into consideration different levels of pesticide use, agricultural production systems in the MCB can be categorized as follows:

Subsistence agriculture: Crops cultivated in this system are generally located in marginal areas. The pest management strategy is primarily based on mechanical control, traditional cultural practices, multiple associate crops, crop rotation, timing, and pest tolerance. Because of sociological and economical circumstances, pesticides are not widely used in these systems.

Low use of pesticide agriculture: Farmers utilizing this production system use pesticides occasionally during periods of the growing season when pests become a problem.

Intensive use of pesticide agriculture: This production system depends exclusively on agrochemicals for crop protection.

According to the national reports (Espinoza González 2000; Hómez Sánchez et al. 2000; MARENA 2000; MINAE 2000), export cash crop intensive farming, the most intensive use-of-pesticide agriculture in the MCB, accounts for 1.48 million hectares, whereas 1.39 million hectares are used for domestic consumption farming, or subsistence agriculture and low-use-of-pesticides agriculture. The data demonstrate that all three systems are extensive and important. Since the basic production strategies of the systems are quite different, the search for best management practices must be considered separately.

In the MCB area, the most important traditional export crops (coffee, bananas, sugarcane, and oil palm) are produced on larger farms (intensive-use-of-pesticide agriculture). These farms are often located in the geographical valleys of the largest river systems in the region, some of which discharge into the Caribbean Sea. Location, coupled with the intricate and efficient natural and anthropogenic drainage systems developed in these production areas, facilitate the mobilization and transport of large quantities of pesticide pollutants from the farm to the Caribbean Sea, especially if these substances are used irrationally and or improperly.

Other crops grown in the region, such as tubers and vegetables (subsistence agriculture) and corn and beans (low-use-of-pesticides agriculture), which are the basis for the family food basket, are generally produced on small family farms. Pesticide use in these systems is generally less because of their less-intensive resource demand. However, since these plots typically are located on marginal hillside land, they contribute greatly to soil erosion, which can also lead to pesticide loss. It is common on the large plantations that the

Table 25.4. Total amounts (TM a.i.) of pesticides used in each country

Pesticides	Nicaragua	Costa Rica	Panama	Colombia	Total
Insecticides	338.06	1,268.60	212.88	2,728.88	4,548.42
Fungicides	662.64	3,355.96	575.19	7,963.83	12,557.62
Herbicides	544.78	1,672.10	900.91	7,746.68	10,864.47
Total pesticides	1,545.48	6,296.66	1,688.98	18,439.39	27,970.51

All values are for imported pesticides except for herbicides in Panama and all pesticides in Colombia, which also include values for pesticides manufactured or formulated for domestic use in those countries.

Table 25.5. Quantities (TM a.i.) and percentages (of total use) of the major pesticides used in each country

Pesticide	Nicaragua	Costa Rica	Panama	Colombia	Percentage of Total
Insecticides					
Malathion	9.18		73.72	704.83	17.3
Endosulfan	8.94		1.36	730.19	16.3
Metamidophos	163.52	111.62	4.67	436.87	15.8
Fungicides					
Mancozeb	133.06	2,350.88	448.10	6,632.18	76.2
Chlorothalonil	146.17	506.49	21.05		5.4
Herbicides					
Glyphosate	105.20	545.26	176.76	3,939.49	44.2
2,4-D	159.78	479.66	356.05	2,259.48	30.0

All values are for imported pesticides except for herbicides in Panama and all pesticides in Colombia, which also include values for pesticides manufactured or formulated for domestic use in those countries. Values do not sum to 100 percent because of the wide diversity of other chemicals used; a.i. means active ingredients.

pesticide producers and the government supervise the pesticide application methods closely. But it appears that the small farmers do not receive the same scrutinized attention.

The dependency of the agricultural systems in the MCB on pesticide use has been discussed at great length in several forums related to pest management. According to the data from the FAO (2001) and National Reports (Espinoza González 2000; Hómez Sánchez et al. 2000; MARENA 2000; MINAE 2000), the quantity of pesticides used in the MCB is extraordinarily high.

The major pesticides used in each country are reported in tables 25.4 and 25.5. With the exception of Colombia, the countries of the MCB depend almost entirely on foreign imports for their supply of pesticides. In Colombia, domestic pesticide production is an important activity for its economy and these pesticides are destined for both the domestic and international markets (Hómez Sánchez et al. 2000).

The major pesticides used each year (table 25.5) in these countries are applied for pest control in a wide range of crops (table 25.6). The major

Table 25.6. Crop use of the major pesticides applied in the countries of the MCB

Insecticides	Crops
Metamidophos	coffee, rice, beans, corn, sugarcane, potatoes, ornamentals, tobacco, sesame seed, peanut, soybean, illegal crops†
Carbofuran	rice, corn, sugarcane, potatoes, banana, pineapple, tobacco, illegal crops
Chlorpyrifos	coffee, rice, beans, corn, potatoes, banana, tobacco, sesame seed, peanut, soybean, illegal crops
Cypermethrin	rice, potatoes, sorghum, illegal crops
Malathion	Rice, potatoes, ornamentals, illegal crops
Terbufos	coffee, sugarcane, banana, plantain, ornamentals
Endosulfan	coffee, rice, sesame seed, illegal crops

Fungicides	
Mancozeb	coffee, rice, beans, potatoes, banana, plantain, ornamentals, tobacco, peanut, soybean, illegal crops
Benomyl	rice, beans, potatoes, banana, peanut, soybean
Carbendazim	rice, potatoes, illegal crops
Chlorothalonil	rice, potatoes, banana, ornamentals, peanut, soybean
Metalaxyl	coffee, rice, potatoes, banana, plantain, tobacco

Herbicides	
Glyphosate	coffee, rice, sugarcane, potatoes, banana, cotton, oranges, heart of palm, ginger, ornamentals
Paraquat	coffee, rice, beans, corn, potatoes, sugarcane, banana, cotton, plantain, ornamentals
Pendimethalin	rice, beans, corn, potatoes, cotton, tobacco, sesame seed, peanut, soybean
2,4-D	coffee, rice, corn, sugarcane
Diuron	sugarcane, cotton, pineapple

†Illegal crops include cocaine, marijuana, and poppy seed.

pesticides such as methamidophos, mancozeb, glyphosate, and paraquat are all used on at least ten different crops in countries in this region.

In these countries, where technically advanced systems of production are applied, the use of pesticides is notoriously high. For example, in Costa Rica, pesticides are applied at a rate of up to 40 kg active ingredients/ha/year in banana plantations (MINAE 2000). In Colombia, 21 percent of the pesticides are used for rice, 19 percent for potatoes, 7 percent for bananas, 6 percent for sugarcane, and 5 percent for coffee. Rice production uses 34 herbicides,

30 insecticides, and 30 fungicides (Hómez Sánchez et al. 2000). In Panama, rice production normally entails the use of a dozen herbicides, 10 fungicides, 6 insecticides, a seed coating, and 2 postharvest insecticides (Espinoza González 2000).

Table 25.7 shows the rate of pesticide application per hectare per year to the principal crops in Nicaragua and Costa Rica. The weighted average for pesticide application in the MCB region of Nicaragua is 0.95 kg a.i./ha/yr (MARENA 2000). In the MCB region of Costa Rica the weighted average for pesticide application is 17.8 kg a.i./ha/yr

Table 25.7. Rate of pesticides applied (kg a.i./ha/yr) to the principal crops in Nicaragua and Costa Rica

Crop	Nicaragua	Costa Rica
Coffee	1.14	6.68
Rice	1.09	13.05
Beans	0.33	2.98
Corn	0.52	3.75
Sugarcane	4.95	2.21
Potatoes	5.99	27.76
Banana		38.86
Sorghum	0.46	
Oranges		11.21
Plantain		8.16
Heart of Palm		11.76
Ornamentals/ Flowers		1.07
Pineapple		26.91
Tobacco	12.36	
Sesame seed	2.46	
Peanut	9.05	
Ginger		3.86
Soybean	14.66	
Weighted Average	0.95	17.8

(MINAE 2000), which is seven times higher than their national average (SEPSA 2000). In Colombia, the value is 8.71 kg a.i./ha/yr (Hómez Sánchez et al. 2000). In the MCB region of Panama the rate is 2.3 kg a.i./ha/yr, which is four times higher than their national average (Espinoza González 2000). The weighted average for pesticide application in industrialized nations such as the United States of America is 1.1 kg a.i./ha/yr (Lin et al. 1995).

Many times advanced technological packages are erroneously associated with pesticide use as the only means of managing pests. Problems of pest resistance due to natural selection, repeated outbreaks of pests due to ecological disturbance, and unbalanced ecosystem conditions due to irrational and indiscriminate use of pesticides are common when this strategy is utilized as an exclusive solution. These conditions generate an uncontrolled upward spiral of pesticide use. With this upward

spiral of pesticide use comes the terminal effect, or what the experts call the "pesticide crisis." It can be described as the stage where an incremental use of pesticides does not yield the desired protection effect, that is, at a certain threshold, no matter how much pesticide is added, the pest damage persists. In this case, the only solution is to abandon the production system.

This situation has been experienced in the MCB with the cotton crop in Nicaragua (MARENA 2000). The problems of unsustainable cotton production in this country have brought into question the industrialized, contaminating, monoculture agriculture that depends on high levels of inputs and is exposed to such risks as climate, pests, and volatile or depressed markets. The persistent and irrational use of pesticides on the cotton crop in the 1970s and 1980s caused soil damage, water contamination, and intoxications in the food chain with serious effects to wild animal and human populations (MARENA 2000). The focus was not to equilibrate and control the pests, but rather to destroy the pests with harsh methods that affected both the beneficial and pest species, thus disturbing the equilibrium of the agroecosystems. Table 25.8 shows the level of cotton production in Nicaragua over the past three decades. The number of hectares in cotton production peaked in 1978 with 212,380 ha harvested. The production steadily declined throughout the 1980s and 1990s. By the latter part of the 1990s and in the first three years of the following decade, only insignificant quantities of cotton were produced in Nicaragua (FAO 2001).

One of the most important causes of entering the path toward pesticide crisis is the traditionally short-term strategic planning for agricultural production, based on quarterly or yearly financial statements. This leads to the unsustainable use of resources to increase yields within a financial projection that matches investment, time to recover that investment, and profit. Recent attempts to reestablish the cotton crop in Nicaragua still have put too much emphasis on maximizing production and yield without measuring environmental costs that this production causes in detriment to sustainability (MARENA 2000). In this strategy,

Table 25.8. Cotton harvest during the last three decades in Nicaragua, in hectares

Years	Average area harvested (ha)
1976–80	154,453
1981–85	101,974
1986–90	56,098
1991–95	18,493
1996–2000	2,402

environmental protection and sustainability are antagonistic to the goal of the producer, maximum profit in the least time. The pressure exerted by the marketing promotion and propaganda compounds this situation. Furthermore, there is little information and technical support for alternative solutions that match the socioeconomic pressures that bear on the private agricultural sector.

There are many reasons for the often excessive and inappropriate pesticide use that occurs in these countries of the MCB. Socially and culturally, people in these countries are unaware of the risks involved in pesticide use. There is a general lack of perception of the dangers inherent in the use of these chemicals (MARENA 2000). Although farmers acknowledge possible contamination of air and water, they are unsure of the pesticide effects on human health and on nontarget organisms such as plants, animals, and fish. Even if they are aware of the dangers, many small producers do not have the resources to buy protection equipment and clothing necessary for safe pesticide application. In addition, they may not have adequate information about treatment of intoxications or accidents that can occur (Hómez Sánchez et al. 2000).

In these countries there is also very little government control of pesticide use, due to lack of operational resources. This results in indiscriminate pesticide use and commercial dominance and pressure of pesticide availability. The government subsidizes the chemical companies with lower taxes and supports farmers who use pesticides by making bank credit more readily available to them. In addition, the governments do not force the chemical companies, or the farmers, to comply with international laws and agreements regarding pesticide applications (MARENA 2000).

The small producers have little or no training in the use of pesticides and technical assistance, and service is not readily available to them. In these countries, few studies have been done that evaluate the cost/benefit analysis of pesticide application, and the effect on public health, the environment, and agricultural productivity. Many of the producers believe that the recommended doses or number of applications of pesticides are simply not adequate for effective pest control and so do not follow the intended instructions. The farmer is attempting to achieve high yields while preventing the risk of infestations of pests or diseases. With the lack of sufficient services and materials for technical training and dissemination of information, as well as the limited development of ecologically sound alternatives to excessive pesticide use, the farmers are not motivated to reduce the level of pesticides that they are applying (Hómez Sánchez et al. 2000; MARENA 2000).

Although data on use pesticide use in the MCB region over the past forty years is not readily available, fertilizer use in these countries over the past four decades has been monitored by the FAO (FAO 2001). In figure 25.6, it is apparent that in Colombia and Costa Rica, consumption of fertilizers is still on the rise, whereas use in Nicaragua and Panama has leveled off. This data can be compared to the pesticide data that is available, amount spent by the four countries over the past forty years on imported pesticides (figure 25.6). In Colombia, Costa Rica, and Panama the amount spent on pesticides has been steadily increasing whereas in Nicaragua, imports have leveled off.

This fertilizer and pesticide data can be compared to the yield data over the past four decades, for four of the major crops grown in the MCB region: bananas, coffee, rice, and corn (figure 25.7). Banana yields increased in the 1960s and 1970s, corresponding to the increase in fertilizer and pesticide consumption observed in Nicaragua, Costa Rica, and Colombia. Yields peaked in the 1980s in Colombia and in the 1990s in the other

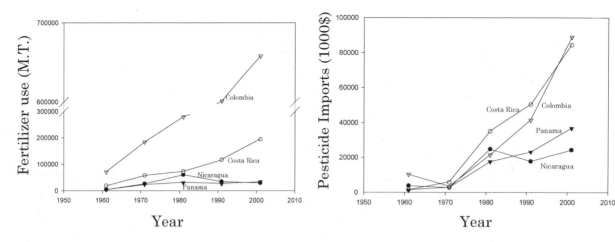

Figure 25.6. Fertilizer use and pesticide imports in Nicaragua, Costa Rica, Panama, and Colombia over the past forty years. Source: FAO (2001).

two countries. Since that time, yields have been decreasing. This suggests that the increases still observed in fertilizer and pesticide use are not resulting in increased crop production.

Similar trends are observed with the coffee and corn yields presented in figure 25.7. The crop yields rapidly increased but then leveled off or decreased since the 1990s. The exception is corn in Nicaragua, which still shows increases in yields into 2001. The reverse is true for rice production where yields have been increasing over the past four decades in all countries of the region except Nicaragua (figure 25.7). One possible reason for the overall decrease or leveling in production may be that the increase in pesticide use is simply luxury consumption and of no further benefit to the crop. It could be that these crops are entering a "pesticide crisis," much the same as occurred with the cotton crop in Nicaragua.

The yields of banana, coffee, rice, and corn, as well as other major crops grown in the MCB region are consistently lower in Nicaragua and Panama than in Costa Rica and Colombia (figure 25.7). This is expected since, as stated previously, both Nicaragua and Panama consistently use lower pesticide application rates than Costa Rica and Colombia (table 25.7). In addition, amounts of fertilizers and pesticides consumed in Nicaragua and Panama are significantly lower than amounts consumed in Costa Rica and Colombia (figure 25.6).

The Project

The Cartagena Convention, which was adopted in 1983 and ratified in 1986 by thirty-three countries, provides the legal framework that guides the regional environmental protection actions in the Caribbean Sea. This convention is applied through three specific protocols: the Oil Spills Protocol; the Specially Protected Area, Fauna, and Flora Protocol; and the Land-base Marine Pollution Protocol.

The United Nations Environmental Program (UNEP) has a specific program (Regional Coordinating Unit of the Caribbean Environment Program of the United Nations—CAR/RCU) for the Caribbean, with offices in Kingston, Jamaica, that oversees the application of the protocols of the Cartagena Convention and Nicaragua, Costa Rica, Panama, and Colombia are contracting parties of this Convention. The four countries have agreed to seek actions jointly to reduce pesticide runoff into the Caribbean Sea under the coordination of CAR/RCU and under the provisions of the Land-base Marine Pollution Protocol.

This project is financed partially through a Global Environmental Facility (GEF) Project Development Fund (PDF) grant. GEF was established in 1990 by the World Bank, the United Nations Development Program, and the United Nations Environmental Program. It provides assistance to the developing countries for investments that would (Pearce and Warford 1996):

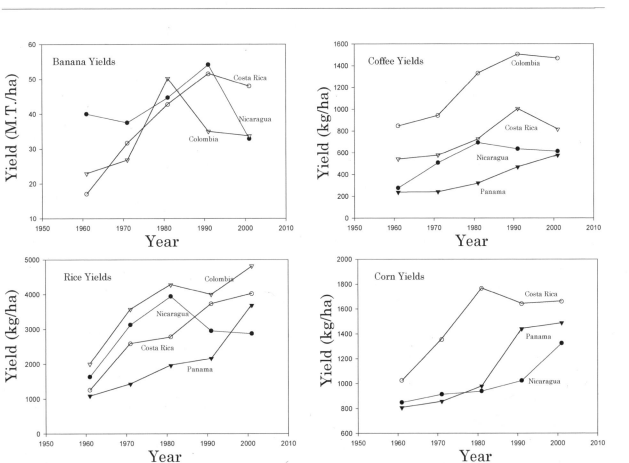

Figure 25.7. Yields of banana, coffee, rice, and corn over the past forty years in Nicaragua, Costa Rica, Panama, and Colombia. Source: FAO (2001).

Protect the ozone layer
Reduce greenhouse gas emissions
Protect international water resources
Protect biological diversity

This regional project qualifies under the objective of protecting international water resources. GEF provides the costs accumulated for the regional benefits of the project and the countries are expected to cover the costs accumulated for the national benefits of the project. Financial participation is also expected from the private sector stakeholders to cover local costs.

Each country has a National Organization, which directs the project at a national level and appoints a national coordinator. The coordinators from the four countries plus a representative from CAR/RCU form a coordinating committee. To facilitate this interaction, CAR/RCU appointed EARTH University as the regional coordinator for the initial phase of the project. An overall steering committee oversees the project, formed by representatives of the World Bank, the Inter-American Development Bank (IDB), the United Nations Environmental Program (UNEP), the Food and Agriculture Organization (FAO), Instituto Interamericano de Cooperación Agrícola (IICA), and EARTH University.

The general objective of the project is to reduce pesticide runoff to the Caribbean Sea by establishing national and regional agendas with the following specific objectives:

Collect and organize available information, and determine areas that need further research.
Identify environmental risks and problems, and determine their causes using a cradle to grave approach.

Recognize best management practices that
can abate the problems, and implement a
program to induce their use.
Establish an institutional organization capable
of promoting and controlling the process.
Develop a regional collaboration program.

There are major hurdles that must be confronted in this project. Although the four countries have a common cause, they are sovereign nations subject to their own legislation, organizational structure, customs, and geophysical differences. Much of the information is scattered, and must be organized and scrutinized. Furthermore, not all the needed information is available, and much about the Caribbean Sea is still a mystery. The horizontal and vertical vastness of the sea is overwhelming and difficult to manage. The complexity and diversity of the ecosystems involved are not well understood. Many of the effects are cumulative and involve not only a spatial element but also a temporal analysis. Therefore, it is very difficult to convince stakeholders to implement policy changes because the cause-and-effect relationship has a time and space lag. Actions taken at a particular place and time may have short-term, medium-term, and long-term effects, and these effects may be evidenced at considerable distances from the source of the cause.

The four participating countries have developed National Reports concerning the problem of pesticide use and contamination of natural water sources (Espinoza González 2000; Hómez Sánchez et al. 2000; MARENA 2000; MINAE 2000), and these reports were discussed with the stakeholders at workshops before the final draft was submitted. From the four national reports, the coordinating committee drafted a regional report (Hernández, Yeomans, and Kasten 2001) that also was discussed with the stakeholders at a regional workshop. The final product was a Project Development Funds (PDF-C) request to the GEF to finance the implementation of the project. This request was approved early in 2002. It is important, once more, to emphasize that the GEF finances actions tending toward a regional benefit. The countries must cover the costs of actions that have only a national benefit.

The Approach to Reducing the Pesticide Runoff

Our project is at its infancy and it may be too early to talk about solutions. However, general concepts and guideline can be suggested at this time. Castro and Jiménez (1999) have visualized the marine pollution problem as a watershed health problem that must be addressed individually for each specific watershed. In other words, it involves local level analysis. Water quality is an indication of the health of each individual watershed. Monitoring water quality indicates the presence and severity of the problem. A clinical analysis is necessary to identify the human actions that are causing the problem in each watershed. Once the causes are identified, then it is necessary to design strategies and a specific action plan to solve the problem, programmed in an incremental manner such that the actions with the most effect are done first. The next step is to calculate a budget and a design a program for the resources to be allocated. Generally, preventive measures are much cheaper than remedial measures (Clites, Fontaine, and Wells 1995). Many preventive measures have a direct cost reduction to the individual user, and are easy to implement as long as the information is available. This part of the analysis is well known and has been done many times because it makes sure that everyone benefits. Although it is not simple, there are methodologies in place and the results are viable.

How Can We Internalize the Externalities?

The information generated is the key to influence decision makers in taking the right steps at the right time and assigning adequate funds to solve the problems. In a free market society, decision makers will maximize profits by identifying an action plan that equalizes marginal benefits to them to the marginal cost of implementing the incremental actions, without considering the effects outside their area of influence. Economists call these outside effects externalities. For example, a farmer will implement an action as long as the benefits he receives are at least equal to the investment that he must make. He is not interested in making an investment that also benefits the downstream stakeholders, unless government regulations force him to internalize the externalities. Since many of the upstream stakeholders are small farmers and the low market prices for their production do not allow for much profit, government regulations may depress the agricultural sector and lead to urbanization and imported food dependency. This is one of the reasons that governments may choose not to enforce such regulations.

Who Should Pay for the Cleanup? An Economic Approach

To internalize the externalities better, it is necessary to identify the benefits at each level—local, national, and regional. In this manner, cost may be allocated on incremental bases and allocated to the direct beneficiary. However, downstream stakeholders are reluctant to pay for actions that do not take place directly on their property unless information demonstrates a direct benefit to them. Since in many cases the benefits are generalized and are difficult to allocate to individuals, stakeholders refuse to pay for a common good. It takes government action to force this internalization through taxes and other tariffs. A similar situation exists on a regional level. National politicians are reluctant to assess taxes to pay for common benefits among multilateral parties. Therefore, the internalization requires regional strategic alliances and help from the wealthy nations, which benefit through the abatement of global effects.

Figure 25.8 shows this concept in graphical manner. It is called "The Sand Clock Concept" because of its shape and ability to rotate 180° for visualization purposes. The circles schematically show the size effect and form an upper conical shape representing the hierarchy of spatial levels of problem analysis. A mirror image is shown on the bottom that represents the hierarchy of spatial-level analysis of solutions over progressively larger areas. As discussed in previous paragraphs, the causes originate at a local level and the impacts are felt downstream, affecting the national level. Then as the pollutants enter the sea, the effects are felt at the regional and global level. As one progresses to a higher hierarchical level, the effects are diluted, the sources are harder to identify, and the impacts may have a longer temporal scale of analysis. In

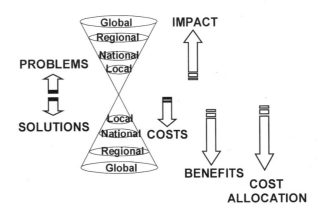

Figure 25.8. The sand clock concept.

conclusion, problem and impact analysis progress from the bottom up, or better yet, from inside to outside. In the same manner, rotating the "sand clock" 180°, incremental solutions begin from the inside to the outside.

If adjustments are implemented to internalize the externalities, the solutions must begin at the local level, such as a farm, and the cost will accrue to the individual farm. But the farmer is attempting to maximize his profits and will implement only that which brings him a direct benefit. If legal actions force the internalization of externalities, the local farmer will probably go out of business because he must assume costs that bring benefits to him only indirectly at the other hierarchical spatial levels. Thus, it is necessary to find mechanisms to compensate the local farmer for these environmental services that he provides to the other hierarchical spatial levels. A national, regional, and global contribution system needs to be introduced to find an integrated solution.

The theory of finding an integrated solution to these problems is well developed; however, the problems of implementation have hardly been solved at this time. Work has recently begun to develop appropriate methods to allocate costs according to benefits. Figure 25.9 demonstrates how this concept works, through macroeconomic principals (adapted from Pearce and Warford 1993). The cost per unit of reduction (y-axis) of an incremental percentage of runoff reduction (x-axis), as indicated by the marginal abatement cost (MAC) curve, assesses the corresponding cost

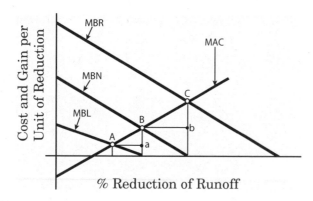

Figure 25.9. Marginal costs and benefits curve. MAC: marginal abatement cost; MBL: marginal benefits locally; MBN: marginal benefits to the nation; MBR: marginal benefits to the region.

of taking a given action. That is, the more you reduce the runoff, the more it costs. The part of the curve that falls below the x-axis represents the implementation of preventive actions that reduce costs. For example, it has been demonstrated that using organic fertilizers in banana production reduces the need for applying nematicides. Thus, the farmer will have a cost reduction because he buys less agrochemicals. Obviously, this is the approach we wish to promote.

The marginal benefit of reducing pesticide runoff, to the local community or farmer, is indicated by the marginal benefits locally (MBL) curve (figure 25.9). For example, this may represent the value of improving the health of the community since the risk of health effects is reduced with each incremental solution. Obviously, this implies that solutions are ranked according to the degree of benefits that they bring. The marginal benefits to the nation and the marginal benefits to the region are represented by the MBN and the MBR curves, respectively (figure 25.9). According to economic theory, an efficient solution is marked by the intersection of the marginal benefit curve with the marginal abatement cost (MAC) curve (Pearce and Warford 1993). At each level, this intersection occurs at a different point on the curve. The solution is found by allocating cost according to benefits. For example, a farmer will pay the costs for programs that provide direct benefits to him. This is shown by the line between the x-axis and point

A. The nation must assume the incremental cost shown by line a-B and the region assumes the cost shown by line b-C (figure 25.9).

In summary, this concept allows the application of an explicit methodology to determine who should pay for the cleanup of pesticides. Since this particular project is being financed partially through a GEF (Global Environment Facility) grant, they will provide the funds to cover the cost differential necessary to reach the marginal benefits to the region. The countries are expected to cover the cost differential between the efficient solution to the local community and the efficient solution for the nation. The private sector stakeholders are expected to cover the costs for a locally efficient solution.

The profitability of the agricultural production systems and its effect on sustainability cannot continue to be regarded as separate and antagonistic strategies. Sound environmental protection criteria should prevail and be incorporated harmoniously into agricultural production systems. Low prices and instability for the export products grown in the region weaken the concept of stewardship. Mechanisms to internalize the cost of stewardship into market prices must be found and applied urgently. The implementation of a program to reduce pesticide runoff requires support of clear regional and national policies, national government programs, and the conscious and responsible participation of the agrochemical manufactures, marketing organizations, local communities, and consumers.

Necessary Actions

The solutions must include social, economic, and environmental components in order to influence sustainable development at all spatial levels. This will require the following actions:

Stakeholders' awareness and understanding of the problem,
Political determination and will to allocate resources, create efficient institutions and laws, and empower stakeholders to decentralize decision making,

International commitment, involvement, and financing especially from more developed and wealthy nations, which are, in many cases, contributing to the conditions that are causing the problem,

The development of an efficient information system and technology transfer, and

The development of a good, solid watershed management system.

Awareness and Understanding

The stakeholders in this project are the farmers, agrochemical distributors, local and national health and environmental agencies, interested NGOs, relevant international agricultural organizations, community organizations, and academic institutions. These stakeholders need to be aware of, and fully understand, the problems, causes, and possible solutions in order to participate in the development of appropriate solutions for their community. This can be realized only through the implementation of an aggressive education and training program at all age levels. It also entails the involvement of the stakeholder in the activities of collecting and analyzing information and in decision making. The active participation has been extensive since the inception of this project. This has helped to develop ownership of the project and it assures the sustainability of the program once the project is over.

National Policy

At the national level, decision makers are aware of the problems and the stakes that are involved if something is not done to abate the problem. This is evidenced by the participation of national agencies of the countries of the MCB in the preparation of the project and by the financial commitment of the governments to the securing of the GEF grant (Espinoza González 2000; Hómez Sánchez et al. 2000; MARENA 2000; MINAE 2000). An excellent information system is a basic requirement so that these resources can be allocated to solve the problem. As well, the people who have a direct stake in the issue make the best decisions and the government agencies have shown they are willing to work with local organizations to help design and control the watershed management systems at the local level. Legislation will have to be reviewed, updated to meet present needs, and above all, efficient mechanisms to enforce the law will have to be put in place.

International Commitment

Wealthy developed nations must assume their share of the responsibility for the problems of pesticide pollution, as it is this group of nations that profits the most from the fabrication and sale of pesticides, and they are a primary consumer of the products. The manufacturers must adopt the industrial codes of conduct, provide technology transfer, and best management practice assistance to the distributors and individual farmers. In one way, the wealthy nations have assumed their share of the cost for the global benefits that they will receive from the reduction of pesticide runoff to the MCB as they have provided the resources necessary for the GEF grant that funds this project.

Solid mechanisms should be established to finance recurrent costs to ensure the sustainability of the program once the project is over. Wealthy nations, through their purchasing power, will have to provide incentives for the application of best management practices by farmers by recognizing price differentials for environmental certifications. Good labor practices that improve the quality of life of the community must also be encouraged and recognized economically. It will require some very creative and innovative systems to address these issues.

Information Systems

Good accurate information is necessary in order to make efficient and appropriate decisions. Much of the available information in this project is scattered and disorganized. Information that is readily available and often quoted internationally has not been validated, and much is speculative. Irresponsibly misinforming customers about the risks that supposedly affect their health, without proper verification, has frequently caused damage to developing nations. It is imperative to introduce good science into the decision-making process though the use of solid data. Data collection should be standardized on a regional basis, in order to develop an adequate confidence level, and should be stored in an accessible and official system.

It is first necessary to collect and introduce this information into a database. The end of the twentieth century and beginning of the twenty-first century have been characterized by the "Information Revolution," due to the advances in the virtual information systems. The Internet has certainly had its effect and is facilitating information and technology transfer. This project will build upon existing information dissemination systems in the MCB such as CEPNET, the Environmental Information Management System, which is a subprogram of CEP. This component will maximize the use of the Internet as a medium for information gathering and dissemination. Activities will be reported on periodically throughout the life of the project and final results will be disseminated and project follow-up will be communicated indefinitely through the CEPNET system. However, many communities within the MCB have no access to these channels of communication. Therefore, it also is necessary to develop alternate information highways that reach places and people with limited or no computer literacy.

Watershed Management

The watershed has been recognized by most national and international organizations as the most adequate spatial division to implement resource management systems. Watershed management integrates water, air, and soil to human activity, recognizing the importance of human intervention needs. It distributes resources in a rational manner to meet the needs of the present generation without endangering the sustainability of the system over time. People who live and work in the watershed make decisions and this increases the probability of making the best decision, at the correct time, with the minimal cost.

The center of the project's activities will be demonstration projects on watersheds of private agricultural lands in each country. The demonstration projects will serve to convey to the stakeholders production alternatives for rational pesticide use. These alternatives will include applying best management practices (BMPs)

according to region for managing watersheds with high levels of pollution, and for identifying and promoting best practices for collection and final disposal of chemical containers and waste products. The production alternatives of the BMPs include good agricultural practices (GAPs) such as integrated pest management (IPM), integrated crop management (ICM), and integrated waste management (IWM), as well as the best harvest, postharvest, and business management practices.

The philosophy and focus of IPMs are aimed at reducing the damage caused by pests through the use of multiple techniques that are appropriate within the social, economic, and environmental context of the region, and that are applied within the principles of precision agriculture. This means that, from a choice of techniques, the grower applies the best action, at the precise time, with the maximum effect, and with the least cost. The use of pesticides is only one of many options that the grower has within those choices.

One of the most important barriers to implementation of IPM is knowledge and information regarding the ecology of pests. IPM begins by preventing the outbreak and controlling populations below a threshold, or point where the population size begins to cause economic loses. This implies that the grower has the tools to identify the organism that causes damage to the crop and must understand the life cycle and levels of populations that can be tolerated. In the past, the research and development resources have been in the hands of the agrochemical manufacturing firms, which have, of course, an interest in selling their products for maximizing their profits in the least time. The use of IPMs offers options for the grower above and beyond the exclusive use of pesticides for crop protection.

The information generated by the demonstration projects will be shared among officials, academicians, and farmers to ensure that the BMPs are well adapted. In order to overcome these barriers to the implementation of BMPs, a basic change in attitude is required, which involves cultural, financial, and technical elements at the local, national, regional, and global level. It is a formidable challenge that will involve a considerable time element.

It will require adopting clear policies that promote the involvement of multidisciplinary teams of experts willing to incorporate the growers in carrying out their research work. To make a change from the traditional approach, it is necessary to assign resources to institutions that are willing to embrace the IPM approach. It may seem like an impossible task. However, it is important to bring to focus the quotation that heads this chapter: "What is lost cannot be recovered, but we can—and we must—change our ways to protect and restore what remains of the natural system that sustains us, if we are to prosper as a species" (Earle 2000).

Recommendations

As previously stated, the project is at its infancy and specific conclusions are premature. However, it is possible at this stage to venture some general recommendations that must be corroborated and expanded as the project proceeds.

It is evident from the previous discussion that the project is very complex and involves social, economic, and environmental elements. Furthermore, it is clear that the analysis, diagnosis, and formulation of solutions must consider different spatial and temporal levels. To be able to manage this large degree of complexity, it is necessary to utilize innovative and cutting-edge tools to collect and organize information, and to formulate decision-making models that can aid in formulating policies and action plans.

In the end, the project can be judged as a success if it facilitates a change in attitude, at all levels, and fosters innovations in the traditional methods of agricultural production. This change requires an evolution toward sustainable agricultural production and commitment by the international community, the national governments, agricultural manufacturing producers and salesman, crop consumers, and farmers. The burden cannot be placed exclusively on one group of stakeholders. All must share in the costs of the program in order to harvest the benefits for all.

Acknowledgments

The authors would like to thank the following people for their assistance in the preparation of this document: Luis Jiménez (Costa Rica) and Jimmy Hernández (Nicaragua), graduates, EARTH University; Edgar Alvarado (Guatemala) and Ramiro de la Cruz (Colombia), professors, EARTH University; and Edmundo Castro, consultant to EARTH University.

References

Carlson, G. A., and M. E. Wetzstein. 1993. Pesticides and pest management. In G. A. Carlson, D. Zilberman, and J. Miranowski, eds., *Agricultural and Environmental Resource Economics*, 268–318. New York: Oxford University Press.

Carson, R. 1962. *Silent Spring.* Boston: Houghton Mifflin.

Castillo, L. E., C. Ruepert, and E. Solís. 2000. Pesticide residues in the aquatic environment of banana plantation areas in the North Atlantic zone of Costa Rica. *Environmental Toxicology and Chemistry* 19:1942–50.

Castro, E., and L. Jiménez. 1999. *Valoración económica de la degradación de las aguas del Golfo de Nicoya: Análisis del sector agrícola.* Heredia, Costa Rica: Universidad Nacional.

Clites, A. H., T. D. Fontaine, and J. R. Wells. 1995. Distributed costs of environmental contamination. In C. Hall, ed., *Maximum Power: The Ideas and Application of H. T. Odum*, 175–82. Niwot: University Press of Colorado.

Contraloría General de la República. 1999. Panamá en Cifras, año 1998.

Earle, S. A. 2000. The water planet. www.seaweb.org/campaigns/danger/water.html.

Espinoza González, J. 1997. Fate and effects of pesticides under tropical conditions: Implications and research needs in a developing country. In *Environmental Behavior of Crop Protection Chemicals: Proceedings of an International Symposium on the Use of Nuclear and Related Techniques for Studying Environmental Behavior of Crop Protection Chemicals*, 93–107. IAEA-FAO, Vienna, July 1996.

———. 2000. Reducción del vertimiento de plaguicidas por escorrentia desde fuentes terrestres no puntuales al mar Caribe, Informe del País. Panama: Autoridad Marítima de Panamá.

FAO. 1995. *World Agriculture: Toward 2010.* New York: Wiley.

———. 2001. FAOSTAT Agricultural Data. http://apps.fao.org/cgi-bin/nph-db.pl?subset=agriculture

Helling, C. S. 1993. Pesticides, agriculture and water quality. In *A Holistic Approach to Water Quality*

Management: Finding Life-Styles and Measures for Harmful Fluxes from Land to Water. Proceedings of the Stockholm Water Symposium, 10–14 August 1992, Stockholm.

Hernández, C., J. Yeomans, and T. Kasten. 2001. Regional Report: Reducing pesticide runoff to the Caribbean Sea. www.cep.unep.org/pubs/meetingreports/GEF-Pesticides/GEF%20Pesticides.htm.

Hómez Sánchez, J., J. Bonilla Arboleda, J. E. Peinado Solano, M. A. Urdaneta Romero, and E. Carrascal Gómez. 2000. Informe nacional sobre el uso y manejo de plaguicidas en Colombia, tendiente a identificar y proponer alternativas para reducir el escurrimiento de plaguicidas al mar caribe. www.cep.unep.org.

Lin, B.-H., M. Padgitt, L. Bull, D. Delvo, and H. Taylor. 1995. Pesticide and Fertilizer Use and Trends in US Agriculture. Agricultural Economic Report Number 717. Washington, D.C.: U.S. Department of Agriculture, Economic Research Service.

MARENA. 2000. Proyecto de Reducción del Escurrimiento de plaguicidas al mar Caribe. Informe Nacional Nicaragua. Ministerio del Ambiente y los Recursos Naturales (MARENA). www.cep.unep.org.

McCarthy, J. F., and L. R. Shugart, eds. 1990. *Biomarkers of Environmental Contamination.* Boca Raton, Fla.: Lewis.

McKay, B., B. K. Mulvaney, and B. Thorne-Miller. 2000. Danger at sea: Our changing ocean. www.seaweb.org/campaigns/danger.

MINAE. 2000. Reducción del escurrimiento de plaguicidas al mar caribe. Informe Nacional, Costa Rica. Ministerio de Ambiente y Energía (MINAE). www.cep.unep.org.

Ministerio Agropecuario y Forestal. 1999. Indicadores Agropecuarios. Boletín Bimensual Año 2 No. 7. Dirección de Estadísticas, MAGFOR. Managua, Nicaragua.

Ministerio de Agricultura y Desarrollo Rural. 1999. Anuario Estadístico 1998. Bogotá, Colombia.

Ogden, J. C. 2001. The Caribbean Coastal Marine Productivity Program (CARICOMP). http://isis.uwimona.edu.jm/centres/cms/CARICOMP/map.html.

Panayotou, T. 1993. *Green Markets: The Economics of Sustainable Development.* San Francisco: ICS Press.

Pearce, D. W., and J. J. Warford. 1993. *World Without End: Economics, Environment, and Sustainable Development.* New York: Oxford University Press.

Piel, G. 1992. *Only One World—Our Own to Make and to Keep.* New York: United Nations.

Pimentel, D. 1997. Pest management in agriculture. In D. Pimentel, ed., *Techniques for Reducing Pesticide Use: Environmental and Economic Benefits,* 1–11. Chichester: Wiley.

———. 1998. Environmental and economic issues associated with pesticide use. In Y. Astorga, ed., *International Conference on Pesticide Use in Developing Countries: Input on Health and Environment. Final Proceedings,* 30–34. San José: Universidad Nacional de Costa Rica.

Ramírez, J. 1998. Consecuencias ambientales del nuevo orden en el sector agropecuario colombiano. Foro Nacional Ambiental, Agro y Medio Ambiente. Fundación Friedrich Ebert de Colombia-Fescol. Bogotá, marzo de 1998.

SEPSA. 2000. Boletín Estadístico No. 11. San José, Costa Rica: Secretaría Ejecutiva de Planificación Sectorial Agropecuaria, Ministerio de Agricultura y Ganadería.

Soto, R. 1998. Monitoreo de las comunidades de algas y lechos de fanerógamas marinas. En Estudio de Caso: Puerto Limón, Costa Rica, Informe Final. Proyecto Regional GEF/RLA/G41. Planificación y Manejo de Bahías y Áreas Costeras Fuertemente Contaminadas del Gran Caribe.

United Nations Environmental Program (UNEP). 1994. Regional overview of the land-based sources of pollution in the wider Caribbean region. CEP Technical Report No. 33. Kingston, Jamaica: UNEP Caribbean Environment Program.

United Nations Population Fund (UNFPA). 2002. The State of World Population 2001. www.unfpa.org/swp/2001/english/index.html.

CHAPTER 26

Neoclassical Economics and Fisheries

Gary Sharp and Charles A. S. Hall

Introduction

Fisheries management and fisheries science have been concerned traditionally with the management of populations of game and commercial species, principally through manipulations of populations, habitat, and, through regulation, harvests. The objective has been, and remains, the maintenance of populations of particular species at levels thought desirable to society. This approach has been in some respects very successful (e.g., for many highly prized game fish such as freshwater trout, largemouth bass, and striped bass). However, although one can find some examples where a region's fisheries have managed to thrive under formal management, these successful fisheries are the exceptions. In particular, many fisheries that at one time or another within the last fifty years produced the major proportions of the global fish catch have passed into commercial or virtual biological oblivion. For example, the National Marine Fisheries Service (NMFS) Report on the Status of United States Fisheries found in 1997 that 86 species are listed as "overfished," 183 species are listed as "not overfished," and 10 species are considered to be approaching an overfished condition based on the criteria specified in the Magnuson-Stevens Act. The status relative to overfishing is unknown for 448 additional species. (NMFS 1997). The most recent statistical analyses of "Status of Fisheries of the United States," compiled up to the year 2000, found that 14 of the 18 most important commercial species for the United States are considered commercially extinct, or in danger of that (NMFS 2001).

Although there is no question that global fisheries are in serious trouble, the degree to which specific fisheries are in decline or danger is a complex and even controversial issue. Myers and Worm (2003) of Dalhousie University in Nova Scotia write, "Industrialized fisheries typically reduced community biomass by 80% within 15 years of exploitation" and, referring to such fishes as cod, halibut, tuna, swordfish, and marlin, "large predatory fish biomass is today only about 10% of pre-industrial levels," that is, since the beginning of large-scale high seas fishing in the 1950s. They find that fishing is now so "efficient" that the population of any species can be caught within fifteen years, some populations disappearing within just a few years. Similar discouraging trends can be found in Pikitch et al. (1997) and Pauley et al. (2002). Fortunately, when these findings have been readdressed by researchers and managers more directly involved, they concluded that the results were not as dire as Meyers and Worm (and others) suggest. Over a year after the fact, and after several efforts to get their comments published, *Nature* finally published "Comments on Myers & Worm," by John Hampton of the Oceanic Fisheries Programme at the Secretariat of the Pacific Community; John R. Sibert of the Pelagic Research Program, University of Hawaii; Pierre Kleiber, of the U.S. Marine Fisheries Service, Pacific Islands Fisheries Science Center; and Shelton J. Harley of the Inter-American Tropical Tuna Commission. These experts, who specialize in tuna fisheries, take apart almost every methodological aspect of the Myers and Worm article. "Fundamentally flawed," "incorrect," "too restrictive" are some of the epithets they use. They conclude that "Myers and Worm do the fisheries community a disservice by applying a simplistic analysis to available data, which exaggerates declines in abundance and implies rebuilding benchmarks." It would probably have paid for Meyers and Worm to have read both of the available Academic Press volumes on tunas by Sharp and Dizon (1978) and Block and Stevens (2001), as well as basic early 1970s

Japanese research by S. Saito, S. Sasaki, Hanamoto, and others (referenced in both volumes) that changed the world of longline fishing after they employed vertical longline techniques to find out where, which, and what sizes of tunas were most abundant and thus most vulnerable to longline gear. The conclusion of all this pointed discussion within the scientific community is that although yes, in agreement with Myers and Worm, there is extreme concern about the commercial disappearance, or the potential disappearance, of many of our traditional fish stocks in light of our tremendous potential for industrialized overfishing, good science must be brought to know, monitor, and model fish populations and the functioning of fisheries.

In addition, there has been a great deal of additional concern about the destruction of the ecosystems within which these fish live, including destruction by fishing itself, for example by the effects of large bottom trawler nets. Aquaculture, which was once believed to be the sustainable solution to feed a growing world's population, can also have disastrous impact on ocean ecosystems (Naylor et al. 2003).

Fortunately, there has been an epidemic of introspection among fisheries scientists since the general recognition during the 1990s that fisheries management actions have been ineffective, if not actually destructive (Garcia and Grainger 1997; Sharp 1992, 1995, 1996, 1997; Hancock et al. 1997). A concise summary of these papers, the contents of the meetings at which they were given, and the literature they summarize is this: conventional fisheries science as implemented in resource management has failed abysmally. Why? Again, the consensus is that relatively few fisheries scientists appear willing or able to implement their commonsensical and often comprehensive knowledge of particular fisheries. Instead they are trained, and in some cases even mandated by their superiors, to apply conventionalized but poorly performing population assessment tools that they learned in graduate school and that have dominated fisheries education and management, rather than on the comprehensive systems approach that is needed. Therefore, little of what is known about any fish species or their related ecosystem or the fisherman's

social system, or about the impact of continuing industrialization of the fishing fleet, is actually applied within the management realm until a crisis occurs. In addition, these scientists often defer to economic models that they may not understand well. The reasons for these failures include the lack of systems training for fisheries managers and the overwhelming power of the political and economic power aligned against the application of the fisheries manager's biological conclusions (Ludwig, Hilborn, and Walters 1993). Within this regime there has been little attention paid to the degree to which the economic framework within which fisheries science and management must operate is adequate or even appropriate for that task.

This chapter brings together a biologist with a comprehensive understanding of the world's major fisheries (Sharp) with an ecologist who over the last three decades has attempted to understand economics (Hall) in an attempt to determine to what degree the failures (and the successes) of fisheries are a function of the increasing intrusion of market economics into fisheries. In a sense, this is a near-impossible job because there are so many ways that fisheries can fail, so that teasing out the effects of markets can be very difficult. On the other hand, it may be useful to determine from those cases that appear to be clear-cut what if any principles might apply. We do not know the degree to which the specific case studies we provide here are broadly applicable, but we think they are. We acknowledge that our conclusions are based on some of the world's large industrial fisheries and not the artisanal fisheries that dominate some regions like West Africa and may be, on balance, more likely to be sustainable (Berkes et al. 2001).

What Are the Requirements for Successful Fisheries?

The requirements of a successful fishery might best be considered as similar to "The Anna Karenina principle," derived from Leo Tolstoy's famous novel (and used in a biological analogy recently in Jared Diamond's *Guns, Germs, and Steel*). According to Tolstoy, "Happy families are all alike; every unhappy family is unhappy in its own way." Thus all sustainable fisheries have similar characteristics.

These include at a minimum a sufficient, productive, and relatively stable stock of fish, an ecosystem that supports them without large fluctuations or degradation, and a fishing capacity small enough so as to not endanger the stock, especially during any time of low abundance. Unfortunately, these characteristics are almost never met, so that unsuccessful fisheries fail each in their own way. What patterns can we see in these failures? We focus on economics while paying attention to other factors.

First, we have to say that historically fish (within which category we include other exploited marine and aquatic creatures) population declines are hardly a recent phenomenon and have had many causes, many initiated and many not initiated by fishermen. These declines have had many implications and manifestations for people. It is only necessary to look to the sixteenth to nineteenth centuries to find fisheries "gold rushes" based on whale oil and seal and otter fur that caused the creation and then loss of many ships, seaside communities, and cultures based on the exploitation of the ocean's resources. When the whales and furbearers were gone, normally within a century, all that was left was fishing for fish. The complete destruction of finfish stocks is a more recent phenomenon, accelerated by growing markets and technical capacities. When these fish are gone, where do folks go? As the coastal and upland systems are co-opted, and as fishers are forced farther out onto the oceans, the likelihood increases that more individuals from the older fishing cultures will opt out, and their cultural ethos and knowledge will be lost. Fishing cultures too must be considered as very fragile, and valuable, if not irreplaceable, global resources. They need to be nurtured and maintained with the same concern that we profess for other endangered biotic resources.

Some Economic Principles

Probably the principal reason that fisheries, at least modern nonsubsistence fisheries, fail is that the raison d'être for catching fish has nothing to do with maintaining stocks, their ecosystem requirements, or even the long-term catch. It is rather the generation of profits. This brings us to economics. Here are some assumptions of contemporary (neoclassical) academic economics, both in terms of the operation of economic systems and as that operation is reflected in academic economics (see Hall 1991 and chapters 1, 4, and 5 of this volume):

1. Humans will apportion their available financial resources to maximize their own psychological well being. These psychological desires can be best met, at least for most matters, through monetary means.
2. Humans are rational, which means in this context self-interested and even greedy.
3. The objective of most human activity and investment is monetary profit.
4. The value of most things can be derived by the intersection of supply and demand in markets.
5. Money now is (much) more valuable than the same amount of money at any future date.
6. The future is not valued as much as the present (related to 5).

In addition, one might add additional assumptions that are associated with market economies but that are probably best considered derivative, often within a political context. These are best considered under the rubric of "efficiency":

1. Unregulated markets generate economic "efficiency," meaning, basically, a "good" use of resources resulting in lower prices than would otherwise be the case.
2. Actions should be taken whenever and wherever possible to enhance efficiency.
3. Governments should interfere with free markets as little as possible.
4. International tariffs should be reduced to encourage world trade. This trade results in efficiency as each region focuses on those economic activities at which they are best.

We consider the above statements about the actions of economics and markets as statements of hypotheses that we will test as best we can.

Finally, there are some important additional concepts that are rarely mentioned in economics but that reflect broader technical changes in society, and that are encouraged in part by the application of neoclassical economics to other domains:

1. Fossil fuel has become cheaper in real (i.e., inflation-corrected) terms.
2. Huge amounts of investment capital have become available around the world.
3. Governments have often subsidized fisheries (this perhaps in opposition to some of the above) in order to maintain "fishing lifestyles" or for other reasons.
4. The economic activity of the world is increasingly concentrated in relatively few multinational corporations, most of which are driven principally by the desire for profit and some of which are larger than most world governments.

It seems to us self evident that essentially all of these principles have at least the potential to operate against rational exploitation of fish, at least most of the time. Yet many economists argue that economics by itself will protect fish stocks from excessive exploitation. As Harden Taylor remarks, "the inexorable laws of economics could curtail the rates of harvesting long before any species of fish was faced with extinction . . . that the fish could recover from whatever we were likely to throw at them and . . . that dollars (were) the real yield" (Larkin 1977). Many of these economists believe that governments should get out of the business of managing fish and allow these "inexorable laws" to manage and even protect the fish. We examine whether this has worked for particular fisheries in the sections that follow. Our methods are simply narratives based on extensive personal knowledge of the history of particular fisheries and of the means of their exploitation and management, and the extensive use of literature in support of our conclusions.

Results of Our Analysis

The next several sections show how the basic economic assumptions have resulted in the destruction of particular fisheries because of the characteristics of the response of real fisheries to free markets that are not captured in the assumptions of that model. We organize our analyses into examining the implications in specific fisheries to the same three groups of economic concepts given above.

This first set of analyses examines the implications of the basic assumptions of neoclassical economics, including initially that humans are (and should be) greedy and self interested on the potential for long-term sustainability of fisheries.

Bluefin Tuna—North Atlantic

Atlantic bluefin tuna (ABT), the largest of the tunas (often approaching 500 kg), were not considered worth fishing for by North American fishermen before 1970 because they were so big and strong that they would destroy fishing gear. The development of the Japanese sushi industry in the 1970s changed all that, and now they are considered seriously overfished. Atlantic tunas are managed under the dual authority of the Magnuson-Stevens Fishery Conservation and Management Act (M-SFCMA) and the Atlantic Tunas Convention Act (ATCA). ATCA authorizes the Secretary of Commerce to implement binding recommendations of the International Commission for the Conservation of Atlantic Tunas (ICCAT). The authority to issue regulations under the M-SFCMA and ATCA has been delegated from the Secretary of Commerce to the Assistant Administrator for Fisheries, NOAA National Marine Fisheries Service (NMFS). Within the NMFS, daily responsibility for management of Atlantic HMS fisheries rests with the Office of Sustainable Fisheries and is administered by the Highly Migratory Species (HMS) Management Division. It is clearly a long way through this abundantly redundant management morass from the fishermen to the decision-making authorities. The story gets even more complicated.

F. J. Mather III, J. M. Mason Jr., and A. C. Jones (1995) concluded that market greed was the principal reason for the destruction of the major stocks of Atlantic bluefin tuna fisheries since 1960 or so. Mather (1974) reported at the International Game Fish Conference (and also reported at

ICCAT Scientific and Statistics Committee meetings in the mid-1970s) about returns from near the North Sea of bluefin tuna tags from fish tagged and released in the western Atlantic during the voluntary tag-and-release program of the recreational fishery off the East Coast of the United States. This confirmed that the Atlantic fisheries needed to consider the resource a mixed stock (i.e., with fish derived from the Mediterranean and from both sides of the Atlantic Ocean), and that it should be managed as such. In the late 1970s, U.S. fishermen began a seine fishery for juvenile ABT as they entered the coastal Atlantic as one-year-olds from their nursery grounds in the Gulf of Mexico and the Caribbean, and older age groups that apparently remained in the western Atlantic until they reached maturity, around age eight. This fishery quickly became the target of ABT management efforts and was shut down before it grew to be a major problem. ICCAT was asked to minimize seine fisheries for immature ABT throughout the Atlantic and Mediterranean, but instead, in the 1980s, ICCAT scientists drew an arbitrary line down the middle of the North Atlantic. This allowed the United States and Canada to make their own management regulations rather than consider the whole Atlantic/Mediterranean ABT resource as a mixed fishery, needing uniform management procedures. Despite the United States' having shut down its emergent seine fishery, the Spanish, French, and Italian fisheries continued harvesting subadult ABT. Thirty-five years later, Block et al. (2005) confirmed the fact that ABT were moving back and forth across the Atlantic, and that eastern Atlantic fisheries were indeed capturing fish from the western Atlantic. Meanwhile, back in the western Atlantic, where the well-known ABT spawning takes place in the spring within the Gulf of Mexico and Caribbean, no effort has yet been taken to minimize fishing effort on the spawners during this period, a seemingly counterproductive failure of concerned management. Berkeley (2001) described the failure of the ICCAT at the Standing Committee meeting on Science and Statistics, and of the ICCAT Commission to address their failures with respect to ABT and other species.

Based on the 1998 revised stock assessment, which showed a serious depletion of ABT, parties at the 1998 meeting of ICCAT adopted a twenty-year western Atlantic BFT rebuilding program, beginning in 1999 and continuing through 2018. ICCAT has adopted an annual total allowable catch (TAC) for the western Atlantic BFT of 2,500 metric tons whole weight, inclusive of dead discards, to be applied annually until such time as the TAC is changed based on advice from the ICCAT Standing Committee on Research and Statistics. The annual landing quota allocated to the United States was set at 1,387 metric tons whole weight. Meanwhile, the various European fisheries and many Asian "flag-of-convenience" fleets went about catching these very valuable fish under "business as usual," out of sight, out of mind. Can you guess who monitors their catches, and landings, when most are transferring their catches to an array of island ports, or at sea, to transport vessels headed for Asian markets? The answer is no one. So we have no idea whether exploitation has actually decreased although it seems very unlikely.

Although the closure of the western Atlantic seine fishery and the minimal catches allocated to the United States and Canada may provide the best example of an oceanic Marine Protected Area, the primary beneficiaries are not the fish but the unregulated European coastal fisheries, along with the multi-flagged Atlantic longline fisheries, whose annual catches recently totaled more than thirty-five thousand tons. In other words, by not considering the entire fish stock and fisheries as a system, the protection of one part of the fish's life has the principal effect of simply improving the ability of others to overfish the same fish.

Bluefin Tuna—Southern Ocean

Reported southern ocean bluefin tuna (SBT) catch had reached eighty thousand tons in the early 1960s. These large catches (which were "regulated" only by the economics of tuna fishing) resulted in the numbers of mature fish dropping to low levels, and by the mid-1980s it was generally recognized that the SBT stock was at a very low level and required rebuilding. That implied that there was a need for a mechanism to limit catches. The main nations fishing SBT, Australia, Japan, and New

Zealand, began to apply strict quotas to their fishing fleets from 1985 to enable the SBT stocks to rebuild. The Commission for the Conservation of Southern Bluefin Tuna (CCSBT) came into being on 20 May 1994, when the Convention for the Conservation of Southern Bluefin Tuna, signed by all three nations, was enacted. The aim of the convention is to ensure the conservation and optimum utilization of southern bluefin tuna through appropriate management. The previous voluntary management arrangement between Australia, Japan, and New Zealand (which had been signed by the three countries in May 1993) was thus formalized when the CCSBT came into force. However, vessels from Indonesia, Korea, and Taiwan, which are not members of the CCSBT, also take significant quantities of SBT. Nearly all the SBT fisheries serve the same markets. It is only on the market floors of, for example, the Tokyo fish market, that one might actually assess the total catches from such diversely monitored fleets and delivery pathways. The nation-by-nation or region-by-region sums have never really been carefully monitored, and reported as such.

The failure of low abundance to limit effort

The logic of the market model says that as the number of fish decline they will not be worth fishing for. But as bluefin tuna abundances have declined (nearly worldwide) their prices have risen in response to their scarcity in the previously developed markets, insuring that fishermen will search longer and harder for the relatively few remaining bluefin. The price of any tuna species is not set at the dockside, or for fresh tuna, but rather for fish products at distant markets in wealthy cities. For example, skipjack tuna is sold in Japan for katsuwobushi, a dried, thinly sliced product that is a daily staple in the Japanese diet. As well, sashimi, prime fish filets of many species of tunas, mahi mahi, amberjacks, and even mackerels, delivered at their highest color and quality, are considered basics—consumed by many at lunch and celebratory meals. The sashimi consumption rate is hardly affected by prices, which range upward for the highest fat content. Other tunas and other fishes are processed for

sashimi, and the relatively recent growing market acceptance for these products in wealthy countries continues to stimulate high exploitation levels for particular species, particularly adult bigeye, yellowfin, and skipjack tuna as well as jack mackerel and mahi mahi.

However, bluefin tuna reign supreme at Japanese high-end sashimi and daily lunch sushi shops. Bluefin tuna are caught in essentially every ocean, landed, graded, and shipped within twenty-four hours, fresh but iced down, from all around the world to Tokyo. Larger quantities of longline-caught bluefin tuna arrive from around the world at the markets, after being caught, bled, and flash-frozen using energy-intensive state-of-the-art technologies. The value of individual fishes are judged at the dock in terms of fat content, color, and general qualities of the flesh—and the demand back home. The prices are greatly enhanced by advertised events at which an individual premium bluefin tuna fish is purchased for sums that started at $15,000 in the 1980s and steadily rose over time to upward of $75,000. In January 1996, an individual bluefin was sold in Japan's local market for a record price of $173,000, about $390 per pound, or about $25 a mouthful. This is during a time when bluefin tuna are considered endangered, particularly in the North Atlantic, where they were once abundant. But these notable market incentives keep the fisheries not only operating, but in some areas expanding in the face of reduced stocks. Lotto, anyone? Clearly, economic approaches working by themselves have not saved the fish stocks or the fisheries.

Abalone

The world's abalone fisheries (*Haliotus* spp., a single-shelled mollusk) have undergone similar gold rushes, and in many locales, from Baja California northward to Oregon, and in the Arabian Sea, they are now severely depleted. Local markets developed and soon evolved into primarily upscale seafood restaurants with specific clientele for what was once merely a subsistence food item. In the mid-1970s, the Asian market began to purchase California shellfish. Local near-shore resources were soon depleted; offshore island populations began to be heavily exploited, causing prices to soar; and most Californians no longer had access to abalone. Other coastlines were soon scoured as well. By the mid-1980s most of these once-plentiful mollusks were dangerously close to non-existent. The U.S. sushi trade is now supplied by abalone farming, where settled spat is raised to 100 grams or slightly larger sizes using natural kelp as food. But this has not helped the wild population, where the desire for them is maintained partly by the continual availability (and hence familiarity with and expectation of) the ranched varieties, and poaching of natural populations is now rampant.

There have been various experiments around the globe to develop abalone substitutes, including treating the flesh of large squid species—and thus providing an analogous texture, but a less satisfying flavor. The Chilean Loco (*Strongomerus bentinkii*), a long-lived carnivorous snail found from southern Peru south to along Chile's extensive rocky coastal shores, was formerly principally a local cultural delight, favored by the older Chilean cultures, particularly the Mapucho. The fisherfolk who harvested these unusual shellfish focused on the larger, older individuals they found hunting for prey within the kelp forests, or algae-covered rocky intertidal zones. It took only a few years, and the economic incentives of a foreign market, to cause a near-collapse of the Loco populations all along the South American coast. A naturally self-sustaining cultural food item became rare, and nearly unaffordable by locals.

Alaska Pollock

One of the most abundant American species is the Alaska pollock, the source for fish sticks and faux crab (surimi). The American fishermen in the Bering Sea get from five to seven and a half cents for a pound of pollock. The big profits are made by company stores, which are owned principally by Japanese conglomerates. The American catch is sold for pennies per pound to Japanese companies for conversion to value-added surimi products such as faux crab, then resold in the United States for dollars per pound. Otherwise, the fish are shipped south to Seattle, where they are turned into fish filets for fast food dispensers. While the main issue for Alaskan pollock is not concern over stock abundance, the species' roles in the larger regional food web and ecosystem dynamics are of direct concern. These issues are of course not in any way reflected in the market price of pollock or its derivatives. This issue is not a stated mission or direct concern of the Magnuson-Stevens Fisheries Conservation and Management Act (M-SFCMA) of 1976, but it should be. This transition awaits true Ecosystem-based Fisheries Management—one of many stated objectives of the more recent Sustainable Fisheries Act of 1996, which was written to address the failings of the M-SFCMA.

Other Species Issues

In any of these or other fisheries rare fish stocks often continue to be caught as nontarget species while fishing for other, still abundant species. For example, there has never existed any particular fisheries for the New England barn door skate, yet this species seems to have been virtually eliminated when they were inadvertently caught in nets targeted for cod or flounders. Similarly, the totuava of the upper Gulf of California is also nearing extinction, from both overfishing and the lack of freshwater flow into the Colorado River and its estuaries, where this species spawned in earlier times prior to the massive development of agriculture and cities in its watershed.

One of the most difficult issues to deal with is exemplified by the well-recognized depletion of three or so *Sebastes* species, particularly bocaccio (*S. paucipinis*), cow cod (*S. levis*), rockfish, and one or two others that just happen to have extremely long lives, if not caught. The problem is that there are at least 30 species of *Sebastes* in every major ecosystem type fished from the Gulf of California, up the west coast of Baja California, into the Southern California Bight, from Point Conception north along the coast to Vancouver Island, and into the Gulf of Alaska, out along the Aleutian Islands, across the North Pacific, down the complex coastline, and the Japanese Island complex, to Korea (Love, Yoklavich, and Thorstein 2002). The other complexity is that the recognizable distinction is that all these *Sebastes* species are internal fertilizers that give birth to live, free-swimming young. Then there is the fact that these free-swimming young at various life stages pass from various locations, ranging from the near shore, grassy areas, kelp beds, and the like into various stage-specific habitats such as shelves, slopes, and deepwater rockpiles and banks. They are not exclusionary. On the contrary, often several species are found at any location—that in the end total over 130 *Sebastes* species. There are also at least four life-history types among the 30 or so species in each region of the ocean. One group, mostly near shore for their entire lives, is fast growing, early developers, with total life spans of about four to six years. The next group is slower growing and matures at about four to six years and lives to about fourteen to sixteen years. The next group lives up to fifty years, with varied maturation ages ranging from eight to sixteen years. The real problem group is the few species that live to be from eighty to over a hundred years old. These too mature over a broad size-age range, but are well known for occasional massive recruitments in local situations, and minimal successes over time in most. Life exists in a continuously varying yet patterned environment.

These diverse life histories tell the working evolutionary biologist that these groups can cope, and have had to cope, with varied periods of successful recruitment in order to thrive. A fish that lives for a hundred years but requires twenty years to reach maturity and that may have only one really successful spawning in its life due to generally unfavorable ocean conditions means that there may be eighty or so years between significant reproductions. Meanwhile, the group of species that lives for six years but can spawn in two may be as viable in the face of fishing pressure as most near-shore pelagic species, such as anchovies. How can anyone go about managing such a massively diverse group, given that they are often found to live in mixed species situations, are often indistinguishable to the fisherman, and are each vulnerable to all nonselective fishing gear? Basically, the market values are similar, and the products often sold under the generic labeling as redfish, rockfish, or even red snapper (Love, Yoklavich, and Thorstein 2002). This complicates management, and single species management is certainly inappropriate. But what do you do, given their massive overlaps and diversities? Management that is responding to market values only makes it worse, as there is little or no species-specific information in the market.

Multinationalization and Globalization

All of the above economic incentives for exploiting and over-exploiting fish are enhanced by the trends of increased multinational corporations and globalization. Although this is particularly a phenomenon of the past quarter-century, it has been important in fisheries since at least the fifteenth-century emergence of the Hanseatic League of buyers, processors, and transporters of North Atlantic fish products. Multinational corporations have no reason to exist except for profits and hence can be expected to make all decisions based on this criterion, subject to any legal and at some level, probably, moral constraints. But there is no mechanism by which moral concerns about overfishing or environmental degradation make it in any important way to affect corporate headquarters or stockholders meetings (except occasionally at street protests as in Seattle in 2000). In fact, when James Wolfson attempted to bring some environmental morality to the World Bank, he was essentially blocked by stockholders who wanted no interference with maximum profits. Fish processors, boat builders, gear salesmen, and fish sellers are not fishers, and they serve poorly the long-term interests of traditional fishing cultures. Individual fish species are not really much of a concern either.

In the examples given above, the principal cause given for the fish stock declines by the experts who study them is simply market-driven greed, with the few exceptions in which lifestyles (i.e., fish life-history patterns) promote their vulnerability. Too often the public gets the message that greedy fishermen initiate these collapses, and that all fishermen are villains. But careful, long-term study of fisheries and their contexts show that this is only rarely the case, because fishing per se is not where the major profits are made in fish trade, particularly since the end of World War II. The price paid for fish, like for other basic raw materials, is continually pushed to as low a value as possible through the phenomenon of many sellers and few buyers. The major wetfish fisheries, herrings, sardines, and anchovies, have landing values on the order of $90 to $100/ton today, while similar prices (corrected for inflation) were paid in the 1940s for these same resources. Meanwhile, since 1972 or so fuel and vessel costs have risen steadily, as technological advances accrued. The profits are made principally after the fish are caught by processors, marketers and in markets, with multipliers from 2 to 9, depending upon the fish being used, and the product(s) created.

Of course, fishermen themselves are not blameless. For example, fishermen initiated the practices of in situ high grading, sorting catches for higher-valued species or parts. Perhaps the most egregious example is that of shark "finning," where the highly valued fins (for shark fin soup) are kept and the living (for a while) rest of the shark is tossed overboard so as not to take up space in the hold (Alverson et al. 1994). It is the same with less-valuable species, which are often shoveled overboard dead or dying. These discards are often small, not yet reproductive, or low-value species that are more often than not unaccounted for in anyone's ledgers. Obviously needed are more sound harvesting procedures wherein valued resources would be caught only in proportion to their reproductive replacement capacities within their local ecological pyramid (Sheldon and Parsons 1967; Sheldon, Prakash, and Sutcliffe 1972; Sheldon, Sutcliffe, and Paranjape 1977; Silvert 1988; Silvert and Platt 1978, 1980).

Market concepts and rationales lead to other problems with maintaining fish stocks. The objective of economic analysis is usually to maximize "present discounted monetary streams," meaning maintaining the largest return to the investor. The "discounted" means that future income is counted for less than present income, so that it is discounted (at usually 5 to 10 percent a year). Thus by this reckoning a fish catch worth $1000 this year is worth more than the same catch next year, which is worth, say, $900 (today) and so on so that the catch a hundred or even ten years from now is worth very, very little. As Clark (1973) points out, this leads to a rationale for catching all the fish now and destroying the long-term income stream! There are of course many counterarguments to this, but because of the dominance of neoclassical economics, which explicitly includes discounting, this strongly influences routine market decisions.

Thus it can be seen from these examples that markets in a sense do what they are advertised to do: they pander to human "rationality"—greed and self interest; they satisfy human psychological desires through monetary means; they generate substantial monetary profit; they allow value to be derived by the intersection of supply and demand curves in markets; and they operate to catch fish relatively quickly, so that money is generated now that is considered more valuable than the same amount of money at some future date. Although there may be market "distortions" through government subsidies and the like, these seem only to exacerbate the existing market system. On the other hand, government regulations may protect the fish. For those who do not like much government intervention, perhaps the best approach is to eliminate subsidies, determine what level of exploitation the fish can accept (perhaps this has to be done annually and perhaps using data from the fisheries themselves through adaptive management), and then perhaps within those limits let free enterprise figure out how the fisheries "should" be regulated. But in conclusion to this section, we see no way in which the market system by itself leads to rational long-term management of fish stocks. Other procedures, more focused on conservation, are needed.

Efficiency

We now examine the second set of assumptions about neoclassical economics to see if fisheries operate to maximize efficiency. Historically, fish such as dried cod or pickled herring were cheap relative to terrestrially based animal protein, and this presumably reflected ancient and historical high abundance of fish and the low cost of catching them, at least prior to the modern industrial subsidy. Unfortunately, it is almost impossible to answer this question now because many fisheries, perhaps most, are highly subsidized by governments. Hence the degree to which the price of fish is still low may or may not be due to the intrinsic properties of the fish and the fisheries. Although many fishing activities turn a quick profit for a few, a careful cost accounting shows that in the long term and over the globe total costs far outweigh many of the short term gains. The FAO (1995) estimates that the global annual fish catch, worth $70 billion, may have been subsidized by governments by as much as $54 billion. Even that estimate includes only a few of many taxpayer subsidies, missing others such as general subsidies for petroleum (Meyers and Kent 2001).

Governments not only subsidize, but they also often regulate to try to protect endangered stocks. Those who advocate free markets often want to eliminate these restrictions. For example, encouragement for turning catch regulation over to markets comes explicitly in "structural adjustment" policies implemented by the World Bank and the International Monetary Fund (IMF). This is done to enhance international trade, including trade in fish. This pressure, for example, led indirectly to demands for increased exports of fish from the rich and formerly stable Argentine hake (*Merluccia* sp.) fisheries despite the clearly expressed concerns of the fisheries scientists that the fish could not stand increased exploitation. Again, many believed that this enhanced world trade and elimination of the role of government would lead to economic efficiency, but it is hard to see how that occurs in this case because the fish stocks and hence the fishermen's livelihood and culture were destroyed.

A classic example of "free markets" (with some subsidy) leading to inefficiency was the subsidized transformation of California's high-seas tuna seine fleet. The fleet in the 1950s was composed of cost-effective midsize, family-operated vessels, of 200- and then 350–750-ton capacities. Even among these the midsize group had been shown to be most economically efficient. Further "development" was based on several changes. The size of the boats increased to the eventual extremes of highly subsidized 1,200- to 2,000-ton-capacity super seiners, which proved disastrous. These decisions resulted from industry subterfuge (and inadequate forethought) that worked to maintain and enhance their own subsidies. In particular, the participants worked to insure that prior participants would be guaranteed fishing rights based on the concept that if there were going to be an annual catch quota (ACQ) used to manage fisheries within the Inter-American Tropical Tuna Commission's yellowfin regulatory area (CYRA), they still would be guaranteed the right to fish. Initially, ACQs were based on the premise that each U.S. vessel that had historical presence in the fishery should be able to make at least one complete full-capacity trip per year, but only if the vessel was in port before the annual quota was filled. That meant that if a vessel put in a productive three- or four-week trip and came back into port before the declared closure date, with anywhere from half to a full load, it would be able to unload that catch and go back out to catch its guaranteed full-capacity load. One can quickly see that a 350-ton-capacity boat at best might land 700 tons from within the CYRA—and then be forced outside the CYRA for the rest of the year. However, a 1,200- or 2,000-ton vessel could manage, under extremely good conditions, to be able to land from 2,400 to 4,000 tons, a truly multimillion-dollar business in those days.

ACQs were set each year based on catch-rate trends. But ownership of the fishing licenses shifted from individuals and fishing families with smaller boats to corporations and unseen investor groups with much larger investment capital and hence larger boats, and with limited interests in resource health. The initial investments were made based on local fishing operations, and smaller boats operated under the economic regime of low diesel fuel costs. After the oil crisis of the early 1970s, none of the larger vessels was profitable, in any realistic terms, and few or none of any new vessels have ever been paid for from their own landings made since their being launched. Nor could the fisheries remain economic with the higher exploitation rates and hence higher competition levels generated by the larger boats. Thus individuals conspired to create fishing conditions that in fact undermined their own economic health. It was not the resource, in this case, that was in decline, but the fleet's overdevelopment and costs of operating these larger vessels that made them uneconomical. Rawitscher and Mayer (1977) concluded that high-seas tuna seining was one of the least productive means of obtaining fish products considering the amounts of energy and goods invested. One way to look at this was that a large tuna boat would leave San Diego with a thousand tons of fuel and return with a thousand tons of fish, of which 80 percent was water!

Things got worse. The typical grocery store sales price for a six-ounce can of light chunk-style tuna was about $.79 in the late 1970s. Today, with the closure of U.S. mainland canneries and internationalization of the tuna canning industry, the tropical tuna products' qualities have slipped, and the sale prices have returned to 1960s values of from three cans for a dollar to $.65 a can. One thing that is clear is that although in some cases economic efficiency (i.e., low price to consumers) may occur over time, any physical definition of efficiency has declined enormously. For example, Brown and Lugo (1981) found that the (food) energy obtained per unit of (fossil) energy input decreased from about 1 to 1 to about 0.3 to 1 from about 1950 to 1980 (and it must be much less since then). The efficiency of fisheries when measured as physical output (in tons, but also in dollars) compared to the input of fossil fuels has continued to decline in recent decades. We can see from this example that the lowered landing values per ton, along with the steady escalation of fuel prices over the same period, will provide a particularly poignant lesson about the idealized "bigger is better" economic models, versus the "small and steady is more durable, and sustainable" models. The pinch on the fisherman is relieved only with politically popular subsidies. In this case there is something to be said for letting markets work rather than continuing the subsidies—as long as the catch restrictions and viable resource populations are maintained.

In the present era of nearly complete divestiture by American tuna boat owners, the corporations whose product lines include highly profitable condiments (e.g., mayonnaise and pickles) that are used in making a tuna sandwich in American households ended up buying the fleets, in order to ensure primary product, even if tuna fishing was carried out at a low profit, or even a loss. The present (2003) landing prices for tropical tunas—that is, skipjack and yellowfin—are well below $300/ ton, creating a major crisis in the industry, as Asian investors had bought into the volume landings for low-value markets and built enormous numbers of

very large seine vessels. Many are going or have gone bankrupt as a result. Today, when you fly over San Diego Bay or other historically active U.S. tuna vessel ports, there are virtually no vessels at the docks, where in the past the entire bay would be lined with vessels in various stages of their fishing cycles. The United States is a very substantial target market, but it is no longer a major producer of tuna products. And the whole process of overdevelopment is shifting to fisheries in developing but highly industrialized countries. For example, Korea builds modern high seas super seiners for investors from developing (and developed) nations, but the crews are not really trained to deal with all that is required to operate these vessels efficiently. After coming up to speed, the landings quickly exceeded the conventional canned tuna markets, and the vessel owners have had to come to agreements about limiting global landings, in order to restimulate the market prices, and that meant shortening, once again, the fishing days at sea for all the participants in these tropical tuna fisheries. Adequate catch regulation for conservation was never the issue, as few or none of these important tropical tuna stocks are overexploited, unlike the highly vulnerable bluefin tuna stocks.

The alternative to oversubscribed fisheries is available, and another tuna fishery in the western Indian Ocean provides an example. During his first summer at FAO, while everyone was away on summer leave, Gary Sharp wrote a descriptive article entitled "Areas of potentially successful exploitation of tunas in the Indian Ocean with emphasis on surface methods" (Sharp 1979). It was a compilation of the experience that he had had over the previous decade or so with fisheries in the eastern Pacific Ocean, developed and developing, that ended in the sad overcapacity scenario described above. Most of the Indian Ocean high seas fisheries, except for the Japanese longline fishery for southern bluefin tuna, were relatively undeveloped. Thus Sharp thought that providing a description of the potential seasonality and localities for various fishing approaches might save many millions of dollars, as well as provide stimulant for those with sufficient experience in high seas fishing to make their move, and try specific times and areas. This all seemed to work out, as the first printing of the report was soon gone, and people from various fishing interest groups began showing up for more insights. This was all described in detail by Sharp (1992).

Several island-based tuna fisheries had been in operation for varying lengths of time. These included the French pole-and-line fishery operated out of northern Madagascar; the Sri Lankan pole-and-line fishery; some small operations from Reunion and Mauritius; and, the oldest of the all, the Maldivian skipjack fishery, operating for over two millennia from the more than one thousand island colonies. That fishery's claim to fame was that the vessels were completely sail-powered, and the fishermen used very specialized techniques for both capturing and maintaining their bait fish, and for their daily fishing activities, which rarely exceeded voyages beyond sight of the island palm trees, or about twelve miles. After a day of successful fishing, a shark would be captured, the boats would head back to their home islands, and the shark would be literally peeled, and the flesh scraped into a paste, for use in attracting baitfishes the following morning. On arrival, the catch was processed, salted, and air-dried by the women and prepared for delivery to buyers in the eastern Arabian Sea, primarily Sri Lanka—as Maldives fish.

In the mid-1970s the Japanese aid agency invested in helping the Maldivians into the modern world of technology by introducing diesel engines into the Maldivian fishing vessels, and working out arrangements to deliver catches to refrigerated pickup vessels. This sounded like a very forward step, but in the long run, it only managed to land the entire Maldives Island system in the petroleum economy, with a new dependency on petroleum suppliers and the Japanese engine and parts manufacturers. FAO sent technical assistants to help the Maldivian fishermen learn how to construct and deploy fish aggregating devices to help increase efficiency, and that worked. Now the problem became how to catch, freeze, and transport to markets enough fish to make the interest on the capital borrowed to build and run all these "modernizations" from bankrupting the Maldivian economy. Decades later, freezer plants and a cannery have been built, but fishermen are leaving their fishing

behind, and using their power boats to transport vacationing Europeans back and forth between the main island airport landing site and tourist resources. The traditional subsistence lifestyle was quickly converted to a fossil fuel–dependent economic struggle.

Meanwhile, the Seychelles Island government was interested in how to benefit from its huge Exclusive Environment Zone (EEZ) (legal fishing zone), and invited the FAO's Indian Ocean Fisheries Development Program (IOFDP) to hold meetings to discuss the development and management aspects of the region's high-seas tuna fisheries. The French and Basque seine fleets had meanwhile been in high competition, fishing off the west coast of Equatorial Africa, and their fisheries were only marginally economical, given distances to markets, and local processing capacities. They contacted the Seychelles Fisheries Authority about setting up test-fishing projects, one based on pole-and-line, the other on high-seas seining. At one of the major IOFDP meetings that ensued, Sharp was asked to help those interested in decision making regarding whether to get involved, in various optional ways, or not. These are difficult issues to begin finding answers to, but Sharp suggested the comparative approach. The first questions needing answers were about the available populations of skipjack, yellowfin, and other tunas. The second set of information needed was about the true dynamics of the region's seasonal ocean, and the requirements for any and all vessels entering the fishery to carry observers, and make and submit reports on catch and ocean/weather conditions on a daily basis. Young French scientists with ORSTOM development research agency got that message and carried out the program, archiving these data from day one. This later proved to be invaluable in interpretations of changes in the catch rate in time and space, and in management decisions that guaranteed this fishery's long-term viability. Thus it was critical to build the (so far) sustainable fishery based on science and not just economics.

The total area of the Eastern Pacific Ocean (ETP) tuna fishery was only slightly larger than the fishable area around the Seychelles (south to Mauritius, eastward to coastal Africa). The region is bounded to the north by the equatorial convergence zone, and the seasonal southward flow of anoxic shoal waters that excludes tunas for much of the year. Since the existing 120 or so vessels catching 200,000 tons of fish from the ETP could not profitably fish year-round, Sharp assumed that about 50 modern seine vessels of about 1,200 tons capacity might not get in each other's way or overfish the resource in this new fishery surrounding the Seychelles. Test fisheries were carried out for several years, with the pole-and-line fishery falling by the wayside for several reasons, while the seiners from both France and Spain found that they were economically successful. Then, all the test fishing was declared over, and all the foreign vessels told to depart the region. Soon thereafter, fifty tickets for access to the fishery were offered by the Seychelles, and the western Indian Ocean high-seas fishery began in earnest. Catches by the two dominant fleets have been different, but their trends are parallel, and as such the two data sets offer lots of information useful in both resource management and economic analyses. Sharp (1992) describes these differences, and compares these fisheries. Since the fishery opened in 1981, there have been few signs of true fishery-driven overexploitation, although catch rates fell for two seasons. These were correlated to the deepening of the thermocline over the region, due to El Niño–related phenomena, and once the thermoclines rebounded, the fishery catch rates went back to normal expectations.

The Seychellois decided not to invest in vessels, but they have made their economic benefits from providing the fishing fleets services, and selling tickets for access, simply because they were attentive when told that no modern seiner had yet paid for itself since the mid-1970s, due to fuel costs and other issues. This is a development success story. The second benefit from the development of this fishery was the shunting of fishing effort away from the West African fisheries, returning them to relative economic viability.

Aquaculture

The contemporary engineering solution for socially developed nations has been, "Let's grow fish in farms." Aquaculture was once perceived as a benign way to feed the world's population (Ryther and Bardoch 1968). Reality has turned out rather differently. These "put-and-take" fisheries require resources, too, such as huge amounts of lower-economic-value but still energy-intensive fishes for feed, and extreme examples of inefficiency are found in some aquaculture, such as for salmon (Folke 1988). The classic losses associated with aquaculture include denuding of previous mangrove forest–covered areas, resulting in related decreases in fish production by local artisanal subsistence fishermen. Beyond this, other devastating consequences affect cultural fishing communities. Closing the production loop in fish and shrimp culture is expensive and requires many resources, including protein-rich food sources and clean water resources. White spot shrimp disease has devastated many formerly rich aquaculture beds in, for example, Ecuador, leaving many useless holes in the mangroves. Today, over 50 percent of the Peruvian-Chilean catch of pelagic fisheries is sold for aquaculture feed, usually in the form of fishmeal. Both fishmeal production and transportation are energy-intensive processes. This makes the transformation of wild fish resources into food for another cultured species for human consumption even less efficient, although the next chapter suggests some other possible technologies. It seems that what is needed is more lucrative markets for direct human consumption of small pelagic fishes, suggesting that what is needed is analogous to Paul Prudhomme's promotion of "blackened redfish," a chef-driven effort to educate people on methods for preparations of these once-ignored species, perhaps by including fried sardines, or in the traditional and delightfully healthy Sicilian-styled baked breaded sardine/anchovy with tomato-garlic sauce. Tasteful solutions abound and could provide more efficient uses of these abundant fishes for human consumption.

When the energy and other costs of contemporary aquaculture are examined, it turns out that salmon aquaculture, for one, is less efficient than even extremely inefficient high-seas salmon trolling (Folke, Kautsky, and Troell 1994). Pauly reviewed the ecological trends within the cultured fish industry and found that unlike the "fishing down the trophic chain" observed in ocean fisheries industries around the world (Pauly et al. 1998), the increases in fish culture, particularly salmon culture, has resulted in a net "fishing up the food chain," in which the protein demands for feed fishes used within these activities has escalated, supplanting the previous trends toward vegetable or alga-based feeds, common in tilapia and catfish culture, that at one time dominated the industry. Effluents of fish farms and fish feeding pens are often quite rich in unutilized protein and metabolic wastes creating pollution that is both wasteful and dangerous. The coastlines of Southeast Asia, China, and Japan are lined with pen-aquaculture sites, and due to the historical lack of concern, much of the near-shore environment has become toxic, anoxic, and fraught with dangerous microbes. There are many other aspects to aquaculture, some that seem to have fewer environmental impacts, which are considered in the next chapter.

Overcapitalization

Probably the principal way that markets generate poor signals for fisheries management—and inefficiency in the use of economic resources—is in the never-ending problem of overcapitalization, also known as excessive (catching) capacity. Excess capacity can result from market signals or poor planning or sometimes also from agency efforts to be overly equitable in implementation of regulations.

The most general case occurs because fishing on an unexploited stock can be extremely profitable. There are many examples of fishing boats returning with $50,000 or $100,000 worth of fish in the hold. Other fishermen or potential fishermen observe that, and the rush to copy the success of the first fisherman is on. A 350-ton-capacity boat might cost upwards of $4 million to build and outfit, so the investment looks very good, especially since federal subsidies were readily available through the 1960 Federal Fishing Vessel Construction Subsidies and Commercial Fisheries Research and Development Act (which made grants to states) as a result of the Stratton Commission's findings. Some examples of this include the early years of the redfish (ocean perch)

fishery off Massachusetts (Campbell 1996), as well as the U. S. tuna seine fleet subsidies that started the "Gold Rush" over high-seas tuna fisheries. All of this was part and parcel of the EEZ deliberations, as undeveloped nations began to plan their participation and began to reap benefits from open-ocean fisheries. One bad result was that in many cases, national governments tended to favor outside investors' fishing ventures in their EEZ's resources over those of their own small-scale and subsistence fishing communities, leading to considerable social distresses. The most recent example is that of Norway's building the largest factory trawler ever, for Irish investors, to be used off West Africa, supposedly to provide fish to markets in those nations in whose EEZs they operated. What about those hundreds to thousands of local subsistence fishermen that will be displaced, or whose resources will be decimated?

Who Wins?

A related phenomenon, perhaps the most general problem leading to overcapitalization, is that when climatic or oceanographic conditions are just right, fish can respond with an extremely strong year class or even a series of them. Fishermen and their backers rush to build boats to take advantage of the abundant fish, but by the time the boats are built the large year class or classes may have been caught—or even have died of old age. The investors in the boats obviously want to get a return on their investment and tend to overfish any remaining fish, including other, smaller year classes, or other less abundant species. It is a recipe for disaster, repeated again and again. More generally, patterns of species abundances shift with the ocean climate. Examples are found in May et al. (1979), Cushing (1982), Sharp and Csirke (1983), Caddy and Sharp (1986), Carpenter et al. (1994), Alverson et al. (1994), Beamish (1995), and Sharp (1995, 1996, 1997).

There has been a recent focus on El Niño and related processes, but the southern oscillation (ENSO) is only one of a suite of environmental patterns that affect marine ecosystems and fish stocks. Durand et al. (1998) undertook extensive research into the causal forcing factors within very noisy ecosystems. Scheffer at al. (2001) describe potential ecosystem perturbations in locations that have reduced resilience due to various causes. We should also by now understand that in natural systems, production-modifying events are not reliably predictable from month to month or year to year, given only catch/landing data to work with, nor are the results even somewhat stable beyond a decade or two for most systems for which we do have records. This issue, and the solution, has been thoroughly described in the recent literature on fisheries forecasts (Klyashtorin 2001; Sharp 2003). Given the conventional wisdom and methods used to manage fisheries, the transition periods between epochs that support different species groups in many ecosystems are not accounted for, causing the mismanagement of both declining and pre-bloom species. Careful tracking of both biological and environmental indicators would definitely improve both resource and market management. Removing the market-based incentives that tend to result in delaying or eliminating the necessary management responses to uncertainty or even clear indicators when they are available is an absolute necessity if aquatic resources are to be sustained and fishing cultures maintained.

The basic message from our perspective is that the market, which in theory sends good signals to investors, in fact generally sends exactly the wrong messages because of the lag time that is of necessity involved. So we too often have yet another classic case of market failure.

Economics

What does economics, as a profession, have to say about these things? Well, of course, that depends upon whom you ask, but probably most economists would agree that at least the perverse, counterproductive subsidies should be eliminated. The lotto-like "I can make it Big Time!" motivations add to the persistent overexploitation-related activities. There would probably be less unanimity about whether whatever free markets that remain should be allowed to determine the level of any fishery. Next we consider how economics, or something akin to it, might be used to ameliorate many if not all the problems described here.

Externalities

All economists are aware of what are called market failures (or perhaps more euphemistically "externalities") where there are real costs of some economic process that are not included in the market price. For example, there is often massive destruction to nontarget species ("by-catch"), which are simply shoveled over the side dead while the economically valuable species, which may be far less in biomass, are cleaned and put into the freezer. Likewise, externalities of other economic activities can affect fisheries. For example, Kawasaki (1983, 1991) and Sharp (1988) point out that at any one 25–30-year period about half of any region's ocean species catches are going up, while the other half of the species are in decline. This is notable even in the top twelve of the world's major fisheries (Klyashtorin 1998, 2001). Is this all due to fisheries? Not likely. But the combination of overzealous fishing along with quasi-cyclical environmental processes that cause some species to have lower recruitment while another group is on the rise can place both in vulnerable situations if fishing effort is not controlled.

We have also barely begun to understand or take into account yet what our responsibilities might be from the perspective of sustaining the functions of aquatic ecosystems. For example, governments and developers facilitate gross manipulation of rivers, lowlands, and wetlands to accommodate agricultural and urban expansion and quick profit-taking schemes over much of the world. This has created mixed blessings ranging from general access to the world's resources and social technologies (e.g., electricity, metal refineries, appliances, indoor plumbing) to virtual disasters for localized eco-dependent species. The ongoing saga of the systematic disappearance of salmon races of the northwestern United States provides adequate examples (Pearcy 1992). We have learned to engineer solutions to many problems in nature, often without adequate regard for the long-term consequences. Most of the manipulations of the world's waterways were done before there was any significant level of environmental awareness, or before records were kept. We may never really know all that has been lost in either the Old or the New World as humans diverted, dredged, and dammed, in efforts to cope with both population growth and natural drought and flood cycles.

Conclusions

We have found in our review of the literature that although other factors, such as inadequate conceptual management models (Larkin 1977; Hall 1988; Downing and Plante 1993), may bring about the demise of fishing populations, unregulated economic activity (and the justification of that activity through the discipline of economics) is sufficient by itself to provide the destruction of many fisheries, either by itself or through exacerbating other causes. This conclusion appears to be reached increasingly by others for fisheries in the developing world (Thorpe, Ibarra, and Reid 2000). Thus we conclude that the "efficiency" that is supposed to occur from the (relatively unregulated) market involved does not in fact occur, and in fact tends to lead to great inefficiency by contributing to the destruction of the resource base.

Is Economics Adequate to the Task?

We believe it extremely important for fisheries scientists to understand the basic underlying problems with the use of what we consider conventional (meaning, essentially, neoclassical) economics. While it is well understood by economists (and of course resource managers) that standard economics does not include the entire cost of producing most commodities in its market price (which relates what people are willing to pay for something with its cost of extracting or producing it), few scientists are aware of the much-deeper problems encountered. These topics have been reviewed and these problems identified and developed much more thoroughly in other publications (Hall 1992, 2000a, 2000b; Hall et al. 2001).

Alternatives to Neoclassical Economics

The first alternative to neoclassical economics is that of ecological economics, as represented by the contents of the journal by that name. While this journal contains many excellent articles, it is not necessarily the alternative we seek, because the majority of the articles are written by economists using traditional economic tools to address problems of the environment including, occasionally, the valuing of wildlife.

The second is that of "sustainable development." Sustainable development again is not an explicit challenge to neoclassical economics but a diverse series of perspectives and plans whose objectives are to hold the cake of undiminished resources (including fish) and enjoy the eating of it too—by definition, development. An important perspective is that "sustainable development" policies rarely examine their objectives in terms of, for example, the nonrenewable fossil fuels that would be required to carry out their sustainable recommendations. Sustainable development means at least three different, often incompatible things to the economists, sociologists, and environmentalists who use the term (Goodland and Daly 1996). A comprehensive analysis for Costa Rica is given in Hall 2000.

The third alternative available at this time is that of "biophysical economics." Biophysical economics attempts to understand real economic systems from a biophysical rather than a social perspective, focusing on the land, energy, and materials required for economic production. Whereas more traditional economics has tended to focus on the importance of human ingenuity for increasing economic production, biophysical economics has tended to focus on the energy and other resources that must be increasingly exploited for additional production to take place (see Cleveland et al. 1984; Ko, Hall, and Lemus 1998). That is the approach we seek for developing a future economics that would be adequate to the task of managing our precious fish. We must start from the perspective of what the real productivity of the resource is, and unlike the Argentine hake case, we must stay inside that. Second, we need to remove subsidies to fishing boats. Third, we need to examine ways of making fishing more labor-intensive and less fuel-intensive, especially with the possibility of increases in fuel prices. Finally, we must simply reduce fishing pressures, let stocks rebuild, then focus on sustainable fisheries. How we can do this in an unregulated market economy we cannot answer.

References

Alverson, D. L., M. H. Freeberg, S. A. Murawski, and J. G. Pope. 1994. A global assessment of fisheries bycatch and discards. FAO Fisheries Technical Paper 339.

Atkinson, L. C. 1982. *Economics*. Homewood, Ill.: Irwin.

Barnett, H. J., and C. Morse. 1963. *Scarcity and Growth: The Economics of Natural Resources Availability*. Baltimore: Johns Hopkins University Press.

Beamish, R. J., ed. 1995. Climate change and northern fish populations. Canadian Special Publication of Canadian Fisheries and Aquatic Sciences 121.

Berkeley, S. 2001. ICCAT: A case study from the Atlantic. In K. Hinman, ed., *Getting Ahead of the Curve: Conserving the Pacific Ocean Tunas, Billfishes, and Sharks*, 31–40. Leesburg, Va.: National Coalition for Marine Conservation.

Berkes, F., R. Mahon, P. McConney, R. Pollnac, and R. Pomeroy. 2001. *Managing Small-scale Fisheries: Alternative Directions and Methods*. Ottawa: International Development Research Centre.

Block, B., S. L. H. Teo, A. Walli, A. Boustany, M. J. W. Stokesbury, C. J. Farwell, K. C. Weng, H. Dewar, and T. D. Williams. 2005. Electronic tagging and population structure of Atlantic bluefin tuna. *Nature* 434: 1121–27.

Brown, S., and A. E. Lugo. 1981. *Management and Status of U.S. Commercial Marine Fisheries*. Washington, D.C.: Council of Environmental Quality.

Caddy, J. F., and G. D. Sharp 1986. An ecological framework for marine fishery investigations. FAO Fisheries Technical Paper 283.

Campbell, D. 1996. Redfish. In C. A. S. Hall, ed., *Maximum Power: The Theories and Applications of H. T. Odum*, 311–30. Niwot: University Press of Colorado.

Carpenter, S., T. M. Frost, A. R. Ives, J. F. Kitchell, and T. K. Krantz. 1994. Complexity, cascades and compensation in ecosystems. In K. Yasumo and M. Watanabe, eds., *Biodiversity: Its Complexity and Role*, 197–207. Tokyo: Global Environmental Forum.

Clark, C. 1973. Profit maximization and the extinction of animal species. *Journal of Political Economy* 81:950–61.

Clark, C. W. 1973. *Mathematical Bioeconomics: Environmental Problems*. New York: Oxford University Press.

Cleveland, C., R. Costanza, C. Hall, and R. Kaufmann. 1984. Energy and the United States economy: A biophysical perspective. *Science* 225:890–97.

Cushing, D. H. 1982. *Climate and Fisheries*. London: Academic Press.

Daily, G. C. 1997. *Nature's Services*. Washington, D.C.: Island Press.

Daly, H. E. 1977. *Steady-state Economics*. San Francisco: W. H. Freeman.

Downing, J., and C. Plante. 1993. Production of fish populations in lakes. *Canadian Journal of Aquatic Science* 50:110–20.

Dung, T. H. 1992. Consumption, production, and technological progress: A unified entropic approach. *Ecological Economics* 6:95–210.

Durand, M. H., P. Cury, R. Mendelssohn, C. Roy, A. Bakun, and D. Pauly, eds. 1998. *Global Versus Local Changes in Upwelling Systems*. Paris: Éditions de l'Orstom.

Ehrlich, P., A. Ehrlich, and J. P. Holdren. 1977. *Ecoscience: Population, Resource, Environment*. San Francisco: W. H. Freeman.

FAO. Various years. Biannual State of World Fisheries and Aquaculture Reports.

Folke, C. 1988. Energy economy of salmon aquaculture in the Baltic Sea. *Environmental Management* 12:525–37.

Folke, C., N. Kautsky, and M. Troell. 1994. The costs of eutrophication from salmon farming: Implications for policy. Journal of Environmental Management 40, no. 73: 182.

Friedman, M. 1953. *Essays in Positive Economics*. Chicago: University of Chicago Press.

Garcia, S. and R. Grainger. 1997. Fisheries management and sustainability: A new perspective of an old problem? In Hancock et al. 1997, 631–54.

Goodland, R., and H. Daly. 1996. Environmental sustainability: Universal and non-negotiable. *Ecological Applications* 6, no. 4: 1002–17.

Hall, C. A. S. 1998. An evaluation of several of the most important theoretical models in ecology and of the data used in their support. *Ecological Modeling* 43:5–31.

———. 1990. Sanctioning resource depletion: Economic development and neoclassical economies. *The Ecologist* 20:99–104.

———. 1992a. Economic development or developing economics: What are our priorities? In M. Wali, ed., *Ecosystem Rehabilitation*, 1:101–26. The Hague: SPB.

———. 1992b. An idiosyncratic assessment of the role of mathematical models in environmental sciences. *Environment International* 17:507–17.

Hall, C. A. S., and M. Hall. 1993. The efficiency of land and energy use in tropical economies and agriculture. *Agriculture, Ecosystems and Environment* 46:1–30.

Hall, C. A. S., 1991. Sanctioning resource depletion: Economic development and neo-classical economics. *The Ecologist* 20:61–66.

Hall, C. A. S., C. J. Cleveland, and R. K. Kaufmann. 1986. *Energy and Resource Quality: The Ecology of the Economic Process*. New York: Wiley-Interscience.

Hampton, J., J. R. Sibert, P. Kleiber, M. N. Maunder, and S. J. Harley. 2003. Comments on Myers and Worm. *Nature* 434 (28 April 2005).

Hancock, D. A., D. C. Smith, A. Grant, and J. P. Beumer, eds. 1997. *Developing and Sustaining World Fisheries Resources: The State of Science and Management*. Collingwood, Australia: CSIRO.

Kawasaki, T. 1983. Why do some fishes have wide fluctuations in their number? A biological basis of fluctuation from the viewpoint of evolutionary ecology. In Sharp and Csirke 1983, 1065–80.

Kawasaki, T., S. Tanaka, Y. Toba, and A. Taniguchi, eds. 1991. *Long-Term Variability of Pelagic Fish Populations and Their Environment*. Tokyo: Pergamon Press.

Klyashtorin, L. B. 1998. Long-term climate change and main commercial fish production in the Atlantic and Pacific. *Fisheries Research* 37:115–25.

———. 2001. Climate change and long term fluctuations of commercial catches: The possibility of forecasting. FAO Fisheries Technical Paper 410. Rome: FAO.

Ko, Y-Y, C. A. S. Hall, and L. L. Lemus. 1998. Resource use rates and efficiency as indicators of regional sustainability: An examination of five countries. *Environmental Monitoring and Assessment* 51:571–93.

Larkin, P. 1977. An epitaph for the concept of maximum sustained yield. *Transactions of the American Fisheries Society* 106:1–11.

Love, M. S., M. Yoklavich, and L. Thorstein. 2002. *The Rockfishes of the Northeast Pacific*. Berkeley: University of California Press.

Ludwig, D., R. Hilborn, and C. J. Walters. 1993. Uncertainty, resource exploitation, and conservation: Lessons from history. *Science* 260:17–36.

Mather, F. J., III. 1974. The bluefin tuna situation. In *Sixteenth Annual International Gamefish Research Conference*, 93–106. Woods Hole, Mass.: Woods Hole Oceanographic Institution.

Mather, F. J., III, J. M. Mason Jr., and A. C. Jones. 1995. Historical document: Life history and fisheries of Atlantic bluefin tuna. NOAA Technical Memorandum NMFS-SEFSC-370.

May, R., J. R. Beddington, C. W. Clark, S. J. Holt, and R. M. Laws. 1979. Management of multispecies fisheries. *Science* 205:267–77.

Myers, N., and J. Kent. 2001. *Perverse Subsidies: How Misused Tax Dollars Harm the Environment and the Economy*. Washington, D.C.: Island Press.

Myers, R. A., and B. Worm. 2003. Rapid worldwide depletion of predatory fish communities. *Nature* 423:280–83.

Naylor, R. L., J. Eagle, and W. L. Smith. 2003. Salmon aquaculture in the Pacific Northwest: A global industry with local impacts. *Environment* 45, no. 8: 18–39.

NMFS. 1999. Our living oceans: Report on the status of U.S. living marine resources, 1999. NOAA Tech. Memo. NMFS-F/SPO-41.

———. 2001. Status of fisheries of the United States. NOAA Report.

NOAA. 2000. Status of the fishery resources off the northeastern United States. Resource Evaluation and Assessment Division Northeast Fisheries Science Center, Technical Memorandum NMFS-NE-115.

Pauly, D., V. Christensen, J. Dalsgaard, R. Froese, and F. Torres Jr. 1998. Fishing down marine food webs. *Science* 229:860–62.

Pauly, D., V. Christensen, S. Guénette, T. J. Pitcher, U. R. Sumaila, C. J. Walters, R. Watson, and D. Zeller, Towards Sustainability in World Fisheries. *Nature* 418:689–695.

Pearcy, W. G. 1992. *Ocean Ecology of North Pacific Salmonids*. Seattle: University of Washington Press.

Pikitch, E. K., D. D. Huppert, M. P. Sissenwine, and M. Duke. 1997. An overview of trends in fisheries, fisheries science and management. In E. K. Pikitch, D. D. Huppert, and M. P. Sissenwine, eds., *Global Trends: Fisheries Management*, 275–78. Bethesda, Md.: American Fisheries Society.

Rawitscher, M., and J. Mayer. 1977. Nutritional outputs and energy inputs in seafoods. *Science* 198:261–64.

Ryther, J. H., and J. E. Bardoch. The status and potential of aquaculture. Clearinghouse for Scientific and Technical Information PB 177-767.

Scheffer, M., S. R. Carpenter, J. Foley, C. Folke, and B. Walker. 2001. Stochastic events can trigger large state shifts in ecosystems with reduced resilience. *Nature* 413: 591–96.

Sharp, G. D. 1979. Areas of potentially successful exploitation of tunas in the Indian Ocean with emphasis on surface methods. Indian Ocean Programme Technical Reports IOFC/DEV/79/47, FAO.

———. 1987. Climate and Fisheries: Cause and effect or managing the long and short of it all. *South African Journal of Marine Sciences* 5:811–38.

————. 1988. Fish populations and fisheries: Their perturbations, natural and man induced. In H. Postma and J. J. Zijlstra, eds., *Ecosystems of the World* 27:155–202. Amsterdam: Elsevier.

————. 1991. Climate and fisheries: Cause and effect—a system review. In T. Kawasaki et al., *Long-term Variability of Pelagic Fish Populations and Their Environment*, 239–58.

————. 1992a. Fishery catch records, ENSO, and longer term climate change as inferred from fish remains from marine sediments. In H. Diaz and V. Markgraf, eds., *Paleoclimatology of El Niño: Southern Oscillation*, 379–417. Cambridge: Cambridge University Press.

————1992b. Climate change, the Indian Ocean tuna fishery, and empiricism. In M. H. Glantz, ed., *Climate Variability, Climate Change and Fisheries*, 377–416. Cambridge: Cambridge University Press.

————. 1995. It's about time: New beginnings and old good ideas in fisheries science. *Fisheries Oceanography* 4, no. 4: 324–41.

————. 1997. It's about time: Rethinking fisheries management. In Hancock et al. 1997, 731–36.

————. 2003. Future climate change and regional fisheries: A collaborative analysis. Fisheries Technical Report, FAO.

Sharp, G. D., and J. Csirke, eds. 1983. *Proceedings of the Expert Consultation to Examine the Changes in Abundance and Species Composition of Neritic Fish Resources*. Rome: FAO.

Sheldon, R. W., and T. R. Parsons. 1967. A continuous size spectrum for particulate matter in the sea. *Journal of the Fisheries Research Board of Canada* 24:909–15.

Sheldon, R. W., A. Prakash, and W. H. Sutcliffe Jr. 1972. The size distribution of particles in the ocean. *Limnology and Oceanography* 17:327–40.

Sheldon, R. W., W. H. Sutcliffe Jr., and M. A. Paranjape. 1977. The structure of the pelagic food chain and the relationship between plankton and fish production. *Journal of the Fisheries Research Board of Canada* 34:2344–53.

Silvert, W. 1988. Generic models of continental shelf ecosystems. *Proceedings of the Ecodynamics Workshop on Theoretical Ecology*, October 1987.

Silvert, W., and T. Platt. 1978. Energy flux in the pelagic ecosystem: A time-dependent equation. *Limnology and Oceanography* 23:813–16.

————. 1980. Dynamic energy-flow model of the particle size distribution in pelagic ecosystems. In W. C. Kerfoot, ed., *Evolution and Ecology of Zooplankton Communities*, 754–63. Hanover, N.H.: University Press of New England.

Thorpe, A., A. A. Ibarra, and C. Reid. 2000. The new economic model and marine fisheries in Latin America. *World Development* 28:1689–1702.

CHAPTER 27

SHRIMP CULTURE IN LATIN AMERICA

An Economic Experiment out of Control,

and the Social Issues of High-tech Solutions

ROD MCNEIL

Introduction

Aquaculture grew rapidly in economic importance for many Latin and South American countries from 1978 to 1998. At least six countries in Latin and South America (Ecuador, Nicaragua, Honduras, Belize, Guatemala, and Brazil) derived over a third of their annual export income from shrimp in the late 1990s. However, the entry of Taura syndrome virus (TSV) in 1989 and white spot syndrome virus (WSSV) from Asia in early 1999 created a series of severe economic issues that came close to bankrupting some countries; for example, the production of shrimp in Ecuador, once the largest shrimp aquaculture producer in the world, fell 75 percent in a single year. In countries such as Ecuador, the value of shrimp had been 52 percent of the total export value balance of trade in 1997, and the loss of 65 percent of the crop production precipitated default on International Monetary Fund (IMF) loans and the failure or closure of virtually every bank in the country (Rosenberry 2000).

A retrospective on the economics of the "shrimp disaster of 1999" (Clifford and Cook 2002) showed that while shrimp disease was the immediate trigger to economic failure of the industry in general and several countries, in particular, the root of the problem extended back over a decade to a foreign money policy that could be supported only if growth in the industry continued indefinitely, in a kind of biological Ponzi scheme. Even more revealing was the fact that the same economic outcome had been produced by the earlier TSV outbreak of 1989. The economic lessons that might have been learned from that were ignored

as developing countries moved toward globalized marketing of one of their principal exports.

Chief among the many economic problems that surfaced was that the IMF loans were made based on a series of unrealistic assumptions regarding the profitability of shrimp production. With the massive increase—7,600 percent between 1978 and 1989—in the monoculture of white shrimp (*Litopenaeus vannamei*), the world supply exceeded demand for shrimp, generating a commensurate and predictable decrease in average price (figure 27.1a). From 1989 to 1999, excessive production had decreased the value of the crop to the point where the interest on debt could not be serviced. This is quite similar to the situation with bananas discussed in chapter 9 and with many other commodities exported by developing countries, such as coffee and peanuts.

The TSV outbreak of 1989 reduced shrimp supplies and stabilized prices for a time. However, it ignored the decreased value margin in the white shrimp fisheries and the biological reasons for the increased likelihood of disease transmission. The IMF continued to loan money to "repair" the losses of the TSV outbreak. The land area involved in shrimp production trebled between 1990 and 1995, at great expense to the salt marsh areas and, to a lesser extent, to natural mangrove areas in the coastal zones of Latin America. The destruction of 35 percent of the mangrove areas (in Ecuador, Panama, Guatemala, Nicaragua, and Honduras) in a 20-year period reduced the production areas for wild shrimp and all but destroyed the small, but stable, shrimp trawl fishery that had been in existence for 150 years. A detailed study conducted by Auburn University has shown that roughly 30 percent of the mangrove forest destruction was directly attributable to shrimp farming development (Massaut 1999). Ecuador, for example, had lost 25 percent of its mangroves since 1970, with an annual deforestation rate of 0.78 percent.

By 1994, prices fell again as production again reached record levels, yet the debt service of the initial IMF loans made in the 1978–92 period remained fixed. By 1998, Ecuador was almost totally dependent on shrimp (20 percent of all Ecuadorian exports, with a record of $872 million) and oil (about 50 percent of all exports) as export products to bring foreign currency into the country, most of which had to go to service previous foreign debt. For every dollar of shrimp production added between 1990 and 1999, growers had to import some $0.68–0.72 worth of foreign goods, such as feed and construction equipment. Thus, the net foreign exchange gained was only about 30 percent of the gross! Shrimp reached an amazing 52 percent of the gross export value for the country (this percentage is related to the $1.6 billion of trade with United States only, not with the total Ecuadorian exports of $4.2 billion), yet the profitability of shrimp production to these countries, even from what had become the largest shrimp-producing export nation in the world, was inadequate to service even the interest on the international debt. The inability to service this debt led the IMF to decline further investment in supporting the Ecuadorian economy in 1998, forcing the closure of all banks and seizure of private assets on deposit to temporarily service the existing debt. This, in turn, eliminated further investment in shrimp farming, and those farms without their own hatcheries could not even afford to restock the farms in the fall of 1998. More than 140,000 jobs were lost in a period of only three months. Farmers who could afford to restock were literally reduced to eating their own crop to survive. By 2002, only 200 hatcheries were active, there were only about 126,000 remaining shrimp workers, and 175,000 ha of shrimp ponds had been abandoned, representing 60 percent of land used in 1998. The shrimp exports had dropped from the record of $872 million in 1998 to $280 million in 2001.

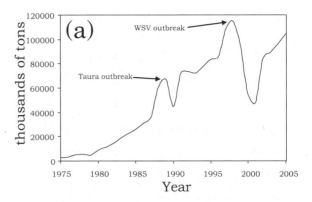

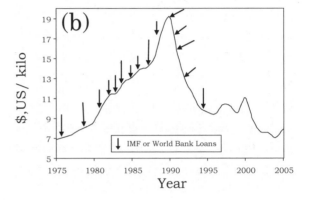

Figure 27.1. (a) Ecuadorian shrimp export production; (b) farm gate price history for Ecuadorian shrimp (21–25 count), prices as of September 30 of each year.

Unlike their response to the TSV, IMF, and WSSV economic disasters of the past, a newly emerging Ecuadorian industry is focused on solving the real biological/environmental problems that precipitated the disease outbreaks and is decoupling shrimp production from the more sensitive estuarine environments (by moving to environments such as salt flats or dry forest areas), by moving toward policies of decreased water exchange, and by increasing biosecurity. But in Ecuador, the salt flats were all occupied by 1995, and the attempt to use freshwater systems have met little success, even adding to the country's woes by generating salt contamination of groundwater supplies. Nevertheless, the implementation of these environmental policies by Latin and South American shrimp-producing countries has allowed the new generation of shrimp growers to recognize the true environmental costs of shrimp production and reduce the direct impact on the environment.

The new generation of shrimp growers in Ecuador certainly has increased biosecurity; however, the production costs have greatly increased for semi-intensive farms from about $6,000–$8,000/ha (1998) to $27,000/ha (2003). This increase in production costs has discouraged small and medium-size growers, so that only large enterprises can afford to continue in the business.

Sadly, this World Bank–sponsored fiasco in Ecuador, followed by IMF foreign investment rescue scenarios, has been repeated in Honduras, Nicaragua, and Panama, as well, in the last three decades. We will look at the shrimp industry and current developing measures, which place greater value and recognition on the true environmental costs of conducting business in a developing country, independent of outside investments focused on global markets. We also examine what the "blue revolution" has contributed and future prospects for better aquaculture technology.

The Cold War, Foreign Aid, and the Blue Revolution

The coastal zone of Ecuador is a rich, biologically productive environment, characterized by the largest estuary of western South America (the Guayas) with extensive mangrove forests and a tradition of artisanal fishing. Shrimp had been a "poor man's protein source" in Ecuador before 1975 (the start of the shrimp boom). Shrimp captured by surf nets, purse seines, scissor nets, and trawlers were used for barter within the country, to help provide a diversified diet. Less than 10 percent of the harvested crop was exported in 1975.

Beginning in 1957, both American and Russian aid began pouring into Central and South America. The two major powers were jockeying for political and economic control of the region. Ostensibly, the goal was the elimination of poverty and hunger, but the means of repayment for their economic development aid was in oil and other valuable natural resources available in abundance in these countries. In Venezuela and Ecuador, the ready abundance of significant oil reserves was particularly attractive to American interests. The reduction in transport costs and the high quality of the Maracaibo oil deposits made trade exchange especially valuable. What America and Russia had, in spades, was agricultural technology of every sort and kind. Through the USAID program, the World Bank, and Soviet programs, Ecuador amassed over $3.7 billion in debt at the highest interest rates of the century (7.5–11.4 percent) in the time period from 1957 to 1972, to begin building the mechanical infrastructure to recover and refine crude oil. This enormous debt looked quite serviceable given the high price of oil in the 1970s. The technological boom actually increased the dependence of these countries on the superpowers for supplies of replacement parts and hardware, unobtainable in the country where the technology was being used.

With the deflation of global oil prices in the Middle East in the early 1980s, the profit available from petroleum could not service the debt accrued, and Ecuador sought relief from the World Bank and the IMF to tide them over, beginning as early as 1974, only one year after the start of the oil crisis.

During the late 1960s and early 1970s a new environmental movement, initially promoted by Ralston Purina, known as the "blue revolution," seemed to hold enormous promise to increase protein supplies significantly through expansion of the science of aquaculture. Just as the green revolution, with improved plant genetics, new culture techniques, and more energy-intensive fertilizers, had more than doubled the available grain production in the 1960s, the hope was that major breakthroughs in aquaculture could increase protein supplies while reducing significantly the environmental pressures created by deforestation for the production of grazing space for cattle and hog production. A key focus of much of this development work began in 1972 and was initially carried out by Ralston Purina at Crystal River, Florida. A key development was the closure of the life cycle of *L. vannamei* and the development of shrimp feeds that allowed relatively efficient growth: feed conversion ratios—FCRs—of less than 2.0 kg of feed per kg of shrimp produced (note that the shrimp is wet weight and the feed is dry weight). Three types of shrimp culture evolved: extensive, semi-intensive, and intensive culture.

Extensive culture use captured wild postlarvae (shrimp larvae born in the wild and captured with scissor nets in the shallows) stocked in shoreline earthen ponds at a density of 5–10 postlarvae per square meter. Water exchange, provided by tidal exchange, amounts to 50–100m³/kg of shrimp production. No feed or aeration is provided. Ponds could be created on salt flats or in mangrove areas with nothing more than a shovel, a machete, and many hours of backbreaking work. Pond sizes vary from 0.5 to 10 hectares. After four months, the farmer places a net over the outlet as the tide is going out and collects what shrimp have survived during the four-month period. Capital investment in such systems was low or nonexistent. Typical yields were in the 0.06–0.5 tons per hectare/cycle. Unless the facility was close to the equator, seasonal temperature changes made more than one cycle a year unlikely. A family group or a group of one to five families would manage the extensive farm (typically 1–50 hectares), and the crops would be used to provide protein in their own diets and provide a valuable trade good for exchange in the local markets.

Semi-intensive culture uses wild captured postlarvae in earthen ponds at densities of 12–25 postlarvae per square meter. Water exchange is provided by fossil-fueled pumping stations or tidal exchange and amounts to 15–30 m³ water/kg of shrimp produced. Formulated feed must be added to support the shrimp production, in excess of the natural productivity of the environment. Under optimal conditions, these procedures can result in as much as 2.5 tons/hectare/cycle. Excavated ponds ranging in size from 4–20 hectares are used, sometimes at a short distance from the sea (1–10 kilometers). Enormous trenches are then constructed to conduct fresh seawater to the farm at high tide. The principle costs of operation included the formulated feed and the energy costs necessary to pump water from the sea into the ponds. In some semi-intensive operations, a commercial hatchery is used to rear the postlarvae used for stocking. Since growth with formulated feeds is somewhat faster, and postlarvae were available more of the year, it became more routine to achieve two growth cycles a year. A semi-intensive farm involves far more people, with construction

workers, hatchery operators, feed transport, and large-scale harvesting with shrimp processing in the local vicinity. Farms have ranged in size from 10 to 5,000 hectares and involve thousands of workers. Due to the relatively low capital investment and early success, semi-intensive culture techniques have produced the majority of environmental damage generated to the coastal areas and the majority of local employment.

In intensive culture, shrimp are stocked at densities of 40–120 per square meter. Formulated feeds and mechanical aeration are used to support the high production potential of the intensive farm. The required investment capital for such a farm is high, at $25,000–50,000/ha for all infrastructure. Water consumption can be lower and more money is spent on recycling water. Typical water exchange rates are in the 4–10 tons/kilo of shrimp produced. With outputs of 5–12 tons of shrimp per hectare per cycle, effective harvest can be prodigious and the potential for large-scale commercial trade realized easily. In the 1970s, the power consumption of such a farm, including hatchery operations, could easily reach 20 KW/ha. Intensive farms almost always have their own hatchery. Typical intensive shrimp farms use only 20–80 hectares of land, so high is their productivity.

Efficient Shrimp Technology Development

In the beginning, before huge international loans and debt, or the international spread of shrimp diseases, shrimp was an important source of high-quality protein for the common man and represented the best of "poor man's protein." While it takes seven kilos of grain to produce a kilo of beef or four kilos of grain to produce a kilo of pork, it only takes 1.4 kilos of grain to produce a kilo of shrimp (Hall, Cleveland, and Kaufman 1986).

The use of specific, high-growth, genetically defined strains of *L. vannamei* has resulted in much faster growth and more consistent feed consumption. Average growth rates increased from 0.74 grams per week in 1998 to over 1.4 grams per week in 2005. Significant improvements in the understanding of shrimp nutrition produced feeds that have reduced FCRs from 2.0 in 1995 to 1.4

in 2005. This improvement in feed utilization has reduced the accumulation of organic wastes dramatically during the growth cycle as well. Water is no longer discharged directly to a receiving estuary or drainage canal but to a settlement lagoon, many of which are operated like waste treatment plants, reducing the oxygen load demand by 90–95 percent.

Recent significant changes in shrimp feed formulations have reduced fishmeal use by at least 50 percent. One of the principle NGO objections to shrimp culture is the use of more fish meal than is generated in shrimp production. In 1999, it took 1.2–1.5 kilos of fishmeal to generate a kilo of shrimp, but movement toward microbial-dominated systems has nitrogen-fixing bacteria "upgrading" the protein value of the system from 18–22 percent protein, from principally grain resources, to 37–44 percent in microbial flocs that are directly consumed by benthic detrital shrimp species (McNeil 2000).

The Beginning of the "Borrowing Your Way out of Debt" Era

In 1974 the IMF proposed shrimp culture as a means of exporting a high-value crop into the very markets where debt relief was needed, and the program was enthusiastically adopted in Ecuador. This model was a semi-intensive one, which entailed the use of shallow ponds varying in size from 4 to 20 hectares and typical farm sizes in the 200–600-hectare range for economy of scale. Characteristically, these ponds were carved out of the natural coastal salt flats and mangrove forests. What the IMF did not tell its new client was that the same "shrimp solution" was being proposed throughout Central and South America.

Although a stable, but poor, artisanal shrimp fishery had existed in Ecuador for hundreds of years, with no impact on the environment other than to the shrimp themselves, the new plan required direct access to ocean waters and a lot of land to achieve its goals. The initial goal was to clear some 12,000 hectares of mangroves and salt flats for the development of 1,000 ponds of 7–12 hectares in size, rearing 5–12 shrimp per square meter. Assuming 60 percent survival, this area was capable of producing over 17,000 tons of shrimp

each year, worth over $400 million. Suddenly, the accrued debt burden didn't look so bad, and the Ecuadorian government accepted a massive IMF funding package, worth $520 million, over a four-year period (1974–78). Mangrove forests disappeared overnight, with the government's blessing. Unfortunately for the environment, the program was initially hugely successful, generating the expected income. The program was expanded yearly, using another $1.87 billion from the World Bank between 1978 and 1989, at which point over 60,000 hectares of mangrove had been removed. The resulting pond area of 72,000 hectares generated over $2.2 billion annually by 1989. By 1985 over 90 percent of the crop was being exported to satisfy the developers' need for more foreign capital and, to a limited extent, service the debt of the oil and shrimp aid programs of the previous twenty years.

What the IMF and World Bank apparently had not adequately considered, despite its deep understanding of macroeconomic issues, was that by proposing the same economic repayment plan for all the countries in Central and South America, the volume of shrimp involved would become enormous. Some of these programs came into being later, but by 1985, eight countries (Ecuador, Venezuela, Colombia, Costa Rica, Panama, Nicaragua, Honduras, and Belize) in the region had shrimp programs funded by IMF. The funding and shrimp programs were known as the "white gold" program. In Ecuador alone, by 1985, the shrimp industry employed 150,000 workers in all aspects of shrimp farming and export. The value of this crop had risen from roughly $1.50 per kilo in 1957 to over $19 a kilo in 1985, and the average Ecuadorian could certainly no longer afford to consume the "rich man's delicacy" produced in his own backyard, inasmuch as 90 percent of the aquaculture production was for export.

But what was not to like in this new "white gold" program? It did generate enormous sums of money in a very short period, utilizing natural resources that are "wasted space" (a common perspective on estuaries). Those who could wrestle shrimp farm permits from the willing government hands could expect to be millionaires within five years in a country where the average annual income was less than $800 in 1980.

Environmental Input

The Guayas River Basin was a natural nursery for the species of interest (*L. vannamei*). A single berried (gravid) female captured in the wild could generate 500,000 offspring and stock 3–4 hectares of ponds, and shrimp farming created a lucrative market for artisanal fishermen: they changed their activities from catching wild stocks for consumption, to selective recovery of gravid females, as well as capturing postlarvae in the shallows, along the margins of mangrove estuaries. An extremely destructive process, the collection of wild shrimp postlarvae destroyed huge quantities of the larval stage of other mangrove forest species. Studies conducted in the 1990s showed that the number of shrimp in wild artisanal collection was less than 9 percent of the total collected. The remaining bycatch was discarded, destroying much of the future stocks of the other species that used the mangrove forests. The few fishermen who tried to continue harvesting wild shrimp found their numbers falling precipitously, and the average size of gravid females in the wild fell from over 100 grams in 1978 to 55 grams in 1985. In a period of less than ten years, half of the artisanal fishermen gave up and went to work on the shrimp farms or processing sheds to earn an income (Browdy and Hopkins 1995). In Ecuador, according to the Instituto Nacional de Pesca (National Fishery Institute), wild shrimp fisheries declined from 4.1 million pounds per year in 1998 to 1.9 million per year in 2002.

Another profound effect of the enormous shrimp industry was the cyclical release of large quantities of concentrated organic wastes during harvest. If these loads could have been released slowly over the length of the growth cycle, perhaps the damage would not have been as great. However, the standard practice in semi-intensive culture in the 1980s and 1990s was to exchange 5–20 percent of the water daily and allow organic waste to accumulate in the pond throughout the entire cycle. Then, at harvest, all the organic waste was flushed into the surrounding estuaries. A five-hectare pond would dump seven to ten tons of high biochemical oxygen demand (BOD) waste into the rivers or discharge streams, sometimes killing everything for miles downstream on its way to the ocean. Since all the farms were harvested at about the same time, once or twice a year, for a period of a month, the receiving aquatic environments were completely altered. This huge bolus of waste would deplete the oxygen upon entering the estuaries, killing much of what was left fighting for survival, in what remained of the mangroves (Avnemelich 2001).

Additionally, numerous other species whose early life stages involve mangrove-dominated estuaries began to disappear. It was becoming increasingly difficult for subsistence survival for the human population living in the littoral regions, and there was a growing awareness that there was something really wrong with the environment where shrimp mariculture was undertaken. But greed is a powerful incentive in the human population, and environmental-balance issues were ignored, while the area of shrimp production area expansion at 30 percent per year continued.

Ironically, the acidity of the soils in mangrove swamps makes shrimp culture difficult there, unless massive amounts of lime are added to the soil after every cycle. Those farmers who prepared ponds on open salt flats had production space that was twice as productive, on average, as ponds prepared from mangrove soils. Fortunately, this lesson was taken to heart, and much of the development after 1992 did not inflict as much damage on mangrove areas, which are much more important as natural nursery areas than the salt flats.

Today, the Ecuadorian government and the shrimp growers of Ecuador have adopted a Code of Practice for Responsible Shrimp Farming, which has stopped many of the destructive practices of the previous two decades. The rate of farm expansion and the number of farms are dwindling as pressures from the globalization of white shrimp production caused a 50 percent price drop in the period from 1998 to 2005. The average farm size dropped from 600 hectares to around 140 hectares, but the old, worn-out, or abandoned farms of the coastal zone still remain. Much of the damage will take millions of more dollars and much time to restore. Where will the money come from to restore the environment?

Socially, the shrimp industry generated ambiguous outcomes. Many thousands of families were displaced from the mangroves and estuarine fishing grounds where they had traditionally made their living. "Gulf pirates," armed people who steal shrimp production in the transportation process between shrimp farms and packing plants, were a social problem during the 1990s. The economic benefits to the national welfare flowed primarily to farm owners and the wealthy, a situation that has not changed. The local people and *comuneros* living around the shrimp farms have not improved their living conditions.

Outbreak of Disease in Shrimp Mariculture

Then, in 1989, a new disease spread like wildfire throughout Ecuador in less than six months. The Taura (TSV) outbreak destroyed 35 percent of the adult shrimp population, and suddenly shrimp mariculture didn't look as profitable. For the small farmer with less than a hundred hectares of ponds, the result was economic ruin, with over half the farms being abandoned with no environmental reconstruction or remediation. Over time, erosion, the mangroves, and the jungle would reclaim seventy-five thousand hectares of land stripped between 1972 and 1985, for the sake of short-term shrimp production.

In 1992, the Ecuadorian industry began to rebuild, but now shrimp survivals were lower and growth cycles longer, due to the endemic presence of TSV and another virus, IHHN (infectious hypodermal and hematopoietic necrosis). Biosecurity was next to impossible due to the scale of the farms and the size of individual ponds. TSV had numerous transmission vectors, through other crustaceans or bird feces, and the proximity of the farms to the shoreline allowed transmission vectors such as crabs to reintroduce the disease back into the ponds. Average postlarvae to harvest survivals dropped from 80–85 percent prior to TSV to 40–55 percent after the disease became endemic. Efforts on the part of national researchers to develop TSV-resistant strains gradually gained

ground over a five-year period and by 1995, survivals were up to 70–75 percent. Production reached its peak in 1998, when total production space reached 180,000 hectares and the annual crop was 253,000 tons of shrimp exported for $1.98 billion (Rosenberry 2000). Unfortunately, to achieve this level of expansion and continue to expand its oil production capacity, Ecuador had borrowed another $12.4 billion from 1963 to 1998, and the debt service alone was almost $2 billion annually (figure 27.2). Note the correlation between the timing of IMF and WB loans in figure 27.1b versus the ability to service debt. With each leveling off in the debt service, in 1978–85 and 1994–96, the number and size of loans doubled. The debt service alone equaled the GDP of Ecuador by the year 1997 (Hemmings 2003). With the decrease in oil and shrimp prices, the increase in oil recovery costs, and the "failure" of the shrimp industry to support even the interest on foreign debt, the country was waiting for the ax to fall. By 1998, Ecuador was the largest shrimp producer in the world and yet the country could not enjoy its success. Prices of shrimp had fallen 35 percent due to oversupply, the net gain of foreign exchange was less and less over time, and the worst was yet to come.

In 1999 Mexico reported an outbreak of an Asian-based shrimp disease to which white shrimp had little or no resistance, the white spot virus (WSV). This deadly disease produced 70–100 percent mortality in the recipient population and was spread by birds, copepods, and crustaceans, at an almost unbelievable rate (50–60 miles a day), throughout the Pacific coastal region of Central and South America. The disease reached from northern Mexico to Guayaquil, Ecuador, in less than eight months. Retrospective genetic research by the University of Arizona has carefully documented the spread of the disease and its point of origin (Lightner 2002). Researchers from the Insituto Nacional de Pesca recognized that in many cases, the quarantine in the imported larvae was not respected.

The disease all but wiped out the wild shrimp and with it the wild postlarval hatchery industry, which supplied 90 percent of all postlarvae to the Ecuadorian shrimp industry. A few hatcheries,

Foreign debt and debt interest in
Ecuador 1963-2003

Figure 27.2. Foreign debt and debt interest in Ecuador, 1963–2003. Boxes represent leveling of debt service.

which had some level of biosecurity (i.e., freedom from pathogen) and were working on developing specific pathogen free (SPF) lines, were able to produce a fraction of what was needed, but charged three times what they had only six months before. Overnight, 65 percent of the industry shut down and total production in 2000 dropped to only a quarter of what it had been the year before.

With the tremendous decrease in export monies and debt increasing at 100 million a month, Ecuador defaulted on its Brady bond interest (the instrument of debt service to the earlier World Bank and IMF loans) in 1999, and the IMF withdrew from discussion of debt deferment. Ecuador closed its banks, 23 percent of which failed in a six-month period of 1999, and seized all assets on deposit. Owners could access and withdraw only 5 percent of their deposits monthly until the crisis passed.

In the Ecuadorian shrimp industry, total production from September 2002 to September 2003 was only 89,000 tons (as compared with 253,000 tons in 1998), and the value of shrimp was at a ten-year low ($12.60 a kilo for 21–25 shrimp per pound). Ecuador fell from the largest producer of shrimp in the world to fifth place, with China, Thailand, Vietnam, and India entering the white shrimp industry after 1999 and exceeding Ecuadorian production significantly. In 2002, Ecuador's current foreign debt stood at $13.4 billion, with an

annual interest debt service of 2.31 billion, which was equal to 117 percent of the GDP. Roughly half of this foreign debt ($7.14 billion) was created by development loans from IMF and the World Bank in a thirty-five-year period from 1963 to 1999 (Traa 2003). A quarter of this money was used specifically for shrimp mariculture development, and half was spent in the development and bailout of the oil industry.

Current Technological Trends

Since the outbreak of WSV, all of Central America has suffered important losses in shrimp production. However, these losses of production were not all bad, as the reduction in availability helped keep prices up slightly. Nevertheless, there have been important lessons learned, and certain advances in shrimp culture may bode well for the future.

The Lessons Learned

One of the first things that we learned was that wild catch shouldn't be used for postlarval supply. The likelihood of the postlarvae's being infected was too great and supplies too small to meet the market demand. In 1998, about 10 percent of postlarvae were supplied by SPF hatcheries, and this percentage rose to over 90 percent in 2003. This relieved the pressure on the wild populations, and surveys showed a 700 percent increase in the wild shrimp population in recent years. With so many farms going bankrupt, those that have reemerged have dwindled significantly in size and intensified. Average farm size has dropped from 650 hectares to less than 70 hectares, and stocking densities have climbed from an average of 12 postlarvae per square meter in 1998 to 60 in 2003. Along with this intensification came a precipitous drop in water exchange and consumption. The high levels of exchange were recognized as an introduction vector for disease as well as a source of pathogens to other citizens, and average water consumption for a kilo of shrimp dropped from 15,500 liters in 2000 to 2,800 liters in 2003 (Rosenberry 2003). The average size of ponds dropped from 12 hectares to less than 4 hectares in only four years. These new, smaller ponds are part of a strong trend toward increasing biosecurity on farms. Inlet water is sterilized with chlorine, inlet screens removed zooplankton or larval crustaceans that might act as disease vectors, and water exchange is only to replace evaporative losses. In Ecuador, shrimp growers are implementing a "green house pond" system, ponds surrounded by bamboo and cement structures covered with plastic to produce a "greenhouse" effect to increase the temperature of the water ponds. According to local researchers and growers, this system significantly reduces WSSV mortality and has been applied successfully, though the installation cost are about $27,000 per hectare.

While all of these environmental and biological changes have aided the industry in fighting back from the brink of total collapse, the economic news is not so good. In the time period from 1999 to 2003, China increased its exports by 8,000 percent (95,000 tons to the USA in the first nine months of 2003), and Vietnam went from no white shrimp exported in 2000 to more than 150,000 tons shipped in 2005. These countries achieved this success by importation and extensive production of an exotic species (*L. vannamei*), originally exported from Ecuador in 1998. Time will tell whether this was a decision that ultimately destroys some portion of the native population of crustaceans or if escaping shrimp generate other unforeseen problems.

Most shrimp-producing countries in Latin America were affected by the TSV and WSSV outbreaks. Brazil was a notable exception, and it did not expend its foreign loans on shrimp culture but rather spent the monies principally on infrastructure development and education. While debt principle was 43 percent of the GDP in 2000, the entry of Brazil into shrimp culture approximately two decades after the rest of the Americas allowed it to avoid many of the environmental/economic errors made in the past. The shrimp industry of Brazil is all intensive, with average stocking densities of 70 pls/sq m and water exchange rates of only 1–4 percent. The country has mandated only the use of SPF postlarvae and imported the best strains from other countries to begin its genetics programs. Brazil rose from no shrimp exports in 1995 to number six in the world, with 65,000 tons of production in the first nine months of 2005.

As of 2003, all of the affected countries of Latin America were recovering from the disease problems of the 1990s at about the same rate, but the debt service created by their earlier loans meant that many could not break even. The concurrent environmental costs associated with the initial means of practicing semi-intensive shrimp culture have added hundreds of millions of dollars of remediation costs to these earlier culture efforts. The WWF estimates the cost of restoring the mangroves lost in the 1975 to 1990 period at $400 million in Central America alone (Sutton 2002).

One Possible Future in Shrimp Culture

Even more intensive systems are under development. Culture systems have been developed with three stages; hatchery (lasting 18 days), nursery (lasting 35–40 days), and growout (lasting 90–95 days). The intensification of stocking density at each of these stages has created significant increases in efficiency and much lower water consumption. The author has developed superintensive microbial floc shrimp systems (SIMFSS) that use stocking densities of 500–700 postlarvae per square meter and results in production levels in excess of 100 tons (wet weight) per hectare in indoor tanks, using recirculation pumps and artificial lighting to mimic estuarine flow and diurnal light levels. Water consumption is only 0.17–0.24 m³ per kilo of shrimp production, and the same water is reused indefinitely. The system has had no waste discharge over a four-year period. These results can be achieved only by shifting the surface area/volume ratio of the system by incorporating in situ biofiltration media called AquaMats (see AquaMats.com), which cleans the water biologically while providing habitat for the shrimp.

AquaMats are designed to mimic natural sea grasses, but with greatly increased surface-to-volume ratios. They are composed of buoyant strips of fibrous polyethylene, with surface areas as high as 240 square meters per square meter of fabric. The fabric is split into strips to simulate sea grasses and provides an excellent surface for the growth of epilithon, to be used as a feed resource and functioning as a biofilter. In addition to the shift in surface area/volume ratios, these systems incorporate specific feeds that are more readily digested and utilize protein resources that significantly reduce the need for fishmeal. We use ground wheat meal, cornmeal, and soy meal to provide the needed protein and amino acid balance. No fish meal at all is used in these systems.

The species of shrimp selected are benthic detrital grazers, so that fecal material, as well as waste feed particulates, are reprocessed by the microbial community and eaten and reused several times (coprophagy) by the shrimp in the length of a growout run (typically 90–95 days). Although some people may recoil at this behavior, it should be pointed out that wild shrimp do this as well. Wild shrimp eat successively smaller particulates generated through successional microbial attack. Spartina detritus, which has been eaten, excreted, and recolonized with nitrogen-fixing bacteria (which enhances its protein content), is then eaten again by a shrimp, which digests the outer coating of protein-rich microbial material and excretes the carbon-rich particulate core (Odum and de la Cruz 1967).

In short, the SIMFSS system is designed to mimic the natural systems in which the species evolved and thereby increase its survival and growth potential. The use of indoor tanks (5–1,800 cubic meters) allows the systems to be built and operated anywhere, perhaps closer to urban facilities and markets, instead of within delicate coastal ecosystems, with significantly reduced biosecurity risks. They have been successfully tested in indoor facilities in Montana, a thousand miles from the ocean with outdoor temperatures of –20° C. The system is capable of full automation and needs only have automated feeders filled once a week.

Development systems by other researchers (Samocha et al. 2001) are less energy-intensive but result in lower yields per unit volume. The Samocha raceway systems can be operated on solar-powered airlifts to provide circulation and aeration with little or no electrical inputs. Even with this significant compromise in power input, it is capable of rearing four times the density of shrimp of conventional intensive shrimp systems. In recent production runs, a commercial grower achieved 45+ tons/hectare/cycle in an inland area of Ecuador.

A Final Perspective

A question raised by the reviewers during the preparation of this chapter was the issue of the environmental versus social acceptability of the SIMFSS system in developing countries. The efficiency of the SIMFSS system is high and its production per hectare is the highest on record for shrimp, exceeding the output of conventional systems twenty times over. Yet, its capital cost is high and its use of manpower very low. SIMFSS may be practical for urban areas, where shrimp are consumed in close proximity to the production facility, but what about its practicality in rural areas?

Is this high technology resolving the most important social issues of the developing world, which often revolve around providing jobs? SIMFSS is another example of our growing trend of producing whatever we need with more fossil-fuel energy and less labor. Is this the right fit for the developing countries of Central and South America? I would have to conclude that it is not. The last thing these countries need is a requirement for further capital to retool the industry for super intensive microbial shrimp systems.

In addition, while a SIMFSS system uses one person to produce thirty tons of shrimp, more conventional systems, working at the high end of the conventional intensive scale, employ twelve to fifteen people to generate the same quantity of shrimp. The generation of twelve times as many jobs has far greater value than the ability to produce more shrimp in less space with fewer people, in a market where the value of shrimp continues to fall. However, we need to make sure that these jobs are not going to be lost due to trial and error in the shrimp industry and to ecosystems collapse. The SIMFSS system may have environmental and economic value in cities where local market demand could consume its production, but we seem to have reached a turning point in the integration of shrimp technology with social and cultural needs. Using the SIMFSS system we can produce shrimp for 25 percent above the cost of the feeds used to grow the shrimp. These costs are almost exclusively for electrical power, as labor costs are so low, relative to output. Thus, the driving impetus is for lower-cost feeds in the SIMFSS system, but we have come full circle. Perhaps the worst-case scenario would be a near-infinite source of non-labor-requiring protein, fueling a population explosion of people who have no function but to consume.

With the development of shrimp export and mass production, imported shrimp became a rich man's delicacy. Now that excess production, through introduction of the same investment program over an entire hemisphere, has resulted in massive quantities of shrimp, prices are headed back to the low levels of thirty years ago, when shrimp were used directly by individuals and on a limited basis for barter and trade. In addition, the interruption of stable production, particularly due to the disease outbreaks of 1989 and 1999, allowed many countries such as China and Vietnam to enter the market, adopt the growth of nonindigenous, benthic detrital species to their use, and effectively compete against the Central and South American production programs. Unfortunately, this took place in spite of the availability of numerous indigenous species that have equal or superior potential for intensive pond culture or SIMFSS culture. These countries were also able to develop this export industry without repeating the environmental development errors that were made in Central America. While shrimp culture in mainland China is touted as a three-thousand-year-old technology, the efficiency, as it was practiced until the 1980s, was so low that it could only function as a subsistence practice or in the creation of a barter good for local trade. The globalization of shrimp technology and trade since 1999 has spread intensive shrimp practice, with radically reduced water consumption worldwide, as a prerequisite of increased biosecurity and cost reduction. The massive move of the world market toward the culture of a single species (*L. vannamei*) has taken place due to its ability to live in crowded conditions and the coprophagic nature of its feeding behavior. *P. monodon* constituted 78 percent of the market in 1998; by 2005, total production was 70 percent *L. vannamei*. When I was in China in 1999, I witnessed entire areas (2,000 hectares in a single week) of rice paddies and *P. monodon* ponds in Guangdong province converted to *L. vannamei* culture. This not only raises questions about the wisdom of monoculture of a single species worldwide,

but also raises questions regarding destruction of resources for the production of other food staples, such as rice. In Vietnam, a 4,500-hectare project was funded for development in 2003 on the premise that "the annual profit per hectare is fifty times greater with shrimp culture than rice culture." Will Asia become the "shrimp bowl" of the world? Who will grow the needed rice? Or do we say to the poor, paraphrasing Marie Antoinette, "Let them eat shrimp?"

Shrimp may yet again become "poor man's protein," but it will not solve the indebtedness generated by the development of the industry or repair the cumulative environmental damage of twenty-five years of misunderstanding and funding misapplication. The rush of Asia to profit from the culture of a single shrimp species may also lead to depletion of other essential food resources. Ecuador and China are both now part of the global shrimp picture. The Chinese proverb, "May you live in interesting times," may well prove to be a pronouncement of the curse of foreign debt in the exploitation of the developing world's natural resources.

I do think there is a way out of this mess, but it requires systems thinking and the use of a social agenda rather than just turning everything over to markets with the sole aim of feeding Americans with numerous insatiable appetites. We have found that AquaMats are also very effective at organic waste treatment because of their high surface-to-volume ratio. They can be used like Jon Todd's biotechnology approach to treat human sewage at about ten square meters of AquaMat per person. One thing that the developing world is not short of is untreated organic waste. Systems can be designed that would deal with sewage and more than pay for themselves by producing shrimp or other suitable species. Water, with secondary levels of treatment, can be combined with shrimp culture and a purge period used after harvest to protect humans from any possible pathogens (no cases are known yet but the potential is there). The systems can be designed to run on solar power with winter supplemental lighting as needed, and to be labor rather than energy intensive. This system has no chance of survival in the free market world as there will always be pressures for intensification and unbound profit. But if human health and waste treatment is given priority, and shrimp production is seen as a side benefit for nutrition and income generation, then truly useful systems might be implemented. This is a true scientific challenge to meet the needs of the developing world in a sustainable way.

References

Avnemelich, Y. 2001. A study of shrimp pond effluent and nitrogen loads in shrimp culture. *Aquaculture* 42, no. 2: 294–307.

Boyd, C. 1990. *Water Quality in Ponds for Aquaculture*. Birmingham, Ala.: Birmingham University Press.

Browdy, C., and J. S. Hopkins, eds. 1995. *Swimming Through Troubled Waters: Proceedings of a Special Session on Shrimp Farming*. Baton Rouge: World Aquaculture Society.

Clifford, H., and H. Cook. 2002. Disease management in shrimp culture ponds, part 3. *Aquaculture* 28, no. 4: 29–39.

Hall, C. A. S., C. Cleveland, and R. Kaufman. 1986. *Energy and Resource Quality: The Ecology of the Economic Process*. New York: Wiley.

Hemmings, R. 2003. IMF Fiscal Policy Advice, IMF Economic Forum, April 23.

Lightner, D., ed. 2002. *Proceeding of the World Aquaculture Society, Shrimp Disease Section*. Beijing: World Aquaculture Society.

Massaut, A. 1999. *Mangrove Management and Shrimp Aquaculture*. Auburn University, Ala.: ICAAE.

McNeil, R. 2000. Zero exchange: Aerobic heterotrophic systems. *Global Aquaculture Advocate* 13, no. 3: 72–76.

Odum, E. P., and A. de la Cruz. 1967. Particulate organic detritus in a Georgia salt marsh–estuarine ecosystem. In G. Lauff, ed., *Estuaries*, 383–88. Washington, D.C.: AAAS.

Rosamond, L., R. L. Naylor, R. J. Goldburg, J. H. Primavera, N. Kautsky, M. C. M. Beveridge, J. Clay, C. Folke, J. Lubchenko, H. Mooney, and M. Troell. 2001. Effect of aquaculture on world fish supplies. *Nature* 413:591–96.

Rosenberry, B. 2000. World shrimp farming 2000, Ecuador. *Shrimp News International*, 25–38.

———. 2003. World shrimp farming 2003, Ecuador. *Shrimp News International*, 154–61.

Samocha, T., A. Lawrence, C. Collins, C. Emberson, J. Harvin, and P. VanWyk. 2001. Development of an integrated, environmentally sound inland shrimp technology. In C. Browdy and D. Jory, eds., *The New Wave, Special Session on Sustainable Shrimp Farming*, 64–75. Baton Rouge: World Aquaculture Society.

Sutton, M. 2002. Healing the wounds: A review of mangrove area restoration in Central and South America. World Wildlife Fund Report.

Traa, B., M. Zermerio, H. Hirshhofer, E. Vesperoni, and M. Rodriguez. 2003. *Ecuador: Selected Issues and Statistics*. Washington, D.C.: International Monetary Fund.

PART SIX

SCIENCE FOR DEVELOPMENT

Doing Better Economics

Economics is far from being only about price in supply-demand space. A vast community of economists (and non-economists) is doing innovative and critical research about the choices made by individuals and society in a world with limited resources. As with other sciences, economics research is quite separate from its operational branch, and economists themselves are some of the first to warn about the weaknesses and incoherencies within their field (see part 1). In this section we give examples of very pragmatic methods that could be used to do better operational economics now. Other methods have already been described in previous sections in this book. Here we expand on how we can capture people's decisions given further space, time, resources, and social constraints, and move closer to the desired situation where researchers actually work with decision makers.

The original great thinker on the cost of productivity was Johann-Heinrich von Thünen, a German farmer and amateur economist. Andrew Nelson and Grégoire Leclerc (chapter 28) ask how well von Thünen's theory of the isolated state, originally devised for Germany before industrialization, applies to the hillsides of Honduras. Can accessibility help us to understand how people today relate to their village and to regional markets, and can these ideas be utilized in guiding development?

Thomas Leinbach (chapter 29) continues this line of thought with an assessment of transportation to rural areas in Indonesia, observing that roads do not necessarily generate the economic benefits to the target population as was intended. He proposes a simple and flexible model for improving the planning of transportation infrastructure. Kathrin Happe and Alfons Balmann (chapter 30) make a comprehensive assessment of the weakness of conventional economics to address complex problems and explain how evolutionary economics and new agent-based methods can be harnessed for agricultural policy design. This offers a very different and exciting approach to economics that reduces the gap between policy makers' and farmers' visions of the world. In chapter 31, Bruno Barbier and his colleagues summarize years of research on bioeconomic models to help orient policy for more sustainable farming systems in several agroecosystems of Africa, Asia, and Latin America. Finally, Juan Rafael Vargas and his colleagues (chapter 32) produce the first input-output matrix for Costa Rica and present realistic policy simulations for better sectorial and regional integration. All these authors are struggling with trying to understand at the most basic level, what does economics mean, how does it relate to biophysical reality and people's motivations, and how can it be used for development?

CHAPTER 28

A Spatial Model of Accessibility

Linking Population and Infrastructure to Land-Use Patterns

in the Honduran Hillsides

ANDREW NELSON AND GRÉGOIRE LECLERC

Introduction

There have been dramatic changes in rural development and local planning in developing countries in the last twenty years. The greater emphasis on economic "liberalization" (that is, neoclassical economics) has seen many national governments cease to be the major providers of services, infrastructure, and facilities. Regional and local levels of government as well as provincial institutions have become more important, seeing themselves as increasingly vested with the responsibility for economic development and employment creation—though not necessarily with the means to carry this out (Dixon-Fyle 1998). All entities associated with development need a way to examine the relation of producers to markets and how these might change with any planned development.

Our interpretation of the patterns of rural development and the spatial relationships of rural economies stems from von Thünen's model of land use, even though the real world is much more complex (Hite 1997). The model says essentially that land use is a function of distance. The simplicity of the von Thünen model is a great advantage in helping to isolate essential relationships and generalize about the fundamental nature of rural economies and their development. Given that local "demand-driven" development is accepted by many economists as the means to make the most efficient use of scarce resources, then von Thünen's theory might be a suitable starting point for grasping local realities and understanding rural economies and their movements.

Rural economies are characterized by a spectrum of social, physical, and agricultural factors and constraints, and neither watersheds nor political units can claim to represent all of these dimensions. People's mobility is critical yet this dimension has been systematically overlooked by the development process, or in the best cases has been oversimplified. It is here that the von Thünen model can play an important role in defining, in a rigorous and reproducible way, the regional extent of rural economies.

Von Thünen

Early in the nineteenth century, amateur economist Johann Heinrich Von Thünen developed a model of land use that showed how market processes could determine how land in different locations would be used. (He was also the first, with Wicksell, to state explicitly the Cobb-Douglas function, a standard in neoclassical economics analysis.) The model is based on the following assumptions:

> The city is a self-sufficient "Isolated State"; hence there are no other cities.
> The city is surrounded by a flat featureless wilderness; hence there are no roads.
> Market price is the same for all producers of a given product.
> Yield is invariant of location, hence climate and soil are constant.
> Transportation costs are proportional to distance and invariant to direction.
> Farmers act to maximize profits.
> (von Thünen 1966)

Von Thünen hypothesized that in an isolated state a pattern of concentric circles would develop with intensive farming nearest, followed by

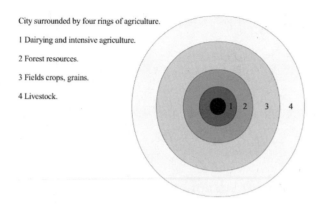

City surrounded by four rings of agriculture.

1 Dairying and intensive agriculture.

2 Forest resources.

3 Fields crops, grains.

4 Livestock.

Figure 28.1. Agriculture patterns around von Thünen's isolated state.

forested areas and timber production, then extensive field crops, and finally ranching (figure 28.1). The von Thünen model is an excellent illustration of the balance between land cost and transportation costs. As one gets closer to a city, the price of land increases. The farmers of the isolated state balance the cost of transportation, land, and profit and produce the most cost-effective product for market.

Reality

In reality few regions are self-sufficient, the terrain in the Honduran hillsides is anything but flat and featureless, soil quality is possibly the most heterogeneous of all biophysical variables, and there is a complex road network permeating the landscape. Von Thünen's neat concentric circles, if they ever existed, are continuously being disturbed, erased, and redrawn. Rural development is about a process of change in time, and the von Thünen model, taken by itself, offers only limited insight into the dynamics of change in remote economies. Certainly the availability of fossil fuels has decreased the importance of close forest resources.

If we interpret the concentric rings as rings of economic distance rather than Euclidean distance, then we can replace distance with some measure of economic cost. If such a definition is to be accepted, however, it must follow that since some places are more remote than others, some places are also more rural than others. However measured, there are degrees of remoteness and degree of "rurality." Since economic distance refers to the costs of overcoming the economic

"friction" of space, being rural means operating under the economic disadvantage of having to overcome costs that are lower in other places that are less rural. And since the costs of overcoming distance are not forever fixed, and indeed are radically altered by innovations in transport and communications, the degree of remoteness—that is, rurality—shifts through time in ways that dictate the economic opportunity of a particular location. This economic cost and its inequity among the population can be termed accessibility, the ease—in terms of time, effort, and cost—with which a need can be satisfied.

Accessibility: Deriving Economic "Catchment" Areas for Markets

Accessibility has been defined as the ability for interaction or contact with sites of economic or social opportunity (Deichmann 1997a; 1997b); there are a multitude of ways in which this intuitive concept has been used in the literature. Goodall (1987) defines accessibility as the ease with which a location may be reached from other locations, Geertman (1995) , Ritsema van Eck, and de Jong (1999) state that the concept of accessibility can be used in rural development policy as an indicator of rural deprivation and as a variable for location analysis. Access is a precondition for the satisfaction of almost any economic need, and certainly for all physical needs, hence accessibility provides a central integrating concept with which to grasp the complex interactions between the subsistence, economic, and social needs of any population (Dixon-Fyle 1998). If the level of accessibility to a market can be estimated then boundaries of the potential catchment areas of the market can be drawn, providing a spatial unit that is related to:

Social and economic aspects such as population pressure, and provision of infrastructure and services.

Physical aspects such as topography, rivers, or barriers.

Agricultural aspects such as land use and land-use change.

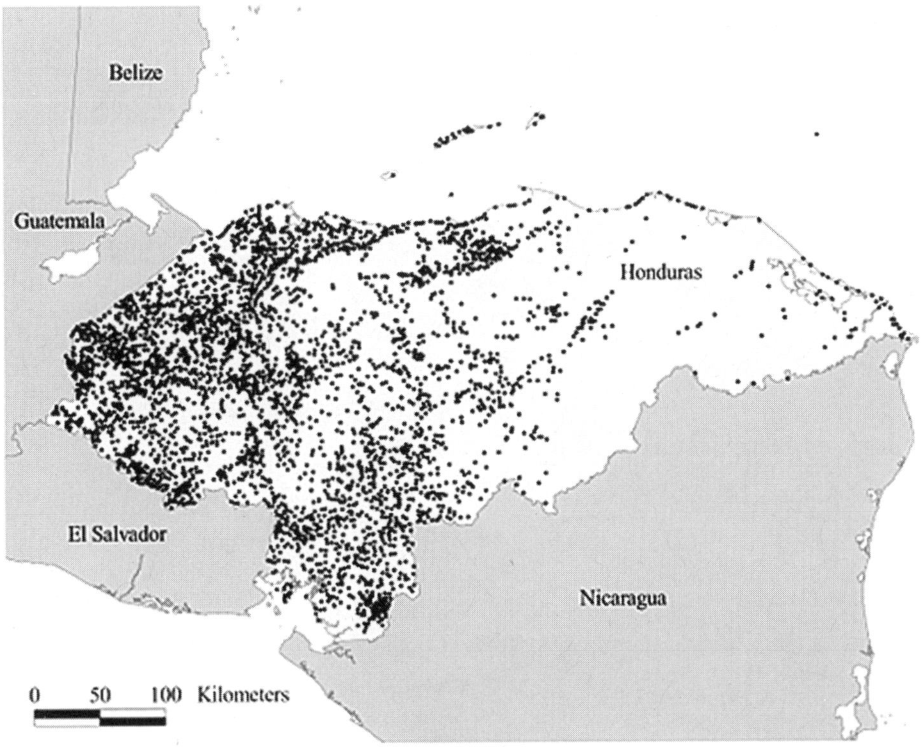

Figure 28.2. The 3,730 aldea centers, from the 1988 Honduran population census.

Geographical information systems (GIS) lend themselves naturally to the computation of accessibility indicators (Ritsema van Eck and de Jong 1999). GIS can represent networks, villages, or facilities and provide functions to compute distances to all spatial units within a region and to define relations among spatial objects. Consequently, certain accessibility measures can be computed using packages such as IDRISI, GRASS, and ArcGIS.

This chapter argues that:
Accessibility can be modeled easily in a GIS environment.
Land use is closely related to market accessibility.
Market catchments are a useful unit of analysis for rural development.

What follows are two case studies of the application of an accessibility model applied to the Honduran hillsides.

Data and Methodology

We present first the data we used and then the methodology we used in the case studies to relate land use to accessibility, and to compare market catchments to farmers' perceptions of town boundaries.

Data

The transport network is represented by a *friction surface* that consists of a regular two-dimensional grid (raster) where each cell in the raster represents a transport route such as roads, railway lines, tracks, or navigable rivers with low values, and relatively inaccessible land and water bodies with high values. We generated the transport network from 1:50,000 topographic sheets containing highly detailed road and river information, including road type and river width. Travel speeds were taken from the literature (Chesher and Harrison 1987; Archondo-Callao and Faiz 1994; Barwell 1996) and from surveys and driving times within Honduras. Slope data were derived similarly from the 1:50,000 map sheets, using 100m contour intervals (and 20m intervals for coastal areas) that were interpolated into a single digital elevation model. Slope was used as a factor to

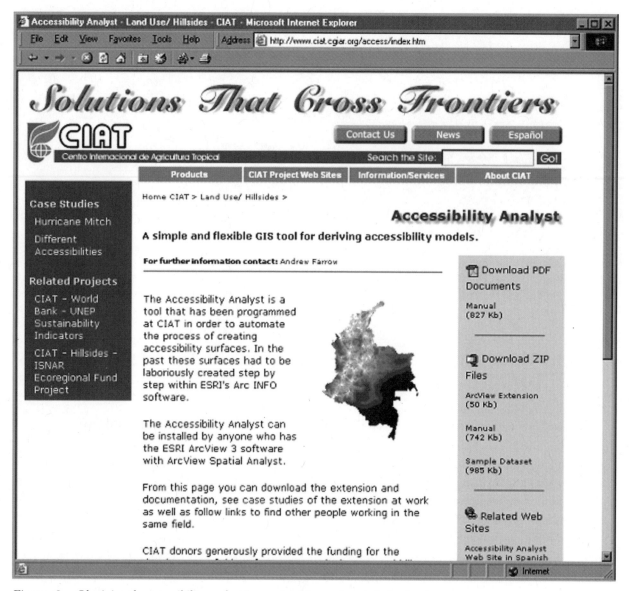

Figure 28.3. Obtaining the accessibility analyst (www.ciat.cgiar.org/access/index.htm).

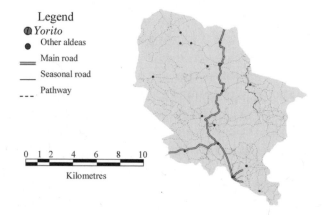

Legend
- Yorito
- Other aldeas
— Main road
— Seasonal road
--- Pathway

0 1 2   4   6   8   10
Kilometres

Figure 28.4. Roads, tracks, and aldeas in the municipios of Yorito and Sulaco.

decrease the maximum speed on steep inclines, assuming that travel speed is reduced for both uphill and downhill travel. We located the markets (towns and villages) on the transport network, which are represented then by a *target* raster. The target data is represented by *aldea* (village) centers (figure 28.2). Additional datasets include official aldea boundaries, digitized by Secretaria de Recursos Naturales y Ambiente de Honduras (SERNA), and 30m-resolution land-cover data, based on classified Landsat TM images from 1986 and 1994.

To validate our village market catchments, we

Table 28.1. Velocity by surface type, transport type, and season used to compute accessibility

Dry Season	Velocity by transport type (km/hr)			
Surface type	Car	Truck	Bus	Walking
Paved road	100	80	60	6
Packed earth road	60	40	30	6
Track or footpath	20	10	—	5
Forested	—	—	—	4
Croplands	—	—	—	4
Bare soil	—	—	—	4
Wet Season	Velocity by transport type (km/hr)			
Surface type	Car	Truck	Bus	Walking
Paved road	80	50	40	5
Packed earth road	40	30	20	5
Track or footpath	—	—	—	4
Forested	—	—	—	3
Croplands	—	—	—	3
Bare soil	—	—	—	3

used georeferenced interviews from an independent study (Ravnborg 2002) aimed at understanding the linkages between well-being and natural resources management. Ravnborg collected data for twelve villages and interviewed a total of 768 Honduran farmers located in three very different regions of Honduras: Rio Saco in the north coast (208 households); Tascalapa in the central highlands (270 households); and Cuscateca in the south (290 households).

For each village, farmers were selected randomly from a list of inhabitants and were asked to fill a questionnaire. In addition each farmer had to locate, on orthophotos and maps, the field that they used for their main agricultural production. The coordinates of these fields were digitized and linked to the database of questionnaire information. The questionnaire also asked for information on the hamlet and on the village to which the farmer claims he belongs.

Testing Van Thünen's Hypothesis Using the Accessibility Model

The accessibility model is based on a GIS cost-distance algorithm that calculates the least-accumulative cost-distance to each market across the transport network and determines the catchment area of each market. The model has been developed by CIAT into a publicly available GIS tool called the Accessibility Analyst (www.ciat.cgiar.org/access/index.htm). This software, a user manual, example applications, and technical notes can be downloaded from the CIAT website (figure 28.3).

Accessibility maps were generated for the CIAT benchmark site of Tascalapa (figure 28.4) with the assumptions on velocity versus surface type, transport type, and season given in table 28.1.

These values were validated by fieldwork at the study site and by compiling travel time information, for both vehicle and foot-based travel. An example travel-time matrix is shown in table 28.2 (travel time is given in minutes). The figures in bold are journeys that were made as part of the verification.

Table 28.2. Selected validation results for dry season by car and by foot (minutes)

	Santa Marta	El Destino	Pueblo Viejo	El Portillo	Yorito	Vallecillos	La Esperanza	Luquigue	Jalapa	La Albardilla	San Antonio	El Desmonte	Las Canas	San Juan	Sulaco	El Jaral
Santa Marta	0															
El Destino	39	0														
Pueblo Viejo	17	22	0													
El Portillo	26	35	12	0												
Yorito	45	8	28	41	0											
Vallecillos	42	18	25	38	10	0										
La Esperanza	109	97	103	116	89	79	0									
Luquigue	59	21	42	55	14	24	98	0								
Jalapa	62	24	45	58	6	26	81	17	0							
La Albardilla	80	42	63	76	34	44	67	32	17	0						
San Antonio	82	45	65	78	30	47	74	29	20	7	0					
El Desmonte	83	46	66	79	30	48	75	33	21	8	5	0				
Las Canas	87	50	70	83	42	52	78	37	25	12	9	5	0			
San Juan	90	53	73	86	45	55	82	40	28	15	12	7	12	0		
Sulaco	87	49	70	82	41	51	78	37	24	11	8	3	8	3	0	
El Jaral	95	58	78	91	50	60	87	45	33	20	17	12	17	12	8	0

Additionally, farmers were asked to estimate the time it took to walk to markets, and this too was compared to the model, although sometimes the responses were vague, and we acknowledge that it is difficult to verify these results fully.

We traveled more than sixty routes, and the average error in predicting the time required for each route was less than 10 percent, with the lowest errors being on routes with flat, good-quality roads and the greatest errors on steep sinuous paths and trails. Most errors were attributed to inaccurate and old road-quality data. For example, the main road passing north-south through the area has been recently repaved with compacted earth and gravel, producing far quicker travel times than the model had predicted. After changes were made to the road database to reflect the current situation, an almost perfect fit was achieved.

Methodology
Study 1

The test site for the first study surrounds Tascalapa. The main road runs north and south through the two *municipios* of Yoro and Sulaco and passes through Yorito and other aldeas. Two land use/ land cover images were available for this region, from 1986 and 1994, as was a 50m-resolution slope map (figure 28.5).

We compared the relation between land use and distance to markets (Von Thünen) with travel time to markets (accessibility). We defined concentric bands of land use based on distance to markets. The distance-to-market map was combined with the two land-cover images to determine the percentage of each land use that was within each distance band to the nearest aldea. For ease of visualization, we combined the land classes to farmland, forested, and other, where "other" can be urban area, degraded land, or bare soil.

We then compared the relation between land use and travel time to markets (accessibility). We defined bands of land use based on time to market, thus changing somewhat the symmetrical nature of the original von Thünen model. We combined the road network and slope map to create a friction surface that was combined with the aldea centers to generate an accessibility map of travel time from each location to the nearest aldea (figure 28.6). This time-travel map was combined with the two land-cover images to determine the percentage of

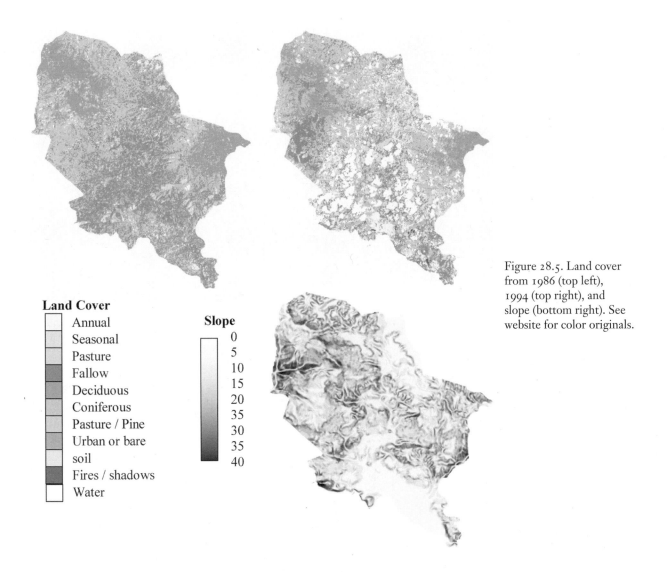

Figure 28.5. Land cover from 1986 (top left), 1994 (top right), and slope (bottom right). See website for color originals.

Land Cover

Annual
Seasonal
Pasture
Fallow
Deciduous
Coniferous
Pasture / Pine
Urban or bare
soil
Fires / shadows
Water

Slope

0
5
10
15
20
35
30
35
40

each land use that was within each time band to the nearest aldea. These percentages are represented as histograms in figure 28.6 for both dates. With both models our hypothesis was that the amount of agricultural land decreases steadily with increased distance from the market, and that the amount of forested land would increase. Additionally we expected urban or degraded land should decrease with distance from market.

Study 2

Our second study compares farmers' perception of location to official aldea boundaries and then to the boundaries of the accessibility market model. We ran the cost-distance algorithm for each of the three sites surveyed by Ravnborg, using the aldea centers as the markets, and computed market

catchments around each aldea. The household locations were compared to the aldea boundaries and the computed catchments by generating a classification matrix and computing Cohen's kappa index of agreement (Cohen 1960), which is the overall accuracy corrected for chance (there is always a possibility that some villages may be classified correctly even if they are distributed randomly).

A test aimed to measure the significance of agreement is Press's Q statistic:

$$Q = \frac{[N - (nK)]^2}{N(K - 1)}$$

Where N is the sample size, n is the number of correctly classified observations and K is the number of groups. Significance is given by the value of

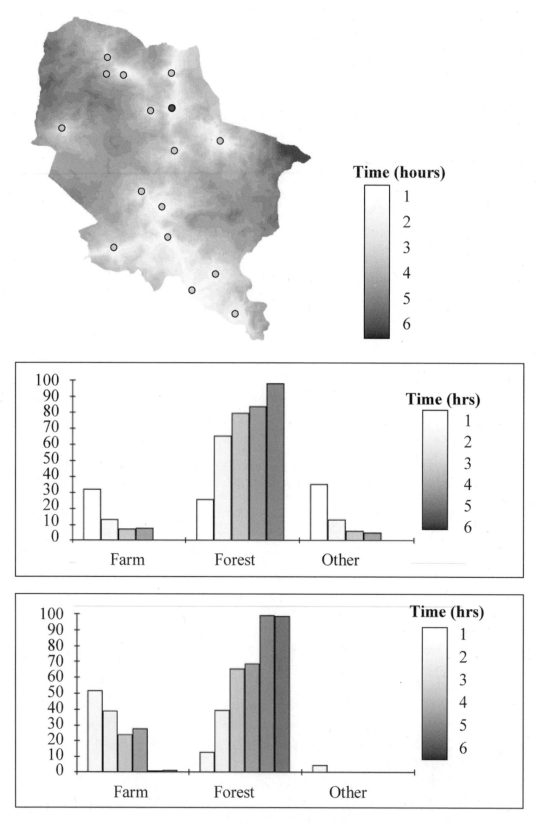

Figure 28.6. Access to aldeas (top); land cover per time band in 1986 (middle) and 1994 (bottom). The horizontal scale in each grouping represents travel time to aldeas.

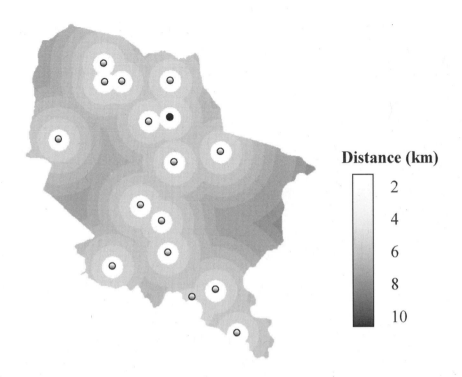

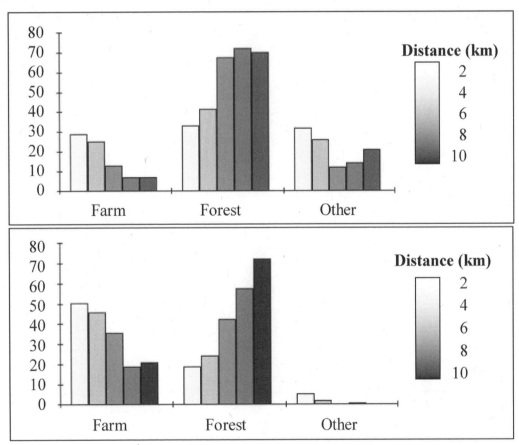

Figure 28.7. Distance to aldeas (top); land cover per distance band in 1986 (middle) and 1994 (bottom).

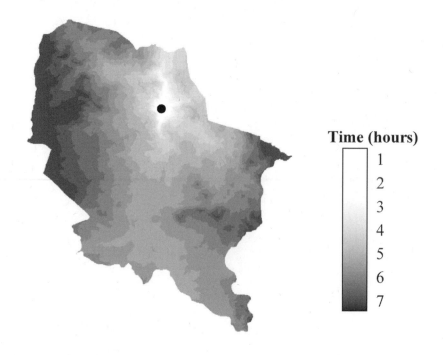

Time (hours)

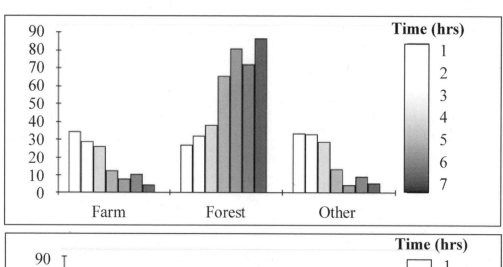

Time (hrs)

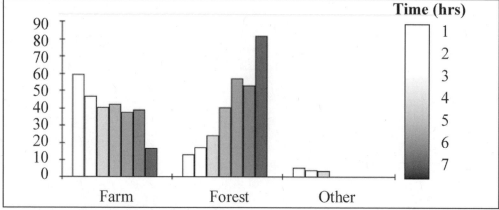

Time (hrs)

Figure 28.8. Access to Yorito (top); land cover per time band in 1986 (middle) and 1994 (bottom).

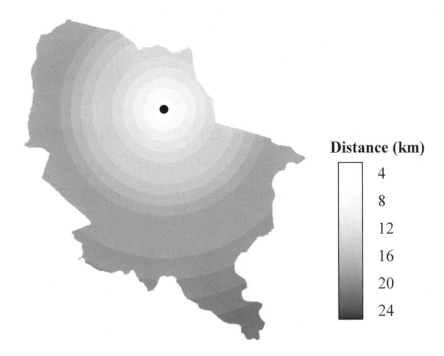

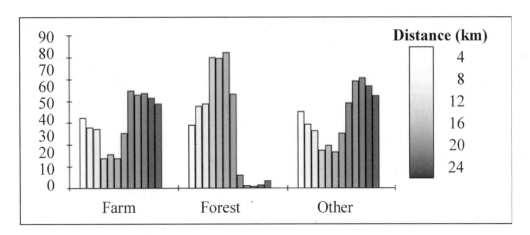

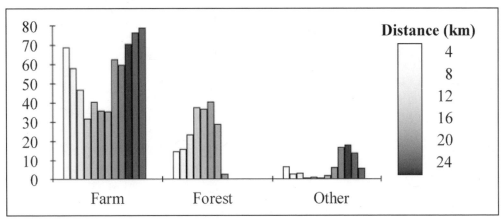

Figure 28.9. Distance to Yorito (top); land cover per distance band in 1986 (middle) and 1994 (bottom).

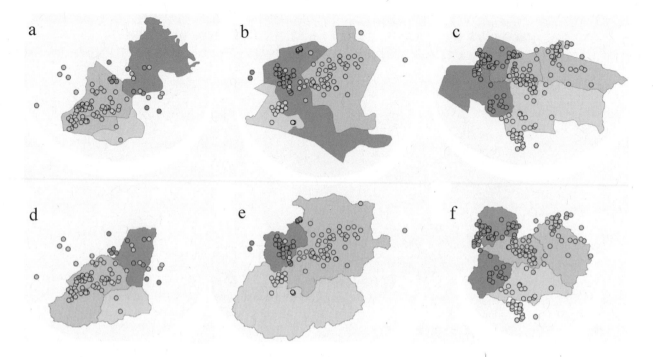

Figure 28.10. Household locations compared to official boundaries (top) and market catchment boundaries (bottom) for Rio Saco (left), Cuscateca (center), and Tascalapa (right). See website for color originals.

the chi square distribution for $K(K–1)$ degrees of freedom. We expected a close correlation between the farmers' perceived location and both sets of boundaries.

Results
Study 1: Land-cover Patterns and Distance/Access to Markets

For the accessibility model, in general we found that:

> The percentage of *farmland* decreases with travel time from the aldea. This is consistent with the von Thünen model.
>
> The percentage of *other* decreases with travel time from the aldea, and is also consistent with the von Thünen model.
>
> The percentage of *forest* increases with travel time from the aldea, and does not peak just beyond the maximum farmland value as had been predicted by the Von Thünen model.

Also an increase in agricultural land at the expense of forested land is evident between the two time periods, with the land that is between two and three hours distant from the aldeas seeing the greatest degree of change. For the distance model, in general we found the same strong trends for all three land classes in both time periods. Again the change from forested to agricultural land is evident between the two time periods, with the land that is between four and eight kilometers distant from the aldeas seeing the greatest degree of change.

The town of Yorito is recognized as being the major local market for this area, and so the experiment was repeated but using only one target market, Yorito. Figure 28.8 shows the travel time in hours around Yorito, and the corresponding land-cover percentages per time band. We see the same trends using only Yorito as a single local market that we did when we considered all the aldeas together—that is, decreasing agricultural land and increasing forested land with increasing time from Yorito. Similarly, we repeated the process for distance from Yorito (figure 28.9). In this case the majority of forested land appears to

Table 28.3. Matrices for comparing the classification accuracy of the official boundaries (upper) with the catchment boundaries (lower)

1a Rio Saco

Code	10803	10806	10822	10824	Other
10803	3 (0.25)	0	4	1	4
10806	0	0 (0.00)	2	0	0
10822	2	1	32 (0.52)	16	10
10824	0	0	3	11 (0.79)	0

Code	10803	10806	10822	10824	Other
10803	4 (0.33)	0	5	0	3
10806	0	0 (0.00)	2	0	0
10822	1	2	32 (0.52)	6	20
10824	0	0	3	11 (0.79)	0

1b Cuscateca

Code	70304	70316	70329	Other
70304	32 (0.89)	2	0	2
70316	7	7 (0.50)	0	0
70329	10	0	50 (0.79)	3

Code	70304	70316	70329	Other
70304	33 (0.92)	1	0	2
70316	0	14 (1.00)	0	0
70329	3	0	59 (0.94)	1

1c Tascalapa

Code	180904	180906	181104	181106	181109	Other
180904	14 (0.93)	0	0	0	1	0
180906	0	15 (0.45)	1	0	0	17
181104	1	9	24 (0.71)	0	0	0
181106	0	1	2	24 (0.71)	0	7
181109	6	0	7	0	27 (0.60)	5

Code	180904	180906	181104	181106	181109	Other
180904	15 (1.00)	0	0	0	0	0
180906	0	14 (0.42)	2	0	0	17
181104	0	1	31 (0.91)	1	0	1
181106	0	0	1	25 (0.74)	0	8
181109	0	0	1	0	36 (0.80)	8

Table 28.4. Overall accuracy between farmers' perceptions of their village and village boundaries.

Users: User accuracy. Kappa: Cohen's Kappa. Q: Press's Q. P: probability of null hypothesis according to Press's Q (i.e. that villages do not fall in the right boundary)

	Rio Saco				Cuscateca				Tascalapa			
	Users	Kappa	Q	P (n = 12)	Users	Kappa	Q	P (n = 6)	Users	Kappa	Q	P (n = 20)
Official	0.52	0.23	34	0.0007	0.79	0.65	105	0	0.65	0.57	240	0
Catchment	0.53	0.26	37	0.0002	0.94	0.90	186	0	0.75	0.70	261	0

be nearer to Yorito than the majority of agricultural land, which exhibits a U-shaped histogram. The same patterns are visible in both years. This single market distance experiment contradicts the von Thünen model.

Study 2: Testing Farmers' Perceptions of Town Boundaries to Market Catchments and Administrative Boundaries

We compare the farm location to the official boundaries and catchment boundaries with the data arranged in one column per site (Rio Saco, Cuscateca, and Tascalapa; figure 28.10). The points, which correspond to the farmer's main production field, are colored based on their location, and are overlaid on the official boundaries (a to c) and then on the generated market boundaries (d to f).

The relations are presented as matrices in table 28.3. The upper section shows the congruencies between the official boundaries (columns) and the farmers' perception (rows), and the lower section shows the congruencies between market catchment boundaries and the farmers' perception. The user's accuracy, which is the percentage of farms falling in the corresponding village zone, is given in parenthesis. It represents the accuracy of the zoning from the viewpoint of the farmer. Table 28.4 gives for each region the overall accuracy, as measured as number of villages assigned correctly to a catchment, and Cohen's kappa index of agreement.

The catchment method gives market boundaries that are systematically more accurate than the official ones. This means that the farmers' perceptions of town boundaries bear more resemblance to the access-derived market boundaries than to the official boundaries.

In Rio Saco (table 28.3a and table 28.4) the overall classification accuracy is low for both boundaries but still significant. The low accuracy here can be partially explained by aldea number 10806 (colored yellow in figure 28.10), since only one household identified itself as belonging to this aldea. In Cuscateca (table 28.3b and table 28.4) and Tascalapa (table 28.3c and table 28.4), accuracy is particularly high. Rio Saco is also in flatter terrain, and this may cause a greater confusion in the sense of place because of better accessibility in all directions—that is, farmers are more mobile. Another possibility, which is also linked to increased mobility, is that the farmer's main field may be located far from his or her house.

Discussion
Accessibility

It is clear that the availability of transport means and services determines the movement of goods, agricultural and otherwise, into and out of communities. Inaccessibility has the immediate effect of causing isolation, but it also has medium- and long-term implications as a constraint on agricultural productivity. Transport is in reality a means to an end, and that end is simply to gain access (Leinbach 1995).

It can be argued that access is a precondition for the satisfaction of almost any need, and that accessibility provides a central integrating concept with which to grasp the complex interactions between the spectrum of subsistence, economic, and social needs of any population. With the concept of accessibility it becomes possible to investigate the degree to which a given community is involved in economic activities. Recognition of the actual accessibility needs of the rural population could lead to an identification of the factors that affect their satisfaction. Using accessibility as an entry point gives us a better idea of what is actually happening from the point of view of socioeconomic development in many critical areas of rural life, and what can be done to improve the situation.

Application
How hurricane Mitch affected access to markets

The access analyst has been used by us and by Farrow and Winograd (2000) to show how the effects of Hurricane Mitch modified accessibility to markets in Honduras and Nicaragua by highlighting the areas that lost accessibility (Leclerc et al. 1998). The application and use of accessibility for policy making and planning is clear from comparing two options of potential reconstruction and the beneficiaries of either option.

Analysis of accessibility and milk markets in Colombia

Farrow and colleagues at CIAT, in collaboration with Tropileche (a consortium that tests and promotes legume-based forages to increase the productivity of both milk and beef in small-scale, dual-purpose farms), have applied the access analyst to investigate the significance of transport costs on the prices received by the farmer and the proclivity to adopt new technologies. This work is still in progress but suggests that insights into effects of accessibility can be studied in order to arrive at global conclusions, probably confirming the fact that other factors besides accessibility are more significant drivers, but that location is important.

Assessing the model

For a spatial model, a factor very much favoring this approach is that the data requirements for accessibility modeling are minimal: a road coverage and a market location would be sufficient. However, the framework is flexible, and many other data sources,

such as rivers, international borders, and topography, can be included if required.

There are several key issues surrounding the market catchments.

1. Each catchment is focused on a resource or market, commonly referred to as a target. Although administrative units are also based around a population center, there are no consistent guidelines or rules that describe their creation from region to region, and they may or may not have any relation to resource or market catchments. The extent of the catchment depends on the road network, which in turn reflects the attractiveness of certain zones such as large cities.

2. Each catchment can be divided into hierarchical bands of accessibility. This makes the catchment a unique type of areal unit, since it is now possible to control the disaggregation process (by splitting the catchment into time bands) as we move to a finer level of detail.

3. They are user-defined, in that the analyst has full control over the boundary generation process; data can be represented in a controlled and specific manner, unlike using administrative units. This is an important concept for addressing MAUP (Modifiable Areal Unit Problem) issues.

4. They are defined by local physical, agricultural, and economic factors relating to accessibility.

5. The units are dynamic in that they are able to adapt with time as the underlying factors influencing them change. Road networks are expanded in some places and become degraded in others. Land cover undergoes dramatic changes as population pressure increases. Crop prices fluctuate, farmers adopt new crops, and markets change.

6. Accessibility is important at local, regional, and national levels and is an inherently scaleable concept. Catchments for local products can be generated, as can catchments for processing plants for

large-scale agricultural production, and finally for commodities such as exported crops as related to access to ports and major cities.

7. Accessibility can be applied to a range of issues, and access to agricultural markets is but one application. For example, health-care provision via midwives and rural healthcare centers of general hospitals can be assessed and compared to infant mortality rates. Access to education can be determined as well as its effect as a constraint on local development. Gender issues could be addressed by focusing on infrastructure and facility siting improvements to minimize the load-carrying work and effort where women bear the larger part of the transport burden. (Dixon-Fyle 1998)

Conclusion

We have presented a new concept for defining and developing economic regions, with roots in the von Thünen model of agricultural economies and land patterns. By using time instead of distance in his model, we incorporate a further degree of real-ism and verify Von Thünen's essential hypothesis.

In our the first empirical study examining this concept, we found that land-use patterns were more closely and more consistently related to travel time than to distance over two time periods and over two spatial scales of analysis. In fact, accessibility is a strong determinant of land-use patterns yet it is poorly taken into account in most economic devel-opment models.

In our second study, we found that the village market catchments based on accessibility were generally consistent with perceptions of local boundaries, particularly in hilly terrain, and were more closely related to farmers' perceptions of lo-cal boundaries than the official boundaries derived from interviews and the 1988 population census. In most countries the area of influence of towns or villages is unknown, and our model can be used for a rapid appraisal (and a quite accurate one in hilly terrain). But the strength of our approach lies more in the possibility to obtain quickly and inexpensively an area of influence (or a market catchment for demand-driven development) for any set of geographical locations.

Accessibility combines biophysical (land cover and terrain), social (population and infrastructure), and economic (market forces, supply and demand) factors. These factors change naturally with time, both on the long term and the short term, and the units adapt with them. Therefore, it is a unique spatial unit particularly well suited to development planning, monitoring, and modeling.

References

Archondo-Callao, R., and A. Faiz. 1994. Estimating vehicle-operating costs. World Bank Technical Paper 234.

Barwell, I. 1996. Transport and the village: Findings from Africa-level travel and transport surveys and related studies. World Bank Discussion Paper 344.

Chesher, A., and R. Harrison. 1987. Vehicle operating costs: Evidence from developing countries. World Bank Publication 374.

Cohen, J. 1960. A coefficient of agreement for nominal scales. *Educational Psychological Measurements* 20:37–46.

Deichmann, U. 1997a. Accessibility and spatial equity in the analysis of service provision. Workshop on Geographical Targeting for Poverty Reduction and Rural Development, World Bank, 11 November 1997.

———. 1997b. Accessibility indicators in GIS. United Nations Statistics Division, Department for Economic and Policy Analysis.

Dixon-Fyle, F. 1998. Accessibility planning and local development: The application possibilities of the IRAP methodology. Rural Accessibility Technical Paper, International Labor Organization.

Farrow, A., and M. Winograd. 2000. Hurricane Mitch. www.ciat.cgiar.org/access/accessibility-case-studies. htm.

Geertman S. C. M., and J. R. Ritsema van Eck. 1995. GIS and models of accessibility potential: An application in planning. *International Journal of Geographical Information Systems* 9, no. 1: 67–80.

Goodall, B. 1987. The Facts on File Dictionary of Human Geography. Facts on File Publication. New York.

Hite, J. 1997. The Thunen Model and the new economic geography as a paradigm for rural development Policy. *Review of Agricultural Economics* 19, no. 2:2–22.

Leclerc, G., E. B. Knapp, A. Nelson, and G. Hyman. 1998. A brief description of the potential of Geographic Information Systems as a tool for decision making in the mitigation of the effects of Hurricane Mitch. CIAT Internal Concept Note.

Leinbach, T. 1995. Transportation and third world development: Review, issues, and prescription. *Transportation Research* 29A, no. 5: 337–44.

Ravnborg, H. 2002. Poverty and soil management: Evidence of relationships from three Honduran watersheds. *Society and Natural Resources* 15:523–39.

Ritsema van Eck, J. R., and T. de Jong. 1999. Accessibility analysis and spatial competition effects in the context of GIS-supported service location planning. *Computers, Environment and Urban Systems* 23:75–89.

Von Thünen, J. H. 1966. *Isolated State*. New York: Pergamon.

CHAPTER 29

RURAL ACCESSIBILITY DECISION MAKING

Issues of Integration, Scale, and Sustainability

THOMAS LEINBACH

Introduction

We are all aware that transportation investments continue to account for a major share of the capital investment of less-developed countries (Wilson 1966; Owen 1987). In fact, up to 40 percent of public expenditure is devoted to transport infrastructure investment, with additional amounts coming from the World Bank and the technical assistance programs of the wealthier countries (Button 1993). These simple facts provide striking evidence of the prevailing recognition of the important role of transport in development. Yet the exact role continues to remain ambiguous and has been subject to recent reappraisals. It is particularly important to ask what directions our inquiries should take.

Specifically, during the past decade some rather significant reassessment of the role of transport in third-world development has been taking place. This has been motivated in part by the concern over the spatial and structural maldistribution of income and inequities in delivering basic needs to predominantly rural nations. Especially now, when in many countries austerity budgets are in effect and projects have been "re-phased" or postponed indefinitely, the exact role of transport has come under close scrutiny (World Bank 1996). Thus a legitimate question then is: what do we really know about the relationship of transport to development? Some development experts even maintain that overinvestment has occurred in the sector and that future funding should be released only when a critical need can be identified. Several trends include increased local participation as well as restoration and rehabilitation of existing systems. In addition, the involvement of the private sector (both commercial enterprises and NGOs) is increasingly being encouraged (e.g., Toh 1989).

Objectives

This chapter has several purposes. First, it presents a number of general observations on the prevailing wisdom and current knowledge regarding the impact of rural transport investment, and it draws attention to the critical issues. Second, it reviews some specific accessibility impacts that might be found commonly in rural developing-world situations and examines a specific context and policy device—the Cash Incentive Rural Works Program in Indonesia. Third, it utilizes one simple planning model for transport investment decisions that has considerable utility and flexibility and that might be applied in a variety of development situations, including those where the growing trend of decentralized decision making is in place. Finally, it offers some comments on new paths that need to be forged in examining the questions of rural transport investment in the context of ecoregional modeling toward long-term growth.

The Impact of Rural Transport Investment

It is well documented that inaccessibility and inefficient transport have important impacts on the productivity and structure of agriculture as a result of the inability to obtain credit and financing as well as higher transport costs for both inputs and products (e.g., Hine et al. 1983a, 1983b). In addition, we suspect that transport is critically interwoven with communication and social change and, moreover, that access has some effect on employment searches and basic-needs acquisition, including the delivery of health services. However, despite the data that document these impacts, too often the intended effect of enhancing rural life falls far short of our expectations or is even counterproductive. Little is known about the ways in which rural transport should be improved or how to deliver benefits to needy populations. A major issue is individual mobility and nonmotorized transport (Filani 1993). Until recently, people's needs have been associated with conventional engineered roads. In addition, too often development needs are more easily seen near urban areas and along main roads, while more remote and inaccessible areas and peoples tend to be ignored (Chambers 1983, 1997). When data are gathered and examined in a rigorous fashion, the results of road impact are too often conflicting and frequently ambiguous (Howe and Richards, 1984).

I start with some general observations. First, local circumstances and environment have considerable bearing on the way roads affect economic and social change. Both the development and the physical environments are critical. Second, new evidence does not sustain continued optimism about the supposedly positive impact of roads on poverty. The general reasons are the rather widespread incidence of land consolidation, the increasing number of landless workers, the decline of local industries in the face of outside competition, and the acceleration of outmigration. Third, road improvements, in contrast to new roads, rarely lead to sharp decreases in the cost of transport, which is critical to stimulate demand. In addition, land tenancy is often a major factor in determining who benefits. If the land is unevenly distributed, the landless or land poor will receive little benefit. But if land is more evenly distributed, road projects often serve poorer households more effectively.

Blaikie and his colleagues (1979) found that with road development in southern Nepal, personal mobility expanded greatly with the new availability of bus travel. Moreover, provincial towns acquired an administrative presence and, as a result, some additional income. But the positive impacts that were expected from these new roads failed to develop. Increased penetration of local markets by Indian goods to some extent destroyed local manufacturing. The roads served to encourage agricultural

imports from the more productive plains rather than exports. Adoption of new technologies and new crops were very limited. The move toward increasing subsistence due to population pressure outweighed any benefits of local commercial development. In short, the construction of roads to help the poor actually worked against them.

Thus the roads had very little net effect on the crucial prerequisites for significant development, namely increasing productivity in agriculture and industry. Why? In large part the answer is that government machinery was not organized to support peasant agriculture and poverty was so severe that farmers could not afford agricultural inputs or indeed even risk innovation. The extent to which development takes place is critically dependent upon the capacity of the local and regional economy and government to respond and reallocate resources. The roads in question made little contribution in Nepal because they did not affect the major determinants of the local political economy, nor did they begin to resolve the basic problems of a predominantly agrarian system. These problems are mounting population pressure, ecological decline, and the meager subsistence production, which results from the peculiar circumstances of the region and its position as a dependent periphery of India.

The Cash Incentive Rural Works in Indonesia

As we know, the strong concern for eradicating rural poverty and eliminating regional inequities has stimulated considerable policy debate. But the matter of how and where to intervene involves very complex questions and decisions. Defining and evaluating benefits from investments continues to perplex decision makers. Obviously, given limited resources, it is critical that investments are made carefully in order to insure that real benefits will accrue.

The following narrative summarizes one rural development program and shows the results of an evaluation of rural road infrastructure development. After it is a discussion that depicts how these evaluations might be turned into a broader "investment-selection" methodology that can be useful where decision makers are often presented with complex problems that have multiple and sometimes conflicting goals.

With ever-present concerns about rural poverty, food shortages, and underemployment, the government of Indonesia has experimented with a variety of rural development instruments. Since the late 1970s, a cash incentive program has been used to deliver cash income supplements (and, before this, food) to the poorest in Indonesian society by using labor-intensive methods. This new cash version had two essential objectives:

provide income injections immediately on
    a temporary basis to some of the poorest
    districts in the country
construct new and rehabilitate old infra-
    structure that would deliver long-term
    benefits

Typical projects included irrigation construction and small bridges, but rural feeder roads were paramount.

An effort was made to determine the impact of the investment from a sample of rural road projects that had been constructed for at least six months. Most of the projects drew regularly scheduled minibus services after the upgrading. This broad expansion of accessibility is sometimes referred to as "the Colt Revolution" in Indonesia, where Japanese-manufactured Colt passenger vans form the vehicle stock for the services. But, in addition, other forms of mobility emerged that had impacts on the movement of goods and marketing of crops. Before the roads, vehicles could not enter many of the areas and transportation service was irregular. But clearly, even after regularly scheduled services were delivered, many families still find such services too costly and continue to use traditional means of transport such as bicycles and back loads.

We often forget that impact of a road depends upon the physical, social, and economic environment through which it passes. Poor agricultural environments where precipitation is highly variable can have a strong effect on the results of road upgrading. As an example, in the wet season commerce is interrupted, but in the dry season traders and consumers are more mobile. In addition, the expansion of cash crops such as simple root crops was quite common in many areas as a result of a new road placement, where previously crops could not be marketed without the road.

In many cases, a general expansion of mobility occurred—distinct increases in trip frequencies to markets were measured. But especially important was a greater awareness as well as increased use of simple medical facilities and especially family planning information available through these simple rural health posts, called *posyandu*. Small local businesses expanded after construction, but many declined and disappeared in a very competitive environment where the consumer field was too small. On the other hand, select small industries were beneficiaries of the access improvement and have endured, in part because of the unique need they fulfill. Simple sugar-making operations and rattan weaving are illustrations of positive economic outcomes that came from the road.

Too often the analysis of the impact of improved accessibility has focused only on economic criteria. But just as commodities flow over roads, so too do ideas and information related to family planning and other innovations. A simple hand-operated threshing machine was one example of an innovation that diffused into the region under improved access. Widespread use occurred as a result of the new roads. But a question of this and other innovations, particularly in densely populated areas, centers on the real benefits when machines displace labor rather than create employment. It was also clear in numerous situations that outmigration from the project area occurred as a result of the improved access and resultant decrease in demand for labor. Both of these situations suggest that the interrelationship between access improvement and information change is not fully understood.

Clear problems and negative benefits also resulted from the construction or upgrading of roads in numerous situations. Too often, roads were placed or upgraded where there was severe competition from other roads with little net effect. In addition, many of the projects had limited population service fields. One interesting example occurred in a road hinterland in Poncol, East Java, that

Locations of Potential Rural Road Projects in East Java, Indonesia

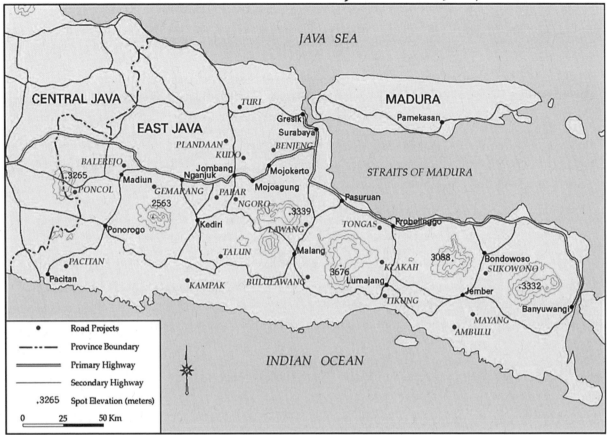

Figure 29.1. Locations of potential rural road projects in East Java, Indonesia.

terminated at the provincial border and was not accessible to a large rural population three kilometers away. This was the result of lack of coordination between provincial governments. The potential benefits were diluted as a result of the lack of maintenance, poor road location, and steep gradients, as well as poor design of even simple bridges.

A Planning Model That Leads Toward Improved Project Selection

Clearly a need exists for improved project selection and planning for specific situations. The immediate illustration is from East Java, Indonesia (figure 29.1). Given the wide and varying impact of development projects and the sometimes conflicting objectives and constraints, how can we select projects that will provide the greatest returns? We must be concerned with the cost of projects, reduction of unemployment, and improving agricultural productivity.

We begin by selecting a set of project variables (table 29.1). These variables are illustrative only and could be changed depending upon the situation and context. Total population in an area and agricultural land are included as well as internal access, integrated development potential, bridge costs, and seasonal unemployment levels. Subsequently, we then needed to derive some attainment or expectation levels (table 29.2). These show the minimum population that needs to be served, the maximum road length per project, the maximum off-season unemployment, and the like. In the case of the first variable we wished to insure that each project would serve a minimum of fifty-five thousand people. We then grouped the nineteen criteria into six separate priority levels (see also table 29.2), where the most critical variables that we must attempt to include are given a priority of P_0. In this illustration, we wish to maximize the total population served and minimize the number

Table 29.1. Road project selection variables

Total population:	aggregate number of people served by all road projects selected for construction.
Threshold population:	requirement of minimum, critical population serving a village within a ten-kilometer band on either side of the proposed linkage.
Total agricultural land:	amount of currently productive wet rice or other agricultural land to be served by the proposed road plus the amount of potential agricultural land or land that may be converted.
Potential agricultural land:	an additional variable created by separating out only the amount of potential agricultural land from the actual cultivated land.
Resource conversion requirement:	a measure of the need within a specific project area to convert, on average, one hectare of potential arable land into actual cultivated land. Measured in man/days (an average working day per individual), the resources required vary and are a function of site, situation, crops to be planted, and other considerations.
Higher order connection:	measure of whether the proposed road project links to a higher-order road and, thus, serves to build up a major exit-entrance portal.
Internal access:	extent to which the proposed road project builds up internal access in the district by connecting up with existing roads.
Integrated development scheme:	whether the proposed road project is part of a "package" of other improvements in the area or whether a complimentary development scheme is proposed for the area.
Daily market distance:	distance to the closest active daily market; the objective is to improve access in districts that already have a nearby market; a road project is to make the market more "usable."
Facilities served:	extent to which proposed road gives access to schools, healthcare facilities, extension offices, and so on.
Road length:	if the road length is excessive (greater than eight kilometers) it will be difficult to maintain.
Bridge costs:	heavy bridge costs reduce funds that could be allocated to construct other projects. Delays in bridge construction often reduce the full use of the project until bridges are completed.
Estate land:	desire to minimize government-owned estate land in project area; projects are intended to serve rural poor; estate road funds should be derived from alternative sources.
Off-season unemployment:	projects should provide temporary wage income for unemployed; high rates of seasonal unemployment indicate need.
Competing road:	a proposed project should not be built in an area where there is a nearby or parallel facility that competes in objectives.
Distance to surface materials:	availability of gravel, stones, and so forth within reasonable distance (under thirty kilometers) of the proposed road project site.
Project costs total:	the combined costs of all projects constructed must not exceed a critical limit.
Self-help level:	projects should be located within areas where there is and has been a strong record of intravillage cooperation in accomplishing goals.
Projects constructed:	a minimum number of projects that must be constructed.

Table 29.2. Attainment levels and goal priorities: Base model

Number	Criteria	Priority level	Attainment level
1	Minimum total population served	P0	55,000
11	Maximum road length per project	P0	8 km
12	Maximum total bridge costs	P0	30 million rupiah
14	Maximum off-season unemployment level per project	P0	35 percent
15	Maximum number of competing roads	P0	3
17	Maximum total project costs	P1	260 million rupiah
19	Maximum number of projects funded	P2	12
2	Threshold population served per project	P2	2,000
3	Minimum total agricultural land served	P2	2,250 ha
8	Minimum number of projects that are part of an integrated development scheme	P3	1
10	Minimum number of facilities served	P3	15
16	Maximum distance to surfacing materials	P3	30 km
18	Minimum percentage of villages that have demonstrated adequate self-help records per project	P3	50
4	Minimum amount of potential agricultural land to be converted	P4	650 ha
6	Minimum number of projects that link to a higher-order road	P4	5
7	Minimum number of projects that improve internal accessibility	P4	7
9	Maximum distance to a daily market per project	P4	12 km
5	Maximum man days available for land conversion	P5	200
13	Maximum amount of estate land included within project area	P5	100 ha

Table 29.3. Goal achievement results: Basic model

Number		Priority level	Weighting factor	Satisfied (Y/N)
1	Minimum Total Population Served	P0	1	Y
11	Maximum road length per project	P0	1	N
12	Maximum total bridge costs	P0	1	N
14	Maximum off-season unemployment level per project	P0	1	Y
15	Maximum number of competing roads	P0	1	Y
17	Maximum Total Project Costs	P0	1	Y
19	Maximum number of projects funded	P1	1	Y
2	Threshold population served per project	P2	1	N
3	Minimum total agricultural land served	P2	1	N
8	Minimum number of projects that are part of an integrated development scheme	P3	1	Y
10	Minimum number of facilities served	P3	1	Y
16	Maximum distance to surfacing materials	P3	1	N
18	Minimum number of villages that have demonstrated adequate self-help records per project	P3	1	N
4	Minimum amount of potential agricultural land to be converted	P4	1	N
6	Minimum number of projects that link to a higher-order road	P4	1	Y
7	Minimum number of projects that improve internal accessibility	P4	1	Y
9	Maximum distance to a daily market per project	P4	1	N
5	Maximum man days available for land conversion	P5	1	Y
13	Maximum amount of estate land included within project area	P5	1	N

Solution One

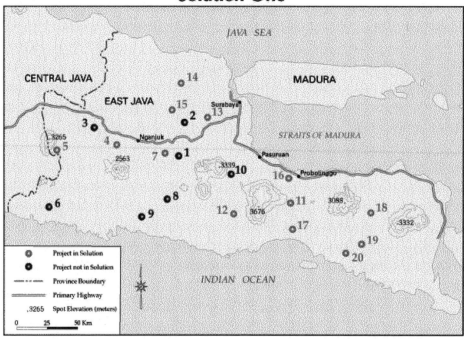

Figure 29.2. Solution one (see table 29.3), based on attainment levels and goal priorities given by table 29.2.

Solution Two

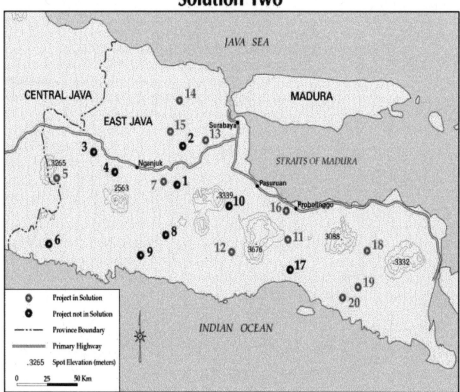

Figure 29.3. Solution two (see table 29.4), with a lower priority given to population (priority assignment changed from P0 to P1).

Table 29.4. Goal achievement results: Second model

Number		Priority level	Weighting factor	Satisfied (Y/N)
1	Minimum total population served	P1	1	N
11	Maximum road length per project	P0	1	Y
12	Maximum total bridge costs	P0	1	Y
14	Maximum off-season unemployment level per project	P0	1	Y
15	Maximum number of competing roads	P0	1	Y
17	Maximum total project costs	P0	1	Y
19	Maximum number of projects funded	P1	1	N
2	Threshold Population Served Per Project	P2	1	N
3	Minimum total agricultural land served	P2	1	N
8	Minimum number of projects that are part of an integrated development scheme	P3	1	Y
10	Minimum number of facilities served	P3	1	Y
16	Maximum distance to surfacing materials	P3	1	N
18	Minimum percentage of villages that have demonstrated adequate self-help records per project	P3	1	N
4	Minimum amount of potential agricultural land to be converted	P4	1	N
6	Minimum number of projects that link to a higher-order road	P4	1	Y
7	Minimum number of projects that improve internal accessibility	P4	1	Y
9	Maximum distance to a daily market per project	P4	1	N
5	Maximum man days available for land conversion	P5	1	Y
13	Maximum amount of estate land included within project area	P5	1	N

of competing roads. Of lower priority is the size of agricultural land made accessible and the minimum number of facilities served.

Solution Procedure

Using a methodology from goal programming, the problem of multiple conflicting goals is solved using an ordinal hierarchy approach: higher-order goals must be satisfied before lower-order goals (Leinbach and Cromley 1983). The solution method also allows us to utilize a weighting factor to determine how much increase in one variable is necessary to offset a decrease in another variable of the same priority level. In the initial solution, thirteen of twenty road projects were chosen for implementation (table 29.3 and figure 29.2). All potential projects in the eastern area were selected based upon the large populations, high rates of unemployment, and low overall bridge costs there. All of the P0 goals were achieved except bridge costs and road length.

In the second solution (table 29.4 and figure 29.3), we attempted to examine the impact of changes of priority assignment. Here the population goal was lowered to P1; that is, a secondary priority was now attached to this variable. The result is that only eleven projects were selected, and this occurred because of the conflict of bridge cost and road length versus other goals in the P0 level. This outcome had been suppressed in the first assessment because projects 4 and 17 had very high population levels. Now although all P0 goals are fulfilled, no P1 goals are. The goal-programming-solution methodology is very general and can be expanded to include additional types of infrastructure projects or other investments in any regional development scheme. Moreover, sensitivity analyses are possible where weights and priority levels may be altered to develop and test particular outcomes given specific objectives such as regional preferences, or policy constraints such as budget limitations.

Sustainability Policies
for Transport Reform

Finally, in a policy vein, it is clear that the notion of sustainability, however we wish to define this term, has become infused in the literature on transport. The World Bank has put sustainability at the heart of a new, more comprehensive transport policy (World Bank 1996). The broad rationale is that rapid changes in the global economy have increased the need for flexibility and reliability in transport services and that individual aspirations for more mobility have generated the need for a greater variety of transport services. But mounting social concern about the degradation of the environment and concerns that transportation may not deliver all the benefits we once thought have increased the need to evaluate transport strategies more carefully. The new expression of these concerns is generally met through a conventional neoliberal assessment of economic and financial sustainability where resources supposedly are used efficiently through competitive market structures, an enabling framework for competition and efficient use of infrastructure. However, not being completely convinced of the efficacy of the conventional neoclassical approach, we choose to use a broader set of definitions of sustainability (figure 29.4). These include:

1. Environmental and ecological sustainability where external effects of transport are taken into account, particularly the adverse consequences of development induced by roads and other networks on forests, wetlands, and other natural habitats.
2. Social and distributional sustainability where the transport problems of the poor are targeted for improvement by improving access to jobs, reducing barriers to the informal supply of transport, and the elimination of gender biases.
3. Economic and financial sustainability where efficient operation, pricing, design, and above all investment are insured. These three dimensions and specific examples are shown in figure 29.4.

While these are magnanimous objectives, there are many barriers to their implementation. Most significant, apart from the realities of the political, social, and economic context of the transport situations, is the lack of real research on a variety of questions assumed in the development of these policies. The issues we have discussed need to be examined in the context of sustainability definitions and resource availability.

Discussion

A common criticism of road investment programs in the third world is that they have concentrated on providing benefits to the richer urban populations and have ignored the needs of the rural poor (Leinbach 1982, 1983a, 1983b). This often occurs because the better-off are more politically vocal, more mobile, possess higher time values, and are more concentrated spatially than the rural poor (Hine 1982:8). Thus decision makers are not provided with information about the disaggregated effects of roads. Who gets richer and who gets poorer? This is especially critical in low-volume traffic areas.

A new conceptual framework may be required to effect a more contemporary approach to the analysis of transport's role, especially in rural development (Jolibois 1991). Such a framework must of course incorporate explicitly economic but equally important political and social, and especially gender, considerations within an integrated dynamic system. The latter factors are important because the majority of the transport movements are not related to economic but rather other activities (Barwell et al. 1985). Such a framework must close the conceptual gap between the traditional way the impact, development, and use of the transport system has been viewed by development agencies and the socioeconomic reality of those transport systems. In this effort, it is clear that micro-scale approaches are going to be much more useful than the macro-scale, holistic view of transport relationships in development. What are the critical elements in this perspective?

It appears, as we review the evidence, that the extent to which development takes place is critically dependent upon the capacity of the local and

THREE DIMENSIONS OF SUSTAINABLE DEVELOPMENT: SYNERGIES AND TRADEOFFS

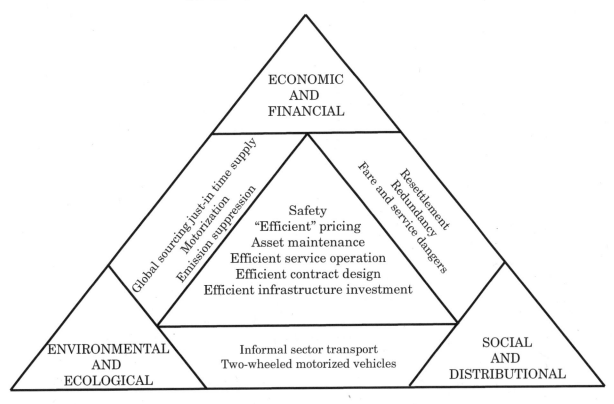

Figure 29.4. Three dimensions of sustainable development: synergies and trade-offs.

regional economy to respond and particularly to reallocate resources. Transport, in order to effect change, must relate to the major determinants of the local political economy and be combined with efforts to resolve problems of largely agrarian economies. These include the lack of entrepreneurship, environmental decline, landlessness, and mounting population pressure.

One useful approach toward achieving some greater understanding of small-scale development situations and especially the role of access may be to explore the utility of variations of the political economy theme. We should perhaps examine the interrelationship of transport with the forms of, and limits to, production in a broader systems analysis. The objective here is to learn how individual producer incentives and accumulation could be enhanced. In this analysis, the key actors and decision-making processes and institutions at the village level may be isolated as key elements in our

new understanding. Within this broad approach many aspects deserve the attention of researchers but several topics stand out as especially worthwhile for case study analysis.

First, it is clear that a deeper understanding must be gained of the concept of rural household travel demand. A basic deficiency of current knowledge is that reliance on market demand models has led to an undifferentiated view of the benefits and costs of work-performance to household members. This approach has emphasized the role of men and thus has ignored the important influence of gender bias at the intra-household level. The fallacy here is the lack of understanding of the transport needs of the subsistence-producing household members who allocate their survival tasks on the basis of contextual factors rather than optimizing market principles. Given a better definition of the real needs of the peasant household, better transportation strategies can be devised, such as those that recognize the main activities and needs of households (Ellis 1988; Bryceson and Howe 1993).

Second, the role of transport as it affects production relations in village situations between landholders and those without land is important. What differences separate these two groups and how does transport inhibit or aid these distinctions?

We now know too little about the broader role of increased access to improved information flow. Although resources, capital, infrastructure, and education are essential, frequently it is the lack of information about a service or an opportunity that constrains change. Careful studies isolating the information impacts of accessibility would be especially useful for investment decisions and policy formulation.

A key element in both rural and urban development is employment. Yet too little information on the role of transport and accessibility in the provision or use of labor is known. Especially useful here would be studies that relate transport to strategies of labor commuting and circulation as well as the search for employment. In this regard women's employment situations, given the simultaneous needs of reproductive and productive activities, are of special interest (Ellis 1993). Even detailed studies of women's labor time allocation have devalued the burden of inadequate transport (Bryceson and Howe 1993). Moreover the matter of employment within the transport sector, especially in rural areas, deserves research attention. This general theme of course supports the well-recognized priority in all developing areas: employment creation.

In addition the control of and accessibility to transport resources remains a largely unexplored area (McCall 1977, 1985). Topics here include the power of local-level or other decision makers to decide the location of networks and the ease of entry of different groups into transport operations (Friedmann 1992). In addition, the constraints associated with the use of transport services and infrastructure by poor people must be better understood. In this vein it is important to reiterate that many of the poor cannot afford even low-cost public transportation and must walk. In rural areas, appropriate vehicles and transport services are frequently not available or affordable for the

majority of people. Too frequently investments in better, but more expensive transportation have tended to reduce the diversity of options, forcing people and goods to conform to the few higher-cost modes rather than utilize the more traditional and affordable means. It is clear that a more diverse system is less susceptible to inefficiency, disruption, and system failure. Transport investment policies should be reoriented in an attempt to accommodate the needs of the poor and often isolated rural people. One avenue that might be more thoroughly explored is schemes that provide low-cost credit for affordable mobility. Moreover, and most important, transport researchers must begin to recognize this more informal dimension of transportation by taking on projects that probe the practical and policy implications of a broader, more diversified and equitable access provision (Replogle 1991).

In order to improve our understanding of the dynamics of the transport relationship, we must focus on the real purposes of development and orient our analyses to capture the ways in which transport interacts with and constrains the basic forces in the development change process. In these efforts economic, political, and social relationships must be examined thoroughly. One new theoretical lens that may hold some promise from a policy perspective is imbedded in the relatively new area of institutional economics (Nabli and Nugent 1989).

One argument that supports this view is that a major underlying cause for the failure of governments to sustain investments in facilities lies with the incentives facing participants in the design, finance, construction, and use of facilities. When road infrastructure deteriorates after construction, it may be assumed that the actors involved in the initial development process were submitting to incentives that essentially rewarded them for actions that resulted in unsustainable investment (Ostrom et al. 1993). It must be stressed that incentives are not simply financial rewards or penalties. They are the positive and negative changes in personal outcomes that individuals perceive and that result from particular actions taken within a set of rules in particular spatial, social, political, and economic contexts. This position assumes that there are reasons for individuals involved in the delivery of transport to do what they do. The choices and decisions that people make regarding the use of services and facilities purposely or inadvertently benefit or harm others because of the interdependence that exists in settlement situations. In other words, individuals who were rewarded to create the road were not rewarded to maintain it.

An additional issue which is already of immense importance as we consider design-making for accessibility is the notion of decentralization. It is clear that decentralization is increasingly important because informed decisions must now be made by local institutions that have had little experience in assessing budgets and complex resource allocation. This is true not only in Indonesia but elsewhere as well. The point here is that the form of transport ownership and operation and especially the delivery mechanisms obviously need further inquiry. Such analysis can also illuminate our understanding of the interrelationship between development (perhaps specifically in this case the changing role of the state) and transport requirements.

Following this line of argument, one possible new approach to viewing the interrelationship between transport and development lies in an enlarged understanding of the institutional bases of transport. This involves an examination of the matter of provision and production of rural and regional facilities and includes questions of rent seeking, joint use, and economies of scale (Ostrom et al. 1993). But more important are deeper inquiries into the individuals surrounding the facilities, the associated incentives and transaction costs. An additional obvious thrust for analysis along these lines is an inspection of institutional arrangements relevant to the structure in its spatial and socioeconomic context.

Conclusion

One prescription for a new thrust in research on transport and development is two-pronged: a "political economy" and a "rational institutional" approach (Leinbach 1995, 2000). We can greatly increase our ability to understand the larger incentive system by including a political economy approach, something that is rarely if ever undertaken when

development is guided by only the neoclassical model. This involves a new examination of development schemes by expanding our concept of production to include the important role of women in local economies; the counterintuitive importance of new roads to bring in competing agricultural products from elsewhere, thus undermining rather than helping the nominal target population; the incentives that drive those who control transport resources; and a deeper understanding of rural household travel demand and factors that influence such demand (Doran 1990; Barwell and Zille 1987). But most critical again are changes in priorities for transport policy that must meet broader human needs instead of mainly those of elite groups as has traditionally been the case (Heggie 1989). While obviously informal transport cannot replace motorized forms, it can serve a high portion of local travel needs. Yet we need to stimulate research in this direction in order for change to come about. But in addition, and not unrelated, it may behoove us to explore the relations between transport and development through a "rational institutional approach" (Edmonds 1982). In this light, our inquiry assumes a strongly behavioral posture where "actors" are pointedly rational and seek to maximize material goals in the face of uncertain information concerning alternative behaviors. But more critically, it assumes that the institutional setting plays a critical role in defining those decision situations. These two approaches do fit together, for the first assumes a deeper understanding of transport needs and constraints. Given this, intervention and delivery strategies must take into account, even in remote rural areas, the institutional connections of accessibility.

References

Barwell, I., G. A. Edmonds, J. D. G. F. Howe, and J. deVeen. 1985. *Rural Transport in Developing Countries.* London: Intermediate Technology Publications.

Barwell, I., J. Howe, and P. Zille. 1987. *Household Time Use and Agricultural Productivity in Sub-Saharan Africa.* Oxford: IT Transport Ltd.

Blaikie, P., J. Cameron, and D. Seddon. 1979. The relation of transport planning to rural development. Development Studies Discussion Paper No. 50, University of East Anglia.

Bryceson, D. F., and H. John. 1993. Rural household transport in Africa: Reducing the burden on women. *World Development* 21, no. 11: 1715–29.

Button, K. 1993. *Transport Economics*. 2nd ed. Aldershot: Elgar.

Chambers, R. 1983. *Rural Development: Putting the Last First*. London: Longman.

———. 1997. *Whose Reality Counts? Putting the Last First*. London: Intermediate Technology Publications.

Doran, J. 1990. *A Moving Issue for Women: Is Low Cost Transport an Appropriate Intervention to Alleviate Women's Burden in Southern Africa?* Norwich: School of Development Studies, University of East Anglia.

Edmonds, G. A. 1982. Towards more rational rural transport planning. *International Labour Review* 121, no. 1: 55–65.

Ellis, F. 1993. *Peasant Economics*. 2nd ed. Cambridge: Cambridge University Press.

Filani, M. O. 1993. Transportation and rural development in Nigeria. *Journal of Transport Geography* 1, no. 4: 248–54.

Friedmann, J. 1992. *Empowerment: The Politics of Alternative Development*. London: Blackwell.

Heggie, I. 1989. Reforming transport policy. *Finance and Development* 26, no. 1: 42–44.

Hine, J. L. 1982. Road planning for rural development in developing countries: A review of current practice. Transport and Road Research Laboratory Report 1046, Crowthorne, England.

Hine, J. L., J. D. N. Riverson, and E. A. Kwakye. 1983a. Accessibility, transport costs and food marketing in the Ashanti region of Ghana. Transport and Road Research Laboratory Supplementary Report 809, Crowthorne, England.

———. 1983b. Accessibility and agricultural development in the Ashanti region of Ghana. Transport and Road Research Laboratory Supplementary Report 791, Crowthorne, England.

Howe, J., and P. Richards, eds. 1984. *Rural Roads and Poverty Alleviation*. London: Intermediate Technology Publications.

Jolibois, S. C. 1991. *Reorganizing Development: A Conceptual Framework for Efficient Rural Transport in LDCs*. Berkeley: Institute of Transportation Studies, University of California.

Leinbach, T. R. 1982. Towards an improved rural transport strategy: The needs and problems of remote third world communities. *Asian Profile* 10, no. 1: 15–23.

———. 1983a. Transport evaluation in rural development: An Indonesian case study. *Third World Planning Review* 5, no. 1: 23–35.

———. 1983b. Rural transport and population mobility in Indonesia. *The Journal of Developing Areas* 17:349–54.

———. 1995. Transportation and third world development: Review, issues, and prescription. *Transportation Research* 29A, no. 5: 337–44.

———. 2000. Mobility in development context: Changing perspectives, new interpretations, and the real issues. *Journal of Transportation Geography* 8, no. 1: 1–9.

Leinbach, T. R., and R. Cromley. 1983. A goal programming approach to public investment decision-making: A case study of rural roads in Indonesia. *Socio-Economic Planning Sciences* 17:1–10.

McCall, M. K. 1977. Political economy and rural transport: A reappraisal of transport impacts. *Antipode* 9, no. 1: 56–67.

———. 1985. The significance of distance constraints in peasant farming systems with special reference to sub-Saharan Africa. *Applied Geography* 5:325–45.

Nabli, M., and J. Nugent. 1989. The new institutional economics and its applicability to development. *World Development* 17, no. 9: 1333–47.

Ostrom, E., L. Schroeder, and S. Wynne. 1993. *Institutional Incentives and Sustainable Development*. Boulder, Colo.: Westview Press.

Owen, W. 1987. *Transportation and World Development*. Baltimore: Johns Hopkins University Press.

Replogle, M. A. 1991. Sustainable transportation strategies for third world development. In *Transportation Research Record 1294*, 1–8. Washington, D.C.: Transport Research Board.

Toh, K. W. 1989. Privatization in Malaysia: Restructuring or efficiency. *ASEAN Economic Bulletin* 5, no. 3: 242–58.

Watkins, J., T. R. Leinbach, and K. Falconer. 1993. Women, family and work in Indonesian transmigration. *Journal of Developing Areas* 27, no. 2: 377–98.

Wilson, G. 1966. Towards a theory of transport and development. In G. W. Wilson, B. R. Bergmann, L. V. Hirsch, and M. A. Kleig, eds., *The Impact of Highway Investment on Development*, 190–218. Washington, D.C.: Brookings Institute.

World Bank. 1996. *Sustainable Transport: Priorities for Policy Reform*. Washington, D.C.: World Bank.

CHAPTER 30

AGENT-BASED SYSTEMS AND POLICY ANALYSIS

Perspectives and Challenges for a New Approach to Economic Modeling

KATHRIN HAPPE AND ALFONS BALMANN

Theoretical Background

Economists have viewed economic processes as the result of interactions among large numbers of individuals ever since the writings of Adam Smith (1778) on the division of labor. Adam Smith was the first to provide ideas of how markets could coordinate the decisions and behavior of many economic actors and "transfer chaos and anarchy on unbridled greed into order and harmony" (Scitovsky 1990:135). The outcome of this self-coordinating property is a "competitive" economic equilibrium, a state of rest in which supply matches demand for all market participants. This "competitive" equilibrium is considered as a benchmark by which to judge outcomes of any other allocation process, and therefore also the outcome of any model (Kirman 1997). The condition to reach market equilibrium is quite weak; it requires only that prices drop in the face of excess supply and that quantities produced decline when prices are lowered (Simon 1996). As Simon also points out, market clearing can be achieved when economic agents are not rational but follow rather simple rules.

To show, however, that these price mechanisms generate an optimal market outcome in the sense of Pareto requires the strong assumptions of perfect competition and the maximization of profits or utility. The essence of optimal competitive market equilibrium—its crucial condition, so to speak—is that all market participants are "rational." This means (among other things) that all actors on the market have a universal knowledge of all possible patterns of exchange on the market (Shackle 1988) and optimize individual utility.[1] In an intertemporal context, the notion that a market is indeed in equilibrium implies that the market will be "cleared" at all possible points in the future. For this to occur, future expected prices, not just current prices, have to be taken into account (Erdmann 1993). The concept of an optimal outcome, together with the "marginal revolution" (in which prices were seen to be derived by the relation of supply and demand "at the margin" meaning at existing conditions) in the second half of the nineteenth century, provided the theoretical and methodological basis for neoclassical economics (Dopfer 2001). Marginal analysis allowed economists to describe an economic problem in the language of mathematics and to apply differential calculus to solve this problem to obtain a unique equilibrium. Starting with this, neoclassical economists have subsequently defined conditions (axioms) for the existence of market equilibria and their stability, such as the existence of property rights, indifference curves, and convex production functions.[2]

Since the 1940s, neoclassical economics has become the dominant paradigm in both economic research and teaching. The use of mathematics to express economic problems has certainly contributed greatly to this fact. However, despite its wide acceptance, economists and others have increasingly criticized neoclassical theory (e.g., Hall et al. 2001; see chapters 1–5.). Criticism mainly concerns the following points:

Economies are hardly ever in equilibrium for longer periods. On many markets, supply and demand fluctuate permanently and they never balance. Markets may even not be cleared ("bought up") at all over longer periods, as is the case on the labor market, for example.

Under certain conditions, an economic system may be in an equilibrium-like state, but one that is suboptimal. Such a system is locked into an inferior state. The reasons for this include the historical path dependencies that make it impossible or unattractive for a system in a particular inferior state to switch to the optimum state (Brandes 1978). Among the reasons for path dependence are network externalities or increasing returns to scale (David 1985; Arthur 1989), but also the power of big corporations.

For some goods (mainly environmental goods), property rights are imperfect (to put it mildly). The result is that individual behavior and socially optimal behavior do not correspond. This is one of the reasons for a number of problems, such as the excessive use (consumption and pollution) of the environment.

Today's economic reality is so complex that the intellectual and cognitive abilities of economic agents are hardly capable of determining lasting socially optimal behavior and putting it into practice.

Another issue is whether economics should be about only social and price issues, that is, whether economics might be equally studied from the perspective of other disciplines such as ecology (Hall 2000; Hall et al. 2001), physics (Stanley et al. 2000; Weidlich 1992), or evolutionary game theory (Mailath 1998; Friedman 1998).

To tackle selected criticisms, some economists have sought extensions in order to make neoclassical theory a better reflection of reality.[3] Game theory, parts of resource and environmental economics, information economics, industrial economics, and new institutional economics all represent such extensions in the vein of the neoclassical paradigm. All of these economic disciplines take central positions in modern economic research, and most have made their way into economics textbooks.[4]

Another group of scholars, however, went farther in that they took the shortcomings of the neoclassical paradigm as a starting point for rethinking the paradigm. Evolutionary economics is one

example of such efforts. The object of analysis in evolutionary economics is economic development and endogenous change, wherever it appears within a system. Following Witt (1987:9), an evolutionary theory of economics has to meet the following criteria:

1. The theory is dynamic: it explicitly covers development over time.
2. Time is historic and irreversible.
3. The theory makes hypotheses about why, how, and when novelty appears within a system.

The majority of evolutionary approaches that fundamentally question neoclassical thinking and do not take it for granted seem to have two things in common: First, they put the understanding of the economy as an evolving complex system at the center of their research (see Alchian 1950; Arthur, Durlauf, and Lane 1997). Second, they are concerned with understanding phenomena at a macro level as the result of the actions and interactions of individuals at the micro level (see Allen 1988; Schelling 1978; Day 1993). Despite the increasing attention that evolutionary approaches have gained over the past years, they have not become as successful and established as neoclassical economics and its modern predecessors.

What are the reasons for this? One reason probably is a similar view of the world that is centered on individual decision making, which is believed by many to be properly taken into account by neoclassical economics (therefore other approaches would look superfluous). Another reason is related to the use of formal analytical mathematics in economic modeling. Modern economics is primarily concerned (at least in theory) with empirically testable formal models that are applied to the economy and economic policies (Colander 2000). Conventionally, economic problems are expressed in terms of an optimization problem, which is solved using differential calculus and results in an analytical solution with either a unique equilibrium or multiple equilibria. The applicability of mathematics to economic problems is what Shackle (1988:214) calls the "toolbox conception of economic theory." It is also what is shown in numerous modern microeconomics textbooks, where economic problems are stated in mathematical terms. Evolutionary (or indeed biophysical or ecological) approaches do not possess a comparable toolbox that is equally standardized.[5] In addition, it is questionable whether this should be the ultimate goal of evolutionary approaches as they explicitly shift their attention away from finding equilibrium solutions toward the description and analysis of complex evolving processes such as the reasons and paths of economic change. A third reason could be seen in the rational-choice assumption, which is the dominant behavioral assumption of modern economics. As game theory shows, the rational-choice assumption allows deducing equilibrium solutions in a comparatively straightforward way (Axelrod 1997). Although it is more or less unquestionable that perfect rationality is not a realistic assumption about individual behavior, the advantage of the rational-choice assumption is that it allows deduction.

In particular, this latter point has been criticized extensively since the 1940s, and authors such as Schumpeter, Alchian, Hayek, Simon, Cyert and March, and Nelson and Winter proposed alternatives to the rational-choice assumption. A key aspect in these propositions is that they focus on some form of individual adaptive behavior. This includes seeing economic actors as heterogeneous and distinct individuals that do not necessarily follow the same decision patterns and that are boundedly rational (Simon 1955, 1996), meaning that they make decisions based on the information available to them, which can possibly even be wrong. As Simon (1955) writes, "Broadly stated, the task is to replace the global rationality of economic man with a kind of rational behavior that is compatible with the access to information and the computational capacities that are actually possessed by organisms, including man, in the kinds of environments in which such organizations exist."

Accordingly, the rational decision making of agents is strongly related to the availability of information in the environment of agents and the capacity of agents to process this information adequately.[6] An important issue, then, is that this information may often be incorrect or woefully inadequate. All of these perspectives are, of course, quite in line with other chapters in this volume, especially the very first one.[7]

A Different Approach: Agent-based Modeling of Complex, Evolving Economic Systems

Besides verbal descriptions and empirical studies, the evolutionary approach has increasingly resorted to numerical methods from mathematics and computer sciences to describe, model, and simulate the complex dynamics of economic systems. Ever more powerful computers and computational tools, most notably object-oriented programming, have facilitated this. In addition, agent-based computational economics is a result of these developments. Agent-based computational economics encompasses the computational study of economies modeled as complex evolving systems of autonomous interacting agents (Conte, Hegselmann, and Terna 1997; Epstein and Axtell 1996; Gilbert and Troitzsch 1999; Axelrod 1997). Agent-based tools permit researchers to extend existing research on the evolution of economic systems in five ways (see Tesfatsion 2001):

Artificial economic worlds can be computationally constructed that are populated with a multitude of heterogeneous agents that interact and develop according to defined internal rules. Within this artificial model world, it is possible to carry out numerous simulation experiments.

A broad range of agent behaviors and interactions can be defined. There is also the possibility that agents adapt their behavior, that is, change their rules, in response to interactions with other agents. Because behavioral rules are not necessarily fixed from the outset of the model, self-organized structures can evolve.

Agents in these artificial economic worlds can coevolve; the individual performance (fitness) of an agent depends on the evolving behavior of other agents.

Artificial economic worlds can grow along a real timeline. This means that the modeler sets initial conditions and subsequently observes the development of the system without acting upon it. This is similar to growing cultures in a Petri dish.

Artificial economic worlds can explicitly be connected to space to analyze land-use changes due to economic activity (Verburg et al. 2004; Parker et al. 2002).

Following Tesfatsion (2001), agent-based computational economics is a methodology that is able to blend tools and concepts from evolutionary economics, cognitive sciences, and computer sciences. This fact also determines the scientific value of the approach, which lies in:

1. the observation of interesting phenomena such as chaos, agglomeration, and path dependence, phenomena that cannot be observed in standard neoclassical models;

2. the possibility to look at economics from a different perspective that is not bound to an established theory and, based on this:

3. the formulation of new research questions that would not have come up with traditional research methods;

4. the construction of new theories on interactions between heterogeneous autonomous agents;

5. the testing and refinement of these theories through simulation experiments, statistical analysis, and interfaces to real data, and

6. the integration with other disciplines in models.

As promising as these points are, they also require careful research that demonstrates more concretely both the advantages and limitations of agent-based computational economics (Tesfatsion 2001:283). It is important to note, though, that the use of the agent-based metaphor in economics does not automatically imply an evolutionary model behind it. It is rather a metaphor that fits the requirements of evolutionary economics probably better than other modeling approaches.

Agent-based Systems
Definitions

Agent-based systems (ABS) or multiagent systems (MAS) originate from computer science, and in particular, from the field of distributed artificial intelligence, which started to form in the early 1980s. The motivation for an increasing interest in ABS research follows from the ability of ABS (see Sycara 1999):

1. to carry out certain tasks and solve problems with computer systems and computer programs that are complex themselves (just compare the features of a word processor from the early 1990s with today's systems). This calls for breaking down large complex programs into smaller parts.

2. to provide solutions to problems where expertise and knowledge are "possessed by individuals who communicate within a group, exchange knowledge and collaborate in carrying out a common task" (Ferber 1999).

3. to provide solutions to problems or explanation of phenomena that can naturally be regarded as a society of autonomous interacting components, like air traffic; but also an economy.

4. to use information efficiently that is spatially distributed.

ABS therefore represents a reaction to these needs. Ferber (1999:4) concludes:

The approach developed here [ABS] . . . takes into account the fact that simple or complex activities, such as problem solving, the establishment of a diagnostic system, the coordination of actions or the construction of systems, represent the fruits of interaction between relatively independent and autonomous entities called agents, which operate within communities in accordance with what are sometimes complex modes of cooperation, conflict and competition in order to survive and perpetuate themselves.

Table 30.1. Properties of agents

Property	Meaning
reactive (sensing)	responds in a timely fashion to changes in the environment
autonomous	exercises control over its own actions
goal-oriented (purposeful)	does not simply act in response to the environment
temporally continuous	is a continuously running process
communicative	communicates with other agents, perhaps including people
learning (adaptive)	changes behavior based on previous experience
mobile	able to move in space
flexible	actions are not given exogenously
character	credible "personality" and emotional state

Source: After Franklin and Graesser (1997)

There is a host of different agent definitions and depending on the type of research and the intended applications of ABS, users choose a different definition.[8] Agent definitions range from an understanding of agents as simple problem solvers (Sycara 1998) to agents that are endowed with a number of properties (Ferber 1999). Franklin and Graesser (1997) have looked at different agent definitions, and based on them they define the essence of agency thus: "An autonomous agent is a system situated within a part of an environment that senses that environment and acts on it, over time, in pursuit of its own agenda and so as to effect what it senses in the future." Still, the authors consider this definition very general, as according to it people as well as thermostats or software could be understood as agents. Therefore, Franklin and Graesser classify agents along certain properties (table 30.1). Accordingly, agents may be usefully classified based on subsets of properties, but the authors consider the first four properties to be the minimum requirements for an agent: an agent should at the same time be able to react autonomously and in goal-oriented ways to signals in the environment.[9]

Although ABS are mainly the domain of computer science and software technology, they have also penetrated other fields of research and practice, like robotics, biology, social sciences, and financial markets (see Luck et al. 2003 for an overview of current agent technology in Europe).

Special Features of Agent-based Systems

Three specific features of ABS are particularly important when applying the agent metaphor to (agricultural) economic systems, namely (1) flexibility, (2) the potential to represent complex emerging structures with heterogeneous and individual behavior, and (3) the integration of spatial aspects.

Building up on the features mentioned at the beginning of this article we shall now discuss in greater depth these features of ABS which in our view are particularly important.

Flexibility

ABS models belong to the class of "bottom-up" approaches. There is no central planner who controls the system as a whole, and hence the behavior of individual agents, at the aggregate level. Instead, regularities at the macro level are the result of local individual actions and interactions among agents. To reflect this, modelers can define agents along a broad range of different properties and behavioral rules.[10] The ABS approach allows endowing agents with a much greater variety of properties and behaviors than more conventional "top-down" approaches. In order to insure consistency between the micro and macro levels, "top-down" approaches require assumptions that are comparatively more restrictive. Heavy reliance is placed on externally imposed coordination devices such as fixed decision rules, rationality, representative agents, and market equilibrium constraints (Tesfatsion 2002). However, from the ABS perspective, it is questionable whether the assumptions mentioned are not too strong to achieve consistency between the micro and macro level. With respect to this, "bottom-up" approaches, and hence ABS models, are more flexible in that the model approach as such does not prescribe any fixed set of behavioral assumptions. Rather, assumptions are set depending on the specific problem. Consider, for example, the relationship between demand and supply. Without doubt, ABS models would require a certain degree of consistency between the micro and the macro level as nothing can be sold that was not produced beforehand. However, to achieve this consistency it is not necessary to impose perfectly rational agents or to assume market equilibrium. This flexibility in particular allows the modeler to implement and analyze the effect of alternative behavioral assumptions such as bounded rationality, or aggressiveness on markets. Accordingly, it is possible to achieve a more accurate model of reality.[11]

Furthermore, the flexibility of ABS extends to the definition of the framework conditions in which agents act and interact. Convex production functions and the existence of perfect markets with perfect knowledge of agents are not necessary requirements to obtain a unique solution of the model, as would be the case with analytical approaches. Nonconvexity is less of a problem since behavior on the agent level is commonly less complex than an adequate representation of behavior at the aggregate level. Because of this, the problem of NP-incompleteness is less severe.[12]

Another source of flexibility is the fact that the modeler creates a model world, and defines rules along which the world and its components develop over time. For example, real biophysical resources and their opportunities and limitations can be represented. The modeler is both a creator and controller of the model world. In other words, the modeler's cognitive abilities can be transferred into a computer model.

To summarize, ABS models are flexible in that they allow the modeler to define the model and set assumptions that are specific to the problem to be studied. Compared to conventional modeling approaches, ABS models increase the spectrum of possible models and assumptions that can be defined.

This greater flexibility in modeling economic actions is very advantageous; however, it requires the modeler to choose assumptions carefully with respect to their kind and quantity. Accordingly, assumptions should be well founded, justified, reasonable, and documented. Any assumption that does not comply with all of these criteria will necessarily make the model and its results less credible. This is important because an audience with at least some economic background will be familiar with standard economic assumptions, which for the most part stem from the neoclassical world. As for the number of assumptions, a highly flexible modeling approach such as ABS bears the danger of overspecification, of making the model too particular. This, however, increases model complexity, which does not necessarily increase the understanding of the real system to be modeled. The more complex and specific a model gets, the more difficult it is to establish a connection between causes and effects within the model and between the model and the target system. This can mean that, when tracing back the computation for formal causes, frequently the cause spreads over the whole system and cannot be attributed to a single causal factor (Edmonds 2000).

Complex structures and emergence

A particular feature of ABS is its ability to generate complex structures that change endogenously, or "from within." This particular property is known as self-organization. Examples are chaos, path dependence, or multiphase dynamics (see Balmann 1995; Manson 2001). A system is called self-organizing if the individual parts of the system interact in such a way that certain structures, including complex structures, arise without external influence (Brandes 1998). Self-organization applies not only to the structure of the system, but also to the speed of change, which is also determined from within and not set externally. If the speed of change is slow, then a system can potentially remain far away from an equilibrium for a long time.[13]

Another property of ABS is what is called emergent structures. Briefly, emergence describes the property that a system is not equal to the sum of its parts. Developments, which we can observe at the macro level, cannot be explained by observing the properties of the individual parts of the system in isolation (Emmeche 1994). They are rather the result of a very large number of interactions and individual actions of the parts of the system. Examples of emerging phenomena are the "invisible hand" that coordinates markets, a flock of birds, or living organisms in general. As fascinating as emergence phenomena may be, they are still difficult to handle in models. Axelrod (1997:4) notes: "Emergent properties are often surprising because it can be hard to anticipate the full consequences of even simple forms of interaction. . . . Some complexity theorists consider surprise as a part of the definition of emergence, but this raises the question of surprising to whom?"

Spatial representation

The agricultural economics profession has recognized the importance of the spatial and feedback mechanisms between economic agents and land use ever since the work of von Thünen and Ricardo. Verburg et al. (2004) underline the potential of ABS in current land-use-change modeling in particular with respect to exploring dependencies between different levels of scale by linking the behavior of individuals to collective behavior. Particularly in agriculture, land use takes a central position. Accordingly, spatial aspects have a direct effect on farm decision making, and therefore also on the economics of the farm. In addition to land value and transport conditions as the common driving force of land-use change, the suitability of land for agricultural production is determined by factors such as soil quality, climatic conditions, and slope that are not explicitly considered in economic models. What could eventually make ABS particularly attractive is the possibility of linking economic models with spatial models to support a better understanding of interdependencies between agent behavior and space in land use systems. There have been a number of efforts to integrate spatial models of land-use change with economic, social, and environmental models (Parker et al. 2002; Berger 2001; Bousquet et al. 1998; Barreteau, Bousquet, and Attonaty 2001; Rouchier, O'Connor, and Bousquet 2001; Janssen 2002).

Goals and Fields of Application of Agent-based Systems

Researchers from different disciplines use ABS models to pursue a variety of objectives. Table 30.2 shows one such classification of applications, according to which the modeling objective could be divided into problem solving and systems analysis. If agents are used as *problem solvers* this mainly concerns the solution of complex problems such as optimization problems. For this, agents can either work together to solve problems that are beyond their individual problem-solving capabilities (distributed problem solving) or, alternatively, each agent separately solves the complete problem (solution rivalry) and the best solution is taken. In distributed problem solving, a problem is decomposed into smaller subproblems, each of which is then solved by an individual agent. A tedious and time-consuming aspect of this process is the decomposition of a global problem into subproblems and the specification of the relation between the subproblem and the global problem. The same applies to the question of a how tasks should be allocated to agents.[14] Solution rivalry follows a different approach in that each agent in a population of heterogeneous agents solves the same problem. A central control agent then collects results and evaluates how well the individual agents solved the problem. The procedure selects bad solutions and replaces them with better or new solutions. This is, in very general terms, the procedure followed in approaches such as genetic algorithms (Holland 1975; Mitchell 1998; Goldberg 1989), genetic programming (Koza 1992), evolutionary strategies (Rechenberg 1973; Schwefel 1977), classifier systems (Holland 1975, 1995), or ant systems (Dorigo, Maniezzo, and Colorni 1996).

Agent-based systems also find applications in the field of *systems analysis* where they are used to study the behavior and development of systems of interacting individuals. Table 30.2 distinguishes three groups of exemplary applications by their

---

**Table 30.2. Examples of references to research using ABS models
in social systems analysis and problem solving**

General problem solving			Social systems analysis		
solution concept	distributed problem solving	solution rivalry	rule-based	normative	artificial intelligence
examples	O'Hare and Jennings (1996), Lesser (1990)	Holland (1975), Goldberg (1989), Rechenberg (1973), Schwefel (1977), Koza (1992)	Conway's "Life," Schelling (1978), Axelrod (1984)	Day (1963), Balmann (1993, 1997), Berger (2000), Happe (2004)	Axelrod (1997), Balmann (1998), Cacho/Simmons (1999), Balmann/Happe (2001), Balmann/Musshoff (2001)

---

solution concept: rule-based, normative, and artificial intelligence. Conway's game of life is one of the simplest examples of the first group. The game generates "emergent phenomena" based on simple rules. A cell located on a grid of cells changes its state according to the states of other cells. The player of the game can study how elaborate patterns and behaviors can emerge from very simple rules that the player defined beforehand. Another well-known example is the work by Schelling (1978), who studies spatial segregation and aggregation phenomena in different societies. The behavioral foundation of his agents is also very simple and based on simple rules such as "search for a new home if too many neighbors belong to another social class."[15] Yet another example of a simple rule-based ABS is Axelrod's (1984) simulation of agents (strategies implemented in a simple computer program) playing in a Repeated Prisoner's Dilemma game. It showed that the well-known tit-for-tat strategy was the most successful in the game. Although this was already proven in the 1950s, Axelrod's model nevertheless contributed significantly to the understanding of how social norms evolve (Anderies 2002).

In the second group of models, agents follow a normative behavior. Most agricultural economic ABS applications are located in this group. An early example of an ABS model based on normative behavior is recursive-programming models (Day 1963; Heidhues 1966; De Haen 1971), which were applied to analyze and forecast dynamic developments in the agricultural sector. The models allow farms agents representing farm types (group of farms) or regions to interact.[16] The farm agents are heterogeneous with respect to factor capacities, technical coefficients, and the definition of the objective function in the linear program underlying each farm agent. In each period, farm production capacities are updated based on previous experience, results of the last period, and external factors influencing the farm (Heidhues 1966). In principle, the models used in Balmann (1993, 1997), Berger (2001), and Happe (2004) follow a similar approach.[17] These models, however, are more complex and consider a multitude of individual farms instead of group of farms to represent an agricultural region. Each of these farms plans production using a linear or mixed-integer program. The factor that differentiates these models most from the earlier models of the 1960s is their explicit consideration of space.

In the third group of models, agent behavior is governed by artificial intelligence. Axelrod, again, gives a nice example for this type of model. Whereas in 1984 he had computer programs competing for the best solution to the prisoner's dilemma, in 1997 Axelrod replaced the computer programs in the 1984 tournaments with strategies generated by a genetic algorithm. For this, he defined a population of so-called genomes, each of which is coded in a binary string consisting of 0s and 1s. If decoded, each string corresponds to a particular solution or strategy that competes with the other genomes for the best solution to the problem. The genetic algorithm then replaces strategies with a worse performance with better ones. This particular property of a genetic algorithm is comparable to a simple type of learning.[18] Sample applications of genetic algorithms in agricultural economics are Cacho and Simmons (1999), who apply genetic algorithms to farm investment behavior in a risky environment. Balmann and Happe (2001) have applied a distributed genetic algorithm to determine equilibrium strategies on a lease market for land. In this model, a genetic algorithm determines the bidding behavior of farms on the land market, and selects for better bidding strategies. Balmann and Musshoff (2001) use genetic algorithms to derive equilibrium investment strategies for real options problems with competing agents.

Agent-based Models for Agricultural Economic Analysis

The preceding section presented some goals and fields of application of ABS. It hence sets out a general framework for an application of agent-based methods. We will now turn to the particular field of agricultural economics. We will first develop a conceptual basis for agent-based models in agricultural economic research. This is followed by an example of an agent-based model of agriculture, based on which possible directions of agent-based research are presented.

The Scope of ABS Models in Policy and Sector Modeling

Agricultural economics is an applied science that deals with two major concerns. The first is to develop a better understanding of a given target system, be it a farm, a region, or the sector, and to project possible future developments of this system. The second concern is to study the various effects of policies on a given target system. In regard to the first points, researchers are particularly interested in finding the (economic, technical, ecological, or social) laws and rules governing the agricultural system. For this, they use models that are located at different levels or scales. Many agricultural system models aim to integrate economic with non-economic aspects of agriculture such as environmental factors (e.g., emissions, nutrient leaching, soil erosion), technical relations, or animal health and welfare. As for the second point, policy analysis, policies are commonly evaluated along specific indicators, such as efficiency, income, or environmental impacts. Developing a good representation of a target system and policy analysis cannot be seen separately from each other, as sound policy analysis requires an appropriate representation of the target system to derive meaningful conclusions. Despite this interdependence we will further our focus on the second concern, policy analysis.

Traditionally, quantitative models have played a major role in agricultural policy analysis. Most of these models view agriculture from a macro perspective (country, sector, or region) or from a micro perspective, that is, the perspective of the individual farm.[19] In the latter case, individual farm models are usually aggregated to derive effects at a higher level of scale such as a region or sector. Such an intermediate-scale approach is useful because if one follows either the macro perspective or the individual farm perspective strictly in policy analysis, one leaves out a number of effects that are situated in between the micro and the macro levels. These effects, such as structural or distributional effects, may nevertheless play an important role when deciding on implementing one policy in favor of another. In this respect, two points appear to be crucial:

1. A pure macro level neglects the heterogeneity of individual agents and in particular their individual behavior. If farms are built into these models, then they are usually treated as aggregates representing a group of farms. Regarding policy analysis, the use of macro models for prediction amounts to an extrapolation of aggregate data patterns into the future, with no, or only a very limited, foundation to the behavior of individual economic agents (Stoker 1993). In that sense, a representative farm alone does not sufficiently account for heterogeneity between farms.

2. Farm-based micro-models look at individual farms or groups of farms. For this, they use individual farm data and simulate the effect of changes in policy on each of these units. As much as certain agricultural policies

affect individual farms' behavior (e.g., direct payments), there is also an aggregate policy effect that can be observed at the regional, sector, or society level. This aggregate effect is the result of individual farmers' decision making (Wossink 1993). In other words, what can be observed at the macro level (e.g., changing market prices or structural change) is the combined effect of individual farm activity that becomes obvious in farm size changes, changes of production technology, change in farm types, or farms quitting production. Because of this, a simple aggregation of micro-level characteristics to represent a region or even the sector does not do. It could not possibly consider the full differences among individual farms, dynamic adjustment processes, and interactions among farms, in brief the genuine complexity of the system.

The conclusion of these two arguments is that an approach is lacking that combines farm behavior and interactions among farms and that includes the aggregate effects in a consistent way. The ABS approach offers some potential to fill this gap as it acknowledges explicitly the contribution of each individual farm in the chosen target system (e.g., a small region) to the outcome at a higher level of scale. This could lead to important new insights about policies, such as the connection between agricultural policies and structural change, while including dynamic effects. Hence, an ABS model of agriculture could overcome aggregation problems because, theoretically, it is possible to model all farms in a region as well as dynamic interactions among them.[20] In this sense, an agent-based model of agriculture would provide one answer to Stoker's (1993) request "to build empirical models that are applicable to the applied question of aggregate data, but retain the feature of modeling behavior at the individual level."[21]

What are specific challenges that agricultural policies pose to modeling? More generally, it is the role of agricultural policies to set framework conditions of the agricultural system. Policies define part of the action space, that is the set of possibilities, in which farms can develop over time, and in which structural change takes place. Agricultural policies affect the system at different points and at different levels of scale. For example, price policies do not affect individual farms directly but through markets; direct payments, on the other hand, are paid to individual farms, and affect markets only indirectly. Thus a good model of agricultural development must capture this environment within which real farms operate.

In the European Union, the agricultural policy framework was pretty much constant until the late 1980s, and if it changed, it did so only slowly. Nevertheless, in recent years, the speed of agricultural and environmental policy change has accelerated considerably. In 2000, the EU introduced the Agenda 2000. Subsequently, in the face of ten new states accessing the EU in 2004, the European Commission proposed another set of policy reforms, known as the 2003 reform of the Common Agricultural Policy (EU Commission 2003). These policies are directed at providing a sound budgetary basis for financing the accession of the new member states. In addition to this, the commission claims to respond to what society demands from agriculture, such as tighter environmental regulations. The key contents of the reform are the following:

1. Direct payments to farmers are decoupled from production allowing the farms maximum flexibility in terms of production decisions.
2. Direct payments to farms are progressively reduced over time (modulation). The increased funds resulting from this action shall be transferred into regional development funds (the second pillar of agricultural policies).
3. The policies intensify the principle of cross-compliance, which states that full financial aids will be granted to farmers only if they comply with defined management requirements and good agricultural practices.
4. The policy responds to society's demand for safe food, environmentally friendly

production methods, and animal welfare.

5. The policy provides a framework in which farmers can act as entrepreneurs.

Already these few points may give an idea about the diversity and variability of agricultural policy. They give an impression of the existing pressure on the agricultural sector to adjust to the policy environment. The points also suggest two things. On the one hand, it can be expected that structural change will speed up. On the other hand, individual local behavior, local interaction, and therefore heterogeneity will become increasingly important.[22] The new Common Agricultural Policy, however, challenges current agricultural policy analysis because, for the most part, policies are no longer located at the macro level (e.g., price policies), but are increasingly farm-specific such as direct payments bound to the person of the farmer. This has obvious consequences for policy analysis models as the focus of analysis is shifting from a global and general perspective to local specific problems at the farm or regional level. Moreover, because of this shift of perspective the complexity of the problems to be studied increases. Meeting the new modeling challenges adequately requires not only methodological advances (as mentioned at several places in this chapter), but equally that modelers look out and apply new methods and techniques, and in particular, the heavy use of computers to answer relevant questions.

The intense use of computers in agricultural economics has a long history that goes back to the 1950s (e.g., linear programming models). Nevertheless, the relative importance of computer-based analyses in agricultural economics research has actually decreased since the 1970s, with computing power being increasingly replaced by theoretical findings (mostly microeconomic and often associated with neoclassical approaches and even ideology). Computers and software packages have become standard research tools for implementing this ideology without fully using the computing capacities that ever more powerful computers could offer for more realistic analysis. It is only with the availability of new computer-based research methods, such as genetic algorithms, neural networks,

and ABS, that computing power has become more important again because of properties such as nonlinearity, stochasticity, or dynamics, which are inherent to many problems of the real world. As was seen before, specific problems such as those posed by agricultural policy analysis require the use of new methods and powerful computers. One such challenge is the handling of data. With numerous databases, the Internet, and better communication channels, the availability of data has increased enormously. However, to integrate this data into models or to build models around data has not become easier.

Summing up, new methodologies, better computers, and highly improved data management provide a window of opportunity for agricultural economic modeling that could possibly lead to a great number of new insights. In principle, ABS models could provide one possibility to fill out this window. Assuming that progress in computing power continues at its current speed, from a pure computing perspective, it should be possible to run computing-intensive simulation experiments in ten years' time. Whether this will make sense depends not only on cognitive abilities but also crucially depends on how to overcome the apparent weaknesses of the ABS approach in general and the model approach presented here in particular.

The Agent-based Agricultural Policy Simulator: AgriPoliS
The model

After having introduced the need for MAS models in agricultural economic research in this section we now turn to a concrete example of an agricultural MAS model. Our initial motivation for AgriPoliS (Agricultural Policy Simulator) (cf. Happe 2004) is to study dynamic effects of agricultural policies on structural change processes in small-scale agricultural regions.[23] Hence, referring to table 30.2, the objective of AgriPoliS is to obtain further insights into the agricultural system. The core of the AgriPoliS model is the understanding of a regional agricultural structure as an ABS. This system, shown schematically in figure 30.1, consists of a number of individual farms that act individually and interact with each other subject to their

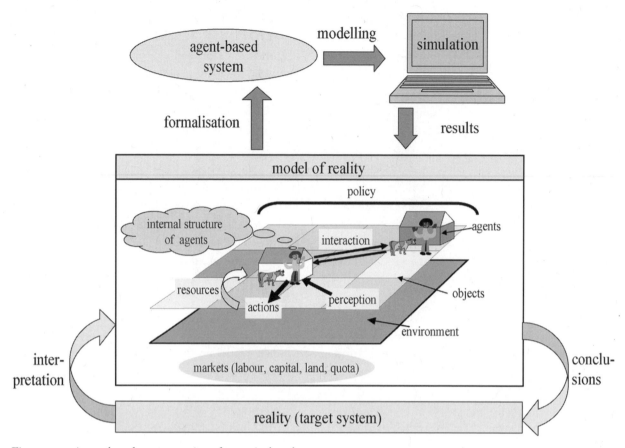

Figure 30.1. Agent-based representation of an agricultural system.

actual state and to their individual environment. This environment consists of other farms, factor and product markets, space, and the technological and political environment. The actions of agents are determined based on an internal behavioral model that we shall discuss in more detail further down in the text. This agent-based model of a real target system can be formalized subsequently as a computer program, which then simulates the evolution of the system. On the basis of the simulation results, conclusions can be drawn for both the model system and under certain conditions, for the underlying target system as well.[24]

Before we present a more detailed description of the AgriPoliS model and its central features, such as the land market, we first want to introduce the kind of agents used in the light of table 30.1. Within AgriPoliS, there are two kinds of agents, farm agents and a land market agent. Farm agents represent agricultural households. They follow a normative behavior by maximizing farm

household income. AgriPoliS farm agents have a number of the properties mentioned in table 30.1. Besides their goal-orientation, we assume farm agents act autonomously, exercising control over their own activities. This means that each farm agent decides individually on the organization and activities of its farm. Furthermore, agents react to changes in their environment. For example, farms react to increasing competition on the land market by adjusting farm organization or, at the extreme, by giving up farming altogether. Farms are also flexible in the sense of table 30.1 because farm variables change from one simulation period to the next. For example, a farm's equity capital changes from one period to the other due to either profits or losses incurred in a period. The second kind of agent, the land market agent, coordinates the allocation of free land to farms willing to rent land. As the land market is implemented as an iterative auction, the land market agent can be interpreted as the auctioneer who collects bids

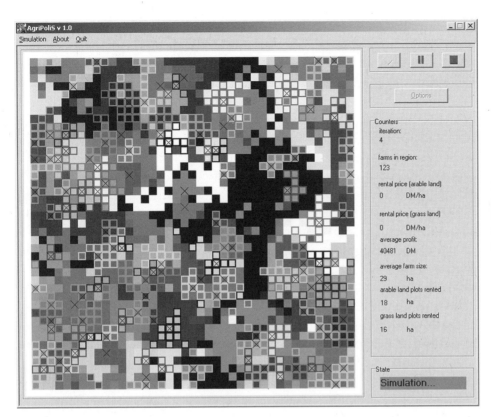

Figure 30.2. Exemplary graphical user interface (GUI) of AgriPoliS. See website for color originals.

from farm agents, ranks them, and allocates the respective land.

In this contribution, we have applied AgriPoliS to study the agriculture and structural dynamics of the Hohenlohe region of southwestern Germany. Hohenlohe comprises about 75,000 hectares of agricultural land. In figure 30.2, this region is represented as a GIS-like grid of about 30,000 cells of 2.5 hectares each.[25] The cells in figure 30.2 represent agricultural land; 75 percent of the land is arable land, and 25 percent grassland. The black cells are fallow land. There are about 2,600 farms in the region, which can be interpreted as agents in analogy to figure 30.1. The location of a farmstead on the graphical user interface is marked with an X. Each individual farm has owned and leased land. In figure 30.2, all land (owned and leased) belonging to one farm has the same color; each parcel of land owned by a particular farmer is also surrounded by a box.

Each farm agent can engage in thirteen production activities (pig fattening, pig breeding, turkeys, dairy cows, beef cattle, suckling cows, crops, sugar beet, rapeseed, and permanent grassland) that are typical for the region. For production, farms can choose between twenty-nine investment options

(buildings, machinery, facilities) of different types and sizes to implement economies of size.[26] Farms can also lease or let land, production quotas, and manure disposal areas. Additional labor can be hired on a fixed or per-hour basis, but farm family labor can equally be offered off-farm. To finance farm activity, farms can take up long-term, and short-term, credit. Similarly, liquid assets not used on-farm can be saved. Farms quit production either if they are illiquid or if the opportunity costs of the production factors used do not cover costs.

If a farm makes an investment, then we assume the investment will affect production capacities for its entire operating lifetime. This means that investments cannot be used for other purposes; their investment costs are therefore said to be sunk. Farms are handed over to the next generation every twenty-five time steps (representing years). If this is the case, opportunity costs of farm family labor increase by 15 percent, which can be interpreted as an investment into agricultural training. And finally, farms differ not only with respect to factor endowment (environmental conditions) and production technology, but also with respect to the management ability of the farmer. To reflect this, we provide each farmrandomly with a so-called management factor that affects the farm's profitability and competitiveness by way of variable production costs.

Production and investment decisions are made simultaneously on the basis of a single-period mixed-integer program, which is updated each period. Even though farms optimize their production program, farm decision making can still be called myopic or boundedly rational because the decision problem of the model farms is highly simplified compared to the real decision problem. For instance, farms cannot communicate directly, cooperate, or merge. They also cannot act strategically, which would imply that farms would base their decisions on a perfect knowledge of all interactions among farms, and the technical and political framework conditions now and in future periods. Because farms are considered by agricultural economists as "boundedly rational," markets coordinate individual actions.

In the main, farms appear to follow adaptive expectations: they adjust to mistakes they made during previous periods. Policy changes known to the farms beforehand are included into the decision-making process one period in advance, and farms determine how they would behave in the next period under changed policy conditions. Furthermore, we assume that the prices of livestock and cereals will continue to follow a slight downward trend.

Before the simulation starts, the location of the farmsteads, as well as the farms' initial endowments with production factors (family labor, machinery, buildings, production facilities, land, production quota, liquid assets, and borrowed capital), are specified. During the simulation, these and other variables change as a result of production, lease, and investment activities. Even though farms do not interact directly with each other, they are connected indirectly via markets for products, land, milk quota, and manure disposal area.

Within AgriPoliS, the land market is of particular relevance, since farms cannot grow independently of land. In Germany, farms grow predominantly by leasing additional land. We therefore consider only a land rental market. Land is available on the market either because farms have

quit farming or because unprofitable land is let for lease by farms still in the business. The land market is implemented as an iterative auction organized by the land market agent. In the auction, each farm determines the plot it wishes to lease. The farm determines a bid for this plot depending on the shadow price for land, the number of adjacent farm plots, and the distance-dependent transport costs between the farmstead and the plot.[27] Adjacent plots and the bid are correlated positively because we assume that economies of size in crop production can be realized with larger field sizes.[28] To reflect this, a markup is added to the bid depending on the number of adjacent plots, which increases the probability that the farm will receive the plot it wishes. Finally, the bids are collected and compared by the land market agent; the farm with the highest bid receives the plot it wishes to lease. This process continues until all land is leased or the bids are zero. The renting process alternates between arable land and grassland. As other costs associated with leasing land, such as taxes and fees, are not considered in the bid formation, the actual rent paid is set at 75 percent of the bid. To avoid strong dynamic effects and a large fluctuation of rents between periods, the rent paid for a plot each period is adjusted toward the average rent paid for newly leased plots.

AgriPoliS furthermore implements technical change in the form of process innovations. With process innovations, farmers usually expect to realize cost savings. In AgriPoliS we implement this relationship by assuming that with each new investment the variable unit costs of the product produced with the investment object decrease between 1 and 1.5 percent. As farms are highly heterogeneous in reality, it is hardly possible to determine the exact cost-saving effect. The labor-saving features of larger investments, which were mentioned above, also represent an instance of technical change.

Data and model calibration

We calibrated both the farm agents and the region to the Hohenlohe region. To initialize the farms we derive so-called typical farms from accounting data of selected real farms in Hohenlohe

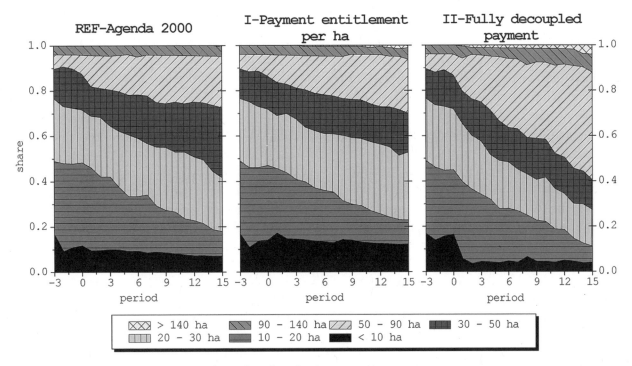

Figure 30.3. Development of farm size classes for selected policy scenarios.

from the 1997–98 financial year.[29] Where data were not available from accounting records, such as data on prices, production costs, and technical coefficients, they were taken from standardized data collections published for other regions or the whole of Germany (KTBL, Landesanstalt für Landwirtschaft, Regierungsbezirk Mittelfranken 2000). The farms selected for Hohenlohe are considered typical for the region; they cover the most important farm types, production activities, and organizational forms of the region. Farms and the agricultural structure in AgriPoliS are calibrated to reflect some key characteristics of the real region. For this, each typical farm is assigned a frequency that takes into account the total number of farms in the region, differentiated by size, farm type, land use, and livestock production.[30] The frequencies are determined by minimizing the weighted quadratic deviation between the total number of farms in the model and in reality (Balmann, Lotze, and Noleppa 1998). In a final step, the now 2,600 model farms, which are based on 12 different typical farms, were further individualized with respect to a number of farm decision variables. The age and kind of buildings, facilities, and machinery, and the exact farm location were initialized at random.

A simulation of the full region (2,600 farms) over twenty time periods takes about ten hours on a PC with a 1.8 GHz processor. During the simulation large amounts of data are generated that show the developments of about ninety farm variables for each farm and the development of the region. The data are then read into data analysis and visualization programs (e.g., Excel, Origin, SPSS, Matlab) and can subsequently be analyzed to answer certain research questions.

Example results

In the following, we show some typical results based on an application of AgriPoliS to policy analysis (figure 30.3 shows a graph of representative results).

The graph on the left shows the development of farm classes under the conditions of the Agenda 2000. One central feature of Agenda 2000 has been the granting of direct payments to farmers as a compensation for market price decreases. As mentioned before, the 2003 reform of the European Union's Common Agricultural Policy has represented a major turnaround in policy making. We simulated a policy similar to the decoupling in the 2003 reform. The key change is to give payments to farms on a historical reference and divide the resulting total direct payment per farm by the farm's hectares to get what is called payment entitlement. The corresponding farm-size distribution is shown in the middle graph. Another, more radical, approach is to decouple direct payments from any farming activity and attach it to the person of the farmer. This is like a lump sum payment to an individual farmer granted irrespective of what the farmer is doing. The effect of this rather severe policy change on the farm size distribution is depicted in the figure on the right. This graph shows that a pronounced and sudden policy change, such as the complete decoupling of direct payments on short notice, may result in significant structural changes that cause many farmers to quit farming.

Further Directions of Agent-based Research in Agriculture

The notion of an agricultural system as a complex adaptive system has existed long before agent-based systems and nonlinear dynamics had been an issue. As was mentioned before, already Day (1963) and possibly many scholars before him understood the agricultural system as a complex system consisting of a large number of individual interacting agents developing over time. In that sense, the ABS interpretation is not new to agricultural economics; however, it had never been taken up explicitly until the 1990s when authors such as Balmann (1993), Bousquet (1994), or Le Page and Cury (1996) developed cellular automata or agent-based models of agricultural or natural resource systems. Assuming that the abstraction presented in figure 30.1 is appropriate for representing an agricultural system, what could be possible starting points for new ABS models or extensions to existing models in the field of agricultural economics? Five possible directions can be identified, which will be discussed in more detail below:

structural development of real regions;
representation of agent behavior;
modeling economies in transitions and also
  farm economies of less-developed countries
  (LDCs);

modeling of organizations;
integrated modeling (using GIS, bioeconomic
  models, combining agent-based modeling
  with biophysical modeling).

Representing the structural development of real regions

Regional structural development has been at the center of the first ABS models in agricultural economics. In particular, the model by Balmann (1997) represents a fictitious agricultural region with a number of farms aimed at exploring the determinants of path dependence in regional structural change. This model allows carrying out simulation experiments on the impact of factors such as sunk costs, higher opportunity costs of labor, and inverse demand structure. Since farms in the model region are fictitious, the model's scope for analysis existed in exploring general patterns of path dependence and their origin within the modeling system. The model AgriPoliS (Happe 2004), as well as the model by Berger (2001), is inspired by the Balmann Model. As shown before, these models have an interface with real data and are calibrated to represent real regions at a particular point in time.

A necessary precondition for modeling agricultural regions in detail is the availability of data. At the farm level, the FADN (Farm Accountancy Data Network) database of the European Union certainly provides a suitable repository of data for different regions that can be used to define typical farming systems. Regional data can also be obtained from statistical offices. For less developed countries or regions, the availability of data may be more limited, if not impossible.[31] This, of course, limits substantially the scope for calibrating the model to real data. In any case, whenever individual data on farms or regions is not available, the modeler has to choose the second-best option, which often also is stylized data or expert knowledge. The case is similar for time series data of farms and regions. Despite the availability of data of good quality, there remains the problem of preparing the data to specify the model farms adequately. This also requires much more detailed data, for example, on prices and technological coefficients, than today's standardized data sources provide. Hence, with respect to the underlying data, there remains a large demand for empirical investigations and data surveys. Whether this will ever be put into practice can be questioned in the face of the ever-decreasing importance of the agricultural sector and the financial requirements of a detailed data survey.

Behavioral foundation of agents

Besides a detailed representation of agents based on real data, another important question is what agents do based on the information available to them. Let us take the example of AgriPoliS. If we take an individual farm agent as the object of analysis, agent behavior is determined normatively using optimization techniques such as linear programming. The objective of a farm agent then is either to maximize profit (or gross margin), or to minimize costs. However, this well-established behavioral foundation of farms poses a challenge to future modeling.

On one hand, it is questionable whether farms really aim to maximize income (Brandes 1985). Especially with respect to agriculture in LDCs other goals such as securing food availability or maintaining social structures (families, villages), appear to be of greater importance. On the other hand, there is the question of whether linear programming is an appropriate method to model farm behavior, having in mind that it can represent only a fraction of the actual decision problem. Weak factors, such as social conditions, cannot be included. Furthermore, the linear programming approach depends on the availability of technical coefficients that quantify the use of a certain resource (e.g., land) to produce an output (e.g., crops). As for development issues, technical coefficients are often not readily available from verified statistical sources, and possibly they are of poor quality.[32]

What are possible alternatives on which to base individual agent behavior? One starting point for an alternative representation of agent behavior is artificial intelligence methods such as genetic algorithms or neural networks (Balmann 1998; Balmann and Happe 2001; Balmann and Musshoff 2001).

Another approach that has been applied by the CORMAS research group in a number of LDCs is to develop model behavior based on field experiments (Bousquet et al. 1999). To do so, researchers first survey users of a common pool resource about individual attitudes about the use of the resource and the way they use the resource. In a second step, the surveyed information is then transferred into the simulation model, which is then simulated. A third approach could be to base model behavior on role-playing games with real agents (Barreteau, Bousquet, and Attonaty 2001). The results of role-playing games may give information about the potential behavior of agents in computer programs. Kellermann (2001), who has developed the agricultural business game PlayAgriPoliS, in which players take the position of a politician or a farmer, follows a slightly different approach. Because players are involved in the game and can influence it, they can observe and experience directly the complex effects of setting particular policies on a system with many agents. This approach may also provide insight into information and communication channels that real persons use in order to make certain decisions. This, in return, could be implemented in model agents.

Economies in transformation and less-developed countries

A further prospective development of ABS models is to apply them to transformation processes such as to agriculture in former communist countries or a number of less-developed countries (LDCs). In these countries, agriculture takes a central position and a large share of the countries' labor force is employed in agriculture. Although they are often applied to countries in transition, it is difficult to apply general equilibrium models to the agricultural sector in these countries. The prime reason for this is that markets are often incomplete, subject to information asymmetries but also to failures. Furthermore, transition countries exhibit a situation that is far away from equilibrium due to explosive demography, heavy migration patterns, and endemic rural poverty. The poor do not have the bargaining power that allows Pareto optimality (or even Pareto inferiority).

Market-oriented reforms that accompanied multilateral trade liberalization and structural adjustment programs in less-developed countries (LDCs) have lead to increased integration of the rich and politically connected farmers of the LDCs to world markets but have left out the immense majority of the agricultural working force. Interestingly, farmers in LDCs receive ten times less in subsidy than European or American ones, yet development banks continue to promote a free-trade model—one that has not survived in developed countries—to LDCs that do not have the instruments to cope with market risk or that cannot compete on a level playing field with the subsidized agriculture of the developed countries.

What becomes clear, though, is that an agricultural system in transition most likely develops far away from the equilibrium (a condition assumed by conventional economics), while embodying strong dynamics that often come about spontaneously and unplanned (e.g., a sudden change of political regime). Because of these properties of transformation processes, an application of general or partial equilibrium models appears to be rather unlikely.

In other words, the case of LDCs is complex and instruments such as ABS have the potential to deal with that complexity, freeing the analyst from the underlying axioms of equilibrium approaches and allowing experimenting with different, locally valid decision rules. These arguments may offer a broad window of opportunity for ABS models, since it is less the objective of ABS models to strive for an equilibrium solution than to model and simulate the complexity and dynamics of a system.

In view of the behavioral foundation of farm agent behavior in the context of LDCs and countries in transformation and the problems associated with optimization it seems to be a turn away from a strong quantitative optimization perspective toward more qualitative research. This involves, for instance, the modeling of local systems and social structures such as villages or cooperatives with the objective to understand the interrelation of the different components of the system. The companion modeling approach followed

by the CORMAS group (Bousquet et al. 1998; Barreteau, Bousquet, and Attonaty 2001), which identifies different "points of view" of the stakeholders involved and subsequently bases the definition of behavioral rules on these, appears to be promising in this respect.

Modeling organizations

In agricultural economic and development research, the ABS approach is not limited to models of sectors and regions. In fact, the ABS approach extends to all issues that involve the organization of different parts in a system, and therefore it extends also to the modeling of specific organizations including companies, families, villages, and the process chain (see Carley and Lee 1998; Carley 1999; Organization Science 1999).

Regarding process chains, agent-based methods could provide a way to model interdependencies between different levels of the system. Large firms can equally be understood as a complex system with different stakeholders (agents) with differing interests. Accordingly, an agent-based model of large firms could, for example, elucidate the process of decision making and facilitate the development of a model of decision making with many stakeholders. Such a model of an organization could become important to understanding decision making in the companies formed by former communist farm cooperatives that have a variety of different stakeholders (e.g., members, employees, lessors, lenders, managers) each following a different objective. A model could investigate stakeholder influence on the decision making and development of the organization. Particularly in LDCs, social organizations such as families or villages seem to have an important influence on decision making in that preserving a stable social organization is at the center of decision making. Making decisions purely out on the basis of optimizing income and profits such as is done with conventional models would therefore neglect a significant aspect of reality in many LDCs.

Integrated modeling

Integrated modeling concerns the combination of models from different disciplines. Berger (2001) gives an example of integrating an economic agent-based model with a hydrological model for an agricultural model in Chile. The model considers return flows of water between different irrigation regions in addition to a large number of individually acting agents that represent farms.[33] In general, the application of agent-based methods to the study of land-use/land-cover change has been growing steadily over the past decade. Agent-based models of land-use/land-cover change combine a cellular model representing the landscape of interest with an agent-based model that represents decision-making entities (Parker et al. 2002).

Problems When Dealing with Agent-based Models

Up to this point we have presented what we think is the scope of agent-based modeling in economics in general and agricultural economics in particular. A scientific approach to modeling requires every modeler (using classical methods or new methods) to be rigorous and to be aware of the possible problems associated with the model and the chosen approach. This also holds for agent-based modeling. Accordingly, in this subsection we shall mention aspects that represent a source of problems when dealing with agent-based methods. One group of problems is of a more theoretical nature, whereas a second group of problems deals with developing ABS models, verifying and validating the model, and getting results across to the audience.

Problems Arising from Theoretical Considerations

One reason for researchers to use ABS models is their ability to reflect the complexity and dynamics embodied in the real system that is the subject of their studies. Accordingly, an ABS model could show some complex behavior itself such as experiencing large shifts in outcome in response to small changes in inputs (Manson 2001). This claim to an ABS model's validity has consequences for handling and analyzing these systems in applied research.

To elucidate some of these theoretical problems, let us assume that a system that shows some kind of complex behavior (e.g., nonlinear dynamics) moves toward what is known as an attractor.[34]

Further, we assume that there is not one attractor but a number of different attractors. If we have no ex ante information about the exact number and topology of possible attractors, it is impossible to anticipate the exact direction in which a system develops. We can only form expectations about future developments that are based on past experiences. Even if a single attractor was known, it does not mean that the system is actually going to move toward this attractor during the period that we observe, or that it is of interest to a modeler. For instance, if a system develops infinitely slowly, no simulation will be able to capture the development of the system. What we observe about a system such as an economy is necessarily always only a part of the whole system. Finally, whether a system is moving toward an attractor or whether it is locked in a transient state also depends on the initial conditions or initialization of the system. If the attractor model is applied to an economic system then an attractor could correspond to an economic equilibrium. The consequence is that an economic system can develop and remain far away from an economic equilibrium (attractor) for a very long time. This phenomenon, for example, provides a reasonable explanation for persisting small-scale family farm–dominated agricultural structures (Balmann 1999). With respect to economies in transition, there is also some strong evidence that they are not in fact in equilibrium.

Coordination and consistency within agent-based systems represent another theoretical challenge. We have seen that ABS modeling follows an inherent "bottom-up" approach. ABS are decentralized systems in which a central planner is absent (if this is what we want) so that agents store information locally and act more or less autonomously. Because individual behavior in economic systems needs to be compatible and consistent (Day 1995) interdependencies between agents need to be defined, either directly (e.g., via message exchange between agents) or indirectly (e.g., via markets). As long as individual agents do not consider these interdependencies in their respective decision problem, the overall system is manageable. The picture gets more complex if agents do include these interdependencies in their decisions—if decisions become strategic, in other words. It states that each agent's decision is no longer determined exclusively by the specific decision situation of the individual agent, but also by the decision situation of—in the extreme—all other agent in all periods. In other words, each agent would have to have a model about the strategic situation and behavior of all other agents, who again have a model of the strategic behavior of other agents. Finding a solution to the strategic decision situation is everything but trivial. For a small number of agents the problem may be tractable, but with an increasing number of agents the problem may not be computable anymore. A solution furthermore depends on how myopic agents are. If all agents see only themselves, if they are extremely myopic, then the overall problem is comparatively simple. At the other extreme are fully rational agents, in which case the problem will most probably not be solved. In principle, there are two ways out. One solution was just mentioned, namely to endow agents with a bounded rationality—that is, to base agent behavior on simple ad-hoc rules that mimic some strategic aspects but reflect a myopic view of agents. This is probably a realistic behavioral assumption. Another solution would be to establish central institutions that facilitate the coordination in a system with a multitude of actors such as markets, auction, and traditions.

Practical Problems and Challenges

ABS modeling efforts have to cope with a number of practical problems that range from model design to required labor and time input to the dissemination of results and acceptance with an audience. In the end, the way to solve these practical problems may contribute significantly to the success and meaningfulness of the model approach. Even though most model undertakings face similar problems, in this section we will discuss them briefly in the light of ABS models. What lies at the background of any modeling approach is the question of what factors make a model approach last—that is, what factors make an approach that appeals to researchers, teachers, and policy makers. Three key factors are model validation and verification, implementation of a model, and the ways in which

a model and results can be disseminated to reach an interested audience.

Verification and validation

The general question to be asked of all models is how well a model represents the underlying target system in its structure and behavior. Verification and validation are two facets of this question. Accordingly, a model needs to be valid and verified in order to produce meaningful results.

Verification is generally associated with the process of testing the software model to ensure the proper functioning of the program (Kleijnen 1995; Manson 2001; Gilbert and Troitzsch 1999, chapter 2). Possible sources of errors are the program syntax and also the logic. Powerful debugging environments, graphical interfaces, or the application of standardized data analysis methods such as regression analysis help in detecting logical errors is. But most of all it is experience and familiarity with the subject itself that avoids most logical errors.

Validation, on the one hand, is concerned with the question of whether the simulation is a good and suitable representation of the target system (Hall and Day 1977; Gilbert and Troitzsch 1999). On the other hand, there is the view that a model's validity can be measured by the model's ability to make good predictions and retrodictions (Moss 2000). Regarding ABS models, the need for validation depends on the degree to which the model is to be used for theoretical reasoning or in applied research. For example, if an ABS model is of a purely conceptual, theoretical, or didactic nature it is difficult to validate such an artificial model against real systems or real data. Hence, the more applied the ABS model, the higher is the need for thorough validation. But this is also not a straightforward procedure, inasmuch as the validation of complex simulation systems generally is a difficult task (Weinschenck 1977; Odening and Balmann 1997; Brandes 1985). Following Manson (2001), the key caveat is the effect of complexity or nonlinear relationships. This is because complex models can generate complex and often surprising model results. Despite this, surprising outcomes cannot be treated as outliers. In any case, outcomes must be validated along the greatest possible number of benchmarks. Hence, complexity is not an excuse for results that cannot be explained. Unfortunately, there is no standardized validation procedure for ABS models. Currently, good validation of ABS models requires use of multiple, complementary methods. Manson (2001) presents different validation and verification techniques such as statistical methods, comparison of model patterns to patterns of real systems, and spatial validation techniques. Kwasnicki (1999) proposes a list of criteria along which to evaluate a simulation model (correctness, consistency, universality, simplicity, fecundity, usefulness).

In addition to these rather "objective" criteria, validation and verification also hinge upon theoretical convictions about the model used. For example, Balmann (1999) identified the combined effect of sunk costs together with economies of scale to explain the persistence of small-scale family farms. However, most agriculture economists accept neither the effect of sunk costs nor economies of scale on a broad basis. As a consequence, the model and its outcome may not be considered valid because it conflicts with these economists' normal assumptions, and they may thus reject it. In the end, only those who are already convinced of the importance of sunk costs and economies of scale will agree with the line of reasoning. This example shows that validation itself is never entirely objective, but depends on the cognitive capacities of both modelers and the audience.

Model implementation and maintenance

Before designing the actual components of an ABS model, it is necessary to decide on whether it is appropriate to develop a new model from scratch or to adapt an existing approach by relevant factors to fit our needs.[35] Recently, different groups undertook a number of efforts to develop modeling platforms for ABS (e.g., SWARM, RePast, Ascape, CORMAS, or the SimCog project) that provide enough functionality to build basically any kind of ABS model.[36] Such metamodeling platforms also have the advantage that agent definitions can be exchanged more easily between models and used in more than one model.

The next step in the modeling process concerns model design and its implementation as a computer program. The model design defines the basic building blocks of the model and how model components interact. Interaction in this respect concerns interaction within the model (e.g., between agents) but also between the model and the user (e.g., by way of a graphical user interface), or external data and the model. To facilitate the design process, there exist a number of tools (e.g., UML) with whose help the model structure and design can be represented. The next step is the actual implementation of the concept as a computer program. Object-oriented programming languages such as C++, Java, and SmallTalk are suitable for agent-based modeling because object-orientation, which is the programming concept of these languages, is very similar to the definition of agents by means of attributes and actions.

Communication and acceptance

A look at agricultural economic models that have been successfully applied to agricultural policy and sector analysis in the past reveals that these models seem to be intuitive to policy makers, and also to other researchers.[37] This applies particularly to the model objectives, the underlying assumptions, results, model design, and documentation. What are the reasons for this? One reason could be that the theoretical background of the model is familiar to the addressees because this is what they may have learned about economics before. As standard economic theory is what is taught and written about, this is most likely what addressees know about economics. In that sense, its axioms represent a kind of common knowledge. This creates a kind of standardization of economics within people's brains and provides a common basis for discussion, or perhaps we should say sometimes a starting place for raising our objections to it.

As we have mentioned at different points in this chapter, ABS model approaches do not show a similar standardization, and may never even reach it because they aim at representing variety. This is a clear disadvantage in terms of communicating a modeling approach. The problem is aggravated by the fact that complex models require long and detailed documentation to lay out all model components. Because of length restrictions, it is difficult to place them in respective journals. What could be achieved though is to generate a general understanding of complexity and dynamics with an audience. This could provide at least a basis for constructive and critical discussion of complex systems modeling approaches. This would also prevent researchers from dismissing complex systems models from the very beginning. Pursuing the development of metamodeling platforms is also a step in the same direction, inasmuch as these platforms make it easier for a broader audience to gather experiences with developing and experimenting with complex systems models in general and ABS specifically.[38]

Communication of ABS, however, is only one side of the problem. Provided that ABS models or complex systems models provide a promising approach for applied policy research, they need to be accepted by addressees that are by their very nature policy makers and other researchers. More efforts are needed to achieve this with ABS because, just as with any other product, the qualities of the new product ABS have to compete on the market with other more traditional approaches. With respect to policy analysis models, the market is quite dense. The fact that ABS provides a consistent approach for regional modeling on the basis of individually acting farms is no comparative advantage in itself.

Hence, ABS models can become relevant only if addressees are convinced not only by the methodological advantages of ABS, but also by the fact that the study of complexity and dynamics pays off. An example from agricultural policy analysis might underline this: conventional agricultural-policy analysis was concerned with different kinds of policies and the effects of these. What did not play a role, though, because it was difficult or impossible to analyze, was the timing of policies—that is, if a policy change were introduced at once or slowly over time. This issue, however, has significant effects on how farms adjust to a policy change, and therefore it also affects structural change and markets.

There also seems to be an increasing demand from policy makers for alternative models to policy analysis that aim to take more account of the complexity of the system and the heterogeneity of actors. With respect to this, Bonnen and Schweickhardt (1998) state, "The analytic power of economic analysis comes from the logical, often mathematical and statistical rigor, and from theory and assumptions that simplify the conceptual framework of the analysis. We are trained to resist movements away from this methodological dispensation. . . . Economists abstract from real-world conditions for the disciplinary purposes, but policy makers must deal with the world as they encounter it."

In his 1990 address to the American Agricultural Economists Association, Warren E. Johnston states, "The recognition of this diversity amplifies the need for careful analysis of more complex issues and problems and certainly challenges those who seek answers for policy and decision makers."

Conclusions

Agent-based methods offer a great number of possibilities for helping see economic reality from different points of view. They offer opportunities to study research questions that would otherwise be difficult or even impossible to analyze with conventional economic methods. Therefore, agent-based methods open up the possibility of finding new answers to both old and new questions. They offer a way to address the complexity of development by relying on common sense, observation, and intuition rather than on neoclassical paradigms. This does not mean that traditional economics is not good per se, but it does mean that it should be more systematically confronted with other approaches. ABS represents one attempt in that direction. What is promising, though, is the fact that in recent years ABS has become an important field of research and applications in computer sciences and complexity studies and is now a common tool in e-commerce (see Luck et al. 2003), or in electricity markets (e.g., Reticular Systems 1999). Despite these developments, agent-based methods have penetrated into the economic discipline only slowly, and even less into agricultural economics. The challenge to agricultural economic and development research is to identify and develop the necessary skills to take up new developments and new methods like ABS. As it is a comparatively new field of research the full scope of use of ABS is not yet entirely explored.

Provided that there is potential for further agent-based research, it is only possible to use these new options and possibilities effectively if they fall on fertile ground. This means that policy makers and researchers in particular should possess at least a basic understanding of complexity, and of the scientific value these approaches would offer. We by no means call for a complete turn away from traditional approaches such as neoclassical economics. We rather think that researchers should be able to move within and between different paradigms and examine the perhaps different policy decisions that might come out of different systems of analysis. This is what serious research calls for: to question existing paradigms constantly and leave them if necessary.

Notes

1. Rubinstein (1998) lists four conditions of the rational man hypothesis: (1) perfect knowledge of the choice problem; (2) a clear preference ordering; (3) the ability to optimize, that is, the assumption that the decision maker has all skills necessary to make whatever complicated calculations are needed to discover his optimal course of action; and (4) the indifference to logically equivalent description of alternative choices.

2. Convexity is a necessary condition for finding a solution to a mathematical problem. It implies that consumers always prefer a mixture of two product bundles to a single product bundle.

3. Lucas (1986) takes a strong opposing standpoint to the claim to better reflect reality: "Economics works surprisingly well, under some conditions, and I think progress is more likely to follow from an understanding of the factors that have contributed to past successes and from trying to build on them than from attempts to reconstruct economics from the ground up in the image of some other science."

4. Colander (2000) even calls for abandoning the term "neoclassical economics" as modern economics substantially differs from what has originally been called "neoclassical economics."

5. Recently, there have been some efforts to at least establish a common theoretical basis (see Dopfer 2001).

6. Brandes et al. (1998) discuss a number of reasons

why it is not necessarily "optimal to optimize." The prime reason is that if a decision problem is sufficiently complex, search costs are high. Accordingly, agents tend to be satisfied with the first solution that fits their individual aspiration level, one that is not necessarily optimal.

7. In principle, transaction-cost economics faces a similar problem because it also assumes that agents are boundedly rational. However, transaction-cost economics uses a trick by making a concrete definition of bounded rationality. Then it asks how this limited knowledge can be dealt with in a rational way, if competitors also behave rationally.

8. On a discussion of agent definitions, see Anderies (2002).

9. This is only one possible agent definition. Other authors (e.g., Ferber 1999) have defined agents in a different way with slightly different properties. For the purpose of this study, the presented classification appears to be the most appropriate.

10. It is not a necessary condition that each individual agent follows a different behavioral pattern, but ABS offers the possibility to implement this if needed.

11. This is not a necessity, though. For a deeper discussion on model abstraction, see Edmonds (2000).

12. NP-incompleteness means that with an increasing number of variables or restrictions, the necessary computing time increases exponentially or as a faculty. An example for this is the traveling salesman problem, where the necessary computing time for an optimization for n locations to be visited increases by n.

13. The concept of self-organization originally stems from the natural sciences (see, e.g., Haken 1988; Kauffman 1993; Odum 1988) and it concerns elementary particles in the first place. Concerning this fact, Lentz (1993) points out that the elements (humans) in social systems are not of a particle nature but complex themselves. Unlike elementary particles, they are intelligent in that they can "plan" structures to a certain extent.

14. Methods like artificial neural networks might help here, because they endogenize the decomposition and specification of the problem. The modeler has to specify respective variables and the kind of neural network to use.

15. Educative agent-based simulation environments, like StarLogo (Resnick 1997), give many other examples. Users can easily run and modify predefined simulations or create new, simple applications.

16. Although the field of agent-based systems did not exist in the 1960s, and hence the terminology has not existed, the group farm or regional farms fulfill the criteria for simple agents. However, the solution was determined

in a single linear program (LP), which also included simple exchange routines. It would have been equally possible to solve a separate LP for each individual farm, but at that time, nobody thought about that.

17. Berger's modeling approach extends and refines the ideas of Balmann's original approach in many respects. Farms follow heterogeneous decision models, and they can communicate explicitly within communication networks. Because water management played an important role in the study region, a hydrological module was added to the model in which water flows are considered in addition to a trade of water rights. The model was initially used to study the adoption of new technologies in a selected region in Chile. Recently, the model is being adapted to water management and land-use problems in Uganda.

18. According to Chattoe (1998), "learning" in this type of models does not correspond to human learning. Humans learn at a different speed and according to different rules. It is less problematic, though, to view this approach as a way to identify Nash equilibria and evolutionary stable strategies (see Dawid 1999).

19. See Heckelei, Witzke, and Henrichsmeyer (2001), which provides an overview of agricultural sector modeling and policy information systems.

20. Happe and Balmann (2002), for example, consider more than 2,500 individual farms.

21. It is interesting to note that Stoker at no place in his survey article mentions ABS methodologies. But at the same time, with his line of argumentation and conclusions, he sets the ground for ABS models.

22. Vertical integration of farms can be viewed as one characteristic in this development. Farms are less interacting on anonymous markets, but increasingly interact bilaterally or with a well-defined number of partners, such as in quality programs, for example. Consequently, a farm's success is increasingly the result of direct interaction with other actors on the market.

23. More detailed technical model documentation can be downloaded from www.iamo.de/dok/sr_vol30.pdf.

24. This point is probably the most crucial and critical one in agent-based modeling as, strictly speaking, we can only draw conclusions within the limits of the model. The quality of conclusions is also critically determined by the model's validity, that is, its ability to map the target system.

25. AgriPoliS is not (yet) connected to a GIS of the region; hence, the distribution of plots is purely random. For reasons of simplification, figure 30.2 shows only 10 percent of the total region.

26. With increasing size, the costs per unit produced decrease and labor is assumed to be used more efficiently.

27. As shadow prices for land can possibly increase with land endowment, it would be desirable to bid for more than one plot at a time. This poses computational difficulties, though. Therefore, in addition to the shadow price for only one plot, we calculate the shadow price for renting eight plots at a time and take the maximum of both as the basis for the rent offer.

28. There are some estimates that production costs of cereals would decrease by 30 percent if the plot size were increased from 2.5 to 30 hectares.

29. An adaptation to the financial year 1998–99 appeared unsuitable because of the extremely unfavorable situation on pig markets.

30. Kleingarn (2002) provides a more detailed description of the database and the calibration procedure.

31. Although data often are available, they are not issued due to reasons of data protection.

32. A study on sustainable farming in the northeast of Brazil carried out at the University of Hohenheim faced the problem that a number of statistical offices and administrations published technical coefficients on, for example, water requirements of certain plants, but these were not coherent with each other.

33. Berger's approach considers a multitude of farms following heterogeneous decision models. In the model farms can communicate explicitly within communication networks. Another application is water management and land use in Uganda.

34. The detection of logical errors in the program is a much more difficult task because such errors may become apparent only by chance or if simulation results do not make sense to the modeler.

35. A model's level of abstraction is mainly determined by the underlying research question—the question to be tackled and answered with the help of the model. Where exactly to place the model in the continuum between abstraction and detail depends on the availability of data, knowledge of the target system, expertise, access to information, modeling skills, and experience (Gilbert and Troitzsch 1999). Hence, one possible conclusion is that the more applied the research question, the higher the detail of the model.

36. The SimCog project (www.lti.pcs.usp.br/SimCog/index.html) aims at developing a metamodeling platform for cognitive agents. The development is based on an ongoing survey of researchers' requirements of ABS simulation platforms. Parker et al. (2002) provide a good synopsis of the other modeling platforms.

37. By success we mean acceptance by the audience and a broad dissemination of results.

38. In the past, we have had numerous discussions about ABS with neoclassical trained agricultural economists. And it often was the case that a great number of them lacked a basic understanding of complexity and dynamics. In our view, this can partly be explained by the fact that these scholars may recognize the existence of complexity in general, but less in their own subject.

References

Alchian, A. A. 1950. Uncertainty, evolution, and economic theory. *Journal of Political Economy* 58:211–22.

Allen, P. M. 1988. Evolution, innovation and economics. In G. Dosi, ed., *Technical Change and Economic Theory*, 95–119. London: Pinter.

Anderies, J. M. 2002. The transition from local to global dynamics: A proposed framework for agent-based thinking in social-ecological systems. In M. A. Janssen, ed., *Complexity and Ecosystem Management: The Theory and Practice of Multi-agent Systems*, 13–34. Cheltenham, England: Edward Elgar.

Arthur, W. B. 1989. Competing technologies, increasing returns and lock-in by historical events. *Economic Journal* 99:116–31.

Arthur, W. B., S. N. Durlauf, and D. Lane, eds. 1997. The economy as an evolving complex system II. *SFI Studies in the Sciences of Complexity* 27. Reading, Mass.: Addison-Wesley.

Axelrod, R. M. 1984. *The Evolution of Cooperation*. New York: Basic Books.

———. 1997. *The Complexity of Cooperation: Agent-based Models of Competition and Collaboration*. Princeton, N.J.: Princeton University Press.

Balmann, A. 1993. Modellierung regionaler Agrarstrukturentwicklungen mittels des Konzepts 'zellulärer Automaten.' *Zeitschrift für Agrarinformatik* 2:34–41.

———. 1995. *Pfadabhängigkeiten in Agrarstrukturentwicklungen—Begriff, Ursachen und Konsequenzen*. Berlin: Duncker & Humblot.

———. 1997. Farm-based modelling of regional structural change: A cellular automata approach. *European Review of Agricultural Economics* 24, no. 1: 85–108.

———. 1999. Path dependence and the structural development of family farm dominated regions. *IX European Congress of Agricultural Economists Organized Session Papers*, 263–84.

Balmann, A., and K. Happe. 2001. Applying parallel genetic algorithms to economic problems: The case of agricultural land market. *Proceedings of IIFET 2000*.

Balmann, A., and O. Musshoff. 2001. Real options and competition: The impact of depreciation and reinvestment. Working paper, Humboldt University of Berlin.

Balmann, A., H. Lotze, and S. Noleppa. 1998. Agrarsektormodellierung auf der Basis 'typischer Betriebe.' *Agrarwirtschaft* 47, no. 5: 222–30.

Barreteau, O., F. Bousquet, and J.-M. Attonaty. 2001. Role-playing games for opening the black box of multi-agent systems: Method and lessons of its application to Senegal River Valley irrigated systems. www.soc.surrey.ac.uk/JASSS/4/2/5.html.

Berger, T. 2001. Agent-based spatial models applied to agriculture: A simulation tool for technology diffusion, resource use changes, and policy analysis. *Agricultural Economics* 25, nos. 2–3: 245–60.

Berger, T., and C. Ringler. 2002. Tradeoffs, efficiency gains and technical change: Modeling water management and land use within a multi-agent framework. *Quarterly Journal of International Agriculture* 41, nos. 1–2: 119–44.

Bonnen, J. T., and D. B. Schweikhardt. 1998. Getting from economic analysis to policy advice. *Review of Agricultural Economics* 20:582–601.

Bousquet, F. 1994. Distributed artificial intelligence and object-oriented modelling of a fishery. *Mathematical Computer Modelling* 2018:97–107.

Bousquet, F., I. Bakam, H. Proton, and C. Le Page. 1998. CORMAS: Common-pool resources and multi-agent systems. *Lecture Notes in Artificial Intelligence* 1416:826–38.

Bousquet, F., O. Barreteau, C. Le Page, C. Mullon, and J. Weber. 1999. An environmental modelling approach: The use of multi-agent simulations. In F. Blasco, ed., *Advances in Environmental and Ecological Modeling*, 113–20. Paris: Elsevier.

Brandes, W. 1978. Zur Konzentration der Agrarproduktion in der Bundesrepublik Deutschland aus Betriebswirtschaftlicher Sicht. *Agrarwirtschaft* 27, no. 1: 1–12.

———. 1985. *Über die Grenzen der Schreibtischökonomie*. Tübingen: Mohr.

Brandes, W., G. Recke, and A. Berger. 1998. *Produktions- und Umweltökonomik*. Vol. 1. Stuttgart: Ulmer.

Cacho, O., and P. Simmons. 1999. A genetic algorithm approach to farm investment. *Australian Journal of Agricultural and Resource Economics* 43, no. 3: 305–22.

Carley, K. M. 1999. On the evolution of social and organizational networks. In S. B. Andrews and D. Knoke, eds., *Research in the Sociology of Organizations:*

On Networks in and Around Organizations, 3–30. Stamford, Conn.: JAI.

Carley, K. M., and J. Lee. 1998. Dynamic organizations: Organizational adaptation in a changing environment. In J. L. Baum, ed., *Advances in Strategic Management*, 269–97. Stamford, Conn.: JAI.

Chattoe, E. 1998. Just how (un)realistic are evolutionary algorithms as representations of social processes? www.soc.surrey.ac.uk/JASSS/1/3/2.html.

Colander, D. 2000. The death of neoclassical economics. *Journal of the History of Economic Thought* 22, no. 2: 127–43.

Conte, R., R. Hegselmann, and P. Terna, eds. 1997. *Simulating Social Phenomena*. Berlin: Springer.

David, P. A. 1985. Clio and the economics of QWERTY. *American Economic Review* 75:332–37.

Dawid, H. 1999. *Adaptive Learning by Genetic Algorithms: Analytical Results and Applications to Economic Models*. 2nd ed. Berlin: Springer.

Day, R. H. 1963. *Recursive Programming and Production Response*. Amsterdam: North-Holland.

———. 1993. Evolution in economic processes: Introductory remarks. *Structural Change and Economic Dynamics* 4, no. 1: 1–8.

———. 1995. Multiple-phase economics dynamics. In W. Takahashi and T. Maruyama, eds., *Nonlinear and Convex Analysis in Economic Theory*, 25–45. Berlin: Springer.

De Haen, H. 1971. Dynamisches Regionalmodell der Produktion und Investition in der Landwirtschaft. *Agrarwirtschaft Sonderheft* 43.

Dopfer, K., ed. 2001. *Evolutionary Economics: Program and Scope*. Dordrecht: Kluwer Academic.

Dorigo, M., V. Maniezzo, and A. Colorni. 1996. The ant system: Optimization by a colony of cooperating agents. *IEEE Transactions on Systems, Man and Cybernetics Part-B* 26, no. 1: 1–13.

Edmonds, B. 2000. The use of models: Making MABS more informative. In S. Moss and B. Edmonds, eds., *Multi-agent-based Simulation*, 15–32. Berlin: Springer.

Emmeche, C. 1994. *Das lebende Spiel: Wie die Natur Formen erzeugt*. Hamburg: Rororo.

Epstein, J. M., and R. Axtell. 1996. *Growing Artificial Societies: Social Science from the Bottom Up*. Cambridge, Mass.: MIT Press.

Erdmann, G. 1993. *Elemente einer evolutorischen Innovationstheorie*. Tübingen: Mohr.

EU Commission. 2003. Council Regulation (EC) No. 1782/2003.

Ferber, J. 1999. *Multi-Agent Systems: An Introduction to Distributed Artificial Intelligence*. Harlow, England: Addison-Wesley.

Franklin, S., and A. Graesser. 1997. Is it an agent, or just a program? A taxonomy for autonomous agents. In J. P. Müller, M. J. Wooldridge, and J. P. Jennings, eds., *Intelligent Agents III: Agent Theories, Architectures, and Languages*, 21–35. Berlin: Springer.

Friedman, D. 1998. On economic applications of evolutionary game theory. *Journal of Evolutionary Economics* 8:15–43.

Gilbert, N., and K. Troitzsch. 1999. *Simulation for the Social Scientist*. Buckingham, England: Open University Press.

Goldberg, D. E. 1989. *Genetic Algorithms in Search, Optimization, and Machine Learning*. London: Addison-Wesley.

Haken, H. 1988. *Information and Self-Organization: A Macroscopic Approach to Complex Systems*. Berlin: Springer.

Hall, C. A. S., ed. 2000. *Quantifying Sustainable Development: The Future of Tropical Economies*. San Diego: Academic Press.

Hall, C. A. S., and J. W. Day. 1977. *Ecosystem Modeling in Theory and Practice*. New York: Wiley-Interscience.

Hall, C. A. S., D. Lindenberger, R. Kümmel, T. Kroeger, and W. Eichhorn. 2001. The need to reintegrate the natural sciences with economics. *BioScience* 51, no. 8: 663–73.

Happe, K. 2004. Agricultural policies and farm structures: Agent-based modelling and application to EU-policy refrom. IAMO Studies on the Agricultural and Food Sector in Central and Eastern Europe 30.

Happe, K., and A. Balmann. 2002. Struktur-, Effizienz- und Einkommenswirkungen von Direktzahlungen. *Agrarwirtschaft* 51, no. 8: 376–88.

Heckelei, T., H. P. Witzke, and W. Henrichsmeyer, eds. 2001. Agricultural sector modelling and policy information systems. *Proceedings of the 65th European Seminar of the European Association of Agricultural Economists*.

Heidhues, T. 1966. *Entwicklungsmöglichkeiten landwirtschaftlicher Betriebe unter verschiedenen Preisannahmen*. Hamburg: Paul Parey.

Holland, J. H. 1975. *Adaptation in Natural and Artificial Systems*. Ann Arbor: University of Michigan Press.

———. 1995. *Hidden Order: How Adaptation Builds Complexity*. London: Addison-Wesley.

Janssen, M., ed. 2002. *Complexity and Ecosystem*

Management: The Theory and Practice of Multi-Agent Systems. Cheltenham, England: Edward Elgar.

Johnston, W. E. 1990. Structural change and the recognition of diversity. *American Journal of Agricultural Economics* 72, no. 5: 1109–23.

Kauffman, S. A. 1993. *The Origins of Order: Self-organization and Selection in Evolution.* New York: Oxford University Press.

Kellermann, K. 2002. PlayAgriPoliS—Ein agentenbasiertes Politikplanspiel. M.S. thesis, Humboldt University, Berlin.

Kirman, A. P. 1997. The economy as an Interactive System. In W. B. Arthur, S. N. Durlauf, and D. Lane, eds., *The Economy as an Evolving Complex System,* 491–531. Reading, Mass.: Addison-Wesley.

Kleijnen, J. P. C. 1995. Verification and validation of simulation models. *European Journal of Operational Research* 82:145–62.

Kleingarn, A. 2002. Anpassungskosten von Agrarpolitikänderungen—Erstellung und Kalibrierung der Datengrundlage für ein räumlich-dynamisches Multiagentenmodell der Region Hohenlohe. M.S. thesis, Humboldt University, Berlin.

Koza, J. 1992. *Genetic Programming: On the Programming of Computers by Means of Natural Selection.* Cambridge, Mass.: MIT Press.

Kuratorium Technik und Bauwesen in der Landwirtschaft (KTBL). Various years. Data collection for agriculture.

Kwasnicki, W. 1999. Evolutionary economics and simulation. In T. Brenner, ed., *Computational Techniques for Modelling Learning in Economics,* 3–44. Dordrecht: Kluwer Academic.

Landesanstalt für Landwirtschaft des Landes Baden-Württemberg. Various years. Deckungsbeiträge für ausgewählte landwirtschaftliche Produktionsverfahren.

Le Page, C., and P. Cury. 1996. How spatial heterogeneity influences population dynamics: Simulations in SEALAB. *Adaptive Behavior* 4, nos. 3–4: 249–74.

Lucas, R. E. 1986. Adaptive behavior and economic theory. *Journal of Business* 59, no. 3: 401–26.

Luck, M., P. McBurney, C. Preist, and C. Guilfoyle. 2003. Agent technology: Enabling next generation computing—A roadmap for agent based computing. www.agentlink.org.

Mailath, G. J. 1998. Do people play nash equilibrium? Lessons from evolutionary game theory. *Journal of Economic Literature* 36:1347–74.

Manson, S. M. 2001. Simplifying complexity: A review of complexity theory. *Geoforum* 32, no. 3: 405–14.

Mitchell, M. 1998. *An Introduction to Genetic Algorithms.* Cambridge, Mass.: MIT Press.

Moss, S. 2000. Messy systems: The target for multi-agent-based simulation. In S. Moss and B. Edmonds, eds., *Multi-agent-based Simulation,* 2–14. Berlin: Springer.

Odening, M., and A. Balmann. 1997. Probleme einer Politikoptimierung: Konsequenzen für die Konstruktion von Agrarsektormodellen. *Schriften der Gesellschaft für Wirtschafts- und Sozialwissenschaften des Landbaues e.V. 33,* 371–81. Münster-Hiltrup: Landwirtschaftsverlag.

Odum, H. T. 1988. Self organization, transformation and systems. *Science* 242:1132–39.

Organization Science. 1999. Special Issue on the Application of Complexity Theory to Organization Science. *Organization Science* 10, no. 3.

Parker, D. C., T. Berger, S. M. Manson, and W. J. McConnell, eds. 2002. Agent-based models of land-use/land-cover change. Report and Review of an International Workshop October 4–7, 2001, Irvine, California.

Rechenberg, I. 1973. *Evolutionsstrategie: Optimierung technischer Systeme nach Prinzipien der biologischen Evolution.* Stuttgart: Frommann-Holzboog.

Regierungsbezirk Mittelfranken. 2000. Deckungsbeiträge, Variable Kosten, Akh-Bedarf der wichtigsten landwirtschaftlichen Produktionsverfahren, inkl. Sonderkulturen. www.regierung.mittelfranken.bayern. de/wir_f_s/wissensw/landwirt/db2000.dbf.

Resnick, M. 1994. *Turtles, Termites, and Traffic Jams: Explorations in Massively Parallel Microworlds.* Cambridge, Mass.: MIT Press.

Reticular Systems. 1999. Using intelligent agents to implement an electronic auction for buying and selling electric power. www.agentbuilder.com/ Documentation/EPRI/index.html.

Rouchier J., M. O'Connor, and F. Bousquet. 2001. A multi-agent model for transhumance in North Cameroon. *Journal of Economic Dynamics and Control* 25:527–59.

Rubinstein, A. 1998. *Modeling Bounded Rationality.* Cambridge, Mass.: MIT Press.

Schelling, T. 1978. *Micromotives and Macrobehavior.* New York: Norton.

Schwefel, H-P. 1977. *Numerische Optimierung von Computer-Modellen mittels der Evolutionsstrategie.* Basel: Birkhäuser.

Scitovsky, T. 1991. The benefits of asymmetric markets. *Journal of Economic Perspectives* 4, no. 1: 135–48.

Shackle, G. L. 1988. *Business, Time and Thought: Selected Papers of G. L. Shackle*. London: Macmillan.

Simon, H. A. 1955. A behavioral model of rational choice. *Quarterly Journal of Economics* 69:99–118.

———. 1996. *The Sciences of the Artificial*. 3rd ed. Cambridge, Mass.: MIT Press.

Smith, A. 1776. *The Wealth of Nations*. London: Skinner.

Stanley, H. E., L. A. Nunes Amaral, P. Gopikrishnan, V. Plerou, and B. Rosenow. 2000. Econophysics: What can physicists contribute to economics? In D. Helbing, H. J. Hermann, M. Schreckenberg, and D. E. Wolf, eds., *Traffic and Granular Flow '99: Social, Traffic, and Granular Dynamics*, 15–30. Berlin: Springer.

Stoker, T. M. 1993. Empirical approaches to the problem of aggregation over individuals. *Journal of Economic Literature* 31, no. 4: 1827–75.

Sycara, K. P. 1998. Multiagent systems. *AI Magazine* (summer 1998): 79–92.

Tesfatsion, L. 2001. Introduction. *Journal of Economic Dynamics and Control* 12:281–93.

———. 2002. Agent-based computational economics. *Artificial Life* 8, no. 1: 55–82.

Verburg, P. H., P. Schot, M. Dijst, and A. Veldkamp. 2004. Land use change modelling: Current practice and research priorities. *GeoJournal* 61, no. 4: 309–24.

Weidlich, W. 1992. Das Modellierungskonzept der Synergetik für dynamische sozio-ökonomische Prozesse. In U. Witt, ed., *Studien zur Evolutorischen Ökonomik II*, 39–63. Berlin: Duncker & Humblot.

Weinschenck, G. 1977. Zur Anwendung der Systemforschung und der Simulation in der landwirtschaftlichen Sektoranalyse. Forschungscolloquium 1977 des Lehrstuhls für Wirtschaftslehre des Landbaus, Kiel.

Witt, U. 1987. *Individualistische Grundlagen der evolutorischen Ökonomik*. Tübingen: Mohr.

———. 1991. Economics, sociobiology and behavioral psychology on preferences. *Journal of Economic Psychology* 12:557–73.

Wossink, A. 1993. Analysis of future agricultural change: A farm economics approach applied to Dutch arable farming. PhD dissertation, Wageningen University.

Chapter 31

Making Tropical Agriculture More Sustainable by Using Bioeconomic Models

Bruno Barbier, Daniel Deybe, Véronique Alary,

and Chantal Line Carpentier

Introduction

Small farmers from the tropics are struggling to sustain their livelihoods while the world's natural and policy environment is changing. Trade liberalization affects many of these farmers differently—often negatively when subsidies and protections are removed, sometimes under the direction of "structural adjustment" programs of, for example, the IMF or the World Bank; in some cases positively when previous policies were biased against agriculture and when a freer access to market expands opportunities. Looking beyond short-term profits, the question of whether the new policies induce more sustainable production systems is still quite ambiguous.

Small farmers are also struggling to adopt new technologies. There seemingly is a large variety of technologies available, but adoption is still low among small farmers from tropical countries. What type of policies and what type of technologies can help improve productivity of poor farmers while maintaining the resource base? To what degree do these new technologies make small farmers beholden to debt, the industrialized countries, and the probable future increases in the price of petroleum and its products?

To answer these questions, one has to study farming systems in some detail and make some predictions about how these systems will respond, change, and adapt to external incentives while population is increasing rapidly even as natural resources are under increasing pressure. Teams of economists and agriculturalists join their expertise to link farming system analysis and natural resources processes with human behavioral models to simulate the dynamics of the farming systems under various scenarios. In this chapter we present a few applications of these bioeconomic models to address the impacts of increasing population pressure, increasing access to markets, and external incentives related to welfare and natural resources management. What are the relations between these factors and environmental degradation? What are the policy and technical options to make these systems more sustainable? In the first part of the chapter, we present the tropical agroecosystems that we studied. In the second, we review the use of bioeconomic models in agriculture. In the third we describe a few applications, and in the last part we present overall results and conclusions.

The Tropical Agroecosystems Studied

Tropical small-scale farming systems are numerous and diverse but can be categorized according to a gradient of management intensity from slash-and-burn to permanent agriculture (Ruthenberg 1980). In this chapter we analyze and compare the fallow systems from the savanna of West Africa, the forest systems of the hillsides of Central America, the rancher system of the humid forest margin of Amazonia in Brazil, and the permanent intensive systems of the subhumid Gangetic Plain of northern India as representative of this gradient of intensification.

In West Africa, increasing population pressure on land should lead, at least according to the Boserup school of thought, to labor and capital intensification and to the adoption of new technologies (Boserup 1965; see chapter 12). Instead, we observe migrations either to less-populated rural areas or to overcrowded cities. Trade liberalization of the mid-1990s was supposed to free farmers from an "inefficient" state, but while the devaluation of an overvalued currency had a positive impact, privatization led to market failures and too often the destruction of these farmers' way of subsistence.

The three African villages studied, located on a north-south transect representing a gradient of increasing rainfall, are typical of their climatic conditions. The Sahelian village of Banizoumbou in Niger (ILRI dataset 1998) was used to predict the future of transhumance in the Sahel (Barbier and Hazell 2000). Increasing population pressure and expansion of cropland makes the traditional transhumance migrations of cattle and sheep from north to south more difficult every year. While most "experts" believe that nomadism has no future, a recent school of thought argues that it is the most suitable human activity for the Sahelian ecosystem (Scoones 1996). The other semiarid village, Kolbila on the Mossi Plateau of Burkina Faso (ICRISAT dataset), is less arid but is located in a much more densely populated region. Agriculture is the main activity, but its sustainability is at risk because of declining biomass and soil fertility. The village of Bala, located in the cotton-producing area of Burkina Faso (CIRAD dataset), is in a more humid region. It is less populated at present, but immigration from the north is increasing population pressure, which induces a shift from slash-and-burn to a more intensive but not yet sustainable system (Barbier and Benoît-Cattin 1997).

In Central America, we analyzed the situation of the communities on the hillsides of Honduras. In addition to being the second-poorest country of the American continent after Haiti, Honduras was hit by a hurricane in 1999, which destroyed a large part of its infrastructure and showed as well how poor management of its upper watersheds has made its valleys vulnerable to floods and landslides. Most of the fertile lowland valleys are used for extensive large-scale ranching, while small farmers struggle on the steep hillsides where the topsoil is eroding rapidly. The five Honduran watersheds where we applied bioeconomic models represent contrasting pathways of development.

Farmers in the Lalima watershed follow a vegetable production pathway, producing principally a large range of vegetables. Overdrafting of the river by irrigation reduces water availability during the dry season (Barbier and Bergeron 1999).

The San Nicolas watershed has become an intensive coffee production and processing area, which generates extremely high levels of water contamination that in turn affect many downstream communities (Barbier et al. 2003). The Río Calán watershed produces vegetables and coffee and supplies water to the downstream city of Siguatapeque and to a large hydroelectric dam (Jimenez et al. 2000). In the Jalapa watershed, farmers produce on steep slopes prone to rapid erosion and are part of the El Cajón watershed, which drains into a dam that generates 60 percent of the electricity used in Honduras (Hernández 2002:642). In the Choluteca watershed, widespread grain production on slopes threatens the sustainability of the shrimp industry downstream in the mangroves of the Golfo de Fonseca (Hernández et al. 2002). The large charge of sediment in the water makes shrimp production much more expensive (Samayoa 2000:647).

In these watersheds, the "pathway of development" type applied by the population has been explained as principally a function of exogenous factors such as agroclimatic conditions, availability of spring water, and access to markets (Pender et al. 1999). The two watersheds that were well connected to markets have progressively expanded their vegetable production. Those located farther from a good paved road or major city have focused on coffee where rainfall is generous and on basic grain if the climate is drier.

In Brazil, the Amazonian forest continues to shrink progressively under pressure from loggers followed by small farmers and finally ranchers. In some areas the Brazilian government is trying to prevent farmers from clearing more forest by allocating plots of a few dozen hectares of forest margin to families, under the condition that they will stay within these boundaries and clear only half of their holdings. One such settlement project takes place on the western southern border of the Amazonian forest (IFPRI dataset) in the regions of Rondonia. The objective of the study was to identify the second-best alternative to slash-and-burn (Carpentier et al. 1999). Is it coffee, timber production, forest products extraction, food crop, cattle ranching, or carbon sequestration? The model was supposed to verify if the new systems are economical and environmentally sustainable.

The Indian study is set in Haryana state in northern India, one of the most productive states of India, and also one of the most populated. In the 1960s and 1970s the green revolution, based on improved germ plasm, chemical fertilizers, and irrigation, transformed the state into a massive producer of rice and wheat. The adoption of new techniques was helped by heavy governmental subsidies to reduce input price and stabilize output prices especially for wheat and rice (Aggarwal et al. 2000; Dorin and Landy 2002). Now that the Indian government is trying to cut subsidies to the agricultural sector, some fear that Haryana's grain production will stagnate. Now that the government wants to reduce subsidies for water and electricity, one has to assess the likely impact on production, poverty, and the environment (Alary 2002:645).

Overall, the comparative study given in this chapter includes nine farming systems in four ecoregions of five countries (tables 31.1–31.3). All except the Indian example are small-scale, semi-commercialized farming systems integrating crop and livestock, using mainly hand tools with little mechanization and irrigation. They are all increasingly integrated to the market, but population pressures and resource degradation are at play.

Modeling Farming Systems and Simulating Their Future

To understand these systems, scientists use the farming system approach to try to disentangle the key variables and identify ways to improve the systems' efficiency in a sustainable and equitable way. Critics argue that applying a systems research approach to actual agricultural systems is too complicated and expensive, and that it has failed to improve the general picture, to predict likely scenarios of changes, or to identify significant new solutions. We argue quite the contrary, that computerized models and geographical information systems (GIS) have in

fact greatly improved our analysis and recommendations, and that in fact the policy failures came from the previous lack of synthesis and coherence used to help understand complex systems, predict their evolution, and identify from these models new sustainable techniques. Models are particularly useful to simulate likely outcomes of new policies or technologies (ex-ante analysis). If modelers do not pretend to be able to predict with very high accuracy, but instead expect only some reasonable approximations of the outcome of key changes, the models still can be extremely useful.

The main models used in this study are behavioral, which means that they try to mimic the behavior of actors. The most commonly used behavioral model is mathematical programming, which maximizes a utility function, usually net income, under constraints of land, labor, capital, and risk aversion. Economists make the hypothesis that once the model is correctly specified, the model behaves similarly to how farmers do in the real world.

Mathematical programming, in its linear form, has been used widely in agriculture to determine the factors explaining agricultural supply and farm incomes under different technologies and policy options (Hazell and Norton 1986; McCarl and Spreen 1998). Policy makers from developed countries increasingly use the results of these models to design policies, to negotiate new farm bills, and even formulate international treaties. Now that the debates about sustainability issues intensify, scientists have started to include environmental components in these models.

Making Models More Environmental

The easiest and most common way to include environmental components in such models is to link some environmental indicators to key activities and to simulate what will be the effect of economic decisions on such things as erosion, water production, contamination, or deforestation. Studies based on this type of models are numerous in the United States (Shortle 1984; Carpentier et al. 1988; Ellis et al. 1991; Dosi and Moretto 1993) but less so in Europe (Flichman 1998). In developing countries, scientists encounter more difficulties in applying these models because tropical

Table 31.1. General characteristics of the farming systems analyzed here

Farming system	Unit	Niger nomads	Burkina central	Burkina cotton	Honduras horticulture	Honduras coffee	Honduras coffee and horticulture	Honduras grain	Amazonia	India rice-wheat
Location		Banizoumbou	Kolbila	Bala	Lalima	Río Frio	Río Calán	Jalapa	Rondonia	Haryana
Region		Niamey	Central plateau	Mouhoun	Central Region	West	Central region	North	Acre and Rondonia	Haryana
Climate		Semiarid		Subhumid	Subhumid, mountainous				Subhumid	Semiarid
Altitude	Masl	300	300	300	800 to 1200	800 to 1200	800 to 1200	700 to 1000	110	
Rain	mm	500	600	900	1200	1200	1200		2000	560
Climate mode		Unimodal			Bimodal	Bimodal	Bimodal	Bimodal	Mono	Bimodal
Vegetation		Steppe	Savanna		Pine tree forest				Rain forest	Grass
Landscape		Flat			Flat				Flat	Flat
Soils		Arenosols	Alfisol	Alfisol	Basaltic ash			Calcareous	Oxisol	Various
Pop. density	km²	34	62	32	65				4	328
Pop. growth	%	3	3	3	2.5	2.5	2.5	2.5	2.4	1.8
Producers		Farmers/Nomads				Farmers /Ranchers			Ranchers	Small
Land tenure		Commons to open access				Private			Private	Private
Crop area/ per capita	Ha	0.5	0.5	1	1	1	1	1	1.4	0.2

Table 31.2. Main activities in the nine farming systems

Farming system	Niger nomads	Burkina central	Burkina cotton	Honduras horticulture	Honduras coffee	Honduras coffee and horticulture	Honduras grain	Amazonia	India rice-wheat
Annual crops	Millet, bean	Sorghum-millet	Cotton-Maize-sorghum	Grain	Maize, bean	Maize	Maize, bean	Rice, maize, bean, cassava	Rice, wheat, mustard, sorghum, cotton
Perennial crops	—	Karite	Karite		Coffee			Coffee, grain	
Livestock	Meat, milk	Draft	Draft, cattle	Draft meat, milk			Meat, milk	Draft, milk	
Trees	Acacia, eucalyptus, bush			Pine tree,	Pine tree, broadleaf	Pine tree, coffee	Coffee, coffee	broadleaf	
Wood use	Fuelwood	Fuelwood	Fuelwood	Fuelwood				Hedges, timber	Fuelwood
Other major activities	Migration	—	—	Wood extraction	Wood extraction	Wood extraction		Brazil nut and wood	

agroecosystems tend to be more complex and less well studied. The pioneers of farming system research in the tropics promoted the use of mathematical programming and a focus on biophysical properties to study the limits and the potential of local farming systems (Ruthenberg 1980; Beets 1990; Benoît-Cattin 1990). Initial attempts started with erosion in Indonesia (Barbier 1988), organic matter in India (Parikh 1991), soil nutrients in Mali (Kruseman et al. 1995), and soil nutrients in Indonesia (Van Rheenen 1996).

It is now relatively common to find farm models that produce indicators of environmental degradation. It is more difficult to build models that include the feedback of natural resource degradation on crop yields because little is known about the effect of erosion or soil fertility depletion on yields and because yield effects over time are confounded by increased usage of fertilizers. A common way to overcome this deficiency is to apply a generic biophysical model for a studied site and then to estimate the relations for a wide range of conditions (Hall 2000). Another solution is to make reasonable assumptions about the relations and to run a sensitivity analysis to identify at which level natural resource degradation really matters, or to compare actual yields over time to what might be expected if there were no erosion,

Table 31.3. Production factors in the nine farming systems

Farming system	Niger nomads	Burkina central	Burkina cotton	Honduras horticulture	Honduras coffee	Honduras coffee and horticulture	Honduras grain	Amazonia	India rice-wheat
Water	—	Lowland	Lowland	Streams	Streams	Streams		—	Wells, canal
Irrigation	—	Gravity	Gravity	Sprinkler		Sprinkler	Sprinkler	—	Sprinkler
Mechanization	—	Donkeys / Weeder	Oxen / plough	Oxen / plough		Oxen / plough		Chainsaw	Oxen, tractors
Fertilization	Manure, estiercol, NPK	Compost, manure, estiercol, NPK	Compost, manure, estiercol, NPK	Compost, manure, estiercol, NPK	Compost, manure, estiercol, NPK	Compost, manure, estiercol, NPK		NPK, fallow and improved fallow	Compost, manure, estiercol, NPK
Tested improved technologies	Pastures	Pastures phosphorus	Pastures phosphorus	—	—			Pasture, animals	Animal (IA)

Table 31.4. Characteristics of the nine models

Farming system	Niger nomads	Burkina central	Burkina cotton	Honduras horticulture	Honduras coffee	Honduras coffee and horticulture	Honduras grain	Amazonia	India rice-wheat
Time frame	Dynamic	Dynamic	Dynamic	Dynamic	Static	Static	Static	Dynamic	One year but recursive for seasons
	Recursive	Recursive	Recursive	Recursive	Static	Static	Static	Recursive	Recursive
Planning horizon	4	5	5	10	1	1	1	15	1
Risk method	Discrete, sequential, stochastic	Target motad	Target motad	—	—	—	—	Mean variance	Target motad

while including (or not) the effects of the increase in fertilizer applications usually seen.

One particular difficulty is that these relations are mostly nonlinear and may involve threshold effects. With mathematical programming it is relatively easy to approximate nonlinear production and damage functions with linear segments (Barbier 1998) or to use nonlinear algorithms directly to approximate natural resource evolution, including thresholds (Barbier and Bergeron 1999).

The Bioeconomic Models Used in This Study

The bioeconomic models used in the studies presented in this chapter are of the mathematical programming sort. Some are dynamic, others static, and they may be applied at the farm, the village, the watershed, or the state level. All the models include the farmers' main activities, such as cropping, animal husbandry, forestry, and migration, and in some cases forestry. The activities are described by their cost, benefit, labor time, variability, and their effect on the activities of others and the environment. The models take into account the constraint of land (area and quality), labor and capital, and in some cases farmers' risk aversion.

The models were "validated," meaning that results of the model were compared with reality and, in several cases, that the model was changed until simulation results become sufficiently similar to farmers' production plans. In all cases, we conducted in-depth farm surveys, sometimes with our laptops and the model brought to the farm to discuss with farmers and to try to understand directly the rationale of farmers' choices. In the vast majority of the interviews farmers explained their choice through economic reasoning similar to the mathematical programming framework used. They mention prices, yields, labor, land, capital, and risk. However, the word "validated" has to be taken with caution because agricultural prices and yields are uncertain and a farmer's behavior is conditioned to a certain level of risk aversion that is difficult to assess. Despite that, models usually reproduce well what farmers do in reality, especially since small farmers from the tropics are under severe constraints and have few alternatives.

Various scales: Farm, village, and watershed modeling

The models we used simulate farming systems at different scales to respond better to the problem at hand and to take into account land or water held in common. The reason we went beyond simple farm level models is that for some resources, such as land, water, or labor, one has to think about a larger level such as village or watershed. In Burkina Faso and Niger, land is held in common or in open access for pastures. The African models are village-level models, but they include distant transhumant pastures so that they capture the possibility of farmers and herders using distant rangeland.

Land use in the Honduran regions we studied is typically divided between private cropland and forest that had been nationalized in the sixties, although actual land use is mixed because sometimes previous owners used forests as pastures. Our Honduran model was designed at the sub-watershed level to include problems of irrigation and in one case contamination by coffee processing plants. In the Amazonian case the model is a farm-level model since land is allocated individually to farmers. When necessary various social groups are distinguished, such as farmers and herders in Africa, and small farmers and ranchers in Honduras. In the Indian case, the model is a regional model with two zones (arid and semiarid areas) to capture the different impacts of water tariff reform and five different types of farming systems in each area (Alary and Deybe 2002). Each farming system is representative of a social group with specific labor and land exchange rules with the other groups.

Natural resources and limiting factors

Natural resources become more important to communities when they become limiting factors of production, as tends to happen over time as population density increases. For soils, the limiting factors perceived by the farmers are amazingly diverse. In the Nigerian Sahel, phosphorus is considered the first limiting factor of crop yields, while in neighboring Burkina Faso agriculturalists incriminate insufficient soil organic matter and to a lesser extent soil erosion by water as agents that decrease their yields. In Amazonia, soil nitrogen is considered the limiting factor of crop yields, while in central Honduras, erosion on slopes and waterlogging on flat soils are major problems.

In most models, the landscape was divided into several spatial land units characterized by altitude, slope, types of soil, and in some cases land tenure (figure 31.1). Each area had an initial set of variables that change through time such as population, soil organic matter, soil nutrients, tree volume, and soil conservation infrastructures. Access to roads and irrigation were changed exogenously according to past investment events or future hypothesis.

For soil organic matter we distinguished three types of stocks: below crops, pastures, and forests. The stock of soil diminishes under crops over time unless the model finds it cost effective to add organic fertilizers or increases the area under pastures and forests. If there is a rotation among the three land uses—for instance, if an area of forest is transformed into cropland—the stock of soil nutrient of the reclaimed area of forest is transferred to the stock of soil nutrients under the crop. This way the model is able to mimic farmers' traditional soil-fertility management.

To improve the understanding and quantification of biophysical processes within an agroecosystem, scientists have produced biophysical models that simulate the cycles of chemicals and organic elements in these systems. In Burkina Faso and Honduras we used the biophysical model EPIC (Erosion Productivity Impact Calculator) developed by Williams et al. (1987) to determine the main contributing factors to yields, such as cropping patterns, soil conditions, and climate. EPIC also computes erosion and its impact using the

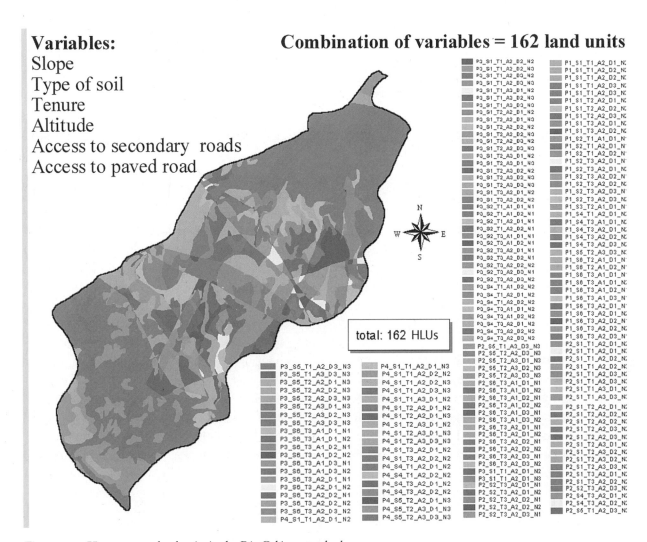

Variables:
Slope
Type of soil
Tenure
Altitude
Access to secondary roads
Access to paved road

Combination of variables = 162 land units

total: 162 HLUs

Figure 31.1. Homogenous land units in the Río Calán watershed.

revised version of the Universal Soil Loss Equation (Wischmeier 1978). Results were found realistic when compared to actual measurements of soil erosion but they were not validated statistically.

Dynamic framework

In each of the five countries at least one model had a multi-annual planning horizon. For example, the Amazonian model has a fifteen-year planning horizon because the solution of the problem at hand is based on the potential of perennials. The discount rates are the interest rates utilized in these areas. We analyzed the sensitivity of the results to changes in the discount rates, but the models were not especially sensitive to changes to the discount rate or

planning horizon. Nevertheless, the higher the discount rate, the slightly less sustainable the systems were in terms of natural resource management.

In each country there is also at least one recursive model, meaning that the results of one simulation become the starting point of a new simulation. The resources that are carried over in a recursive way are animals, food reserves, money, area under different kind of land uses and its content in soil organic matter, soil nutrients, and arable soil depth. With a recursive framework, a model can predict a very long pathway into the future. For example, the Brazilian model takes the result of year 5 as a starting point for a new run. Repeating the run five times helps to predict what will happen in twenty-five years. The other recursive models realize the operation every year but predict farther into the future because we wanted to assess the effect of long-term population growth.

Farmers' risk-aversion behavior

Risk aversion is included in most models except in Honduras, where interannual risk was considered relatively low. In Burkina Faso and in India, the target motad method (Trauer 1983) allowed us to include the income variability in the constraints. The Sahelian model includes a sophisticated discrete stochastic programming framework that is a decision-tree formulation and a mean-variance formulation in the objective function. In Brazil, the risk aversion was modeled by a mean-variance method.

Results by Agroecosystem

For each site we ran a different type of model with different options under contrasted scenarios. The comparison of the sites helped draw a more coherent picture of the situation and what can be done to make agriculture more profitable and more environment-friendly. We tested various options, such as payment for environmental services to farmers to improve their land use.

West Africa: Intensification or Migration?

The simulations in the three villages suggest that intensification of agriculture (for example through the use of fertilizers or irrigation) is much more effective in the subhumid regions (around 1000 mm) than in the semiarid region (less than 700 mm). Intensification in the Sahelian area yields little improvement in our model of crop production. The various techniques tested are not likely to make a difference in the near future because the climate is dry and irregular, soil fertility is depleted, and irrigation is particularly expensive in this typically flat landscape of West Africa.

Opportunities are much more favorable in the southern villages of Burkina Faso, where maize, cotton, peanuts, rice, and animal production are much higher and more regular from year to year. As a consequence, we think that government should let the current movement of migrations from the less favored and more populated north to the more favored and less populated south of the Sahelian countries continue. The cost of maintaining many farmers in the degraded land of the Sahel is too high.

However, even on the more favored land, sustainability is a challenging proposition. In particular, it proves difficult to shift to permanent agriculture because soils require too much organic matter to maintain biological fertility and structure, and production of much-needed compost or manure is hampered by lack of crop residues and animals. The model suggests that once the arable area is cultivated, per capita income will drop, even if farmers adopt several new soil conservation techniques. We predict that for most villages of this ecosystem, once the cropped area is cultivated, soil fertility will decline. Farmers will have to come back to a short fallow system (the ley system, described by Ruthenberg 1979). Meanwhile, a large fraction of farmers will have to migrate to the still important but less populated areas.

According to our simulations, the future of nomadism in the Sahel is less pessimistic than predicted by most observers. Even if rapid population growth and cropland expansion make the lives of herders more difficult, our simulations show that the conversion of pastures to cropland does not mean a loss of potential forage, since millet straw, beans, and weeds are reasonable substitutes for pastures. Thus, crop expansion means a change of access rather than a loss of forage. However, if world prices for grain continue to decrease, it is probable that millet production will become less attractive to farmers in the Sahel. As imported grains are becoming increasingly more competitive and as farmers find more off-farm activities, they will rely more on food purchases than on homegrown millet. They most certainly will intensify their temporary or definitive migrations to southern countries and to cities. In the long term we believe that the area of millet will decrease, and that extensive nomadic cattle rearing is still the most viable and sustainable alternative for the Sahel. The land will probably support fewer people directly, but whether the people will suffer depends upon what occurs in distant cities.

The Hillsides of Honduras:
An Untapped Potential

The situation in Honduras is not that different from the situation of West Africa, even if the landscape is hilly, climate is more temperate, and population density lower. The situation is similar in terms of the level of poverty, the inadequate rainfall (a long dry season), and a reliance on basic grains, and also similar in that farmers are tending to diversify into vegetable or cash crops and in farmers' efforts to acquire draft animals and cattle.

In Honduras, the impact of population pressure is similar to that of West Africa as per capita agricultural incomes decline progressively as the human population increases. New farmers will work on more marginal land or become workers for larger farms as they have no other choices. Our model confirms that increasing population pressure can induce a more sustainable agriculture when population density or soil fertility reaches some threshold, but also that there is not enough economy of scale to lead to higher incomes.

But because Honduras is still not as densely populated as West Africa, rural population growth is also not likely to have as disastrous consequences and there is still enough space to increase the cropped area, even if it is on steep hillsides. We do not envision a critical population crunch. Hillsides will almost certainly remain in coffee production even if world prices are currently very low because of structural overproduction that could last a few more years. Despite its poor quality and hence low price, Honduran coffee has comparative advantages because of its low production cost. Wages are low, and coffee produced under shade requires fewer external inputs. In addition, Honduras can target the market of ecological coffee, and with a little coordination, efforts from coffee-producer organizations could avoid the current price penalty for its poor quality. A first step to improve the sustainability of hillside farmers is to control the effluents of coffee processing. There is still a future for coffee production in Honduras.

One possible valuable alternative to coffee production is vegetable production. In Lalima, coffee has been replaced by vegetable production and in Río Calán vegetables are expanding fast while coffee harvesting is decreasing. In Central America, vegetable production can go beyond the tiny domestic market, since exports to Salvador and the United States are increasing. Hillsides of Honduras still have many unused favorable areas with abundant springs. Vegetables can be grown on small plots and even steep slopes by small farmers.

But our simulations show that in the long term, vegetable production in mountainous areas can have a heavy environmental cost since vegetable fields are more prone to erosion than traditional maize-bean associations that cover the soil better. Among the land conservation techniques tested, grass strips were found to be cheaper than terraces and live barriers. Small incentives could help reduce erosion. However the direct economic benefits of land-conservation practices in general are low to the farmers, explaining their low adoption. We also tested some components of organic farming without chemical fertilizers. Simulations show that without chemical fertilizers, production and incomes would decrease substantially even if farmers increase organic fertilizers. Erosion would increase, too, because farmers would switch to more extensive techniques and would extend cropland on steeper slopes.

For the large chunk of Honduras, where vegetable production is not an option because there are no streams, nor coffee production because it is too dry, maize and bean farming, usually in association, are the main farm activities possible. For such regions the outmigration of farmers seems difficult to reverse. There is, however, a case that can be made for paying those communities for environmental services such as carbon sequestration, flood prevention, and production of clean water. Figure 31.2 shows an example of various scenarios under water supply in the Río Calán watershed. Honduran upper watersheds need to be managed better since the small valleys are very prone to floods and some of these valleys are intensively cultivated for export fruits or shrimp. According to our simulations, even modest environmental payment could easily help some communities invest in more environmentally friendly activities instead of most erosive annual crops.

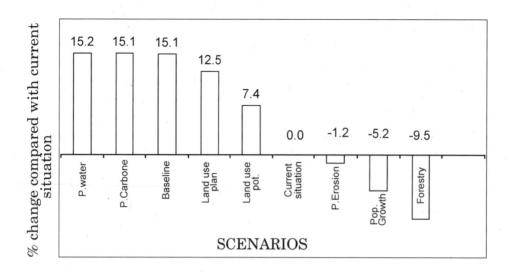

Figure 31.2. Change in water supply in Río Calán watershed by scenario.

Forest Margins in Amazonia: A Case for Ranching?

The Amazonian farming systems show some similarities with the African subhumid system in that cropping of annual crops is hardly sustainable. The mineralization of soil organic matter is too rapid to allow sustainable cropping. After a few years, cropped areas of the southern Amazonia invariably turn into grassland. The best option for Brazilian farmers is still ranching. The simulations show that the government's proposed fifty-hectare-lot project, every Brazilian small farmer's dream, is large enough for one family to sustain a decent living through ranching. Cropping exclusively is not a sustainable option because the traditional slash-and-burn methods would mean a complete deforestation of the fifty-hectare holding in a few decades. The simulations also show that coffee production would be cost-effective only with a sharp increase in the price of coffee so that farmers could attract the necessary workers for the harvest. Carbon sequestration could become an option, but a relatively high price per ton of carbon would be required to keep the fifty hectares under forest. Similarly, the sustainable forestry alternative is not cost-effective because it would require a much higher price for timber products.

Northern India: Cutting Subsidies

The Haryana state farming system is different from the previous three regions we analyzed in that the climate is quite temperate, the population density is much higher, and the use of inputs and irrigation are widespread. Many consider the green revolution particularly successful in Haryana. The drawback of this intensive system is increasing soil salinization by canal irrigation, eutrophication of water bodies, and a decrease in the water table because of excessive pumping in tube wells for crop irrigation. The reduction of subsidies on phosphorus and potassium while maintaining subsidies on nitrogen had induced an imbalance between these elements in the soil, which induces more leaching of nitrogen into streams and the aquifers. Thus, although the intensification of the production system has meant that the very high population level and growth has not led to starvation it is not clear that this is a long-term solution.

The simulations show that cutting the fertilizer subsidies might harm the poorer farmers since smaller subsidies will reduce irrigation and fertilization. Poorer farmers are also likely to compensate for the reduction in subsidy-based income with increasing sales of milk, which might be at the expense of family food security. Some economists argue that making farmers pay the "right prices" (that is, the nonsubsidized price) for inputs such as fertilizers will help them make more efficient use of those resources, which will in turn reduce environmental problems. Certainly anything that increases the price of inputs will decrease their use, which may have environmental benefits but at the expense of the poor farmer's livelihood.

Comparison Among Farming Systems

The farming systems of West Africa, Honduras, Brazil, and India are comparable in terms of farm type: all are small and poor, with few other opportunities and a pressure to shift from an unsustainable extensive fallow system to a more permanent and sustainable one. In some ways these systems are quite similar (each has only one rainy season and cereal production dominates). They differ most importantly in their respective population pressure, which explains a great deal of the cropping intensity (Ruthenberg 1979). In Amazonia, low population density and hence large per capita availability of land leads to slash-and-burn and very extensive fallow systems; in Burkina Faso and Honduras, medium population density leads to a fallow system; in Niger, higher population density leads to the ley system (short fallow); and in India, high population density requires an intensive multicropping system.

One major result of our prospective simulations is that integration of crop and livestock is not sufficient to compensate for the decline of soil fertility under permanent cropping. The addition of manure is beneficial but is not enough by itself, because chemical fertilizers are required to allow permanent cropping. Most of our scenarios strongly suggested that population growth would reduce farmers' incomes. The results show decreasing per capita incomes as new farmers cultivate more marginal land or become landless despite the availability and even the adoption of new techniques, contrary to Boserup's assertion that population-driven intensification increases per capita income. Population growth induces an intensification process only when the arable area of cropland is entirely cultivated. Until then there is little benefit in adding extra labor or capital per hectare. Land intensification increases income per unit of land but not per worker. When land becomes scarce, farmers tend to migrate to less-populated areas rather than invest in land improvement structures.

However, the results do show that tropical conditions are not hopeless for agricultural intensification. Production can be increased significantly with additional inputs and new technologies can make a significant difference—if they can be afforded. If there is no new technology available to farmers in the area it will be difficult to compensate for the diminishing amount of land, even with increasing yields. So although these people can probably continue to survive, the rural poor are likely to become even poorer and more poorly fed.

Per capita income can increase with new markets such as vegetables, coffee, cotton, or animal products such as milk. However, most rural areas have limited access to urban markets and thus find only a limited number of options to diversify production beyond what is already cultivated in the region. Our models showed good response to the development of new markets, especially when the market for basic grain is stable enough to help farmers buy grain and thus reduce their own production.

Another finding is that in forested areas in Amazonia and on the hillsides of Latin America, payment for environmental services can be a viable alternative to grain production. It can hardly become an alternative to vegetables, but it can be compatible with coffee growing. If coffee production can be combined with payment for supplying clean water, communities located in forests can develop new types of activities related to tourism.

Conclusion

The scenarios produced with these bioeconomic models (BM) have proved to be more realistic than some earlier analyses using simply economic or sociological approaches alone because they take into account the severe constraints facing tropical farming systems. Farmers, extension agents, and researchers found the scenarios produced by the models close to reality, recognizing that the predictions for some models already occur in more advanced or more populated areas from within the same ecoregion. The bioeconomic models proved their usefulness in understanding complex realities and helped draw a coherent picture from abundant research results accumulated through time by agronomic research in these sites. There exist many more of these data-rich sites in tropical countries, where bioeconomic models can help generate useful technical and policy recommendations. Meanwhile, all investigators and especially all policy makers must recognize that biophysical constraints, including those from population growth, soils, and rainfall, are real and are pressing in on the poor of much of the world. Without recognition of this fact and a use of it in efforts to help the poor, our best efforts will be doomed to failure.

References

Aggarwal, P. K., R. Roetter, N. Kalra, C. T. Hoanh, H. Van eul Keelen, and H. H. Laar, eds. 2000. Exploring land use options for sustainable increase in food grain production in Haryana: Methodological framework. Systems Research for optimizing future land use in South and South-East Asia. Los Banos, Philippines, International Rice Research Institute.

Alary, V., and D. Deybe. 2002. Impacts of different water tariff reforms on rural livelihood and water and public resource in India: The case of Haryana Producers. Biennal Conference of the International Society for Ecological Economics, Sousse, Tunisia.

Barbier, B. 1998. Induced innovation and land degradation: Results from a bioeconomic model of a village in West Africa. *Agricultural Economics* 19, nos. 1–2: 15–25.

Barbier, B., and M. Benoît-Cattin. 1997. Viabilité d'un système agraire. *Economie Rurale* 239:12.

Barbier, B., and G. Bergeron. 1999. Impact of policy interventions on land management in Honduras: Results of a bioeconomic model. *Agricultural Systems* 60:1–16.

Barbier, B., and P. B. R. Hazell. 2000. Declining access to transhumant areas and sustainability of agro-pastoral systems in the semiarid areas of Niger. In P. B. R. Hazell, ed., *Property Right and Collective Action.* Washington, D.C.: IFPRI.

Barbier, B., R. Hearne, J. Gonzales, A. Nelson, and O. Mejia. 2003. Trade-off between economic efficiency and contamination by coffee processing: A bioeconomic model at the watershed level in Honduras. XXV IAAE Conference, Durban.

Barbier, E. 1988. The economy of farm level adoption of soil conservation measures in upland Java. World Bank Environment Division Working Paper No. 11.

Beets, W. C. 1990. *Raising and Sustaining Productivity of Small Holders in the Tropics.* Alkmaar, Netherlands: Agpe.

Benoît-Cattin, M. 1990. Essai de modélisation mathématique des systèmes agraires et systèmes de culture tropicale. Recherche opérationnelle et développement. Montpellier: Agropolis.

Boserup, E. 1965. *The Conditions of Agricultural Growth: The Economics of Agrarian Change Under Population Pressure.* New York: Allen and Unwin.

Carpentier, C., S. Vosti, and X. Witcover. 1999. A farm level bioeconomic model for the western Amazonian forest margin. Washington, D.C.: International Food Policy Research Institute. EPTD Discussion Paper.

Carpentier, C. L., D. D. Bosch, and S. S. Bathie. 1988. Using spatial information to reduce costs of controlling agricultural nonpoint source pollution. *Agricultural and Resource Economics Review* (April): 72–84.

Dorin, B., and F. Landy. 2002. *Agriculture et alimentation de l'Inde: Les vertes années (1947–2000).* Paris: INRA.

Dosi, C., and M. Moretto. 1993. Nonpoint-source pollution control, information asymmetry, and the choice of time profile for environmental fees. In C. S. Russell and J. F. Shogren, eds., *Theory, Modeling and Experience in the Management of Nonpoint-Source Pollution,* 91–122. Boston: Kluwer Academic.

Ellis, J. K., D. W. Hugues, and W. R. Butcher. 1991. Economic modeling of farm production and conservation decision in response to alternative resource and environmental policies. *Northeastern Journal of Agricultural and Resource Economics* 20:198–208.

Flichman, G. 1998. Modelling agricultural and environmental policy using a bioeconomic approach. *Metu Studies in Development Journal* 25:61–74.

Hall, C. A. S. 2000. ed. *Quantifying Sustainable Development: The Future of Tropical Economies.* San Diego: Academic Press.

Hazell, P. B. R., and R. D. Norton. 1986. *Mathematical Programming for Economic Analysis in Agriculture.* New York: Macmillan.

Hernández, R., F. López, s. Riveria, and B. Barbier. 2002. Escenarios de simulación de la tierra del uso de la tierra en la cuenca del rió Choluteca. *Tatascan* 14, no. 1: 13–29.

Jimenez, A., B. Barbier, and s. Riveria. 2000. Escenarios de desarrollo en la cuenca del rió Calán: Optimización del uso de la tierra. *Tatascan* 12, no. 2: 43–64.

Kruseman, G., R. Ruben, H. Hengsdijk, and M. R. Van Ittersum. 1995. Farm household modelling for estimating the effectiveness of price instruments in land use policy. *Netherlands Journal of Agricultural Science* 43:111–23.

McCarl, B. A., and T. H. Spreen. 1998. Applied mathematical programming using algebraic systems. http://agrinet.tamu.edu/mccarl.

Parikh, K. S. 1991. *An Operational Definition of Sustainable Development*. Bombay: Indira Gandhi Institute of Development Research.

Pender, J., S. Scherr, and G. Duran. 1999. Pathways of development in the hillsides of Honduras: Cause and implications for agricultural production, poverty and sustainable resource use. EPTD Discussion Paper 45.

Ruthenberg, W. 1980. *Farming Systems in the Tropics*. Oxford: Oxford University Press.

Scoones, I., ed. 1996. *Living with Uncertainty: New Directions in Pastoral Development in Africa*. London: International Institute for Environment and Development.

Shortle, J. S. 1984. The use of estimated pollution flows in agricultural pollution control policy: Implications for abatement and policy instrument. *Northeastern Journal of Agricultural and Resource Economics* 13:277–85.

Tauer, L. W. 1983. Target motad. *American Journal of Agricultural Economics* 65 (August): 606–10.

Van Rheenen, T. 1996. *Quantifying Farming Systems: A Multiple Optimisation Approach*. Wageningen, Netherlands: Wageningen University.

Williams, J. R., C. A. Jones, and P. T. Dyke. 1987. EPIC, the Erosion Productivity Impact Calculator. Temple, Tex.: U.S. Department of Agriculture, Agricultural Research Service, Economics Research Service, and Soil Conservation Service.

Wischmeier, W. H. . 1978. *Predicting Rainfall Erosion Losses: A Guide to Conservation Planning*. Washington, D.C.: U.S. Department of Agriculture.

Chapter 32

Using Input-Output Analysis
to Analyze the Economy of the
Grande de San Ramón River Basin in Costa Rica

Juan-Rafael Vargas, David Cardoza,

Rodrigo Briceño, and Henry Vargas

Introduction

Input-output analysis is an important tool for understanding the economy of any region or country. It was originally designed during World War II by the Russian Nobel laureate Wassily Leontief, then working in the United States, to make sure that when a tank or similar machine was being built, the final product would not be held up by the lack of some small part—for example, the right kind of washer for a tread. The idea was to follow all of the requirements for "final demand" backward through society to see what was needed for each subsystem, which parts for each of those, and so on. This tool of economic analysis helps the understanding of the interindustrial relations for any economy, and it has been applied widely. It has also been modified to examine the total energy use and the total pollution produced for various products of an economy (Hannon 1982), and new applications are found every year. It can be especially important for developing countries with limited industrial resources because so many components of their economy must be imported, and these imports are very expensive. This is especially crucial when attempting to determine the impacts of some program designed to generate foreign exchange. For example, nearly half the money earned from Costa Rican bananas went to pay for the industrial products required to generate the average banana—and that had to be imported.

Input-output economics is a poorly developed field among Central American scholars, and regional analysis is limited by data availability. This chapter presents the first regional input-output table for Costa Rica. We show how the table was built and some economic policy simulations that were done using it.[1] The results, both the successful construction of the matrix and the applications, suggest that similar efforts should be performed elsewhere. Better national and regional policies could be developed if we had this tool performing well.

In order to assess the linkages of this regional economy with the rest of the country (and world), we need to organize specific details of its economic production system. We use the four-digit International Standard Manufacturing Classification (ISIC) of national output-generating activities as our benchmark. This breakdown level has been used for other types of studies, and quite stable coefficients have been obtained. Almost all international work on manufacturing economics uses the classification, which allows an increasing number of hypotheses and models to be evaluated and compared.

Two principal economic entities are calculated: final demand, which is what the final consumer buys, and intermediate products, which are economic goods or services one sector buys from another in order to construct final demand goods or services. The "value added" is how much more the products of a process are worth compared to the value of the input components. The matrix shows the monetary quantity of each component of the modern part of the economy that is purchased from other components. It was built on the basis of 1995 constant price accounts. That was done because of greater availability of secondary data for that year due to surveys done by the Dirección General de Estadística y Censo (Census Bureau) and the Instituto de Investigaciones en Ciencias Económicas (University of Costa Rica Economic Research Institute) and data collected by the PRODUS Research Group for the Grande de San Ramón River Basin.

The national 1991 input-output matrix was transformed using the RAS mathematical algorithm.[2] That procedure was followed because building an input-output table is an extremely data-intensive procedure. It allowed for the use of data compatible with sectoral transactions of the region. This process uses control totals as suggested by Stone (1961). The intermediate consumption data are generated from the total of the column control variables. The row vector is the gross production value (GPV) and the imports required because the final demand sector is needed as input into the mathematical algorithm.

The four-digit ISIC data for money earned by wage earners were assigned to the county totals from the Caja Costarricense del Seguro Social (CCSS) database. The other data source was the national households survey (EHPM) for 1995. From all that data, the structure of the intersectoral transactions matrix was built. The chart contains thirty-six sectors: six agricultural, twenty-two manufacturing, and seven service, with the government as an independent sector (table 32.1). The procedures for undertaking these calculations are shown in many books, including Abraham (1969). The components that compose the value added are salaries and wages, residual entrepreneur's profit (capital's income), and indirect taxes. They are taken from the 1995 survey (EHPM) given by the DGEC as well as the statistics provided by the CCSS for that year. The intermediate consumption data were obtained from the statistics provided by the IICE.

Methodology

The river basin, with an area of 1,850.7 km², is the most important area economically of the western Central Valley. It is made up of six counties: San

Ramón, Grecia, Atenas, Naranjo, Palmares, and Valverde Vega. The total population was 199,718 inhabitants in 1995. The Grande River Basin matrix is composed of thirty-six sectors that are broken into the main economic sectors such as agriculture, industry, services, and the government. The matrix is developed from 1995 data, and it is in millions of colones current for the year in question.

Added Input-Output Matrix

The economic activity in any region is better understood by adding up the input-output matrix into three sectors: agriculture, industry, and services (Barros and Lessa 1979). It shows the main economic sectors as each including numerous activities. In turn, it integrates many small and a few large firms. Both the linkage and the relative strength of the industries become clear from that picture. They buy from each other (by column) and sell (by row) to other firms and to consumers at home and outside the basin (both in Costa Rica and overseas). The column and row totals are the same, and they add up to the GPV. Table 32.1 shows intermediate goods and final demand. The latter is made of consumption, capital goods, and exports.

The matrix could also be broken into four quadrants. The first details final demand, made of private consumption, public consumption, investment, and the total regional exports. The latter includes those that go to other counties outside the region and the ones that are ultimately sold outside Costa Rica. The second quadrant includes the interindustry transactions that could be interpreted as a production function. The third shows the value-added items: wages, profits, indirect taxes, and sectoral imports. They are primary inputs that are not produced within the system.

Although indirect taxes are not part of added value,[3] they are included for computational reasons. They assure the equality between the rows (inputs) and columns (outputs) on the transactions matrix, as stated above. It also allows tax collections to be part of possible policy simulations while showing their consequences on the regional economic structure. Therefore, adding intermediate consumption to wages and profits yields total value before taxes. Those taxes should

Table 32.1. Río Grande de San Ramón: Input-output matrix, 1995 (10^6 Colones)

Sector	Agriculture	Industry	Services	IS	FD	EXP	GPV
		II				I	
Agriculture	4.19	13.7	.02	17.92	21	4.48	43.4
Industry	5.48	.86	.96	7.3	19.18	14.81	41.3
Services	4.11	4.19	4.99	9.99	12.05	.59	22.65
		III				IV	
IP	13.78	15.45	5.97	35.21	52.25	19.89	107.35
AV	24.5	14.3	15.64	54.45			
IMP	5.12	11.54	1.03	17.69			
GPV	43.4	41.3	22.65	107.35			

IP: Intermediate purchases; IS: Intermediate sales; EXP: Exports; AV: Added value; FD: Final demand; GPV: Gross production value; IMP: Imports.

Source: Briceño, Cardoza, and Vargas (1997)

be net of subsidies because they are for all firms in the basin.

Another way to see the addition by columns is to recognize that the prices involved are not the producer's final prices, because they have to pay indirect taxes or to receive subsidies to place their goods in the market. Once net taxes have been added, these are the prices the producer asks for its products at its gate. Still, these prices are not those that the buyers pay. Storing, transport, and commercialization costs need to be added. Once that is done, the final buyer's price is set.

The fourth quadrant shows the total value of the intermediate sales, final demand, and regional exports. The total of the rows add to intermediate purchases, added value, and imports of the region. This quadrant yields accounting consistency of the input-output model. The row totals of intermediate consumption, added value, and imports are equal to GPV. For the columns, total intermediate sales, final demand, and exports are also equal to the GPV. Consistency is therefore built in. It is shown in the demand and supply equation for the Grande River Basin:

Demand = Supply

$$\sum_{j=1}^{n} X_{ij} + Y_i = X_i \qquad j = 1,2,3,\dots,n$$

$$35.21 + 72.14 = 107.35$$

National product = National Income

$$\sum_{i=1}^{n} Y_i - \sum_{j=1}^{n} M_j = \sum_{j=1}^{n} VA_j$$

$$72.14 - 17.69 = 54.45$$

Two major features are especially important in the region, and they come out of the data in the matrix:

A. The sector that generates the largest gross production value is agriculture, with a production of 43,400,000 colones, representing 41 percent of the regional total. Manufacturing is second with 41,302,000 colones (38 percent). Services account for 21 percent of the region total with 22,650,000 colones. This pattern is different from the country as a whole, where services make up the largest sector and agriculture the smallest. The latter not only supplies products for the population's consumption, but also provides the principal inputs to agroindustry. Agriculture also makes the largest intermediate purchases (15,452,000 colones).

Table 32.2. Río Grande's economic structure 1995: Economic sectors (billions of current colones)

Production schedule   **Production destiny**

Agriculture

	Absolute	Percent		Absolute	Percent
Intermediate consumption	13.78	32	Intermediate sales	17.92	41
Added value	24.5	56	Final demand	21	48
Effective production	38.28	88	Exports	4.48	10
Regional imports	5.12	12	Gross production value	43.4	100
Gross production value	43.4	100			

Industry

	Absolute	Percent		Absolute	Percent
Intermediate consumption	15.45	37	Intermediate sales	7.3	18
Added value	14.31	35	Final demand	19.83	48
Effective production	29.76	72	Exports	14.17	34
Regional imports	11.54	28	Gross production value	41.3	100
Gross production value	41.3	100			

Services

	Absolute	Percent		Absolute	Percent
Intermediate consumption	5.97	26	Intermediate sales	9.99	44
Added value	15.64	69	Final demand	12.06	53
Effective production	21.61	95	Exports	.59	3
Regional imports	1.03	4	Gross production value	22.65	100
Gross production value	22.65	100			

Source: Briceño, Cardoza, and Vargas (1997)

B. The primary sector generates the largest value added, with nearly 24,500,000 colones, which represents 45 percent of the region's total. Services, accounting for 15,643,000 colones, is next with almost one-third of the total value added. Manufacturing generates only 26 percent, which is 14,309,000 colones. The largest agricultural value added comes from labor engagement in coffee, sugarcane, and staples. A resulting feature is the large employment multiplier; in other words, there are many people employed per unit of economic activity in agriculture. This is sometimes missed by many development agencies, which promote policies to increase labor productivity, thinking that will lead to "efficiency," but in fact leading to unemployment and a larger use of fossil fuel, among other consequences.

Furthermore, agriculture has a relatively low requirement for imported inputs, a feature clearly seen on the matrix. The last outstanding feature is large export values for both coffee and sugarcane.

The reason for a large service sector in a relatively rural region is the relative importance of banking services, transportation, construction, and electricity as inputs required by the other sectors. Furthermore, the commercialization margins are not part of intermediate consumption for the output generating branches, and that is reflected in the producing prices in the matrix. As to general government, its production value is mostly made up of the employees' wages, plus some purchases of goods and services.

Economic Structure of Sectors

This section goes into a deeper assessment of the

productive features of the region and its economic structure. The agricultural sector generated gross production value of nearly 43,400,000 colones. It purchased 4,192,000 colones from the same sector. Tools, fungicides, and similar inputs are bought from the manufacturing sectors for 5,484,000 colones. The services sector sells 4,106,000 colones, mostly in electricity, transport, banking services, and so on.

Table 32.2 shows the structure of the productive sectors and its destination. Intermediate consumption adds up to 13,782,000 colones. The agricultural sector generates 24,500,000 colones in value added, about 56 percent of the total gross value of the agricultural production of 38,290,000 colones. The imports are equal to 5,117,000 colones, representing approximately 12 percent of the GPV of the agricultural sector. (This also includes the imports needed for the intermediate requirements, both from overseas and from the rest of the country.) Agricultural imports are nearly one-third of the total regional imports; it is the second largest importing sector, after manufacturing.

Agriculture generates total intermediate sales of 17,918,000 colones, which means 41 percent of GPV. Twenty-three percent of these intermediate sales were sold to the same sector. Services bought 21,000,000 colones (1 percent), and the manufacturing firms purchased 13,704,000 colones worth of agricultural products (76 percent). This is important. It shows the link between the activities of the agricultural and the manufacturing sectors. There are obvious economic policy consequences of that pattern.

Final demand consumes nearly 48 percent of gross production value (21,002,000 colones). It is the flow of goods used to satisfy the regional needs. Exports from this sector represent approximately 10 percent of the GPV (4,480,000 colones). There is an exports-imports deficit worth 637,000,000 colones.

The same analysis can be made for the remaining two regional sectors in the matrix in table 32.2. Manufacturing is the sector that generates the most intermediate consumption. It is worth 15,453,000 colones, namely 43 percent of the total

intermediate consumption. As already mentioned, most of its buying is done at agricultural firms (88 percent of the total purchases). Services are 27 percent of intermediate consumption. It shows a trade balance surplus worth 2,633,000 colones. Coffee and sugar exports are the main sources of that trade surplus.

Linkages

Input-output analysis helps explain the degree of interaction within an economy. To do so, there is a need to measure the degree of linkage. The first step is to distinguish between backward linkages and forward linkages. Backward linkages show how strong a buyer one sector is relative to the others. That effect can be seen along the columns. Forward linkages tell how good the sector is in providing inputs to other sectors. Its effect is appreciated through the rows.[4]

Methodologically, the linkages between one sector and the others are based on the direct and indirect requirements that are obtained from the inverse of Leontief's matrix. It is denoted by the following equation:

$$X = (I - A)^{-1} F + (E - M)$$

where
    X = Gross production value
    A = Technical coefficients Matrix
    F = Final Demand Vector
    E = Exports Vector
    M = Imports Vector

The backward linkages are defined as the sum of the direct and indirect input requirements[5] from each column—for example, how much from the entire manufacturing industry is required to generate a million colones worth of agricultural output. It accounts for the demand a given industry makes for others' inputs to produce a unit. In mathematical notation, it is denoted as the sum of the Kij elements for each element from the Leontief's matrix:

$$\sum_{i=1}^{n} K_{ij} = K_j \ (j = 1,2,3,\ldots,n)$$

where Kij represents the elements from the inverse

Table 32.3. Río Grande de San Ramón:
Total requirements of the productive sectors, 1995

Sector	Total linkages			
	Backward	Rank	Forward	Rank
1. Coffee	1.4	9	1.81	3
2. Sugarcane	1.42	7	1.59	5
3. Basic grains	1.44	6	1.43	7
4. Cattle raising	1.62	5	1.28	9
5. Forestry and fishing	1.03	31	1.27	10
6. Other agricultural products	1.36	11	1.36	8
7. Meat and milk production	1.13	21	1.01	27
8. Edible oils	1.08	25	1.01	25
9. Coffee processing	2.05	1	1.04	19
10. Grain mill products	1.31	14	1.04	20
11. Bakery products	1.17	19	1	35
12. Sugar	1.77	2	1.23	12
13. Other manufactured products	1.1	23	1	32
14. Drinks	1.03	30	1	34
15. Tobacco products	1.08	26	1	33
16. Textiles and clothing	1	36	2.28	2
17. Shoes and leather	1.37	10	1.08	17
18. Wood and paper	1.35	12	1.07	18
19. Printing and paper	1.01	35	1	31
20. Chemical products	1.19	17	1.01	23
21. Tires	1.09	24	1.01	26
22. Rubber and plastic	1.06	28	1	30
23. Glass and ceramics	1.33	13	1.08	16
24. Construction materials	1.01	34	1.26	11
25. Basic metals	1.02	33	1.16	13
26. Electrical goods	1.06	27	1.01	24
27. Transport equipment	1.02	32	1.02	22
28. Other manufactures	1.1	22	1	29
29. Construction	1.66	3	1.01	28
30. Banking, finance, and insurance	1.21	16	1.02	21
31. Trade	1.06	29	1.08	15
32. Transport	1.41	8	1.12	14
33. Services	1.63	4	3.54	1
34. Electricity	1.22	15	1.77	4
35. Housing ownership	1.17	20	1.53	6
36. General government	1.18	18	1	36

Source: Briceño, Cardoza, and Vargas (1997)

Leontief's matrix and n the number of sectors.

Forward linkages are the sum of the technical coefficients (the requirements for direct and indirect products) of each row. It measures which products of a specific branch are necessary as inputs for the production of one unit of output. In mathematical notation:

$$\sum_{j=1}^{n} K_{ij} = K_i \quad (i = 1,2,3,\dots,n)$$

The actual data include the imported inputs. The production function interpretation would have been best modeled if only domestic production part is recognized as a different input. It would mean intermediate inputs are taken from the market for Armington aggregates into the production of regional output. The available breakdown does not allow treating domestic technical coefficients by themselves.

Table 32.3 shows the total requirements of the economy of the Río Grande region. The thirty-six sectors have been ranked according to the total requirements of each branch. Coffee processing (9) is number one for backward linkages, with a requirements level of 2.05 units. That means no other economic sector produces more indirect activity in the region. That is very important for economic policy considerations. The second place is for sugar (12) with 1.77. Construction (29) is third with 1.66. The fourth place is for services (33) with 1.63 and it shows a strong backward linkage.

Services (33) shows the highest forward linkages with total requirements of 3.54. Textile and clothing (16) is the second with 2.28. Coffee (1) with 1.81 and electricity (34) with 1.76 are third and fourth. These sectors reflect how important a supplier each of the sectors is.[6]

This analysis of the total requirements shows how the regional economic system is interrelated. Agricultural sectors—namely, coffee, basic grains, and sugar—provide the main inputs to processing intermediate products or final products. That is linked directly to manufacturing. Likewise, the service sectors score high, especially transportation and distribution of regional goods. Electricity is important for both household and manufacturing consumption. Banking shows significant forward linkages, too. Construction and inputs for construction are important in building infrastructure.

Applications

Building the input-output matrix was important on its own. It was a pioneering task for Costa Rica. Furthermore, it was a crucial element in the understanding of how production took place in the region, as well as revealing interactions among production units. Yet, those features are not as interesting as the policy experiments. They provide a deeper look at the river basin and spell out the tasks public policy at the region faces. Most of the exercises are applications of Leontief inverse matrix.

The first case elaborates a demand model application for coffee and sugar processing. To make the simulation for coffee and sugar processing the following assumptions were needed:

> The most important assumption for this simulation was that the regional economy has inertial behavior; it will continue to act as it did in the past.
>
> All export calculations were based on annual average prices, since international prices vary almost daily.
>
> FOB prices for 60 kg coffee sacks were the basic figure for the impact multiplier, while those for sugar were FOB prices referred to 50 kg bundles. The prices are done in dollars.
>
> The behavior of the international prices shows a cyclic tendency that is seen clearly if a long historical series is observed. This assessment of the effect that changes in international prices of the two major export products have on the regional economic structure shows the large interdependence effects that exist within the region.
>
> All the assumptions for the input-output analysis were valid, as no additional restriction was needed.

Table 32.4. Simulated shock in coffee prices: Principal effects in the regional economy, 1995 (in millions of colones)

Sector	GPV	18% reduction Absolute	18% reduction Percent	25% increment Absolute	25% increment Percent	30% reduction Absolute	30% reduction Percent
Region	107,353	−4,715	−4.4	6,548	6.1	−7,858	−7.3
Coffee processing	16,122	−2,296	−14.2	3,188	19.8	−3,826	−23.7
Coffee	16,311	−1,676	−10.3	2,327	14.3	−2,793	−17.1
Textiles	11,001	−298	−2.7	414	3.8	−496	−4.5
Services	8,060	−195	−2.4	270	3.4	−324	−4
Electricity	3,282	−148	−4.5	206	6.3	−247	−7.5

Source: Briceño, Cardoza, and Vargas (1997)

The simulation started from:

$$X = [I - A]^{-1} D$$

Then,

$$X = [I - A]^{-1} \Delta D,$$

where the changes in production are given by changes in the final demand and:

X = Sectoral gross production values

$$\Delta X = [I - A]^{-1} \Delta D,$$

D = Final demand vector

Simulating Shocks on Coffee and Sugar Prices

Three scenarios were developed based on historical performance of each branch. For the case of coffee processing, the first case assumes an 18 percent reduction in the international price, assuming an identical behavior to the 1991–92 crop. The second scenario, quite optimistic, assumes an increase in prices of 25 percent, half of the increase that actually happened in the 1993–94 crop (as a consequence, among other factors, of the frozen temperatures in Brazil). The third scenario could be termed as pessimistic, assuming a 30 percent price reduction, based in the accumulated reduction during the 1991–93 crops. The activities most affected in all three simulations are coffee processing, coffee production and textile, and clothes. The fourth and fifth places are services and electricity sectors. The absolute reductions measured in millions of colones can be seen in table 32.4. Magnitudes that at first seem very large often are not if scaled to their relation to GPV. A more realistic interpretation is obtained.

The 18 percent drop in prices yields reductions in output in the sectors coffee processing, coffee, textile and clothes, services, and electricity of 14.2 percent, 10.3 percent, 2.7 percent, 2.4 percent, and 4.5 percent, respectively. The decrease generated as a consequence, a 4 percent reduction in the regional GPV, is quite large, especially when one realizes that it is just one of many sectors affected.

Our second analysis was an assessment of the effect that changes in international prices of the two major export products have on the regional economic structure. It showed the large interdependence effects that exist within the region.

Three similar scenarios were performed for the sugar production. The first one assumed a 7 percent reduction in the international trading prices, on the basis of a behavior similar to that of the 1991–92 harvest. The second scenario, an optimistic one, assumed a 19 percent increase in prices similar to that of the 1994–95 harvest. The third scenario is a pessimistic one, supposing a 48 percent prices reduction, which places prices at the 1987 level, under the assumption that the preferential market quota will decrease.

Table 32.5. Simulated shocks in sugar prices:
Principal effects in the regional economy of Río Grande de San Ramón,
1995 (in millions of colones)

Sector	7% reduction		19% increment		48% reduction	
	Absolute	Percent	Absolute	Percent	Absolute	Percent
1. Sugar	−98.24	2.21	266.66	6	−673.66	15.16
2. Sugarcane	−44.05	2.13	119.57	5.78	−302.07	14.6
3. Services	−14.09	.12	38.25	.47	−96.64	1.2
Regional total	−172.97	.16	469.5	.44	−1,186.11	1.1

Source: Briceño, Cardoza, and Vargas (1997)

The absolute reductions, measured in millions of colones, are shown in table 32.5. At first sight, those magnitudes seem large. Relation to GPV provides better scaling and shows reasonable terms. For the three simulations, the largest consequences are on sugar processing, sugarcane agriculture, services, and electricity.

A 7 percent price reduction yields a 0.16 percent reduction on the regional GPV. The sugar sector decreased 2.21 percent, sugarcane dropped 2.13 percent, and services activities are 0.12 percent smaller. The reduction has relatively minor consequences on the region. The results show important features of the region: sugar activity is limited to a couple of counties with small backward and forward linkages. That sets limits to the sector as anchor of an economic development policy.

Simulating Air Pollution

The Leontief approach that we give here is also useful in assessing some environmental impacts. Input-output analysis is quite appropriate for that task. Air pollution is a good starting point, and it allows us to show how measuring damage could be crucial for policy measures enactment. It has been a common practice for many environmentally conscious groups to complain about pollution in third world countries. Yet, often the evidence is not there. The second law of thermodynamics provides the argument that indeed it is there. Only the data are needed. Input-output economics could link air

pollution with production and allow us to show that pollution is a crucial issue. The following step in the analysis will be to study what kind of economic growth would generate the least environmental impact. Public policy needs that assessment.

It is clear that air pollution is not the number one environmental issue in Costa Rica and that the Río Grande River Basin, which is a mostly rural region, is not the highest priority in the country as far as cleaning the environment is concerned. Yet, being able to do such assessments for a well-defined and small enough region is important for academic and policy reasons. Montiel and Vargas (1994) did such an analysis for the whole country, but that is too large a region, given that Caribbean winds blow away most of the pollution except for highly polluted San Jose. Of course, there is not just one appropriate measure of the environmental deterioration and recently there has been concern in Costa Rica for natural preservation because of the increases in the degradation of natural resources and in ecotourism.

The main offering of input-output economics in this sense is an accounting system that can incorporate environmental accounts explicitly. That it could be applied for Costa Rica and more importantly for the region studied is crucial. It can be used to make much more comprehensive assessments that would support social, economic, and ecological policies. More generally, the input-output approach is an appropriate economic framework for analyzing the interrelations between the environment and the economy. It can be enlarged to include natural resource flows from the environment as well as natural inputs on economic activities. Measuring the flow of residuals from the production and consumption activities is needed to shape public policy.

Other approaches are available. Bartelmus, Stahmer, van Tongeren (1989) and United Nations (1993) have used the satellite charts methods. This consists in separating the independent satellite charts from those that are in the input-output tables. It is complex, to say the least. A second method is the one Leontief and Ford (1972) applied to the United States. It consists of adding a pollution matrix to the regular input-output matrix. It is simple enough and the assumptions are clear and straightforward.

The present application is meant to quantify air pollution caused by the productive sectors of the region, with an alternative way of treating a global problem from a regional perspective. The present simulation will also allow detecting which sectors generate the largest emission of air pollutants. Five types of pollutants are studied: nitrogen oxides, sulfur oxides, carbon monoxide, particles, and hydrocarbons.

Leontief and Ford (1972) registered the total emission of the those five air pollutants for the 1967 American economy, using emission data developed directly in an industry-by-industry study. In a later work, Montiel and Vargas (1994) quantified these coefficients for the Costa Rican economy according to the structure of the input-output matrix. Granted, these are not the only elements that damage the atmosphere, but all are important, and most of the air quality indexes explicitly take them into account.

For the present study it is assumed that the direct air pollution coefficients for each regional activity are the same ones Montiel and Vargas estimated for Costa Rica. There are no regional industry-specific air pollution coefficients so we use very general values. The total pollution coefficients are captured on the following input-output related matrix system:

$$X = E\,[I - A]^{-1}$$

where:

X = Matrix of total pollution coefficients by sector

E = Matrix of direct pollution coefficients by sector

$[I - A]^{-1}$ = Leontief's inverse matrix

Table 32.6 orders each productive sector according to its emission of pollutants. The construction materials sector, grain milling sector, and construction sector are the main generators of particle pollutants. The basic metals, rubber, and plastic industries pollute most when sulfur oxides are the case in point. The largest hydrocarbon producers are sectors 31, 32, and 34. For carbon monoxide pollutants, basic metals sector, transport sector, and electricity sector lead the field.[7]

The pollution coefficients used differ from native Costa Rican technological characteristics but they are the only estimates available. Revision and sensitivity analysis is mandatory. For instance, the electricity sector appears as one of the biggest producers in three of the five pollutants, although in fact Costa Rica produces much of its electricity from hydroelectric power. This result would be valid for those years when fossil fuel-derived electricity generation has been significant.[8] Otherwise, that statement could not be made. Furthermore, all thermoelectric plants are outside the Basin and it is unlikely the wind will bring those pollutants in.

The main contribution of our analysis is to establish the fundamental relationship between production and pollution at activities-specific measured levels. It also needs to be stated that household pollution is entirely absent from our analysis because of the production bias of input-output economic analysis. But similar studies could be made for any other pollutant type or economic activity. This would allow corrective policies applications according to the severity of damage caused to the environment (for example, taxes, prohibitions, and other command and control approaches).

Table 32.6. Sector ranking by increase in pollutant level, Río Grande de San Ramón, 1995

	Rank				
Sector	Part	SOx	HC	CO	NOx
1. Coffee	16	7	6	6	8
2. Sugarcane	15	6	8	8	4
3. Basic grains	22	4	13	12	18
4. Cattle raising	10	3	11	13	16
5. Forestry and fishing	33	8	35	28	35
6. Other agricultural products	13	5	16	11	15
7. Meat and milk production	26	20	31	33	34
8. Edible oils	30	23	28	32	30
9. Coffee processing	18	9	7	7	9
10. Grain mill products	2	18	19	20	23
11. Bakery products	19	22	20	21	24
12. Sugar	12	11	5	5	5
13. Other manufactured products	32	24	27	30	27
14. Drinks	35	28	34	34	28
15. Tobacco products	23	34	24	24	18
16. Textiles and clothing	36	36	36	36	36
17. Shoes and leather	14	30	15	18	13
18. Wood and paper	24	17	18	19	20
19. Printing and paper	4	21	26	27	29
20. Chemical products	9	13	14	15	14
21. Tires	31	27	25	23	25
22. Rubber and plastic	28	2	21	25	22
23. Glass and ceramics	7	29	10	14	7
24. Construction materials	1	12	33	35	32
25. Basic metals	6	1	30	1	31
26. Electrical goods	27	19	23	10	21
27. Transport equipment	34	33	32	26	33
28. Other manufactures	25	32	29	31	26
29. Construction	10	10	4	4	6
30. Banking, finance, and insurance	21	25	17	17	10
31. Trade	29	35	1	29	19
32. Transport	8	14	2	2	1
33. Services	11	16	9	9	2
34. Electricity	5	15	3	3	3
35. Housing ownership	20	26	12	16	11
36. General government	17	31	22	22	12

Briceño, Cardoza, and Vargas (1997)

Conclusion

The input-output matrix is a simple and very useful instrument for regional economic analysis. This chapter shows that it was possible to build the table for regional analysis in a developing country. In order to do so, a relevant group of statistical economic series for the region was developed from readily available data. For the first time in history, we had regional economic accounts in Costa Rica, and these allowed us to undertake these analyses.

The matrix enables the assessment of the regional economic structure and interactions. It yielded accurate measurement of forward and backward linkages. That scheme shows the economic structure and its interrelations in a very clear manner. The importance of that result for economic policy is quite large. By itself, employment and output multipliers allow either municipal or national governments to develop job-creating programs. It could also assess the impact of any proposed program on production or employment. Before the development of the matrix, the best most officials could do was an educated guess. This pioneering effort shows that a developing country, like Costa Rica, has the data infrastructure necessary to build such a matrix, which in turn reinforces government policy options.

The scenarios presented in this chapter are still preliminary and should be complemented by additional studies. Two of them show what effects world economic events have on a small region in a third world country. The issues of commodity prices are important and the calculation shows interesting productive links within the region. The air pollution case is relevant, and it gives a new quantitative sense to that important issue. Never before has such an analysis been carried out at regional level in Latin America. The input-output matrix is a useful instrument to determine where to look, and to single out what may be important. It has a powerful exploratory power, and it allows vastly better evaluation of development policies than pure neoclassical economics would have done.

Notes

1. This work reports results from Briceño, Cardoza, and Vargas (1997). It was part of the PRODUS research program. The support Rosendo Pujol provided, as well as unconstrained support from Merck Foundation, is gratefully acknowledged.

2. The RAS method is better explained at length in Instituto de Investigaciones en Ciencias Económicas (1985:28–34).

3. Lora (1987) presents a detailed analysis.

4. Instituto de Investigaciones en Ciencias Económicas (1985).

5. These are part of what in technical terms is known as Leontief's inverse matrix.

6. If the reader wanted to see what activities follow in order of linkage importance (backward and forward) he or she would have to continue with the analysis previously mentioned with each one of the matrix branches.

7. The emission of nitrogen oxide appears in the first place for sectors 32, 33, and 34 because they are the only ones that have direct coefficients of air pollution. This can be seen on the regional input-output matrix; see Briceño, Cardoza, and Vargas (1997).

8. In normal years, more than 90 percent of electricity on the national grid is air pollution–free hydroelectricity.

References

Abraham, W. I. 1969. *National Income and Economic Accounting.* Englewood Cliffs, N.J.: Prentice-Hall.

Ahmad, Y., S. El Serafy, and E. Luts, eds. 1989. *Environmental Accounting for Sustainable Development.* Washington, D.C.: World Bank.

Barros, A., and C. Lessa. 1979. *Introducción a la economía.* Mexico City: Siglo XXI.

Bartelmus, P., C. Stahmer, and J. van Tongeren. 1991. Integrated environmental and economic accounting: Framework for an SNA Satellite System. *Review of Income and Wealth* 37, no. 2: 111–48.

Briceño, R., D. Cardoza, and H. Vargas. 1997. Construcción de una matriz de insumo-producto para la cuenca del Río Grande de San Ramón: Un análisis de encadenamientos intersectorales. B.A. thesis, University of Costa Rica.

Costanza, R. 1991. *Ecological Economics: The Science and Management of Sustainability.* New York: Columbia University Press.

Dirección General de Estadísticas y Censos. 1984. *Censo de la población.* San José, Costa Rica: DGEC.

———. 1995. *Encuesta de hogares de propósitos multiples: Modulo de empleo.* San José, Costa Rica: DGEC.

————. 1996. *Costa Rica: Calculo de la población por provincia, cantón y distrito al 1° de enero de 1996*. San José, Costa Rica: DGEC.

Hannon, B. 1982. Analysis of the energy costs of economic activities: 1963–2000. *Journal of Energy Systems Analysis* 6:249–78.

Instituto de Investigaciones Económicas. 1985. *Cuentas nacionales e insumo-producto en Costa Rica: Primeros pasos para una actualización*. Heredia: University of Costa Rica.

Leontief, W. 1936. Quantitative input-output relations in the economic system of the United States. *Review of Economics and Statistics* 18, no. 3: 105–25.

————. 1941. *The Structure of the American Economy, 1919–1929*. New York: Oxford University Press.

Leontief, W., and D. Ford. 1972. Air pollution and the economic structure: Empirical results of input-output computations. In A. Brody and A. P. Carter, eds., *Input-Output Techniques*, 3–26. Amsterdam: North-Holland.

Montiel, N., and J. R. Vargas. 1994. Desarrollo económico y medio ambiente. *Revista Ciencias Económicas* 14, no. 2.

Stone, R. A. 1961. *Input-Output and National Accounts*. Paris: OECD.

United Nations. 1993–94. *Integrated Environmental and Economic Accounting: Handbook of National Accounting*. New York: United Nations Press.

PART SEVEN

SCIENCE FOR DEVELOPMENT:

Working with Decision Makers

In this section, we address an arena where scientists usually do not like to venture: the uneasy place where tough decisions that have an impact on real people are taken. At the policy-making level, decisions involve evaluating options (usually one option, sometimes more), selecting the best one, devising a strategy to negotiate with other policy makers, and acting (this is when there will be some impact on populations and the environment—or not), and all this with deadlines pressing and political interests showing up. None of this is what led most scientists into science. But the public pays for most basic science, and the public and its representatives have done so mainly with the promise that somehow there will be a payback for their investment. Some scientists understand this. Others do not but should.

Scientists, however, are careful and meticulous by nature, and they tend to be very conservative when they have to make a definitive statement that has irreversible consequences. Most scientists are somehow pleased when a theory, even their own, is proven wrong, because it means they are closer to the truth and that a mistake will be avoided in the future. And future research might get them closer to whatever that truth is. So uncertainty (which can translate to indecision) is part of the scientist's culture. But decision makers do not want uncertainty, and they often do not understand a scientist's reticence in providing them one. What, after all, are scientists paid public money to do?

Therefore, when a minister asks a scientist for advice—say, "Where should I develop agriculture?"

—the reply will generally be something like, "It depends." Such an answer is not very useful to a decision maker, who will then quickly turn to an economist who will give him an answer right away, plus an "accurate" estimate of the cost and benefit of the decision in dollars. Consequently, it was difficult to find, within our network of colleagues at least, natural scientists who actually took the risk of working with influential decision makers and who would write about their experiences for this book. We did find a few.

Chapter 33 describes a venture with the Costa Rican ministry of agriculture to explore how land-use tools such as the ones described in chapter 15 can support technical assistance for conservation agriculture. Chapter 34 gives the viewpoint of a professional of the Canadian International Development Agency who worked closely with scientists and community leaders on watershed projects process in Honduras. Chapter 35, whose coauthors include past agriculture and rural development ministers in the government of Colombia, uses a complex systems framework to unfold a new multilevel rural development planning process that is taking place in Colombia. Perhaps this is the ideal situation: find decision makers who are willing to work directly with scientists and the converse. Chapter 36 focuses more on methodology, explaining how to operationalize a flexible representation of poverty measures for an improved dialogue between stakeholders and for better targeting of investment toward populations that need it the most.

Chapter 33

Toward Sustainable Agricultural Development in Costa Rica

Roles and Complementarities of Technical Assistance and Science

Pieter M. Dercksen and Hans G. P. Jansen

Introduction

Over the past two decades, degradation of the natural resource base and the resulting negative effects on agricultural productivity and rural development in Costa Rica have become an issue of increasing concern to a wide range of stakeholders. The latter include not only environmentalists but also national and regional policy makers, plantation owners, cattle farmers, and small- and medium-scale farmers practicing mixed crop farming and raising livestock. About 52 percent of the Costa Rican population lives in areas classified as rural, and about 20 percent of these depend on agriculture or related activities (SEPSA 2000). In Costa Rica, loss of soil fertility is a major form of natural resource degradation, and the two most serious threats to soil fertility and productivity include soil erosion caused by excessive water runoff and chemical contamination, resulting in loss of soil organic matter, destruction of soil structure, and elimination of biological soil activity (Pimentel et al. 1995; Jeffery, Dercksen, and Sonneveld 1989). The majority of farmers in Costa Rica live in hillside areas where they farm sloping lands and report significant decreases over time in crop and animal productivity and an ever-increasing need for external inputs such as chemical fertilizers and animal feed supplements to avoid further productivity decreases (Hall 2000). For example, the Puriscal region was once an important basic grain-producing zone in the country, but decreasing productivity and concomitantly increasing production costs have already stimulated migration of farmers to other zones with more fertile soils and less sloping lands.

In an attempt to address this situation, the government of Costa Rica has increased its efforts to promote sustainable land use through the execution of a range of farm-level technical assistance programs. One of the most widely known and longest running of these programs is the Soil and Water Conservation Program (SWCP) of the Ministry of Agriculture and Livestock (MAG). This program, initiated in 1984 in cooperation with the Food and Agriculture Organization of the United Nations (FAO) and with major support from the governments of Italy (1984–89, first phase) and the Netherlands (1992–97, second phase), is now entirely executed by the MAG. Its major achievement to date is the development and application of a number of innovative concepts to assist small- and medium-scale farmers in making appropriate land-use decisions and conserve their land resources, all of which take as their departure point the multifunctional character of their agricultural production systems. This approach also confirmed the reality and complexity of the soil degradation processes and the importance of not only biophysical aspects but also socioeconomic considerations in planning and implementing conservation agriculture (FAO 1996; Hall et al., 2001). The need was recognized explicitly for an interdisciplinary focus as well as participatory design and implementation of conservationist production technologies that enable farmers to produce in an economically and environmentally sustainable manner (FAO 1998).

On the other hand, after numerous (but largely unsuccessful) efforts to increase farmer adoption of soil and water conservation (SWC) measures in the past, it became clear by the early 1990s that important adjustments needed to be made in agricultural extension strategies. The need for a better understanding of the farmers' biophysical as well as socioeconomic environments became increasingly evident. As a result, the SWCP shifted its focus from the localized implementation of soil conservation measures toward the development of an integral, interdisciplinary, and participatory methodology for land use and SWC planning. A number of technical concepts as well as a methodology for planning, implementing, and disseminating technologies for sustainable development of production systems were developed and implemented on a pilot scale in a number of areas such as Tierra Blanca in the watershed area of the Río Reventazón, Labrador de San Mateo in the watershed area of the Jesús River, and Cedral in the watershed area of the Río Aranjuez.

Even though the basis for a continuing program of conservation agriculture in Costa Rica is now firmly established, many questions still remain, particularly with respect to the technical and socioeconomic feasibility of large-scale adoption of conservation agriculture. In addition, it was realized increasingly that efforts aimed at its widespread adoption have to take account explicitly of the fact that different scale levels (watershed, subregion, region, and nation) each present their own conditions, opportunities, and constraints. Consequently, a firm belief developed that for the successful application of a program aimed at widespread introduction of conservation agriculture, methodologies and tools would be needed that enable an all-compassing technical and socioeconomic analysis of the potential impact of proposed land use and technology recommendations. It was felt that the application of such tools would enrich the orientation of the local, regional, and national planning processes, as well as assist in the selection of appropriate technical options and policy measures at different scales. Practical experiences of local technology generation needed to be connected with technical assistance programs within an overall research program that would generate methodologies and tools designed for the exploration or prediction of the technical and socioeconomic impacts of technology application at various scales.

This would assist extension technicians and farmers in developing and improving criteria for the identification and analysis of promising production activities and sustainable technologies. In addition, it would facilitate the formulation and realization of local, regional, and national agricultural policies, which in reality are often defined on the basis of rather incidental and local information.

In Costa Rica, the development of interdisciplinary methodologies and tools for the evaluation of land use at various scales has been the major thrust of an extensive research and education program called REPOSA (Research Program on Sustainability in Agriculture) led by Wageningen University of the Netherlands, in collaboration with CATIE (Tropical Agronomic Research and Higher Education Center) and MAG in Costa Rica during the period 1987–98. This program has brought traditional agronomic scientists together with social scientists and policy makers with the explicit charge of implementing the results of scientific research—and then using scientific research itself to examine the degree to which the policy objectives were realized. The relevance of these tools for agricultural policy formulation has been demonstrated through training sessions for extension technicians and other land-use analysts. Both the technical aspects and practical policy applications using the tools developed by REPOSA have been published widely in both local media (Jansen 1996; Jansen et al. 1997; Stoorvogel, Jansen, and Jansen 1995) and in the international scientific literature (see Bouman et al. 2000 and chapter 15 of this book). Moreover, in 1996 REPOSA started an intensive collaboration with the National University (UNA) through a research and training project "Agrarian Policies for Sustainable Land Use and Food Security in Costa Rica" (Roebeling et al. 2000) with financial support from the embassy of the Netherlands in Costa Rica. This project developed some of the land-use analysis tools of REPOSA further and trained UNA staff in their technical aspects and use for policy analysis. Finally, in 1997 REPOSA, in collaboration with MAG and the UNA, began a new project that focused on the application of some of its land evaluation tools at the watershed level through a case study in the watershed of the Río Aranjuez. This project also involved a major training component, this time focused exclusively on MAG staff. Although the objectives of the MAG-FAO and the REPOSA projects were clearly different (the former contributed to the development of sustainable agriculture through practical work at a farm level, while the latter focused on innovative research that placed sustainability in a wider context of multiple disciplines and scales), it was recognized that combining the experiences of both programs can contribute significantly to the creation of a new technical, interdisciplinary, and interinstitutional framework on which a dynamic, adequately oriented national program for conservation agriculture can be built.

New Insights in Soil and Water Conservation: Conservation Agriculture

In Costa Rica, most agricultural technicians and many farmers are already familiar with the concept of SWC in one way or another. Various types of conservation measures have been practiced traditionally in coffee plantations, and SWC has been included in the technical assistance program of the national extension system since its establishment in 1948. Most SWC measures were aimed at runoff control (Dercksen 2001; Dercksen, Solórzano, and Cubero 1994; Shaxson 1995), which was felt to be the first need, since precipitation in most regions is high, varying between 1,500 and over 5,000 mm per year. The construction of physical works for water diversion or retention was promoted as the best solution to the generation of high amounts of runoff water. Such measures included not only hillside ditches, diversion channels, and bench terraces, but also stone or vegetation barriers. In most cases, contour planting also formed part of the recommended package. These measures were generally labor-intensive and expensive, particularly for farmers who did not already possess the essential construction materials such as stones or cobbles needed for the protection or reinforcement of physical works. Runoff water was diverted to natural channels, roads, or rivers, and in most cases the water was loaded with sediment since no further soil protection measures were applied to the land situated between the conservation works. However, sealing of superficial soils and detaching of soil particles continued, leading to reduced water infiltration capacity of the soils and to a further increase of runoff water. Furthermore, the destructive effects derived from raindrop impact were not controlled, so that most of the aforementioned measures had virtually no impact on soil productivity and did not result in appreciable yield increases (Jeffery, Dercksen, and Sonneveld 1989; Shaxson 1995; FAO 1996; Dercksen 2001).

Despite the very limited success of the application of these measures during a number of decades, the first efforts to introduce changes in the technical strategy with respect to SWC did not take place until the initiation of the second phase of the MAG-FAO project. In 1992, a start was made with the identification of practices aimed at an integrated control of the soil erosion process, which basically consisted of addressing three phases: raindrop impact, soil sealing and soil particle detachment, and transport of soil particles by runoff water and sedimentation. The focus of SWC strategies shifted completely, from a nearly exclusive emphasis on the construction of physical works toward a focus on erosion control through the identification and application of appropriate management measures, which comply with technical principles able to address these three development phases of the soil-erosion process. These principles include the establishment and promotion of soil cover for the reduction of raindrop impact; the sealing of soils to reduce detachment of soil particles; the increase of water infiltration and reduction of runoff water, aimed at decreasing the transport of soil particles; and an increase of soil organic matter content for improvement of soil structure, infiltration, and soil fertility. Much attention was also paid to the reduction of soil and water contamination caused by soil erosion and the indiscriminate use of fertilizers, herbicides, and insecticides (FAO 1996). Moreover, within the extension services it was realized slowly that in order for SWC measures to continue to be used by farmers, they should comply with the need to increase productivity and farm profitability in the short to medium term (i.e., they should reduce unit production costs by increasing crop production per unit of land), given most farmers' risk aversion and relatively short time horizon.

The year 1992 thus marked the start of the paradigm shift in Costa Rican SWC circles (from physical works to SWC management). In the years that have passed since 1992, it is now generally accepted that control of the first phase of the erosion process through the increase and maintenance of adequate soil cover is essential for an efficient SWC (Dercksen 2001; FAO 1998). Covering the soil with vegetation or its residues reduces soil particle detachment, improves water infiltration, reduces runoff, and promotes biological activity, all of which lead to an increase in soil organic matter and soil fertility. The practical experiences with the new technical approach obtained in farmers' fields and its emphasis on the first phase of the erosion process have led to a reduced need for physical works, which now increasingly play a complementary role in SWC and in which soil management is now regarded as the central component. Given the generally high costs of physical structures for SWC, the application of this new SWC strategy has led to a significant reduction in total costs for SWC per unit area. Moreover, in virtually all cases the reduction of soil productivity has been halted or soil productivity even increased, as expressed by incremented crop yields that are a direct result of improvements in fundamental soil characteristics such as higher percentage of soil organic matter, higher retention of soil moisture, and increased availability of soil nutrients. The shift in strategy for SWC has stimulated a significant improvement in the proportion of farmers reached by the extension services who apply SWC measures in their fields (FAO 1998).

Adequate soil cover can be achieved in different ways. In Costa Rica, farmers who practice SWC stopped burning crop residues and often use (leguminous) cover crops in rotation with main crops, in order to produce large amounts of crop residues for spreading on the fields' surface. Alternatively, farmers may intercrop food crops with cover crops or cash crops. These cropping practices are combined with the application of minimum tillage involving the replacement of the disk plough by the chisel plough or zero-tillage practices involving direct seeding over existing crop residues. In yet other cases, soil cover is promoted through weed management and an economic and environmentally adequate management of crop residues (FAO 1997a). The use of drip irrigation systems in dry areas and the application of improved seeds are other frequently applied technical options that contribute to the improvement of soil cover and crop yields. On the other hand, the government of Costa Rica strongly promotes a program for the development of organic agriculture, which aims at serving the growing demand for organic products from national and international markets, while complying with the technical principles of SWC, as well as the requirements with respect to the use of agrochemicals. Although the development of organic agriculture usually is associated with yield reductions, especially during the transitional phase between traditional and organic management, as well as high prices for quality certification, additional costs are in most cases more than compensated for by higher prices for organic products. These examples represent the integrated approach that forms the basis of SWC implementation. They show how soil management aims at the provision of an adequate soil cover, improved soil fertility and soil biology, improved water retention in soils, increased crop diversification, the reduction of plant diseases through crop rotations, and the interplanting of cash crops for improved economic benefits. Rather than isolated practices, the new strategies for SWC are seen increasingly as an integral part of conservation agriculture that promotes changes in entire production systems that have major implications in a variety of technical aspects and fields and in which adequate soil, water, and crop management together play a major role.

Participatory Planning for Conservation Agriculture

During the first year (1992) of the second phase of the execution of the MAG-FAO project, farmers and technicians were inclined to continue with the then-accepted concepts of erosion control, implemented through a traditional extension

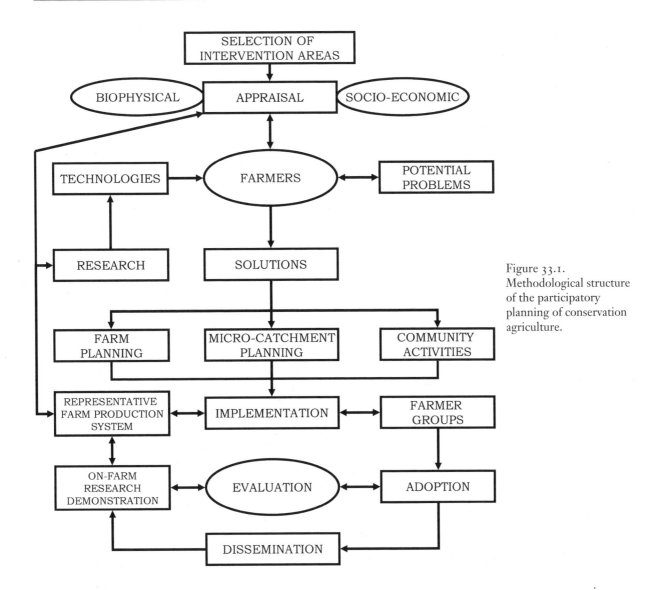

Figure 33.1.
Methodological structure of the participatory planning of conservation agriculture.

methodology based on the transfer of research-generated knowledge to extension technicians and from extension technicians to farmers. The transition toward the implementation of the new technical strategy and the increase of the adoption of integrated technologies was rather slow initially (Dercksen 2001). However, a few years of experience with intensive training of participating farmers on SWC techniques and related concepts, in combination with on-farm testing of a substantial number of field measures identified over the years on the basis of thoroughly analyzed biophysical and socioeconomic information of local production systems, resulted in the creation of a large body of experience in SWC among extension technicians and farmers alike. Finally, an estimated

total of twenty thousand farmers were reached by the extension service and personnel of local NGOs through the execution of practical training courses in the field and the implementation of dissemination campaigns and the use of the communication media (radio and television programs, video presentations, and the like) at the national level (FAO 1997b). During this process, both extension technicians and farmers became increasingly convinced that a systematic, integral methodology for participatory planning for conservation agriculture has a large potential to benefit farm productivity and farmers' welfare. This methodology (figure 33.1) consists of a series of steps and allows for the explicit and immediate incorporation of farmers' know-how as well as their perceptions of problems related to agricultural production and possible solutions to these problems. The methodology uses instruments such as applied research on farmers' fields with active participation of farmers themselves, thus contributing to the improvement of their capacity to analyze problems and identify promising solutions based on the technical principles of conservation agriculture while simultaneously taking explicit account of the economic benefits of proposed technological interventions. The participatory methodology for conservation agriculture replaces the traditional system that largely consisted of the presentation of standard recommendation packages. The latter often represented isolated practices that typically failed to recognize the multidisciplinary character of agricultural production systems and their associated opportunities and problems.

The new methodology for implementing conservation agriculture was initially developed in eight pilot areas with small groups of farmers (about two hundred farmers in total). Each of these areas is representative of different combinations of biophysical and socioeconomic conditions found in the rural areas of Costa Rica (table 33.1 and figure 33.2). Pilot areas were selected using reconnaissance surveys as well as more-detailed soil- and land-use studies (Van Enckevorth 1994, 1995; Vásquez 1989). Selection criteria included a wide range in biophysical variables such as climate, topography and soil characteristics, farm management considerations (such as agronomic, soil, and crop management variables), and socioeconomic aspects of the most relevant production systems such as coffee, vegetables (potatoes and onions), and mixed farming systems involving basic grains (maize, rice, beans), extensive livestock, and fruits (orange, melon). Information on farm management included data collected through formal and quantitative socioeconomic field surveys, as well as qualitative information based on informal discussions with farmers (Trujillo and Azofeifa 1994–96). The information assembled included detailed data regarding the use of technologies, itineraries of farm management operations, and major problems that limited the development of sustainable agricultural production. The various types of

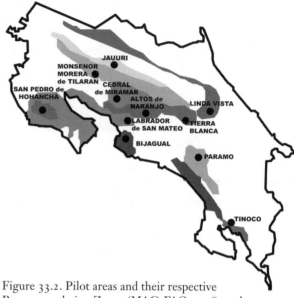

Figure 33.2. Pilot areas and their respective Recommendation Zones (MAG-FAO 1996); scale approximately 1:4,000,000.

complementary information assembled enabled the development of the next step, which included the identification of possible solutions and promising technical options, as well as the establishment of action plans to be executed at the farm, micro-watershed, and community levels. The methodology includes participatory workshops for the determination of follow-up and evaluation activities, aimed at the identification of the necessary adjustments to the development process as well as the determination of the need for new technologies to be developed through research in farmers' fields or on experimental stations. In addition, the methodology provides a mechanism that aims at a continuous gathering of the information necessary for retroactive decision making and interaction between farmers and technicians, as well as for the determination of research priorities. Finally, it enables farmers to develop improved farm administration skills and the capacity to perform simple cost-benefit analyses of alternative soil, crop, and livestock management practices.

An example of the information developed and used in the participatory process of improvement of production systems is given in tables 33.2–33.5. Experiments on farmers' fields for improved livestock management and reduction of soil degradation in the area of Tilarán (MAG-FAO project;

Table 33.1. Characterization of pilot areas of the MAG-FAO project

Pilot area	Coordinates	Principal biophysical characteristics	Principal production systems / soil conservation measures / socioeconomic conditions
Tilarán, Hector Morera (143 ha)	10° 26′ 44″ to 10° 27′ 53″ 85° 55′ 57″ to 85° 56′ 50″	640–840 meters above sea level; Typic Ustrivitrands; slope 8–60 percent; limitations related to fertility (low in N, P, Zn, K and organic matter), soil depth stoniness, erosion risk; climate: precipitation 2,120 mm/yr, dry spells of > 3 months/year, strong winds; mean annual temp. 23.6° C	Principally pastures; basic grains, vegetables, coffee, tubers, and fruit trees. Application of hillside ditches, stone barriers, live barriers, contour planting, pasture improvement and cattle rotation, windbreaks (trees). Small farmers (2–5 ha), milk, tuber, and coffee production for local markets, basic grains and vegetables for auto-consumption and local markets. About 50 percent of farmers work off-farm for extra income.
Altos de Naranjo (275 ha.)	9° 59′ 54″ to 10° 00′ 44″ 84° 26′ 12″ to 84° 27′ 26″	920–1,340 meters above sea level; Typic Ustropepts; slope 30–75 percent; fertile soils, with minor limitations (low in P and Zn); additional limitations related to soil depth, stoniness, and erosion risk; precipitation 1,800 mm/yr, dry spells > 3 months/yr, strong winds; mean annual temp. 23.7° C	Principally coffee and pastures; basic grains (maize and beans), sugarcane, and vegetables. Application of hillside ditches and live barriers. Some farmers apply soil cover between coffee plants (weed management). Small farmers (0.5–5 ha), coffee production for local and international markets, milk and meat for local markets, vegetables for local markets and auto-consumption. About 33 percent of the farmers work off-farm for extra income.
Cedral de Miramar (367 ha)	10° 14′ 17″ to 10° 15′ 68″ 84° 40′ 51″ to 84° 42′ 25″	900–1,420 meters above sea level; Andic Eutropepts and Alfic Udivitrands; slope 8–60 percent; fertile soils (although low in P and Zn), with minor limitations related to stoniness, soil depth, and erosion risk; precipitation 3,500–4,000mm/yr, dry spell about 2 months/yr.; mean annual temp. 20° C	Mainly pastures and coffee; basic grains (maize, beans), vegetables and fruit trees. Application of hillside ditches, bench terraces, individual terraces, live barriers, contour planting, windbreaks, some soil cover in coffee and fruit tree plantations (*Arachis pintoi*). Small and medium farmers (2.5–115 ha), coffee production for local and international markets, milk, meat, fruits and vegetables for local markets, and basic grains for auto-consumption. About 7 percent of the farmers work off-farm for extra income.
Jauúri	10° 27′ 10″ (185.5 ha) to 10° 28′ 40″ 84° 37′ 10″ to 84° 38′ 30″	250 meters above sea level; Typic Distrandepts; slope 15–30 percent; medium fertile, well-drained soils (low in P, high organic matter content, high infiltration rate), with minor limitations related to stoniness and erosion risk; precipitation 3,560 mm/yr, no clear dry spell, most rainfall between the months of June and December; mean annual temp. 25° C	Principally basic grains (beans and maize) and pastures. To a minor extent tubers, banana, and tropical fruits. Appli-cation of hillside ditches, live barriers, contour planting. Small farmers (2–5 ha), basic grains and milk for auto-consumption and local markets, tropical fruits and bananas for local markets. About 17 percent of farmers work off-farm for extra income.
Labrador de San Mateo (296 ha)	9° 56′ 12″ to 9° 56′ 15″ 84° 37′ 68″ to 84° 37′ 71″	50–160 meters above sea level; Ustic Palehumilts and Ultic Paleusalfs; slope 0–15 percent; Low to medium fertile soils (moderately low Ph, low in organic matter, low in N, P, K and Zn), with major limitations related to heavy texture, low infiltration rate, stoniness, soil depth and erosion risk; precipitation about 2,300 mm/yr, dry spell > 3 months/yr; moderately strong winds; mean annual temp. 26.5° C	Mainly basic grains (maize, beans, rice); fruit trees, peanuts, and to a minor extent pastures, vegetables, and melon. Application of live barriers, stone walls, windbreaks, and contour planting. Small farmers (2–5 ha), basic grains for auto-consumption and local markets, fruits, peanuts, and melon for local markets. About 50 percent works off-farm for extra income.

(continued on next page)

Table 33.1. Characterization of pilot areas of the MAG-FAO project (cont'd)

Pilot area	Coordinates	Principal biophysical characteristics	Principal production systems / soil conservation measures / socioeconomic conditions
San Isidro de Hojancha (216.5 ha)	9° 59' 54" to 10° 00' 44" 84° 26' 12" to 84° 27' 26"	400–825 meters above sea level; typic Haplustalfs; slope 15–90 percent; medium fertile to fertile soils (although moderately low Ph, low in P, K and Zn), with major limitations related to heavy texture, low infiltration rate, high erosion risk; precipitation about 2,200 mm/yr, dry spell > 3 months/yr; moderately strong winds, mean annual temp. about 27° C	Principally pastures. To a minor extent basic grains (maize, beans, rice), coffee, vegetables and fruit trees. Application of minimum and zero tillage for planting of basic grains (maize and beans), hillside ditches, live barriers, and contour planting. Small farmers (2–5 ha), basic grains, milk, meat and vegetables mainly for auto-consumption and local markets, coffee and fruits for local markets. About 95 percent of the farmers work off-farm for extra income.
Bijagual de Turrubares (250 ha)	9° 42' 28" to 9° 43' 48" 84° 33' 43" to 84° 34' 55"	440–588 meters above sea level; Ustic Haplohumults; slope 3–75 percent; low fertile soils (low Ph, low availability of Ca, P, K and Zn), with major limitations related to heavy clay texture, very low infiltration rate, high erosion risk; precipitation about 2,700 mm/yr, dry spell > 3 months/yr; mean annual temp. about 25° C	Principally pastures and tubers. To a minor extent basic grains (maize and beans), vegetables and fruit trees. Application of hillside ditches, live barriers, and contour planting. Improved pastures in some areas (*Brachiaria brizantha*). Small farmers (5–7 ha), principal farm income from tuber cultivation for local market and export and livestock, basic grains and vegetables mainly for auto-consumption. About 60 percent of the farmers work off-farm for extra income.
Tierra Blanca de Cartago (152 ha)	9° 54' 10" to 9° 55' 08" 83° 54' 45" to 84° 53' 48"	1,820–2,080 meters above sea level; Ustic Humitropepts; slope 3–30 percent; fertile soils (medium pH, low availability of P, Zn, Mg), with major limitations related to high erosion risk, stoniness, soil depth; precipitation about 1,470 mm/yr, dry spell about 3 months/yr; mean annual temp. about 15.4° C	Mainly vegetables (onions, potatoes, and carrots) and pastures. In the dry season some vegetables and beans where irrigation is available. Application of hillside ditches, some live barriers and wind breaks. Contour planting is rare and seedbeds are frequently situated into the slope direction. Intensive soil tillage is common. Small farmers (0.5–10 ha), vegetable, milk and meat production for local markets, beans and maize for auto-consumption. About 30 percent of farmers work off-farm for extra income.

Pilot areas are representative for larger areas with similar characteristics, denominated as recommendation zones (see also figure 33.2). Soil classification according to the Soil Taxonomy (Soil Survey Staff 1992).

based on data from Tilarán, Monseñor Hector Morera, Guanacaste; see also table 33.1) included the introduction of pasture legumes and the application of enclosures for cattle rotation and pasture management. Tables 33.2–33.4 illustrate the technical and economic parameters of a small livestock project; table 33.5 illustrates the expected environmental impact of these practices with reference to the technical principles of conservation agriculture.

Tables 33.2–33.5 show that the project certainly is financially profitable, but only after six years. On a per-year basis in case of the traditional technology (without project situation), annual operational costs are covered with the production of at least 2.9 liters of milk/cow/day [col. 86,788 / (5 cows × col. 40) × 150 days]. In the case of introduction of the proposed improvements, the break-even milk yield increases to 3.1 liters/cow/day [col. 269,712 / (12 cows × col. 40) × 180 days]. This is mainly the result of the increase in labor costs for milking, animal feed and medicines, and fertilizing of pastures. In 1994, agricultural wages were about col. 1,000/working day. In the without-project situation, returns to labor are about col. 5,500 per working day [(net benefits + wage payments) / 30 days]

Table 33.2. Farm situation with and without project

Price of milk (col./1)   40.00
Price of calves (col./animal)   18,000

	Without project		With project
Pasture type *Arachis*	*Estrella africana* with few enclosures		Mixture of *Estrella africana* and *pintoi* with many enclosures; fodder bank with sugarcane
No. of calves sold per year		4	9.6

Parameter	Unit	Quantity	Quantity
Farm area	Hectare	4	4
Enclosures	No.	4	24
Stocking rate per ha	Animal Unit	1.2	3
Stocking rate (total per farm)	Animal Unit	6	14.4
No. of double-purpose cows	No.	5	12
Milk production	L/cow/day	5	5
Calving rate	%	80	80
Calf production	No.	4	9.6
Milk production left to calves	%	25	25
Lactation period	Days	150	180
Type of labor		family	family

Costs are in 1994 colones (1 USD = col 157)

Table 33.3. Investment costs

Parameter	Unit	Without project Quantity	Without project Costs (colones)	With project Quantity	With project Costs (colones)	Incremental difference
Establishment of enclosures (every ten years)	no.	4	124,670	24	266,360	141,690
Cows (double purpose)	animal unit	5	400,000	12	960,000	560,000
Establishment of legume (every ten years)	hectare			4	122,733	122,733
Establishment of fodder bank of sugarcane (every ten years)	hectare			0.15	32,525	32,525
Total investment costs			524,670		1,381,618	856,948

Table 33.4. Operational costs

Parameter	Unit	Without project		With project		Incremental difference
		Quantity	Costs (col.)	Quantity	Costs (col.)	
Annual basis:						
Salt and minerals	kg	274	13,688	657	32,850	19,162
Sugarcane extract	gallon	70	5,100	82	6,010	910
Concentrates	kg	450	13,500	630	18,900	5,400
Medicines	colones		24,500		58,800	34,300
Labor for fence maintenance	working days	5	5,000	15	15,000	10,000
Labor for milking and herd management	working days	25	25,000	90	90,000	65,000
Fertilizing of pastures	kg			800	44,800	44,800
Replanting of fodder crop	colones				3,352	3,352
Total annual operational costs			86,788		269,712	182,924
Every eight years:						
Fencing	colones		40,560		87,760	47,200
Every ten years:						
Poles for fencing (every 10 years)	colones		35,100		78,000	42,900

Table 33.5. Incremental profitability analysis

Year	0	1	2	3	4	5	6	7	8	9	10
Income from meat (sales of animals)	72,000	172,800	172,800	172,800	172,800	172800	172,800	172,800	172,800	172,800	172,800
Income from milk sales	150,000	432,000	432,000	432,000	432,000	432,000	432,000	432,000	432,000	432,000	432,000
Total income	222,000	604,800	604,800	604,800	604,800	604,800	604,800	604,800	604,800	604,800	604,800
Incremental investment costs (col.)	856,948										
Operational costs (col.)											
Annual operational costs	86,788	269,712	269,712	269,712	269,712	269,712	269,712	269,712	269,712	269,712	269,712
Incremental fencing costs (every 8 years) Incremental poles costs (every 10 years)			47,200 42,900								47,200
Total costs that vary (col.)	86,788	359,812	269,712	269,712	269,712	269,712	269,712	269,712	269,712	316,912	269,712
Net benefits (col.) 135212	-611,960	335,088	335,088	335,088	335,088	335,088	335,088	335,088	287,888	335,088	
Incremental cash flow (col.)	-747,172	199,876	199,876	199,876	199,876	199,876	199,876	199,876	152,676	199,876	
Opportunity costs of capital (based on Zuniga 1996)	8%										
Net present value (after 5 years) (col.)	78,849.38										
Net present value (after 6 years) (col.)	47,106.40										
Net present value (after 10 years) (col.)	440,676.18										

Table 33.6. Expected impact of improved livestock management project according to the principles of conservation agriculture

Principles of conservation agriculture	Expected impact
Increase of soil cover	+, Direct
Increase of infiltration	+, Indirect
Reduced runoff water	+, Indirect
Improved soil fertility and soil organic matter	+, Indirect
Reduction of soil and water contamination	+, Indirect
Increase of productivity*	+, Direct

*See Tables 33.2–5
+, Direct = direct impact
+, Indirect= indirect impact
Source: Vieira (1997)

---

or over five times the wage rate. In the without-project situation, returns to labor decrease slightly to about col. 4,100 per day [(net benefits + wage payments) / 105 days] but with the advantage that the farmer is able to use some 75 days more of his labor on his own farm. Since opportunities with respect to off-farm labor are limited in the Tilarán area, improved technologies that are labor-intensive offer good prospects to raise farm incomes.

The positive environmental effects mentioned in table 33.6 include the increased soil cover, which results from cattle rotation, elimination of overgrazing, improved pasture growth through the application of fertilizer, and improved root development in less-compacted soils. A better pasture development leads indirectly to the improvement of the infiltration rate in the soils and increase of soil organic matter, which consequently contributes to improved soil fertility conditions, such as water and nutrient retention capacity. Improved infiltration leads to runoff reduction and the decrease of water contamination by sediments, organic matter, and remaining fertilizer.

Institutional Aspects and Legislation for Soil Conservation and Management

The experiences of the MAG-FAO project and the gradual development and application of this new methodology for conservation agriculture based on multidisciplinary concepts and participatory extension led to the conclusion that in order to institutionalize and further disseminate the new approach at the national level, an adequate operational system would be needed, including new ways of intraministerial coordination between the major technical divisions. The latter are the Agricultural Extension Division, the Agricultural Research Division, and the Plant and Animal Protection Division. Each of these three divisions operates at the central (i.e., national) as well as regional level, respectively through their headquarters in San José and eight regional offices, one in each region defined on the basis of both geographical and administrative criteria. The regional offices are managed by regional directors and have both extension and research personnel. They are complemented by eighty-four agricultural services agencies (ASAs), each with on average only a couple of extension workers. The ASAs represent a national network of small local institutions, which have been designed to provide technical assistance to the farmers. This is done through the execution of field visits, organization of training courses and participatory workshops, introduction of new technologies, and exchange visits between farmers of different areas. On the other hand, ASAs play an important role with respect to the enforcement of local farmers' organizations and the coordination with regional institutions that are involved in agricultural development. The daily execution of the participatory planning of conservation agriculture is done at this level.

At the country level, 580 extension workers are together responsible for supplying technical assistance to some 30,000 small and medium farmers. However, in most cases the extension agencies cooperate with local and regional farmers' organizations such as the National Coffee Institute (ICAFE), cantonal agricultural centers, various chambers such as the Chamber for Livestock, cooperatives, and other nongovernmental organizations that work in the field of agricultural development. Research is executed by the Agricultural Research Division, making use of the operational infrastructure described above. Research activities are carried out on farmers' fields as well as on a few experimental stations; the latter are used for training purposes as well. In order to be able to implement the conservation agriculture program adequately, most extension technicians received substantial training on the subject. In several cases training courses included technicians of nongovernmental organizations, farmers' organizations, universities, and other training institutes including the National Training Institute (INA), the Costa Rica Technological Institute (ITCR), and the University of Costa Rica (UCR).

From the methodological structure of the participatory planning of conservation agriculture (figure 33.1), it becomes clear that the extension component plays a fundamental role not only in the dissemination of the core concepts to farmers but also in the provision of the information necessary for adequate planning of the research program. The methodology of participatory planning for conservation agriculture implicates a demand-driven research component, a concept that requires the continuous attention and changes in the attitudes of both researchers and extension technicians. Rather than continuing with the traditionally practiced top-down approach, the success of the new approach depends crucially on both researchers' and extension technicians' willingness

to develop integrated actions and joint activities, such as the execution of farmers' workshops and the conducting of research on farmers' fields in close cooperation with farmers themselves. Although substantial headway has been made with respect to the improvement of the participatory character of the planning process by integrating farmers' perceptions of new technologies in their farming systems and taking account of farmers' reasons and motivations for decision making when analyzing problems in the field, traditional working methods, based on the principles of traditional extension (top-down) methods, widely prevail and changes in attitude and mode of operation are achieved only gradually. The introduction and consolidation of the necessary changes is an ongoing process, and the program of conservation agriculture continues with the application of the participatory planning process at the farm level. The local successes obtained on small and medium farms in the area of conservation agriculture have led to an increasing awareness of the necessity of coordinated interinstitutional interaction in order for the methodology of participatory planning of conservation agriculture to be adopted as a basic concept for the orientation of the technical and social roles of the institutions involved.

A prime example of a successful effort to institutionalize the technical, strategic, and operational aspects of participatory planning of conservation agriculture was the establishment of Law 7779 for Land Use, Land Management, and Soil Conservation, approved in 1998 (Government of Costa Rica 1998; Dercksen 1999). The adoption of this legislation confirms the national political support for participatory planning of conservation agriculture and the associated concepts in order to restructure the agricultural sector in Costa Rica. Law 7779 allows for the decentralization of conservation agriculture activities through the establishment of local and regional committees. These committees are composed of representatives of the Ministry of Agriculture and Livestock (MAG), the Ministry of Natural Resources and Energy (MINAE), local and regional political entities (mainly municipalities), farmers' organizations, and other relevant governmental and nongovernmental organizations. The law explicitly recognizes that its implementation requires training of farmers and technicians, to be executed in selected representative pilot (micro) watersheds. In addition, the law provides for economic incentives to farmers who realize sustainable land use and who commit to soil and water conservation. This can be done by applying the basic technical principles for the identification of appropriate management measures to achieve SWC along the lines discussed in this chapter (FAO 1996). On the other hand, the law also stipulates sanctions that can be imposed in cases where farmers do not comply with the established rules for improved land use and cause soil erosion, soil and water contamination, or other negative on-site and/or off-site effects. It is the responsibility of the agrarian tribunals to process all matters that originate through the application of this law. Finally, apart from training activities for farmers and technicians, the law establishes an inspection system that is executed by land-use specialists, who are entitled to inspect and certify land-use activities and conservation agriculture practices implemented by individual farmers or farmers' groups. These specialists are organized in Committees for the Inspection and Security of Natural Resources (COVIRENAS, established by executive decree 26923-MINAE) and are trained by the MAG and the MINAE, even though they do not necessarily belong to the institutes of the public sector.

However, with respect to the institutional and organizational requirements for the execution of the national program of conservation agriculture, reference has to be made to the negative effects of the implementation of the various structural adjustment programs implemented in Costa Rica from the late 1980s onward. As a result of these programs, the number of extension and research personnel of the MAG has been reduced by about one-third, and various ASAs in the regions were closed down. These measures resulted in the reduction of the technical assistance capacity to small farmers, since most of the released technicians found employment in market-oriented agricultural enterprises that do not cater to small subsistence-oriented farmers, and that lack the necessary grade of organization and financial means to purchase private extension services. The effects of these structural adjustment policies have almost certainly led to an increase in rural poverty and groups of small subsistence farmers abandoning agriculture while migrating to the urban areas.

Although there are important initiatives to improve the access of smallholders to private technical assistance, such as the execution of training programs in organic agriculture for farmers and technicians, such initiatives often depend on international donor funding. To the extent that they depend on public resources, the latter have gradually diminished over time in response to structural adjustment and a general lack of national funds. There is a clear need for the government to invest more in the training of both extension technicians and farmers, since this will be essential to the future of the national program of conservation agriculture and for farmers' ability to comply with the national environmental legislation.

Transfer and Extrapolation of Experiences

As mentioned earlier, the development of a methodology for participatory planning of conservation agriculture was based on technical and operationally practical experiences in a number of pilot areas. The latter were selected on the basis of a variety of biophysical and socioeconomic characteristics and spread over different agroecological zones on the basis of criteria such as soil type, range in altitude, climate, and major vegetation and land-use types. Additional selection criteria related to the applicability of improved technologies outside the pilot areas were also included, to make sure that the characteristics of the farmer groups and their production systems would be representative for larger geographical areas. These areas, called recommendation zones (Van Laake 1996), are characterized by similar agroecological conditions, similar production systems, and similar potential for dissemination of specific technologies, all of which would facilitate the extrapolation of the results obtained in the pilot areas. These recommendation zones also formed the basis for the planning of a horizontal training program of farmers and technicians. Under this program, trained extension technicians of the ASAs responsible for the implementation of conservation agriculture in the pilot areas are able to transfer local experiences directly to colleagues and farmers in neighboring zones. A generalized example of the type of recommendation zones used in Costa Rica is given in figure 33.2.

Tools for Land-use Analysis and Planning of Conservation Agriculture at Different Scales

The development of a national program for conservation agriculture in Costa Rica has led to a significant, although not yet massive, adoption of a number of more sustainable agricultural production technologies for a variety of production systems managed by small-scale and medium-scale farmers in the country. Most of these technologies are developed for specific crops and production systems and typically require certain investments as well as adjustments in land use and technology use. Since most of these requirements imply an increase in risk for the farmers who adopt the new practices, involving investments in new equipment, time for training and experimentation at the farm level, sometimes lower production levels during the first years, and often insufficient information with respect to demand for products and market prices, it is now realized increasingly that further development and expansion of the conservation agriculture program should make use of complementary planning methodologies that allow the local planning process to be embedded in, and consistent with, the overall agricultural development strategies at the subregional, regional, and national scales. Such methodologies should be of a multidisciplinary character and able to take explicit account of both biophysical and socioeconomic requirements and implications of a wider adoption of conservation agriculture technologies and associated adjustments in land use. Moreover, such methodologies should be capable of evaluating the impact of agricultural policy measures in terms of economic sustainability and environmental indicators at different scales including the local, subregional, regional, and national levels. The methodologies could then be used for the exploration and prediction of the likely

effects of policy decisions such as the introduction of economic incentives for the generation of environmental services in sustainable production systems, introduction of taxes on the use of pesticides, and improvements in the road network. A framework, most likely computerized, that would enable relatively quick development and evaluation of alternative policy scenarios and that would include and integrate socioeconomic data such as production costs, market prices, product demand and supply, supply of labor, and costs and benefits of alternative land uses and technologies with implications of the latter for sustainability and the environment, would substantially reduce the risk of policy failure through improving the planning process for policy makers, private-sector entrepreneurs, farmers' organizations, and extension technicians. Such analysis could be developed based in part on existing biophysical models of crop production (Hall 2000, chapter 14).

As mentioned before, the REPOSA (WU-CATIE-MAG) project has developed a coherent set of tools for land-use analysis and agricultural policy formulation that can be applied at different scales, using the Atlantic Zone of Costa Rica as its first and largest case study (Bouman et al. 2000). The best-known (and arguably the most important) element in this tools package is a methodology called SOLUS (Sustainable Options for Land Use; see chapter 15; Bouman et al. 1999; and Jansen et al. 2005). SOLUS is a methodology for subregional and regional land-use analysis that can be used to explore the effects of alternative land-use options and technologies in terms of both their economic impact as well as their effects on sustainability and the environment over a relatively long time horizon (twenty to thirty years). In this way SOLUS is able to depict clearly and quantify the various trade-offs involved in moving from one type of land use and technology to another. SOLUS consists of three main components (see figure 15.3 in this book): (1) a bioeconomic agricultural sector model of the linear programming (LP) type that incorporates the labor market as well as a multimarket structure for commodities and that includes both socioeconomic and biophysical constraints; (2) models of the expert-system type (called technical coefficient generators or TCGs) that define large numbers of production activities, each of which is characterized by a specific technology; and (3) a geographic information system (GIS) to store and manipulate georeferenced data information of both biophysical and socioeconomic nature. The LP model selects the optimal combination of production systems and technologies by maximizing the income generated by the agricultural sector in the region (Schipper et al. 2000). The expert systems in the TCGs quantify the economic (yields, labor use, input costs), sustainability (soil nutrient balances), and environmental (quantities of pesticides used and their environmental impact, emission of various greenhouse gasses) effects of a large number of production systems at the plot level for cropping systems, pastures, forestry, and livestock. These production systems include actual systems currently in use by farmers as well as improved systems that have shown to be viable but are not (yet) widely adopted (Hengsdijk et al. 1999). GIS is used to reference spatially biophysical and economic data that characterize the subregion or region, to create input files for the TCGs and for the LP model, to store and reference spatially LP model output, and to create maps of both input and LP output data (Jansen et al. 2005).

The SOLUS methodology is a powerful tool for measuring the economic (farmers' incomes), sustainability (soil conservation), and environmental (e.g., effects of pesticides and gas emissions) implications of a national policy for conservation agriculture at various scales. Even though SOLUS was originally developed for the Atlantic Zone of Costa Rica, its tools and models are sufficiently generic to allow its implementation in other regions with different biophysical and/or socioeconomic conditions. For example, SOLUS may be used to analyze the regionwide effects of the application of improved livestock management in silvipastoral systems in the Central Pacific region or the application of zero-tillage practices in irrigated rice cultivation in the Chorotega region. On the other hand, in addition to their role in the SOLUS methodology, the TCGs can be used as standalone tools and are useful for decision support at the farm and plot level. In particular, they could

be used and amplified within the context of the program of conservation agriculture. For example, they can be used to quantify the trade-offs among economic (short-term yield and income) and sustainability indicators (soil nutrient mining, erosion) at the field level for a variety of conservation technologies, or to explore the relative importance of inputs in production systems and technologies through cost-benefit analysis. While cost-benefit analysis may support decisions made at the farm level (e.g., with respect to the efficient application of different inputs), the trade-offs among different farmer objectives can be made explicit to identify alternative production options and allow more balanced decision making with regard to new production systems in conservation agriculture (Bouman et al. 1998; Hengsdijk, Nieuwenhuyse, and Bouman 1998).

Another important development in the area of decision support methodologies concerns the joint REPOSA-UNA effort to develop a framework that can be used for making more precise predictions about the likely short-term (< 5 years) effects of policy measures on farmers' land-use decisions (see figure 15.4). This framework is based on the explicit incorporation in the SOLUS methodology of farmer behavior in individual optimization models for representative farm types (as opposed to a single optimization model for the entire subregion or region in the original version of SOLUS). Even though each of the farm-type models is of the LP type, they differ significantly in terms of their overall structure, objective function, resource endowments, and other boundary conditions. In addition to the original SOLUS methodology, the REPOSA-UNA adaptation is also of interest to the national program for conservation agriculture since it is designed for modeling behavior on the farm level while at the same time enabling the modeling of aggregate behavior of producers and consumers at higher spatial scales (region or nation; see Roebeling, Jansen, et al. 2000; see also chapter 15).

Researchers and other stakeholders, ranging from farmers to regional policy makers, are increasingly becoming aware of the need for close interaction and dialogue in agricultural sector development. This is demonstrated by the fact that, in 1997, MAG expressed strong interest in exploring the development options for the watershed of the Río Aranjuez in the Central Pacific Region by making use of the SOLUS methodology. This interest also confirmed the growing institutional awareness of the need for the use of advanced planning tools at different spatial scales, including the level of the watershed. This new collaboration at the watershed level in a new region presented a unique opportunity for both researchers as well as local MAG field extension workers and technicians to apply their knowledge in the fields of soil science, land evaluation, soil and water conservation, GIS, and biophysical and socioeconomic analysis of production systems in an integrated manner by adapting and applying the SOLUS framework at the watershed level. The training provided by REPOSA and UNA staff included the application and adaptation of technical coefficient generators (Hengsdijk 1999) and the development of an LP model for the analysis of land-use options in the watershed (Saénz et al. 1999). Compared to the application of SOLUS to the Atlantic Zone, its application in the Aranjuez watershed required the development and operationalization of two new sustainability indicators, soil erosion and water runoff. The resulting adaptation of SOLUS resulted in the design and evaluation of a number of policy scenarios, which were discussed extensively among MAG extension technicians and a wide range of local stakeholders (Mera-Orcés 1999).

The results of the exercise in the Aranjuez River watershed area contributed to a better understanding among the regional and local MAG personnel of the complexity of using models for policy analysis and for prediction of the effects of decisions made by policy makers on local farming systems. A number of highly interactive training sessions conducted by REPOSA and UNA staff gave participants the opportunity to broaden their technical and conceptual knowledge base with respect to the multidisciplinary character of production systems while building on their practical and theoretical experience gained as a result of their participation in the earlier MAG-FAO project. Specific experiences obtained included developing technical coefficients

for conservation technologies and incorporating them into the TCG framework, designing and operationalizing relevant sustainability indicators, working with optimization models, and analyzing the outcome of different scenario runs. The exercise contributed to the testing of the SOLUS methodology in a different environment and at a different scale than the subregional or regional level. The practical application of the methodology at a scale level with which extension personnel are familiar also forced the participants to think through the decision-making process by farmers further, thus highlighting a number of factors that are overlooked frequently by technicians and high-level decision makers alike. As an example, the exercise revealed that the cultivation of organic coffee in the watershed of the Río Aranjuez, an alternative option promoted by the government's national program for organic agriculture, is not attractive to farmers because market prices for this product are too low to be competitive with coffee produced with traditional technology and the high labor requirements of organic coffee are difficult to satisfy. The experience thus confirmed that there is a great need to execute technical assistance in a participatory way in order to be able to analyze correctly farmers' perceptions and motivations that play such a pivotal role in the adoption of conservation effective agriculture.

In summary, the joint application of the SOLUS methodology in the Río Aranjuez watershed by researchers and local stakeholders confirmed the usefulness of planning methodologies that allow for explicit inclusion of farmers' objectives, opinions, and expert knowledge of technicians, and the matching of local desires regarding agricultural development with subregional, regional, and national realities and priorities for the agricultural sector.

Final Thoughts

In Costa Rica, large-scale adoption of conservation agriculture has thus far been limited for a variety of reasons. Farmers usually have strong reservations with respect to innovative forms of management of their crops and soil and water resources, and often are inclined to return to their traditional management practices, especially in those cases where no adequate technical assistance and consistent follow-up are given. Many technicians are trained in traditional ways and need to change their top-down extension methodology into a participatory one. However, this requires a consistent analysis of production systems, participatory identification and application of new technologies, and their economic and environmental validation in close cooperation with farmers. Technical "improvements" may be rejected by farmers for a variety of reasons, all of which can be identified through proper analysis of technical and economic information generated in the field. However, this is only possible when both technicians and farmers insist on the consistent execution of the methodology described earlier in this chapter, including continuous measurement of relevant field indicators established on the basis of the technical principles for conservation agriculture. None of the farmers in Tilarán would have adopted the proposed system based on improved pastures, legumes, and livestock management using enclosures and cattle rotation without having been able to gradually introduce these changes on their farms, analyze their economic and environmental benefits, and discover that the system increases milk production while at the same time reducing the need to work outside the farm, saving land and generating soil improvements.

For a successful transition toward a more competitive and environment-friendly agriculture based on the principles of conservation agriculture, we consider it necessary that MAG internalize the methodology for the participatory implementation of conservation agriculture and train its personnel in the use of tools and methodologies for sustainable land-use analysis on different scales, including the SOLUS and/or REPOSA-UNA methodologies. The latter may provide important new insights before resources are invested in the promotion of conservation technologies (such as zero-tillage rice cultivation) that require high initial capital investments beyond the financial carrying capacity of most farmers. These methodologies may be of great value when it comes to, for example, explaining the decreasing fertilizer-use efficiency at the national level, a phenomenon that has been found for virtually all major crops in Costa Rica (Hall et

al. 2000). In our example (table 33.3) of the "with project" situation, the use of fertilizer is introduced. This measure, however, represents only one isolated component of a range of improvements, which form part of an integrated management system; we consider that fertilizer-use efficiency in Costa Rica can be improved through the adoption of integrated land, water, and crop-management practices based on integrated farm-management plans. In such cases, policies could be developed that identify research needs; improved crop, soil, and water-management systems and improved extension instruments, all of which facilitate higher production levels; improved product quality; and positive environmental impacts.

Conclusions and Recommendations

1. Costa Rica's national soil and water conservation program has generated a wide range of technical and operational experiences that have culminated in new insights in soil and water conservation; led to the definition of new concepts for the identification and dissemination of sustainable agricultural production technologies; and stimulated the development of a new participatory extension strategy and planning methodology for conservation agriculture.

2. Traditional soil and water conservation concepts, with their narrow focus on combating soil erosion through the establishment of expensive highly localized physical works, largely have been abandoned and replaced with erosion control as an integral part of the management of entire production systems. Technologies for SWC are now identified on the basis of technical principles derived from the analysis of the consecutive development phases of the water erosion process, socioeconomic factors in relation to production systems, and the potential of various technologies to comply with the multiple objectives of farmers.

3. The new participatory methodology for the planning of conservation agriculture provides for the possibility of increasing the adoption of sustainable agricultural

production technologies through a sequence of consecutive processes consisting of planning, implementation, evaluation, and follow-up. This process improves the selection of technologies and their adaptation to local conditions greatly. It also leads to appropriate identification of research priorities through the analysis of interdisciplinary information and results of practical experiments on farmers' fields.

4. The dissemination of technologies for conservation agriculture in Costa Rica has been accelerated through a process of horizontal transfer of experiences gained by technicians and farmers working together in ASAs in pilot areas, to technicians and farmers located in recommendation zones, which are characterized by similar biophysical conditions and production systems.

5. Efforts aimed at increased adoption of sustainable agricultural production technologies and corresponding changes in land use and management of production systems should be linked with tools and methodologies for sustainable land-use analysis on different scales, including the SOLUS methodology for explorative regional land-use analysis and the REPOSA-UNA methodology for predictive farm-type analysis. The experience obtained with the application of these methodologies at the watershed level has shown that recommendations given to farmers have to be considered within the possibilities and limitations dictated by their biophysical and socioeconomic conditions, as well as within the context of regional and national agricultural policies and developments. The promotion of the cultivation of organic coffee mentioned in this chapter is a good example where the application of these methodologies could have saved considerable effort, time, and other resources that were spent trying to pursue inappropriate recommendations. Adequate use of the SOLUS and/or REPOSA-UNA methodologies may provide important new

insights before resources are invested in the promotion of expensive conservation technologies such as zero-tillage rice cultivation or the installation of structures for artificial climate and plant disease control (tropical versions of glasshouses). Both these technologies are interesting from a conservation point of view (reduced soil erosion, control of the use of water and biochemicals) but require considerable financial capital and therefore may not be feasible from a socioeconomic point of view.

6. The MAG program of conservation agriculture needs to incorporate and stimulate the development and use of complementary tools for land-use analysis and planning of conservation agriculture at a local, subregional, regional, and national level. The activities generated in 1997–98 in the watershed of the Río Aranjuez deserve an adequate follow-up and should also be developed for other areas where the potential impact of the conservation agriculture program is considered large. Research aimed at the adjustment of methodologies for the areas concerned, as well as the further development of models at the farm, subregional, regional, or national levels, should involve not only MAG's Research Division but also other national research institutes with relevant expertise, such as the UCR (University of Costa Rica) and the UNA.

7. Relatively easy-to-use expert systems that enable rapid and relatively simple biophysical and socioeconomic evaluation of agricultural production technologies at the plot level (such as the TCGs in the SOLUS and REPOSA-UNA methodologies) are promising stand-alone tools to be used for decision support by extension technicians and farmers alike.

8. The use of computer-based methodologies for land-use evaluation allows for the analysis and design of optimal land use and management at the national level while enabling focusing in on the regional and local (field) levels. In order to generate useful

results and give these instruments an essential function in the planning process at the various scale levels, it has to be stressed that there is a need for a highly interactive work strategy, which involves the continuous exchange of relevant data between local extension workers and regional and national planners. This process enables a frequent update of the results obtained from the use of these methodologies, thus allowing for the adjustment of agricultural policies at the different levels concerned.

9. Finally, at the institutional level, the participatory methodology for the planning of conservation agriculture requires a fully integrated programming of research and extension activities. This has important implications, especially for the functioning of MAG's extension and research divisions. Given the facts that (1) MAG's institutional structure allows the implementation of such a working strategy; (2) the institution has the advantage to be present at a national, regional, and local level; and (3) the full implementation of conservation agriculture is backed up by adequate legislation for conservation agriculture, there are no barriers left for the two divisions to work together to the fullest extent possible in order to contribute to a more sustainable agriculture in Costa Rica.

References

Bouman, B. A. M., H. G. P. Jansen, R. A. Schipper, H. Hengsdijk, and A. Nieuwenhuyse, eds. 2000. *Tools for Land Use Analysis on Different Scales*. Dordrecht: Kluwer Academic.

Bouman, B. A. M., H. G. P. Jansen, R. A. Schipper, A. N. Nieuwenhuyse, H. Hengsdijk, and J. Bouma. 1999. A framework for integrated biophysical and economic land use analysis at different scales. *Agriculture, Ecosystems & Environment* 75:55–73.

Bouman, B. A. M., A. Nieuwenhuyse, and H. Hengsdijk. 1998. PASTOR: Version 2.0 users guide.

Dercksen, P. M. 1999. Panorama del desarrollo de la legislación agroconservacionista en Costa Rica. Memorias de la V reunión bienal de la red latinoamericana de agricultura conservacionista, Florianopolis, Brazil.

———. 2001. Costa Rica: Strategy, principles and instruments for the development of conservation agriculture. First World Congress on Conservation Agriculture, Madrid.

Dercksen, P. M., N. Solórzano, and D. Cubero. 1994. Participatory soil and water conservation planning for sustainable productivity in Costa Rica. *Proceedings of the 8th ISCO Conference*, 1042–50. New Delhi: ISCO.

FAO. 1996. Serie: Agricultura conservacionista. Tema I: Conceptos y enfoque. Un enfoque para producir y conservar. Proyecto fomento y aplicación de prácticas de conservación y manejo de tierras en Costa Rica (MAG-FAO). San José, Costa Rica.

———. 1997a. Serie: Agricultura conservacionista. Módulo II-7: Opciones técnicas para cumplir con los principios de la agricultura conservacionista. Proyecto fomento y aplicación de prácticas de conservación y manejo de tierras en Costa Rica (MAG-FAO). San José, Costa Rica.

———. 1997b. Serie: Agricultura conservacionista. Módulo III-2: Técnicas e instrumentos de extensión y comunicación. Proyecto fomento y aplicación de prácticas de conservación y manejo de tierras en Costa Rica (MAG-FAO). San José, Costa Rica.

———. 1998. Informe terminal. Proyecto fomento y aplicación de prácticas de conservación y manejo de tierras en Costa Rica (MAG-FAO). San José, Costa Rica.

Government of Costa Rica. 1998. La Ley de uso, manejo y conservación de suelos. Ley no. 7779 de 30 de abril de 1998. La Gaceta No. 97, 21 de mayo de 1998. San José, Costa Rica.

Hall, C. A. S., ed. 2000. *Quantifying Sustainable Development: The Future of Tropical Economies*. San Diego: Academic Press.

Hall, C. A. S., C. Leon, W. Ravenscroft, and H. Wang. 2000. Temporal and spatial overview of Costa Rican agricultural production. In C. A. S. Hall, *Quantifying Sustainable Development*, 349–401.

Hall, C. A. S., D. Lindenberger, R. Kummel, T. Kroeger, and W. Eichhorn. 2001. The need to reintegrate the natural sciences with economics. *Bioscience* 51, no. 8: 663–73.

Hengsdijk, H. 1999. LUCTOR-Aranjuez: Sistema de experto para cuantificar sistemas de cultivo en la cuenca Aranjuez. Report No. 140, REPOSA, Turrialba, Costa Rica.

Hengsdijk, H., B. A. M. Bouman, A. Nieuwenhuyse, and H. G. P. Jansen. 1999. Quantification of land use systems using technical coefficient generators: A case study for the Northern Atlantic Zone of Costa Rica. *Agricultural Systems* 61:109–21.

Hengsdijk, H., A. Nieuwenhuyse, and B. A. M. Bouman. 1998. LUCTOR.: Land Use Crop Technical Coefficient Generator. A model to quantify crop systems in the Atlantic Zone of Costa Rica; version 2.0. Quantitative Approaches in Systems Analysis 17. Wageningen, Netherlands: AB-DLO/PE-WAU.

Jansen, H. G. P. 1996. Uso sostenible de la tierra en Costa Rica. *Guía Agropecuaria de Costa Rica* 12, no. 26: 15.

Jansen, H. G. P., B. A. M. Bouman, R. Schipper, H. Hengsdijk, and A. Nieuwenhuyse. 2005. An interdisciplinary approach to regional land use analysis using GIS, with applications to the Atlantic Zone of Costa Rica. *Agricultural Economics* 32:87–104.

Jansen, H. G. P., A. Nieuwenhuyse, M. Ibrahim, and S. Abarca. 1997. Evaluación económica de la incorporación de leguminosas en pasturas mejoradas, comparada con sistemas tradicionales de alimentación en la Zona Atlántica de Costa Rica. *Agroforestería en las Américas* 4, no. 15: 9–13.

Jeffery, P. J., P. M. Dercksen, and B. Sonneveld. 1989. Evaluación de los estados de la erosión hídrica de los suelos en Costa Rica. Proyecto MAG-FAO/GCP/COS/009/ITA. Informe técnico 2-E. Rome: FAO.

Mera-Orcés, V. 1999. Evaluación de la transferencia de la metodología SOLUS (de REPOSA) al Ministero de Agricultura y Ganadería (MAG), Costa Rica. Report no. 138, REPOSA, Turrialba, Costa Rica.

Pimentel, D., C. Harvey, P. Resosudarmo, K. Sinclair, D. Kurz, M. McNair, S. Crist, L. Shpritz, L. Fitton, R. Saffouri, and R. Blair. 1995. Environmental and economic costs of soil erosion and conservation benefits. *Science* 267:1117–23.

Roebeling, P. C., H. G. P. Jansen, R. A. Schipper, F. Sáenz, E. Castro, R. Ruben, H. Hengsdijk, and B. A. M. Bouman. 2000. Farm modeling for policy analysis on the farm and regional level. In Bouman et al., *Tools for Land Use Analysis on Different Scales*, 171–98.

Roebeling, P. C., F. Sáenz, E. Castro, and G. Barrantes. 2000. Farm household modelling for agrarian policy analysis and appraisal: A case study in the Atlantic Zone of Costa Rica. In W. Pelupessy and R. Ruben, eds., *Agrarian Policies in Central America*, 76–102. New York: Macmillan.

Sáenz, F., R. A. Schipper, H. Hengsdijk, R. Azofeifa, and H. G. P. Jansen. 1999. Análisis del efecto de políticas agrícolas sobre el uso de la cuenca del río Aranjuez. Report no. 139, REPOSA, Turrialba, Costa Rica.

Schipper, R. A., B. A. M. Bouman, H. G. P. Jansen, H. Hengsdijk, and A. Nieuwenhuyse. 2000. Integrated biophysical and socioeconomic analysis of regional land use. In Bouman et al., *Tools for Land Use Analysis on Different Scales*, 115–44.

SEPSA (Secretaria ejecutiva para la Planificación del Sector Agropecuaria). 2000. Estadísticas sobre el desempeño sectorial. San José, Costa Rica.

Shaxson, T. F. 1995. Planificación participativa para la conservación, uso y manejo de los suelos y aguas. Informe del consultor. Proyecto fomento y aplicación de prácticas de conservación y manejo de tierras en Costa Rica. San José, Costa Rica.

Soil Survey Staff. 1992. *Keys to Soil Taxonomy*, SMSS. Blacksburg: Virginia Polytechnic Institute and State University.

Stoorvogel, J. J., D. M. Jansen, and H. G. P. Jansen. 1995. El Programa Zona Atlántica: Un paso hacia el desarrollo sostenible. *Agricultura & Ganadería* 4:20–21.

Trujillo, J. M., and R. Azofeifa. 1994–96. Aspectos socioeconómicos de las áreas piloto del Proyecto MAG-FAO. San José. Costa Rica.

Van Enckevorth, P. L. A. 1994–95. Estudios de suelos y capacidad de uso de las áreas piloto del Proyecto MAG-FAO. San José. Costa Rica.

Van Laake, P. 1996. Los ámbitos de recomendación de las áreas piloto: Proyecto fomento y aplicación de prácticas de conservación y manejo de tierras en Costa Rica. San José, Costa Rica.

Vásquez, M. A. 1989. Cartografía y clasificación de suelos de Costa Rica (1:200,000). Proyecto MAG-FAO. Rome: FAO.

Vieira, M. J. 1996. Matriz de relaciones entre los procesos de degradación de las tierras y opciones tecnológicas. Proyecto fomento y aplicación de prácticas de conservación y manejo de tierras en Costa Rica. Rome: FAO.

———. 1997. Aspectos de producción y conservación de suelos y agua en áreas ganaderas. Conceptos y Técnicas. Proyecto fomento y aplicación de prácticas de conservación y manejo de tierras en Costa Rica. Rome: FAO.

Zuñiga, N. 1996. Estimación de la tasa de interés promedio. *El Financiero*, 22–28 January 1996.

CHAPTER 34

Watershed Scales and Levels

Experiences with Projects in Central America

Gaston Grenier

Introduction

The staff of the Canadian International Development Agency (CIDA) dedicates a lot of effort to make development assistance more effective. While supporting natural resource management projects in the past, CIDA has dealt with difficulties in attempting to classify the land on the basis of the needs of the stakeholders. In most cases, the data collected by research assistants were used to produce very detailed reports and maps with little participation of the stakeholders. These projects failed to deliver the anticipated results. In other cases, the local stakeholders were not able to make the link between the land-use plans and their own benefit. For a donor institution like CIDA, it took only a few failures to decide to eliminate land-use planning projects from the aid portfolio. Currently, the number of such projects is very small.

Yet certainly land use and land-use planning has to be an important part of effective development aid. This brief chapter focuses on the need for the development of new technologies and methodologies that will enable greater participation of stakeholders in the management of natural resources. It is based on lessons learned in watershed projects funded by CIDA in Central America. The projects discussed are located in Honduras (five projects), Nicaragua (three projects), and Costa Rica (two projects). The strategy of these projects is to use the needs of the stakeholders at various levels as a basis for classifying all or part of the watershed area. The parameters of the watershed are classified in space and time according to available data. In general, climatological and hydrological series, where they exist, are given as tables. We map some physical and soil characteristics, slope, natural resource distribution (forest, agriculture, wildlife) and economic

and social conditions of the population. We make an effort in all the projects to classify the land use with the participation of the stakeholders, and to demonstrate ex ante the virtual reality of improved land-use planning with instruments such as crop guides, crop input-output models, cash-flow projections, and financial viability indicators. We also attempt to illustrate the various ecological benefits and environmental services the watershed provides to local communities.

Stakeholder participation requires some preparation from the local populations as well as for the surveying team. Surveying teams must come prepared to recognize the competency of the local *campesinos* in classifying their own land. "Experts" who believe that the only approach is to plan everything ahead of time with beautiful maps and project plans describing the optimal land-use pattern are at risk of producing virtual products and no more. It is important that local participants, farmers and their families, be exposed to the beneficial results of improved land-use planning through demonstrations, projections, training, and the like.

Methodology

To illustrate this process we present two cases at different scales:

(1) The preparation of farm-level land use plans by extension workers with the participation of farmers. This is done for the agroforestry farming system component of the CIDA Hardwood Forest Development Project in the North Coast of Honduras.

(2) The preparation of territorial unit plans for use in the Arenal Watershed of Costa Rica.

The steps for farm land-use planning in Honduras were:

1. Preparation of the farm sketch. This step involves the collection of available information concerning the farm: family composition, manpower, land tenure, housing, current crop and animal production patterns, current infrastructure and equipment, economic balance sheets, geographical location, and data on elevation, climate, and hydrology. In addition, farmers locate crop and forest areas, watercourses, farm roads, fences, and the like on a rough map. Thus we have both a biophysical and a financial worksheet so that we can construct integrated analyses.

2. Mapping the current land use: This step implies the preparation of the farm land-use boundaries, noting them relative to a point of reference and the associated changes in terrain slope. Transects of the farm are delineated, and land-use information is collected along them.

3. Generation of the slope map on the basis of the data collected along the transects.

4. Mapping of potential land use: A map of potential land use is derived from soil depth and slope data. Land is then classified into seven categories of potential use: (a) without crop limitation, (b) with crop limitation, (c) grazing land, (d) permanent crops, (e) nonrestricted lumber production, (f) restricted lumber production, and (g) areas that need protection.

5. Mapping of discrepancies between recommended and actual land use: Maps illustrating the differences between recommended and current land use are made. These maps allow the farmers to see the management plan as it relates to their own present farm. This map translates the virtual reality of the discrepancies between the desired and actual land use at the farm level.

6. Development of the management plan: Criteria for the management of land are based on the needs of the farmer and made

in consultation between the farmer and the extension worker. This consultation takes into consideration the economic viability of the various cropping systems and their contribution to the resolution of any conflicts between the recommended and the present land-use patterns. From its onset and throughout the planning process the farmer must be informed of the economic and technical aspects of the cropping, livestock, and agroforestry systems presented.

Figure 34.1 shows an example of participatory planning maps for a watershed of the CIDA Hardwood Forest Development Project in the North Coast region of Honduras.

We next illustrate classification of the land-use capacity, land-use potential, and land-use condition with maps developed for an area of the Aranjuez River micro-watershed of the Arenal watershed in Costa Rica. This classification scheme was elaborated from a list of eleven characteristics classified by the experts of the Arenal Conservation Authority during a planning process consisting of five steps:

1. Making baseline survey, diagnosis, and sectorial projections
2. Drafting solutions to perceived problems identified in 1 or elsewhere
3. Consulting and deciding what has to be done
4. Making a plan of action
5. Executing that plan

One reason by which this process differs from the previous one is the diversity of the interests of the stakeholders of the Aranjuez River micro-watershed that need to be expressed. The variables used to classify the watershed area were: geology and geomorphology, climatology, hydrology, soils, forest resources, biology, socioeconomy, agriculture and livestock, institutions, archaeology, and the existing mapping framework.

Typically, potential and conflicting-use maps are produced from the top based on technical criteria defined by experts, which are often close to

(a) ACTUAL LAND USE MAP   **(b)** POTENTIAL LAND USE MAP

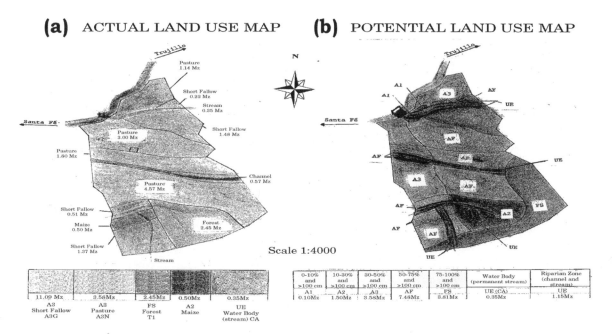

Scale 1:4000

0-10% and >100 cm	10-30% and >100 cm	30-50% and >100 cm	50-75% and >100 cm	75-100% and >100 cm	Water Body (permanent stream)	Riparian Zone (channel and stream)
A1 0.10Mz	A2 1.50Mz	A3 3.58Mz	AF 7.48Mz	FS 3.81Mz	UE (CA) 0.35Mz	UE 1.15Mz

(c) LAND USE CONFLICTS MAP

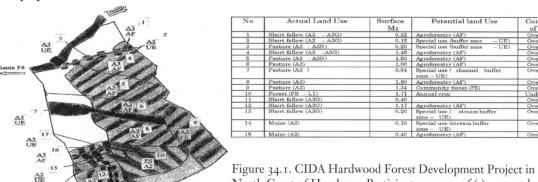

No	Actual Land Use	Surface Mz	Potential land Use	Conflict of Use
1	Short fallow (A3 - A3G)	0.22	Agroforestry (AF)	Overused
2	Short fallow (A3 - A3G)	0.15	Special use (buffer zone - UE)	Overused
3	Pasture (A3 - A3N)	0.20	Special use (buffer zone - UE)	Overused
4	Short fallow (A3 - A3G)	1.45	Agroforestry (AF)	Overused
5	Pasture (A3 - A3N)	1.50	Agroforestry (AF)	Overused
6	Pasture (A3)	1.00	Agroforestry (AF)	Overused
7	Pasture (A3)	0.64	Special use (channel buffer zone – UE)	Overused
8	Pasture (A3)	1.80	Agroforestry (AF)	Overused
9	Pasture (A3)	1.34	Community forest (FS)	Overused
10	Forest (FS - L1)	1.71	Annual crop	Underused
11	Short fallow (A3G)	0.40		Overused
12	Short fallow (A3G)	1.17	Agroforestry (AF)	Overused
13	Short fallow (A3G)	0.20	Special use (stream buffer zone – UE)	Overused
14	Maize (A2)	0.10	Special use (stream buffer zone – UE)	Overused
15	Maize (A2)	0.40	Agroforestry (AF)	Overused

Figure 34.1. CIDA Hardwood Forest Development Project in the North Coast of Honduras: Participatory maps of (a) current land use; (b) potential land use; (c) potentially conflicting land use.

useless in a real situation. For Honduras, the plans were negotiated between the technicians and the farmers, but only a few parameters could be taken into account properly.

Results and Discussion

In the case of the land-use approach for the development of individual farms, the planners have concluded that the plans for each farm might permit the eventual classification of most of the watersheds. They felt that this approach should be undertaken even if this approach is expensive and has to be subsidized. However, more than ten years after the inception of the project in Honduras, and even after having tested land-use classification through multidisciplinary teamwork and by defining all the land-use patterns in the watersheds, there has been very little use of the plans and little adoption of the proposed cropping systems.

We have concluded that a chief reason for this failure is that the number of parameters used to classify watershed areas is generally limited and that many of the most important variables are left out. Those parameters used tend to be the easiest to measure by the planners and stakeholders. Consequently, if virtual representation of planned agroforestry systems appears to be a very important component of both the management and decision-making processes among the most interested stakeholders—the farmers—and if new mapping and imaging technology might improve the quality of such representations, we must admit that we are undertaking such analyses mostly using the wrong information. In aid projects, budget and time constraints often limit the capacity of those involved in project implementation to innovate methods that might get the more appropriate information. Such needed parameters include the relation of the watershed area to markets, the flow of information within the area, the distribution of the political power and cultural characteristics, micrometeorological and microbiological data, and so on. But these are available only in exceptional situations.

Moreover, very little has been done to incorporate the rate and acceleration of change in the area: population dynamics, organization and networking, nature dynamics, market development, rate of deterioration, capital accumulation, and so on. To determine the level of these parameters is difficult and more applied research is needed. One interesting possible tool is the development of very inexpensive laptop-based mapping systems by Eric Dudley (see Hall 2000, appendix).

One hypothesis that could explain the limited number of parameters used in the plans is that the scales of measurement for little-used but important parameters are either very large or very small, and consequently they cannot be captured and used by the main stakeholders. New tools must be developed in order to transfer the scale of the parameters to something perceptible to the users. For someone with very little school education, a curve on a sheet of paper may not be a very convincing tool. We have begun the development of new customized indicators to define the socioeconomic parameters and new modes to visualize their dynamics. Computers have improved the capacity of researchers and planners to classify spatial information, but the application of these technologies to watershed and micro-watershed areas is still very limited. For example, at the very micro level, mapping of spatial information can be very useful when applied to pest management supported by micrometeorology, precision farming, and simple devices for the evaluation and testing of water quality and soil microbiological activity. But this will require the development of new sensors. Perhaps in time we will be able to develop computer projections similar to what Hall (2000) did for Costa Rica or what Barbier (chapters 13 and 31 of this volume) did for Honduras and other countries, so that farmers and planners could see the immediate implication of their decision or possible decision.

Conclusion

The virtual representation of watersheds and/or their subdivisions, such as a farm plot, on portable computers is an important management tool. The technology enables the stakeholders in natural resource management projects to appraise the present, or perhaps through modeling, future, condition of their land and its potential more accurately. It requires the classification of watershed characteristics. Currently, only a small number of parameters are taken into consideration in watershed classification in the CIDA projects considered. The main difficulty lies in the lack of instrumentation and methodology for the measurement of a number of important parameters in the field at the scale needed. Simple and inexpensive tools must be developed to enable farmers and extension workers to deal with these difficult scales. CIDA and aid agencies in general, although they acknowledge the importance of an orderly stakeholder participation in development projects, do very little to translate this intention into practice. The weakness of actual approaches and the small impact of good science in the field should be addressed in a new adventure where scientists and decision makers work hand in hand.

References

Hall, C. A. S., ed. 2000. *Quantifying Sustainable Development: The Future of Tropical Economies*. San Diego: Academic Press.

CHAPTER 35

A Systems Approach to Planning as a Mechanism for Rural Development in Colombia

Nathalie Beaulieu, Jaime Jaramillo, Juan Lucas Restrepo,

and Jorge Mario Díaz

Introduction

In Colombia, a country confronted with serious governance issues, much hope is placed in multi-level decentralized planning at the level of territorial entities as a mechanism to achieve sustainable and equitable development. Colombia is one of the most advanced countries in Latin America in the development of legislation on territorial planning, partly as a result of the serious governance problems it faces due to long-standing armed conflicts. It is also one of the most decentralized, having seen a rapid increase in the proportion of its public expenditures made by territorial entities in the last fifteen years (Porras Vallejo 2003). However, the country is still in the early stages of a learning process on decentralized planning. As expected, planning has not been the panacea some of its advocates had hoped for, and many improvements need to be made to its practice. The search for improvements should be oriented not so much toward the mechanisms and practices themselves but in the mindsets needed from citizens and leaders to allow planning to take them where they want to go. We make an analysis of the situation in Colombia from the perspective of rural development, examining empirically what works and what does not while hoping to prevent any discouragement about planning, and we make a few recommendations about practices that could help change mindsets. We also think that development officers, governments, and civil society in other countries can benefit from understanding the Colombian context and the lessons learnt up to now.

To link the concepts of planning and development explicitly, we need to go back and define what

development means for us. We also agree with the definition given in chapter 3 that *"Development is the process of change toward those conditions desired by those targeted."* However, one might ask, "change of what?" and "who is targeted?" Planning is the process where players of development define their desired conditions and determine the conditions they would like to change and how they will achieve that change. Participatory planning occurs when those individuals and institutions effected take part in the planning, synchronizing their goals and actions. Planning adds a component of direction and intention to the process of change; without intentions, change can occur in many directions, but not necessarily in a way that gives satisfactory results for everybody. It helps reduce the uncertainty with regard to attaining goals while accepting that uncertainty will always remain. It is about making choices in an uncertain environment and sometimes guessing (or making hypotheses) about the consequences, and learning as the consequences unfold. In addition to this, the questions asked during planning, which includes hypothesis generation and testing, evaluation, monitoring, and day-to-day decision making, create a bridge between science and development. Scientists and information providers can link to planning processes directly or indirectly, focusing their research and information collection toward development needs.

In Colombia and in many other countries, governmental planning is conducted at various administrative levels, and serves as a platform for many organizational processes. Colombia is one of the few Latin American countries where municipalities are required by central governmental legislation to conduct territorial planning, over a time span that is significantly longer than the political mandate of the administration. Politicians of many other countries who are implementing legislation regarding territorial planning are seeking to learn from the Colombian experience. However, many people have doubts about the effectiveness of planning processes, although the need for planning is obvious. As both a cause and a result of this ineffectiveness, planning is unfortunately often considered as a bureaucratic exercise to fulfill a legal requirement. It is much practiced but little taken advantage of. The more recently mandated participatory nature that it has acquired through the legal requirement for public consultation has increased its potential considerably, while creating expectations that are most often underfulfilled. Scientists and information providers who count on planning to have an impact on development and poverty alleviation often feel that the chain is broken, that the relay between players is not working as it should. Plans are not used as management tools, decision makers do not have the culture of using information for important decisions (which can be exacerbated by a lack of relevant information), or different plans are totally unarticulated between administrative levels and even within the same administration. Many people have lost faith in planning, stating that it simply does not work, or are frustrated in the process.

However, many of us who have taken part in successful participatory planning experiences are filled with hope and are convinced that the process can have extremely positive impact on development at every scale. But what makes the difference between successful and unsuccessful planning? We think that by considering planning as a mutual learning process rather than a control process from above, individuals, groups, institutions, and governments will be more motivated to indulge in it and will profit from it much more. In this chapter, we will propose a systems approach to planning as a learning process. We think that the systems that compose our society will be able to learn how to improve their functioning to reach their goals, overcoming development obstacles that are most often the same obstacles to effective planning and learning.

A Systems Approach to Planning

In his book *Smart Thinking in Crazy Times*, Ian Mitroff (1998) states that the inefficiency of many institutions results from them trying to solve the wrong problems. This occurs when decision making concentrates on only part of the problem, considers only a very limited range of options, and does not consider their consequences on all the interest groups. His approach for smart thinking therefore includes recommendations on how to think with a systems approach, to consider the various interest groups involved, to expand the limits of the problem and the range of possible options. He insists on the necessity of integrating different points of view to avoid falling in the trap of solving a false problem. He mentions that, while making a decision, it is always better to consult representatives of the interest groups themselves, but when none of these are available, it is possible to generate or imagine a variety of points of view. He presents techniques allowing decision-makers to imagine the points of view of noninfluential interest groups that could be against their decisions. Governmental and community planning, on the other hand, provide excellent opportunities to combine different points of view without having to generate or imagine them. Thanks to the requirements of participation in most planning laws and of the constitutions of democratic countries, planning processes have the excuse and the obligation to integrate the points of view of real-life players in vivo. Actors and decision makers, however, need to develop skills in listening, learning, and thinking to be able to take advantage of these exchanges.

But what is a systems approach, and how can it help us in planning? We review some basic apects of a systems approach that are essential for understanding how we can use it in assessing and improving the conditions of development in Colombia. A system is simply an organized set of interacting components. These in turn are hierarchical in that they are composed of a series of smaller sets or components (or subsystems), and that the system itself forms part of a larger set (or supersystem). Systems are dynamic and their state changes with time. There are interactions among their components and among their hierarchic levels.

It is fairly obvious to see how governmental hierarchies, most institutions, and social and biophysical processes can be described as systems. A systems approach allows simplifying the description of complex hierarchical arrangements, where an exhaustive description would be overwhelming because one finds another series of hierarchical organizations upon looking at any component in detail. It is especially useful when one needs to describe or enhance the interaction among components or between levels. The most important defining characteristics of systems include emergence, hierarchical control, and communication (Clayton and Radcliffe 1996). Emergence refers to the fact that each level has properties that cannot be explained solely by referring to the properties of its components. Through hierarchical control, each level promotes or constrains the actions of the level below. Systems can also have important self-control (or self-correction) mechanisms and are even perceived as having "self-design" (Odum 1988, 1994). Systems must have an adequate degree of control through natural selection or properly functioning social organizations, or they will not survive. Excessive control can limit their ability to adapt to new conditions, and insufficient control reduces their ability to determine outcomes in normal conditions. Communication allows the transfer of information for regulation, and functions principally through feedback loops. A good review of the early thinkers in applying systems theory to social issues is given in Hammond (2003).

There is a hierarchy of goals in social systems, and the goals of a given level usually include some control of the level below. In social systems, it is important for component-players to understand the whole-system goals they are serving, and it is also important for whole-system coordinators to have their goals be synchronized with the goals of the component-players. Any component has three types of goals: to sustain and improve itself, to contribute to the goal of the level above, and to assist in the goals of levels below by coordinating its own components and to insure that they have the conditions necessary to fulfill their responsibilities, including resources, interactions, and security. Synchronization and communication of

goals are some of the most important functions of a good leader (Sharma 1998). Absent or incomplete goal synchronization causes conflict, discontentment, slower progress toward the goals, or all of these, and can even lead to the destruction of the governing system at the next higher level. But interaction among players does not limit itself to control and goal synchronization. Most complex goals need contributions or actions from a variety of players, in a variety of levels. Interactions are also necessary to synchronize these actions and to allow the output of some components to become the inputs of others.

One of the most important features of living systems, including organisms, ecosystems, and social systems, is their capacity to adapt to a change in external conditions. This adaptation is done through a process of iterative evaluation of how the actual situation compares with the desired ones, which can be represented by figure 35.1. The big circle in the center represents feedback loops, through which actions are adapted in function of the evaluation of conditions, conducted through some kind of monitoring. Because many of the examples of systems in this chapter refers to cars, we used the Colombian *chiva*, a bus used in rural areas, to symbolize the system that undergoes the feedback loops. In this figure, the interrelationships between components and levels are represented by the word "partnerships."[1]

There are two types of feedback loops, positive and negative. Positive feedback loops are self-enforcing; they occur when a process encourages even more of the same process. They can be described as either "virtuous" or "vicious" cycles, respectively, if the increasing condition is desired or not. Examples include population growth (more people produce more babies), composite interest at the bank (more money yields even more interest, which if plowed back into the capital yields ever more interest), soil erosion (eroded soils are less covered by vegetation and are therefore more susceptible to erosion), violence (creates vengeance and more violence), and the growth of a cancerous tumor. In some cases positive feedbacks often lead to systems instability, and although sometimes they should be encouraged up to a certain point,

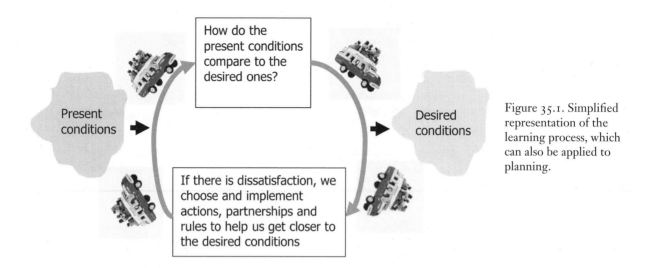

Figure 35.1. Simplified representation of the learning process, which can also be applied to planning.

in others they should be slowed down or avoided. Negative feedback loops are the ones that allow systems to restrain certain activities and to control the excessive progression of positive feedback loops. In systems generally they tend to lead to stability and sometimes inertia. We use them when we ride a bicycle, to keep the bicycle from dropping to one side or from going too fast while going down a hill. Negative feedback is required to maintain resource exploitation within the limits of the productivity of nature. The immune system, limiting the growth of cancer tumors in a body, can also be seen as using negative feedback. Meadows (1997) mentions that reducing the gain around a positive loop is usually more powerful than strengthening negative loops. When driving a car, it is more effective to control speed by moderating pressure on the accelerator rather than letting the car go too fast and then applying the brakes.

Self-correction mechanisms, when successfully functioning in lower levels, can allow systems to save considerable energy in control. In our example on cancer, healthy cells have an internal mechanism that limits their growth, which they lose when they become cancerous. In social systems, the most important self-correction mechanism is the personal "conscience," which is related to one's paradigms, values, and principles. This self-regulation is possible when one is able to identify with higher-level goals and synchronize or compromise lower-level goals in function of them. For example, again while driving a car, one's goal might be to get to work

in the morning while minimizing the time spent on the way. However, when we see a red light, we are likely to stop even if we compromise our goal of arriving quickly. We will stop even if it is unlikely that a police officer, an agent of the official controlling mechanism, will be present to punish us. We know that if we do not, we might cause an accident that would hurt another or ourselves. And besides, we have another higher-level goal, which is to be part of a society where people respect each other's rights. These higher-level goals, which we share, have a priority over our individual goals. In any case, we have considered the presence of traffic lights on the way to work in our hypothesis of how long it will take us, so we have already accepted the fact that it will take us longer than if we were alone in the city. However, not everybody thinks in this way, and we sometimes have very pressing goals that are stronger than our civic ones. This justifies the presence of official regulation and control mechanisms such as police or, broadly speaking, institutions.

North (1994) defines institutions as "the formal rules (constitutions, statute and common law, regulations, etc.), the informal constraints (norms of behavior, conventions, and internally imposed codes of conduct) and the enforcement characteristics of each. Because they make up the incentive structure of a society they define the way the game is played." He mentions that "Institutions are created by humans to structure human interaction in order to reduce uncertainty in pursuit of their goals (of those making the rules) in social, political and economic exchange."

Development involves change in institutions, which can be triggered through a variety of mechanisms. Meadows (1997) writes that leverage points "are places within a complex system (a corporation, an economy, a living body, a city, an ecosystem) where a small shift in one thing can produce big changes in everything." She lists and describes a series of possible places to find leverage points, the most important being the mindset or paradigms that lead the system. This is followed in importance by the goals of the system, then by the power of self-organization, the rules of the system, information flows, powerful positive feedback loops, regulating negative feedback loops, material stocks and flows, and, last, a category she calls "numbers" or parameters, which correspond to adjustments to details in the functioning of a system but will not change its overall behavior.

Planning with a systems approach implies first and foremost the ability to define the system's desired future conditions, setting whole-system goals, understanding how subsystem goals can contribute to the major goals, and understanding how the system's goals are included in a supersystem's. To be able to do this, it is necessary to understand society as a system, to identify which supersystems it is a component of and which subsystem its components are. Planning also involves allowing components and levels to communicate so they can synchronize their goals and their actions, matching the actions of one with the needs of others, both from the top down and from the bottom up. Planning also involves putting into practice a variety of mechanisms or actions to attain those multiple goals, thus making hypotheses in the process of choosing them. It involves periodically adjusting mechanisms and actions in function of their effects and of external conditions. It includes setting control and self-correction mechanisms, paying special attention to the vicious circles we want to avoid. It includes identifying and facilitating the necessary feedback loops for both the control and the hypothesis testing for adaptation. An important advantage of a systems approach to planning is that the same principles apply at every level, from the

individual to the family, the enterprise, the association, village, municipality, country, or international organizations. From this and from the aforementioned definitions by North (1994), we can deduce that planning is an approach that can be taken to induce institutional change, as long as we use it to discuss what is the game being played and how we would like it to be played.

Planning the Right System for Colombia
Desired Future Conditions

A good place to look for national-level "desired future conditions" for Colombia is in the 1991 constitution, in the Colombian legislation, and in the national development plans. The constitution defines Colombia as "a social state of rights, organized as a unitary republic, decentralized, participatory and pluralist." The paradigms behind this constitution are of equality, participation, and peace. In general, the Colombian legislation and policies also state rules and means to achieve desired conditions; they often correspond to an ideal situation that is different from the present one but toward which the rules are expected to lead society.

The National Development Plan developed at the start of the mandate of the present president Alvaro Uribe Vélez (PRC 2002) defines the desired country as a "community-state." It aims at a participatory state that involves citizens in the achievement of social goals, a state that manages and invests public resources with efficiency and austerity, a decentralized state that privileges regional autonomy with transparency, political responsibility, and community participation.

With respect to rural development, the previous government of Andrés Pastrana had promoted a visionary exercise called "Agrovisión Colombia 2025," conducted by institutions of the agricultural sector, leading to the definition of desired future conditions and the means to get there (PRC 2000). The resulting document describes the desired Colombia for 2025 in the following terms: "The country enjoys sustained growth, maintenance of peace and social coexistence. A full democracy is at work in all spheres of human activity, with an efficient social and political control by its citizens. Rural areas enjoy opportunities and life conditions that are equivalent to those enjoyed by the rest of society. The economic system is sustained in a culture of competition and favors the creation and the development of dynamic markets. Nonetheless, the State intervenes to regulate and orient the equitable distribution of the benefits of development while guaranteeing the respect of political and citizen rights." The means chosen in the Agrovisión exercise to achieve a dynamic and competitive rural economy is to create specialized regions, to orient agricultural production toward tropical products for export, and to create efficient production chains to produce high-quality products with high added value. These would be made possible by:

> a generalized educational development in rural areas, which guarantees that the agents adopt quality decisions in their economic, political, and social activities;
> high and increasing scientific and technological capacity, which guarantees dynamic innovation;
> a large, pertinent, and timely offer of information, which allows persons and organizations to make optimal decisions;
> coherent institutionalism, which provides a climate of certainty and stable rules, promotes and develops markets of goods and factors, encourages a sustainable and efficient use of natural resources, and stimulates the development and the disposition of human and organizational capital;
> an adequate provision of infrastructure, services, and public goods by the state.

It would be possible to have discussions about how much growth and international trade is desired and how government will intervene to equitably distribute the benefits of development and guarantee the respect of political and citizen rights, and debates about how specialized we want regions to become (risking a loss of diversity), and what proportion of production should be aimed at exportation. However, the elements listed above seem like reasonable desired future conditions and are compatible with the other desired conditions previously

described in other plans or programs and in the 1991 constitution. The present government is presently coordinating the development of regional agendas for research in agriculture and livestock, which should contribute to achieve this vision.

Rural Development in Colombia as a System

Rural development includes all of the activities and processes that take place in rural areas, and includes their interaction with cities. It comprises many productive activities other than agriculture and livestock, and involves all economic sectors. Consequently, the players involved are very numerous; they include both actors and stakeholders, and any individual, group, or institution can be one, the other, or both, depending on the situation and the decision to be made. *Actors* are those who can influence the future conditions and *stakeholders* are those who are affected by the actions of the actors or by the resulting conditions. Because Colombia is part of larger systems (human society, the international community, the biosphere), the distribution of roles among players in Colombia is very much affected by the international context and by historical events.

One of the most important recent factors determining the international context is the structural adjustments imposed by the International Monetary Fund (IMF) as conditions for receiving financial support from international financial institutions. These adjustments encourage decentralization and the downsizing of central governmental programs. Decentralization, which had already started in Colombia in the 1960s but was accelerated in the 1990s, involves the transfer of administrative, technical, fiscal, and regulative responsibilities to other levels of governments or other players. It was encouraged not only by the international context but was also demanded by territorial entities to ensure more legitimacy and accountability of the governments (Porras Vallejo 2003). The popular street demonstrations that preceded the revision of the constitution in 1991 are another indication that decentralization was strongly desired in Colombia (Oliva, Bès, and Hernandez 1998). Another important consideration is the fact that these decentralization adjustments were promoted after the end of the Cold War, during a time when strong central governments were, on the contrary, strongly encouraged (Costa et al. 1998) and heavily funded by the World Bank in the case of countries aligned with the Western Bloc. This tendency toward decentralization, following a heavy centralization of governmental services, somewhat complicates the sharing of responsibilities, as we will see later. But clearly, for good and for bad, political fashions are part of the external environment and must be considered (and perhaps eventually modified) in a systems view.

Another international factor that greatly affects rural development is the globalization of the economy. Incidentally, Echeverri Perrico and Pilar Ribeiro (2002) consider that globalization and decentralization are simply different aspects of the process of transferring responsibilities of the state, either to higher or to lower administrative levels. Through these processes, national governments have delegated or abolished many controlling mechanisms. Although allowing more flexibility, this lack of control also has some consequences on the distribution of resources and in addition we have seen an enlargement of the gap between the rich and the poor (Cusack 1998). At the international level the competitiveness of developing countries, in which the IMF impedes subsidizing agriculture and industry, is greatly threatened by developed countries where agriculture and industry are heavily subsidized (Kroeger and Montanye 2000). Now international organizations such as the United Nations (UN), federations of states such as the European Union, the World Trade Organization (WTO), and international treaties of commerce such as NAFTA are creating new regulation and control mechanisms, sometimes overruling national policies on the protection of the environment and of labor rights.

In any case, we see decentralization as an opportunity to improve rural development, by transferring responsibilities and economic resources to power structures that are closer to the rural population. In terms of governmental administration, three types of "territorial entities" are defined in the Colombian constitution. There are thirty-two departments, 1096 municipalities, 603 indigenous reserves, and four districts. The word "territorial" implies that administrations have responsibilities over their entire territory, both rural and urban, and it implies that they are responsible for all sectors of development. A large part of the investments for infrastructure and human resources for rural development are now required from departments and municipalities, who get their financial resources from direct taxes as well as through transfers from the central government. The hierarchic units of the social-political system correspond to the administrative level of representation of the territory and its population, which are separated physically by political-administrative boundaries. The responsibilities are distributed, at least in theory, as a function of which level and which player can best do the job. Rural development responsibilities are perceived as much wider than governmental ones and are shared with the private sector, universities and research institutions, the media, nongovernmental organizations (NGOs), community-based organizations, farmers' unions, and individual producers and consumers. Many decisions are taken at the family and individual levels (what to consume, what to produce, where to live, and so forth), which have their corresponding responsibilities (and thus power) and have an impact on regional and national development.

Organizations Sharing the Responsibilities of Rural Development

The distribution of responsibilities between central government, departments, and municipalities still suffers some ambiguities but will be clarified, with luck, through the Ley Orgánica de Ordenamiento Territorial, which the national congress has discussed various times but still has not approved. Municipal administrations, led by the mayor, are responsible for coordinating education and health services (using financial transfers from the central government); enabling public services such as water supply, electricity, and garbage disposal (often through private companies); constructing local roads; and providing recreation facilities and cultural activities for the population as well as rural technical assistance. Departmental administrations, led by the governor, have the responsibility of coordinating municipal activities over the department and of serving as an interface between municipalities and the national government. They receive some financial resources through transfers from the national government and play a certain role in financing infrastructure for health and education. They also fund the construction and maintenance of departmental-level transport infrastructure such as roads or ports. Departments and municipalities in which there are natural resources exploitations (for example mines or petroleum) receive special taxes or *regalías*. Municipalities are the most local level of government, but villages and urban neighborhoods have their form of local organization and leadership through community-based organizations, called *juntas de acción comunal*. These are represented at the municipal level through the association of *juntas*, which usually meets frequently and addresses local issues with municipal authorities.

We mentioned that one of the responsibilities of municipalities is to provide direct rural technical assistance (or "extension") free of charge to small producers, and as a charged service to medium producers. This service is supposed to be provided either through a municipal unit of technical assistance (UMATA), where extension agents are municipal public servants, or through contracts with private companies or individuals. This technical assistance is potentially extremely important for rural development because it is the means of transfer of new production options to small and medium producers. It is also meant to be the means of feedback from producers to the Colombian agricultural science and technology system, communicating their needs for research and technology, as well as any local success in innovation. When given the resources to do their work properly, rural extension agents are usually the most effective interfaces between the municipal administration and the rural inhabitants. Not only do they assist farmers with agronomical problems, but they also help them organize associations and links with markets, help them with various forms of financial arrangements, and promote the investment of the municipality's financial resources in infrastructure

to support local production.[2] In addition to actively participating in municipal planning itself, helping out with the logistics of rural planning workshops and transmitting input from rural inhabitants to the municipal administration, rural extension agents can play a very important role in helping rural inhabitants with their own planning. Departments, through their secretariat of agriculture, have the responsibility of monitoring the effectiveness of municipal rural assistance. In general the functioning of UMATAs is not satisfactory, which is probably due to a lack of staff commitment toward rural technical assistance, rather than because of the relevance of the UMATA concept in itself.

In Colombia, environmental control is insured, at least in theory, by autonomous, regional corporations (CARs). These regulate the exploitation and the extraction of natural resources in their regions of authority, provide permits for use and exploitation of natural products and mineral and forest concessions, as well as incentives for forest regeneration such as the forest incentive certificate (CIF).[3] They apply fines to those who do not respect environmental law. They also participate actively in educational campaigns and research. They sometimes fund specific environmental projects in their area of influence. They are funded through transfers, by municipalities, of 5 percent of the collected land taxes. They can also generate their own financial resources by providing certain charged services such as water, electricity, technical assistance, and information.

At the regional level, Colombia previously had regional councils of economic and social planning (CORPES) until January 1, 2000. These had been created in 1985 to allow the regions more autonomy; establish permanent coordination links among national, departmental and municipal institutions, especially relative to planning; and insure the participation of the regions in the preparation of the regional plans, which were supposed to be included in the National Development Plan. These political entities have not been renewed beyond their last mandate, defined in 1996, but the creation of new regional structures is included in the Ley Orgánica de Ordenamiento Territorial, such as autonomous planning regions (RAP) and territorial regions

(RET), which would assume similar competencies and roles to the CORPES. An important debate will have to take place, however, about the way of using this regional mechanism, because the CORPES were heavily criticized for being ineffective.

Large producer unions (often referred to as *gremios* in Colombia), sometimes having a national span, play a very important role in the organization of productive chains and the management of *parafiscal* funds. The latter are funds that are managed by the national treasury, to which the members of the unions contribute and which are reinvested in research, development, training, credit, and other activities for the benefit of the sector. These unions also influence a variety of other policy instruments, such as the guarantee of minimum prices to producers, obtained through discussions with the Ministry of Agriculture and Rural Development.

The national government is represented by the president of the republic. Legislative aspects are covered by the National Assembly and the Congress. The execution of legislation and other types of policy is insured by the various ministries and national departments, which are all relevant to rural development. The Ministry of Agriculture and Rural Development (MADR) provides the policy framework for research and development and production and credit mechanisms, in coordination with other ministries. It comprises a large set of distinct entities that manage the research and technical development component for agriculture and livestock, offer development programs, and develop policy. In 2003, four of these entities were merged into the Colombian Institute of Rural Development (INCODER), which now assumes responsibilities of coordinating activities related to fisheries and aquaculture, land improvement through drainage and irrigation, and land reform, as well as integrated rural development.

The National Department of Planning (DNP) provides leadership in the planning of the nation's spending as well as of the economic and social development of the country, through the multisectoral coordination of the different initiatives discussed in the National Council of Economical and Social Policy (CONPES). This department has a division especially devoted to agrarian development, and another one devoted to territorial development. Other extremely important ministries are the Ministry of Transportation, the Ministry of Interior and Justice, the Ministry of the Environment, Housing and Territorial Development, the Ministry of Finance and Public Credit, as well as the Ministry of Social Protection, covering both health and labor considerations. Each of these ministries has its counterparts at the departmental level, and in some cases at the municipal level, through specific secretariats of these territorial administrations. The MADR regularly consults with the departmental secretariats of agriculture through the Consejo Nacional de Secretarías de Agricultura.

Agricultural research is conducted by a National Agricultural Research System (NARS) composed of national agricultural research institutions, universities, the private sector, rural extension services, and farmers and their organizations, as well as other representatives of civil society. Science and technology in the agriculture and livestock sector are provided by CORPOICA and by national research centers known as the "CENIs," which are centered on a particular crop or production system such as sugarcane or coffee. CORPOICA is a corporation that was created to strengthen and reorient research and technology transfer related to agriculture and livestock, with strong links and participation from the private sector. Since the creation of CORPOICA, the role of the older Instituto Colombiano Agropecuario (ICA, the national institute of agricultural and livestock science) has been restricted mostly to the prevention, control, and mitigation of sanitary, biological, and chemical risks that affect agricultural and livestock production. This system conducts forums to insure that agricultural research is focused toward the needs of society. These national forums are included in a regional plan for all of Latin America and the Caribbean, called FORAGRO. Long before regional forums were created in the mid-1990s, some coordination of research in Latin America was (and continues to be) insured by the Interamerican Institute for Agricultural Cooperation (IICA). The diverse regional forums in the world participate in the Global Forum on Agricultural Research (GFAR). International centers of the Consultative Group for

International Agricultural Research (CGIAR) have the role of providing methods, scientific results, and technology, especially oriented toward the alleviation of hunger and poverty. Two centers have strong activities in Colombia, the International Center for Tropical Agriculture (CIAT), based in Cali, and the International Center for Maize and Wheat (CIMMYT), based in Mexico. MADR and CORPOICA have a cooperation agreement with both of these centers.

Financing opportunities are coordinated through the Fondo para el Financiamiento del Sector Agropecuario (FINAGRO). This fund was created in 1990 in response to a need of the agricultural sector of Colombia to have an autonomous and specialized entity that could manage resources for credit, which were previously dispersed in various organizations. One of its most important lines of credit is the associative loan, a mechanism to finance activities or production projects run by associated producers, which must include at least 50 percent of the small or medium producers. To be eligible for the program, they must have organized the sale of their products through anticipated contracts and respond to the obligations of credit. Given the fact that small and medium producers often do not have a demonstrated paying capacity or sufficient collateral to provide as a guarantee, the government created the Fondo Agropecuario de Garantías (FAG), a fund that covers the guarantees of up to 80 percent of the loan for small producers, up to 60 percent for medium producers, and up to 50 percent for large producers.

The Formalization of Planning in Colombia

We can see that the desired future conditions need contributions from a variety of players. All of the players within the Colombian system have planning requirements or at least opportunities, either official or nonofficial, and through participation have the opportunity to influence the decisions taken at levels above. Monitoring and evaluation gives these players the opportunity of validating the hypotheses they made during planning, by looking at what has worked and what has not, thus using the scientific method. Some planning

mechanisms are even required by law in various administrative levels, such as the development plans or Planes de Desarrollo (PD) and the longer-term territorial plans or Planes de Ordenamiento Territorial (POT).[4] Because of their existence at various administrative levels, these offer the possibility of articulating actions between levels and articulating the various components of a given level. In Colombia, development plans are carried through at the municipal, departmental, and national levels. For the moment, territorial plans are required legally only at the municipal level, but the Ley Orgánica de Ordenamiento Territorial will make them required at the departmental level as well. Municipal territorial plans have a time span of twelve years and cover three times the constitutional mandate of mayors. They are strategic planning efforts where the municipal administrations have to set a series of norms, actions, programs, and projects at short, medium, and long term, and they must generate spatial plans over their legal territory. In addition to the longer time span, their other novelty with respect to development plans is that maps are used to represent the spatial distribution of natural threats and risks; areas with specific restrictions or potentials for land use; areas with cultural, historical, or environmental patrimony; and the present and desired distribution of infrastructure. But like the development plans, territorial plans are a multisectorial effort and have to include all the social, economic, cultural, and environmental activities, both in the rural and urban areas. These plans also have to project how financial resources will be distributed.

A development plan is required by law from each new administration in the first four months of the exercise of its functions. They are therefore repeated after each election, every four years. Like the territorial plans, they express a series of programs, projects, and norms, but only the ones to be carried out during the mandate of the administration in question and determine how the financial resources will be used.

Development plans necessarily have to be linked to the territorial plans and thus determine short-term and local actions consistent with long-term regional objectives. Development plans are comprehensive and multisectorial, but include a series of sector-based programs that can themselves include specific action plans. These sector-based programs need to be articulated with the corresponding sector-based programs of the administrative level above. For example, at the municipal level, the development plan (Plan de Desarrollo Municipal, PDM) includes the municipal agriculture and livestock program (Programa Agropecuario Municipal, PAM), which itself includes the plan for rural technical assistance or Plan de Asistencia Técnica Directa Rural. The agricultural plans of all of the municipalities within a department are then coordinated by the departmental secretariat of agriculture. By law, municipalities are required to invest a minimum proportion of their budget in rural areas,[5] and the development plan is the mechanism allowing rural investments to be identified specifically.

In Colombia, the political-administrative units are defined by the Ley Orgánica del Plan de Desarrollo (law 152 of 1994), which establishes the planning and controlling authorities for the national level and the territorial entities in the following manner:

The planning authorities are:

> At the municipality level: the mayor (highest planning authority); the municipal council of government, which has to work in the formulation of the plan, in coordination with the municipal administration and other entities working in the municipality and any specialized office or secretariat, for example the municipal unit of rural technical assistance.
> At the departmental level: The governor (highest planning authority); the departmental council or government; the planning secretariat, administrative department or office, which have to work jointly on the formulation of the plan in coordination with the other secretariats and administrative departments, decentralized departmental or national entities who operate in the territory and any other specialized office.

At the national level: the president; the highest authority of the national planning administration; CONPES; the National Department of Planning (DNP), which runs the secretariat of CONPES, follows the directions given by the president, and coordinates the formulation of the plan with the ministries, administrative departments, and territorial entities. DNP and the ministries of finance and public credit insure consistency in national budgets, coordinating with other ministries and administrative departments.

The authorities that control planning processes are:

> In the municipality: the Municipal Council, responsible for approving the territorial plan, development plan, and all norms related to planning and social and economic development; the Municipal Planning Council, and the Council for Territorial Planning, both consultative councils that group representatives of civil society not only for the formulation of plans but also for monitoring and evaluation. The Municipal Council of Rural Development (CMDR) is in charge of developing and monitoring the agriculture and livestock program and the plan for rural technical assistance.
> In the department: the Departmental Assembly, responsible for approving the departmental development plan and the norms related to economical and social development and planning, with the consultative Departmental Council of Planning.
> In the nation: the development plan is approved by the Congress of the Republic and the National Council of Planning (CNP), which is composed of representatives of the territorial authorities, indigenous groups, ethnic minorities and women, and of various economic sectors, and representatives of other interests such as the cultural, educational, ecological, and community-based ones.

Figure 35.2 shows a few historical milestones relative to decentralization and planning in Colombia (many of the dates taken from Oliva, Bès, and Hernandez 1998).

National planning efforts have led to extremely valuable plans, thanks to planning legislation and the 1991 constitution, which encourages participation and plurality. Another participatory exercise akin to planning are the *trochas ciudadanas*, or citizen paths, organized by the CNP in preparation for the presidential elections. These are a means for civil society to give advice to the presidential candidates on what they should include in their campaign and how they should tackle certain political, social, and environmental issues. Two of these have been held up to this writing, the first in 1998 and the second in 2001, leading to documents that are available to the public. They are conducted through meetings with members of the civil society, NGOs, and the government in territorial entities, as well as in forums and meetings with experts. Participants explain what kind of country they want to live in and what their suggestions are. The documents present the different points of view, and in the case of issues that are controversial, which position the CNP takes.

Another extremely effective participation mechanism has been the Consejo Comunal de Gobierno, held every Saturday in a different city, usually a departmental capital, and broadcast live on national television and radio. These meetings group many of the stakeholders of rural development, including leaders from regional corporations, departmental and municipal governments, community-based organizations, farmers' and workers' unions, environmental and women's groups, and many more, who interact with the president and representatives of all of the ministries. For each sector, the ministries present reports of national programs and indicators for the department in question. Questions are then raised by the stakeholders, who usually suggest mechanisms to attain the objective (or solve the problem) they raised. The suggestions are then discussed live, usually leading to some kind of engagement by the ministry to investigate the different options raised in the meeting. Although there is a moderator to control the length of the interventions, these meetings are largely facilitated by the president of the country himself, who asks the ministers to respond to such and such a question, and gives them "homework" on things to investigate or solve after the meeting. These meetings have an extremely positive impact on people's motivation at every level. In many cases, in preparation for the meetings, leaders hold meetings with their communities to discuss their intervention. Many people in the area concerned by a given council meeting watch or listen to "the show," and therefore are exposed to the deliberations. They often continue the deliberations with their colleagues or friends after the meetings. People feel legitimately concerned, and they often see or hear their community or union leader speaking on the radio and appearing on television. They hear about the issues that concern them and about the different efforts being deployed. At some level these meetings reflect a real use of the scientific method because if some mechanism is not working then the agencies involved hear about it directly from the people affected, as long as there is no censorship or manipulation of interventions.

Learning to Fill the Gaps between Actual and Desired Conditions

While the last section talked about the progress that was made in terms of planning in Colombia, this section describes what still needs to be achieved. A detailed diagnosis of the effectiveness of rural development, describing the actual conditions and using statistics, is out of the scope of this chapter although we refer readers to Vargas del Valle (2002) for an appraisal of past rural development programs, to World Bank (2002a) for a report on poverty, and to World Bank (2002b) for an analysis of country assistance strategies. With the violence that still thrives in Colombia today, and with the poverty and social inequalities that remain, it is obvious that Colombia has not yet achieved its desired conditions. Although planning has made important contributions to development, many groups of the population still feel excluded from the goals of policy decisions, especially the poor, the populations of rural areas, and youth.

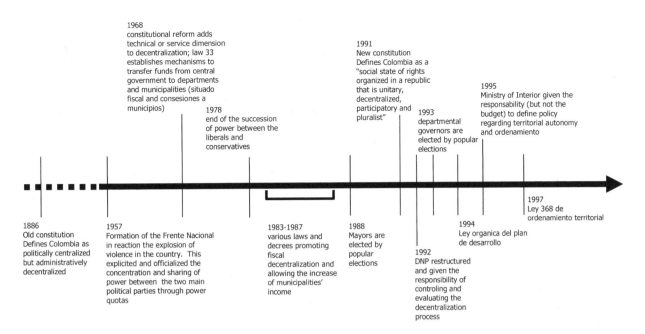

1968
constitutional reform adds technical or service dimension to decentralization; law 33 establishes mechanisms to transfer funds from central government to departments and municipalities (situado fiscal and consesiones a municipios)

1978
end of the succession of power between the liberals and conservatives

1991
New constitution Defines Colombia as a "social state of rights organized in a republic that is unitary, decentralized, participatory and pluralist"

1993
departmental governors are elected by popular elections

1995
Ministry of Interior given the responsability (but not the budget) to define policy regarding territorial autonomy and ordenamiento

1997
Ley 368 de ordenamiento territorial

1886
Old constitution Defines Colombia as politically centralized but administratively decentralized

1957
Formation of the Frente Nacional in reaction the explosion of violence in the country. This explicited and officialized the concentration and sharing of power between the two main political parties through power quotas

1983-1987
various laws and decrees promoting fiscal decentralization and allowing the increase of municipalities' income

1988
Mayors are elected by popular elections

1992
DNP restructured and given the responsibility of controling and evaluating the decentralization process

1994
Ley organica del plan de desarrollo

Figure 35.2. Time diagram of decentralization and planning in Colombia.

Territorial planning has been, for municipalities, the first serious long-term planning effort. Law 388/97 and its corresponding decrees established June 2000 as a deadline for the approval of territorial plans, basic plans, and schemes. However, by the middle of 2003, only 740 of the 1096 municipalities had their plans approved (Porras Vallejo 2003). Sixty-eight were still in the process of formulating them, and the remaining plans were in the process of approval. For many municipalities, the delay in the elaboration of the plans was caused by a lack of technical and economic resources. Other causes include a lack of political will, insufficient capacity for management of leaders, problems with governance and public order, or simply a lack of interest in the process.

One of the leftovers of central planning is the fact that municipal planning and departmental planning are often perceived as homework given by central government. Indeed, the guidelines for the preparation of these plans are written by the central government, which is perceived by Costa et al. (1998) as a form of centralized control. Municipalities must have their plans examined and approved by the level above, and the examination is often more on issues of form than content. The goal of the planning exercises—which is to articulate goals, actions, partnerships, and control mechanisms toward desired future conditions, to make choices, and to self-organize—is often set aside at the expense of an intermediate goal, which is to comply with the requirements. As an indicator of this, the elaboration of plans is often contracted out to consultants who coordinate citizen participation (often also only to comply with the requirement from central government) but with little participation from the administration itself. Plans elaborated in this way are not used as a learning and management tool. Plans of different administrative levels are very rarely articulated, and development plans often are not articulated with territorial plans. Although clear guidelines for planning from the central government are necessary, each level has to take genuine ownership of its planning processes, with an appropriate attitude that encourages learning.

As we mentioned before, municipal units of technical assistance (UMATAs) are structures created through decentralization. It seems logical to have rural technical assistance planned, prioritized, and managed at the municipal level, which is the level of government closest to the rural population. However, these units have been heavily criticized for being inefficient or for being used as political instruments by individuals of the administration to return political favors. In many cases, the units exist to satisfy the legal requirement of having them, but the extension offices are not given the necessary human and financial resources to conduct the necessary visits in rural areas and give satisfactory services to beneficiaries. The units are often seen as ends in themselves rather than means to achieve development goals. As a result of this, it is not uncommon to hear the statement "rural technical assistance does not work" or comments on the inadequateness of municipalities to coordinate such a service. Planning and monitoring of rural technical assistance by its beneficiaries is one of the ways to improve this use. The municipal development plan (PDM) includes the municipal agriculture and livestock program (PAM), itself including the municipal plan for rural technical assistance. The elaboration and regular monitoring and evaluation are supposed to be conducted by the CMDR, which includes representatives of the beneficiaries themselves. There has been, unfortunately, an overly relaxed attitude with respect to these planning, monitoring, and evaluation mechanisms, and the vast majority of municipalities do not have functional CMDRs. The Ministry of Agriculture and Rural Development, having recognized the importance of rural technical assistance and of its planning, monitoring, and evaluation, has organized a vast training campaign, following the revision to the legislation on the subject. However, municipalities must become fully conscious of the role of these units in the rural development of their territory, take ownership in the planning of their activities, and distribute responsibilities and resources accordingly.

Oliva, Bès, and Hernandez (1998) mention that difficulties in decentralization come from both the fact that central government is reluctant to let go of some of its responsibilities, and on the other hand that territorial entities often do not have the capacity to take them on. Taking on new responsibilities is a learning process, filled with obstacles and temptations that can sidetrack the process. Citizens also often do not take their due share of power. Participation refers not only to individual citizens, but also to institutions and organizations.

Colombia has seen a rapid increase in public participation, as many participatory practices are encouraged by the central government. Participatory planning is not a theoretical concept anymore, and the country has this year organized its seventh national symposium on the subject. However, in practice, there is great variation in the quality of participation. Two major related factors influence this quality. The first is the willingness of leaders to give their components some autonomy (thus transferring some of their power to them); the second is the willingness of the components to assume more autonomy and the associated responsibility. Organizations still interact more with the central government than with each other, and expect the central government to take many responsibilities. This is also true in many municipalities and departments. The articulation between the actions of components and the self-organization of many groups could be very much improved. The central government continues to contribute to rural development, but projects are often decided on a case-by-case basis , leading to very specific impacts. On the other hand, a large part of the investments made by central government or policy responds to pressures of influential groups. There is no general rural development policy aimed at improving the livelihoods of the rural population of the entire country.

Governmental planning and the management of territorial entities are extremely vulnerable to the political game. Often, power alternates between opposing parties from one mandate to another, and a given party tends to hinder any project that has been started by the other party, even if it actually contributes to the goals of the same population they are supposed to represent. In addition to the individual interests that politicians are vulnerable to, the desire to win (not necessarily an election; it can be a debate or a popularity survey) distorts politics a great deal, even if the only thing at stake is a person or a group's ego. Winning the election, or having the party be reelected, becomes the main objective and not a means to achieve development goals.

Chapter 37 of this book talks about "the elephants in the living room." In the political context of Colombia, the elephants are not only the relentless population growth emphasized in that chapter but also all the illegal activities and processes that influence economies and decisions, which will most probably not be specifically mentioned in any plan. They create powerful obstacles to planning and the use of information, because they are not officially permitted. They include corruption, traffic of narcotics, contraband, armed groups, the illegal use of natural resources, and any influence to benefit particular groups while possibly disfavoring large part of the population. In Colombia the huge financial resources available to those associated with illegal drugs is a particular problem, but not the only one.

We tolerate and live with these processes out of convenience, obligation, or fear. When formal processes are dysfunctional, too complicated, and too expensive or when laws are impossible to respect, we see the development of parallel processes that are sometimes illegal and often at the edge of illegality. We see parallel justice systems when people cannot trust the official justice. We see parallel administrative systems, or accelerated channels, when the official channels are too slow or restrictive. We see parallel commercial links to avoid paying import or consumer taxes. When personal consciences do not intervene, and when a law cannot be enforced well, irregular activities develop, sometimes simply because the illegal ways are easier and less costly. Then, these processes are very difficult to legalize. Information and any type of diagnosis showing the process and the lack of law enforcement become unwelcome, both by law authorities and by the actors involved. Whatever the situation, information and stakeholder participation are unwelcome when there is something to hide. Corruption not only causes an important leakage of resources outside the system, but it also undermines both official control and self-correcting mechanisms, potentially leading the system into chaos. Powerful illegal actors infiltrate political systems to drain public resources and gain control over justice mechanisms. In a system that is sufficiently dominated by these "parallel" processes, there is a natural selection for leaders. The honest people tend to avoid politics, and the ones who want to access political leadership

often have to fulfill conditions imposed by the "parallel" actors.[6] In Colombia, armed groups still heavily persecute and often kill political leaders or candidates who do not want to go along with their plans. Many consider the drug traffic in Colombia, and the delayed response of the judicial system, to have seriously damaged the values of many Colombian institutions and individuals.

Colombia's new National Development Plan, presently in the process of approval by the congress, has a special chapter on improving the state's transparency and efficiency. Proposed improvement measures include improving salaries of public servants while having higher standards for their recruitment and promotion, encouraging the monitoring of municipal finances by citizens through the formation of *veeduría* committees, the development of an "online government" where contracts and public expenditures would be accessible to the public, and a modification of the procedures for assigning contracts for public goods, infrastructure, and services (PRC 2003). A very pragmatic approach to combating corruption in cities, which we believe can also be applied to rural municipalities, has been proposed by Klitgaard et al. (2000). This approach is being used in a number of Colombian municipalities.

Describing the Obstacles with a Systems Approach

What can go wrong in a social system? Meadows (1997) mentions that the paradigms or mindsets underlying the system are the most important factor in the determination of its outcomes. How can the logic of the players influence these outcomes? Schwartz (1996) draws the main lines of a method to explore, mentally, scenarios of possible futures. He suggests the drawing of different plots from a series of driving forces, and even suggests considering different types of logic that can greatly influence how futures might evolve. He mentions that three main logics show up constantly in modern times, which he calls respectively "winners and losers," "challenge and response," and "evolution." These are useful to explore possible futures, but they can also give us insight on the reasons why we observe certain behaviors.

How logic can affect system outcomes

In the "winners and losers" logic, players are polarized in opposing sides that seek control of resources, domination of the economy, power to decide, or simply victory. The entire logic is based on competition, and conflict is inevitable, although sides often find a balance in power. This logic is usually found in present political systems, where democracy is expressed through voting, because only one given party or candidate can win an election. Such a logic is especially dangerous when the overall goals are forgotten and when winning becomes the main goal. Under a winners-and-losers logic, the most motivating factor is the presence of an enemy, which can be a person, group, or country, or even a problem such as poverty, drug traffic, pollution, or terrorism. If there is no enemy, people under this logic will create one, base their actions on combating it, and will argue for support based on the fear of it.[7] An example illustrating the importance of the outcomes of this logic was the Cold War, which influenced international and national politics and justified the support of repressive dictatorships. Even the American space exploration program had a competitive logic behind it, as the principal motivation for the United States was to get to the moon before the Russians. Although such a logic can be motivating to the point of doing extraordinary things (such as flying to the moon or beating sports performance records), it is detrimental to the development of society as a whole. This logic unfortunately continues to be promoted by the United States with the war on terrorism. The United States also funds a war against drugs in Colombia, labeling this funding as aid. The adoption of a winners-and-losers logic by producers and consumers is, in some way, one of the assumptions of models constructed in neoclassical economics, in the sense that players are assumed to search for their own benefit only. Because these models have been used to explain the behavior of the economy in many (but far from all) circumstances, the assumptions of competitiveness and selfishness have mistakenly been taken for values that should be adopted. Competitiveness and the quest for self-benefit are necessary, but they are dangerous if not balanced by a sense of responsibility toward the rest of the system.

A somewhat extreme but very common form of the winners-and-losers logic is the one of domination and submission. One group seeks domination over another to be able to exploit it or obtain benefits from this unequal relationship in force. In Colombia, armed groups dominate entire territories to obtain illegal taxes and different groups fight each other to expand their domain. Domination patterns exist between sexes, races, castes, social classes, countries, and even hemispheres. De Leener et al. (1999) attribute poverty to "the domination of a center and the submission of its periphery to unique points of view. The center nourishes its legitimacy and exploits the periphery by devaluing it." In their view, decentralization is a process of taking consciousness of—and attenuating—these domination patterns, not only between central government and territorial entities, but in any type of group. Although some might argue that domination is inevitable in this world, we think that it is a question of mindset and that it is possible and beneficial to think more in terms of the complementarity of the different components of society.

The type of plot that Schwartz calls "challenge and response" refers to the adjustments and reactions of a person or group to a series of difficulties or changes in conditions. Many of the examples given by the author are from Japan, where the word "optimism" means "having enough challenges to give life meaning." Development can be seen, in this logic, as the improvement of the person or group after overcoming the successive challenges. Schwartz mentions that when companies adopt this type of mindset, even only in planning exercises, they start looking at each difficulty as an opportunity to learn and take consciousness of the importance of being able to count on the public to work with them to solve problems.

The "evolution" plot described by Schwartz considers that conditions change gradually from one state to another and that certain conditions, such as technology or urban construction, grow in a biological fashion. These plots always evolve in one direction, usually either growth or decline.

However, with a planning point of view, we can see that systems are unlikely to go in the desired direction if they do not know where they want to go:

The system can be dominated by a winners-and-losers logic and lose sight of its desired conditions. The inclination to win or to be the best can divert its attention and completely sidetrack the system and its players. This is what often happens in political rivalry between parties.

The system can benefit from a "challenge to response" logic, but if it loses sight of desired future conditions, it can be perpetually adjusting without necessarily improving.

The system can be obsessed with the evolutionary logic of growth, leading to the depletion of resources and to dangerous, self-enforcing, positive feedback loops, which can then lead to serious coordination problems.

A lack of sense of responsibility

In addition to inadequate logic, systems can suffer from social values related to a lack of sense of responsibility. We mentioned earlier that each level has three types of responsibility: toward itself (to take care of itself and eventually grow), toward the top (to contribute to the goals of its supersystem) and toward below (to ensure that its components have the necessary conditions to fulfill their goals, thus to contribute to the goals of the level in question). In addition to this, each level has lateral responsibilities, consisting of not harming or interfering with the activities of other players, and ultimately working in a complementary way with them. We will refer to this as "360-degree responsibility." Everybody acts both as a component and as a coordinator (or leader) in different circumstances. Even an individual who is not in a situation of leadership has to coordinate the parts of his body and his possessions. In social systems, the coordinating bodies of the different levels are composed of individuals who are given the responsibility of representing a group and facilitating interactions within it. There are coordination and leadership problems when:

Leaders are not conscious of their coordination responsibilities and are more concerned with their individual interests, either material (leading to corruption) or emotional (which can lead to manipulation or egocentric behavior that is against the interest of the group);

leaders forget any one of their types of responsibility.

One of the causes of lack of sense of responsibility toward the rest of one's system is the obsession for growth. Meadows (1997) pointed to the fact that growth is often seen as an important leverage point, but that it is usually manipulated in the wrong direction. Economic growth is encouraged by current macroeconomic policy, and we have seen that it has become a goal and even an obsession for some. For those in a position of economic power but also with a social responsibility, growth offers a way, in theory at least, to maintain or increase their own wealth while helping others. However, many studies have shown that economic disparity tends to increase with higher growth. It is officially accepted by society that the main goal of corporations and private companies is to make profit, although many question these values. Yet encouraging uncontrolled growth in social systems may be more like taking away the body's immune system against cancer, and removing the cell's self-control mechanisms with regard to multiplication. Actors that are obsessed by growth and not concerned with development systematically use their economic power or are forced to modify or neutralize legal control mechanisms, in legal or illegal ways. The more they grow or accumulate resources, the more they have power to affect their surrounding to allow them to continue doing the same (self-enforcing, positive feedback loop). Large corporations and economic interests use their influence on policy, in a perfectly legal manner, through the financing of political campaigns and through lobbying. Illegal actors such as mafias, armed groups that extort public resources, or just plain criminals, use either force or bribery to overcome legal controls. Once a system is sufficiently infiltrated by processes related to growth obsession, it is extremely difficult to reverse the situation through only military or judicial actions. We need to keep in mind that the growth of armed groups and mafias, criminality in general, and unfair trade are themselves often only symptoms of a social illness. We will go nowhere by attacking them without attacking the causes of the illness, which lie in our exclusionary logic and deficient sense of responsibility. On the other hand, as Klitgaard et al. (2000) point out, the problem of corruption cannot be tackled only with a moralistic approach of the type "If we were all responsible citizens there would be no corruption." Institutions that want to get rid of corruption need to take very concrete prevention measures such as reducing opportunities coming from very complicated procedures, and avoiding situations where a person or group has the monopoly and the discretion in offering certain services or making certain decisions.

In his provocative book, Diakité (2002) describes some of Africa's development obstacles, most of which are also found in Colombia. He mentions that the most important change needed is with culture, and that we need to act on mentalities. For him, the most determinant factor of underdevelopment is the culture of the possibility of rapid and easy gain, which tends to undermine values of sustained effort, rigor, patience, and humbleness. It tends to maintain the culture of assistance. The heavy foreign aid that Africa received during the Cold War, without any conditionality or requests of accountability, has contributed to enhancing this culture of easy and quick gain. It is important to note, however, that this culture is also enforced in the northern occidental capitalist environments, where easy gain was (legally) achieved in the 1990s through the stock exchange, currency transactions, and investments in high-yielding pension plans, and where the CEOs of large corporations and movie and sports stars make millions of dollars per year. Recent scandals in the United States and with multinational corporations remind us that illegal channels to quick and easy gain are not restricted to developing countries.

Problems can also arise when feedback loops are missing or are not working properly, compromising control mechanisms and learning processes.

This can happen because of either a lack of human or financial resources or a lack of will to learn or control certain activities. "There is a systematic tendency on the part of human beings to avoid accountability for their own decisions. That's why there are so many missing feedback loops" (Meadows 1997). Here again, the lack of sense of responsibility is a determinant factor. Another cause of dysfunctional feedback loops is when communication channels are too numerous and participants are confused. Sometimes, sectorial policies are inconsistent with each other and players receive contradictory messages. Fear is another important cause of missing feedback related to justice, and is used by illegal actors to continue their activities.

Mindsets and Planning Practices for Development

The obstacles to development are not always as obvious as an elephant in the living room. They are sometimes small and insidious, like cockroaches in the kitchen. As we mentioned before, the most important leading factors in systems are the paradigms or mindsets from which the goals and controlling mechanisms emerge. These paradigms include the values and principles of people at all levels and unspoken but well-integrated rules. These rules are much more determining than any of the ones included in the legislation. If we want equitable development to happen in Colombia and elsewhere, we need a change of "ways of thinking" (mentality, culture, paradigms, mindsets), which is undoubtedly one of the most difficult tasks. But how can planning help encourage ways of thinking that can facilitate development? We think that planning, through the reflections and the discussions it involves, can help develop the sense of connectedness and responsibility required for development. Rather than recommend a "way of thinking," here is a checklist of things to consider during planning, based on the discussion of the previous section:

> Does every level understand its own long-term desired future conditions and goals? Does it understand the goals of other players and levels?

Do leaders effectively represent their components, and do they exhibit a 360-degree sense of responsibility?

Do the components of a system understand the complementarity of their roles and actions in achieving common goals, and do they act accordingly?

Which are vicious circles that we want to avoid, and which are the control mechanisms used? Are the self-control mechanisms working properly, if not, why?

Are plans being used as learning and management tools?

Are the communication channels within and outside the group working properly, and is the necessary information available?

We must mention that the most important mind shift can be achieved by changing the mental picture that leaders and citizens have of society and their community. Indeed, our behavior is determined by our mental picture of the world (O'Connor and Seymour 1990). If we visualize society as a system and understand the role of the different components and the interrelation of processes, our behavior is bound to be affected.

In addition to this, there are some "ways of thinking" that should simply be avoided: the winners-and-losers logic, the obsession with growth, and the culture of quick and easy gain. In the next subsections we comment on practices that can be used during planning that can help participants become more conscious about these issues. Active participation is needed for all of these practices. Various participatory planning methodologies can be used in this sense. For example, the "soft systems methodology" (Checkland and Scholes 1990) uses systems-thinking principles for community-based groups. A simple participatory planning method called "Visions-actions-requests between administrative levels" (Beaulieu et al. 2000; Beaulieu, Jaramillo, and Leclerc 2002) addresses the definition of goals and complementary actions. Other participatory methods will be mentioned along the way.

Understanding Goals and Desired Future Conditions

We mentioned previously that development requires a logic of progression toward long-term, collective goals. However, we often confuse means and ends, and the desired outcomes or desired future conditions are too often absent from planning or from the prescriptions coming from different forms of policy. "We have substantial technical knowledge about probing means and strategies to reach objectives, but we know much less about probing ends" (Forester 1999). This probing of ends is what vision-based planning methodologies aim for (Lightfoot, Alders, and Dolberg 2001; Green, Haines, and Halebsky 2000). Any form of reflecting and discussing about "desired future conditions" can lead us to have a long-term goal attitude. How would we like to see society (or our municipality, community, family, business) in five, ten, or twenty years? How would we like to see future generations? Developing a common vision of desired future conditions is different from coming up with a "vision statement," a technique often used in business management. The set of desired future conditions can be quite long, and should include all of the participants' input and all points of view. Technical devices can help in this such as the computer visualizations given on the CD that comes with Hall (2000).

There are three reasons why it is more effective to discuss "desired future conditions" rather than "problems." The first is that it is often much easier to find agreement on desired future conditions than it is on the means to get there and on the obstacles in the way. Indeed, each actor can have a different contribution to the goal, and a given problem situation can have various causes that are all important and related. The second reason is that defining the desired future conditions can allow a better inclusion of diverse contributions into the process of change, and thus allow a variety of players to take part in it. The third reason is that discussing a vision of a desired future also has a positive psychological effect on participants, in comparison with the discussion of obstacles (Bhatia et al. 1993; Lightfoot and Okelabo 2001). Participants feel excited and motivated to do what they can do to reach their dream, and the discovery that their dream is shared by other influential actors brings them optimism.

When discussing obstacles or problems that are under the sphere of responsibility of participants of a meeting, these participants usually feel attacked and take an unproductive, defensive attitude. In general, focusing on obstacles tends to discourage people. To motivate action, problems must be made into objectives (O'Connor and Seymour 1990). Unless we keep in mind the desired future conditions, we can become trapped into thinking that our goals are simply to overcome the obstacles. We can focus on these and forget to go where we want to go. Although overcoming obstacles is necessary, obstacles lead to goals that are intermediate and that must lead to a higher-level goal of reaching the desired conditions.

However, as Forester (1999) points out, the quest to learn about "what we should want" and about "value" can be manipulative. To paraphrase him, planners and politicians can use these exercises as "dialogical boot camps" to help participants in meetings to *really* know what they want. Indeed, another way of obtaining common goals is for leaders to convince their followers to share theirs. Here again, learning and exploring common goals can be used either aiming at genuine deliberation or at manipulation. These discussions will lead to positive development only if leaders and powerful actors have a 360-degree sense of responsibility.

Even if common goals and desired future conditions can be found, that does not mean that they will take the system to where it will be best in the long run. In terms of territorial planning, leaders and facilitators of the planning process have to consider a range of issues and a variety of options and have a long-term perspective. The observation of similar cases in other sites, the consideration of scientific results, and eventually the use of simulation models can be very useful to explore the long-term consequences of the means considered by the group (see Hall 2000 for many examples for Costa Rica).

It is also important to be realistic and to understand that the desired future conditions will not be achieved overnight. During planning, the stages of progression toward the desired future conditions can be defined, and indicators can be chosen to be able to determine, in the future, in which stage we are. It is fundamental not to get discouraged because a policy or institutional mechanism does not work right away, and not to jump to hasty conclusions that they do not work.

360-degree Sense of Responsibility

As we mentioned in previous sections, each system has to realize that it has responsibilities in various directions: it must insure its own sustainability and improvement, it has to contribute to the goals of the larger systems that it is part of, it has to insure that its components have the conditions necessary to fulfill their goals, and it must work accordingly with the other components of the bigger system. This applies to both public and private institutions.

In social systems, the necessary attitude can be encouraged through any practice where system representatives deliberate about their respective goals with representatives of their components and with representatives of the larger systems they are part of. A first change in mindset can simply come through being more conscious of the needs and aspirations of the other players and levels, and by realizing that they exist, thus expanding our mental picture of the society we live in. However, this is often not enough to guarantee a sense of responsibility, and for any decision that has to be made, it is important to analyze the consequences of the decisions on the various directions in the system (above, below, and laterally). One must look for solutions or actions that allow all directions of responsibility to be fulfilled. Once a group agrees on general common goals, the challenge remains to find the most appropriate means to get there, thus finding intermediate goals that do not exclude, repress, or harm any of the players or the environment. This is the least obvious, but is very much worth trying.

Planning can help players discuss the rules and control measures to ensure that the different responsibilities are fulfilled. Planning can also help individual players distribute their time and resources between their different responsibilities, which are usually compatible but require different activities.

Complementarity of Actions

Systems can work either in partnerships or in complementarity with others, leading to a collective reaching of higher-level goals. Finding common goals does not mean homogenizing points of view. On the contrary, including different and contrasting points of view in the discussion of common goals encourages a variety of contributions often necessary to reach the desired conditions.

Practices that can help actions of different players to be complementary include any type of discussion where participants state what they can do to reach the common goals, and describe the contribution needed from other players, either at the same or at a higher hierarchic level. These discussions offer an opportunity for leaders and influential groups to expand their mental concept of their social and environmental systems. As we mentioned in the previous subsection, they become more aware of the needs and contributions of other players through personal contact and discussions, and their mental picture of "us" expands unconsciously. They are also obliged to think of long-term implications of their actions, which also helps them expand their mental picture.

Even when governments try to please all stakeholders, by offering programs, funding opportunities, and incentives within the limits of their resources, they will have limited impact if they do not enable interactions among the various players of the territory. Within the framework of decentralization, governments have a greater role in enabling than providing services (Helmsing 2002). Consulting stakeholders separately and then deciding to whom they should distribute resources will not have the same effect as a fully interactive participatory process where players can discuss with each other, establish common goals, and enable the matching of contributions of ones with the needs of others. Thinking systematically can improve the enabling role of governments, if they consider themselves as catalysts of the interactions between players rather than as the center point of "you request, I provide" relationships. A helpful practice

to promote interactions is to have participants express their possible contributions to the common goal, and then express their demands or expectations from other players. Facilitating or enabling institutions (or the group members themselves) then form or coordinate partnerships as ways to match contributions with needs.

Participatory planning exercises should encourage capacity building for groups to continue to act even in the absence of facilitators. Groups should aim for self-reliance, but not at disconnectedness from external institutions and other players. When done in a fully participatory way, planning gives the less-influential groups the opportunity to organize themselves, gain access to information, and seek support from other influential groups or higher administrative levels to support their initiatives. In a logic of winners and losers and power struggles, leaders and influential actors can feel threatened by this, which is one of the reasons why some do not insist too much on the participatory component of planning. However, when there is a convergence of goals, increased organization and external support become an enormous advantage. The convergence of goals mentioned earlier then becomes a practice that facilitates participation, and participation itself enables the convergence of objectives. The vicious circle of opacity and individual objectives can be turned into a "virtuous" circle of openness and mutual objectives.

Encouraging Self-control Mechanisms in Components

Control includes all mechanisms that either promote or restrain certain actions. Norms and legislation define actions that are acceptable or not, but planning also has to foresee what should be done when norms and laws are not respected. Control does not only restrain itself from actions that are illegal but applies to any process that should be moderated. In social systems, very special care must be taken with control mechanisms, because if they are dysfunctional, players either lose consideration for the rules or lose trust in the controlling institutions or individuals. As we mentioned previously, an adequate degree of control must be found, because too much control can impair actions of the level below, but too little control can lead the system to chaos. What needs to be strictly avoided is control for the sake of it. It is much more efficient to encourage self-control mechanisms than to apply control mechanisms continuously from the top.

One way to encourage these mechanisms is to have players fully understand the goals that are aimed at. Control mechanisms include official and unofficial rules, but if their objectives are not well understood by players, the desired results will not be obtained. In the case of restrictive rules, players always seem to find ways to go around the restrictions, and in the case of incentives, there are almost always abuses. However, the behavior of those who fully understand the ends of a given set of rules is usually too compliant even when it is against their short-term and individual interests.

Sometimes the "ways of doing" follow a number of implicit rules and contribute to a larger definition of "institutionality" (North 1994). It is very important to develop such "ways of doing" in order to have functional processes without being dependent on a leader or facilitator. Such forms of organizing allow groups to conduct meetings, share tasks, communicate, and resolve problems even when they have no official leader or when the leader is absent. Through these rules and "ways of doing," part of the control of the leader above is "decentralized" and transferred to the players of the level below, who also take part of the responsibility. The good functioning of these forms of organizing requires trust among players, not only trust in their honesty but also trust in their capacity to fulfill their engagements. These can take time to become fully functional, as participants must learn to function in that way, but once the codes of practice are well integrated, they can apply them in new working and organizing relationships. These relationships, codes, and ways of doing are also part of social capital (Pretty 1998; chapter 22). However, a manipulative leader can shatter these organizational links with the (sometimes unconscious) objective of gaining exclusive control of its components. If leaders expect their followers to follow rules without repression, they have to set the example and respect them themselves.

If the components do not have the conditions necessary to reach their own goals and to participate in the higher-level goals, they are less likely to follow the rules and to make any contributions, especially if they feel that the higher levels are not concerned with their well-being. This is illustrated by the rise in criminality that accompanied the rise of urban poverty in many countries. Society has to turn to repressive control measures against members that have inadequate conditions and that feel abandoned by it, and thus feel no responsibility toward it.

Using Plans as Learning and Management Tools

As we have seen, learning can happen through attentive monitoring and evaluation, in a continuous process of follow-up and adjustments to plans. Plans must be used as management tools and not considered as ends in themselves. However, the follow-up to planning has to be made simple, or else it can make management heavy, inflexible, and discouraging for participants. Effective monitoring and evaluation procedures can consider both the actions conducted and their effects. Monitoring and evaluation includes verifying the effect of actions and allowing players to learn from successes and failures and to adjust activities and norms included in the plan. It is also an opportunity for the individuals and organizations that participated in the planning to continue to work together in a regular fashion and to develop operational linkages, and an opportunity to collect information that will be useful for future plans. In this sense, what we are advocating is, again, to make the entire process more scientific (using explicit objectives as hypotheses and testing their results) and additionally to include the tools of systems science (especially feedback loops) to make the entire process more powerful and effective.

Administrators and civil society councils should use the evaluation of previous plans as a basis for the diagnosis of any new plan. To simplify monitoring and evaluation and the articulation between plans, plans should have clear goals and desired future conditions, and have identified indicators of progress. Where possible, planning and follow-up should work as much as possible with existing institutions, committees, councils, and other structures to avoid duplication and having members of these entities attempting to undermine the new efforts.

Local learning groups, related to but not necessarily dependent upon governmental structures, can be created by community residents, and can be supported by local governments. These can include participatory research and experimenting groups, machinery rings, co-marketing groups, and community food cooperatives (Pretty 1998). One can find various reports of exploration of local learning processes in East Africa to help farmers and extension workers cope with the decentralization and privatization of agricultural extension services in Lightfoot, Alders, and Dolberg (2001). One can also find methodological suggestions, which include elements of vision-based planning. Participatory monitoring and evaluation is an important component of collective learning processes. Learning alliances can be created between groups and various institutions (Lundy 2002), and stimulate complementary activities that could not be conducted only locally.

Exchanging Information

Information is an important input to planning, inasmuch as feedback loops depend on it. With the word "information," we include any observations, data, documentation, maps, information systems, and decision support tools that can be generated by diverse individuals or institutions. But to be useful, this information has to be fed into one of the active feedback loops used for learning and self-control.

In many cases, decisions are adequately taken based on intuition and local knowledge, which is itself fed by a multitude of feedback loops through learning processes. Local knowledge and intuition are based on the experience of people and on the information accumulated and interpreted in their minds over time. In many cases, especially where there are no conflicts of opinion, local knowledge and intuition are sufficient. However, there are opportunities when additional information is necessary, for example where there is a divergence of opinions or when there is uncertainty on what should be done. In these cases, diagnoses that are based on the players' perceptions need to be supported by trustworthy information from secondary sources, surveys, or measurements. External or new information can become extremely useful to expand the range of options being considered, and to explore the consequences of these options. However, in situations of power struggles, less-influential players such as poor rural people often do not have the same opportunities to access information as the more influential players. We need to develop mechanisms to facilitate this access to help rural players increase their capacity to be able to use external information effectively.

However, all of us have seen or experienced situations in which information is accumulated without being used efficiently for planning or decision support. Sometimes, much energy is spent in digitizing, organizing, correcting, and updating information, and then when particular information is needed for a particular decision, we find that it has not been included in the database. Sometimes, we are in a situation where the need for the information that we are collecting has not been defined clearly. To prevent the blind accumulation of information, we must carefully define the questions to which we want to respond. There are two types of questions arising in planning, the ones for monitoring and evaluation and the ones for defining (or adjusting) actions, partnerships, and rules. The monitoring and evaluation questions, which can lead to the formulation of indicators, include "How far are we from the desired conditions?" "Why is the present situation the way it is?" "How would the situation be if the present tendencies were maintained?" "What is being done about it, and how is that helping?" "How are our partnerships working out?" Are the present rules well adapted to the situation, and are they allowing us to function properly?" The questions for defining actions, partnerships, and rules include "Which are the conditions that we want to improve, and what are the available options?" "Which are the most appropriate actions for a given place?" "Which would be the best location for a given option?" "What would happen if we chose such and such a strategy?" Geographic information can become very useful when working over an extension of land, ranging from a single property to a village, a country, or a continent. It should however be used by local players in a learning and empowerment process, rather than having these players simply participate in a planning process that is managed by technical professionals (D'Aquino et al. 2002).

There is, however, one source of information that must be considered by all planners and participants at the start, namely, all previous plans and any records of their monitoring and evaluation.

Information is useful to answer questions related to development, but it can also help to strengthen the relationships between institutions and players, because it can be shared at a very low cost. However, we need policies that facilitate rather than restrain the accessibility to information. Indeed, the lack of resources has impaired the publication of some information or has forced some institutions to fund their operations through selling information. But part of national planning could consist of determining which information is of primary importance for the country's development and should be considered as a public good. In Colombia, statistics and data derived from census surveys are provided or commercialized by the National Administrative Department of Statistics (DANE). Basic maps and information on topography, land tenure, land use, and land-use potential are provided by the Instituto Geográfico Nacional Augustín Codazzi (IGAC), which is now a branch of DANE. Information relative to hydrology and climate are provided by the institute of environmental studies, IDEAM, which is a branch of the Ministry of the Environment, Housing and Territorial Development. Information on prices of agricultural products is provided by, among other organizations, the Corporación Colombia Internacional, the Bolsa Nacional Agropecuaria, MADR, and DNP. Regional corporations often have lots of information on their region; sometimes they sell it, but many times they are not able to share it thereafter because the rights are reserved to the institution that purchased it. A general consideration of the needs to make data from different ministries compatible is provided in Hall (2000, chapter 7).

Another important source of information for development officials is the scientific community.

However, development players usually find that the results of scientific research are not accessible to them or are available in forms that they cannot understand. Scientific results usually go through a chain of simplification and extension before they trickle down to local players. Scientists and local players are seldom in direct communication, except in specific development-oriented research, usually done in specific localities. Planning can serve as a very practical mechanism to allow scientists and development players to interact and define hypotheses and questions together. Scientists can take part in support groups to the commissions that do the follow-up and monitoring to plans and to learning groups, thus learning together with the players in an exciting way. However, scientists tend to avoid linking directly with politics, often because they distrust the political system or because they fear that politicians will use their results in a political battle between parties or to increase their popularity.

Conclusions

Colombia has some of the most explicit legislation in Latin America in terms of participatory planning. While planning and development are inseparable, leaders and individuals in Colombia and many other countries need to accompany the existing practices, methods, and laws with mindsets that allow development of society as a system. These include:

Having a logic oriented toward achieving long-term, collective goals and reaching desired future conditions;

Having a 360-degree sense of responsibility;

Understanding the complementarity of their roles and actions in achieving common goals;

Favoring control mechanisms (with a preference toward self-control rather than control from above) to moderate undesirable, self-enforcing processes;

Using the scientific method to generate objectives as explicit hypotheses, and then testing whether or not these objectives were achieved, enhancing feedbacks to increase the probability that they indeed become enacted;

Recognizing that growth by itself should cease to be the goal, but rather specific goals should be identified and then growth should be examined as to whether it contributes to this goal or not.

Simple deliberative and goal-oriented planning practices can help reinforce these mindsets. These include the discussion of long-term desired future conditions, the contribution that each individual or group can give toward the goals, and what contributions they expect from others. Coordinators at different levels can use the contributions and expectations of their components to articulate complementary actions within each level and among levels. Extremely important practices include using planning as a continuous management and learning process. Control processes and learning require fluid communication and exchange of information.

In the scope of globalization, these mindsets should also have to prevail at the international scale, but the international context is (like many local and national ones) very much affected by a winners-and-losers logic, an obsession for economic growth, and the search for quick and easy gain. The effect that the international context has on local conditions is extremely important, but it does not make local planning useless. Indeed, through planning, groups can realize that an important part of the decisions that affect their development is under their control. The local attitude can also determine the local effect of external processes and factors (including corruption). Nonetheless, a global-level reflection—and why not call it planning?—is needed, in which the affected rural stakeholders must participate.

Development, either specifically rural or in general, results from a complex series of actions from very diverse social players. These players define their actions in decision-making processes that are conscious or not, collective or individual. They can make decisions in two types of contexts, either in some kind of planning or in solving problems as they arise. Decision making by territorial or political institutions constitutes, for scientists

and information providers, an opportunity to put their results to the service of development and management of natural resources. For them, it is an entry point, a link in the chain between research and development to which they can hook on. The scientific contribution to social objectives can be facilitated by planning processes; it is more difficult for scientists to contribute to solving problems as they come along, in which case the urgency seldom leaves sufficient time to consider different options, look for relevant information, or communicate questions to the scientific community.

In Colombia, we expect to be able to develop an interactive link between research and local development through a network of support to municipal and departmental planning. CIAT and the Ministry of Agriculture and Rural Development have been collaborating on this issue, and will soon set up a network principally aimed at supporting the planning and monitoring of rural technical assistance and technology transfer, in the scope of municipal management. We expect these initiatives to help rural communities and ourselves reach desired future conditions of better livelihoods and better communication between administrative levels as well as between rural communities and scientists and extension agents. At least that is one of our hypotheses, and by trying this out and watching what happens, we will be able to validate or refute it.

Notes

1. A very similar figure is used by O'Connor and Seymour (1993) to represent the learning process in their introductory book on neurolinguistic programming, a set of psychological techniques that aim at helping individuals to improve their personal and professional results through improving their mental perceptiveness, flexibility, and communication skills. This set of techniques also uses a systems approach and can be applied at other levels than the individual person.

2. A decree of December 2002 expands the obligations of the rural technical assistance with respect to law 607 of 2000, to include these contributions to the organization of farmers and rural inhabitants in general.

3. The Certificado de Incentivo Forestal was created through law 139 of 1994 and is regulated by decree 1824 of 1994.

4. This law defines for Colombian municipalities three types of territorial plans, in function of the number of inhabitants, in the following manner: Municipalities with fewer than 30,000 inhabitants conduct a scheme or Esquemas de Ordenamiento Territorial (EOT); those with between 30,000 and 100,000 inhabitants conduct a basic plan or Plan Básico de Ordenamiento Territorial (PBOT); and those with more than 100,000 inhabitants conduct a Plan de Ordenamiento Territorial (POT). However, municipalities can choose to conduct a plan corresponding to a larger population than the one they have.

5. Indeed, law 60 of 1993 states that municipalities must invest, in rural areas, a proportion of transfers from the state for social programs that is at least as much as the proportion of rural inhabitants, and that in areas where the rural population exceeds 40 percent, this proportion must be increased by 10 percent. This law was modified by the law 751 of 2001, but this modification does not affect this requirement to invest in rural areas.

6. German Castro Caicedo (2002) describes how in the departments of Arauca and Casanare, with large oil exploitations, political leaders are forced to give a significant part of the oil taxes to both guerillas and paramilitaries, and that they have to agree to this before they are even allowed to present themselves to elections. This is only one example of the influence that illegal groups have on politics.

7. Part of the logic of this approach can be found in the title of John Stockwell's book *In Search of Enemies*. Governments, especially those saddled by failing domestic policies, manufacture enemies to rally their citizens behind them.

References

Beaulieu, N., J. Jaramillo, and G. Leclerc. 2002. The vision-action-requests approach across administrative levels: A methodological proposal for the strategic planning of rural development. Internal report. Cali, Colombia, and Montpellier, France: CIAT/MTD.

Beaulieu, N., J. Jaramillo, G. Leclerc, S. Pabón, M. Gómez, and C. A. Quirós. 2000. Propuesta metodológica para el componente participativo del ordenamiento territorial, basada en el desarrollo de una visión común. Report. Cali, Colombia: CIAT.

Bhatia, A., C. K. Sen, G. Pandey, and J. Amtzis. 1993. Participatory tools and techniques, appreciative planning and action: APA. Context paper eight of capacity building in participatory upland watershed planning, monitoring and evaluation, a resource kit. Rome: FAO.

Castro Caicedo, G. 2003. *Sin tregua*. Bogotá: Editorial Planeta Colombiana.

Checkland, P., and J. Scholes. 1990. *Soft Systems Methodology in Action*. Chichester: Wiley & Sons.

Clayton, A. M. H., and N. J. Radcliffe. 1996. *Sustainability: A New Systems Approach*. London: Earthscan.

Costa, F. J., A. G. Noble, A. K. Dutt, and R. B. Kent. 1998. Currents of change: Urban planning and regional development. In A. G. Noble, F. J. Costa, A. K. Dutt, and R. B. Kent, eds., *Regional Development and Planning for the 21st Century*, 1–17. Aldershot, England: Ashgate.

Cusack, C. 1998. Future trends: Globalism and regionalism. In A. G. Noble, F. J. Costa, A. K. Dutt, and R. B. Kent, eds., *Regional Development and Planning for the 21st Century*, 365–378. Aldershot, England: Ashgate.

D'Aquino, P. 2002. Le territoire entre espace et pouvoir: Pour une planification territoriale ascendante. *L'Espace Géographique* 1:3–22.

De Leener, P., E. Ndione, J. P. Perrier, P. Jacolin, and M. Ndiaye. 1999. *Pauvreté, décentralisation et changement social: Éléments pour la reconstruction d'une société politique*. Dakar: Editions ENDA GRAF.

Diakité, T. 2002. *L'Afrique & l'aide, ou Comment s'en sortir?* Paris: L'Harmattan.

Echeverri Perrico, R., and M. Pilar Ribero. 2002. *Nueva ruralidad: Visión del territorio en Latino América y el Caribe*. Bogotá: IICA.

Forester, J. 1999. *The Deliberative Practitioner: Encouraging Participatory Planning Processes*. Cambridge, Mass.: MIT Press.

Green, G., A. Haines, and S. Halebsky. 2000. *Building Our Future: A Guide to Community Visioning*. Madison: University of Wisconsin Extension.

Hall, C. A. S., ed. 2000. *Quantifying Sustainable Development: The Future of Tropical Economies*. San Diego: Academic Press.

Hammond, D. 2003. *The Science of Synthesis: Exploring the Social Implications of General Systems Theory*. Boulder: University Press of Colorado.

Helmsing, A. H. J. 2002. Decentralization, enablement and local governance in low-income countries. *Environment and Planning C: Government and Policy* 20:317–40.

Klitgaard, R, R. MacLean-Abaroa, and H. Lindsay Parris. 2000. *Corrupt Cities*. San Francisco: Institute for Contemporary Studies and World Bank.

Kroeger, T., and D. Montanye. 2000. An assessment of the effectiveness of structural adjustment in Costa Rica.

In C. A. S. Hall, *Quantifying Sustainable Development*, 665–94.

Lightfoot, C., and S. Okalebo. 2001. Vision-based action planning: Report on a learning process for developing guidelines on vision based sub-county environmental action planning. Montpellier, France: International Support Group, Development Support Services.

Lightfoot, C., C. Alders, and F. Dolberg, eds. 2001. *Linking Local Learners: Negotiating New Development Relationships Between Village, District and Nation.* Amersfoort, Netherlands: International Support Group (ISG), Agroforum.

Lightfoot, C., M. Fernandez, R. Noble, R. Ramírez, A. Groot, E. Fernandez-Baca, S. Okelabo, et al. 2000. A learning approach to community agroecosystem management. In C. Flora, ed., *Interactions Between Agroecosystems and Rural Communities*, 131–55. Boca Raton, Fla.: CRC.

Lundy, M. 2004. Learning alliances with development partners: A framework for scaling out research results. In D. H. Pachico and S. Fujisaka, eds., *Scaling Up and Out: Achieving Widespread Impact Through Agricultural Research*, 221–34. Cali, Colombia: Centro Internacional de Agricultura Tropical (CIAT).

Meadows, D. 1997. Places to intervene in a system. *Whole Earth*, winter 1997.

Mitroff, I. 2001. *Smart Thinking for Crazy Times: A Guide to the Art of Solving the Right Problems.* San Francisco: Berret-Koehler.

North, D. C. 1994. Economic performance through time. *American Economic Review* 84, no. 3: 359–68.

O'Connor, J., and J. Seymour. 1993. *Introducing Neuro-Linguistic Programming.* London: Aquarian Press.

Odum, H. T. 1988. Self-organization, transformity and information. *Science* 242:1132–39.

———. 1994. *Ecological and General Systems: An Introduction to Systems Ecology.* Niwot: University Press of Colorado.

Oliva, C., M. Bès, and R. Hernandez. 1998. La decentralización en Colombia, nuevos desafios. www.iadb.org/regions/re3/codes1.htm.

Porras Vallejo, O. A. 2003. La política de decentralización y ordenamiento territorial en Colombia. Paper delivered at the Taller latinoamericano sobre territorio y desarrollo sostenible, Cali, Colombia, 18–21 June.

Pretty, J. 1998. *The Living Land.* London: Earthscan.

PRC (Presidencia de la República de Colombia). 2000. Agrovisión 2025. Ministerio de Agricultura de Colombia, Santa Fé de Bogotá.

———. 2002. Bases del Plan Nacional de Desarrollo 2002–2006: Hacia un estado comunitario. Santa Fé de Bogotá.

Schwartz, P. 1996. *The Art of the Long View: Planning for the Future in an Uncertain World.* New York: Doubleday.

Sharma, R. S. 2003. *Leadership Wisdom from the Monk Who Sold His Ferrari: The 8 Rituals of Visionary Leaders.* London: Hay House.

Vargas del Valle, R. 2002. Colombia: Propuesta de estratégia para promover el desarrollo en las zonas rurales. Banco Interamericano de Desarrollo, Bogotá.

World Bank. 2002a. Colombia Poverty Report. Report No. 24524-CO, Santa Fé de Bogotá.

———. 2002b. Memorandum of the president of the International Bank for Reconstruction and Development and the International Finance Corporation to the executive directors on a country assistance strategy of World Bank Group for the republic of Colombia. Report No. 25129-CO, Santa Fé de Bogotá.

CHAPTER 36

IMPROVING POVERTY-REDUCTION POLICIES, PART 2

Contrasting and Harmonizing Representations

GRÉGOIRE LECLERC

Introduction

It is fascinating to find how little is known about poverty measurement and how unreliable poverty estimates are, after decades of massive investments in poverty-alleviation programs. It is as surprising to see that poverty is still extremely widespread and endemic in the world.[1] It is perhaps this proportion of the population for which the green revolution or structural adjustments have had no effects—or have had negative ones—and that is still as poor or poorer as it was decades ago. The World Bank, a key actor in helping developing countries to reorganize and invest in their growth, has followed the advice of an army of very talented economists and implemented well-known strategies with roots in neoclassical economic theory. In recent years, though, the World Bank has realized that poverty alleviation and development were not as successful as expected and that a new rural development strategy was needed. I do not think its decision to rethink its approach to development is only a question of public relations; it is also the result of a genuine interest in poverty alleviation.

Participatory poverty assessments (PPA), which were popular in the 1990s, have brought a new dimension in the picture: the poor were finally asked to say something about what poverty is. While past PPA efforts were generally restricted to the scale of the community, recent research is addressing methodological issues of combining qualitative and quantitative poverty-measurement methods (Ravallion 2001; Ravnborg 1999; Carvalho and White 1997; see chapter 20). Discrepancies between results of independent qualitative and quantitative approaches are to be expected (Bergeron, Morris, and Medina Banegas 1998; McGee 1999; Kanbur

et al. 2001), and the question is no longer to decide which is the best one but to see what each approach can bring to a better understanding of the situation and a better operational setting. An elegant way to combine qualitative and quantitative indicators is to convert the former into a utility function that is then included in an econometric model (Van Praag 1968; Ravallion and Lokshin 2001). The combination of qualitative and quantitative approaches in an iterative process of hypothesis formulation, survey design, measurement, representation, and socialization should lead to a much better solution than each one taken separately.

Two schools of thoughts are currently associated with poverty appraisal efforts (Christiansen 2001). So-called *quantitative poverty assessments* follow a logical positivism paradigm, where there is a single, external reality that can be captured by proper analysis of "hard" data and then transferred to the poor via policies and investments. *Qualitative poverty assessments*, on the other hand, suppose multiple perceptions of reality and imply a commitment to empowerment, which puts them in the traditions of interpretivism and constructivism. At the extremes of these schools of thought one can find, on one hand, a universal dollar-a-day poverty threshold that determines the faith of foreign aid money, and on the other hand an opposition to positivism, which dooms poor communities to remain unique and misunderstood. While chapter 20 tends to favor a positivist view by quantifying perceptions of well-being, this chapter is more in the domain of constructivism.

In chapter 20 I proposed simple ways to compute poverty indexes derived from traditional expert advice as well as from PPAs. Many methodological bottlenecks are avoided by using raw, unit-level census data instead of aggregated data. At the same time, having access to a gold mine of data and having the flexibility to produce poverty indexes tailored to specific needs carries an unexpected side effect: a feeling of anguish in front of this complexity and the multiplicity of choices (Tufte 1997; Tukey 1977; Fisher 1986). To increase the distress even more, I added the spatial dimension, that is, poverty maps used either to communicate a message or to find spatial patterns to target our interventions.

Honduran officials have worked hard to develop targeted poverty-alleviation programs, with uneven success. With Honduras as a backdrop case study, I show here that simple, practical alternatives to business-as-usual poverty analysis are not farfetched. I present several methods to contrast or harmonize different representations of poverty (by varying indexes, aggregation levels, and map classification choices) and illustrate the effect these representations may have on poverty-alleviation policy. I examine the effect that the choice of poverty indicator has on the efficiency of targeted policies, namely, that the money invested in poverty-alleviation programs actually reaches the poor. I complete the case study by outlining the functionalities of a simple, user-friendly interface to raw census data, one that allows various representations to be generated from and explored freely on the World Wide Web. I also give a few examples of spatial analysis methods that can be applied to disaggregated data to gain insights on the determinants of poverty.

Materials and Methods
Poverty Indicators from the Honduras Population, Housing, and Agriculture Censuses

In chapter 20 I introduced the Honduras unit-level census and GIS databases and showed how one can compute and map poverty indexes at various levels of aggregation. In a first step, we adopted a traditional approach and showed how a strict unsatisfied basic needs (UBN) index can be constructed from the variables found in the population and housing censuses. This was illustrated with an index that consisted of a linear combination of three indexes (housing, services, non-land assets) and was labeled UBN3. Then we added a variable related to education attainment to the UBN3 index, making it more similar to UNDP Human Development Index, and called it UBN4. Aggregation was done by counting the number of households in an aggregation unit having an UBN index in the poorest quintile. These headcount indexes (labeled PUBN3 and PUBN4) were mapped for village, municipality, and department by choosing a classification by quantiles of the distribution (suitable for use in a targeted allocation of funds scheme), and a double-ended chromatic scale to highlight extreme values (i.e., poorest and richest). It was made clear that the choice of census variables, the acceptable threshold (poverty line), and the weights for combining them into a single index were somehow arbitrary (i.e., our "expert" choice) and that any individual may come up with a combination that better suits his or her experience or needs. It was also evident that PUBN3 and PUBN4, although very closely related by construction, were not as highly correlated as I would have expected, and that the maps produced showed marked dissimilarities (figure 20.4).

In a second step, I introduced the results of an independent study (Ravnborg 1999), which was a PPA that was designed to enable the extrapolation of poverty indicators that were defined based on the perceptions local informants have of households in their community. Ravnborg (1999) found eleven indicators that were a priori valid for three Honduras departments, and I explained how I extracted proxies of these indicators from raw census data. In this case, I had to use all three censuses (for a total of nine proxies to Ravnvorg's indicators) to have a picture of poverty consistent with the PPA. The resulting well-being index (*WBI*) was averaged at village, municipality, and department level, and was mapped using the same quantile classification and double-ended chromatic scale, for consistency. In addition to standard choropleth mapping I introduced a new plot (the geographical starplot) where the value of the nine proxy indicators can be assessed at once in geographical space (figure 20.7). This was an example of how mapping can be used to convey multidimensional information in a snapshot.

Indicators have to be obtained and summarized for as many purposes as there are decision makers. In practice, though, aggregation often means oversimplification: we go from extremely detailed census information to gross summary statistics (e.g., mean income by department) that dilute the underlying complexity. There is no technical constraint to giving full access to the census data to all, with a palette of aggregation procedures that will capture complexity while preserving anonymity (Duke-Williams and Rees 1998; Dale 1998). However, much effort is still needed to provide user-friendly aggregation and summary *methods* instead of the usual summary *data*.

In this chapter, I examine how the choice of indicators and aggregation levels can change the composition and meaning of poverty profiles. I give several examples of possible uses of raw information to locate clusters of poor villages, analyze factors related to poverty, and anticipate the impact of targeted investments.

Matching Perceptions and Highlighting Spatial Patterns

For several centuries, researchers have investigated ways to link the display of data (and information) in map form (and other forms) from various perspectives and for various purposes (Monmonnier 1996; Tufte 1983, 1990, 1997). In recent years, some consensus about general semiological guidelines seems to be taking shape (Brunet 1997; Tufte 1983; Monmonnier 1996; Brewer and McMaster 1999), but most map users and producers, with the exception of some census and statistics bureaus, are unaware of the advances in this active field of research. Clearly, today's GIS mainstream packages would benefit from introducing more clever data classification and display techniques available in some small noncommercial packages (Mazurek 2002). Dissemination of statistical government digital data in a better, understandable, and unbiased way is also a subject of concern (Carr, MacEachern, and Scott 2000). I would recommend spending a great deal of effort in providing each map with a

detailed explanation in clear text, stressing limitations and warning about possible misuses.

Thematic maps offer a powerful opportunity for matching perceptions and representations and for stimulating dialogue. We have to be aware that the most popular thematic map format for displaying statistics—the choropleth—carries an intrinsic bias by default (Monmonnier 1996), and comparing maps made with different biases rapidly can become nonsense. The name *choropleth* comes from the Greek *choros*, "place," and *plethos*, "large number, magnitude, or size." A color is applied to each region to represent a range of values. The impact of a colored region, therefore, is a product of its color and the area of the patch to which it is applied. Therefore, many say that it is more suitable for mapping relative variables (e.g., normalized by area). However, we see numerous cases of choropleth mapping of absolute variables (e.g., counts), the map being intended to be used as a spatial table and not for detecting spatial patterns (this is how we used these maps in this chapter and in chapter 20). Dot maps (in which each region is represented by a colored circle of fixed or variable radius) could be more appropriate in this case.

One can obtain different choropleth maps that appear drastically different—even when the data represented are the same—by changing the class breaks. Thus it is very easy to "lie" (that is to say, to show a particular viewpoint) with a particular poverty map, and the users have to be aware of the power of visual representation. There is no reason to be satisfied with one precooked poverty map when affordable information technology is there to help experiment with several indexes and several representations.

The great flexibility now available in the selection of indexes and of map categories is both a blessing and a curse. Without guidance, an inexperienced user will be overwhelmed rapidly by the numerous possibilities to specify indicators, data ranges, and categories; in addition, it is very easy to fool an observer by classifying data in a way that will bias the interpretation. The classification of continuous data (which is also an aggregation procedure) is a delicate operation because it poses two problems: giving a meaning to the classified map by choosing a classification method, and by making the implicit assumption that the data and the spatial units within a class are homogenous.

Data can be classified based on rough statistical techniques (e.g., quantiles, nested means, equiprobability, clinographic) and more complex ones that highlight patterns in their distribution with or without considerations of spatial contiguity (Cromley 1996; Lark 1998; Murray and Shyy 2000). These patterns can then be examined and contrasted to gain new insight (or more confusion) on poverty causes or trends. This flexibility is possible as long as the raw data are available, which is often not the case, especially with published historical data. In fact, the occurrence of fixed representations vastly exceeds the variable ones (i.e., ones that use raw data that the user might reinterpret), mainly because of the limitations of traditional presentation media. Consequently, we will have to cope, most of the time, with fixed representations such as official poverty maps, and we need a way to put them side by side (Van Beurden and Douven 1999). However, it is possible to classify raw data such as the well-being index (*WBI*) in a way that minimizes the difference with data from independent sources.

To do so, I have adapted a method described by Cromley (1996) for finding optimum data classification for choropleth display, which in turn builds on the pioneering work by Jenks (Jenks and Caspall 1971; Jenks 1976, 1977). The original concept is simple and elegant: categories are constructed from raw data in a way that minimizes a cost function with respect to user-defined strategies. The strategies selected by Cromley (1996) offer a wide range of possibilities to a user who wants to explore the data for their specific purposes, and there is no restriction for adding other strategies. Instead of the Lagrange multiplier relaxation method proposed by Cromley (1996), I used the genetic algorithm minimization procedure described by Burns (1998). Genetic algorithms are a flexible alternative that is robust to local minima; they will not necessarily find the absolutely best optimum solution but one close to the optimum even for complex problems, such as the ones requiring integer programming for which other optimization methods often fail.

This strategy can be exploited to find a data classification that best matches another one (e.g., a reference) to be able to compare two representations while minimizing their differences. This is a new application of the technique where the goal is not to minimize a cost function inherent in the data, but to minimize a cost function with respect to an independent map used as a reference. I have implemented several strategies to adjust a dataset to a reference map with a number T of categories, based on the contingency table constructed from the reference map and a map with variable class breaks. In the case of ordered categories (and when we expect the order to be the same—as in the case of poverty indexes) the measure of similarity between both maps can be judged by either tabular accuracy or Cohen's kappa index of agreement (Cohen 1960), which is a tabular accuracy corrected for agreement by chance (necessary in case the size of the classes is not uniform). When one compares maps for which the order of the classes is unknown a priori, I suggest using the Rand index corrected for agreement by chance (Hubert and Arabie 1985), while minimizing the total table error or the mean of errors for individual classes.[2] By using a weighted index such as weighted kappa (Cohen 1968; Naesset 1996), it is possible to account for internal variability of the map utility, either because of known errors in one or several categories, or to put emphasis on certain classes (e.g., the very poor category).

Results

Representations of Honduran Poverty

I mapped the indicators PUBN3, PUBN4, and *WBI* at various levels of aggregation, using legend categories defined by quantiles of the data and a double chromatic scale. The multiple dimensions leading to the *WBI* were also represented via geographical starplots, which is a promising way to represent data with little bias (figure 20.7).

Because geometric shapes and large masses of colors inevitably attract our eye, it is tempting to start an ad-hoc analysis of the regional patterns that appear on a choropleth map with a given legend and a given level of aggregation, which can easily lead to invalid conclusions (Monmonnier 1996). In several Honduran official publications, we see a reference to a "Poverty Belt," which appears as a ringlike suite of poor municipalities around the country's capital, Tegucigalpa. One may ask: what is special about these municipalities? Is there some connection or correlation between these munici-palities? Or some drain of neighboring resources by the rich Tegucigalpa? Or are they just suburban slums? In fact, this is due to a visual artifact that quickly disappears by a change in legend catego-ries. Choropleth maps based on optimum classi-fication strategies (which quantiles are not) are much better for the purpose of finding patterns in our data distributions.

The regional picture becomes more synthetic as we aggregate at municipality and department levels, but many villages that appear as poor on the village-level map end up being merged on the map into a municipality or department that is not poor overall, especially if this area contains a city. Thus there is an increasing probability of inefficient tar-geting (and conflicts) as we decrease the level of detail. Regional targeting is also improved by using finer-resolution maps that enable better municipal-level targeting. Government funding allocated based on department-level targeting will need to be redistributed nonuniformly within the municipality (e.g., at the municipality level) when there is a large variation of poverty profiles within a department (e.g., Choluteca; see figure 36.1). In this context, an alternative to a data table to represent poverty profiles at different scales can be obtained by fol-lowing the work of Carr et al. (1998), who suggest the simultaneous display of geographical informa-tion and box plots. Figure 36.1 shows, for each department highlighted on the micro-maps on the left, the distribution of village-level *WBI* for each municipality. One can immediately evaluate, for each department, the overall *WBI* and the inequali-ties within each department and municipality, and analyze regional patterns. For example, one can see that the overall well-being is greater in Yoro than in Valle, and that within Yoro some municipali-ties are much better (or worse) off than others. In the first case we are looking at inequalities among municipalities, while in the second case we see that within a given municipality a lot of villages are much better (or worse) off than others (i.e., we are characterizing inequalities among villages within

municipalities). In this case the inequalities among villages in most municipalities are much lower in the Valle department than in Yoro.

The policy-making world is populated mostly by people who have more experience in interpret-ing a table of summary statistics than a map. With the pitfalls of choropleth maps and the difficulty policy makers have truly integrating data in mul-tiple dimensions (and in a regional context), it is easy to understand why data tables are preferred (and perhaps it is better that it has been like that). Carr's work (Carr, MacEachern, and Scott 2000) is a good example that shows that it is possible to generate both representations—that is, maps and statistics—together for improved interpretation and decision making.

Issues for Policy Design
Indicators and aggregation issues
I cannot emphasize enough how critical is the choice of poverty measure and the scale of analy-sis for planning. McGee (1999) has also studied the correlation between locally derived well-being rankings and the standard poverty targeting by the Colombian government, and concludes that the optimum for social policy delivery is probably a combination of both approaches (McGee 1999).[3] Table 36.1 shows the correlation coefficients that I obtained between PUBN3, PUBN4, *WBI*, and official data (FHIS 1992) from the Honduras Social Fund for Social Investment (FHIS, its Span-ish acronym) at various aggregation levels. It gives an overview of the degree of compatibility between various representations of poverty and how this perception changes (or persists) with the level of aggregation. For example, a policy maker who is using department-level data can see how well this data reflects village-level data, and therefore get a quick assessment of possible impacts, at the village level, of a targeted policy that would be based on department-level data. One can immediately see that correlation is low in general, and that PUBN4 (the compound index that includes housing, ser-vices, non-land assets, and education) is more consistent across scales than the other poverty measures (which does not automatically imply that it is a "better" indicator, just a more uniform one).

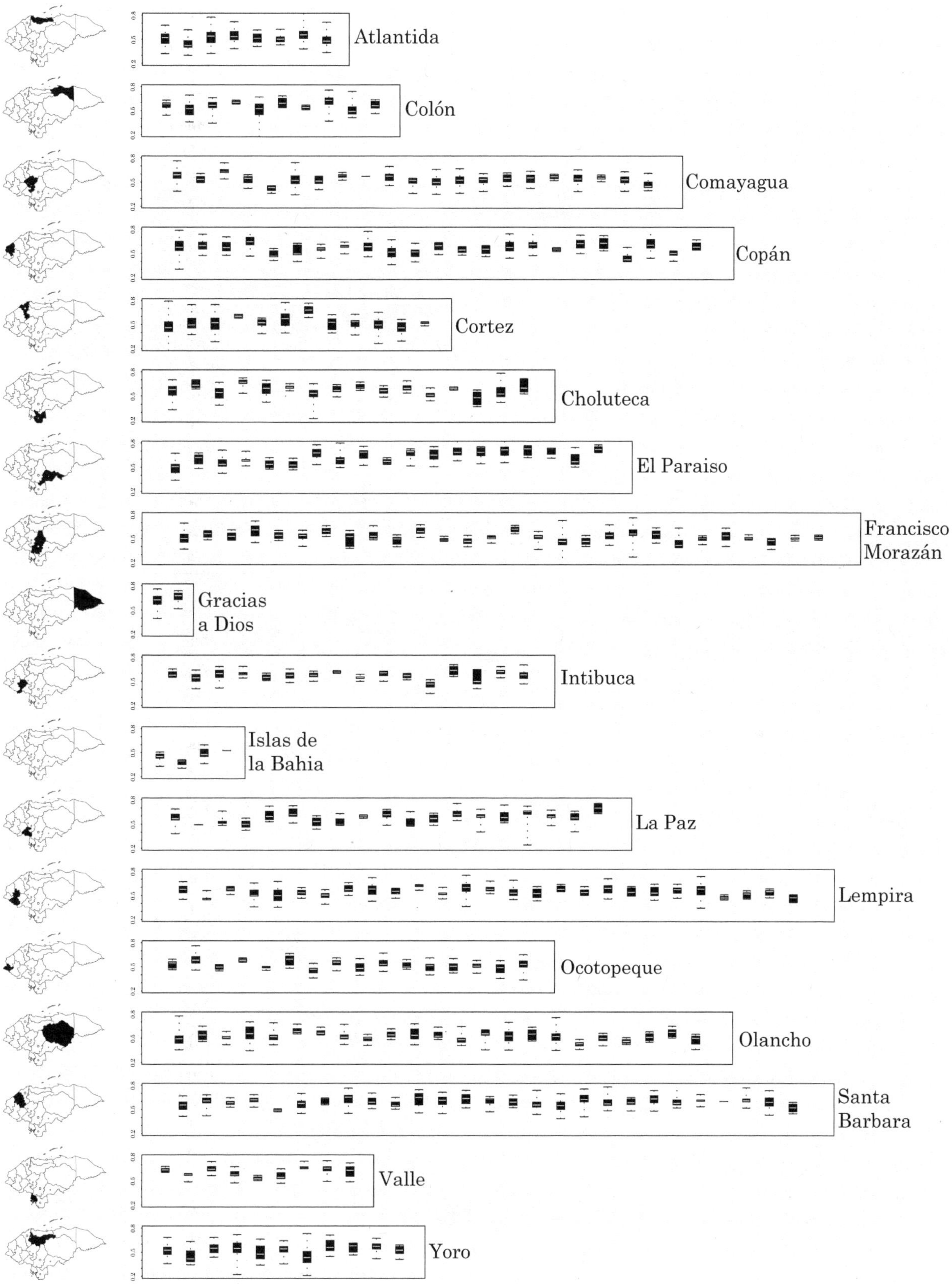

Figure 36.1. Poverty profiles (*WBI*) for all villages, by municipality and department (black areas on left micromaps). These box-plots show the wide variability of different villages within each municipality, and the variability among municipalities and departments.

Table 36.1. Correlation matrix between several poverty measures at various aggregation levels

		Village			Municipality				Department			
		WBI	PUBN4	PUBN3	WBI	PUBN4	PUBN3	FHIS	WBI	PUBN4	PUBN3	FHIS
Village	WBI	1										
	PUBN4	0.38	1									
	PUBN3	0.44	0.84	1								
Municipality	WBI	0.60	0.31	0.30	1							
	PUBN4	0.28	0.67	0.47	0.43	1						
	PUBN3	0.29	0.53	0.50	0.48	0.91	1					
	FHIS	0.28	0.36	0.40	0.46	0.65	0.78	1				
Department	WBI	0.37	0.31	0.24	0.62	0.43	0.43	0.35	1			
	PUBN4	0.22	0.61	0.34	0.33	0.81	0.63	0.42	0.55	1		
	PUBN3	0.24	0.57	0.36	0.38	0.77	0.66	0.49	0.63	0.96	1	
	FHIS	0.23	0.47	0.35	0.38	0.66	0.63	0.59	0.63	0.83	0.92	1

Cells in the upper right are shaded proportionally to the correlation coefficient (given in the lower left), i.e., darker cells mean correlation is higher. Correlations greater than 0.5 appear in bold).

It is amazing to find such a low correlation between the same indicator given at different aggregation levels, for example, 0.36 between department and village level PUBN3. This gives an idea of the local relevance of a policy design based on aggregated data.

Several authors have emphasized the problem of low correlation between different poverty measures. Boltvinik (1996), after an exhaustive review of poverty measurement methods, concludes that "the choice of the measuring method determines the level of poverty and the policies required to address it." In a case study in Ivory Coast (Glewwe and Van der Gaag 1988), seven indicators of human well-being were computed from household data, and target population computed from these estimates; the authors found that there was little overlap between population identified as poor according to each measure. For Venezuela, maps of poverty indexes based on economic indicators were found to differ significantly from the ones based on data-driven composite indexes (Baker and

Grosh 1994). Therefore, it is not unfair to say that policies are typically more related to an empirical choice by decision makers and analysts than to evidence driven by robust data analysis, a situation that I would like to see change in the future.

Classification issues

Three "official" poverty maps used by the government of Honduras are displayed in figure 36.2: the 1994 map used by FHIS (figure 36.2a), and two maps that appear in the most recent poverty reduction strategy paper (RH 2001), one from SECPLAN, which is based on 3 UBNs computed from the 1988 population and housing census (figure 36.2b) and one from the seventh schoolchildren's height census for ages six to eight (1997; figure 36.2c). There is a large agreement between figure 36.2a and 36.2b, which reveals the weight of the population and housing census in the FHIS map. However, categories from both maps have been defined in a way that emphasizes poverty: if we look at the original data used by FHIS before aggregation (FHIS 1992), we find that what is considered "acceptable" or "average" corresponds to a FHIS poverty index between 0 and 0.3 while the "very bad" category applies to indexes above 0.5.[4] The same is almost true for figure 36.2b: a municipality will be considered as "poor" when more than 40 percent of households have three UBNs. Figure 36.2c displays an index of the population risk for chronic malnutrition, another facet of poverty that is not taken into account by UBNs. Food security is, however, one of the eleven well-being indicators obtained by Ravnborg (1999) but for which, unfortunately, no equivalent was available in the three censuses to which we had access.

For consistency, we chose the same chromatic pattern for all the poverty maps displayed in the two parts of this paper.[5] However, the official maps are all using shades of red exclusively, which strongly suggest that nothing is going well in Honduras. There is no doubt that Honduras is a very poor country, but it seems that the data suggest lower levels of poverty than those of the government reports. The effect of color in the design of maps has been known for several centuries, and the first ever poverty map also used a color scheme that conveyed a suggestive meaning (Booth 1902).[6] In effect, Booth's colored maps served as a summary and translation of the data and so was designed to be easily understandable by anyone. It is clear that we need to think much more about the spatial dimensions for displaying the data and the color dimensions for maps of data, and in general to devise better ways for simplifying and synthesizing and formalizing our representations of poverty (Tufte 1983, 1990, 1997).

When we look at all our different poverty maps at the same time, however, consistent patterns seem to emerge. For example, it becomes clear that the western part of Honduras—the departments of Choluteca, Valle, Intibucá, La Paz, Lempira, Ocotopeque, Copan, and Santa Barbara—suffers from much higher poverty than the rest of the country. This is consistent with a recent reanalysis of several existing studies, which found that poverty tends to be concentrated in the departments of the southwest (Choluteca, Valle, Intibucá, La Paz, and Lempira), in which three-quarters of the combined

(a)   *FHIS*

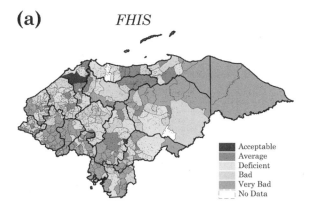

(b)   *SECPLAN (3 UBN)*

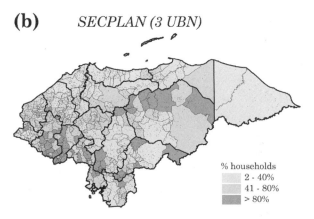

(c)   *Schoolchildren's Height Census*

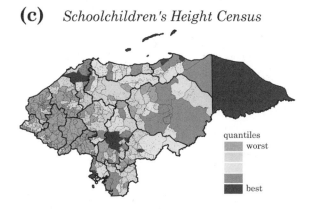

Figure 36.2. Three official poverty maps for Honduras: (a) the 1994 map used by FHIS, based on two UBNs and on malnutrition; (b) map from SECPLAN, based on three UBNs computed from the 1988 population and housing census (from RdH, 2001); (c) map of the malnutrition risk from the seventh schoolchildren's height census for ages six to eight (1997; RH 2001). See website for color originals.

populations have income below the poverty line (Paes de Barros et al. 2000). On the other hand, a popular belief about "marginality" of the northern zone of Honduras (read: concentration of poverty and isolation) is not noticeably sustained by the data or its different renditions.

This stresses the importance of understanding fully the concepts behind the indicators used, their distribution, and their aggregation. Handling this complexity is made easier by enabling the construction of poverty measures and representations to adjust to our specific needs (or to our capacity to induce change) in a flexible yet controllable way. However, one should be able to assess how representations match, in particular between scales, because conflicts arise from decisions, and decision makers at various levels use data at various scales and aggregation levels (Van Beurden and Douven 1999). My opinion is that the scale of the village and of the municipality are the most appropriate in the context of decentralization.

Figure 36.3 shows our results obtained from two applications of the optimum classification strategy described in the methods section. On the left, we used the FHIS map as a reference, then produced maps from the PUBN4 and *WBI* that maximize the overall kappa index of agreement between the two maps. We see that in the case of PUBN4 and *WBI*, we have a 47 percent and 39 percent improvement, respectively, over the match that we would have obtained with a random map. On the right, we show maps that minimize the total within-class variation so that the overall variation is explained by the classification as much as possible (the group mean for a given class represents the best individual values within the class). The cost function of this strategy is given by:

$$c = \sum_{j} \sum_{i \in G_j} (X_i - \overline{X_i})^2$$

where X_j corresponds to data within class G_j (proportion of poor).

Forcing the municipal *WBI* map to resemble the one from FHIS (maps on the left of figure 36.3) gives a result that was expected: it emphasizes poverty in Honduras, with a prevalence of very poor municipalities. One can immediately see

that targeting with this FHIS classification would miss a large number of rural municipalities from the viewpoint of the *WBI*. In the case of PUBN4, the "forced" map shares similar characteristics to FHIS's in the western part of the country, but there are significantly fewer municipalities that appear as "acceptable" (0.22–0.305), and more in the category "deficient" (0.305–0.69). Perhaps FHIS should include more indicators in its poverty map in order to account for various paths out of poverty that are somehow taken into account by the UBN4. The "forced *WBI*" map generates many more municipalities classified as "very bad" (0.536–0.72).

Various mapping approaches have different strengths and weaknesses. The optimum classification approach provides a picture that is less biased as we move across different poverty indicators (rightmost maps of figure 36.3). The *WBI* map presents less clustering than the other two, while PUBN4 shows large clusters in the poorer and richer categories, and little emphasis in the middle category. There is more consistency among the three maps concerning the categories representing the wealthier/better-off, which suggests that the poverty indicators used by FHIS and UBN4 correspond more to the rich than to the poor! Likewise, one has to keep in mind that if one finds that households with observable poverty-related attributes are geographically concentrated, this does not necessarily mean that there are poor areas, that is, spatial poverty traps. Strictly speaking, this would be revealed by an econometric analysis of household data that would include spatial variables (Ravallion and Jalan 2002).

The fact that the *WBI* map generates smaller patches seems to indicate that regional effects are less sizeable than we may expect for the rural poor in Honduras. This implies that in order to consider geography in poverty analysis and targeting, spatial variables will have to be updated and accurate. Ravallion and Wodon (1999) have found, in a study of household data in Bangladesh, that there are sizeable spatial differences in the returns to given household characteristics, which (if it applies to Honduras) would result in the observed diffuse geographical clustering of the *WBI*.

The degree of similarity between a reference

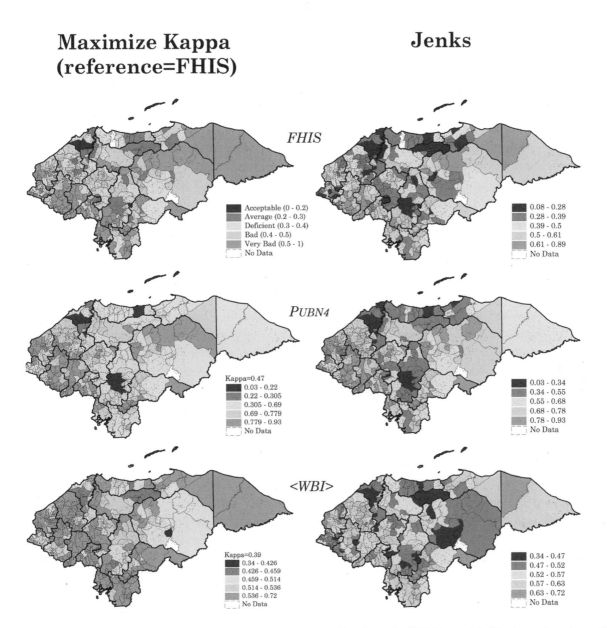

Maximize Kappa (reference=FHIS)

Jenks

FHIS

Acceptable (0 - 0.2)
Average (0.2 - 0.3)
Deficient (0.3 - 0.4)
Bad (0.4 - 0.5)
Very Bad (0.5 - 1)
No Data

0.08 - 0.28
0.28 - 0.39
0.39 - 0.5
0.5 - 0.61
0.61 - 0.89
No Data

PUBN4

Kappa=0.47
0.03 - 0.22
0.22 - 0.305
0.305 - 0.69
0.69 - 0.779
0.779 - 0.93
No Data

0.03 - 0.34
0.34 - 0.55
0.55 - 0.68
0.68 - 0.78
0.78 - 0.93
No Data

<WBI>

Kappa=0.39
0.34 - 0.426
0.426 - 0.459
0.459 - 0.514
0.514 - 0.536
0.536 - 0.72
No Data

0.34 - 0.47
0.47 - 0.52
0.52 - 0.57
0.57 - 0.63
0.63 - 0.72
No Data

Figure 36.3. Various representations of poverty at the municipal level, i.e. the FHIS (unsatisfied basic needs and nutrition), our PUBN4 (unsatisfied basic needs and education), and the locally derived well-being indicator (*WB*I). On the left, legend categories are constructed to minimize Cohen's kappa with respect to the FHIS map. On the right, we use the optimum classification strategy of Jenks (1976) to emphasize patterns in the data.

map and another map that is "forced" to match the reference, or between two maps using the same optimum classification strategy, gives an indication of the degree of similarity of each representation, and therefore the likeliness of conflicts that may arise by using one over the other.

Discussion

In the previous sections I have introduced general methods to represent the spatial patterns of

poverty, and I have shown some implications of the distortions to decision making resulting from the ways that aggregation and optimum classification of Honduras poverty are currently undertaken. In this next section we extend the analysis further and introduce new aspects of the use of microdata (i.e., highly disaggregated data, such as household surveys or censuses) through two application examples. In the first example, access to microdata allows one to anticipate the effect of a policy in a targeted investment context. In the second application, I describe the experience I have had with my colleagues in accessing and processing microdata through the World Wide Web.

A Simulation of the Prediction of the Impact of Poverty-targeting Programs

In Honduras, government poverty-alleviation strategies involve social spending for improving human capital and integrating the poor into the macro-economic framework (RH 2001). The government uses two approaches; the first is targeted toward the poor, and the second is uniform—that is, the same policy is applied independent of wealth. In targeted investments, the government must find where the poor are, and then they need to know if they are having any impact. The main targeted social investment program is administered by the FHIS, an entity created as a safety net added onto an aggressive structural adjustment program initiated in 1990. Founded by decree in 1990, FHIS was conceived as a social-compensation instrument directed primarily at alleviating poverty in the short term. It received clear instructions to use statistical information to target, monitor, and evaluate activities. The fund was originally conceived as a temporary agency, but its mandate was extended in 1994 and again in 1999 until 2012. Resources are allocated through demand-driven small-scale projects with more resources per capita being allocated to the poorest areas. FHIS is structured around four programs: (1) infrastructure, (2) basic need, (3) credit to the informal sector, and (4) credit and technical assistance.

To improve the targeting of its programs, FHIS developed a municipal-level poverty map based on indicators of unsatisfied basic needs (FHIS 1992; RH 1994, 2001) and started to use it as early as 1990. This was done in collaboration with Honduras Secretaria de Planificación, Coordinación y Presupuesto (SECPLAN). This was the first time census data was used for a detailed poverty study in Honduras. In 1994 FHIS produced another map as an unweighted sum of three indicators: the percentage of households without access to water, the percentage of households without access to basic sanitation, and the children's malnourishment rate.

As programs were being implemented different weights were given to the indicators (i.e., 40 percent to water, 20 percent to sanitation, 25 percent to malnourishment of children) and the allocation of resources changed accordingly (Von Gleich and Galvez 1999).

In the period 1990–95, the basic needs program invested $21.3 million out of the total poverty-alleviation budget of $65 million to the 118 poorest municipalities (Webb, Woo, and Sant'Anna 1995) in 646 subprojects that were executed by NGOs. Targeting helped FHIS succeed in helping the poor in areas not reached by social services delivered by the state (through uniform programs), and a decrease of the proportion of households lacking the basic needs addressed by FHIS has been observed.[7] FHIS chose to target at the municipal level because it often groups ethnohistorically related populations and because it represents the basic democratic perspective. There was a plan to produce poverty maps at a finer level as early as 1994, in a number of units (2,000–3,500) close to the village level, which was a major challenge at the time.[8]

Our approach would help target investment by anticipating the perception by the poor of actual poverty-reduction strategies. As an example, we analyze how targeting by FHIS gives different results from what would result from targeting based on well-being perceptions (i.e. the *WBI*). This is equivalent to running two parallel prioritizing exercises, one by FHIS and one by a group of poor people, and contrasting the results (which would eventually lead to a negotiation of tradeoffs). The indicators chosen by FHIS are quite different from the ones that were derived from local perceptions. If the poor themselves had had the opportunity of doing the exercise, they would have chosen something closer to our *WBI* maps. We can therefore examine how these different perceptions can be harmonized. As mentioned above, the FHIS basic needs program has funded projects in the poorest 40 percent of municipalities of the country (according to either their 1990 or 1994 poverty index).

Given various ways to contrast perceptions of targeted investment, one can quantify the degree of "hits" and "misses" on the target population of a policy based on a given perception. Two viewpoints are then compared: the one taken by the policy and related investments, and the one of the target population. For example, we can assess the impact of FHIS investments on the rural poor (according their index) by taking our *WBI* as the measure of poverty of the target population and estimating how they match.[9] If we take this particular example we would have three situations: (1) *coincident targeting*: the situation where a municipality would receive funding for social investment because it is considered poor in terms of the FHIS indicator, and the target population would perceive itself as poor (as estimated by *WBI*); (2) *leakage*: the situation where a municipality would receive funding for social investment because it is considered poor in terms of the FHIS indicator, but the target population did *not* perceive itself as poor; (3) *undercoverage*: the situation where a municipality would *not* receive funding for social investment because it is *not* considered poor in terms of the FHIS indicator, but the target population in fact perceived itself as poor (as estimated by *WBI*). The maps of figure 36.4 show how social investments by FHIS or *WBI* would be distributed in the 40 percent of poorest municipalities.[10]

Using the same example (FHIS targeting and impact measured by measuring coincident targeting with *WBI*) a synthetic measure of impact can be obtained by counting, for a given target of poor municipalities (according to FHIS ranking), the number of poor households for which targeting is coincident with local perceptions (according to *WBI* ranking), and divide this number by the number of poor in the targeted municipalities according to local perceptions. The variation of this impact measure in function of the target threshold (percentage of poor municipalities in which to invest) is displayed on the graphs at the bottom right of figure 36.4, for rural poor target (top-left graph) as well as rural *and* urban poor target (bottom-left graph). The dashed line corresponds to the case of a uniform (i.e., nontargeted) policy, and the dotted line to the case of perfect targeting (e.g., FHIS targeting policy based on the same index as the one used for targeting). Deviation above the dashed line

indicates the improvement over a uniform policy that would be expected by using a given poverty index for targeting.[11] On the leftmost graph we look at a situation close to the actual one: targeting with FHIS, while the poor perceive themselves differently, according to the *WBI*. On the rightmost graph, we look at the reverse situation: how the impact of a policy that would be based on *WBI* would be perceived by a target population whose actual poverty would be more in agreement with the FHIS index.

If we look at the leftmost graphs of figure 36.4 (i.e., the expected impact of a policy based on FHIS) we find only a small improvement over a uniform (or random) policy from the viewpoint of the perceptions of the rural poor. However, if we assume that the *WBI* applies to all poor, including urban ones,[12] the improvement would be minimal in the case of the worst 40 percent of municipalities, and we would see a worsening for the better-off! Targeting with the *WBI* (rightmost graphs) seems to be a much better alternative overall in the case where the FHIS criteria is used to measure the target population: it provides a significant improvement of impact over a uniform or random strategy for both the rural and urban cases.

The capacity to estimate the effect of uniform versus targeted social investments can help the implementation of an effective Honduras poverty-reduction strategy, which at this time seems to be moving in favor of uniform investment strategies, in the very tradition of neoclassical economics (RH 2001). The "politically naive" models of targeted investments (everyone agrees that giving more money to the poor is a good thing) or uniform investments (because of assumed neoclassical economics efficiency) could be vastly improved by adding a political feasibility constraint, such as that proposed by Gelbach and Pritchett (1997), in which the total budget to allocate to pro-poor policies varies with the priorities of voters.

A User-friendly Database in Practice

We believe that three factors have contributed to an underuse of census data in Honduras. First, there was no mechanism to insure that the central government's actions would actually be

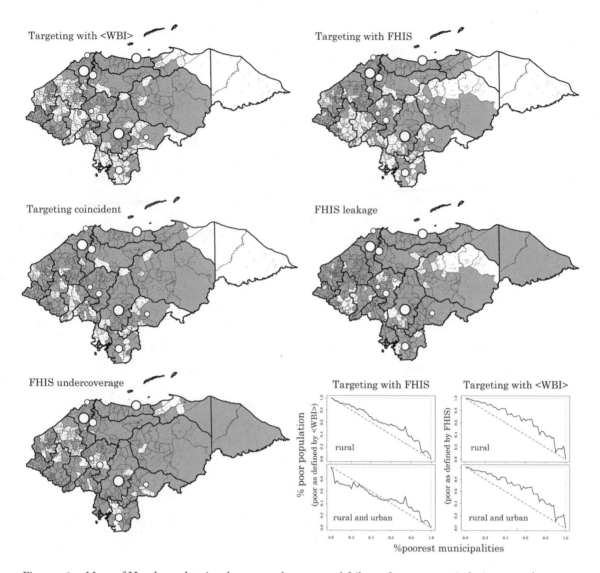

Figure 36.4. Maps of Honduras showing the expected success and failure of two poverty indexing procedures. Municipalities are highlighted in white if they are among the poorest 40 percent, according to *WBI* (targeting with *WBI*); if they are among the 40 percent poorest according to FHIS (targeting with FHIS); if they are poor according to FHIS and to *WBI* (targeting coincident); if they are poor in terms of FHIS but not in terms of *WBI* (FHIS leakage); if they are poor in terms of *WBI* but not in terms of FHIS (FHIS undercoverage). On the bottom right, ex-ante impact plots: plots of the number of poor (urban and rural) potentially reached (y axis), as measured by one indicator, by a policy that would target a given proportion of the poorest municipalities (x axis), as measured by another indicator.

implemented at the village level, so the need for data at this level has never been a pressing issue.[13] Second, processing and publishing data and maps have traditionally made for tedious work, which implies that since the exercise had been done once by the central government there was no one to reconsider the need to generate an alternative map afterward. Nationwide household and village-level databases can become very cumbersome to manage and difficult to interpret, partly because of the traditional high costs of the data-processing

infrastructure, which is especially difficult to afford for a developing country. Third, the old adage "information is power" is probably key to many who have little interest in sharing their information with the rest of the civil society. Information technology helps to address the first two factors, but can become problematic in the third case. Thus there is a need to mandate that the data be made publicly available.

Those who use data to help decision making do not often perceive its limited availability as a constraint. Few decision makers are aware of the implications of working with data that is chosen and aggregated by someone else for some other purpose. In addition, the data are aggregated to a scale imposed by predefined boundaries, which leads to a phenomenon known as the "ecological fallacy" (Robinson 1950; Openshaw 1984). The ecological fallacy arises when area-level aggregate statistics are used to obtain information that is subsequently assumed to apply at the level of individuals. Openshaw and Taylor (1981) showed that changing the boundaries of the areas within which data is aggregated has a drastic effect on the results of statistical analysis of this aggregated data, which questions the validity of any analysis done based on data for predefined administrative units. However Tranmer and Steel (1998) propose an approach that allows for within-area homogeneity and correct aggregate-level statistics. Recently, these authors have shown that a multilevel model (i.e., with data aggregated at various levels) preserves the variation at a given level provided other levels are included in the model (Tranmer and Steel 2001). Therefore, it is always better to use the finest scale possible and be very careful when working with aggregated data.

Information technology is now mature enough to permit the design of user-friendly databases to simplify operations and provide smaller and lighter, aggregated data sets according to fixed or user-defined areal units. The pioneering work of Openshaw and Turton (1995) and Turton and Openshaw (1995) demonstrated the feasibility of a low-cost system to query, interpret, and process raw census data (in this case the 1991 UK SAR). The existence of open source software communities, combined with the arithmetic increase of computer performance/price ratio and internet bandwidth, provide a unique opportunity for people in developing countries to process and share its data efficiently and at low cost.

In just three weeks two students have programmed a Web interface to demonstrate to our partners the feasibility of a low-cost, secure system that allows a nonexpert user to process raw census data (Bleuse and Vallejo 2001). Processing options include: (1) the generation of summary statistics (mean, standard deviation, min., max.); (2) headcount indicators (percentage of variable X with respect to variable Y); (3) Composite indicators (weighted linear combination of several variables); (4) user-defined SQL query; (5) help/tutorial; (6) metadata. Queries can be performed on any of the census variables, and aggregation levels range from *caserio* to village, municipality, and department[14]; results are downloadable. Possibilities for such a simple interface are countless. For example, it would make it easy for an institution such as FHIS to target infrastructure investments by computing (option 3 above) a village-level distribution of housing types based on a user-defined housing quality index from roof, floor, and wall type. It also allows for sensitivity analysis, by providing the flexibility of varying the composition of indexes and their level of aggregation, which results in a better appreciation of the robustness, or lack thereof, of the results (and therefore of the policy that is derived from these results).

In case the Honduras government decides to provide access to only a sample of individual census records, such as in the 2 percent sample of anonymized records (SAR) of the UK (Dale 1998), sample size should be large if we are interested in village-level information, given the number of small rural villages in Honduras (75 percent have a population of less than a thousand). However, a sample of this size will not be small enough to preserve anonymity (Duke-Williams and Rees 1998). In this case, one could embed the SAR (or better: the raw data) in the data processing, which would correct aggregate-level statistics in a way that is invisible to a user (Tranmer and Steel 1998; Charlton 1998; Williamson et al. 1998). Duke-Williams and Rees (1998) give useful recommendations about safe strategies for publishing census data. In that case, methods for processing data would be provided as well; it would be important to provide assistance in selecting a method and understanding its domain of application.

The combination of Apache (the Web server), MySQL (the RDBM manager), and PHP (the Web interface to MySQL) has proven to be a powerful, easy-to-implement, stable, and free alternative to large commercial systems. National statistics or planning institutes of developing countries may have the financial resources, which are often obtained by contracting a loan with a development bank, to rely on an expensive system and therefore may not be interested in the risk associated with open source and free software. Smaller organizations such as municipalities (more and more, in an increasingly decentralized world), could implement a low-cost Web-based RDBM system with subsets or anonymized samples of the census raw data, in addition to their own data. In any case the support of the open-source community may be more appropriate than the one that large corporations are selling.

Although the Web is currently flooded with "dumb" map servers, few applications in statistical cartography have seen the light of day, and they are mostly experimental ones (Andrienko and Andrienko 1999; Peterson 1999; Cartwright 1999; Carr, MacEachern, and Scott 2000; Winter and Neumann 2000; Gaborit 2000). Statistical cartography involves complex design constraints: Internet bandwidth, concurrent processes, display resolution and swiftness, choice of statistical routines and graphical representations. While giant technological progresses are happening in the Internet world, the best opportunities for developing countries are still pieces of code running on a personal computer (Gondard and Mazurek 1999; Mazurek 2002). Nevertheless, improvements in technology will not preclude us from understanding better the cognitive process involved in the production, reading, and use of a statistical map (see Mark et al. 1999 for a review of cognitive models of geographical space).

Such systems will have to be stuffed with data aggregation and data mining tools and a capacity to define new areal units, in order to give to people with diverse interests the security and freedom needed to make sense of the large amount of information that represents raw census and small-area data sets (Fisher 1986). There are many more ways to aggregate data than proportions and univariate statistics: Gini coefficients, concentration index, location index, shift and share analysis (Krumme 1969) add a lot to the understanding of socioeconomics. Complex microeconomic studies can be

realized on the basis of raw census data (King and Bolsdon 1998; Deaton 1997).

Because of the connection between the local and the regional the best practice is to work with various aggregation levels simultaneously (Subramanian, Duncan, and Jones 2001; Morehart, Murtagh, and Starck 1999; Tranmer and Steel, 2001). Examples of multiscale analysis with village-level PUBN3 and PUBN4 can be found in Leclerc, Nelson, and Knapp (2000), for one, detecting the presence of child mortality hotspots, and the correlation of poverty with environmental risk, which analysis can be done reliably only with small area data. Turton and Nelson (2001) have also studied mortality rates in Honduras by applying tools of the Geographic Analysis Machine to raw population census data (Openshaw 1987; Openshaw et al. 1987).

Adding Data-mining Capacity for Knowledge Discovery

As stressed before, the choice of aggregation scale matters as much as the choice of indicator. Aggregation at predefined scales such as administrative units imposes a great deal of difficulty when cause-effect relationships are sought. With poverty data mapped at the village level, however, geographical analysis becomes more reliable. Then any correlations between poverty and other variables such as environment ones, if any, will appear more clearly. I will briefly introduce two methods for geographic analysis that have been tested on a range of problems, including poverty, to show the potential of microdata (highly disaggregated data such as poverty data mapped at village level) for multiscale analysis. The first one allows computing the probability of finding poor villages based on an independent variable. The second allows detecting geographical clusters of poverty, that is, spatial poverty traps.

Poverty and environmental risk

In this example, we start with a classic hypothesis: "poverty is related to environmental risk." We use the PUBN3 and PUBN4 as poverty indicators, and water budget as an indicator of environmental risk and an approach inspired by Skidmore (1998). Given a map of categorical variables used as explanation of poverty, $N(i)$ the total number of villages—and $N_p(i)$ the number of poor villages—that that are located within a map category i, the excess probability of being poor is given by:

$$P(i) = \frac{Np(i)}{\sum_i Np(i)} - \frac{N(i)}{\sum_i N(i)}$$

In other words, we start with a map containing a certain number of categories (here we have five categories corresponding to meaningful water budget ranges), we count the number of poor villages within each category, and compare the proportion with an estimate of what it should be if there was no correlation (i.e., random distribution). If the number of villages exceeds what is expected from random sampling in this area, we conclude that a village has a non-null probability of being poor if located in this area. The results obtained by averaging the probabilities computed from monthly water budget maps are shown at the bottom of figure 36.5. On the starplots of figure 36.5, we find that probabilities (about 5 percent in the case of PUBN3) are higher when the poverty index chosen is PUBN4 (about 10–15 percent). This is surprising: education should not, a priori, correlate well with water budget![15] In addition, we see from the starplots that there are more poor villages in areas and periods where the water risk is nonexistent (the green lines) in potentially very productive areas. This may have a simple explanation: children form a good part of the working force in Honduras's agricultural areas, and the number of dropouts is alarmingly high. In fact, the World Bank financed a basic education project with the Honduras Instituto de Desarrollo Agrario in 1995, the strategy of which was as follows: "To reduce the high dropout rates among rural children, the project . . . will adjust the school calendar to take into account the harvest period in agricultural regions." Our spatial data analysis technique has permitted us to highlight this more complex phenomenon.

Spatial clustering

Our second example is the application to Honduras census data of the Geographic Analysis Machine (GAM) (Openshaw 1987; Openshaw et al. 1987), a powerful public-domain tool that has been developed to identify significant spatial clustering from point data. It has been applied, for example, to the difficult problem of locating significant clusters of rare disease cases. It is essentially a multiple statistical testing on a population distributed in points in space. GAM works by examining a large number of circles of varying sizes distributed on a regular grid covering the area of interest. The radius of the circles determines the scale of analysis. Two sets of data are retrieved from the points falling in each circle: one set represents a population "at risk," and the other set represents the population of cases for which we want to determine if there is significant spatial clustering. Then a test of significance is applied to compare both distributions. In the case of poverty, we may use the number of households as population at risk (of being poor), and the number of poor households for which we want to test for significant spatial clustering. If there are significantly more poor people than suggested by the sampled population,[16] the degree of significance is assigned to the location corresponding to the center of the circle. The procedure is repeated for all circles, and this generates a surface representing the degree of significance of clustering. Figure 36.6 (a and c) shows the results obtained for the village-level PUBN3 and PUBN4 for circles with up to 20 km radius. These maps highlight significant clusters (i.e., poverty hotspots), which tend to be found in the southwest, which suggests that we have a closer look at this region. They can be used to study the possible correlations of poverty with any independent variables at a similar scale. In figure 36.6 (b and d) we show the result of GAM applied to identify hotspots where data was not sufficient to compute the UBNs. In this case, we see that they correspond essentially to densely populated areas. Figure 36.6 (e and f) shows the location of hotspots of illiteracy in men and women; subtracting the two maps gives the hotspot distribution of illiteracy gender imbalance (figure 36.6g). One could systematically process a large number of indicators this way to identify areas that require immediate attention.

Turton and Nelson (2001) have also studied mortality rates in Honduras with a version of GAM

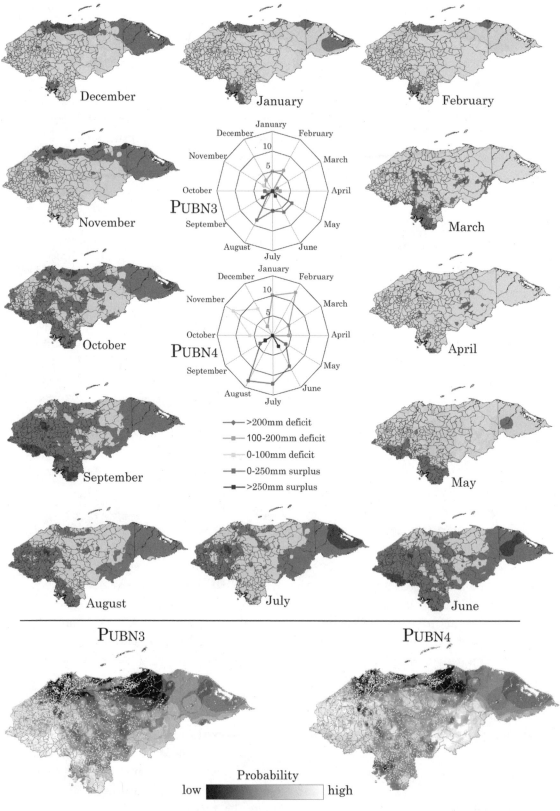

Figure 36.5. Probability of finding a poor village (using poverty index PUBN3 or PUBN4) within a given water budget class (outer ring of maps). (a) Probability maps: the lighter the shade the higher the yearly average probability. (b) Radar plots: monthly probability by water budget category (the color of the lines corresponds to the one of the water budget map legends). See website for color originals.

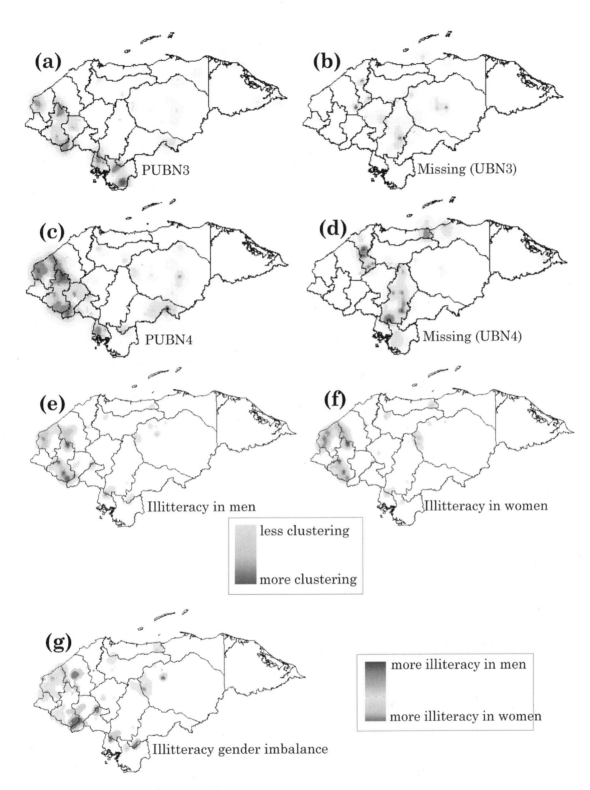

Figure 36.6. Geographic Analysis Machine (GAM) analysis applied to the village-level PUBN3 and PUBN4 (a and c) and to the proportion of village data that was missing to compute the UBNs (b and d). Illiteracy in men (e) and women (f). (g) Illitteracy gender imbalance: map (e) minus map (f). Darker areas correspond to more significant clustering.

that accounts for other dimensions, in addition to the geographical coordinates, such as time (Openshaw 1994:5). McGill and Openshaw (1998) have combined GAM with artificial life techniques (flocks) for computationally efficient pattern detection algorithms.

Conclusion

The observed divergence of the paths to poverty-alleviation policy and action that are taken by different development actors calls for more participation, negotiation, and learning (Brock, Cornwall, and Gaventa 2001; McGee and Brock 2001). Many new initiatives invest heavily on horizontal networking (some with participation of the poor) with an emphasis on information and communication technology. Therefore, I have explored ways to bring together different perspectives on poverty, with a focus on quantification, data processing, visualization, and use. I have tried to demonstrate the great value-adding potential of microdata such as raw censuses and presented examples on how the research products and information technology can be mobilized to bring transparency and rigor to the process. My goal was not to find the causes of poverty or explain its distribution (we think Hondurans are much better positioned to do so) but to provide the means to reduce or at least control the inevitable *lie*—deliberate or not—carried by data, maps, and statistics, and the conflicts that these biases generate. I wished to provide tools for those who need an alternative to neoclassical economics for making decisions about how to attempt to deal with poverty. Simply dumping money into an area with the hope that some will find its way to the poor is very different from being able to find and explicitly target the poor and communicate with them. This chapter attempts to show how that might be done.

The new Honduras poverty-reduction strategy, a requirement of the World Bank and IMF program that somehow includes an emphasis on the need for government responsibilities for policy design and social investment, foresees an increased role of municipalities, communities, and NGOs, as well as the private sector, in poverty reduction. It does not address specifically the way information technology will be harnessed to help this emerging process of practical democracy. I hope that this chapter provides elements of an answer that will prove useful, especially in the context of the 2001 population and housing census, a gold mine of important information that no player in Honduras can afford to underutilize.

Acknowledgments

Apache, MySQL, PHP, and S-PLUS are registered trademarks.

I thank the Dirección General de Estadística y Censo of Honduras for providing the unit-level census data used in this study; and SECPLAN, which provided the georeferenced village database and FHIS poverty data. Special thanks to Nicolas Bleuse and Sergio Vallejo, who developed the Web interface to census data in record time, and to Andrew Nelson for GAM analysis. I appreciate the commitment of the Institut de Recherche Pour l'Ingénierie de l'Agriculture et de l'Environnement (CEMAGREF), CIRAD, and IRD, which hosted me in their Montpellier installations. Hubert Mazurek from IRD was key in introducing me to statistical cartography.

I would like to acknowledge the contribution of Stan Openshaw, who has generously put into the public domain several spatial analysis tools that he has developed.

This work has been partly funded by the Consultative Group for International Agricultural research, the Dutch Trust Fund for methodological support to ecoregional programs, and the Inter-American Development Bank.

Notes

1. Of course, there are other factors that affect people's wealth; however, we should not be too proud of our science if it directs poverty alleviation programs to the wrong people.

2. It is also possible to relax the constraint on the number of classes.

3. In fact, both approaches give different results. It is safer to combine them than to select one or the other.

4. This number corresponds roughly to the percentage of households with unsatisfied basic needs.

5. We use a double-ended pattern, a sequence of colors from blue to orange, where the saturation for the two

hues is greatest for rates at the extremes of the rate distribution.

6. The Booth poverty map uses the following classification:

> Black: Lowest class. Vicious, semicriminal.
> Dark blue: Very poor, casual. Chronic want.
> Light blue: Poor. 18s. to 21s. a week for
>   a moderate family
> Purple: Mixed. Some comfortable others poor.
> Pink: Fairly comfortable. Good ordinary earnings.
> Red: Middle class. Well-to-do.
> Yellow: Upper-middle and upper classes. Wealthy.

7. Surprisingly, school education, which was strongly addressed by FHIS projects, was not one of the indicators used for their poverty maps.

8. We have not heard about the existence of this map, but FHIS seems to be moving to village-level targeting (RH 2001).

9. This is indeed close to the actual situation in Honduras.

10. Note that FHIS considers total poor (urban and rural) whereas the WBI concerns only local perceptions by the rural poor.

11. We suppose that targeted investments are uniform within a municipality.

12. This is, strictly speaking, incorrect; in effect, the sampling for defining the well-being indicators, as well as for computing them from the census, was restricted to rural villages.

13. This is changing with decentralization of responsibilities to municipalities and the increased involvement of NGOs, in all sectors including the ones related to poverty reduction (RH 2001). However, while the issue of empowerment of local decision-makers is becoming key to sustainable development, only the central government has access to disaggregated census data and the capabilities to process it.

14. To enforce privacy, the minimum aggregation level is the caserio.

15. Remember that PUBN4 is identical to PUBN3 except that it includes an extra indicator related to education.

16. Suppose that the number of poor corresponds to a random sampling of the population of households. Then we can say that there is no significant clustering.

References

Andrienko, G. L., and N. V. Andrienko. 1999. Interactive maps for visual data exploration. *International Journal of Geographical Information Science* 13, no. 4: 355–74.

Baker, J. L., and M. E. Grosh. 1994. Poverty reduction through geographic targeting: How well does it work? *World Development* 22, no. 7: 983–95.

Bergeron, G., S. S. Morris, and J. M. Medina Banegas. 1998. How reliable are group informant ratings? A test of food security rating in Honduras. Discussion Paper No. 43, Food Consumption and Nutrition Division, IFPRI.

Bleuse, N., and S. Vallejo. 2001. Mise en place d'une interface web Pour interroger la base de données des recensements du Honduras. Rapport Technique Mastère SILAT, CIAT.

Boltvinik, J. 1996. Poverty in Latin America: A critical analysis of three studies. *International Social Science Journal* 148:245–60.

Brewer, C. A., and R. B. McMaster. 1999. The state of academic cartography. *Cartography and Geographic Information Science* 26, no. 3: 215–34.

Brock, K., A. Cornwall, and J. Gaventa. 2001. Power, knowledge and political spaces in the framing of poverty policies. Working Paper 143, Institute of Development Studies.

Brunet, R. 1987. *La carte: Mode d'emploi*. Paris: Fayard.

Burns, P. J. 1998. S poetry. www.burns-stat.com.

Carr, D. B., A. MacEachern, and D. Scott. 2000. Digital Government Quality Graphics research project. www.geovista.psu.edu/grants/dg-qg/intro.html.

Carr, D. B., A. R. Olsen, S. M. Pierson, and Y. P. Courbois. 1998. Boxplot variations in a spatial context: An Omernik ecoregion and weather example. *Statistical Computing and Statistical Graphics Newsletter* 9, no. 2: 4–13.

Cartwright, W. 1999. Extending the map metaphor using web delivery multimedia. *International Journal of Geographical Information Science* 13, no. 4: 335–53.

Carvalho, S., and H. White. 1997. Combining the quantitative and qualitative approaches to poverty measurement and analysis: The practice and potential. World Bank Technical Paper 366. Washington, D.C.: World Bank.

Charlton, J. 1998. Use of the census samples of anonymised records (SARs) and survey data in combination to obtain estimates at local authority level. *Environment and Planning A* 30:775–84.

Cohen, J. 1960. A coefficient of agreement for nominal scales. *Educational and Psychological Measurement* 20:37–46.

———. 1968. Weighted kappa: Nominal scale agreement with provision for scaled disagreement or partial credit. *Psychological Bulletin* 70:213–20.

Cromley, R. G. 1996. A comparison of optimal classification strategies for choroplethic displays of statistically aggregated data. *International Journal of Geographical Information Science* 10, no. 4: 405–24.

Dale, A. 1998. The value of the SARs in spatial and area-level research. *Environment and Planning A* 30:767–74.

Deaton, A. 1997. *The Analysis of Household Surveys: A Microeconomic Approach to Development Policy.* Baltimore: Johns Hopkins University Press.

Duke-Williams, O., and P. Rees. 1998. Can census offices publish statistics for more than one small area geography? An analysis of the differencing problem in statistical disclosure. *International Journal of Geographical Information Science* 12, no. 6: 579–605.

FHIS (Fondo Hondureño de Inversión Social). 1992. *Presupuesto de inversión 1992–1993.* Tegucigalpa: Presidencia de la República de Honduras.

Fisher, F. M. 1986. Statisticians, econometricians, and adversary proceedings. *Journal of the American Statistical Association* 81:277–86.

Gaborit, G. 2000. La cartographie dynamique sur le Net avec SVG. http://svgmap.free.fr.

Gelbach, J. B., and L. H. Pritchett. 1997. More for the poor is less for the poor: The politics of targeting. World Bank Policy Research Working Paper 1799. Washington, D.C.: World Bank.

Glewwe, P., and J. Van der Gaag. 1988. Confronting poverty in developing countries: Definitions, information, and policies. LSMS Working Paper 48. Washington, D.C.: World Bank.

Gondard, P. and H. Mazurek. 1999. *El espacio andino: Territorio, sociedad, economía.* Lima: IRD.

Hubert, L., and P. Arabie. 1985. Comparing partitions. *Journal of Classification* 2:193–218.

Jenks, G. F. 1976. Contemporary statistical maps-evidence of spatial and graphic ignorance. *American Cartographer* 3:11–19.

———. 1977. Optimal classification for choropleth maps. Occasional Paper No. 2, Department of Geography, University of Kansas.

Jenks, G. F., and F. C. Caspall. 1971. Error on choroplethic maps: Definition, measurement, reduction. *Annals of the Association of American Geographers* 61:217–44.

Kanbur, R., R. Chambers, P. Petesch, N. Uphoff, F. Bourguignon, D. Sahn, C. Moser, et al., eds. 2001. *Qualitative and Quantitative Poverty Appraisal: Complementarities, Tensions and the Way Forward.* Contributions to a workshop held at Cornell University, 15–16 March 2001.

King, D., and D. Bolsdon. 1998. Using the SARs to add policy value to household projections. *Environment and Planning A* 30:867–80.

Krumme, G. 1969. Identifying regional economic change: A variation of the theme "shift and share." *Canadian Geographer* 13, no. 1: 76–80.

Lark, R. M. 1998. Forming spatially coherent regions by classification of multivariate data: An example from the analysis of maps of crop yields. *International Journal of Geographical Information Science* 12, no. 1: 83–98.

Leclerc, G., A. Nelson, and E. B. Knapp. 2000. Extension of GIS through poverty mapping: The use of unit-level census data. In M. Kokubun, S. Ushida, and K. Tsurumi, eds., *6th JIRCAS International Symposium: GIS Applications for Agro-Environmental Issues in Developing Regions*, 163–82. Tsukuba, Japan: JIRCAS/MAFF.

Mark, D. M., C. Freska, S. Hirtle, R. Lloyd, and B. Tversky. 1999. Cognitive models of geographical space. *International Journal of Geographical Information Science* 13, no. 8: 747–74.

Mazurek, H. 2002. CABRAL 1500: Logiciels de cartographie statistique. User's manual, Version 1.0–2.0.

McGee, R. 1999. Technical, objective, equitable and uniform? A critique of the Colombian system for the selection of beneficiaries of social programs, SISBEN. IDPM Working Paper No. 57, Institute for Development Policy and Management, University of Manchester.

McGee, R. and K. Brock. 2001. From poverty assessment to policy changes: Actors and data. Working Paper 133, Institute of Development Studies, Brighton, England.

McGill, J., and S. Openshaw. 1998. The use of flocks to drive a geographic analysis machine. www.geocomputation.org/1998/24/gc24_01.htm.

Monmonnier, M. 1996. *How to Lie with Maps.* 2nd ed. Chicago: University of Chicago Press.

Morehart, M., F. Murtagh, and J-L. Starck. 1999. Spatial representation of economic and financial measures used in agriculture via wavelet analysis. *International Journal of Geographical Science* 13, no. 6: 557–76.

Murray, A. T., and T-K. Shyy. 2000. Integrating attribute and space characteristics in choropleth display and spatial data mining. *International Journal of Geographical Information Science* 14, no. 7: 649–67.

Naesset, E. 1996. Use of the weighted kappa coefficient in classification error assessment of thematic maps. *International Journal of Geographical Information Science* 10, no. 5: 591–604.

Openshaw, S. 1984. Ecological fallacies and the analysis of areal census data. *Environment and Planning A* 16:17–31.

———. 1987. An automated geographical analysis system. *Environment and Planning A* 19:431–36.

Openshaw, S., and P. J. Taylor. 1981. The modifiable areal unit problem. In N. Wrigley and R. J. Bennett, eds., *Quantitative Geography: A British View*, 60–69. London: Routledge.

Openshaw, S., and I. Turton. 1996. New opportunities for geographical census analysis using individual level data. *Area* 28, no. 2: 167–76.

Openshaw, S., M. Charlton, C. Wymer, and A. W. Craft. 1987. *A mark I geographical analysis machine for the automated analysis of point data sets. International Journal of Geographic Information Science* 1:335–58.

Paes de Barros, R. 2000. Honduras: Un diagnóstico social. Rio de Janeiro: IPEA.

Peterson, M. P. 1999. Active legends for interactive cartographic animation. *International Journal of Geographical Information Science* 13, no. 4: 375–83.

Ravallion, M. 2001. Can qualitative methods help quantitative poverty measurement? In R. Kanbur et al., eds., *Qualitative and Quantitative Poverty Appraisal: Complementarities, Tensions and the Way Forward*. Contributions to a workshop held at Cornell University, 15–16 March 2001.

Ravallion, M., and J. Jalan. 2002. Geographic poverty traps? A micro model of consumption growth in rural China. *Journal of Applied Econometrics* 17:329–46.

Ravallion, M., and M. Lokshin. 2001. Identifying welfare effects from subjective questions. *Economica* 68:335–57.

Ravallion, M., and Q. Wodon. 1999. Poor areas, or only poor people? *Journal of Regional Science* 39, no. 4: 689–711.

Ravnborg, H. M. 1999. Assessing rural poverty: A practical method for identifying, extrapolating, and quantifying local perceptions of rural poverty. Cali, Colombia: CIAT.

RH (República de Honduras). 1994. *Honduras, Libro Q: Potencial, potencialidad y focalización municipal*. 2nd ed. Tegucigalpa: República de Honduras.

———. 2001. *Estrategia para la reducción de la pobreza*. Tegucigalpa: República de Honduras.

Robinson, A. H. 1950. Ecological correlation and the behavior of individuals. *American Sociological Review* 15:351–57.

Subramanian, S. V., C. Duncan, and K. Jones. 2001. Multilevel perspectives on modeling census data. *Environment and Planning A* 33, no. 3: 399–417.

Tranmer, M., and D. G. Steel. 1998. Using census data to investigate the causes of the ecological fallacy. *Environment and Planning A* 30:817–31.

———. 2001. Ignoring a level in a multilevel model: Evidence from UK census data. *Environment and Planning A* 33:941–48.

Tufte, E. R. 1983. *The Visual Display of Quantitative Information*. Cheshire, Conn.: Graphics Press.

———. 1990. *Envisioning Information*. Cheshire, Conn.: Graphics Press.

———. 1997. *Visual Explanations*. Cheshire, Conn.: Graphics Press.

Tukey, J. W. 1977. Some thoughts on clinical trials, especially problems of multiplicity. *Science* 198, no. 4318: 679–84.

Turton, I., and A. Nelson. 2000. Honduras mortality: The effect of location and time. Paper presented at the international workshop: Scale effects in decision making for ecoregional development, 4–6 July 2000. San José, Costa Rica.

Turton, I., and S. Openshaw. 1995. Putting the 1991 census sample of anonymised records on your Unix workstation. *Environment and Planning A* 27:391–411.

Van Beurden, A. U. C. J., and W. J. A. M. Douven. 1999. Aggregation issues of spatial information in environmental research. *International Journal of Geographical Information Science* 13, no. 5: 513–27.

Van Praag, B. M. S. 1968. *Individual Welfare Functions and Consumer Behavior*. Amsterdam: North-Holland.

Von Gleich, U., and E. Galvez. 1999. Pobreza étnica en Honduras. Report, Unidad de Pueblos Indigenas y Desarrollo Comunitario, Banco Interamericano de Desarrollo.

Webb, A. K. V., L. K. Woo, and A. M. Sant'Anna. 1995. The participation of non-governmental organizations in poverty alleviation: A case study of the Honduras social investment fund. World Bank Discussion Paper 295. Washington, D.C.: World Bank.

Williamson, P., M. Birkin, and P. Rees. 1998. The estimation of population microdata using data from small area statistics and samples of anonymised records. *Environment and Planning A* 30:785–816.

Winter, A., and A. Neumann. 2000. Cartographers on the Net: Scalable vector graphics. www.carto.net/papers/svg.

Chapter 37

Chapter 37

Postscript

The Elephants in the Living Room

Charles A. S. Hall and Grégoire Leclerc

Anyone who has managed to make it through this book, or indeed any significant part of it, must be pretty tired of learning about the many failures of conventional economics and of economic development to date, the remaining problems of the poor and of the environment, and the rather diffuse and perhaps insufficient biophysical tools that we bring to bear on making development work. We think that we owe the readers, especially those from the developing countries themselves, a summary of what we think we have learned from the previous chapters, along with a set of rules by which development might be undertaken so that people actually benefit. We wish to emphasize that these, too, are not offered as a necessary prescription for success, but rather as an alternative viewpoint that we think might be very useful for increasing the probabilities for success while avoiding the almost certain prescriptions for failure that we, and others, believe are characteristic of many development plans to date. This might be considered a rather extreme statement, but while we were finishing this book, the important and thoughtful developmental ecologist William Easterly came out with another book that chronicles, again, the many failures of development despite the West's investment of some \$2.3 trillion (Easterly 2005). What is most astonishing to us is what we believe this book has shown in many chapters and in many ways: that the most important issues in development, and the most important scientific tools in our arsenal for possibly designing some kind of development scheme that has a chance of working, are not even on the agenda of most development plans or in the toolboxes of the development agencies. We call these failures to include or focus on the obvious non-economic issues the "elephants in the living room," meaning that there is something very large and very obvious, but that no one talks about out of embarrassment or ignorance, because of their academic training, or just because it seems too difficult to handle.

Elephants and Scientists

We are two older natural scientists who have been involved with development issues for most of our lives. We have watched much of the less-developed world become economically poorer (or at least not richer when that should have been the case), more dependent upon resources from outside their boundaries, more beholden to policies designed by others far away and, generally, much more disparate in their own internal distribution of wealth. In addition, we have watched an enormous diminution of environmental quality, both in terms of resources that support economies directly and, in addition, resources not so closely connected with the economy. This is despite the fact that we have spent much of our lives in association with institutions whose purpose has been to improve the lot of the poor. It is not that there have not been successes. In fact there have been many, but even these have mostly just passed the poor on by.

Our experiences and those of our colleagues are found throughout this book. We think that there are many reasons for hope that we can do a better job. Obviously, we think that science and the scientific method (as applied to both natural and social sciences, and our preference, which is for a synthesis of both) make for a more powerful tool than ideology for guiding development. What follows are some explicit things that we think we have learned from our lives and especially from writing and editing this book.

1. Beware of "silver bullets" (the mythical tools of the Lone Ranger, a mythical horseman of the old American West familiar to most older Americans). If some development scheme looks too good to be true (as with shrimp in Ecuador, textiles in Costa Rica, and uranium in Niger), it probably is. While such schemes can bring large immediate profits, they are often of a very limited net value when viewed over a longer period, and they tend to encourage increased reliance on expensive and often politically constraining imports rather than true development. As we elaborated in detail in part 1, we think that a great deal of the economics that has been used to guide development is fatally flawed, and it is only by replacing or supplementing conventional economics with good natural science and a systems approach that we can have any hope of achieving lasting—and, at least to some degree, sustainable—development goals.

2. As part of this, good economic analysis usually should have a spatial component. But, in the world of one economist whose work we do like, "there is almost no spatial analysis in mainstream economics" (Krugman, 1995). Many chapters here and in Hall (2000) show how spatial economics can be done.

3. While we are extremely suspicious of much theory within conventional neoclassical economics, we do believe in many prudent and important practices that are part of good economic and financial standards. These include fiscal discipline, watchdog agencies on public and private corruption, and good business accounting standards.

4. Investments must be looked at from a longer time perspective, implying the need to modify or even stop using discounted analysis. For countries without fossil fuels and/or an industrial base, the requirements of foreign exchange to pay for the inputs that the investments will probably entail must be looked at very carefully. For example, investing in nontraditional crops or ecotourism, which many view as very desirable alternatives to conventional investments, implies large expenditures for agrochemicals or minibuses and the fuel to run them, Western-standard bathroom fixtures and water heaters, and so on while shunning local, low-cost, or original initiatives. Whether such approaches can be sustained in a future of almost certain increases in the price of oil is doubtful.

5. In the same vein, a very important concept is that of net foreign exchange—that is, the amount of money gleaned from an operation after the expenses have been paid. For example, in Costa Rica, about one dollar's worth of petrochemicals is required to grow bananas that would fetch two dollars at dockside. So although in the 1990s bananas generated about $600 million a year of foreign exchange for Costa Rica, the country gained only about half that when corrected for the cost of the inputs.

6. The scale of investments is also critical. "Microcredit," or small loans, often to women, have shown some important positive results.

7. The "West," including scientists from the West, often brings in great ideas for generating "solutions" to age-old problems. Sometimes there is a certain arrogance to this, whereas the local people, unsophisticated in "modern" methods of agriculture or resource management, may actually have a better plan for long-term resource management, including simply not having the tools to overexploit the resource base. For example, a great deal of Western agricultural expertise went into developing the agriculture of Costa Rica, and it indeed raised productivity, but only at the expense of making the country nearly paralyzed by its needs for agricultural inputs (Hall 2000). But indigenous knowledge is not necessarily adequate either, as shown by Tainter

(1989) and Diamond (2004), both of whom chronicle the collapses of numerous earlier societies when their culture, rather than being adaptive as is often assumed, was often quite maladaptive. It is not very popular now to talk about environmental limits but such constraints have operated powerfully in the past, often wiping out whole civilizations, and they will do so again, perhaps on a rather larger scale. There is no guarantee that development will work, that sustainability will be found, or even that cultures will persist. And nature simply does not care.

8. Scientists are (mostly) smart, honest, rigorous, and dedicated. Because of that, they are just a little difficult to work with and quite hopeless at decision making. But they have a wealth of approaches, methods, and tools and are more than willing to contribute to make a better world.

9. When planning development, do not let the "invisible hand" take care of everything. It will not. Things must be thought out very carefully.

10. Be very wary of "free" aid that cannot work without a continual purchase from outside your borders of fossil fuel, parts, replacements, and so on. Such "free" aid has destroyed many of the economies that we have studied.

11. And, of course, we, like others, stress the importance of good and open government, a free press, and so on, so that questions of who gets the benefit of whatever development takes place are well discussed and understood.

The Most Important Conclusion

We have reviewed the many failures and some successes of development programs. In this we join the assessments of many others, mostly economists, who also conclude that whatever development has promised it has done so in only a very small proportion of the countries that need success. Meanwhile, the economies of most of the world's poorer people limp along, with the people

muddling through often extremely difficult circumstances. A very few success stories exist where a developing country with (or with access to) valuable resources, a well-functioning political system, and hard-working and educated people has found a special niche: Japan with microelectronics and small, well-made, and efficient automobiles; Korea with these things and heavy industries such as shipbuilding; Hong Kong and Singapore with trade; Malaysia with natural gas and oil palms. According to many economists, the rest of the world simply has to find a niche where they have "competitive advantage." We think that there are few such opportunities for most developing countries, and when there are some, it is often at the expense of sustainability. The world has watched as one prescription for ending poverty after another has failed or barely succeeded—and, if so, often with many unintended and undesirable consequences. A particular problem is that relatively few things that the world wants from the market are not already fully developed. The tropics do indeed supply much of the developed world with "breakfast": coffee, tea, bananas, sugar, oranges, and so on. But finding a new niche is tough. Costa Rica invested heavily in bananas with U.S. aid and then found that the United States had also been encouraging Ecuador to do the same, so the world market is flooded with cheap bananas. Then Europe stopped buying bananas from either place, choosing to buy only from former African colonies. Coffee is every tropical country's salvation—except that world demand is nearly flat and many more countries have entered the growing game.

Meanwhile, the environments of most of these countries, and of the earth as a whole, have continued to degrade, often horribly. Poor people in the past at least had clean water and breathed clean air, and they often had access to a decent patch of soil or some fish to be able to eat. Now, as shown in, for example, chapters 13 and 14, even that is increasingly unavailable to poor people.

One of our main conclusions is that most of the economic tools that have in the past been used for guidance of development work much more in the minds of those who believe in them than in practice. Chapters 2 and 3 reviewed the once-famed Domar and Rostow models, which were found completely wanting when their effects were subject to explicit assessment. In general, for us as scientists it is astonishing that so many economic models or ideas have so much credibility with so little validation or justification for their use. In fact, those countries that are most successful at development—including, incidentally, the United States long ago, Korea and Malaysia more recently, and China today—are successful because they did not follow the modern prescription, including the tenets of neoclassical economics—among them, no trade barriers. Why many development advisors should continue to advocate models that obviously do not work is a mystery to us.

What is it that can work, then? Most fundamentally, we believe that the process of development for a locality, region, or country must be undertaken more or less as follows. Quite frankly, we do not know if this will work, for as empiricists we have not had the opportunity to observe it, and it flies in the face of all previously advocated development schemes. But here goes:

1. Feed the people, and do that with human labor. With the exception of highly industrialized nations, little can be done without insuring first that the populace is fed. This has several advantages: first agriculture is, or should be, relatively labor-intensive. Countries with surplus, unutilized labor are likely to have trouble on their hands. This means that one of the most important aspects of development is that you do not want to increase labor productivity unless you have a good plan to absorb that surplus labor. This is, of course, the opposite of what most development plans call for.

2. If possible, reduce the imported energy intensity of the agricultural (and other) economy. Do this in a way that reduces labor productivity, and accept that. Fossil fuels are expensive in much of the world, and they are especially expensive in terms of foreign exchange. They are likely to become much more expensive within coming years or decades. Points 1 and 2 are related, because a main way to keep labor employed is not to replace its function with energy-intensive chemicals or machines. Sometimes it is not possible to do this in increasingly open markets, so more thought needs to go into whether "free trade" delivers all that its advocates suggest.

3. Educate the people. Do not stop until 100 percent of the population is literate. Talk openly about sex, birth control, the role of a woman, and oppression of various sorts. Develop and nurture scientists, agronomists, and engineers at least as much as economists and policy people, or, ideally, develop them together. Maintain high-quality national systems of meteorology, hydrology, soil analysis, and so on to monitor the basic conditions and resources of a country and of the world. Experiment, observe and listen, be critical. Apply a systems approach to solve the country's problems and build a better future.

4. Remember that successful development can encourage large families and undermine that development.

5. Prevent war and armed conflicts at all costs: there is no need for enemies in development. Poverty and latent conflicts cannot be ignored; the opinion of civil society matters. Manipulation, dictatorship, and corruption should not be tolerated. Tolerance of other cultures is essential.

We have also offered some prescriptions as to how we might make the process of development better through the use of science. These include, especially, the use of spatial tools that allow us to understand how different economic policies might have very different results in different landscapes. But we have no illusions about the limitations of what we propose. Science and its tools are really quite powerless in the face of at least four enormous problems, or "elephants," any of which can completely destroy our efforts.

The first and largest elephant in our living room is that the production of wealth has to be examined relative to how many people will share it. Perhaps the largest reason that development has failed is that in general it is extremely difficult for any nation to achieve sustained economic growth of 3 percent a year. If population growth is 4 percent a year, then per capita wealth (technically, income) will decline. It is that simple. Our own research has taken that relation a step further. Since for most countries the generation of wealth has a close to one-to-one relation with the use of energy, we can say that where the population increase is more rapid than the growth of energy (and, incidentally, the infrastructure to use it well), wealth decreases. Where the population growth is slower than the growth in energy use, per capita wealth increases (see figure 5.1). We have found almost no exceptions to this relation (see table 5.1), but its importance seems to have escaped all economists. For the future, let us call this the Hall theory of growth (as Grégoire Leclerc names it, honoring his colleague Charles Hall). Empirically, it is clearly much more powerful than the Harrod-Domar or Solow models.

The importance of population growth was taken for granted by early investigators into development, but according to Sachs (2002) fell out of favor when revisionist social scientists in the 1970s began to emphasize the importance of "human capital" (education, access to technology, and the like). In addition, there have been powerful political movements in the United States that have taken population off the global agenda and attempted to supplant it with free-market ideology. Chapter 12 tests one of the concepts of these revisionists and finds their theories not supported by data from Nepal. A more recent and much wider analysis by Birdsall, Kelley, and Sinding (2001) found exactly what the title suggests: *Population Matters*. The misery that has been visited upon the world because population growth fell off the agenda of development agencies (with more than a little help by the anti–family planning political forces in the United States) over the last thirty-odd years can only be considered criminal.

The second elephant is the issue of how long the availability of cheap petroleum will last. We have shown in great detail how economic development is extremely strongly correlated with the use of energy, which for most countries means imported petroleum. The price of oil in the year 2000 was more or less as inexpensive as it had ever been (when corrected for inflation), although as of 2006 the price was increasing, which certainly hurt the economies of most developing nations. Oil will never run out, but cheap petroleum will almost certainly within a generation and probably much sooner (Hallock et al. 2004; ASPO websites). We have documented the critical importance of energy in development (Ko, Hall, and Lemus 1998; Tharakan, Kroeger, and Hall 2001; Hall et al. 2003), as have many others. We have also documented how that oil is used in many aspects of development and even general economic activity in Costa Rica in Hall (2000). When the cheap oil is gone, as will happen, all bets are off.

The third elephant is the issue of the bottom line. Whatever we (or nations, or NGOs, or other entities) might wish to do to improve the standard of living of the poorer people in the world, those people must face enormous pressures that often work against them that come from large financial entities that are working to improve their own bottom line by shaping trade rules and developing policies. It is our opinion that many unscrupulous people hide behind neoclassical economics to justify their exploitation of others. Given the power of establishment economics in our universities, it is hard to see how to change this, but it is probably our first priority.

Finally, the fourth elephant in our living room is our own collective ignorance. We recognize that we, the editors and authors of this book, do not have all of the answers or maybe even any substantial part of them. But we do think it critical to open much more the discussion about how we go about the business of development, including using to a much greater degree the tools of the scientific method including putting forth policies as testable hypotheses, and the inclusion of natural science in an arena generally left to economists alone.

We hope that this book is a start in that direction.

References

Birdsall, N. A., C. Kelley, and S. W. Sinding. 2001. *Population Matters: Demographic Change, Economic Growth, and Poverty in the Developing World*. New York: Oxford University Press.

Diamond, J. 2004. *Collapse: How Societies Choose to Succeed or Fail*. New York: Viking.

Easterly, W. 2005. *The White Man's Burden: Why the West's Efforts to Aid the Rest Have Done So Much Ill and So Little Good*. New York: Penguin Press.

Hall, C. A. S., ed. 2000. *Quantifying Sustainable Development: The Future of Tropical Economies*. San Diego: Academic Press.

Hall, C. A. S., P. Tharakan, J. Hallock, C. Cleveland, and M. Jefferson. 2003. Hydrocarbons and the evolution of human culture. *Nature* 426, no. 6964: 318–22.

Hallock, J., P. Tharakan, C. Hall, M. Jefferson, and W. Wu. 2004. Forecasting the limits to the availability and diversity of global conventional oil supplies. *Energy* 29:1673–96.

Ko, J. Y., C. A. S. Hall, and L. L. Lemus. 1998. Resource use rates and efficiency as indicators of regional sustainability: An examination of five countries. *Environmental Monitoring and Assessment* 51:571–93.

Krugman, P. 1995. *Development Geography and Economics Theory*. Cambridge: MIT Press.

Perkins, J. 2004. *Confessions of an Economic Hit Man*. San Francisco: Berrett-Koehler.

Sachs, J. 2005. *The End of Poverty: Economic Possibilities for Our Time*. New York: Viking Penguin.

Tainter, J. 1990. *The Collapse of Complex Systems*. Cambridge: Cambridge University Press.

Tharakan, P., T. Kroeger, and C. A. S. Hall. 2001. Twenty-five years of industrial development: A study of resource use rates and macro-efficiency indicators for five Asian countries. *Environmental Science and Policy* 4:319–32.

Contributors

FRÉDÉRIC ACHARD is a research scientist with the European Commission Joint Research Centre (JRC) in Ispra, Italy, where he has coordinated portions of the Tropical Ecosystem Environment Observations by Space Project (TREES). His research interests include the development of observation techniques for global and regional forest monitoring and the assessment of forest-cover changes in the tropics and boreal Eurasia. He received his PhD in tropical ecology and remote sensing from Toulouse University, France.

VÉRONIQUE ALARY has an engineering degree in agronomy and a PhD in agricultural economics. She is now a researcher at the Centre de Coopération Internationale en Recherche Agronomique pour le Développement (CIRAD). Her main field of research is the analysis of farmers' decision making and the impact of policies on the agricultural supply and farms' livelihoods. Her working experience includes research in Cameroon, Mali, India, and North Africa.

SUSAN ALLAN is a community development practitioner. Her primary interest is to support practitioners and organizations to strengthen the impact of their development work with communities. She has worked with government agencies and community organizations in Australia, the Philippines, the United Kingdom, and Peru. She has an MSW from the University of Queensland, Australia.

ALFONS BALMANN is the executive director of the Institut für Agrarentwicklung in Mittel- und Osteuropa (IAMO) in Halle, Germany. He studied agricultural economics in Göttingen, where he also did his PhD. He is senior researcher at the Humboldt University in Berlin and has many publications on structural change, real options, and genetic algorithms.

BRUNO BARBIER is an expert on applied bioeconomic modeling, currently working at the Centre de Coopération Internationale en Recherche Agronomique pour le Développement (CIRAD). He has worked for the International Center for Tropical Agriculture and lived in Honduras and Burkina Faso. He received his PhD from the Ecole Nationale Supérieure d'Agriculture in Montpellier, France.

FELIPE BARITTO is chief of the modernization and institution-building program for the socioeconomic development plan of the southern region of Monagas, a technical and financial cooperation agreement established between the European Union and the Bolivarian Republic of Venezuela. He is also a professor at the School of Environmental Engineering, Universidad Gran Mariscal de Ayacucho.

RICK E. BEAL earned a PhD in biochemistry from SUNY Buffalo and has taken additional environmental courses at SUNY's College of Environmental Science and Forestry in Syracuse. He currently directs the ESF in the High School Program, bringing high-quality environmental programs to high schools in upstate New York.

NATHALIE BEAULIEU is programme officer at the International Development Research Center. She contributed to this book when she was part of the rural planning group of the institute of rural innovation at the International Center for Tropical Agriculture in Cali, Colombia. She is a civil engineer with a PhD in remote sensing who has specialized in participatory planning, with work experience in Latin America and Africa.

Gilberto Páez Bogarín is an agronomist and statistician with a large experience in research and teaching on applications of experimental and quantitative methods. He has occupied several high-profile positions, including director general of CATIE (1981–84) and IICA director and representative in the United States, Costa Rica, the Dominican Republic, and Brazil. He is now a scientific advisor to the government of Paraguay and contributes to various projects in the MERCOSUR.

Johan Bouma is professor emeritus at Wageningen University and Research Center. He works on precision agriculture, land-quality indicators, and pedo transfer functions, and is active in the field of transitions in agriculture toward sustainability.

Rodrigo Javier Briceño is a health economist for Sanigest International and professor of economics at the National University of Costa Rica.

Sandra Brown has a PhD from the University of Florida. A former professor of forestry at the University of Illinois, she has worked for the Environmental Protection Agency and Winrock International. She has long experience in planning, developing, implementing, and managing research projects focusing on estimating and modeling the stocks and flows of carbon in forests and the environmental and human factors that influence them, which has resulted in more than 160 publications.

Jorge Calvo is a researcher specializing in fisheries at the Center for Austral Research, located at the southern tip of Argentina.

Henry Vargas Campos is an economist at the Banco Central de Costa Rica as well as a national accounts consultant. He is also a professor of economics at the Universidad Nacional de Costa Rica.

Chantal Line Carpentier joined the Commission Nord-américaine de Coopération Environnementale (CNACE) in May 2000 as manager of environment, economics, and trade sector program. She has a diploma in agricultural engineering from McGill University and a PhD in agricultural and environmental policy from Virginia Polytechnic Institute.

Mamadou Maï K. Chetima is a doctoral student at Cornell University. His research interests are related to crop and animal systems and food security in the Sahel, West Africa, specializing in system dynamics modeling, applied economics, and environmental information science. His working experience includes research and development project planning with the National Agricultural Research Institute (INRAN), ONG Karkara, and the Ministry of Environment and Desertification Control in Niger.

Pieter M. Dercksen is an independent consultant in the field of sustainable agriculture and rural development with emphasis on conservation agriculture. He is based in Costa Rica and has worked in Asia, the Middle East, and Latin America with the FAO and the Dutch government. His most recent activities are related to the promotion of payment of environmental services for agricultural projects. He received his MSc in physical geography from the Free University in Amsterdam.

Daniel Deybe is seconded to the Policy Aspects of Research and Sustainable Development Unit of European Commission's Research Directorate General, mainly dealing with projects on land use and sustainable development. He is the former head of the Economics, Policies, and Markets Program of the Centre de Coopération Internationale en Recherche Agronomique pour le Développement (CIRAD). He has worked in the United States, Africa, and Asia.

JORGE MARIO DÍAZ is a consultant on rural development and institutional capacity building. In previous years, he has worked for the Colombian government as director of the agrarian department at the National Department of Planning and as director of policy at the Ministry of Agriculture and Rural Development.

AARON DUSHKU has been consultant for the World Wildlife Fund, Geographical Modelling Services, Clark Labs, and Winrock International. He studies issues of land-use change and its implications for carbon storage. He received a master's degree in GIS for development and environment from Clark University.

WOLFGANG EICHHORN is professor of economics at the University of Karlsruhe, Germany. His publications in leading international journals range from pure and applied mathematics on statistics to economic theory and insurance science. He has been a guest professor at numerous universities in Europe and North America.

HUGH EVA is a research officer at the European Commission's Joint Research Centre in Ispra, Italy. He specializes in the use of remotely sensed data for mapping fires and forests in tropical ecosystems and has published two land-cover maps of South America derived from satellite imagery. He was the Latin America coordinator of the TREES project, which was set up to monitor and measure changes in the tropical forest belt using remote sensing. He holds a PhD from the Catholic University of Louvain-la-Neuve.

CLAUDIO GHERSA is an agronomist and landowner based in Buenos Aires. He has done graduate study at Oregon State University on sustainable agriculture and is working on making Argentine agriculture more sustainable.

JOHN GOWDY received his PhD from Vanderbilt University. His many studies in economics emphasize the physical and environmental aspects of economics, and he is now working on the economics of sustainability.

GASTON GRENIER was trained in agricultural engineering and business administration and has worked for many years as a consultant in these areas. He has led CIDA-funded rural development activities in Honduras and been director of the CIDA Sahel and Ivory Coast regional program. He is now head of the board of WARDA, the Africa Rice Center.

AILEEN GUZMAN is a PhD student in the College of Environmental Science at the State University of New York, majoring in risk assessment and systems. A native of the Philippines, she is studying the resource requirements of the growing city of Manila. Her research interests are remote sensing and GIS, water resources management, sustainable development, and climate change.

CHARLES HALL is ESF Foundation Distinguished Professor at the College of Environmental Science and Forestry, State University of New York. He received his PhD from the University of North Carolina. He has undertaken many systems studies of rivers, estuaries, and forests, as well as of energy and economics, usually combining empirical studies of anthroposystems with simulation modeling. He is now working on the consolidation of a new field of research: biophysical economics.

MYRNA HALL is assistant professor at the College of Environmental Science and Forestry, State University of New York. She specializes in geographical modeling and urban ecology. Some of her major research projects have been simulating the retreat of glaciers in Glacier National Park and examining the rates and patterns of land-use change and tropical deforestation in Brazil and Bolivia, as well as modeling the impact of land-use change on the water supply of New York City.

KATRYN HAPPE is a senior researcher at the Institut für Agrarentwicklung in Mittel- und Osteuropa (IAMO) in Halle, Germany. She holds a PhD from the University of Hohenheim in Stuttgart. She does research on agent-based modeling, structural change, multifunctional agriculture, agricultural policy analysis, and efficiency analysis.

ALEXANDER HERNANDEZ is currently a PhD student in the Department of Forest, Range and Wildlife Sciences at Utah State University. His research deals with remote sensing and GIS modeling of ecological thresholds in semiarid areas of the intermountain region of the United States. His work experience has primarily been in Honduras with some spatial analysis applications carried out in El Salvador, Nicaragua, and Costa Rica.

CARLOS E. HERNÁNDEZ is a civil engineer with a PhD in resource development from Michigan State University. He was chief project engineer for the supervision and coordination of design and construction of the EARTH University campus at Las Mercedes, Costa Rica. He is the director of that school's Daniel Oduber Campus.

DEAN HOLLAND has a PhD in the social sciences and specializes in adult learning and participatory approaches to agricultural research. He has studied action-learning systems for farmers and researchers in the Philippines and Peru. Dean works for the nongovernmental organization Greening Australia, exploring ways to link the private sector, public sector, and civil society to better manage natural resources.

HANS G. P. JANSEN is research fellow and coordinator of the Central America Office at the International Food Policy Research Institute (IFPRI) in San Jose, Costa Rica. A native of the Netherlands, he has lived in Asia, Africa, and Latin America, carrying out research on farming systems, livestock, vegetable systems, and sustainable land use. He has been a consultant to the FAO, the Dutch government, and development banks. He holds a PhD in agricultural economics from Cornell University.

JAIME JARAMILLO is a specialist in environmental management and works with Petrotesting in Villavicencio, Colombia, on the production of biofuels. From 1999 to 2004, he was a specialist in rural planning in the International Center for Tropical Agriculture's land-use program and rural innovation institute.

TIM KASTEN is chief of the Natural Resources Branch of the United Nations Environment Programme (UNEP) in Nairobi, Kenya. Before that posting, he was deputy coordinator of the UNEP Caribbean Environment Programme in Kingston, Jamaica, and worked for the U.S. Environmental Protection Agency in its water and hazardous waste programs.

RON KNAPP retired after twenty years with the Consultative Group on International Agricultural Research (CGIAR). His research interests and experience center on the spatial analysis of soil-crop systems and environments, including computer modeling and decision support systems, applied crop production, and farmer decision analysis. He currently serves as chairman of the technical committee for the USAID-funded Soil Management CRSP. He holds a PhD in soil science from Washington State University.

JAE-YOUNG KO received his PhD from the State University of New York in Syracuse. His research interests include ecological economics, the interconnection of environment and energy, resource and waste management, industrial ecology, environmental and energy policy, and sustainable development. Most recently, he has been involved in environmental and energy issues along the Gulf Coast of the United States.

TIMM KROEGER holds a PhD from the College of Environmental Science and Forestry, State University of New York. Having worked on issues related to reducing the air pollution of Lima, Peru, he is now an economist for Defenders of Wildlife in Washington, D.C.

REINER KÜMMEL studied physics at the universities of Darmstadt and Frankfurt. He worked as a research assistant to John Bardeen, who twice obtained the Nobel prize in physics, at the University of Illinois, Urbana. He taught physics at the Universidad del Valle in Cali, Colombia, and since 1974 he has been a professor of theoretical physics at the University of Würzburg.

GRÉGOIRE LECLERC holds a PhD in applied physics from Sherbrooke University, Canada. As a senior scientist with the International Center for Tropical Agriculture (CIAT), he developed methodologies and tools for natural resources management in Latin America. He is a senior scientist with the Centre de Coopération Internationale en Recherche Agronomique pour le Développement (CIRAD). Based in Senegal, he works on participatory modeling and ecological economics of nomadism in the Sahel.

THOMAS R. LEINBACH is a professor of geography at the University of Kentucky. His interests focus on industrialization, technology, transport, and regional development, especially in Southeast Asia. A current interest is the theme of e-commerce and its role in firm value chains and their competitive advantage. He holds a PhD in economic geography from Pennsylvania State University.

DIETMAR LINDENBERGER teaches energy economics at Cologne University and is manager of the Institute of Energy Economics there. He consults on energy industry and policy for the German federal government and the European Commission, and has published widely in the field of energy economics. He holds a PhD in economics from the University of Karlsruhe.

JOEP C. LUIJTEN has a PhD in agricultural and biological engineering from the University of Florida. He has been a consultant to the International Center for Tropical Agriculture (CIAT) and the United Nations Environmental Program (UNEP), working on projects that involved the application of GIS technology and modeling tools for improving water and land resources management in Latin America and the Caribbean.

PABLO DANIEL MATOSSIAN is a businessman, entrepreneur, and lecturer in finance in Buenos Aires and Bariloche, Argentina.

ROD MCNEIL is an independent inventor and aquaculture specialist. He worked in chromatography and optics, then expanded his interests and expertise over the years into many facets where technology and environmental concerns interface. He is the inventor of, among many other things, "aquamats," an artificial aquatic substrate that, in its different forms, has many applications to erosion control, waste treatment, and raising organisms such as shrimp.

ORLANDO MEJÍA is involved in research in GIS analysis and agricultural impact assessment. Before working as research assistant at Michigan State University, he served in the Honduran Ministry of Agriculture, the International Center for Tropical Agriculture (CIAT), and the Pan American School of Agriculture in Zamorano, Honduras.

ANDY NELSON is a geographer and postdoctoral research fellow in the Global Environmental Monitoring Unit of the Joint Research Centre of the European Commission. His interests include multiscale spatial analysis combining socioeconomic and environmental data and global mapping and generation of key spatial datasets for population, transport, accessibility, and terrain modeling. He holds a PhD in geography from the University of Leeds.

CLARA OLMEDO has worked as a teaching assistant and research assistant in the Universidad National de la Patagonia Austral (UNPA) in Argentina. She has studied the labor market problems of her native Patagonia, and the results helped to design public labor policies there. She holds a master's degree from the State University of New York, Binghamton.

RUDRIKSHA RAI PARAJULI has a master's degree from the College of Environmental Science and Forestry, State University of New York. Her research focused on the impact of population growth on the potential of Nepal to feed its growing population. She is a program officer for the Mountain Program of the World Wildlife Fund in Nepal.

CARLOS LEÓN PÉREZ has a master's degree from the Kennedy School of Government at Harvard University. He worked for many years for the Costa Rican Ministry of Agriculture and Livestock. He is now director of Fundación Neotrópica, a conservation and education foundation based in Costa Rica.

MARIO PIEDRA holds a PhD in agricultural economics from Louisiana State University. He has been a researcher and lecturer at the International Center for Tropical Agriculture and other schools and institutions in Central America. Currently he is the director of the Continuing Education and Outreach Program at EARTH University in Costa Rica.

DAVID PIMENTEL received a PhD in entomology from Cornell University, where he is a professor of ecology and agricultural science. His research spans the fields of basic population ecology, ecological and economic aspects of pest control, biological control, biotechnology, sustainable agriculture, land and water conservation, natural resource management, and environmental policy. He has published more than five hundred scientific papers and twenty books and has served on many national and governmental committees.

HELLE MUNK RAVNBORG received her PhD in 1993 from Roskilde University Centre in Environment, Technology and Social Studies. She is currently a senior research fellow at the Danish Institute for International Studies in Copenhagen. She has undertaken research on poverty, on watershed management, and on collective action in natural resource management, in Colombia, Honduras, and Nicaragua.

JUAN LUCAS RESTREPO is a counselor with the Colombian government on issues related to coffee and is a negotiator for Colombia for the treaties on free trade in America. He has worked for the nation's government as vice minister of agriculture, as director of the agrarian department at the National Department of Planning, and as director of policy at the Ministry of Agriculture and Rural Development.

SAMUEL RIVERA has a PhD from Utah State University and is a natural resources management specialist with long experience in forestry, watershed management, and training-research methodologies. His work has concentrated on Central America and issues related to forest management, erosion control practices, water quality, and watershed management. He is currently a project specialist for the Canadian International Development Agency (CIDA) in Honduras.

DAVID CARDOZA RODRÍGUEZ is professor of econometrics at the Universidad Nacional de Costa Rica. He is also an economist at the Contraloría General de la República de Costa Rica.

JORGE RUBIANO is an agronomist with a PhD in geography from Leeds University. His experience is mainly in watershed management and development plans for rural areas. He recently joined the International Center for Tropical Agriculture and is involved in several projects relating to environmental services supplied by water systems.

LAURA SCHMITT has an undergraduate degree in environmental sciences from Brown University. She is completing her PhD at the College of Environmental Science and Forestry, State University of New York.

JEROEN SCHOORL is assistant professor at Wageningen University and Research Center in the Netherlands. He holds a PhD from the same university. He works on the development of landscape-process and land-use-change models.

GARY D. SHARP is a fisheries biologist with a PhD from the Scripps Institute of Oceanography. He specializes in the biology and population responses of exploited fish populations to climate and ocean changes. He has worked with various national and international research and forecast institutions to provide insights into both natural and anthropogenic forces, local, regional, and global, that affect ecosystems.

Juan-Rafael Vargas holds a PhD in economics from the University of Pennsylvania. He is a professor of economics at the Universidad de Costa Rica. He is editor of *Revista Ciencias Económicas*, anchorperson of *Economía y Sociedad* on Channel 15, and a researcher in the university's PPPI program.

Tom Veldkamp holds the chair in Soil Inventory and Land Evaluation at Wageningen University and Research Center in the Netherlands. His research themes and interests range from geology and geomorphology to the interactions and feedbacks of soils and land use in the context of global change. Within the Netherlands, he studies transitions in agriculture toward sustainability.

Jane Yeomans has a PhD in soil microbiology and biochemistry from Iowa State University. She works in the Office of Research at EARTH University in Las Mercedes, Costa Rica, and is involved in various special projects in waste management and water quality. She also teaches physics, environmental sciences, and sustainable food systems there.

INDEX

The letters *f*, *t*, or *n* following a page number refer to a figure, table, or note on that page.
The number following the *n* is the note number.